ART
of the 20th Century

Ruhrberg · Schneckenburger · Fricke · Honnef

ART

of the 20th Century

Edited by Ingo F. Walther

Part I

PAINTING

by Karl Ruhrberg

TASCHEN

KÖLN LONDON MADRID NEW YORK PARIS TOKYO

© 2002 TASCHEN GmbH
Hohenzollernring 53, D-50672 Köln
www.taschen.com
Edited by Ingo F. Walther, Alling
Project management: Juliane Steinbrecher, Cologne
Translation: John William Gabriel, Worpswede;
Ishbel Flett, Frankfurt; Fiona Elliott, Edinburgh;
Frances Wharton, Cologne
Cover design: Angelika Taschen, Cologne

Printed in Spain
ISBN 3-8228-1362-1

Contents

Painting
by Karl Ruhrberg

Prologue to Modernism

The Magic of Light
The Janus Face of Impressionism

A balloon floated over the Paris World Fair of 1867 and perched in its gondola was a man named Nadar, photographer, aeronaut, and caricaturist. In Oslo one can still see the captive balloon, floating in the upper right-hand corner of a painting that was executed the same year by Edouard Manet, *View of the World Fair* (ill. below), a painting which now hangs in the National Gallery in the Norwegian capital. Nadar's real name was Gaspard Félix Tournachon; the *nom de plume* reflected an awareness of his worth and mission. He was befriended with the artists who, as a group, would later be known as Impressionists. This term was meant to ridicule the apparently haphazard and half-finished character of their "snapshots" in painting, whose significance the photographer Nadar intuitively recognized. Seven years after the World Fair, from April 15 to May 15, 1874, Nadar made his premises at 35, Boulevard des Capucines, on the right bank of the Seine near the Opera, available to the painters for an exhibition.

The previous year, 1873, Claude Monet had depicted the boulevard from a window high above, giving the crowds hurrying along the pavement the blurred, schematic look of an early photograph. Here, in the midst of sophisticated nineteenth-century Paris, where

Nadar enjoyed a reputation in high society, his painter-friends at last had an opportunity to show their pictures. These pictures had been repeatedly rejected by the jury of the official Salon exhibitions, or had been hung so disadvantageously that their fresh, bright colors blossomed in obscurity. Nadar's Impressionist show was the first unjuried exhibition ever. Admission cost fifty centimes, the catalogue one franc. The artists themselves had made the selection of paintings on display; no carping art expert was permitted to exclude anyone in the name of an academic tradition betrayed.

It was no coincidence that a photographer was among the few people who realized the artistic rank of these painters and their new approach to reality. Like his artist-friends, Nadar attempted with the means of his metier to capture the excitement of the unique, unrepeatable moment on a photographic plate. He, too, saw the world from a long, all-encompassing view, probably encouraged by his flights in the balloon.

All early photographs had a coarse-grained texture that very much resembled the brushwork of Impressionist paintings. This is seen to good effect in the very first photograph in the world, the picture taken in 1826 of the town of Châlons-sur-Saône by Nicéphore Niepce,

"One morning one of us had run out of black; and that was the birth of Impressionism."
PIERRE-AUGUSTE RENOIR

Edouard Manet
View of the World Fair 1867, 1867
Oil on canvas, 108 x 196 cm
Oslo, Nasjonalgalleriet

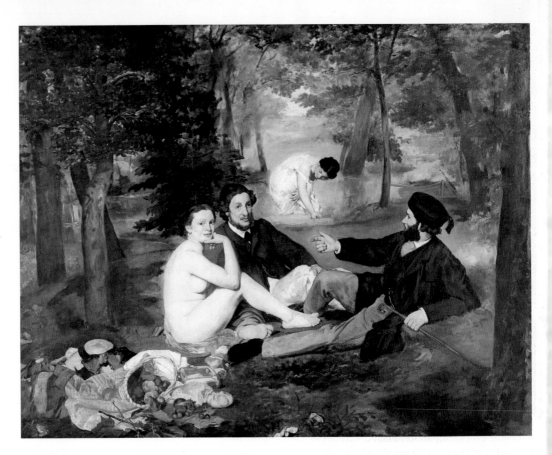

Edouard Manet
Le Déjeuner sur l'herbe, 1863
Oil on canvas, 208 x 264 cm
Paris, Musée d'Orsay

a landowner and amateur scientist. Niepce made the photo from the window of the chemical laboratory he had installed at his estate, Gras, outside his home town. The image was made on a zinc plate covered with light-sensitive asphalt. When the plate was rinsed with lavender oil and petroleum, the portions of the surface that had not been hardened by exposure to light were washed away. This lent the image a grainy irregularity, a sort of visual vibration which, though unintended, recalled the sketchy rendering of vegetation and sky combined with solidly depicted houses found in the similar motifs of a painter like Camille Pissarro.

The final decade of the waning century witnessed preparations on all hands for a revolution in the visual arts, a conscious revolt against tradition and established taste. Vincent van Gogh painted under the searing sun of Arles; Paul Gauguin and Emile Bernard, working at Pont-Aven in Brittany, founded a movement they called "Synthetism" the Norwegian painter Edvard Munch showed his work at the Association of Berlin Artists; James Ensor completed his provocative *Entry of Christ into Brussels in the Year 1889*; Parisian art dealer Ambroise Vollard showed the paintings of Paul Cézanne; and the Impressionists by this time had made their public breakthrough. Thus began what has come to be known as the "Heroic" epoch in the history of modern art.

The prologue to this chapter had been prepared in the spring of 1874, when Monet, Alfred Sisley, Pierre-Auguste Renoir, Edgar Degas, Armand Guillaumin,

Berthe Morisot, and Cézanne joined forces in Nadar's studio. But one important name was missing. Manet, though venerated by his colleagues as the painter of *Le Déjeuner sur l'herbe* (ill. above) and *Olympia* (Paris, Musée d'Orsay), though he had shown fifty works in his own pavilion at the 1867 World Fair, was not an Impressionist of the first hour. His once-rejected paintings had since found entry to the official Salon, where even Renoir (ill. right), with his still quite conventional *Lise with a Sunshade* (Essen, Museum Folkwang), and Monet with his Honfleur seascapes, had also enjoyed first recognition.

The Bourgeois Geniuses

While Manet's colleagues admired him, they also were envious of his public success. In a sense they were revolutionaries against their own will, for most of them were honest, upstanding citizens from humble backgrounds. Only Manet and Degas were born into the upper-middle class, and represented the type of the educated, urbane, quick-tongued Parisian. Henri de Toulouse-Lautrec's family belonged to the French aristocracy. None of these artists could be called social revolutionaries or barricade fighters like Gustave Courbet, the great realist who was jailed after the smashing of the Vendôme Column during the Paris Commune. Although those who could avoided military service during the Franco-Prussian War of 1870/71, Monet, for one, later became a close friend of Minister President

Pierre-Auguste Renoir
Le Moulin de la Galette, 1876
Oil on canvas, 131 x 175 cm
Paris, Musée d'Orsay

Georges Clemenceau, whose militancy earned him the nickname of "The Tiger." It was the rejection, scorn, and derision poured upon them by press and public that transformed this loose group of artists into secessionists. They had a simple message to convey, and wanted to be understood. The fact that they were absolutely misunderstood struck them as an embarrassing misfortune. The notion of purposely shocking the bourgeoisie was far from their minds. It was Monet's picture *Impression – Sunrise* (p. 10), a depiction of the sun shimmering

Edgar Degas
Dance Studio of the Opera,
Rue le Pelletier, 1872
Oil on canvas, 32 x 46 cm
Paris, Musée d'Orsay

Claude Monet
Impression – Sunrise, 1872
Oil on canvas, 48 x 63 cm
Paris, Musée Marmottan

Page 11 above:
Lovis Corinth
The Lake of Lucerne in the
Afternoon, 1925
Oil on canvas, 57.5 x 75.5 cm
Hamburg, Hamburger Kunsthalle

Page 11 below:
Max Liebermann
Munich Beer Garden, 1884
Oil on canvas, 95 x 69 cm
Munich, Bayerische Staats-
gemäldesammlungen,
Neue Pinakothek

through dawn mists, that gave Louis Leroy, critic of *Le Charivari,* the opportunity to deride the group as "Impressionists," although this term actually says very little.

Like the Roman god Janus, guardian of gates and doorways, Impressionist painting has two faces. It makes no attempt to plumb the meaning of existence. It reflects the colorful surface of life, strives to record the beauty of surface appearances as seen in changing lights and seeks, to capture the charm of the moment. It is very much of this world, secular rather than transcendental. Impressionism represents the culmination and end-point of illusionistic painting, which since the beginning of the age of perspective in Renaissance Florence had dominated European art and habits of perception. But as every style has the tendency to flip over into its opposite when it reaches its apex, Impressionism at the same time represents the root of modernity in art. It had already begun to reflect the vagaries of human perception and its relativity to times of day and changes of place; it provided the materials for an anti-illusionistic art, the technical, formal, and, tentatively, even the theoretical underpinnings for advances to come. Impressionism liberated color to the point of autonomy, and it took the dissolution of traditional form to the verge of an atmospheric, shimmering veil behind which the objects depicted vanished, ushering in a "non-objective" art.

Cézanne, a loner who obstinately worked *sur le motif* in and around the southern French town of Aix-en-Provence, sought a harmony of color and form in a self-contained art "parallel to nature." Gauguin left his family and his stockbroker's career for the South Sea island of Tahiti, where he hoped to find a lost paradise and a new, unspoiled innocence in painting. Georges Seurat and Paul Signac developed with scientific acumen and great patience a style called Pointillism, in which the subject was rendered in tiny dots of unmixed paint which came together in the eye of the spectator to reveal figures and scenes.

In the work of the Impressionists and their successors painting was once again taken back to its original sources: pure color *and* pure form. It was liberated from every literary and allegorical reference. With the addition of van Gogh's obsessive passion for subjective expression, Impressionist painting laid the groundwork for all that was to come.

"I Paint What I See"

Impressionism marked the birth of subjective art. Not the "what" of the motif but the "how" of its depiction came to decide the rank and value of a painting. "I paint what I see and not what others deign to see," said the young Manet when he was still a pupil in the atelier of Couture. It was no longer the individuality or originality of the subject that counted but the personality of the artist who rendered it, with his own, unique and specific touch. A portrait by Manet, said the writer André Malraux, contained more of the painter than of the person portrayed.

Impressionism in painting conveyed a certain view of life that was also reflected and refracted in the music of the period (Claude Debussy), in its literature (Marcel Proust), and in its philosophy (Henri Bergson, Friedrich Nietzsche), all of which bore witness to the increasing secularization of art.

Despite its worldly, seemingly rational character, Impressionist painting was the result not of systematic research but of spontaneous experience. The example had been set long ago, by the great Spanish masters Diego Vélazquez and Francisco de Goya, by French artists Eugène Delacroix and "Père" Corot and the Barbizon masters of the *paysage intime* (intimate landscape) who had taken their cue from 17th-century Dutch art, foremost among them Charles Daubigny, the first painter to work primarily out-of-doors. Yet even they were overtopped by the dynamic figure of Gustave Courbet, whose realism swept the brown gravy of complacent studio painting off the canvas once and for all time. Among many others, Courbet too was an immediate precursor of Impressionism.

The history of Impressionism has yet to come to an end. Not only the triumphant success of recent retrospectives – 960,000 people saw the 1996 Monet exhibition in Chicago – indicates the continuing currency of the style, which, like all great art, resists the tooth of time. More importantly, Impressionism has continued to influence the development of 20th-century painting down to the present day. The term "abstract Impressionism," coined to describe the abstract landscapes of a Jean-Paul Riopelle or a Jean Bazaine, is only one of countless examples.

From France into Germany

The full-fledged German Impressionism of the trio Max Liebermann, Max Slevogt, and Lovis Corinth (ill. right and p. 12) cannot be said to have brought any crucial innovations, perhaps with the exception of Corinth's late work. The style reached Germany with a delay of fifteen years, when artists in France had long begun to distance themselves from a stream that had since found widespread acceptance. While German artists enthusiastically adopted the vibrant illumination of French Impressionism, they apparently did not feel comfortable with it until it was toned down by an admixture of Dutch nineteenth-century landscape painting. The Mediterranean *joie de vivre*, the brilliantly orchestrated palette found in the best paintings of the French Impressionists are sought in vain in the work of their German followers.

German art nevertheless owes a debt of gratitude to the trio of Liebermann, Slevogt, and Corinth. Inspired by the naturalistic and unliterary landscapes of the Worpswede and Dachau groups, and by the relaxed brushwork of Hans Thoma, Wilhelm Leibl, Carl Schuch, and Wilhelm Trübner, the German Impressionists mounted a concerted attack on the chauvinism of academic art during the Wilhelminian era. That

Max Slevogt
Flowering Lilacs, c. 1921
Oil on wood, 54 x 66 cm
Frankfurt/Main, Städelsches
Kunstinstitut und Städtische
Galerie

Paris (Berlin, Nationalgalerie), which reflects a view of the typical German soldier as a hero with a heart who, when he happens not to be occupied in defeating the French, sings Schubert, plays the "Appassionata", or just muses on the deeper meaning of life.

It was against such sentimental idealization that the shrewd and skeptical intelligence of Liebermann revolted. A realist in both his art and life, he was instrumental in the founding of the Berlin Secession, which reflected his critical opposition to the official art policies of the day more than his acceptance of innovative alternatives. The uproar caused by the exhibition of Edvard Munch's symbolic, but shockingly honest paintings in the Architects' Building of the Association of Berlin Artists in 1892 was only a secondary cause. Liebermann did not make avant-garde artists of the secessionists. They were not progressive, only open to the new and unusual, convinced that it had to be given a chance, and to fight for it if necessary. Being Germans, these artists naturally cleaved to the idea of a deeper meaning which art must make visible. Content and message were just as important to them as form. This is why they remained basically conservative, all except for Corinth, whose dramatic late work – culminating in the self-tormenting, psychologically penetrating, Rembrandesque self-portraits, the incredibly impassioned Walchensee landscapes, and the religious depictions in the manner of an *Ecce homo* – shows at least as many Expressionist as Impressionist traits. The Expressionists themselves were soon to have ominously nationalistic arguments marshalled against them, even by Corinth himself, and to feel the brunt of Liebermann's *grand seigneurial* obstinacy.

Berlin, upstart younger sister of the French capital, produced the outstanding personality in this development, Max Liebermann, should come as no surprise, for Impressionism was essentially a metropolitan art. And in the German metropolis, the middle class was experiencing a growing democratic sense of its importance which led it to rebel against the court and its apologists. First among these was Anton von Werner, the highly praised painter of the Foundation of the German Empire in the Hall of Mirrors at Versailles, and of *Base Quarters outside*

The Painting of Pure Reason
Seurat and the Neo-Impressionists

Although Georges Seurat died at a young age, he was the most significant of those artists who are lumped together in art-history books as Post- or Neo-Impressionists. Seurat himself would have preferred to have his and his friends' style known as "Chromo-Luminarism," or painting in color and light. The terms Pointillism (painting in dots of color set next to one another) or Divisionism (painting in separated areas of color) are likewise more precise than Neo-Impressionism, a term coined by the critic Félix Fénéon, which the young painters accepted out of respect for their erstwhile mentors. "Once again artists appear with books under their arm," wrote the eminent German critic Julius Meier-Graefe around the turn of the century, implying that it was theoretical writings by artists and physicists that had sparked the new departure. Seurat learned from the great colorist Delacroix, who had already strongly influ-

enced the Impressionists, that dabs of different colors, when seen from a certain distance, would merge into *valeurs* of great brilliance and freshness in the eye of the viewer.

Other stimuli came from the color theories of the scholars Dave, Blanc, Helmholtz, Sutter, and Rood, but especially from Michel Eugène Chevreul's doctrine of "simultaneous contrasts." The artists gathered to discuss such theories in the branch of the Goupil art dealership headed by van Gogh's brother, Theo. Seurat, just over 25, argued with Signac, four years his junior, his most faithful follower and soon to become the spokesman for the movement. The debate was occasionally joined by Toulouse-Lautrec, Gauguin, or Bernard, and by the always receptive and open-minded patriarch Pissarro. Cézanne, however, had to be admired largely at a distance.

The Haughty Cartesian

There can be no doubt that the artists gathered around the young, taciturn, aloof and almost haughty Seurat, a disciple of Cartesian philosophy, believed themselves to be the heirs and continuators of Impressionism. Yet is it equally clear that their investigations and meditations unavoidably led them ever farther from the source. Impressionist spontaneity, the naive abandonment of a Renoir or a Monet to the joys of the sensuous life, were not for Seurat. Manet and Degas appealed to him more. Like him, they had made untiring studies in an attempt to detect the formal canon, the hidden geometries, the intellectual framework beneath the surface of the paintings of a Hans Holbein, a Raphael, Nicolas Poussin, or Jean Auguste Dominique Ingres, and to precisely analyze the complimentary contrasts and tapestry-like brushwork of Delacroix.

The more instinctive than rationally controlled division of light into the colors of the spectrum practiced by the Impressionists ran counter to Seurat's rigorous intellectuality and to his belief in the benefits of the natural sciences, which he shared with his contemporaries and which was so characteristic of the latter half of the nineteenth century, with its deep mistrust of the irrational. Also, something within Seurat revolted against the tendency of Impressionist painting to destroy form. He strove for a permanence in art, an art that was decorative in the best sense of the word, an "art in function" which did not retire to the easel painting as the be-all and end-all of art. We are witnesses to the exciting spectacle of a painting technique that had fully matured into a style, which then, thought through to its logical end and taken in practice to the extreme limits of its

possibilities, suddenly turned into its opposite. Seurat completed the process begun by Théodore Géricault, continued by Delacroix, and brought to maturity by the Impressionists – the gradual dissolution of planes of color into ever tinier color particles. But what with the Impressionists was the result of spontaneous visual experiences became with Seurat an exact scientific method.

The effects of this systematization were to extend all the way to the abstractions of the Netherlandish group, "De Stijl," headed by Piet Mondrian. Seurat did not paint outdoors any more. He reverted to the age-old tradition of sketching outdoors and painting in the studio, which in Seurat's case was a study and laboratory in one. But his approach to color was anything but traditional. Instead of mixing paints on the palette (with the exception of the adjacent colors of the spectrum), he would place them carefully, dab by dab, side by side on the canvas, based on scientific analyses of light and the doctrine of simultaneous contrasts.

The mixing of pigments practiced by the Impressionists appeared to the Neo-Impressionists to make the colors seem too material, too "dirty." By keeping them pure, they hoped to dematerialize them, make them convey the disembodied brilliance of the light spectrum. The process of mixing was now to take place on the retina of the viewer's eye, and thus the viewer was cautioned not to approach the canvas too closely. This radical formulation of the Impressionist approach once again demanded an alteration of visual habits. And in this case, too, the result was that an unknowing public stuck their noses right into these curious pictures and were blinded by their brilliant luminosity. Fénéon, the

Georges Seurat
A Sunday Afternoon on the Ile de la Grande Jatte, 1884–1886
Oil on canvas, 206.4 x 305.4 cm
Chicago (IL), The Art Institute of Chicago

Neo-Impressionists. Through optical mixture (mixture in the eye of the observer) of these pure colors, whose relationship to one another can be varied at will, an infinite number of hues can be obtained, from the most brilliant to the greyest. Every brushstroke that is taken pure from the palette remains pure on the canvas."

These words have a cool, scientific tone that reflects as much detachment from the artists' own activity as from the vociferous attacks of their opponents. One was too sure of one's mission to be unsettled by criticism. The finished painting was the result of patient work, which, in Seurat's case, sometimes extended over a full year's time; it was "constructed" according to laws which stood on a level with the most advanced physics of the day, laws which could be confirmed by any one who cared to. The process of painting was no longer subject to the vagaries of emotional sensations or personal temperament. The subjectivity of Impressionism had flipped over into objectivity. Now, colors were *set* like the notes in music.

The vibration of Impressionist colors was linked to form, and the resulting compositions once again possessed stability. In a painting like Seurat's famous *Sunday Afternoon on the Ile de la Grande Jatte* (p. 13), a moment in time is lent permanence, instead of passing in a fleeting impression. The figures of the strollers, composed of thousands of dots that congeal into shapes, take on a almost symbolic meaning, for despite their period clothing, they also represent a certain human prototype. There is nothing naturalistic about their depiction. In this picture a silent happiness takes on painterly form: "L'art c'est l'harmonie," art is harmony. Later artists' aspirations would extend, in Mondrian's words, to making art contain a "universal harmony."

critical apologist of the new movement, accordingly reminded his readers that it was not advisable to sit in the middle of the brass section if one wished to hear a symphony.

The Neo-Impressionist Conception
"With these colors, mutually tinged and lightened with white," Seurat's friend and heir Signac described the Neo-Impressionist method, "an attempt is made to achieve the richness of the sunlight spectrum with all of its tones. An orange that blends with yellow and red, a violet that tends towards red and blue, a green between blue and yellow are, with white, the sole elements of the

Creative Intelligence
Seurat died of meningitis at the age of 31. His early death prevented the compilation of his ideas and studies into a coherent theory. His friend Signac (ill. above), who lagged far behind him as a creative artist, made up for this lack with his 1899 book, *From Delacroix to Neo-Impressionism*. Decades before speculations about painting machines, computer art, and holography, this book only served to show, however, that no theory, no matter how perfect, and no method, no matter how sophisticated, could replace the creative human being. It was precisely, this, which Signac and his colleagues and followers had hoped would be possible. Neo-Impressionism in its most logical, didactic form aimed at establishing a binding doctrine, a normative aesthetic, those notorious "objective criteria" which do not exist and cannot exist as long as art remains alive. Once Neo-Impressionism itself became a dogma, its vitality was inevitably sapped.

Paul Gauguin
The Birth of Christ
("Te Tamari No Atua"), 1896
Oil on canvas, 96 x 128 cm
Munich, Bayerische Staats-
gemäldesammlungen, Neue
Pinakothek

In Search of a Lost Paradise
The Work and Legend of Paul Gauguin

No greater contrast is conceivable than that between the cool-headed, bourgeois, scholarly Seurat and the adventurer, speculator, and prophet of art, Paul Gauguin. The only thing they shared in common was a quest for lucid form in painting, which they believed had been lost and which they attempted, by quite different methods, to restore.

Gauguin was not only a great painter, he was also a great actor. The play in which he performed the leading role was the legend of his own life. When in 1902 he considered returning to Paris from the Marquesas Islands in the South Pacific, his friend Daniel de Monfreid, for whom Gauguin had painted his famous, deeply resigned self-portrait in 1896, replied with merciless frankness: "You must not come back. You enjoy the immunity of the great dead .... You have gone down in art history." The year after, on May 8, 1903, at about eleven o'clock in the morning, Gauguin died in Atuona, on Hiva-Oa, in the South Pacific. His dissolute life, extreme poverty, a heart condition, alcohol, and finally, the "French disease," had broken the spirit and ruined the body of this seemingly indomitable, athletic man.

Born in 1848 in Peru, the son of an opposition journalist and a French-Peruvian mother, Paul spent a restless childhood in the country where some of his ancestors on his grandmother's side had served as viceroys. His father had died on the passage from Europe. Gauguin entered the merchant marine, became, like the poet Charles Baudelaire and the painter Monet, steersman's mate, discovered in Rio de Janeiro the exotic charm of the South American landscape, and finally, returning to Paris, entered the employ of a renowned Parisian financing firm on Rue Lafitte, the same street on which the famous and clever art dealer, Vollard, would later reside. Successful market speculations made Gauguin a prosperous man. He married the lovely daughter of a respected Danish family, Mette Gad, and had money enough to amass a significant collection of Impressionist art. Twelve years later the amateur painter, the stockbroker and father of five who had been smitten by Impressionism, threw everything to the wind and decided to live only for art. Disgusted by the satiety and complacence of European civilization, Gauguin set off on his quest for a paradise lost, first going to Panama and Martinique, then to villages in Brittany (Pont-Aven and Le Pouldu), and finally to Tahiti and the Marquesas Islands.

Gauguin died indigent and alone, banned from the memory of his respectable wife, who was unable to forgive him the fate he had brought upon her and their children.

"With this painting, I tried to make everything breathe faith, quiet suffering, religious and primitive style and great nature with its scream."
PAUL GAUGUIN

Paul Gauguin
Exotic Legends
(Contes barbares), 1902
Oil on canvas, 131.5 x 90.5 cm
Essen, Museum Folkwang

"Painting is the most beautiful of all the arts; in it all feelings are summed up, looking at it each viewer can, through his imagination, create a novel; one single glance can engulf the soul in the most profound memories, a slight effort of memory and everything is summed up instantly. A complete art that sums up all the other arts and completes them."
PAUL GAUGUIN

The Clandestine Classicist

This story of an artist's life, as if right out of a Holly-wood movie, has long distracted attention from the aesthetic qualities of Gauguin's work. Nor was he himself entirely without blame for this. Gauguin called himself a barbarian or wild Indian once too often for us not to believe him, particularly in view of the exotic milieu depicted in his South Pacific paintings. In truth he was never a primitive at all; nor was he an amateur, even in his earliest attempts. For all their awkwardness in detail, his Impressionist works evince an astonishingly high degree of sophistication, and a fine sense of the decorative. Formally speaking, Gauguin is a clandestine classicist, albeit without the perfectionistic smoothness usually associated with this term.

Gauguin's compositions have a strictly balanced framework of horizontals and verticals to which the harmonious rhythms of the groups of figures remain subject. The sensuous curves of the many bronze-skinned Maori girls he depicted (ill. above) are stylized into flat, unmodelled forms which reflect the "Cloisonnism" developed in Pont-Aven, a style based on the leaded contouring between the panes of stained-glass windows, which lends the figures their solidity of outline.

More important to us today than his ambitious but vain attempt to combine the innocent sensuality of the heathen world with the ascetic humility of Christianity into a new, "synthetic" myth, is Gauguin's genius for planar composition. *Te Tamari No Atua* (p. 15), a depiction of an island girl lying on her cot, a manger with oxen and a dog behind her, two helpers in the background, mother and child encompassed by a gleaming

aureole, is still as moving today as when it was painted. Yet its charm does not lie alone in the shifting of the manger from Bethlehem to Tahiti, nor in the somewhat sentimental idea of "Virgin Mary among the Natives."

More important is the transformation of the touching story into a grand, classically serene composition, based on horizontals and verticals and a balanced harmony of colored planes, and supplemented by abrupt shifts in perspective which lead to a unification of various levels of reality within a *single*, coherent image. This principle, soon to be taken to its extreme by Pablo Picasso in *Les Demoiselles d'Avignon* (p. 69), would become a crucial element in 20th-century art.

The Would-Be Fresco Painter

Gauguin's talent predestined him to be a painter of frescoes, but it was a talent that went unused. It was the Symbolist Pierre Puvis de Chavannes, whose attenuated figures inspired Gauguin (and from whom he later attempted to distance himself), who received the mural commissions for which Gauguin waited in vain. This was really his fundamental artistic tragedy. "Be concerned with the silhouette form of each object," Gauguin had written, very much in line with turn-of-the-century tastes, and, "One must always feel the plane, the wall; tapestries need no perspectives."

Gauguin's ideas of form are independent of the exotic South Pacific milieu. They come out just as clearly in the paintings from Brittany, where Gauguin and Bernard (p. 14), who would later bitterly claim priority, announced their theory of "Synthetism". This term implied a return to the basic elements of all visual creation, including the intrinsic value of the material used for the painting. The artists sought a new, ornamental, two-dimensional arrangement of simplified forms and figures with emphasized contours. By express analogy to music, they experimented with pure, unmodelled, colored "notes" or "sounds," which, like line, were to be independent of the natural model. Above and beyond this, they wanted to fill their paintings, once again, with poetic content.

Gauguin's œuvre, too, bore traits of the poetic symbolism of the period, but he was outspoken in his advocacy of representing sensations and emotions solely through abstraction, through line, form and color. The analogies between music and painting were more important to Gauguin than to the Neo-Impressionists.

Georg Wilhelm Friedrich Hegel's concept of the musical in *all* of the arts, his emphasis on the absolute, non-representational character of art in general, found its painterly realization in the art of Gauguin, who envisioned making "music in colors." Where this could not help but lead in artistic terms becomes clear from decisive passages in Gauguin's letters and writings: "I am no painter after nature." – "There is only drawing." – "Pure color, one must sacrifice everything to it." – "The artist may deform if his deformations are expressive and beautiful." Or even more concisely: "Do not work after nature. Art is abstraction."

No Art without History

The art of Gauguin points as far back into the past as it does forward into the future. Javanese art and Egyptian reliefs, the Buddha figures of India and the Parthenon frieze, Japanese woodblock prints and medieval church windows, Melanesian sculpture and Oriental ceramics, Breton crucifixions scenes and Aztec idols, Early Renaissance Italians and the early Manet, Puvis de Chavannes and Degas – all contributed to the formation of Gauguin's style. By the time of his mature period he had diverged from the strict flatness of his Breton motifs and begun arranging the composition in layers, from foreground to background, in the manner of a bas relief. As

these historical references indicate, not even a "revolution" in art can come about by arbitrary decisions made in a historical vacuum. Such revolutions generally make an appeal to traditions which have been forgotten or have not received their proper due.

Gauguin's immediate influence can be seen in the arabesques of a Toulouse-Lautrec, and the path he opened led to the art of the "Nabis," from the ecclesiastically-minded Maurice Denis and Paul Sérusier to the more secular Pierre Bonnard and Edouard Vuillard. His legacy was taken up by Art Nouveau and by Munch, and through Munch it was passed on to the graphic art of the German Expressionists. Gauguin's commitment to the musical quality of pure color anticipated Henri Matisse and the Fauves, even Wassily Kandinsky; his abstract-organic forms were taken up and developed by Hans Arp and Joan Miró.

Truth beyond Beauty
Van Gogh: Painting as Dramatic Action

Van Gogh's paintings now fetch prices reaching into the two-digit millions. During his lifetime, however, this man sold only one picture, from his mature period, *Red Vineyard* (Moscow, Pushkin Museum). It was bought while it was part of an exhibition of a group known as the "Les Vingt" (The Twenty) in Brussels, for 400 francs. The purchaser was Anna Boch, who was herself an artist, and the sister of a Belgian poet-painter whom van Gogh had portrayed in Arles. Van Gogh's career certainly does fit the popular notion of the "neglected genius", and its exploitation in movies and novels has reduced it to a cliché.

The year of the artist's death, Albert Aurier described him and his career in the *Mercure de France* in understanding, if quite pathetic, words. Even in the

eyes of his painter-friends – from Gauguin to Toulouse-Lautrec and Signac – he was basically a stranger, whose greatness remained concealed behind his wooden, ungainly peasant exterior. Only his younger brother, Theo, recognized Vincent's genius and understood the alienation it entailed from the world around him. An employee of the Paris art dealership Goupil, Theo fought for his brother's recognition where he could. But it was in vain. Vincent's artistic and human tragedy was too much for his reserved, sensitive brother to bear. Despite a first public success at the "Salon des Indépendants" and the congratulations of Pissarro and Gauguin, Vincent ended his life in summer 1890 with a pistol shot. Six months later, on January 29, 1891, Theo followed him.

"I experience a period of frightening clarity in those moments when nature is so beautiful . I am no longer sure of myself, and the paintings appear as in a dream."
VINCENT VAN GOGH

Vincent van Gogh
Wheat Field with Ravens, 1889
Oil on canvas, 50.5 x 103 cm
Amsterdam, Rijksmuseum Vincent
van Gogh, Vincent van Gogh
Foundation

Speaking in Pictures

The son of a Dutch pastor, Vincent became a painter because he had failed as a preacher. Because speech would not obey him, in about 1880 Vincent began to draw, and then to paint. Despairing of the coldness of civilized life, he was one of those artists who were condemned to an existence in the hell described by Arthur Rimbaud. Van Gogh's unfulfilled longing led to that panic fear of life which is at the bottom of the "speechlessness" of modern man. His urgent need to communicate broke through in a precipitate series of visual statements. From the dark, earthy tones of *The Potato Eaters* (Amsterdam, Rijksmuseum Vincent van Gogh) to the sinuous arabesques and luminous colors of the Arles, Saint-Rémy-de-Provence, and Auvers-sur-Oise series, van Gogh's life's work was done within the incredibly short period of five years.

It was a superhuman effort that destroyed him. At the apex of one of his creative spells, which gripped him as if in a delirium, he attacked his idolized friend, Gauguin, with a razor, and immediately thereafter turned the blade on himself and severed his right ear lobe. Van Gogh was committed to the mental asylum in Saint-Rémy, then transferred to Auvers, where he came under the care of his eccentric benefactor, Dr. Paul Gachet. His suicide brought to a close the tragedy of an artist whose attempts to find himself ended in self-destruction.

Between Order and Anarchy

With van Gogh, for the first time in the history of the early modern movement, we come upon an artist who was not a Frenchman. Though far from achieving the painterly perfection of his compatriot, Rembrandt, van Gogh was filled with a comparable passion and depth of feeling. In fact his expressive urge was so strong that traditional forms could not contain it, so he changed and bent them to his will. The expressiveness of his excited, writhing lines, a brushwork so violent that it sometimes verges on brutality, the rustic roughness of his art distinguished it fundamentally from that of Gauguin, the Parisian, who tempered his conscious primitivism with the rules of classical harmony.

The incessantly moving, agitated forms in van Gogh's painting correspond to the processes of nature, ever in flux. Its sometimes harsh dissonances, its precariously maintained balance between order and anarchy, are very Germanic in character, despite the fact that van Gogh took his point of departure in French Impressionism and also occasionally used a flat, as it were spaceless composition inspired by Japanese woodblock prints. But the dynamic quality of his art was definitely Nordic as opposed to Mediterranean in origin. Van Gogh looked "into the heart of the people" for his motifs, as he wrote to his painter-friend Anton van Rappard. His ideal in this regard was Jean François Millet, who in turn had been influenced by Honoré Daumier.

In contrast to Impressionism, van Gogh's painting was not an art of acceptance but an art of protest, not indifferent to society and its ills but critical of them, especially in his early period of depictions from the milieu of the poor and underprivileged. Apart from the Provençal landscape, on which he did not yet exclusively focus, van Gogh painted people at their humble repast, denizens of poorhouses, old men, mail carriers, women neither beautiful nor rich, barges, worn-out boots, cane-seated chairs, dreary night cafés "where you can go insane and commit crimes," third-class waiting rooms, hospitals, and, of course, the mental asylum. The anxiety of the rootless, homeless human being, born of a sense of the emptiness and meaninglessness of life, found lasting visual expression in van Gogh's work.

For van Gogh, painting a person or object no longer meant giving a faithful reproduction of appearances. His concentration of form, agitation of line, and intensification of color not only suggested an exterior world shaken to its foundations, but also reflected his own, extreme experience of the anxieties and fears of the period, which broke out of him with explosive force. This is the source of the tremendous disquiet that permeates van Gogh's œuvre. Unlike Impressionism, his is an art that radically questions the culture from which it emerged, that transcends the traditional value system of moral and aesthetic categories. And unlike the Impressionists, and even Gauguin, van Gogh is no longer concerned with beauty, but with truth alone. Truth is found neither in palaces nor on Tahiti; it is found on the streets of Arles, in the faces of plain people, even in the mental asylum.

The Last Dutch Master

The imagery of this last of the "Dutch masters" in the wake of Rembrandt has none of the static calm of the art of his friend, Gauguin. It is dynamic. Everything seems in perpetual motion. The process of painting becomes a dramatic act, and its record is still there on the canvas for all to see. An early example of Action Painting, in other words, though done under quite different circumstances from the "dripping" of a Jackson Pollock or the gesticulations of the latter-day Wild Painters or Neo-Fauves. The traces of making remain evident in the finished work, since van Gogh made no attempt to smooth down his convulsive brushstrokes or sweeps of the palette knife, or to blend the pure colors squeezed out of the tube direct onto the canvas. His pictures are unretouched. For him, technique and mastery of the craft were a means to an end: "Let us try to plumb the mysteries of technique so deeply," van Gogh wrote to van Rappard, "that people will crowd around and swear to heaven that we have no technique."

Such words illustrate the stance of this extremely unclassical artist to whom perfectionism was entirely foreign. His attitude is also reflected in the commonplace, disregarded things he chose as motifs. As he wrote in 1883, he even considered using materials from a junk

Vincent van Gogh
Starry Night, 1889
Oil on canvas, 73.7 x 92.1 cm
New York, The Museum of
Modern Art, Acquired through
the Lilly P. Bliss Bequest

pile "as models." A direct path leads from such decisions to the present-day treatment of materials in art. Van Gogh's humble, empty wooden chairs are distant relatives of Joseph Beuys's *Fat Chair* (p. 553). Not virtuosity but expression, the communication of subjective emotion, was the aim of van Gogh's work. The passionate individualism of a great and lonely man beset by self-doubt shaped this œuvre. Every slashing stroke of the brush or pen eloquently attests to this.

Despite the unleashed color in his paintings, to which he gave an unprecedented luminosity, van Gogh was above all a gifted draftsman. It is primarily the energy of his line that lends his work its eminently expressive force. Especially in his later years he drew and "spoke" with color, and not only in the black of the contours. Now, line, as it has no volume, can be called the abstract element in visual art. Any painting style that is dominated by line will tend to abstraction. Even van Gogh once toyed with abstraction, though he soon abandoned the idea. "When Gauguin was in Arles," he wrote to Emile Bernard, "I let myself, as you know, be tempted into abstraction once or twice, in the 'Berceuse' and the 'Woman Reading a Novel.' At the time abstraction seemed an interesting path to me. But that is bewitched ground, my friend! And in no time you run up against a wall."

It was not such fleeting experiments in abstraction that marked the significance for the future of van Gogh's art and personality. Rather, it was the autonomous, formative and deformative power of his line, his ability to combine untrammelled expression with decorative appeal, that strongly influenced his followers (sometimes to their own detriment) from Jugendstil to the social-critical artists of the 1920s and 1930s. Perhaps the most moving homage ever paid to a father of modern art was that paid to him by Francis Bacon. The British artist's series of van Gogh variations is painterly evidence of a rare affinity of spirit that overleaps the barrier between past and present centuries (p. 331).

Van Gogh's yearning for redemption, his suffering from the world as it is, his final yielding to the self-destructive forces that lurk within us, what Paul Klee called his "exemplary tragedy," the fire of his palette – all these made the Dutch artist a forebear of European Expressionism. "When no one else knew how to go on, he found a wide road for the future," said Pablo Picasso. This future is our present day.

"It is the excitement, the honesty of a man of nature, led by nature's hand. And sometimes this excitement is so strong that one works without noticing it – the strokes of the brush come in quick succesion and lead on from one to the next like words in a conversation or letter. Yet one should not forget that is not always so and that in the future too many despondent days without any inspiration will follow." VINCENT VAN GOGH

World Art from the Provinces
Paul Cézanne: the Primitive of a New Art

One of the pioneers of international modern art was a man who lived in the provinces of southern France, and who only left the country once – to visit western Switzerland just across the border, in 1891. His name was Cézanne. The decisive phase of his career, whose effect is still undiminished today and whose influence hardly any major twentieth-century artist was able to avoid, played itself out largely at a distance from the busy metropolis of Paris. It was the period when Cézanne painted in the rural seclusion of Aix-en-Provence, outdoors, "in front of the motif": Mont Sainte-Victoire (ill. right), which he had in front of his eyes every day; at the country estate of his parents, Jas de Bouffan, which he inherited and later sold (ill. below); in the immediate vicinity of his house in the Château Noir; outside his studio in the Lauves hills north of town; and in the Bibémus quarry. Cézanne painted Provencal peasants and petty bourgeois, and painstakingly arranged still lifes.

In early years Cézanne travelled widely through France. That his work found no favor with the academic judges was almost obligatory for a pioneer of the new vision at the end of the nineteenth century. It hurt him as deeply as the continual rejection of his pictures by the selection committees of the official Salon exhibitions, as the end of his friendship with the author Emile Zola, or the denial of the Cross of the Legion of Honor. The naturalistic writer instinctively rejected the aesthetic, anti-illusionistic tendency of the new approach that emerged ever more clearly in Cézanne's work.

In the figure of the painter Lantier in his novel *L'Œuvre* (The Work), a counterpart to Balzac's *Chef-*

Paul Cézanne
House with Red Roof. The Premises of Jas de Bouffan, c. 1887
Oil on canvas, 73.5 x 92.5 cm
Germany, private collection

d'œuvre inconnu (The Unknown Masterpiece), Zola gave a scarcely veiled portrayal of his former friend as a negative hero, a failed artist whose theorizing had ruined his creative powers. The author's misunderstanding precisely marked the break between an illusionistic art that conscientiously describes reality and a non-illusionistic painting "parallel to nature" as envisioned by Cézanne. In coming decades his approach would paradoxically lead, as Walter Hess notes, "from the most humble inquiry into nature ... to 'abstract' painting." Cézanne himself sensed the profound changes that were soon to take place in art. "Perhaps I came too early," he said to his friend, the young writer Joachim Gasquet. "Someone else will do what I have been unable to do. Perhaps I am only the primitive of a new art."

The Painter as Constructor

"Réalisation" was the concept most crucial to Cézanne – the realization or achievement of his own ideas of form, inspired by an immediate confrontation with nature, but without slavish reproduction of appearances. His aim was to achieve harmony, but not a harmony that was given *a priori*. The harmony Cézanne strove for had first to be "constructed," and instead of denying the existence of tensions between divergent forces, it would reconcile such contrasts by means of "the right placement of color gradations," or in other words, through conscious design.

By his own testimony, Cézanne wanted to be a "classical" artist. Yet it would be mistaken to view his retiring personality and the time-transcending serenity of his art, which was intended to make visible "a timeless existence divorced from genesis and decay," as evidence of a lack of feeling or temperament. His wild and uncontrolled early work, influenced by the southern French painter Adolph Monticelli, with its depictions of murder, revolt, rape, and orgiastic wish-dreams, reveals that Cézanne was basically a Baroque, passionate man. At the mercy of a overrich imagination and tormented by an inferiority complex, he was incapable of overcoming his innate shyness and difficulty in meeting people. It took an incredible amount of self-discipline for Cézanne to subject these chaotic impulses to the order of his will. As so often in art history, the originality of his style was able to develop only in resistance to an apparently predestined path. The Baroque component in Cézanne's character becomes entirely clear when he enthuses, in face of the pictures of the great Venetians, especially Tintoretto and Paolo Veronese, "All tones interpenetrate, all forms revolvingly interlock. This is coherence."

No one after the Venetians of the 16th century was more exclusively a painter than this college-educated, middle-class, patois-speaking citizen of Aix. Drawing interested him only in so far as it contributed to painting. Cézanne's aim was nothing less than to transform the world into an image on canvas. The means to this end was not line but color. "Nature is… not on the surface," he said, in a typical and compelling blend of sober objectivity and pathos, "it is in the depths. Colors are an expression of these depths on the surface. They rise from the roots of the world."

"My Canvas 'Joins Hands'"

In order to give shape to the world in a landscape, in a bowl of fruit, a group of anonymous people, or in a portrait, Cézanne first had to organize color according to strict laws. In contrast to the Impressionists, he did not attempt to visualize the reflection of light *from* the surface of things but light itself as manifested *in* the colors of things. The charm of atmospheric effects left Cézanne cold. His art was devoted not to the changing appearances of the outside world but to its unchanging being or essence; instead of capturing the fleeting moment it strove for permanence.

Although his brushwork, like the Impressionists', had a finely articulated "molecular structure," it did not dissolve forms, having the effect not of nervous dispersion but of calm concentration. Cézanne built up his pictures with infinite patience, in a process, according to Gasquet, in which twenty minutes might pass between one brushstroke and the next. He gradually brought contrasts into harmony, until a dense, gapless weave of colors had emerged. When he was satisfied

with the result, "My canvas 'joins hands,'" he would say. "It holds firm."

This wonderfully characterizes Cézanne's deductive working method, progressing gradually from the small to the large. A fine texture now replaced the hitherto usual composing of a picture by establishing contours, volumes, and spatial relationships. Cézanne's pictorial architecture provided the source of abstract art, from the Platonistic geometry of the Cubists to the monochrome painters of recent days, who like Cézanne, do not compose a painting but weave it out of fine textures, like a tapestry. Every one of the French artist's pictures is like a world unto itself. Crossed tree branches, a boulder, a wall, or a house facade mark the limits of this world; we as viewers remain outside. We are not drawn into the image as we are into pictures based on an illusion of perspective depth. This fact points to the autonomy of Cézanne's painting. It is not dependent on nature, but, as he himself said, exists "parallel" to it, a creation of equal value, based on its own laws. Such visual barriers as the ones just mentioned even occur in the still lifes and portraits. The edge of a table, an easel, or a palette shut off the world of the picture from the world of the viewer. The effect is further underscored by Cézanne's waiver of depth relationships and plastic modelling. The pictorial space is defined solely by rich and subtle gradations of incorporeal color. Instead of using paint to *model* figures and objects, he *modulates* the paint with the aid of half and quarter tones as a composer modulates his theme by changes of key.

2 The World as Symbol

The Art of the Initiates
Symbolism and its Consequences

Artistic styles that were heavily dependent on content, on ideas, were long out of fashion after the last war. It was not until the rediscovery of the Pre-Raphaelites, of the Nabis, of Gustave Moreau and Arnold Böcklin, that symbolism in the widest sense began to gain a more just appreciation. Despite its sources in the Romantic era, the Symbolist movement met with great distrust on the part of a generation that had been surfeited with ideology in art, especially in Germany. Although the reaction is understandable, it is not just. For without Symbolism and its practitioners modern painting would look very different; nor, in fact, would there be an autonomous art of the kind we know.

Symbolist painting goes back to two disciples of Gauguin, Paul Sérusier (ill. right) and Maurice Denis (ill. below). It was anticipated in the work of the idealizing neoclassicist Puvis de Chavannes, and in that of Odilon Redon, the first "modern" painter of supernatural and subconscious themes. From Paris and France Symbolism spread to Switzerland, informing the work of Ferdinand Hodler, and to Norway, influencing that of Munch. The notion of a pure and absolute art cropped up as early in Symbolist painting as it did in the

poetry of a Mallarmé or Verlaine. The visual image was considered independent of reality, self-contained and self-explanatory; that is, reflecting nothing but the subjective ideas of its maker. Color and form were used to translate thoughts and sensations into visual terms. It is one of the numerous paradoxes of art history that it was precisely this bond between idea and image that lent the painting a previously unprecedented degree of autonomy and independence of the natural model.

It was also a Symbolist, of all people, who said, "One must remember: a picture, before it is a warhorse, a nude woman, or some anecdote or other, is first and foremost a flat surface covered with colors in a certain order." These revolutionary words were uttered by Maurice Denis as early as 1890. Art therefore need not, as the German naturalistic poet Arno Holz maintained, have "the tendency to be nature again." It can be a creation based solely on intrinsic principles, corresponding to the artist's imagination and subject to his will to form.

Historically, Symbolism was a reply to the increasingly materialistic and mechanized life of the burgeoning Industrial Age and to the empirical, naturalistic art that uncritically reflected this development. The visual "nationalism" of Impressionist art was countered by the Symbolists with an emphasis on spirituality and an acceptance of the mysteries of existence. *Intuition*, introspection and inspiration, became the new magic word of the *Initiés*, the initiates of Symbolism, who rejected mere *artistry*. The major group in the movement, founded by Sérusier in 1888, called themselves "Nabis," a Hebrew word meaning "enlightened one" or "prophet". The creative power of imagination once again came into its own. The Romantics had earlier believed in it.

The practice of art again received a metaphysical consecration. William Blake and Philipp Otto Runge, in close contact with the poets and philosophers of the period, had already spoken of "symbolic color" and "pure forms." Runge, like the poets Novalis and Ludwig Tieck, realized that interrelationships existed between mathematics, music, and color in art. His painting *The Lesson of the Nightingale* (Hamburg, Kunsthalle) was intended to be the same thing "as a fugue in music." In his studies for the unfinished cycle on *The Times of Day*, Runge developed an enigmatically coded picture-writing, symbolic hieroglyphs, which would be taken up

Maurice Denis
The Muses or In the Park, 1893
Oil on canvas, 171.5 x 137.5 cm
Paris, Musée d'Orsay

by later artists. Already in the early 19th century the Romantics sought a way to bridge the gap between mind and matter, the spiritual and the perceptual, between ideal and reality.

The alienation of the individual from society had begun. Gifted and dissatisfied loners withdrew ever further from an increasingly commercialized world; artists, who saw themselves as belonging to the elect, set themselves off from "the madding crowd." The gap between artist and audience grew apace.

The Enigmatic World

All of this was a consequence of an increasing sense in the 19th century of the inadequacy of scientific explanations of the workings of nature and society. Too much still remained an enigma. Previous bases of social consensus, from religion to common sense, had begun to crumble away. Only the individual could hope to find some solution for the problems of life, alone in his study or studio. This was the source of the private, even hermetic character of art and the artist's life in the Romantic period. The artist came to be seen, and to see himself, as an elect person, a seer or prophet; and consequently art became a surrogate religion, a development that sooner or later could not help but lead to art for art's sake. Capar David Friedrich painted a ghostly ship, called *Hope,* stranded in a sea of icefloes (Hamburg, Kunsthalle).

European nihilism and the melancholy of the modern artist had their roots in Romanticism, which in in turn largely anticipated the philosophy of Symbolism and the course of its representatives' lives. With Gauguin the night thoughts of the Romantics burgeoned into a nausea with civilization. Rimbaud no longer mourned the loss of paradise, instead offering his readers the experience of *A Season in Hell.* Baudelaire wrote a book of poems called *The Flowers of Evil.* With him the Romantics' sufferings at the state of the world turned into a surfeit, a deadly ennui in face of it all.

The Symbolist painters, rediscoverers of the Romantic arabesque, the music of color, the symbolic form, developed in different directions. Some, like Sérusier and Denis, although they were artistic disciples of the heathen Gauguin, became the founders of a new ecclesiastical art in a Catholic vein. Another, the Belgian painter Jan Verkade, joined the artists' brotherhood in Beuron Monastery. Hodler, the Swiss, adopted a more secular artistic ethic, beholding solely to the human individual, the society in which he lived, and the history that had shaped it. Art, he believed, should fill existence with beauty, which would make people better and more capable of living in peace with each other.

Hodler embodied the idealistic strain within Symbolism, for he believed with unshakeable naivety that art could be a universal language, understandable to all and therefore capable of reconciling nations. For artists like Hodler, art was meaningful only when it fulfilled a social function, not when it attempted to be self-

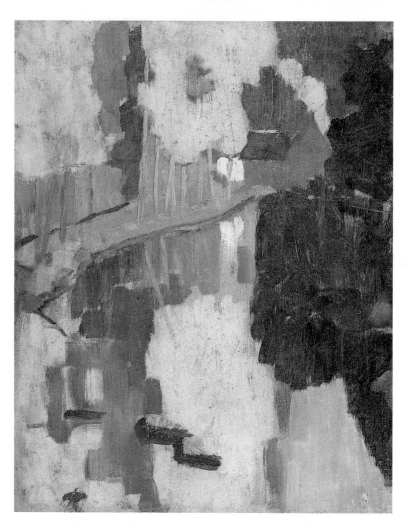

sufficient. Other painters, such as the incomparable colorist Bonnard and his colleague Vuillard, although they too originally belonged to the Nabis circle, took a less sentimental, more skeptical view of the mission of art.

Attempts to improve the world and religious zeal were equally foreign to them. And they were foreign to Marquis Henri de Toulouse-Lautrec. On withered legs that had been injured in a fall from a horse as a youth, Lautrec explored his personal version of Rimbaud's hell in the bordellos and sleazy cabarets of Montmartre. The scope of Symbolist art originally reached from Toulouse-Lautrec's reports from the demi-monde to Sérusier's devoutly spiritualized imagery. It cannot be gainsaid that the painters who turned most radically away from the original Symbolist idea of redemption through art produced work which, in terms of quality and significance, outstripped the meaningful but often sweetly decorative paintings of their religious counterparts. Today Sérusier, whose brilliant philosophical mind was already appreciated by his fellow-students at the Paris Academy, and Denis, the co-leader of the Nabis, are valued perhaps less as painters than as thinkers and theoreticians who sparked a renascence of ecclesiastical art.

Félix Vallotton
Bath on a Summer Evening, 1892
Oil on canvas, 97 x 131 cm
Zurich, Kunsthaus Zürich

Symbolism, unlike German Expressionism or French Cubism, was not a movement striving for stylistic unity, but a mental and spiritual attitude that permitted many variants. It stands as proof of the absolute superiority of France – that is, of Paris – in the art-historical situation at the close of the 19th century. The French metropolis was not only the production plant and market for the naturalistic, empirically oriented arts but the center of the Symbolist reaction against their hegemony. The movement began in 1891, with the first exhibition of Impressionist and Symbolist painting at a newly opened gallery, the Le Barc de Boutteville.

Art becomes Literary

Again the pendulum swung back to a literary art. Symptomatic of this development was the cooperation of visual artists with a spate of new and important journals, *Plëiade, Décadent, Vogue, Plume, Mercure de France*, and *La Revue Blanche*, which published the graphic art of the Symbolist painters. The art dealer Vollard published a series of now-famous deluxe books, limited editions to which both the worldly and pious Symbolists alike contributed illustrations. Henry van de Velde, Dutch artist and Art Nouveau architect, he too an adept of dynamic, sinuous line, ornament and arabesque, designed the editorial offices of the *La Revue Blanche*. An occasional visitor there, by the way, was a taciturn man from the far north of Europe by the name of Edvard Munch.

The sharp contrast between Impressionist and Symbolist art theory is well-illustrated by the statements of

Albert Aurier, an admirer of Gauguin, published in *Mercure* in 1891: "The work of art must be, firstly, 'ideational'; secondly, symbolistic, because it expresses an idea in forms; thirdly, synthetic, because it describes these forms and these signs in a generally understandable way; fourthly, subjective, because the object is never considered an object per se but rather as a sign for an idea which is expressed through the object; fifthly, decorative, because the original decorative painting, as practiced by the Egyptians and very likely also by the Greeks and primitive peoples, is nothing other than a simultaneously subjective, synthetic, symbolistic, and ideational manifestation of art."

One can see that the Symbolists too had their venerated ancestors. Under the generic heading of "traditionalism" they interpreted Egyptian, ancient Greek, and early Italian Renaissance art in an arbitrary manner suited to their own needs. The concept of the decorative, understood to mean simplified forms enlivened by arabesque contours and a color harmony of pure and broken hues, received a considerable re-evaluation. Again artists, true to Verlaine's demand that poetry be "music above all else," began speaking of "notes" and "chords" in painting, as Gauguin had done before them and as Kandinsky would subsequently do. Unlike many a later purist, the Symbolists were not ashamed to admit that art could be ornamental, even though it was primarily idea. Thus it was very much in conformance with the Symbolist aesthetic that the applied and graphic arts, not highly valued by the academies, experienced a new flowering.

The long forgotten and only recently rediscovered Swiss artist Félix Vallotton (ill. left), a highly intelligent man with a fine sense of design whose style combined a moderated Art Nouveau sinuosity with a subtle color range, helped revive the technique of the woodcut. The art of lithography was brought to an unprecedented peak of perfection by Toulouse-Lautrec and others, the tradition of tapestry-making was revived, and poster design became an art in its own right. Surpassing the fly-sheets and copper engravings of earlier days, the new graphic arts brought greatly improved possibilities of producing and distributing quality works of art and publications.

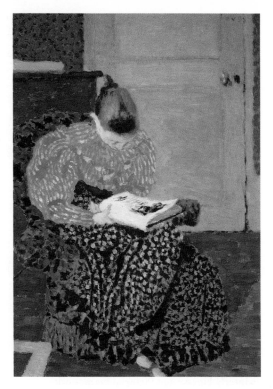

Moreover, the Nabis and Symbolists now received the mural commissions for which a Gauguin had waited all his life in vain. Vuillard was asked to decorate the Palais de Chaillot in Paris, near the Eiffel Tower, and the Palace of the League of Nations in Geneva, a project to which Denis also contributed. The formal approach of the Symbolist artists was perfectly suited to fresco paint-ing: a simplification of form to the point of conscious "primitiveness," and a preference for expansive, two-dimensional, depthless planes of the kind found in Japanese prints or Egyptian art. Despite their emphasis on heightened color and arabesque contour, which they took to the verge of Expressionist distortion, the Sym-bolists strove for aesthetic harmony, an "abstract" order within the depiction. To this extent they kept the her-itage of Cézanne and Seurat alive in their art, despite the very different aims they pursued. Gauguin's former Pont-Aven disciples Sérusier and Denis announced their return to the religious wellsprings of art: mysti-cism, legend, allegory and dream. They also maintained ties with the more or less dubious sects and groupings of the period, whether cabbalist, theosophical or occult, including the Rosicrucians and their Richard Wagner cult. As in the preceding Romantic era, the wisdom of the East once again attracted followers, and artists pro-claimed their allegiance to the *Elan vital* described by philosopher Henri Bergson, the superiority of intuition over intellect.

In sum, the entire epoch yearned for redemption. Many artists and poets, like the drinker Paul Verlaine, fled into the saving arms of the Catholic church. Yet Symbolist painting in France managed to escape a "gothic" look, with its proliferation of detail and vague-ness. Its structural framework remained lucid, coherent, and disciplined. This was due not least to the artists' adoption of mystical numerology, their revival of the "sacred proportions" which already in the Middle Ages had led to a combination of clarity of thought with med-itative absorption, and which appeared to the devout artists to represent the ideal form of an *imitatio dei*, or imitation of God. Their reverence for the right angle, the horizontal and vertical as "pure axioms of the spirit," anticipating Piet Mondrian and the aesthetic of De Stijl, also played a key role in the maintenance of pictorial order.

Pierre Bonnard
Female Nude in the Bathtub,
c. 1937
Oil on canvas, 94 x 144 cm
Germany, private collection

Pierre Bonnard
The Breakfast Room, c. 1930/31
Oil on canvas, 160 x 113.8 cm
New York, The Museum of
Modern Art

Page 27:
Pierre Bonnard
The Toilette, c. 1908
Oil on canvas, 119 x 79 cm
Paris, Musée d'Orsay

Painterly Finesse and Pictorial Framework

Bonnard and Vuillard, who founded the Nabis after Sérusier's visit to Gauguin, have best withstood the test of time precisely because they soon ceased to conform to the group's doctrinaire principles. Their compositions are highly daring, revealing the influence of Japanese prints – indeed Bonnard was titled the "Nabis très japonard." They love apparently random but actually carefully calculated overlappings of form, and often cut off objects and even the limbs and heads of figures at the canvas edge. This lends their pictures the charm of the accidental, without jeopardizing the harmony of an art of extreme sophistication and exquisiteness.

Vuillard's style is consciously two-dimensional (p. 25). Its planar decorum and rich ornamentation, emphasizing the rare and exquisite, often lends his paintings the appearance of a fine tapestry. Bonnard, taking his cue from the late Monet, developed Impressionist color to the peak of refinement. His palette is subdued yet retains a vibrant intensity. Landscapes, figures, and objects appear as if behind a diaphanous veil, their shimmering contours rendered in subtle gradations of hue, the whole suffused by an incredible range of values, an exciting glissando of color. A wonderful cool blue, a richly gradated white are contrasted to luminous warm color chords. The art of Bonnard, the retiring former lawyer, has a tantalizing grace, exudes an irresistible but never cloying perfume, which is counterpointed by a decisive and daring composition derived from Degas and rife with significance for developments to come. In contrast to the Impressionists, Bonnard did not paint spontaneously (pp. 26 f). He corrected his pictures again and again, sometimes working for years on a single painting or series of paintings without ever being satisfied with the result. Yet his art has all the carefreeness and seeming effortlessness of a Mozart symphony. It celebrates leisure, the pleasures of the good life; it shows beautiful people surrounded by beautiful things, a world apparently unburdened by cares or labor. But again, the lyricism and charm of these idyllic "moods" were the result of endless, self-critical, even pedantically obsessive effort.

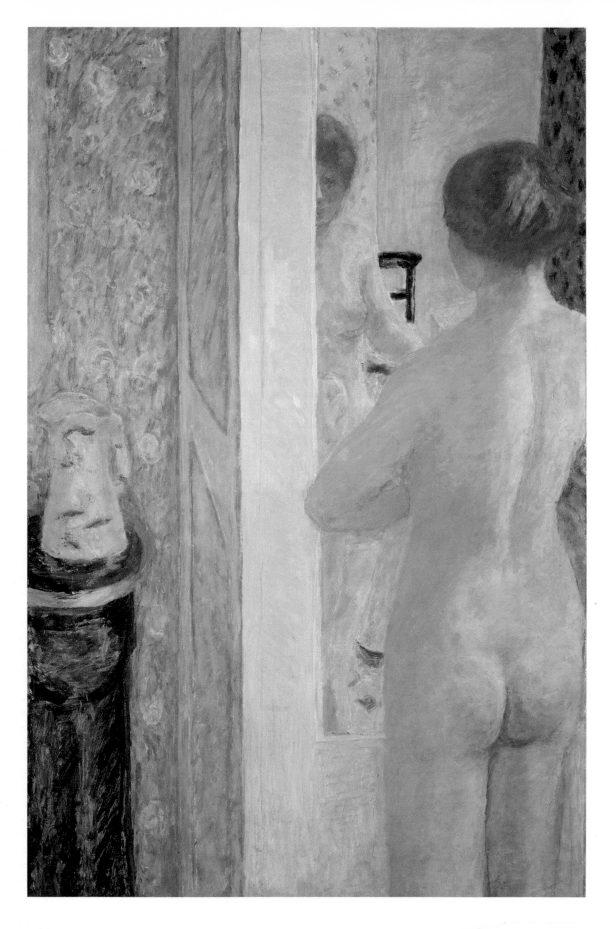

Bonnard did not stop at correcting pictures that already hung in exhibitions or even museums, clandestinely, if necessary. His apparently so unrevolutionary, unobtrusively tranquil painting was a late blossoming of the French cultivation of the medium, and yet it was also full of potential for the future, as the shy, retiring artist was evidently aware. "The abstract is a component of art," Bonnard said, and summed up his experiences in the proud yet modest statement, "The path is open, but the work of art still remains to be created." This bourgeois *intimiste* was not the unoriginal Post-Impressionist successor which for decades he was considered to be. In the quality of their *peinture*, Bonnard's pictures need not fear comparison with those of the great Matisse, and in their visualization of ideas by means of a balanced asymmetry of pictorial framework, they early anticipated things to come.

A Closed Society
Henri de Toulouse-Lautrec and the World of Montmartre

"Nothing for it, nothing for it, I must play the deaf mute and batter my head against the walls – yes – and all for an art that eludes me and will never encompass all the terrible things I have endured for its sake… Ah, dear grandmother, you are wise not to give yourself over to painting as I do. It is worse than Latin if you take it as seriously I do."

HENRI DE TOULOUSE-LAUTREC

The lives of most of the Symbolist painters took a different course from those of the poets of the period – the morbidly melancholy Baudelaire, the Rimbaud who abandoned poetry for the active life, the alcoholic Verlaine. But for one painter, Henri Marie Raymond de Toulouse-Lautrec (ill. below), life was truly "A Season in Hell". Much as the label would have angered him, he too was a Symbolist, if not in the sense of holding to any rigid aesthetic or ideological doctrine. He was a Symbolist in the sense that all of the figures he painted or drew – prostitutes, *grisettes*, singers, dancers, dandies, apaches, pimps, gentlemen about town – we "representative" of a certain type of person, products of an era that was on the verge of discovering the dubious, absurd aspect of human existence. In the feeling of having been abandoned by God, people let themselves go, plunged into sin and licentiousness, for a greed for life is the reverse of a fear of life.

The painting of this man, who suffered by proxy the fate of his own and the succeeding generation, is great, precise, and clairvoyant art. In it the expressive force of the linear arabesque was put in the service of the depiction of human character. Toulouse-Lautrec jettisoned the historical and mythological ballast that had

Henri de Toulouse-Lautrec
A Dance at the Moulin Rouge,
1889/90
Oil on canvas, 115 x 150 cm
Philadelphia (PA), Philadelphia
Museum of Art, The Henry
P. McIlhenny Collection in
Memory of Frances P. McIlhenny

encumbered previous figurative art. He was inspired by
the Modern Style, the English source of Art Nouveau
and Jugendstil, but he far transcended its self-conscious
play of line, its tendency to the sheerly ornamental, and
its programmatic symbolism. Toulouse-Lautrec's paintings, drawings, and posters are suffused with reality,
based on precise observation. In his skilled hands the
denizens of Montmartre, the cabaret and circus people,

the habitués of bars and bordellos, are transformed into
symbols of themselves. Toulouse-Lautrec's art is simultaneously realistic and symbolic. The figures are
stripped of accidental detail and reduced to the essence
of character. Though sometimes verging on caricature
or even overstepping the line, these figures, for all their
individuality, have an emblematic presence. They are an
essence distilled from reality by a great artist.

Ferdinand Hodler
Night, 1890
Oil on canvas, 116 x 299 cm
Bern, Kunstmuseum Bern

Art as a Philosophy
Ferdinand Hodler: Swiss Symbolist

Born into a tradesman's family in Gürzelen, canton
of Bern, Hodler left home at the age of 19 and went to
Geneva, in French-speaking Switzerland. His art, intellectual, laden with problems, and rather heavy-hand-
edly symbolic, was destined to have almost no echo in
France. In Germany, on the other hand, it was readily
taken up, especially by the Munich Circle of Symbolists
around the poet Stefan George. This is not surprising in
view of the fact that in the land of poets and thinkers,
painting has always involved a deal of cerebration. Hodler
occasionally went too far in this regard. His depth of
thought, his penchant for allegory and tendency to mys-
tify life and organic processes, almost spoiled the effect
of the very paintings he considered his best: *Spring*
(Essen, Museum Folkwang), *Eurythmy, Dialogues with
Nature, The Chosen One* (all Bern, Kunstmuseum), and
Gaze into the Everlasting (Basel, Kunstmuseum).

This was the entire impressive series that had begun
in 1890, with *Night* (ill. above). In an extreme heightening of the Romantic notion of symbolic form, Hodler
here transformed form itself into an ideology. Through
symmetry of composition, a parallel arrangement of

figures in vertical or horizontal rows, a palette rife with
symbolic meaning, a rhythm of dignified movements,
a contained passion of facial expression, and a serene
pathos, he attempted to achieve a new and convincing
monumentality. Hodler sought to unify the sensual with
the spiritual in his art.

"Parallelism," the technique Hodler developed to
create monumental effects by sparing means, without
having to resort to masses of figures, perhaps cannot
entirely convince a contemporary eye, which tends to
see only the forced look of the poses. Nonetheless, the
Swiss artist demonstrated that monumental history
painting free of academic sentimentality was indeed
possible at the beginning of the twentieth century. Also
significant are Hodler's portraits and his light-flooded
late landscapes, melancholy views of Alpine nature without a sign of human life. The soaring mountain ranges,
the parallel bands of water, land and sky that seem virtually to continue beyond the canvas edge, convey the
grandeur of the wide open spaces and possess the force
of form and line reduced to the essence and cleansed of
all anecdotal detail.

*"Light in the evening is a harbinger
of the night. In a picture, one can
add to this light and I act according
to the logic of this law of a unified
light. I did not want to render a
night effect, but rather a more general, deeper feeling."*
FERDINAND HODLER

3 The Break with History

Youth Wipes the Slate Clean
The End of the Historical Definition of Art

"Thus some artists believed they could find a new source of ornamentation, or even the lost principles of modern style, in various linear combinations. These attempts seem to have been inspired to a certain extent by the graceful, wary movement of Japanese line, which has so happily influenced linear ornament. Without a doubt, in the decorative arts drawing has experienced an enrichment in new kinds of linear coils and developed a manner, in which can be found something of the charming pliancy and sound decorative understanding of oriental motifs." MARCEL BING

No one would think of judging the artistic style of our own period by looking at the design of the subway entrance on the next corner. Around 1900 people did just this. Those who visited the Paris World Fair at the start of the new century and prepared to descend the stairs to the Métro had before their eyes an example of the formal language of a new art. The cast-iron ornamentation of the recently installed Métro entrances contained in a nutshell the unified opposites out of which the style had been shaped. Known as Art Nouveau in France, the Modern Style in England, its country of origin, and Jugendstil in Germany, where it came to full flower, the style combined a playful use of plant-like, intertwining lineatures with an appreciation of the fitness of the materials to the design. Floral ornament burgeoned during the early phase of Art Nouveau. The later, more geometric phase, dominated by the outstanding personality of the Belgian artist, designer and architect Henry van de Velde, marked its end. The generic term for the style in the German-speaking countries derived from an important illustrated magazine, *Jugend* (Youth), published from 1896 by Georg Hirth in Munich. The name is itself a kind of statement of principle. It embodies the carefree freshness of the innovative stream of art that set out to expose what Friedrich Ahlers-Hestermann called the "stylistic masquerade" of the 19th-century Historical Revival styles. All over Europe it wiped the slate clean, sweeping away knickknacks and furbelows of the Victorian variety in England, of the Wilhelmine variety in Germany, and

of the post-Napoleonic variety in France. In Spain, with Antoni Gaudí, it brought forth a neo-Baroque renascence in architecture. Everywhere it cast off the burden of traditions to proclaim a new beginning. The link between art and publishing points to the literary element in this youth movement in art, which laid claim to creating not only a new aesthetics but a new ethics as well.

Social Reformers

Art Nouveau set itself the task of radically changing the human environment. The young artists wanted to fill the world with beautiful things, and to fight for the maintenance of individuality in the face of an increasingly technologized society. Technology was to be "humanized," machines were to be made the servants, not the masters, of man. At the beginning of the century the protagonists of Art Nouveau already tackled an issue that still concerns us today: how to bridge the gap between artist and audience, between individual and society. They too showed a penchant for the Gesamtkunstwerk, a comprehensive work of art that would take effect on everyday life, indeed that would make life itself a work of art, an idea from which a direct path leads to Joseph Beuys's postulate that everyone is an artist.

The pacemakers of the Art Nouveau movement were originally painters. But indicatively they soon turned to architecture or to the previously so belittled arts and crafts, in order to facilitate the dissemination of their ideas. They became builders and designers, van de Velde of Belgium, Joseph Maria Olbrich of Vienna, August Endell of Munich (whose influence led beyond Art Nouveau to Kandinsky), the northern German Peter Behrens, the southern German Richard Riemerschmid, and their many followers. Hermann Obrist, a natural scientist who studied sculpture, even found his specific form of expression in embroidery. This choice of medium illustrates the paradoxical blend of social utility and elitist exclusiveness that characterizes the style. "We must use the snob in order gradually to reach the people," stated the painter Otto Eckmann. His credo sheds light on the problematic nature of the entire movement, for by the time Art Nouveau actually came "to the people", it had been distorted almost to the point of unrecognizability by manufacturers of mass products who speculated on its popularity.

Adolf Hoelzel
Abstraction II, c. 1913/14
Oil on canvas, 52 x 61 cm
Stuttgart, Staatsgalerie Stuttgart

"I am not interested in myself as the 'object of a picture'. In this respect, I am more interested in other people, particularly in women, and even more in other appearances. I am convinced, that I as a person, am not especially interesting. When you look at me, you see nothing special. I am a painter who paints day after day from morning until night. I paint figures and landscapes, seldom portraits." GUSTAV KLIMT

Gustav Klimt
The Kiss, 1907/08
Oil on canvas, 180 x 180 cm
Vienna, Österreichische Galerie
im Belvedere

Yet even more than in painting and drawing, Art Nouveau came into its own in architecture and interior design. With the Darmstadt artists colony of 1899, the first Gesamtkunstwerk encompassing city planning, architecture, sculpture, painting, and applied art was conceived and realized. The most original talents of Art Nouveau would have nothing to do with the easel painting, which to them seemed the quintessence of an elitist and hermetic art for art's sake. Similar considerations would later be aired in the program of the Weimar Bauhaus. Indicatively, it was an architect, Walter Gropius, who was nominated as director of the new school of art, and that on recommendation of van de Velde.

Art as a Surrogate Religion

In Germany especially the ideological weight that Art Nouveau was expected to bear finally brought it to its knees. What was basically an honorable and well-meaning attempt to completely redesign the human ambience, including finding the best possible form for household appliances, ultimately issued in a development that, for all its beneficial results, proved incapable of resisting the onslaught of kitsch. The movement finally ended in a mass production of pseudo-Art Nouveau products that discredited the style for decades to come. However, this should not be allowed to blind us to the immense historical significance of the Modern Style and its continental offshoots. Not only did it give the *coup de grâce* to the endless historical revivals of the late 19th century (what Karl R. Popper terms "historicism"), but it replaced them by a new, independent sensibility to form, born of the spirit of the contemporary age, and by so doing it paved the way for revolutionary directions in modernism. In England the development, inspired by John Ruskin and William Morris, who themselves revived aspects of past art, especially Gothic, had already come to a standstill by the time it was peaking in Germany. British artists, perhaps more conservative in attitude, sought a compromise between tradition and innovation; the reformers remained at bottom artisans, and they rejected the machine as the destroyer of handcrafted quality goods. In consequence, the English aesthetic reforms petered out before they had hardly begun.

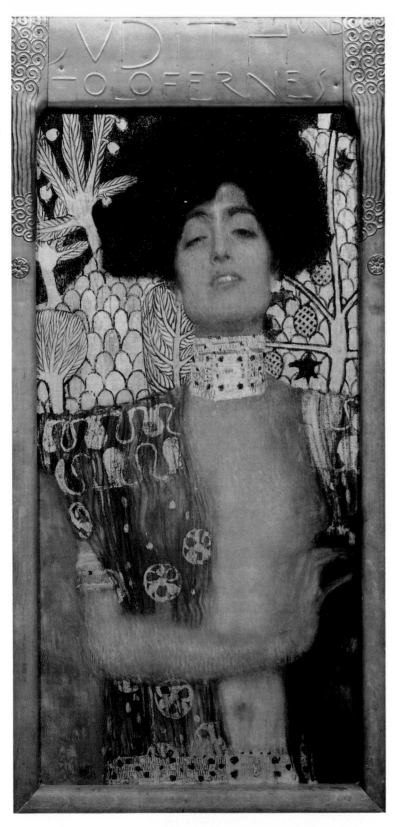

Gustav Klimt
Judith I, 1901
Öl auf Leinwand, 84 x 42 cm
Wien, Österreichische Galerie
im Belvedere

They invented a new brand of planar ornamentation, which initially depended largely on the natural forms of plants and flowers but which gradually developed towards abstraction and autonomy, while at the same time taking on more sculptural volume. Van de Velde provided a tectonic structure for the style. In general, Art Nouveau described a path from a contemplative and amusing glass bead game with free forms to a constructivist seriousness and utility. It would lead to the stark buildings of Adolf Loos, the Viennese Secession architect, who proclaimed that ornament was a crime. Other artists of the movement had begun to dream of a public that no longer asked about the "motif" or "subject matter" of a picture but were ready to lose themselves in the mellifluousness of line as in the melodies of music. The painter Adolf Hoelzel (p. 30) began to think about a theory of harmony as applied to colored forms, and he also experimented with black and white figurations transformed entirely into ornament.

The affinities of Art Nouveau with contemporaneous French painting are obvious. The formal language of the style was not exhausted in the sophisticated, hothouse late Mannerism of the English illustrator of Oscar Wilde's *Salome*, Aubrey Beardsley. It also appeared, as suggested above, in the sinuous flamelike play of line in van Gogh's cypresses, and in Seurat's and Toulouse-Lautrec's arabesques. Many major artists of the late 19th and early 20th century were influenced by Art Nouveau.

The Perfume of the Vamp

An important and highly idiosyncratic variant of the new style emerged with the Viennese Secession, founded in 1898 by Gustav Klimt, who was the most gifted painter in the group (pp. 31 f). This great decorative artist, whose proliferating paintings and subtle, supple, erotic drawings stood in sharp contrast to the purist architecture of his fellow-Secessionists Loos and Otto Wagner, was the first and most significant depictor of the manhunting vamp, the *femme fatale* of the *fin de siècle*. Klimt's sensuous female figures embedded in rich ornamentation studded with gold and jewel-like colors represented the type of the courtesan, which would find widespread dissemination with the advent of film. One might even say that if Renoir created the popular image of the Parisian woman, that of the vamp was created by Klimt.

Yet Klimt's depictions entirely lack the existential seriousness, the passion sometimes pitched to the point of hate, which the theme "woman" took on with an artist like Munch. Klimt's sophisticated world, with its atmosphere of drawing-room wildness, influenced the young Oskar Kokoschka, the Austrian Expressionist and belated heir of the Baroque. Art Nouveau prepared the ground for the growth of many considerable talents and a few major painters, but it did not itself really produce any. This fact points up the greatness and the limitations of the movement that emblazoned on its banners "Youth!" and "New!"

In the other countries of Europe the movement away from tradition took place all the more rapidly and radically, if with varying results. Artists discovered the expressive potential of the organic, freely curving line.

James Ensor
The Entry of Christ into Brussels
in the Year 1889, 1888
Oil on canvas, 258 x 431 cm
Malibu (CA), The J. Paul Getty
Museum

Masquerades
The Haunted Realm of James Ensor

In November 1949, a lonely old man died at the age of almost ninety in the attic of his house in the fashionable Belgian resort Ostend. James Ensor, son of a Flemish mother and an English father, had outlived the major phase of his work by nearly five decades. By the time the once-derided painter of ghostly masquerades, a latter-day heir of the Netherlanders "Hell Breughel" and Hieronymus Bosch, received a knighthood from the Belgian royal house at the age of seventy, Ensor's visionary force had long deserted him, and he had become a reclusive eccentric.

Ensor's fantasies are records in painting of a profound anxiety that pervaded the art and lives of many artists around the turn of the century. His work is suffused by deep skepticism in the face of a materialistic world. With the sensitivity of a seismograph Ensor registered the cracks in the glossy surface of a prospering bourgeois society which would soon tumble into the abyss of the First World War. His demons, grinning skeletons, and eerie masks were omens of approaching disaster. In *The Entry of Christ into Brussels in the Year 1889* (ill. above), the apocalypic imaginings of the artist, translated from personal experience into general terms, take on exemplary form. Like the painter himself in many of his portraits (ill. right), the figure of Christ is surrounded by masqueraders who attempt to pull him along with them as the crowd streams towards us out of the picture. These are bourgeois ghosts, normal everyday citizens revealing the brutal, snobbish, demonic or macabre side of their nature, accompanied by a skeleton, a mummer of the devil with his retinue in train.

Reality dons a mask, becomes wierd and strange, the ground is pulled out from under the artist's feet – isolating him, leaving him alone with his mistrust of the real world around him, and with an anxiety that causes him to see nothing but death and decay everywhere. The

"Oh, one must see them, the masks beneath our great opal sky! Smeared with horrible colors, moving wretchedly, their backs crooked, pathetic figures, horrified figures, outrageous and shy at the same time, scolding and bickering."
JAMES ENSOR

James Ensor
Portrait of the Artist Surrounded by Masks, 1899
Oil on canvas, 120 x 80 cm
Antwerp, private collection

hues and prismatic reflections of Impressionism, intended to give a perfect illusion of real appearances, were made to serve the ends of a non-illusionary, and disillusioned, art. As the world around him grew darker, Ensor's palette grew brighter. But if we look more closely, we see that this brightness consists of myriad gradations of opalescent hues that suggest the colors of decay and putrefaction, processes that are also evoked by the increasingly loose, disintegrated texture of the painting surface. The light in these pictures seems bleached, producing a pastel tonality that is occasionally heightened by accents of bright, disturbing yellow and harsh, toxic red. Even in face of Ensor's most beautiful paintings and etchings, whose technical mastery recalls Rembrandt and whose themes recall Goya or Jacques Callot, one doubts the wisdom of one's first reaction of spontaneous pleasure. This doubt is justified. Signs of dissolution are even found in Ensor's landscapes. A print like "Peculiar Insects," which the artist has given his own and a woman-friend's faces, anticipates Kafka's nightmarish tale *The Metamorphosis*, in which a salesman, Gregor Samsa, wakes up one morning to find himself transformed into a giant beetle.

Ensor was neither an Impressionist nor a Symbolist. Nor did he found a school, though many Expressionist and Surrealist artists learned a great deal from him. Emil Nolde's ecstatically religious imagery, at least in terms of color scheme, goes back to Ensor just as much as does the masquerade realm in many paintings by Karl Hofer or the invocation of overwhelming inhuman forces in the visions of graphic artist Alfred Kubin. Ensor's hallucinatory art was continually threatened by an influx of dissolution, his brushstrokes disintegrated beneath his hand. Like Monet's *Haystacks* and Turner's watercolors, such paintings as Ensor's *Crushing of the Rebel Angels* (Antwerp, Koninklijk Museum voor Schone Kunsten) belong to the forerunners of Abstract Expressionism and L'art informel.

Redeemer is at the mercy of the raving crowd, a Don Quixote, a tragic fool whose approach is watched with veiled curiosity by the actors on the market stage, for someone *this* unworldly is hard to believe.

As early as Redon (ill. above), an artist saw reality, nature turn demoniacal, as eerie, phantasmagorical creatures emerged from apparently innocuous bouquets of flowers. But what the French artist achieved by "literary" means, Ensor translated into pure line and form. He unmasked society by letting it don the masks of its own choosing, revealing the underlying attitude to life of the epoch in compelling and disturbing imagery.

Ensor employed painterly means developed in Impressionism. This adds another paradox to the many that characterize his art. The luminous, shimmering

Life unto Death
The Crisis of Modern Consciousness in the Work of Edvard Munch

Anxiety can be a spur to creativity, as the work of Ensor shows. That of Munch reflects the crisis of modern consciousness with even greater intensity. In his case, too, the personal experiences of a depressive nature corresponded with the pessimistic basic mood of the era.

Already as a boy Munch was confronted by the death that inevitably closes life's cycle. He was only five when he lost his mother to tuberculosis. A sister died a short time later, and a third became insane. Edvard's father, a melancholy man, was a doctor who treated the poor of Oslo, so misery was a continual guest in the Munch household. The sensitive young man feared to

succumb to the family fate; an aunt suggested that painting would be a good way to take his mind off such depressing ideas. She thereby showed him the way to articulate his oppressive anxiety.

It cannot be denied that Munch's artistic uniqueness, the factors in his work that made him a pioneer of modern painting, were closely linked with his personal circumstances. For confirmation we need only compare the works of his early period, up to 1908, with those he painted after the Danish physician, Dr. Daniel Jacobson, had cured him in a Copenhagen clinic of the obsessions that had led to a near-fatal nervous breakdown.

Suddenly his paintings showed no more despairing
young girls on *The Day After*, no panic-stricken men and
women, no sick children, no dead and dying, no storm-
whipped, darkly ominous landscapes. From then on
Munch depicted only scenes from normal, everyday life,
farmers, fishermen and workmen, horses before the
plow, peaceful stretches of countryside.

Munch had recovered his health and his ability to
cope with life, but this regained power also entailed a
loss of hallucinatory vision and nervous sensibility. Yet
to the end he remained an artist of remarkable expressive force. The caesura in his development did not lead,
as it did with Ensor, to an abrupt decline in imaginative
capacity. Even at an advanced age Munch produced
works as compelling as the self-portrait in which he
depicts himself, tall and emaciated, his face seemingly
already beyond the grave, standing shaky-kneed and
with arms dangling helplessly at his sides next to a
grandfather clock that shows his hour has come (Oslo,
Munch-Museet).

La Boheme in Oslo

Munch had his first lessons with Hans Olaf Heyerdahl
and Christian Krogh in Oslo. Then, in 1885, he travelled
to Paris for a three weeks' stay. By the time he returned
home he had learned the Impressionist technique of
painting in brilliant colors on a white canvas, instead of
on the traditional dark ground. His association with
Hans Jäger, a writer who had shocked the good citizens
of Oslo with a novel so sexually explicit that it was
promptly banned, brought Munch into contact with
Oslo's Bohemian scene. (The city was at the time still
known as Christiania.) The artists there had distanced
themselves as far from the self-satisfied bourgeoisie as
they had in Paris, and they protested against the commercialization of industrial society in a life-style as
unconventional as they could manage.

This period saw a second incident that emotionally
injured Munch so deeply that he never recovered, and in
fact that made him incapable of marriage. The unfaith-

fulness of a girl he loved led him, the tall man with the
chiselled features whose looks fascinated women, to
view females as vampires, and love for them as a fatal
attraction.

The year 1889 found Munch in Paris for the second
time. He went to exhibitions of Impressionist, Neo-
Impressionist, and Symbolist art, and frequented the
editorial offices of *Revue Blanche*, where he met Toulouse-Lautrec. Munch discovered the magic of line,
admired Gauguin's ability to compose in flat planes of
musically modulated color, but did not imitate his
approach. Instead, he transposed the aesthetic insights
gained in Paris into his own, Nordic realm of "nocturnal
brightness," as Werner Haftmann has put it. For
Munch, form was not an end in itself but a means to
translate his visions into painting, to make them manifest on canvas. Munch turned his most intimate and private feelings outwards. But his Paris experiences did provide him with the formal framework within which his
revelatory, confessional art could unfold. French painting saved him from sentimentality, self-pity, and from
submersion in the sheerly literary.

Munch had an especially strong influence on German art. The arabesques of Jugendstil went back to the
curvatures in Munch's painting, such as the waves of
color surrounding the panicked figure in his *Scream* of
1893 (p. 35), which would subsequently be translated into
graphic ornaments. The German Expressionists learned
from Munch to transform their inmost sensations into
painting, to reduce the human figure and the landscape
to essentials shorn of all superficial detail, to subordinate form, at the price of deformation, to the artist's
urge to expression, and to reveal the reality hidden
beneath the surface of things.

Edvard Munch
Puberty, 1894
Oil on canvas, 151.5 x 110 cm
Oslo, Nasjonalgalleriet

Edvard Munch
The Dance of Life, 1899/1900
Oil on canvas, 125.5 x 190.5 cm
Oslo, Nasjonalgalleriet

Expression and Form

The Fauves and their Classic Representative
Matisse and his Circle

They used colors like "bombshells" that would discharge light, said André Derain, one of the painters who figure in histories of 20th-century art under the heading "Fauves", Savages or Wild Men. No wonder Parisians shielded their eyes in horror when they saw the Fauves' first group show, in 1905, in the main room of the Salon d'Automne, or Autumn Exhibition, which had started two years previously.

It was Louis Vauxcelles, the by no means hostile critic of *Gil Blas*, who made the legendary quip, *Donatello parmi les fauves* (Donatello among the savages). By "Donatello" he meant a bland neoclassical sculptor by the name of Marque. The savages whose pictures threatened Monsieur Marque's Florentine-style torso of a child were Henri Matisse, Albert Marquet, Derain, Maurice de Vlaminck, Othon Friesz, Henri-Charles Manguin (ill. right), Charles Camoin, Jean Puy, Louis Valtat, and Georges Rouault. A year later the earnest, always somewhat secretive Georges Braque and the insouciant Raoul Dufy, the Rossini of art, became the final members of the group.

Its spokesman and undisputed master was Matisse. In 1909, four years after the scandal at the Autumn Salon, he formulated his credo: "What I dream of is an art of balance, of purity and serenity devoid of troubling or depressing subject matter, an art which might be for every mental worker, be he businessman or writer, like an appeasing influence, like a mental soother, something like a good armchair in which to rest from physical fatigue." The title of one his early key works, which summed up the experiences of Neo-Impressionism, was borrowed from Baudelaire: *Luxe, calme et volupté* (a title whose literal translation is misleading, and might better be paraphrased as *Beautiful Things, Peace of Mind, and Sensual Pleasure*). These aims can be seen to characterize Matisse's entire œuvre, because they represent a program: creation of art as the highest mental and spiritual form of luxury.

A Culinary Art
How was it possible that a style of painting that had, in Bertolt Brecht's term, "culinary" aims, an art intended not to be "troubling" but to "appease," should have provoked contemporary viewers and critics to such an extent? Their anger was directed not only at the two

Henri-Charles Manguin
Jeanne with Sunshade, 1906
Oil on canvas, 61 x 50 cm
Bielefeld, Kunsthalle Bielefeld

"Fauvism shook off the tyranny of Divisionism. It could not live in too orderly a household. So they broke out into the wild, to use simpler means that would not suffocate the spirit. At this moment, the influence of Gaugin and van Gogh came into play. These were the ideas of the time: constructing with coloured surfaces, searching for intensity through colour effects – the material is unimportant. Light is no longer smothered but finds release in the vibrant interaction of the brilliantly coloured surfaces."

HENRI MATISSE

painters who outdid the savages in savagery – Derain shooting his "bombshells" of color into the audience, Vlaminck, the "barbarian," squeezing the paint straight out of the tube onto the canvas. It was also and equally aimed at Matisse and his paintings *Open Window at Collioure* (New York, John Hay Whitney Collection) and *Woman with Hat* (private collection; both 1905). It was the Fauves' reliance on the elemental, on the effects of pure color independent of natural appearances and on a radical simplification of form, that struck the public as primitive and wild. The exquisite sophistication of the style was beyond their perception.

The blue-violet hat worn by the lady in the portrait (Madame Matisse), topped by a colorful, fantastic feather ornament, the brick-red and cobalt blue hair, the green, yellow and pink face, red and orange neck, green skirt and glove, the upper part of the dress glowing in variations of green, violet, pink and yellow, then the echo of all of these combinations in the expansive, loosely rendered planes of the background – all of this went so far beyond Impressionism, which people had only recently become accustomed to. The wings of the *Open Window* and the bluish-green and reddish-violet

Othon Friesz
Snow in Munich, 1909
Oil on canvas, 64 x 80 cm
Moscow, Pushkin Museum

"This woman, symbolising the eternal woman: a flighty, often fatal bird, going through life with a flower in her hand, in quest of a vague, mostly terrible ideal. Always moving on, treading everything underfoot, even geniuses and holy men. This dance is danced, these mysterious wanderings played out before the staring eyes of gaping death and the executioner with his sword." GUSTAVE MOREAU

Gustave Moreau
The Apparition (Salome),
1874–1876
Oil on canvas, 142 x 103 cm
Paris, Musée Gustave Moreau

walls clearly show how Matisse draws together the dabs and touches of Impressionist renderings of things into broad, comprehensive planes. By the same token, the twining ivy is no longer depicted in a Neo-Impressionist technique but with a loose, ornamental brushwork that presages the arabesques of the artist's late work. The view of the sea with light playing across its surface and the boats on the beach likewise shows a tendency to generous flat planes and concentration of form.

Matisse's admiration for Signac, spokesman of the Neo-Impressionists and president of the Salon des Indépendants, led him to follow him to Saint-Tropez in 1904. The town, yet to be discovered by high society, was at that time still a reasonably-priced idyll for artists with little money. The brilliant sunlight and the luminosity of the sea, they felt, could no longer be depicted by naturalistic means, nor could the means of the now-accepted Impressionism do them justice. "One must give a correspondence to sunlight through a rich, polychrome orchestration, through passionate translations which must always begin with the experience of nature and whose results and theories emerge from an enthusiastic search," Othon Friesz (ill. above) here described the essence of Fauvism. The transformation of reality into aesthetic form merged with the sensibility of the artist. As Matisse emphasized again and again, "I am unable to distinguish between the feeling I have for life and my way of expressing it."

It was their youthful enthusiasm that distinguished the Fauves from their somewhat pedantic Neo-Impressionist predecessors. They painted with greater verve, infusing form with expressiveness. The harmony which Matisse above all, but also the young Derain, strove for even in their storm-and-stress period, was achieved not by subduing color values and combinations but by lending colors emotional values and reducing forms to the simplest terms. A sense of depth and space was now engendered by the color juxtapositions themselves, rather than by perspective devices or *trompe l'œil*. "That was the point of departure of Fauvism," stated Matisse. The paintings of Cézanne provided key impulses. Beginning with Impressionism, the Provencal artist had given color an independent status, while at the same time – in contradiction to the Impressionist aesthetic – pulling the strokes of paint together to form colored fields, and thus preventing it from dissolving into a vague atmospheric evocation.

"I Am the Bridge…"

Gustave Moreau (ill. below), a Symbolist long scorned as a *décadent* and only recently rediscovered, was a hallucinatory dreamer like Redon, but his dreams were inspired not by nature but by the gaslights in his own studio. Moreau is not only recognized as the mentor of the young talents who came to be known as Fauves, but highly regarded as a predecessor of Surrealism. He quickly realized what the work of his pupils Matisse, Rouault and Marquet held in store. "They will simplify painting," Moreau stated, and precisely defined the role his imaginative, anti-positivist stance would play: "I am the bridge over which some of you will go."

Simplification of form did not imply a simplistic approach. Gauguin had shown this with his decorative planes of color, and even Manet, long before, had already ended the compromise between painting and sculpture by emphasing the two-dimensionality of the canvas. The painters gathered around Matisse were, in addition, inspired by the early French "Primitives" and their brilliant color schemes.

Henri Matisse
Luxe, calme et volupté, 1904/05
Oil on canvas, 98.3 x 118.5 cm
Paris, Musée d'Orsay

Matisse and Marquet began to paint in pure colors as early as 1898. For a time the overweening figure of Signac suppressed all other influences. Convinced of his mission to provide a normative aesthetic for painting, he took the fledgling Fauves firmly under his wing. But Matisse, in paying his reverence to Signac's doctrines, simultaneously overcame them. *Luxe, calme et volupté* is a good example (ill. above). The placement of the dabs of paint seems Pointillistic only on first glance. Looking more closely, we see that Matisse's coloration is much more intense and luminous than that of Signac, the silvery shimmer of whose paintings Matisse initially so admired. The greater freedom of his paint application is also evident. Matisse subjects Seurat's and Signac's scientific thoroughness to imagination, breaks the objective rules by putting them to the test of his subjective, personal view. The pastoral scene of the painting – six nude women and a clothed man on a beach – evokes not a timeless Arcadia but a very up-to-date, localizable idyll in the vicinity of Saint-Tropez just after the turn of the century. The composition has nothing in common with Nicolas Poussin's dark, Greco-Roman style arcadias of death. It does, however, possess classical harmony, the horizontals on the far shore replying to the emphatic vertical of the slender tree trunk in the foreground, which in turn is echoed by the mast of the sailboat in the center. The diagonal of the beach in the foreground ties the oppositions together; the counterpoint

of the standing or seated, reclining or moving figures finds an echo in the curves of the bay and in the flowing lyrical rhythm of the hills in the background. This diagonal is repeated several times, in the branches, bands of light, and an inclining mast.

The brilliant mosaic of color is firmly locked in a carefully designed framework, in the spirit not only of Seurat but, and especially, of Cézanne, who literally built his paintings. It was his example that saved the French "Expressionists," with their need to give emotion free rein and their trust in intuition, from falling into sentimentality or formlessness. When the Fauves distorted things or figures, they did so for decorative reasons, not for the sake of sheer emotional expression. They knew very well that Oceanic and Black African sculpture was not a "primitive" art in the sense of being unskilled, but that the distortion found in it was a conscious device.

Cézanne and van Gogh

With Matisse and Marquet, aesthetic discipline was innate. A wonderful early example of this in Marquet's work (p. 40) is his treatment of a theme popular since Monet's days and also addressed by Manguin – that of the flag-decorated streets of France on July 14th, Bastille Day. The nervous rush and bustle of Monet's picture, the ecstatic palette-knife sweeps of van Gogh, have here given way to quiet, lucid planes. The only "savage" fea-

"I never left the object. The object is not interesting in itself. It is the environment which creates the object. Thus I have worked all my life in front of the same objects which continued to give me the force of reality by directing my spirit towards everything that these objects had gone through for me and with me. A glass of water with a flower is different from a glass of water and a lemon. The object is an actor: a good actor can have a part in ten different plays; an object can play a different role in ten different paintings." HENRI MATISSE

Albert Marquet
The Beach of Fécamp, 1906
Oil on canvas, 51 x 61 cm
Paris, Musée National d'Art
Moderne, Centre Georges
Pompidou

ture – from a contemporaneous point of view – is the brilliant colors of the flags, especially the vermilion gleaming against the dark house walls. The composition, on the other hand, is almost geometrically rigorous. (The theme would have to wait for Raoul Dufy to recover the character of a fleeting "impression".)

The case is different with the two Fauves from Chatou, André Derain and Maurice de Vlaminck. Their idol was not Cézanne but van Gogh. The admiration they felt for the Dutch artist for a few years united their very different temperaments, Derain, was the scion of a rich merchant family and humanistically educated, Vlaminck, was a rough fellow, born near Les Halles, whose parents were itinerant musicians. Vlaminck earned his living as a street fiddler, farmhand, novelist and professional cyclist before his paintings began selling well enough to support him. He was the only real "wild man" among the Fauves, and Derain, equally energetic but much more sensitive, found his stormy temperament irresistible. In Chatou color did not blossom, it veritably exploded, in unmixed vermilion, cobalt, chrome yellow, and Veronese green. Throughout his long life – Vlaminck died in 1958 at the age of 82 – he evidently never suffered an attack of self-doubt. In his memoirs, paraphrasing a famous saying of Louis XIV, he coolly declared, "I am Fauvism." Vlaminck had apparently forgotten that, as mentioned, Matisse and Marquet had already begun in 1898 to work in pure colors, and that Matisse was respected by his colleagues as a superior mind who had given Fauvism its aesthetic and intellectual foundation. Painterly instinct played a

Maurice de Vlaminck
Sailing Boat on the Seine, 1906
Oil on canvas, 54.5 x 73.5 cm
Private collection

"Do you know a painter who has invented a color different from those that compose the solar spectrum?"
ANDRÉ DERAIN

André Derain
Drying Sails, 1905
Oil on canvas, 82 x 101 cm
Moscow, Pushkin Museum,
I. A. Morosov Collection

greater role than intellect in Vlaminck's art. And his unpolitical character led to his sympathizing with the Nazis during the Occupation.

"Raphael is the Greatest"

Derain was too astute and well-educated to remain a Fauve for ever. This becomes apparent when we compare his *Boats in Collioure* (ill. right) with the *Rhône Barques* of his idol, van Gogh. Van Gogh addresses the subject with all the rustic directness of a Dutchman; Derain's picture, for all the vitality of its palette, its daring perspective, and simplification of form, reveals a nervous sensibility and a sure taste. The ease and fluency of the brushwork is a fine example of French painting culture. Derain's Fauvist paintings combine the vehemence of a Vlaminck with the culture of a Matisse. The Pointillist technique of dividing colors and the Fauvist technique of making them cohere are blended into a high-spirited and joyous style. Derain's landscapes of Saint-Tropez, Collioure, and London not only belong to the masterpieces of his relatively brief Fauvist period; they also represent the apex of his œuvre. In contrast to the Impressionists, Derain always concerned himself with "the solid, the eternal, the whole", and resisted the Impressionist temptation to be satisfied with shimmering atmospheric effects. This covert classicism, even present in the pictures in which color is completely unleashed, is typical of Derain's art.

André Derain
Boats in Collioure, 1905
Oil on canvas, 60 x 73 cm
Düsseldorf, Kunstsammlung
Nordrhein-Westfalen

Raoul Dufy
Sailing Boat at Sainte-Adresse,
1912
Oil on canvas, 86.4 x 114.3 cm
New York, The Museum of
Modern Art

Georges Braque
L'Estaque, 1906
Oil on canvas, 50 x 61 cm
Private collection

His classical tendencies, if not his final turn to a stylized realism, are already recognizable in Derain's brilliant early work. Like Cézanne to Poussin, Derain professed his allegiance to Raphael. "Raphael is the greatest of misunderstood artists", he declared, "Raphael alone is divine." Following his wild years Derain became a preacher of moderation, proportion and harmony, turning from a revolutionary into a conservative, even into a political conformist who, during France's darkest hours, betrayed not only his artistic but his humanistic principles by sympathizing with the Nazis. But one crucial point is essential to make: Derain was the first European artist to discover the expressive power of African sculpture, which he collected and to which he drew Picasso's attention. This, as we know, opened a new and far-reaching path for modern art.

Music in Colors and Architecture in Painting

Moreau's students and the Castor and Pollux of Chatou were joined in 1905 and 1906 by three further painters: Georges Braque, Raoul Dufy, and Othon Friesz. In the year of scandal, 1905, Dufy saw Matisse's *Luxe, calme et volupté* at the Salon des Indépendants, and thereupon immediately forswore Impressionism, deciding in favor of form over "mood." Dufy went with Marquet to paint in the Le Havre vicinity, while Braque joined Friesz in Antwerp. Dufy's charming art, which in later years would become overly ingratiating and elegant, combines in its best examples the virtues of Impressionism with those of Fauvism. *The Beflagged Street* (ill. right) shows this combination to good effect. The solid arrangement of lucid, carefully juxtaposed planes of color is counterpointed by the lissom depiction of the ebb and flow of life on the street. Dufy's style is always evocative of motion, invariably retaining something of the Impressionist snapshot. It exists on the sunny side of life, reflecting uncomplicated, mundane situations and sophisticated social gatherings and sports with equal ease.

Braque is deeper and has more substance. As decisively as he reveled in pure color at the beginning, he just as determinedly never allowed color to shake his control of his craft. Every brushstroke was carefully considered, every accent of color precisely placed; his compositions, for all their painterly freedom, had a classical balance and harmony. He was more ascetic and rigorous than his friends, and he used his enormous skills with more circumspection. Braque's pictures are always *built*, even when, as in *L'Estaque* (ill. left), he lavishly scatters flecks of color like jewels over the surface. In view of such paintings the transition to Cubism is not as surprising as it would seem when comparing brilliantly colored Fauvist paintings with the reserved greyish-brown hues and formal regularity of Cubist compositions. The possibility of thinking in painting, an idiosyncrasy of the athletic ex-boxer Braque, had indeed been demonstrated by the Fauves, especially by Braque's idol, "Professor" Matisse.

Raoul Dufy
The Beflagged Street,
Le Havre, 1906
Oil on canvas, 81 x 65 cm
Paris, Musée National d'Art
Moderne, Centre Georges
Pompidou

barous era. Living a simple life in the midst of post-war prosperity and luxury, Matisse drew sustenance and joy from his art even in an old age marked by sickness and frailty. When his brush hand would no longer obey him, he began cutting his arabesques with scissors out of paper, as if immersed in a glass bead game.

"I no longer ask whether and how long my works will outlast me," Matisse told Gotthard Jedlicka, who visited him in his hotel room in Cimiez, in the hills above Nice, his retirement home. "What I create, what I shape, has its meaning in the fact that I create it, that I shape it; is fulfilled in the enjoyment my work gives me – my work? My play? I play, and fulfil myself in play; and must a game outlast the player? Isn't its meaning to fulfil itself in itself? The purest player is the child, because it is one with the game. I too play, with the scissors, like a child, and I ask just as little as a child does what will become of the game that gives me such delightful hours." Out of this game, begun because he was no longer able to paint, grew a late work, a manifestation of an outstanding genius independent of medium and tools, his *gouaches découpées*, among the purest and most beautiful imagery in the art of all time (p. 44).

Kees van Dongen
Nude of a Young Girl, c. 1907
Oil on canvas, 100 x 81.5 cm
Wuppertal, Von der Heydt-
Museum

Intelligence and Sensibility

The same clarity of thought, the same "fervor," as Braque used to call his contained passion, informs the work of by far the most outstanding Fauvist and one of the very greatest artists of the 20th century: Henri Matisse. The scope of his creativity only became apparent after the "pioneer period" at the start of the century, at a time when the force of his Fauvist friends' work was not increasing. Without the encouraging atmosphere of the group and its collaboration, the other talents – like most of the German Expressionists in a similar situation – began gradually to produce work of less substance. This is true of the cultivated Marquet, and of the significant loner, Rouault. Another fine talent, Dutch artist Kees van Dongen, even eventually became a fashionable portraitist to Parisian society (ill. right).

For Matisse, on the other hand, the "wild" days were only the overture to a life's work in painting, drawing, printmaking, and sculpture that is one of the supreme manifestations of Western art in the 20th century. Intellectuality and sensuality, inspiration and artistry, color and form, decoration and expression, tradition and contemporaneity, all exist in an exemplary balance in Matisse. He achieved something that only the greatest in art can achieve: Like a tragedy by William Shakespeare or a comedy by Molière, like a Michelangelo sculpture or a Rembrandt painting, Matisse's art speaks equally to the layman and to the connoisseur. It lends pure, spiritual form to the gratuitous beauty of things. Working untiringly down to the final days of his long life, Matisse demonstrated in this century of catastrophes that painting, even after 1900, is still capable of giving people joy. If Renoir can be called the painter of an "unconscious" happiness, Matisse is the painter of a conscious happiness, maintained in the teeth of a bar-

HM 53

Henri Matisse
Spray of Leaves, 1953
Gouache cut-outs, 294 x 350 cm
Los Angeles (CA), Wight Art
Gallery, University of California

Old Truths in a New Light

As described in Heinrich von Kleist's essay, *On the Marionette Theater*, Matisse's work and personality followed a path from knowledge through infinite experience to emerge as a second naivety. The quiet revolutionary never denied the influence that the great masters of the past and non-European cultures had had on his style. In his Paris apartment hung paintings by Renoir and Cézanne, and Courbet's *Young Women on the Banks of the Seine* (Paris, Musée du Petit Palais). He admired El Greco and Rembrandt, the Sienese artists Duccio di Buoninsegna and Piero della Francesca, Japanese woodblock prints, and Manet. Matisse knew that the liberation of color was primarily the achievement of the Impressionists, the heirs of Delacroix. He early recognized the significance of Gauguin for his own development. He paid his respects to the Pointillists Seurat and Signac, he admired Cézanne and revered Redon, whose influence is seen in many a Matisse still life of flowers. Matisse frankly admitted the importance of his confrontation with Islamic art, with Persian miniatures in particular, which helped determine the decor and arabesques of his mature work.

Henri Matisse
Spanish Woman with
Tambourine, 1909
Oil on canvas, 92 x 73 cm
Moscow, Pushkin Museum,
S. I. Shchukin Collection

"The artist only sees old truths in a new light," stated Matisse, "because there are no new truths."

Matisse loved to study and to learn from others. He took Moreau's advice literally, going both to the museums and into the streets. When he was already a well-known painter, reports his German student Hans Purrmann, Matisse continued to attend night courses at a school of decorative art. This stupendous assiduity was the source of his outstanding craftsmanship. Matisse's drawings are like shorthand records of reality. A few contours allowed him to capture the essence of his model. Out of a handful of colored planes and sparing arabesques he would evoke the figure of a musing girl, an interior, the view through a window. In paintings like these the tension between self and world seems to have been overcome. *Joie de vivre*, the title of a painting that made Matisse undisputed leader of the Fauves when it was shown at the Salon des Indépendants in 1906, might stand as a motto over his entire œuvre (Merion, Barnes Foundation). In canvases such as *The Dance, Spanish Woman with a Tambourine, Harmony in Red, Lady in Blue* (pp. 45 f), and many others from all phases of his career, sensations are raised to an art form in its own right.

"I am the Model"

Maurice Denis recognized the originality and rank of Matisse's art at an early date. "What we have here," he wrote in 1905, "is a painting wrest away from all randomness, painting per se, pure painting.... What is going on here is the quintessential search for the absolute."

Matisse found "the absolute" in the ornamental designs of an oriental carpet or in a bouquet of flowers, in a seascape or in the face of a girl, in the sensual, ani-mal magnetism of his odalisques (from whom, by his own admission, he would have taken to his heels had he met them in real life). Matisse already played with abstract form. In this regard he went much further than his German students Hans Purrmann, Rudolf Levy, and Oskar Moll. They adhered closer to the motif, their lyricism was more direct, and they had no qualms about evoking "moods." "I am the model" – this self-confident declaration of Matisse's would never have occurred to them.

Hans Purrmann
Still Life, 1908
Oil on canvas, 80 x 99.5 cm
Berlin, Nationalgalerie,
Staatliche Museen zu Berlin –
Preussischer Kulturbesitz

Purrmann's style combined the decorative with the structural, Matisse with Cézanne (ill. above). The artistic substratum of his career – apart from the superb paper cut-outs – is the Chapel of the Rosary in Vence, the building of which was partially funded by the artist himself. It, too, is a Gesamtkunstwerk, for Matisse not only decorated the chapel but designed it as well. From an early age, the artist did speak of a "kind of religious feeling" he had about life. This feeling found its artistic expression in the symbolically abbreviated wall-paintings of the Matisse chapel, which depict the Passion of Christ, the Virgin and Child, and St. Dominic in contour drawings.

Artistic reason and a Romanticistic sense of order and proportion came to fulfillment and reached the limits of their potential in the œuvre of this scholarly artist, who enjoyed talking about art almost as much as painting.

With the Fauves and their classic representative Matisse, "the solar adventure of modern art", as Jean Leymarie emphatically calls it, began an adventure which nevertheless, as we know, had its dark, penumbral side as well. Before leaving Matisse, a brief note on his sculpture is in order (p. 428). Few as the number of his works in this medium is, they represent much more than a marginal note to his œuvre. In fact, the only major twentieth-century painter to have surpassed Matisse as a sculptor was Picasso.

Victory over "Satan's Sun"

The quintessential painter of the dark side of man, of evil, despair, and decay, but also of pity and redemption, the prophesy of a victory over *Satan's Sun* – the title of a famous novel by Georges Bernanos – was Georges Rouault. He exhibited with the Fauves at the 1905 Salon d'Automne, but despite the aggressiveness of his early work he was not really one of them. He had no wish to be a "renowned luminary of revolt and negation." Like Matisse and Marquet a student of Moreau's, in fact his favorite student, Rouault was the most passionate religious artist of the twentieth century. His protest against the hypocrisy of pre-First World War society and the dry, boring art of the academies was not an exuberant revolt against tradition, no cheerful firing-off of colored bombshells à la Derain or Vlaminck. Rouault's resistance to the status quo had other reasons, rooted in his profound Christian faith.

"Anybody can rebel. But to obey in silence an inner calling, to search lifelong without impatience for the means of expression adequate to us – that is much more

"If there had been beautiful church windows as in the Middle Ages, I might not have become a painter."
GEORGES ROUAULT

Georges Rouault
The Holy Face, 1933
Oil and gouache on paper,
91 x 65 cm
Paris, Musée National d'Art
Moderne, Centre Georges
Pompidou

Georges Rouault
The Old King, 1937
Oil on canvas, 76.8 x 54 cm
Pittsburgh (PA), The Carnegie
Museum of Art

difficult," said Rouault, and he did not speak lightly. He lived and worked according to this insight. The formal concentration and the expressiveness of Rouault's painting were modelled on the late Rembrandt. His seemingly self-illuminated phosphorescent colors, shining through thick relief-like layers of impasto and heavily contoured as if with leading, were oriented towards the stained-glass windows of Gothic cathedrals.

Slatterns instead of Seraphim

Rouault was still far from the religious themes of his later period when he exhibited with the Fauves. At least it appeared so. His paintings, in acid, cool bluish-greens counterpointed by a livid greyish-red and overlaid with brittle grids of blackish-grey, depicted prostitutes, clowns, and – taking his cue from Daumier – the malicious faces of philistines and corrupt judges. Nausea and anger suffuse these significant early canvases of Rouault's, not the cool detachment or indifference with which a Toulouse-Lautrec dissected society. The light that would illuminate the later paintings was still concealed, the artist was still polemicizing, mounting an

attack on the venality and vices of humankind. In this phase of his work Rouault was still more of a social critic in the vein of Goya or Daumier than a proclaimer of Christian redemption.

Icon Painter of a Late Civilization

Rouault's painterly invocation of an ideal early Christianity did not begin until 1930. In a process that frequently extended over years, he applied layer after layer of paint to the canvas until he felt that the right hue had been found. The primary – and primal – hues of green, blue, red and yellow, gripped within black contours like the colored panes of church windows within leading, strive for metaphysical sublimity. Their lavish impasto seems pervaded by deep melancholy. Evening shadows lie over silent landscapes; the faces of the figures are careworn, marked by life's sorrows. The hope of redemption is not announced with the jubilation of glad tidings, but simply stated as a humble expectation. The Christianity proclaimed in Rouault's paintings is a burdensome one, chiliastic, borne up by the belief in the coming of the millennium (p. 47).

Sensation and Ecstasy
Northern German Expressionism

A protest against academic art stands at the beginning of art history in the 20th century. The first revolutionary phase came to an end when many erstwhile rebels were offered teaching posts and themselves became professors at art schools. The eminent German critic Werner Haftmann already cautioned, at mid-century,

against the danger of the emergence of an "abstract academy," implying that abstract art could not be taught without a basis in painting craft, and that any attempt to do so would only lead to a pseudo-revolutionary eclecticism. Similar warnings were expressed by American critic Harold Rosenberg in his essays, "The Tradition of the New".

Many a student was astonished when his or her teacher, an acknowledged pioneer of modern art, assigned drawing from life as the first step towards becoming an artist. But though the fact has long been overlooked, the teachings and practices of the past were not without meaning for the leading personalities in late-19th and early-20th-century art. They learned from them, and their protest against them – or against their all-too dogmatic application – formed the precondition for their life's work. This statement holds not only for art since the Impressionist period. It holds for the realist, Courbet, in France, as it does for the German idealist who worked in Rome, Hans von Marées. It also applies especially to Käthe Kollwitz, the socially critical, expressively naturalistic denouncer of proletarian mass poverty, genocide, and chauvinism. Kollwitz's passionate empathy, her motherly yet harsh commitment, lends her graphic art an affinity with Munch. Her expressive style, for all its naturalism, points forward to German Expressionism, at the beginning of which stands the figure of another, very young, motherly woman, who, a few weeks after the birth of her long-awaited first child, left

"A great simplicity of form, that is something wonderful. I always tried to give the heads that I painted or drew the simplicity of nature. Now I have a deep empathy for how I can learn from the heads of antiquity."
PAULA MODERSOHN-BECKER

Paula Modersohn-Becker
Self-Portrait with an Amber Necklace, 1906
Oil on canvas, 62.2 x 48.2 cm
Basel, Öffentliche Kunstsammlung Basel, Kunstmuseum

this world at the age of only 31 with the words, "How sad." This was Paula Modersohn-Becker (p. 48 and ill. right).

Though a native of Saxony, Paula Modersohn-Becker belongs for art historians in the context of the artists' colony of Worpswede, a village near Bremen in northern Germany. It was here that a new, lyrical landscape painting emerged, in reaction to the hectic and increasingly inhumane milieu of the industrial cities of the period. The artists' protest took the form of a retreat. In the midst of the noise and smoke of a world in the making, they sought an island of calm, accepting reality only in those aspects that conformed to their romantic, youth-movement ideals.

One of the artists active in Worpswede was the landscapist Otto Modersohn. Paula Becker would marry him in 1901. Modersohn, at the time more famous than she, was the only one who recognized her talent at an early date. Paris, as it had for the young poet Rainer Maria Rilke, became the second pole of Modersohn-Becker's life. She marvelled at the lucid planes in Gauguin's paintings, at the energy of the contours, the musicality and glow of his palette. Yet despite her admiration for him, for the self-taught painters of Brittany, and for Böcklin's nature symbolism, Modersohn-Becker felt intuitively drawn to the formal rigors of Cézanne. Little by little she worked to make the forms in her painting cohere into flat planes, inexorably turning away from romantic charm and Impressionist "atmosphere". She reduced the "natural" appearances of landscape and figure to their formal essence; she emphasized her tectonic planes of color with strong outlines. Modersohn-Becker had ceased to describe things and had begun to express them. The aspects of the Worpswede style that remained alive in her work reflected the caring side of her nature, her love of the simple life and of plain people, of whom she felt herself one. Her personal feelings, her love, her desire for a child, and the universal themes of fertility and motherhood, accordingly became the principal subjects of her art. "Sensibility" was transposed into painting, albeit in a more subjective way than Matisse envisaged. Thanks to her unsentimental, generous, rigorous sense of form, the subdued glow of her colors, and an honesty of feeling that prevented her work from ever growing cloying, the small number of major paintings that Paula Modersohn left to posterity, especially her self-portraits and pictures of children, have a simplicity and immediacy of presence that sometimes recalls the magic of Egyptian portraiture.

The Northern German Eccentric

Emil Nolde was the outstanding representative of a new, expressive art that emerged in northern Germany. Not that he himself attached any importance to such labels. A farmer's son from Schleswig-Holstein, the most northern of the country's provinces, all he wanted to be was a painter, and obstinately to go his own way. It was destined to be a long and rocky road, and when it

seemed that every obstacle had been overcome, Nolde himself erected new ones. He had arguments with the influential art dealer Paul Cassirer and the eminient critic Meier-Graefe; he missed no opportunity of making himself disliked. Nolde railed at the French and the Jews, despite his own depictions of Christ, his disciples and figures of the Old Testament as Jews in his religious paintings, and he let his German nationalism be known at every opportunity. Yet Nolde felt ill at ease among people. At the same time he suffered under his own isolation, which only his first wife, the Danish actress Ada Vilstrup, shared with him tenaciously despite protracted illness. Not even the company of like-minded artists was something Nolde could stand for long. He left the Dresden Brücke group after only a year and a half. His naive hope that the National Socialists would appreciate his art, which he felt was truly and essentially German, rooted in the soil and nourished by the lifeblood of his rural homeland, was cruelly disappointed. In 1937 Nolde found himself in the company of the "degenerate artists" vilified by the Nazis. His paintings were removed from public collections and sold off for a pittance. Finally he was officially forbidden to paint at all.

There is no other German painter whose medium for the depiction of appearances and emotions was so exclusively color. Emil Hansen, a native of the village of Nolde, took on the name of his birthplace after his marriage in 1902. Nolde pretended to despise the Impressionists who came after Manet. Yet his first major paintings of flowers and gardens were little else than a dramatized and intensified continuation of the Impressionist treatment of color, a translation into German, as it were, in which van Gogh played the role of intermediary. This implied a turning away from the decorative

Paula Modersohn-Becker
Seated Nude with Flowers, 1907
Oil on canvas, 89 x 109 cm
Wuppertal, Von der Heydt-Museum

"I want the to give colors intoxication, fullness, excitement, power By trying to forget Impressionism, I wanted to conquer it. In the process I was conquered. We must work with assimilated, digested Impressionism."
PAULA MODERSOHN-BECKER

Emil Nolde
Whitsun, 1909
Oil on canvas, 87 x 107 cm
Berlin, Nationalgalerie,
Staatliche Museen zu Berlin –
Preußischer Kulturbesitz

"Colors, the painter's material. Colors in their essence, crying and laughing, dream and happiness, hot and holy, like songs of love and eroticism, like hymns and magnificent chorales. Colors vibrate like the silvery pealing of bells and bronze tones. They herald happiness, passion and love, soul, blood and death." EMIL NOLDE

outward charm of Impressionist painting in favor of a passionate introversion, or, in psychological terms, a cathexis with the things that struck his eye. Yet Nolde would have to become almost 40 years old before he had developed his technical means to the point of being able to paint what moved him and be satisfied with the results.

At the beginning of his path towards an original style stood an interior, sumptuously painted in delicate gradations a little in the manner of Bonnard and showing Ada reading in the center, a surprisingly tender homage to his beloved wife with the allusive title of *Spring in the Room* (1904; Neukirchen, Stiftung Seebüll). In the subsequent period Nolde's color, not uninfluenced by his "Brücke" friends, experienced an extreme heightening of intensity. His floral pictures contained final reminiscences of the subdued, tone-in-tone values of the Dachau "landscapists" with whom Nolde had worked, and of Franz von Stuck, the idol of Munich, whose allegories, however, now ceased to interest him. But even these works represented only a transition. Nolde's finest achievement, as he himself knew, came with his series of religious depictions. It began in 1909, and with two major works at that: *The Last Supper* (Neukirchen, Stiftung Seebüll) and *Whitsun* (ill. above). The nine-part altar painting *The Life of Christ* (1912; Neukirchen, Stiftung Seebüll) and the triptych *Maria Aegyptiaca* (1912; Hamburg, Kunsthalle) marked the cul-

mination of the theme. By way of *The Tribute Coin* (1915; Kiel, Kunsthalle), *The Philistines* (1915; Essen, private collection), *That Ye May Not Become as the Children* (1929; Essen, private collection), the series led to *The Great Gardener* of 1940 (Hanover, Sprengel Museum), which brought a surprisingly lyrical note into the late work.

Ecstatic Religiosity
In these canvases an ecstatic religiosity breaks through, an emotion whose fervor goes back to the influence of Matthias Grünewald and whose psychological penetration derives from Nolde's admiration for Rembrandt. The sublime and the grotesque, the sacred and the profane, despair and transfiguration exist side by side in these works as in the paintings of the medieval "Primitives."

Nolde's violent and conscious barbarism comes out even more strongly in the secular figurative compositions, which depict dancers and pierrots, dubious characters from Berlin nightlife (ill. right), and men and women living out their animal instincts. Demonic masks, inspired by Ensor, lend destructive primal forces visual presence. The compelling power of Nolde's approach is also manifest in the paintings of lonely marshes, dunes, clouds and sea. His express aim was "a new evaluation of nature, with the infusion of personal soul and spirit." The medium for this was heavy impasto

paint, which embodied that "primal-utterance character" of nature spoken of by Wilhelm Worringer, a leading German art historian, in connection with Expressionism in general. What took shape here was not
"beautiful, purified nature but the enigmatic, unarticu-
lated reality which never loses the threatening character
of being haunted by spirits."

The blood-and-soil miasma rising from some of
Nolde's paintings still awakens unpleasant associations.
Not all of his works give a satisfactory answer to the
question of artistic mastery of the forces of chaos. Yet
the most beautiful imagery this artist gave to the world
will certainly survive: his watercolors painted on damp
Japan paper, with their diaphanous veils of interflowing
colors. In the best of these, floral subjects and landscapes, Nolde's strength blends perfectly with aesthetic
delight and a masterful technique.

Christian Rohlfs

Late watercolors also marked the culmination of the
work of another artist from Holstein, Christian Rohlfs
(ill. right). His long career, which belonged both bio-
graphically and artistically as much to the late nineteenth as to the early 20th century, is an indication of the
fact that Expressionism was not the result of arbitrary
individual decisions but represented a Europe-wide
movement.

Christian Rohlfs
House in Soest, 1916
Tempera on canvas, 80 x 100 cm
Private collection

Emil Nolde
In the Café, 1911
Oil on canvas, 73 x 89 cm
Essen, Museum Folkwang

A fall from a horse, tormenting years of being bedridden, followed by the amputation of his right leg, made Rohlfs incapable of taking up farming. His father finally agreed to let him try to make his way as an artist. Rohlfs's earliest work was in the *plein-air* mode, a very noble and solidly crafted landscape art in the tradition of the *paysage intime* of the school of Barbizon in France and The Hague in the Netherlands. This was the favored style around the turn of the century in Weimar, where the young artist came of age.

Rohlfs was 48 years old when he discovered his interest in Impressionism. The ensuing paintings were suffused with dramatic passion in the manner of van Gogh. The "script" of his brushwork grew grainier, heavier, more dynamic – in a word, more expressive. *Birch Woods* of 1907 (Essen, Museum Folkwang), done at the age of 58, records the artist's transition from the rendering of an *impression* to a striving for *expression*, from Impres-

sionism to Expressionism. Though here the borderline was still vague, soon the decision would be made. The impulse came from Nolde, whom Rohlfs had met in Soest in 1905. There emerged a series of vibrantly colored cityscapes with church spires, depictions of farmhouses, and – again influenced by Nolde – compositions with Biblical figures. Though Rohlfs never succumbed to Nolde's fervency, he did often similarly distort figures to the point of grotesqueness. As he grew older, his work gained in artistic discretion in proportion to its decline in visionary force. Rohlfs's paintings possess a strange, shimmering translucency. Towers and walls seem no longer able to rely on their own stability, begin to waver, to disintegrate. This instability corresponds to the vibrato of the color. It embodies a striving for spirituality, but at the same time it represents a sign of growing doubt about the solidity of the foundations on which the world rests.

The Struggle for a New World
The "Brücke" Painters and their Utopia

In 1905, the same year as the public uproar over the Fauves in Paris' Salon d'Automne, four young men in Dresden founded a group called "Brücke" (Bridge), planting the seed of German Expressionism. Their names were Fritz Bleyl, Erich Heckel, Ernst Ludwig Kirchner, and Karl Schmidt. They were later joined by

Ernst Ludwig Kirchner
Potsdamer Platz, 1914
Oil on canvas, 200 x 150 cm
Berlin, Nationalgalerie,
Staatliche Museen zu Berlin –
Preussischer Kulturbesitz

Page 53:
Ernst Ludwig Kirchner
The Red Tower in Halle, 1915
Oil on canvas, 120 x 90.5 cm
Essen, Museum Folkwang

Max Pechstein and Otto Mueller, and, for a time, by Nolde. The four had come to Dresden to study architecture at the college of technology there. In their spare time they painted and drew, with an enthusiasm inspired by Nietzsche and his *Zarathustra* (from which the group's name also derived) that initially stood in for solid training in art. They started from scratch, refusing to consider attendance at an academy. On the other hand, they had no Moreau as mentor to support them, nor a Pissarro to provide understanding and encouragement. Just the opposite: Corinth, who was more of an Expressionist than an Impressionist even in his mature years, denounced the new style with a complete misjudgement of its essence as "un-German" and "intellectualist".

What brought the Brücke painters together and kept them together for eight years, until they dispersed in 1913, was a belief in a new brotherhood of man, a solidarity which only young people, artists in particular, could bring about. Only in a commune, by collective effort, thought the Brücke artists, could the storms of the period be weathered, could a plan for a new and better world, indeed a new type of human, be conceived and implemented. Van Gogh had already dreamed of such an artists' commune, and had temporarily been able to interest Gauguin in the idea. But finally the obtuseness of his contemporaries, the strong individualism of French artists, and the eccentricity of his own personality, doomed his attempts to failure.

What van Gogh and Gauguin had not succeeded in doing 17 years previously in Arles came to pass in an

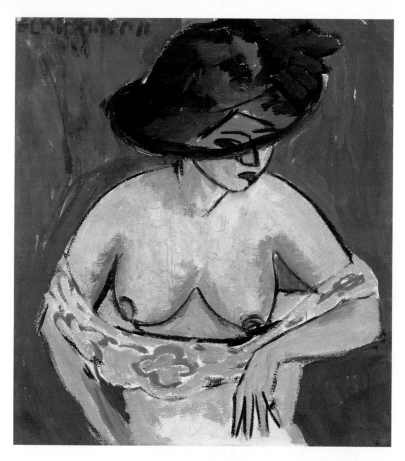

Ernst Ludwig Kirchner
Female Half-Length Nude
with Hat, 1911
Oil on canvas, 76 x 70 cm
Cologne, Museum Ludwig,
Haubrich Donation

*"My wife always says that I never
again accomplished another
painting like this of a woman, and
here jealously plays a slight role,
because there are also some very
beautiful nudes of her. But perhaps
she is right insofar as in this painting
for the first time a profound love
for the female figure comes forward,
and such a thing can happen only
once."*

Ernst Ludwig Kirchner

empty shoemaker's shop on Berliner Strasse in Dres-
den-Friedrichstadt, which Heckel had converted into a
studio. The four friends not only collaborated in their
work, they lived together and shared their daily chores
and cares. The impetus that bore them up had its source
in this sense of community. Left to themselves, none of
them would have had the power to touch off this powerful movement. For decades, admittedly, observers and
critics abroad, whether French or American, considered
German Expressionism a Gothic-Teutonic aberration,
a violent would-be art that lacked every sense of fine
execution and formal balance. Now that this view has
been honorably corrected on both sides of the Atlantic,
the enthusiasm for the *Furor teutonicus* in painting has
reached such a level that for a time even the generation
that could have been the Expressionists' grandchildren,
the Wild or Neo-Expressionist painters, were swept
up in it.

Expressionism in the broader sense is a timeless
phenomenon in art. It is found among the Pacific
islanders and the Aztecs, in Africa and in Gothic cathedrals, in medieval manuscript illuminations, in Grünewald and El Greco. Spiritual depth and a link with
the metaphysical, the invisible and intangible, have
characterized German painting and sculpture from its
earliest days. But this is only part of the story. German
Expressionism at the beginning of the century was a
committed art. In literature even more than in the

visual arts, it was closely allied with the revolutionary
socialist movement. In contradistinction to most Neo-
Expressionists of the 1980s, the original Expressionists
not only wanted to create art, they set out to create a
new ethics.

In other words, German Expressionism was
political at its source. This statement holds especially for
the poets and writers who strove for reconciliation and
cried in the face of a spreading barbarity, "Oh, Humanity!" But it also holds in the wider sense of the term
"political" for the Expressionist painters. Admittedly
their commitment was less ideologically defined than
that of the writers, not linked with any doctrinare world
view, and for that reason less subject to perversion by
party-political considerations. The utopian ideals of the
Brücke artists were expressed in the visionary terms of
the contemporary youth movement. Kirchner later
desired his name not to be mentioned in connection
with this "silly youth stuff," but in 1906 he thought
differently. "Putting our faith in development and in a
new generation of creators and art lovers," he wrote in
the Brücke manifesto, "we call upon all youth to unite.
We, who possess the future, want liberty of action and
thought with respect to the hidebound older generation. Anyone who honestly and directly expresses what
urges him to create is one of us." These words clearly
indicate what distinguishes the German Expressionists
from their French counterparts, the Fauves, despite all
they share in common. It is a far cry from this militant
youthful idealism to Matisse's epicurean idea of an "art
of balance, of purity and serenity devoid of troubling or
depressing subject-matter."

Where Matisse wished to convey tranquillity and
"detached pleasure," the German Expressionists set out
to excite and incite the public; where the former avoided
the problems of modern life, the latter plunged into
them. The balance for which Matisse strove, the Expressionists set out to upset. Purity seemed suspect to them.
They empathized with the "impure," the miserable and
downtrodden of the earth. They wanted to smash the
old world in order to build a new one from its ruins.
Instead of a new aesthetic, they proclaimed a new,
ethically founded stance. They sought a new and immediate relationship to reality. Their art strove for
inward truth rather than for outward beauty.

The Brücke artists were carried along by the current
of an agitated and exciting era in which one artistic sensation, one discovery followed on the heels of the next.
They admired Munch, especially his woodcuts, though
Munch's pessimism and Strindbergian misogyny held
no appeal for them. Even more they admired the early
medieval German masters, whom Kirchner, as the first,
had seen in Nuremberg. Van Gogh's luminous impasto
colors and sinuous contours confirmed the Brücke
artists in their own expressive urge. From Art Nouveau
they had learned that line was an independent element
with the aid of which subjective feelings and personal
temperament could be visualized. Gauguin's escape

from civilization corresponded to the scorn they felt for a satiated and hypocritical turn-of-the-century society, and his undoctrinaire handling of color and plane impressed them as much as the Neo-Impressionists' analysis of the spectrum. The Brücke painters found their Tahiti in the Dresden Museum of Ethnology, embodied in Black African and Polynesian sculpture. The experience gave them courage to employ distortion as an artistic means.

"For a Humane Culture"

The rapidity with which the characteristic Brücke style emerged is astonishing. The paintings of these temperamentally so different men initially looked very much alike. Their common program obscured the individuality of the Brücke members, whose full freedom and originality would unfold only in the course of the years. Out of the passionate brio of their brilliant, occasionally somewhat slapdash concert of color the personal idiosyncracies of the players gradually emerged. There were the dynamic, primitivistic compositions of Karl

Schmidt, who called himself Schmidt-Rottluff after the town near Chemnitz where he was born. There was the hieroglyphic formal canon of Kirchner, the sensitive professor's son from Franconia. There was the more gentle, lyrical and introspective imagery of Heckel; Mueller's "earthly paradise", which the reticent loner found in Bohemia and Eastern Europe; Pechstein's powerful figurations; and the religious visions of the Nordic Nolde.

No one can remain a revolutionary for life. As Kirchner emphasized as early as 1913, in his chronicle of the Brücke, disagreement over which finally broke up the group, it struggled for a humane culture "uninfluenced by the current streams, Cubism, Futurism, etc." Almost unnoticed by themselves the Brücke artists had become increasingly conservative, and each now decided to stick to the path he had disovered and felt was right. Similar to the Fauves, the elan of storming the barricades of convention could not hold the Brücke together for more than a few years. Agreeing to disagree, the artists went their own ways.

"It is not right to judge my pictures according to the standard of what is true to life, for they are not depictions of certain things or beings but rather are themselves independent organisms, comprised of lines, planes and colors. They only contain natural forms insofar as these are a necessary key to understanding them. My pictures are allegories, not portraits."
ERNST LUDWIG KIRCHNER

Ernst Ludwig Kirchner
Winter Moon Landscape, 1919
Oil on canvas, 120 x 121 cm
Detroit (MI), Detroit Institute of Arts, Gift of Curt Valentin

Loners

Kirchner had set off on his own long before the Brücke disbanded, following a path none of the others could, or wished to take. He was the only one in the group who was not satisfied with the autonomy of color and form they had achieved, despite the fact that for a few years he was strongly influenced by the Fauves and had antedated some of his paintings to prove the innate tie between French Fauvism and German Expressionism. Kirchner's development eventually led him far from what is generally understood under the blanket term "German Expressionism". His art, rife with tensions, contradictions, and audacities, eludes every stylistic label. Despite his temporary identification with the collective, Kirchner was fundamentally a loner. The continual mental strain under which he lived, compounded by the dashing of his hopes in the First World War, the postwar years, and the Nazi terror, brought about a series of nervous breakdowns. In the end, illness and despair caused Kirchner to take his own life in 1938, in Switzerland.

Kirchner's mental state is reflected in the proliferating abundance of visions and configurations in his art, its obvious tendency to the apocalyptic, the harsh incisive "barbarian" of its palette, and in the use of distortion as a means to express passionate emotion. The conscious primitivism is combined in a remarkable way with sophistication of technique and enigmatic, hieroglyphic symbolism. Kirchner's angular, hatched or restlessly sweeping contours, nervous and as if charged with electricity, reveal a tremendous strain between intellectuality and sensuality, a trait that distinguishes his major work very clearly from that of his friends. His career can be seen in terms of two main phases, marked on the one hand by his fascination with the "inferno" of the big city, and on the other by the idyllic if precarious balance between man and nature seen in the forbidding Alpine landscapes of Switzerland, where, after a serious breakdown, Kirchner temporarily found peace of mind in 1915. These two phases were those of his preceding "street scenes" and of his Swiss imagery from 1917 onwards.

Between Heaven and Hell

A key trait of Kirchner's œuvre is its formal reconciliation of opposites and contrasts. His is not a literary or illustrative art. What Kirchner does is translate reality, overt and covert, into forms and colors on the painted surface. In early years, inspired by his somewhat naive belief in the social efficacy of art, he set out to destroy illusion and penetrate to the core of appearances. Superficial beauty was anathema to him. "How fundamentally different is Germanic from Romanic art," he said, falling into the vocabulary of Teutonism. "The Romanic artist obtains his form from the object, from the natural form. The German artist creates his out of imagination, inner vision, and the forms of visible nature are to him only symbols.... For the Romanic artist, beauty lies in appearances; the other sees it behind things."

Kirchner's beginnings still stood under the spell of van Gogh's agitated brushwork and palette-knife technique. As with all of the Brücke artists, Neo-Impressionism, Art Nouveau arabesques, the Nabis Vuillard and Vallotton, even Toulouse-Lautrec, as well as Polynesian sculpture left their traces on his style. Munch also played a role, but less in terms of form and design than in terms of his disquieting moods. All of these influences were amalgamated very early on with Kirchner's own personal approach. Sooner than his friends he found himself, and together with them, out of the ruins of academic conventions, developed the Brücke style with its luminous, expansive passages of color, its emphasized contours, and its lapidary simplifications of form. Kirchner's nervous hieroglyphics began to emerge at an early date. His abrupt changes in perspective, changes of vantage point, sharp overlappings, and compositional audacities in the form of characteristic V, N and X-shaped configurations, also announced themselves. In his renowned 1914 painting of cocottes on *Potsdamer Platz* in Berlin, these features were brought to full mastery (p. 52).

Metropolis and Mountains

The street scenes reveal Kirchner to have been a fascinated and precise observer of big-city life. These paintings, which include the impressive cityscape *The Red Tower in Halle* of 1915 (p. 53), belong to the most superb accomplishments of his career, ranking alongside such masterpieces as *Female Half-Length Nude with Hat* of 1911 (p. 54), the ambiguous *Circus Rider* wonderfully

Karl Schmidt-Rottluff
Farm in Dangast, 1910
Oil on canvas, 86.5 x 94.5 cm
Berlin, Nationalgalerie,
Staatliche Museen zu Berlin –
Preussischer Kulturbesitz

Karl Schmidt-Rottluff
At the Station, 1908
Oil on canvas, 70 x 92 cm
Vienna, Österreichische Galerie
im Belvedere

inscribed in an ornamental oval (1914; Saint Louis Art Museum), and the scathingly frank self-portrait, probably influenced by Heckel, *The Drinker* (1915; Nuremberg, Germanisches Nationalmuseum). A second culmination came later with Kirchner's monumental depictions of the Alpine environs of Davos, Switzerland. His *Stafelalp in Moonlight* of 1919 (Dortmund, Museum am Ostwall) is suffused by a tantalizing magic. Nature becomes demonic, a symbol of itself. The spiritual affinity to Romantic art, especially that of Caspar David Friedrich, is obvious.

This is equally true of *Winter Moon Landscape* (p. 55) of the same year, whose expressive color scheme is very compelling. After the mid-1920s many of Kirchner's paintings begin to take on a rather cheerful air that calls to mind posters or children's book illustrations. Here the limitations of his art become apparent, as does his dogged attempt to visualize in painting such phenomena of the physics of light waves as interference and polarization. The result is a disjunction of forms that inadvertently recalls Picasso, much as Kirchner himself resisted such comparisons; the difference being that Picasso achieved double the artistic effect with half the intellectual effort. The all-too emphasized cheerfulness of some of the late canvases is not entirely convincing, in view of Kirchner's medical history and psychological state. He suffered from a progressive intestinal illness, increasingly oppressive apocalyptic visions ("The angels strewing the plagues from their bowls – aren't they the airplanes dropping gas bombs?"), and recurrent premo-

nitions of death. "Have a lot planned for this summer," he wrote in 1937. "Maybe it will be my last?" It was his last.

Of equal rank with his major paintings are Kirchner's watercolors, drawings, and above all, his graphic art. The woodcuts are among the finest imagery in his entire œuvre. With the aid of this technique Kirchner attempted to curb and lend valid form to the unique, nervous lineatures of his drawings, which had a spontaneous flow akin to handwriting. Kirchner's extraordinary craftsmanship and his love of experiment served him well in this regard, as they did in every graphic medium he employed.

Monumental Landscape
The graphic art of Schmidt-Rottluff, the first in the Brücke group to make lithographs, likewise stands on a level with his painting. The woodcut technique compels an artist to simplify, to eliminate superfluous detail and concentrate on the essentials of a face or a landscape. This is why the woodcut was so well adapted to the Expressionist style in general, and to the energetic character of Schmidt-Rottluff in particular. The one who suggested the name for the group and convinced Nolde to join it, Schmidt-Rottluff had perhaps the most consistent career of all of the Brücke artists, although it cannot be denied that, like them, he did his best work during the early *Sturm und Drang* period of critical engagement with the ills of the era. Beginning with a dramatized version of Pointillism, Schmidt-Rottluff

"I really feel a pressure to create something that is as strong as possible. The war has really swept away everything from the past. Everything seems weak to me and I suddenly see things in their terrible power. I never liked the type of art that was simply appealing to the eye, and I have the fundamental feeling that we need still stronger forms, so strong, that they can withstand the force of the crazed masses."
KARL SCHMIDT-ROTTLUFF

Max Pechstein
The Fishing Boat, 1913
Oil on canvas, 190 x 96 cm
Berlin, Brücke-Museum

developed a monumental, cohesive, symbolic style of landscape painting in which a new sense of nature, derived from a protest against modern urban civilization, found expression (p. 57). Instead of the interesting motif he sought an unsullied natural environment, and found it, with the other Expressionists, in the village of Dangast on the North Sea, in the Dangaster Moor, in Norway, on the Baltic island of Fehmarn, in the hamlets of Alsen and Nidden near the seacoast.

After the First World War Schmidt-Rottluff produced work suffused by deep melancholy and embittered resignation. His *Self-Portrait with Hat* (1919; private collection) is a key painting of Expressionism. The artist has no qualms about extending distortion to include his own features. One eye is large, the other small; one is open, the other as if blind; the face is skewed; the colors are violently dissonant, translating the disturbed harmony into aggressive contrasts. The man depicted here has lost all illusions. He is a marked man, struck to the core by the experience of the first great catastrophe of our century. The optimistic faith in the future of his rebellious years has vanished, to be replaced by disappointment and skepticism. In the

Erich Heckel
Crystalline Day, 1913
Oil on canvas, 138 x 114 cm
Munich, Bayerische Staatsgemäldesammlungen, Staatsgalerie moderner Kunst

course of the years Schmidt-Rottluff's style would grow increasingly tranquil, as a strong tendency to the decorative, influenced by Fauvism, came to the fore. His compositions grew more serene, reflecting a striving for a balance of opposing forces, a harmony. Thus Schmidt-Rottluff gradually became a classical modernist.

Expressionism and Dostoevsky

The retreat into a natural idyll took on even clearer form with Erich Heckel, the most sensitive and melancholy of the Brücke friends. The idea of "vicarious" suffering, rooted in Christian ethics and ecstatically heightened under the influence of Fiodor Dostoevsky, was one of the essential traits of Expressionist literature and art, and it found perhaps its most concise embodiment in Heckel's imagery. The *Two Men at a Table* (Hamburg, Kunsthalle), confined in a tiny room, tormented, mutually distrustful, and suffering, behind them the image of Christ stretched out supine on the cross, is a compelling document of this mental attitude.

The lyrical side of Heckel, whose palette rarely rose to the fanfare of the other Brücke artists, came out most purely in the early landscapes suffused with morning light, as in Crystalline Day (p. 58 below). Heckel perhaps belonged to Expressionism more by historical contingency than by virtue of his personality. Yet a painting like the deserted Canal in Berlin (Cologne, Wallraf-Richartz-Museum) shows that Kirchner was not the only one to master the nervous touch, the "hieroglyphics" of form, and that influence among the Brücke artists during their collaborative years was certainly mutual.

The tranquillity of Heckel's late work in painting and graphics, which, by way of the Neue Sachlichkeit and a decorative Fauvism took on an increasing restraint and balance, seems to confirm the assumption that even the Futurist-influenced passion of the early period reflected little more than a youthful revolt on Heckel's part.

As so often happens in art history, the Brücke artist who enjoyed most contemporaneous success later came to be considered one of its lesser exponents: Max Pechstein. In his paintings the brashness and crudeness of Expressionism seem to lack metaphysical reference, being more straightforward, direct, and intellectually less demanding. Though Pechstein's art has elemental force, it is more decorative than that of his friends, despite the fact that some of the superb achievements of his Brücke and post-Brücke periods can certainly

stand beside theirs. Examples are *Girl in Red under a Sunshade* (Darmstadt, Hessisches Landesmuseum), *The Fishing Boat* (p. 58 above), and *The Green Sofa* (Cologne, Wallraf-Richartz-Museum).

"Gypsy" Mueller

More significance attaches to the thematically limited but formally interesting work of Otto Mueller, whose lyricism enriched the brass band of Brücke color by the haunting notes of a shepherd's flute. Mueller's origins were long shrouded in obscurity. His mother was rumored to have been an "abandoned gypsy child," and he himself, wrote Werner Haftmann, was "short and slender" with the "melancholy eyes of the gypsy." The artist's sister was less prone to mystification. Mueller's mother, she wrote in her memoirs, was "born out of wedlock to a Bohemian servant girl" and later put up for adoption. She was described as a "pretty, brown-skinned Bohemian woman" with "black hair and dark eyes" – no mention of gypsies here.

In 1924 Mueller travelled with his divorced wife and his new wife through Dalmatia and Bosnia. Three years later found him wandering alone through Hungary and Romania. It was here that he made his personal contribution to the time-honored theme of German Romanticism, "man and nature." He lived among the homeless and portrayed their girls in the midst of the countryside, giving them something of the grace of plants, awkwardly innocent and lascivious at once, like

"My art cannot be bought. I will not exchange my feeling for any earthly treasure. Other people might run themselves ragged for money, fame and honor, but I am not taking part in this. I would rather lie on the grass under blooming flowers, let the wind caress me, listen to the hustle and bustle of the people – this gives me strength and amuses me – and dream away the day."
OTTO MUELLER

Otto Mueller
Female Nudes in Open Air,
c. 1920
Distemper on burlap, 86 x 111 cm
Wuppertal, Von der Heydt-Museum

Erich Heckel
Windmill at Dangast, 1909
Oil on canvas, 70.7 x 80.5 cm
Duisburg, Wilhelm Lehmbruck
Museum

Gauguin's Maori women. Sensibility and gesture arise from a simple, unbroken feeling for life and an elemental sensuality. Unburdened joy fills these images of naked children of nature, playing among the dunes, in the reeds, under trees, in the water. Mueller painted with distemper on rough burlap, in subdued, matte colors. This gives his pictures their strangely muted atmosphere (p. 59).

In later years Mueller's palette grew darker. Now he began to portray his gypsies as outcasts and pariahs, dispossessed by destiny and society. In the pictures of lovers the coexistence of sexuality and death, happiness and damnation is emphasized. Gypsy mothers with child and their "providers" are given a nimbus, and thus characterized as relatives of poor Mary from Nazareth in the Bethlehem stall. Religious ideas are transposed into a secular, proletarian context – not always successfully, it must be admitted.

One of the happier results of the Neo-Expressionist wave of the 1980s was that attention was drawn to the sculptures of the original Expressionists, not only to those by sculptors such as Ernst Barlach (p. 413) or Wilhelm Lehmbruck (pp. 414 f) but to those by painters, like Kirchner (p.423) and Schmidt-Rottluff (p.424). Though the great expressive force of these works was pointed out as early as 1931 by Alfred H. Barr, Jr., founding director of the Museum of Modern Art, New York, they had been almost completely forgotten for decades.

A Belated Heir of the Baroque
Oskar Kokoschka: Viennese Expressionist

"How do I define a work of art? It is not an asset in the stock-exchange sense, but a man's timid attempt to repeat the miracle that the simplest peasant girl is capable of at any time, that of magically producing life out of nothing."

OSKAR KOKOSCHKA

Oskar Kokoschka grew up among the circle of Klimt and the Viennese Secession, and owed his first advancement to the architect Loos. He developed into one of the finest portrayers of human beings the century has seen. His early portraits were of an eerie clairvoyance, justifying commentators to describe them, perhaps a bit pathetically but at bottom correctly, as X-ray pictures of the human soul and character. No doubt the artist's own self-tormenting disquiet, a reflection of the disquiet of the age, played a role here, but this alone cannot explain why the portraits have the appearance of painted hallucinations.

Kokoschka's models often refused to recognize their likenesses. "One day he asked me whether he could draw me," reported one of his "victims" in the journal *Kunstblatt* in 1918. "The picture was finished in twenty minutes – but what a picture it was! Three months in jail would not have been too much for the 'damage to my good name and reputation' he caused me. The drawing was published in *Sturm* which was the leading German avant-garde art journal of the day. It was published by Herwarth Walden, a passionate advocate of modernism of every variety who had begun his career as a poet and composer. Walden had brought Kokoschka to Berlin in 1910. It was probably also he who coined the generic term "Expressionism," the first time a new movement had been given a name that was not derogatory in intent.

Kokoschka's 'Second Sight'

Professor Auguste Forel, the famous Swiss natural scientist of whom Kokoschka painted a still more famous portrait in 1910, was another dissatisfied sitter. Neither he nor his family accepted the portrait, and they refused to purchase it. It was especially the "dead" right eye in the scholar's careworn face, and his "convulsed" hands, which gave cause for indignation. Two years later Forel suffered a stroke, which resulted in paralysis of one side of the brain. Kokoschka, with the "second sight" of his nervous sensibility, had quite unconsciously anticipated the disaster. Another man he portrayed, the reviewer and essayist Peter Scher, reported that during the sitting Kokoschka's brush penetrated the surface of his face, producing a "pretty grim-looking" convict's mug. Years previously Scher had actually "sat" in a more unpleasant context, namely in jail, where he had been put for insulting a government minister and where he had had to weave reed mats. Scher had told Kokoschka nothing of this episode, but the artist found out about it nonetheless, as the portrait was being done.

At the time, Gustav Mahler was composing his monumental, brilliantly disjunctive symphonies, which both quoted the past and anticipated the future. Hugo von Hofmannsthal was sadly but presciently invoking the downfall of the Austro-Hungarian monarchy at the heart of Europe. Arthur Schnitzler, in Sigmund Freud's footsteps, was describing the "vast land" of the human psyche. Arnold Schönberg's ecstatic early work was emerging, while on the other hand, the public were suppressing their anxieties about the moribund state of the empire in the charming company of "sweet maidens" at the operetta. An awareness of this historical background is necessary to understand Kokoschka's idiosyncracies, which distinguished him from all the other Expressionists.

The psychological penetration and nervous agitation of the early portrait masterpieces correspond to the technique employed (ill. above). The paint application is thin, the color schemes are subdued. The handle of the brush has been used to inscribe intertwining, eerily gleaming lines into the wet paint surface, and entire areas have been applied with the fingers and hands – Kokoschka got beneath the skin in more senses than one. That the result is an "expressive art" goes without saying. But the sophisticated quality of Kokoschka's style, which is also evident in the linear webs of the lithographs, stands in sharp contrast to the neo-primitivism and merciless distortion of the German artists.

The Austrian was a passionate painter. The extent to which he suffered from his own failings and the fragility of the era, from the struggle between eros and reason, is indicated by the affair of the doll, which began in 1920,

when Kokoschka was a professor at the Dresden Academy. He had a life-size artificial dummy manufactured, based precisely on the principles of the female anatomy. It was to serve as his "life's companion," accompanying him wherever he went, even to the theater. A maid was hired to work the doll. Yet hardly had the doll been delivered, that the whole affair was over. Anyone who has seen the portraits of the young Kokoschka will realize that the episode represented an extravagant outbreak of despair, rooted in bitter disappointments in love and in a feeling of terrible loneliness. The background was as follows: Though a pacifist, Kokoschka had volunteered for war service. It was the only way he saw to escape from Vienna and from the tantalizing Alma Mahler, artists' muse and later the wife of architect Walter Gropius and writer Franz Werfel. The daughter of the Viennese landscape painter Emil Jakob Schindler, Alma was married at the time to Gustav Mahler. Her relationship with her much older, greatly admired husband, who moreover died prematurely, did not fulfil the beautiful, passionate woman. Then she met Kokoschka. The years with him "were a single violent love-battle," wrote the companion of so many great men in her candid memoirs.

"The Bride of the Wind"

The results of this love-battle were depicted by Kokoschka, distilled into a symbol of the eternal struggle between the sexes, which he considered preordained by fate. The picture is called *Die Windsbraut*, or *The Bride of the Wind*, the German term for "whirlwind" or "hurricane" (p. 62). The woman, who bears a portrait likeness to Alma Mahler, lies asleep, her body half beside, half over that of the sleepless man. His eyes gaze emptily from deep sockets; the face is sunken, the skin stretched like parchment over the skull and hanging in shreds from the body, which seems to be decaying, almost a skeleton. The uncanny scene plays itself out in an infinite, indeterminate space through which the

Oskar Kokoschka
Portrait of Herwarth Walden, 1910
Oil on canvas, 100.6 x 69.3 cm
Stuttgart, Staatsgalerie Stuttgart

Oskar Kokoschka
Dresden Neustadt, 1922
Oil on canvas, 80 x 120 cm
Hamburg, Hamburger Kunsthalle

Oskar Kokoschka
The Bride of the Wind, 1914
Oil on canvas, 181 x 221 cm
Basel, Öffentliche Kunstsamm-
lung Basel, Kunstmuseum

couple is whirled as if caught in a vortex. As in Romantic art, love and death appear here as siblings, but the underlying message is not "death and transfiguration" but horror and damnation. As the feverishly sweeping forms and curving brushstrokes show, this artist is indeed a belated son of the Baroque, an era that was more conscious of the equivocal nature of human existence, its fragility and mortal dread, than a public familiar only with the worldly opulence of Baroque festivities and operas is perhaps aware. Not only El Greco's spiritual Mannerism but also Symbolist art contributed to this major work of Kokoschka's, which anticipates significant stylistic changes. From now on the paint would be used in a more definitely painterly way. Linear, graphic elements would lose importance, and the paint, instead of being diluted to watercolor thinness, would be applied in thick impasto, though the brilliance of French and German Expressionist paintings was neither equalled nor desired. Kokoschka's color chords have more of a Symbolist subtlety and reserve.

Cities Portrayed

For a time Kokoschka continued to work in this allegorical vein, but suddenly he gave up his professorship in Dresden and vanished without a word of farewell. His profound restlessness impelled him to a vagabond life, and as he explored the world, he painted its great cities, whose feverish confusion mirrored the state of his own mind. Kokoschka generally depicted cities from a high vantage point, which permitted him to gain an overview, a comprehensive image of their physiognomy and character as a whole. Thus his city views, the glory of his mature period, are themselves a species of portrait. And they, too, like every great work of art, contain an element of the autobiographical. The overcharged tension of Kokoschka's early period is released, the colors gain in intensity. This development began early, with the views of Dresden and the Elbe River painted after 1920 (p. 61). But now the impassioned expression that invoked heaven and hell gives way to an impression, although it is one dramatically suffused with the energies of the restless wanderer and his adventurous life.

Denounced by the Nazis as degenerate, Kokoschka emigrated to England, where he found himself almost as misunderstood as during his early years in Vienna. He painted passionate appeals to the conscience of mankind, which are humanly deeply moving but aesthetically not always convincing. After the war, Kokoschka attained a calm and serene late style. But though his technical mastery remained as strong as ever, his visionary force diminished. The innovative paths marked out by younger artists Kokoschka declined to follow.

Universal Anxiety and a New Acquiescence
Meidner, Morgner, Schiele and Late Expressionism

Thirty years ago, during the opening ceremony of an art festival in Recklinghausen, Germany, the speaker was interrupted by a loud remark from the audience. It came from the artist whose work was being discussed, and who wished to draw attention to the fact that he was still alive: "I'm here – Meidner!" Apparently the speaker was unaware that the subject of his obituary was in the room. Ludwig Meidner (ill. right) was born in 1884 in Bernstadt, Silesia. An eccentric and willful man, Meidner continually swam against the stream, and his later years were overshadowed by loneliness and poverty. Expressionist pathos and a veritably manic compulsion to self-depiction, despair at the state of the world and at his own situation, embittered criticism and hate of man's inhumanity to man, marked the work of this restless Jewish artist. Although his œuvre is not flawless, it certainly represents a significant document of recent history.

Meidner experienced the first half of the 20th century as an apocalyptic age. Ensconced in his humble attic-studio in Berlin before the outbreak of World War I, he painted visions of the Last Judgement and the end of the world. "Sometimes I feel like hopping out of the window, down four storeys," Meidner wrote in his autobiography. "When I'm half awake I die many terrible deaths, but I know that I shall come into divine bliss again nevertheless…. I'm going to throw myself under a train, so its wheels can run screaming into my serene skull – ! Into a momentous, grand death – !" Even down to the punctuation, such statements are suffused with an ecstatic acceptance of the "twilight of humankind", "fall and scream," an apocalyptic mood, and also a touch of self-pity, are reflected in Meidner's words. As a painter he stood under the spell of van Gogh, and affinities with the early Kokoschka are also apparent. Wildly sweeping lines, extreme distortion of features in the portraits, jumbled perspectives in the cityscapes, where the buildings seem shaken by an earthquake and on the verge of collapsing, where the ground is pulled out from under our feet and the sky goes up in flames or disintegrates before our eyes – and in the midst of this chaos, man, alone and forlorn: Meidner himself.

Tragic Fragments: Egon Schiele

A universal anxiety and a deep mistrust of one's fellow men likewise suffuse the work of Egon Schiele, who, like Kokoschka, emerged from the orbit of the Viennese Secession. Schiele transposed the hot-house eroticism of Klimt, who was twenty-eight years his senior, into a more aggressive and tragic mode. In his hands the suave ornamentation of the Viennese variant of Art Nouveau became nervous and agitated, and finally, with Expressionist heightening, it took on an angular sharpness.

While Schiele's palette remained subdued, the broken hues were often interspersed with glaring accents of red. Like Kokoschka, Schiele was a hypersensitive personality and a prophet of the imminent European catastrophe. For him, as for the allied soul of the visionary poet, Georg Trakl, life was constantly lived in the face of death. Even Schiele's mercilessly frank erotic depictions reflect this state of mind. Especially in the drawings, as Wolfgang Fischer notes, the "burning unfulfilled sexual-

Ludwig Meidner
The Burning City, 1913
Oil on canvas, 66.5 x 78.5 cm
St. Louis (MO), St. Louis Art
Museum, Bequest of Morton
D. May

Egon Schiele
Summer Landscape (Krumau),
1917. Oil on canvas,
110.3 x 138.9 cm. Private collection

Egon Schiele
Reclining Woman, 1917
Oil on canvas, 96 x 171 cm
Vienna, Leopold Collection

"My existence, my decay, transposed to enduring values, must bring, sooner or later, my strength to other strongly or more strongly developed beings, like a living revelation of religion… I am so rich that I must give myself away."

EGON SCHIELE

Egon Schiele
Lovers, 1913
Pencil, tempera and oil on paper, 48 x 32 cm
Turin, Galleria Galatea

ity of the nudes and embraces" finds expression. It seems grotesque, but these depictions caused Schiele to be labelled a "pornographer," on which charge he even spent almost four weeks in jail in 1912. What they in fact embody is the suffering involved in sexuality, the night side of the relations between male and female, as described in the work of Freud (ill. above and below).

A more tranquil contrast to the figurative work is seen in Schiele's cityscapes, with their idiosyncratic perspectives and enigmatic, melancholy mood (p. 63). Here the borderline to abstraction is reached, if not overcome. "Painting is not enough for me," the artist wrote, "I know that one can create qualities with colors." Schiele's grandiose œuvre was destined to remain a fragment. He died on October 28, 1918, of Spanish influenza, the same illness to which his pregnant wife, Edith Harms, had succumbed three days previously, and which had taken the life of Klimt before them.

Like Schiele, the life and work of Wilhelm Morgner, born in Soest, Westphalia, in 1891, were prematurely cut short. The artist was killed in action near Langemarck in 1917. Morgner was not a precocious artist like August Macke, from whose carefree brilliance he was worlds apart. He was a contemplative, melancholy man whose path vanishes into obscurity. Influenced by van Gogh, Morgner depicted rural subjects, such as farmers working in fields stretching to a far horizon. As regards technique, he initially employed an ornamentally based, somewhat heavy-textured Pointillism in compositions reminiscent of Hodler. The "Sonderbund" exhibition, held in Cologne in 1912, brought a decisive confrontation with the work of the Brücke, the Cubists, and the Blauer Reiter. The despairing invocation of humanity that suffuses Expressionist poetry is also found in Morgner's fervently religious imagery. Passionate color combinations – culminating in the illuminated glow of the figurative ornament in his major work, *Entry into*

Jerusalem (ill. right) – a swirling agitation of forms, and trenchant critique of human failings, are characteristic of Morgner's art. His *Astral Landscape* recalls the adoration accorded to a monstrance. Morgner was on the path to abstraction, although how far he would have travelled it had he lived, no one can say.

Man as a Lump of Clay

The principal representative of Flemish Expressionism, an earthy version of the style that took its point of departure in the early van Gogh of *The Potato Eaters*, was Constant Permeke, a Belgian. In his dark-hued paintings of plain people and rural life, human beings seem formed of the same clay they work, predestined to bear the burden of a laborious life (ill. below). Permeke's forceful, brusquely simplified style divests Expressionism of its usual aggressiveness and turns it into a medium to convey monumental calm. Influences of Cubism, of the French neoclassical realism of Derain and followers, and of Picasso's neoclassical period, are all detectable in the original and powerful paintings of Permeke.

Unlike the work of the Fauves, that of the German Expressionists called the real world in question, for it had its origin in protest. Over the years the force of this protest diminished, partly out of disappointment, but partly from a newly felt need for acquiescence with the status quo. Ultimately this turn to the positive led, with the Brücke painters – and in an Impressionist variation

with Kokoschka – to a brand of realism characterized by heightened colors and reduced forms, a style in which years of experience found application. This path, marked out by the original protagonists of Expressionism, was taken by their followers as well. Among them was Lasar Segall, a Jewish artist born in Vilna who spent his later years in Brazil (ill. above); Werner Scholz, who adopted Expressionism under the influence of Nolde and the Brücke; and César Klein, who gained his reputation especially as a designer of theater sets.

A special case is that of the Rhenish Expressionists, a group of artists that originally referred to themselves as "Young Rhineland". The style reached a sort of culmination in the vociferously socially critical work of Gert H. Wollheim, who later emigrated to the United States; the

stark, black and white visions of Otto Pankok; and the work of artists who were temporarily part of the scene, such as Otto Dix, Max Ernst, and the Cologne "Progressives" around Heinrich Hoerle and Franz Wilhelm Seiwert in Cologne.

It was a Dutchman, Jan Thorn-Prikker, who established the first links between the Rhineland and international contemporary streams in art. At the time the region was still provincially preoccupied with its illustrious past, represented by the Düsseldorf School of the nineteenth century, whose influence had spread to Scandinavia, Russia, and even to New York (Hudson River School). Thorn-Prikker's symbolistic, semi-abstract murals and window designs translated influences of early Christian art, the Nabis, the Orphic Cubists, and the Blauer Reiter into a formal language of considerable originality (p. 66).

Mention should also be made of Jankel Adler, a Polish Jewish artist who, before persecution drove him into exile, lived for an extended period in Düsseldorf, where he met Paul Klee (p. 66). His style initially oscillated between Klee and Picasso, until expressive renderings of the natural scene and a subjective depiction of his personal experiences helped him develop a more rigorous, nobly hierarchical approach to composition. Individual traits were reduced to the prototypical, while subjective feelings were objectified. Adler's later paintings possessed a reserved earnestness that brought an Eastern European note into the generally decorative tendency of French-inspired Rhenish art.

An Attempt to Break through to God

"Paintings have their time," wrote Carl Linfert. Put differently, pictures and their styles are by no means random, ahistorical products. Expressionism was a European movement whose conceptual source lay in the feverish unease of the years preceeding the First World War, and in the optimism with which parts of the younger generation reacted to this malaise. All over the continent artists began to revel in pure color and dynamic composition – in Paris and Dresden, in Berlin and Vienna, even in the provinces far from the acknowledged centers of art. Key aesthetic and artistic streams and developments do not take place in a vacuum; they are embedded in actual, historical circumstances.

Expressionism, which we shall confront again under very different premises and in a different form in the Munich artists group Der Blaue Reiter, was not only a temporary direction. It represented an artistic and human stance which was to prove lastingly viable despite

Jankel Adler
Woman, 1928
Gouache, watercolor, sand and distemper on cardboard, mounted on wood, 62 x 46 cm
Tel Aviv, Adam Eyal Collection

the vicissitudes of time. In Expressionism the imbalance between emotion and reason was righted, the claim of the creative mind to make independent artistic decisions beyond all questions of utility, social conformity, and scientific principles, was strongly confirmed. The expressive art of the early century was an initial attempt to mount resistance to the automatism of industrial and commercial life, to set a dynamic lawlessness against the ossified laws, rules and regulations of the era. The Expressionists' distortion or deformation was not an attack on human dignity, just the opposite. All of their critique of the times, all of their distortions and screaming colors aimed at one thing only: "The most profound, presciently sensed meaning of all Expressionist art is … an attempt to break through to God, through all of the barbed wire entanglements of the laws of nature," as Wilhelm Worringer put it in 1919, with the pathos of a war-torn period.

However, it should not be overlooked, especially in the case of Expressionist architects, that their preference for the grand gesture and monumental demonstration contained a certain latent danger, which continues to exist to this day. Their pathos had ideological underpinnings, and the vocabulary of their theoretical writings in part anticipated the big words which a quite different political movement was soon to mobilize. Today, with the advantage of hindsight, certain crypto-fascist traits can be detected in the pithy pronouncements of the Expressionists, though one cannot in justice hold their spokesmen responsible for the terrible vulgarization to which their ideas were subsequently subjected. We are approaching a discussion, which is by no means closed even today.

Jan Thorn-Prikker
Madonna among Tulips, 1892
Oil on canvas, 146 x 86 cm
Otterlo, Rijksmuseum Kröller-Müller

Classicism and Imagination

The Calm after the Storm
Cubism, or Classical Modern Art

"Action equals reaction" – this axiom of physics also holds in a general way for art. We have seen how Cézanne attempted to rescue form from complete disintegration into Impressionist dots and commas of paint. Though the Fauves never forgot Cézanne's example, their prime concern was to liberate color, to use it in its purity and brillance. This concern, initially at least, forced considerations of form into the background. With the Expressionists outside France, the urge to turn their inmost feelings outwards, to exorcise their ghosts, even led to a destruction of form. The reaction to this came with Cubism, in which not feeling and sensation, but reason and design predominated. Yet the two opposing tendencies shared something in common – an elimination of traditional *trompe l'œil* effects. Instead of fooling the eye, the Fauves and Expressionists sought subjective truth in color, and the Cubists sought it in form. The fundamental problem they faced was how to depict three-dimensional objects on the two-dimensional plane of the canvas without resorting to perspective illusion.

A little over a year after the great Fauves show at the 1905 Salon d'Automne in Paris, Pablo Picasso tackled this problem for the first time. He began in spring 1907 and that same summer presented the result to his friends: *Les Demoiselles d'Avignon* (p. 69). The now-legendary painting depicts five nude female figures with rough-hewn, angular bodies and schematic faces in the manner of primitive Romanistic Catalan frescoes. The Picasso noses of the four figures shown frontally or in three-quarter profile are bent to the side, pressed into the plane; the bodies are unmodelled, devoid of volume. This exoticism had no formal significance as such; Picasso always defended himself against the inference that he had been influenced by African art, which the Fauves had discovered. The fact is that in May or June he had visited the Ethnographic Museum at the Palais du Trocadéro, and – like Matisse and Derain before him – he had been impressed by the African sculpture there. Whether he actually later altered three figures in *Les Demoiselles* (two on the right, one on the left) or even repainted them or changed their sequence under the influence of this experience, remains uncertain. Nevertheless, the similarities to African art reflect an inner affinity, which was confirmed, at least, by the artist's visit to the Trocadéro. In addition, the expressive ugliness of the masks points to something else: the innate expressive traits in Picasso's personality. Among other things, he was heir to the tradition of Spanish Realism, whose combination of harshness and ecstatic mood strongly shaped the Andalusian artist's approach.

Picasso was the most significant "expressionist" painter of the century, in the sense of the dramatic events that played themselves out on canvas after canvas. Yet this circumstance is not central to *Les Demoiselles*. More crucial are the technical means with which the artist forces the masks (which in this regard diverge from African sculpture) into the two-dimensional plane and elicts an impression of volume and mass not by means of light-dark contrasts, or chiaroscuro, but through long parallel strokes of green or blue-black. These parallel hatchings are found only in the faces of the two figures on the right. They amount to the earliest document of Cubism. This feature was so radical and strange that even Picasso's friends, the poets and writers Guillaume Apollinaire, Max Jacob, and André Salmon (who eventually suggested the picture's title) did not initially understand the painting, and Braque was prompted to say that Picasso apparently wanted to give people "kerosene to drink." Nevertheless, this shock ultimately led to Braque's conversion: the Saul of the Fauves became the Paul of the Cubists.

Picasso and his Crew

Les Demoiselles, by the way, had initially been conceived in quite different terms. It was to include figures of men, a student and a sailor, dining in the company of ladies from the Carrer d'Avinyo (Avignon Street) in Barcelona. The fruit in the foreground – grapes, pear, apple, melon – remain over from the original composition. Its scene was a Barcelona brothel well known to Picasso and his friends. "Le Bordel d'Avignon" was accordingly Picasso's chosen title, which shifted the events depicted from Avignon Street to the town of Avignon itself. But André Salmon, reportedly to the artist's displeasure, decided a title less offensive to genteel ears would be better. As Picasso later told his friend and dealer Daniel-Henry Kahnweiler, he and his confreres made ribald jokes about the whole affair, and

"In 1908, Picasso showed a few paintings in which there were some simply and firmly drawn houses that gave the public the illusion of these cubes, whence the name of our youngest school of painting. This school has already aroused passionate discussion. Cubism can in no way be considered a systematic doctrine; it does, however, constitute a school, and the painters who make up this school want to transform their art by returning to original principles with regard to line and inspiration, just as the Fauves – and many of the cubists were at one time Fauves – returned to original principles with regard to color and composition."
GUILLAUME APOLLINAIRE

"This time, in 'Les Demoiselles d'Avignon', they said I'd put the nose on sideways, but I had to paint it that way to show it was a 'nose'. I was sure that later they would come to see that it was not the wrong way round."   PABLO PICASSO

assigned starring roles to Max Jacob's grandmother, the artist Marie Laurencin, and his current girlfriend Fernande Olivier as "The locked-up ladies of Avignon". This anecdote reveals the faunlike and clowning side of Picasso's nature, though of course it says little about the significance of the painting in the history of Cubism.

The "Bateau-Lavoir" (Laundry Barge), a dilapidated studio building located at Rue Ravignan 13 between Place Pigalle and the top of Butte Montmartre, was a Noah's ark for Picasso and his Bohemian "crew" between 1903 and 1912. "Painters, sculptors, writers, humorists, actors, laundresses, seamstresses, and itinerant vegetable dealers" lived there, reports Fernande Olivier in her memoirs. "It was an icebox in winter and a sweatbox in summer, and the tenants met at the only water faucet with pitcher in hand." The artists worked and partied, loved and starved there, until finally an angel of grace appeared, in the figure of Gertrude Stein, rich American poetess and exacting muse of so many artists of the first third of the century, from Matisse and Picasso to Sherwood Anderson and Ernest Hemingway. But what above all appeared at the Bateau-Lavoir was a

intellectually tempered mysticism, which nevertheless had something fanatically determined about it. A cold flame burned the breasts of these artists. They behaved like the members of a religious order, a brotherhood that knew that it was far in advance of the times, and therefore that its thinking and the results of its inquiries would not be understood by its contemporaries. "Philosophers of form," Klee termed the Cubists.

This is why the protagonists of the style, Picasso and Braque, kept their products out of the public discussion as long as they could. They initially showed their pictures only with Kahnweiler, a young German-Jewish dealer from Mannheim who had come by way of England to Paris, opened a gallery on Rue Vignon, and, with somnambulistic sureness, had taken up the Cubists in an exclusive choice he never would have reason to regret. At Kahnweiler's gallery they could expect connoisseurs or at least interested viewers, and avoid the obloquy that had been poured on the heads of the Impressionists and Fauves. Kahnweiler made the Cubists' retreat from the public eye possible by agreeing to take their entire production, without stipulating fixed periods for delivery. Thus their intellectually reflected conceptual art was enabled to come to maturity slowly, more or less in peace and quiet, in a process of hard, concentrated work. This indicates how entirely different the artists' daily lives were from their activity in the studio. As members of the wild Montmartre *bohème* they were part of "Picasso's crew," but as painters they labored with extreme concentration and persistence to find solutions to the tasks they had set themselves.

Cézanne, the "Protective Mother"

At the beginning of this development stood Cézanne, whose paintings had made a deep impression on the future Cubists at the memorial exhibition held in the 1907 Salon d'Automne. "He was like a protective mother to us," Picasso admitted in a conversation with Kahnweiler. Cézanne had once said, "The eye absorbs… the brain produces form." Still, it would be mistaken to consider the outsider from Aix the only ideal of the Cubists. It is true that his canvases "joined hands," that is, were composed of a dense interweave of strokes that resisted Impressionist dissolution of form. But it is important to remember that Cézanne, despite mentally preconceiving the forms in his paintings, ultimately derived them from color. The Cubists approached this problem from a different angle, and with different means. As Kahnweiler said, they wanted "simply to give a precise image of bodies on a flat plane, without illusion of any kind." In contrast to Cézanne, and in even greater contrast to the fanfare colors of the Fauves, the Cubists subdued their palette. In the early years it was comprised of only greys, ochers, browns, a dark saturated green, and an occasional accent of bright red. The forms were abbreviated, geometrically simplified, condensed. At first, plastic volume was not dispensed with, but instead of being suggested by illusionistic

Pablo Picasso
Study for "Les Demoiselles d'Avignon", 1907
Watercolor on paper, 17.5 x 22.5 cm
Philadelphia (PA), Philadelphia Museum of Art

form of painterly expression that can be considered the classical art of the 20th century.

Cubism reacted in a way quite different from Expressionism to the anxiety and disquiet, the crisis of faith and lack of roots that emerged from European nihilism. It raised no protest and staged no revolt, nor did it naively proclaim "back to nature" as the way to salvation. In the face of chaos, Cubism set out to create a new order, an arrangement of silent signs on canvas. An extreme degree of objectivity was combined in this early form of "conceptual art" with a strange, brooding,

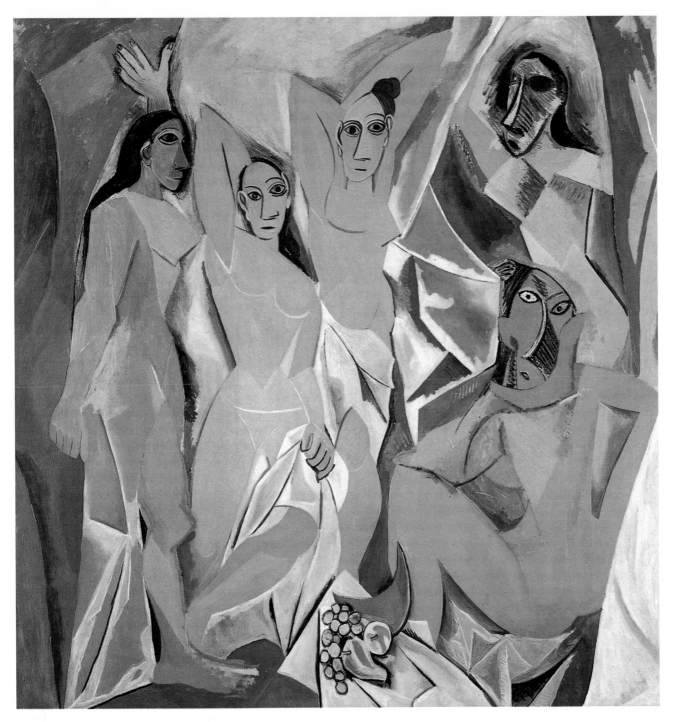

shadowing it was evoked by passages of flat modelling. Braque came back from L'Estaque with paintings from which the bright Mediterranean atmosphere had vanished, but which contained what were clearly cubic shapes (p. 70). These were the elements that gave the style its name, and it was again the critic Vauxelles who coined it, when he described the unusual works as "cubistic bizarreries." (Albert Gleizes pointed out to Daniel Robbins that another critic, Louis Chasserent, spoke as early as 1906 of "cubism," but this was in connection with Jean Metzinger and Gleizes.)

The magic of light and atmosphere was sacrificed to clarity of form, as everything unreal, vague and undefined was banned from Cubist pictures. Their subjects were quite commonplace: houses, trees and rocks, bowls, fruit, vases and musical instruments. "The vase gives emptiness a form, as music does silence," said Braque. Instead of seeking the particular, the Cubists concentrated on the general, on the unchanging essence of things rather than on their transient appearance.

The compositional planning this involved went far beyond Cézanne, who wished to dispense neither with

Pablo Picasso
Les Demoiselles d'Avignon, 1907
Oil on canvas, 243.9 x 233.7 cm
New York, The Museum of
Modern Art, Acquired through
the Lillie P. Bliss Bequest

Georges Braque
L'Estaque, 1908
Oil on canvas, 60.3 x 50.2 cm
New York, The Museum of
Modern Art

Georges Braque
Fruit Bowl and Glass, 1912
Charcoal and papiers collés,
62 x 44.5 cm
Private collection

light nor with the bluish hues things take on when seen from a distance. Picasso's paintings of the Spanish village Horta de Ebro of 1909, like Braque's concurrent landscapes, showed buildings and setting in terms of highly reduced, cubic configurations. The terracing of hills and houses perfectly suited the pictorial architecture for which Picasso and Braque strove. The forms of nature, subjected to man's needs, played an only marginal role.

In Braque's hands even the elaborate ornamentation of Sacré-Cœur cathedral was transformed into a monument of tectonic rigor and formal logic. *Chiaroscuro* returned to Cubist painting for a while, but not in order to produce striking effects of illumination, but to emphasize the sculptural modelling of the simple cubic forms. Interruptions of contour at the meeting-point of two planes provided transitions, softening the harsh light-dark contrasts at the edges of the outlines. The separate shapes, despite their reduction to geometric blocks, seemed to interpenetrate like

crystalline growths. This mitigated the rigidity of the compositions and lent them a painterly vibrato which already anticipated the facetting of Analytic Cubism. The well-nigh monotonous colors, limited to ocher, reddish-yellow, and greenish-grey, also represented a feature very typical of early Cubism – a puristic rigor of palette. Color was not allowed to detract from the principal theme. That theme was form.

The Silent Revolution
In the following period, from 1910 to 1912, the large, simplified, condensed form began to be divided into smaller and smaller parts that resembled the facets of a crystal. Figures were taken apart, then reassembled on the plane and made to cohere by pulling together the light reflections on various parts of the body. In the famous *Girl with a Mandolin* (New York, The Museum of Modern Art), done in 1910, the corporeal character of the figure is still retained, despite the formal disassembly of figure and instrument and their integration in the geometrical facetting of the picture plane. This analytical procedure gave the development a direction that could not help but lead to a final break with traditional habits of perception.

What occurred during these years was the silent revolution of Cubism, apparently unsensational but rife with consequences. Anti-illusionism was taken by the Cubists to its logical end, producing results that became obligatory for European art for a long time to come. In keeping with the great self-consciousness of a late culture, Cubism was an intellectual art. The theory on which it rested is no easier to understand than the analytical paintings themselves. But a brief outline might be of help. We shall set aside the scholarly debate on whether the theory came first or the artists, progressing from insight to insight in the course of painting.

70 PAINTING

"What attracted me in particular –
and became the main direction in
Cubism –was the materialization of
this new space that I sensed. So I
began concentrating on the still life,
because the still life possesses a tactile
space one might almost describe as
'manual'… For me, this corresponded to a wish I had always had
to touch a thing rather than simply
to look at it. This space attracted me
so much because the quest for space
was foremost a Cubist quest. Color
played only a minor role. The only
aspect of color that interested us
was light; light and space are closely
related and we dealt with them
together." GEORGES BRAQUE

Georges Braque
The Portuguese, 1911
Oil on canvas, 116.5 x 81.5 cm
Basel, Öffentliche Kunstsamm-
lung Basel, Kunstmuseum

Probably both views are correct, because in an art as
conceptually oriented and technically difficult as
Cubism, it is almost impossible to separate idea from
realization, perceptual critique – influenced by the new
perceptual physiology and psychology of the 19th century – from the practical struggle with problems of form.

Their restless search very clearly reflected the epistemological doubt over truth of sensory perception
which was characteristic not only of early Cubism but
of the entire century, including its science. The evidence
of the eye came to be considered only an "optical illusion", unreliable, a misrepresentation of facts. The eye

Georges Valmier
Abstract Composition, c. 1920
Oil on canvas, 116 x 82.5 cm
Private collection

Georges Braque
Atelier II, 1949
Oil on canvas, 131 x 163 cm
Düsseldorf, Kunstsammlung
Nordrhein-Westfalen

recorded only external appearances, and could not penetrate to the core of things. But it was this core with
which the painters were concerned, an essence which
they hoped to define and represent in paint on canvas –
which amounts to the same thing. "Writing does not
mean describing, painting does not mean copying," said
Braque. But according to the Cubists it was precisely
copying, to put it simply, which illusionistic painting in
all its varieties since Giotto had done. Picasso and
Braque now proceeded to draw their conclusions. They
ceased painting objects "as they saw them" and began
painting them "as they thought them," as Maurice Raynal put it in his essay "What is Cubism" of 1913. "This is
precisely the law which the Cubists have taken up again
and expanded and codified under the heading of 'the
fourth dimension'." They broke objects open, flattened
them out and deprived them of volume and the illusion
of a surface skin; they no longer looked at a table, a
chair, a vase, a glass or even a human being from a single
vantage point only but from several vantage points.
They walked, as it were, around things, and what they
saw in the process was supplemented by what they knew
about these things, and their knowledge, in turn, was
supplemented by experience.

This process ultimately led to the simultaneous
depiction of various aspects of reality. Different views of
the same object seen at different points in time were
represented together, as in a multiple exposure photograph. This amounted to bringing the factor of time
into an art that intrinsically was very static and intended
to emphasize permanence, a principle that – under
other conditions and with different aims – would soon
be adopted and ramified by the Futurists. The painted
image, as Carl Einstein put it, now developed "out of a
cadence of tectonic planar forms." Apollinaire spoke of
a pictorial space with a "reversed perspective." The light

sources in these paintings were not detectable, light and
shade remained ambivalent in nature. The image was
capable of accepting anything that could be translated
from three-dimensional volume into two-dimensional
surface, while dispensing with an illusion of depth.
Compositional harmony was engendered by a well-

considered juxtaposition of contrasts, which led to the
"plastic," relief-like effect Kahnweiler described. The
Cubist method was akin to that of counterpoint in
music.

The Thing in Itself
In this way the Cubists, instead of reproducing the
appearance of an object, hoped to penetrate to what
Plato (and Picasso) called the underlying "idea" and
what Kant called "das Ding an sich," or the thing in
itself. Instead of representing more or less accidental or
partial aspects of reality, in other words, they strove to
represent reality itself, based on a new conception
of space and time. Optical illusion would be replaced
by "true vision," the "lie" of visual perception by the
definition of a new, comprehensive reality. "Defining a
thing means putting the definition in its place," was
Braque's terse equation.

So the definition of a thing was the thing itself. By
means of exact analysis, these artists attempted to bring
back into painting a reality that had grown so complex
and ramified that it could be stated only in terms of
formulae. In making such statements, color would only
stand in the way. It would have brought a sensuous factor into this strict, logical art, in which something of
Kant's philosophical rigor was revived. "The senses
deform, the mind forms…. There is no final certainty
except that the mind grasps," stated Braque. Thus
Picasso and Braque, in their analytical period, limited
themselves largely to grey, ocher, and brown. But these
grisailles were so subtly gradated, so rich in intermediate
tones, that they took their place among the most
exquisite manifestations of European painting.

The implicit purism of this radically anti-percep-
tual, in a way even iconoclastic art that hermetically
sealed itself off from sensation-hungry curiosity, can be

as little denied as the purism of its life-long prophet and brilliant interpreter, Kahnweiler. The famous art dealer early on stated the opinion that painting was a written language that invented symbols or characters which it was the task of the viewer to decipher. Truly, the hermetic language of Cubist pictures is not easy to read. The painters themselves sensed this, and as simplicity is often a sign of maturity, as soon as they felt certain of their technical means they began to give the public visual hints, suggestions of recognizable things, which at the same time served to interpret the subject matter of their paintings. For example, Picasso's *Souvenir du Havre* (Basel, private collection) of 1912 contains a number of references to reality, memories of an apparently enjoyable and somewhat "wet" journey with Braque – boats' rigging, seashells, rippling waves, and above all, drinking glasses.

The introduction of letters of the alphabet into their paintings emphasized the Cubists' fundamentally anti-illusionistic stance. These characters served as orientation points within the non-perspective space. In their search for the true, unadulterated local color of objects, the painters' fanatical love of truth led them to begin to imitate the textures and colors of materials, and soon even to insert actual materials such as wood, marble, or printed wallpaper into their works. This supplemented the painted surface by new, tactile values. These works, collages and *papiers collés*, were not intended ironically or meant to disparage past art as were those of the Dadaists and Surrealists of a later period. Rather, they represented visible and tangible elements of reality,

"things in themselves," which in this way were introduced into art. In addition, non-aesthetic materials – Braque soon began using sand, wood shavings, and twine – offered a chance to elicit effects of depth without recourse to tabooed perspective, because a surface could be built up in the manner of a low relief, in which the planes advanced or receded solely by dint of the contrast between their color or textural values.

"Don Juan, or The Love of Geometry"

With these works, into which brilliant colors again entered, began a turn away from Analytic Cubism. The new direction led to what is known as Synthetic Cubism, a style just as intellectual but less complicated than its predecessor, and therefore more easily accessible. In this new phase a third artist joined the pioneers Picasso and Braque. This was Juan Gris, actually José Victoriano Gonzáles, like Picasso a Spaniard, and one of the most sympathetic figures in the history of modern art, a "minor" painter but a great one. Gris was a handsome man who loved to dance. His friends nicknamed him "Don Juan Gris" because women found him almost irresistible. Nevertheless, no scandalous stories about him have come down to posterity, for the same discretion that is such a signal trait of his art characterizes his life as well. Of all the Bateau-Lavoir artists Gris had the hardest time. He was so poor that he had to draw cartoon series in order to survive. This cost him a great deal of time, but he watched and waited. When he was finally in a position to concentrate on his own work, Gris first oriented himself towards Analytic Cubism, concentrating, as in his famous 1912 portrait of Picasso, on the form-engendering and form-dissolving qualities of reflected light. Yet soon Gris developed an original approach. Unlike his friends, he did not take Cézanne as

Juan Gris
Still Life with Pipe and Newspaper (Fantomas), 1915
Oil on canvas, 60 x 72 cm
Washington, National Gallery of Art, Chester Dale Fund

"I work with the elements of the intellect, with the imagination. I try to make concrete that which is abstract. I proceed from the general to the particular, by which I mean that I start with an abstraction in order to arrive at a true fact."
JUAN GRIS

Juan Gris
Still Life (Violin and Inkpot), 1913
Oil on canvas, 89.5 x 60.5 cm
Düsseldorf, Kunstsammlung Nordrhein-Westfalen

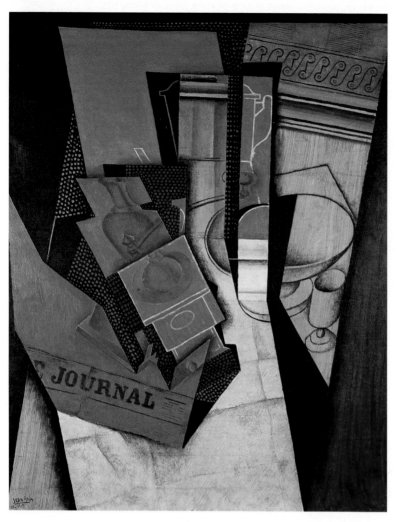

Juan Gris
Le déjeuner, 1915
Oil and charcoal on canvas,
92 x 73 cm
Paris, Musée National d'Art
Moderne, Centre Georges
Pompidou

Fernand Léger
The Stairway, 1914
Oil on canvas, 130 x 100 cm
New York, The Museum of
Modern Art

a point of departure. He turned the Aix master's methods upside down, as it were, first designing an abstract, tectonic pictorial structure and then inserting objects into it. Instead of creating abstractions, Gris rendered the abstract concrete. "Cézanne made a cylinder out of a bottle," he once stated; "I make a bottle out of a cylinder."

In the still lifes done by this method, mathematics and poetry are combined, as in music (p. 73 and ill. above). Gris's palette is completely liberated and independent of the local colors of things, strong and at times brilliant. This reconsideration of the importance of color had also taken place with Picasso and Braque, initially in their collages. As regards form, the ideal configuration of an object or figure was now no longer arrived at in a long process of analytical investigation and division into component parts, but projected according to the artist's imaginative idea. In contrast to Cézanne's method of working "in front of the motif," or from life, this process involved and relied on memory. Perceptual experience was no longer conceptualized; rather, a mental conception was rendered perceptible. Instead of dividing a whole into parts (analysis), the artists began

combining parts into a whole (synthesis). What was retained from the earlier approach was the purely planar character of the painting, whereby three-dimensional objects were tilted up into the two-dimensional plane. This was the final consequence of Cézanne's perspective distortion, in which the composition was subject to the laws of form alone. It is a feature of Cézanne's still lifes that still strikes the naive observer as awkward, because the fruit bowls, knives, pitchers and jugs seem on the verge of slipping down the inclined plane of the table and falling to the floor. The ascetic, brooding greyish-browns of the Analytic paintings remained a memory. Though the palette of Synthetic Cubism did not reach the brilliance of Impressionism, not to mention Fauvism, its subtle, subdued hues presented a feast for the eye, and the compositions were understandable without undue intellectual effort. Gris – until his premature death – and Braque set out to explore the new style in all its variants.

Braque in fact became the classical representative of late Cubism, a man whose work reflects the culture of French color and form in an incomparable harmony. Only an occasional misjudgement in format, or a discrepancy between still-life calm and the agitated movement of sometimes life-sized figures, made slight smudges on the lucid mirror of Braque's œuvre. Its intellectual stance is closely allied with that of the great French still-life painters from Chardin to Cézanne. "I am not a revolutionary painter," admitted Braque. "I do not seek exaltation – excitement is enough for me." After the stormy years of his beginnings, Braque became one of the great and profound conservatives of the age.

The Sunny Side of Technology

Cubism was originally suffused with mistrust of human perception of the reality of the visible world. In the work of Fernand Léger, it became an art of acceptance (pp. 75–77). The heavyset, awkwardly charming grandson of Norman farmers and son of an animal breeder, Léger praised the glories of the technological world in a quite unintellectual, somewhat naive way. His favorite shape was the tube or pipe, which led Vauxelles, godfather to so many major artists, to nickname Léger a "Tubist." For a time Léger was a convinced communist, and dreamed of a popular art for all. His late, prototypical style, perhaps the purest formulation of socialist realism because it was entirely without ideological blinders, represented the utopia of a "proletarian Olympus." That it was destined not to be understood by the people for which it was meant was a personal disappointment for Léger, but one he shared with many avant-garde artists.

Léger, too, was helped by Cézanne out of the dilemma that faced the successors of Impressionism. But as the early *Nudes in a Forest* (Otterlo, Rijksmuseum Kröller-Müller) already shows, Léger's reading of Cézanne differed greatly from that of the other Cubists'.

Fernand Léger
The City, 1919
Oil on canvas, 230.5 x 297.8 cm
Philadelphia (PA), Philadelphia
Museum of Art

*"A work of art must be significant in
its own time, like any other intellectual manifestation, whatever it may
be. Painting, because it is visual, is
necessarily the reflection of external
conditions, not psychological ones.
Every painting must allow for this
momentary and eternal value,
which will make it last beyond the
period of its creation."*
FERNAND LÉGER

Fernand Léger
Woman with Book, 1923
Oil on canvas, 116.2 x 81.5 cm
New York, The Museum of
Modern Art, Nelson A.
Rockefeller Bequest

The Proletarian Olympus

The work of this great French artist leads, by many
byways, far away from Cubism and very close to the
concerns of the present day. During his time of service in
the First World War, Léger felt a brotherly attachment
towards the farmers, navvies, miners, and sailors in his
unit, saying "their plain-spokenness and their argot were
my language." But as an artist what intrigued him the
most were the guns and equipment that the soldiers
used. He saw clearly that in this merciless realm, human
beings were degraded to a marginal role.

This changed fundamentally during the postwar
years, as Léger began to project his "proletarian Olympus." The gods with whom he populated it were plain,
even vulgar, earthbound, apparently insentient figures,
which nevertheless possessed a strange greatness and
dignity that were more than superficial. Humanity,
the people in their simplest, typified form, were celebrated by a man who permitted himself no emotion, no
attempt at psychological penetration. "Psychic expression was a too sentimental affair for me," Léger commented in a note of 1917. Yet it was precisely his waiver
of the heroic pose and the superhuman factor that
enabled him to create imagery of compelling force in
which people and things are reduced to brief, lapidary
signs.

The way in which Léger carried out this reduction
and condensation was initially still influenced by his
"Tubism." The human body continued to be treated as a
machine, a configuration built of pipes and levers. In
subsequent years, however, organic forms began to play
an increasing role, particularly in his paintings of aver-

As he himself said, the painting is "a battle of masses,"
in which giant, robot-like figures move through a proliferating jungle of tubular trees. This dynamic approach
to composition would continue to inform subsequent
paintings, which in addition had large areas of bright
color inserted between the abstracted, tubular figures.
The landscapes, figurative compositions, still lifes, and
stair motifs of the pre-World War I period were all
reduced to strongly contrasting, geometric bodies
whose volumes, instead of being flattened out, are
especially emphasized. The palette of bright blue, red,
yellow, and green was employed as a constructive
rather than a coloring factor, and the hues possessed
a metallic hardness. The early Léger took Cézanne's
famous saying literally, transforming everything that
came into his hands into cones, spheres, and cylinders.
Whatever he painted took its place in a mechanized
world.

Nor did this change in the coming years, during
which Léger became the founder of a *nouveau réalisme*.
His formal discipline, the binding logic of his pictorial
architecture – or rather, structure – made this engineer
among artists into a classic. "One of his pictures is titled
'Homage to Louis David'," remarked Kahnweiler; "that
says everything." He was right, for David, the painter of
"The Horatian Oath," was a revolutionary who metamorphosed into a neoclassical court artist to Napoleon.
David's perfect execution expunged every trace of
painterly luxuriance. But that disturbed the socialist
Léger as little as did David's change of camp. All he was
interested in was his great predecessor's ability to construct a painting. The admiration of the self-confessed
proletarian artist for the extoller of the French Revolution and then of the tyrant who brought it to bay, indicates how little aesthetic issues have to do with philosophy or political stance.

*"I worked for two years to make 'La
Grande Parade'. I study everything
ponderously. I work extremely
slowly. I don't know how to improve.
The more I examine myself, the
more I see that I am a classical artist.
I undertake lengthy preliminary
work. First I make a number of
drawings, then I make gouaches
and finally I turn to the canvas, but
when I start on it, I am 80% certain. I know where I'm going."*
FERNAND LÉGER

Fernand Léger
The Pause, on a Red Ground, 1949
Oil on canvas, 114 x 148 cm
Biot, Musée National Fernand
Léger

age people involved in leisure-time activities. Léger
depicted them at the circus or on an excursion into the
country, among flowers and trees and clouds like fluffs
of cotton wool which were just as graphically simplified
as the expressionless faces and chunky figures. The
subdued lyricism of these scenes stands in contrast to
the harsher mood of depictions from the realm of labor,
showing farmers and workers and engineers to whom
the machine is not alien but familiar. Solidarity among
simple people, anticipating the brotherhood of man in
a classless society, are the themes of this phase. Thanks
precisely to their restraint and understatement, these
paintings represent an epic eulogy to the advantages of
a technological existence.

As this implies, Léger attempted to refute the
supposed incompatibility of nature and machine. In still
lifes of incomparable formal simplicity he juxtaposed
flowers and bolts, clouds and cogwheels, dichotomous
elements and symbols of one and the same world.
Pop artists like Roy Lichtenstein learned much from
these paintings. To Léger, to fall into cultural pessimism
or protest against the status quo would have seemed
an escape from reality.

Thus, without becoming unfaithful to himself,
Léger developed from a Cubist into a realist. He also
went through an abstract phase when he designed
murals in collaboration with his friend, the architect
Le Corbusier, and others. But for him abstract art had
a serving function. It was "applied art", a means of deco-

rating large surfaces, perfectly suited to interpreting and
heightening architecture, what Léger himself termed
"architectonic" art. Because of his great simplification
of form and the brilliance of his color planes – the
transparency of the flowing colors behind the contours
was inspired by Broadway's neon signs – Léger was
predestined to be a muralist. It is no accident that his
influence on Mexican mural painters such as Diego

Fernand Léger
La Grande Parade, 1954
Oil on canvas, 299 x 400 cm
New York, Solomon R.
Guggenheim Museum

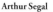

Arthur Segal
Harbor in the Sun, 1918
Oil on canvas, 91.5 x 109.5 cm
Zurich, Kunsthaus Zürich

Albert Gleizes
Composition
(Madonna and Child), 1930
Casein on canvas, 146.4 x 114.6 cm
Private collection

Rivera and José Clemente Orozco, as well as on Pop Art and poster design, was second to none. But Léger was too straightforward and honest not to realize that abstract art was beyond his scope.

However, he respected those who thought differently: "Only a few creative artists and knowledgeable connoisseurs can maintain the high level of this art," he said. "In this height also lies its danger. But make no mistake: This form of art arose from an inner necessity. It had to emerge, and it will endure."

Reaction against Picasso and Braque

Like Léger, Robert Delaunay's painting led far from Analytic Cubism. An admirer of Kandinsky as representative of the "great abstract," Delaunay was the restless, rebellious spirit of Section d'Or, (golden mean), a group of Cubist heretics founded by Jacques Villon. Meeting on Place de l'Alma or in Villon's studio, the group discussed the golden mean and – based on Platonist ideas revived by Symbolism – ideal proportions of measure and number on which a "pure painting" could

Jean Metzinger
At the Cycle Race Track, c. 1911/12
Oil and collage on canvas,
130.4 x 97.1 cm
Venice, Peggy Guggenheim
Collection

André Lhote
The Rugby Players, c. 1917
Oil on canvas, 148 x 179 cm
Private collection

be based. Above all, color again became a key issue. These concerns reflected a decided opposition to the primacy of form and abstention from color in the work of the Cubist grand masters Picasso and Braque. They did not attend the group's gatherings, but Gris did. He must have been interested in the formal considerations aired there with regard to new subject matter. The others present were mostly Cubists of the second

Roger de La Fresnaye
The Conquest of the Air, 1913
Oil on canvas, 235.9 x 195.6 cm
New York, The Museum of
Modern Art, Mrs. Simon
Guggenheim Fund

Marie Laurencin
Two Girls, 1923
Oil on canvas, 65.5 x 54.5 cm
Tokyo, Bridgestone Museum of Art

hour, who developed more or less personal versions of the style and above all popularized it. These included Jean Metzinger and his associate Albert Gleizes, a metaphysician who linked up with Symbolism and finally, like Delaunay, arrived at abstraction. Also active in the group were Gleizes's friend, Henri Victor Le Fauconnier, the estimable Polish artist Louis Marcoussis, and the intelligent André Lhote (ill. below and p. 78).

For other artists such as the great Dada chief Marcel Duchamp, Francis Picabia, František Kupka, and Léger, the Section d'Or was only a waystation. Also occasionally present was Marie Laurencin, the painter of a sophisticated yet sensual, joyful Arcadia populated by charming girls, an Arcadia which entirely lacked the fateful shadows of Poussin's (ill. above). The sensitive Jacques Villon, actually Gaston Duchamp, a brother of Marcel Duchamp, adopted an axiom of Leonardo da Vinci's, according to which the imaginary lines that connect a subject with the artist's eye form a pyramid. This pyramid determined Villon's compositions, which were just as reserved and lyrical as the pastel, translucent bloom of his palette (p. 78).

Delaunay (pp. 80, 81) attacked the new aesthetic issues with much greater energy than Villon. He began by studying the structural laws of Gothic architecture,

Louis Marcoussis
Still Life with Jug, 1925
Oil on canvas, 33 x 41 cm
Saint-Etienne, Musée d'Art
Modern

as reflected in his paintings of Saint-Séverin, the church of Parisian professors and students. In 1909 Delaunay arrived at a theme that would concern him through long series of paintings: the Eiffel Tower. He discovered the hidden dynamism of this apparently so static structure. By means of shifting and overlapping vantage points, by disassembling and reassembling the bril-

Jacques Villon
Young Woman, 1912
Oil on canvas, 146.8 x 114.7 cm
Philadelphia (PA), Philadelphia
Museum of Art

Robert Delaunay
Circular Forms, 1930
Oil on canvas, 128.9 x 194.9 cm
New York, Solomon R.
Guggenheim Museum

liantly engineered giant toy, Delaunay achieved a vital pictorial rhythm that wonderfully embodies the skyward thrust of this symbol of modern engineering. The dramatic effect is heightened by the simple geometry of the buildings staggered around the tower, and by the rounded cloud formations interpenetrating the iron web. With this series Delaunay vehemently broke out of the hermetically sealed still-life world

of Analytic Cubism, and brought color back into its own. It is as if he had grown tired of the philosophizing and visual riddles of the analysts and thrown himself head-first into the pulsating life of the big city.

Hymn to the Sun

This is actually overstating the case, for Delaunay was actually a clear, exact thinker. His great achievement was to have discovered a way to compose a picture using color, a way diametrically opposed to formal analysis. Color became Delaunay's principal theme. He investigated its intrinsic laws, allowing him to engender rhythm and movement simply by juxtaposing complementary colors, red against green, blue against orange, yellow against violet. These colors then reproduced the effects of light on canvas. Delaunay was the first painter to play the color spectrum as if it were a musical scale. Though a practical application of Chevreul's speculative color theory and its doctrine of "simultaneous contrasts," Delaunay created painted poetry. Apollinaire suggested a name for it, "Orphism." Delaunay's palette reached a degree of luminosity unprecedented in art. Light, the rays of the sun, the disembodied glow of the colors of the rainbow, suffused Delaunay's entire œuvre. The world of the first technological revolution, with its towers, airplanes, and balloons, appeared there flooded with light and filled with hope for the future.

Robert Delaunay
The Windows, 1912
Oil on canvas, 92 x 86 cm
Chicago (IL), Morton G.
Neumann Collection

Delaunay's brilliant art found its loveliest and most delicate formulation in his *Window Paintings*. The compositions are determined by prismatic colors, luminous and transparent, rich in gradations and transitions. This abstract Cubism, as the artist himself termed it,

eventually led to complete abstraction. This point was reached with the *Formes circulaires*, the circular forms of the following two years. The circular or rotating movement of colors ultimately became Delaunay's sole theme. "As long as art does not detach itself from the object, it remains description," he wrote in an essay, "Concerning Light" (Über das Licht), published in 1913 in Herwarth Walden's *Der Sturm*. Delaunay drew his conclusions from this subjective insight. The liberation of color he achieved between 1910 and 1916 must have filled him with indescribable joy. The artist's triumphant happiness conveys itself to anyone who sees this imagery, pure and seemingly divested of all earthly ties.

Subsequently Delaunay returned to objective depiction. But in his late years, not without the influence of his wife, Sonia Terk (ill. above), geometry once again triumphed. The paintings became flatter, more ornamental, sometimes even slightly poster-like. The period in which Delaunay, according to an unpublished manuscript by Gleizes, played "with sun and moon like an amazed child," was over. The predominant shape was now the disk, as the fundamental model of the simultaneity of light and motion. The compositions were lent a dynamic character by means of dissolving the spectrum of the color wheel. "A painting formed according to the laws of this organization is a microcosm adapted to the rhythms of the macrocosm," Delaunay explained. The rays of his brilliant palette extended even to the neighboring countries, where they influenced, among many others, the artists of Der Blaue Reiter. Their effect has been felt down to the threshold of the present day, especially in the work of major American painters.

The range of Cubist influence, including that of its "Orphist" opposition, may be seen in the work of František Kupka (ill. below and p. 82), a native of Czechoslovakia. After beginning in a style allied with Art Nouveau and Symbolism, he too produced compositions of abstract color wheels, then later advanced to architectural structures of rectangular shapes arranged in a way that recalls musical fugues. For Kupka the work of art represented "an abstract reality," which "demands that it be formed of invented elements. Its concrete meaning derives from the combination of

Sonia Delaunay-Terk
Electric Prisms, 1914
Oil on canvas, 250 x 250 cm
Paris, Musée National d'Art Moderne, Centre Georges Pompidou

Robert Delaunay
Eiffel Tower (The Red Tower), 1909
Oil on canvas, 133.7 x 90 cm
New York, Solomon R. Guggenheim Museum

"Simultaneous contrast ensures the dynamism of colors and their construction in the painting; it is the most powerful means to express reality." ROBERT DELAUNAY

František Kupka
Cathedral, 1913
Oil on canvas, 180 x 150 cm
Washington, Jan and Meda Mladek Collection

morphological primal images and the architectonic conditions intrinsic to its own organism." Kupka went to France at an early date. Yet in Prague, too, a group of artists developed a relatively independent variant of Cubism, surely influenced by visits to Kahnweiler, Picasso, and Braque. Miroslav Lamac designated it "Cubo-Expressionism," and quite aptly so. For unlike classical Cubism of the French variety, Czech Cubism combines an expressive tendency with the crystalline forms which would come to represent its basis. This is particularly evident in the work of Otokar Kubin and Emil Filla, but also in that of the early, Futurist-influenced Antonín Procházka, and in that of Josef Čapek and his writer-brother Karel, who refused from the start to be pinned down to Braque's and Picasso's Cubism of the pioneer years. This led in 1912 to a break with Filla and his followers.

Francis Picabia, who would experiment in virtually the full gamut of avant-garde styles, was at the time producing ornamental abstractions in a subdued color range from which every memory of the things and experiences that had inspired them had been expunged. Picabia demanded "a painting based on pure imagina-tion, which recreates the world of forms on its own strength." Marcel Duchamp, in contrast, depicted a *Melancholy Boy in a Train* (Venice, Peggy Guggenheim Foundation) and his renowned *Nude Descending a Staircase* (p. 129), later spoofed in America as an "explosion in a brickworks." These are dark, dreamlike images in which the movement of the young man being shaken by the vibration of the train and that of the woman walking down stairs are depicted in an eerie simultaneity of their separate consecutive phases. In terms of formal approach, these paintings of Duchamp's should be viewed in the context of Italian Futurism, as should, incidentally, Villon's *Marching Soldiers* (Paris, Musée National d'Art Moderne).

More Ascetic than the Ascetics

Many artists of the twentieth century, obsessed with the idea of purity of means and truth of depiction, fought not only illusion in visual art but everything that smacked of sensuality, emotion, or individualism. They crusaded against these with all the zeal of Martin Luther against the Pope. Their goal was a supra-individual, absolute painting, which subjected all phenomena

"The creative ability of an artist is manifested only if he succeeds in transforming natural phenomena into 'another reality'. This part of the creative process, can be considered an independent element, and if conscious and developed, it hints at the possibility of creating a painting. It can thus charm or move the onlooker without disturbing the organic color of natural phenomena." FRANTIŠEK KUPKA

František Kupka
Amorpha – Fugue in Two Colors, 1912
Oil on canvas, 211 x 220 cm
Prague, Národni Galeri

that rested on deceptive visual perception to a rigorous, rational order. This visual order, as Kupka already demanded, must realize itself independently of nature. Thus Cubism produced its fundamentalist reformers. These were Amédée Ozenfant (ill. above right) and Edouard Jeanneret, who, as an architect, became famous under the name Le Corbusier (ill. above left). The two joined battle against what they considered the "degeneration" of classical Cubism into the merely decorative.

Like all apostates Ozenfant and Jeanneret were even stricter than the church founders. From now on, they declared, verticals and horizontals were to be the sole bases of a pictorial geometry controlled by reason, precise, and capable of validation like a scientific experi-

ment. Their ideal was the perfection of the machine, an instrument of modern civilization produced and mastered by the human mind. Acceptable subjects were few – everyday mundane things rendered in straight-forward colors, to ensure that no sensuous charm, deco-rative fillip, or insinuating motif should detract from the mathematical harmony. The aim of this abstinence was a sort of normative visual poetics, its result an austere, didactic art out of a test-tube – "Purism" in painting. This was the name attached to the entire stream. Its cool harmonies – thanks not least to Le Corbusier – soon took effect in architecture, but its underlying ideas also remained vital in painting. In 1938 Ozenfant opened an art school in the United States which would prove extremely influential.

Assault on Tradition
The Brief but Violent Earthquake of Futurism

The intellectual roots of the "art of the future" con-ceived in Italy can be traced back to the European nationalism of the years prior to 1914, which inexorably led to the disaster of World War I.

The rigorous attitude of the Futurists, iconoclasts and image-makers in one, had its source in the feeling of being excluded from the European art discussion. Since the 18th century and Giovanni Battista Tiepolo, Italy had produced no artist of truly European rank. Its young intelligentsia, unable to explain the sudden decline of creative powers in a country that had led the

world for centuries, were enraged. From the art journals flourishing in neighboring nations and the Venice Biennale, established in 1895, they knew of the advances being made elsewhere. An urgent need to play a role, to regain international importance in art, heightened to fever pitch by chauvinism and a naively positivistic faith in progress, produced the brief but far-reaching blos-soming of Futurist art. "Italy has been the great market-place for old-junk dealers long enough," declared the author Filippo Tommaso Marinetti in his *Futurist Manifesto* of 1909, which was followed the next year by

Luigi Russolo
Dynamism of a Car, 1912/13
Oil on canvas, 106 x 140 cm
Paris, Musée National d'Art
Moderne, Centre Georges
Pompidou

"We declare that the world's magnificence has been enriched by a new beauty: the beauty of speed. A racing car whose hood is adorned with great pipes, like serpents of explosive breath – a roaring car that seems to ride on grapeshot is more beautiful than the Victory of Samothrace.- We stand on the last promontory of the centuries!... Why should we look back, when what we want is to break down the mysterious doors of the Impossible? Time and Space died yesterday. We already live in the absolute, because we have created eternal, omnipresent speed."

F. T. MARINETTI

Gino Severini
Dancer + Ocean =
Bouquet of Flowers, 1913
Oil and collage on canvas,
91 x 60 cm
New York, private collection

an artists' manifesto signed by Giacomo Balla, Umberto Boccioni, Carlo Carrà, Luigi Russolo (ill. above), and Gino Severini. An excerpt: "We want to liberate [Italy] from the countless museums that blanket it like countless churchyards."

The ground for the movement was prepared, in Italy as elsewhere, by literary men – Giovanni Papini, the author-artist Ardengo Soffici, and above all, Marinetti – as well as by committed journals such as *Leonardo* or *Voce*. It was through the latter that the Futurists became familiar with Cubism. Their uncompromising desire to give Italy a new cultural self-confidence made any means to this end seem justified. Long before Mussolini, the Futurists and those who paved the way for them sung the praises of imperialism, and extolled war as a sublime and purifying bath in bullets – "the sole hygiene for the world." Besides advocating war, they celebrated the cruelty and harshness of an unjust life, which was a battle in which the strong would prevail over the weak, and sought adventure for its own sake. Even art, stated the Futurists, could "only be violence, cruelty."

Naturally this led them to believe in intuition as the source of all art, a doctrine that, in Italy, went back to Benedetto Croce. The Futurists revelled in the heady feeling produced by the powers of technology, especially an intoxication with speed, which led to Marinetti's proverbial saying that a racing car was more beautiful than the Nike of Samothrace. Dynamism, motion, speed were the incantatory formulae of the Futurists, and not surprisingly, this very dynamism would lead with the velocity of a racing car to the fascism of the amateur race-driver Mussolini. Other traits the Futurists shared with the future *Duce* were the extravagance of their demands, and a propagandistic celebration of force that completely misjudged the actual power relationships of the day. Artistically the movement came to an end the moment it compromised itself by collaborating

with fascism. By that time its key surviving representatives, Severini and Carrà (Boccioni had died in 1916, after a war injury and a subsequent fall from a horse) had long turned to aims of an entirely different nature.

Orgy of Destruction

Such considerations might well ruin one's pleasure in the pictures produced by this aggressive movement, which was unscrupled in both its methods and aims. Yet Futurism also engendered a number of major works which are capable of making one forget the well-nigh terrorist boasting of the manifestos. Then, too, things look different after the bitter experiences of a century than they did in 1909. This was the year of Marinetti's publication of the *Futurist Manifesto* in the then still progressive *Le Figaro* of Paris. In the name of the future, Marinetti advocated that libraries, museums, and universities, and by implication, the entire European tradition, be destroyed at the earliest possible date. The trauma of an undigested past, in this case the great Italian artistic tradition, lay heavy on the minds of its descendants and provoked a – fortunately only theoretical – orgy of destruction. Freed of the invisible chains in which their ancestors had fettered them, they strode optimistically into the future. Their intoxication was short-lived. Yet it remains an historical fact that while Futurism throve, Italy again became a serious partner in the European art discussion. In 1912, the Bernheim-Jeune gallery in Paris gave the Futurists not only an opportunity to show their work but a chance to describe what distinguished their position from that of Cubism. Put briefly, this amounted to stasis (Cubism) versus dynamic movement (Futurism). As this exhibition travelled to London, Herwarth Walden organized, that same year, a Futurist retrospective in his Berlin gallery, Der Sturm.

Noise and confusion, provocation and excitement at all costs, were the characteristic traits of Futurist agitation. In the long run they began to grate so on the nerves of the sensitive Gino Severini, who was initially influenced by Seurat's Pointillism, that he repeatedly exhorted his comrades to please calm down. Their obtrusive vitalism was not only verbal but visual. Inspired by Analytic Cubism, the Futurists focussed on the simultaneity of various views of a motif, but instead of depicting it in a state of immobility they showed it in rotating, plunging, or thrusting motion. Motion itself, or rather, the various phases of its process, were to be immediately visualized in a painting or sculpture. This intention was achieved in its mildest form by Severini, a cultivated colorist who, even in his Futurist work, never entirely lost touch with Neo-Impressionism in his many paintings of balls and ballerinas. The dynamism of his very effective compositions is lyrically subdued, formally disciplined, and, to this extent, clearly influenced by the aesthetic of classical Cubism. No wonder that, in the 1912 show, it was Severini's work that most appealed to the French audience (p. 84 and ill. right).

Dynamism and the Fourth Dimension

A more energetic embodiment of Futurist ideas was achieved by Umberto Boccioni. "I wish to paint the new, the fruit of our industrial age," he noted in his diary. Boccioni employed powerful, plastic forms that eventually led him to sculpture, and an expressive palette that far transcended Neo-Impressionism. He also developed what he termed a "dynamics of the human body," which however was impressively contained in controlled form. Cézanne and Cubism stood at the beginning of this style. States of excitement and emotional moods entered the picture in Boccioni's renderings of *The Street Revolts* (New York, The Museum of Modern Art) or *The Street Penetrates the Building* (p. 86 above). Here the forms grow transparent, interior and exterior interpenetrate, are depicted in simultaneous overlaps, as are the events taking place in the building and the street. The fourth dimension, time, enters the scene – or at least this was the artist's intention. The viewer was to be spirited "into the midst of the picture." A tumultuous unrest, the hectic nervousness of urban life, but also the intoxication of speed, become painterly events in Boccioni's work. And this even though the striving to depict motion – before the invention of "moving pictures" and long before kinetic art – was ultimately foiled by the immutable stasis of the painting surface.

Though Futurism was able to represent the course of a motion diagrammatically, in a way similar to multiple-

Carlo Carrà
Interventionist Demonstration
(Patriotic Celebration), 1914
Tempera and collage on cardboard,
38.5 x 30 cm
Milan, Mattioli Collection

Gino Severini
Portrait of Paul Fort, 1913/14
Collage on canvas, 81 x 65 cm
Paris, Musée National d'Art
Moderne, Centre Georges
Pompidou

Umberto Boccioni
The Street Penetrates the
Building, 1911
Oil on canvas, 100 x 106.5 cm
Hannover, Sprengel Museum
Hannover

Umberto Boccioni
Dynamism of the Human
Body, 1913
Oil on canvas, 100 x 100 cm
Milan, Civico Museo d'Arte
Contemporanea

Umberto Boccioni
Dynamism of a Soccer Player, 1913
Oil on canvas, 193.2 x 201 cm
New York, The Museum of
Modern Art, Sidney and Harriet
Janis Collection

exposure photographs, the depiction motion itself escaped its means. Faithful depiction of motion had to wait for the film, which had been pointed the way by the instantaneous sequential photographs of Eadweard Muybridge and the "chronophotography" of Etienne-Jules Marey, also of key significance to the Futurists. To today's eyes a runner with ten legs or a horse with twenty might seem rather jejune, especially as the Futurists' express aim was to render reality more closely than their predecessors. But being surfeited with flickering electronic media imagery, we realize that such criteria are beside the point. What counts, apart from the continuing effects of Futurism's elan, is above all the degree of its aesthetic success.

Futurist work that still deserves undivided attention includes the relatively static and often almost entirely abstract paintings of the oldest protagonist of the movement, Giacomo Balla (ill. right and below); the *Dancers* by his pupil, Severini; and especially the energy-charged compositions of Boccioni with their dynamic distortions. Severini came, by way of a return to Cubism, to the neoclassical style so widespread in the 1920s and 1930s, before, in old age, he began to recapitulate Futurist motifs. Carlo Carrà authored a manifesto of *Total Painting*, a sort of multimedia art comprising colors, tones, noises, and odors. Yet basically he was a covert classicist, whose roots in Giotto and Paolo Uccello are evident in his superb metaphysical paintings.

Giacomo Balla
Form Cries "Viva Italy", 1915
Oil on canvas, 134 x 188 cm
Rome, Balla Collection

"Futurism, predestined force of progress and not of fashion, creates the style of flowing abstract forms that are synthetic and inspired by the dynamic forces of the universe."
GIACOMO BALLA

Giacomo Balla
Dynamism of a Dog on a Leash
(Leash in Motion), 1912
Oil on canvas, 90.8 x 110 cm
Buffalo (NY), Albright-Knox Art
Gallery, Bequest of A. Conger
Goodyear

His friend, Giorgio De Chirico, though he was among the founding fathers of Futurism, likewise retained a stronger allegiance to *Pittura metafisica*. This phase brought forth his finest works, before he turned to a more realistic style shot through with occasional references to earlier approaches.

Total or multimedia art, simultaneity, dynamism, depiction of movement and speed, an interlocking of interior and exterior worlds, a painterly interpretation of feelings – these are the Futurist ideas which survived the movement itself, whose only direct follower of any significance was Enrico Prampolini, a skilled theater painter and later abstractionist (ill. above). These ideas lastingly inspired not only Italian art but spread throughout Europe and beyond. Far-reaching innovations and a number of good paintings were all that remained of the revolt of chauvinistic intellectuals, of which some later distanced themselves from the militancy of their early years. Everything else vanished, like ostensibly dynamic fascism and its ephemeral *aeropit-*

tura, or painting in an airplane, which today is little more than a curious footnote to art history.

"Standing on the top of the world, we once again fling our challenge to the stars," the Futurists declared in their manifesto. Their great exhibition of 1986 in Venice not only documented the vital force of the movement in every medium of art (painting, sculpture, poetry, music, theater, and dance), it also pointed out its intellectual and aesthetic wellsprings (for instance, in the Pointillism of Seurat) and its far-reaching consequences from Russian Cubo-Futurism to the Op Art and Kinetic Art of our own day.

The consequences, too, were multi-disciplinary. They related to music, in the form of *musique concrète*, to the theater, as well as to attempts to link art with technology and life with art. "Power to the artists!" demanded Marinetti in 1919, because they had the ability to "artistically suffuse life and make life itself into a work of art." The affinity with the later demands of a Lucio Fontana or a Joseph Beuys is obvious, as is the attempt to infuse visual art, especially sculpture, with energy and dynamism. As regards sculpture, the Futurists were the first artists ever to advance the notion that all materials were fundamentally of equal value. The inclusion of the factor of time in art likewise went back to Futurist conceptions. Kurt Schwitters's proliferating "MERZ" structure (p. 461) would have been as unthinkable without them as the dynamic sculptures of Norbert Kricke (p. 495) or the accumulations of the Nouveaux Réalistes.

"Paris, You, My Second Vitebsk!"
Marc Chagall and the Jewish Outsiders

One is the hero of sentimental artists' legends; the second is extremely popular; the third was unjustifiably almost entirely forgotten until a just few years ago. All three shared in common a Jewish background and an artistic home, Paris. They were an Italian and two Russians: Amedeo Modigliani, of Livorno; Marc Chagall, of Vitebsk, and Chaïm Soutine, of Smilovich, near Minsk. The three were linked with Cubism by the circumstance of sharing, with Léger, a dismal studio in the vicinity of the Paris stockyards in Vaugirard. Other links with Western European streams in art were more or less accidental, although it cannot be gainsaid that formal and technical skills acquired in Paris gave them the means to express their feelings, indeed to overcome the traditional Jewish ban on image-making. All three elude stylistic classification; each stands as an original figure alongside the mainstream of developments. For all three men, as Chagall said, art was foremost a state of mind, and only secondarily a problem of form. What the very different pictures of these three Jewish artists share in common is an overabundance of emotion, which in Modigliani and Chagall is accompanied by a lyrical charm that is hard to resist.

Modigliani, son of an upper-middle class family, kept alive the Tuscan tradition of *disegno*, masterful drawing, which Vasari described as the "active creative principle in the visual arts." (ill. right and p. 90). Like the Picasso of the pre-Cubist Blue and Rose periods, Modigliani was fascinated by Lautrec's arabesques, traces of which are found in his early work. The great Romanian sculptor Constantin Brancusi encouraged him to create idol-like, elongated figures. Modigliani was also influenced by the expressive force of Black African sculpture, and ultimately he submitted himself to the gentle yoke of Cézanne's formally concentrated figurative painting. Cézanne's color also gave him pointers. Modigliani's art was rooted in a brotherly love for social outcasts and outsiders, one of whom he felt himself to be. The eccentric friends with whom he debated and drank, his girlfriends, poor, half-starved children of

"By the way, I try to formulate with the greatest clarity the truth about art and life, in the way that I experienced it occasionally through the beauties of Rome and since I saw the inner connection, I will try to reveal it..." AMEDEO MODIGLIANI

Amedeo Modigliani
The Peasant Boy, c. 1918
Oil on canvas, 100 x 65 cm
London, Tate Gallery

Amedeo Modigliani
Nude on a Blue Cushion, 1917
Oil on canvas, 65.5 x 100.9 cm
Washington, National Gallery
of Art

Amedeo Modigliani
The Bride and Groom, c. 1915/16
Oil on canvas, 55.2 x 46.4 cm
New York, The Museum of
Modern Art

Page 91 below:
Marc Chagall
The Cattle Dealer, 1912
Oil on canvas, 97 x 200.5 cm
Basel, Öffentliche Kunstsamm-
lung Basel, Kunstmuseum

the Montmartre and later Montparnasse milieu, were
Modigliani's models. He depicted them with the clairvoyant vision of the drinker and drug-taker, one of the
last Bohemians of the century – a tall, handsome man to
whom women were magnetically attracted, but also a
sick and wasted man, unable to manage the money his
family sent him.

Modigliani was a latter-day Mannerist, the painter
of overelongated, willfully distorted figures with long
necks and close-set, introspective, sometimes empty
eyes in masklike faces. The charm of his art lies less in its
palette than in its drawing. Modigliani's line has a lyrical
beauty that occasionally verges on the overelegant. In
what one commentator calls his "human still lifes" the
finest tradition of Sienese-Florentine art survives, something of the melancholy grace of Sandro Botticelli,
heightened by a touch of Matisse.

A far cry from the aura of lasciviousness that surrounds Modigliani's nudes is the art of Marc Chagall.
The shy, stuttering son of a Russian clerk from Vitebsk,
in 1910 he came to the bustling avant-garde center of
Paris, his head full of colorful dreams and tales from the
village and ghetto. Chagall's art drew sustenance from
this humble world, where his memories and desires
were at home, continually returning to the great events
of little lives: birth, love, marriage, death. The highest
praise Chagall could think of affording Paris was to
exclaim, "There it is! Paris, you, my second Vitebsk!"

Apart from his meeting with the famous theater designer Léon Bakst, Russian schools had little to offer Chagall. Like many Western prophets of a new art, he was refused entry to the state art school. Yet in Paris he found immense inspiration. Chagall made friends with the author of "simultaneous poetry," Blaise Cendrars, with Max Jacob and Apollinaire. He became acquainted with Modigliani and above all with Delaunay, whose brilliant Orphism confirmed his own, folkloristic, colorful approach. Chagall delved into the aesthetic issues of Cubism, which helped give his painting a solid structural framework. But despite the abundance of impulses from outside, Chagall remained true to his own origins, which were rooted in the Chassidic love of storytelling, in Jewish pantheism with its faith in the indissoluble link between God and men, which makes believers capable of working miracles.

Chagall's paintings accordingly evoke a world full of miracles that happen every day – in lovers' bedrooms, at the inn, on the streets of Vitebsk, even under the Eiffel Tower. Even though he adopted a Cubistically austere style and employed simultaneous effects, he basically remained a Russian-Jewish storyteller. Yet Chagall cannot be called a narrative artist, at least during his best years, for he had the ability to transmute his fantastic tales directly into pure painting. This is why the Surrealists revered him as a predecessor, the artist who introduced the metaphor into modern painting, as André Breton said. The austere still-life subjects of the Cubists, their tables, glasses, bowls, and guitars, held little interest for Chagall.

Even his famous Cubist composition *The Drinking Soldier* (ill. right) tells a story. The soldier is so tipsy that he feels his cap is flying off his head, as he sees a vision of a couple dancing on the table in front of him. This is

Marc Chagall
The Drinking Soldier, 1911/12
Oil on canvas, 109 x 94.5 cm
New York, The Solomon
R. Guggenheim Museum

Chagall himself and a Russian girl – an image of remembrance. Chagall made the mundane appear "miraculous". That was the aim of his estranging effects, which include physical manifestations of sheer joy. An example is the picture in which he and his fiancée and later wife, Bella, float blissfully through the air; another is the wellwisher at *The Birthday* (ill. above), who is filled with such joy that he leaves the floor, his back to his girl, his head bent backwards at an angle only love could permit, offering a kiss. Then there is the *Violinist*, hovering over the rooftops of Vitebsk as he plays, in the background a haloed figure passing across the sky, watched by a man with three heads in the foreground – a saint's legend in modern embodiment. Finally, there is the face of Chagall's *Rabbi*, enigmatic and inscrutable, broodingly spiritual, marked by the millennia-old torments of his people and its divine revelations.

Chagall's painting and his very painterly graphic, illustrations to Gogol, Lafontaine, and the Bible, transgress the borderline of the visible and tangible realm. To that extent his art is surreal, as few similarities it otherwise bears to the intellectual, consciously shocking juxtapositions of Surrealism proper. Color is used symbolically, especially the all-pervading, mystical violet, but also Chagall's luminous red, shimmering green, cerulean blue, or blue-green oxide. This exciting color range intrigued the Expressionists, who, like the Surrealists, and to a lesser degree the Cubists, considered Chagall their brother in spirit.

In 1914 his paintings were shown at Walden's Sturm gallery in Berlin, and had a resounding success. The poet Ludwig Rubiner even went so far as to tell the artist, "Your paintings have initiated Expressionism. They draw high prices. But don't expect to receive the money Walden owes you. He is not going to pay you a thing, because he maintains that fame should be enough for you."

"I Am Certain that Rembrandt Loves Me"

Evidently Chagall did not bother much about the commercial side of art. "I am certain that Rembrandt loves me," he wrote in his autobiography. Chagall admired Cézanne almost as much as the great Netherlandish artist. His involvement with Cézanne helped him develop a formal framework to contain his apparently freely and spontaneously composed imagery, a rational check on the irrational tendency of Chagall's visions.

He was an extremely prolific painter, and constantly recapitulated certain themes around which his thinking and feeling revolved. Rarely did anything new or unprecedented enter this circumscribed world. In the 1930s and 1940s, horrified by the fate of the Jews under Nazi terror, Chagall's form and color grew agitated and wild, and he depicted a number of crucifixions. The *White Crucifixion*, done in 1938, evoked evils perpetrated and anticipated those to come. It is a key image of the epoch.

Marc Chagall
The Seine Bridges, 1954
Oil on canvas, 115.5 x 163.5 cm
Hamburg, Hamburger Kunsthalle

The death of Chagall's first wife, Bella, in 1944, triggered a series of paintings charged with memories of the past. Previously, in the 1930s, the artist had discovered the beauty of flowers in southern France. Not all of the resulting paintings were of equal quality. Especially in his late years, Chagall was not always able to avoid the pitfalls of sentimentality, the anecdotal, and the all-too ingratiating.

Apocalyptic Landscape

The art of Chaïm Soutine (p. 95), still not accorded the respect it deserves, is darker and more ambiguous than Chagall's. One of many children born into a tailor's family in a hamlet near Minsk, Soutine basically remained a homeless wanderer throughout his life. The wild fire that suffused the shy, hypercritical painter broke out in a series of apocalyptic landscapes blazing with Expressionist-Fauvist color, in depictions of slaughtered oxen, in portraits and paintings of choirboys transfused with melancholy and forlornness, but also sometimes partaking of sly humor. Soutine's art is nourished by the heavy, glowing sumptuousness of the paint, which he applied to the canvas spontaneously, almost without preliminary drawing, sometimes directly from the tube. Werner Haftmann has pointed to Soutine's

Moïse Kisling
Kiki of the Montparnasse, with Red Sweater and Blue Scarf, 1925
Oil on canvas, 92 x 65 cm
Geneva, Musée du Petit Palais

affinities with the visionary aspect of German Expressionism. But even more relevant is his position between two artists separated by decades in time: van Gogh, and the great American from Holland, Willem De Kooning.

The high-strung erotic art of Jules Pascin, born in Bulgaria to a Spanish-Jewish father and an Italian mother, also belongs in this context (ill. above). His sexual themes and celebration of *la dolce vita* were only the other side of a deeply depressive character. Pascin's mental torment came to a head when he realized that he had sacrificed his eminent gifts as a draftsman to the demands of fashionable society. Seeing no way out, Pascin hanged himself in his studio on the eve of a vernissage.

With these artists, among whom must be counted the realistic Polish painter Moïse Kisling (p. 94), began the Jewish contribution to figurative painting in the 20th century. Paris brought to light the imagery slumbering in the depths of a people whose religion precluded the making of images. Modern Israel, though eager to close the gap, for a long period had little to set beside the early contribution of the Jewish members of the Ecole de Paris and that of two major American artists of Eastern Jewish origin, Mark Rothko and Barnett Newman. However, as developments in recent decades indicate – from the influential work of the former Klee student Ardon to Yaacov Agam, Kadishman, and younger artists such as Rafi Kaiser, Zvi Goldstein, Serge Spitzer, et al. – a great deal has changed since then.

Henri Rousseau
The Snake Charmer, 1907
Oil on canvas, 169 x 189.5 cm
Paris, Musée d'Orsay

Dreams of Compelling Magic
Henri Rousseau, his Contemporaries and Followers

"I don't know whether you feel the way I do, but when I am in these hothouses and see the strange plants from exotic lands it seems to me that I am entering a dream. I feel like a quite different person."

HENRI ROUSSEAU

When eager amateurs open a paintbox, every day becomes a Sunday. And what charms us about the works of these Sunday, weekend, or naive artists is the carefree, holiday mood they lend to reality. "For your true, dyed-in-the-wool Sunday painter, art is not a heartfelt concern, it is heartily indifferent to him," as someone aptly said. Naive artists have saved for our problem-laden era something of the innocence of the anonymous folk art which was submerged by the great European styles in fine art. The fact that such outsiders have even been noticed at all is a consequence of that search for a lost innocence that began with the discovery, in the early years of the century, of the supposedly primitive art of exotic peoples and distant times. It was so much public interest as that of intellectuals and artists that brought to light the imaginative masterpieces of unassuming amateurs.

This first happened, like so many other firsts of the period, in Paris. There resided a man by the name of Henri-Julien-Félix Rousseau, an employee of the *Douane*, or municipal customs bureau, whose life,

despite the many legends that have grown up around it, lies largely in obscurity. He stood at the inception of the history of what Kandinsky termed the "great reality", as whose representative in an era growing increasingly unreal Kandinsky described Rousseau. But he was also a dominating figure whose art remains unsurpassed in its poetic abundance and visionary force.

Rousseau's personality combined naivety with great intelligence; his simplicity was that of a prophet of the people, a seer. The exotic atmosphere of his tropical forests was once thought to reflect memories of a trip to Mexico, though this is now disputed. More probably, Rousseau's vegetation originated from the exhaustive studies he made in the Jardin des Plantes. A police report alludes to sinister affairs, and due to actively abetting fraud on the part of a bank official, Rousseau narrowly missed actually being sent to an exotic land: Cayenne and its penal colony. We know that he gave lessons in recitation and the violin, in order to keep his head above water after an early retirement. Also on record is the legendary banquet which Picasso gave in honor of the *Douanier* at the Bateau-Lavoir. Rousseau took the occasion to insure his host that both were great painters, he, Rousseau, in the modern style, and Picasso in the Egyptian style. According to a report by Gertrude Stein, who was present with her entourage, as were Max Jacob, Apollinaire, André Salmon, Marie Laurencin, and others, the gratified Rousseau slept through most of the boisterous party.

This odd fellow was revered almost as a household saint by the artists and writers of Bohemian Montmartre as the great primitive of a late era, despite the fact that his pronouncements often made them laugh. Apollinaire inscribed a farewell poem on his gravestone with an engraving tool, and Constantin Brancusi and the painter de Zarate later deepened the lines and made them weatherproof. It was a well-earned honor for Rousseau, who lived his entire life in poverty and whose paintings, hardly had he passed away, began to fetch astronomical prices. He far surpassed every *peintre naif* who went before him, nor has any matched him since. Except for his artist-friends, who recognized him as one of their own, Rousseau's rank was initially appreciated only by Wilhelm von Uhde. It was the German collector and tireless discoverer and his 1928 exhibition of Rousseau, André Bauchant, Camille Bombois, Séraphine (Louis), and Louis Vivin finally sparked public interest in naive art.

Strolling through the Impressionist collections in the Musée d'Orsay in Paris, one may suddenly stop short, transfixed by eyes as if from a dream, gleaming among tropical vegetation. Snakes coil in the trees, on the lakeshore, around the shoulders of a dark-skinned woman. The forms of everything are very precisely rendered, yet still unreal, surreal, fixed like symbols. The scenery is spirited into a timeless intermediate realm, where dream and reality merge indistinguishably. This is a picture by the eccentric Douanier Rousseau, called *The Snake Charmer*, an incunablum of pure realism (p. 96). The late jungle paintings, visions of compelling magic, are the major works of Rousseau, some of them, incidentally, executed with amazing sophistication. Yet his less fantastic motifs, mundane suburban landscapes and figure groups, are reduced in the same way to essentials, concentrated into monumental emblems. The process lends the group pictures, stiffly posed like family photos in an album, a timeless aspect, such that the humor of the awkward rendering flips over into sublime dignity. Rousseau's works are archetypes, images from the source of all imagery. An incredible instinct for the expressive power of color, for the arrangement of planes in space, and for formal structure, lends them their outstanding quality. Hermann Broch once justifiably spoke of Rousseau's "mythical naiveness."

Another extraordinary talent, more obsessive than naive, was Séraphine Louis. She was Wilhelm Uhde's cleaning lady, and he discovered her talent more by chance. A rare case among amateur artists, Séraphine showed little concern with the outside world, painting only her visions – phantasmagorical shrubbery, foliage, flowers and fruit, partaking of both heaven and hell, with angels' and devils' eyes meeting our gaze. Beset by voices and ghosts, Séraphine escaped the coils of evil lusts in painting and prayer. Her works are the traumatic

Henri Rousseau
Myself, Portrait-Landscape, 1890
Oil on canvas, 143 x 110 cm
Prague, Národni Galeri

Séraphine
Paradise Tree, c. 1929
Oil on canvas, 195 x 129 cm
Paris, Musée National d'Art
Moderne, Centre Georges
Pompidou

visions of a woman who suppressed carnal desires and devoted her life to the Virgin Mary (p. 97).

The other painter to whom Uhde drew the attention of Paris and the world was less complex and more down to earth. André Bauchant (ill. below left) depicted Greek landscapes and allegories, in which "the village postman cheerfully marches alongside Vercingetorix." Camille Bombois brushed flat planes and brilliant colors next to one another on canvas with the hard grip of a veteran wrestler (ill. right). Louis Vivin, conscientious as a diligent boy, painted his churches stone by stone, and if the result did not look natural enough, he added a little more plaster to the paint (p. 99 below).

The five Parisian artists have since been joined by a great company, in France as elsewhere. To list only three of the more serious European *naïfs*: first, Adalbert Trillhaase, a depictor of scurrilously demonic, fanatically pious hunting scenes and Bible stories. Second, a respectable Dutch hotel owner, horse breeder, and rider called Jan van Weert, who started painting when he was seventy because the pictures he had bought had gotten lost and the walls looked so bare. His specialty was Dutch mail coaches in landscapes of the changing seasons. Third, there was Stepan Generalíc, whose military subjects soon, unfortunately, became all-too routine. These three were accompanied by scores of others, known and unknown, not to mention the increasing numbers of *faux naïfs* that came in their wake. Active on the other side of the Atlantic were a

number of American folk artists, whose tradition began in the 19th century with the sign-painter and itinerant preacher Edward Hicks. Morris Hirshfield, who was born in Poland, had a careful technique and his paintings – particularly of female nudes – were rich in ornament. This is apparent, for example in *Girl in the Mirror* (p. 99 above). Grandma Moses, an original who lived to be 100, was for the time being the last famous link in the chain (ill. above). Like van Weert, the rugged farmer's wife was over seventy when she first picked up a brush, to depict memories from which ugliness and evils may be expunged, but which celebrate the glories of the simple life with great humility and peace of mind.

A Painter of Montmartre

Some of the same qualities are found in the best paintings of a resident of Montmartre, Maurice Utrillo. He stands at the borderline that separates the "naive" from the "professional" artist. Ultimately he was something of both. Maurice was a shy, weak, and above all neglected boy, to whom his love-hungry mother was not always able to devote enough time. A feeling of being abandoned, shut off from the world, augmented his hereditary propensity. Maurice drank and painted. He became the portraitist of Montmartre (ill. below). In keeping with his background he began with Impressionism, under the tutelage of his mother, whom Degas had taught to paint. But Utrillo had a heavy hand. His division of colors was not methodical, and his art, at least in the early years, lacked all perfectionistic fluency. Artistic problems did not interest him much anyway. Utrillo simply wished to realistically paint the environs in which he lived, not to create art. Impressionism struck him as the best way of approaching reality – apart from the fact that he knew no other. But reality includes the feelings and moods of the person who perceives it. Utrillo projected such sensations into his pictures. This is the source of their melancholy, occasionally somewhat sentimental poetry, and of the mellowness of their color, especially in the "white period" with its subtle gradations between white and grey. "White and silence are what one must paint," Utrillo told Florent Fels, "the color of the barracks, the hospitals, the prisons. My life has run its course in these houses of the lost, in the midst of the white of misery .… . It is not jolly being a cursed painter [*un peintre maudit*]."

"Montmartre, with your small town corners and your alleys of the Bohème – how may stories could b written about this quarter... I will always feel well when I am close to you, when I sit my my room and paint a picture with whitewashed houses." MAURICE UTRILLO

6 The End of Illusion

Painting as an Inner Necessity
The Blauer Reiter, Kandinsky, and the Spiritual in Art

The most radical revolution in painting since the Renaissance was set underway not by a fiery young rebel but by a distinguished middle-aged man, who at thirty would have become professor of national economics at Dorpat University had he not decided for a career in art instead. His name was Wassily Kandinsky, born in 1866 in Moscow, died in 1944 in Neuilly-sur-Seine. Though his intellectual and artistic life came to fulfillment in Western Europe, a very Russian yearning for the "great mother," Moscow, and the golden glow of her domes never left him. It is idle to debate the question whether or not Kandinsky was the inventor of the abstract painting which dominated the art scene for a full fifty years of the century. Other artists could justifiably claim priority: Kupka, the Lithuanian painter Mikolajus K. Čiurlionis, Adolf Hoelzel of Germany, the American Arthur Dove (ill. below), Katharina Schäffner of Prague, not to mention the Art Nouveau practitioners Henry van de Velde, Hermann Obrist, or August Endell. Surely the earliest theoretical and practical approaches to abstraction can be found in the streams represented by the above names, if we disregard even earlier but ephemeral examples that lead from Leonardo da Vinci and the perspective manuals of the 16th century down to Lawrence Sterne's *Tristram Shandy* illustrations,

Mikolajus Konstantinas Čiurlionis
Star Sonata. Allegro, 1908
Tempera on cardboard,
72.2 x 61.4 cm
Kaunas, Museum Čiurlionis

Arthur Dove
Holbrook Bridge, Northwest, 1938
Oil on canvas, 63.5 x 89 cm
New York, Roy R. Neuberger
Collection

Victor Hugo's gouaches, and certain Italian examples in the 19th century.

Čiurlionis, who began as a musical prodigy, was primarily a Symbolist painter of dreamlike fantastic landscapes, but he also translated symphonic sounds and structures into "abstract" paintings (ill. right). The first picture of this type emerged in 1905. Hoelzel transformed landscapes and figures into free, rhythmic ornaments, while Schäffner expressed moods and passions through lines alone. Kupka, who came out of Symbolism, painted his first abstract picture, based on Art Nouveau ornamentation, in 1910/11, certainly without knowing of Kandinsky's concurrent experiments. Yet none of the attempts named really went beyond the experimental stage, transcended the merely ornamental, or, most importantly, had a logical theory behind them. This ultimately holds for Hoelzel as well, who, with Kupka, was among the most significant of the forerunners of abstraction. His work was a prelude to the transition, which remarkably began at a number of different places almost simultaneously, without the painters' initially being aware of each other's development – with Delaunay and Kupka in Paris, with Kandinsky in Munich, and with Mikhail Larionov in Moscow.

The time was ripe for an art of signs and symbols in a world that was growing more complex seemingly by the day. Any attempt to cope with or explain this complexity had to fall back on formulae. In this regard, the

Page 100:
Wassily Kandinsky
Two Ovals
(Composition No. 218), 1919
Oil on canvas, 107 x 89.5 cm
St. Petersburg, Russian State
Museum

Marianne von Werefkin
Self-Portrait I, c. 1908–1910
Tempera on paper, 51 x 34 cm
Munich, Städtische Galerie im
Lenbachhaus

Wassily Kandinsky
Murnau – View with Railway and
Castle, 1909
Oil on cardboard, 36 x 49 cm
Munich, Städtische Galerie im
Lenbachhaus, Gabriele Münter
Foundation

artists' experiments paralled developments in other
fields, particularly science and technology. These
included, on the one hand, color theory, emerging in
the wake of Newton, Euler, Huyghen, and the early
"color piano" of Castel; light theory, cosmology,
morphology, and quantum mechanics. On the other,
there was the development of photography and methods of reproduction, continuations of the Romantic
artists' investigations into correspondences between

painting and music, color and sound. Psychology and
psychonanalysis had more importance for Surrealism,
which was emerging almost concurrently with abstraction.

It was Kandinsky's historical achievement to have
recognized these interrelationships both as an artist and
as a theoretician, and to have been the first to methodically investigate them. The Russian was the undisputed
leader of the group of Munich artists who called themselves "Der Blaue Reiter," (Blue Rider), not Franz Marc,
the now-popular painter of creaturely fates, not the
radiant boy August Macke, and certainly not Klee, who
was still at the beginning of his development. With the
Blauer Reiter, German Expressionism entered its
second, as it were aristocratic, phase. This loose union of
very different temperaments and diverse personalities
was not concerned, as the Brücke artists of Dresden initially were, with improving the world and reforming
society. Their aim, as announced in the title of the essay
Kandinsky wrote in 1910 and published in 1912, was
On the Spiritual in Art (Über das Geistige in der Kunst).
As Franz Marc wrote to his wife from the front, "Precisely 'pure' art concerns itself so little with the 'others',
bothers so little about the 'purpose of unifying mankind', as Tolstoy says, pursues no purposes at all, but
is simply a metaphorical act of creation, proud and
entirely 'of and for itself'." This amounted to a clear
rejection of the positivistic, materialist thinking of the
19th century.

The Hour of Pure Abstraction
Nothing could be more mistaken than to consider these
artists, who wished to be neither reformers nor revolutionaries, a group of level-headed intellectuals. Kandinsky and Marc in particular, much like the Romantics
before them, saw art as being closely related to religion.
Kandinsky's thinking was rooted in an emotional Christianity of the Slavic variety, and Marc's thinking and
feeling grew out of a highly imaginative and decidedly
Romantic sense of nature, which prompted a yearning
for purity and redemption. The most important crite-
rion of all artistic activity for the Blauer Reiter members
was – in Kandinsky's phrase – "inner necessity." With
their art they hoped to set the viewer's mind in sympathetic vibration, not upset it by distorting and radically
reducing their motifs like the rebellious architecture students in Dresden.

Far from the Brücke's converted railroad station
and the scene of their famous and riotous "Dresden
Fests" at the Baroque Fürstenhof, the artists in sophisticated Munich preached not neo-primitivism but
profound contemplation and sensibility. In Kandinsky's
eyes, fundamental emotions such as love, lust, and
anxiety were "material," that is, vulgar emotions, and as
such had no place in art. He intended to strike more
sensitive chords in the human soul. The art of the Blauer
Reiter, with the exception of the uncomplicated and
worldly Macke, tended to the transcendental, meta-

Wassily Kandinsky
Untitled, 1910 (1913)
Pencil, watercolor and India ink on
paper, 49.6 x 64.8 cm
Paris, Musée National d'Art
Moderne, Centre Georges
Pompidou

physical, the realm of pure mind. Despite all its emotionality, it was informed by a philosophical strain. It was an art of thinking painters for twentieth-century man. Inspiration was subjected to rational control; no attempt was made to pretend that innocence and naivety had not been irrevocably lost. Pure realism could be found only among a few, truly naive sorcerers of painting like Henri Rousseau. For the others, above all Kandinsky, the hour of pure abstraction, what he called the "great abstract," had come.

The aesthetic revolution did not break out suddenly. It was prepared for over a long period, and Kandinsky was almost 45 years old when, between 1910 and 1913, he advanced to abstraction. His famous "first abstract watercolor," dated by the artist to 1910, was long considered the incunabulum of abstract painting (ill. above). However, it was likely not rendered until about 1913, as recent stylistic and technical investigations appear to prove.

Other members of the Blauer Reiter were Alexei von Javlensky, a former lieutenant in the Russian hussars, and his painter-wife, Baroness Marianne von Verefkin (p. 102); Kandinsky's pupil and long-time companion Gabriele Münter; Adolf Erbslöh; Alexander Kanoldt, who later developed a neo-classically tinged, sharp-focus "magic" realism; the graphic artist Alfred Kubin; the French Cubist Henri Le Fauconnier; Karl Hofer for a time; and finally, Macke and Marc. If we include Heinrich Campendonk and Lyonel Feininger, who participated in the 1913 "Deutscher Herbstsalon" (German Autumn Salon) the ranks of the late Blauer Reiter are complete. Kandinsky also introduced the composer Arnold Schönberg, who occasionally painted, to the group.

A Bavarian Coffee Party

The differences of character, and of intellectual and aesthetic goals, were too great for the group to last long. For a few years conservative Munich witnessed a phalanx that, picking up where Jugendstil left off, strove for a new European art. They mounted significant exhibitions of the great French artists, were attacked as "un-German" and "pro-Western" by the pious and patriotic Vinnen of the Worpswede artists' colony (and sadly also by Käthe Kollwitz), and suspected of "wheeling-dealing" by no less than Meier-Graefe. In the meantime the critics took their usual potshots at "incurable madmen," "shameless bluffers," and "boom profiteers," thereby enriching the vocabulary of the brown-shirted iconoclasts soon to come.

Then an event occurred which is not uncommon amongst contentious artists – a great and resounding quarrel. When Erbslöh and Kanoldt decided they could no longer follow Kandinsky's innovations, he and his Bavarian friend Marc drew their conclusions. They resigned, and began planning an almanach to explain their secessionist views to the public. As a title they chose *Der Blaue Reiter*, after a motif of Kandinsky's. It was collaborative work on the almanach, co-edited by Kandinsky and Marc and published in 1912, that brought the group into being. In addition to pictures

"As has been said often enough, it is impossible to make clear the aim of a work of art by means of words. Despite a certain superficiality with which this assertion is leveled and in particular exploited, it is by and large correct, and remains so even at a time of the greatest education and knowledge of language and its material. And this assertion – I now abandon the realm of objective reasoning – is also correct because the artist himself can never either grasp or recognize fully his own aim."
WASSILY KANDINSKY

Wassily Kandinsky
Improvisation "Klamm", 1914
Oil on canvas, 110 x 110 cm
Munich, Städtische Galerie im Lenbachhaus

and articles by Kandinsky, Marc, and Macke, reproductions of work by Klee, Kubin, Cézanne, Matisse, Delaunay, Picasso, Rousseau, Kirchner, Nolde, Kokoschka, and Hans Arp, the almanach contained compositions by Schönberg, Alban Berg, and Anton Webern. As the participation of composers indicates, the group viewed the issues of form and expression in the visual arts in connection with music. What Gauguin had intuitively sensed, was now methodically investigated – the process of synesthesia. "Music and painting are basically the same – you only have to have the organ" to detect it, Marc wrote home from the war.

Rarely have conversations over the coffee table had more momentous consequences than those concerning the almanach, which took place at Marc's house and of which he gave an excited and somewhat subjective report. From that point on, Germany became an equal partner with France on the European art scene for twenty years. Though the First World War brought a painful caesura, and Macke and Marc were killed, the development continued until the rise of the Nazis to power in 1933 abruptly ended it.

The anecdote about how Kandinsky arrived at abstract painting has often been told, not lastly by the artist himself. He came home in the evening twilight, saw one of his paintings, turned ninety degrees and standing on its side, and did not recognize it. It seemed to him, that this was the work of a stranger, but he liked what he saw. What Kandinsky saw were only colors and forms, "suffused by an inner glow." He realized that painting had to become independent of material objects, that representations of them would be detrimental to his art. Yet abstraction was at first no dogma for him. Suggestions of objects break through again and again in the paintings of subsequent years: horses and riders, boats, angels with trumpets, church cupolas, hills and valleys, above them the sun or moon. These are fragments of memory, abbreviated signs, but they do originate from the visible world. A strong tension arises between the objective forms and the free composition of amorphous shapes and colors, making these works among the most beautiful the great Russian artist ever did, and giving them a place of prominence in his œuvre.

Moscow and "Lohengrin"

Kandinsky had to travel a long path before achieving this breakthrough. In Russia, he had been deeply impressed by Rembrandt in the Hermitage in St. Petersburg, and by Claude Monet's *Haystacks* and Richard Wagner's *Lohengrin* in Moscow. Wagner's opera seemed to him to musically reflect the resplendent colors of the Russian capital. For the first time he realized the possibility of expressing such sounds through color and form, an idea that basically made him decide to take up art and abandon what was a very promising academic career. Kandinsky began painting very novelistic, narrative pictures of a Romantic character which went back to Russian folk art. They teemed with figures, were ornamental and colorful as fairy tales; many were infused with the Romantic charm of the Middle Ages, to which was later added the influence of European Symbolism and Art Nouveau. These works, sentimental in the best sense, hardly suggest the revolutionary developments to come.

The final liberation of color came at Murnau, a Bavarian village on a lake, Staffelsee, where Kandinsky lived with his pupil, Gabriele Münter. His pictures, still very Impressionistic in approach, gradually grew ever more passionate, as the impasto strokes merged to form planes of color. The subject matter – landscapes and figures – was increasingly simplified in the manner of the German Expressionists and the French Fauves, whose work Kandinsky had seen in Paris. The artist submitted to the principle of the flat surface, gradually expunging every naturalistic and impressionistic detail. Byzantine splendor intermingled with European design in color. Other impulses came from Bavarian glass painting with its simple forms and strong colors. The motif was now only the occasion, not the theme of the painting, whose means – form, color, plane – grew increasingly autonomous. By reducing outward appearances to their essence, Kandinsky hoped to bring out the character of their painting as an entity independent of the natural model. Through the psychological effects of color even more than through its physical effects, Kandinsky hoped to touch the soul of the viewer. In his own words, "In general, then, color is a means to exert a direct influence on the soul." Using the analogy of a piano, he went on, "Color is the key. The eye is the hammer. The soul is the piano, with many strings."

Kandinsky envisaged playing on the piano of the soul. In his programmatic treatise, *On the Spiritual in Art*, of 1912, he outlined a tablature of the inherent values of colors and forms. These were fundamental patterns capable of infinite variation and combination, studies for a sort of thorough bass of painting, which Kandinsky considered desirable and possible as a supplement to Goethe's color theory. Colors, he explained, could be cold or warm, light or dark, bristling or smooth, soft or hard. The tension between blue and yellow represented the poles of cold and warm, spirituality and passion. When the tension was released by mixing them, the result was green, the color of calm. White had the effect of "great silence," black sounded like "a dead nothing-

"Every work of art is the child of its time, often it is the mother of our emotions. Thus, every period of culture produces its own art, which can never be repeated. Any attempt to give new life to the artistic principles of the past can at best only result in a work of art that resembles a stillborn child." WASSILY KANDINSKY

Wassily Kandinsky
In the Blue, 1925
Oil on cardboard, 80 x 110 cm
Düsseldorf, Kunstsammlung
Nordrhein-Westfalen

ness after the extinguishment of the sun," grey was "soundless and immobile," Saturn red coveyed the impression of power, energy, joy, and triumph, and cinnabar or vermilion was "like a constant, glowing passion." Forms, too, had their intrinsic character and mood. The circle, one of Kandinsky's favorite shapes, represented perfection or wholeness, while a semi-circle resting on its straight edge signified tranquillity and an upright triangle represented energy. Yellow was the "triangle color," blue the color of the circle. In the case of forms, direction played a key role. For instance, a triangle pointing upwards had a very different significance, and elicited a very different mood in the viewer, from a downward-pointing triangle. The same was true of lines: horizontality meant calm, an upward course meant joy, a downward course meant sadness. The energy with which lines were drawn, their width and direction of taper, also had their psychological connotations. Kandinsky's theory marked the beginning of the development of an entirely new vocabulary for talking about art. In turn, painting became a sort of written

Wassily Kandinsky
Sky-Blue, 1940
Oil on canvas, 100 x 73 cm
Paris, Musée National d'Art
Moderne, Centre Georges
Pompidou

language that had to be learned to appreciate it. Its words were colors and forms, its punctuation marks lines. In the course of time, Kandinsky envisaged, these symbols would call forth in the viewer's mind images or conceptions as precise as those elicited by common every-day words, like tree, sky, man, flower, and sea.

Like speech, but above all like music, painting was seen to possess rhythms, a certain mathematical precision, repetitions, and leitmotifs. A hierarchy of artistic means no longer existed, each being of equal value, like the twelve tones of the musical scale of Schönberg, whose formal theory confirmed the artists' investigations. The Russian composer Alexander Skriabin attempted to heighten the effect of musical notes by supplementing them with the corresponding colors. Macke had notes played on the piano to match the hues of his palette. As in music, inspiration and structuring, feeling and calculation came together in painting. Kandinsky's goal was to make the viewer's soul vibrate, like a sounding board, by means of the sounds of colors. He remained true to this aim even in his later, more dogmatic period, when during his years of teaching at the Bauhaus his paintings grew ever less expressive and more rigorous, controlled, and mathematical.

Before this phase of artistic development lay years spent in Russia during and after the First World War, from 1915 to 1921. The works of the period, not least as a result of Kandinsky's intellectual and aesthetic involvement with Constructivism, were initially very contradictory and heterogeneous. Kandinsky's own ideas and theory made little impression on his Constructivist colleagues, such as Alexander Rodchenko and Ivan Puni. The invitation to return to Germany and teach at the Bauhaus came as a godsend.

Kandinsky was convinced that the world of colors and forms rose from the depths of the human soul, like music. Although ordering colors and forms into a composition was a rational and necessary process, the source of the artist's means and activity was subconscious. His work was neither pure ornament, lacking in content, nor was it the result of pure calculation. Kandinsky energetically denied the accusation of formalism, nor would he condone talk about abstract wallpaper patterns or of meaningless, dry geometry. "Every means is sanctified, as long as it is inwardly necessary," he explained, in the moral categories of the German phrase, *Der Zweck heiligt die Mittel*, which were very typical of him. "Every means is sinful, as long as it does not stem from the wellspring of inner necessity … . Nothing is more detrimental and sinful than seeking form violently." For Kandinsky every form had its "inner content," and was "the expression of this content." Content was made up, firstly, of the personality of the artist, and secondly, of the spirit of the epoch in which he lived. Thus Kandinsky painted pictures of the "world within," mental images he saw with unusual vividness and clarity, the eidetic gift.

Painting and Physics

Another development that found entry into his imagery was the revolutionary new physics and its view of the universe, a development Kandinsky followed passionately and very knowledgeably. The results of this interest are best seen in the paintings of his "period of genius," from 1910 to the First World War, many of which are in the collection of the Städtische Galerie im Lenbachhaus, Munich. These *Improvisations, Compositions,* and – more rarely – *Impressions,* with their swirling, streaming, form-engendering and form-dissolving brushwork, their sometimes controlled and sometimes explosive outbreaks of unleashed color, their nervous, microbe-like webs of line, represent Expressionism taken to its logical conclusion.

It is difficult not to see a primary and conscious connection between the atomization of the pictorial plane and the findings of atomic physics, just as a perhaps unconscious link can be detected with the political catastrophe then coming to a head in Europe. Marc wrote while in the army that such pictures should be painted before a war, whereas in its aftermath, the thing was to confront chaos with a constructive order. Kandinsky did both.

Kandinsky's later compositions reflected his conviction that the ultimate abstract form in any art was number, an idea related to medieval and symbolist numerology. Yet while they were methodically designed and calculated, the best of these paintings temper mathematics with poetry. The artist's "inner necessity," that is, his creative gift, transfuses even their rigorous shapes and

arrangements, rendering them transcendent, raising them to the level of signs and symbols capable of pointing beyond themselves. In the late years following upon Kandinsky's emigration in 1933 to Neuilly, near Paris, his work began to be populated with playfully biomorphic shapes that recalled Surrealism and the imagery of Miró, and whose lyric joyfulness pointed back to Kandinsky's early predilection for Russian folk art.

The Popular "Cultural Bolshevik"

A less hermetic, less encoded world opens up before us in the work of a painter of whom, in a reversal of Klee's lament, it could be said that "A people supported him." This is Franz Marc, whose paintings the Nazis had to remove from their "Entartete Kunst" (Degenerate Art) exhibition because their "degeneracy" attracted crowds of admiring Aryans. Marc's continuing popularity, however, rests largely on a misunderstanding. Everybody enjoys his motifs, animals, and the lyrical, metaphysical aspect he lends them. We appreciate him emotionally and sentimentally, and tend to overlook his aesthetic gifts (ill. above and p. 108).

Marc was more than one of the most sympathetic figures in the history of modern art. He was an uncompromising artist who, with Kandinsky and his other Blauer Reiter friends, threw himself wholeheartedly into the campaign against public incomprehension. "The writers, at least, have managed to make the public accept that the moon can very well stroll into a room," he wrote in a note concerning *The Limitations of Art.* "One is even permitted to wear a sun in one's heart,

Franz Marc
Large Blue Horses, 1911
Oil on canvas, 102 x 160 cm
Minneapolis (MN), Walker Art Center, Gift of the Gilbert M. Walker Fund

"In this time of the great struggle for a new art we fight like disorganized 'savages' against an old, established power. The battle seems to be unequal, but spiritual matters are never decided by numbers, only by the power of ideas."

FRANZ MARC

Franz Marc
In the Rain, 1912
Oil on canvas, 81 x 105 cm
Munich, Städtische Galerie im
Lenbachhaus

Franz Marc
The Poor Land of Tyrol, 1913
Oil on canvas, 131.5 x 200 cm
New York, Solomon R.
Guggenheim Museum

Platonic notion by which Marc understood neither conceptual art nor allegories but meaningful symbols or signs which contained reality in distilled form. And the ideas represented, he hoped, would be capable of encouraging community. In view of Marc's present worldwide popularity, such visions are easily misunderstood, as if he had conceived of an "art for all," in anticipation of certain agitprop slogans to come. Any such inference would miss the point entirely. It is enough to quote a statement of Marc's, made in the spirit of Kandinsky: "The coming art will be our scientific principles become form…. We will live in the 20th century in the midst of strange faces, new images, and unheard of sounds. Many who do not possess the inner fire will freeze, and feel nothing but a coldness, and escape into the ruins of their memories."

A Dreamer's Pathos

Marc's notion of a "community" was an elite receptive to "the spiritual in art," a sort of worldly brotherhood which would carry its ideas into the future without regard for the real, social ills of the day. His pathos was more fanatical, less tempered by intellect, than that of his older friend, Kandinsky. Marc's dream of a better, purer world, which he saw prefigured in the insentient creaturely life of animals, is a notion to which we owe many of his wonderfully crystalline, luminously colored paintings, which hover between objectivity and abstraction. But of course this visionary enthusiasm, like all overheated idealism, contained within itself the danger of a blindness to reality. Marc considered the First World War, whose victim he became in 1916, as Macke had before him in 1914, to be an unavoidable inferno through which men had to pass before entering the better world he dreamed of.

Marc learned from Delaunay's color theories, from the Cubists' distillations of objective form, and from the Futurists' prismatic facetting of form and inclusion of the element of time in painting. But it was under Kandinsky's all-powerful influence that he arrived at an abstract order, if one that appeared somehow unfinished and occasionally still too beholding to the ornamental. Marc's œuvre remained a promising fragment, cut short by his untimely death. He pursued the pure, crystalline form, but was not given enough time to find it. The series of his major works began in 1911, only three years before his death, with *Three Red Horses* (Cincinnati, private collection), in which he succeeded for the first time in employing color as a symbolically expressive device. In *Tower of Blue Horses*, a 1913 composition now lost, Marc approached very closely to his crystalline ideal.

From this point on his style became increasingly differentiated. The forms began to overlap, were prismatically divided, became ever farther removed from nature. The motif was subordinated to the arrangement of forms on the plane, and only the colors were still suffused with that "mystical inwardness" which the artist

bring the stars down to earth, etc. But just let a painter try to hang the moon up in a drawing room, lay it on a table, etc. Some things have been allowed by decree, such as putting wings on a horse; but you have to write 'patented by Berceuse' underneath it." Marc, too, sought a "universal painting" in which the dilemmas of life would be resolved in a harmony of creation. But he took a different path from his Russian friend, who at least had studied with a comparative outsider on the Munich scene, Franz von Stuck. Marc's background was in the academic painting of the city, and his father had been an artist before him. At bottom, Marc was a brooding, melancholy man, a religiously inspired idealist who suffered from the imperfection, or – as he himself would have said – from the impurity of the world and its loss of metaphysical meaning. This was the source of his conviction that the *Nur-Bild*, or painting in itself, was not sufficient. Rather, artists should represent "ideas," a

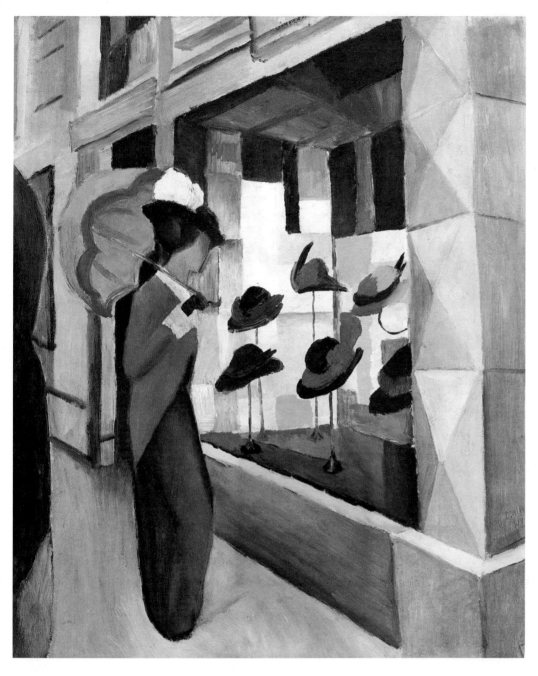

"It is a tremendous effort for me to paint and I exert so much energy when I am painting that I am always very tired afterwards. I tear the paintings stroke for stroke from my brain. Really. I am actually very lazy. If I have torn out my nerves, however, then these canvas rags should also be worth something, at the very least my energy has been spent on them. They can be appreciated by whoever pleases.
I paint, paint, paint and am deeply happy when my eye sinks with the light into the darkness of the forest or trembles above the meadows and finally dreamily follows the clouds in the distance. Every day a new happiness is experienced, a new joy. I want to use the days now as much as I can. I always feel the urge to work."   AUGUST MACKE

August Macke
Hat Shop, 1914
Oil on canvas, 60.5 x 50.5 cm
Essen, Museum Folkwang

attempted to make visible. *The Poor Land of Tyrol* (p. 108 below) is a harsh, forbidding landscape with bare, rugged mountains, humble dwellings, martyrs' crosses, emaciated, shaggy horses, and a ruffled eagle perched on a bare limb – Marc's apocalypse, an ominous, depressing picture. It proves that Marc was no innocuous painter of pastoral idylls.

Ariel among the Expressionists

The most radiant and vital figure among the Blaue Reiter artists was August Macke, born in Meschede, Westphalia, in 1887, active in Düsseldorf and Bonn in the Rheinland, and at Tegernsee in Bavaria, died in action in Champagne, France, in 1914 (ill. above and

p. 110). Macke was not metaphysically interested like his friends, to whom he was introduced by his bride's uncle, the collector and art patron Bernhard Koehler. As time went on he grew increasingly alienated from Kandinsky, nor was he sparing of criticism with respect to the "intellectual painting" of his older friend, Marc. More important to Macke than the spiritual in art was sensuousness of color and harmony of form; he remained true to the beauties of this world. Macke had a great lust for life, and attempted to project it into his art. Influences worked on him through the eye, not the intellect. Macke involved himself in the pre-1914 directions in painting in an entirely carefree, open way, tirelessly experimenting, accepting and rejecting. The brilliancy of his palette was

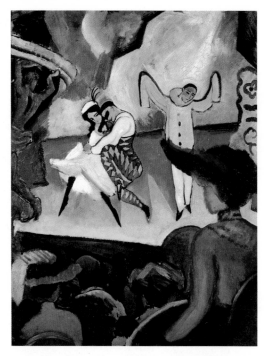

Below:
August Macke
Lady in a Green Jacket, 1913
Oil on canvas, 44 x 43.5 cm
Cologne, Museum Ludwig,
Haubrich Collection

Right:
Heinrich Campendonk
In the Forest, c. 1919
Oil on canvas, 83.8 x 99 cm
Detroit (IL), Detroit Institute
of Arts

of forms to tubular shapes. Macke even tried abstraction, though it certainly suited his temperament least of all approaches.

Macke's style combines the insouciance of Impressionist art with the formal logic of a Seurat. His unmythical, worldly approach made him the most romantic of German painters in the 20th century. Unlike Marc, Macke was not still struggling to find himself when he died – he had reached early maturity. Macke's gifts came to full flower within the space of only two years, in marvellous landscapes with figures, his favorite theme. His finest accomplishment then came with the Tunesian watercolors, the fruit of a trip to Africa undertaken with Klee and Louis Moilliet in 1914. There is nothing in 20th-century German art to compare with the transparent beauty of these works, the unprecedented, luminous major key of their palette, their melodious grace of form. Macke's paintings are the final reverberation of a period from which he took leave in a depiction of the mobilization, presciently titled "Farewell."

A Modern "Old Lower Rhinelander"

Inhabitants of the Lower Rhine region are known for a temperament almost as meditative and melancholy as the peoples of Eastern Europe. Heinrich Campendonk, a native of Krefeld, is a case in point. Recruited by Marc for the Blauer Reiter in 1911, Campendonk came by way of Cézanne to Cubism, whose formal clarity he adopted, but not its subject matter or subdued palette.

inspired by Marc and the early Kandinsky, but even more strongly by Delaunay's color-circles and window paintings. In terms of form, Macke was intrigued by the lucid logic of Cubist composition, for a time by the dynamics of Futurism, and finally, by Léger's reduction

Campendonk's work blends a tendency to narrative, relating folk legends in a popular tone, with a strongly ornamental bent. Yet despite this narrative character his pictures are static, as if all movement were caught in suspended animation. The colors in the early work are brilliant and luminous, but later their fire is subdued, and they sometimes verge on the saccharine (ill. above). Campendonk was more naive than his friends; basically he remained a conservative, in the tradition of Lower Rhine landscape art. Driven out of his post at the Düsseldorf Academy in 1933, he died in Amsterdam in 1957, a highly honored but embittered and lonely man.

Cavalry Officer and Mystic

More important to the group than Campendonk was Alexei von Javlensky, a former Russian cavalry officer with a great zest for life who gradually discovered the contemplative, mystical side of his nature. Javlensky's prime theme was the human face, into which he projected all the intensity of his sensibility. As the glowing colors and heavy, simplified contours indicate, the artist was concerned not with the individual but with the general in the human aspect. The wide-open eyes, filled with a melancholy ecstasy reminiscent of medieval manuscript illuminations, transfix the viewer. "I am less interested in searching for new forms," said Javlensky; "but I do wish to become more 'profound'." This he achieved with the aid of color, which, more definitely than with the other Expressionists, was infused with a symbolic character. Javlensky envisioned heightening the luminous chords of Fauvism and the passionate fire of van Gogh's palette into a metaphysically expressive color. As regards form, by the end of his career he had reduced it to a few, sweeping contours, and to horizontal and vertical strokes to indicate the facial features. The

face became an apparition, with all sensation and emotion as it were turned inwards. Javlensky's long series of "Meditations," variations on this single theme, can have a slightly wearying effect, but this should not prevent us from admiring his exquisite still lifes and his few landscapes. The involvement with landscape led, during the First World War and thereafter, to impressive compositions of lapidary simplicity and ingenious lyricism (ill. above right and p. 112).

Another member of the Blauer Reiter, as well as of its predecessor, the "Neue Künstlervereinigung," was the graphic artist Alfred Kubin. His reputation as an invoker of the demonic, dark side of human nature was already established when he joined the group. Compared to his drawings and prints, Kubin's work in painting was less significant. More important was the work of Kandinsky's pupil, Gabriele Münter. She represented the rare case of a naive artist who attended an art school and whose work nonetheless retained a wonderful freshness and unaffectedness. Münter's early paintings were primarily landscapes and still lifes done during the years spent with Kandinsky in Murnau. Their instinctive dis-

Alexei von Javlensky
Still Life with Vase and Jug, 1909
Oil on cardboard, 49.5 x 43.5 cm
Cologne, Museum Ludwig,
Haubrich Collection

Alexei von Javlensky
Evening, 1929
Oil on cardboard, 53 x 32.7 cm
Private collection

tillation of form and brilliant colors were inspired as much by Javlensky as by Kandinsky, to whom Münter owed her artistic development but whose intellectual approach remained foreign to her (p. 111). She is said to have discovered the indigenous glass paintings whose bright, folkloristic colors gave so much to the Blauer Reiter. Münter's best works stand on a level with those done concurrently by her friends.

With the outbreak of the First World War, the his-

tory of the Blauer Reiter came to a close. Macke and Marc were killed in action; Kandinsky, threatened with internment as an enemy alien, fled by way of Switzerland to Russia; Münter, driven by her own demons, wandered restlessly through Europe. The final reverberation came with the founding in 1924 of "The Blue Four" – Kandinsky, Klee, Javlensky, and Feininger, all of whom were masters at the Weimar Bauhaus and by that time internationally known.

Design of a Possible World
The Exemplary Art and the Exemplary Life of Paul Klee

"At one time, people used to paint things that could be seen on Earth, things they liked looking at and would have liked to see. Now we make the reality of visible things apparent and in doing so express the belief that, in relation to the world as a whole, the visible is only an isolated example and that other truths are latently in the majority. Things appear in their extended and manifold sense, often seemingly contradicting yesterday's experiences. The aim is to reveal the fundamental idea behind the coincidental."
PAUL KLEE

Among the circle of writers and poets who gathered in Jena during the early Romantic period, Friedrich Hardenberg-Novalis was the most thoughtful and imaginative, and yet also the most reserved. In his writings reality was transformed into a symbolic cypher; to speak with Klee, he was "not graspable this side of the grave." For all his personal kindness, Novalis was surrounded, like Klee, by an aura of unapproachability. Existing in his "intermediate realm," he remained in closer touch with the wellsprings of creativity than his colleagues. The purity of his nature, the ineffable profundity of his writings, and the precision of his thought made Novalis the tacit moral authority for his friends, a man who set standards, just as, in our own century, Klee set standards for the artists of the Blauer Reiter, the Bauhaus, and many others in their wake. In Klee's work, the Enlight-

enment and early Romantic era were revived, with an authentic zeal that had nothing in common with the lip-service paid by so many to that movement. Klee was a "Romantic with an exact, conscientious sense of form," who, as Werner Haftmann has shown, admired not only Novalis and Friedrich Schlegel, Runge and Friedrich, but also Goethe and the philosophical painter and physician Carl Gustav Carus. Klee's world was no idyll. He was not a painter-poet who told fairy tales in miniatures with a Surrealist touch. We should not allow ourselves to be deceived either by his generally small formats or by his conscious primitivism, which was merely a reflection of that extreme sparingness of means which marks "ultimate professional insight." In Klee's case, too, Cézanne was the mentor par excellence.

As in Novalis's texts, we find a unification of oppositions in Klee's work. Mysticism and logic, poetry and mathematics, day and night, metaphysical and physical realms, the visible and the invisible, the conscious and the unconscious, childlike naivety and aesthetic sophistication, death and life, the organic and the inorganic, East and West, order and anarchy, irony and commitment, are often simultaneously present.

For Klee, the making of art was a simile for the creation of the world. Like Goethe, whom he considered the "only bearable German," and whose experience of nature seemed allied to his own, Klee attempted to capture nature in terms of primal images; and like the poet, the artist discovered "analogies to the universal design in the tiniest leaf." On an early trip to Italy, undertaken with the Swiss sculptor Hermann Haller, Klee was intrigued less by the legacy of visual artists – with the exception of Leonardo – than by the structural principles of Italian architecture, which he saw as a continuation of natural laws by human hands, and by the fantastic aquatic flora and fauna in the Naples aquarium. Between these two poles lay the garden, organic nature domesticated and shaped by man, which inspired many of Klee's finest pictures. And it was between these two poles, those of construction and imagination, that his rich œuvre slowly and continually developed.

The Scholarly Artist

Klee's personality was informed as much by Novalis' striving for wholeness, the endlessness of an undivided creation, as by Goethe's sense of harmony, proportion, and perfection. Like the poet, Klee was artist and scientist in one. "An artist must be so much – poet, natural scientist, philosopher," he noted in an early diary entry. Nor was this said lightly. Klee's precise knowledge in the fields of natural science, world literature (he read the Greek classics in the original), in philosophy and music,

surpassed that of many a specialist. He was a scholarly artist, a *pictor doctus*. What with Novalis remained a fragment, life and work, Klee brought to fulfillment. When he died in 1940 at the age of 60, of cardiac paralysis brought on by a terrible disease, a hardening of the skin caused by measles, Klee had accomplished his life's work.

Two writers have been mentioned with whom the artist felt allied and whose different characters he in large part embodied within himself. It might have been even more to the paint, however, to speak of two composers. For Klee not only possessed a great literary gift, as his writings show; he was also an outstanding connoisseur and performer of music. Born in 1879 in Münchenbuchsee, near Bern, to a German music teacher and his music-loving Swiss wife, Klee long vacillated between a career in music and art. According to his own record, he finally decided on painting because as its development was not so far advanced as that of music, his own contribution might be more important and necessary to painting. In music he loved Mozart and Bach above all. Bach's sense of form, the strict principles of his musical architecture, are as present in Klee's work as the grace of Mozart and the suggestion of something demonic just beneath the surface. As in Mozart's case, connoisseurship alone does not suffice for an understanding of Klee, who was

*"Nature can afford to be wasteful
everywhere, but the artist has to be
extremely thrifty. Nature is almost
dizzyingly talkative, the artist must
be taciturn. – If my things sometimes give a primitive impression,
then this can be explained by arising
from my discipline which seeks to
reduce to a few steps. It is only thrift,
the final professional know-how,
actually the opposite of true primitivism."*
                    PAUL KLEE

comparably able to retain artistic quality despite an
enormous productivity that was almost unprecedented
in modern art – his own catalogue of works encompasses nearly nine thousand items.

Klee's talent was soon recognized. His first Munich
teacher, Heinrich Knirr, already prophesied that he
would achieve something out of the ordinary. The
famous "Böcklin-German," Franz von Stuck, also
thought highly of Klee. Alfred Kubin, the draftsman of
the wierd and ghostly, was his first purchaser. Kubin felt
a kindred spirit in the drawings and prints of Klee, who
had yet to begin to paint. Although Kubin was right, he
recognized only part of the younger man's personality,
his tendency to the bizarre and eerie, to the sarcastic and
ironic. Kandinsky, long a co-teacher with Klee at the
Bauhaus, was proud of having recognized Klee's genius
at first sight, although around 1910 Klee had produced
only a thin œuvre consisting almost entirely of drawings
and graphic works. Also, he had destroyed many of his
early attempts. Klee needed a long time in which to find
himself: "There should be no hurry when one wants so
much," he noted in his diary. For a time Klee even toyed
with the thought of devoting himself to sculpture. He
actually did produce a few idol-like, grotesquely wierd
sculptures, but this was to remain an episode.

Strict Rites

Klee's drawings and etchings showed an early propensity
towards a unique, Manneristic lineature which varied
reminiscences of Symbolism and Jugendstil in a very
personal way. They were satirical not for the sake of

being satirical but out of "distaste in view of the higher
things." Klee's humor is often acid and cruel, and the
laugh it prompts is uneasy. Many of the distorted,
insect-like creatures contain a half-digested "Gothic"
aspect. Some of them are perhaps too intellectual, too
indirect, requiring translation and a knowledge of literary allusions in order to understand them.

In the course of time Klee overcame his latent illustrative tendency. For years he had devoted himself to
illustrating Voltaire's *Candide*, intrigued as he was by its
clarity of diction and well-turned plot. When people
later asked him for illustrations, he usually requested
them to choose something suitable from among those
he had already done. Glass paintings, many in a negative
process, and white drawings on a black ground, a few of
them colored, were the next of Klee's areas of study. In
the course of his career he was so tirelessly to investigate
every nook and cranny of art that in the end there was
no unexplored territory, no problem of craft, that found
him without a solution, no theme to which he could not
apply the perfect technique. The material side of art was
indeed just as important to him as the ideal. Nor did he
ask himself the idle question as to the priority of form or
content. With Klee, the two always remained in balance.
Down to carefully prepared patina and artificial mildew
marks on the paper, there was nothing uncalculated or
uncontrolled about Klee's art.

"The Call of Color"

For many years the watercolor technique served Klee
primarily as a means to define the entire color scale with

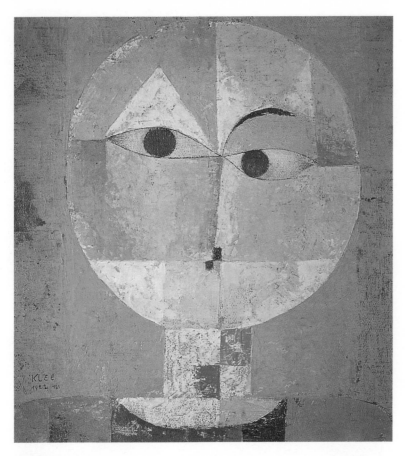

Paul Klee
Senecio, 1922 (181)
Oil on gauze with chalk ground;
original yellow frame, 40.5 x 38 cm
Basel, Öffentliche Kunstsamm-
lung Basel, Kunstmuseum

Page 117 above:
Paul Klee
Highroad and Byroads, 1929 (90)
Oil on canvas on a stretcher,
83.7 x 67.5 cm
Cologne, Museum Ludwig

Page 117 below:
Paul Klee
Insula dulcamara, 1938 (481)
Colored paste and oil on
newspaper, mounted on burlap
on a stretcher; original frame,
88 x 176 cm
Bern, Kunstmuseum Bern,
Paul Klee Foundation

The path to his liberation of color had been theoretically paved by Delaunay, whom Klee had met in Paris.
The influence of Orphism is evident in many of the
watercolors done in Kairouan and other places. *South
Wind in Marc's Garden* (1915; Munich, Städtische Galerie
im Lenbachhaus), for instance, was clearly stimulated
by Delaunay's window paintings. Klee has loosened the
Cubist rigor of the composition by introducing slight
irregularities and hardly detectable shifts, a method he
would retain, particularly in the incomparable major
work, *Highroad and Byroads* (ill. right), a fruit of his trip
to Egypt in 1928/29. Even during his years of collaboration with Kandinsky, Oskar Schlemmer, and Feininger
at the Bauhaus, Klee's idiosyncrasies always remained
somewhat beyond the law, as it were. For "genius is the
defect in the system," stated the conscientious system-
builder, who knew that genius was the only thing that
could neither be taught nor learned. This is why Klee's
pictures, no matter how constructed they seem to be,
are never lifeless. The "defect in the system" keeps them
vital.

Orient and Occident

Kairouan made Klee into a painter. The experience of
the holy Moslem city moved him so deeply that he
returned home through southern Europe as it were with
his eyes closed, in order to retain his impressions
unblurred. Klee had found a second artistic home in
Tunisia. The strange mixture in his painting of sophisticated Western and exotically Oriental elements is one
source of its charm. This blend began to take shape in
Tunisia, the significance of which is only comparable to
that of Egypt, where Klee, as mentioned, travelled in
1929. Kairouan gave him color and pictorial architecture; Egypt gave him the experience of a timeless coexistence of permanence and transience.

Klee's work did not begin to develop in full freedom
until 1914. But it led to an œuvre that, second only to
Picasso's, profoundly influenced contemporary art all
the way down to Conceptual Art. Klee's imagery teems
with symbols, which with time grew increasingly simplified and essential, condensing like crystals. Although he
always proceeded from a visual experience of plants, animals, or humans, of the natural or man-made environment, and ultimately of death – which for him was
always present in life – Klee's art, like his elusive personality, exists on a plane beyond the everyday. It reflects
nothing visible, but – to use the artist's most famous
phrase – it makes visible.

Painting is Script

His art is a very original creation, a both imagined and
carefully calculated design of a possible universe beyond
the one we know. From there, Klee hoped, perhaps the
imperfection of all previous art could someday be overcome, and a work created "of a really great scope, covering the entire elementary, objective, substantive and stylistic territory." Similarly to Cézanne, Klee considered

all its transitions and gradations between black and
white, and to explore the influence of color and light on
effects of depth. This was self-abnegating laboratory
work, which Klee performed with great conscientious-
ness and superhuman patience, trying and testing, musing and meditating like a medieval craftsman, lost to the
world and not expecting immediate, tangible results
because he had no definite goal. Only a man of great
self-assurance could have undertaken such labors. Quietly confident of his mission, after a stormy youth Klee
consciously brought order into his private life by marry-
ing Lilly Stumpf, a Munich pianist, creating an atmosphere conducive to the development of his art.

The artist was well-prepared when, at the age of 34,
while travelling in Tunisia with his painter-friends
Macke and Moilliet, "the call of color" reached him.
This was not coincidentally in Africa, to which his
ancestry on his mother's side extended back. Klee felt at
home there. Those who knew him said that in his young
and middle years he had something of the appearance
and gaze of an Arab about him. The cubic, both austere
and fantastic architecture of the Arab settlements, the
brilliance of the Mediterranean light, the intense colors
of Tunisia, struck Klee with the force of a revelation.
"Arabian Nights as an extract with ninety-nine percent
reality content," he decided. Spontaneously he discovered a way to create a synthesis between actual and pictorial architecture.

himself the "primitive of a new sensibility." He passed through many way stations on the road to his distant destination. In keeping with his temperament, he depicted not so much being as becoming, not the blossom but the process of blossoming, not the river but the process of flowing, not the tree but its growth, as Haftmann said. Arrows, punctuation marks, numbers and arabesques facilitate the reading of Klee's pictures; they provide orientation, point out directions, set signals, but without entirely answering the pictorial riddle. One is put in mind of Kahnweiler's early remark to the effect that painting was script, hieroglyphics.

In the last years of the artist's life his formats grew larger and the imagery starker, more monumental. This was partially the result of Klee's illness, which began in 1935. The drawings grew increasingly lapidary and more like writing, frequently recalling Chinese or Japanese calligraphy. "Variations on the theme of drawing the final line," Georg Schmidt once called Klee's last series of works. The theme of death indeed comes strongly into the foreground, as seen in the compelling *Angel of Death* (Basel, Kunstmuseum), done in the final year of his life, as well as in many other paintings and drawings. The late works represent a summing-up not only in autobiographical terms but in aesthetic ones as well. For the dark, threatened nature of human existence was always present in Klee's work. His very last painting (p. 115) was a still life with vases, pitcher, a sculpture, a flower-decorated table, and a moon. At the lower left, on a white field, one sees Jacob wrestling with the angel and a cross, as if Klee himself had decided, now it is enough.

7 Revolt and Poetry

"Scarecrows against Reason"
The Dadaist Revolt

Even today many people still look upon Dadaism as a nihilistic monster, sheerly destructive in intent. This is an over-simplification. The European cataclysm of the First World War made it impossible for artists, in so far as they were committed and felt responsibility, to escape into philosophy, because the war had made all big words and resounding phrases seem suspect. The only possible reaction was a radical one. Dada, even in its negation, was an offshoot of Western bourgeois thinking. The movement had nothing to do with Bolshevism, despite certain parallel, ephemeral, and soon suppressed streams in Eastern Europe and in Soviet Russia immediately after the October Revolution. As for nihilism, most Dadaists did not propagate it but merely registered its existence.

Their revolt unified a range of international artists and writers of solid middle-class origin, free-thinking individuals from New York to Zurich, from Cologne to Paris, from Berlin to Hanover, with reverberations felt in London, San Francisco, Moscow, Budapest, and Tokyo. No stream of 20th-century art was as global as Dada. Dada journals were published in Switzerland, Italy, the Netherlands, Germany, Austria, Hungary, Serbia, Romania, Poland, and the United States.

The Dada revolt was an expression of disgust, anxiety, and despair in face of a world in which "everything works fine, but people don't any more," as author Hugo Ball put it. Ball was one of the spiritual fathers of the Zurich branch of the movement and, indicatively, later a convert to Catholicism. The mass slaughter of mechanized warfare had far outstripped anything envisaged by the pessimism of the preceding age. Dada drew its conclusions from the insanity of an unquestioning faith in progress, and proceeded to celebrate the triumph of the absurd. Dada was more than the horseplay in which it occasionally manifested itself. It was a revolt of vitality against ossification, of liberty against doctrine, of the irrational against the "reason" of politicians and war speculators, a despairing attempt to survive destructiveness by destroying. As Max Ernst said, during his period of activity as "Minimax-Dadamax" in Cologne, Dada was a profoundly pacifist reaction to "the mess of this idiotic war." It was a frontal attack on "the civilization that produced it," including the language and visual imagery of that civilization, including its "eternal values," including the Venus de Milo and Mona Lisa, whom Duchamp embellished with a moustache. Subsequently Dada made attempts at reconstruction, which were viewed with skepticism by Ernst, because, as he said, you cannot "glue parts of an exploding grenade together."

All thinking, writing, and painting that side-stepped the hopelessness of the historical situation, attempted to ignore it, prettify it, or even to justify it, became the target of ruthless criticism, which did not stop short at the artists' own bourgeois heritage and the art it stood for. Dada was not a style, not a philosophical or aesthetic program; it was a series of individualistic, anarchic acts made in reply to a collective and terroristic world, "an outbreak of joy in life and fury," to again quote Ernst. It was an outbreak full of aggressiveness, of elan, activity, and movement, whose vitality put the entire past in question. Declaring "the best of all possible worlds" to be an old wive's tale, Dada stuffed it into the garbage can of a pre-Beckett "End Game," without being able to offer an alternative or even wishing to. Dada was the manifestation of a despairing attempt of free individuals to maintain their integrity in a regimented world whose regimentation had led straight to Armageddon.

Each Dadaist fought a lonely battle, even as member of a group, whether in Zurich or Berlin, in Cologne or Budapest, but especially in Hanover (Kurt Schwitters) and New York (Man Ray). This was both the movement's strength and its weakness, for it finally led to a dispersion of forces (which in any case never had a real chance of preventing the lemmings from throwing themselves into a new and even deeper abyss). By definition, Dada could never have become a mass movement. This is why it is completely mistaken to accuse these artistic individualists, as some have, of having unwittingly paved the way for political terrorism. Ultimately, the intellectual elite remained isolated. "The cynicism of the Dadaists is a mask," said the painter, sculptor, and poet Hans Arp; "the Dadaist suffers from the delirium of the human delusion of grandeur that began with the

"jolifanto bambla ô falli bambla
grossiga m'pfa habla horem
égiga goramen
higo bloiko russula huju
hollaka hollala
anlogo bung
blago bung
blago bung
bosso fataka
ü üü ü
schampa wulla wussa òlobo
hej tatta gôrem
eschige zunbada
wulubu ssubudu uluw ssubudu
tumba ba – umf
kusagauma
ba – umf"   HUGO BALL

George Grosz
Republican Automatons, 1920
Watercolor, ink and India ink on
cardboard, 60 x 47.3 cm
New York, The Metropolitan
Museum of Art

Sophie Taeuber-Arp
Vertical-Horizontal Composition,
1927/28
Oil on canvas, 11 x 65 cm
Locarno, Museo Civico Castello
Visconti

World War of 1914." This mask often bore the grimace of
the slanderer, joker, or clown, the agent provocateur
who – as in Beckett's plays – proclaims his truths under
cover of a fool's cap.

Nevertheless, with the aid of elements of Futurism
(and of its Russian version, Ego-Futurism), of Expressionism, Duchamp's first "ready-mades," Kasimir
Malevich and Alexei Alexeivich Morguniov's prome-
nade of wooden spoons, and Alfred Jarry's *Ubu Roi*,
Dadaism did attempt to make a new beginning from its
lost outpost. This could only succeed if first the past was
smashed to smithereens.

The Debunking of Western Civilization

The official date of the birth of Dada was December 5,
1916. It was on this day, in respectable Zurich, that the
"Cabaret Voltaire" opened, an "association of young
artists and literary men," as an innocent newspaper
article put it, "whose aim it is to establish a center for
artistic entertainment." The word "dada," which first
appeared in April of that same year in Ball's diary, was
reputedly discovered by him and Richard Huelsenbeck,
poet and later psychiatrist. As the two were leafing

Hans Arp
Configuration (Navel, Shirt and
Head), 1927/28
Painted wood relief, 145.5 x 115.5 cm
Basel, Öffentliche Kunstsamm-
lung Basel, Kunstmuseum,
Emanuel-Hoffmann Foundation

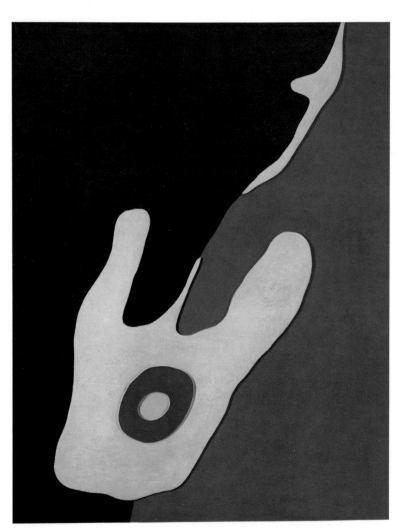

through a German-French dictionary in search of a
striking stage-name for a female singer, they came across
the children's word "dada," which means "hobbyhorse"
or "giddyup," but also "Hottentot." And it was like
Hottentots, at least in the eyes of the good citizens of
Zurich, that the artists behaved – Ball, Huelsenbeck,
Tristan Tzara, Arp from Alsace, and Marcel Janco, an
artist from Romania. They had all been driven to Zurich
by the war, with which they wanted nothing to do, and
they all refused to believe in the "meaning of history."
They set up "scarecrows against reason," as Arp put it,
and reacted to common sense with noisy and provocative nonsense: simultaneous poems, spoken or roared in
unison; a "Bruitism" borrowed from the Futurists; performances accompanied by cacophonous musical enter-
tainments; shocking manifestos; poetry composed of
grunts and squeaks; Arp's profound tomfoolery in verse;
attacks on the church; and an Expressionistic, sentimental appeal to the best in humanity. The primal, childish,
primitive, and also the factor of random chance, were
held up scornfully in the face of officially sanctioned
culture.

During the sometimes boisterous, sometimes sarcastic activities undertaken by these critical and intellectual
artists, activities which also reflected a radical self-criti-
cism, something new came to light – what became visible now was the poetry of the absurd and grotesque, the
charm of the illogical and paradoxical. These artists discovered the unconscious mind and the dream as sources
of a new reality and artistic inspiration. In the course

of breaking down traditional forms and styles Dada obtained new materials for art. Though they rejected all perfectionism and wished to start with a clean slate, the Dadaists again and again made surprising finds, with the result that – as subsequently would often happen – their anti-art ultimately developed into a new art form. Despite repeated attempts, art in the 20th century has been unable to escape itself.

Everybody Likes a Good Joke

Not everything about Dada was an expression of protest, reflected a philosophy, or better, an anti-philosophy; nor did Dada ever become an ideology. Many of the movement's explosions were touched off by nothing more than a sense of fun, the enjoyment of play innate to *homo ludens*. They were manifestations of a pure love of practical joking, subject to no rules or compulsions. "Dada is against the compulsory form of the German school essay," wrote Arp, the kindliest, most visionary, and most disciplined of the Dada leaders. "But Dada is for dreams, colorful paper masks, kettle drums, sound-poems, concretions, *poèmes statiques*, for things that are not far from picking flowers and making bouquets." Or, as a later artist associated with Pop, Claes Oldenburg, would put it somewhat more bluntly: "I am for an art that is political-erotical-mystical, that does something other than sit on its ass in a museum."

Apart from Janco and from Arp's first wife, Sophie Taeuber, the poet, sculptor and painter was the only one of the Zurich group to develop a style which had a lasting influence on contemporary art, as well as on poetry in both the traditional and the Dadaist sense. Arp had his origins in abstract painting, knew Kandinsky, and had participated in the 1913 "German Autumn Salon." In Zurich he broke with geometric abstraction and took up impulses from Cubist collage, but in place of rigorous design he set "controlled chance." Arp put together existing things made of various materials as they came into his hands, mixing organic with geometric shapes, and mounted them on the surface, as it were in the order of their appearance (p. 120). His montages of unaltered fragments of *objets trouvés* have the strangely tantalizing magic of a chaos contained. In the playful relief-compositions of free-form colored shapes we already find the plantlike, organic configurations and the formal concentration that would become characteristic of Arp's work in painting and sculpture. Aesthetic and natural forms have become one in this imagery, which has "grown like a fruit."

Sophie Taeuber-Arp was likewise a mild and kindly person (p. 120). Though her imagery was strictly geometrical, it was filled with a cheerful mood. Using circles, squares and rectangles in light to luminous colors, she played a sensitively poetic glass-bead game. Janco (ill. above), who would later emigrate to Israel, where he made a considerable contribution, at the time concentrated on watercolors, crayon drawings, and mostly varicolored reliefs of a great richness and harmony of form, an abstract pictorial architecture built up of fragments of objects and natural phenomena. Seen from today's vantage point, Janco's art has mellowed, now appearing more appealing than provocative.

Hannah Höch
My Home Mottoes, 1922
Collage and India ink on paper,
32 x 41.3 cm
Berlin, Galerie Nierendorf

On the Barricades

In Berlin, Dada took on the aspect of a revolutionary uprising. The members of the group uncompromisingly expected to make an immediate effect on politics. They attacked Church and State in no uncertain terms. "Chief Dada" Johannes Baader, while attending a service in Berlin Cathedral, replied to the pastor's rhetorical question, "What does Jesus Christ mean to us today?" by announcing loud and clear, "To your sort, He doesn't mean a damn thing!" Raoul Hausmann wrote a

Manifesto Against the Weimar Approach to Life, George Grosz scoffed in biting drawings at the "home front," at war profiteers and brothel frequenters, militarists and speculators, before turning to more idyllic subjects after his emigration to America. Grosz's art of the period was more realistic to the degree that the Dadaists' striving to make a difference in day-to-day Berlin politics was more direct than in Zurich. But in Berlin, too, artists and especially writers explored the realms of the unconscious and automatism, polemicizing at Freud the while. In the visual arts, a group gathered around Hausmann (ill. below), Hannah Höch (p. 121 and ill. left), Grosz, the brilliant agitator John Heartfield (ill. below) and his brother Wieland Herzfelde, aimed at what they termed a "satirical hyper-realism" and carried considerably more weight than the abstractionists. Aesthetic consequences arose especially from their experiments in photomontage, by means of which a theme could be represented from various vantage points, in different perspectives, and with daring juxtapositions of form and content. These devices alienated reality so strongly that the shocked viewer was confronted with the mundane transmuted into the extraordinary, in a sense even into the surreal, and was forced to cope with it whether he accepted or rejected what he saw. This new technique, often used in combination with pithy, satirical texts, has retained its revolutionary effect down to the present day, and that not only in an aesthetic sense. Photomontage remains the strongest weapon in the hands of the politically committed artist. A straight line runs from John Heartfield to Klaus Staeck.

John Heartfield
Hjalmar, or the Growing
Deficit, 1934
Photomontage, 54 x 38 cm
Berlin, Akademie der Künste,
John-Heartfield-Archiv

Raoul Hausmann
Tatlin at Home, 1920
Collage and gouache, 41 x 28 cm
Stockholm, Moderna Museet

Page 123 below:
Max Ernst
Fruit of a Long Experience, 1919
Painted wood relief, 45.7 x 38 cm
Geneva, private collection

À L'HEURE DE L'OBSERVATOIRE — LES AMOUREUX

Dadamax of Cologne

In Cologne, Max Ernst was the outstanding Dada figure (ill. below and pp. 138, 139, 141). In his early collages he arbitrarily pieced together fragments of reality, rearranged separate elements taken from technical drawings into an astonishing, unreal but convincing mechanical world, created a completely new system of references among things, and by so doing, paved the way for Surrealism. "Deranged!" people cried, and they were right in a sense they perhaps did not realize. By dictionary definition, Ernst truly "upset the arrangement, order, or operation" of these painstakingly rendered machines, removing the components from their normal context and placing them in a new one, and giving them a new meaning which is often underscored by the title of the collage.

The literary factor so crucial to Surrealism was anticipated by Ernst as well. His early *Pietà, or Revolution by Night* (1923; London, Tate Gallery) depicts a boy with curly blond hair, clad only in shirt and trousers, perched on the arm of a moustachioed, derby-hatted gentleman standing in front of a wall out of which projects, at the right, a shower head. In the background is the outlined figure of a tall, bearded man at whom the boy gazes, and whose aristocratic air contrasts strongly to the frumpiness of the man in the hat, uncomfortable in the role of the Virgin. In *Saint Cecilia*, the figure of the title appears walled in, seated on a movable framework, as a dove shoots vertically into the air towards a triangle formed of three balls, open at the bottom and suspended at the top by a string from a fourth ball, which in turn is affixed to the sky. Dreamlike images without apparent logical coherence, unconscious associations, are made visible in such paintings. It was not symbols Ernst depicted, but magical signs. In the first post-war years he also depicted quite different subjects, openly intended to provoke. One was *The Virgin Spanking the Christ Child before Three Witnesses* (Cologne, Museum Ludwig), which was done in 1926 and caused a scandal in Cologne two years

later. With this visual satire, alluding to the "Chastized Cupid" of antiquity and to Christian depictions of the life of Jesus – the three witnesses, by the way, are Breton, Paul Eluard, and Ernst himself – the artist liberated himself from the traumatic memory of a "pious" spanking once received from his father. In addition to remi-

Man Ray
Observatory Time – The Lovers,
1932–1934
Oil on canvas, 100 x 250.4 cm
Longport-sur-Orge, William N.
Copley Collection

The Rope Dancer Accompanies Herself With Her Shadows

*"Throughout time painting has
alternately been put to the service of
the church, the state, arms, individual patronage, nature appreciation,
scientific phenomena, anecdote, and
decoration.
But all the marvellous works that
have been painted, whatever the
sources of inspiration, still live for us
because of absolute qualities they
possess in common. The creative
force and the expressiveness of painting reside materially in the color
and texture of pigment, in the possibilities of form invention and organization, and in the flat plane on
which these elements are brought to
play."*   MAN RAY

niscences of the Mannerism of Pontormo or Parmi-
gianino and of De Chirico's metaphysical painting,
Ernst's work contains early anticipations of the Surrealist scenario.

From Dada to Merz

In business-like Hanover the movement produced a late
and marvellous blossom in the work of Kurt Schwitters.
"It was Schwitters who spoke the last Dada word," wrote
Georges Huguet in the catalogue of the unforgettable
exhibition "Fantastic Art, Dada, Surrealism," held in
1936-37 at the Museum of Modern Art, New York, which
had been founded seven years previously. The activities
of the "Société Anonyme," established by Man Ray
(p. 123 and ill. above) and Duchamp in 1920 and supported by the Schwitters enthusiast and tireless advocate
of European modernism in the United States, Katherine
S. Dreier, had laid the cornerstone for the early fame in
America of Schwitters' "one-man Dadaism", to use
Werner Schmalenbach's term.

Schwitters was also a poet, the author of *Anna
Blume*, which caused a scandal in 1919. Influenced by
Hausmann's consonant-poem *fmsbw*, the *Ursonata*,
(primal sonata), was the quintessence of all stammering,
roaring, yet wonderfully metrical, phonetic poems. This
experimental poet happened to be a tall, well-built man.
According to his friend, Hans Richter, after the war
Schwitters was even able to hold at bay a belligerent
group of officers of the guard in the still-militant garri-
son town of Potsdam solely through his eloquence and
the magnetism of his extremely gentlemanly, quite
unbohemian personality. During the war, in which he

had "upheld the Fatherland... in an office," Schwitters
used his desk job to jumble the files and thereby help
men accused of insubordination, defeatism, or deser-
tion to escape punishment.

Using a collage technique that employed objects
and materials of the most heterogeneous description,
Schwitters created a highly individual "world view," an
anti-ideology he called *Merz*. This word, like Dada, was
a chance find. It emerged in the course of making a collage which included newspaper clippings, one of which
was an advertisement for the "Privat- und Com-
merzbank." After it had been torn and pasted over, all
that remained was the word-fragment "merz." Schwitters's unconventional view was born and christened
simultaneously. Down to the last years of his career,
everything was transformed under Schwitters' hand
into *Merz*. He naturally also applied the term to the
fantastic structure he built in his Hanover house at 5,
Waldhausenstrasse. Made, like his pictures, of materials
found by chance, random remainders of everyday life
supplemented by lumber, plaster, and oil paint, the
Merzbau gradually proliferated upwards story by story.
Schwitters worked intensively from 1920 to 1936 on this
endless column of longing, whose full title was *Merzbau
with the Cathedral of Erotic Misery*. Schwitters considered
this fantastic architectural object to be the quintessence
of his life's work, or at least the bass that underlay the
melody of his œuvre. Nothing – except for the death
of his wife, Helma – hurt the artist more deeply than
the news that the *Merzbau*, which he had had to leave
behind on his escape from Nazi persecution, had been
destroyed in an air raid.

Kurt Schwitters
Merz Picture 9 b (The Big Me
Picture), 1919
Collage, oil and gouache on
cardboard, 96.8 x 70 cm
Cologne, Museum Ludwig,
Ludwig Collection

The reconstruction of the original *Merzbau* in
Hanover (p. 461), a visual and architectural manifestion
of Schwitters' life-long yearning for a unification of all
the arts, was one of the high points of Harald Szeemann's memorable 1983 exhibition "Der Hang zum
Gesamtkunstwerk" (The Penchant for the Total Work of
Art). Schwitters would surely have been gratified by this,
because the notable and notorious "penchant," a key
feature of the art of this century and the last, was just as
much a part of his work as *Anna Blume* and the long
series of pictorial collages. The *Merzbau*, in that it went
far beyond the use of previously scorned materials in art,
marked the ultimate transcendence of the traditional
borderlines of painting.

In spite of Picasso's significant sculptural work, the
approach introduced by Schwitters remained the exception in the first half of the century, gaining followers
only after mid-century. This is precisely why the early
example of the universal artist, prototype of *homo ludens*,
is so important. It was in keeping with Schwitters' personal penchant for the Gesamtkunstwerk that, being also
an excellent typographer and publicity man (on his own
behalf as well as others') , he not only produced the
Merzbau but envisioned a *Merz Revue* and a *Merz The-*

Kurt Schwitters
Construction for Noble
Women, 1919
Assemblage, 103 x 84 cm
Los Angeles (CA), Los Angeles
County Museum of Art

ater as well. *Merz* was nothing more than an identifying
word; it pointed to the irrational because it had nothing
substantial to designate and owed its discovery to
chance. Yet it became a fetish, like the nonsensical con-
sonant sequences of the sound-poems and the things
and materials of which Schwitters made collages – and
especially after his confrontation with the Dutch De
Stijl movement-reliefs and three-dimensional objects.
Merz is the signet of the unutterable that eludes language.

"Art," explained Schwitters not without pathos, "art
is a primal concept, sublime as the godhead, inexplicable as life, undefinable and gratuitous." Art has no message; its message is the art itself: "Every line, color, or
form has a certain expression. Expression can only be
given by a certain combination, but it cannot be translated. One cannot formulate the expression of a picture
in words, just as one cannot paint the expression of a
word, such as the word 'and'." This amounts to a rejection of any attempt to translate visual realities into
verbal terms. A waiver of all illusion, including the ideological variety, and a commitment to abstraction are key
factors in Schwitters' otherwise traditional aesthetic.
Though his artistic products may have shocked the
bourgeoisie, he was basically a bourgeois at heart, for
whom art was art and nothing else. Socially or politically
committed art was a contradiction in terms for Schwitters. "The art we strive for," he declared, of all places,
in an article on the subject of "proletarian art" in 1923
(other contributors were Theo van Doesburg, Arp,
Tzara, and the critic Spengemann, a friend of Schwitters') – "Art is neither proletarian nor bourgeois.…
What we are preparing… is the all-inclusive work of art,

which is exalted above every poster, be it made for champagne, Dada, or communist dictatorship."

As Schwitters' collages of paper, wood, fabric, tin, wire, and sackcloth show, the materials used in art are of little significance. This should be recalled when one feels irritated by Beuys's fat or felt, Dieter Roth's cheese, or by the wilted leaves, coal-dust or pollen employed in the work of the *Spurensicherer*, trace or cluefinding artists. Going far beyond the Cubists and their collages, Schwitters discovered the covert poetry of the trivial, of disdained and discarded everyday things, in a way that radically questioned traditional values. Under his hand street-car tickets, baby-carriage wheels, tin cans, yellowed newspapers, string, hair, nails, and rotten roots were transmuted into another reality, a visual reality of compelling magic (pp. 125–127).

The magical power of Dadaist objects reached a culmination in the work of this solo Dadaist, this brilliant junk collector who was a mediocre academic painter, a culmination that far transcended Dada as a movement out to *épater le bourgeoisie*. Schwitters rehabilitated, even nobilitated, enfranchised things. He possessed a childlike innocence, receptivity, and imagination, which enabled him to look at commonplace things with a fresh eye and be astonished by them. He discovered them anew, as if they had never existed before. But already as his eye took things in, he changed them, and by playfully manipulating them he infused them with a new meaning, an innate dignity. Combined with this candor was the shaping will of the intelligent artist, an extraordinary sensibility, and an inexhaustible imagination that accepted the existence of contradiction and paradox. Added to these, Schwitters was gifted with an innate sense of humor, which was never injurious and remained forgiving in the face of every provocation, and had its source in his basically melancholy nature.

Kurt Schwitters
Merz Picture 32 A. (The Cherry Picture), 1921
Assemblage, 91.8 x 70.5 cm
New York, The Museum of Modern Art

The works of later styles that relied on the autonomy of materials; styles such as L'art informel and Arte Povera, the many and various attempts to unite painting and sculpture, Pop Art, the neo-Dadaist streams of yesterday and today, typography, and literary experiments – all of these quite clearly owe key impulses to the direction taken by Schwitters'. Much of the art that emerged in the post-war period can be traced back to his inspiring example, not least the revival of the idea of the comprehensive, multi-disciplinary work of art, at which Schwitters aimed with his three *Merzbau* projects in the knowledge that they were destined to remain utopian.

"I called my new way of creation with any material 'merz'. This is the second syllable of 'Kommerz' [commerce]. The name originated from the 'Merzbild', a picture in which the word 'Merz' could be read in between abstract forms. It was cut out and glued on from an advertisement for the Kommerz und Privatbank." KURT SCHWITTERS

Transcending Boundaries: an Interim Report
Marcel Duchamp, Non-Conformist and Prophet

Just as, after 1945, there was a lively and varied neo-Dada scene whose effects are still being felt, there was a proto-Dada scene around the outbreak of the First World War. It emerged in New York, which at the time could not even dream of ever advancing to become the world center of visual art. With the Armory Show of 1913, the city was just beginning to bring the avant-garde movements of the day and their key works to the United States. However, there was one person who predicted the development that would reach its first culmination only three decades later: Marcel Duchamp. "If only America would realize," he said in an interview with the journal *Current Opinion*, that the art of Europe is over, dead –

and that America is the land of the art of the future, instead of trying to build all it does on the foundation of European traditions."

Although the American parallel to European Dada was over by the early 1920s, leaving deep traces but sinking no roots – causing Duchamp and his artist-friend Man Ray to return to Paris in 1921 – his vision of the future was something of a self-fulfilling prophecy. For hardly another artist did more for the art of the future through his public activity and inspiring influence behind the scenes than the war-weary visitor from France. Duchamp was originally part of a group of anti-war emigrés from various European countries, voluntary

"The criticism of modern art is a natural result of the freedom given to the artist to render his individual view. I consider the barometer of the opposition to be a healthy indicator of the depth of the individual expression. The more hostile the criticism, the more encouraging for the artist." MARCEL DUCHAMP

Marcel Duchamp
The Passage from Virgin to Bride, 1912
Oil on canvas, 59.4 x 54 cm
New York, The Museum of Modern Art

Marcel Duchamp
The King and Queen Surrounded by Swift Nudes, 1912
Oil on canvas, 115 x 128.3 cm
Philadelphia (PA), Philadelphia Museum of Art, Louise and Walter Arensberg Collection

Page 129:
Marcel Duchamp
Nude Descending a Staircase, No. 2, 1912
Oil on canvas, 147.5 x 89 cm
Philadelphia (PA), Philadelphia Museum of Art, Louise and Walter Arensberg Collecion

photography of Etienne-Jules Marey, and perhaps also to visual ideas of the type that early appeared in Kupka's work. The significant series begins with *Dulcinea* (1911; Philadelphia Museum of Art), and leads by way of the *Portrait of an Actress* (Philadelphia Museum of Art) and the depiction of the veritably vibrating *Sad Young Man in a Train* (Venice, Peggy Guggenheim Foundation) to the various versions of *Nude Descending a Staircase* of 1912, the second version of which was a *succès de scandale* at the Armory Show (p. 129).

The Passage from Virgin to Bride (ill. left), done in autumn 1912 in Munich, already anticipates *The Large Glass*, just as the various versions of the *Chocolate Grinder* (p. 130) and the *Nine Masculine Forms* mounted between two panes of glass (1914-15; Milan, Arturo Schwarz Collection) point the way to the mechanical and anthropomorphic figures of the "bachelor Machine" with the irionic title, *The Bride Stripped Bare by Her Bachelors, Even* (p. 458). Duchamp worked on this key piece for eight years – or ten, counting the pre-

liminary studies – before he finally declared it "definitively unfinished."

By the same token, Duchamp's entire œuvre, complex and full of arcane allusions to his many and varied interests (literature, music, mathematics, physics, mechanics, folk culture), eludes final definition. Every attempt at interpretation – and there have been superb ones – has remained as incomplete as his major work, which impressively manifests Duchamp's final abandonment of painting (his last picture had been done in 1918, for Katherine S. Dreier, his most important patron apart from the Arensbergs). This residue of enigma, which remains just as inexplicable as the texts of the Symbolist outsider Raymond Roussel, which Duchamp read with passionate interest, points to the presence of two elements of early Romanticism. The first of these is Romantic irony, which Duchamp heightened to a Dadaist peak in works such as the reproduction of the Mona Lisa which he "improved" by adding a moustache and an obscene abbreviated title, *L.H.O.O.Q.* (*Elle a*

exiles who lived in the midst of the New York business world and apparently tried to numb their despair over a hopelessly corrupted humanity in a series of wild parties. The leaders of the group, in addition to the intellectual rigorist Duchamp, included his closest friend, Picabia of the ever-changing masks. Their American hosts were Alfred Stieglitz, photographer and art promotor from his gallery at 291 Fifth Avenue, and collector-poet Walter Arensberg and his wife, Louise.

Back in Paris, Duchamp had initially involved himself with Impressionism and the art of Seurat. The resulting Fauvist and especially the Cubist-influenced canvases already exhibited an extraordinary painterly talent, in terms of their sophisticated color values and their mastery of difficult compositional problems. Moreover, these works pointed to the intellectual independence of Duchamp, who immediately abandoned an approach as soon as he had understood it. Repetition wearied him to the point of disgust. With Duchamp, boredom always led to a decline in activity – or, as he himself termed it, to laziness, for what really impelled him was curiosity. The only thing that really interested the artist Breton called the most intelligent man of the period was *creatio ex nihilo*, creative work that started from zero, from scratch. This is why the most significant of his periods in painting, the productive involvement with Cubism, was soon at an end.

Duchamp's independence and willfulness were already apparent in the paintings that combined variations on Cubist design and color with depictions of phases of movement. These were not, as was long assumed, primarily influenced by Futurism, which Duchamp said he did not particularly value, although his dynamic canvas with the ironic title *The King and Queen Surrounded by Swift Nudes* (ill. right) was presumably painted after a visit to a Futurist exhibition. Rather, the approach relates to the motion-sequence

NU DESCENDANT UN ESCALIER   MARCEL DUCHAMP

Marcel Duchamp
Chocolate Grinder, No. 1, 1914
Oil, thread and pencil on canvas
primed in black, 65 x 54 cm
Philadelphia (PA), Philadelphia
Museum of Art, Louise and Walter
Arensberg Collection

Jean Crotti
The Clown, 1916
Mixed media on glass, 35.1 x 23.2 cm
Paris, Musée d'Art Moderne de la
Ville de Paris

chaud au cul). The second Romantic factor is the fragmentary, provisional, open-ended nature of the artist's
work. He radically questioned all supposedly eternal
values, and was sadly yet cheerfully aware that all certainties and systems were nothing but speculation, if not
a great swindle. Duchamp believed God was an invention of man; yet he nevertheless finally decided that it
was better to believe in such things after all, because it
would help one to die "happier".

The "eternal value" of painting was also suspect to
Duchamp. During the ten years in which he devoted
himself exclusively to playing chess – with some international success, even – he not only gave up painting
but also gave up art of any kind. Nor did he do anything
to quash the rumor that, since the mid-1940s, he had as
good as given up art entirely, while in reality he had been
working for twenty years on his legacy, an enigmatic
environment of diverse materials (from wood, velvet
and stones to plexiglass, a gas lamp, and a motor)
visible only through two peepholes in a door. Its title:
Given: 1. The Waterfall, 2. The Illuminating Gas (Etant
donnés: 1° la chute d'eau, 2° le gaz d'éclairage). Forced
into the role of voyeur, the spectator sees a naked female
figure in three-quarter view, her pubic hair shaved off,
holding a gas burner in her hand. Her arm is covered
with dry twigs. In the background is a wooded landscape, with a lake and waterfall. All of the means
Duchamp ever employed are present in this initially
shockingly naturalistic, but actually allusively encoded
scene, as is his latent eroticism, which culminated in the
brash demand that a "visual coitus" should take place
between viewer and painting or object of art. This postulate was truly the precondition for Duchamp's final
work, which, despite its superficial naturalism, is even
more complex, ambiguous, and enigmatic than the
Large Glass.

This ostensible anti-artist, as is well known, was also
the inventor of the "ready-made": a *Bicycle Wheel*
mounted on a stool (p. 457), a mass-produced *Bottle
Rack*, a urinoir titled *Fountain* and signed "R. Mutt"
(p. 459). Duchamp put these banal things in a gallery or
museum environment and declared they were works of
art. However, such acts did not mean he had ceased
being an artist. He was "rien qu'un artiste," he himself
said two years before his death. Duchamp was no iconoclast. What he attacked was not art but the abuse of art,
the boredom caused by repetition, the emptying of all
meaning caused by hypocritical pathos, and the decline
of the work of art to the status of a commodity.

By the same token, Duchamp's radical critique had
its source in an extraordinarily high, ambitious, even
utopian conception of art, and in the ironically or sarcastically veiled insight into the impossibility of its realization. Only in a mental exchange between the work of
art and the viewer, in Duchamp's imaginative "coitus,"
could an experience of beauty and of one's own individuality still be had. The fragmentary character, the unfin-

ishability, if you will, of the major works are a clear indication of this belief. And so the question remains open
whether the work of Duchamp's last twenty years represents a document of final success or of an ultimate failure to fulfil his own exacting demands.

Cushioned by the privileges of his upper-middle-
class background, Duchamp persisted in his aim of
resisting commercialization and rapid success. "When I
think of all the young people," he told Pierre Cabanne,
"who absolutely want to have a one-man show by the

time they're twenty! And believe that that in itself would make you a great painter!" And the "consulting museum authorities," in Duchamp's eyes, were "the art dealers."

Duchamp inspired the art of his and our own times like no other. This holds equally for America and Europe, although he himself considered a society without art a possibility, "a state … perhaps not so nice … but conceivable". The move away from pure abstraction can be traced back largely to Duchamp's influence. Pop Art, which he liked because it waived distortion and abstraction and brought "finished things" into the picture, Op Art, Conceptual Art, all learned from Duchamp, and even the famous visualized statement of Beuys', "The silence of Marcel Duchamp is overrated," reflects an intensive involvement with his predecessor. Above all Duchamp demanded that art be intelligent, wrote Allan Kaprow, father of the Happening, which Duchamp by his own admission would like to have invented himself.

Duchamp was far in advance of his time. With him began what is known as "the expanded arts", the crossing of borderlines between media, the interdisciplinary approach that blurs the distinctions between painting, sculpture, artistically designed spaces ("installations" or "environments"), and object. But above all, Duchamp introduced a reflective art, an art of indirect allusion, including literary and philosophical allusion, which for a thinking artist like Duchamp – as for René Magritte in his footsteps – was just as naturally a part of the work as the mobilization of the viewer. The viewer was chal-

lenged to enter into a dialogue with the work, completing it with his imagination by giving mental associations free rein. With Duchamp began a chapter in contemporary art history that no one could have conceived of before him. In a dialectical shift unparalleled in modern art, Duchamp's years of relinquishing artistic production in favor of reflection triggered creative impulses on the part of great numbers of artists, down to the next and following generations. Hardly ever before or after has uncompromising analytical thinking had so far-reaching creative consequences.

The Columbus of Art

If Duchamp was a systematic thinker, Francis Picabia was an eccentric experimenter. The quiet concentration of the chess player stood in sharp contrast to the unrest of his anarchic friend. As Picabia's early Orphic-Cubist canvases show, he was one of the most gifted painters of the early century. By conventional standards, he was also one who squandered his talents by sampling style after style and rarely taking enough time to bring any one of them to maturity. Picabia was unconcerned about such judgements, for his heart was in experimentation. What he had done yesterday held no interest for him today. After beginning in the purist style of Section d'Or, he had gone into Orphism. A stay in New York in 1915 was followed the next year by his founding, in Barcelona, of the journal *391*, an offshoot of the New York Dada journal *291*, which sparked discussions on Dada in the group and eventually led to contacts with Paris Dada. Picabia

Francis Picabia
Cacodylic Eye, 1921
Oil and collage of photographs, postcards, and papers on canvas, 148.6 x 117.4 cm
Paris, Musée National d'Art Moderne, Centre Georges Pompidou

Francis Picabia
Udnie, 1913
Oil on canvas, 300 x 300 cm
Paris, Musée National d'Art Moderne, Centre Georges Pompidou

"Francis Picabia is the Christopher Columbus of art. His philosophical composure, his creative play and his technical cold-bloodedness have not been matched by anyone. He steers his ship without a compass. He has discovered the 'concrete islands' on which the 'abstract gentlemen' eat each other."

HANS ARP

PARADE AMOUREUSE

Francis Picabia 1917

created female portraits out of hairpins and matches, landscapes with trees out of steel springs, painted female nudes on targets – the renowned *Spanish Night* (Cologne, Museum Ludwig) – or on black and white striped backgrounds. His colors were sparing, his materials unusual (pieces of wood, gold and silver powder). The *Portrait of an American Girl in a Naked State* (private collection) consisted of a spark plug. For Picabia and his colleague, Man Ray – as later for the French artist, Arman – the alarm clock was a "symbol of perfect humor."

Picabia, too, was a machine fetishist, as exemplified by *Love Parade* of 1917 (ill. left). The machine gave rise to a new mythology; the "sexual frenzy" of pistons and levers became a dynamic, erotic symbol. The new myths that grew up around technology were multifarious, extending even to the science-fiction legend of flying saucers. Picabia's versions of the myth represented an attempt to affirm the new world of the machine, more intelligent and less aggressive than the Futurists'. Literary quotations pointed to the foundations on which his art, or anti-art, rested, for it was intended to discredit the classical heritage. After the fallings-out among the Dadaists in 1921, Picabia shifted his allegiance to Surrealism, but his restless spirit soon took him down a different path. Later he even made essays in abstraction before returning to objective depiction

again, producing some imagery of a fashionable eroticism that bordered on kitsch. The experiments and youthful glee in discovery of the man whom Arp called a "Columbus of art," if one who always "sailed without a compass," led to successes and failures that have provided a lasting stimulus to younger generations of artists down to this day. A prime example is Sigmar Polke, who was strongly influenced particularly by Picabia's abstract "polka-dot paintings" of the late 1940s and early 1950s.

Picabia can be seen as a key Dadaist figure, despite the fact that a large part of his wilfully contradictory œuvre, inspired by movie magazines, emerged outside the Dada orbit, and that he practiced a hollow, trivial realism in the 1940s in a dubious political accord with the Vichy Regime, before turning to a style that approached abstraction and even, in the late dot-paintings, L'art informel.

Man Ray, painter-photographer and the most significant American Dadaist of the New York group, experimented with arrangements of objects placed on photographic plates and exposed in the darkroom. These "Rayographs" were taken up by László Moholy-Nagy at the Bauhaus, and provided key impulses to artistic photography to come. In cinema, the abstract films produced by the Berlin painter Hans Richter and the Swedish artist Viking Eggeling have lost little of their compelling force even today.

"Artists are afraid; they whisper in each other's ears about a boogey man which might well prevent them from playing their dirty little tricks! No age, I believe, has been more imbecilic than ours."
FRANCIS PICABIA

Melancholy and Loneliness
Giorgio De Chirico and Metaphysical Painting

The heyday of Futurism was brief. One of its leading advocates, Carlo Carrà, turned away from the movement in 1917, on the force of a meeting with Giorgio De Chirico at a field hospital in Ferrara. De Chirico was born in 1880 to Italian parents in Volos, Greece, the point from which the legendary Argonauts set sail. Celebrated by Apollinaire in Paris as one of the most astonishing young painters he had met, De Chirico, even before the war, had concerned himself with ways to overcome Impressionism, the art of lovely surfaces, and to penetrate to the "inward meaning of things." De Chirico and Carrà set out to formulate the aesthetic of a *pittura metafisica*, a painting that would project onto canvas metaphysical spaces suffused by deep melancholy, great loneliness, and lurking anxiety. The changeover from Futurist to Metaphysical painting was a radical one. Obtrusive dynamism was replaced by an oppressive, silent immobility, and a "materialistic" representation of subject matter by a metaphysical, arcane symbolism. Turning way from Impressionism, whose nervous, agitated surfaces had been adapted by Futurism, the Metaphysical painters looked back to the mas-

ters of the Early Renaissance in Italy, to Uccello, Masaccio, and Piero della Francesca and their precise delineation of figures and objects, their carefully calculated if perplexingly unreal perspectives.

At the time Carrà was in a clinic being treated for a nervous disorder. When the doctors saw his and De Chirico's paintings, they agreed that the two artists were direly in need of recuperation. This episode is symptomatic, for the traumatic anxiety of the period, the feeling of continual threat, of emotional emptiness and lonliness, found compelling expression in the work of Carrà and De Chirico.

De Chirico, who died in 1978 at the age of nearly 100, came to develop his style in almost complete independence from the different directions in painting that were most influential at the time. Indifferent to Impressionism, Fauvism and Futurism, he admired the then so belittled Arnold Böcklin and Max Klinger, the almost surrealistic painter, sculptor and graphic artist and author of the *Spaziergänge* (Perambulations) and the fantastic *Glove* series of etchings. De Chirico studied with Klinger during his early years in Munich.

"I remember one vivid winter's day at Versailles. Silence and calm reigned supreme. Everything gazed at me with mysterious, questioning eyes. And then I realized that every corner of the palace, every column, every window possessed a spirit, an impenetrable soul. I looked around at the marble heroes, motionless in the lucid air, beneath the frozen rays of that winter sun which pours down on us without love, like perfect song. A bird was warbling in a window cage. At that moment I grew aware of the mystery which urges men to create certain strange forms. And the creation appeared more extraordinary than the creators."
GIORGIO DE CHIRICO

Francis Picabia
Love Parade, 1917
Oil on cardboard, 96.5 x 73.7 cm
Chicago (IL), Morton G.
Neumann Collection

"As for me, I am calm, and I deco-
rate myself with three words that I
wish to be the seal of all my work:
Pictor classicus sum."
GIORGIO DE CHIRICO

The formal logic of De Chirico's pictorial architecture goes back not to Cubism but to the early classical
period of Italian art. The scenes in his paintings are likewise classically Italian. They are inspired by the city
squares in Ferarra, a somber, melancholy town redolent
with memories of past celebrations, as well as by squares
in Turin and Florence, open spaces devoid of human
life, populated only by faceless sculptures that cast long
shadows. Monotonous arcades open out like gaping
maws of the void; the abrupt, exaggerated perspective
with its eerily foreshortened lines and close vanishing
points creates an ominous vacuum and a sense of unreality. On the horizon one sometimes glimpses a loco-
motive or streetcar, ghost trains from the underworld –
reminiscences of De Chirico's father, who was a railroad
engineer.

These are Kafkaesque scenes, suffused with melancholy colors, with green, ocher and grey predominating.
International tourist attractions take on a demonic cast,
things and objects develop a wierd and disturbing life of
their own. The expressive force of the empty, silent spaces
is further increased when the sculptures are replaced by
tailor's dummies, *manichini*, phantom figures made of
leather and wood. Shadows are cast across the squares by
unidentifiable light sources, and in the midst of this
emptiness the *manichini* take on an anonymous, idol-like
presence. The alienation from familiar scenes is complete. De Chirico's displacement of real things into a new
context in which they appear incongruous and unexpected engenders a sense of shock and disillusionment.
The viewer is forced to perceive a dreamlike, secondary
reality, and to become involved in interpreting it. This
paradoxical, illogical juxtaposition of disparate things,
which De Chirico said was invented by Nietzsche,

would later become the foundation of the Surrealist aesthetic. Nietzsche and Schopenhauer, wrote De Chirico
in his programmatic essay, "We Metaphysicians" of 1919,
"were the first to teach what a profound meaning the
non-sense of life has." Good artists, he added, were
"philosophers who have overcome philosophy."

In De Chirico's metaphysical interiors we find collections of the most heterogeneous objects – fragments
of Greco-Roman sculpture, rubber gloves, plaster casts,
fruit, vegetables, cookies, and scientific apparatus, particularly of the mathematical variety. Behind or between
them there is empty space, which in the course of time
would grow increasingly cut off, bounded, as if the artist
had begun to fear the icy breath of nothingness he himself had invoked. The compositions became more complex, but also less clear and more confusing. One senses
a touch of psychological insecurity in such pictures. In
fact, by 1925, when the Surrealists trimphantly caught up
with him, De Chirico had long passed beyond metaphysical painting. As early as 1919 he had already advocated a return to tradition, thus introducing a widespread development in post-World War I art. De
Chirico began to copy Renaissance masters, especially
of the 15th century, and to praise the great colorists up to
Renoir, especially the Renoir of the pre-Impressionist
years. In the same year as his "We Metaphysicians", De
Chirico wrote an essay that would prove decisive for
things to come. Entitled "The Return to Craftsmanship", its penultimate sentence read "Pictor classicus
sum". With this De Chirico not only sealed his return to
the old masters but also his rejection of his epochal early
work. Nevertheless it disturbed him greatly that Carrà,
in his essays on pittura metafisica, neglected to give him,
De Chirico, credit for helping to invent the style.

Giorgio Morandi
Still Life, 1956
Oil on canvas, 35.5 x 35 cm
Bologna, Galleria Comunale
d'Arte Moderna

Giorgio Morandi
Still Life, 1946
Oil on canvas, 37.5 x 45.5 cm
London, Tate Gallery

Although more skeptical than in the immediate postwar decades of the notion of a "will to art" as advanced by Alois Riegl, we have broken ourselves of the habit of reproaching artists for not practicing something they never intended. While De Chirico's best works of the 1920s, 1930s and beyond do have a restorative, retrospective tendency, they also possess a great, intrinsic originality. Carrà's "metaphysical" œuvre is closely allied to that of his friend of the early period, who later so bitterly denounced him as an ungrateful imitator. Yet while his work deserves all respect, it rarely achieves the aesthetic logic and compelling poetic force of De Chirico.

A significant variant on metaphysical painting was produced by the like-minded Bolognese artist Giorgio Morandi, whom the rigorous and autocratic De Chirico admired without considering him a true metaphysician. Even more than his landscapes, it is the masterful, enigmatic still lifes of this outstanding painter and draftsman, rendered in subdued colors against indeterminate backgrounds, that discover ever-new painterly and poetic aspects in the simple shapes of mundane things such as bottles, bowls, funnels, cups. Morandi's finest works need not fear comparison with those of Chardin (ill. above).

The Omnipotence of Dreams
Surrealism – From André Breton to the Present

With de Chirico, classical scenes were transformed into nightmarish visions. Surrealism raised this sort of visualization of the unharmonious, dissonant side of human existence to the status of a program. Their inclusion in literature and visual art of the irrational, paradoxical, and absurd had been prepared for by the Dadaist revolt. The Surrealists, led by the writers André Breton, Paul Eluard, and Pierre Reverdy, set out to bring system into anarchy. The first *Surrealist Manifesto* was published in 1924, the second in 1930. The Surrealists marshalled many and diverse ancestors to legitimate their endeavors: Bosch, Breughel, Giovanni Battista Piranesi, the creator of labyrinthine dungeons; the Swiss painter of nightmares Johann Heinrich Füssli (who later, in Eng-

land, became Henry Fuseli); another Englishman, William Blake; the Goya of the *Caprichos* and the *Horrors of War;* the French artists Redon, Henri Rousseau, and Moreau, mentor of the Fauves; and finally the early Chagall, Klee, a few works by Léger, the Romanian sculptor Brancusi, and more. The *poètes maudits*, or condemned poets, from Rimbaud and Baudelaire all the way back to Lautréamont and Marquis de Sade, were also invoked. That Dada was also a key precursor was something the Surrealists tended to gloss over, despite the great influence of Duchamp. Recent research has brought to light the connections between Surrealism and historical Mannerism, drawing new attention to artists such as Giuseppe Arcimboldo, court painter to

"Surrealism is based on the belief in the superior reality of certain forms of previously neglected associations, in the omnipotence of dream, in the disinterested play of thought. It tends to ruin once and for all all other psychic mechanisms and to substitute itself for them in solving all the principal problems of life."
ANDRÉ BRETON

Page 136:
Carlo Carrà
The Enchanted Room, 1917
Oil on canvas, 65 x 52 cm
Milan, private collection

Rudolf II in Prague, who in a way anticipated the grotesque black humor of the Surrealists.

Max Ernst once said that his art was as unharmonious and inconsistent as his life. In fact for the Surrealists the notion of lending harmony to chaos, of idealizing reality, was a lie, and the idea of the creative artist as a *creator mundi* was a "superstition," in Ernst's view, a sad relic of the myth of creation. More, to limit artistic depiction to the realm of consciousness would be to curtail intolerably the abundance of existence. Citing the insights of psychoanalysis – despite the fact that its founder, Freud, did not appreciate their art – the Surrealists proclaimed the significance of the unconscious mind, of hallucination and dream and states of intoxication and ecstasy, which, they stated, were just as real as the experiences of conscious life. To bring to light previously repressed feelings and images, and thus to visualize the whole of human existence, including its absurd contradictions, its terrors and underlying humor, regardless of social taboos – that was the mission the Surrealists set themselves. They approached the task either passively, as a sort of medium, as in the case of Max Ernst; or actively, as a free-floating, all-knowing, self-styled genius, as in the case of Salvador Dalí.

Surrealism, pronounced Breton, was "pure psychic automatism." That is to say, the Surrealist artist would delve below the level of the conscious mind with its controls and inhibitions, and "automatically" reproduce what his subconscious inspiration dictated to him. He would submit to no morality, repress none of his deepest desires or instincts, because the Surrealist inhabited a value-free realm in which evil, ugliness, cruelty, instinct, paradox, the grotesquely comic, even the satanic, had as much right to exist as the good, true and beautiful. Such ambitious ideals could, of course, be put into practice only partially. The underlying principle was an acceptance of anarchy.

It was thus no wonder that the Surrealists' connection with the radical political Left, especially with the ex-communicated revolutionary Leon Trotsky, proved untenable in the long run. Although the Surrealists considered the existing social order outmoded and hypocritical, they set out, if not to overthrow it, at least to discredit it with every means at their disposal. But they had no desire to be pressed into a new ideological straitjacket. To these artists, with their anarchical love of liberty, their extreme individualism, and their fundamental refusal to submit to the rules of any collective, the humorless totalitarian doctrines took on an increasingly ominous aspect.

On the other hand, the free-floating attitude of Dalí, eccentric provocateur and immoralist, had quite different consequences. Despite his friendship with the Spanish poet Federico García Lorca, who was later mur-

Max Ernst
The Rendezvous of Friends,
1923/24
Oil on canvas, 129.5 x 193 cm
Cologne, Museum Ludwig

Max Ernst
The Entire City, 1935/36
Oil on canvas, 60 x 81 cm
Zurich, Kunsthaus Zürich

dered by the Fascists, and despite his visionary premonitions of the atrocities of the Spanish Civil war as a prelude to the cataclysm of 1939–1945, Dalí toyed for a time
with the affinity he felt with the personality of Adolf
Hitler. In Hitler's delusions of grandeur Dalí saw – perhaps naively, perhaps opportunistically – certain parallels to his own narcissistic, masochistic, and paranoiac
tendencies. Even the apocalyptic visions of this superb
mannerist and Surrealist eclectic were presented with a
certain coquetry, with a demonstration of virtuosity
from the exalted position of Dalí's "critical-paranoiac"
stance, and entirely without moral commitment. Dalí
was not even entirely unsympathetic to Generalissimo
Franco, who was ultimately responsible for García
Lorca's brutal execution, which long made the artist a
controversial figure, even in his home town of Figueras
in Catalonia. His Surrealist colleagues of the early period
not only reviled Dalí, they cast him out of the group –
at least personally. As far as his art was concerned, they
did not like to do without it in their exhibitions.

The systematization of anarchy envisaged by Breton
was a typical Surrealist paradox, a contradiction in
terms, which was almost impossible to realize in practice. What could be realized, on the other hand, was a
merging of the visual with the literary, of form with content, something which was much doubted at the time
and later, with the triumph of pure painting and abstraction, was condemned outright as mere "illustration."
The finest of the Surrealist painters were precisely those
who were able to overcome Breton's contradiction in
terms by translating their subconscious visions and dis-

coveries directly into a new pictorial structure with little
loss of their fantastic character. This structure served to
hold together an abundance of highly diverse mental
associations and pictorial sensations. Max Ernst managed this difficult process in a more intellectual way, and
Miró in a more playful, spontaneous way.

Other and lesser artists, especially among the following generation, were unable to solve this crucial problem
of Surrealism, and remained bogged down in the indiscriminately destructive or the decoratively illustrative.
This led to an underestimation of Surrealism that lasted
for decades. For a time it even seemed as if Surrealist
shock tactics had definitively lost their vitality. It also
seemed that interesting after-effects of the kind that
undoubtedly occurred in poetry, in the work of René
Char and Paul Celan, for instance, were not to be
expected in the visual arts. Dalí's virtuoso opportunism,
his profitably toyings with the snob-appeal of sophisticated society, appeared to confirm this judgement, as
did the platoons of unoriginal camp-followers of Surrealism in both Europe and the United States. In the
meantime, however, we know that such sweeping gener-
alizations are bound to be wrong. Gifted painters like
Roberto Matta and Wifredo Lam were already at the
peak of their powers, and younger artists like Konrad
Klapheck, Rebecca Horn, and Jannis Kounellis were on
the verge of developing innovative and wittily ironic
variations on the Surrealist theme. That the transitions
were gradual between Surrealism and Abstract Expressionism on both sides of the Atlantic is now also common knowledge.

*"Therefore, when one says of the
Surrealists that they are painters of
an always changing dream reality,
this does not mean that they paint
what they have dreamed (that
would be descriptive, naive naturalism) or that each one constructs his
own little world out of dream elements, in order to behave amicably
or in an evil way, (that would be
a 'flight from time') but rather,
that they move freely, bravely and
naturally on what is physically and
psychologically certainly a real ('surreal') – even if not yet adequately
defined - border area between the
inner and outer worlds."*

MAX ERNST

kind, with a few additions from the artist's hand, were transformed into natural objects or phenomena. A pattern of parallel bands of grain might become a cleft in a rock-face, and a knothole might be seen as a bird hovering with outspread wings. The stripes of its body merged into a circular head, prompting a mental association with *The Origins of the Pendulum Clock*. Oil paintings, too, could be textured in a similar way, by contrasting various spontaneously rendered free forms. Ernst's images of forests composed of tubelike or serrated shapes were done in this manner. A variation known as grattage involved scratching textures into the painted surface; later pictures were done by "decalcomania," a technique discovered in 1935 and perfected by Oscar Dominguez (ill. below), a Surrealist from Teneriffe who took his own life on New Year's Eve of 1957/58. In this method, a surface covered with wet paint was pressed onto the painting surface, then removed, leaving fantastic, swirling patterns that evoked landscapes of moss, water, rocks, and coral reefs. These patterns set off a chain reaction of creative ideas in the artist's mind.

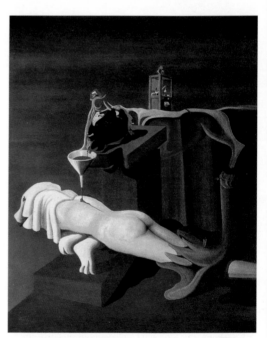

Max Ernst's Phantasmagoria

A key part of the Surrealist catechism was Hippolyte Taine's dictum, "The painting, like the perception it reproduces, is hallucinatory by nature. The hallucination, abnormal as it may seem, is the essence of our mental life." Since no artist could continually have hallucinations or be cognizant of the hallucinatory nature of everyday perception, he had to provoke his imagination, inject into its oyster, as it were, the grain of sand which would become the pearl of inspiration. Only by this means could the process of "psychic automatism" Breton spoke of, the process of drawing or painting as if in a "state of trance," be set underway. Max Ernst, based on his Dada experiments, discovered new methods of inducing this enlightened state, techniques by which controlled chance was introduced into the creative process. Continuing the Cubist collage approach, and with an eye to Lautréamont's famous poetic confrontation of a sewing machine and an umbrella on a dissecting table, Ernst juxtaposed disparate, mutually alien visual elements within a new and strange context. His intention, as he once wrote to Franz Roh, was to "generate an electric or erotic tension. The result was discharges or high-tension currents. And the more unexpected the elements brought together [e.g., gun barrel, beetle mimicry, lace petticoat], the more surprising were the sparks of poetry that leapt the gap."

After collage came frottage, a technique based on Ernst's chance discovery of the charm of wood grain in the floorboards of a hotel room. Seeing strange images in the grain, the artist placed a sheet of paper on the floor and rubbed over it with a soft pencil or crayon. The resulting patterns might evoke waves on the sea, and when the sheet was placed over a phonograph record and rubbed again, its grooves became the rising sun on the horizon. Surprising configurations of this

Using these and similar invocatory formulae Ernst created an ambiguous world of imagery, eerie or joyful, dreamily romantic or magically grotesque, in which things of the most diverse description merged without transition: the human with the animal, the animal with the vegetable, the organic with the anorganic. Out of a protoplasm of moss-like forms emerged ominous giant figures that strode towards the dwellings of men: *The Horde* (Amsterdam, Stedelijk Museum). A collection of intertwining, polyp-like shapes, rendered with realistic precision and fitted with birds' heads, became a *Monument to the Birds* (1927; private collection).

An obscenely swelling configuration with three heads, a bird, human, reptile, and monster mammal in

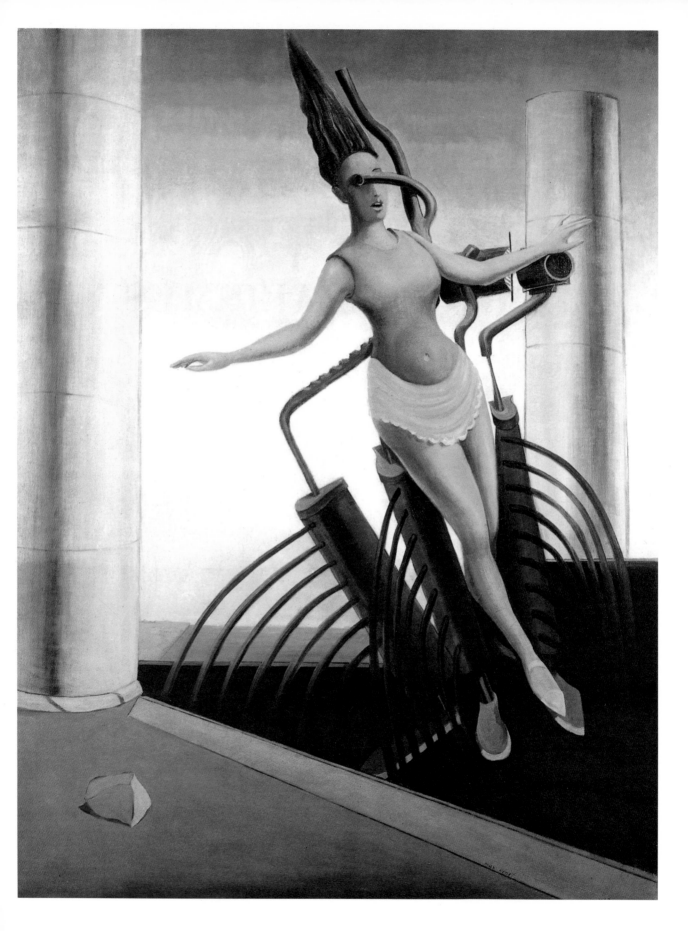

one, "automatically" paints a picture with a hand growing out of its polyp arm: *Surrealism and Painting* (1942; New York, CPLY Art Trust), a grandiose visual translation of Breton's programmatic essay of the same title. *Head, Egg, and Fish* (1925; private collection), painted as if in relief on a wall, is a metaphor for primeval evolution, the seed of life coming to light out of chaos. *Loplop, Chief of the Birds*, becomes a sort of controlling authority, the artist's alter ego, symbolic figure of the subconscious id and the conscious ego both, which in Ernst's case interpermeated and intermerged.

Ernst's phantasmagoria are quite realistic in detail, yet entirely unreal in their combination of disparate elements, their manneristic ambiguity, their inclusion of chance and subconscious imagery. The borderline between external and internal worlds, matter and mind, is transcended, as is the distinction between various periods, for in Ernst's work there is no such thing as development or progress from one phase to the next. The border-lines are vague, and they would remain so to the end of his career. Ernst's inventiveness surpassed that of any other artist of Surrealism, with which only a part of his œuvre was directly associated. A waiver of the traditional sources of artistic inspiration, an objective depiction, and fantasy are combined in a unique way, even in those works which at first sight seem so clear and real, such as the renowned *The Rendezvous of Friends* (p. 138). Only on second glance do we realize that past

"The painting develops before my eyes, unfolding its surprises as it progresses. It is this which gives me the sense of complete liberty, and for the reason I am incapable of forming a plan or making a sketch beforehand."   YVES TANGUY

Yves Tanguy
The Five Strangers, 1941
Oil on canvas, 98.1 x 81.3 cm
Hartford (CT), Wadsworth
Atheneum, The Ella Gallup
Sumner Collection

and present (Max Ernst and Dostoievsky, Raphael and De Chirico), real and unreal, day and dream, the living and the dead also have their rendezvous here in this ghostly, airless space.

Much more limited by comparison was the visual vocabulary of Yves Tanguy, a former seaman who decided to devote himself entirely to art after being deeply impressed by a De Chirico painting. Against milky, vague, misty or opalescent, unbounded backgrounds Tanguy set carefully rendered shapes, part animal, part mechanical, evoking things that do not exist in the real world, but which consciously or unconsciously surely reflect the artist's early fascination with menhirs. Tanguy depicted the dreamlike configurations brought forth by his imagination in an almost illusionistic manner, then abandoned them to the wastelands of an unbounded environment in dream landscapes of a high degree of abstraction (pp. 140, 142).

The Obsessions of Salvador Dalí

Tanguy's seemingly infinite perspectives returned, in a later twist of the spiral, in the much more veristic and descriptive landscapes of Dalí. More than any other Surrealist, Dalí raised the factors of absurdity and simulated

insanity to a principle. The disgusting and obscene, the satanic and monstrous, were presented in a veritably theatrical way. Dalí's technique was brilliant, Old Masterly, correct to the point of pedantry. Yet he used the perfectly rendered naturalistic detail to convey content of a monstrous, unnatural nature. Bloated, decaying limbs form gates of horror, rattling skeletons stuck on posts, emaciated female figures with bellies like chests of drawers, stand starkly against ominous horizons. The essence of this art, what Dalí termed "paranoiac critique", was a hallucinatory exaggeration of sexual, sadistic, masochistic, and compulsively neurotic ideas. According to the artist, blood, decay, rot, and excrement were key components of a painting approach which – like Surrealism in general – continued and ramified the anti-aesthetic principles of Dada in that it was intended to be understood not in the traditional sense, but in the sense of a demonstration and analysis.

Yet Dalí's art in particular obviously displays an abundance of historical references and allusions, especially to Mannerist painting, and ultimately, it too was unable to escape the inevitable transformation of anti-art into a new, as it were "positive" form of art. The clownish, grotesquely comic traits in Dalí's art, intended

Salvador Dalí
The Persistence of Memory
(Soft Watches), 1931
Oil on canvas, 24 x 33 cm
New York, The Museum of
Modern Art

"Soft clocks: they are nothing else than paranoiac-critical, gentle, and extravagant Camemberts outside of time and space."
SALVADOR DALÍ

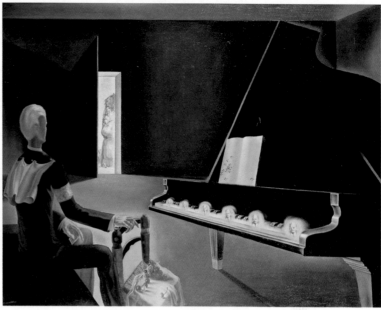

to provoke the complacent, whether of the middle-class or the ideological Left, should not be overlooked. They formed the humus in which the flowers of evil grow. In fact the "satanists," from de Sade through Lautréamont to Baudelaire and Rimbaud, provided as much material for Dalí's pictures as they did for Luis Buñuel's films.

Still, there is no doubting the originality of many of Dalí's pictorial inventions. Examples are the eerie and ironic depiction of soft and drooping clocks in the painting *Persistence of Memory* (p. 143), the apocalyptic figure of the *Burning Giraffe* (1936/37; Basel, Kunstmuseum), or the *The Enigma of Wilhelm Tell* (1933; Stockholm, Moderna Museet), which due to the resemblance to Lenin of the Swiss idol transformed into a cannibalistic anti-hero, caused a scandal among the left-leaning Surrealists – a typical instance of the inevitability of the conflict already mentioned between artistic individual and political collective. However, these and other masterpieces stand opposed to many paintings that exhibit more speculation and empty virtuosity than true obsession and intuition – not to mention the mass editions of facile to slipshod prints and faddish knick-knacks which Dalí sadly also produced.

The Catalan artist is a paragon example of the exhibitionistic self-actor who benefited for decades from brilliant career management. His chief manager was Gala, the woman Dalí took away from Paul Eluard and who jealously guarded over him for more than fifty years. It was only when, with increasing age, Gala began to loosen the reins a bit that her husband fell into the clutches of business-wise secretaries and dealers. That success is not always an insurance of rising quality becomes sometimes cloyingly obvious in the late work of the eccentric and knowledgeable eclectic, even though in middle and old age Dalí again and again pro-

duced a significant work, such as *The Temptation of St. Anthony* (1946; Brussels, Musées Royaux des Beaux-Art), executed in 1946 for a Hollywood competition. Another theme on which Dalí rang many and compelling changes was *The Angelus* by Jean François Millet, a theme whose pious to murderous complexity involved Dalí from his boyhood years to the very end.

Salvador Dalí
Dream Caused by the Flight of a Bee Around a Pomegranate, One Second Before Awakening, 1944
Oil on cavas, 51 x 40.5 cm
Madrid, Museo Thyssen-Bornemisza, Fondazione Thyssen-Bornemisza

Salvador Dalí
Partial Illusion. Six Apparitions of Lenin on a Piano, 1931
Oil on canvas, 114 x 146 cm
Paris, Musée National d'Art Moderne, Centre Georges Pompidou

Salvador Dalí
Mae West's Face which May Be Used as a Surrealist Apartment, 1934/35
Gouache on newspaper, 31 x 17 cm
Chicago (IL), The Art Institute of Chicago

Page 144:
Salvador Dalí
Apparatus and Hand, 1927
Oil on wood, 62.2 x 47.6 cm
St. Petersburg (FL), The Salvador Dalí Museum, formerly Collection E. and A. Reynolds Morse

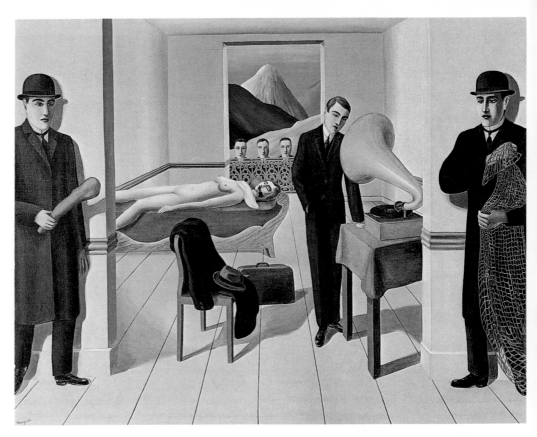

René Magritte
The Threatened Murderer, 1926
Oil on canvas, 150.4 x 195.2 cm
New York, Collection, The
Museum of Modern Art,
Kay Sage Tanguy Fund

René Magritte
Time Transfixed, 1939
Oil on canvas, 147 x 98 cm
Chicago (IL), The Art Institute of
Chicago

Surrealism in Belgium

Surrealist pictures tell stories. This is why for many Surrealists a literary idea, an art-theoretical or philosophical commentary, were more important than the actual painterly execution. The intellectually most impressive example of this is the work of René Magritte, a Belgian artist who continued Duchampian notions in painted form. Instead of bringing the aspect of the surreal into his pictures, Magritte built riddles out of components of reality, pointing up its absurdity in the process. Magritte's picture-puzzles are intellectual games that at the same time call reality radically in question. Not an invocation of the unconscious is his theme but the discomfiting of the viewer and his habitual perception, by means of the confrontation, anticipated by Lautréamont, of disparate, uncompatible, mutually alien elements. By so doing Magritte intended to make us stop and think about the nature of reality and our tacit assumptions concerning it, as well as about art and processes of perception in general. Magritte admired the work of his great idol, De Chirico, he said, because of the "superiority of poetry over painting and the diverse painting styles" it evinced. The aesthetic device Magritte used to engender a magical, poetic transmutation of the mundane and to jog the viewer out of his complacency was that of surprise. This effect took the form, in the early, "criminalistic" paintings, of turning familiar situations upside down: in *The Threatened Murderer* (ill. above) the murderer is the victim; in *The Amusement* (Düsseldorf, Kunstsammlung Nordrhein-

René Magritte
The Treachery of Images, 1928/29
Oil on canvas, 62.2 x 81 cm
Los Angeles (CA), Los Angeles
County Museum of Art

Westfalen) a girl consumes a bird; in *The Sleepwalker* (1927; Essen, Museum Folkwang) the title figure walks through a nocturnal room lit by a streetlamp.

Magritte's conception of an interplay of painting and poetry, subject and idea, magic and reflection, comes out most clearly in the works in which the subject depicted is verbally denied its identity. The most famous is the painted pipe captioned *Ceci n'est pas une pipe,* or This is not a pipe (ill. above). The prob-

lem was redoubled and intellectually sharpened when Magritte repeated the theme forty years later, shortly before his death. This time the picture of the pipe with its negating caption was placed on an easel, within a larger picture containing a larger pipe floating in empty space. Its ironic title: *The Two Mysteries* (1967; New York, Mr. and Mrs. Terry Semel Collection). In both cases it is pointed out that a painted pipe is not a real one; the floating pipe in the later canvas refers

Frits van den Berghe
Le Beau Mariage I, 1928
Oil on paper on wood, 64 x 48.5 cm
Private collection

Gustave de Smet
The Blue Divan, 1928
Oil on canvas, 145 x 115 cm
Private collection

Paul Delvaux
Phases of the Moon, 1939
Oil on canvas, 139.7 x 160 cm
New York, The Museum of
Modern Art

once again to this fact, but it is not any more real or tangible than the original pipe, but only a two-dimensional depiction of it.

Similar trains of thought are evident in Magritte's pictures within the picture, such as that of a weight-lifter whose bald head is apparently identical with one of the two weights he is lifting, or in the canvas *The Human Condition* (1933; Washington, National Gallery), where the "actual" view through a window merges with a

painted section of the same view standing in front of the window on an easel. This picture within the picture effect corresponds to an ambiguous and ironic device that goes back to the Romantic era, that of the theater within the theater, in which the question as to reality and illusion is asked with the same, veritably philosophical force.

The other classical Surrealist of Belgian origin was born a year before Magritte: Paul Delvaux. Originally an

Paul Delvaux
The Blue Train, 1946
Oil on canvas, 122 x 244 cm
Private collection

Expressionist influenced by Permeke, Delvaux, like Magritte, had a confrontation with the painting of De Chirico that proved decisive. Yet unlike Magritte, Delvaux relied heavily on imagery from the subconscious mind, especially imagery of an erotic nature. His musing, pale nudes perambulate with empty gaze, sometimes observed by voyeurs alive or dead, through cool, moonlit, imaginary cityscapes in the neo-classical manner, occasionally set off by a De Chirico-like steam engine. The air seems to stand still in the silence of this imaginary realm, in which sexuality and death, ghostly life and waxwork petrifaction, community and loneliness, nightmare and ennui coexist (ill. left).

In this context a brief look must be taken at the so-called Surrealist phase of Picasso's work. After all, the Spanish artist did participate in 1925 in the first Surrealist exhibition at Galerie Pierre in Paris, because he sympathized with the aims of the group and its revolutionary elan, including its then-leftist ideology. It was a similar mood to that which produced Picasso's expressively magical symbolism, though unlike the Surrealists proper and despite his protean liberty in the choice of painterly and sculptural means, Picasso always cleaved closely to reality. Alienation effects and arbitrary combinations of disparate and contradictory elements, a submission to dream and the Freudian unconscious, were things that held no appeal for Picasso. The distortions in his work had a quite different meaning.

Joan Miró's World

The "psychic automatism" of Breton, which continued to affect *informel* work of Georges Mathieu and the ecstatic drawings of the painter-poet Henri Michaux, found its purest expression in the work of another Spaniard, the Catalan artist Joan Miró, though his style was only partially Surrealist-influenced. Miró's paintings have since achieved considerable popularity. Though it would be cruel to ruin the naive pleasure people find in his fantastic universe of signs, it would be equally wrong to treat Miró as a decorative artist, a teller of lightheartedly grotesque tales populated by strange configurations in vivid colors. He not only painted canvases like the delightful *Harlequin's Carnival* (p. 150), but also the eerie *Head of a Woman* (Los Angeles, private collection) of 1938, a huge and belligerent insect who calls Kafkaesque metamorphoses to mind. Miró's world is not consistently cheerful and sunny; it is occasionally overclouded by something uncannily magical. What distinguishes him from the majority of his contemporaries – including Klee, to whom he owed much – is Miró's ease and originality of invention. He did not need to work through any oppressive visual compulsions in order to arrive at the "second naivety" of the modern artist. Although he oriented himself to historical models such as the Dutch masters, Miró, like the artists of aboriginal cultures, drew on a universe of signs and symbols that was essentially inborn.

Joan Miró
Person Throwing a Stone at a Bird, 1926
Oil on canvas, 73.7 x 92.1 cm
New York, Collection, The Museum of Modern Art

Miró's development was extremely logical. The early landscapes, done around 1920, reveal an unspoiled eye for reality and the freshness of vision of a Sunday painter. The compositions and rendering of details are rigorous and painstaking, but they already show a tendency to stylization in which the forms are sharply juxtaposed – a Spanish realism curbed by Cubism. Already one sees graphic lineatures beginning to snake playfully across the plane, and numbers appear like magic signs. Such pictures anticipate much of what is to come – a

"Immobility fascinates me. This bottle, this glass, a big stone on a deserted beach – these are motionless things, but they set loose great movements in my mind. I don't feel this with a human being who changes place all the time in an idiotic way. People who go bathing on a beach and who move about touch me much less than the immobility of a pebble." JOAN MIRÓ

Joan Miró
Nocturne, 1935
Oil on copper, 42 x 29.2 cm
Cleveland (OH), The Cleveland Museum of Art, Mr. and Mrs. William H. Marlatt Fund

Joan Miró
The Poetess, 1940
Gouache and turpentine paint
on paper, 38.1 x 45.7 cm
New York, private collection

another. As the years go by, the organic elements, derived from the primeval forms of plasma, would come increasingly to dominate Miró's imagery. The circle, his favorite shape, took a place of prominence, whether in pure or irregular form. Human, animal, and vegetable configurations, sun, moon, and stars, began to whirl and intermingle until it became impossible to distinguish them.

Although these configurations are obviously far removed from the realm of everyday perception, they nonetheless retain an individual physiognomy. Their features cover a particular gamut of expressions, all the way from carefree, childlike joy to a barely concealed demonism. Sharp saw-teeth, pointed claws, grisly suction cups, and grasping, amoeba-like creatures point up the fact that one enters the realm of such hybrids of imagination and reality only at one's own risk.

A reliance on chance and on existing objects and materials also played a role with Miró. He learned these techniques from the sculptures of Arp, whose spontaneously engendered organic forms gave Surrealism its most decisive turn in the direction of abstraction. The Surrealist object became a fetish for Miró as well. In his later years he tended, not always advantageously for his painting, to the monumental, reducing forms to the utmost, to signets floating on an expanse of canvas. But that this emblematic art was ultimately nothing other than condensed reality, in both the physical and poetical sense of the word, is revealed by Ernest Hemingway's remark that everything he knew about Spain, Miró had painted – harsh landscape, hot sun, and the bullfight.

reduction of real objects to abstractions, of real scenes to excerpts, emblems. A tree trunk becomes a cone, a plowed field an undulating ornament. But unlike the rigorous paintings of the Cubists, this reduced reality contains an admixture of the fantastic. The crowns of trees sprout eyes, ears grow out of their trunks, a magical triangle is a pyramid, face, and treetop in one. Organic and anorganic forms are set in effective contrast to one

Joan Miró
Harlequin's Carnival, 1924/25
Oil on canvas, 66 x 93 cm
Buffalo (NY), Albright-Knox Art
Gallery

Page 151:
Joan Miró
Ladders Cross the Blue Sky in a
Wheel of Fire, 1953
Oil on canvas, 116 x 89 cm
Private collection

Joan Miró
Personages and Dog Before the Sun, 1949
Tempera on canvas, 81 x 54.5 cm
Basel, Öffentliche Kunstsammlung Basel, Kunstmuseum, Emanuel-Hoffmann Foundation

André Masson
In the Forest, 1944
Oil on canvas, 56 x 38 cm
Buffalo (NY), Albright-Knox Art Gallery

Page 153 below left:
Léopold Survage
Surrealistic Composition with Fish and Figures, 1917
Oil on canvas, 92 x 73 cm
Geneva, Musée du Petit Palais

Page 153 below right:
Toyen
Slumbering Woman, 1937
Oil on canvas, 81 x 100 cm
Private collection

his "psychograms" and Jackson Pollock's drip paintings (pp. 268 ff).

Visions of massacre and inexorable destruction are likewise suggested by the excited and exciting canvases of Arshile Gorky, an Armenian born in Russia who, ill and disappointed, committed suicide in New York at the age of 44. Like Masson's, Gorky's significant and only belatedly appreciated work continued and transcended Surrealism, to take a key place within the Abstract Expressionism of the New York School (p. 278).

The paintings of Richard Oelze, born in Magdeburg, Germany, in 1900, are those of a loner who submitted to no Surrealist dogma. His *Expectation* (ill. right) caused a furor when it was shown in the famous exhibition, "Fantastic Art, Dada, Surrealism," held at the Museum of Modern Art, New York, in 1936. While Oelze's style drew on the lyricism of the German Romantic era, it was a lyricism grown ominous and ghostly. His landscapes show fantastic grottoes and caverns under clouded, endless skies, populated by bizarre, enigmatic figures, animals, plants and spirits with bloated or decaying forms, the whole suffused by subdued, as it were twilight colors, delicate gradations of grey, brown and rose. This hallucinatory realm appears as if behind veils, and over it lies a pall of decay. Like Masson's work, Oelze's macabre depictions of enchanted, romatically surreal locales reflect the anxieties of the age in visual terms.

International Surrealism

Like Miró, André Masson was initially influenced by Cubism. His master was Gris. Yet the stringent composition of the Cubists with its lucid, structural emphasis was soon inundated by a nervous, passionately dynamic network of lineatures that was a direct expression of the artist's mental state (ill. right). This excited, emotionally agitated mood suffuses Masson's œuvre. The paintings of his most significant period, before and after 1930, read like a confirmation of Breton's Surrealist dictum: "Beauty will be convulsive, or it will not be at all."

Masson was highly receptive to the cataclysms and cruelties of the age. The battle of all against all, whether in the animal kingdom, among humans, or even between the sexes, became a trauma for him, and he painted in an attempt to rid himself of it. The result was a strange mythology of destruction: fish fighting one another, birds killing one another, and erotic confrontations that seemed to verge on murder. The experiences of Masson's youth, the First World War, the Spanish Civil War, the Second World War, escape and persecution, the inexorable chain of catastrophes shaped his automatic calligraphies, which during an American sojourn during the war, became feverish and garish. The incredible mental tension under which he stood was impossible to bear in the long run, which perhaps explains Masson's turn back to an Impressionist approach influenced by William Turner, in which he produced pictures of a surprisingly tranquil, reserved lyricism. Yet his earlier automatic technique continued to have an effect on other artists, down to Hans Hartung and

Surrealism, like the fantastic architecture of the Spaniard Antoni Gaudí, is an unclassical art par excellence, a protest against the norm. To that extent it represents a timeless human possibility, a further tributary of the romantic stream that runs through the history of ideas. With this introduction, we can turn to a loner who, though he had nothing to do with Surrealism as a programmatic movement, did apply an essential part of its methods and insights to his art. The English painter, Graham Sutherland transformed landscapes and naturally occurring forms into disagreeable objects, the *objets désagréables* so crucial to the Surrealists. Angular, thorn-studded configurations grow out of half-moon shapes or are imbedded in them; the two halves of a bare, broken branch become threatening elephant's tusks, and a distorted face appears at the point of the break. Sutherland's *Thorned Head* (done in several versions) has a bird's head with a half-open sickle shape containing spear-sharp configurations from another world, half evil birds in a thorny nest, half thistle. The nature mystique in the artist's best works engenders not familiarity but unfamiliarity, alienation, fear. Yet this creative phase was relatively brief. Sutherland also did a number of impressive portraits, including one of the author

*"With respect to my thorn pictures,
I can say, that I was thinking of the
crucifixion... and that I was thinking about thorns, about wounds that
come from thorns."*
GRAHAM SUTHERLAND

Somerset Maugham (ill. left). The most famous of his portraits was that of Winston Churchill, which achieved late fame for a rather sad reason – Lady Churchill burned it because it was not sufficiently "like" her husband.

If Sutherland was connected with Surrealism by elective affinity alone, two further artists took up its aggressive tendencies as immediate followers: Roberto Matta of Chile, and Wifredo Lam of Cuba. Matta's enormous canvas *Being With* of 1946 caused a sensation at documenta 2 in 1959, because it proved that supposedly moribund Surrealism still had a great deal of life left in it. The fact that the new wave ran in the opposite direction, no longer from Europe to America but vice versa, was no coincidence. In art as in literature we have repeatedly seen how America takes up European tendencies, emancipates and transforms them, then exports them back to the Old World. "Ping-pong," Pontus Hulten has aptly termed this process of exchange in the history of ideas.

In the work of Matta there is no attempt made to disguise either his critical engagement or his direct reference to current realities. Our technology-suffused existence, including missile launching pads and the experience of space travel, take on painterly presence. The industrialized world becomes a laboratory, an experimental station, with man delegated to playing the role of robot or test-tube product. The human figure in Matta's work appears surrounded by machines, piping and capsules which man himself has created. The machinery, in turn, seems to take on a creaturely life of its own, threatening or tormented, suspended in a mesh of steel rods and levers, the whole teeming with eerie, bristling, insect-like configurations. Matta's colors are cool and thinly applied, his compositions rigorous and graphic; yet at certain points hot, fiery hues in heavy impasto shine out (p. 155).

"I tried to pass from intimate imagery, forms of vertebrae, and unknown animals, very little known flowers to cultural expressions, totemic things, civilizations."
ROBERTO MATTA

Roberto Matta
Bringing Light without Pain, 1955
Oil on canvas, 200 x 300 cm
Brussels, private collection

It is a long path from Duchamp's or Picabia's cult of the machine to Matta's critique of technology and its effects. His critique is radical, and its tone sarcastic and bitter. It is easy to see what side Matta stands on – that of the disadvantaged and dispossessed. The Chilean artist's themes make him a sort of "Hell Breughel" of our own age. Whether you take the serious, silent wall paintings (Matta worked for Le Corbusier as an architect for a few years) or the visions of outer space, the dramatic "paintings of anger and protest," Matta's attempt to face up to a complex and frightening reality and to change his and our lives through art remains impressive.

Wifredo Lam's Chinese father lived to the age of 108, when he died of a fall from a horse. His son inherited this vitality and invested it in a painterly œuvre of great puissance. Lam had Chinese, African, Indio, and European blood in his veins, which is as evident in his paintings as the influence of Picasso. They are populated by figures half-human, half-animal, armed with sharp implements and scythes, performing their dark rites in impenetrable jungles in which hybrid creatures and heads lurk at every turn. Like all of Surrealism, Lam's compositions are not without a touch of grotesquerie and black humor. In his paintings the myths of primitive African and South American tribes are reformulated for the contemporary age, for Lam's nocturnal beings symbolize the jeopardy of human life in a world echoing with war cries and the screams of innocent victims (p. 156 above left).

Another artist who belongs within the orbit of Surrealism is Josef Šima, a Czech painter who, like many Eastern Europeans, spent his formative years in France.

In 1935 he travelled with Breton and Eluard to Prague, establishing first contacts between Czech and French Surrealists. Sima's highly sensitive, poetic, dreamlike compositions delve into the secrets of the universe and also – under the influence of Carl Gustav Jung's psychology – explore the depths of the unconscious mind, whether the subject be "Europe," rendered as a double female torso, *The Fall of Icarus*, or a simple *Landscape* (p. 156 below).

Roberto Matta
Untitled, 1971
Oil on canvas, 206 x 160 cm
Private collection

On the Margins of Surrealism

Another, if less substantial variant of Surrealism was the now almost forgotten "fantastic realism" of the Vienna School, which emerged from the academy class of painter-writer Albert Paris Gütersloh. That this neo-manneristic style arose in Vienna was no coincidence, nor was the influence of nearby Prague and its history, particularly the phase represented by Rudolf II and Giuseppe Arcimboldo. That the group of five artists had as mentor an author who also painted is reflected in the literary bent of their work from the start. Apart from Arcimboldo, they drew inspiration from the art of the late Gothic period, from the Danube School, from the Venetians Gentile and Giovanni Bellini and Carlo

Crivelli, from the Netherlanders Hieronymus Bosch, Pieter Breughel and Joos van Cleve, from the Fleming Joachim Patinier, the Symbolist Moreau, and even the Pre-Raphaelites – indeed a large bite to digest from the history of art.

It must be said that the style of the Vienna School, whether of Ernst Fuchs, Erich (Arik) Brauer, Wolfgang Hutter, or Anton Lehmden, gradually became increasingly facile and superficial. There was "absolutely nothing… new about it," stated critic Uwe M. Schneede. "The ingredients of this marketable mixture of shallow mannerism, high-flown kitsch, and quasi-religious profundity were already musty when they returned in the works of these Viennese artists: a saccharine symbolism, a defused Surrealism, a dolled-up mythology, and exhausted pictorial means." The only member of the group to make a name for himself in the serious art scene was Rudolf Hausner, a thoughtful and painstaking artist whose incessant self-investigations explore the borderline between reality and imagination, which, in Hausner's own words, "continually tend… to intermerge" (ill. right).

More significant for the later history and effects of Surrealism was the work of Hans Bellmer, which, despite his early contacts with the Surrealists and his friendship with Max Ernst, Man Ray, Yves Tanguy, and Paul Eluard during the French emigration, did not find the attention it deserved until after 1945 (ill. below) – more precisely, until the participation of this brilliant graphic artist in the great Surrealism demonstration of 1947. Bellmer's erotic obsessions between dreaming and waking, his fantastic labyrinths out of which leads no Ariadne's thread, visualize, as Herbert Pée notes, "the inferno of the instincts" in a way that recalls Hieronymus Bosch.

The erotic theme appeared no less subtly, if much less directly in the paintings, collages, and objects of the fascinatingly beautiful Meret Oppenheim. In her case the aspect of the absurd was addressed straightforwardly, by means of a combination of disparate and contradictory realities, materials and iconographies that, strictly speaking, were mutually exclusive.

A quite different case is represented by Gerhard Altenbourg, an East German artist who died in an accident shortly before the reunification of the country in 1989. An isolated loner in the then GDR, Altenbourg anticipated the mode of the drawing as an autonomous work of art, a theme to which much space was justifiably devoted at documenta 6 in 1977. His profoundly romantic imagery bears as much affinity to Klee – who also relied on many Surrealist devices – as it does to programmatic Surrealism proper. The image, whether a head, a figure, or a landscape, was developed without a

pre-conceived plan, if not entirely "automatically." The narrative or literary elements in Altenbourg's works, their enigmatically distorted, fundamentally indecipherable configurations, their mixture of conscious and unconscious promptings, and the poetic "christening" of spontaneously emerging imagery, all point back beyond Surrealism to the Romantic era – up to and including the scurrilous jesting of a Jean Paul. As the richly nuanced, indeed sometimes oversumptuous palette of many of Altenbourg's watercolors, gouaches, and tempera paintings indicates, this born draftsman was also a gifted colorist (p. 368).

In the United States, Surrealism never dominated the art scene as it did for a time in Europe, and this despite the 1937 exhibition "Dada, Fantastic Art, Surrealism," despite the presence of many war emigrés (including Ernst, who in 1946 married Gorky-student Dorothea Tanning), and despite the pioneering art of Gorky himself. Surrealist influences, which ranged from Gorky to C.G. Jung, were ultimately turned in a quite different direction, as seen for instance in Pollock or De Kooning. It should not be overlooked, however, that

Dado
The Massacre of the Innocents,
1958/59
Oil on canvas, 194 x 259.5 cm
Paris, Musée National d'Art
Moderne, Centre Georges
Pompidou

Ivan Le Lorraine Albright
The Farmer's Kitchen, c. 1933/34
Oil on canvas, 91 x 76.5 cm
Washington, National Museum
of American Art, Smithsonian
Institution

infusions of Surrealism altered the style of precisionist, socially critical realists such as Ivan Le Lorraine Albright (ill. above right) or Peter Blume in the direction of the fantastic.

Surrealist tendencies in the art of the Eastern Bloc countries of the day were long subjected to political repression. As a result, to give only two examples, the Ukrainian artist Alexander Tyschler was unable to retain the visionary force of his early painting, and Dado felt himself compelled to abandon Yugoslavia for Paris (ill. above left). However, one need only take an even cursory look at the contemporary Eastern European scene

to realize that the love of the super-real and fantastic can never be entirely suppressed.

The imagery of Balthus, the brother of the esoterically erotic painter-writer Pierre Klossowski, whose family came from Poland, is situated in the twilight zone between Surrealism and an almost magical realism, which is not blatant but psychologically subtle. Indicatively the aging Rilke admired the young prodigy Balthus, who soon augmented the sensibility of a Far Eastern painter by a precision of detail and a logic of composition which went back to illustrious artists of the past, from Piero della Francesca in the Renaissance

Louis Soutter
Abel, 1937–1942
Gouache and India ink on paper,
64.8 x 49.8 cm
Napa (CA), Hess Collection

Adolf Wölfli
St. Adolf Diamond Ring, 1913
Pencil and crayon on paper,
98 x 74.7 cm
Bern, Adolf Wölfli Donation

Balthus
The Street, 1933
Oil on canvas, 195 x 240 cm
New York, The Museum of
Modern Art, James Thrall Soby
Bequest

to Courbet's 19th-century naturalism. Until the 1960s Balthus enjoyed the reputation of a rather decadent painter for a small coterie, who, however, paid well for his works. With their elegantly subdued palette, at first a bit on the dark side, but then becoming lighter, more pastel, these interiors and figures are marked by a silent, dreamlike tranquillity. The girls in Balthus' pictures are not yet women, but no longer girls; they possess an ambivalent sexuality between innocence and vice, which, often underscored by obvious devices, fills the scenes with a lasciviousness that recalls the salons of Marcel Proust. Balthus's sophisticated painting technique partakes of the surreal, though certainly not of doctrinaire Surrealism. It calls to mind theater scenes in suspended animation, tableaux in which the familiar grows strange and mundane reality takes on the vividness of dream (ill. above).

It is a far cry from this intelligent, sophisticated, high-strung erotic art to the works of those painters who occupied the twilight zone between delusion and reality, and in whom the Surrealists' interest was sparked by Hans Prinzhorn's collections and writings, foremost his 1922 book, *Bildnerei der Geisteskranken* (The Picture-Making of the Mentally Ill). Space permits reference to only three exemplary figures: Friedrich Schröder-Sonnenstern, Adolf Wölfli (p. 158 below right), and Louis Soutter (p. 158 below). The youngest of the three, who

styled himself "Friedrich the One and Only," was a restless if entirely benign wanderer, who later became the victim of unscrupulous forgers of his eccentric colored-pencil works. The second, Wölfli, was a compulsive sexual criminal. The third, Soutter, a failure in normal life, was committed to an asylum by his family when, bitterly disappointed and abandoned by wife and friends, he returned from America to Europe at an advanced age. For all three artists, spontaneous visual creativity served to help them overcome the speechlessness into which their inability to adapt to the norms of society had forced them. Their aggressive, anarchic allegories were a visible sign of the suffering of the social pariah from the coldness and indifference of the age, from unchanneled sexuality, from the lack of meaning in their own and others' lives, and from the plight of the poor and outcast. Schröder-Sonnenstern's garish drawings, Wölfli's visual rebuses, Soutter's fingertip-paintings emerged from the same subconscious depths that played such a key role in Surrealism. But in their case, there was no simulation of states of madness as advocated by Breton as a means to "reunite dream and waking states, insanity and reason" (T. Spoerri), no artificially induced intoxications or ecstasies. If their imagery moves us, it is because it emerged immediately and uncensored, without aesthetic calculation, from the depths of their troubled souls.

"Every time that I have placed the last brushstroke on a painting, I am overcome by the idea that I have forgotten everything that I knew about my art and will have to discover everything anew. It is as if you wake up, have to write a speech, and then realize that you cannot recall the simplest rules of grammar."
BALTHUS

Kasimir Malevich
Suprematism, c. 1917
Oil on canvas, 80 x 80 cm
Krasnodar, Lunatscharski-
Museum

Abstraction and Reality

Russian Revolutionaries and Dutch Iconoclasts
Suprematism, Constructivism, and "De Stijl"

It is an age-old dream of artists, that the creation of a better and more beautiful environment will further the emergence of a new and more noble type of human being. This utopian idea has metaphysical roots, in that it is related to religious doctrines of salvation. Such dreams have retained their effect down to the present day, especially among architects. That 20th-century architecture was profoundly influenced by an anti-individualistic style of art which claimed to establish a new universal order is therefore not surprising. Russian "Suprematism" and its successor, "Constructivism," as well as the Dutch movement, "De Stijl," were rooted in an attempt to change the world and to create a functional, normative art. All the artists involved in both movements – with the exception of Kasimir Malevich – rejected the traditional concepts of the fine arts as being sufficient unto themselves. Both movements envisioned a universal, collective art for all, an applied art in the best sense, far removed from all individualism and subjectivity. No greater contrast to the fantasies and ecstasies of the Surrealists is imaginable. Russian Constructivism, especially its Suprematist phase, rooted in pre-revolutionary anarchism and later condemned by Lenin, might be characterized as the "romantic" side of the movement, while the Dutch variant represented the "classical" side with its idealistic and spartanic emphasis. Suprematism and Constructivism had a tendency to the infinite and absolute, Suprematism exhibiting a more mystical, pathetic strain and Constructivism a more futurological, technological one. The artists of De Stijl oriented themselves towards the exactly defined and delineated plane. But whether it was the dynamic pictorial structure of the Russians or the static one of the Dutch, all strove for the greatest good for the greatest number, a utopian striving which is symbolically reflected in the themes of their works.

The widespread belief that two different and mutually alien cultures existed in Europe was an untenable hypothesis long before the political upheavals of the late 1980s and early 1990s. It was disseminated as opium for the people on both sides of the Iron Curtain during the Cold War, which had been touched off in February 1945 by the notorious Yalta Conference. Art was enlisted by the opposing ideologies as an instrument of political propaganda, chauvinistic Socialist Realism on the one side, and on the other abstract art, which was touted as a symbol of Western freedom. One plain fact tended to be overlooked: that officially sanctioned art was not the only art that existed beyond the border, and that neither

"It has become clear to me that new frameworks of pure color-painting should be created, constructed at color's demand; and, secondly, that color should leave the painterly mixture and become an independent factor, entering the construction as an individual of a collective system and individual independence."
KASIMIR MALEVICH

Kasimir Malevich
Suprematist Painting, 1915
Oil on canvas, 101.5 x 62 cm
Amsterdam, Stedelijk Museum

the Eastern European dictatorships nor the Soviet Union under Stalin had been able to completely suppress it. European art history in the 20th century, as Riszard Stanislawski points out, rested on "reciprocal inspiration," on a continual exchange of ideas between East and West. The question of priorities is moot, because they continually changed. This was first brought to widespread public attention in the late 1970s and early 1980s by "Paris-Moscow," an exhibition curated by Pontus Hulten and shown at the Centre Pompidou in Paris and at the Pushkin Museum in Moscow.

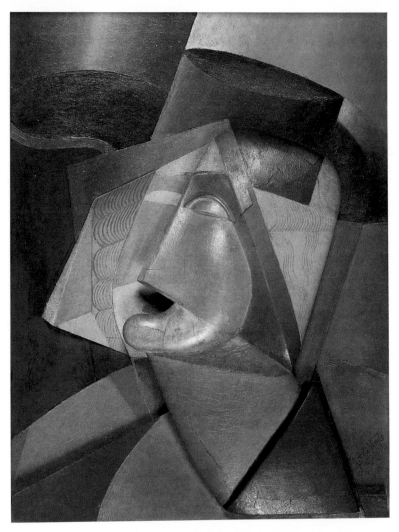

Alexander Archipenko
Woman with Hat, 1916
Oil, metal, papier maché and
gauze on wood, in wooden frame,
35.5 x 26.5 cm
Private collection

*"The forms of suprematism, the
new realism in painting, are already
proof of the construction of forms
from nothing, discovered by intuitive reason."*

KASIMIR MALEVICH

Not only the Jewish art tradition but also that of the Slavs, which was subjected to alien influences, Byzantine and European, for a millennium, attained a new self-awareness only in our own century. This liberating moment came suddenly, ten years before the October Revolution of 1917. Shchukin and Morozov brought paintings by Cézanne, Gauguin, the Fauves and Cubists to Russia; Russian artists travelled to France and Germany. These events could not remain without consequences. Kandinsky made the final step towards absolute abstraction; Chagall lent the imageless world of Jewish legends and myth visual concreteness; Leon Bakst made Russia's most significant contribution to the theme of the stage set as a work of art. Alexander Archipenko (ill. left) and above all Vladimir Tatlin, subsequent designer of the famous *Monument to the Third International* of 1919/20 (p. 444), created the first abstract sculptures, reliefs and objects, Tatlin as the result of an early involvement with Picasso's collages in space, which he transformed into three-dimensional works in wood, glass and metal.

The first programmatic art of Russian origin was practiced around 1911 by Mikhail Larionov, founder of "Rayonism" (French *rayonner* = radiate), a style based on Futurism and Cubism which sought to liberate color and form. Flecks and rays of color, corresponding to the Futurists' lines of force, were arranged into self-sufficient compositions entirely independent of the motif. Initially these works were completely free-form, with no trace of figurative allusion (p. 163 below).

The year 1913 marked the publication of the *Rayonist and Futurist Manifesto*. Working in collaboration with his wife, Natalia Gontsharova, who did not approach so closely to complete abstraction as he did (p. 163 above right), Larionov also continued to paint in a starkly simplified figurative vein and designed sets for Sergei Diaghilev's Russian Ballet. While Larionov's innovative ideas initially remained an episode, they, and his magnetic personality, nevertheless had a great influence on his Russian colleagues.

On the Verge of Nothingness: Kasimir Malevich

Kasimir Malevich (pp. 160, 161, 164, 165), like Tatlin, fell especially under Larionov's spell, though he was destined to far outstrip his mentor in terms of audacity, influence, and gifts of design. Malevich has gone down in art history as the initiator of Suprematism. This awkward neologism was intended to express a very simple aim: to lend supremacy to the basic means of art, color and form, over the mere depiction of phenomena of the visible world. It is important to know that Malevich spoke in this connection of the "supremacy of pure sensation." This reveals the romantic tendency of his thinking and art, and excludes the possibility of considering his paintings the result of purely intellectual processes. Though Malevich was indeed fascinated by the beauty of mathematical forms, he wished to infuse them with passionate emotion, with a sense of what he

As surely as the French paintings bought by Russian collectors Mikhail Morozov and Sergei Shchukin greatly influenced the early Russian avant-garde, there is no denying that Western abstract painting would be an entirely different thing without Čiurlionis, Kupka, and Kandinsky, or De Stijl without Suprematism and Russian Constructivism. Also, the work of many emigrés who achieved fame in the West was clearly rooted in Eastern traditions. This is just as true of the Romanian sculptor Brancusi as of the Russian artist Chagall, or of the Polish-born painter Roman Opalka, not to mention Vitali Komar/Alexander Melamid and Ilya Kabakov, who years ago exchanged Russia for the blandishments of the American West. The long, in part politically conditioned absence of Eastern European art from Western museums has tended to blind us to this circumstance, as has the facile "naturalization" of the works of Eastern artists in Western cultural scenes. The question whether what Thomas Strauss calls the "avant-garde as idea" emerged in Eastern or Central Europe need not concern us. Western and Eastern avant-gardes simply cannot be separated.

called "the solemnity of the universe." The expanses of the backgrounds in his paintings, the vibrating textures that seem to continue virtually into infinity and the concise visual signs that float in front of them, correspond to the amplitude of Malevich's sensibility. Passion and scientific accuracy (Malevich apparently drafted his trapezoids and ellipsoids under the influence of Tatlin's material constructions) combined in his work with an ecstatic invocation of a New Age to come. Admittedly the Russian artist knew that this was a goal that could only be approached but never reached. The meaning of his revolutionary painting lay in the journey, the process of moving towards the infinite, towards that zone of "non-objective" perfection in which the oppositions between man and nature, mind and matter would be overcome.

Ivan Puni
Suprematist Composition, 1915
Oil on canvas, 94 x 65 cm
Amsterdam, Stedelijk Museum

Natalia Gontsharova
The Harvest, 1911
Oil on canvas, 92 x 99 cm
Omsk, Museum of Fine Arts

Mikhail Larionov
Rayonism, 1912/13
Oil on canvas, 52.5 x 78.5 cm
Ufa, Baschkirski Muzei

Kasimir Malevich
Suprematist Composition, 1915
Oil on canvas, 49 x 44 cm
Ludwigshafen, Wilhelm-Hack-
Museum

Ivan Kliun
Suprematism, 1915/16
Oil on canvas, 89 x 70.7 cm
Moscow, Tretyakov Gallery

*"The square is not a subconscious
form. It is the creation of intuitive
reason. It is the face of the new art.
The square is a living, royal infant.
It is the first step in the pure creation
in art. Before it, there were naive
deformities and copies of nature."*
KASIMIR MALEVICH

Malevich was the first artist to seriously attempt to achieve absolute painting, cleansed of every objective reference and allusion. He aimed at "a new reality of color, understood as non-objective pictorial creation. The forms of Suprematism have the same life as the forms of nature. This is a new pictorial realism, purely pictorial, because the reality of mountains, sky and water is absent. Every real form is a world, and every pure painting surface is more alive than a painted or drawn face, out of which a pair of eyes and a smile stare." That Malevich was one of the first artists to discover the expressive potential of empty space, the void, was no coincidence – the experience of flying had opened his eyes to it.

Initially impressed by the Nabis, Vuillard, Bonnard, and Vallotton, Malevich later involved himself with

Fauvist and Cubist art. An undertone of Russian folk-lore is present in all his early paintings, whether they represent a woman and man on a village street, a man carrying a heavy sack, or a couple dancing the polka. The colors are luminous and heavy, the forms ponderous and rustic, and the compositions are suffused with the humor of a Gogol. Then the artist began to bring his temperament under control. The forms of the human figure and natural scene were condensed, then subsequently geometrically abstracted to produce an autonomous pictorial order. Behind these pictures one senses the presence of Léger, as one senses that of Gris behind Malevich's superb *Head of a Peasant Girl* (1912/13; Amsterdam, Stedelijk Museum). This imagery laid the groundwork for Suprematism.

It was evidently in 1913 that Malevich painted his famous – and notorious – *Black Square on a White Ground* (cf ill. left), entirely independent of European developments and influences. First exhibited in 1915 at the latest, the canvas was the first in the long series of "last paintings" subsequently done in the course of the 20th century, symbols of artists' final detachment from the visible, exterior world. Malevich invoked the "naked, unframed icon of our age." His asceticism, driving him to the borderline of nothingness, reached its culmination in 1917 with the white-in-white painting *White Square on a White Ground* (New York, The Museum of Modern Art). These manifestations profoundly influenced modern developments down to Clyfford Still, Yves Klein, and monochrome painters such as Robert Ryman, Piero Manzoni, and Raimund Girke, all the way to the painterly œuvre of Jannis Kounellis, one of the key representatives of Arte Povera, which has since expanded into the mythical dimension.

Kasimir Malevich
Black Square on a White Ground,
dated 1913; executed after 1920
Oil on canvas, 106.2 x 106.5 cm
St. Petersburg, Russian State
Museum

Malevich's triangles, rectangles, crosses and trapezoids are magic, dynamic signs that hover within seemingly infinite spaces. It is this tendency to endlessness and dynamic motion that distinguishes these works from those of the De Stijl group, which are composed by reference to the delimited plane surface. The meditative, even mystical lyricism of Malevich's paintings ("I didn't invent anything," he said, "I just felt the night within myself and sensed the new thing I call Suprematism") stands in contrast to the practical nature of his architectural models, which fundamentally influenced 20th-century architects, Frank Lloyd Wright among many others. Apart from Malevich, whose Suprematism temporarily or permanently cast its spell over many major Russian artists – his later wife, Nadeshda Udalzova, Nikolai Suetin, Ivan Kliun (p. 164), Ivan Puni (p. 163), Pavel Mansurov, Alexander Rodchenko (p. 166), Lyubov Popova (ill. right), the Cubo-Futurist Alexandra Exter (p. 166) and others – Tatlin and above all El Lissitzky emerged as key influences. Tatlin was the founder of Constructivism, in comparison to Suprematism, a much more worldly movement oriented towards technology and its applications. Tatlin's, Rodchenko's, Vassili Ermilov's and many others' abstract, mechanistic paintings and reliefs made of glass, wood, metal and concrete inspired the sculpture of the brothers Naum Gabo (pp. 406, 452 f) and Antoine Pevsner (pp. 450 f). Later "kinetic art," from Alexander Calder (pp. 468, 471, 473) to Jean Tinguely (pp. 499, 506–508) and Nicolas Schöffer (p. 582), can also be traced back to Constructivism. Its representatives felt a deep-seated disappointment with the existing world, its outmoded systems and unjust hierarchies;

Alexander Rodchenko
Composition without Objects, 1918
Oil on canvas, 53 x 21 cm
St. Petersburg, Russian State
Museum

they sensed the emergence of a new, technological age
and expressly wished to help shape it. Their work is an
impassioned profession of the beauty of technology,
which in their eyes established new human values and
represented a hope for the betterment of the lot of the
proletarian masses.

The "Proun" World of El Lissitzky
El Lissitzky (pp. 167 f) joined the Suprematist-Construc-
tivist group shortly before its historical exhibition of

Alexandra Exter
Abstract Composition, 1917
Oil on canvas, 86 x 70 cm
St. Petersburg, Russian State
Museum

Varvara Stepanova
Man Playing the Drum, 1920
Oil on cardboard, 44 x 31 cm
Moscow, Pushkin Museum

1919, which summed up its achievements to date and
pointed towards a new, revolutionary future. Two years
later, Lenin's announcement of a "New Economic
Policy" abruptly, and quite unrevolutionarily, cut off
this future before it could begin. Thus the cornerstone
was laid for that simple-minded backwardness in which,
cemented by Stalin's enthronement in 1932 of Socialist
Realism as the only true proletarian mass art, official
Russian art would find itself for decades to come.
Heroic maidens, super-soldiers, and noble, self-sacrific-
ing workers replaced genuinely revolutionary Russian
Soviet art, which was outlawed and officially disap-

peared from the scene. Still, the undesirable works of art were not destroyed, as they were under the Nazis; they were put in storage, out of which they gradually began to re-emerge even before *glasnost* and *perestroika*.

Lissitzky, too, advocated a New World, but a "world of objects" which was to be created by the artist. He outlined an entirely new frame of reference in his pictures, which he called *Prouns* (Russian *pro unovis* = for a

renewal of art). The forms in Lissitzky's compositions are rhythmically arranged, seeming virtually to move along different planes, horizontal, vertical, or diagonal, suggesting interlocking spaces. The intrinsic dynamism of these compositions is very striking, and quite different from the static orders of the Dutch artists. Also obvious is the revolutionary aim of Lissitzky's art. Despite being bitterly disappointed by Lenin's verdict, he remained convinced throughout his life that a revolutionary art could be realized within a revolutionary, proletarian society. This belief was shared by his friends, the film and theater directors Vsevolod Meyerhold, who was executed in 1940; Alexander Tairov, who adjusted to the circumstances before it was too late; and Sergei Eisenstein, whose films were suppressed. Another staunch believer in the cause was poet Vladimir Mayakovsky, whose disappointment over its forsaken ideals led him to commit suicide in 1930.

Lissitzky's emigration to Western Europe was a result of external compulsion. For him, art was ultimately nothing but a "way station to architecture." At

this point Russian Constructivist thinking overlaps with that of De Stijl, but even more so with the concept of architect Walter Gropius, the first director of the Weimar Bauhaus. It was an attitude Lissitzky tirelessly advanced in Western Europe, and not even the lung ailment which forced him to recuperate in Davos and eventually led to his pre-mature death was able to break his courage. Lissitzky influenced abstract film, typography, photography (László Moholy-Nagy), and finally – through the famous "Abstract Cabinet" in the Provinzialmuseum, Hanover, which was destroyed in the Third Reich, and through his design of the Soviet pavilion at the Pressa Exhibition in Cologne in 1928 – he furthered the creation of an innovative type of museum and exhibition: the "living museum".

Almost every major progressive artist in Europe of the 1920s, from Arp to Schwitters, from Piet Mondrian to the architects Ludwig Mies van der Rohe and Jacobus Oud, knew and valued the energetic Russian, who had introduced his and his friends' work for the first time in 1922, at Galerie van Diemen in Berlin. Yet despite the

Olga Rozanova
Composition without Objects, 1916
Oil on canvas, 62.5 x 40.5 cm
St. Petersburg, Russian State Museum

El Lissitzky
Composition, 1919
Oil on canvas, 71 x 58 cm
Kiev, Museum of Ukranian Art

El Lissitzky
Proun 19 D, c. 1922
Gesso, oil and collage on plywood,
97.5 x 97.2 cm
New York, The Museum of
Modern Art, Katherine S. Dreyer
Bequest

*"Constructivism demonstrates that
the border between mathematics
and art, between a work of art and
an invention of technology, cannot
be ascertained."*
El Lissitzky, Hans Arp

El Lissitzky
Proun 99, 1924
Oil on canvas, 129 x 99 cm
New Haven (CT), Yale University
Art Gallery

Piet Mondrian
Composition No. II. Composition
with Blue and Red, 1929
Oil on canvas, 40.3 x 32.1 cm
New York, The Museum of
Modern Art

and was therefore essentially static. The paintings of the group are like blueprints for the design of a better future. Their art is limited to contrasts of horizontals and verticals brought into equilibrium; their palette is limited to the three primary colors, blue, red and yellow, augmented by the "non-colors" black, white and grey. In the context of architecture, according to Mondrian, space corresponds to the non-colors and materials to the colors. This implies total abstraction, the elimination of the last trace of memories of or references to the visible world, an overcoming of nature (Barnett Newman to the contrary. The American artist, whose European father-figure was Mondrian, once stated that the Dutchman's rigorous paintings were still too "naturalistic" for his taste, because their rectilinear composition, abstract as it might seem, was ultimately derived from nature).

strong impulses that proceeded from his work, Lissitzky ultimately did not succeed in planting the seed of Constructivism in the narrower sense in Western European soil. He was and remained a Russian; his friends, even the Socialists who politically sympathized with him, remained Western Europeans. For all the aesthetic rapprochement and mutual inspiration these kindred spirits shared, their differences remained stronger than their similarities. The conflict between pure form and a new class consciousness was, so to speak, intrinsic to the Constructivist project itself. The conflict between formalists and activists had already broken out in the young Soviet Union, and it continued until the disintegration of the empire.

Why this was so becomes rapidly apparent when we compare Constructivism with De Stijl, two directions which on first sight have the look of twins. De Stijl is not anarchistic but bourgeois in spirit. It represents an aesthetic reaction on the part of people conditioned by living in a countryside wrested from the encroachment of the sea, a symbol of the superiority of the ordering and building human mind over the brute forces of nature. Not a covert imitation of nature was the thrust of "Neoplasticism," as the new Dutch style in painting was known, but a creative activity out of the ordering spirit which is also embodied in nature. Peace, harmony, and discipline were the characteristic factors of this art, and a totally harmonious world its utopian goal. Mondrian, the greatest of the De Stijl artists, envisaged in art the formulation of a universal ideal of happiness, whose prophet he considered himself. "He spent his entire life in this utopian future," said H.L.C. Jaffé. Mondrian's essay, "Neoplasticism," was dedicated to "the man of the future."

Suprematism and Constructivism, in that they reflected revolutionary political thought in Russia, were essentially dynamic in character. The aesthetic of De Stijl, developed in 1917, at the peak of the European cataclysm of World War I, reflected a longing for peace,

The Harmony of Geometry: Piet Mondrian

For Piet Mondrian the elimination of the real and visible was not only an aesthetic requirement but a philosophical tenet. De Stijl set out to create a pure art composed of pure elements, whose man-made order would be set against the wild proliferation of nature and the twisting, curving or interrupted lines of natural forms. It is not surprising that this ascetic art emerged in Holland, the land of Calvinism and the Iconoclasts, the classic country of the bourgeoisie and its values. And in art, after all, Holland is not only the homeland of Jacob van Ruisdael and Rembrandt, but also that of Pieter de Hooch, Jan Vermeer of Delft, and the architecture painters Pieter Saenredam and Emanuel de Witte.

PM '25

Piet Mondrian
Gray Tree, 1912
Oil on canvas, 78.5 x 108.5 cm
The Hague, Haags Gemeente-
museum

The protagonists of De Stijl, apart from Mondrian, were Theo van Doesburg (pp. 171, 172), who in 1917 founded the journal *De Stijl* and thus gave the movement its name; Bart van der Leck; the Hungarian artist Vilmos Huszár; and the Belgian painter and sculptor

Piet Mondrian
Composition No. 6, 1914
Oil on canvas, 88 x 61 cm
The Hague, Haags Gemeente-
museum

Georges Vantongerloo (p. 171 above). They were later joined by César Domela (p. 172), by the German artist Friedrich Vordemberge-Gildewart (p. 173), by the architects J.J.P. Oud, Cornelis van Eesteren, Gerrit Rietveld, Jacobus van t'Hoff, and others. What the majority of these men shared in common was a pious Calvinist background. In personality and appearance they hardly conformed to the general notion of the revolutionary artist. They were disciplined men with a tendency to asceticism, in both their life and art. Mondrian's life and thought call to mind those of a Chinese sage, despite his very Western penchant for sarcasm, which helped him cope with self-abnegation, and an enjoyment of physical movement which inspired the passionate jazz dancer Mondrian in the syncopated, staccato rhythms of the *Boogie-Woogie* paintings he did in 1940, after fleeing from German air raids to New York (p. 171 below right).

In addition, a series of paintings emerged during the final years of Mondrian's life in America which are among the finest works he left to posterity. These are panels on which the conventional media of oil, pencil and charcoal are combined with apparently carelessly applied, partially thumbtacked strips of adhesive tape – a technique hard to reconcile with the image of the painstaking purist, but which brings a vitality into the strict classicism of the compositions that even surpasses the rhythms of the dance-inspired paintings. America, Mondrian once told his friend, Sidney Janis, an influential dealer and collector, America had permitted him to work more rapidly than in Europe. Yet the experimental spontaneity of the taped canvases was not achieved at

"I see a flower. It gives me a sensation of the beautiful. I wish to paint it. At this moment I see the whole subject – flower – changed."
GEORGES VANTONGERLOO

Georges Vantongerloo
Composition, 1917/18
Oil on canvas, 36 x 54 cm
Paris, Musée National d'Art
Moderne, Centre Georges
Pompidou

the expense of precision. Their relaxed, unroutine character points back to the material collages of the Cubists on the one hand, and on the other points forward to Robert Rauschenberg's or Jasper Johns's employment of mundane and trivial materials.

Personal vanity was unknown to the De Stijl artists; what they strove for was anonymity. Their attitude was

does develop powers that in turn determine culture as a whole."

The De Stijl artists felt their philosophy confirmed by the perfection of the machine, by the increasing tendency of modern man to live in groups and collectives (political parties, trade unions, associations), and by the anonymity of the modern labor and industrial process.

Theo van Doesburg
Simultaneous Counter-
Composition, c. 1929/30
Oil on canvas, 50.1 x 49.8 cm
New York, The Museum of
Modern Art

Piet Mondrian
Broadway Boogie-Woogie, 1942/43
Oil on canvas, 127 x 127 cm
New York, The Museum of
Modern Art

socialistic to the extent that they envisioned a collective art for all. Only such an art seemed capable of upholding universal harmony in the face of rampant individualism. Not that the Dutch artists saw themselves engaged in the class struggle, however. "Art, as we understand it," stated van Doesburg, "is neither proletarian nor bourgeois. Nor is it determined by social conditions; but it

Every form of imitative, naturalistic painting, in their eyes, had been taken ad absurdum by photography. As early as 1921, Rodchenko had drawn his conclusions from this insight and bid painting farewell with a monochrome *Triptych in Pure Colors*, that a revolutionary new architecture developed out of De Stijl's rectilinear, harmoniously proportioned compositions beholding to

Theo van Doesburg
Pure Painting, 1920
Oil on canvas, 130 x 80.5 cm
Paris, Musée National d'Art
Moderne, Centre Georges
Pompidou

César Domela
Neo-Plastic Composition, 1924/25
Oil on canvas, 82 x 67.5 cm
Private collection

old architecture painters, and in that of the Hague
School, which itself looked back to the Golden Age of
17th century Dutch art, Mondrian painted Impressionist and Pointillist-influenced landscapes and still
lifes. He then began to simplify the curving lines of such
subjects until an abstracted, fundamental pattern
emerged in which the interrelationships of form took
precedence over the subject depicted. While he was
aided in this process by the Analytical Cubism he had
studied at the source, in Paris, Mondrian still adhered
too closely to the subject to divorce his Cubist abstractions entirely from nature. Soon he had reduced his grey
and ocher-hued compositions to a system of verticals
and horizontals; but even these still seemed to relate too
closely to the external world. Mondrian realized that
pure, universal beauty could be achieved only by
expunging every memory of subject matter, in a complete harmony of a small number of colors and shapes
simplified to the utmost – in compositions that were
not abstracted from nature but represented a counter-
image to nature. Thus he proceeded from a practically
monochrome Cubism, based on elliptical shapes, to
compositions of rectangular planes that virtually continued beyond the canvas edge, compositions whose colors, in order to expunge every last trace of illusion, he
began in 1920 to reduce to red, yellow, blue, and black
and white.

the Platonic notion of an ideal, geometric beauty, seems
a matter of course. The "pure" relationships discovered
by the painters were applied to architecture and translated into three dimensions. "In view of Constructivism
who would have predicted," asked Johannes Cladders,
"that even the skyline of our old cities now no longer
looks Gothic but Constructivist?"

Van Doesburg later turned away from painting in
favor of architecture. The change was symptomatic. In
1920 he had visited the Bauhaus in Weimar, where he
triggered a fundamental reorientation. It was due not
least to Van Doesburg's influence that Gropius and the
Bauhaus masters abandoned the mystical, speculative
pathos of the founding years in favor of a new objectivity
and sobriety, less ambitious but definitely more practically effective. Le Corbusier, too, concerned himself
with the ideas of De Stijl, which provided him with
essential stimuli and confirmation of his own approach.

When van Doesburg died in 1931, the optimistic
movement lost impetus, as indeed its positivistic attitude and belief in the power of rational thinking to
shape the future had already been shaken by revolutionary developments in science, especially in physics. Persecution and repression at the hands of the fascists
brought the *coup de grâce.*

Any outstanding artist, despite a pledge to create an
anti-individualistic, undramatically harmonious art for
all, is bound to transgress the bounds of the collective.
This holds for De Stijl as well, in which the outstanding
artist was Mondrian. After preludes in the style of the

Mondrian once reported that he had first seen this
method in the work of Bart van der Leck, who, however,
applied the Neoplastic palette and formal repertoire to
figurative subjects (p. 173 above right). With Mondrian,
the canvas became an impersonal panel, conducive
to meditation. The intellectual foundations for this
development had been laid by the philosopher M.H.I.
Schoenmakers, whose ideas were an odd mixture of

mysticism and mathematics. In his philosophical interpretations of vertical and horizontal lines, of figures and formulas, Schoenmakers attempted to explain the universe and make it understandable in concrete terms.

Mondrian's rejection of individual sensibility and the artist's personal touch was rigorous. Like Malevich with his squares, Mondrian not only reached but overstepped the extreme borderline of art as previously understood. At this point we come up against the inexplicable quality, the secret contained in this so rationally and rigorously calculated Neoplasticist style. For the seemingly so impersonal, collectivist artist Mondrian, the constructor of beautifully simple patterns of form and color, was not only a mystic like Schoenmakers, he was also a prodigy of technical uniqueness. That no one, not even the most brilliant of forgers, is capable of copying Mondrian's paintings is a ridiculous, if indicative, statement. But his works can easily be distinguished from the apparently so similar ones of the other De Stijl artists even by the layman. Mondrian was the only one of them who achieved that perfect proportion and harmony, divorced from all drama and sentiment, for which all of them strove.

De Stijl's Continuing Influence

The aesthetic of De Stijl was adopted and ramified by Vordemberge-Gildewart (ill. right), the German member of the group, who resisted Mondrian's dogmatism. He escaped the tyranny of Mondrian's vertical-horizontal as well as van Doesburg's diagonal color-field borders and, inspired by the dynamic factor introduced by the latter, lent the rigorous style more freedom and sensibility despite retaining a great sparingness of means.

Carl Buchheister of Hanover also maintained close contacts with De Stijl (p. 174 above left). Yet his works of the 1920s, when Hanover was a center of Constructivist art, showed just as close ties to the Russians' concept of an art for the masses, as indicated by his reproduced

paintings of mid-decade. Also, Buchheister used a greater range of colors and shapes than the Dutch artists, lending his flat compositions a certain vibrancy. A few of his works, which were more diverse and full of contrasts than long assumed, even anticipated tendencies of Action Painting and monochrome art.

Outstanding specimens of the Constructivist approach were also produced by Erich Buchholz (p. 174

below), who in the final phase of his long career distanced himself from his pre-1933 artistic activity and wasted much time in post-war Berlin launching cranky attacks on contemporary developments. In addition to paintings, painted reliefs, and sculptures based on the circle, square, and narrow rectangle, Buchholz too pro-

Carl Buchheister
Composition Blue Square,
1926–1933
Oil on plywood, 65.5 x 52.5 cm
Münster, Westfälisches Landes-
museum

Hans Richter
Autumn, 1917
Oil on canvas, 79 x 63 cm
Zurich, Kunsthaus Zürich

duced designs for architecture and the stage, did commercial work and designed industrial products. Walter
Dexel (p. 175 above left) was a native of Munich who in
1933 gave up art for almost thirty years, as a result was
long forgotten, and only a few years before his death in
1973 was given the appreciation he deserved. By way of
Cubism and its German-American transformer,
Bauhaus master Feininger, Dexel arrived at sparingly
Constructivist cityscapes from which figurative references did not entirely vanish until the artist finally
adopted a more stringently abstract approach.

Hans Richter, a Dadaist of the first hour in Zurich
(1916), became a protagonist of the abstract film.
Throughout his life one of the most intelligent and energetic witnesses to 20th-century developments, Richter
returned late in his career to painting, in a style that
oscillated between strict, Cubist-influenced composition and suggestions of Surrealist anarchy (ill. above).

De Stijl remained viable not only in architecture but
in art as well. The line of development leads, with many
variations and changes of theme, from the Paris group
Abstraction-Création, founded in 1931, to which Vordem-
berge also belonged, through Auguste Herbin, Ben
Nicholson, and Victor Pasmore, to the kinetic art of
sculptor Nicolas Schöffer, the painting in light of *Zero*,
the monochrome painters, and finally to the Op Art of
Victor Vasarely and others. Also related to the De Stijl
context are the stringent squares of Josef Albers and –
in a creative reaction to Albers – American Color Field
painting, all the way down to diverse recent developments such as the work of Helmut Federle, Niele
Toroni, or Peter Halley (p. 390).

The influence of the German members of De Stijl,
in addition of course to contacts with neighboring Holland, was important to Belgian artist Victor Servranckx,
whose monochrome grisaille *The Squarest Rectangle*
would have been unthinkable without Malevich's pioneering composition.

A Glance at Eastern Europe

Even more important were the continuing effects of
Suprematism and Constructivism in Eastern Europe,
especially in Poland. In 1924, three years after Lenin's
verdict, a Constructivist group called "BLOK" was
founded there by Henryk Berlevi (who had met El
Lissitzky in 1921), Vladislav Strzemiński, and Henryk

Erich Buchholz
Relief Painting, 1922
Oil on wood, 60.4 x 45 cm
Cologne, Museum Ludwig

Stazevski. Berlevi became known for his development
of "Mechanofaktur," an ostensibly universal system,
based on the ideas and works of the Russian Constructivists, with the aid of which art could be produced
according to mechanical principles. Berlevi, too, soon
went west, to Paris (1928), and he also returned repeatedly to Berlin (p. 176).

Strzemiński (ill. right), born in White Russia and
seriously wounded in the First World War, was in 1919
already participating in the activities of the Moscow
Constructivist avant-garde. In 1922, after his marriage to
Katarzyna Kobro (p. 449), an important sculptress he
went to Poland. There, Strzemiński not only became a
founding member of BLOK but, later, with Stazevski
and others, of the group "a.r."; he was also that rare case
of an artist who established a museum. The Sztuki
Museum in Lódz, which subsequently, under the directorship of the polyglot Riszard Stanislavski, would
maintain contacts with the West under political conditions of the most difficult, owed its founding to
Strzeminski's initiative.

In the mid-1920s, in parallel with Russian Suprematism, Constructivism, and Cubo-Futurism, he worked
out the theory of "Unism," which "defines the image as
a self-referential entity." There followed "Architectonic
Compositions," pictures composed of elementary geometric forms, "based on a system," as Janini Ladnovska
says, "of mathematical calculations, substrates of compositions in space for which Strzemiński developed his
own theory." Subsequently, before being ostracized for
his criticism of Socialist Realism, the artist executed his
After-Images of Light.

likewise influenced by the art of Malevich and Lissitzky at an early date. His untiring search for new expressive potentials in many fields, from painting to photography, design, typography, and kinetic sculptures incorporating the element of light, will be discussed in detail in another context.

In the 1980s younger artists, who could have been their grandchildren, picked up the thread of the Constructivists' achievements in East and West. The first syllable of the abbreviation "Neo-Geo" (Neo-Geometry) points up the eclectic character of tendencies in post-modern art and its, so to speak, late-Hellenistic situation. In contrast to the pioneering avant-gardes, today's artists refer consciously to historical styles, not out of a belief in a new art capable of shaping the future but with a skeptical to cynical knowledge that such utopias are illusory.

Henryk Berlevi
Mechano-Faktura, 1924
Gouache on paper, 98 x 81 cm
Lódz, Muzeum Sztuki

Strzemiński's serial method, his equilibrium of color and line, and his resolution of the dualism of flat surface and three-dimensional form into a "unistic" entity, all had far-reaching consequences, not only for the international Zero movements of the 1960s but also for developments of a very recent date. The same holds, if to a lesser extent, for the work of Stazevski (p. 175 above right), who endeavored to combine the principles of Mondrian's Neoplasticism with those of Unism into a synthesis.

Turning to Hungarian abstraction, the pacemakers in the field during the 1920s were emigrés living in Vienna and Berlin, such as the painter-poet Lajos Kassák (ill. right), known as "steersman of the vanguard," and his temporary partner, Sándor Bortnyik, who was influenced by Popova.

Moholy-Nagy, the Hungarian Bauhaus master in Weimar and later in Chicago, at the New Bauhaus, was

Lajos Kassák
Pictorial Architecture, 1922
Oil on cardboard, 26 x 24 cm
Cologne, Museum Ludwig,
Donation Peill

Art with a Social Mission
The Artists at the Bauhaus under Walter Gropius

"Architects, sculptors, painters, we all have to return to the crafts. 'Art as a profession' does not exist. There is no real difference between the artist and the craftsman. The artist's task is an intensified version of the task of the craftsman."
WALTER GROPIUS

The attempt to build a mystery cult around art is age-old. As Max Ernst already scoffed, art had been raised to the status of a religion, and the artist to that of a Chosen One whose inspiration represented an act of grace. It was under such conditions that art, especially since the 19th century, developed in a world apart, Elysian Fields far removed from the social realities, and in the process lost its social function and responsibility. This development culminated in an ominous, hybrid aesthetic idealism which bore a close relationship to the sense of mis-

sion felt by the statesmen and generals of the day, and thus ultimately if indirectly contributed to the justification of war.

The First World War, which even Franz Marc viewed as an inferno that must inevitably preceed the making of a better world, swept such ideas away in a carnage of a horror never before seen. The notion of an art sublime and exalted above reality proved to be a self-delusion. To re-establish art's "bond with society" – in Hugo von Hofmannsthal's phrase – to give it social tasks to per-aesthetic usefulness in designing the environment. The Bauhaus teachers were no longer professors but "masters of form," that is, artisans, but artisans who in the design of prototypes included considerations of mass production from the start. The machine was no longer looked upon as a threat to art but a welcome helper. Free, applied, and industrial design enjoyed equal status at the Bauhaus; the hierarchy of the arts was overcome; functional art became teachable and learnable.

Many of the most significant artists of the day contributed to the realization of this conception. Klee taught glass painting and weaving, and while at the Bauhaus he wrote the *Pedagogical Sketchbook*, one of the most important theoretical and epistomological source texts in modern art. Kandinsky taught analytical drawing and developed out of this experience a normative, rigorously methodological textbook on composition, *Point and Line to Plane*, His path from the expressive idiom of his early period to a poetic geometrical style reflected not only Kandinsky's confrontation with Russian Constructivism, but also the development of pictorial thinking at the Bauhaus. Gerhard Marcks

"The geometrical form is that form that can be the best comprehended and defined. Its basic elements are the circle, the square, the triangle. The germ of every possible form is in these form elements. Visible to those who look – invisible to those who do not."   JOHANNES ITTEN

Johannes Itten
Meeting, 1919
Oil on canvas, 105 x 80 cm
Zurich, Kunsthaus Zürich

form, and finally to overcome the division between fine and applied art, became the goals of the Bauhaus, established in Weimar in 1919 by the architect Walter Gropius. There was to be no more art for art's sake; art was to become a responsible activity. Painting, sculpture, the crafts, and industrial design were to become integral elements of architecture, the mother of all the arts which encompassed them all. The well-functioning building, designed to make people's lives easier and happier, became the focus of a utopian conception of a new and better world. As it had in Russia and Holland, the vision of a lucid and functionally beautiful environment for a classless society stood at the inception of developments in Weimar.

The young architect's enthusiasm was so infectious that everyone Gropius asked to participate in helping build the "cathedral of the future" agreed to take part. The historic model for the Bauhaus was the anonymous community of artists and craftsmen of the medieval building guilds; its immediate model was Jugendstil, and its offshoot, the "Deutscher Werkbund," founded in 1907. Influences from Constructivism and De Stijl also played a fruitful role. Van Doesburg, Lissitzky, Gabo, even Malevich came to Weimar; writings by Mondrian, van Doesburg, and Malevich were published in the series of "Bauhaus Books." At the beginning, the Bauhaus philosophy was a seemingly incompatible mixture of sober objectivity and romantic, Expressionist-style idealism, but gradually practical, functionalistic thinking gained the upper hand. One of Gropius' first acts, and main achievements, was to eliminate the hierarchic organization of the traditional academy. Classes were transformed into workshops, in which the students, starting from scratch, were asked to investigate materials of all types with an eye to their practical and

Georg Muche
Composition with Black and Green Form, 1920
Oil on cardboard, 71.5 x 53.8 cm
Bonn, Kunstmuseum Bonn

(p. 416), a relatively conservative sculptor, headed the ceramics department; painter and art teacher Johannes Itten (ill. above left) taught the basic preliminary course; and artist Oskar Schlemmer ran the workshop for wall painting (murals), and later also the sculpture workshop and the Bauhaus Stage. Feininger was nominated by Gropius as early as 1919 for the first masters' council, and headed the printing shop, if only for a brief period.

Gropius was not enough of a doctrinaire to share Klee's opinion that genius represented a "defect in the system." He was aware that the great individual, even

*"And I know now that if I develop
my best abilities in the manner
appropriate to them, – if I try to
come to an honest and thorough
understanding of the meaning of
my life – then it is right for me to
become a painter. My talent lies
in the expression of my life and
creative power through light, color
and form. As a painter I can convey
the essence of life."*
LÁSZLÓ MOHOLY-NAGY

though he might subordinate himself and his activity
to service to the community, would still overstep its
boundaries, and that it was in fact the "defect" of genius,
unteachable and unlearnable, that justified the educational system by calling it into question. Gropius would
not countenance work at the Bauhaus being submitted
to any uniform style. He permitted Klee to tell his students that quality in art could never be a norm, or be
pressed into a formula; rather, quality was something in
the process of becoming, and every artist had to create it
anew, as the product of aesthetic and intellectual effort.
Based on his insight, Gropius retained the great individualists on the faculty even when the decision to make
strict functionalism the guideline for Bauhaus work
became final, and thus the priority of architecture over
visual art was established. This decision prompted the
idealist Itten, the Expressionist and former member of
the *Sturm* theater Lothar Schreyer, the sculptor Marcks,
and the painter Georg Muche (p. 177) to leave the
Bauhaus, in that order.

The story of the Bauhaus' odyssee as a result of
political pressure from the Right is familiar. After being
forced to move to Dessau in 1925, it was driven in 1932
by the National Socialists to Berlin, where Hermann
Goering irrevocably closed the school as "a hothouse of
cultural bolshevism." But political pressures were not
the only reason for its demise. Internal dissolution had
begun much earlier. Gropius relinquished his office in
1928; other faculty members, including Moholy-Nagy,
architect Marcel Breuer, Schlemmer, and Klee followed
suit. Gropius's successor, Hannes Meyer, was a committed socialist and a strictly functionalist architect under
whose aegis the crisis deepened. The last director of the
school, architect Mies van der Rohe, a protégé of

Gropius, no longer had time to attempt to re-establish
the unity of the arts that had stood at its inception.

The importance of the Bauhaus for painting lay
above all in the systematic analysis of its means and the
basic research into its applications which the Bauhaus
achieved. The Bauhaus books were among the most significant art-theoretical writings of the period. Their
authors represented the new type of the conscious and
methodical creative person who took responsibility for
his work and was almost as much of a scientist as an
artist. The influence of the teaching activities of
Kandinsky, Klee and Schlemmer was extraordinarily
great. It continues to this day, even though its effects
may not be so visible as those of the Bauhaus architects
on international building all the way down to the Post-
Modern reaction.

The Man of the Day after Tomorrow

The fundamental premise of the Bauhaus, to experi-
mentally investigate the nature of materials, was put
into practice most thoroughly by Moholy-Nagy (ill. left
and below). Like Kassák and others of his countrymen,
Moholy-Nagy had emigrated from Hungary after the
counter-revolution, going initially to Vienna. He had
been called by Gropius to Weimar in 1923. A Constructivist and founder of the group "MA", Moholy-Nagy
earned himself the title "man of the day after tomorrow." Many a subsequent avant-garde artist was an heir
to Moholy-Nagy; many a light-show, many a rotating
kinetic wall-object dependent on the effects of shadow
and light, and many an image made of glass, was a
variant or continuation of what began at the Bauhaus.
Moholy-Nagy was the spiritual father of several generations of artists. A gentle man with a tendency to melancholy, he took seriously the hypothesis of Konrad

Fiedler, formulated in the 19th century and much in advance of its time, that the inception of all artistic activity was the creation (as opposed to the imitation) of reality. For Moholy-Nagy this meant the reality of the times and the environment in which he lived. He tested materials for their applications in art with the curiosity of a child and the experimental ardor of an aware intellectual. Things we take for granted and thoughtlessly use every day became in his hands the substance of aesthetic design: wire, paper, bits of fabric, razor blades. This activity went back to Cubist and Constructivist collage techniques, as well as to the Dadaist-Surrealist ready-made, but at the same time it went beyond these. As Giulio Carlo Argan says, Moholy-Nagy's materials became "the new primal matter of a formal construction" consisting of triangle, cube, circle, and rod-shape. The artist also continued Man Ray's photomechanical experiments, producing montages, negative prints, X-ray images, depictions of moving bodies by means of photographic series, photograms, etc.

Such experiments still play a role today in the attempts of many artists to capture reality by means of photographs altered by overpainting, extreme enlargement, or blurring, as in the case of the early Gerhard Richter, Chuck Close, or the Photorealists, who, so to speak, built their imagery over fragments of reality. These experiments were also fruitful for kinetic art, and art that relied on the effects of light. They eventually led Moholy-Nagy to begin experimenting in the medium of abstract film. As early as 1929 he had attempted to combine light, form and color, in an object entitled *Light Prop*. His series of experiments eventually led to the *Light Space Modulators* (p. 454) created in the United States, where in 1937, after his second emigration, the Hungarian artist founded the New Bauhaus in Chicago. The *Light Space Modulators* were three-dimensional constructions of transparent planes, among which light and shade played in wonderfully sophisticated and surprising ways. Moholy-Nagy "painted" with plastics, such as plexiglass, Galalith, and Neolith; but after the *Telephone Paintings* on enamel of 1922, which with the aid of color charts and graph paper he had executed in a factory according to his telephone instructions, the artist also "painted" with light – an art of far-reaching consequences, especially in the field of theater.

This combination of spontaneous experimentation with the materials of a new century, technical and artistic sophistication, and an intellectual, constructive method, quite aptly describes the range of all the work at the Bauhaus, whose poles were marked by a tendency to the folkloristic and naive on the one hand, and on the other by a commitment to the machine and technical perfection.

Besides Moholy-Nagy, it was especially Josef Albers whose activities definitively turned the Bauhaus, after it had sloughed off all remainders of Expressionism, towards a constructivist art in the service of architecture. Influenced by De Stijl, Albers's work exhibits an extreme reduction of form to a lapidary, geometric idiom rendered with extreme painterly and technical perfection. And like Moholy-Nagy, he consciously did a great deal of commercial work and contributed significantly to the development of industrial design. Yet his major paintings, the series of *Homages to the Square* (ill. above and p. 180), have nothing at all to with applied art. Hardly another artist of our era demonstrated more compellingly than Albers that the most elementary things are ultimately inexplicable. As the philosopher Ludwig Wittgenstein said, everything we see could just as well be different. Everything we can describe at all could be different as well. There is no order of things *a priori*. Albers's œuvre corroborates Wittgenstein's insight, painting by painting. His works are like traps into which the viewer is repeatedly tempted to fall. The sense of insecurity they instill is great, and the proof they give of the fallibility of perception is irrefutable. This aspect of irritation, Albers's illustration of the existence of the irrational by rational means, his demonstration of the fact that there are no finally valid solutions but only permanent change, infinite variation, all indicate that at bottom Albers remained a European despite living and achieving his finest work in the United States. But he was no formalist who produced multiple art. He justifiably insisted not only on the originality but on the variety of his visual inventions. Every realization of an idea, he believed, was a one-off, unique work.

The combination of perceptual possibilities is as endless in Albers's structural constellations in painting as it is in his tectonic graphic art. The aggressiveness of

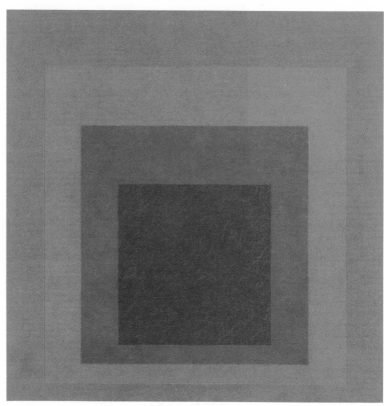

Josef Albers
Homage to the Square, 1964
Oil on canvas, 121 x 121 cm
Bottrop, Josef Albers Museum

"As 'gentlemen prefer blondes', so everyone has a preference for certain colors and prejudices against others. This applies to color combinations as well. It seems good that we are of different tastes. As it is with people in our daily life, so it is with color. We change, correct, or reverse our opinions about colors, and this change of opinion may shift back and forth." JOSEF ALBERS

Josef Albers
Homage to the Square:
Ritardando, 1958
Oil on canvas, 76.2 x 76.2 cm
USA, private collection

Antonio Calderara
Untitled, 1963
Oil on wood, 36 x 36 cm
Laufen, Collection A. R.

*"Practical exercises demonstrate
through color deception (illusion)
the relativity and instability of
color. And experience teaches that
in visual perception there is a discrepancy between physical fact and
psychic effect."* JOSEF ALBERS

these visual manifestations and the eye's inability to ultimately fix them, are almost painfully evident, both physically and mentally. The economy of means, precision
and concentration of Albers's imagery stand in inverse
relationship to the effectiveness of each variant. The
same holds for the colors, whose values alter depending
on the adjacent colors, and are subject to a continual
temperature and climatic change from warm to cold,
cold to warm. Mixed with grey, they appear de-material-
ized, floating as if in a mist, the borderlines blurred; the
hues appear to advance and recede in space, and the eye
cannot hold them. In Albers' *Squares*, as in his prints,
plane and space are reciprocally perceived. This effect is
created entirely without personal touch, but with a high
degree of objectivity and sensibility. "I paint as thinly as
Breughel," Albers once told a visitor to his New Haven
studio, which he called the smallest workroom in the
world. Painting after painting was done here on a plain
deal table. He wanted to "realize," not "express" himself, the artist added, because while he had learned to
think and see, he had not learned "art." Albers never
took the second step before the first; his pictorial thinking was oriented towards practice. He did not formulate
his variations on the basis of any preconceived system,
or subject them to any *a priori* theory. Rather, his
approach and teaching were the result of experience,
empirical trial and error. To recognize the originality of
Albers's œuvre, a sensibility for nuances is required. It
was like with the cook, the artist once jocularly put it.
Sometimes she used more salt, sometimes less. That
made the great difference.

The Human Being in Space

The Bauhaus theory of harmony and proportion was
related to that of the Renaissance, with the difference
that instead of positing a finite space defined by the laws
of perspective, it posited an infinite space for which
these laws no longer held. This distinction points up the
problem faced by another Bauhaus teacher, the painter
Oskar Schlemmer. Schlemmer was one of the last mas-

ters of perspective in art history. His major theme was
what he termed "the human being in space." The
strange mixture of constructive and sentimental, soberly
realistic and romantically expressive tendencies that
marked the early years of the Bauhaus, was also present
in the personality of Schlemmer. At happy moments, he
once said, he had to physically compel himself not to go
about indiscriminately "embracing people." In the face
of official Bauhaus doctrine, Schlemmer believed paintings were "revelations of the divine through the medium
of man, known as 'the artist,' a language of forms and
colors mystical in origin." This stands opposed to the
diary entry, "Not laments over mechanization, but an
enjoyment of precision.... If the artists of today love
machinery and technology and organization, if they
want the exact instead of the vague and fuzzy, this is an
instinctive escape from chaos and a yearning to give
shape to our era...."

This wonderful and complex man, subsequently
defamed by the Nazis as a "cultural Bolshevik," kept
alive the heritage of the great Renaissance masters of
perspective, and in their wake that of Hans von Marées,
the German in Rome whose forte was the idealized
human figure in the landscape. Impressed by Seurat and
also by Cubism, whose analysis of form he, however, did
not adopt, Schlemmer reduced the human figure to its
basic geometric elements and set it in relationship to
the surrounding space. Every individual feature was suppressed in favor of the prototypically human. Schlemmer's figures were representatives of a noble type, generally appearing in groups, part of a community yet
nonetheless alone, thoughtful, proud, and introspective.
The *Five Men in Space* (1928; Stuttgart, private collection) and the *Bauhaus Stairway* (ill. right) embody
Schlemmer's classically idealistic conception to perfection. His murals and reliefs in the workshop wing of
the Weimar Bauhaus were destroyed in 1930, by order of
the National Socialist government of Thuringia at the
behest of the notorious Paul Schultze-Naumburg, who
called them "exercises devoid of artistic value."

Schlemmer's murals strove for a harmony of actual and imaginary space, an absolute equilibrium. The wall surface, he believed, should be rendered transparent and thus be virtually eliminated, permitting the ambient space to be continued within the picture. The perspectives of actual and pictorial spaces would flow into and interpenetrate each other – an idea of indisputably utopian grandeur. Admittedly, the contradiction between objective imagery rendered in perspective terms and an architecture that was growing increasingly dynamic and flexible proved well-nigh impossible to

overcome. When Schlemmer turned to easel painting it was ultimately as a stop-gap, since all of his work and its tendency to monumental scale revealed the urge to design for the architectural setting.

Schlemmer's conception of "the human being in space" found its purest expression in his theater work. Here the space-creating imagination of the artist, who was also a talented amateur dancer, could freely unfold. Parts of his famous *Triadic Ballet* (1922), to which Paul Hindemith wrote a new score for mechanical organ in 1926, were already performed in Stuttgart during the war, at a regimental entertainment in 1916. He was inspired to the ballet, said Schlemmer, by Seurat's painting *Le Chahut* (Otterlo, Rijksmuseum Kröller-Müller). "In Seurat's painting the most vigorous movements of dance are achieved through stringent forms (straight-lined, decisive)," Schlemmer noted. An intellectual basis, or preliminary design, as it were, was provided by Heinrich von Kleist's essay "On the Marionette Theater". The

mechanical artificiality of the marionette became the model for Schlemmer's abstract dance, which attempted to avoid all sentiment because the expression of feelings, according to Oscar Wilde's ironic apercu, becomes further removed from art the more real the feelings are. With the aid of highly abstracted masks and costumes, that is, of sheer artificiality, Schlemmer hoped to unite the Dionysian aspect of dance with its Apollonian one, the sensual with the spiritual.

Another covert romantic with a superbly lucid mind was Lyonel Feininger (pp. 182, 183), born in New York to German parents who were both musicians, a child prodigy on the violin, and later a gifted player of Bach and composer of respectable fugues. Feininger began his career as a successful caricaturist, but, as he said, had no intention of being "condemned to create in perpetual travesty." In 1906 he discovered the quiet beauty of Thuringian villages and their architecture, which he would later depict in a famous series of paintings. That

Oskar Schlemmer
The Dancer – The Gesture, 1922/23
Oil and tempera on canvas,
200 x 130 cm
Munich, Bayerische Staats-
gemäldesammlungen,
Staatsgalerie moderner Kunst

Oskar Schlemmer
Bauhaus Stairway, 1932
Oil on canvas, 162.3 x 114.3 cm
New York, The Museum of
Modern Art, Gift of Philip Johnson

"Since my childhood, the church, the mill, the bridge, the house – and the cemetery – have aroused deep and reverential feelings in me. They are all symbolic..."
LYONEL FEININGER

Lyonel Feininger
Before the Rain, 1927
Oil on canvas, 45 x 80 cm
Hamburg, private collection

same year saw his second trip to Paris; in 1907 Feininger cancelled all his journalistic contracts to devote himself exclusively to painting from then on. His meeting with the circle of German students of Matisse (Levy, Purrmann, Moll) and with Delaunay, and his confrontation with the disciplined imagery of Seurat, brought first and strong impressions of the new developments in art. The crystalline compositions of the Cubists strengthened Feininger in his conviction that he was on the right track. He described his aim as "a passionate longing for rigorous spatial design – without painterly intoxication of any sort." This longing was one that was shared by Gropius and the Bauhaus, where Feininger's influence, by the way, was not so much in the capacity of a teacher as in that of a free artist whose example set standards.

From his experiences on the shores of the Baltic, that "tranquil sea," and of the landscapes of central Germany, through which he hiked and cycled, Feininger distilled a highly original pictorial architecture, reducing the forms of churches or sailboats to overlapping crystalline shapes rendered in increasingly translucent hues. A Latin lucidity and a Gothic-Romantic mystery, occasionally tinged with irony – especially in the accessory figures – entered into a unique blend in this imagery. Over the years Feininger heightened expression and form to monumentality. The thirteen *Gelmeroda* canvases of the 1920s, symbols of the church's striving towards heaven, metaphors of a longing for the infinite expressed in the finitude of crystalline form, have a logic of composition, a transparency of structure, that recall the fugues of Bach. These works were the culmination of Feininger's development. Many of the best and loveliest examples of his style are found among the delicate watercolors and prints, especially the woodcuts, the finest of which possess an intimacy, force, and quality of form quite on a par with the major oils.

Lyonel Feininger
Village Pond in Gelmeroda, 1922
Oil on canvas, 86 x 112 cm
Frankfurt/Main, Städelsches Kunstinstitut und Städtische Galerie

In later years, particularly after his return to the United States, Feininger's lucid crystalline style of the mature European period made way for a more romantic approach in which the contours grew vaguer, more blurred, recalling the work of Turner, which had impressed Feininger early in his career. The further removed in space and time he became from the land of Romantic art, the more romantic his painting grew. *Gelmeroda* continued to preoccupy Feininger's mind in America, where initially he felt out of place and was plagued by homesickness, until his work began to receive the honors it had enjoyed in Europe. It was characteristic that he should have translated the vertical gigantomania of Manhattan into a Gothic mode although he was here unable to achieve the lucid spirituality of the transparent compositions of the earlier years.

Page 182:
Lyonel Feininger
Gelmeroda IX, 1926
Oil on canvas, 108 x 80 cm
Essen, Museum Folkwang

Return to the Visible World
The Wave of Realism after World War I

Mario Sironi
Self-Portrait, 1913
Oil on canvas, 51.5 x 49 cm
Milan, Civico Museo d'Arte
Contemporanea

Mario Sironi
The Truck, 1917
Oil on cardboard, 90 x 80 cm
Milan, Pinacoteca di Brera,
Jucker Collection

In the years following the Armistice many painters began to abandon the aesthetic speculations that had done so much to advance art during the pre-war period. An emphasis on the purely formal aspects of art suddenly appeared dubious to them, as if it represented a retreat, conscious or not, from a responsibility to society, a refusal to face up to the abuses of power. Many of these artists shared with their peers at the Bauhaus a sense of duty to society, even if they expressed it in quite different terms. Feeling themselves belated heirs to the Enlightenment, they used expressionistically heightened or caricatural means to unmask the ills of the post-war era and the venality or shallowness of its representatives. Abstraction was no help in this regard, since their aim was to "show" in the Brechtian sense, to record and document realities, and to penetrate beneath their surface to reveal the motives and mind sets that had led to the European disaster. These artists were filled with a sense of mission – to prevent such a war from ever re-occurring. They pointed accusing fingers, intervened in political affairs, in depictions of disabled veterans, trench warfare, profiteers and prostitutes and brutal crimes. They launched merciless Jeremiads in paint, yet all the while remaining skeptical of the efficacy of art to really make a difference.

Such was the background to the widespread return to realism in the early 1920s. It provided the impetus for Grosz's depictions of the post-war world in terms of the obscene scrawls on latrine walls, as it did for Beckmann's ballad of human cruelty, *The Night* (p. 195), an image that far transcended its temporal reference to become the period's most superb and horrifying evocation of the beast that lurks in man.

The war pictures of Otto Dix, in contrast, resist ideological definition, having more the character of a disillusioned analysis than a pillorying of society's ills. By the same token, the socially critical art of the realists and verists of the day is marked by a kind of inverted idealism, which perhaps never before in history had had so much reason for disillusionment with society. The pitfalls of a committed, polemical art are well known. They were frighteningly demonstrated in the socialist, fascist, and vulgar-Marxist pseudo-realism that flourished before and after World War II in both Western and Eastern Europe. Art of this ilk can easily degenerate into propaganda.

In Italy and France after 1918 a return to the visible world as a reaction to the storm and stress of the pre-war period set in as well. The shape it took, however, differed profoundly from the aggressive social criticism of German artists. The Latin countries witnessed an attempt to create a new order.

In Italy this development was encouraged by the neoclassicism of De Chirico and Carrà, but also by the classical Renaissance heritage which was an integral part of Italian artists' environment. Morandi's reinstatement of the transcendental dignity of commonplace things also played a role. In 1918 the first issue of *Valori Plastici* (Plastic Values) appeared, with an editorial that programmatically demanded the revival of traditional values in art. "We want Italian painting to find its way back to order, method, and discipline, and to attain to solid, tangible form," wrote Carrà, the erstwhile Futurist. The mobility and dynamism of Italian art were suspended for years to come. The "noble simplicity and quiet grandeur" of the ancient Greeks, Johann Joachim Winckelmann's leitmotif for German classicism, well describes the efforts of Italian artists during the 1920s, which were largely conservative to reactionary in thrust. This regressive tendency was furthered by a group of artists who called themselves *Novecento Italiano* (Italian 20th Century), at whose first public showing Mussolini gave a speech.

Felice Casorati
Noon, 1922
Oil on wood, 119.5 x 130 cm
Trieste, Civico Museo Revoltella,
Galleria d'Arte Moderna

20th-century experience, these images from the distant past re-materialized in the Alexandrine world of Campigli's imagery.

The painting of Felice Casorati (ill. above) was inspired by the sophisticated Jugendstil eroticism of Klimt and disciplined by the idealistic symbolism of Puvis de Chavannes and the Pre-Raphaelites. Though he subsequently achieved a simplified planarity in the manner of Gauguin, Castorati's work, like that of many of his countrymen, points up the fact that Italian art in the wake of Futurism and *Pittura Metafisica* was long overrated. Another case in point is Gino Bonichi, alias Scipioni, a Roman artist who died at an early age. His expressionist style, inspired by El Greco, was infused

Massimo Campigli
Women with Gloves, 1937
Oil on canvas, 73 x 92 cm
Private collection

A return to the figure, to monumentality, to traditional values, coupled with a rejection of Impressionism and decadence, and of the supposed effeminacy and cosmopolitanism of critical art – all this seems very familiar, calling to mind as it does German art under Hitler or the anti-formalist ideology of Stalinism. Yet while Italian aims may have been similar, that country never developed the official, aggressive philistinism nor the merciless persecution of non-conformism that reached such horrifying levels in Germany.

Yet nothing revolutionary could be expected from Italian art from that point on, either. Mario Sironi (ill. left), the former Futurist and war volunteer turned metaphysical artist, attempted in the work of his post-vanguard years to depict alienated man in an industrial landscape heightened to the point of archaic monumentality, a bleak world into which the pathos of Nordic Expressionism also entered.

Massimo Campigli (ill. above) brought buried realities back to light in a different, one might say cultural-historic way. Beginning with Cubism, then influenced by the monumental, Ingresque and archaic figuration of Picasso, Campigli discovered the charm of defunct cultures – Etruscan and Arabian, the hieroglyphs of Egypt, the frescoes of Pompeii, and the mosaics of Ravenna. Ironically refracted, viewed through the spectacles of

Rudolf Schlichter
Portrait of Margot, 1924
Oil on canvas, 110.5 x 75 cm
Berlin, Märkisches Museum

with religious ardor and suffused with the somber reds of Dante's Inferno. The vehement expressionist painting of Luigi Spazzapan, finally, bordered on abstraction and anticipated developments to come.

Neue Sachlichkeit

The return of the Italian painters to a view of the real and tangible world through the veils of history had consequences throughout Europe, particularly in Germany. The aesthetic results, however, were more modest than

the achievements of the critically realist camp. Their style derived its name from an exhibition mounted in 1925 by G.F.Hartlaub, then director of the Mannheim Kunsthalle, to which he had been soliciting contributions since 1923. Neue Sachlichkeit – variously translated as New Objectivity, Sobriety, or Austerity – brought together 124 works by 32 artists. Their re-investigation of late medieval painting, of 15th-century Italian art, of the simplified, comprehensive plastic forms of Ingres' and David's neoclassicism, said Hartlaub, led to an emphasis on the "autonomy of the objects in our environment." These things were depicted in sharp focus, with almost microscopic attention to detail, and often without regard to their interrelationships. All motion was brought to a stand-still. Painting reverted to a static state. "Magic Realism" was Franz Roh's term for this new austerity.

Viewed historically, Hartlaub's and Roh's names for the movement had a very different thrust, which sparked a terminological debate that has continued to the present day. The many attempts to find a common denominator for the diverse artistic personalities and aesthetic approaches involved finally resulted in a compromise. Their differences notwithstanding, art historians have agreed on the term "Neue Sachlichkeit". The exaggerated focus in which things and figures were rendered occasionally lent the paintings of the movement a well-nigh surreal look – that magical quality to which Roh referred. Christian Schad's portraits, or Alexander Kanoldt's bleak suburban landscapes punctuated by telegraph masts of 1930, are key specimens of the style, in whose orbit Dix and Grosz, inspired by Metaphysical Painting, also temporarily moved. At this period Grosz produced compelling depictions of the loneliness of mass man, de-individualized, lost in cold and empty urban ambiences, pictures that need fear no comparison with those of Carrà or De Chirico.

Some artists' fascination for the object – in the dispassionate dissections of a Schad (ill. right), even humans themselves became objects – led in the long run to immobility and even petrifaction, as is seen in the work of Kanoldt (ill. below) and of Georg Schrimpf (p. 186 below). With Kanoldt, this tendency even brought a dalliance with National Socialism, whose pseudo-classical aesthetic proved too tempting for the passionate admirer of Ingres. The kitsch-mongers of the Haus der Deutschen Kunst were already lurking in the wings, and their triumph would not be long in coming.

More progressive, and thus of more lasting importance, was the socially critical variant of Neue Sachlichkeit. Seeing reality through disillusioned eyes, it was to that extent anti-illusionistic. Its major representative,

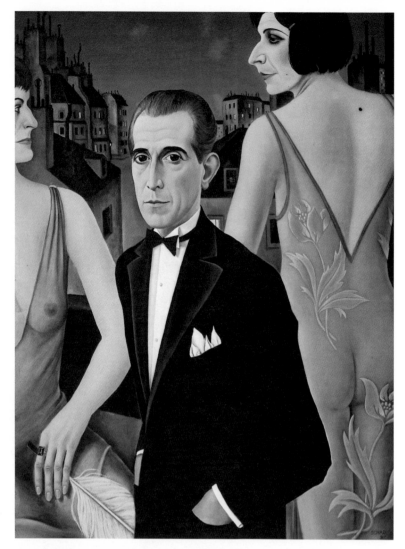

Christian Schad
Count St. Genois d'Anneaucourt, 1927
Oil on wood, 86 x 63 cm
Hamburg, private collection

Otto Dix, was born in 1891 into a laborer's family in Untermhaus near Gera. Like the other artists of the movement, Dix was inspired by a confrontation with the Old Masters, especially Albrecht Dürer, Lucas Cranach, Hans Baldung-Grien, Grünewald, Hans Holbein, and Botticelli, though his first key works, done in wartime, still showed a strong Futurist influence: *The Cannon* (1914; Düsseldorf, Kunstmuseum) and *Self-Portrait as Mars* (1915; Freital, Haus der Heimat). In his masterly portraits Dix combined painstaking attention to detail with a manneristic refinement, seen in the elongated figures and eloquent gestures. The intriguing thing about these pictures is the application of a grand, Old Masterly technique to banal, proletarian or prurient subject matter. Dix's portraits of children, depicted with crystal clarity and an infallible eye for character (and with a side glance at Runge), likewise evince a typical and paradoxical mixture of detached observation, empathy, and harsh irony. Though partaking of European nihilism in the wake of Nietzsche, this amalgam bears traits of early Romanticism as well. These traits would come to the fore later, when the aging Dix turned to

Alexander Kanoldt
Still Life with Jugs and Red Tea-Caddy, 1922
Oil on canvas, 77.5 x 88.5 cm
Karlsruhe, Staatliche Kunsthalle

Otto Dix
Metropolis (triptych, central panel), 1927/28
Mixed media on wood, 181 x 200 cm
Stuttgart, Galerie der Stadt Stuttgart

"Nobody wants to look at it. What is it all supposed to mean... the old whores and the old , worn out women and all of life's cares? ... It doesn't make anybody happy. No gallery wants to exhibit it. Why do you even bother to paint it?!"

OTTO DIX

landscapes, flowers, animals, and figures, depicted in a somewhat rough-hewn, expressively heightened style, and in a range of bright colors. Works such as the *Portrait of the Artist's Parents* (ill. right), that of his brother-in-law, Dr. Koch (1921; Cologne, Museum Ludwig), or the portrait of the author Theodor Däubler (1927; Cologne, Museum Ludwig), who is depicted as a prophetic figure of veritably Old Testament proportions, a tragic colossus looming up before the neoclassical columns of the Brühl Terrace in Dresden, belong among the truly great works of the epoch.

Despite such outstanding, absolutely frank and in no way idealized portraits, which include that of Johanna Ey, maternal protector of Düsseldorf artists (1924; Kunstmuseum Düsseldorf), Dix gave his very best in the unsentimentally analytical, mercilessly revelatory imagery devoted to the First World War and its after-

math. In the etching cycle *Der Krieg* (War), as in *The Trench* of 1923, an oil destroyed in the Second World War, Dix depicted devastation, decay, and horror in nightmarish, well-nigh surrealist visions that finally buried the legend of the glory of dying for one's country. The mood of the postwar period was embodied in the *Metropolis* triptych of 1927/28 (ill. above), whose middle panel shows tuxedo-clad heroes of the ambivalent Golden Twenties dancing the Charleston with their playgirls, as on the flanking panels other flappers strut past crippled war veterans begging on the street. Dadaist attempts such as *Seaman Fritz Müller of Pieschen* (1919; Turin, Museo Civico) also belong in this context. As Otto Conzelmann justifiably points out in his otherwise resentment-biased book *Der andere Dix* (The Other Dix), the merciless anatomist of war, painter of eroticized Old Testament stories and recorder of the violent sexism of the period, as exemplified in *The Rape-Murderer,* escapes classification in terms of any philosophy or ideology.

Dix himself, in an interview in 1965, laconically remarked that he and his friends in Dresden in 1919 were "all nihilists." He viewed the war as an inexorable natural catastrophe, experienced all its horror on the front lines, and depicted it with an almost terrifying mixture of fascination and cruelty, a mixture that is as closely allied to the Nietzschean will to power as it is to Ernst Jünger's *Stahlgewitter* (Storms of Steel). In his war diary Dix wrote, "War, too, must be seen as a natural occurrence." The images of unmitigated horror, whose dynamic quality gave way in later depictions to an almost monumental statuesqueness, as in the triptych *War* (1929-32; Dresden, Gemäldegalerie) and the battlefield landscape of *Flanders* (1936; Berlin, Nationalgalerie), encompassed the dialectic of creation and destruction, growth and decay. Although Dix's approach followed in the footsteps of a Goya or Callot, his execution, as Paul Ferdinand Schmidt notes, was characterized by a "fanatical cold-bloodedness." His paintings also bear obvious affinities with the apocalyptic poetry of the period, with Georg Trakl (whose suffering under human cruelty, unlike Dix's, led to self-annihilation), with Georg Heym and Gottfried Benn. Stylistically, the art of these years is marked by an unprecedented combination of hyper-real precision of detail with comprehensive, coherent composition, and a palette that is morbidly manneristic in atmosphere.

It is no wonder that Dix's work rankled the National Socialists no end, as they had the conservative, nationalistic critics before them. Yet it is precisely the unsenti-

mental detachment of his technically superb and largely emotionless style that contributed to lending the major works of Dix a permanence that his later paintings by no means achieved.

The Skewered Philistine

To "skewer" the philistine on his pencil-point – that was what George Grosz envisaged as he transmuted his early, metaphysical scenes into radically verist depictions. By means of exaggeration to the point of razor-sharp cari-

George Grosz
To Oskar Panizza, 1917/18
Oil on canvas, 140 x 110 cm
Stuttgart, Staatsgalerie Stuttgart

George Grosz
The Pillars of Society, 1926
Oil on canvas, 200 x 108 cm
Berlin, Nationalgalerie, Staatliche
Museen zu Berlin – Preußischer
Kulturbesitz

*"I see the future development of
painting taking place in workshops,
in pure craftsmanship, not in any
holy temple of the arts. Painting
is manual labor, no different from
any other; it can be done well or
poorly."* GEORGE GROSZ

cature, Grosz pilloried the hopeless state of the post-war
world. He succeeded so well in this bitter task that average Germans were soon characterizing the unscrupulous legislators, businessmen, and military men among
them, with their stiff collars, bull necks, and helmets,
simply as "Grosz types". His pictures and person
accordingly became the target of virulent attacks, not
excluding attempts on his life.

Even in his oil paintings, Grosz remained a draftsman foremost. The means he used to simultaneously
depict various aspects of the urban inferno were derived
not only from the anonymous "artists" of public lavato-
ries but from Futurism and Dadaism. After his early
period, Grosz continued to create significant oils, one of
the finest of which was his eerie and anarchistic *To Oskar
Panizza* (ill. above). It shows a ghostly procession seemingly tumbling downwards through a canyon of top-
pling buildings, rendered with Futurist dynamism and a
Futurist simultaneity of chronological events. As Death
crouches on the coffin, downing a shot of schnapps, a
moon-faced preacher waves a crucifix, ill-boding masqueraders stumble past, and in the background a carriage passes across and over the pandemonium. Like this

canvas, Grosz's portraits, exemplified by the moving
depiction of the writer Max Herrmann-Neisse (Mannheim, Städtische Kunsthalle), have survived the period
of their making. Grosz must be credited with the historical achievement of having confronted the legend of the
Golden Twenties with the reality of Weimar, that so
unstable and jeopardized republic.

Max Beckmann's Masks

Important as the artists just discussed were, they were
outshone by a contemporary who was one of the century's greatest: Max Beckmann (pp. 191–195). Recognized early in his career, after leaving the Berlin Secession group, Beckmann for a time pursued similar thematic and stylistic paths to Dix and Grosz, but as the
years passed he attained to a depth they could not reach.
Beckmann was a lone wolf who belonged to no group or
trend, a man who began to employ the stylistic means of
Expressionism long after Expressionism, as a project,
was over. More, he ceased to indulge in the self-analysis,
the psychic exhibitionism of the Expressionist painters
after once mercilessly evoking, in his 1917 *Self-Portrait
with Red Scarf* (p. 194), the shock and consequent ner-

vous breakdown to which his experience of the brutality of war had led.

Later Beckmann concealed his mental torment behind impenetrable masks, be it the tragic mask of the visionary in *Self-Portrait with a Crystal Ball* (1936; private collection), the self-confident one of the *grand seigneuer* in *Self-Portrait in a Tuxedo* (1927; Cambridge, MA, Busch-Reisinger Museum), the aloof and self-critical mask of the performer in the circus of the world in *Self-Portrait with Horn* (1930; private collection), or the symbolically enigmatic mask of the ancient Greek hero in *Odysseus and Calypso* (1943; ill. above).

Increasingly, reality was translated into mythical ciphers, despite the fact that Beckmann always took actual experience, moments of vision, as his point of departure. He painted what he saw; but as his early, long under-rated, grandiose and pathos-filled visions of veritably Baroque drama already showed, Beckmann was anything but a naturalistic artist. Late in his career he would caution his students against the mere imitation of nature, saying that it was a wonderful chaos, and that it was the artist's task and duty to lend order to it. The translation of reality into color and form, the transposition of space onto the two-dimensional plane, were in Beckmann's eyes the only "true abstraction" in art. Abstraction for its own sake, the sheer play of non-signifying form, he considered inadmissible.

The older Beckmann became, the less importance he attached to the particular experience that led to a painting. What counted more was the working through of a subject once chosen to lend it historical depth. This power to transform a subject was a gift that revealed itself early in his career. It already appeared full blown in the still quite realistic vision of terror and aggression

The Night (p. 195). Murderous thugs have broken into the attic apartment of a family, where they coolly perform their grisly work in front of a black, gaping void, silent, indifferent, inescapable. That the scene plays in a postwar city is apparent only from the style of dress; it might just as well be set in ancient Rome, in the Middle Ages, in a Nazi concentration camp, on the Congo, in Cambodia, Chile, or the Balkans. Horror at the demoniac and destructive side of human nature, including the artist's and our own, takes on oppressive presence in this image.

Beckmann's triptych *The Departure* of 1932/33 (p. 192) contains autobiographical references. It reflects the artist's own role and his view of the relationship between the sexes, but it also can be seen as a premonition of Beckmann's own destiny, his emigration from Germany when the Nazis came to power. At the same time the painting, as always with Beckmann, alludes to contexts of a much wider nature. In one study, by Friedhelm W. Fischer, *The Departure* is interpreted as a re-staging of the myth of the Flood as a purifying and renewing force. On the middle panel, against the backdrop of Beckmann's so beloved sea, a group of people stands in a boat, preparing to cast off: a veiled, super-human female figure in a mythical mask; a human woman holding a child in her arms; a ferryman, his face half hidden; and the crowned figure of a king, who releases fish from his net. The two flanking panels contain images of cruelty:

Max Beckmann
Odysseus and Calypso, 1943
Oil on canvas, 150 x 115.5 cm
Hamburg, Hamburger Kunsthalle

Conrad Felixmüller
Death of the Poet Walter Rheiner, 1925
Oil on canvas, 185 x 129 cm
Los Angeles (CA), Los Angeles County Museum of Art

Max Beckmann
The Departure (Triptych), 1932/33
Oil on canvas, wing panels
215.1 x 99.5 cm,
central panel 215.5 x 115 cm
New York, The Museum of
Modern Art

"Departure. Yes, departure from the deceptive appearance of life to the things themselves that matter, behind the appearances. But, in the final analysis this applies to my pictures…" MAX BECKMANN

executioners and their victims, situations and places one leaves without ever being able to forget them. World and anti-world, the noble and the base, darkness and light, brutal reality and mythical transfiguration, all are given compellingly concrete form in these three images.

Another triptych, *The Argonauts* (ill. right), definitively completed only a day before the artist's death ("Not a single brushstroke more," Beckmann wrote), likewise shows a group of people preparing to depart. On a platform above the ocean stand two adolescent figures: Orpheus, crowned with a wreath, his lyre at his feet, and Jason, on his arm the wryneck, the bird given him by Aphrodite, whose cries would send Medea into a passion of love. Behind the youths, an old man clambers up a ladder out of the sea, pointing out the direction to be taken by the heroes of the legendary ship "Argo." On the left panel we see a painter, whose gestures suggest Beckmann but whose physiognomy resembles van Gogh, standing at an easel and depicting the sword-bearing, voluptuous Medea. She is seated on a mask that bears Beckmann's features. On the right is a group of girls playing music, very contemporary-looking girls whose beauty corresponds to the American ideal, which intrigued Beckmann. These are modern representatives of the antique choir. Jason, too, is a 20th-century adolescent, classically noble of feature but with the athletic

physique of a football player. His hair is ruffled by the wind, a wind which, according to the artist's friend Erhard Göpel, represented "the cooling breeze of the plateaus of the Beyond" to Beckmann. Göpel has also pointed out that *The Argonauts*, like many major works of this outstanding artist, is so multifarious in meaning that it permits of any number of other interpretations. Moreover, it includes messages that can only be expressed through color and form, messages which, like the content of all great painting, cannot be translated into verbal terms.

The most intriguing thing about Beckmann's paintings is the way present, past and future flow into one another and interpentrate. Yet every scene in the artist's universal theater was based on a real situation. In the case of *The Night* it was the horror of the post-war period in Germany; in that of *The Departure* it was the artist's personal fate; and even *The Argonauts* played a role in Beckmann's own life – they were the group of friends who shared his exile in Amsterdam. In Beckmann's work the present is rendered permeable to the winds that blow from the underworld and the world beyond; each painting, the triptychs above all, becomes a universal metaphor. Precisely by taking a biographical or historical situation and transcending it, rendering it timeless, Beckmann permits time to permeate the image. This is the fourth dimension, of time past, lost, then remembered, recovered again. Beckmann himself described what he felt in the process of painting as follows: "For me, translating three into two dimensions is a magical experience, in the course of which I momentarily capture that fourth dimension after which my entire being seeks."

What is incomparable about these symbol-laden compositions is that they are neither painted literature nor are they burdened by that fatal profundity which is the besetting sin of German art. The key to understanding them, accordingly, is not speculation but precise observation and knowledge of their background. Beckmann's paintings amount to an exact if mythically transformed record of the state of human affairs during a particular period of history, a deeply penetrating and illusionless interpretation of human behavior in situations of extremity.

Beckmann's portraits, not only of himself but of others, are taciturn as well. The sitters wear masks, which conceal their inner-most thoughts instead of revealing them. The loneliness of man in society, or, again, the isolation of humans within the cage of the self, finds expression in many of Beckmann's works. It is there in the hopeless attempt of Calypso to prevent, with melancholy tenderness, the departure of Odysseus,

whose thoughts are already far from her (*Odysseus and Calypso*); it is there in *Apache Dance* (1938; Bremen, Kunsthalle), where the man, his eyes flashing victory, carries off the half-willing, half-violated woman, much as Perseus does Andromache in the *Perseus* triptych of 1941 (Essen, Museum Folkwang).

Executioners and their victims, persecution and escape, despair and new-found hope, the dereliction of man in an infinite space "whose foregrounds one continually has to fill up with a little rubbish so one cannot see their terrifying depths so clearly.... This endless lostness in eternity. This aloneness" – all of these Beckmann depicted, and thus gave his own sense of life and of the reality of the century and its historical and mythical background a visual expression as precise and compelling as that of Picasso.

Along with Picasso, Beckmann is one of the greatest expressive realists of the modern age, a painter who spoke in parables, a moralist and metaphysician who, despite the fact that the people in many of his pictures appear captive, imprisoned, believed that art could play the role of helper and liberator of humanity, that through form, the many ambiguities of life could be resolved, as Beckmann told his students a few months before his death. An idealist without illusions, in other words, who let neither the chaos of the century nor of

Max Beckmann
The Argonauts (Triptych), 1950
Oil on canvas, wing panels
189 x 84 cm,
central panel 203 x 122 cm
Washington, National Gallery of
Art, Gift of Mrs. Quappi-Mathilde
Beckmann

"The old man in the center panel who is climbing out of the sea on a ladder is a god who shows the young men the way to a better world – the way to a higher level of consciousness, above earthly life. There is a strong wind; sun and moon are darkened, two new planets are just being created."

MAX BECKMANN

Max Beckmann
The Night, 1918/19
Oil on canvas, 133 x 154 cm
Düsseldorf, Kunstsammlung
Nordrhein-Westfalen

human history, nor hateful persecution at the hands of sub-human supermen, deter him from fulfilling his mission.

Metaphysics and Painting

As fascinating as is the existential background of Beckmann's art, we must not forget its technical side, the mastery of which cost him a great struggle. Beckmann was born in Leipzig, Saxony, to parents who had moved there from Lower Saxony. His early paintings were characterized by Baroque theatricality and a certain allegorical overloading. By learning to discipline these tendencies and to place his virtuosity in the service of concentrated expression, Beckmann became the dominant figure in German art of the 20th century. This fact was only belatedly recognized in the United States, and only recently in France, the classic land of *bonne peinture*. That Beckmann holds a position of prominence among the very greatest painters of the century, of whatever nationality, can no longer be gainsaid. Although his major works still reflect a graphic tendency, the heavy, containing contours are not only entirely integrated into the painterly whole but have become a painterly element *sui generis*. Their expressive force corresponds perfectly with the sonorous color chords of Beckmann's palette.

Joyless Silence

Another lone wolf among German artists, if for entirely different reasons, was Karl Hofer (p. 196). He was a truly tragic figure. Hofer spent three years in a French internment camp during World War I, and during World War II, a single night's air raid on Berlin cost him the major part of his life's work, which he subsequently attempted, despairingly and not always successfully, to reconstruct. Hofer finally died during – not to say of – one of those embittered debates on the primacy of abstract or objective art which were such a depressing feature of the postwar decades.

The decisive aesthetic experiences for Hofer were the idealizing figurative painting of Hans von Marées and the constructively logical painting of Cézanne. The classicist among modern German artists, Hofer was an idealist disillusioned by bitter experience. His subject matter was influenced by a journey to India, where he was deeply moved by the sight of girls whose gentle, awkward grace was apparently entirely unselfconscious.

Hofer's figures, both his young men and his young women, live in a world that has turned inwards, alone and self-contained, melancholy and joyless, as if musing on their own isolation and mortality. A note of sentimentality sometimes creeps in, whether the subject be the silent suffering of the creaturely or of the intellectu-

Max Beckmann
Self-Portrait with Red Scarf, 1917
Oil on canvas, 80 x 60 cm
Stuttgart, Staatsgalerie Stuttgart

Marcel Gromaire
Sailor in Clear Grey, 1930
Oil on canvas, 55.5 x 46 cm
Private collection

ally aware life. *The Poet* (1942; destroyed by fire), hand raised in a gesture of warning and invocation, gliding in a boat over dark water before an empty, nocturnal horizon, was one of Hofer's most compelling images. His poet was brother to Charon, ferryman of the underworld, fearlessly traversing the terrible void.

Hofer's landscapes are as forlorn as his figures. In the finest of them, done in Tessin, his otherwise dry, matte color begins to shine. The stringently harmonious compositions, like a few of the still lifes, reveal an affinity to the principles of Cézanne, although considerable variations in quality appear across the œuvre as a whole.

Mention has been made of the return to realism of French artists such as Léger and Derain. But this return, as with the Italians and some of the Germans, was not to the classical Renaissance. Derain, for instance, took his point of departure in the Gothic art of Avignon. A less important expressive realist, Marcel Gromaire (ill. right), was influenced by Léger, his socialist outlook and themes from the life of workers and peasants, rendered in a toned-down Cubist style. In general, post-World War I French realism exhibited a stronger reaction than elsewhere in Europe to current historical events, which led to a defusing of Cubist formal ideas. This development gained significance in Europe only when it began

Karl Hofer
Circus People, c. 1921
Oil on canvas, 148 x 118.5 cm
Essen, Museum Folkwang

to be reflected in Picasso's neoclassical phase. Paris – or better, the Paris Abstract International of the post-World War II years – put not only all realist art but all figurative art out of the running for years, because every artist who considered himself progressive was convinced that abstraction represented the epitome of art, an epitome which, illogically, they thought would last to Kingdom Come. The course of history, as it almost always does, has impressively proven the prophets wrong.

Groups and Individuals

Neorealist tendencies were noted, if still only in passing, at Harald Szeemann's documenta 5, held in Kassel in 1972. "Art is returning to itself," announced the imaginative exhibition curator with a sure instinct for current issues and emergent trends. What he meant by this was artists' reaction to their disappointment over the abortive political commitments of 1968, their return to a new brand of *l'art pour l'art*, to more personal concerns, even to a new ivory tower, as a result of the painful insight that art, by itself, is not capable of changing the world.

Another key if long underrated exhibition date was more significant than the documenta in this context. This was "22 Realists," shown in 1970 at the Whitney Museum in New York, a hodgepodge of diverse streams within an over-arching development which had little more in common than a programmatic advocacy of figuration. At the very least, this neorealism had the beneficial effect of leading to a rediscovery and re-evaluation of earlier realist painting in the orbit of Neue Sachlichkeit and Magic Realism in Europe. In the United States, artists began to recall their own realist heritage of the 1930s and 1940s, the American Scene in all its variants, from the admired Edward Hopper to the socially critical Ben Shahn.

Franz-Wilhelm Seiwert
Knockin'-Off Time, 1925
Oil on burlap, 200 x 140 cm
Hamburg, Hamburger Kunsthalle

young artists, who, as socialists, envisioned an art for the urban masses. Accordingly, Hoerle's and Seiwert's key scenarios and *dramatis personae* were taken from the industrial world of manufacturing plants and laborers. The paintings of these two combine in a highly idiosyncratic way realistic and constructivist elements, derived both from Neue Sachlichkeit and from Constructivism and Léger. The figures are impersonal, indeed de-personalized, standing for entire social strata or human types – male and female workers, farmers, disabled war veterans. In Seiwert's case, religious motives initially entered the picture as well. In 1922 he painted an image of *Christ in the Ruhrgebiet* (Cologne, private collection).

Heinrich Hoerle
The Contemporaries, 1931
Oil on plywood, 120 x 200 cm
Cologne, Kölnisches Stadt-
museum

In Germany, whose realist scene was not without influence on the Americans, artists realized that Neue Sachlichkeit was not represented by Dix and Grosz, nor even Kanoldt and Schrimpf alone. Salient rediscoveries were made among the group of Cologne "Progressives," Heinrich Hoerle (ill. above right), his friend Franz-Wilhelm Seiwert (ill. above left), and Anton Räderscheidt. These artists had separated from the Cologne Dada group around Ernst and Baargeld, as we have seen, because their antics appeared too bourgeois to the

On a wall in the background of the painting was inscribed, "What you have done to the lowliest of my brethern, that you have done to me." In front of the wall stood a gnomelike figure with protruding eyes and a steel helmet and – already at this early date – a swastika, blood-spattered symbol of the still-preventable rise of "Arturo Ui" alias Adolf Hitler. The warnings of Hoerle and Seiwert, who died young, proved to be as vain as their attempts to make themselves understood to those whose cause they championed.

Anton Räderscheidt
Self-Portrait, 1928
Oil on canvas, 100 x 80 cm
Private collection

Franz Radziwill
Water Tower in Bremen, 1931
Oil on canvas, 80 x 99.5 cm
Private collection

Bruno Goller
Large Show-Window, 1953
Oil on canvas, 150 x 115 cm
Düsseldorf, Kunstsammlung
Nordrhein-Westfalen

Heinrich Maria Davringhausen
The Black-Marketeer, 1920/21
Oil on canvas, 120 x 120 cm
Düsseldorf, Kunstmuseum
Düsseldorf im Ehrenhof

Karl Hubbuch
Hilde Twice, 1923
Oil on canvas, 150 x 77 cm
Munich, Bayerische Staats-
gemäldesammlungen, Neue
Pinakothek

Räderscheidt's theme was the loneliness of the individual in a collectivized society, for which he found memorable formulations in depictions of elongated figures in urban settings of forbidding emptiness (p. 197 below left).

Realist groups formed everywhere in Central Europe at this period, not only in Germany but in the Scandinavian countries, in Austria and Switzerland, and within Germany, not only in Cologne but in Berlin and Munich, Hannover and Dresden, where first tentative steps were taken in the direction of a socialist realism untrammeled by party discipline. There were also loners like Franz Radziwill (p. 197 below right), who lived in the North Sea hamlet of Dangast. Though he temporarily fell under the spell of fascism, Radziwill depicted eerily abandoned cityscapes overflown by insect-like aircraft which almost prophetically predicted the imminent disaster of World War II. The rediscovery of such artists began in 1961, sparked by a show at Haus am Waldsee, Berlin. Eberhard Marx, sensing the deflation of the "wild" painting of the 1950s, L'art informel and Tachism, mounted a retrospective of realism under the same title Hartlaub had chosen almost 35 years previously in Munich: Neue Sachlichkeit. Since this time, artists of the second echelon have also been given their due: Gustav Wunderwald, known as "Berlin's Utrillo," who was also much in demand as a stage designer; the social critic Karl Hubbuch (ill. left); Heinrich Maria Davringhausen of Munich (ill. above right); Carlo Mense, later active in the Rhineland; Dresden artists Hans and Lea Grundig and Wilhelm Rudolph; Carl Barth of Düsseldorf; and the Swiss Niklaus Stoecklin, to name only a few. Other realists such as Oelze, Höch, or Julius Bissier (p. 199 below) soon turned to other concerns, to create œuvres of great individuality beyond Neue Sach-lichkeit and Magic Realism.

Links with these styles are also evident in the work of Bruno Goller, a Düsseldorf original who, like his student Konrad Klapheck, went far beyond these 1920s sources. The son of a milliner, Goller succumbed to the magic of objects early on. The things in his initially soft-contoured, then increasingly harsh and flat compositions – ladies' hats above all, but also dresses, parasols, ribbons, bows and jewellery – unfold a strange inner vitality of compelling charm that is tempered by a bizarre, ironic humor. Goller's people and accessories tell stories, or their own personal story, like the coquettishly smiling hat mannequin surrounded by hats and ribbons in *Large Show Window* (p. 198 above left). Quite real props of everyday life, these things seem far removed from reality in Goller's art. His treatment of banal objects – umbrellas, jackets, armchairs, hatstands, or even numerals and monumental ears – anticipated

the more pragmatic approach of Pop, whose protagonists in Germany accordingly admired the self-effacing old gentleman as one of their forerunners.

A cool, ironically sparkling humor also suffuses the paintings of Klapheck. He loves the well-ordered, light-flooded interiors of Vermeer, the classicism of Poussin, but also admires – apart from his mentor, Goller – the Surrealists and Dadaists. With painstaking accuracy Klapheck depicts banal things, transforming and alienating them in the process into actors in the human comedy, by placing them in unfamiliar situations or combinations, or raising them to the plane of the super-real. An old-fashioned typewriter, monumentalized, becomes *The Weapon of Earnestness* (Essen, collection Ruhnau) and a masculine sex symbol in one. Bicycle bells without caps sound a silent *Memento Mori* (Essen, private collection). A sewing machine embodies *Female Logic* (Estate of the Artist). A *Sex Bomb and Her Companion* (Wuppertal, Von der Heydt-Museum) are incarnate in a curvaceous hand-shower fixture and a static, vise-like object that wonderfully persiflages empty-headed machismo. Metallically gleaming drill-presses, marching like robots toward the viewer out of a lurid background, proclaim *The War* (ill. above). Unimpressed by the more or less dominant abstract streams of the period, Klapheck has continued to follow the highly individual path he chose for himself early in his career.

Precision is also the salient trait of the work of Domenico Gnoli (p. 200 above left), an Italian artist whose life was prematurely cut short. Gnoli's detail-obsessed, ornamentalized banal objects occupy an intermediate zone between Magic Realism and Surrealism. The things he paints are items of apparel, like shoes and shirts, suits and ties, things closely related to the human beings who either do not appear at all in the picture or are shown from the back, and thus rendered anonymous. By isolating these things and blowing them up to large scale, Gnoli reveals their covert and threatening

Konrad Klapheck
The War, 1965
Oil on canvas, 145 x 200 cm
Düsseldorf, Kunstsammlung
Nordrhein-Westfalen

"I do not use objects as symbols, but instead I paint them as well as I can and then see what they say to me. In the end, paintings are cleverer than their creator and exceed his expectations." KONRAD KLAPHECK

Konrad Klapheck
The Logic of Women, 1965
Oil on canvas, 110 x 90 cm
Humblebæk (Denmark), Louisiana
Museum of Modern Art

Julius Bissier
22nd May 61, 1961
Egg-oil tempera on canvas,
43.5 x 48.5 cm
Düsseldorf, Kunstsammlung
Nordrhein-Westfalen

Domenico Gnoli
Man with Two Elevations, 1964
Oil and sand on canvas, two parts,
149 x 72 cm each
Cologne, Museum Ludwig,
Ludwig Donation

Ben Shahn
Miners' Wives, 1968
Tempera on cardboard,
122 x 91.5 cm
Philadelphia (PA), Philadelphia
Museum of Art

enigmatic quality. In their immediacy of presence,
Gnoli's works are symbols of the emptiness and imper-
sonality of modern life.

The American Scene

After the First World War artists in the United States
became painfully aware of their dependence on Europe.
Amidst the political outcry to "dump Wilson," who had
not been able to gain acceptance for his "Fourteen
Points" in the Treaty of Versailles, America rediscovered
the benefits of "splendid isolation". Its artists began to
gain a new self-confidence based on an appreciation of
their national identity. After Black Friday in 1929 and the
ensuing Great Depression, many of them turned to
socially critical themes. The American Way of Life,
whether idealized or in its unsensational aspects as
reflected in the existences of commonplace people, the
poor and dispossessed, the black minority – Barbara
Rose has spoken in this context of the boredom and
emptiness of life in democracy – became fit subjects for
art. From the first significant attempts of American
artists to emancipate themselves from the European tradition, embodied in the Ashcan School of the turn of
the century, this development led to Precisionism and
Regionalism, and finally culminated in the work of
Edward Hopper. After learning a mastery of color and
light in Paris, Hopper returned home to apply his skills
to the American Scene, depicting the countryside but
above all the loneliness of the big city in works of a
stature unique to that point in American art.

The Ashcan School, composed of John Sloan,
George Luks, George Bellows and others, made the first
attempt to introduce the subject of the metropolis into

Marsden Hartley
Portrait of a German Officer, 1914
Oil on canvas, 173 x 105 cm
New York, The Metropolitan
Museum of Art, Alfred Stieglitz
Collection

the short history of American art. Ben Shahn (p. 200), born in Lithuania, brought to the United States at the age of eight, was an admirer of Dix and Grosz who, apart from working as a photographer, was assistant to the great Mexican revolutionary painter Diego Rivera. This background is evident in both the subject matter and the style of Shahn's paintings, which consciously departed from the then-dominant hedonism of Paris. Shahn was the most committed social critic among the American artists of the day and continued the tradition of the Ashcan School. He achieved fame through a cycle devoted to the life and death of the Italian-American anarchists Sacco and Vanzetti, who, based on a scandalous verdict were executed for murder on insufficient evidence – a macabre foreshadowing of the persecutions for "un-American activities" at the hands of Senator Joseph McCarthy in the 1950s, at the onset of the Cold War.

Shahn, like Grosz, basically remained a graphic artist foremost. His colors, in accordance with the theme, were initially subdued, and later took on a lighter brilliance. His precision was certainly influenced by photography, but in later years Shahn relinquished detail for a more generous, if occasionally somewhat decorative treatment of form. His paintings derived their suspense from a contrast between relatively small-scale figures and expansive backgrounds, while the aggressive mood of the earlier compositions gradually made way for a more elegiac atmosphere.

Charles Sheeler (p. 202 below right), leading light among the Precisionists, who included Charles Demuth (p. 202 above right) and Ralson Crawford, was likewise a photographer, an excellent one, whose prints now hang in many museums. The flat, reduced forms in his compositions were surely derived more from photography than from Cubism, the influence of which many American critics see as seminal to the Precisionist approach. More important to the group, astonishing as it might seem, was Duchamp. His unaltered "ready-mades" pointed up the covert magic of the simplest, most unprepossessing objects, of the very type that Sheeler, Demuth and their friends depicted in simplified, planar terms and in strong color. As Horst Richter notes, there is little connection with Cubism to be seen here, but all the more with Pop Art (if not with latter-day neo-realism), whose protagonists not incidentally had Duchamp's sympathy.

The celebrators of the American Scene – of provincial America, far from New York and the East Coast – were at home in the South, West and Midwest. Their protest against the dominance of the "European Babylon" of New York would bear fruit decades later in West Coast art, but also in the highly original work of artists from Edward Kienholz to Bruce Nauman, or the light-modulating styles of Robert Irwin, Doug Wheeler, and Ron Cooper (of whom Irwin, best known in Europe, has probably the most complex œuvre to his credit). Yet in the case of almost all the isolationist painters of the

Joseph Stella
Battle of Lights, Coney Island, 1913
Oil on canvas, 192.5 x 213.5 cm
New Haven (CT), Yale University
Art Gallery

Thomas Hart Benton
People of Chilmark, 1920
Oil on canvas, 166.5 x 197.3 cm
Washington, Hirshhorn Museum and Sculpture
Garden, Smithsonian Institution

rural life back then, their regional limitation led to artistic narrow-mindedness. Only the *American Gothic* of Grant Wood (p. 203 above) – the title of a double portrait of elderly Babbitts in front of a neo-Gothic wooden chapel, rendered in an ironically tinged style schooled on the precisionism of Flemish masters – or occasionally the rustic power of Thomas Hart Benton (p. 201), Pollock's teacher, still deserve serious interest.

In the work of Edward Hopper, however (ill. below and p. 203), American realist painting achieved a level before World War II which justifies placing Hopper and his work beside the best Europe had to offer in the field in the 1920s. It is no exaggeration to say, as does Wieland Schmied, that Hopper's art was the painterly equivalent of the major American literature of the period, from John Dos Passos to Theodore Dreiser, Sinclair Lewis, or William Faulkner. Hopper's evocations of the isolation of big-city dwellers in bars, diners, trains, even in the theater or cinema, at railroad stations, gas stations, in their own humble front yards and homes in the country or suburbs, reveal a superb execution, mastery of the effects of light and shade, and great coloristic quality, derived from the artist's thorough study of French painting. Even more, the theme of isolation, loneliness, and lack of purpose in life, sometimes mitigated by an evocation of life's small joys, is distilled into memorable pictorial symbols, and occasionally even into legends. His mastery of the craft permitted Hopper to simplify his compositions and waive all merely anecdotal detail. What speaks to us from his works is compassion, empathy with the fates of normal, commonplace people, with life in a mass society, which ultimately throws the individual back upon himself or herself.

A key if stylistically unclassifiable position in the American Scene, and indeed in 20th-century painting as whole, is held by the work of Georgia O'Keeffe (p. 204 above right), who died at the age of almost 100 at her lonely residence in rural New Mexico. Hers' is a position between abstraction and realism, between America and Europe. Married to Alfred Stieglitz, photographer and promotor of avant-garde art in New York, O'Keeffe doubtless drew much inspiration from European art, not least from Kandinsky, but she nevertheless always remained herself and indubitably American. The organic, biomorphic shapes in her work, derived from plants, landscapes, even human faces, combine a concentration on symmetry with the painterly effects of loosely brushed passages, ornamental spiral forms, and pastel gradations. It is enough to compare a rigorously stylized seashell of 1926 with a spirally rotating, constructive "Abstraction" of the same year, to become aware of the strangely intermediate position of O'Keeffe's art between autonomous abstraction and what has been termed "relativizing realism."

Art of Revolutionary Fervor

A special case, which outstripped the American Scene in terms of drama and monumentality, which indeed represented a diametrically opposed approach, was the expressive realism, or better, the realistic expressionism, of the Mexican revolutionary painters José Clemente Orozco, Diego Rivera, and David Alfaro Siqueiros. The list could be extended by an artist who shared their tradition but did not reach the pitch of their political com-

mitment, Rufino Tamayo, the author of a mural on the UNESCO building in Paris (ill. below left).

The starkest form of this "transcendent realism" is found in the work of Orozco, a Creole who had lost an arm, was frequently ill-humored, but always effaced himself in favor of his art. As early as 1926, his collaborator, Rivera, called Orozco Mexico's greatest artist (p. 205). He was also, despite certain affinities with

Picasso, the most original painter of the group, a man who, though well-versed in European painting, came down most clearly on the side of the art of his own country, from the Mayas to colonial Baroque, and lent it an inimitable identity. Orozco's panels, and above all his murals on the struggles and passions of his people, on the battles and victories of the Mexican revolution, are a rare example of the fact that monumental history painting of a clearly revolutionary bent is still possible in the 20th century. His multiple-figure compositions are filled with tumultuous drama, doubtless derived not only from Mexican traditions but from an awareness of Expressionism and the expressive realism of a Picasso. But these influences are transmogrified into an aggressive, obsessive style with an inimitable, personal stamp. Orozco is not afraid of pathos, even of sentimentality on occasion, courageously taking risks that lesser artists would avoid.

Rivera's painting, dynamic if formally more tranquil by comparison to Orozco's furor, is likewise at its monumental best in the fresco medium. It reveals the European influences, from the orbit of Modigliani and Apollinaire, of Picasso, Braque, and Gris, even of the frescoes of Giotto, which Rivera overcame by an enormous act of will without ever quite being able to forget them.

Siqueiros (p. 207 below), the third in the league of painting revolutionaries, stood even more decisively on the side of the wretched and the poor, especially of the Indians. To "socialize artistic expression with the aim of eliminating individualism" was his express intention. Like his friends Orozco and Rivera, the latter of whom he met in Paris in 1921, Siqueiros took his point of departure in the aesthetic and ideological doctrines of the revolutionary graphic artist Posada and the founder of

the "Indian Renaissance," Dr. Atl (alias Gerardo Murillo). But unlike them, he wholeheartedly accepted the role of political propagandist, activist, and educator of the people. Despite his many commissions, Siqueiros even occasionally relinquished artistic activity entirely in favor of grassroots political work. Nevertheless, he managed to introduce a number of technical innovations, such as the systematic use of new tools like the airgun. These he put in the service of a rapid, propagandistically effective, "current" painting which was capable of keeping pace with the political developments of the day.

Diego Rivera
Nude with Calla Lilies, 1944
Oil on hardboard, 157 x 124 cm
Mexico City, Emilia Gussy de
Gálvez Collection

José Clemente Orozco
The Soldiers' Wives, 1926
Oil on canvas, 70 x 100 cm
Mexico City, Museo de Arte
Moderno

José Clemente Orozco
Zapatistas, 1931
Oil on canvas, 114.3 x 139.7 cm
New York, The Museum of
Modern Art

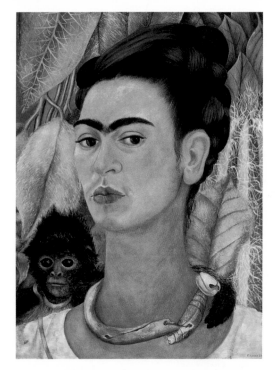

Frida Kahlo
Self-Portrait with Monkey, 1938
Oil on hardboard, 40.6 x 30.5 cm
Buffalo (NY), Albright-Knox
Art Gallery, Bequest of A. Conger
Goodyear

Diego Rivera
The Arsenal – Frida Kahlo
Distributes Arms, 1928
From the cycle: "Political Vision
of the Mexican People" (detail)
Fresco, 203 x 398 cm
Mexico City, Secretaría de
Educación Pública

The confrontation at the Düsseldorf Kunsthalle in 1995 of 50 each drawings and paintings by Siqueiros and Pollock, who worked together in New York in 1936, shed a new light on both artists. In the engaged realist's laboratory, the later painter of "drip" abstractions learned the technique of letting paint drip from a stick while moving around the canvas lying on the floor.

An important rediscovery was the work of Frida Kahlo, Rivera's wife, who long stood in the shadow of her dominating husband (ill. left). The moving paintings of this long-suffering artist are socially critical without being aggressive. They are images of compassion, documents of human warmth, in which a merciless frankness obviates every tendency to sentimentalism.

The flowering of Mexican mural painting, which was not without influence on North American art, began in 1922 with the execution of murals for the Escuela Nacional Preparatoria by the trio of Siqueiros, Rivera and Orozco. These were followed by many other frescoes which are now the pride of Mexico City. Unlike many like-minded European artists, the Mexicans had the satisfaction of being understood by those to whom their art was addressed – and sometimes even by their artistic and political opponents, which involved them in a great deal of trouble despite their popularity. Although they were political artists and convinced of their mission, they never subordinated themselves to any party line, not even Siqueiros, who was a convinced communist. That saved them from compromise, not to mention those acts of submission which watered down or even ruined the work of so many of their colleagues. The later, often embarrassing concessions of the erstwhile Russian revolutionary painter Alexander Deineka to the Stalinist version of Socialist Realism may stand as an example.

Concessions of a less drastic nature are seen in the work of the Sicilian artist Renato Guttuso. Like the Mexicans, he too remained a convinced socialist, if of the Italian stamp – a Eurocommunist, in other words, even holding the position of senator from 1976 onwards. And like them, Guttuso was one of the major realists of the years before and after mid-century. A certain insecurity, engendered by his attempts to conform to the doctrines of Socialist Realism, which he basically accepted, is reflected in the irritating inconsistency in the quality of Guttuso's work over long periods. Nevertheless, despite a verism that shows parallels to the work of neo-realistic film directors like Roberto Rossellini, Guttuso never descended to shallow naturalism. For that he was too widely travelled, and involved in too lively an exchange with the best in the art of the period.

The pictures which brought him first fame reflect, apart from an innate expressive tendency, a continual coming to terms with a range of contemporary styles, on the basis of a schooling in the Italian tradition. This is impressively attested by one of Guttuso's major canvases, *Caffè Greco* (pp. 207, 208), a scene in which the

"At a certain point, the painting itself gives the orders. One starts a painting with the idea that one will control it, that one will do what one wants. But somewhere along the way one realizes that the painting has made its own laws. These are independent of one's own thoughts and force one either to do or to refrain from doing certain things. This is based on a logic that arises from the forms, but not only from them."   RENATO GUTTUSO

Renato Guttuso
Caffè Greco, 1976
Oil on canvas, 282 x 333 cm
Cologne, Museum Ludwig,
Ludwig Collection

David Alfaro Siqueiros
Death and Funeral of Cain, 1947
Acrylic on wood, 76 x 96 cm
Mexico City, Museo de Arte
Alvar y Carmen T. de Carillo Gil

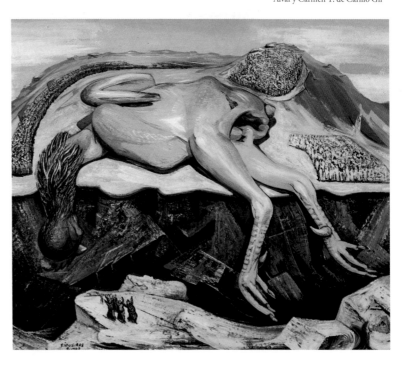

worlds of the living and the dead mingle. De Chirico and André Gide, Duchamp and Buffalo Bill, lesbian girls and Japanese tourists, a female head by Picasso and the Apollo of Belvedere, hold a rendesvous in this realistic phantasmagoria related to an actual place and conceived at that place. Beyond this, a key historical event that altered world consciousness, the Paris revolt of May 1968, which very nearly led to Charles de Gaulle's demise, found its most compelling artistic formulation in a work by Guttuso.

Guttuso's achievement notwithstanding, political-critical realism in the West produced no works that in terms of artistic rank could be set beside the best of Futurism prior to World War I and of Verism in its wake – not to speak of the prostituted productions that were churned out in such masses in Stalin's Soviet Union and Hitler's Germany. Even the Paris May had few artistic consequences, although its manifestations profited greatly from new, spontaneous forms of art and theater such as the Happening and the Living Theater. In West Germany, the most effective contribution to a politically engaged critical realism has been that of a Heidelberg attorney-at-law, Klaus Staeck, with his photograph-based posters and postcard series.

It is surely no coincidence that a relatively critical postwar realism should have emerged in Spain. There, artists were largely in agreement in their protest against

Renato Guttuso
The Takeover of Land by Sicilian
Peasants, 1949/50
Oil on canvas, 265 x 344 cm
Dresden, Gemäldegalerie Neue
Meister, on loan from the
Akademie der Künste

Eduardo Arroyo
Blind Painters, 1975
Oil on canvas, 221 x 180 cm
Zurich, Crex Collection

the Franco regime, even though many of them – if not
most, such as Antoni Tapiès, for instance – set themselves goals in which their political conviction played
little part. One is reminded of Herbert Marcuse's reply
to students clamoring for an agitprop art during the
unquiet late 1960s and early 1970s: Though Courbet, as a
political man, participated in the razing of the Vendôme
Column, said Marcuse, you couldn't tell this from his
pictures.

Among the critical realists of Spain, Juan Genovés
and Rafael Canogar hold places of prominence, Genovés with compelling figurative symbols of political vio-

lence and persecution, often set in stark contrast to
empty spaces, and Canogar with photocollages and later
three-dimensional figures (often headless torsos) representing anonymous victims of political persecution and
torture, demonstratively placed before empty walls.
"Equipo Cronica", founded by Manuel Valdes and
Rafael Solbes in 1964 – four years before the Paris May –
employs overpaintings of reproductions of famous historical works from Goya to Picasso and Lichtenstein
and uses the collage technique to update these images
and place them in the service of the current political
debate.

A special niche on the Spanish scene is occupied by
Eduardo Arroyo, a writer and journalist who lives in
Paris. In his graphic and painterly work the actual is
blended with the unreal, the real with the surreal, primitivistic simplification with intellectual metaphor. In
one painting a man in a suit hops on his head down the
stairs, his face a palette, indicating his role as painter. A
dog and cat, in the form of a rubber collage, lie on the
pavement in Berlin-Kreuzberg. "The Last Optimist"
represents Julio Alvares del Vayo, minister of state of the
Spanish Republic before the advent of Franco, his *Shoes
of Exile* multiplied to five, the broad smile in the circular
portrait he holds like a shield in front of his face in the
full-figure depiction fixed in a grimace. Flecks of color
hover before the eyes of Arroyo's *Blind Painters* (ill. above
right), and he depicts himself as *Robinson Crusoe* (1965),
clad in skins and a feathered hat, seated in a chair that,
while comfortable, is obviously located on a desert
island. In a three-panel picture, Janek Walczak, the
boxer, though apparently beyond his prime and looking
apprehensive, strikes a fighting pose in the center, while
at the left a skinny black opponent raises his guard and
at the right, a pair of gloves and a deflated punching ball
hang on the familiar nail. As one can see, a telling, liter-

Erró
Venus, 1975
Oil on canvas, 130 x 97 cm
Aachen, Ludwig Forum für
Internationale Kunst

ary wit, not unlike Magritte's but more related to current events and concerns, is one of the prime tools of Arroyo's unacademic painting. "Panama," his biography of the boxer Al "Panama" Brown, long held a place on the non-fiction bestseller list.

Political commitment is expressed more directly and without literary trappings in the work of the Icelandic artist Erró, who distills his equally straightforward and sarcastic political vocabulary from comic books and posters, and recombines the elements by means of painted collage (p. 208 below).

The work of the Swedish-American artist Öyvind Fahlström, though it likewise relies on comic-strip clichés, is more ambiguous, indirect, and allusion-charged than that undertaken by Erró. Hovering in an area between Pop and New Realism, Fahlström's compositions give pointed intellectual expression to an enigmatic humor rooted in the Dadaist and Surrealist tradition (ill. right). Taking a convinced pacifist position during the Vietnam War, the artist waived the expression of the emotions it aroused in him, instead he marshalled facts and data that were intended to attack the war-mongers and educate the viewer. Those he criti-

cized and those effected by the inhumanity of government, Fahlström hoped, would both "understand and be injured" by his imagery. In a few cases he certainly succeeded in this; but for the masses Fahlström's work remained a message that did not reach them.

A completely different approach to a critique of social conditions is evident in the work of Columbian artist Fernando Botero (ill. left). Botero reveals the "discrete charm of the bourgoisie," of ecclesiastical and political leaders, by means of fine painting and the device of the blow-up. Masterpieces of art history from Raphael to Peter Paul Rubens are as little immune from this process as presidents and cardinals. Admittedly, however, the sometimes frivolous, if ultimately gentle humor of Botero's depictions of this literally inflated society, along with the brilliance of their execution, do blunt the point of his attack.

Öyvind Fahlström
Roulette, Variable Painting, 1966
Oil on photograph, paper, vinyl, cardboard, magnets, 152.5 x 166 cm
Cologne, Museum Ludwig, Ludwig Donation

Fernando Botero
The President, 1969
Oil on canvas, 267 x 135 cm
Munich, Bayerische Staats-gemäldesammlungen, Staatsgalerie moderner Kunst

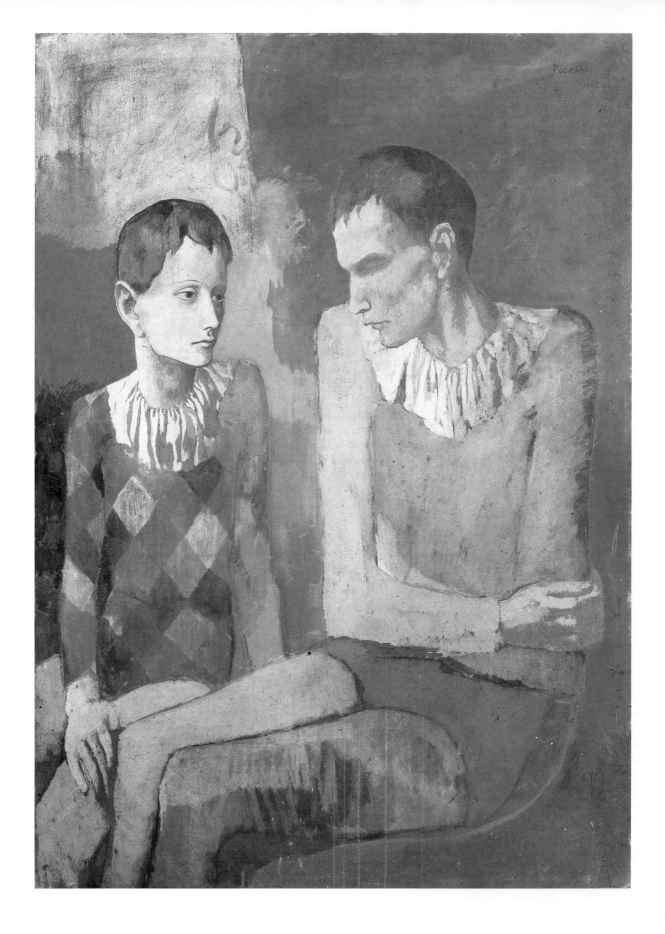

The Face of the Century

Painting as a Dramatic Act
Pablo Picasso: an Artist and his Legend

It is no easy task to become a monument to oneself during one's lifetime. For many artists who do so, it leads to ossification and a decline in their creative powers. If there was one painter of our times who was an exception to this rule, it was Pablo Picasso. Born in Málaga, Andalusia, Pablo was the son of Doña Maria Picasso y Lopez and Don José Ruiz Blasco, an academy instructor and later professor in Barcelona. Even far into his eighties, this small, great man with the blazing eyes continued to excite controversy. It is common knowledge that at an advanced age, Picasso married the beautiful young Jacqueline Roque, who later was unable to get over his death, and that before and between his two marriages he had several mistresses. It is also common knowledge that Picasso distorted the human anatomy in his work, occasionally deforming the human image to the point of monstrosity; that he was able to paint and draw quite realistically, even classically, and yet seldom chose to. In the meantime the experts have declared Picasso a Proteus, comparing him to the ever self-transforming, oracular "sea-ancient" of antiquity. For some a god, for others Picasso was the symbol incarnate of Hans Sedlmayr's *Der Verlust der Mitte* (Loss of the Center) – thus the title of the conservative art historian's influential book – and his diagnosis that the melancholy of the modern artist was due to his having lost touch with God.

Although Picasso never had a private student, he did unwittingly found a school that has incomparably affected art in our century, whether by acceptance or rejection of his work. The number of his followers and imitators is legion. Even the violence with which many painters attacked their father-figure after 1945, especially during the 1950s, only goes to show how difficult they found it to emerge from his shadow. The greatness of Picasso, someone aptly said back then, could be measured by the number of debates he was capable of triggering. Most of the doubters, though, have long since turned from Sauls to Pauls, a conversion that was encouraged by the gradual revelation of the scope and diversity of Picasso's œuvre, in sculpture as well as in painting and graphic art.

One of the most important exhibitions of the early 1990s was "Picasso. Die Zeit nach Guernica" (The Period After Guernica). This presentation convincingly disproved the legend of the late Picasso's faltering imagination, a legend to which even William S. Rubin, a friend of the artist and curator of the otherwise breathtaking retrospective held in 1980 at the Museum of Modern Art, New York, in honor of Picasso's 100th birthday, still paid tribute. Rubin, as if embarrassed by the late work, discussed it only in passing. How erroneous this was became entirely obvious in 1992, at the exhibition named above. Shown in Berlin, Munich and Hamburg, it began with the year 1937, when Picasso painted *Guernica* (p. 217) for the Spanish Pavilion at the Paris World Fair – the epoch-making canvas that remained homeless in Franco's Spain, enjoyed a refuge in New York, and now has found its final place, unavailable for loan, in Madrid. Post-modernism, which has relativized the concepts of innovation and the avant-garde, has confirmed the re-evaluation of Picasso's late work from the standpoint of the present day.

It is truly exciting to watch the aging Picasso, entirely oblivious of avant-garde ambitions, in full control of his incomparable painterly means, doing what he will with colors and forms, unashamedly quoting himself and the greats of art history as the whim takes him. As if providing a running commentary on his own career, the old painter spreads out before our eyes his decades of experience with a dazzling abundance matched by no other artist of the era. The best of these late and latest works possess a freshness of invention, a precision of execution, and a brilliancy of attack which attest to the unbroken force of an imagination of unbounded scope. Compelling evidence is found in paintings such as *Le Déjeuner sur l'herbe* after Manet (1961; Paris, Musée Picasso), *Great Profile* (1963; Düsseldorf, Kunstsammlung Nordrhein-Westfalen), the lovely, tenderly melancholy *Portrait of Jacqueline* (1964; heirs of Jacqueline Picasso), the bucolic *L'Aubade* (p. 218), the ironically insouciant double portrait *Musketeer and Cupid* (1969; Cologne, Museum Ludwig), or the *Musketeer with Pipe* (p. 218).

The Human Drama

Beneath the artist's stylistic leaps and masquerades one can detect a basically quite logical development, driven by a sensibility that reacted seismographically to changes in the world around it, and with a dramatic vehemence intended to be immediately effective. Picasso once scoffed at the aestheticism of Impressionist landscapes

Pablo Picasso
Acrobat and Young Harlequin, 1905
Gouache on cardboard, 105 x 76 cm
Private collection

and their subtle records of changing light, calling them mere "weather reports." In every transformation he went through, Picasso remained a great realist. His sense of reality was Spanish in origin. Instead of being satisfied with beautiful appearances, he painted to get under people's skin. As his friend, Eluard, once said, Picasso was after the truth hidden beneath the surface. He never painted for the sake of painting alone. Picasso aimed to depict the adventure of life, the human drama. This is why, as close to abstraction as some of his works came, he rejected abstract painting in the narrower sense.

"Abstract art is nothing but painting. Where is the drama in that?" Picasso asked Christian Zervos, editor of *Cahiers d'Art*, in 1935. With this in mind it is no wonder that Picasso gave up Analytic Cubism when he decided the style had become too scientific, too hermetic. Picasso was no pure artist; he wanted his pictures to have an effect. "Some day we should be able to paint pictures that are capable of curing a person's toothache," he once said, in a wonderful understatement that aptly described what moved him to paint. Although he was capable of painting, and above all of drawing, not only as correctly but as beautifully as any Old Master, Picasso's art is not slick or facile; it is rough, disquieting, harsh, dramatic, and often provokingly grotesque and sarcastic.

The restlessness that drove him and determined the course of his life was also the agent that moved his art.

Pablo Picasso
Harlequin, 1915
Oil on canvas, 183.5 x 105.1 cm
New York, The Museum of Modern Art

Hardly any other painter gave himself over so completely to the adventure of art, to working without the benefit of the safety-net of convention, and that to a ripe old age. This was the source of Picasso's incessant stylistic changes. Master of every skill and artistic means, he was capable of transforming himself from year to year, even from month to month, week to week, day to day. Picasso shifted effortlessly from the dramatic to the lyrical mode, from the classic to the expressionistic, from realism to symbolism, Cubism to Surrealism. He continually altered his standpoint and point of view, uncovering ever-new aspects of his motifs. Picasso knew that an artist, due to the fast rhythm of the modern age, could not put all of himself into a single masterpiece, but had to express his vision in terms of series. This is why he did 15 versions of *The Women of Algiers* after Delacroix, and a full 58 versions of *Las Meninas* after Velázquez (Barcelona, Museu Picasso).

Rather than proceeding on the basis of a pre-considered plan, Picasso let himself be led by intuition. " I never know what will come up next," he said, and admitted that he sometimes made a hundred studies in a single day. The rapidity of his production was predicated on a somnambulistically sure hand. This entailed an unbelievable concentration, a meditative process of painting in which the external world was completely shut out. No one dared to disturb Picasso at his work. The few people he permitted to watch, such as the English painter and collector Ronald Penrose, report that he worked in absolute silence.

Picasso thought with his hands; his experiments were seldom or never a testing of pre-conceived theories, but unconscious practice. Reflection came later. As intelligent as he was, Picasso left theorizing to others. He did not set much store in explanations. And if something remained obscure, all the better. "Everybody wants to understand art," he told Zervos. "Why don't people try to understand the songs of a bird? Why do people love the night, flowers, everything around us, without needing to understand them?"

In his œuvre Picasso traversed the entire range of expression and form in modern painting, discovering countless new provinces. But he never sacrificed reality to pure, aesthetic form or self-satisfied revellings in color. His manner of working immediately and entirely from the promptings of his unconscious was a sign of his freedom of spirit and ultimately of a great tolerance, which touchingly expressed itself in Picasso's enthusiasm for the work of other artists, especially younger talents, even if they were no more than mediocre. Throughout his life, Picasso encouraged young artists and never discouraged them. This attitude reveals the apparent arbitrariness and inconsistency of his continual stylistic changes to have actually been a logical process, independent of fashion and fleeting period styles. The only thing that was capable of making Picasso feel insecure was his self-doubt, which, after all, is a sign of the critical, creative mind.

Master of the Line

Yet the Spaniard could also be as gentle as a Rococo painter, as enamored of decor and ornament, in love with the beauty of human beings and landscapes untouched by strife and conflict. Many still lifes, Mediterranean scenes, bucolic drawings, but above all the series of female portraits, glowing with gem-like color, document Picasso's artistic mastery in this field (p. 214). They show him looking upon the bright side of life, which he continually needed to compensate his sense of the omnipresence of death, so compellingly and terrifyingly embodied in his depictions of bare animal skulls. The clowning, faun-like side of Picasso's nature also had its source in this struggle with darkness. That

Eros and Death, joy and tragedy are siblings, is more clearly revealed in Picasso's work than in that of any other artist of our times.

"In modern painting, every brushstroke has become precision work," the great draughtsman once said. Despite his brilliant facility, Picasso had to struggle over and over again for decades to achieve this precision anew. The drawings and prints illustrate the scope of his accomplishment. Like Kirchner's woodcuts, Picasso's etchings and lithographs stand on an artistic par with the oils. Many of them, like the drawings, possess the quality of originals, since rather than representing preliminary studies to larger works, they are autonomous works of art in their own right. There are very few paint-

Pablo Picasso
Guernica, 1937
Oil on canvas, 349.3 x 776.6 cm
Madrid, Centro de Arte
Reina Sofía

ings in Picasso's œuvre that were done on the basis of an existing drawing. More often, drawings were "copied" after paintings. However, there were numerous reciprocal relationships between the two media as regards the artist's stylistic development, although their various phases did not always coincide in time. The "naturalism" that appeared in the paintings in about 1918 was already pre-figured in the drawings of 1914-15; the influence of Ingres vanished from the paintings in 1923-24, while remaining evident in the drawings and prints thereafter.

The idiosyncrasies of the artist's personality and working process are just as clearly evident in the graphic work as in the painterly. Picasso always worked spontaneously, letting technique and style of treatment be prompted by the subject at hand. "A picture is not conceived and determined in advance; while you're doing it, it follows the changeability of the idea," is how he himself once put it.

"I'm no pessimist, I don't abhor art," Picasso bravely stated during a period of deep self-abhorrence, "because I couldn't live without devoting all my time to it. I love it as my sole purpose in life. Everything I do in connection with art gives me the greatest pleasure." A Mediter-

ranean enjoyment of everything life has to offer, a heathen optimism and love of the pleasure of creation, found immediate expression in Picasso's graphic art. But neither did Goya's countryman suppress the night side of life, struggle and death, when addressing the copper plate, lithographic stone, or – in later years – the linoleum block. It is truly the whole Picasso that one encounters in the graphic œuvre. Concentration and infallible sureness of line, sovereign mastery of every technique, the intensity of expression already familiar from his painting, the sense of the decorative that lent charm to his not always practical but invariably original ceramics – all these made Picasso one of the most significant draughtsmen and printmakers of all times.

His sculptural work was no less inventive than his graphic art. In this field, too, the Spaniard was a pioneer. Not his compatriot, González, first used iron as sculptural material, but the friend whom González had agreed to help in his experiments. And when Picasso decided to make a ready-made, the results, thanks to his boundless imagination, far surpassed those of his Dadaist-Surrealist models. Not satisfied with a mere gesture or a demonstration that existing banal things could be art, he transformed them into true works of art, quite unlike Duchamp's fetishes. Picasso would take a bicycle saddle, turn it point downwards, attach handlebars to the broad end – and there was a *Bull's Head* with horns (p. 479). A configuration of this kind witnesses to the probity of Picasso's insight that the decisive factor for his art was not seeking, but finding.

"In the distorting mirror of art, reality appears undistorted." Kafka's famous statement applies perfectly to Picasso. It is the face of the century that looks out at us from the lifework of this great artist.

10
Between Revolt and Acceptance

The Unknown in Art
The New Realities of Abstract Painting

Abstract art has survived any number of obituaries. True, abstraction is no longer considered the only viable style of painting, as it still was in the 1950s. But if a so unconventional and independent-minded abstract artist as Gerhard Richter can state, "Abstract paintings are fictitious models, because they illustrate a reality which we can neither see nor describe, but the existence of which we may deduce," this insight shows that the paths of abstract painting have yet to be travelled to the end.

Born around the year 1910, abstraction passed through an adolescence that was uneventful as far as broad public resonance was concerned, then, in the mid-1940s, celebrated a belated post-revolutionary triumph. Starting from its headquarters, Paris, where it had been imported by Dutch, Russian, and German emigrés, abstraction conquered not only Europe but the entire Western world. For twenty years it reigned undisputed. The innate internationalism of abstract art, ignoring all national borders to overleap oceans and continents, seemed at the time to justify the concept of world art. Yet in hindsight, now that its dominance has waned, abstraction can be seen to have encompassed an enormous range of signs and symbols that reflected a changing, and still changing, world – despite the time-honored veracity of Hugo von St. Viktor's dictum, "The sign cannot be the truth, even though it be a sign of the truth." That entire legions of abstract camp-followers and *bons vivants* have disappeared into the void of oblivion, and that what seemed meaningful yesterday is meaningless today, is part of the painful process of "becoming classical" which every era of art history must go through.

The bias of the arguments advanced against non-objective painting over the decades becomes quite obvious in hindsight, now that the smoke has settled over the battlefield and we can play the role of detached observer. Abstraction was neither levelling nor productive of uniformity, it neither eliminated individuality nor abolished beauty, neither destroyed the human image nor caused the "death of ornament" or lost contact with reality. It led neither to fundamentalistic stultification nor to anarchistic excess. To judge the enormous scope of expressive possibilities inherent in abstraction it is enough to set the crosses and squares of a Malevich beside the revellings in paint of a Pollock, the piously

decorative painting of an Alfred Manessier beside the despairing rages of a Wols. A tension like that between the representatives of the various brands of "abstract", "non-objective", "non-figurative", "absolute", or "concrete" art – or whatever the inadequate category may be – such polar, mutually exclusive oppositions like those between Platonic geometry and the controlled chance of gestural paint orgies, have been exhibited by no other stream in 20th-century art, neither by Fauvism nor Expressionism, Cubism nor Realism, not even by Surrealism.

Nicolas de Staël
Figure on the Beach, 1952
Oil on canvas, 161.5 x 129.5 cm
Düsseldorf, Kunstsammlung
Nordrhein-Westfalen

Alberto Magnelli
Dialogue, 1956
Oil on canvas, 130 x 162 cm
Rome, Galleria Nazionale
d'Arte Moderna

*"The idea 'object' will be abandoned
but the idea 'volumes', the idea light,
and the idea 'color' will be maintained: same determination and
same impurity; the manifestation
'object' has disappeared but ... the
work remains objective in its means,
in its technique: it is not correct to
call this work abstract."*
AUGUSTE HERBIN

Auguste Herbin
Midnight, 1953
Oil on canvas, 161.5 x 114 cm
Zurich, Kunsthaus Zürich,
Association of Zurich Friends
of Art

The same distance separates the whirling, atomized forms of the early Kandinsky from Mondrian's right angles as separates Classicism from Romanticism, Apollo from Dionysus. Every direction in modern art temporarily issued in abstraction, and every one returned on a higher revolution of the spiral to transcend itself: Impressionism and Expressionism, Cubism and Surrealism, Dada and, for a time, even Verism in its harshest, most brutal form: solipsistic *l'art pour l'art* with an impassioned social commitment. It would almost seem as if in the years after 1945, European art of the first half of the century, in its post-revolutionary, as it were already "post-modern" phase, had attempted to marshal all its powers once again before temporarily abandoning the field to its American student, in whose hands it had for decades placed the means of self-realization with which he then proceeded to overcome his mentors and make New York instead of Paris the world capital of art.

The Second Modern Movement
The change of scene – or rather, preparations for it – came during the period of the Second World War. The shifting of props on the avant-garde stage was merely an external sign of a profound transformation that took place in the minds of artists and their audience. With the outbreak of war, the classical epoch of modern art came to an end; a second modern movement, which is still underway, began. The 1940s marked the watershed. In 1937 the notorious "Entartete Kunst" (Degenerate Art) exhibition took place in Munich, and in 1939 the works of the defamed artists were sold for a pittance at an auction in Lucerne. The great emigration began, first within Europe, then to the United States. The era of utopias and closed systems, which despite trenchant criticism and unmistakable signs of the approaching catastrophe still retained an idealistic belief in the improve-

ment of man and his world, came irrevocably to an end. Now, art, whether abstract or figurative, is always a reply to reality. It is no wonder that in a confused, agitated, brutalized world the reply should have been ambivalent. Out of the chaos of the "incubation period," as art critic Laszlo Glozer has characterized the years between 1939 and 1945, emerged the radical propositions of a new art, in the face of which one can no longer allege that all of the decisive arguments in the 20th-century art discourse were advanced by 1910, and that what came after 1914 was merely repetition or, at best, variation.

For the avant-garde, "the Second World War... cannot be considered a divide," says Glozer, but represented a "hinge-point." And he adds, "The collision of modernity with current history surely had one effect: the motif of liberty was made public, became a leitmotif of reception.... Thus began a new phase in the history of effect – that of perceived, received modernity."

The "revolution of modern art," in Sedlmayr's phrase, no longer played itself out within the aesthetic realm alone, but advanced into society. Just short of a decade later the 1968 Paris May revolt would signal changes in political and social consciousness whose effects can still be felt today. After 1945 the avant-garde emerged "from the phase of limited experiments, out of private circles and initiatives, into the exposed status of public attention; out of isolation into what may not have amounted to general popularity, but did represent a solemnly underwritten legality."

Another point Glozer makes is the "internal alteration in the framework of avant-garde art" that took place during the war years and the years of crisis that preceded them: "The new art which emerged from this as early as the 1940s, while it was rooted in the epoch-making achievement of the avant-garde, actually resulted from immediate concern," reflected artists' experience of the shock-waves that shook "the value systems of civilization, culture and art."

The work of Wols in Europe, and of Pollock in America, seismographically recorded these shock-waves, as different as their intellectual positions and their results may have been. Such is the background, along with the sense of a new-found freedom and a belief that art could overcome all national barriers to embrace the globe, against which the temporary triumph of post-war abstract art should be seen.

Beginnings in Silence

The abstract tidal wave gathered force in silence, in part even in underground exile. Stalinist, Nazi, and – in lesser degree – Italian fascist terror, which had degraded art to an instrument of state propaganda, had interrupted a development in full flow, initially in Russia, then in Germany. In Italy the caesura was not so grave, because Mussolini not only understood nothing about L'art brut – unlike the artist and architect *manqué* Hitler – to an extent admitted this failing. How dependent art is on liberty is indicated by the astonishing fact that the decades of Stalinist and fascist tyranny, despite immense official support for conformist art, produced not a single painting or sculpture that has remained in the awareness of the cultured world.

Writing in Germany today, one cannot emphasize this fact enough, because a dangerously simplifying, ostensibly "objectifying" historiography is in the process of reducing the unparalleled brutality of the National Socialists to a "normal" level by pointing out atrocities committed by others elsewhere. In this connection belongs the attempt to convince today's public, especially young people, that, since we all know "anything goes", something in the nature of substantial art existed in Nazi Germany. The only reply to this is to state, categorically, that it did *not* exist. German art between 1933 and 1945 was produced in exile, or, to a lesser extent, in the "inner emigration." Klee, Kirchner, and Beckmann, to name only three, were driven from the country. Max Ernst lived in France from the 1920s onwards and later was compelled to emigrate a second time, to the United States. Schlemmer's *Window Pictures*, Willi Baumeister's *Eidos* series, and finally Nolde's *Unpainted Pictures*, all were executed under the protection of courageous friends and out of the public eye. Ernst Wilhelm Nay's *Lofoten* canvases were done in Norway. Artists such as Otto Freundlich, who fell into the hands of Hitler's henchmen, were murdered.

The works of the persecuted and suppressed are now very much in the public eye, hanging in museums all over the world, not lastly in Germany. German art of the period between Hitler's takeover of power and his demise is thus fully represented. The art that was offi-

Otto Freundlich
Composition, 1932
Oil on canvas, 161.5 x 130 cm
Basel, Öffentliche Kunstsammlung
Basel, Kunstmuseum

Bram van Velde
Painting, 1960
Oil on canvas, 130 x 195 cm
Private collection

Camille Graeser
Translocation II, 1969
Oil on canvas, 120 x 120 cm
Napa (CA), Hess Collection

Max Bill
Four Double Colors, 1967
Oil on canvas, 80 x 80 cm
Bern, Kunstmuseum Bern,
Anne-Marie and Victor Loeb
Donation

cially tolerated and furthered during the Third Reich falls into the category of kitsch. These paintings (and writings) exhibit those "contradictory elements" which Saul Friedländer has unmistakably called by name in his essay *Kitsch und Tod* (Kitsch and Death): "... support of the existing order of things on the one hand, and of death and destruction on the other.... Here the visions of harmony, there the firestorms of the apocalypse; here the flower-wreathed girls and snow-capped peaks of the Bavarian Alps, there the heroes' dirge of the Feldherrn-halle, the ecstasy of the twilight of the gods, and the visions of the end of the world."

Fritz Glarner
Relational Painting, Tondo 36,
1954/55
Oil on composition board;
diameter 104 cm
USA, private collection

Unlike the field of literature, that of the visual arts produced no artist of rank under Nazism or fascism. Not even Hitler himself was satisfied with the results of his policies. And when a gifted young artist like Arno Breker submitted himself to the reigning ideology, artistic decline was the price he paid.

In the former Eastern Bloc, too, only Krushchev's *Thaw* brought remarkable talents back to light, in Poland, then-Yugoslavia, then-Czechoslovakia, and elsewhere. Many of these artists linked up with dormant traditions, or with dominating tendencies in the West; some adopted abstraction, others, like Strzemiński and Stazewski, even provided impulses to the Western vanguard ("Zero"). Their formal idiom had often been developed in the underground, and not without danger to themselves.

In France, abstraction remained a relatively weak tendency during the years between 1920 and 1940. At least it presented no serious rival to the great masters Picasso, Braque, Léger, or the Surrealists, especially as Delaunay, painter of the Eiffel Tower and *Views from a Window*, who had not only approached the frontier of abstraction but crossed it several times, returned in later years – like Villon and, temporarily, Herbin – to a more or less definite objectivity. What was on view in Paris at that period in the way of abstract painting was a weak reflection of things that were happening outside France – something for connoisseurs and adepts, and for a few artist-colleagues who even tried their hand at it for a time, before hesitating and returning to the objective world.

The French sense of reality long resisted the infiltration of utopian universal harmonies à la De Stijl and Slavic romanticism à la Kandinsky. Malraux, once a Marxist author, later a conservative and minister of culture under de Gaulle, long successfully hindered the acquisition of a Mondrian for the Musée National d'Art Modern in Paris. French artists eschewed abstract painting until they saw that *bonne peinture* in the French tradition was possible even using non-objective forms, and that abstraction was not only, as they somewhat one-sidedly imagined, either frenetic, uncontrolled action or a drawing-board art that extolled the benefits of technology, the submission of the individual to the mass, of man to the machine, of painting to architecture. The Parisian individualists either rejected the idea of painting with a function, as industrial design or applied art or advertising, or they remained initially distrustful and aloof. After all, the metropolis of modern art had long courageously hindered the penetration of functionalist architecture – apart from a few Art Nouveau arabesques and that giant tinker-toy, the Eiffel Tower – into its grand 18th-century design. Saint-Ouen and La Défense were still undreamt-of.

The "Liberation"

Credit for the emergence of an independent abstract painting in France must ultimately be given not so much to Kandinsky and Mondrian as, astonishingly, to Klee, the "level-headed Romantic" from Germany. Roger Bissière, teacher of Manessier and Jean Bazaine, in his maturity an "abstract intimiste", admired Klee, as his paintings clearly indicate. Bissière also published a portion of Klee's theoretical writings in French translation, which is to say, shorn of myth and mystery, he picked brilliance and grace notes out of the nocturnal obscurity. Manessier, in turn, placed these transformed elements in the service of his Christian symbolism. What preceded this development was abstract painting at second-hand, post-revolutionary exploitation of revolutionary ideas, not comparable in terms of formal power or intellectual intensity to the pioneering works of a Kandinsky, Mondrian, or Malevich.

The gradual subversion of the objective Ecole de Paris continued without much ado, but with consequences that were all the more far-reaching. In 1924 the energetic van Doesburg organized the first Paris exhibition of the De Stijl group. In 1930, shortly before his

death, he began editing the programmatic journal *Art Concret*. As mentioned, the Dutch artists rejected the adjective "abstract." They spoke of "concrete" art, explaining that color, form and plane were quite concrete values which represented a reality in themselves. In 1929 the first comprehensive show of Kandinsky's works went on display in Paris, followed a year later by the first international exhibition of abstract art. With it, the discussion on the aims of the new painting got officially underway in the world capital of art of the first half of the 20th century.

A group called "Abstraction-Création" was formed, laying the foundation for the international abstract Ecole de Paris. Developments were considerably advanced by the move to Paris of the Russian sculptor-brothers Pevsner and Gabo, by Kandinsky's flight there from Nazi Germany, and also by Mondrian's activity, the presence of Arp and several Surrealists, and finally by the infiltration of Russian Constructivist and Bauhaus ideas.

The fascination exerted by these ideas proved to be extraordinarily strong. "Liberation" was the operational word, as it had been for the revolutionaries around 1910. Color and form were at last given full autonomy as values in themselves; "purity of means" became an axiom. It was not until the 1940s that the concept of Nouvelles Réalités, or new realities, cropped up, and was subsequently applied to literature as well.

"Loss of the Center" and "Atomization"

But the new art had many opponents. Their oft-reiterated arguments were that its purism was "inhumane" and "despairing," and that it would lead to sheer, chaotic anarchy. This led to the hypothesis of the "loss of the center," of the "rootlessness" of abstraction or the "empty void" in which it floated. Critics accused abstract art of being an obscure affair addressed only to experts, called its concepts arrogant, arcane, and self-serving, said it aimed at disintegrating the visible world, called it a conspiracy of the intelligentsia against the poor, helpless public. As one can see, the defaming arguments remained the same, while the object – or lack of

"Art for me has always been abstract motion. Abstract motion excels over physical or naturalistic motion in its speed and feeling of exhaltation. Everything is motion, everything moves. There is no fixed point in the universe." OLLE BAERTLING

an object – to which they were addressed, changed. The Jeremiads and pamphlets could just as well have been directed against later styles, such as L'art informel, Action Painting, Minimal and Conceptual Art – and in fact, although the vocabulary was different, this is exactly what came to pass.

The title of Sedlmayr's book, *Loss of the Center,* became just as much of a slogan as that of Max Picard's essay, "Atomization in Modern Art". In the eyes of these cultural pessimists, the key artists of the first half of the century and their predecessors were, roughly speaking, not diagnosticians of the despairing or hopeless state of the world, but themselves partly responsible for it. In other words, not those who created the situation were guilty, but those who described it or drew critical conclusions from it – who supposedly fouled

their own nest. Then as now, the conservative critics called for a return to lost values, not realizing that a return was impossible because the clock cannot be turned back.

Rarely has a stream in art triggered so much debate, embittered on both sides, as has abstract art. Instead of concentrating on the visual evidence, the colors, forms, and rhythms of the pictures involved, the opponents of abstraction mounted polemics and issued pamphlets, which its advocates answered with the provocative exaggerations of a camp fighting against prejudice. Both sides fell into an error that has long been avoided in discussions of music: They asked about the meaning of abstract painting and attempted to explain it in verbal terms, forgetting that painting, like music, is a nonverbal language.

"The work of art is an independent organism, on a par with nature and in its deepest inner essence without connection with it... insofar as nature is taken to be the visible surface" of things, wrote Wilhelm Worringer at the beginning of the century in his book *Abstraktion und Einfühlung (*Abstraction and Empathy, 1908), clairvoyantly written – as a dissertation – before abstract art in the narrow sense even existed. The debate for and against abstract art that set in after 1945 was unparalleled in terms of obstinacy and duration, even our so eminently polemical century.

From the vantage point of the present day this seems all the more surprising because of the fact that as the abstract wave subsided, it grew increasingly obvious that while the non-objective painting of mid-century may have had an evolutionary character, it was certainly not revolutionary any more. The occasional cry of "Dump Picasso!" or "Down with geometry!" was harmless by comparison to the revolt against the Academy, the aesthetic revolution, that took place at the start of the century.

Cosmopolitans of Art

The story of the emergence of the Ecole de Paris was not an exciting, suspenseful drama; it was the story of a gradual, hesitant, as it were "trans-avant-garde" digestion of impulses that came from outside. Slavic influences mixed with Germanic and Latin ones; currents from all over Europe flowed into the city on the Seine. There was formed the type – later to be so bitterly criticized – of the "cosmopolitan of art," for whom national traits and ties ceased to be of importance, who absorbed stimuli wherever he found them, for whom the concepts of "blood" and "soil" had been emptied of meaning.

Indicatively the pioneers of the School of Paris were not French. Vordemberge-Gildewart, heir of De Stijl and Constructivism, was a German, as was the painter-sculptor Otto Freundlich (p. 221). Freundlich, born in Stolp, Pomerania, in 1878, was discovered by the Nazis in his hiding-place in the Pyrenees in March 1943, deported to Poland, and died a short time later as an

inmate in Maidanek. Stylistically, Freundlich was influenced by Delaunay and his chromatic colors. The De Stijl followers Félix Del Marle and César Domela (p. 172) came to Paris from Belgium and Holland. Alberto Magnelli was an Italian, more precisely a Florentine. As his Cubist-derived, architecturally rigorous compositions indicate, not even abstract art can exist in a void, cut off from every relationship to history. In Magnelli's somewhat dry paintings, links with the Renaissance architects Leon Battista Alberti and Filippo Brunelleschi, with Uccello and Piero della Francesca, are clearly evident (p. 220 above).

With Ruler and Compass

Among French painters, Auguste Herbin was the first to seriously adopt a rigorous abstraction in which he expunged every memory of the visible world seen in his earlier work (p. 220 below). Herbin practiced pure geometry, establishing relationships between the elementary, flat forms of triangle, rectangle, circle, and arc segment. There were no half-tones, gradations, or gradual transitions in Herbin's compositions. Though they represented an interesting and highly skilled beginning, they already contained the end of strict geometrical abstraction, that intellectual glass bead game aimed at plumbing the secrets of proportion and number – facile, perfectionistic shapes of poster-like two-dimensionality which, in the hands of lesser talents, stiffened into dry-as-dust academicism.

Ben Nicholson
February 1959 (Half Moon), 1959
Oil on canvas, 160 x 149 cm
Private collection

"After all, every movement of human life is affected by form and color; everything we see, touch, think and feel is linked up with it, so that when an artist can use these elements freely and creatively it can be a tremendously potent influence in our lives." BEN NICHOLSON

Atanasio Soldati
Composition, 1934
Oil on canvas, 103.5 x 57 cm
Milan, Civico Museo
d'Arte Contemporanea

Adolf Fleischmann
Abstract, 1959
Oil on canvas, 96.5 x 78.7 cm
Private collection

responsibility, the same thoroughness, and the same striving for truth, devoid of all bravado, that underlay his service as a national councillor. In all his œuvre – whether in painting, sculpture, or industrial design – one finds nothing half-hearted. Everything is right, everything fits, everything is as intelligent as it is precisely calculated. Bill's work was inspired by a fascination with numbers. Its aesthetic appeal derived from the harmony of exactly balanced relationships of form and color. For him, an aesthetic configuration was the result of mathematical, verifiable thinking, a brain-game. Bill took the ideas of the Bauhaus to their logical conclusion. Whether painting or sculpture, in which he was perhaps more successful (p. 456), art for Bill was no longer the creative act of an individual but a means to the super-ordinate end of designing a more humane environment.

Precise construction of a painting based on geometric principles was likewise the guiding idea of Camille Graeser (p. 222). For him the painting was a *creatio ex nihilo*, a configuration without relation to the world of objects, but shaped in analogy to the laws of musical composition. Like Kandinsky, Graeser spoke of the "musical sound" of a painting, which could be achieved solely through proportion, and the values of color, form, and line.

Richard Paul Lohse (p. 223), who since 1942 has concentrated exclusively on perpendicularly oriented color fields, is the most rigorous of the concrete artists in the wake of Constructivism. His visual thinking is marked by considerations of a social nature, for he envisions the concrete utopia of a harmony between man and his environment. Like Bill's, Lohse's variation-rich sequences and arrangements of colored forms are based on numerical relationships, which determine both the

Herbin's approach, like the later one of Vasarely, not only inspired Op Art, it also set off a new wave of concrete painting, along the lines of the concept of "concretion" coined by van Doesburg and Arp. In this context mention should be made of a later group, the "Zurich Concretes," which included Max Bill, Paul Lohse, and Camille Graeser. For Bill (p. 222), first rector of the Ulm School of Design in the 1950s, there was no hard and fast line between fine and applied art. In his eyes the design of a chair, a folding table, or an electric socket was just as significant a task as composing a painting or sculpture. Bill approached every task with the same sense of

Alfred Manessier
Crown of Thorns, 1951
Oil on paper, mounted on canvas,
58 x 48.5 cm
Essen, Museum Folkwang

Gustave Singier
Window on the Sea, 1957
Oil on canvas, 210 x 170 cm
Rome, private collection

"And to yield to one's wonderment
requires a necessary precariousness.
But no less precarious the continuing
awakening to preserve expressive
harmony." PIERRE TAL-COAT

relation of the fields and color groups to one another, and their relation to the format as a whole. Despite this veritably ascetic formal discipline, which is surpassed only by Albers's *Homages to the Square* (p. 179), Lohse's rigorous compositions appear to push beyond the edges of the canvas. And despite the waiver of any trace of individual touch, the brilliancy of their colors lends them a vibrant, quasi musical lyricism.

The Belgian Victor Servranckx (p. 223) moved the orbit of the Paris group "Abstraction-Création" centered on Ozenfant and Le Corbusier. He was also intrigued by Léger. Contacts with Eastern European Constructivism and even to Dutch De Stijl, on the other hand, were scant. Still, Servranckx's thinking was dominated by the Constructivist ideals of an elimination of the border-line between fine and applied art, and a linking of art and life. More strongly than other concrete artists he was fascinated by the world of machinery, to whose functional precision he attempted to create an equivalent in painting – pictures in whose autonomous color-shapes it is difficult to detect their source of inspiration.

A different case is that of Ben Nicholson, a British painter whose second wife was the sculptress Barbara Hepworth. Both of Nicholson's parents were artists. His father, Sir William Nicholson, was a very highly regarded Post-Impressionist in his day. Out of opposition to his parents the young Nicholson soon defected to Cubism, to Braque and above all Gris, whose cool, structural thinking deeply impressed him. At the age of 40 Nicholson met Mondrian, a meeting that determined his subsequent development.

Nicholson (p. 225) attempted to combine the De Stijl idea of a universal harmony with the structural principles of Cubism, within an autonomous, non-illusionistic pictorial space. In his sensitive drawings, sparing line is used to trace the mystery of cathedral portals, the complicated structure of vaulting, and the beautiful forms of commonplace things. From this point Nicholson's path led him to abstract compositions in which occasional reminiscences of objects appear, what Her-

bert Read calls "last vestiges of reality." The motifs are reduced to a few, basic shapes: rectangle, circle, and sometimes the abbreviated form of a lovely pitcher or jug. Nicholson's "geometric lyricism" draws sustenance from a formal tension between straight line and curve, between abstract, artificial configuration and fragment of the visible world. His palette is subdued; Nicholson's compositions, inspired by musical and architectural forms, are not seldom executed white in white or grey in grey. Occasionally he raises the picture plane into low relief, and emphasizes the play of light and shade.

Geometric painting of every variety was disseminated all over the world. It found adherents in Italy (Atanasio Soldati; p. 225), in Sweden (Olle Baertling; p. 224), in Germany (Adolf Fleischmann; p. 226), in Brazil (Almir Mavignier). Yet few of its later proponents were able to match, let alone surpass, the innovative force of its pioneers and classical representatives. But one thing should not be forgotten: The intellectual effort and rigorous focus of the Platonists of modern art, by harking back to the Egyptians, the early Greeks, the Early Renaissance, to Chardin's and Poussin's well-considered pictorial frameworks, as well as to ancient human symbols such as the labyrinth, zigzag, plait, spiral, etc., liberated these artistic means from the yoke of non-aesthetic, anecdotal encumberments. As Thomas Mann said in *Doktor Faustus* with regard to the twelve-tone scale in music, geometric abstraction "reinstated [composition] in its mean." In another place Mann wrote,

Pierre Tal-Coat
Passage to the Bottom of the
Canyon, 1956
Oil on canvas, 190 x 195 cm
Paris, Musée National d'Art
Moderne, Centre Georges
Pompidou

Jean Le Moal
Autumn, 1958–1960
Oil on canvas, 130 x 81 cm
Paris, private collection

Roger Bissière
Grey, 1958
Oil on canvas, 116 x 89 cm
Paris, private collection

Maurice Estève
Vermuse, 1958
Oil on canvas, 100 x 81 cm
Private collection

"Organization is everything. Without it there is absolutely nothing, least of all art." This might have been the credo of the geometric abstractionists. Their art was the expression of a revolt of European rationality against uncontrolled emotion, of cool objectivity against factitious sentimentality, of order against anarchy. The perfect form they sought for, to speak with Plato, seemed to represent "that which always is." Against the backdrop of the rampant irrationality that led to the second world catastrophe, this attitude surely had its historical significance. Franz Marc would probably have shared it.

Yet what the geometricians of modern art ended up designing was the construction plan for an abstract-utopian world, hermetically sealed, without direct connection with nature or with the social reality of the era. In the long run, this purist ivory tower naturally proved uninhabitable. The alternative nature *or* abstraction was too dogmatic and absolute to be viable. Artists remembered that art, realistic or not, could never be pure repre-

Jean Bazaine
The Clearing, 1951
Oil on canvas, 120 x 96 cm
Private collection

Gérard Schneider
Opus 87 B, 1955
Oil on canvas, 116 x 89 cm
Paris, private collection

sentation, that its aim and essence was not quotation but transformation and formal design. Back then Bazaine, soon to become one of the leading figures in the *tradition française* movement, pointed out that even Jan van Eyck was a great abstract artist in so far as it was not verisimilitude that determined the rank of his work but the quality of its form and color.

"Inventing the World"

Perhaps it speaks for itself that the Fronde against Platonism in painting first gathered force in France. It was there that the notion of Nouvelles Réalités first began to circulate. Artists realized that what one cannot see can nevertheless be real – as, in our own day, Gerhard Richter has once again expressly pointed out. It was physics that served to open artists' eyes to the complex structure of matter and its ambivalent nature. Perpetual truths were relativized, and two world wars did their part to once and for all destroy the naive trust in traditional, immutable values.

According to the proponents of the New Realities, conventional, realistic painting only represented the appearance and surface of things, not their essence or core. Out of this negative insight they drew the positive conclusion that it must be possible to "invent a world," a pictorial world which, on the one hand, was both more true than illusory appearance, and on the other, not so far removed from reality as was geometric abstraction. This world of imagery would be based in equal measure on the visual and mental experience of the artist, which, freely translated and independently of "natural" colors and forms, would take shape in paint on canvas as the artist's own creation, a Nouvelle Réalité .

The artist would no longer depict an immediate impression but the echo or resonance it set up in his mind and imagination. Klee had already progressed far in this direction: *Flora on Sand* (1927) was the title of a watercolor composed of irregular squares and a few rectangles in luminous hues.

Thus the retreat of art from reality, its escape into utopia, was at least partially reversed, for a critique of contemporary conditions was not attempted. The

horrors of the Second World War and its aftermath, artists believed, were simply too monstrous to allow for direct depiction in art. These were the years in which Theodor W. Adorno's proclamation that after Auschwitz, no more poems could be written, was considered an incontrovertible truth. Until poets, not least one who had been immediately involved in the Holocaust, Paul Celan, proved the invalidity of yet another absolute statement.

Maria Elena Vieira da Silva
Theatre of Gérard Philipe, 1975
Oil on canvas, 162 x 130 cm
Colmar, Musée d'Unterlinden

Maria Elena Vieira da Silva
Breton Festival, 1952
Oil on burlap, 92 x 72.5 cm
Private collection

*"When I am in front of my painting
and palette, there is a constant
effort; a little more white, a little
more green, it is too cold, too warm,
lines that ascend, that descend, that
meet, that part. This means so much
in painting and so little in words."*
MARIA ELENA VIEIRA DA SILVA

French Tradition

In 1941, Jean Bazaine mounted in Paris an exhibition titled "Twenty Painters in the French Tradition." Apart from the initiator, the participants included Alfred Manessier, Léon Gischia, Maurice Estève, Edouard Pignon, and Jean Le Moal (p. 227). The express reference to their national tradition could be understood as a gesture of resistance in several respects: firstly, as resistance to the military occupation of France by a foreign power, Germany; secondly, to the domination of foreigners in the abstract Ecole de Paris; and thirdly, as resistance to the geometric abstractionists' "un-French" disdain of *bonne peinture.*

Roger Bissière (p. 228) had paved the way for the traditionalists. The paintings of Bazaine reflected a closer affinity to the landscapes of Impressionism (pp. 228, 229) than to the influence of Cubism or to certain Klee-inspired paintings by Bissière himself. As he himself put it, he let "the subject disappear as an object" in order to "justify it as form." In other words, an impression of nature was replaced by a painterly system of chromatic and formal rapports or correspondences. Bazaine did not work on the basis of any pre-conceived plan; he let his hand follow his inspiration. The fundamental element was always color, which for him possessed space-creating and atmospheric qualities in one. Bazaine's sophisticated palette reveals the influence of Bonnard, while the atmosphere in his canvases was Impressionist in origin.

"The potential today seems to me to lie in nonobjective art, because through it the painter can best find his way back to reality and to an awareness of that which is essential in it." The words are Manessier's, and they precisely express the mood of those post-war years in which abstract art triumphed, with an exclusiveness which it is nowadays difficult to grasp.

For the Christian artist Manessier (p. 226), the regaining of a lost reality represented the certainty of salvation in the midst of a transient world. The form this reality took was the pictorial symbol. Painting thus became an act of meditation, a path to an awareness of self and of man's position in the world. Manessier depicted the *Passion* as a solemn arrangement of abstract symbolic black configurations against a red ground, signs representing the instruments of martyrdom against a hue that underscored the deep seriousness of the theme. But unfortunately Manessier's artistic skills were not always up to the profundity of the task he set himself.

The work of Maurice Estève has proven more lasting (p. 228). A series of brilliantly colored still lifes and interiors, executed with bravado and daring in the choice of unconventional croppings, was the first culmination of his career. The second was a series of ornamental and architectonic abstractions in luminous, sometimes somewhat garish colors – blue, red, green, yellow. Estève's work, too, is based on actual visual experiences, memories and recollections of which appear in the compositions. Reality is transformed and rearranged into islands, continents, fields, and bars of color.

A position between abstraction and objectivity is occupied by the free figuration of Charles Lapicque, who has produced a number of interesting paintings employing abrupt changes in perspective and graphically structured autonomous color (p. 229). Later Lapicque let his compositions be dominated by pure color, and waived the integration of color configuration and motif – with highly varying success, it must be admitted.

The tension between abstraction and objectivity reaches a peak in the œuvre of Nicolas de Staël, who was born in St. Petersburg, Russia, in 1914 and ended his life in 1955 by jumping from a window in Antibes. Instead of would not be mistaken to see a connection between the weave of her transparent architectural visions and the figures enmeshed in imaginary spaces in Alberto Giacometti's paintings (ill. below), although these admittedly far surpass da Silva's in terms of force of vision and pictorial realization. Yet her filigree imagery likewise expresses a fundamental feeling of the epoch: the anxiety of modern man, his fear of being caught in the labyrinth of a world over which he has lost control, the prime symbol of which is the big city, New Babylon.

Expressionist Art in the Abstract Mode

The development of abstract art after the war led from puristic objectification based on mathematically calculated form, through an autonomous realm of signs suffused with memories of nature, to issue finally in a depiction of subjective feelings and sensations, mental reflections of artists' experiences of reality – an abstract expressionist art, in a word, which culminated in L'art informel in Europe and Action Painting in the United States.

At the beginning of this new development stood the work of a German artist, Hans Hartung, a native of Leipzig (p. 232). His checkered biography reflected the notorious restlessness of the period. Like every truly

Alberto Giacometti
Head of a Man
(Diego Giacometti), 1951
Oil on canvas, 73.3 x 60.3 cm
Private collection

addressing the issue of "objective or non-objective" in his painting, De Staël attempted to overcome this unproductive alternative and re-create a lost unity. His work accordingly unfolded between the poles of abstraction and objectivity, tending first more to the one, then to the other, before the dialogue was interrupted in mid-sentence by his suicide on the Côte d'Azur. De Staël had by no means spoken the last word in his art. His late works were no longer as powerful and encrusted with spatula passages as the earlier canvases, as seen in the *Football Players* (done in various versions), which is painted in more fluent, lighter strokes of the brush and palette knife, larger in format, and indicative of the artist's return to an emphasis on the subject (ill. above and p. 219). But the late works also show that De Staël was not able to solve his self-posed problem, which Werner Schmalenbach defines as "measuring the boundless with the dimensions of painting." The artist apparently must have felt that he had arrived at a dead end, despite the fact that the sophisticated beauty of his relaxed, free, quite unconventional compositions would suggest that, on the contrary, he was on the verge of developing innovative pictorial possibilities.

The enormous range of approaches covered by the generic term abstract painting is illustrated by a comparison between the apparently so dynamic work of De Staël and the labyrinthine urban visions of the Portuguese artist Maria Elena Vieira da Silva (p. 230). If the paintings of the unhappy Russian seem like a transmutation of the intellectual principles of Cubism into a vitalistic, almost barbarian emotionalism, the hallucinatory world of da Silva is rooted in Surrealism. Perhaps it investigations Hartung's innate musicality, his intensive scientific interests, and his feeling for poetry served as curbs on his emotionality. As early as 1922 he was already working in an abstract idiom. What especially intrigued him about these studies was the personal touch, the "handwriting" of the artist, as an immediate expression of his temperament. "The deeper we immerse ourselves in our own personality," Hartung said, "the more clear and convincing will be the image we can give of our inmost selves, but also, the more comprehensive our expression will be." This remark amounts to a credo, a dedication to self-imaging. Hartung found a method to achieve this which was very much his own: the psychograph in painting, the spontaneous record of emotional and mental states ranging from euphoria to depression. A polished technique enabled Hartung to retain differentiation and precision even when working under extreme emotional tension.

Against usually light, loosely brushed backgrounds the artist set sheaves of dark, linear, agitated strokes that recorded an existential moment. Hartung painted these psychographs with great energy and sometimes as if in a trance. The procedure, by analogy to Surrealist theory and practice, was automatic in nature. Complex experiences, desires, and ideas flowed together under Hartung's hand to congeal into a pictorial sign. Dramatic accumulations, collisions, overlappings, and corrections resulted, concentric force-fields alternated with nervous lineatures, heavy paint passages with graphic inter-

Hans Hartung
T 1956-9, 1956
Oil on canvas, 180 x 137 cm
Paris, private collection

Hans Hartung
T 1962-U 4, 1962
Oil on canvas, 180 x 111 cm
Private collection

original German artist, Hartung, who had his first public exposure in Dresden in 1931, soon ran into trouble with the Gestapo after Hitler came to power. The critics Will Grohmann and Christian Zervos, in a memorable German-French collaboration involving some very clever maneuvering, assisted Hartung in leaving the country. Like many others before him, Hartung too became a Parisian painter. His identification with his host country went so far that he volunteered for the Foreign Legion in 1939 and subsequently fought with de Gaulle in Africa. In 1944 Hartung lost a leg in fighting near Belfort, and the year after he was awarded French citizenship. That a man who lived so uncompromising a life should have adopted an expressive approach to painting is no wonder, particularly as Hartung stemmed from a country in which expressionism of one kind or another was not only a period style but a fundamental artistic tendency.

Accordingly, after initially exploring the mysteries of Rembrandt, Hartung gravitated to Kokoschka, Nolde, Marc, and not least, to Kandinsky. In the course of his ships of asymmetrical color fields. The palette, at first subdued and tone-in-tone, over the years unfolded a stronger, sometimes festive brilliance in passages effectively contrasted to darker color fields. Though the minor key is sometimes sounded, it is rarer than a brilliant major chord. What distinguishes Poliakoff's paintings from those of his Cubist predecessors, apart from their generally intense palette, is the unclassical treatment of forms, which often appear to virtually extend beyond the canvas edge or penetrate into the plane from outside, the way the forms interlock, and their limitation to a comparatively narrow range of shapes. In recent years Poliakoff's accomplished painting has again been accorded the respect it deserves, as indeed the entire abstract Ecole de Paris has come in for a juster appraisal, after having been first over-rated, then underrated, during its heyday.

Pierre Soulages
Painting 10th September 1953, 1953
Oil on canvas, 195 x 130 cm
New York, private collection

Pierre Soulages
Painting 21 June 1953, 1953
Oil on canvas, 195 x 130 cm
Private collection

weaves. In these dynamic hieroglyphs the artist's personality was laid bare.

Later Hartung's approach grew calmer, the pictorial signs lighter, more graceful. His fan-like configurations, when successful, had something of the spiritual charm of Far Eastern calligraphy. Brushstrokes were incised into the surface as negative shapes, and with the aid of a new spray technique, dark clouds of color expanded across the canvas – the image became a meditational panel.

Perhaps even more compelling is the earnest and powerful expressive abstraction of Pierre Soulages, whose work has recently come in for a re-evaluation (ill. above and right). Early on in his career, Soulages began to concern himself with archaic and early Romanistic art, and some of the dignity of that era has accordingly entered his dynamic abstractions. Using a special spatula, the artist set monumental swathes of a shimmering black derived from Manet against monochrome, often light backgrounds which suggest boundless space, achieving impressive effects of contrast. "The waiver of the loquaciousness of line," Soulages formulated his artistic credo, "corresponds to a waiver of the loquaciousness of color.... I was always of the opinion that the more limited the means are, the stronger the expression will be."

The Russian artist Serge Poliakoff (p. 234) set out to develop the principles of Cubism and De Stijl into an original idiom. While graphic networks initially were employed to lend stability to the compositions, soon they began to rely solely on sophisticated inter-relation-

Serge Poliakoff
Red, Blue and Black – Abstract
Composition, 1957
Oil on canvas, 115 x 89 cm
Saarbrücken, Saarland Museum

Serge Poliakoff
Composition, 1950
Oil on wood, 130.5 x 97.2 cm
New York, Solomon
R. Guggenheim Museum

Farewell to Subject Matter
Abstract Art in Germany

In Eastern Europe, even in the former Soviet Union after the final enthronment by Stalin in the early 1930s of Socialist Realism as the sole officially sanctioned style, painters and sculptors continued to work in an abstract vein, despite the fact that it could cost them their career or even their liberty. One of the key groups that has since come to Western attention is "Movement," headed by kinetic and performance artist Lew Nusberg. The existence of this group alone disproves the orthodox Marxist hypothesis that abstract art of whatever variety can flourish only in a capitalist climate. No one continues to believe such hypotheses now that "actually existing" pseudo-socialism has crumbled, especially as Socialist Realism, in its shallow, doctrinaire form, had long since discredited itself as absolutely petty-bourgeois. The Hungarian communist Vasarely and the Hungarian

socialist Schöffer, who both lived in France and were leading representatives of abstract painting, have since had museums devoted to their work in their native country. In Russia, too, the realization is growing that Suprematism and Constructivism represented the truly revolutionary art. In Poland, the Muzeum Sztuki in Lódz has long since become one of the most significant international centers of classical and contemporary modernism.

That abstract art can signal resistance against an all-powerful tradition grown stultified in academicism, resistance against empty conventions and normative aesthetics, but also against political bullying, became evident in Germany between 1933 and 1945. When the war ended, a non-objective art came to light which stood on a par with European developments on all sides – a small cultural miracle that the world registered with some bafflement. To many people at the time in Germany, abstract art seemed like a beacon light of freedom in a period of total repression. This position was taken at one of the first of the subsequently famous Darmstadt Talks in 1950 by the artist Willi Baumeister, during a debate with the orthodox art historian Sedlmayr on the topic of *The Human Image in Our Era*. At that period, heated debates between representatives of figurative and abstract art became an international phenomenon.

Romantic Idealism

The path of Willi Baumeister (ill. right) to what he termed "absolute painting" was a long one. Born in Stuttgart, Baumeister was no child prodigy, as little as was his ideal, Cézanne, with whom he shared in common a sedentary and superficially uneventful life. In terms of his visual thinking Baumeister had an affinity with Klee, whom he admired as much as he did Miró. What ultimately concerned him was the unknown, the never-before-seen, the unheard-of. To his mind, these could take on material shape only in abstract painting. "Abstract forms," said Baumeister, "can contain, retain or absorb real forces.... Non-objective manifestations of the human spirit are open to the transcendental. Objective depictions are always more or less burdened by the earth's gravity, and their pinions are not free." This metaphysical, romantically tinged idealism was anchored in Baumeister's work by a formal discipline which he owed to an intensive study of Seurat, Cézanne, Cubism and Constructivism, as well as by an emotional reserve which consciously kept its distance from the fervors of Expressionism. In every phase of his diverse career, clarity and harmony were Baumeister's foremost concerns.

Baumeister was a fellow-student of Schlemmer, and his most important teacher was Hoelzel, who addressed himself to the problem of abstract rhythms and color chords at an early date. Baumeister's early figurative works were related, in terms of spirit and aesthetic, to Hans von Marées and Cézanne. After the First World War, searching for a new order in the face of general chaos – as Marc had written in his war letters – Baumeister came to Constructivism, to Le Corbusier's and Ozenfant's Purism, and especially to Léger. While his theme remained the human figure, he subjected it to a harsh, stringent geometric, mechanical order. Thereafter the artist abandoned traditional brushwork, adding sand to the oil paint to produce rough, low-relief surfaces. The painting, Baumeister believed, must become a solid, constructed, final entity. The *Wall Pictures* of those years can be described as designs for an as yet non-existent architecture.

But these rigorous montages did not remain Baumeister's last word. Elements of the fantastic, the surreal entered the compositions of the – still figurative – *Sport Pictures*. As this theme itself suggests, static pictorial frameworks were now superseded by painterly evocations of movement. The final turn to "The Unknown in Art," as Baumeister titled a manifesto written

Willi Baumeister
Bluxao V, 1955
Oil on cardboard, 130 x 100 cm
Hamburg, Hamburger Kunsthalle

Willi Baumeister
Safer, 1953
Oil on canvas, 65 x 54 cm
Stuttgart, Archiv Baumeister

Fritz Winter
Motive Forces of the Earth, 1944
Oil on paper, 29.5 x 21 cm
Ahlen, Fritz-Winter-Haus

"My art does not legitimize itself through elements that lie outside the realm of art. Its meaning can be comprehended – experienced – by looking at the elemental painting."
ERNST WILHELM NAY

age-old messages in terms of a very contemporary, invented visual language.

Towards the end of the artist's career came the *Montaru* and *Monturi* canvases, usually dark in hue and dominated by deep black, more rarely colorful and carefree in mood. With these works, at the zenith of his maturity, Baumeister created his own, personal, pictorial myths. In the course of time black came increasingly to dominate the compositions, like an ominous pall. No one can say whether a premonition of death was manifested here. Perhaps not even the artist himself knew, for concurrently with the dark compositions he produced many of a festive, sometimes even brash joyousness of color. In Baumeister's œuvre as in so many others, a love of life and melancholy went hand in hand.

In contrast to the works Baumeister produced during his emigration within his own land, the paintings Schlemmer did in the same situation – *Views from a Window into a Neighbor's Window*, he called them – record a turn to reality and a waiver of what he sarcastically termed the "picassible abstract." Yet reality, only a slice of which was accessible to the persecuted artist, was mystified, spiritualized, drawn inwards. Everything, Schlemmer declared, boiled down to the old question, "... what is truth? The truth of art – the truth of nature." A turn to the spiritual, to the transcendental in art becomes just as obvious in Schlemmer's attitude as the rejection of superficial reality in the case of Baumeister.

An intermediate position in this context was occupied by Fritz Winter. Although his early abstract compositions of the 1930s were still "burdened by life," Winter's dark, somber formulations strove beyond the finite and earthbound towards the infinite and universal. A romantic mystique of nature and a longing for transcendence were the sources of Winter's art. His best-known series, the *Motive Forces of the Earth* (ill. left), comprising forty small oils on paper, was, like Schlemmer's "window pictures", done during the period of worst persecution. The "degenerate" artist, who nevertheless was inducted into the army, was taken prisoner of war by the Russians, and not released until 1949, did the *Motive Forces* in 1944, during a home leave to recover from a wound. The travails of a life spent first as a coal miner, then as a front-line soldier, entered into these unusually condensed works. They nonetheless maintain a balance between emotional tension and spiritualized form, to become compelling visual symbols of the immutability of motive forces that emerge from the depths into the light, as the seething colors emerge from dark, earthy brown.

Color as a Formative Element

The art of Ernst Wilhelm Nay, the first German abstract painter to achieve international recognition after 1945, was rooted in Expressionism. That Nay began with a semi-abstract realism in subdued tones, toyed with Surrealism, then was influenced by Kirchner and Munch, who took Nay under his wing in Norway, is hardly evident from the works of his maturity. Their spiritual atti-

towards the end of the war and published in 1947, indicatively began during the period of his persecution.

In the footsteps of Malevich, Baumeister produced figurations floating free in space, which he called "ideographs". From here the artist's path led to the series of *Eidos* paintings, in which amoeba-like configurations hover in front of abstract pictorial spaces. These works document the last possible step in the process of the reduction of natural phenomena to abstract forms. After this, Baumeister developed a personal hieroglyphic picture-writing which was inspired by pre-historical and early historical art, by paleolithic rock paintings, by the art of indigenous peoples, of early Babylon and Egypt, archaic Greece and the Far East. "Memories" of lost cultures and their magical symbolism, rising from the unconscious mind, were freely translated into new pictorial signs. The Gilgamesh Epic and the Old Testament inspired Baumeister to an abstract re-formulation of tude and palette are no longer introverted and Nordic, but definitely marked by a Western optimism (ill. right).

Nay began emphasizing the dynamic aspect of painting early on. In his landscapes and figures he favored the general over the individual. The *Lofoten* canvases, based on the life and environment of Norwegian fishermen, stood at odds with the officially ordained naturalistic style in 1930s Germany. The compositions combine an expressively nervous rhythm, recalling Kirchner's hieroglyphics, with a concise reduction of form to essentials. Over the following years, particularly shortly before and after the end of the war, Nay heightened his palette to orchestral brilliance. There emerged incredibly rich compositions in which the subject was detectable only in alienated form, as mythical memory or inspiring stimulus. These works of the so-called "Hecate" period are among the finest Nay ever produced. This imagery creates the impression of an exquisite ornamental tapestry, shot through with dreamlike eyes, rare butterflies, and precious fans. Ellipses and discs also appear, but these forms do not yet play the dominating role they would in Nay's later paintings. At this point the artist still based his compositions on an underlying, supporting graphic grid. Subsequently he would set the color discs free, to hover and dance, interlocked or overlapping, across the pictorial plane.

The freedom with which Nay handles purely painterly means in his mature work, his openness to all their possibilities, up to and including the decorative, are rare in German art. The element of the musical, of the dance, plays an essential role here. The dynamic shapes convey no mental associations; the colors and rhythms of Nay's compositions do not signify anything beyond what is contained in their wonderfully differentiated chromatics. Here, color is no longer used as a means of expression but as an autonomous pictorial value. Color also determines the non-perspective space

of the image. The colored shapes appear to advance and recede, descend and ascend; cool and warm hues, heavy and light configurations, are counterpointed with great refinement. The temptation into which this "pure" painting runs the risk of falling is evident: repetition,

Ernst Wilhelm Nay
Daughter of Hecate I, 1945
Oil on canvas, 98 x 85 cm
Private collection

Ernst Wilhelm Nay
Blue Flood, 1960
Oil on canvas, 190 x 340 cm
Cologne, Museum Ludwig,
Donation Peill

Hann Trier
Staccato, 1959
Oil on canvas, 130 x 162 cm
Düsseldorf, Mannesmann A.G.

Georg Meistermann
Being Torn, 1952/53
Oil on canvas, 150 x 220 cm
Germany, private collection

ing- board, "space-plans", "ground-plans", and "scaffoldings" – imagery that reveals an impetuous personality subjecting itself to intellectual control.

Hann Trier (ill. left) is one of the few German and European abstractionists of the early post-war period whose work has lost none of its drive. The theme of his early canvases was motion, including the mechanical variety. "Sewing", "typewriting", "talking of the devil", "writing in the wind", but also the flustered fluttering of wings in a dovecote, were evoked in painterly and graphic abbreviations of dynamic rhythm and explosive force. The nervous clattering of typewriter keys, the zig-zag lines of hems, the strokes of the needle were translated into a visual code in which objective references were still detectable. Trier's sparkling irony had little in common with the existentialist end-of-the-world mood of Tachism, with which his work was roughly concurrent. Trier's path led him from what, speaking flippantly, one might call life's little dramas to true poetry in painting. Although the rhythmic articulation of the picture plane and the blending of graphic structure and

routine, mere tasteful arrangement. Nay occasionally succumbed to this temptation. Perhaps this explains why he subsequently introduced more ruggedness and unpredictability into his compositions by breaking up the disc form, before, towards the end of his life, surprisingly turning to a decidedly two-dimensional, generously simplified ornamental approach.

Like that of Nay, the painting of Georg Meistermann (ill. right) established a point of orientation for contemporary German art in the immediate post-war years. In addition, Meistermann brought new life into secular and ecclesiastical glass painting, and was an eloquent advocate of the rights of art and artists. The visible world, ensconced in his early work behind harsh graphic grids, was later translated into signs and symbols, hieroglyphic messages from a world the in process of becoming. Ovid's *Metamorphoses* took on a visual presence. *Fish Wants to Become Bird* (1952; Cologne, Museum Ludwig) is a typical work of this period. In a subsequent phase Meistermann showed himself to be a rigorous architect of the picture, who designed, as if on a draw-

colored form remained characteristic of his art, the motion and machine pictures were followed by word, script, and dance paintings, which from 1955 onwards were executed with both hands simultaneously, tracing the rhythms of the artist's body movements. Here the theme of the labyrinth, crucial to Trier as to many of his contemporaries, already made its appearance. Trier was also an influential teacher, one of whose students was Georg Baselitz.

The Abstract International
Non-Objective Painting around the World

The first and decisive phases of the 20th-century revolution in art can be connected with particular nations: Fauvism and Cubism with France, Futurism with Italy, Expressionism with Germany, Suprematism and Constructivism with Russia, De Stijl with Holland, and so forth. The only exact statement one can make about the second great wave, that of abstraction after 1945, is that it

originated in Paris. After that, non-objective painting immediately burgeoned into an international phenomenon. Its principles were adopted and put into practice for some time to come by the finest talents around the world, whether in Paris or Berlin, Rome or Cologne, Milan or Copenhagen, London or New York, Tokyo or Rio de Janeiro.

The phenomenon cannot be explained solely by reference to the advantages and disadvantages of the unprecedented dissemination of information through exhibitions, world trade, newspapers, radio and television, or tourism. Nor is it enough to cite the effects of clever marketing and the adaptability of dealers, as little as their not always beneficial influence can be denied. The vocabulary of abstract painting was taken up by artists around the world as if the salvation of their soul depended on it. Let us recall that prior to 1914, experiments in abstraction were going on at various places in Europe almost concurrently, without the mutual knowledge of the artists involved – Kandinsky, Čiurlionis, Kupka, and Malevich, to name only a few. And after the harshest phase of the Cold War, when the Iron Curtain began to lift, the world realized that even in the countries of Eastern Europe, abstract art had continued to exist despite its ostensibly "subversive character" and its "capitalist formalism".

Even the quintessential land of the classical tradition, Italy, fell under the sway of abstraction and, for the first time since the heyday of Futurism, it re-entered the European art discourse. That Italian artists too were concerned not with *l'art pour l'art* but with *l'art pour l'homme* is indicated by the association of artists working in highly diverse styles into a "New Front of the Arts," which was formed in 1947. Abstract painters such as Renato Birolli, Giuseppe Santomaso, and the vehemently expressive Emilio Vedova, temporarily rubbed shoulders with dyed-in-the-wool realists like Renato

Guttuso. The ambitious, indeed utopian goal of the group was nothing less than to bring about an unprecedented synthesis of the opposing streams. That, in view of the extreme individualism of the artists involved, simply could not work in the long run. Their idealistic initiative was doomed to failure like so many others in art and politics which attempt to set signposts for a new beginning by sloughing off the burden of the past.

In 1951 an exhibition took place that struck European art critics as an absolute sensation: "astratta e concreta." Birolli, in politics a socialist, was among the leading fig-

Emilio Vedova
Non dove '87 (Tondo –1–), 1987
Oil on wood, diameter 280 cm
Napa (CA), Hess Collection

Emilio Vedova
Cosmic Vision, 1953
Tempera on plywood,
82.8 x 55.5 cm
New York, The Museum
of Modern Art, Blanchette
Rockefeller Fund

ures (p. 239). Birolli rejected the doctrinaire ideology of communism with the same fervor as he had previously protested against the narrow-minded art policies of fascism. By way of landscapes and figurative paintings Birolli gradually approached free abstraction, but even here, his passionate temperament prevented him from losing touch with nature and humanity. He remained an expressive, dramatic realist whose art always took its point of departure in experience.

The same is true of the more reserved painting of Giuseppe Santomaso (p. 239 above right). The palette of his early, abstract landscapes was suffused with the light of Venice, while the paint handling revealed the influence of the Ecole de Paris, especially of Hartung. Later Santomaso would blunder into the well-worn paths of an "informal art", grown fashionable and facile. Antonio Corpora, too, envisaged a revival of the "dialogue with nature," before he, too, succumbed to the superficial charm of amorphous, non-referential paint structures (p. 241 above left).

A quite different case is the art of Vedova. The Venetian is a painter of enormous force, matched by his imposing stature, who has made by far the greatest Italian contribution to Abstract Expressionism (ill. above and left). In the 1950s Vedova was celebrated as the star among the Tachist and L'art informel artists, although this label was always misleading. "My works are full of structures", he says. "These structures are the structures of my consciousness." This confessional tendency is an integral part of Vedova's personality and work, which has never drifted into the merely aesthetically pleasing and has retained its committed character.

Painting as an Adventure

For Vedova, painting is an adventure, which includes a willingness to take risks. He sets out to depict the problems of human beings who, in Heidegger's memorable term, are "thrown" into existence as a dog throws its young, and to protest against the absurdity and cruelty of contemporary life. Vedova's pictorial space possesses a Baroque depth (he knows his Venetian art from Tintoretto to Tiepolo very well). It is a space without beginning or end, into which break vibrating, ecstatic rhythms of black swaths set against the empty white of the canvas. Although the dynamism of his compositions recalls Futurism, Vedova will have nothing of this. He insists that he does not illustrate movement. The movement in his paintings emerges from himself, from the gestures of his arms and the movements of his body – which, by the way, determines the scale of his canvases – in a word, from his passionate temperament.

When Vedova transgressed the borders not only of the easel painting but of painting per se, using primitive means – paint on unprocessed rough wood or particle board – to produce large-scale objects titled *Plurimi di Berlino* which were shown in 1964 in the hallowed halls of the documenta, both the art trade and a large part of

Antonio Corpora
Untitled, 1950
Oil on canvas, 70 x 60 cm
Italy, private collection

Giuseppe Capogrossi
Superficie No. 305, 1959
Oil on canvas, 74 x 61 cm
Germany, private collection

the public and critics withdrew their support. For many years thereafter the official art discussion passed over Vedova in silence. Then, with the expressionist tendencies of the 1980s, the realization spread that Vedova's work had set standards in the field of gestural painting. The *Plurimi* have since become incunabula of an unconventional, innovative object art.

Another, half-forgotten Italian artist was remembered in the context of subsequent developments: Giuseppe Capogrossi (ill. above). His work is characterized by an ornamental picture-writing consisting of simple signs, some invented, others derived from pre-historic models. It was the New Ornamentation or Pattern Painting of some years ago that led to a rehabilitation of Capogrossi.

Just as the Italians must bear the sweet burden of their Renaissance and Baroque painting, so must the Dutch cope with the glory of their 17th-century middle-class art. Rembrandt and Vermeer, van Gogh and Mondrian mark the poles of the great arena in which Dutch art has moved down to the present day. The feeling of liberation that suffused the entire nation after 1945 communicated itself to the first post-war art of Holland, which was principally expressive in thrust. This is seen in the Dutch members of the "Cobra" group (a name composed of the first two letters of Copenhagen, Brussels,

Corneille
The Discovery of the Island, 1965
Oil on canvas, 81 x 65 cm
Private collection

Pierre Alechinsky
Alice Grows, 1961
Oil on canvas, 205 x 245 cm
Private collection

and Amsterdam), which exhibited in 1949 at the Stedelijk Museum in Amsterdam. Their tendency to free, occasionally rough-and-ready action painting came out most clearly in the work of Karel Appel (p. 243 above right). Appel's compositions in brilliantly colored, thickly applied impasto, inspired by Surrealist automatism, were initially populated with hybrid figures derived from folk art, primitive art, or the naive and grotesque L'art brut of the early Jean Dubuffet. In their racy way, Appel's figures even occasionally recall the more spirited *dramatis personae* in the dream landscapes of Paul Klee, and particularly of Joan Miró. Connections to the mythical Nordic realm of trolls and poltergeists are also evident. In the course of time Appel turned to an increasingly abstract expressionistic approach, but without ever entirely eliminating objective allusions. For years now Appel's work has sadly been declining in substance.

More reserved and controlled than Appel's is the work of Corneille (p. 241). The convoluted formal structure of his labyrinths and the rudimentary, emblematic, parcelled character of his architectural and landscape

compositions perfectly embody the linking of abstraction with figuration for which the Cobra artists initially strove. It was not until the advent of Tachism, L'art informel, and Action Painting that they made the step to total abstraction.

The Belgian member of "Cobra" was Pierre Alechinsky (p. 241). Alechinsky's early compositions teemed with abstract symbols that recalled vegetation, earth and rock formations, held within a structural framework. But gradually, under the influence of his friends, the artist's gestural brushwork grew increasingly free, expressive, and agitated. Ghosts and spirits, demons large and small, began to populate a picture plane covered with energetic swaths of paint and scurrilous graphic ciphers. But Alechinsky's expressionist phase lasted only a few years. Influenced by Japanese calligraphy his painting grew more tranquil, yet the oscillation between abstraction, non-naturalistic objectivity, and fantastic, sometimes ornamental figuration has remained characteristic of the artist's approach down to the much more facile work of recent years.

Impassioned Expression

The outstanding member of "Cobra" was Asger Jorn, a Dane (pp. 243, 244). Jorn received his first strong impressions from Munch and Nolde, and like that of the German artist, Jorn's iconography was drawn to a large extent from the realm of Nordic myth, with its legendary creatures, its trolls and gnomes. But perhaps even more important was Jorn's confrontation with the imagery of Max Ernst and Paul Klee. What he learned from Surrealism was above all the spontaneity of *écriture automatique*, or automatic writing (which also concurrently influenced American Action Painting), as well as the blending of the worlds of day and night, reality and dream. The vehemence of Jorn's attack, the frenzy of his gestures, and the visionary imagination that flows into his imagery, all set his work above that of his friends. His impulse to destroy form arises from an ingrained disgust with the perfectionism of a merely aesthetic, tasteful art lacking in all critical thrust, and with the self-satisfied complacency of art-lovers who demand no more. The aggressively satirical element in Jorn's art is not to be overlooked.

Yet despite the wildness of his brushwork, Jorn's explosions of form and color never lead to amorphousness. His work is marked by a characteristic balance

"Let's suppose that the first colour I apply to the canvas is red. Now, that action determines everything else that happens to the painting. After that I could put yellow on it, and some blue; then I might perhaps obliterate the red with black, and the blue would perhaps become yellow, and the yellow purple, while the black changes to white. Obviously anything can happen. But the whole fascinating process began with that first red, and if I hadn't begun with red, the whole painting would have been different. Is there a system, is there order, in this chaos?"
KAREL APPEL

Asger Jorn
Loss of the Mean, 1958
Oil on canvas, 114 x 146 cm
Ghent, Museum van Hedendaagse
Kunst

*"True realism, materialist realism,
lies in the search for the expression of
forms faithful to their content. But
there is no content detached from
human interest."* ASGER JORN

between abstraction and objectivity, whereby the objective reference was more strongly emphasized in the earlier work than in the later, in which free form and unleashed gesture dominate. As the artist says, "No work of art can emerge that does not represent, in and of itself, an alienation with respect to the existing 'real' or 'normal' exterior world." The figures that emerge from Jorn's agitated color fields are imaginary figures which are held up to the superficial "reality" of visible appearances. The levels of reality are shifted here – the visible world grows unreal, while the unreal world of dream is revealed to be the reality "behind things."

This impassioned expressiveness represents the diametrical opposite to "concrete" art. For the politically committed Jorn, art must have an immediate effect on life, not by attempting to enlist scientific rationalism to its own ends, but by projecting an imaginative counterworld to the existing one. This attitude led to an embittered dispute with Max Bill, and to Jorn's temporary participation in the provocative actions of the "Situationists," a politically extreme left-wing group whose German headquarters was then in Munich, where a group called *Spur* (Trace) formed around Heimrad Prem, Lothar Fischer, and H.P. Zimmer. Prem, who ultimately lost faith in a renaissance of painting out of the spirit of spontaneity, and Uwe Lausen, who was also involved in the group's activities, ended by taking their own lives.

The outstanding figure in British painting of the period was Ben Nicholson. But the pioneer of pure abstraction in that country was Victor Pasmore (p. 245 below). After following in the footsteps of Bonnard by cultivating a sophisticated style *à la française*, Pasmore came for a time under the influence of Piet Mondrian. Robin Denny, Richard Lin, Roy Ascot, and Mary

Carl-Henning Pedersen
The Flying Red Horse, 1941
Oil on canvas, 84 x 101 cm
Herning (Denmark),
Herning Kunstmuseum

Martin in her later phase, all rang changes on Pasmore's images of a right-angled, ideal world. But geometric abstraction never became entirely acclimatized in Great Britain. The then-influential, formally stringent canvases of the Scottish artist William Scott, with their symbolic signs and vibrant, sophisticated palette, already anticipated Action Painting, while Alan Davie's work (ill. right) pointed at this early date in the direction of a new figuration and neo-Expressionist tendencies to come.

Quite a different case was that of Stuart Davis, the leading figure among the few abstract painters in the United States who worked in a more geometric than Surrealism-derived style (p. 246). Davis's work has only recently begun to attract greater attention in Europe. He began his career as a realist and a successful one, having already been represented in the renowned Armory Show of 1913. In thematic terms Davis was attracted by the everyday situations and trappings of modern life, and he accordingly worked as a cartoonist for various periodicals. Stylistically, he came by way of an involvement with Matisse to Cubism, whose ascetic palette, however, he did not adopt.

From there Davis's development led logically to geometric, structurally oriented abstraction. Yet references to the visible world remained present in the allusive pictorial signs that enlivened his landscapes and still lifes. A tendency to schematize was just as evident here as the artist's love of the contemporary urban scene with all its bright and garish color and syncopated rhythms. Impulses from Davis's work spread in various directions. In formal terms, they led via Cubism – particularly in Léger's version – to the American abstraction of the late 1930s onwards. And in terms of content, Davis's use of trivial subject-matter and bright colors had an influence on Pop Art (which in turn owed much to the late Léger).

In the classical painters' land, Spain, a progressive, free art remained viable even during the period of the Franco dictatorship. Though Picasso – not only an artistic revolutionary but a member of the French Communist Party – Gris, Miró, and González carried little weight in their home country, and the decades between the two world wars passed rather uneventfully in artistic terms, immediately after 1945 the situation changed radically. Influenced not lastly by remarkable art journals, developments that had taken place in the rest of Europe were rapidly disseminated in Spain, for the Franco government made no concerted attempt to intervene. The first abstract artists' group was founded in 1948, in Saragossa, and only a few years later Constructivism and "Magic Abstraction" had triumphed across a broad front. When in 1957 the group "El Paso" formed in Madrid and dedicated itself to *pitura informal*, the Spanish version of L'art informel, artists of European rank came on the scene. With the likes of Tàpies and Antonio Saura, Spain again had a voice in the European art discourse.

Alan Davie
Entrance for a Red Temple
No. 1, 1960
Oil on canvas, 84 x 68 cm
London, Tate Gallery

The Omnipresence of Tradition

"The present, for an Austrian, is his tradition," writes the Austrian critic Wieland Schmied. "He feeds on it like Hundertwasser, dissects it like Hausner, attempts to expunge it like Rainer... Austrians occupy themselves with themselves, not with the world." This omnipresence of tradition, especially the Baroque tradition, a cult of the past revolving around the glory of the Austro-Hungarian Empire, plus the massive attacks of the erst-

Victor Pasmore
Transparent Construction,
1959/60
Plexiglass and wood, 76 x 81 cm
Vienna, Museum moderner Kunst

while revolutionary, Kokoschka, on abstract art, did not create a climate conducive to the development of abstraction in Austria. Nor has it ever come to play the dominating role there that it did in other European countries. Yet it existed nonetheless. The diverse and varied work of Arnulf Rainer and action painters like Markus Prachensky will be discussed in another context. Josef Mikl initially oriented himself to Mondrian, but then developed squares and rectangles into elaborate labyrinths and gestural configurations in a range of modulated colors, without sacrificing the link to the constructive, architectural basis of his work. Mention must also be made in this connection of the work in painting and sculpture of artist-friends Herbert Boeckl (ill. below) and Fritz Wotruba (p. 491), whose influence

as teachers has been especially great, contributing substantially to the receptiveness of the Austrian scene to contemporary developments in painting and sculpture. Boeckl's "coded idiom," especially in the early work, was embodied in a painterly form both sensitive and expressive, and his "color islands," as W. Hofmann has said, "can be read as metaphors for spatio-physical energies." Boeckl's late work stands under the spell of Cézanne, to whose art he opened his students' eyes, thus fostering the spread of abstraction in the Alpine republic.

The transition from Klimt's Jugendstil arabesque to the episodic "New Ornamentation," which had a brief revival in American "Pattern Art," is recorded in the work of Friedensreich Hundertwasser, especially in his early work. Hundertwasser was probably the first environmentalist and Green among the artists of our era (p. 247). With his "mould manifesto", he protested against the monotony of soulless functionalist architecture and its "walls with holes," proclaiming individual "window rights" and propagating the benefits of cows grazing on planted roofs. Now that the friend of the Dalai Lama has become a successful party-lion and has been able to put his architectural suggestions into arguably successful practice, it is difficult to recall the scandal caused by Hundertwasser's early projects, such as the transformation of the interior of the Hamburg School of Art into a thread-like labyrinth. In his relevant works, based on the spiral as a perpetually recurring fundamental form, the world metamorphoses into a fairytale garden and at the same time into a critically ironic mirror of the times, and Klimt's celebration of the vamp takes on the character of a morbidly erotic mythology not without sarcastic, self-ironic, and eroto-manic traits.

The cultural link between Poland and Western Europe goes far back in history, and it has never entirely broken. In comparison to other Eastern Bloc countries, Poland has enjoyed a relatively great cultural liberty, even at the height of political repression. In the 1920s, as mentioned above, the "Blok" and "Praesens" groups –

founded by Berlevi, Stazewski, and Strzemeński, and materially influenced by progressive architects – maintained contacts with Malevich and Mondrian, and fought to keep abstract art viable, even into the years after 1945.

Polish artistic thinking might be briefly described as extremely volatile, imaginative, and ready to resist ideological and aesthetic doctrines at all times. These characteristics are reflected in the diverse œuvre of Tadeusz Kantor (ill. below right), as they were in that of his universalist like-minded predecessor, Stanislaw Witkiewicz (ill. below left). From an early date Kantor was equally intrigued by art and theater. In 1943 he participated in the establishment of an illegal underground theater in

Cracow. In 1945 he became a member of the "Young Sculpture" group. In 1947 Kantor even became an academy professor, though he was fired just two years later. After that began a collaboration with an artist he admired, Maria Jerema, with whom he worked more or less out of the public eye.

Kantor was the vanguard artist par excellence, unceasingly changing, always on the move. His relatively brief phase of painting in a L'art informel vein was already over by the mid-1960s. But everything Kantor did thereafter – producing his own *musée imaginaire*, creating assemblages, *emballages* and objects, organizing happenings, but above all working in the field of theater – had its source in this abstract, gestural approach. In his

Friedensreich Hundertwasser
The Great Way, 1955
Polyvinyl acetate on two joined strips of canvas primed with chalk and zinc white, 162 x 160 cm
Vienna, Österreichische Galerie im Belvedere

Friedensreich Hundertwasser
Grass for Those Who Cry, 1975
Mixed media, 65 x 92 cm
New York, private collection

Stanislaw Witkiewicz
The Struggle, 1921/22
Oil on canvas, 99 x 106 cm
Lódz, Muzeum Sztuki

Tadeusz Kantor
Painting, 1959
Oil on canvas, 86 x 99.5 cm
Warsaw, Muzeum Narodowe

pictures as in his theater work Kantor rendered visible his idea of "hot abstraction," as a process, a departure into a new freedom. To this extent he was one of the most consequential representatives of gestural abstraction in either East or West.

In the former Czechoslovakia, where visual art has always had close ties with Surrealism and Fantastic Realism, abstract painting did not come to play a dominant role despite the great Czech model of Kupka. In addition, tentative artistic connections with the outside world were brutally severed in 1948. It was not until the 1960s that representatives of tendencies opposed to official Socialist Realism were able to dare public exposure. None of the later abstractionists has enjoyed a world acclaim like that of the poet and collage-maker Jiří Kolář. Yet although Kolář's visual alphabet-poems, related to concrete poetry, occasionally verge on abstraction, they constitute only a small portion of his œuvre.

In Hungary there was, and is, a continuation of the Constructivist stream initiated by Moholy-Nagy, Kassák, Vilmos Huszár (p. 173), and Sándor Bortnyik. The influence of Vasarely and Schöffer is likewise evident. Constructivist links are apparent in the various

phases of the work of László Lakner, who now lives and teaches in Western Europe (ill. above). While Lakner's early style was a critical realism with Surrealist overtones, his current reputation is based on "Script Portraits" of famous and anonymous people from past and present, executed in rich and delicate nuances on canvases and unstretched fabric. The series was largely inspired by illegible scrawls on building walls and subway graffiti seen during a stay in America. In the meantime, Lakner has considerably advanced his combination of highly cultivated painting and script or calligraphy. In his works sensibility and intelligence, autonomous form and allusive, ambiguous message merge into a compelling pictorial unity.

Geometry as Grammar

The dissemination of the international language of abstraction did not remain limited to Europe and the United States. Japanese artists, for instance, were influenced by it as well. During the heyday of the Ecole de Paris it was Koumi Sugaï who attracted particular attention, with Far Eastern pictographs monumentalized in a Western manner (ill. left).

Even in the Soviet Union abstract tendencies were not entirely suppressed, as the skilled and very original painting of Vladimir Weisberg indicates. Beginning with Cézanne, Weisberg came by way of analyses of coloration and structure to an incomparably sensitive transparency of barely detectable transitions, a veritably "invisible," metaphysical painting in which all objectivity is dissolved in a hovering, unreal space. Unlike many of his colleagues, Weisberg did not succumb to a Western-influenced eclecticism despite – or perhaps because of – his opposition to official art doctrine.

The abstract wave also inundated Latin America, South Africa, the Philippines, India, Egypt, Syria and

Israel. This was not necessarily always positive, because it tempted many artists in these areas to forsake their tradition, deny their identity, and become mere imitators of a foreign art which they practiced at second-hand. It is not unjustified to view this process as a reflection of cultural colonialism, which led to an unfortunate loss of originality. Luckily many artists of the younger generation have since become conscious of their own roots.

"Geometry," said Apollinaire, who had an infallible sense of emerging new developments, "geometry is to visual art what grammar is to the writer." The mastery of this grammar and the development of ever more liberated forms, all the way down to Abstract Expressionism, has given artists complete freedom in dealing with their medium. That is perhaps the most significant gain which the great epoch of the Abstract International brought to art.

The Gentle Anarchist
Wolfgang Schulze: a German Artist in Paris

"A life-changing decision of the kind made by Rimbaud or Gauguin is no longer feasible in the present and future; the character of the era precludes it," wrote the conservative sociologist Arnold Gehlen in his book *Zeitbilder* (Pictures of an Era). The author should have known better. A few years prior to the publication of his reactionary commentary on contemporary art, a destiny had run its course in Paris that was comparable to Rimbaud's, indeed comparable to any of the artists' fates in that city's "heroic" period. Admittedly the protagonist was no revolutionary, no angry young man in the Romantic style who, disgusted with civilization, set out to find an earthly paradise in India or the South Seas. He was a negative hero who, rather than challenging fate, suffered it: escape, persecution, hunger, loneliness, and finally, self-destruction.

Carl Jakob Burckhardt, deeply impressed by the first "exhibition of the works of a certain Wols" in late May 1947, at Galerie Drouin, Paris – a show that went practically unnoticed by critics and public – understood the "quality of the era" much better than Gehlen. "Under what tensions an era must stand," Burckhardt wrote to the Swiss critic and essayist Max Rychner, "in which something of this nature is possible...!"

Indeed, something of the nature of Wols's mature work would have been impossible in any other era. Attacking the canvas or sheet with the brush, scratching through the paint with its handle, working at the highest emotional and physical pitch, this artist produced in the mid-1940s a series of images whose dynamic sheaths of line and nervous, filigree strokes, as Werner Haftmann recognized, established "a completely new brand of painting at one fell swoop." Preceded and paralleled by Hartung's psychographs and Jean Fautrier's *Otages* (Hostages), Wols's paintings introduced to Europe the second wave of uncompromising and illusionless modernity, as Pollock's paint frenzies did to the United States. Georges Mathieu, himself later a successful Tachist who made spectacular public demonstrations of his calligraphic rapidity, immediately recognized the significance of the forty oils on display at Drouin. "Forty

masterpieces!" Mathieu wrote. "Every one more shattering, thrilling, sanguine than the next – an event, without a doubt the most important one since the works of van Gogh.... It was like forty moments from a man's crucifixion...."

Alfred Otto Wolfgang Schulze, alias Wols, born in 1913 in Berlin, came of an upper-middle-class public servant's family. His father, a cultivated man who loved music above all else, was president of the State Chancellery in Saxony. Wolfgang inherited his father's musical gift, but not his practical sense. Restlessly on the move, he studied one subject, then another, tried his hand at fish-farming, photography, the violin. Schulze enrolled at the Frobenius Institute in Frankfurt to study ethnology, then applied to the Bauhaus, which was then located in Berlin and entering its final phase. Moholy-Nagy advised him against enrolling, and suggested he go to Paris instead, which he eventually did. Schulze was so accomplished a violinist that Fritz Busch, the German conductor who later emigrated to England, said he would find him a position as concert master. And after Hugo Erfurth had seen the photographs done by the

"The image can be in rapport with nature like the Bach fugue with Christ; such a case is not a re-copy but an analogous creation."
WOLS

Wols
Painting, 1944/45
Oil on canvas, 79.7 x 80 cm
New York, The Museum of Modern Art, Gift of Dominique and John de Menil

Wols
Le Bateau ivre, c. 1945
Oil on canvas, 90 x 73 cm
Zurich, Kunsthaus Zürich

eighteen-year-old, he told Schulze he had nothing more to learn. He earned a meager living as a photographer in Paris before becoming the official photographer for the 1937 World Fair. It was at this period that the artist adopted his pseudonym. As his wife, Gréty, recalls, a telephone operator who did not understand her husband's unfamiliar German name, simplified it to Wols. And Wols it remained.

Quiet, friendly, and highly sensitive, lost in musings and meditations, reading Meister Ekkehard and the Chinese philosophers, Novalis and Kafka, Poe and Rimbaud, Shelley and Lautréamont – when he didn't happen to be playing the violin – Wols soon found many friends despite the distance he felt between himself and other people. Among these friends were Miró, Max Ernst, Calder, Tzara, and Simone de Beauvoir, but above all her life companion, Jean-Paul Sartre, who to the end continued to help Wols where he could, when others had forgotten him or given him up. As long as he could afford it, Wols was a generous host, giving what he had without a thought for tomorrow. His love of the exquisite extended to fine dining. It was a terrible irony of fate that in the end, weakened by alcohol and the rigors of withdrawal treatment, Wols died of food poisoning.

"For a Painting You don't buy Hamburger"
Under the pressure of internment in various camps – uwanted in Germany, Wols was suspect in France as an "enemy alien" – he began to drink heavily in 1940. Eventually he needed alcohol as a stimulant when recording his confessional autobiography in paint, his hopes and despairs, his desires and privations. "We had no wood and could not make a fire," Wols's widow recalled. "So he sat down and painted both, the wood and the fire. He

always painted his dreams like this, the good ones and the bad." As his situation grew worse and worse, Wols's œuvre developed as it were in private. He had never wanted to be a professional artist. He would rather have kept all his paintings himself. "For a painting you don't buy hamburger," Wols said.

Despite his unusual intelligence and many talents Wols tended to follow the promptings of emotion first. The necessity of some order in his life, some planned career, had no appeal for him. He remained a stranger in the world of realities, a homeless and rootless vagrant in the spirit of François Villon, the type of the vagabond reborn in the 20th century.

This young man, who aged early, unwittingly triggered the most violent change in the history of modern art, which was surely not lacking in revolts and protests. Wolfgang Schulze was the father of Tachism (French la tache = spot, mark) in the narrower sense, and of L'art informel in the wider sense – that style of gestural or action painting which revolted against the formalism of the abstract academy, brought sensuousness back into art by letting the paint run free, splashing and dribbling it onto the canvas. Tachism openly embraced chance, the irrational, the unpredictable, and the urges of the subconscious mind. It was the protest of passionate human feeling against the supposed objectivity of constructed, calculated art, of spontaneity against routine, of a romantic against a classical frame of mind.

Yet Wols's works signalled more than an art-historical watershed. They showed the artist turning his inmost feelings outwards, bringing his entire personality into play, revealing the plight of a man alone, reliant only on himself, and – in the Existentialist phrase – thrown into existence, as a representative of, witness to, and victim of the times. This could not have been done with the aid of traditional forms or styles. These had to be swept aside, to make way for the emergence of a new, unprecedented pictorial structure. The new structure went far beyond Surrealist *écriture automatique*. It was Wols' role as a witness, his abandonment of himself to the painted image, that gave his late work an exemplary significance beyond all purely aesthetic categories.

Filigree Dream Cities
After Expressionist beginnings, Wols produced expressive works that were sited on the permeable border-line between non-objective painting and Surrealism. "Everything I dreamed took place in a big and very beautiful unknown city," the artist once said. The works on paper of the 1930s still contained many literary references. Filigree dream cities and landscapes evoked Kafkaesque realms, in which Baudelaire's *Fleurs du mal* flourished as well. Ghostly figures, humans and zoomorphic creatures in process of dissolution, populated streets and squares depicted with a fragile, microscopically precise lineature and in nuances of sometimes morbid color. The real mingled with the surreal, the organic with the constructive, in paradoxical combination.

Wols
The Blue Phantom, 1951
Oil on canvas, 73 x 60 cm
Cologne, Museum Ludwig

As time went on, the world of appearances grew increasingly vague. As the elements in Wols's compositions became ever more autonomous, there emerged "interior worlds," images of eerie and enchanting fantasy. Parallel lines, overlappings, rotations, and interweaves were combined into configurations that distantly recalled natural phenomena. Vortexes, spirals, branchings, sinuousities, proliferations and growths called microscopic enlargements of animal and vegetable structures to mind. Many Wols' paintings were in fact inspired by photographs of biological micro- and macro-structures, as well as by telescopic photographs, of spiral nebulae, for instance. His own photographs of animal cadavers, which had already influenced a number of fantastic drawings, also entered the work in oil.

Wols's photographic œuvre, done between 1932 and 1941, holds an independent position alongside his watercolors, drawings, and oils.

In his little more than 80 paintings Wols tirelessly experimented with unusual techniques. For instance, he would let several layers of thinned paint flow into one another and congeal, producing a dense interweave of textures, then would scratch or score the paint with a brush or sharp tool to reveal the ground beneath. At this period, the night side of life assumed compelling presence in these spontaneous, feverishly nervous paintings. Occasionally, anxiety and a sense of threat took on fantastic, surrealist shape, as in *Blue Phantom* (p. 251), done during the last year of the artist's life. The scoriated, martyred skin of his paintings was Wols's own.

Painting as a Voyage of Discovery
Tachism, L'art informel, L'art autre

Art-historical labels seldom sit comfortably. They are convenient tokens we use when talking about art, simply because they have become widely accepted. Cases in point are the names given to the records of a revolt against the Platonism of the Abstract International: Tachisme, L'art informel, Abstract Expressionism, Action Painting, or simply, *un art autre*, a different art. The gestural painting and sculpture so designated can look very diverse, but it appeared at about the same time and out of the same impulse in Europe and America, without the mutual knowledge of the artists involved.

Here again, the operative term was "liberation." Liberation from rules, liberation from the traps of formalism, from conformity in abstract disguise, but also from the burden of the tradition that even the classical modernism of the first half of the century had since formed.

Artists said farewell to the illusion that art could contribute to changing and improving the world. Put positively, this implied a new, ideologically resistant liberty on the part of the self-reliant individual, which in artistic terms took the form of a trust in vital, flowing paint, impulsive line, spontaneous gesture, and raw, unaesthetic materials.

The link between gestural abstraction and Surrealism, above all its automatic writing, is obvious. But the influence should not be overrated, because spontaneous painting based on the promptings of the subconscious mind involved primarily process and technique, and only secondarily the content and substance of the works. The gestural approach can be traced far back into the past, not only back to Dada and the abstract expressionism of the early Kandinsky, but even back to the *Haystacks* and *Water Lilies* of the late Monet, to Turner's watercolors, to the topographical drawings of Leonardo da Vinci, and finally – among the Germans – to Romanticism, to Albrecht Altdorfer, to the Danube School. Also discernable in the broad range of gestural abstraction is a renewed search for an unsullied innocence beyond the sophistications and strictures of the civilized world. This attitude led to a recourse to the authenticity of the visual symbols of pre-historical cultures. It also led to a new approach to landscape, in which artists penetrated beneath the surface to create a sort of structural geology in paint and other, unconventional materials, applied in heavy layers to the point of three-dimensional relief. "It used to be we came from nature to art," said the German gestural painter Bernard Schultze back then: "Now we come from art to nature." In this context also belong the "mental landscapes" of many L'art informel painters, which had an early fore-runner in the remarkably atmospheric, if sometimes sentimental

Jean Fautrier
The Gentle Woman, 1946
Oil, pastel and India ink on paper, mounted on canvas, 97 x 145 cm
Paris, Musée National d'Art Moderne, Centre Georges Pompidou

Jean Fautrier
Tormented Man, 1942
Oil on paper, 80 x 115 cm
Paris, private collection

paintings of August Strindberg, playwright and amateur artist.

Seldom before in art history have painters so frankly expressed their personality, their anger, joy, or sadness. Jean Paulhan, chief editor of the glorious *Nouvelle Revue Française,*in an early "Eulogy to Non-formal Art," not only acknowledged its great seriousness but declared that it possessed the dignity of the tragic. Other interpreters, in contrast, spoke of a moral neutralization of art, of an escape from the "compulsion to make a statement." The paradox of these contrary readings is resolved when we realize that the best works of the protagonists of gestural abstraction, from Wols to Tàpies, stood firmly in a definite historical context. They were in part dramatic, in part silent painterly records of a damaged life, of human dereliction and despair, and of the widespread speechlessness of the period.

L'art informel was the last European artistic current to have had its inception in Paris, and it was soon to be joined by a massive influx from America. Immediately after the liberation of France, Galerie René Drouin, on the narrow Rue de Visconti, showed paintings by Wols, Fautrier, and Dubuffet. There followed, in 1948 to 1950, exhibitions at Galerie Facchetti of the Americans Pollock, Mark Tobey, Clyfford Still, and Robert Motherwell. It was above all Pollock, and his method of dripping paint from a can onto a canvas on the floor, who confirmed the French artists in their approach. The tendency was soon adopted in Germany by the Munich "Zen" group, the short-lived "Quadriga" group in Frankfurt, and by "Gruppe 53" in Düsseldorf. It Italy it was represented by "Movimento Arte Nucleare."

Art without Consolation

Like the painting of the emigré Wols, that of Jean Fautrier is well described by Jean Paulhan's reference to the tragic dignity of L'art informel (pp. 252–254). In Fautrier's case, it was not so much his own personal suffering as that of others that stood in the forefront. *Les Otages* (The Hostages) was the collective title of a series of thirty paintings done between 1943 and 1945 which made Fautrier famous. They are heads with vaguely suggested features formed of plastic material (*hautes pâtes*) and lightly worked over in oil.

The artist and his friends always put great store in the statement that *informel* tendencies had been anticipated in Fautrier's work as early as 1928, which, indicatively, was a year before he interrupted his artistic activity for all of a decade. Thirty at the time, Fautrier made illustrations for Dante's *Inferno,*images in the "black manner" and white "glaciers" in a free-flowing, form-dissolving approach whose surfaces were suffused with sinuous lineatures. "The Fautrier of 1928 already had within himself the visionary force, the innovative technique of the Fautrier of 1943," wrote André Verdet. At any rate, the gestural and expressive elements of later works were clearly present at this time.

More important than the question of priority – which Fautrier claimed over Dubuffet with respect to the relief-like, built-up surface as well – is the question of artistic substance. In Fautrier's case, this has been given its due only in recent years. This significant painter had been forgotten twice over, once in the 1930s, and again after L'art informel had lost its dominant position. Fautrier himself remained a lone wolf, but his work

"No form of art can depict feelings if a piece of reality is not included in it. No matter how tiny, how imperceptible this suggestion may be, this irreducible part is like the key to the work. It makes it readable, it illuminates its meaning, it opens the deep, essential reality of the aesthetic perception, which is true intelligence."
JEAN FAUTRIER

Jean Fautrier
Head of a Hostage, 1945
Oil on paper on canvas,
35.5 x 26.5 cm
Private collection

*"Painting operates through signs
which are not abstract and incorporeal like words. The signs of
painting are much closer to the
objects themselves. Further, painting manipulates materials which
are themselves living substances.
That is why painting allows one to
go much further than words do, in
approaching things and conjuring
them."* JEAN DUBUFFET

Jean Dubuffet
Road with Men, 1944
Oil on canvas, 129 x 96 cm
Cologne, Museum Ludwig,
Ludwig Donation

whiplash lines are set against an indeterminate background and are certainly irregular in character, but not
amorphous. Some paintings even have titles like *Small
Construction* or *Perpendicular Lines*. But Fautrier's most
far-reaching contributions were the use of compact,
plastic materials and the introduction of an open pictorial structure. What is not found in his work is the free
fluxes of paint, raised to autonomous formal and expressive values, seen in Wols and other L'art informel artists.

Poetry of the Commonplace

Dubuffet (pp. 255, 256) became famous much more
rapidly than Fautrier. After a checkered life he finally
decided, in 1942, to give up his business career and
devote himself to art. This was a year before Fautrier
began painting his *Otages*. Prior to his decision Dubuffet
had already discovered a new and unspoiled originality
and authenticity in the picture-making of the mentally
ill, of naive artists and children, which he collectively
called L'art brut, or raw art. Such impressions contributed materially to his nevertheless highly conscious
and intellectually considered neo-primitive works of the
1940s and 1950s, with which Dubuffet ironically
protested against elegant *peinture* and traditional, supposedly eternal values in art. He discovered the poetry
contained in plain materials, in the commonplace
things of everyday life, in the banal existences of human
beings, animals, and plants.

Initially perfectionism of any sort seemed suspect to
Dubuffet. Nor was he interested in the unusual. Banal
things, seen wherever you look – chalk scribblings made
by children on the pavement, rough-surfaced stones,
muddy soil, dried and cracked – sufficed Dubuffet
entirely. In the pseudo-naive, carefree and ironic style
developed from such impressions the artist in 1947
portrayed a series of contemporary intellectual heroes,
including Fautrier, Michaux, the critic Michel Tapié,
and Pierre, the son of Henri Matisse, under the collective title *Lovelier Than You Think*.

Dubuffet rehabilitated the trivial in a way quite
different from the later Pop artists, many of whom, such
as Claes Oldenburg and Eduardo Paolozzi, greatly
admired him. Instead of deriding the commonplace, he
attempted to discover its hidden poetry, and to arrange
"rich and sublime festivities." He did so without the
aid of exquisite colors or sophisticated forms. The picturesque seemed equally suspect to Dubuffet as good
taste and culture did as a whole. He did not believe in
the *homo aestheticus*, saying "As far as the superiority of
the scholar or the precious sophisticate over the next
best farmhand is concerned, I have my doubts."

For the Dubuffet of the early and probably most significant phases, there was no color, but only matter: "I
am thinking of paintings," he said, "that are quite simply
made of the original, monochrome ooze, without variation of any kind, neither in tone nor in hues, not even
in gloss or arrangement, and whose effect would derive
solely from the many types of sign, trace, and vital

set an example and proved highly influential, even
across the Atlantic – Jackson Pollock and Willem De
Kooning were deeply impressed by the *Otages*. Fautrier's
œuvre is rebellious, disquieting, and at the same time
hermetic, not easily accessible and discouraging to
those who think abstract art can be taken in at a glance.
Not only a committed artist but a difficult, hot-tem-
pered man, Fautrier prompted Paulhan to dub him
l'enragé.

The consistency with which Fautrier broke with traditional forms and techniques was quite unmatched.
His skepticism was radical. He was not only one of the
earliest but one of the most significant representatives of
that disillusioned second wave of modernity that began
to sweep away classical modernism just before mid-century. The *Otages* are a key case in point. Done under the
impression of war atrocities, they show tormented, tortured, deformed heads, and in the images of the series of
Objects and *Naked Ones* the remains of dismembered,
decaying bodies as well.

It is precisely the anonymity of the victims, the
waiver of a direct reference to visual appearances in
favor of vague suggestion, that lends these images their
dignity and authenticity. Form and color combine into
a sign, a shockingly grisly if sometimes sardonically
grotesque, alienated symbol of reality. In the following
years, as the shock subsided, Fautrier again began tentatively to try a more aesthetic approach. The dense material of the paintings developed into relief, the palette
grew lighter, more buoyant.

Unlike the forms in the works of most of the other
French gestural painters, the color forms in Fautrier's
paintings do not appear to extend beyond the canvas
edge. His rectangles, squares, and spontaneous,

Jean Dubuffet
Smeared On Man, 1955
Oil on canvas, 116 x 89 cm
Private collection

Jean Dubuffet
Amorous Propositions, 1967
Vinyl on canvas, 130 x 162 cm
Private collection

intermittently, it continually turns, going off into emptiness, taking and giving and taking, and it incessantly emits its filament, which breaks off and is reknotted and whose ends dangle down all over the place. – And you can paint this filament. It's marvellous!"

Dubuffet's painting seems suspended between reality and dream, actual and mental experience, and his figures are wittily ambiguous. Accordingly, his art holds an intermediate position between abstraction and objectivity. Dubuffet has created his own fantastic reality out of a belief, as one commentator says, in "the magic miracles of materiality," which for him is true nature. He is a primitive who uses the advancement of the chemical industry for his atavistic incantations, and who announces that art is meant not for the eye but for the mind alone.

As early as the 1950s Dubuffet turned to other, more graphically oriented techniques. By combining lithograph and ink impressions in their negative form, concrete details from reality were alienated through surprising juxtapositions. The graphic elements of these assemblages of printed material also found entry into the oil medium, determining the texture of the *Legends*. By comparison to the rawness of Dubuffet's early L'art brut, these images appear more gentle, even almost decorative, in terms of theme, color and style. Yet in comparison to the *Landscape Tables*, the *Landscapes of the Mind*, the *Philosophical Stones*, the amorphous, practically unstructured *Textures* and *Topographies*, the absurd plant collages, and not lastly the *Materiologies*, Dubuffet's *Legends* and the ensuing *L'Hourloupe* series have lost something of the latent demonology and especially the tactile character of the early works, while becoming more light-hearted and carefree in character.

In a word, Dubuffet's pictorial idiom gradually became more puzzle-like, more ornamental. This ornamental rhythm of cellular signs was then applied to sculptural and architectural projects (such as the group of trees on Chase Manhattan Plaza, the enamel garden in Otterlo, the "Villa Falbala" in Périgny-sur-Yerres). From abandoned works on paper, finally, Dubuffet composed his *Théâtre de mémoire* (Theater of Memory), assemblages intended to capture moments of thought, made in the belief, as the artist says, that "visual memory is more vivid than merely cognitive memory." It was "rich and sublime festivities" that Dubuffet celebrated in his late work. It had little more to do with the earlier "ecstasies of commonness." The sworn enemy of the culture business had become a brilliant arranger of form, an aesthete.

Painting as an Actionistic Show

As Dubuffet's example indicates, only those practitioners of L'art informel could hope to survive the period who retained the capacity for change and further development. One of them, Georges Mathieu, recognized the problem early on. "The so-called avant-garde," he said, "is basically only a working-out and statement of

impression which the hand leaves when it works pulp." Employing tar, cement, plaster and stones, Dubuffet produced ambiguous, insouciantly ironic imagery in which tables might double as landscapes, textures metamorphose into tiny idols, gnomes or demons, animals or people, into a *Tumult in the Sky* or a *Metaphysical Landscape*.

There lives on in such pictures a memory of forgotten things which we pass by without noticing. "The glance is very mobile," the painter says, "it leaps quickly from one object to the next, flares up and goes out a thousand times a second, stops and begins again. Then,

Gaston Chaissac
Composition with Face, 1961
Gouache on paper, 31 x 21 cm
Hamburg, private collection

Enrico Baj
The General, 1969
Appliqué, 146 x 114 cm
Paris, Musée National d'Art
Moderne, Centre Georges
Pompidou

new forms, a short time before these become part of a tradition." Yet Mathieu's insight could not save his paintings, not to mention his spectacular, and surely also speculative actions as a quick-sketch artist, from oblivion. As a showman who knew how to beguile an audience, Mathieu briefly seemed to have stepped into the shoes of Dalí, whose irrationalism, however, the intelligent and well-educated Frenchman eschewed. Like a fencer, Mathieu threw his whole body into the process of painting (p. 258). His extremely effective and telegenic demonstrations sometimes recalled circus performances. Moustachioed and clad in bizarre costumes, Mathieu attacked canvases of often huge proportions. The act of painting itself was so "interesting and exciting," he thought, that it deserved to be demonstrated for all to see.

What Mathieu publicly demonstrated was action painting in pure form. His virtuoso performances, though perhaps only superficially brilliant, did make entirely clear what was at the bottom of L'art informel of the Tachist variety and the Action Painting concurrently developing in the United States: painting itself had become the subject of painting, the strokes and flows of paint had become its "content."

In Mathieu's case these configurations consisted of dynamic, as if electrified, signs with a calligraphic character. Yet unlike Chinese or Japanese calligraphy these pictographs, which naturally had their source in Surrealist automatic writing, did not communicate content or encourage meditation but were purely dramatic, even theatrical in nature. This was not changed when Mathieu, using the title of an exhibition he organized in 1947, said he wished his painting to be understood as "lyrical abstraction."

Jean-Paul Riopelle (p. 259), a Canadian artist in Paris, likewise began as an "automatic" painter in the footsteps of the Surrealists and Expressionists. Soon, however, he turned to a more controlled, if still vivid style, using spatula and palette-knife to apply thick impasto over paint brushed or dripped on the canvas to produce textured, mosaic-like surfaces. The pictorial order was based on serial procedures and the interlocking of color fields. The canvases exhibited no composition in the narrower sense, having no center of interest, no beginning nor end. The paint textures seemed arbitrarily cut off at the canvas edge, as if they would other-

Zao Wou-ki
Untitled, 1962
Oil on canvas, 130 x 160 cm
Private collection

Georges Mathieu
Capetians Everywhere, 1954
Oil on canvas, 295 x 600 cm
Paris, Musée National d'Art
Moderne, Centre Georges
Pompidou

*"Evolution in art is produced by the
saturation of the means of expression
(significations) and their replacement by new means, of which the
efficacy is unknown at the moment
of use. The significance of these new
means assumes a necessity, a structuring of the pictorial material, such
as that realized to a lesser degree in
psychical or biological facts."*
GEORGES MATHIEU

Henri Michaux
Untitled, 1970
Watercolor on paper, 50 x 31.5 cm
Private collection

wise continue into infinity. Riopelle's approach was
based not on the laws of harmony but on the principle of
the series. Just as, in Monet's late *Water Lilies*, the subject almost vanishes behind the veils of paint, Riopelle's
non-objective imagery inadvertantly calls up memories
of objects. The picture becomes a landscape of paint
whose finely articulated textures recall the earth seen
from the air. Yet rather than abstracting from an experience of nature, Riopelle too came back to nature
through art. The impasto application and the furrows
separating the color fields give many of his paintings a
rough, relief-like surface. Not surprisingly, the artist
later made attempts in sculpture. The dynamic character of mutually opposed energies and color gradations
lends Riopelle's canvases a high degree of gestural
expressiveness, and his mastery of color placement lends
them an unusual coloristic quality.

Although the Belgian painter-writer Henri Michaux
(ill. left) belonged to the Paris scene, he was not a Tachist
in the narrower sense. However, the contemporary tendency drew much attention to his drawings and paintings. For the poet, who was self-taught as a painter,
painting and drawing were a means to overcome speechlessness, to make visible what could not be expressed in
words: "Can't they see," he asked, "that I paint in order
to leave words behind…?" Another thing Michaux, the
great traveller, wanted to leave behind was the visible
world, and the laws of logic as well. What interested him
were "the spaces within," the inner man, to the exploration of which he devoted a lifetime of work, untiringly
investigating the dialectic of word and image, both
of which he understood as writing, script. Michaux
attempted to expand his consciousness with the aid of
drugs, such as mescaline, and to record the visions he
experienced. For him, free will was "the death of art."

Jean-Paul Riopelle
Composition, 1954
Oil on canvas, 97 x 162.5 cm
Berlin, Nationalgalerie,
Staatliche Museen zu Berlin –
Preußischer Kulturbesitz

Construction and Destruction

Another "anti-artist" like Dubuffet, at least in terms of the use of unconventional materials, was Alberto Burri (p. 260). But after abandoning abstract painting in 1948, the Italian artist took a quite different path. A former physician, who did not begin to paint until his internment in an American prisoner-of-war camp, Burri made pictures out of burlap bags, sheets of wood and iron, and various plastics, which he crumpled and folded and burned with a torch. The results were compositions of both rustic force and great sensibility, whereby the charm of the rough surface was consciously included in a play with materials inspired by Schwitters. Above all,

the burlap images accentuated with color, which possessed a latent classicism in which Constructivist, and especially Cubist influences were clearly apparent, brought Burri rapid success. Their raw, material nature was consciously opposed to the perfection of "fine painting." The expressive force of the compositions was increased by the roughly stitched textiles, their apparently random folds and wrinkles, and by the shadows cast by loosely dangling ends. The "wounds," "scars," and "sutures" may contain reminiscences of the artist's earlier profession, but they without doubt represent an attempt to come to terms with his experiences as a medic during the war.

Simon Hantaï
Untitled, 1973
Acrylic on canvas, 243 x 232 cm
Paris, private collection

Jean-Paul Riopelle
Virevolte, 1953
Oil on canvas, 81 x 65 cm
Private collection

The burning red in many of the burlap pictures evokes the idea of festering wounds, just as the black craters in other works – including some executed in plastics – call up strong associations with the smell of burning and decay, apart from the immediate association with the moon's surface. When Burri built picture-objects of boards, the impression of a boarded-up world was inescapable, despite the fact that the artist would not hear of such interpretations. Perhaps his most compelling works were those in which the picture surface was hermetically sealed off with pieces of sheet iron. These somber, often almost pathetically serious works – picture, relief, and object in one – had a great influence on Jannis Kounellis.

Alberto Burri
Sack 5P, 1953
Mixed media and collage, 150 x 130 cm
Città di Castello, Fondazione Palazzo
Albizzini, Collezione Burri

Right:
Alberto Burri
Sacking and Red, 1954
Burlap, glue and vinyl on canvas,
86 x 100 cm, London, Tate Gallery

The factor that proved seminal for the following generation of artists was above all the suspenseful dialectic in Burri's art between constructive form and destructive dissolution of form. This combination completely transcended the principles of L'art informel. Not only Kounellis (pp. 362, 558 f) and Arte Povera, but a number of American image- and object-makers, profited from this step forward.

Burri's compatriot Roberto Crippa (ill. left) initially involved himself with an action painting in which wild, whirling spirals predominated, before attaining to a new classicism in relief paintings, collages of wood, iron, canvas, and paper.

Tellurian Landscapes

Perhaps the most significant representative of L'art informel in the wake of Wols, as well as of material-oriented painting, is Antoni Tàpies of Spain (pp. 261, 262). Tàpies' works are informed by a great, organizing artistic intelligence. The emotions that enter them tend to be of the quiet and meditative nature, rather than of the volcanic so characteristic of other gestural abstractionists. Instead of acting out his inmost urges in the arena of the picture, Tàpies consciously orders the plane in terms of expansive, often empty passages and simple, generous forms, that have been given an ordered structure.

Roberto Crippa
Untitled, 1962
Collage on wood, 200 x 200 cm
Private collection

The impulses he received from his great compatriots Picasso and Miró, from Klee and the Surrealists, declined in importance as his career progressed. Tàpies creates his own personal reality – pictorial landscapes whose formal tension derives from a contrast between empty, silent spaces and shaped configurations, between positive and negative, between projections and depressions, between chance and order, freedom and control. Some of the artist's works put one in mind of crumbling walls, inscribed with enigmatic markings reminiscent of Assyrian or Egyptian pictographs, which elude rational explanation but nonetheless seem to bear witness to lives once lived in some distant past. Others reveal primeval landscapes, lost continents, the ground plans of buried fortifications, craters and sand dunes, blown by winds off the ocean.

These are not metaphysical but tellurian landscapes, very much of the earth in that they point far back in time to forms of pre-existence on our planet. Often dark, dun, apparently monochrome but actually shot through with an extraordinarily subtle range of color, Tàpies's paintings seem removed from the context of current time. They possess a strange dignity and serenity, and suggest a positive reaction to the enigmas of the universe, which we know are insoluble despite nuclear fission, space travel, gene technology, and futurological predictions. Tàpies creates "counter-images," the replies of a thinking artist, on the one hand, to the restlessness and high-tech euphoria from which we both suffer and know to be our future, and on the other to the permanently lurking threat of nothingness.

As with Fautrier and the early Dubuffet, materials – plaster, cement, sand, clay, paint mass – play a key role in the Catalan artist's work. While human beings may not appear in the form of figures, the human presence is there, in the form of traces left by the hand, inscribed or impressed on the surface. Tàpies thus might be called an early forerunner of *Spurensicherung*, trace or clue-finding art, which later emerged particularly in Germany. He also has had an unmistakable influence on the purism of Minimal Art, on Arte Povera and its approach to materials, and finally on Process Art.

Tàpies's compatriot, Antonio Saura, also began in a Surrealist style (p. 263). But in contrast to Tàpies, the son of a Jewish mother and an Arabian father is a radical socialist and abstract expressionist. He lets his convictions and sufferings flow untrammelled into stark black and white imagery composed of ragged forms in which demons seem to lurk. "The canvas is a battlefield without limits," says Saura, and his early pictures looked the part. Later the forms grew simpler, and an earthy brown supplemented the black and white. Yet the expressive energy, the directness of the painterly statement of protest against an unjust world order remained.

Discovering the poetry in previously overlooked materials has been the concern of Jaap Wagemaker, a Dutch artist and outsider who has stood somewhat in the shadow of the Cobra group (p. 263 below). His

Above:
Antoni Tàpies
Grey Relief in Four Parts, 1963
Mixed media, with sand, on canvas,
150 x 217 cm
Cologne, Museum Ludwig

Below:
Antoni Tàpies
Matter on Wood and Oval, 1979
Mixed media on wood,
270 x 220 cm
Private collection

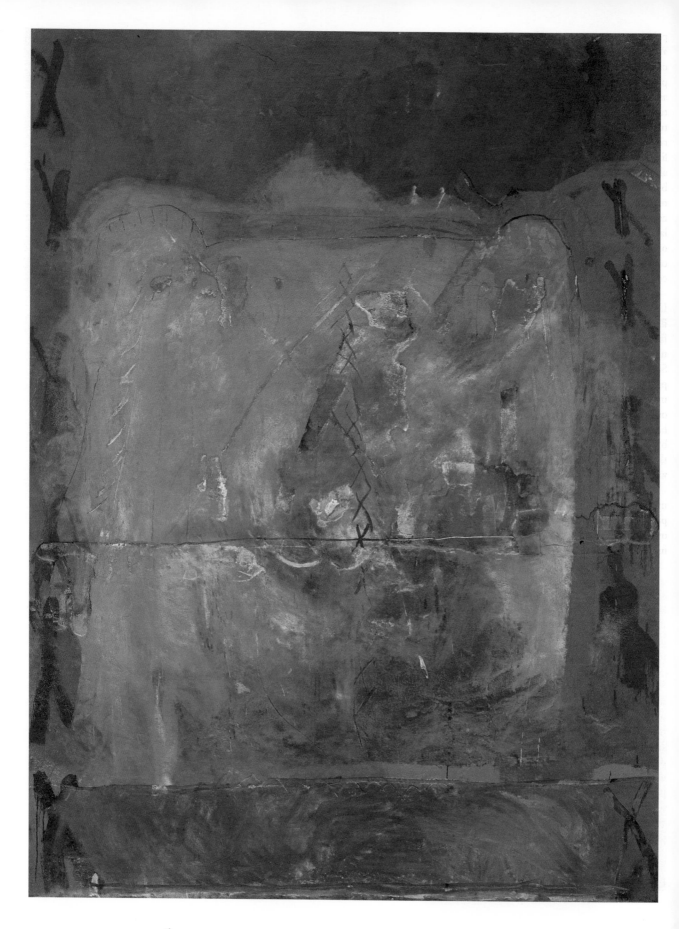

paintings, built like masonry into painted reliefs, evoke a world in process of transformation. Wagemaker cements stones and twine onto canvas, sometimes supplementing them with unprepossessing materials such as rags, textile scraps, stucco, and base metals. The structures of the artist's "primeval landscapes" are less spiritual, more earthy and secular than those of Tàpies. The colors tend to remain in the range of earth tones, but like so many of his colleagues of this period, Wagemaker also investigated the expressive potential of a silent black. Viewing his works one is put in mind of lakes, mountain chains, great plains, deserts, and volcanic craters in a planetary – or more rarely, inter-planetary landscape. Forms penetrate into the picture plane from outside, strive beyond its edges, or describe labyrinthine circles. A forceful sense of design holds the often harsh contrasts in equilibrium.

The leading German representatives of Tachism and L'art informel have survived better than most of their French counterparts. This is probably largely due to the fact that they recognized the pitfalls of spontaneous gestural painting early on. The oldest of these artists, Emil Schumacher, combines a thoughtful intelligence with painterly energy and a vulnerable sensibility. Schumacher's canvases (pp. 263, 264) are "landscapes" without direct reference to the visually perceived world, tellurian "landscapes of the inward man." The artist veritably digs into the paint as if it were a matter of opening the earth's crust to discover what the injury to matter will bring to light.

Schumacher's art is disillusioned, but not despairing. As he himself says, his pictures are those of a "happy painter" who has wrest them out of a struggle with his own doubts. They are serious, inquiring, and skeptical, in keeping with the experience of a generation of

Antonio Saura
Tani, 1962
Oil on canvas, 162 x 130 cm
Private collection

Below left:
Emil Schumacher
For Berlin, 1957
Oil on canvas, 170 x 131 cm
Frankfurt/Main, Deutsche
Bank Collection

Below right:
Jaap Wagemaker
The Living Desert, 1957
Mixed media, with sand, on
canvas, 90 x 75 cm
Germany, private collection

Page 262:
Antoni Tàpies
Brick-Colored Relief, 1963
Mixed media, with sand,
on canvas, 260 x 195 cm
Düsseldorf, Kunstsammlung
Nordrhein-Westfalen

Emil Schumacher
Terrano XII, 1990
Oil on wood, 170 x 125 cm
Private collection

Jean Miotte
Deliverance, 1960
Oil on canvas, 73 x 92 cm
Cologne, Museum Ludwig,
Haubrich Collection

Karl Otto Götz
Painting of 8.2.1953, 1953
Mixed media on canvas,
175 x 145 cm
Saarbrücken, Saarland Museum

of deep black or earthy brown, applied over the paint layer or shining through from the ground. Schumacher works at full pitch, both physically and mentally. A dialectic of painterly surface and masterfully distributed graphic accents, of shapes and negative shapes, lends the artist's work an extraordinary tension and concision. The process of painting itself, as a decidedly unliterary theme of visual thinking and acting, becomes an existential symbol in this vital imagery. "The measure of the picture," says Schumacher, "is the force that dictates the path of the line."

This corresponds to French painter Jean Miotte's statement that "painting is an act, a sequence of movements one bears within oneself, whose source is one's inner being." This emphasis on the active, immediate nature of the painting process well characterizes Miotte's approach, a free-form lyrical abstraction beholding to the Ecole de Paris, Tachism, Abstract Expressionism – in a word, to L'art autre. The artist is just as familiar with the American scene as with the European. In this regard his highly original work, which since the mid-1990s has exhibited a marked reduction of color accompanied by a sense of expanding space, mediates between streams on either side of the Atlantic (ill. below).

painters whose relevant work began only after 1945 and who, unlike their predecessors after 1918, felt no temptation to exorcise chaos by means of signs and emblems of a new order. The younger generation lived in *Sodom* (Hagen, Karl-Ernst-Osthaus-Museum), as one of Schumacher's early encrusted landscapes is titled, a landscape in fiery reds that emerge from the heavy integument of paint as if secreted from a wound.

Not all of the artist's images are so marked by pain. Many are dominated by a wonderful, subtly glowing, spiritualized blue, which, however – as in other cases the red and orange – is shot through with darker gradations,

Labyrinths

With his tendency to philosophical musing and introspection, Bernard Schultze is a quintessentially German artist (p. 265 right). An excellent draftsman whose graphic skill remains evident in his painting, Schultze traces his roots back through Surrealism to German Romanticism, all the way back to Grünewald, the Danube School, and late Gothic. As the eye roams through his allusive, richly configured landscapes in two or three dimensions, it is confronted with *Les fleurs du mal* in poisonous hues. Not coincidentally, the French Symbolists and the German apocalyptic poet Georg Trakl are amongst Schultze's favourite writers, who himself writes poems. His visionary, labyrinthine landscapes, though populated with demons and horrors, are shot through with irony and a sometimes Chaplinesque humor that create detachment. The ancient Vanitas motif is re-interpreted out of the chiliastic consciousness of a late

culture and the hallucinatory vision of a belated Alexandrine, the aesthetics of the ugly re-formulated in modern terms. As regards palette, green and red in all variations and nuances dominate. These do not have the brilliance seen in Italian, English, and above all French painting; they are greyed, more morbid, sometimes to the point of evoking decay. Many Schultze paintings are nocturnal pieces, phantasmagorias without beginning or end, visionary landscapes that exist on a level beyond the real.

The flowing paint not only soon penetrated beyond the canvas edge, it burgeoned into full three dimensions. The next step was the emergence from the tangle of proliferating lineatures and flux of color of hidden figures – Schultze's *Migofs*. In these figures the eerie and ominous threat lurking in the darkness of the human unconscious was brought to light. They confront us with the leering mask of man stripped naked, reduced to a creature. Yet the crippled, decaying appearance of Schultze's figures is mitigated by signs of new, proliferating growth. In his rich and very fresh late work the color chords become surprisingly light, proving that the

artist is no pessimist with regard to the world's future. He describes his attitude as that of "existential optimism." "I am certain," Schultze says, "that nature will go on, it will grow and proliferate as it does in my paintings, even if someday humans should have ceased to exist."

In the fairy-tale world of Ursula, Schultze's wife, dangers lurk just beneath the carefree surface (ill. above left). Her work is more strongly beholding to Surrealism than her husband's. In stippled brushwork and inked line she relates tales of glory and mystery that emerge from subconscious depths and play themselves out in a twilight realm populated by good and bad fairies, humans, animals, plants, and strange legendary creatures. Painterly sophistication and a love of story-telling combine, not without sarcasm, in images whose precious shimmer occasionally recalls medieval miniatures.

Gerhard Hoehme (p. 266 below) is perhaps the most meditative figure among the German gestural abstractionists. He has also travelled the longest road. Hoehme intends his pictures – and not only the "Roman Letters"

Ursula
It's me. So what?, 1995
Oil on canvas, 147 x 98 cm
Hamburg, private collection

Bernard Schultze
Apparition, 1990
Oil on canvas, 120 x 90 cm
Private collection

– to be *read*. Despite his early revolt against the "tyranny of the rectangle," despite his triumphal discovery of color as energy, as a simultaneously mental and material principle, Hoehme has remained an introverted artist to the point of self-flagellation. He allows line literally to emerge from the painted surface or painted object, as a "feeler" extending from the imaginary pictorial space into the actual, surrounding space. Hoehme has altered himself, his thinking and imagery more visibly and more frequently than other German artists of the period, exposing himself and his work to the highest risks. His imagery demands that the viewer complete it in the process of viewing. "Paintings are not on canvas," Hoehme states, "they are in the human" who makes and sees them.

Early Action Painting

If the label of "action painter" fits any German artist in the L'art informel orbit, then it is Fred Thieler (ill. right). After a late start due to political discrimination in the Third Reich, Thieler became an influential mentor and respected role-model for entire student generations at the Berlin School of Art. In keeping with his belief that painting is his only way of life, he concentrates on the

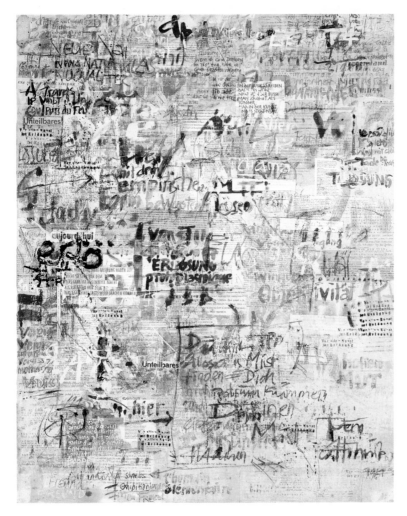

dynamic painting process, using a limited range of color and occasional admixtures of rough-and-ready collage. Everything he experiences, victories and defeats, euphoria and depression, finds immediate entry into Thieler's imagery. Marked by a difficult life, he chose gestural abstraction because, as he says, "You can't live with ideologies."

Karl Otto Götz paints with even more rapidity than Thieler, sometimes even finishing a canvas in a matter of minutes (p. 264 below right). The process has been frequently described. First "the initial strokes are quickly set with thin, dark paint on a light ground, as pattern and ground." Then new textures are created by drawing a rubber scraper across the wet paint. Finally Götz uses a dry brush to inscribe linear skeins into the wet surface. The imagery is the result of long and intensive premeditation, followed by a rapid execution that balances on the razor's edge between success and failure. Götz's action painting is based on a Surrealist concept: "Use psychic automatism and paroxysm to catch the miracle by the tail!" The work demands extreme concentration on the artist's part. The high risk involved determines an acceptance/rejection ratio of about 1:15 or 1:20. Götz has been able to derive continually new and interesting formulations by patiently exploring this dynamic process.

According to K.R.H. (Kurt Rudolf Hoffmann) Sonderborg, who was born in the Danish town of that name (p. 267), the ecstatic rhythms in his work reflect a spiritual longing, an artistic transformation of personal experience, an answer to realities seen and heard – in a jazz cellar, at Hamburg harbor, in prison, on Stromboli, or in Rome. His pictorial means are emblems of his own

Tachism and L'art informel was Winfried Gaul, whose Tachist works were extraordinarily sensitive in terms of palette and a structure that had the effect of being potentially unbounded.

Despite post-war deprivations, the period was one of abundance in painting, in France as well as Spain, in Italy and especially in Germany. If one were to name the smallest common denominator of L'art informel and gestural abstraction, it would probably be the artists emphasis on color and its expressive potentials, which reflected a faith in the continuing meaning of painting. What characterized the "young wild painters" of the 1950s, immediately in the wake of the calamity of the Second World War, was the compelling intensity of their pictorial structure and a high degree of existential concern and thoughtful skepticism, accompanied by a waiver of myth, self-assertive posing, and nationalistic and religious attitudes.

While the effects of European gestural abstraction on the whole were enormous, as regards its influence on and exchange of ideas with the American scene, its German representatives played only a modest role. Not even Wols was duly recognized across the Atlantic until the mid-1980s. The revolt against the academy which opened new roads to art was only one manifestation of the extraordinary intellectual ferment of a period dominated by restless spirits in every field.

K. R. H. Sonderborg
Composition, 1959
Oil on cardboard, on canvas,
107.5 x 70.5 cm
Bonn, Kunstmuseum Bonn

existence, and at the same time something entirely different. There is a Sonderborg painting of 1980 in which, far transcending current gestural tendencies, the diagonally or horizontally rotating strokes seem to come to rest, condensing into a stringent sign. The image is "trace art" of a very special brand. Its title: *Trace of Andreas Baader* (later abbreviated by the artist to *Trace A.B.*). We see the contour of the damaged ceiling molding in the terrorist's cell in Stammheim Prison; an irregular triangle marks the position of his body under the bedsheet. Sonderborg has projected into the image his shock at the mysterious circumstances surrounding Baader's death, and his sympathy for the prisoner's plight. It is a painting of compassion as well as of impassioned commitment, a political painting of compelling force, but without the slightest trace of propagandistic bias or hate.

To render emotions visible in which the temperament and personality of the artist were expressed, was also the goal of Peter Brüning, who died young (ill. right). Brüning employed color with great reserve and delicacy. In his early paintings it served primarily to convey impulsive, spontaneous, yet intellectually controlled gestures that embodied Brüning's characteristic lyrical and dramatic sensibility. During his L'art informel phase, his procedure was related to the serial music of the period, with whose composers and interpreters he maintained close contacts. Later Brüning turned to other themes: street scenes and a painterly cartography. Another German artist who soon left the orbit of

Peter Brüning
Untitled, 1961
Oil on canvas, 129 x 97 cm
Private collection

The Paris-New York Shift

America Overcomes Europe
Mid-Century Painting in the USA

The years around mid-century were important not only chronologically but stylistically, for they marked a profound shift in the development of visual art. This process, in contrast to the period preceding World War One, took place in a rather more evolutionary than revolutionary way. Nevertheless, the art being done around the world after mid-century differed fundamentally from that which had gone before. The outbreak of World War Two and the subsequent war years marked a fissure between the end of the first modern movement and the beginning of its successor.

The disillusion that artists felt in the face of total war, a disillusion that had often led them to abandon their last remaining ideals, long ruled out a naive enthusiasm of any sort in art. After 1945, we look in vain for high-sounding programs, and find only very few optimistic manifestos. The metaphysical idealism of the Zero movement and its initiators, Yves Klein and Lucio Fontana, was the exception that proved the rule. Except during an interim period in the late 1960s, hardly any artist still dared to conceive of art as a vehicle of ideology. Few wished to emulate the results of the more or less strict government regulation of art in the Eastern Bloc countries and Maoist China. Liberty of artistic practice became the fundamental tenet.

As economic prosperity returned to the post-war world, the demand for art increased. In the West the consumption of art, in all its positive and negative aspects, soon reached a level no one could have predicted. Modern art became a public, and popular, affair. The improvement of printing and reproduction methods, up to and including the dubious advance of producing art works in series, brought contemporary art to strata of the population which it had never before reached. The museums and exhibition venues began to attract undreamed-of numbers of visitors, a tendency that is still on the upswing at this writing.

The circle of collectors, connoisseurs, and afficionados of contemporary art grew ever larger. Governments, churches, and communities began, if hesitantly and not always sure of their aesthetic ground, to make contacts with artists and to award commissions. These institutions were joined by banks and businesses which recognized the image-promoting potentials of art. There commenced a process of integration that has continued

"The modern artist, it seems to me, is expressing an inner world – in other words – expressing the energy, the motion, and other inner forces."
JACKSON POLLOCK

Jackson Pollock
Black and White, Number Five, 1952
Automotive lacquer on canvas, 142 x 80 cm
Private collection

and grown stronger to this day, but which has also brought problems of a different and perhaps unexpected kind along with it. What successful artists have had to fear most, since the 1980s at the lastest, is a benevolent embrace that threatens to crush creativity, since it entails adaptation to market mechanisms and something most people, not only artists, find hard to resist – the temptation to make a quick buck.

Now that America has once again begun looking to Europe, and the German-Italian "trans-avant-garde" has had a spectacular success both in New York and London, it has become easier than in previous years to imagine the dominant influence which Europe once exerted over American art before its emancipation.

Jackson Pollock
Number 4, 1950
Oil, enamel paint and aluminum paint on canvas, 124.1 x 94.3 cm
Pittsburgh (PA), The Carnegie Museum of Art, Gift of Frank S. Kaplan

Jackson Pollock
Guardians of the Secret, 1943
Oil on canvas, 122.8 x 191.3 cm
San Francisco (CA),
San Francisco Museum of Art,
Albert M. Bender Collection

"My painting does not come from the easel. I hardly ever stretch my canvas before painting. I prefer to tack the unstretched canvas to the hard wall or the floor. I need the resistance of hard surface. On the floor I am more at ease. I feel nearer, more a part of the painting, since this way I can walk around it, work from the four sides and literally be in the painting. This is akin to the method of the Indian sand painters of the West.
When I am in my painting, I'm not aware of what I'm doing. It is only after a sort of get acquainted' period that I see what I have been about. I have no fears about making changes, destroying the image, etc., because the painting has a life of its own. I try to let it come through. It is only when I lose contact with the painting that the result is a mess. Otherwise there is pure harmony, an easy give and take, and the painting comes out well."

JACKSON POLLOCK

Since the 19th century, masterpieces of European art had continually flowed to America, thanks to the unparalleled financial resources of collectors who wished to embellish their business empires with culture. The influence of Europe on American artists was equally strong, and it continued well beyond the 19th century and far into the twentieth. Many of them, such as Hopper, studied in Europe, above all in Paris. What resulted artistically from this confrontation of the New World with the Old was for the most part eclectic, if not imitative. Many Americans in Paris, beginning with Symbolism, Fauvism, or Cubism, launched into their own more or less convincing variants of tendencies current on the Paris scene.

This changed fundamentally in the course of the 1940s, as artists in America, especially in New York, grew increasingly confident of their own powers. The next decade brought a growing awareness in Europe that an exchange of roles had taken place. There was no denying that American artists had shaken off European tutelage. The overwhelming vitality of the huge canvases of the Action and Color Field painters made the pictures of the abstract Ecole de Paris seem tasteful but substantially modest products of an aging culture.

The superb exhibition "Fifty Years of Modern Art," shown at the Brussels World Fair of 1958, passed the European development in review once again; but in the American pavilion, Europeans saw themselves confronted with an independent new art, above all with painting of compelling power and undoubted originality. Previously, the Basel Kunsthalle had shown, for the first time in Europe, "The New American Painting," an exhibition compiled by the Museum of Modern Art. What announced itself here became a reality with

breathtaking speed. Within the next few years New York had supplanted Paris as the world center of the arts.

Beginnings in 1913
The long road to the emancipation of American art from Europe began in 1913, with the legendary Armory Show. As in Paris with the Impressionists, it was a photographer who took the initiative in the art world of New York after the turn of the century. Just as Nadar had mounted the first exhibition of Impressionist paintings at his studio on Boulevard des Capuchines, Alfred Stieglitz presented the first shows of avant-garde art in America at his studio at 291 Fifth Avenue. Stieglitz showed Rodin's drawings, causing a great scandal, then works by Cézanne, Matisse, Rousseau, Picabia, and Constantin Brancusi. His studio became the focus of New York Dada. Yet the reactions of American audiences and critics, despite their freedom from overweening tradition, were every bit as biased as those of their European counterparts. Instead of calling avant-garde artists "Hottentots in starched shirts" or "paint-spattering monkeys" as in Paris, they were termed a "black gang" or, in the case of a group of socially critical painters, the Ashcan School.

As Herbert Frank has pointed out, the situation of the American artist attempting to cast off the fetters of an inflexible tradition was even more difficult than that of his Old World colleagues: "Even though the young Impressionists felt like 'pariahs' because the official Salon remained closed to them, they nevertheless lived in an educated society that revered art as a high cultural good … In a nation that had battled to escape its colonial past, on the other hand … all that counted was

Jackson Pollock
Search, 1955
Oil and enamel paint on canvas,
146 x 228.6 cm
Private collection

efficiency of action and hard-headed, practical think-ing. While science, in so far as it served progress and furthered industrial development, enjoyed high esteem, the significance of art and literature had not even entered the average American's field of vision."

But there were above-average Americans as well, such as unbiased and impassioned collectors of the type embodied by the Stein family, especially the poet Gertrude and her brother Leo. The significance of these men and women cannot be over-estimated, for in Amer-ica, as initially in Europe, it was neither public institu-tions nor government departments that interested themselves in modern art, but private citizens.

Arthur B. Davis, president of the Association of American Painters and Sculptors, founded in 1912 and comprising 25 members, saw the *Sonderbund* exhibition held in Cologne, Germany, that same year. Together with his friend, Walt Kuhn, he went through consider-able organizational and diplomatic effort to bring a selection of 500 works of art to the United States. In order not to confront visitors with entirely unfamiliar art straight off, the selection began with Ingres and Delacroix. It was by no means without gaps and revealed Davis's predilection for Symbolism. Then too, tactical considerations made it necessary to include a further 500 works, by more or less traditionalistic Amer-ican artists. The resulting show caused a scandal nonetheless. Davis had expected this, even hoping it would boost interest in his project. By the time it ended, the "International Exhibition of Modern Art" had attracted 75,000 visitors to the Armory building in New York City, and in Chicago it even drew 200,000. Only in conservative Boston did the public stay politely aloof.

The critics wailed once again about the "end of art," but visitors bought pictures nonetheless. A total of 200 European paintings from the show remained in the United States. The taboo that had previously been attached to modern art was broken, even though some time was still to pass before the seeds sown by Davis would sprout in artistic practice. The First World War and its aftermath then interrupted this development.

Influence of the Museum

Sixteen years after the Armory Show, in 1929, the Museum of Modern Art was founded in New York. Once again, the initiative had come from the private sector. Although according to its statutes, the museum was to accept only certified and proven works of art, it revolutionized museum practice in a manner similar to the Hannover Museum headed by Alexander Dorner, who was subsequently driven from Germany by the Nazis. In addition to fine arts, the so-called applied arts, including photography, film, architecture, and design, were given their own departments at the Museum of Modern Art. The traditional ideal of the museum as a treasury for the benefit of connoisseurs and scholars was replaced from the very start by the idea of a vital, democratic art institution. At the Museum of Modern Art, works of art were not understood to be rare and precious objects but reflections and examples of real life.

According to its founding director, Alfred H. Barr, the museum's two supporting pillars were Paris and the Bauhaus. The expansion of the collection, down to the immediate present, was conducted on the basis of Barr's motto that the museum man must be right up front, but still one step behind. In other words, he should follow

"I approach painting the same way I approach drawing, that is direct – with no preliminary studies."
JACKSON POLLOCK

current developments with great attention, without succumbing to the temptation of making the collection into a bazaar of novelties. The "MOMA" has fared quite well under Barr's principles, even though acquisition policy in the field of contemporary art, including American contemporary art, may have been initially somewhat hesitant. At any rate, the influence of the museum and its incomparable collections, as well as that of its associated or succeeding institutions, has materially furthered the appreciation and acceptance of 20th-century art in the United States.

As collecting activities continued to burgeon in America, the revolutionary development of a painting independent of and surpassing European models unfolded in relative obscurity. Though the beginnings of the "Pacific School" in the Northwest – a school, by the way, which its revered mentor, Mark Tobey, called an "invention of the critics" – went back to the year 1930, the final breakthrough of emancipated American art on a national, and soon international level had to wait until 1952. This was the year in which the Museum of Modern Art introduced the New York School, including Pollock, Rothko, Still, and others, in an exhibition titled "15 Americans."

New York Becomes a Capital of Art

In the following period American painting, with irrepressible elan and brash self-confidence, began to play the leading role in world art it would continue to hold until the 1970s. A Paris art dealer of the rank of Daniel Cordier, furtherer of Surrealist and post-Surrealist art, closed his gallery at the time, saying the French capital had become an amusement park for tourists and its art scene had declined into insignificance. In the meantime, people interested in art registered everything that was happening in the New World, especially in New York, but later also on the West Coast, with the same eagerness they had previously reserved for Paris. Not only European artists but European collectors, dealers, and museums began to increasingly orientate themselves towards developments in America.

As the abstract Ecole de Paris produced ever more aesthetic variations on earlier pioneering achievements, the Americans disproved the still widely held hypothesis that abstraction was a uniform, monotonous style. The contrasts between the delicate picture-writing Mark Tobey derived from East Asian calligraphy and the explosive gestures of a Willem De Kooning, between Pollock's frenzied Action Painting and Rothko's or Barnett Newman's serenely meditative panels, could not have been greater. But despite their differences, the American artists of these formative years all shared key things in common: a mixture of vitality and sensibility unprecedented in the art of this century, the ability to lend their works, even the meditative abstractions, the character of immediate reality, and a democratic sense of the social mission of an art which, by definition, was meant for all. The notion of an esoteric existence in an ivory tower would have seemed absurd to most of these artists. Only the late Ad Reinhardt (p. 293) of the *Black Paintings* represents a certain exception, though it should not be forgotten that their creator was also an art theoretician and a political man whose polemics could be scathing.

Painting as a Process

All the artists later labelled Abstract Expressionists shared the need to express themselves through the immediate, spontaneous act of painting. The old idea of the artist as a representative of his contemporaries took on a new, pragmatic meaning in their works, a meaning entirely devoid of the neo-mystical pathos that would reappear in the mature phases of a Rothko and especially a Newman. In Action Painting the gesture and resulting brushstroke express themselves rather than any extraneous meaning; the process of painting represents the content of the picture. In such works the temperament and character of the artist, his joys and despairs, are revealed immediately, without recourse to the intermediary steps of developing a motif. This is especially true of Jackson Pollock.

Pollock once said that he did not want to *illustrate* feelings but to *express* them, spontaneously and immediately, without obfuscating technique. One is put in mind of van Gogh, who likewise wanted to "forget" technique and cause "people to flock together and swear by everything sacred that we have no technique." Pollock's paintings, in which chance and principle converge, in which the vital recklessness of the frontier pioneer meets the neurotic vulnerability of civilized man, are not projections but manifestations of life (pp. 269–274).

The works of Pollock's early phase are done in a livid and somber semi-expressionist style with manneristic traits, recalling El Greco. For a time, the artist was excited by the bright-hued art of the American Indians and their picture-writing, then by the monumental expressiveness of the Mexican revolutionary muralists Rivera, Orozco, and Siqueiros. Surrealism, at least Miró's version, and the quasi-Surrealist phase in Picasso's œuvre left their traces on Pollock's approach as well.

Pollock's painting is a dramatic art of expression. Even where Cubist formal elements still play a role and an ornamental planar arrangement is still strived for, in every square inch of the canvas covered with thick impasto to the point of low relief one senses the artist's impassioned attempts to express his inmost self, to find pictorial signs for a sense of life that oscillated between exuberance and anxiety. In place of the ancient myths we find archetypal symbols from the psycho-analysis of C.G. Jung. (Due to alcohol problems Pollock was under

Jackson Pollock
Frieze, 1953–1955
Oil and aluminum paint on canvas,
66 x 218 cm
Merion (CT), private collection

"The modern artist is living in a mechanical age and we have … mechanical means of representing objects in nature such as the camera and the photograph. The modern artist, it seems to me, is working and expressing an inner world – in other words, expressing the energy, the motion, and other inner forces … the modern artist is working with space and time, and expressing his feelings rather than illustrating …"
JACKSON POLLOCK

Jackson Pollock
Blue Poles, 1953
Oil, automotive lacquer and
aluminum paint on canvas,
210.8 x 488.9 cm
Canberra, Australian National
Gallery

psycho-analytical treatment for a time.) Every striving for objectifying distance gave way to untrammelled subjectivity. Yet when Pollock attempted to give form to his personal despairs, visions, and neurotic fears, he was acting in proxy for America and an entire epoch. When he launched out in "search of a symbol" with the aid of daring abbreviations, one can see a parallel with related attempts in Europe. In a similar way as for the Surrealists, mythology was equated with the unconscious mind, what Lawrence Alloway has called the embodiment of the buried life.

The highroads and detours Pollock took in search of himself, of an art original and without parallel, are paved with pictures of greatly varying quality. His obsession with finding true originality in the midst of an over-civilized, perfected, and regimented environment led in 1947 to a momentous decision. He decided to use a

Willem De Kooning
Merrit Parkway, 1959
Oil on canvas, 228 x 204 cm
Private collection

Page 275:
Willem De Kooning
Woman I, 1950–1952
Oil on canvas, 192.7 x 147.3 cm
New York, The Museum
of Modern Art

method with the aid of which he could give shape to his inmost nature without recourse to conscious design. As he had seen Siqueiros do, Pollock spread a length of canvas on the floor and let paint drip onto it from the brush or straight out of a tin can. The principle of "dripping" was born, permitting the direct transmission of the artist's thought and act into painting, by means of what Max Ernst had called "controlled chance." Pollock himself explained that working on the floor gave him a sense of being closer to the painting, more a part of it. He could walk around it, work on it from all four sides, and literally "be in the picture." The Indians in the West, he added, worked in a similar way on their sand paintings. The logical consequence of Pollock's approach, by the way, was not appreciated by Siqueiros.

With immense concentration, precise observation of the paint trails, and a series of rapid decisions, there emerged the "web of paint" which came to be Pollock's trademark. Many paintings were done as if in a trance. The results have an astonishing density and an often baffling logic. The crucial factor is the artist's ability to combine spontaneity with a sense of form, to make "a lyrical statement of the highest subtlety" even using extremely robust means on enormous formats. This singular ability is just as evident in the brightly colored works in which the surface is covered with dense layers and textures, as it is in the more sparing black and white images, in the small formats as in the monumental canvases.

The contradictions contained in the American character, tensed between the brute force of the pioneer and the neurotic wavering of the modern city-dweller, become a visual event in Pollock's imagery, as does the contrast between the tradition-laden Old World and a New World struggling for cultural self-definition. This contrast is well illustrated by comparing the chamber music in painting of a Wols with the explosive fortissimos of Pollock's Abstract Expressionism.

Willem De Kooning
Woman VI, 1953
Oil on canvas, 174 x 149 cm
Pittsburgh (PA), The Carnegie
Museum of Art, Gift of G.
David Thompson

Willem De Kooning
Untitled, 1970
Oil on parchment, on canvas,
182.8 x 107.9 cm
Private collection

"The attitude that nature is chaotic and that the artist puts order into it is a very absurd point of view, I think. All that we can hope for is to put some order into ourselves. When a man ploughs his field at the right time, it means just that."

WILLEM DE KOONING

Unity of Life and Work

An at least equally important representative of Action Painting, with whom Pollock exhibited as early as 1942, and who even surpassed him in terms of the multifarity and intellectual depth of his rich œuvre, was Willem De Kooning. Eight years younger than Pollock, De Kooning was born in Rotterdam. After an apprenticeship in Holland and Belgium, he decided he wanted to go to America, and arrived there without papers after a fantastic odyssey as a ship's machinist and seaman. After beginnings in a figurative style, De Kooning came under the influence of Miró and his friend, Arshile Gorky, and began to depict an inner, pre-existent world, independent of historical reference and external experience. But the more mastery he gained over his means, the more this "landscape of the soul" receded into the background.

The realistic allusions vanished, and expressive color came to determine the non-perspectival pictorial space. The shapes broke up and appeared to shoot beyond the canvas edge. The content of such paintings lay in the making visible of the painting process, the artist's actions themselves, although the series of *Women*, complex, idol-like or demonic female figures, and such painting titles as *Suburb in Havana* or *Merrit Parkway* (p. 274), indicate that references to things seen and experienced were never entirely expunged from De Kooning's abstractions.

Indeed De Kooning always retained the right of artistic decision and resisted being labelled an Abstract Expressionist by producing obviously figurative works, unconcerned by the confusion his *Women* caused among experts (pp. 275, 276). This open-endedness of artistic stance corresponded to the openness of de Kooning's gestures, the unfinished look of his forms. His paintings are metamorphoses of the visible world and, at the same time, of his own mental and emotional world. Since these realities changed as incessantly as the artist's relation to them, his art eludes all stylistic classification. Transformation and change are the dominant factors in the imagery of this eminently gifted painter. These were the source of the amazing richness of form and expressive gesture in his work, which encompasses the poles of explosive drama and free-flowing, serene, comparatively sparing movements, as seen in his late work. De Kooning's style is incredibly vital, and holds a tense equilibrium between unleashed expression and compositional precision. Perhaps this is due to his having learned a lesson from the Cubists, before – at the suggestion of Gorky – letting himself be inspired by Surrealist automatism. Basically there are only two themes in De Kooning's work, of which he made free

Willem De Kooning
Untitled XII, 1982
Oil on canvas, 177.8 x 203.2 cm
Private collection

variations between abstraction and objectivity in numerous series: landscape and figure. Yet his life's work, which includes remarkable, grotesquely demonic sculptures inspired by Auguste Rodin and Matisse, is perhaps richer in metamorphoses and contrasts than that of any other artist working in the latter half of the 20th century.

The œuvre of Philip Guston, whom Gerhard Mack has called "the studio painter among the Abstract Expressionists who has probably the deepest roots in the Western painting tradition," oscillates between abstraction and figuration. In 1968, after a show at the Jewish Museum, New York, Guston decided to deal solely with concrete objects from that point onwards. The combi-

Philip Guston
Courtroom, 1970
Oil on canvas, 170.2 x 327.6 cm
Private collection

Arshile Gorky
The Liver is the Cock's Comb, 1944
Oil on canvas, 183 x 249 cm
Buffalo (NY), Albright-Knox Art Gallery, Seymour H. Knox Foundation

nation of social critique and caricatural elements in his later work is more than obvious. A good example is the threateningly extended index finger pointing at a hooded Ku Klux Klan member and an amalgam of painter's easel and painter's feet in *Courtroom* (p. 277).

Bradley Walker Tomlin arrived by way of an involvement with Cubism, Surrealism, and calligraphy at a specific variant of Abstract Expressionism that occasionally recalls the work of Mark Tobey. His painting style is not as vehement as Pollock's, to whose circle he belonged. Tomlin's rhythmically repeated, sometimes interwoven colored points, lines, and cross-configurations in subdued hues have the weightlessness of a dance and a lyrical atmosphere (p. 279 above left).

The Surrealist tendency remained stronger in the imagery of De Kooning's friend and contemporary Arshile Gorky (ill. above and left), who committed suicide in his mid-forties after a cancer operation and an automobile accident. Initially influenced by Miró, Picasso, and Léger (who had temporarily emigrated to the United States), and later by Matta and Tanguy, Gorky arrived at his personal style in the early 1940s – a biomorphic abstraction with Surrealist reminiscences. It was only quite late in his career that the native Armenian managed to slough off a certain symbolic overloading and begin treating colors and forms in a freer manner. The canvases done after this transition, with their exquisite, European-influenced coloration and wonderfully vital configurations that emerged in the process of painting, are among the finest and most influential examples of American painting during the period of its emancipation. In Europe, Gorky's significance still remains to be discovered.

The great vitality of Action Painting, its drama and pathos, come out full-blown in the large-format black and white paintings of Franz Kline (p. 279). The theme of his art is the direct and immediate record of power-

Arshile Gorky
The Betrothal, 1947
Oil on canvas, 127.5 x 100 cm
New Haven (CT), Yale University Art Gallery, Katherine Ordway Collection

fully sweeping gestures, broad bands of force emerging from nodes of energy to meet and clash across the pictorial field. Unlike Pollock, Kline tended to control the painting process rather than yielding to the promptings of his unconscious. His decision to limit himself to black and white, which were again supplemented by colors towards the end of his career, had its source in parallels between drawing and painting. Kline made numer-

ous brush drawings whose elements he then frequently transferred to canvas. His monumental signs are neither symbolistically encoded references to covert content, nor are they based directly on things seen or experienced, despite the fact that Kline began in an objective style in which allusions, say, to bridges or cityscapes were still detectable. Kline's mature painting takes place, if you will, in the present moment; it is an event arising from the artist's act. The resulting configurations bear their meaning within themselves. Kline's vehement strokes, a far cry from the delicacy of East Asian calligraphy and more closely related in terms of color and gesture to Goya, Daumier, Toulouse-Lautrec, or Picasso, have an expressiveness of sometimes archaic force. Whether limited to black and white or, as in the late work, containing incursions of harsh blue, red, or green,

Above left:
Bradley Walker Tomlin
Number 5, 1949
Oil on canvas, 177.5 x 96.2 cm
USA, private collection

Above right:
Franz Kline
New York, N.Y., 1953
Oil on canvas, 201 x 128.5 cm
Buffalo (NY), Albright-Knox
Art Gallery, Gift of Seymor
H. Knox

Franz Kline
Untitled, 1957
Oil on wood, 46 x 53.5 cm
Private collection

Clyfford Still
Painting, 1951
Oil on canvas, 237 x 192.5 cm
Detroit (MI), Detroit Institute
of Arts

Sam Francis
Blue, 1954
Oil on canvas, 144 x 89 cm
Hannover, Niedersächsische
Landesgalerie

Clyfford Still
Untitled, 1953
Oil on canvas, 236 x 174 cm
London, Tate Gallery

the paintings seem to contain the artist's personality in essence. Kline's canvases represent seminal contributions to America's self-image.

The ethical claims of American painting prior to the advent of Pop Art come out very clearly in a letter of Clyfford Still. American painters were now obligated to take unprecedented action, Still wrote, not to illustrating worn-out myths or contemporary alibis. They must assume full responsibility for what they did, and greatness would lie in the depth of insight and the courage with which they realized their own ideas. Questions of communication were presumptuous and secondary, Still added. Only when the viewer ceased looking at a painting as into a mirror, searching there for his own fears and hopes, would he be able to recognize and participate in the problems of the work.

Still's painting (ill. left and above) derives its tension from a contrast between large surfaces of textured dark paint into which narrow, tapering wedges of lighter color are inserted. The drama of his large-format canvases is lower in key than that of other Action Painters. The drama withdraws into the image with the restrained gestures. These nevertheless convey an exciting energy, manifested in an impasto paint application which lends Still's paintings a vibration, an emotionally charged vitality. As with the other Action Painters, Still's theme is the painting process itself.

Less problematic, apparently, are the methods and results of Action Painting in the work of the almost twenty years younger Sam Francis (ill. left and below). In his painting, too, which initially stood under Pollock's influence, the act of translating emotion into color becomes a painterly event. Francis's paintings, too, have no other content than the paint configurations themselves. At first the artist favored a reserved palette, tending to monochromy. White or black islands or clouds of paint, interspersed with stimulating passages of color, covered the expansive surfaces in an irregular arrangement full of visual sensations which were a source of continual surprise. Meditative calm spoke from this imagery as much as an ebullience that revelled in its own vitality.

In the course of the years France steadily heightened the brilliance of his colors to the point where they obtained what amounted to a luminosity. Transparent blue, red or yellow announced that life, and painting, were a sheer joy. The sweepingness of the gestures was reined in by the artist's sensibility and his sophisticated sense of color. Francis has repeatedly lived and worked in Paris, and he is perhaps the most French of the American Action Painters. The latent threat to his art lies in the temptation to succumb to a luminous, Fauve-inspired palette whose jewel-like exquisiteness occa-

sionally verges on the all-too lovely and decorative. This threat is happily avoided in the late, meditative images, inspired by Far Eastern thought, in which sparing but focused color passages stand in contrast to expansive, empty spaces.

Jack Tworkov
West 23rd, 1963
Oil on canvas, 152.7 x 203.2 cm
New York, The Museum of
Modern Art

"I live in a paradise of hellish blue balls – merely floating, everything floats, everything floats – where I carry this unique mathematics of my imagination through the succession of days toward a nameless tomorrow." SAM FRANCIS

Sam Francis
Round the World, 1958/59
Oil on canvas, 274.3 x 321.3 cm
Private collection

Robert Motherwell
Elegy to the Spanish Republic
No. 34, 1953/54
Oil on canvas, 203 x 254 cm
Buffalo (NY), Albright-Knox
Art Gallery, Gift of Seymour
H. Knox

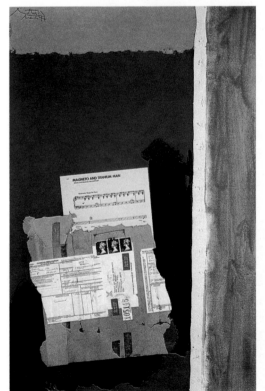

Robert Motherwell
Titanium Man, 1977
Collage and acrylic on canvas,
91.4 x 61 cm
London, Paul McCartney
Collection

The attempt of American artists to jettison the burden of the European heritage and develop their own
expressive potential began during the 1940s, initially
without much hope of attracting the attention or support of their countrymen. For ten years, reports Robert
Motherwell, American artists went their own lonely
way without the participation of the art public.

European Influences

This situation was not easy to bear, particularly for the
highly educated and cultivated Robert Motherwell (ill.
above and left), who had been deeply impressed by
European art. Picasso and Matisse, Surrealism and
Dada cast their spell over him – Kurt Schwitters and
Hans Arp more strongly than Max Ernst or Dalí. Motherwell's cultivated treatment of color, as in the subtle
monochromy of the *Open* pictures, was French in origin. Soft-spoken and reserved, Motherwell generally
held aloof from the loudly proclaimed neo-primitivism
of his colleagues. But to find his own way, he too first
had to forget Paris. The moral impulse of American
painting was especially strongly embodied in Motherwell's personality and work. As he once said, he thought
the laws of painting were in the first place ethical, and
only then aesthetic in character.

The artist involved himself with the human issues of
the era in more than philosophical terms. Motherwell's
long and impressive series of *Spanish Elegies* were dedicated to the Spanish Republic destroyed by Franco. The

highly reduced formal idiom of these compositions combines symbolic force with the subjective decisions of Action Painting. Their author, who also made significant and original contributions to the art of collage, possessed a sensibility and power of imagination, a critical eloquence and a sureness of judgement that made him one of the major artistic intermediaries between America and Europe.

Action Painting in the United States has repeatedly been classified under the rubric of Abstract Expressionism. Although the term is not entirely false, it is not quite correct either. There was nevertheless one bridge,

"Art is not only the eye; it is not the result of intellectual considerations. Art is strictly bound to inherent laws dictated by the medium in which it comes to expression. In other words, painting is painting, sculpture is sculpture, architecture is architecture." HANS HOFMANN

one direct link between European and American expressionism, in the person and œuvre of Hans Hofmann, a native of Bavaria (ill. left and p. 283). Hofmann's reputation had already been established by 1915, when he opened a school of painting in Munich. There he taught a number of American artists, including the later famous sculptress, Louise Nevelson. In 1930 Hofmann was a guest instructor at the University of California at Berkeley, whose museum now holds an extensive collection of his works. The following year he settled permanently in the United States. As an original artist and a teacher Hofmann contributed decisively to the emergence and spread of a self-confident American art, and pointed the way for many students who subsequently became prominent. His School of Fine Art in New York has justifiably been termed the "cradle of contemporay American art."

The sources of Hofmann's mature style, after Impressionist beginnings, lay in the aesthetic revolution that swept Paris from 1905 to the First World War. Picasso and Braque, Matisse and Delaunay, were his great models. Later, after Hofmann's return to Germany, strong impulses came from Expressionism, especially from the Blauer Reiter group. It was in coming to terms with Matisse and above all with Kandinsky that Hofmann found his own, personal style, which culminated in what he termed the "push and pull" of colors, the ability of juxtaposed colored shapes to evoke space, and the currents of energy that emerged from them to virtually overcome the picture boundaries. The daring

Hans Hofmann
Veluti in Speculum, 1962
Oil on canvas, 216 x 188 cm
New York, The Metropolitan
Museum of Art, Gift of Mr. and
Mrs. Richard Rodgers

Cy Twombly
Untitled, 1968
Oil, crayon and pencil on canvas,
172.2 x 228.5 cm
Formerly Saatchi Collection,
London

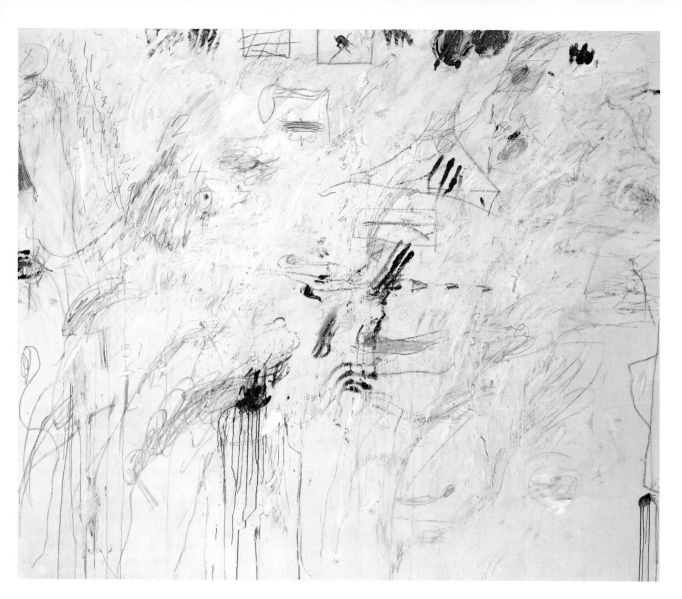

and self-confidence with which Hofmann overcame European painting without ever entirely losing touch with it, was a source of enormous encouragement to American artists. His compositions are equally marked by what one commentator terms "the tension between boundless space and sign-like shape," and by the generative capacity of color to determine form.

The art of Cy Twombly, who lives in Italy, is extremely complex, and full of allusions and associations and references that are not easily deciphered (ill. above). Twombly, too, comes from Action Painting, but over the years he has developed both formally and substantially away from its robust vitalism and drama. The nervousness of his idiom, inspired by grafitti, recalls the linear networks of Alberto Giacometti's paintings, while the compositional device of strewing or dispersing signs and marks across the surface bears a debt to Jackson Pollock's all-over approach. Using references from mythology and literature, from Marquis de Sade to John Keats and the writings of Goethe in Italy, the European-

influenced "primitive of a new path" exemplifies the dominant themes of Eros and death, sexuality and violence, in an allusive graphic-painterly code which tends to conceal more than it reveals. Twombly's sensitive, calligraphic touch ties the loose weave of the compositions into a unity. Again, as occasionally during the early period of L'art informel, a significant artist understands painting as a kind of writing or script, if a largely hermetic one.

Color as Visual Theme

Helen Frankenthaler comes from the sphere of influence of Hans Hoffman, and like the great abstract expressionist mentor, she holds an intermediate position, if of a different kind (p. 286 below). Beginning with the early Kandinsky, but also with Pollock, Gorky, and of course Hoffman, Frankenthaler developed a very personal version of Action Painting which was less dramatic than that of her predecessors. A lyrical tendency, as well as hints of things seen, especially landscapes, have suf-

Cy Twombly
Untitled (Roma), 1962
Oil, crayon and pencil on canvas,
199 x 240.5 cm
Private collection

"Every line is thus the actual experience with its unique story. It does not illustrate; it is the perception of its own realization."
Cy Twombly

Morris Louis
K S I, 1959
Acrylic on canvas, 264 x 438 cm
Essen, Museum Folkwang

fused her work from the start. Frankenthaler also invented a technique that proved seminal for American painting beyond Abstract Expressionism – the soak stain technique, in which thin paint is used on unprimed canvas. This permitted the artist to unify

color and support, content and form, in strict two-dimensionality.

Morris Louis (ill. above and p. 287) and Kenneth Noland adopted Frankenthaler's technique and developed it into styles variously known as Color Field Painting and Post-Painterly Abstraction. In these, the oil medium takes on a surprising diaphanousness, flowing almost as freely as watercolor and appearing light-suffused and immaterial even on the large format. The two painters may additionally have been inspired by the especially beautiful light over the city of Washington, D.C., where they both worked for a considerable period. Open space, suggested by the unprimed canvas surface, plays just as important a role in their approach as the painted configuration. With his *Veil* paintings, in which thin acrylic paint seems almost to blossom across the surface, Louis showed himself a master of the new technique, occasionally employing the principle of controlled chance to determine the paint flow.

During the final years of his life, in allusion to American Indian motifs, Louis created arrow-shaped paint configurations running parallel from top to bottom of the canvas, and above all the "Unfurlings," enormous horizontal formats in which the paint bands flow diagonally across the unprimed canvas, leaving either the center or the edges free. The unique technique and the huge formats of these works give rise to the impression that the images hover between materiality and immateriality, between two-dimensional extension and three-dimensional depth.

The painting of Albers-student Kenneth Noland is more rigorous and geometrical than Louis' (p. 287 above). Initially Noland concentrated on symmetrical configurations – circles, crosses, V- and X-shapes. The treatment of the basic elements, involving subtle irregu-

Helen Frankenthaler
Blue Caterpillar, 1961
Oil on canvas, 297.5 x 174 cm
Collection of the artist

Morris Louis
No. 180, 1961
Acrylic on canvas, 226 x 186 cm
Pasadena (CA), Pasadena Art
Museum

(p. 286). Jensen's strong-hued, finely articulated color fields combine painting with intellectual games and numerological principles. Among the younger painters who have been influenced by the Color Field approach, Al Held stands out particularly (p. 290). After initial *Signal Paintings* inspired by American Indian ornament and employing bright, almost garish color, Held turned to large-format canvases in which architectural or constructivist shapes were rendered in stringent black and white.

Meditation not Action

The sensibility of which American painting is capable comes out most clearly in the work of Mark Tobey (p. 288). In many respects Tobey's painting is the diametrical opposite to the expressive frenzy so typical of the Action Painters. The experience of the First World War ingrained in him a deep abhorrence of the destructive cruelty of which Western man is capable. Tobey turned to the wisdom of Asia, and travelled extensively in the Near and Far East. He spent a long period in a Zen Buddhist monastery, but resisted the temptation to identify completely with the doctrines taught there. The experience of Chinese and Japanese art, gained in collaboration with a Chinese artist-friend, revealed to Tobey the expressive potentials of line, as an autonomous force independent of, and indeed opposed to, the element of

larities and barely perceptible gradations of hue, created the impression of rotating, vertical or horizontal motion. Later works tended to strictly parallel, linear bands extending across cinemascope-like formats, apparently

without beginning or end, and creating an inextricable bond between painted motif and support. Noland's subject was, and remains, color itself – hence the absolute neutrality, or non-referentiality, of the parallel bands. The important thing in painting, says Noland, is to find a means to express color without destroying it, by retaining its value independently of the pictorial systems, be they supra-real, Cubist, or structualist.

The achievements of the Color Field painters in going beyond Abstract Expressionism have brought the work of many other, previously little-known artists to light. Prime among the older of these is Alfred Jensen, who was born in Guatemala and grew up in Denmark

volume. Practice in ink drawing, calligraphy, and Sumi painting confirmed and ramified Tobey's approach.

As early as the middle of the 1930s he produced his first *White Writings*, which were likely Tobey's most significant and personal contribution to contemporary art. Their densely interwoven lineatures, their infinitely varied graphic textures and patterns, combine stylistic characteristics of East Asian calligraphy with Western content and form. Tobey's works are gestural abstractions in the sense of possessing a form-dissolving tendency and relying on the aleatory principle, that is, on a play with controlled chance. Finely articulated, rhythmical compositions built up of – mathematically speaking – infini-

Kenneth Noland
Via Blues, 1967
Oil on canvas, 229 x 671 cm
Pasadena (CA), private collection

Mark Tobey
Harvest, 1958
Oil on canvas, 91.4 x 61.6 cm
New York, private collection

Mark Tobey
Radiant City, 1944
Oil on canvas, 49.2 x 36.1 cm
New York, private collection

tesimal strokes replaced compositional arrangements
intended to be taken in at a glance. These images challenge us to stop and consider – to contemplate, in the
full sense of the word. As the artist himself said, they are
"more Oriental than American."

The reference to reality comes out more clearly in
Tobey's city pictures. The flickering of neon signs, the
termite-like swarming of traffic and pedestrians, the
hum and sparkle of life in the urban jungle are all evoked
in the linear webs of these compositions. Tobey did not
like big cities; he disdained the arrogance of their inhabitants and feared that one day the United States would
be "gradually swallowed up by New York" like France
was by Paris. Accordingly the artist retired in later years
to Basel, Switzerland, where he died.

"We may well realize," wrote Konrad Fiedler at the
end of the last century, "that the eye is there not only to
furnish us with images of things present outside ourselves, but that with the act of perception, something
emerges within ourselves which is capable of independent development by ourselves." Applied to art, this
implies that a painted image which exists in the finite
world can communicate something infinite, when we as
viewers mentally and perceptually enter into the space
of the image. This insight informed the mature work of
Rothko and Newman, the major artists among the
American Color Field painters. Both of them came of an
Eastern Jewish background, and both went through a
Surrealist and an Abstract Expressionist phase before
arriving at a meditative form of image which corresponded to the profundity of their thinking and feeling.

Alfred Jensen
Sphinx of the South, 1960
Oil on canvas, 183 x 117 cm
Napa (CA), Hess Collection

To counter a sense of dissatisfaction with the world by advancing an optimistic utopia aimed at improving the world, as Mondrian did with his notion of "universal harmony," seemed to Newman not very productive. In his eyes, the art of his European father-figure, flat, geometric, right-angled, was ultimately a secular, non-transcendental "untragic" art. Consequently it remained impermeable to the "sublime," which Newman attempted to evoke in his canvases. For him, Mondrian's painting was a derivative rather than a direct, primary art, because it still contained too much "natural reference," even the right angle being a "natural form." The transcendental experience for which Mondrian strove, according to Newman, was no longer possible of realization in a Europe burdened by the weariness of old nations.

This explains Newman's intensive involvement with the "primitive" art of the American Indians, and also his emphasis on content over and above form. By attempting to achieve a sort of second naivety, Newman hoped to regain ritual magic and dignity for art. As for many of his colleagues, Robert Goldwater's book *Primitivism in Modern Art* (1938) was of similar significance for him as Wilhelm Worringer's *Abstraction and Empathy* was for German artists prior to the First World War.

Abstraction, for Newman, had nothing to do with geometry (pp. 289, 290). His categorical demands on art were that, first, its language had to be abstract; secondly, its dynamic had to be ritual will; and thirdly, its goal must be vision and enlightenment. In place of beauty as a reference to the known and visible, Newman, influenced by the philosophy of Baruch de Spinoza and Edmund Burke, truth and the sublime. In place of mediated effect, immediate experience became the goal of his painting. The picture would thus became a conveyor of a perceptually experienced, materially graspable idea, the result of a pictorial thinking that was both radi-cal and deeply emotional. This thinking manifested itself primarily through color, in the color *field* which would become a color *space* when, as the artist stipu-lated, the viewer approached closely enough to the pic-ture and, forgetting traditional, habitual perception, entered into the luminous color plane produced by applying layer upon layer of thin paint. The viewer's willingness to enter the picture, believed Newman, must be complete and uncompromising. He should have no

Barnett Newman
Vir Heroicus Sublimis, 1950/51
Oil on canvas, 242.2 x 513.6 cm
New York, The Museum of
Modern Art, Gift of Mr. and Mrs.
Ben Heller

"What is the explanation of the seemingly insane drive of man to be painter and poet if it is not an act of defiance against man's fall and an assertion that he return to the Adam of the Garden of Eden? For the artists are the first men."
Barnett Newman

Barnett Newman
Who's Afraid of Red, Yellow and
Blue I, 1966
Oil on canvas, 190 x 122 cm
New York, private collection

possibility to orientate himself within actual space, and, in the case of the large formats, no chance to see the whole image at once, for the sublime required no compositional order. Still, Newman's compositions do have an ordering factor. Instead of Mondrian's right angle we find the "zip," a linear, sometimes vaguely contoured vertical, like a section of an endless ribbon.

Working with the Entire Space

Only pure idea had meaning, declared Newman. Yet this Platonic notion was translated into art with the aid of the materiality of painting, if admittedly, unlike the much younger Frank Stella, Newman did manage to deprive the painting of its concrete, objective character. Communicating signs and symbols were entirely excluded. The reality of secular and transcendental experience merged into a third quality – the painted image. What Newman strove for was to make the experience of the painter coincide with the experience of the viewer. Reflection outside the painting would be

Barnett Newman
Chartres, 1969
Oil on canvas, 305 x 290 cm
New York, private collection

Al Held
Untitled, 1960
Oil on canvas, 152.3 x 106.7 cm
Private collection

replaced by direct participation within the painting's own space. And the painting would contain no references to anything that had gone before. It would be its own, self-contained message. As Newman put it, instead of working with the remainders of space, he would work with the entire space. And concerning the sublime, he believed that we create it outside of ourselves, outside our feelings.

Mark Rothko pursued similar goals (pp. 291, 292). Unlike Beckmann, who attempted to "make the invisi-

ble visible through reality," Rothko attempted to make space visible through color, and without reference to external reality. Like Newman, he believed that the "tragic experience" was the only source of art. Yet in contrast to Newman, Rothko did not emphasize the flat plane to convey the space-evoking effects of color. He employed rectangular bands or blocks, blurred at the edges, and seemingly floating in an indeterminate space. Rothko's sense of space had its origin in actual experience, that of the expanses of the open countryside in America, more particularly in Oregon, where the artist was confronted with a seemingly endless space which gave him the sense that his own ego had vanished. From a high vantage point Rothko looked out over an empty landscape covered with white fog. In the milky veil that spread out through space, in this void of earth and mist, there suddenly appeared a tiny dot – a car. Rothko was overcome by a feeling of his own meaninglessness. He never forgot this experience and this feeling. And accordingly, his works represent variations on the theme of infinity. His paintings can be mentally continued beyond the edges of the canvas; what the endless vertical was for Newman, color virtually flowing over and beyond the canvas edge was for Rothko. Like Newman's, his "abstract icons" with their veiled appearance that recedes from the inquisitive eye, that conceals more than it reveals, are counter-images to reality, the result of "transcendental experiences." In their serene, silent way they draw the viewer into spaces that appear suffused with light from some hidden source. This light refers to the artist's "transcendental experiences". The colors are an emanation of light, rising up, as Cézanne said, "from the roots of the world."

Believing in the metaphysical properties of color as he did, Rothko, though he admired Matisse, grew angry when anyone called him a "brilliant colorist." Like the paintings of many Jewish artists, Rothko's may well contain a covert image of the invisible God of whom the religion forbade images to be made, not even if one were

Mark Rothko
Untitled, 1957
Oil on canvas, 143 x 138 cm
Private collection

Mark Rothko
Red, White and Brown, 1957
Oil on canvas, 252.5 x 207.5 cm
Basel, Öffentliche Kunstsamm-
lung Basel, Kunstmuseum

Mark Rothko
Untitled
(Seagram Mural), 1959
Oil and acrylic on canvas,
183 x 153 cm
Washington, National Gallery of
Art, Gift of the Mark Rothko
Foundation

Theodoros Stamos
Infinity Field Cretan Riztika
Series, 1983
Acrylic on cotton wool,
167.6 x 152.4 cm
Napa (CA), Hess Collection

overcome by the "fear of nothingness." It would seem to be just this fear which Rothko's hovering forms conceal like the curtains in a synagogue – for void and infinity go hand in hand.

Beuys once said, "Humans must learn to transcend their reality. They have to create a spiritual vehicle with which they can reach a completely different standpoint in the universe." Rothko and Newman both created just such a "vehicle." Using the means of painting on canvas they transcended the medium just as much as they did the dogmatic tenets of the religion of their fathers. Perhaps the most impressive evidence of this is seen in Rothko's nocturnal paintings in the chapel in Houston, dedicated to all confessions, and Newman's sculpture *Broken Obelisk* outside (p. 497), a wonderfully moving unity of art and architecture flooded with the brilliant light of the American Southwest.

More opaque by comparison to Rothko's transparencies are the colors in the paintings of his friend, Theodoros Stamos (ill. below). Stamos's art is less metaphysically oriented, and unlike the dissolved contours and gradual transitions in Rothko's paintings, Stamos employs forms that despite their irregularity are more decisively articulated.

The Black Monk

Ad Reinhardt (p. 293), author of the *Black Paintings*, which he intended to be the last paintings anyone could make, was an outspoken opponent of all mystification in art. This brought him into conflict with Newman, who was just as acute an analyst and sharp-tongued debater as Reinhardt. Reinhardt's painting is conceivable only as the product of a late culture. Yet despite its high degree of objectification and elimination of all personal touch, despite the artist's rigorous rationality and cool control, his puristic works lead back in an inim-

Ad Reinhardt
Abstract Painting, Blue, 1952
Oil on canvas, 190.5 x 71.1 cm
Pittsburgh (PA), The Carnegie
Museum of Art

Ad Reinhardt
Abstract Painting, 1958
Oil on canvas, 274.5 x 101.6 cm
Fukuoka (Japan), Fukuoka
Museum of Modern Art

itable, irresistably logical, and highly individual way to something extremely elementary – to black, a color or non-color whose capacity of evoking depth is concealed beneath the flat, impenetrable surface.

The late paintings of the "black monk," as someone dubbed the artist, whose combativeness also came out in acerbic caricatures, approach the zero point, the borderline to the no-longer-visible. In this regard Reinhardt's works can be seen in the context of other contemporary

developments both in America and Europe, developments that led to the founding of the "Zero" group in Germany, of "Nul" in the Netherlands, and of "gruppo t" in Italy; to the *Homages to the Square* by Josef Albers (whom Reinhardt admired); to Yves Klein's monochrome blue, red or gold canvases and "invisible paintings"; and finally, to Rothko's and Newman's color field canvases. Links can also be traced back into the past, to the classical rigor of Cubism (which for Reinhardt

Adolph Gottlieb
Blast # 1, 1957
Oil on canvas, 228 x 114 cm
New York, The Museum of
Modern Art

because it is negative. In the words of the Protestant philosopher Paul Tillich, "The negative lives from the positive it negates."

Looking at the *Black Paintings*, which much to Reinhardt's pleasure are not reproducible, requires concentration and a specific sensibility. As late as 1971 a well-known art scholar could still maintain that Reinhardt's minimal tone gradations over-taxed the eye's ability to adapt. Opposed to this stands the simple experience that viewers, especially younger viewers, are inexorably drawn to the silent black panels. Reinhardt's rigorous rejection of everything non-classical, of the mystical and sentimental, his absolute purism, were uncompromising. Abstract art, he declared, had its own integrity, not some kind of "integration" with something else. Every combination, mixture, addition, vulgarization, or popularization robbed abstract art of its essence and compromised artistic conscience. Art was free, Reinhardt said, but "not a free-for-all." In his anachronistic opinion, art could not gain the world without doing harm to its own soul.

Thus Reinhardt proceeded systematically, through the rigor of his aesthetic as through his uncompromising rejection of the art business, to block his own path to success. He was not to experience it until shortly before his death, in 1965, when younger artists discovered Reinhardt as one of the few older artists who were important to them. The Conceptual artist Joseph Kosuth (p. 535) took Reinhardt's "art-as-art" ideology beyond the confines of painting with his doctrine of "art as idea as idea." Although Reinhardt himself knew that the younger generation of Minimal and Conceptual artists had started "from the same point" from which he once had, he soberly realized that they had not begun directly with his work and theory.

represented the major aesthetic event of the century), to Piet Mondrian and De Stijl, to Malevich and his Suprematism.

Black – capable of infinite variation even without the cold-warm distinctions produced by adding primary colors – Reinhardt's black is not a phenomenon of the dark-light contrast. Rather, it is a phenomenon of light itself (whereby the opposite, white as a source of darkness, does not hold). Light is an immanent quality in the *Black Paintings*. They have absorbed it. Their light does not impinge from some hidden external source, as in Rothko's works. Reinhardt's black has extinguished all form. The internal cross-shaped or tripartite divisions occasionally detectable in the compositions – more clearly in earlier ones than in later – have no formal, let alone symbolic, meaning. Reinhardt was greatly amused by attempts to read into the cross shape, which long predates Christianity, something in the nature of a nihilistic Christian view. He used the sparing interior forms only as aids to articulating and differentiating the black field. Black includes all colors; it means *everything* precisely

William Baziotes
The Web, 1946
Oil on canvas, 76.2 x 71.1 cm
Ithaca (NY), Herbert F. Johnson
Museum of Art, Cornell University

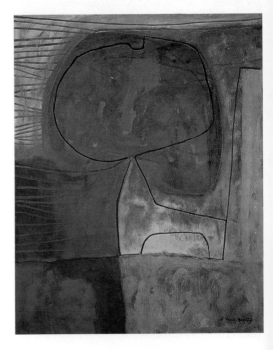

The world as darkness, Reinhardt noted in his lapidary diction; hidden, meaning beyond. It was in 1966 that he made his famous remark that he was doing "the last painting which anyone can make." Nevertheless,

Reinhardt at no time ever postulated the end of art. So might his œuvre represent a concrete utopia, the "principle of hope" – or does it stand for its negation? With Reinhardt, many questions remain open.

Meditation and Motion
European Reactions to Abstract Expressionism

A reaction to unleashed gestural abstraction, in this case of the Cobra group and Tachism, was as inevitable in Europe, as it had been in the United States. Weary of the existential skepticism of the post-war years, artists drew their conclusions from the altered situation, the new economic and political optimism of the late 1950s and early 1960s. The role of the neglected genius lost its attraction. Instead of trusting posterity for recognition, artists turned to the living, sought success in the here and now. In contrast to American Action Painting and its vital, outgoing expression of liberation from the past, Tachism, for all its gestural frenzy, had taken the European path inwards, a path that led it back through Expressionism all the way to the Romantic period in art.

The flagging spontaneity and drama of orthodox Tachism were now confronted with a primarily lyrical painting, serene and optimistic, sustained entirely by light and color. Young artists began to distrust the emotionally charged gesture; yet neither did they turn to the opposite, Constructivist pole, because an art of well-ordered stasis, they believed, could do justice neither to the flexible, continually changing environment nor to the relaxed attitude to life in the early 1960s. The excited dynamism of yesterday was sublimated to a vibrato of color. A limitation to a single hue, either clearly dominating or used in a range of gradations, set a painterly counterpoint to the garishness of the consumer world. The inundation with visual stimuli, the visual pollution of the contemporary environment, was beginning to make itself felt even back then, and the idea of countering it with "pure," sensitive artistic formulations was a not unimportant motive. But instead of the world-weariness and nausea that informed Tachism, the paintings of the monochrome artists showed a fine sense of the beauty of color and its enlivening, encouraging qualities, whether they defined color, like Otto Piene, as "light and energy" or as "sensibilized matter" like Yves Klein. "The nuances," proclaimed Piene, then head ideologue of the Düsseldorf "Zero" group, with all the pathos of his new-found faith in light, "the nuances stimulate our breathing and heighten the force of our colors."

In place of seething cataracts of paint there came a new order based on reduction as an artistic principle; in place of dramatic coloristic effects there came a limita-tion to subtle effects of light and dark, light and shade, or to a gradual differentiation of one and the same tone, or even to black and white. The geometrically constructed, hierarchic composition was replaced by an egalitarian structuring of color fields, without a center of interest, arranged by means of regular modules, facets, grids, or screens, whose regularity might be enlivened by condensation or relaxation, rhythmical displacements, color syncopations, points of calm, delay, or acceleration. The center of this movement was a group of three artists in Düsseldorf called "Zero": Otto Piene, Heinz Mack, and Günther Uecker. They were encouraged by the Frenchman Yves Klein, confirmed by the Italian Lucio Fontana, and inspired by the Munich group "Zen" around Rupprecht Geiger (ill. below), Willi Baumeister, Fritz Winter, Rolf Cavael, and Theodor Werner.

The protest against Tachism began in 1957, with exhibitions lasting only a single evening in Piene's and Mack's studios. The first Zero manifesto was published the following year. Although these artists respected the *élan vital* of a Pollock and the existential mysticism of a Wols, they defended themselves zealously against the claim that art must be an expression of the age. If it were, stated Piene, an artist would be no more than a

"Red is 'the' color. Red is beautiful. Red is life, energy, potency, power, love, warmth, strength. Red gives you a high."

RUPPRECHT GEIGER

Rupprecht Geiger
Red Painting 1961, 1961
Oil on canvas, 190 x 145 cm
Munich, Städtische Galerie
im Lenbachhaus

Otto Piene
Venus of Willendorf, 1963
Oil and smoke on canvas,
150 x 200 cm
Amsterdam, Stedelijk Museum

Heinz Mack
Large Triad (Chromatic
Constellation), 1993
Acrylic on canvas, 230 x 180 cm
Private collection

Page 297 above:
Heinz Mack
White Rotor, 1960
Wood, glass, motor,
153 x 153 x 22.2 cm
Collection of the artist

Page 297 below:
Günther Uecker
Nail Construction, 1962
Nails, canvas and wood,
60 x 52 cm
Venice, Peggy Guggenheim
Collection

"reporter." Zero frankly and, at the time, quite anachronistically believed that, "the Platonic ideal, that the beautiful is also true and good, is not forgotten." On the other hand, the "dullness" of L'art informel color was "a sign of the dullness of the person, the dullness of his consciousness." Zero's path thus logically led from subjective gesture to a practically anonymous objectivity, from Existentialism to Structuralism, from post-war pessimism to the more buoyant visions of the Kennedy era. There was no place in Zero's program for the brooding melancholy which Sedlmayr had supposed to be an essential trait of the modern artist. It was only in the later works of Uecker, with their silent earnestness, that the shadow side of life once again came into its own.

The Medium of Light
For the time being, the three artists agreed among themselves that an art of subjective confession, of suffering under the ills of the world and under one's own frailties and failings, must be supplanted by an art of affirmation, an art that vibrated in sympathy with the rhythms of the universe – and with those of modern civilization. This fundamental attitude corresponded to a turn to life-giving light as a new medium of art.

The "New Idealism" derived from this attitude, Piene's and Mack's romantization of light, was something Uecker, who had joined the group in 1958, could not accept. Yet in the beginning he, too, dreamed of a new, "empty man", a human being without history and therefore without prejudices, capable of liberating himself from the Western trauma of war and holocaust, "prepared to go to another planet". The depressing unimaginativeness of the subsequent real-life astronauts, which was a far cry from the cosmic visions of a Yves Klein, was quite as unpredictable back then as the insane notion of making space a theater for military confrontations.

Back then color was celebrated as an emanation of light. What next step could have been more obvious than to paint monochrome pictures, stage light ballets, and – more philosophically – to understand art as "an articulation of natural forces: light, fire, smoke, wind," as Wieland Schmied said? One night in a Düsseldorf artists' pub, Piene asked the rhetorical question, "Why shouldn't a painting have just one single color? Why not paint a red picture?" Well, over the years Piene painted not only red but yellow, white, and brown pictures, introduced the grid structure into art, worked with smoke and fire, and, in the footsteps of Moholy-Nagy, he made light dance, before shifting to work in three dimensions (ill. left).

Mack very early on attempted to escape from simultaneously flat and illusionistic two-dimensionality and make the picture plane vibrate with life. The result was a series of extremely sensitive and painterly *Vibrations*, done during the pioneer years of the Zero group (p. 297 above). But once he had discovered the charm of reflected light, after having stepped on a thin metal sheet that lay on a carpet and picked up an impression of its texture, Mack was bound to abandon painting, at least for a time. Already in 1963, four years before differences among its members led to Zero's dissolution, Mack painted what he thought would be his last picture, and became a sculptor and creator of light-suffused and illuminated objects. In the meantime Mack has in fact

returned to painting, and that in intense colors; but he still holds fast to his aim of producing concrete sculptural and architectural examples of a better and more sensible design of the human environment, in both the secular and ecclesiastical domain (ill. above). The optimism and belief in the future of the early Zero years continued to inform such all-encompassing projects, as they did works that embraced space like Mack's Sahara project and Piene's famous rainbow over the Olympic Park in Munich.

Uecker was born in Mecklenburg, in north-eastern Germany. Before emigrating to the West he received strong impulses from the Eastern European avant-garde, which was tolerated in communist Germany until 1951. Kasimir Malevich and his Polish student, Vladislav Strzemiński, impressed Uecker especially, while the Expressionists appealed to him mainly for their uncompromising stance and absolute personal dedication to their art.

The emergence of Uecker's mature visual approach (ill. right) came in the mid-1950s, when he rejected content in painting in reaction to the ideological illustrations of Socialist Realism. Reflecting his personal situation, Uecker painted *Dirt Pictures* using his fingers. Subject matter was replaced by the texture of impasto paint, the covert poetry of a mundane material. To intensify the low-relief texture and the vibration of the surface Uecker began to incorporate various everyday objects into the paint. One of these objects was the nail – the principal medium of Uecker's future art was discovered. Initially he used nails no differently than paint, as one working material among others. Then the medium became the message, a means to create sensitive, pictorially structured plays of light and shadow which inexorably draw the viewer's eye to them. By means of the color white, which includes all other colors of the spectrum, the nail was virtually dematerialized, to finally become a fetish, tool, and vehicle of an idea at once. It also became the cross Uecker has to bear, because the process of driving thousands of nails puts enormous demands on his physical and mental energy. Corrections are out of the question. If a mistake is made, the work is ruined.

This high degree of risk and Uecker's acceptance of it lends his work a profound seriousness and the character of a perpetual self-experiment, whether he makes two-dimensional paintings or static and kinetic objects, whether he modulates light by means of sinuous rows of nails, metal rods, or *Plantations*, designs temporary installations related to a specific site, or paints meditative watercolors. The initial, rather naive optimism of the Zero manifesto: "Zero is silence, Zero is the beginning, Zero is round, Zero rotates," soon dissipated, and for Uecker, it never returned. Reality caught up with him. "A post-war generation is becoming a pre-war generation," he wrote in a proclamation against war. This disillusioned insight helps us remember that Uecker's fundamental subject is "not art and life, but life and death." This can only imply that in the incessant transformation of the eternally same – time, which does not flow, but *is* – Uecker's artistic rituals place the human being opposite the picture or object, in an imagined center, not as image but as measure of all things.

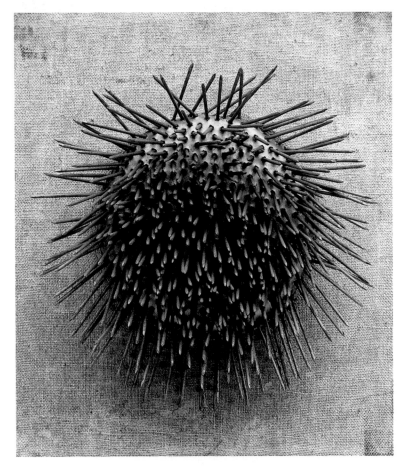

Yves "Le Monochrome"

Though he was no older than his German friends, Yves Klein must be considered the father-figure of the Zero movement (pp. 298–300). In the eyes of the enthusiastic Otto Piene, he was even the "present incarnation of the saint, prophet, messiah." Had "Yves le Monochrome" lived longer, he would almost certainly have been accorded a special status and been venerated as an idol, like the later Joseph Beuys.

Yves Klein
ANT 63 (Anthropométrie), 1961
Pigment and synthethic resin on paper on canvas, 153 x 209 cm
Private collection

"What is blue? Blue is the invisible becoming visible... Blue has no dimensions. It 'is' beyond the dimensions of which other colors partake."
YVES KLEIN

Klein was a fascinating personality: a not very tall, rather chunky man with dark, melancholy eyes, a visionary and manager, a showman and mystic, an activist and a philosopher. Before he appeared on the scene most people believed that Mondrian's universal geometric harmony and Malevich's *Black Square* marked the extreme borderline of what painting was capable of formulating (Reinhardt's *Black Paintings* were as yet unknown in Europe), but Klein by far transcended this belief. Together with a chemist-friend he tirelessly experimented to find that deep, matte, luminous ultramarine blue that would enable the artist to simultaneously make visible the material and spiritual qualities of color and to make these accessible to the contemplative viewer. Klein's monochrome panels, initially flat, later built up in relief with the aid of sponges, covered with brushed or rolled-on layers of "IKB" (International Klein Blue), and later with gold and more rarely, red, divided the art world into two camps, Klein believers and scoffers. The former considered him a genius, the latter a charlatan. From his exhibition of "sensibilized matter," consisting of blue pigment in a special fixative, one of the many paths of the imaginative artist logically led to the "invisible painting." In 1958, at the Iris Clert gallery in Paris, in whose empty, white rooms there was nothing to see, Klein exhibited the principle of immateriality, of the increment of undefinability that is always present in painting even if it cannot be seen. This was more than an artist's prank. The show represented a formulation in "painting" of the silence of the unutterable which was such a salient trait of the current historical situation.

Eventually Klein painted with fire and light, making images that flared up, guttered out, and sank back into silence. He and his friends Arman and Pascal divided up the world among themselves; Klein signed the sky; in collaboration with the architect Werner Ruhnau he conceived of air-conditioning for great geographic territories of the planet. Klein composed a *Monotone Symphony* using a single note, and sold *The Immaterial* for a specified amount of gold leaf, half of which he threw in the Seine. From 1960 onwards, after his meeting with the Nouveaux Réalistes around critic Pierre Restany, Klein made impressions on paper in metaphysical blue of nude, quite physical female bodies, or created negative images using a spray gun.

It may be going too far to view these *Anthropometries* as a "sanctification of the flesh", as a knowledgeable admirer of Klein has done. There is no overlooking the element of heathen mysticism in the romantic and idealistic thought and actions of the artist, who was influenced by Zen Buddhism and the occult doctrines of the Rosicrucians. Beyond doubt, however, is the significance of this restless spirit, whose influence has continued far beyond his short life to extend even to the Conceptual Art of our own day. Klein's cooperation with the New Realists, with the sculptors Jean Tinguely and César, with object-maker Daniel Spoerri, "accumulator" Arman, packaging artist Christo, and décollage-artist Raymond Hains, was not as surprising as it might appear on first sight. For just as Klein worked with real pigments, all of these artists worked with real things from everyday life, from eyeglass frames through typewriters all the way to the remains of a meal on an artist's table. They, too, were ultimately concerned with reinstating the dignity of the commonplace, with a synthesis of the material and the immaterial, if without the metaphysical sublimation which Klein alone strove for, and which led him to hope that, with the aid of art, "a new and grand world civilization of the beautiful" could be realized.

Space Brought to Light

If Yves Klein was a father-figure to his same-age Zero friends, the Argentine-born, thirty year older former sculptor Lucio Fontana (pp. 300, 301) was more like a close relative whom they admired from a respectful distance. It is to him the German group owed its finest collaborative work, the kinetic light-in-space installation *Hommage à Fontana*, which was among the sensations at documenta 3 in 1964. Founder in the 1930s of the Italian branch of Abstraction-Création in Paris, Fontana in 1946 authored a *Manifesto blanco* (White Manifesto), in which he developed synaesthetic ideas that only much later would become an artistic reality, in his own work

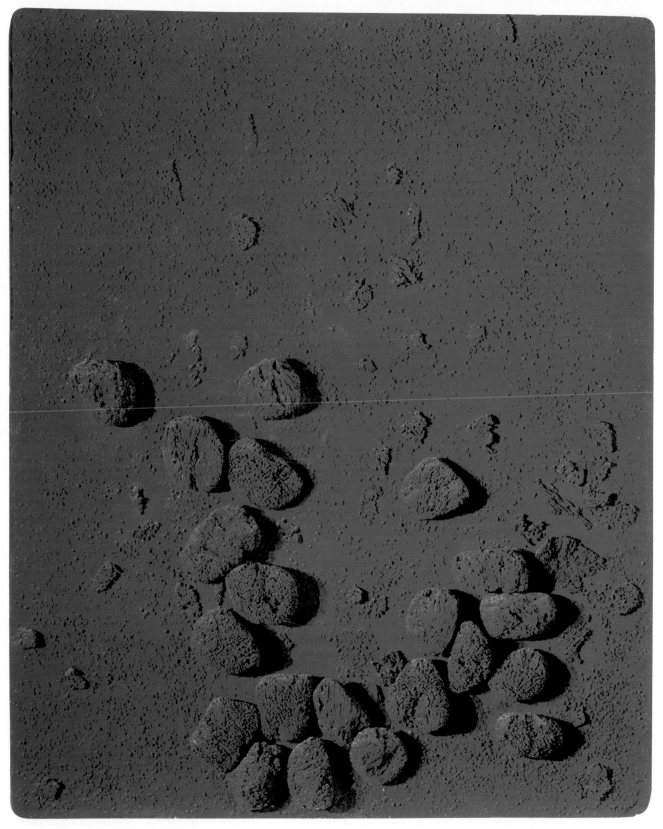

Yves Klein
Blue Sponge Relief (RE 19), 1958
Pigment in synthetic resin on sponges, gravel,
and composition board, 200 x 165 cm
Cologne, Museum Ludwig, Ludwig Donation

Yves Klein
Monochrome Blue IKB 48, 1956
Oil on wood, 150 x 125 cm
Stockholm, Moderna Museet

"To sense the soul, without explanation, without words, and to depict this situation – this, I believe, is what led me to monochrome painting."
YVES KLEIN

it to enter the piece through its openings. And as early as 1951 he used fluorescent tubing to create a sign in space which already anticipated things to come – the new art genre of the environment, the interior space designed to function as an image, as well as the employment of new, industrial materials.

The Dream of the *Gesamtkunstwerk*

Zero was more than a group of German artists and their French and Italian friends and relations. In accordance with their cosmopolitan attitude, the movement soon burgeoned into an international phenomenon, sending out branches as far as Japan. The "Nul" group in the Netherlands, "gruppo t" in Milan, the French "Groupe de la Recherche d'Art Visuel" around kinetic artist Julio Le Parc – none would have existed without Zero, and naturally without Yves Klein. The 1960s were a period, as Jürgen Claus has said, of an "expansion of the arts", a period of border crossings among the classical genres of painting, sculpture, and print-making, of an inclusion of light and motion, word and sound, in works of art which, borrowing a term from science, came to be called interdisciplinary. Material contributions to this development were made by Zero and its predecessors in continuing and expanding upon historical attempts – among them some of the Futurists, Dadaists, Constructivists, and a few of the Bauhaus masters, such as Kandinsky, Schlemmer, Moholy-Nagy. It was no coincidence that Piene, Mack, and Uecker, like Fontana, penetrated into the third dimension, or that Klein, in his ideas and activities, even went a step farther to advance into the domain of the imaginary. Behind all these experiments stood the old artists' dream of the Gesamtkunstwerk, the work of art that would embrace and reconcile mind and matter, include the world and at the same time transcend it.

and others', if not to the extent and with the impact Fontana had envisioned. The manifesto demanded that color and space, light, motion, and sound, be brought into correspondence. Taking the first step of letting space penetrate the two-dimensional picture, or of opening it out to the surrounding space, Fontana – who was already fifty at the time – simply punched a hole in the canvas (*Buchi*) or slit it with a knife (*Tagli*). In his eyes, this seemingly rough-and-ready solution of the problem of space was no act of destruction, but rather an act of liberation. The material surface had to be violated in order literally to make room, to create space, for the visualization of an idea.

Evidently, like that of Yves Klein, Fontana's art is a conceptual art, in which the idea is more important than the way in which it is put into practice. This is reflected in the titles of the works: *Concetto Spaziale* (Spatial Concept) for the paintings, *Scultura Spaziale* (Spatial Sculpture) for the sculptures. The object, whether painting or sculpture, has a merely mediating function. For the artist, the color of the canvas and the aesthetic arrangement of incisions or holes in it, and the perforations in the sculpture, serve in the first place as "aesthetic explanations" of his ideas to the public. The consistency of these ideas is well illustrated by Fontana's flat sculptures, which instead of displacing space allow

Lucio Fontana
Concetto spaziale – Attese, 1965
Watercolor on canvas, five incisions, 100 x 81 cm
Private collection

In the course of his short, restless life, Italian artist Piero Manzoni (ill. below) came by way of late L'art informel, Tàpies and Dubuffet and the New Realists, to the white, actually colorless works he accordingly titled *Achromes*. These pieces go beyond Klein's cosmological monochrome blue works to the extent that every reference to anything outside them is eliminated, and the white canvases, wads of cotton wool or plastic balls, sheets of glass or fiberglass, rounds of rabbit fur or cubes of straw, signify nothing but themselves. The minimalistic forms occasionally even arise from the innate characteristics of the materials. "Infinity," says Manzoni, "is strictly speaking monochrome, or, better still, destitute of color…"

Similarly to Yves Klein, Manzoni then stepped beyond the confines of the picture frame to put his signature on human bodies, eggshells, or the notorious tin cans containing *Merda d'Artista* (Artist's Shit). He declared the air in a balloon to be *Artist's Breath*, called a balloon, a stand, and an air pump in a wooden box a *Body of Air*, drew a line 7200 meters long and proclaimed – in a less mystical, more neo-Dadaistic way than Beuys – the border-line between life and art nonexistent. In 1961 Manzoni erected the *Pedestal of the World* (p. 509). In its radicality his œuvre belongs only partially and conditionally to the painting medium; basically, it eludes all classification. During his brief career Manzoni approach passed through the way-stations of L'art informel, Nouveau Réalisme, Neo-Dada, Happening, and Fluxus and Zero.

The most significant representative of the European Zero movement in Holland, Jan Schoonhoven (p. 302 below), was a deserter from L'art informel. In keeping with Dutch level-headedness, he tended more to the concrete than to the utopian. And unlike the sensitive Belgian monochrome painter, Jef Verheyen, Schoon-

hoven had absolutely no interest in color. The objectification of the work of art was the main aim of this intelligent purist. "Zero," Schoonhoven said, "is above all a new conception of reality, in which the role of the artist is reduced to a minimum. The absence of any preference for certain places and points in the work is important for Zero, and necessary in order to bring the isolated reality into evidence. In practice this means a serial edifice, arranged in ranks, an order that avoids preferences."

Schoonhoven's stringent œuvre developed without breaks or leaps, because he remained true to the principles he had once found correct. The changes in his exact, geometric idiom based on the effects of light and shade and intermediate between painting and sculpture, took place gradually and step by step, reflecting a great intellectual and aesthetic discipline. This procedure explains the richness of detail in Schoonhoven's work, which is thus never boring despite its rigorous logic.

If color does not exist for Schoonhoven, for Gotthard Graubner it is the paramount theme (p. 302 above). In early years he was erroneously classified as a monochrome painter and associated with Zero, with whose members he had friendly contacts. Actually Graubner's palette was more polychrome, more rich in gradations, than that of perhaps any other painter of the

Lucio Fontana
Spatial Concept: Marriage in Venice, 1960/61
Oil on canvas, 152 x 154 cm
Cologne, Museum Ludwig, Ludwig Donation

"The subconscious molds the individual; it completes and transforms him, giving him the guidance which it receives from the world and which he from time to time adopts."
LUCIO FONTANA

Piero Manzoni
Achrome, 1962
Stones and white color on canvas, 75 x 60 cm
Private collection

Gotthard Graubner
Color-Space Body, Diptych, 1977
Oil on canvas over synthetic wool,
248 x 248 x 15 cm (each)
Cologne, Museum Ludwig

day. What linked him with Zero was an understanding
of color as an emanation of light. In an early phase of his
career he described his paintings with a striking simile,
calling them "trampolines of light."

The two-dimensional *Color Spaces* of the young
Graubner were followed by canvases titled *Color Bodies*
(or *Cushion Paintings*) that were lent a haptic quality by
means of padding. Then the artist combined the two
approaches to produce *Color-Space Bodies*, manifestations in color of the infinite, which confronts the viewer
of the painting, surrounds him, and into which he mentally and meditatively enters. In a different way than
Yves Klein – much more painterly and less conceptually
– Graubner lends physical presence to the metaphysical,
visibility to the invisible. "My paintings expand as the
illumination increases," the artist says, and "when it is
extinguished, so are they. Beginning and end are interchangeable. They do not describe a condition; they are
transition." In the process of painting Graubner
attempts to "forget, make quiet, fall silent, exclude the
self."

In the *Color-Space Bodies* the diaphanous flux of
modulated color gradations, rich in nuances and values,
is itself the space-creating element. The paint relies on
the body of the canvas only as a support, not as a plastic
volume in its own right. It was only logical that Graubner also produced works on folded or combed paper in
which the play of light and shadow is a key element.
Under the impression of the light and atmosphere over
Venice, where he represented Germany in the 1982
Bienale, the artist's colors have grown lighter and more
luminous, and the contrasts stronger. The interactions
of color, made visible with great sensibility, continue to
be the salient theme of Graubner's mature work. He is
one of the few German painters who is a major colorist.

Jan Schoonhoven
R 72–27, 1972
Cardboard, paper and distemper
on wood, 200 x 130 cm
Düsseldorf, Kunstmuseum
Düsseldorf im Ehrenhof

The Fascination of the Trivial
Pop Art and Nouveau Réalisme

No other designation of a stream in 20th-century art has entered common usage to the extent that Pop Art has. Daily experience seldom offers a chance to describe something or someone as "expressionistic" or "cubistic." True, a situation or joke might be called "surrealist," but this is rare, and tends to be an in-group usage. The term "pop," in contrast, has become a byword. It is applied to anything from music to hairstyles, from fashion to appliance design, from film to advertising, all of which owe a great deal to Pop Art.

The whole range of American trivial culture is present in a collage by British artist Richard Hamilton, titled *Just What Is It That Makes Today's Homes so Different, so Appealing?* (ill. right). Done in 1956 for the legendary London exhibition "This is Tomorrow," the image includes a body-builder and a pin-up girl, television set and tape recorder, Ford emblem and canned ham, comic poster and ancestral portrait, vacuum cleaner and movie-ad, a huge all-day sucker brandished like a tennis racket (and bearing the inscription "Pop"), and a photo enlargement of a crowded beach, all beneath a ceiling formed by a section of the globe. Like the exhibition itself, this work emerged at a time when the first string of Pop Art in England, the "Independent Group," initiated by sculptor Eduardo Paolozzi and Hamilton himself, had long since disbanded. Nevertheless Hamilton's collage became the programmatic image of British Pop.

The collage reveals three things: first, a mixture of fascination and irony with respect to the symbols of American affluence; second, the significance of collage as a typical Pop technique, derived from Cubist, Dadaist, and Surrealist practice; and third, the intelligence and sophistication of a composition rife with allusions and ambiguities. These stand in crass contrast to the banality of the theme. The ongoing debate about the origin of the term "Pop Art," which is generally ascribed to the critic Lawrence Alloway, need not concern us here. The fact is that the young Paolozzi, who lived in Paris at the time and was as impressed by Dada as by variants of Surrealism all the way to Dubuffet, already used the term "Pop" in 1947, in one of his early collages.

But even more important than the influence of Dada or Surrealism on Pop was that of Duchamp, who was the first to exhibit ordinary, "ready-made" objects in the gallery and museum context, and who irreverently drew a moustache on the sacred symbol of Western art, the Mona Lisa. Other sources of inspiration were the collages and "Merz" constructions of Schwitters, and the late Léger of the "Proletarian Olympus" with its accompanying, everyday attributes. Pop Art not only made trivial subject-matter worthy of aesthetic treatment and – especially in America – monumentalized it through the device of the blow-up, it also increasingly

Richard Hamilton
"Just What Is It That Makes Today's Homes so Different, so Appealing?", 1956
Collage on paper, 26 x 25 cm
Tübingen, Kunsthalle Tübingen,
Prof. Dr. Georg Zundel Collection

Richard Hamilton
Trafalgar Square, 1965–1967
Oil and photograph on wood,
80 x 120 cm
Cologne, Museum Ludwig,
Ludwig Donation

Jean Hélion
The Wrong Way, 1947
Oil on canvas, 113.5 x 146 cm
Paris, Musée National d'Art
Moderne, Centre Georges
Pompidou

Peter Phillips
Purple Flag, 1960
Oil, collage and wax on canvas,
213 x 184 cm
London, private collection

reflected on the icons of mass culture in an intelligent and critical way.

Thus the term Pop Art, unlike its source, the popular or folk art of vernacular culture, is basically a misnomer. Nor, despite its continuing interest for young artists, does Pop retain much vitality today. No doubt the then-young artists who conceived Pop intended it as a style that would appeal to wider audiences. And, after long years of dominance on the part of abstract art of all brands, Pop was received with a kind of relief when the initial shock had subsided. (The reaction to the Neo-Expressionism of the 1980s would be similar.)

Still, the revolutionary changes in form and theme that Pop introduced into painting and, later, into sculpture – its revival of subject-matter, its intrusion of the commonplace into the hermetic realm of abstract art after 1945 – ultimately did not bring about an integration of fine art into mass society. Pop's addressees, like those of Léger's proletarian realism, did not respond as expected to the style's negation of compositional and thematic hierarchies, the egalitarian, as it were democratic tendency of its original, non-derivative imagery. Despite its enormous indirect effect on mass culture, Pop Art never stood a chance of becoming as truly pop-

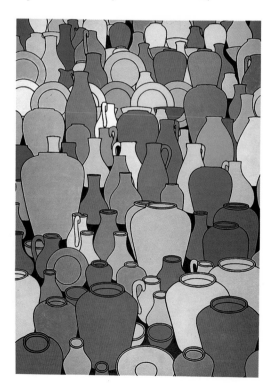

Patrick Caulfield
Pottery, 1969
Oil on canvas, 213.5 x 152.5 cm
London, Tate Gallery

Joe Tilson
OH!, 1963
Oil on canvas, 125.5 x 94 cm
Boston (MA), The 180 Beacon
Collection

ular as pop music or pop fashion design. And when a large German town, Hannover, put Niki de Saint Phalle's fat and happy *Nanas* on its streets (p. 520), a loud popular outcry was the result. In other words, the direct effect of art, as so often in the past, initially remained limited to a circle of connoisseurs and experts – even though this circle had considerably expanded in the meantime.

Banal Subject-Matter – Sophisticated Means

The elitist appeal of Pop becomes understandable as soon as we realize that despite its populistic thrust, the style ultimately oriented itself to Duchamp's demand that art be intelligent first and foremost. Thus although Pop subject-matter was banal, its aesthetic means were generally not. Pop was a style in keeping with the level of consciousness of a late culture; its apparent simplicity was actually artificial to the highest degree. In this case, the medium was not the message at all, contrary to the then widely accepted theory of Canadian popular philosopher Marshall McLuhan. Pop Art, too, was an art of critical, detached reflection, not only on the part of the artist producing it but on the part of the audience contemplating it. This is clearly evident in the British version of the style, which emerged almost simultaneously on both sides of the Atlantic, and initially without mutual influence.

While the more pragmatic American Pop artists drew much direct inspiration from advertising, where many of them had originally made a living, in England a revolutionary new theory of art preceded its practice by many years. There, also, the term Pop Art did not so much refer to the style itself as to what it depicted: the symbols of mass production and consumption, from Mickey Mouse to the cult of packaging, from Hollywood movies to science fiction novels. The protagonists of British Pop envisioned a contemporary art that would be as vital and diverse as contemporary life itself, including its banalities. They threw open the doors between art and everyday living, between art and kitsch, hoping to create a new unity in diversity, an art accessible to everyone, beyond the barriers of education and class.

At the beginning of developments in Britain stood two, basically opposing influences. On the one hand, artists there were intrigued by the intellectual ideas of Duchamp and the Surrealistic mind-games of Magritte, as mediated by Paolozzi and Hamilton. On the other, they were filled with naive admiration at the "American way of life", its promise of Frigidaires and swimming pools for all. This ambivalence ran through the works of early British Pop, whether by Hamilton or David Hockney, Ronald B. Kitaj or Peter Phillips (p. 304), all of whom oscillated between acceptance and rejection of the things they depicted. Then too, since they were in revolt against the mainstream art of a Henry Moore or a Graham Sutherland, young British artists as it were began with a clean slate. In the United States, in contrast, direct links existed with Duchamp, who was living

"I don't mind a picture having a story as long as the beginning and the end exist within the four edges of the canvas. A picture is only finished when it is self-sufficient. The title should not be a synopsis."
ALLEN JONES

Allen Jones
Perfect Match, 1966/67
Oil on canvas, three parts, 280 x 93 cm
Cologne, Museum Ludwig,
Ludwig Donation

Peter Blake
On the Balcony, 1955–1957
Oil on canvas, 121.3 x 90.8 cm
London, Tate Gallery

David Hockney
Le Parc des Sources, Vichy, 1970
Acrylic on canvas, 214 x 305 cm
Paris, private collection

in New York, and with Action Painting, from which the great predecessors of Pop, Jasper Johns and Robert Rauschenberg, emerged.

The brash unconcern of the Americans was beyond the British, who felt the weight of tradition on their shoulders. Their initial enthusiasm was soon and increasingly supplanted by thoughtful reflection. The œuvre of Hamilton reveals this development very clearly. Even his icon of British Pop mentioned above, with its conglomeration of status symbols of affluence, already shows the artist's ironic detachment from his theme, and from the means employed to depict it. This critical attitude grew more pronounced over the years, culminating in Hamilton's contrast of an ultra-hip but brutal "swingeing" London to the "swinging" London of popular cliché, illustrated by the arrest of Mick Jagger and his gallerist-friend Robert Fraser in 1968.

In Hamilton's imagery, the collage technique is developed to perfection, combining traditional materials with the latest from the field of plastics and synthetics. But unlike the statements of his American counterparts, Hamilton's are usually not straightforward but ambiguous and encoded. Mass society and its idols, from movie star to astronaut, are criticized by means of alienation. The range of emotions in Hamilton's work extends from empathy with the fate of stars who, victims of their own artificial personae, cancel themselves out on press photos like Marilyn Monroe (*My Marilyn*, 1964; Cologne, Museum Ludwig), to sheer derision of sophisticated and hypocritical advertising methods in a pastel-hued image of two models in a *Soft Pink Landscape* (1972; Budapest, Magyar Nemzeti Múzeum). In this invocation of springtime the voyeuristic view, and the seductive quality of the toilet paper in the foreground, play the key role.

In contrast to Hamilton, the sculptor Paolozzi (p. 518), whose *Bunk* collages, films, and neo-Dadaist word-puzzles made him a forerunner of Pop, soon turned to concerns beyond the style. The younger Peter Blake, in *On the Balcony* (ill. left), a depiction of four children surrounded by emblems of high and low culture rendered with dead-pan seriousness, created a key image of British Pop. These kids are representatives of a society being confronted, as it were in a state of innocence, by the phenomenon of mass production of both physical and cultural goods. Blake's painting also bafflingly makes us conscious of the problem of original versus imitation, for instead of being an actual collage, it is a painted one. Blake, moreover, was the first Pop artist, far in advance of Andy Warhol, to depict the idols of young people at the time, idols whose unprecedented popularity was mediated to the extent that it would not have been possible without the techniques of mass visual reproduction represented by the new media of film and television. It is indicative that Blake never saw in person the star he depicted so many times, Elvis Presley, for, as the artist admitted, he was more a fan of the legend than of the person.

Ronald B. Kitaj
The Ohio Gang, 1964
Oil and oil crayon on canvas,
183.1 x 183.5 cm
New York, The Museum of
Modern Art, Philip C. Johnson
Fund

*"There will always be skylarks; even
a few nightingales. But arts are not
only the human equivalent of the
song of the singing birds."*
RONALD B. KITAJ

Below:
Sidney Nolan
Glenrowan, 1956/57
Ripolin on hardboard,
91.4 x 122 cm
London, Tate Gallery

Profundity and Playfulness

An intellectual opposite pole to Blake's "popular art" is
seen in the painting of Ronald B. Kitaj (ill. above), an
admirer of Ezra Pound who was born in Cleveland,
Ohio. Unlike the other artists of British Pop, Kitaj was
familiar when he came to London with American
Action Painting and the intermediary styles of
Rauschenberg and Johns. His imagery, instead of taking
its point of departure from the mass media, has its roots
in history. This is indicated by subjects such as *Rosa
Luxemburg's Assassins* (1960) with its allusive visual quote
of the features of German Field Marshal Helmuth von
Moltke; *Isaak Babel Riding with Budjonny* (1962); or
Austro-Hungarian Foot Soldier (1961; Cologne, Museum
Ludwig). Without a knowledge of the historical context,
these images remain largely cryptic.

Kitaj's style, derived from Abstract Expressionism,
has a technical refinement that surpasses that of his
friends. It is only his occasional use of vertical or horizontal series of disconnected images, the combination
of image with typography, or the collage principle trans-

David Hockney
Pearblossom Highway,
11–18 April, 1986
(second version)
Photographic collage, 198 x 282 cm
Los Angeles,
The J. Paul Getty Museum

"Best of all I like handmade pictures; consequently, I paint them myself. They always have a subject and a little bit of form. Balancing the two makes me, I suppose, a traditional painter."
DAVID HOCKNEY

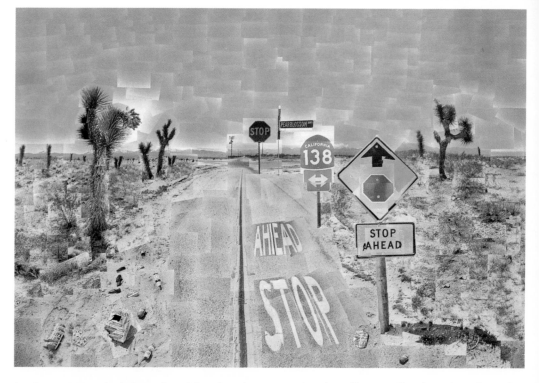

Alain Jacquet
Le Déjeuner sur l'herbe, 1964/65
Silk print on canvas, two parts,
175 x 195 cm
Canberra, Australian National
Gallery

Martial Raysse
She, 1962
Fluorescent paint on cardboard
and photograph, 182.5 x 132.2 cm
Cologne, Museum Ludwig,
Ludwig Donation

lated into painting, that link Kitaj's work loosely with Pop, making it hard to contradict him when he says he is not really a Pop artist. His basically arcane, difficult paintings with their abundance of literary allusions and covert references give free play to mental associations. They are certainly not naive, let alone easy to understand.

Understanding comes easier with David Hockney, the clever golden boy of the movement (ill. above and p. 306). Stylistically, especially in his early work, Hockney owed a great deal to Kitaj. Yet as his often-quoted statement shows, "I paint what I like, when I like, and where I like," the problem-laden, historical themes of his older friend, despite Hockney's intelligence, were not for him. In this respect, Hockney considers himself a traditionalist. One of his prime concerns is an understandable visual idiom in the context of a new figuration. Still, Hockney's approach is not illusionistic. The

"The painting of a flag is always about a flag, but it is not more about a flag than it is about a brushstroke or about a color or about the physicality of the paint, I think."
JASPER JOHNS

Jasper Johns
Three Flags, 1958
Encaustic on canvas,
76.2 x 115.6 x 12.7 cm
New York, Whitney Museum
of American Art

figures are abbreviated, sometimes ironically caricature-like pictorial signs.

Also characteristic of his early work is a combination of painting and script, a contrast of painted passages to the primed or unprimed canvas, and an obvious enjoyment of storytelling. *Flight into Italy – Swiss Landscape* (London, private collection) tells of an automobile trip with friends that was over much too soon for the artist's taste; *A Man Thinking* (London, The Arts Council of Great Britain) shows thoughts materializing like clouds above the figure's head; *We Two Boys Together Clinging* (London, The Arts Council of Great Britain) is fully explained by the title (all works 1961/62).

That Hockney is an excellent draughtsman becomes obvious from a glance at his early drawings and prints. In the mid-1960s his painting style began to grow more realistic, and the comparatively harsh contrasts and juxtapositions of the earlier compositions became rare. Hockney's approach and attitude are equally at home in the homo-erotic and high society coteries of California. His work proclaims that it's great to be alive, if your life is anything like his. Still, his style is suffused by a very British, subdued irony, which for a time prevented the sun-drenched images from slipping into superficiality. This sadly cannot be said of all the paintings of Hockney's most recent period.

Allen Jones (p. 305) developed his style out of a free play of form and color inspired by De Kooning, producing polychrome configurations that bore only oblique references to objective reality. His intention, as Jones once wrote to critic and curator Uwe M. Schneede, was to show that the surface of the picture was primarily a reflection of the artist's ideas. Jones later diverged radi-

cally from this conception, which was quite incompatible with Pop principles, to create a series of obsessive painted and sculpted depictions of his high-breasted, long-legged wife as a sex symbol. These cannot be said to have advanced his art.

Schneede has repeatedly pointed to the fact that, the British Pop artists subjected the means of painting to intensive investigation and questioning, thereby employed combinations of disparate images in a way reminiscent of Surrealism, and included a conceptual factor that was inspired by Duchamp. This penetrating, questioning thoughtfulness is also characteristic of the work of the American artist Jasper Johns.

Johns and Rauschenberg – The Pathfinders
Jasper Johns (pp. 309–312) fits into the category of Pop no better than does Robert Rauschenberg. Yet both paved the way for Pop Art, producing in the process a body of painted and graphic masterworks whose outstanding quality was matched by no other artist of their generation, nor even by older artists such as Roy Lichtenstein. They perhaps found a near-equal in the object-maker Claes Oldenburg, who, like Johns and Rauschenberg, came from Action Painting and had little more in common with Pop than a raising of the trivial to aesthetic status (following cues from Cubist collage and Dadaism), a negation of hierarchic orders in art, and a Surrealism-derived simultaneous presentation of disparate, mutually contradictory imagery. Particularly in Oldenburg's early work, the borderline between painting and sculpture was still permeable, but as his career proceeded, the three-dimensional object came increasingly to the fore (pp. 515, 516).

Jasper Johns
Edingsville, 1965
Oil on canvas with objects,
173 x 311 cm
Cologne, Museum Ludwig,
Ludwig Donation

With Johns, too, a neo-Dadaist inclusion of actual,
everyday things and utensils (newspapers, rulers, wire,
forks, shovels) plays a key role. External reality dis-
turbingly intrudes into the reality of the painted surface.
Sublime themes and pleasing visual illusions produced
by tricks of perspective are entirely absent from Johns's
work. The border-line between the reality of the thing
depicted and the reality of the depiction blurs; the picture becomes an object in its own right. The artist's subject-matter is taken exclusively from the context of the
conventional, the mundane, with which we are all familiar and to which we therefore pay hardly any attention.
The motifs are meaningless patterns, as it were. If they
again become capable of rousing our interest, it is
because of the alienation Johns subjects them to. This
process runs counter to every received scale of values,
whether thematic or aesthetic. Johns is concerned only
with value-free facts, and commonplace things have the
inestimable advantage of being impersonal and neutral.
And since they already exist, there is no need to invent
them – numerals and letters of the alphabet, targets,
maps, wooden slats, banal patterns on building walls or
the sides of delivery vans. It is in keeping with the banality of such motifs that the human figure hardly occurs in
Johns's imagery at all, unless it be in the form of fragmentary casts or – even rarer – summarily painted contours of human limbs.

All of this sounds very pragmatic, and surely reflects
a no-nonsense approach to reality that is perhaps typically American. Yet it is what Johns does with his superficially banal themes that lends his art its unquestionable rank. For instance, the American flag remains the

Jasper Johns
Field Painting, 1963/64
Oil on canvas with objects,
183 x 93.3 cm
New York, collection of the artist

Since the 1980s, similarly to the late Picasso, he has
begun deriving inspiration from his own previous oeuvre, returning to motifs, techniques, and materials of
earlier works and combining these with new experiences
and insights gained from an involvement with space and
materials, history and current events. Naturally in an
artist of such great productivity as Rauschenberg, a certain unevenness of quality is unavoidable.

His love of quotation has always been complemented by a joy in experiment. Rauschenberg's optimism was admittedly considerably dampened in connection with an ambitious, naively visionary attempt to
build a bridge between art and technology in the "EAT"
series, begun in 1966. The industrial sponsors of the project soon lost interest when they discovered it was not
going to pay.

The immediate result was an artistic and personal
crisis which, although it kept Rauschenberg out of the
headlines for a considerable period, did not prevent him
from conceiving, in 1984, an even more ambitious project aimed at nothing less than facilitating international
understanding through cultural exchange: "Rauschenberg Overseas Culture Interchange," or "ROCI" for
short. The artist invested all of his money in this project,
and when the monster travelling exhibition and associated trips to Chile, Mexico, Cuba, China, Japan, the former Soviet Union, and to Berlin immediately after the
Wall came down, threatened to exhaust his funds,
Rauschenberg broke with his long-time dealer Leo
Castelli and sought aid from the equally legendary and

controversial billionaire Armand Hammer and from the
Knoedler Gallery.

ROCI proved that Rauschenberg's maintenance of
artistic detachment, his demonstrative waiver of pathos
and the grand gesture, had nothing to do with moral
indifference, let alone with the cynicism – real or
feigned – of the work of his friend, Warhol. Though he
was unable to cure the world's ills with his courageous
undertaking, Rauschenberg did do the utmost one individual can to bring diverse and divergent people and cultures together. His artistic ethos was manifested not
least in his waiver of the use-value of things, recalling
that of Tinguely, but without going to the other extreme
of making a fetish of the everyday and commonplace. It
was also and particularly manifested in the multiplicity
of meaning and the openness of an art which critic
David Galloway has termed "polyphonal."

There may have been greater inventors in the history
of art than Rauschenberg. He was never an avant-garde
artist in the long over-rated, post-modern sense of the
term. In his thinking, love of experiment and quotation,
Rauschenberg was, precisely, a "combiner," someone
who retained his independence and freedom of movement in an era dominated by the specialist. He always
remained a loner, who was able to combine great sensitivity to the realities of the day with visionary imagination – a utopian without illusions. In his late paintings
and objects Rauschenberg drew the sum of a long and
rich visual experience. Yet though still vital and not
without inventiveness, they reveal a shift of emphasis

towards aesthetic appeal and elegance of execution, while not denying or falsifying the real world in which we live.

Fragments of Reality

James Rosenquist (ill. above) is still another example of an American artist whose roots were in Abstract Expressionism. Yet for him a quite different and more mundane experience proved crucial – making his living as a painter of movie billboards. Perched high above the New York streets on a rickety scaffold, the expanse of surface to be covered right in front of his nose, Rosenquist mechanically filled it in with garish colors, often working as if in a trance. The realistic depiction, seen in extreme close-up, turned into an abstract pattern. This was the insight Rosenquist exploited in his own work in painting. The resulting visual irritation, seen in the large-format later paintings and environments, was intentional.

Rosenquist presented fragments of reality, outsized, often larger than life, clearly defined. Yet instead of being isolated and mutually independent as with Rauschenberg, each fragment was always interlinked with those surrounding it. One and the same excerpt from reality – a paintbrush, an automobile grille, a hair dryer, a mountain of spaghetti, a movie star, a jet fighter – can simultaneously function as the central motif in one field of the painting and as the transitional context in another. Every passage of Rosenquist's compositions, unlike those of his Pop colleagues, is related to the next,

interlocked, interdependent. The things represented do not stand for themselves alone, but are part of a general context of meaning. Indicatively, Rosenquist's closest friends during the heyday of Pop included abstractionist Ellsworth Kelly, but none of his fellow practitioners of Pop.

Unlike his great forerunner, Rauschenberg, Rosenquist had no intention of bridging the gap between art and life. He drew a clear dividing line between them.

James Rosenquist
Horse Blinders (detail), 1968/69
Oil and fluorescent paint
on canvas and aluminum,
23 parts, 275 x 2530 cm
Cologne, Museum Ludwig,
Ludwig Donation

James Rosenquist
Look Alive
(Blue Feet, Look Alive), 1961
Oil on canvas, 170.2 x 148.6 cm
Private collection

Larry Rivers
Africa I, 1961/62
Oil on canvas, 184.2 x 163.8 cm
Private collection

Jim Dine
Five Feet of Colored Tools, 1962
Oil on canvas with objects, 141.2 x 152.9 x 11 cm
New York, The Museum of Modern Art,
The Sidney and Harriet Janis Collection

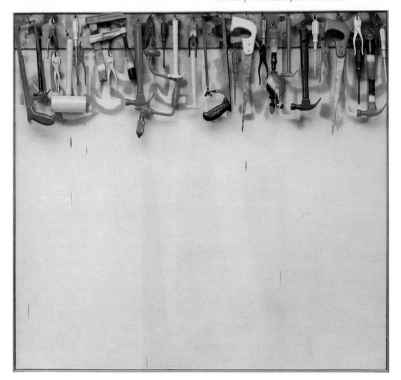

Instead of setting out to depict existential experiences, Rosenquist attempted to convey a new brand of experience to be had within the artificial domain of advertising and consumerism. When he depicted a cigarette ad with Joan Crawford – again, in a monumentalized excerpt – he produced not a portrait of the famous movie star but a reproduction of her image as manipulated for advertising purposes. Such pictures function on several levels of meaning, showing a woman who, already stylized into a mass idol, is in turn manipulated and degraded into a marketing motif aimed at increasing sales.

What Rosenquist painted during his most prolific years did not reflect the rapprochement between political and artistic intelligence that seemed possible during the brief Kennedy era. Rosenquist's skepticism remained unaffected by wishful thinking of this kind.

Larry Rivers (ill. left) is a lone wolf who eludes the category of Pop. His artistic activities began not in the field of painting but as a jazz saxophonist. Rivers went on to study music at the renowned Julliard School in New York, before, intrigued by the portrait of a cellist by Braque, he spontaneously decided to become an artist. This was in 1945, when Rivers was twenty-two. He also admired Richard Lindner, and repeatedly referred to his inspiring influence, saying that he felt a spiritual relationship to the older painter. Although he also respected Oldenburg, Rauschenberg, and Warhol, Rivers always remained an outsider on the scence and went his own way. As even his earliest paintings of the 1970s reveal, the artist drew sustenance from the imagery of commercial art, out of whose clichéd depictions he developed his own, personal visual ideas. What distinguishes Rivers from the protagonists of Pop Art is a close and continuing link with the wellsprings of Abstract Expressionism as manifested in the energetic gestures of a De Kooning. One might say that Rivers's work eludes all stylistic or art-historical labels.

Is Pop Art a Brand of Genre Painting?

Jim Dine (ill. left and p. 319 above), who left the United States in 1967 for London, said just a year later that he thought a great part of what went by the name of Pop Art in America was really genre painting – a pretty facile show-business-type thing. Not that he would deny anything he himself or others had done, Dine added, it was just that Blake and Hockney did this sort of genre painting much better. Like most of his colleagues and friends, Dine came from Action Painting. With Allan Kaprow (p. 319 below), Oldenburg, and others he was involved in the expansion of this actionistic, gestural art form into the actual, public space, that improvised, borderline-transcending art and artists' theater that, as the "Happening", not only went down in history but, like "Pop", became a household word. The happening, moreover, provided the spark that set off the still more improvisational Fluxus movement, the occasionally self-flagellating tendency known as Body Art, the black masses of the Viennese Actionists, and the more disciplined and ritualized "performance." These later developments deserve emphasis when discussing Dine, because the enormous enthusiasm with which he threw himself into the New York art scene would later give way to a profound skepticism.

This doubt with respect to excesses of earlier days led Dine to a creative involvement with the art of the Old World, all the way back to the Egyptians, and away from what Wieland Schmied has termed the "rustical directness of America." But before this came to pass, Dine's irrepressible enjoyment of whatever he was doing – whether painting or making objects or both in one – found expression in a blithely bright palette and especially in his favorite and often-varied motif, the heart. For a time Dine seemed to be the most carefree of Pop artists, and his paintings and objects possessed a degree of concreteness lacking in those of the others. This lay in Dine's respect for craftsmanship, and a lifelong love of simple, basic tools, a love he had inherited from his Polish grandfather. It was to him that Dine ascribed the greatest influence on his work – before, in 1959, he met Kaprow, Oldenburg, Johns, Rauschenberg, and Robert Whitman in New York.

Like that of many American artists, Dine's work frequently reveals an interplay between actual and painted objects. This device had a certain tradition in the United States, going back historically to the *trompe-l'œil* painting of John Frederick Peto and William Harnett in the 19th century (which Johns also admired). For Dine, the canvas was a final point of connection with unreality, while the object – whether shovel, saw, or bathrobe, or, later, the torsos and statues of antiquity, up to the Hellenistic period – generally remained an actual, concrete thing. The tension in Dine's very personal variant of Pop Art long derived from a visualization of this dichotomy. Then a new motif appeared: the landscape. But despite the painterly emphasis of this more conventional imagery, the concrete object still played a role. Hammer, axe, brush, or spatula kept the memory of the artist's grandfather's workshop alive.

Tom Wesselmann (p. 320) perhaps risked more than most Pop artists from the start. He put all his money, if you will, on a single, limited theme: the clichés of advertising, personified by woman as a secularized Eve, equipped with the corresponding attributes: invitingly open mouth, dazzlingly white teeth, swelling breasts, supplemented by ripe oranges and a filter cigarette conveying the dual meaning of phallic symbol and secular *memento mori*. The blatant sexuality of Wesselmann's imagery is ice-cold; his females are merely anonymous, sales-boosting sex objects, whether the inticement be to take up smoking, use paper tissues, or buy a bathtub with shower. This viewpoint also makes itself apparent elsewhere. Other status symbols like the automobile appear in a monumentalized form and spirited into an artificial world in which everything natural seems turned to plastic, even a summer landscape with living people.

Jim Dine
Pleasure Palette, 1969
Oil, glass, paper on canvas,
152 x 102 cm
Cologne, Museum Ludwig,
Ludwig Donation

Allan Kaprow
Baby, 1957
Assemblage: composition board,
linen strips, paper, metal foils,
synthetic paints, India ink,
282 x 306 x 97 cm
Vienna, Museum moderner Kunst

Tom Wesselmann
Bathtub No. 3, 1963
Oil on canvas, plastic, objects
(bathroom door, towel, laundry
basket), 213 x 270 x 45 cm
Cologne, Museum Ludwig,
Ludwig Donation

Wesselmann's subject-matter is less complex than that of his Pop colleagues. Perhaps it was too limited to provide a long-term yield. Also, the decorative tendency in his work was always strong, and the irony not always sharp enough, to prevent the border-line between detachment and affirmation from becoming blurred. The *Outcuts* of later years, their palette saccharine sweet and their schematized figuration stale, provide sad evidence of the fact that no one can produce Pop Art on an assembly-line basis for an entire career without detriment to his own better talents.

The case is different with Roy Lichtenstein (pp. 321–323). The oldest of the American Pop artists, he also, with Warhol, was one of the most influential, his approach affecting both sub-cultural and mainstream visual thinking in his own country, in Europe, and even here and there in the Middle and Far East. A glance at

Tom Wesselmann
Great American
Still Life No. 2, 1961
Oil on canvas, 120 x 120 cm
Pasadena (CA), Pasadena Art
Museum, Gift of Fred Heim

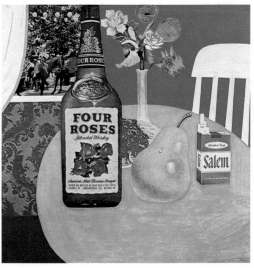

the billboards of most any city, or into the display windows of its boutiques, supermarkets, drugstores, even banks, will suffice to show what I mean. What advertising once provided to Pop Art in the way of inspiration, it has long since harvested many times over. Basically, this conversion process took the same course it did earlier, when Picasso and Mondrian were trivialized and introduced on the popular level, in the design of home interiors, in advertising, or in printed dress patterns. But the feedback of a style whose principal theme was already the banal and mundane was much more strikingly evident than the subliminal influence of Mondrian or the De Stijl group.

Lichtenstein contributed as much as Warhol to this feedback effect. He monumentalized the comic strip and, with the mixture of fascination and irony so typical of Pop Art, lent comic-book heroes and heroines the same visual dignity that his great idol, Léger, had lent to the world of the anonymous working-man. Yet Lichtenstein also turned the tables on high art, stripping the mythical trappings from the sublime and sacred icons of Western culture, from the Greek temple to Monet's *Rouen Cathedral*, from Picasso and Mondrian to the brushstrokes of Abstract Expressionism, by dis-solving them all into the sterile dot patterns of commercial printing methods.

The Covert Classicist

Still, it was no coincidence when the American art historian Diane Waldman mentioned the name of Ingres in connection with Lichtenstein, even before the allusive and no longer so revolutionary work of his mature period had emerged. Lichtenstein is in fact a covert classicist, with a highly developed sense of form. His pictures combine a concise, pointed simplicity with "elegant sophistication and intellectual precision," as Waldman notes. To characterize the American artist's œuvre in a single word, one could do worse than choose the

Roy Lichtenstein
Explosion No. 1, 1965
Lacquered metal, 251 x 160 cm
Cologne, Museum Ludwig,
Ludwig Donation

title of an 18th-century book by Comtesse de Noailles, *Exactitudes*. This term fits Lichtenstein's work from the beginnings to recent years, when his approach began to show a certain expressive relaxation.

It is in keeping with this penchant for precision that, besides Ingres, Dutch artists Mondrian and van Doesburg, leaders of De Stijl, have played as important a role in Lichtenstein's artistic thinking as the Cubists in general, and Picasso and Léger in particular. Naturally his thoughts reach back even further, to Cézanne and his rigorous pictorial structure. And it is surely no coincidence that Egyptian pyramids and Greek temples are

Roy Lichtenstein
Whaam!, 1963
Oil and magna on canvas,
two parts, 172.7 x 421.6 cm
London, Tate Gallery

Roy Lichtenstein
M-Maybe (A Girl's Picture), 1965
Magna on canvas, 152 x 152 cm
Cologne, Museum Ludwig,
Ludwig Donation

Page 323 above:
Roy Lichtenstein
Figures in a Landscape, 1985
Oil and magna on canvas,
243.8 x 279.4 cm
Private collection

Page 323 below:
Andy Warhol
Do it Yourself (Landscape), 1962
Acrylic on canvas, 178 x 137 cm
Cologne, Museum Ludwig,
Ludwig Donation

submitted to the same Ben Day process as barns, hot dogs, or balls of twine. Even when the subject is expressionistic art – by Marc or Heckel, even Picasso – Lichtenstein reduces it to apparently straightforward but actually highly sophisticated configurations full of irony, and rife with a multiplicity of allusions and covert homages.

Since the 1970s at the latest, Lichtenstein's art has been an "art about art", an art for connoisseurs – and for artists. The quiet, distinguished gentleman from Long Island celebrates a timeless, detached classicism.

An Art of Conformity

Pop Art, decreed veteran Dadaist Hans Richter, was not an art or anti-art of protest like Dada, but a record of artists' acceptance of and conformity with contemporary consumerism. In Richter's view, Pop Art was nothing more than a derivative, neo-Dada style. Yet criticism of existing social and political conditions, let alone the notion of improving them through artistic protest, was far from the minds of the protagonists of Pop. Thus

Richter decried a lack of commitment where none was intended.

Let us list some of the characteristics of genuine Pop Art: the blow-up; an isolation or serial presentation of motifs; a waiver of expressiveness and individual touch in favor of an impersonal style; a limitation of subject-matter to actual commercial commodities and mass media imagery; a congruity of motif and style; a preference, as in advertising, for brand-new objects (as opposed to the worn and used ones employed by Johns and Rauschenberg); a waiver of all ideology, critique, and metaphorical reference; and finally, a favoring of technical reproduction processes. In view of these factors, Richter was correct to speak of Pop as an art of conformity or affirmation. Its characteristics are reflected in the purest and most radical form in the work of the man whose name has become a synonym of Pop Art, even among people who could care less about art in general: Andy Warhol (pp. 323–326).

Warhol went beyond even the "completely mechanical and removed style" of which Lichtenstein spoke, a style in which complicated manipulations led to a translation of the original motif into an autonomous image. Warhol proceeded differently. His piles of Brillo boxes, for instance, were not manipulated but simply left in their original state, without alteration on the artist's part. The only sign of his personal choice was the arrangement of the pyramid, with the largest box on top. There is an evident similarity here with the activity of the decorator or designer, and hence with advertising, in which Warhol began his career. Here the object – unlike, say, Johns' bronze beer cans – was not alienated by transposition into another material or by painterly treatment.

Johns, who was two years Warhol's senior, once stated that when you made one object out of another, there was no change, just two objects. Now this no longer held. With Warhol, a Brillo box remained a Brillo box, and a pyramid of Campbell soup cans remained just that. Even in his silkscreen prints of a single or a hundred soup cans, their identity remained intact, apart from slight irregularities in printing. But above all, the factor of mass production and interchangeability was made visible, with an added ironic twist when Warhol used the same serial reproduction process to banalize the Mona Lisa under the title *Thirty are Better Than One* as he did to portray Jackie Kennedy or Marilyn Monroe.

Everything, in other words, could be mechanically produced and repeated *ad infinitum*. The idea of gratuitous beauty was reduced by Warhol to the cool statement that "An artist is somebody who produces things that people don't need to have but that he – for some reason – thinks it would be a good idea to give them." The marketing of art was wholeheartedly accepted: "Business art is the step that comes after Art. I started as a commercial artist, and I want to finish as a business artist ... and good business is the best art." In this state of affairs memory and history naturally had no place. "I have no memory," stated Warhol. "Every day is a new day, because I can't remember the day before. Every minute is like the first minute in my life." He tried to remember, but couldn't, which was why he was married to his cassette deck. Like it, Warhol stated, his memory had a button marked "erase."

Reporter of the Era – Portraitist of Society

Values, feelings, seemed not to exist for Warhol. He registered race riots, suicides, airplane crashes, the atomic bomb, the electric chair with the same cool detachment that he brought to registering soup cans, revolvers, flowers and Brillo boxes. The medium was either newsprint or photography, which for Warhol, who occasionally saw himself in the role of a camera even when he was not using one, was just as important as film. This held true even in cases where a photo transferred to canvas was used as only one of several compositional elements.

There has been much debate about whether Warhol was truly the detached, cold-blooded reporter he made

Andy Warhol
Triple Elvis, 1962
Silkscreen print on canvas,
208.3 x 299.7 cm
Formerly Saatchi Collection,
London

Andy Warhol
Silver Disaster, 1963
Acrylic and silkscreen
on canvas, 203 x 203 cm
Zurich, Galerie Bruno
Bischofberger

Page 325:
Andy Warhol
Twenty-Five Colored
Marilyns, 1962
Acrylic on canvas, 209 x 170 cm
Fort Worth (TX), Modern Art
Museum of Fort Worth,
The Benjamin J. Tillar

himself out to be, or whether his show of emotionlessness concealed a fundamentally moralistic attitude. The issue becomes irrelevant in view of what the intelligent cynic and eccentric jet-set favorite did during the last years before his unexpected death. Now not only were his motifs banal, but so was their slapdash and careless execution. It was as if Warhol felt tempted to see how much a consumption-oriented, snobbish art scene would accept from its undisputed star without ruining his reputation. This was his parting shot.

Or perhaps not, in view of the last paintings Warhol left behind. These are not only done with virtuoso technique, they reveal a well-considered conception which is perfectly suited to the motif (such as the head of Lenin). This elusive eccentric, who concealed his true self and real intentions behind a – naturally equally well-considered – silence and a series of masks, down to the white wig of his final years, never revealed his secret. So with respect to Warhol's work and personality, we are forced to rely on speculation to a greater degree than in the case of almost any other 20th-century artist. But one thing does stand out clearly: his significance as an innovator who provided fresh impulses to practically every field of visual art, and, especially, his importance as a portraitist of late-capitalist society. The cool, seemingly

"With silkscreening, you pick a photograph, blow it up, transfer it in glue onto silk, and then roll ink across it so the ink goes through the silk but not through the glue. That way you get the same image, slightly different each time. It was all so simple – quick and chancy. I was thrilled with it." ANDY WARHOL

Richard Lindner
The Meeting, 1953
Oil on canvas, 152.4 x 182.9 cm
New York, The Museum
of Modern Art

merciless detachment with which Warhol saw behind its masks, particularly in the high society photo series, lends his oeuvre the character of a dispassionate and disinterested stock-taking of our era. In his imagery, future archaeologists digging into the 20th century will find a rich yield.

Fascinated by a New Babylon

The opposite tack to the serial methods of Lichtenstein or Warhol is represented by the painstaking technique of Richard Lindner, a German-Jewish painter born in Hamburg in 1901 (ill. above and p. 328). Lindner experienced the escalation of racism and anti-Semitic violence in Munich and Nuremberg, and was able to escape at the last moment by way of Paris to New York.

His style and technique were beholding to the Neue Sachlichkeit of Otto Dix, Christian Schad, or – to a lesser degree – of the early Balthus, while the aggressiveness of a George Grosz remained foreign to Lindner. The themes of his imagery were initially inspired by the writings of Frank Wedekind and Bertolt Brecht. But then the life and times, the desires and dangers of New Babylon cast their spell over Lindner. As obvious as his European origins remained, this circumstance brought him into proximity with Pop Art. In terms of subject-matter, this proximity was reflected in an emphasis on the trivial (targets, slot machines, and toys, which

recalled the artist's Nuremberg period), in a brash palette (Lindner, too, worked in advertising), and in a coolly detached depiction not only of things but of human beings. Lindner's figures, often derived from the milieu of prostitutes and gangsters, seem emotionally isolated from one another. They act like marionettes, yet they also symbolize certain fundamental human traits. To woman, the artist ascribes the dual role of demon and mother, goddess and whore. In any case the females in Lindner's visual world are superior to the males, in keeping with his belief that in fact women are the strong sex, and not the "pitiable" men.

What fundamentally distinguishes Lindner's paintings from those of the Pop artists is an alienation of reality by means of distortion and a collage-like dissection of objects and figures, an interpretative symbolism, and a painstaking, precise, and patient execution which recalls the Old Masters. Lindner's painting, in a word, is American art shaped by Europe.

Radical Realism in Paris

The use of "components of reality" to produce art, advocated by Rauschenberg, was ramified by a group founded in Paris in 1960 on the initiative of critic Pierre Restany: the Nouveaux Réalistes. The most logical development of this approach over the years took place in the work of Arman (p. 328 below). After starting as a

Andy Warhol
Big Torn Campbell's Soup
Can (Black Bean), 1962
Acrylic on canvas, 183 x 137 cm
Düsseldorf, Kunstsammlung
Nordrhein-Westfalen

Richard Lindner
Telephone, 1966
Oil on canvas, 178 x 152.5 cm
Nuremberg, Kunsthalle Nürnberg

Daniel Spoerri
Hahn's Dinner, 1964
Objects and makings of a
dinner for 16 persons,
on wood panel, 200 x 200 x 38 cm
Vienna, Museum moderner Kunst,
formerly Hahn Collection

Arman
Ciment en Si, 1973
Destroyed guitar in cement,
90 x 60 cm
Private collection

gestural, Tachist painter, the high-strung artist soon began to make three-dimensional objects out of unaltered, everyday things, which he called *Accumulations*. This eventually led to an involvement with prefabricated industrial parts (*Accumulations Renault*). When Arman collected items of daily use and embedded them in clear fiberglass resin to create a portrait of their owner and his habits, the resulting non-formal arrangement was not

without a certain painterly effect. But when he enclosed a number of plastic hands in a polyester torso, he not only transcended the border-line of sculpture, but evoked a symbolic message reminiscent of Surrealism (hands penetrating into a body). Perhaps in reaction, Arman then began to limit himself to a simple presentation of accumulations of real, mundane, sometimes discarded objects (eyeglass frames, paint tubes, water pitchers) which evinced no recognizable incursion on the artist's part. The representation and the thing represented were identical; reality itself became image; the borderline between external reality and aesthetic reality was rendered permeable. Existing things became aesthetic objects.

Daniel Spoerri (ill. below), author of a *Topography of Chance*, fixes traces of life at a certain moment, by attaching, say, the remains of a meal or a party to a board, producing *Trap Pictures* that brought time to a standstill. A table top became a memento; one fleeting second between life and death took on the quality of permanence. Spoerri also is a collector of situations, including verbal ones, considering words to be excerpts of biographical processes. Found objects that fall into his hands by chance continually inspire the artist to new, original, and profoundly witty arrangements, which he sometimes expands into ironic and critical environments like his famous *Musées sentimentaux*. In the meantime Spoerri has ceased to make *Museums* or *Traps*, having recently begun to cast his tables in bronze. He had "now reached an age when an artist has to work in bronze if he wants to be taken seriously," Spoerri self-ironically replied to the question whether Dadaist gestures were now to become museum-worthy art. Nor were such perennial themes as death any longer taboo. Yet as Hans Peter Schwerfel remarks, Spoerri relegates even this theme to "the curiosity cabinet of life, to prevent art from becoming deadly boring."

Raymond Hains (ill. above left), Jacques de la Villeglé (ill. above right), and Mimmo Rotella (ill. below), reversed the principle of collage by tearing off the top layers of billboard posters to reveal the "new realities" concealed beneath. These *décollages*, in Hains's case at least, were concerned not so much with art as with a critique of hypocritical advertising methods. The same not follow the American tendency to value-free depiction but mercilessly pilloried the ills of consumer society, of war and inhumanity. Even though he occasionally returned to pure painting, Vostell's commitment remained strong and obvious.

In this connection mention must be made of two artists who like no other took art out of the museum into the open air, be it a stretch of countryside or an urban site: Christo & Jeanne-Claude (ill. left). Although Christo initially earned his living as a portraitist, he is not primarily a painter but a superb draughtsman and collage-maker. The artist began to alienate commonplace objects of daily use by wrapping them in paper or fabric, which lent them a strangely poetic aura. The ambitiousness of Christo and Jeanne-Claude's ideas already became apparent in 1962, one year after the Berlin Wall was built, when they erected a barricade of brightly colored barrels across the Rue Visconti in Paris. In 1995, six years after the German-German border was opened, Christo and Jeanne-Claude were finally able to realize an idea they had tirelessly pursued for almost a quarter century – their dream of wrapping the Reichstag Building in Berlin (p. 550).

Never before had artists encouraged so many people to think about contemporary art and its meaning, in an entirely relaxed and unpretentious way, than Christo and Jeanne-Claude. This is why they cannot be passed over in this chapter on painting. At first sight it may seem surprising that apart from Christo, Yves Klein, the painter of sheer blueness and the void, should have been one of the leading figures of the group. Yet he, too, in an œuvre that combined the material and the immaterial in an inimitably personal way, in his emphasis on the pure, physical presence of color, and in the impressions of living human figures on paper or canvas, the *Anthropometries* (p. 298), made a crucial contribution to the application of the theory of reality, if for Klein reality always included the transcendental.

Christo
Wrapped Reichstag, Berlin, 1993
Collage: pencil, fabric, twine,
photo by Wolfgang Volz, pastel,
charcoal, crayon, technical data,
tape, 30.5 x 77.5 and 66.7 x 77.5 cm
New York, Cyril Christo Collection
© Christo 1993

method was used for similar reasons for a time by German artist Wolf Vostell (p. 329), who became the European father of the happening. In his work in a Pop vein and his major, socially critical environments, Vostell did

The Damaged Life
The Realism of Francis Bacon

The œuvre of Francis Bacon, who was born in 1909 to English parents in Dublin and lived in London until his death in 1992, holds a special place in 20th-century art. Self-taught, Bacon began to paint in the 1930s, like his countryman, Graham Sutherland, under the influence of Surrealism and the distorted figuration of Picasso. Yet since he destroyed most of this early work, it was only after the Second World War that Bacon began to find international recognition. Immune to the various modernist isms and fads, he remained true to figurative painting for over half a century, to be become arguably

the most significant and complex realist of the period. What Kafka once said about Picasso applies perfectly to Bacon's work: "In the distorting mirror of art, reality appears undistorted."

Bacon was an admirer of the pioneers of photography and film, Muybridge and Eisenstein. Muybridge's experimental photo sequences on the movements of humans and animals, and above all the close-up image of a woman screaming in Eisenstein's film, *Battleship Potemkin*, left clear traces in his work. These influences are apparent in the inter-twined male figures of many

Francis Bacon
Study for Portrait of
van Gogh III, 1957
Oil and sand on canvas,
198.4 x 142.5 cm
Washington, Hirshhorn Museum
and Sculpture Garden,
Smithsonian Institution

Francis Bacon
Study after Velázquez's Portrait of
Pope Innocent X, 1953
Oil on canvas, 153 x 118 cm
Des Moines (IA), Des Moines
Art Center

paintings, as they are in the series devoted to Popes, mouths agape and enclosed as if in a cage. These went back to the superb portrait of Pope Innocent X by Velázquez (Rome, Galleria Doria Pamphilj), a picture Bacon never wanted to see in the original because he felt he could never hope to match such an achievement (ill. below). The artist often worked from photographs, but considered that painting possessed the great advantage of a texture that was much more direct and intensive in effect than that of photography.

Bacon obstinately insisted, despite his polemics against abstraction, that his art was devoted to primarily aesthetic aims. Yet the imagery itself and the often unconventional means used to make it – throwing paint or paint-soaked rags, scrubbing brushes, or whisk brooms at the canvas – reveal an underlying theme: the precariousness of the human condition. "I think art is an obsession with life," said Bacon, "and after all, as we are human beings, our greatest obsession is with ourselves. Then possibly with animals, and then with land-scapes." Seen thus, Bacon's Popes, and even the cruci-fied Christ, become our contemporaries. Since accord-ing to Bacon there are no new myths, an artist must con-tinually reinterpret the old ones – far from all traditional religiosity.

Like Picasso, Bacon employed the device of distor-tion, of both visible aspect and hidden essence, in his figurative and portrait works. But unlike Picasso, he used distortion not for dramatic ends but presented it as the frightening result of his diagnosis of reality. His pic-tures, beyond their outstanding artistic quality and extraordinarily disciplined form and composition, are compelling, precisely observed documents of an era as reflected in an immensely fertile imagination. Bacon did not moralize; he merely pointed out the state of humanity, provided an "image of the phenomenon."

His conscious waiver of commentary, interpretation, and any deeper meaning we as viewers may read into his work reflected Bacon's laconic objectivity and his rejec-tion of storytelling and what he called "illustrational"

Francis Bacon
Study for Self-Portrait (Triptych),
1985/86
Oil on canvas, 198 x 147.5 cm (each)
London, Marlborough
International Fine Art

*"In my case all painting – and the
older I get, the more it becomes so –
is accident. So I foresee it in my
mind, I foresee it, and yet I hardly
ever carry it out as I foresee it. It
transforms itself by the actual paint.
I use very large brushes, and in the
way I work I don't in fact know very
often what the paint will do, and it
does many things which are very
much better than I could make it do.
Is that an accident? Perhaps one
could say it's not an accident,
because it becomes a selective process
which part of this accident one
chooses to preserve. One is attempting, of course, to keep the vitality of
the accident and yet preserve a continuity."* FRANCIS BACON

painting. The damaged life, damaged existence, are
evoked by purely painterly means. Terror and horror,
destruction and the destroyed, tortured human and gut-
ted animal are presented not sadistically but dispassion-
ately, for if Bacon's imagery is tormented, so is the reality
it reflects. The anxieties and fears given shape on canvas
are our own, and were those of the artist. The precariousness of life and reality are invoked by means of historical and contemporary figures – including Bacon
himself and many of his friends – whose contours blur
and dissolve, whose faces are distorted or obscured by
shadows. Equally at home in the upper and the underworld, Bacon always told the truth about what he saw.

From this point of view, Bacon's involvement with
van Gogh as a prime example of the isolated man and
artist becomes clear. Although he later distanced himself from his many variations on van Gogh's *Painter on
the Way to Work* (formerly Magdeburg, Kaiser-Friedrich-
Museum; destroyed in World War II), as he did from his
portraits of the Popes, Bacon must have felt van Gogh to
be a kindred spirit. The series, brilliant in color and executed with an expressive gesture unusual in Bacon, represent stations of the cross in an everyday setting. The
third study (p. 331) shows the lonely painter as a ghostly,
shadowy figure in the landscape, pausing under a tree
on his way to work to escape the burning sun. Even in
this static pose, the figure appears restless and unsettled,

the face barely recognizable and the body seemingly on
the verge of dissolution.

In later years Bacon repeatedly painted triptychs and
series of variations on a theme. He himself explained the
reason, saying "...in the series one picture reflects on the
other continuously and sometimes they're better in
series than they are separately because, unfortunately,
I've never yet been able to make the one image that sums
up all the others." It is perhaps a phenomenon typical of
our troubled century in which the whole has disappeared from view, that the substance of an artist's lifework can no longer be distilled into a single work, but
only revealed through a series of works. In this regard,
too, Bacon was a child of our times.

Lucian Freud (p. 335 above right), grandson of Sigmund Freud, once portrayed Bacon. His predominant
theme, like Bacon's, is the human being, male and
female – their anatomy and physiognomy, including his
own. Refusing to work with professional models, Freud
depicts only people to whom he has a personal relationship, not least his daughters, because they, he says, need
be ashamed of nothing. Freud's canvases bear an affinity
with Bacon's, not so much in terms of painterly
approach and composition as in terms of existential attitude. In this regard, his Jewish descent and emigré's
experiences surely played a role that should not be
underestimated.

Bernard Buffet
Woman with Bathtub, 1947
Oil on canvas, 209 x 109 cm
Private collection

Francis Gruber
Female Nude in a Red Cardigan,
1944
Oil on canvas, 115 x 89 cm
Paris, Musée d'Art Moderne
de la Ville de Paris

Page 335 below:
Philip Pearlstein
Female Nude in an Armchair,
1977/78
Oil on canvas, 182 x 244 cm
New York, Brooklyn Museum,
J. B. Woodward Fund

Investigation into Reality
Aspects of Neo-Realism

The discussion about realist tendencies in post-war art is still in its beginnings. The range and obvious differences in approach and quality of the works shown in 1970 at the Whitney Museum's "22 Realists", mentioned above, already suggested that realism and naturalism were different things. Yet instead of attempting to define the fundamental differences in terms of form and content, methods and results, in the approaches of painters and sculptors working in a realistic vein, most critics continued to lump them together, and do so still. But what do the early portraits of American artist Chuck Close, with their naturalistic reference alienated by means of format, camera focus, and painterly alteration, have in common with the European sensibility and covert romanticism of Franz Gertsch's figure paintings, which capture an entirely new lifestyle? What links the homogeneous sharp focus and frozen immobility of the urban scene as depicted by photo-realist Richard Estes with the cool, manneristic nudes of Philip Pearlstein (p. 335 below)? What relationship can be established between the overpainted photos of the early and middle periods of German artist Gerhard Richter, who was never a photo-realist, and the archetypical, mundane, Joycean situations depicted in a superbly complex technique by Canadian artist Alex Colville? The melancholy nudes of Stanley Spencer have as little to do with photo-realism as Pearlstein's canvases. They are painterly documents of resignation and human alienation (p. 335 above left). The same can be said of the expressive tristesse of Frenchman Bernard Buffet's images of suffering (which, however, soon declined into mannerism), or of the emaciated nudes of his countryman, Francis Gruber, done as early as the 1940s and 1950s (p. 334 right).

If we were concerned with a simple copying of photographs without formal or interpretative alteration, Neo-Realism would truly be easy to pigeonhole. But its major protagonists make the task difficult, even those for whom the photograph – or photo series – is as important a tool as the sketchbook is for other painters. Accordingly, their creative work already begins with the choice of motif, their selection from photographs they have usually made themselves, sometimes with a manipulated camera. Naturally these artists have profited from the achievements of professional photography, which, like modern painting, tenaciously fought for aesthetic autonomy, a struggle in which many visual artists served as pacemakers. The development of color photography also played a key role in this process. In discussing the issue of artists' reliance on photography, we should recall that the Impressionists already drew inspiration from the static, black and white daguerrotypes of the day, and translated them into something entirely different. The influence of technically and thematically expanded photography on Duchamp and Dadaism is also a matter of record. So there is nothing amiss in a painter's employment of the new medium in choosing and preparing his motifs. And this holds not only for realistic painters, when we consider the reciprocal influences between "subjective" photography and abstract art.

The Magic of the Real

The paintings of Richard Estes (p. 336) have a hyper-real effect which is beyond the capacity of the naked eye, and even of the camera, no matter how sharply focused. This is achieved by means of distributing the focal points of various photographs over the entire canvas surface, and rendering every square inch of it with equal precision. Nearby and distant things are seen with equal clarity. A combination of the blow-up, derived from Pop Art,

Stanley Spencer
Seated Nude, 1942
Oil on canvas, 76.2 x 50.8 cm
Private collection

Lucian Freud
Night Portrait, 1976/77
Oil on canvas, 71 x 71 cm
Private collection

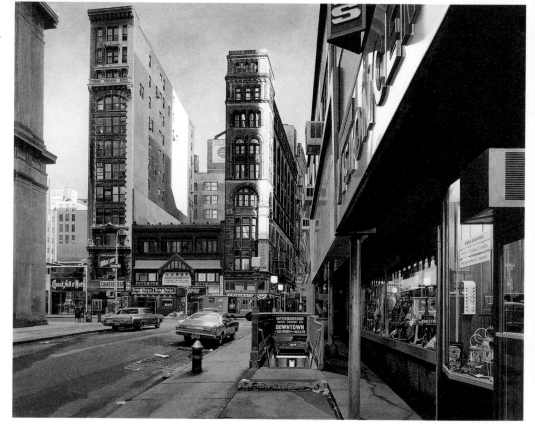

Richard Estes
Downtown, 1978
Oil on canvas, 122 x 152 cm
Vienna, Museum moderner Kunst,
on loan from Ludwig Collection

Richard Estes
Victory Theater, 1968
Oil on wood, 82.6 x 61 cm
Boston (MA), private collection

with a painstaking depiction of natural and artificial illumination and reflections, lends a soundless stasis to the everyday scene of food shops and glitzy entrances, automobiles and reflecting glass facades. Estes's imagery has a timeless magic that distantly recalls Metaphysical Painting. In face of many of his works one is inadvertently put in mind of the provocative statement of the "black monk," Ad Reinhardt, that "art is always dead" – that is, exists in a vacuum, beyond life. As so often, the extremes meet; two diametrically opposed positions tacitly coincide.

In accordance with his stance as an artist, Estes considers photography a preparatory, auxiliary means. Instead of providing a subject, the photograph, as he says, merely gives the best pointers to the theme he wants to paint. For all their apparent faithfulness, Estes's motifs undergo a degree of imaginative transformation unmatched by most other photo-realists employing related subject-matter. This holds for the California artists Richard McLean, Don Eddy (p. 337 above), and Ralph Goings (p. 337 middle), as it does for Brooklyn-born Robert Cottingham (p. 337 below). Cottingham, who, like Rosenquist, began his career in commercial art, transposes the Pop principles of close-up and fragmentary excerpt of reality into the terms of a Pop-inspired neo-realism.

The case is different with Malcolm Morley (p. 338). Morley divides the photographic image into a grid pattern of small rectangles, and rotates it, with the canvas, through 180 degrees. In other words, if in a different way than the later Baselitz, he turns the picture upside down and makes it illegible in order better to concentrate on the painterly detail. Unlike Estes, Morley works in thick, heavily textured impasto, which serves to alienate the mundane subject, be it telephone book or picture postcard. The thing reproduced and its reproduction are no longer identical, the quotations are ambivalent, as indicated by the devices of crossing out, crumpling, or ripping Morley occasionally uses. His concern is not with an illusionistic representation of the visible, but with with an analysis of it, what the artist himself terms "the anatomy of illusion." What this in turn implies is that Morley's true theme – again, like Baselitz's – is painting per se. The more or less arbitrary motif is merely the occasion for painting. Or, as Morley puts it, his intention is to "paint painting." As one can see, this has as good as nothing more to do with photo-realism as pure, straightforward representation – though the artist's later paintings seemingly indicate a certain insecurity, if not a crisis, in his development.

Howard Kanovitz points out that the term "realism," introduced into the discussion on visual art by Courbet, has yet to be adequately defined. As he justifiably adds, there is neither a realist school nor group in the present period. For Kanovitz, realism in painting consists in recognizing something we have never really seen, a shocking piece of visible and psychological reality which cannot simply be limited by the wish to paint things as one sees them.

Kanovitz employs photographs and drawings as preliminary studies for his pictures. The photo serves primarily as an aid to memory, rather than as a conveyor of the visual idea. The decisive thing is the selection of the thematic elements which are to enter the painting. Kanovitz convincingly points out the external and underlying similarities of Neo-Realism with a concurrent stream whose aims were quite different: Conceptual Art. Both, he says, often employ photographs, both are concerned with processes, with "how something is done and expressed."

As with Morley, Kanovitz's central theme is the relationship of reality to illusion, their points of convergence and divergence, even though he approaches the theme by means of a quite different technique and conception. That like all the relevant Neo-Realists he is not concerned with mere illustration is indicated by Kanovitz's express reference to Baroque illusionism, the "illusion of an illusion." Although a painting such as his famous *Vernissage* (p. 338) is still clearly influenced by Pop Art in terms of palette and characterization of figures, and possesses ironic, socially critical aspects including a metaphorical evocation of the emptiness of the people's talk by means of a diffuse background, it also contains elements of the unreal, which would play an increasing role in the artist's work.

Trompe-l'œil painting soon no longer sufficed Kanovitz. But he did turn his experience in this field to

Don Eddy
Private Parking III, 1971
Acrylic on canvas, 122 x 167.5 cm
Private collection

Ralph Goings
Plumbing-Heating Pick-Up, 1969
Oil on canvas, 114.5 x 162.5 cm
Private collection

Robert Cottingham
Carl's, 1975
Oil on canvas, 198 x 198 cm
Aachen, Ludwig Forum für
Internationale Kunst

Malcolm Morley
Vermeer, Portrait of the Artist in
His Studio, 1968
Acrylic on canvas, 266.5 x 221 cm
Private collection

points out, "provides only the mode of perception and conditions" for such works. Painting, in contrast, provides "the aesthetic means of transforming the protocol of the photographic method" – which, in Close's case, supplants the natural vision of the eye – "point by point into a quasi-abstract image, which maintains its autonomy between the color-field painting of Ryman and the media absolutism of Warhol."

That the painting process was the basis of Close's portrait series became ever more obvious, sometimes blatantly so, during the 1980s. The resolution of the faces into small, equal-sized color fields of varying texture was occasionally achieved at the expense of internal cohesion and compositional logic, and thus of quality. The brief phase of *Finger Paintings*, in which Close worked with blurring effects, carried more conviction than the finely articulated monumentality of the subsequent oils.

The Strangeness of the Everyday

At this juncture we should take a brief look at the sculptors working in a hyper-realist style. John De Andrea, who depicts friends in highly intimate situations, expressly says that photographs do not suffice him in representing his sole theme, the absolute individuality of every human being. As he is concerned with immediacy foremost, de Andrea feels that any intervening medium would destroy it.

Duane Hanson, too (p. 514), requires the presence of living models for his work. His theme, says Tilman Osterwold, is "the strange everyday," or, in the artist's own words, "just that fixed moment." Where movement ceases, time stands still. It has entered the painted figures with their utensils that are always the same. Their faces and bodies, silent, motionless, contain their entire life's story. Psychological reality is revealed to view through the physical presence of the sculpture. For Hanson, art is at once an aesthetic product and a document. In contrast to the great environment-maker

good use in expanding the flat image into three dimensions, by combining painting and object, linking the concrete with the imaginary, as for instance by framing a romantic landscape in an actual French door. Even more compelling was an interlinking of transparent visual levels, a combination of the disparate recalling Magritte, consisting of an open grand piano and seat in front of window-wall casting a shadow and standing in water: *The Grandiose Piano* (1987; Berlin, private collection). Here the mythology of everyday life entered a poetic phase in Kanovitz's work.

The extremely enlarged, manipulated photo-portraits on canvas by Chuck Close (p. 339 above) likewise evince surprising links between the radical photo-realism he practiced for 25 years and conceptual, analytical painting. "Photography," as Manfred Schneckenburger

*"I am now making paintings and
sculptural works which involve my
interest in appearance, illusion,
and character. I use a precisionist
approach, crystallizing my images so
that they go beyond realism into an
area that is similar to trompe-l'œil.
I use my own photography as the
source of my painted images."*
HOWARD KANOVITZ

Howard Kanovitz
Vernissage, 1967
Acrylic on canvas, 212 x 426 cm
Cologne, Museum Ludwig

Chuck Close
Self-Portrait, 1968
Acrylic on canvas, 274 x 213 cm
Minneapolis (MN), Walter Art
Center, Art Center Acquisition
Fund

Chuck Close
Linda, 1975/76
Acrylic on canvas, 273.5 x 212.5 cm
Akron (OH), Akron Art Museum

Edward Kienholz (pp. 511, 512), Hanson resorts neither to surrealistic or symbolic reference, nor to anonymity. The painting of his figures, clothed in their personal attire, and the photographic precision of their detail, place his work in an intermediate position between painterly and sculptural Neo-Realism.

The pictures of Canadian artist Alex Colville (ill. below) bear more affinity to the American Precisionists of the 1930s than to photo-realism. His perfect compositions are based on an abundance of sketches and studies, which are first brought into an abstract, geometric scheme before drawings are made from the live model and proportioned according to the planned format. Only then does the slow and patient process of painting begin. Layer upon layer of thinned paint is applied to a primed wooden panel, and the opaque surface finally sealed with transparent lacquer. The process can often take months.

Colville has devoted intensive study to European painting. According to him, it took him many years to digest the impressions gained during two days spent in the Louvre. Yet he has also been deeply impressed by the American Luminists, and not least by Hopper. Colville's paintings are proof of the fact that a realism of content need have nothing in common with naturalism, that the serious realist does not unthinkingly reflect reality, but analyzes it. It is this analytical cast of mind, Colville is convinced, that permits him to discover "myths of mundanity" – on the banks of the River Spree, by the seaside, in the circus, at sports events, on a boat or a highway, in a meadow or a swimming pool, in a telephone booth or a bedroom. Colville insists that the mythical aspect of everyday life is not reserved for authors of the secular rank of a James Joyce, but that the contemporary painter can have access to it as well.

"The Saga of Man"

Colville's silent images are static. Yet practically all of them tell a story, in a brief, concise plot that does not always have a resolution. Fundamental human situations are their both simple and complex themes: loneliness, isolation, parting, work, leisure, estrangement, love. The only subliminally dramatic, often melancholy laconism of content corresponds to the absolute precision of form by which it is conveyed. Like hardly another artist, Colville maintains the difficult balance between imagination and sober calculation, formal interest and social commitment. Behind the realistic surface of his imagery lurks the surreal – but a surreal that lacks every trace of theatrical staging or borrowing from psychoanalysis, whose new myths Colville deeply mistrusts.

Alex Colville
Truck Stop, 1966
Acrylic on composition board,
91.5 x 91.5 cm
Cologne, Museum Ludwig,
Ludwig Donation

Franz Gertsch
Medici, 1971
Dispersion on canvas,
400 x 600 cm
Vienna, Museum moderner Kunst,
on loan from Ludwig Collection

Franz Gertsch
Johanna II, 1986
Tempera on unprimed cotton,
330 x 290 cm
Napa (CA), Hess Collection

Michelangelo Pistoletto
Demonstration No. 2, 1965
Collage on polished steel,
215 x 120 cm
Cologne, Museum Ludwig,
Ludwig Donation

Page 341 above:
Jacques Monory
Murder No. 10/1, 1968
Acrylic on canvas,
195 x 315 cm
Humblebæk (Denmark),
Louisiana Museum of Modern Art

Page 341 below:
Gerhard Richter
Ema – Nude on a Stairway, 1966
Oil on canvas, 200 x 130 cm
Cologne, Museum Ludwig,
Ludwig Donation

Harald Szeemann once spoke of "exaggerated American realism" as opposed to the "more humane European" variety, as manifested in the work of Swiss artist Franz Gertsch. With Colville, engagement and detachment hold a balance. With Gertsch, something else enters the equation – a romantic outlook like that reflected in the contemporary new lifestyles of young people and artists in particular. Everyday situations in their lives are Gertsch's predominant theme. Like De Andrea and Hanson in their own way, Gertsch needs human proximity, a closeness and familiarity with those he depicts. This sense of nearness is underscored by his, as it were, pointillistic technique, which discloses two different types of experience, depending on whether one views the painting from a close or a distant vantage point. Seen close up, the surface offers the aesthetic experience of a masterful, sumptuous *peinture*, while from a distance, it congeals into a figurative scene of amazing vitality.

Pictures of Pictures

According to Gertsch (p. 340 below left), what he paints are "pictures of pictures," in which "the something (the realistic image) should be as immaculately present as the nothing (the white canvas)." This, indicatively, is followed by a reference to the immaculateness of the ultramarine blue sky of Yves Klein. Gertsch's painting derives its tension from the dichotomy between idea and reality. Even in his later, large-format woodcuts, begun in 1986, reality is always the theme, even though the immediate visual experience has given way to memory, and the main role is no longer played by human figures, individuals or groups, but by landscape and nature.

To integrate external reality, the viewer's surroundings, into the reality of the image, and ultimately to negate the borderline between life and art, was the aim of the early *Mirror Paintings* of Michelangelo Pistoletto – photographed figures applied in a collage manner to a polished steel plate (p. 340 below right). The Italian artist has continued to pursue these aims in his later sculptures and environments.

In contrast, French artist Jacques Monory (ill. above) spirits his semi-naturalistic pictorial sequences to a dreamlike realm by means of monochrome blue grounds, while his countryman Jean-Olivier Hucleux paints his enigmatic pictures of human and automobile cemeteries from projected slides.

If we now turn to the work of Gerhard Richter (pp. 341–343), it is with the hope that no one will be tempted to classify his work as realism in the narrower sense. The German artist's painting is many-sided, many-layered, and functions on multiple levels of meaning. In order to at least suggest the complexity of Richter's work, let me quote a comment of Georg Schmidt, the eminent Swiss museum curator, to the effect that for him, Mondrian was a great realist.

And Richter himself, in an interview, stated pointedly, "Don't you understand? That which we flippantly call reality is not there and not real for as long as it has not become reality through art. In other words, art never makes a statement about reality, but is itself the only reality which is there." Some years later, in connection with his more recent gestural abstractions, the artist formulated his expanded definition of reality thus: "Abstract paintings are fictitious models, because they visualize a reality which we can neither see nor describe but which we may nevertheless conclude to exist. We attach negative names to this reality: the un-known, the

Gerhard Richter
Sea Piece, 1975
Oil on canvas, 200 x 300 cm
Private collection

Gerhard Richter
Swimmers, 1965
Oil on canvas, 200 x 160 cm
Stuttgart, Froehlich Collection

un-graspable, the in-finite, and for thousands of years we have depicted it in terms of substitute images like heaven and hell, gods and devils. With abstract painting we created a better means of approaching what can be neither seen nor understood, because abstract painting illustrates with the greatest clarity, that is to say, with all the means at the disposal of art, 'nothing.' ... This ist not an artful game, it is a necessity; and since everything unknown frightens us and fills us with hope at the same time, we take these images as a possible explanation of the inexplicable or at least as a way of dealing with it."

These words give us a sense of the higher unity in which Richter's work is contained, despite its undeniable diversity and its real or apparent contradictions. In all its reflections and refractions, from the involvement with Socialist Realism at the beginning to the monumental products emerging from Richter's studio today, his oeuvre revolves around the inexhaustible theme of "reality," a reality that is never ultimately comprehensible – unless in the form of the reality of art itself, which Richter calls the "highest form of hope."

Thus painting is the Archimedian fulcrum of this born painter. In it is reflected his entire experience of reality, positive and negative, general and personal. Richter's reply to experience always takes the form of a painted image – whether a conceptual one like his minimalistic color panels or grey-in-grey paintings, an ironically romantic one like the landscapes of the late 1960s and early 1970s, or an expressive one in the black, white and grey cityscapes or the grandiose *Alpine Panorama* of 1968. These were followed by overpainted photographs, which introduced Richter's relevant work after his move to Western Germany, by a vehemently gestural approach in the recent works, or by the structurally more reserved movement of the abstract *London Paintings* of the late 1980s. Richter forsakes none of these painterly positions, reserving the right to return to them at will.

His work is the work of an artist who is always on the move, searching, he is continually inquiring into reality and calling it into question. In Richter's work the disquiet and insecurity that marks an Alexandrine, late culture, as well as skepticism and doubt, and the artist's ironically tinged melancholy and moments of subdued happiness, have been turned to creative ends.

Gerhard Richter
S. D. I., 1986
Oil on canvas, two parts,
320 x 400 cm
Napa (CA), Hess Collection

Gerhard Richter
Facade, 1997
Oil on Alucobond, 100 x 90 cm
Private collection

Painting as a Mind-Game

Provoking the Eye
Op Art and the Crossing of Borderlines

The simultaneity of oppositions in the field of art-making is no new phenomenon. It is met with in almost every epoch of art history. Thanks to today's pluralistic thinking, the number of diverse and sometimes mutually exclusive tendencies co-existing on the scene is especially great. Pop Art and Neo-Realism, too, were paralleled by a movement with quite different aims. As their representatives were developing an art determined by life and the outside world, including all its banality,

there were other artists devoting themselves, put simply, to issues inherent to art.

The opposite pole to Pop Art is marked by Optical, or Op Art, which drew inspiration from Albers and, farther back in time, from the Pointillism of Seurat and the Orphism of Delaunay. We recall that Seurat's dot patterns in the colors of the spectrum had compelled the viewer's eye to pull them together, to condense the dots into a composite color and form. This was a complex

"I draw from nature, I work with nature, although in completely new terms. For me nature is not landscape, but the dynamism of visual forces – an event rather than an appearance." BRIDGET RILEY

Bridget Riley
Current, 1964
Emulsion paint on canvas,
135 x 150 cm
New York, The Museum of
Modern Art, Philip Johnson Fund

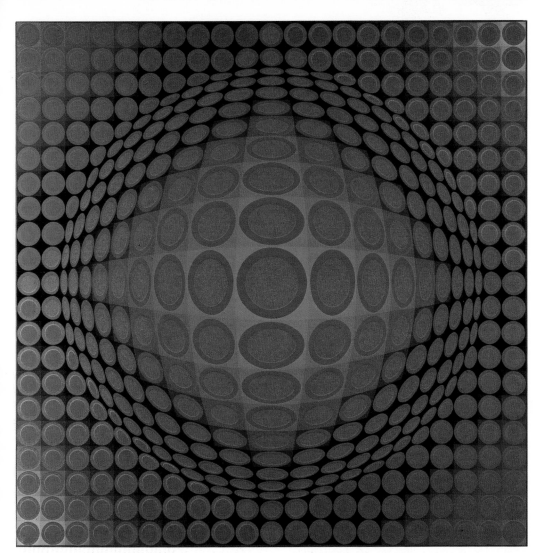

Victor Vasarely
Vega 200, 1968
Acrylic on canvas, 200 x 200 cm
Private collection

and demanding perceptual experience, especially as Seurat's pictures evinced a dichotomy between a surface composed of finite paint particles and a linear composition of veritably classical harmony. Delaunay then went one step farther, with his "simultaneous contrasts" of color, and with a simultaneity of static and dynamic forms, whose "synchronous motion" for him represented the "drama of the universe."

The extreme demands made on the eye by Seurat and Delaunay were taken by representatives of Op Art, in various ways, to the verge of the bearable, and sometimes even beyond. It was Albers who pointed the way. Habitual perception, he realized, could be upset by forcing the eye to take in two contradictory, normally mutually exclusive perceptions at once, by relying on what he termed the "interaction of color." In Albers's paintings and colored prints this effect took the form of a continual oscillation between spatial and planar perception; in the black and white drawings and prints it took the form of a continual flipping back and forth between positive and negative, convex and concave.

Albers's imagery gives the eye no respite. The colors and shapes resist every attempt to definitively fix them. Moreover, as the artist realized, a color will change in intensity or hue depending on the neighboring color. This is what lends the seemingly so simple forms in his painting, including the square, their flickering, ambiguous appearance. This effect is basically the theme of Albers's painting. What it makes visible is the contradiction between the physical fact and the psychological effect. If we are willing to enter Albers's work, we find it capable of inducing doubt as to the dependability of our entire perceptual experience.

Optical Bafflement

This attack on perceptual habits was mounted with even greater force by the London artist Bridget Riley (p. 344). Her concept, Riley once said, in a seeming contradiction in terms, was the open, planar space, a multi-focal space of the kind found, for instance, in Pollock. What this implied was a space without a compositional or perspective focus or center. It took the form of "all-over"

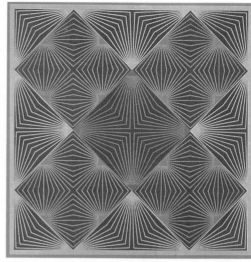

Victor Vasarely
PAUK-SP, 1968/69
Oil on canvas, 150 x 150 cm
Private collection

Richard Anuszkiewicz
Luminous, 1965
Acrylic on canvas, 61 x 61 cm
Los Angeles (CA), Mr. and Mrs.
Melvin Hirsch Collection

compositions inspired by Pollock's, but entirely lacking in Pollock's dramatically emotional gesture. The optical irritation or unrest caused by Riley's pictures is purely visual in nature. Admittedly, changes in tempo, condensation or relaxation of the patterns of stripes, dots, wavy lines, triangular or rectangular shapes, the virtual movements and countermovements and stasis or dynamics of the pictorial elements, evoke a suspenseful if non-relational expressiveness, which, however is always kept under formal control. Riley understands the counterpoint and polarization in her imagery to represent formal parallels "to our emotional life."

Apart from drawing inspiration from the Pointillists and Impressionists (especially Monet), and admiring the universal harmony of Mondrian, Riley has been influenced by van Gogh and the Futurists. Every one of her paintings has its own specific character, despite the fact that all individual touch has been expunged in an effort to make her art as objective as humanly possible. The perceptual irritation it causes, and the pictorial energies

with which it is suffused, demand great, unflagging concentration on the part of the viewer. Riley's imagery requires no interpretation, because the message is all there on the surface, challenging us as viewers to analyze its effect upon our perception.

Victor Vasarely (ill. above left and p. 345) studied with Bortnyik at the Budapest Bauhaus. Unlike Riley, he strove to give his artistic experiences, which ultimately derive from Constructivism, an exact, scientific and theoretical basis. From early on Vasarely was intrigued by networks, webs, and weaves of all types, all the way from isobathic maps of the earth to looms and "patterns of the kind used for many printing processes, also railway nets, lines of force, circuits and their complex systems – all of them coordinates of fascination," in the artist's own words.

This early fascination was the source of Vasarely's attempts to overcome individualistic painting dominated by the artist's personal touch, his rejection of the original work and its aura in favor of reproducible models based on the *unité plastique*, Vasarely's endlessly changeable and interchangeable fundamental form of the "work of art in the age of technical reproduction." The use of serial procedures reflects Vasarely's conviction that a work of art must be repeatable and capable of being produced in as many copies as required, whether it be in two dimensions or three, or even a kinetic work. "If the art product," he says, "does not break through the constrictions of an elite of connoisseurs, art is doomed to death by suffocation." The means to ward off this danger, Vasarely believes, is the mass production and dissemination of art.

This conviction also made Vasarely one of the key pacemakers of multiple art. In the late 1960s and early 1970s, when widespread political and social change seemed imminent, the reproduction of art and concomitant reduction in price, as Günther Gerken notes, promised a "broader and more direct effectiveness than that of the one-off museum piece.... In the work of art

Yaacov Agam
Life is a Passing Shadow, 1969/70
Painted relief, 81 x 117 cm
Private collection

which has lost its character as a prestige object, true intellectual values, not influenced by market value, prevail." As we now know, this wonderful hope was illusory. The masses did not cooperate. The aura, originality, and exclusiveness of a work continue to determine its market value.

The approaches of Riley and Vasarely mark the poles of Op Art and its possibilities: the former cleaving to two-dimensionality and to the importance of the original work despite all attempts at "objectivity," the latter striving to produce the "democratic" multiple and to negate the border-lines between genres in an attempt to create a social art for all.

Intermediate positions were held by artists such as the Venezuelans Jesús Rafael Soto and Carlos Cruz-Diez, by Israeli painter and sculptor Yaacov Agam, by the American Richard Anuszkiewicz, by Wojciech Fangor of Poland or Almir Mavignier of Brazil. Soto's work (ill. right), according to his own testimony, had its source in the desire to "make Mondrian's works appear to be in motion." In front of monochrome, usually low-relief surfaces Soto mounted thin metal rods attached to nylon filaments, which were set in motion by the slightest air currents. The intersection of the sometimes parallel, sometimes opposing lines created a visually irritating effect known as Poggendorf's Illusion – a line that meets another at an acute angle appears interrupted in its course.

Soto's mixture of flat painting with relief already anticipated the three-dimensional kinetic art of a Schöffer, in its – likewise Mondrian-influenced – constructivistic form, or the art of a Jean Tinguely, with its ironic, "black" romanticism. Agam's paintings (p. 346 below) are divided by angular lamella. Their colored shapes change in appearance as the viewer moves back and forth in front of the picture. They become broader, then narrower, until the image either opens out to reveal its multi-colored aspect, or condenses into a black, textured plane.

Changes in the vantage point of the viewer and in the impinging light are employed in a similar way by Cruz-Diez from Venezuela (ill. right), a former designer. In the case of Anuszkiewicz (p. 346 above right), optical bafflement is induced by juxtaposing straight with radiating lines, which appear to cause the former to curve. Mavignier sets the picture plane in vibration by means of a permutation and the progression of equidistant sequences of elements of various size and hue. The former industrialist François Morellet (p. 348) employs the means of painting, relief, sculpture, and occasionally blends of all three, combined into simple, fundamental structures, to produce his precisionistic works, which are sometimes conceived for the architectural context. Constructivist elements are combined here with elements of Minimalism and Conceptual Art.

What all Op artists share in common is a relinquishment of any fixed vantage point on the part of the viewer, which, together with a multi-focal composition, compells the eye to ever-fresh perception. This is underscored by an elimination of the artist's personal touch, in an attempt to concentrate solely on the objective, optical event taking place on the surface. The visual unrest of Op Art reflects an urge not only to keep the eye moving but to set the work of art itself in motion. This process, which led to Kinetic Art, can be seen to good effect in the development of Heinz Mack's work. From the early, still painstakingly rendered serial *Vibrations* it led by way of *Light Columns* in the Sahara Desert to plastic, kinetic pieces, which integrate the aleatory factor and the effects of light interference in an aesthetic play of light seemingly infinite in variation.

Jesús Rafael Soto
Large Vibrating Panorama Wall, 1966
Rome, Galleria Nazionale d'Arte Moderna

Carlos Cruz-Diez
Physichromie No. 326, 1967
Wood, plastic and oil paint, 120 x 180 cm
Cologne, Museum Ludwig

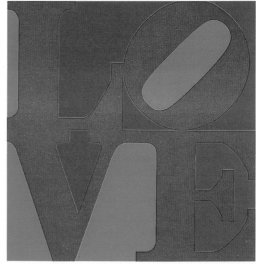

Jean Dewasne
Paris Paris, 1953
Oil on canvas, 130 x 195 cm
Paris, Galerie Denis René

Robert Indiana
Love, 1967
Oil on canvas, 85.5 x 85.5 cm
Seattle (WA), private collection

During the latter half of the 1980s, triggered by Mikhail Gorbachev's ultimately abortive attempt to reform the Soviet Union's ossified sociopolitical system, there suddenly came to light works of art of an originality and diversity, and occasional radicality, which Western observers would not have thought possible under the circumstances. Though it had been obvious for years that orthodox Socialist Realism was on the defensive, the high level of knowledge of Western trends on the part of younger Russian artists in particular came as a great surprise. Under quite different political conditions, these beginnings have continued to bear fruit to the present day.

A Painting is a Painting is a Painting
Minimalist and Conceptual Painting

According to conventional wisdom, every significant proposal in 20th-century art was not only advanced but put into practice during the early modernist period, and every subsequent development was merely imitative, repetitive, or, at best, an eclectic variation on previous achievements. If this were true, every innovative tendency that preceded today's Post-modernism and the "politically correct" statements of the final days before the millennium would have to be judged uncreative and derivative, and be stamped with that mark of Cain, the

"I chose geometry because of its neutrality, the system, that would make me restrict the arbitrary nature of my decisions."
FRANÇOIS MORELLET

François Morellet
From Yellow to Violet, 1956
Oil on canvas, 110.3 x 215.8 cm
Paris, Musée National d'Art Moderne, Centre Georges Pompidou

prefix "post." In that case Wols and Jackson Pollock would be Post-Expressionists, the Pop artists Post-Dadaists, Gotthard Graubner's color-spaces Post-Romantic.

But things are not that simple, for as George Kubler has said, "No formal sequence is ever truly completed in an exhaustion of all its possibilities in a consistent series of solutions. A re-evaluation of all problems under new conditions is always possible, and sometimes indeed topical."

F. N. Mennemeier's statement that "deconstruction is always, or should always be, a construction as well," applies to those tendencies that revived long-forgotten Constructivist ideas and considerations. Among these were Hard Edge Abstraction, Minimal Art, and certain aspects of Conceptual Art and the analytic, conceptual

Robert Mangold
Four Color Frame Painting
No. 3 (pink, yellow green, red, green), 1983
Acrylic and pencil on canvas,
335.3 x 213.4 cm
Formerly Saatchi Collection,
London

Agnes Martin
Untitled VIII, 1981
Acrylic and graphite on canvas,
183 x 183 cm
Formerly Saatchi Collection,
London

Richard Artschwager
Untitled, 1970
Liquitex on Celotex with
aluminum frame, 72 x 62 cm
Private collection

Robert Indiana
The American Dream I, 1961
Oil on canvas, 183 x 152.7 cm
New York, The Museum of
Modern Art, Larry Aldrich
Foundation Fund

Ellsworth Kelly
Blue Red, 1965
Oil on canvas, 165 x 381 cm
Private collection

Ellsworth Kelly
Red Blue Green Yellow, 1965
Oil on canvas (floor section on
composition board), 222 x 137 x 222 cm
USA, private collection

painting associated with it. An outstanding representative of the latter is Agnes Martin (p. 349 above right). Her sensitive paintings and drawings, in which abstract forms were increasingly reduced to serial, horizontal or vertical grid schemes, not only had a great influence on the younger generation but anticipated Minimalist and Conceptual tendencies to come.

American artist Ellsworth Kelly (ill. above and below), who, like his countrymen Robert Indiana (pp. 348, 349) and James Rosenquist, was a friend and student of Martin's, was painting similarly "minimalistic-concrete" pictures long before the terms were coined to describe a style. A key trait of Kelly's painting is its waiver of all referential content. The picture, reduced to a painted surface and its support, stands only for itself. Painting and subject are one. The support determines the shape and extent of the paint surface; painted contours are replaced by the edges of the various numbers of smaller canvases joined together into a whole.

The simplicity of the late Matisse' cut-outs, and occasionally the brilliance of their color, were at the back of Kelly's lapidary statements. Yet the stark contrast between deep black and intense white has also intrigued him. The stringency of his pictorial structure is occasionally mitigated by irregular, geometric apertures. In their object-like character and format, particularly in the case of the *Shaped Canvases*, many of Kelly's works transcend the borderline between painting and sculpture. Kenneth Noland's later paintings, in which parallel bands of color merge completely with the picture support, also belong in the context of Hard Edge Abstraction.

From Purism to Baroque
Frank Stella, too (pp. 351, 352), considers his paintings to be objects, saying that "only that which can be seen there is really there." In the early 1950s he began making

"black paintings" whose surface was articulated by series of narrow, parallel lines in which the light color of the canvas shone through. The stringency of this lineature was toned down by a visual effect of vibration, caused by the varying degree of lightness of the lines and an occasional blurring over by black pigment. For all the objectivity of his approach and methodicalness of the painting process, this feature revealed the artist's emotional involvement in his work. Then came, in the 1960s, Stella's black *Shaped Canvases*, followed by paintings in vivid color employing matte and glossy fluorescent paint to produce an interplay of surface effects. A certain link with tradition is evident even in Stella's minimalistic work, despite his own disclaimers. At this period he still insisted that there was no going back, and asked why any artist would involve himself with things that were "over and done with". Yet subsequently Stella would involve himself, very intensively, with Matisse, for whose sumptuous and sensuous painting he expressed a clear admiration that ran very much counter to current trends. His main interest, Stella coolly admitted, was to do what is popularly known as decorative painting, really close to life, if under "unequivocally abstract premises." Decorative, that is, in the sense as it applies to Matisse. Delaunay's disks of color and Oriental art also left a deep impression on Stella, although his color range of the late 1960s, by comparison to that of the *Concentric Squares* and *Labyrinths* of preceding years, extended to include broken and subdued hues.

The covert Baroque tendencies in Stella's thinking, only suggested in the early, black canvases, emerged full-blown in a series of works begun in the 1970s. These were aluminum reliefs whose basic elements derived from the curved templates used by Danish shipbuilders, followed by more finely articulated, tightly interwoven ornamental pieces with an even stronger emphasis on three-dimensionality and painted surfaces inspired by

Frank Stella
Ctesiphon III, 1968
Fluorescent acrylic on canvas,
300 x 600 cm
Cologne, Museum Ludwig,
Ludwig Donation

American Indian art. Then Stella launched into painted montages of a veritably Baroque vitality and abundance, diametrically opposed to the purism of the early work. Reminiscences of primitive and native American art, which Stella collects, were combined here with quotations from and references to Western European models. Occasionally these three-dimensional paintings – or rather, painted objects – burgeon out into theatrical spaces complete with painted sets and wings. Within

this compilatory, quotation-rife art and its blend, so typical of a late culture, of apparent naivety with a high degree of historical awareness, a certain gradient in quality is evident. In view of some of Stella's works one inadvertently thinks of Pattern Art, that decorative style which, in the hands of its lesser representatives, so strongly recalls lengths of printed dress fabric. Exceptions are talented artists like Robert Kushner (p. 353 above) and Miriam Schapiro (p. 353 middle).

"My painting is based on the fact that only what can be seen there is there. It really is an object. Any painting is an object and anyone who gets involved enough in this finally has to face up to the 'objectness' of whatever it is that he's doing." FRANK STELLA

Jules Olitski
Strip Heresy, 1964
Magna on canvas, 266 x 207 cm
Private collection

Larry Poons
Untitled P26, 1974
Oil on canvas, 197 x 155 cm
Private collection

Robert Kushner
Sail Away, 1983
Various fabrics and acrylic on
canvas, 221 x 523.2 cm
Courtesy Holly Solomon Gallery,
New York

Miriam Schapiro
I am Dancing as Fast
as I Can, 1985
Acrylic and fabric on canvas,
228.6 x 365.8 cm
New York, private collection

Rosemarie Trockel
Hammer and Sickle, 1986
Wool, 130 x 150 cm
Stuttgart, Collection Südwest LB

The Painting as Object

The attempt to transform the painting into an object, by radically reducing the element of form and expunging personal touch, leaving only an opaque surface as smooth as a mirror, takes on extreme form in the perfectly executed works of Robert Mangold (p. 349). Mangold's unusually shaped panels, divided into regular segments, combine highly sensitive painting with precisely delineated graphic elements, recently usually elliptical in form.

The first comprehensive exhibition of Minimal Art to be seen in Europe took place at The Hague, Düsseldorf, and Berlin in 1968/69. The catalogue listed ten sculptors and object-makers – Carl Andre, Ronald Bladen, Dan Flavin, Robert Grosvenor, Donald Judd, Sol LeWitt, Robert Morris, Tony Smith, Robert Smithson, and Michael Steiner – but not a single painter. The work of these artists, which extends into space, defines it, and requires the environment, whether architecture or landscape, for its effect, likewise evinces lines of connection with Conceptual Art (Andre, LeWitt) and with Land Art, which took art out of the museum and into the open spaces.

The death of painting, was a simplistic hypothesis very much in vogue during the 1960s and early 1970s and continues to be pronounced, against all odds, even today. Still, there is no denying that many of the most spectacular events in art since that time have taken place outside the field of painting. And the painting of that period was not exactly popular. This would have its consequences.

Yet even during the heyday of forbidding Minimal sculptural monuments, of Land Art and "Individual Mythologies", of the tumultuous celebration of the supposedly new media of photography, film, television and video, the period of Body Art and the Happening and Fluxus movement and its offshoot, the Performance, of Beuys's expanded definition of art, and of naive attempts to break out of the vicious circle of studio-gallery-museum – even during those years in which "Attitudes Became Form", paint continued to be applied to canvas.

Robert Ryman
Director, 1983
Oil on fiberglass with aluminum
holders, 235.6 x 213.4 cm
Formerly Saatchi Collection,
London

Raimund Girke
Contrast, 1992
Oil on canvas, 200 x 220 cm
Essen, Museum Folkwang

Analytical Paintings

The common denominator of "non-relational" painting
is the artist's reflective attitude, a profound questioning
of his own medium, and a strict refusal to countenance
subject-matter or content extraneous to the image per
se. This analytical, conceptual approach to painting was
based, on the one hand, on Duchamp's example and
theories, and, on the other, on the puristic attitude represented by Barnett Newman, Ad Reinhardt, and Yves
Klein, whose conceptualism the non-relational painters
even surpassed.

While Jules Olitski's lyrical canvases (p. 352), spray-
painted layer upon layer, have earned him the sobriquet
of the "first Abstract Impressionist," Robert Ryman's
works (ill. left) have proven to be the most highly logical
among those of analytical painters. As early as the late
1950s Ryman was already producing white paintings,
which, seen in isolation, was not all that sensational,
considering the fact that even representatives of L'art
informel, such as Tàpies, had worked in a similar vein.
Yet thereafter Ryman began to make use of the painter's
basic materials. The effect of the canvas texture was
included in the effect of the white painted surface.
Materials such as steel, aluminum, copper, fiberglass, or
cardboard, used as supports, emphasized the object-
character of the works. The paint application, however,
continued to be highly variable. Dense textures alternated with loose, regular or irregular ones, thick
impasto alternated with smooth application, opaque
surfaces with transparent. Yet the term "planned painting" is only conditionally applicable to Ryman's
approach, because despite continual intellectual control
his temperament and moods do become evident in the
final image. Ryman relies a great deal on his emotions,
he once said in an interview, doing the things he considers right, preferring to follow his intuition rather than
relying on preliminary testing.

Raimund Girke (ill. left) is not an analytical thinker
like Ryman, nor is he a mystic of chromatic abstraction,
as Brice Marden, following in Newman's footsteps, was
at least for a time. Girke illustrates no theories, saying
that he does not intend to "sacrifice painting for an
idea." "The material remains the determining factor," he
adds, and not merely a means to demonstrate a concept.
Everything Girke paints appeals to the senses, and bears
the unique, personal mark of his hand. Although as
tenacious in his use of the color white as Reinhardt was
in his adherence to black, the German artist's works
have none of the hermetic quality of the American's
Black Paintings. Reinhardt's black seals off the colors it
contains. In contrast, Girke's white seems to expand and
contract, appears open, continually changing. In a
word, it appears to breathe.

English artist Alan Green (p. 355 above) takes a stance
exactly opposite to that of Rauschenberg. While the
American heightens the real character of the image by
integrating actual elements of reality, Green believes
that a picture done by purely painterly means has a bet-

ter chance of belonging to the real world than a reproduction of external reality. He, too, considers the
painted image to be a concrete, autonomous object. The
minimal means he employs are contemporary to the
extent, he says, that they correspond to the "minimal
radius of action" of human beings in an endangered
world marked by dependencies and compulsions.

Art About Art

Unlike Green and the representatives of Shaped Canvas
painting, Jerry Zeniuk (p. 356 below), an American born
in Hamburg, does not wish his paintings to be thought
of as objects. His work records the return of art to its

achieved the color value and sense of diffuse space
which correspond to his idea of painting. The result is a
contemplative, subtly nuanced color-space which
appeals immediately to the eye, and has no need of theoretical underpinning. In later works this rigorous purism
would give way to a stronger emphasis on agitated surfaces and forms. The contemplative panels of Alan
Charlton (ill. below) are radical abstractions untainted
by academicism, which struck exhibition organizer
Christos M. Joachimides as being suffused by a
"Beckett-like loneliness."

The chromatic color-field paintings of American
artist Brice Marden (p. 356 above), whose surfaces

Alan Green
Pink Rectangles to Grey, 1994
Oil on canvas, three parts,
70 x 210 cm (overall)
London, Annely Juda Fine Art

Alan Charlton
Horizontal Painting in
7 Vertical Parts, 1996
Acrylic on canvas, 157.5 x 373.5 cm
London, Annely Juda Fine Art

roots, after the failure of the campus revolt, in the wake
of Vietnam and Watergate. He has set himself the task,
Zeniuk says, of finding out what painting really is. There
could be no clearer statement of the intention to recall
the fundamental premises of art, and to return to its
basic elements. This reflective attitude on the artist's
part, this making of "art about art," not only entails a
slow, patient process of painting. With an intensity that
takes nothing for granted and sometimes verges on
masochism, Zeniuk applies, without a pre-conceived
plan, layer upon layer of paint until he believes to have

absorb rather than reflect light, are a different case
entirely. The thinking of Barnett Newman has left clear
traces in Marden's work. Like Newman, Marden strives
for an imageless religiosity. The rhythm of the propor-
tionally related rectangular fields, diagonal or parallel
structures, and anthropomorphic curvatures, and the
alternation of color values between light and dark in his
work, are seen by the artist as corresponding to human
emotionality. What he paints, Marden says, has nothing
to do with things existing in real space, though it does
with illusion – illusion understood as the realization of

the abstract character of the perceptions we have of real things. He does not paint "trees and flowers," says Marden, though he does employ a "landscape image." Marden considers the artist's role to be that of a mediator between man and the invisible, mystical forces behind all things. Rational calculation and religious sensibility blend in his thinking and his work.

Jerry Zeniuk
Untitled Number 193, 1996
Oil on canvas, 188 x 233 cm
Bonn, Kunstmuseum Bonn

Color and Space

The œuvre of the Beuys student "Blinky" Palermo (p. 357 below) remained only a fragment, due to his premature death. Like many artists working in a minimalistic vein, Palermo was impressed by Constructivism. It speaks for the broad-mindedness of his teachers, Bruno Goller and above all for that of Beuys, that they did not attempt to suppress this then quite unopportune preference, but encouraged its further development. Palermo's approach combined a treatment of the painting as an autonomous object, manifested especially in the series of metal paintings begun in 1972, with a sensitivity to the surrounding space, to which his works – apart from the sketches and miniatures – almost always related. It is unfortunate that none of the pieces realized and installed in actual spaces has survived, although reconstructions do exist.

In a process of logical reduction, every allusion to the human figure vanished from Palermo's paintings as they grew increasingly simple and more concentrated. In the end neither composition nor surface texture remained – only clearly defined, stark color fields, as if made one with the support. These were the result of a painstaking and ingenious painting process in which layer after layer was applied over a white ground, in the course of which the original conception was intuitively revised again and again. The aim of his work, according to Palermo, was to arrive at a sequence or chord of color which he could neither have conceived nor imagined when beginning work.

Page 356 above left:
Brice Marden
Red Yellow Blue, 1974
Oil and wax on canvas,
three parts, 188 x 183 cm
Formerly Saatchi Collection,
London

Page 356 above right:
Imi Knoebel
Untitled, 1987
Acrylic on screw-mounted wood
panels, 250 x 170 cm
Private collection

Shusaku Arakawa
Untitled, 1964/65
Mixed media on canvas, two parts,
247 x 161 cm (each)
Cologne, Museum Ludwig,
Ludwig Donation

For another student of Beuys, Imi Knoebel (p. 356 above), the eye-opening experience was Malevich's Suprematism, particularly his *Black Square*. As for his friend Palermo, both the object-character of the painting and the establishment of a relationship between it and the surrounding space are constituitive for Knoebel. Compellingly manifested in his environment-related

evinces a blend of the minimalist structures of the early works with a strong, if controlled, palette, as he continues to transgress the borderlines between the genres.

An even higher degree of such conceptualism is seen in the work of Shusaku Arakawa (ill. above), a Japanese artist living in New York. The painting in the above illustration belongs to a series entitled *Diagrams*.

installations, these factors already became evident in the constructive, minimalist phase of Knoebel's work, which culminated in a first installation at the Düsseldorf Kunsthalle (now in the Museum Ludwig, Cologne). Subsequently the artist's sensitive purism occasionally made way for a brilliant coloration inspired by Matisse, irregular formats, and especially for the expressive, gestural approach seen in the installations and a few of the paintings. Knoebel's most recent phase

Arakawa's allusive imagery combines graphic and painterly elements with literary and philosophical references on the basis of an abbreviated, evocative sign language. The open character of his paintings is consciously fragmentary, and eludes final definition, for the "mechanism of meaning" is inconstant and continually changing. It permits of numerous, sometimes mutually contradictory interpretations, to the point of logical inversion. The viewer is challenged to participate in the

Blinky Palermo
Points of the Compass I, 1976
Acrylic on aluminum, four parts;
26.7 x 21 cm (each)
Cologne, Museum Ludwig,
Ludwig Donation

On Kawara
June 2, 1971
Liquitex on canvas, 26 x 33 cm
Private collection

unravelling of Arakawas's pictorial codes, which, suggesting an awareness of the provisional nature of all knowledge, allow great latitude for mental association. The use of various sign systems (words and images, plans, photographs, and real objects) increases this effect still further. All identity between the things depicted and the depiction itself is negated. Behind such pictorial mind-games the shades of Duchamp and Magritte are detectable. The step from Arakawa's work to Conceptual Art is a small one.

Roman Opalka (ill. right), a Polish artist who lives in France, since 1965 has been painting rows of numerals in acrylic on canvases of identical format, beginning with one and now far into the millions. These traces of his own life, diaries in paint, he calls "details." Day by day, week by week, month by month, and year by year, they mark the stages of a silent drama, the drama of the artist's own existence, whose vicissitudes are subtly reflected in the character of the brushwork. In addition, since 1972 has been recording a litany of numbers on tape, and making a daily self-portrait photograph. Even when he is on a trip, the sequence of literally existential numerals is not interrupted, though here the medium is drawing. Opalka's numerals are painted in white on grey, a grey that is lightened from canvas to canvas by adding one percent more white. Dieter Honisch has pointed out a link between this unprecedented attempt to bring a life of isolation in the studio into a pictorial unity and the *unism* of Strzemiński, the Polish Constructivist who – going beyond Malevich – posited a

Roman Opalka
Detail 1-35327, 1965
Tempera on canvas, 196 x 135 cm
Łódz, Muzeum Sztuki

unity of structure and image, figure and ground, form and color. Opalka has devoted himself entirely to a unity of art and life, expressed in the form of a work in progress.

On Kawara (p. 358 above), a countryman of Arakawa's who likewise makes his home in New York, has also made his own life the theme of his art, which far transcends the borderline of painting to enter the field of Conceptual Art. Kawara records the places he goes to, what he reads, the people he meets, and current events both public and private such as "Sit-in on Times Square" or "Taeko Kissed Me". He telegraphs his friends telling them what time he got up and that "I'm still alive." Time and space are Kawara's theme. In a multi-volume work he noted down "A Million Years", the painterly yield of which exercise were works on identical formats to each of which Kawara devoted six or seven hours a day. Despite the difficulty of his work of recent decades, it should not be forgotten that the Japanese artist was among the few of any nationality who, in the early 1950s, reacted immediately and compellingly to the horrors of the Second World War, especially the terrible consequences of the atomic bomb attacks on Hiroshima and Nagasaki. The destruction and deformation of the human face found shocking and visionary expression in Kawara's *Death Masks*.

German artist Hanne Darboven (ill. below) produces non-linguistic writings, serially arranged in lines and columns of numbers, letters, and calligraphic motions. Johannes Cladders has aptly described this imagery as "antedating the computer" and as issuing from a "programming office... in which the material is, so to speak, made palatable to electronics." Darboven's endless theme is the course of time, which she treats not only in terms of abstract, encoded formulations which require an index to understand, but in terms of references to actual current events. The works of this major representative of Conceptual Art ascetically radicalize our understanding of painting as writing. In Darboven's oeuvre time is not only represented but subjected to critical commentary by means of enciphered abbreviations, occasionally interspersed with documentary, actual figures and events.

The work of French artist Daniel Buren (ill. above), actually conceptual in thrust, has sparked debates on whether he is really a painter or not. In 1967, on the occasion of the "Salon de la Jeune Peinture", Buren and his friends Olivier Mosset, Michel Parmentier, and Niele Toroni, issued a flyer that listed all the characteristics of painting as traditionally defined. Then, in conclusion, they stated, "...since painting means painting with reference to aestheticism, flowers, women, eroticism, daily milieu, art, dada, psychoanalysis, war in Vietnam, WE ARE NOT PAINTERS." This total rejection corresponded, in positive terms, to a reduction of painting to basic structures. Buren employs alternating bands of color and white, set in regular, impersonal sequences on awning material, plastic sheet, paper or sailcloth.

Daniel Buren
Untitled, 1972
Dispersion on striped fabric,
150 x 140 cm
Private collection

Hanne Darboven
Request Concert – 144 Poems, 1984
Ink and offset printing on paper, greeting cards (collage),
1008 sheets, each 29.7 x 21 cm (detail). Berlin, Busche Galerie

Günther Förg
Untitled (Lead Painting), 1986
Acrylic on sheet lead on wood,
three parts, 120 x 90 cm (each)
Germany, private collection

From a regatta with striped sails on Lake Wannsee in Berlin to a presentation in the museum or the public domain, such works aim at altering and artistically accentuating the environment by means of "painterly" incursions. Buren's space at the 1986 Venice Biennale, like that of his German colleague, Sigmar Polke, justifiably won an award, for it was one of the few highpoints of this artistic miscellany.

A quite different approach is seen in the conceptual painting of Gerhard Merz. The reality of monochrome paint is confronted with the reality of the experience of other peoples and times, lending visual presence to a cultural climate. This is manifested, for instance, in

Merz's provocative juxtaposition of a color chart with popular and frequently cloying images of the Zeitgeist, such as an eagle, nude, flower, or tango dancers. In more recent years the artist has turned to paintings and installations whose rigor recalls Malevich and Mondrian, and occasionally Futurist architecture.

In a similar spirit, if with different aims, Günter Förg (ill. above) contrasts color fields of strict two-dimensionality to reproductions evoking spatial experiences, in works that combine the media of painting, drawing, and photography. Förg also addresses actual spaces, producing installations that reflect the influence of Palermo.

Purists and Prophets
Painting by Sculptors and Object-Makers

"The depiction as illusion – in my opinion this is one of the achievements of European painting, at least in this century." Mario Merz

We should now take a glance at a few important artists who, though they have not devoted themselves primarily to painting, have provided crucial impulses to the medium, and have moreover expanded the border-lines of art itself.

Michael Heizer, with Walter De Maria and Robert Smithson (who died young in an airplane crash), is one of the major representatives of Land Art. This movement, bringing art out of the museum, has left human traces on environments of every description, but preferably desolate, remote places. Examples are De Maria's *Lightning Field* (p. 547), Heizer's *Earthworks* (p. 545), Smithson's *Spiral Jetty* (p. 546), and James Turrell's *Light Crater* in the American Southwest. Heizer is also an excellent draughtsman. As a painter, he admires Matisse and Bonnard. He works on carefully primed canvases using napped rollers to achieve a vibrant interplay of

dense and attenuated textures. Even though Heizer's paintings are done in a city studio, the light and expanse of the landscapes in which he creates his earthworks remain present in them.

Nancy Graves (p. 568) began her artistic activity as a painter before turning to sculpture and objects. Since the 1970s Graves has been painting again. While her three-dimensional works are devoted to discovering and presenting traces of pre-historical eras and lost cultures of the earth, her paintings deal, on the basis of scientific documentation and satellite photographs, with interplanetary spaces. Graves's imagery is a composite of free variations in which topographical elements mingle with abstract passages and graphic improvisations.

Sol LeWitt (pp. 528, 529) is not only one of the major representatives of Minimal Art, but a forerunner of Conceptual Art. In keeping with his realization that when the idea for a work has formed in the artist's mind and its final configuration is determined, the execution happens blindly, LeWitt has his *Wall Drawings* carried out by assistants. Their work is admittedly checked by reference to the artist's ink drawings, which, as plans, have the same value for him as the finished works.

These linear black and white drawings consist basically of horizontals, verticals, and forty-five degree diagonals, rendered with varying pressure and composed to produce varying densities of surface. The black is supplemented by color variations achieved by systematically mixing the elementary colors of yellow, red and blue, as used in printing processes. Both the colored and black and white drawings are transferred directly to the wall, whose material character, dimensions, and architectural design the artist accepts as integral parts of the image. On the other hand, he is disturbed by the fact of being beholding to the architect, and being dependent to a great extent on the givens of the site.

The work of American Minimalist Richard Tuttle (ill. right), who might be termed a contemporary Precisionist between abstraction and objectivity, draws on elements of painting, sculpture, and object, sometimes in a single work. Plain, unprepossessing materials are employed to produce radically simple yet poetic configurations, a highly abbreviated shorthand for landscape, script, and objects which frequently has humorous overtones. These configurations are attached to the wall or placed on the floor, without frame or pedestal, in arrangements that may appear arbitrary but are actually carefully planned. Formal and substantial correspondences play just as important a role in the arrangement as the precise distance of the objects from one another, their relationship, and finally their composition in space by the artist or according to his instructions.

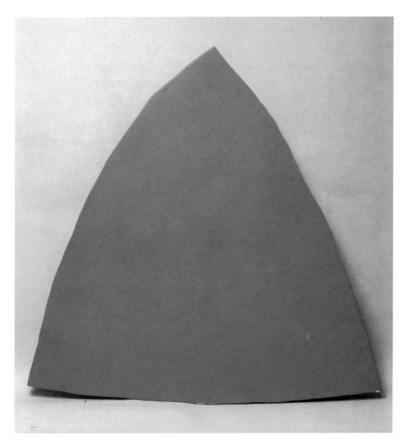

Richard Tuttle
Mountain, 1965
Acrylic on canvas and wood,
116 x 119 cm
Cologne, Museum Ludwig,
Ludwig Donation

Prophet of a New Sensibility

The dialectical pictorial thinking of Mario Merz (ill. above) is even greater in range. A native of Turin, Italy, Merz became famous as one of the key protagonists of Arte Povera, an art employing common materials whose ordinariness stands in inverse relationship to the intellectual richness of the works. Merz first attracted attention to himself with transparent igloo-shaped constructions whose configuration established a link between exterior form and interior space or content. These pieces

had been preceded by intensive early experiments in painting, attempts to go beyond Picasso and beyond the realism-abstraction dichotomy.

Arte Povera, announced Merz, represented an entirely new possibility of creating art. Certain links with Minimal and Conceptual Art were nonetheless evident. Also, Harald Szeemann was justified in including Merz, at documenta 5 in 1972, among those artists who attempt, in highly diverse ways, to establish a link between past and present by creating new myths – what

Mario Merz
Painter in Africa, c. 1981
Dispersion and oil on canvas,
neon tubes, 240 x 940 cm
Cologne, Museum Ludwig,
gift of Dr. Reiner Speck

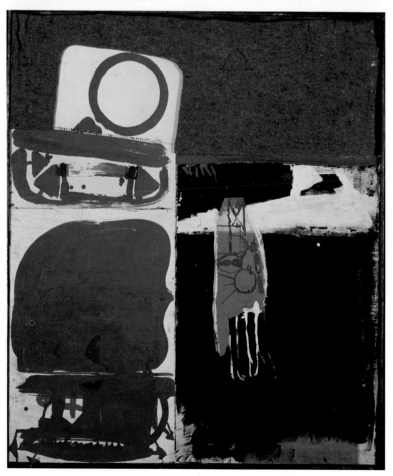

Szeemann termed "Individual Mythologies". But it is only at the point where Merz's work crosses the borderlines of current trends that the intellectual and aesthetic depth of his imagery and objects, based on an invocation of buried, archetypal life forms and forgotten primal imagery, becomes evident.

Merz does not understand avant-garde thinking as a faith in aesthetic progress which is blind to all that has gone before. For him it involves a rediscovery and re-evaluation, in the context of contemporary awareness, of buried myths and insights. These are the building blocks for the artist's models of a new and more humane world in which the powers of the imagination, as opposed to sterile rationality, are again given their due. This existential approach and his belief in the concrete utopia of a liberated society make Merz a kindred spirit with Beuys. They also give him the right to call himself and his confreres the "true Futurists."

Merz's element is not what is dead in the past but what remains vital. This is manifested, for instance, in the numerical progressions of Pisan mathematician Fibonacci (c. 1180–1240), and in the artist's employment of materials such as neon, fruit, and bundles of brushwood. Merz emphasizes that everything he does, including objects and installations, has its source in painting. Just as interior and exterior merge in the igloos, his painting activity, resumed in the mid-1970s, encompasses history and current events, myth and reality, rational thought and vision – but also life and death ("Memento mori," states Merz, "is always ever-present in life"). For him Fibonacci's spiral becomes Ariadne's thread, capable of leading us out of the labyrinth of our social and personal constrictions.

This existential optimism is foreign to the paintings, objects, and static installations of Jannis Kounellis (ill. above), a Greek artist who since 1956 has lived in Rome. Although determined by memory and history like Merz's work, Kounellis's hermetically seals off any path to, or view of, the future. Considering himself a painter foremost, Kounellis is concerned with finding out what images are still possible at this point in time. He attempts to point out the lack of binding values caused, in his view, by the demise of the bourgeoisie and the standards and order it once represented and maintained.

In view of Kounellis's multifarious and ambiguous œuvre – from the painted letters and musical notes to the blind masks, maskings, and montages employing fire, smoke, and lead – it becomes obvious that the theory of the avant-garde as a blithe and optimistic project no longer holds as our century approaches its end. Kounellis's concern takes on visual shape in enigmatic, associative symbolic forms that elude all definition, forms that oscillate between fleetingness and permanence, between being and nothingness. With these Italian artists, political – and poetic – commentary is not merely a footnote to their oeuvre but an integral part of it.

The Last Utopian

This is true, in an even more fundamental way, of the most outspoken advocate of an expanded definition of art, Joseph Beuys (p. 362 below), who died in 1986. Beuys's personality and work exhibited an exemplary congruence between life and art that was singular in the present period. It resulted from the holistic, evolutionary thinking and feeling of a man who united all the contradictions of our era within himself in an attempt to overcome them, to reconcile reason with imagination, myth with reality, enlightenment with magic, history with the present day.

Space does not permit us to more than touch on the unparalleled career of this draughtsman and painter, sculptor, object-maker, environment, Happening, Fluxus and Action artist, co-founder with Heinrich Böll of the "Free International College of Creativity," this both deeply political and religious man. Beuys's profound, melancholy yet optimistic, very complex and very German artistic activities, whose roots can be traced back to the magic symbolism of pre-history, go far beyond his often-cited predilection for the Gesamtkunstwerk. Beuys envisioned a society, as Peter Iden notes, "in which art would enter a synthesis with and be borne up" by society, "society as a sculpture of humane potentials," just as earlier, Christian thinkers envisioned a community in which art would enter a synthesis with and be borne up by faith.

Beuys's incredibly sensitive work in drawing and painting, straightforward, consciously avoiding virtuosity and sophistication, combining the chthonic with the cosmic, already contained the visual thinking and the design of this "possible world" in a nutshell. Beuys's teacher at the academy, Ewald Mataré, who neither could nor would accept the path his master-student took, once imagined Beuys declaring, "I've had enough of the aesthetic work of art; I'm going to make a fetish." This applies not only to Beuys' sculptures and objects, from *Eurasian Staff* to *Queen Bee*, but to the majority of his drawings and marvellously beautiful watercolors as well. Restrained, with lineatures of hypersensitive fragility traced on commonplace, sometimes scrap papers, these indeed often recall a "footprint in the sand," as Mataré said.

The results of Beuys' study of natural history, his marshalling of totemistic animals (hare, stag, elk, wild goat, raven, bee), nomadic legends, rose and cross, heathen and Christian figures and symbols, anthroposophical astral figurations, shamanistic accoutrements, heat machines, sleds, women in the moors and very contemporaneous demonstrators – all appeared in the drawings, which seemed like preliminary exercises for subsequent work in three dimensions and actions in the public domain, in so far as they were not actually dispassionate, precise notations of intellectual and formal considerations.

The romantically visionary, magically evocative art of Beuys, his charismatic personality and face marked by a war wound and intellectual effort, the logic of all his actions, not only inspired and influenced many of his students and colleagues, but shaped the image of the contemporary German artist in the world's mind.

The traditional border-lines between the genres of art which Beuys broke through, are unlikely ever to grow impermeable again. In a television program after his death, one of the panel members asked what would remain of "Beuys after Beuys," of the transitory portion of his œuvre, which naturally could not be reduced to static pictures or objects.

Beuys himself gave the answer during his lifetime, when he shed doubt on the much-touted "eternal value" of works of art, including his own. In his view, every work he did was a model, a model of an idea. "Because these products," Beuys said, "are really just records, documents, outgrowths of this process of becoming conscious, just as I consider products in general to be outgrowths of thoughts."

A contrast to Beuys's critical faith in the future is seen in the deeply pessimistic formulations of Dieter Roth (ill. above), a painter, graphic artist, object-maker, film-maker, and poet who invokes the transience and insignificance of earthly things. Roth's "Collected Works" comprise many volumes, to some of which he applies the period's favorite four-letter word and its meaning: *Early Writings and Typical Shit, Still More Shit*, etc. The artist's chiliastic mood is also reflected in his choice, for many paintings and objects, of perishable materials (sausage, cheese, chocolate), which are enclosed in glass, plexiglass, or plastic sheet. Unlike Beuys, Roth advances a radical critique of the era and its art which contains no hope for the future. This radical skepticism, however, is implicitly countered by an excellent graphic and painterly œuvre that reveals only little of the melancholy which lurks behind the veil of Roth's sarcasm.

Dieter Roth
Untitled, 1976/77
Photograph and mixed media on
canvas, 177 x 241 cm
Stuttgart, Galerie der Stadt
Stuttgart, Courtesy Galerie
Buchmann, Basel

Page 362 above:
Jannis Kounellis
Untitled, 1959
Oil on canvas, 200 x 200 cm
Munich, Goetz Collection

Page 362 below:
Joseph Beuys
King's Daughter Sees Iceland, 1960
Watercolor and oil on paper,
on felt, under glass,
in metal frame, 114 x 98.5 cm
Cologne, Museum Ludwig,
Ludwig Donation

13 Beyond Utopia

Between Vanguard and Reaction
Painting on the Verge of the Millennium

Beuys was the last utopian in contemporary art, at least for the time being. His visionary thinking reflected an unshakeable idealism which no clash with reality was able to quell. A traditionalist and avant-gardist in one, Beuys both invoked the distant past and prophesied a future determined by artistic sensibility. The barriers have since been rebuilt along the frontiers of utopia; the future is a book with seven seals.

pass was not a rebirth but a rediscovery and further development. Traditional painting found many and talented adherents among the younger generation of artists. In the meantime, the new media have become generally accepted, and the work being done in them has grown a great deal more professional thanks to the example of outstanding artists such as Nam June Paik, Vito Acconci, Jürgen Klauke, Rebecca Horn, Nancy

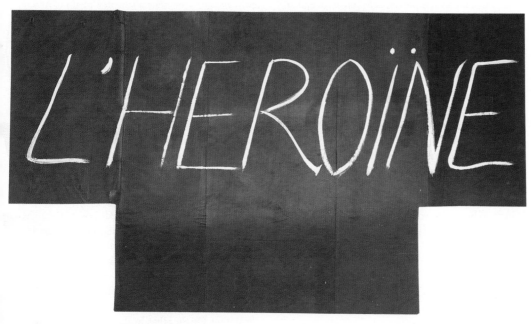

"Each work is a whiteness; the conscious recognition of the simultaneous state of a moment filled with longing, anxiety, curiosity, fear, death, the remembrance of every pertinent impetus nameable and unnameable. Friends living and dead, friends I used to know. The disillusionment with their loss."
JULIAN SCHNABEL

Julian Schnabel
L'Heroïne, 1987
Gesso on tarpaulin, 259 x 457 cm
Germany, private collection

In America, liberal and socialist minds have metamorphosed into conservatives. This is a period of adaptation, in which Herbert Marcuse's conception of "repressive tolerance" has taken on new currency under circumstances quite different from the late 1960s. "Wild" gestures, whether understood as such by their authors or not, no longer excite anyone, unless Richard Serra's austere, silent monuments (pp. 541–543) or, in a different key, Jeff Koons's kitsch sculptures (p. 571) can be said to have temporarily disturbed the peace in America or Europe.

The 1980s have been widely described as having witnessed a rebirth of painting. The term is badly chosen, because painting never died. What actually came to

Hoover, Dan Graham, Ulrike Rosenbach, Bill Viola, and many more (pp. 576–619). A naive fascination by the technological trappings of the new media has given way to familiarity, and their employment no longer seems sensational. Film, video, and performance have long since been accepted as welcome enrichments of the artist's methods and tools. No reasonable person would now consider playing them off against painting or sculpture, especially since many performance, video, and film artists also paint and draw with accomplishment (Klauke, Johannes Bernhard Blume) or create objects or environments (Horn, Paik), or like Astrid Klein or Katharina Sieverding are outstanding photographers who incorporate painterly elements in their

Georg Baselitz
Self-Portrait Disaster, 1987
Oil and pastel on canvas,
250 x 200 cm
Napa (CA), Hess Collection

Jürgen Klauke
Stutter + Stammer/Oblong, 1992
24 parts
Watercolor on paper,
41.5 x 55.5 cm (each)
Düsseldorf, Galerie Bugdahn
und Kaimer

work. By the way, it is striking how great a role women play in the field of the new media.

There was also a further, quite obvious reason for the return to painting mentioned above. This was a certain weariness of the austere purism of Minimal Art and of the intangibility and rarification of the projects of Conceptual Art, with which, incidentally, some of the later wild or neo-expressionist painters had been intensively involved. As in other epochs of art history, this weariness was provoked not so much by the major protagonists of these styles as by the sheer unoriginality and boringness of the work of their countless camp-followers. The story of spontaneous, gestural painting took no different course.

As in the field of the new media, in that of the supposedly new painting the sheep had been separated from the goats by the middle of the 1980s. Whether their work had a neo-expressionist, gestural, or meditative thrust, the best of the young artists ceased to follow well-worn paths, being just as little willing to sacrifice

their intellects to the god of sensuousness as to accept an ideology of progress that degraded avant-gardism to "avant-garditis." The conservative, retrospective character of the dominant tendencies in painting until just a few years ago – from the Italians' new myths to Anselm Kiefer's ambivalent coming to terms with the German past, from Julian Schnabel's decoratively elegant exploitation of variously textured materials (velvet, burlap, carpets, even animal skins) to the banalities of "free figuration" (p. 365) – apparently did not dazzle young artists to the point of forgetting that inertia and endless repetition are the death of art.

Dead End or New Freedom?

Manfred Schneckenburger, two-time head of the documenta, has aptly described the situation of painting (and its offshoots in sculpture) in the past decade. Speaking in an interview, he said, "Free disposal over every style, or the waiver of style, though weakly evident throughout the 20th century, is now penetrating into uncharted territory ... . What we call 'modernism' was essentially determined by two ideas: On the one hand, by the notion of art finding its way back to itself – culminating in [American critic and theoretician] Clement Greenberg's puritan teleology of painting as the self-critique of painting. On the other, by the perpetual opening of art into non-art (slogan: 'art as/is life'), Peter Bürger's leftist theory of the avant-garde. The one path ran linearly and evolutionarily; the other repeatedly subjected art to revolutions. Both paths made it meaningful to speak for 120 years of an avant-garde, both made art appear dynamic and innovative. And both have issued in the static eclecticism of post-modernism – in a dead end, or a new freedom? It is too early to give a diagnosis, let alone a prognosis. But it would also be wrong to overlook the sharpness of the caesura."

A good example of the development is Jürgen Klauke, a definitely vanguard artist whose obsessive drawings, as Werner Lippert notes, express "a mental world interested in findings of sexual identity and their

Raimer Jochims
In Memory of Kandinsky,
1991/92
Acrylic on composition board,
96 x 135 cm
Bonn, Kunstmuseum Bonn

Johannes Grützke
Existence Ponderers, 1996
Oil on canvas, 200 x 180 cm
Berlin, Ladengalerie

Bernhard Heisig
The War Volunteer, 1982–1986
Oil on canvas, 150 x 120 cm
Berlin, private collection.
Courtesy Galerie Brusberg, Berlin

communication phenomena," and whose sometimes ironic (*Post-Modernism, Please Like Me, Zweitgeist*), sometimes existentially concerned performances, photo sequences, and paintings represent a salient contribution to an expansion of artistic possibilities. Even an artist with such credentials could say of himself, "I am a classical artist, a traditional artist."

The story of the new expressiveness in art after the Second World War did not begin with the new myths of the Italian "Trans-Avant-Garde," as its prophet, Achille Bonito Oliva dubbed it, or Arte Cifra, as it is otherwise known. Nor did the story begin with the "Wild Painting" of the Berliners or the "Bad Painting" by the bad boys of Mülheimer Freiheit in Cologne, nor even with their idols, Baselitz and Penck. The new expressiveness emerged much earlier, with European and especially German L'art informel of the Tachist brand, and with American Abstract Expressionism or Action Painting.

The Germans in particular – Schultze, Schumacher, Hoehme – never denied their recourse to Romanticism and Expressionism. It must be recalled that in the 1950s, historical Expressionism, all the way to Beckmann, was considered a German aberration on both sides of the Atlantic. Then the formerly so denigrated traits of savagery and irrationalism were rediscovered, and for a time extolled, from Paris to New York and Los Angeles, from Tokyo to Moscow. And again, the pendulum swung back.

There can be no doubt that the magic of Beuys's personality and work helped lead to a revision of prejudices with regard to German art and artists, despite the fact that Beuys was certainly no eclecticist or Neo-Expressionist, let alone a Neo-Fauve or Wild Painter. Still, his œuvre could hardly have emerged anywhere other than in Germany, perhaps nowhere else than in the Lower

Rhine region near the Dutch border, a region that has produced many profound minds.

Nor is it perhaps a coincidence that Baselitz and Penck, the two pioneers of the new German expressively gestural painting, like Richter, Polke, Graubner, Uecker, Hoehme and others, came from the former German Democratic Republic. It was there that Willi Sitte, with his Baroque super-abundance, and the earnest Silesian-born Bernhard Heisig (ill. above), with his teeming figurations, not only continued the Expressionist tradition but ramified it in a very personal, individual way. After

Wolfgang Mattheuer
After Sunset, 1987
Oil on canvas, 170 x 200 cm
Germany, IBM Collection

all, the memory of Expressionism was never entirely expunged during the years after 1945, not even during the period of political regimentation.

Yet Expressionism was taboo in East Germany when Georg Kern from the town of Deutsch-Baselitz (thence his assumed name) came to West Germany in the late 1950s. It was not until the early 1960s that those who toed the political line, Sitte, Heisig, and also Wolfgang Mattheuer (p. 367), the painter of intellectually reflected, mildly surrealist daydreams, and the virtuoso

neo-mannerist Werner Tübke (ill. above), whose social criticism was schooled on Bosch, Dürer, Mantegna, and Rubens, gained courage and began undermining the ossified principles of Socialist Realism.

This also holds, under quite different artistic premises, for the outstanding painter-draughtsman Gerhard Altenbourg (ill. below), who took his point of departure in Klee. All of these artists – including Penck, who was long influential in Dresden – paved the way for a younger, ambitious generation of East German artists.

When Baselitz arrived in then West Berlin, his teacher became Hann Trier, the Rhineland abstractionist who worked with both hands simultaneously. Baselitz's earlier idols were Corinth and Heckel, but also Ferdinand von Rayski, the great 19th-century portraitist. This list was not a bad basis for the artist who – apart from being a superb draughtsman and printmaker – was to become the prime representative of a gestural, expressive, ostensibly new painting which had strong and never-denied roots in tradition.

In the Beginning was Scandal

Yet before he became prominent, Baselitz first had to cause a bit of a scandal. In 1961, together with his artist-friend Eugen Schönebeck, he issued a first "Pandämonium" manifesto, followed by a second a year later, and proclaimed the advent of the age of "Pathetic Realism." At this period emerged truly savage paintings in an expressive and provocative semi-realist style, blasphemous and frankly obscene: *The Big Night Flushed* (1961; Cologne, Museum Ludwig), *Christmas* (1964; Cologne, Museum Ludwig), *The Hand of God* (1964/65; Bonn, Kunstmuseum). These violent works were done in protest against an abstraction grown sterile and academic, but even more, they pilloried the pride and prudery of Germans under the Economic Miracle. The moral reaction was not long in coming. *The Naked Man* (Berlin, Kleihues Collection) and *The Big Night Flushed* – a grotesquely deformed depiction of an adolescent with oversized head and monumental penis – were confiscated by the police, who released them only after a two-year long court case. It is unfortunate that Baselitz later distanced himself from his early, explosive paintings, saying he considered them "too pubescent."

Georg Baselitz
Night Meal in Dresden, 1983
Oil on canvas, 280 x 450 cm
Zurich, Kunsthaus Zürich

"The art-work comes into being in the artist's head, and it stays in the artist's head. There is no communication with any public whatsoever. The artist can ask no questions, and he makes no statement; he offers no informaion, message or opinion. He gives no help to anyone, and his work cannot be used. No social or personal situation will govern, influence, prevent or make inevitable, the end product."
Georg Baselitz

Georg Baselitz
The Great Friends, 1965
Oil on canvas, 250 x 300 cm
Cologne, Museum Ludwig,
Ludwig Donation

A. R. Penck
Untitled (Group of Friends),
1964/65
Oil on composition board,
170 × 275 cm
Cologne, Museum Ludwig,
Ludwig Collection

Georg Baselitz
The Forest Upside-down, 1969
Oil on canvas, 250 × 190 cm
Cologne, Museum Ludwig,
Ludwig Donation

Yet of course the rebelliousness and spontaneous anger of youth cannot be conserved. It is understandable that the artist ultimately made painting for its own sake, regardless of motif, his principal theme. In order to prove that a well-painted picture remains just that even if you rotate it through 90 or 180 degrees, Baselitz, as everyone knows, began to turn his figures and landscapes upside down. But what was initially a baffling move, a programmatic demonstration, in the long run became rather routine, not always to the advantage of an on the whole impressive œuvre. Baselitz is a superb technician, a master of differentiation and variation, based on an alternation of cool and warm colors, condensed and loosely rendered passages, painterly drama and tranquillity. The key difference between his imagery and abstraction consists in his retention of subject-matter, as a structural element and as a means of control, to prevent the image from slipping into a mere, arbitrary pattern. In the meantime, Baselitz has tried doing without the spectacular headstands of his figurative and abstract elements. The experiment has produced a number of compelling images which seem to indicate that he has no intention of resting on the laurels of his international fame.

A.R. Penck emigrated from East Germany twenty years after Baselitz. Influenced by Rembrandt and van Gogh, Penck also came under the spell of Expressionism early on. This is seen in his ghostly and ironic depiction of a group of friends (ill. above), including Wolf Biermann, Jürgen Böttcher, Baselitz as a specter, and the artist himself, with Picasso's head on a gnomish body. Apart from the obviously Expressionistic features of brilliant coloration and grotesquely distorted figures, forms that would become characteristic of Penck's subsequent work already appear – anticipations of a pictographic idiom of a part pre-historical and archetypal, part technological nature. These reflect the autobiographical references so important to Penck (a pseudonym adopted from the name of a 19th-century scientist), as well as the diversity of his interests, from philosophy, poetry, theater, dance and music to technology and its information systems. Not least, the symbols embody Penck's ambitious endeavor to create a symbiosis of rationality and irrationality, logic and imagination, which would find expression in the following, analytical "System" and "World" paintings, and especially in the artist's attempts to set objective "Standards." In 1978, looking back on his own development – and probably on that of his namesake – Penck, writing under still another in a series of pseudonyms, Ypsilon, declared the attempt to create a universal language of signs a failure. Yet the validity of the steps on the path towards his unreachable goal was not denied. For Penck, as for many of today's artists, there is no one, definitive style, nor does he have any qualms about eclectically exploiting history and art history. In this sense his work is clearly the product of a late culture and its existential doubts. The pitfall Penck faces is the tendency, seen in recent years, for his enigmatic pictographs to slip into mere decorativeness, patterns on the wall.

Jörg Immendorff, who met Penck in 1977 and launched German-German art activities in collaboration with him, has long developed beyond the one-dimensional, narrowly leftist ideology conveyed by the neo-primitivism of his early years. Yet this has deprived his work of none of its polemical force, having only added to the substance of Immendorff's critical involvement with German history and its oscillation between hope and despair. Combining a narration of personal experiences with references to historical situations and

events, the artist's paintings and sculptures link anecdote with symbolism and allusion in a graphic and immediately appealing style in which even grotesque exaggeration is wholeheartedly accepted. One of Immendorff's major projects, a momentous series on the theme of *Café Deutschland* (ill. below), while inspired by Guttuso's *Caffè Greco* (p. 207), expands its theme and applies it in a bitter and disillusioned way to the division of Germany, and by allusion to the division of the world into East and West, and the deformation of thinking to which it led.

A. R. Penck
Me, in Germany (West), 1984
Dispersion on cotton,
600 x 1200 cm
Cologne, Museum Ludwig,
Ludwig Collection

Jörg Immendorff
Café Deutschland I, 1978
Acrylic on canvas, 282 x 320 cm
Cologne, Museum Ludwig,
Ludwig Collection

Nibelungs Never Die...

Anselm Kiefer, too, concerns himself intensively with
recent German history and its fallacious myths. Yet for
him, this history reveals aspects very different from
those addressed by Immendorff. It is rooted in myth,
based on a diffuse ideology derived from realms far distant in space and time, and marked by their irrational
invocation. Kiefer does not rely on eye-witnesses or
records, but attempts to come to terms with the fascination of the evil and irrational, including their sources, by
conducting his own personal investigation, in which a
capacity for empathy plays a key role.

In 1970 Kiefer began a series of heroic landscapes
and heroically symbolic subjects, followed by studies
devoted to Richard Wagner, the Nibelungs, and Parsifal.
These complex themes were translated into imagery of
a compelling and evocative pathos whose ambivalence
and open-endedness left much room for the viewer's
own personal associations. Ultimately these canvases
evoked the intextricable bond between positive and
negative, good and evil. Kiefer's series on the theme of
Scorched Earth, his heroic interiors (*Parsifal*; London,
Tate Gallery), and countrysides infused with history like
Sand of the Marches of Brandenburg (ill. below), have a
symbolically charged subjectivity that permits of various
interpretations. Only rarely in recent art has an immediate, historical reference been stated so clearly as in the
artist's depiction of *Operation Sea Lion*, the planned but
never implemented German invasion of Great Britain,
preparations for which Kiefer has take place in a bathtub.

One cannot always be certain about what dominates
in Kiefer's work – whether he is more overwhelmed by
pity and regret, or by the power of myth and the irrational. His paintings, incredibly dense in texture and
executed in unconventional combinations of materials
(emulsion, oil, acrylic, shellac, epoxy, sand and straw),
are thus subject to misunderstanding, especially in the
current climate of a simplistic historical revisionism in
Germany.

Anselm Kiefer
Margarethe, 1981
Oil and straw on canvas,
280 x 380 cm
Formerly Saatchi Collection,
London

The seriousness of Kiefer's deeply thoughtful, complex, and very German painting, and the outstanding quality of his œuvre as a whole, cannot be doubted. Nevertheless, in face of his imagery, one is inadvertently put in mind of playwright Heiner Müller's laconic and hardly controvertible statement, "Germany is still playing the Nibelungs."

A quite different thrust, if one not without its own evocative magic, is seen in the work of Horst Antes (ill. right), who is six years Kiefer's senior. Antes's reputation was established by his "cephalopods," human figures condensed into heads and feet, which he depicted in a long series of variations. Like his subsequent, formally and technically much more stringent gabled houses of the 1960s, Antes's figures convey an underlying, subtly stated metaphysical message. His detachment from figurative realism, among whose first representatives in Germany Antes was in younger years, became obvious at the latest in the strange, dwarfish creatures with usually super-posed eyes in over-large heads, which he depicted until the early 1980s.

These figures have since vanished from Antes's work, despite his later, very intensive involvement with the magical, spiritualized heads of Javlensky. Yet he does reply, as if in counterpoint, to the Russian artist's imagery, with reduced, geometric shapes derived from house walls and roofs. Antes's intellectual and aesthetic stance is also reflected in his collecting activity, which ranges from mundane objects like school primers and milk jugs to the art of the indigenous peoples of America and Australia.

"I am the People that Paints!"

Even before the 1970s were out, Berlin artists organized a "Biennale" exhibition to protest against the lack of attention their work was receiving, because it ran counter to the mainstream trends on the German and international art scene. Their eloquent spokesman was Markus Lüpertz (p. 374 below). Those politically if not artistically wild years witnessed a debate at the academy

"I have always been interested in surfaces – once could call them synonyms for something. … Reality never interested me. I put my expressiveness into my painting and made a specific fantasy visible. I aim for meaningless, cold painting."
MARKUS LÜPERTZ

Horst Antes
Blue Figure: St. Francis of Assisi,
1961–1964
Oil on canvas, 100 x 80 cm
Private collection

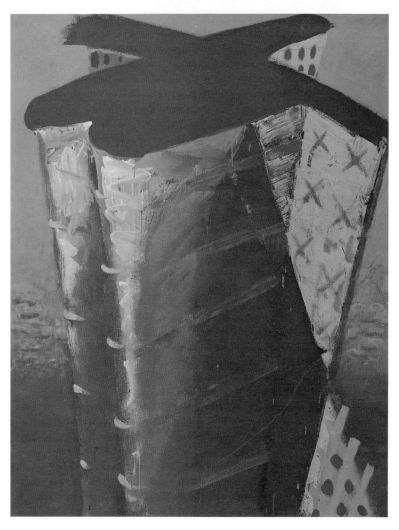

in which Lüpertz' colleagues, styling themselves representatives of the people, polemicized against the ostensible "crypticness" and "elitism" of contemporary art. Lüpertz replied with the unanswerable declaration, "I am the people that paints!" Shortly thereafter Lüpertz's work began to receive national and international acclaim.

Lüpertz' statement reflects the fact that he has worked as a miner, streetsweeper, wrestler, and soccer player. His self-confidence is unmistakably reflected in his style, which he terms "dithyrambic." Though not wild – Lüpertz dislikes being described as a prominent forerunner of the Berlin "vehement" painters or Neo-Fauves – his painting is suffused by an untragic, euphemistic pathos and a great vitality of attack, and yet it also shows an amazing sense of compositional balance and differentiation of color values. For Lüpertz art takes place on the surface without the aid of materials other than paint, which only load down the image. This is why he will have no truck with Kiefer's straw or Schnabel's crockery sherds. Nor do particular motifs have any intrinsic meaning for Lüpertz. They merely provide him with an occasion for the act of painting, which is basically his sole theme, despite his occasional quotation of events in history or art history. Though a brilliant speaker and debater who has no qualms about extolling himself and being extolled as a "master," Lüpertz is equally candid about his debts to other artists, such as the retiring Werner Gilles, about whom Lüpertz has written a book.

Karl Horst Hödicke (ill. right)) had an enormous personal and aesthetic influence on the development of "vehement" painting in Berlin. He worked intensively in the drawing medium, made films, involved himself with Dada, Neo-Dada, Décollage, Pop Art, and Neo-Realism before deciding to concentrate on expressive painting. Hödicke's artistic intelligence, and a mastery of craft gained through tireless experimentation, have proven to be immensely stimulating to younger artists. Despite certain weaknesses in the primitivistic paintings of recent years, his work, both topical and retrospectively involved with history and myth, represents an outstanding contribution to German contemporary art.

It cannot be denied that most of the Berlin painters around Hödicke were politically abstinent by comparison to their immediate predecessors, the critical "Berlin Realists." A more aggressive and cynical approach, far from political utopianism if not without overtones of Bloch's principle of hope, is seen in the work of the brothers Albert and Markus Oehlen (ill. right), Werner Büttner, and Martin Kippenberger (ill. right). The former band musicians, who also share literary ambitions and witty, acerbic painting titles in common, reject autonomous painting as an end in itself, and address topical subjects and issues of contemporary society. They thus continue a tradition that extends from William Hogarth and Goya to Beckmann's ambiguous pictorial parables.

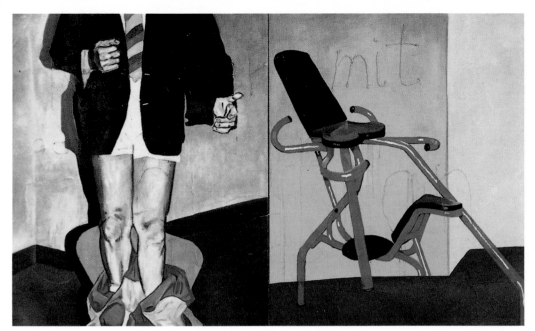

Page 374 above:
Rainer Fetting
Van Gogh and El Train, 1978–1981
Acrylic on canvas, 200 x 250 cm
Collection of the artist

Page 374 below:
Markus Lüpertz
Babylon Dithyrambic I, 1975
Oil on canvas, 162 x 130 cm
Eindhoven, Stedelijk van Abbe
Museum

Martin Kippenberger
Down with Inflation, 1984
Mixed media on canvas,
160 x 266 cm
Germany, private collection

"Truth is Labor" was the illuminating title of a joint exhibition mounted by Büttner, Kippenberger, and Albert Oehlen in the mid 1980s. Though they still fundamentally adhere to this attitude, the improved quality of their painting in recent years indicates that craft no longer plays a subordinate role.

Among the former members of the Cologne group "Mühlheimer Freiheit," Czech artist Jiri Dokoupil was long the most fascinating figure before withdrawing from the limelight. A good soldier Schweik with a paintbrush, Dokoupil has a chamelionlike ability to change his palette, forms, and media seemingly overnight. Walter Dahn, another member of the group, has shown more consistency. His breakthrough with vehemently painted if sometimes rather obvious imagery was followed by a much more considered phase marked by intense, frequently experimental investigation into the means of painting and its themes. Increasingly sensitive and variable, Dahn's work indicates that for all its modernity, it stands in the Romantic tradition which reached its aesthetic and intellectual culmination in Caspar David Friedrich.

K. H. Hödicke
Melancholy, 1983
Synthetic polymer on canvas,
230 x 170 cm
Nuremberg, Kunsthalle Nürnberg

Albert Oehlen
Untitled, 1988
Oil on canvas, 187 x 137 cm
Germany, private collection

Per Kirkeby
Untitled, 1983
Oil on canvas, 200 x 350 cm
Napa (CA), Hess Collection

More significant on the international scene, and more typical of the oscillation of contemporary art between skepticism and an utopian, spiritual vision, are the work and personality of Danish artist Per Kirkeby (ill. above). Not only a painter and sculptor, Kirkeby is also an essayist, novelist, film-maker, and even Arctic explorer – the quintessence of a late Alexandrian personality. The remarkable thing about his painting œuvre is that Kirkeby's admiration for great masters of the past such as Turner, Poussin, and Monet provides a catalyst for his painting without leading to eclecticism. "Paint-ings are always a strange reproduction of other paint-ings," he says, and one might add, on a higher turn of the spiral. It is astonishing to see how Kirkeby's coloris-tically sophisticated, light-flooded, structurally highly differentiated mature approach engenders a sort of "sec-ondary nature," suffused with nature's extreme, chang-ing moods yet nonetheless highly artificial in the best sense of the term.

Stylelessness as a Principle

The Italian movement known as Arte Cifra was likewise a reaction to the previous phase, in more than one sense of the word. One of its leading representatives, Sandro Chia (ill. below), summed up the process as follows: "From 1972 to mid 1975 I did something different – magic conceptualism, an attempt to get to the roots of the creative phenomenon. I wanted to find the zero point at the bottom of the creative process. But zero doesn't exist. Zero is a fiction.... When I started to paint again in 1975, it was a complete new beginning. I felt like someone recuperating from an illness." Similarly, Enzo Cucchi (p. 377 below) definitively renounced a belief in artistic progress when he stated, "We are pre-historical."

Cucchi distanced himself from what he called the "conceptualistic approach" of German artists and their "problem of historical retrospection," as seen in Kiefer's work. Yet he also distanced himself from America, say-ing it was "still much too young" to possess a memory, which for Cucchi is a necessary part of the process of image-making. As he sees it, history is "a memory. Memory comprises recollections.... This does not nec-essarily mean we have to take history literally.... I prefer legend.... Yet I understand what is behind this devotion to myth and history [on the part of artists such as Kiefer]: it's Europe.... The last word on painting will not be spoken by America, but by the 'Old World'..."

Sandro Chia
L'Ammazzapreti, 1983
Oil on canvas, 160.6 x 180.3 cm
Private collection

If we add a clear affirmation of subjective feeling, a dislike of "too much intellect" in painting, and finally the rejection of a consistent or binding style –"Inconsistency, your style is art," says Chia – we have pretty much listed the motives behind post-modernism. History becomes a grab-bag to dip into, eclecticism a principle. Art with a moral message, such as Arte Povera, is considered repressive and masochistic. The sensations experienced in the labyrinth of one's own inner being, and a subjective, private interpretation of history and mythology, become the central theme of the trans-avant-garde. Painting is sufficient unto itself.

It need no longer justify either itself or the new symbolism of its idiom: "The fall of the sacred social [orientation] corresponded to a rise of the ego...," states Germano Celant. "The 'correct' place becomes the private realm, the privileged precinct of an inner monologue, where needs become facts."

The conservative thrust of this change in attitude is obvious. Artist's replies to the visual pollution of our environment are no longer formulated in rigorous, aesthetic terms but in imagery of a highly personal and enigmatic nature. "This painting," wrote Ingo F. Walther about a *Picture sans Title* by Francesco Clemente (p. 378 above), "seeks no link with the external world; rather, it reflects the painter's inner realities." The pitfall of this neo-expressionist approach, which achieved rapid success, consists in its banalization of what is by definition significant, which occasionally takes it over the border into the superficially decorative.

Mimmo Paladino
Tango, 1983
Oil on canvas, with painted frame
and assemblage, 143 x 143 cm
Private collection

*"Every day a painting explodes over
the earth and on the shore a feeling
rises and falls with the waves flows
onwards and breaks upon the land."*
ENZO CUCCHI

Enzo Cucchi
Un sospiro di un onda, 1983
Oil on canvas, 300 x 400 cm
Courtesy Galerie Bruno
Bischofberger, Zurich

Francesco Clemente
Untitled, 1984
Oil on canvas, 274 x 477 cm
Private collection

Mimmo Paladino (p. 377 above) and Nicola De Maria do not deny their experience in abstract and conceptual art in their paintings, objects, and installations. De Maria's sensitive works and Paladino's intelligent play with metaphors are based on a much more complex and controlled conception than the approach of their countrymen. Their multifarious, highly associative imagery, combining references to concrete situations with fantastic, sometimes archaic formulas and mystical

to figurative expressionism, and to multi-layered painting grounds fraught with symbolic signs and mythical allusions. The influence of Miró and Tàpies is evident in terms of style and themes, while in terms of approach, Pollock's gestures and the materials of Arte Povera play a key role. The pictures of Frederic Amat, Miquel Barceló (ill. below), and the abstractionist José Maria Sicilia are marked by energetic attack, while Chema Cobol practices a rather overladen expressive surrealism, and signs and figures dominate in the canvases of artists such as Victor Mira, García Sevilla, Guillermo Paneque, and – in a more reserved, somewhat ennervated way – in those of María Gomez.

Unlike the Italians, Spanish and Germans, Frank Auerbach, a Berlin-born artist who lives in London, was not an initiator of the neo-expressionist wave. Rather, his work was overtaken by this development, which finally opened the eyes of people outside England to the specific qualities of Auerbach's painting. Inspired by late Expressionism, his landscapes, portraits, and figurative compositions are executed in heavy impasto, in a limited range of subtle gradations occasionally punctuated by more brilliant, even searing tones, applied with sweeping, spontaneous strokes of palette knife or broad brush. "Painting," says Auerbach, "is... a moral act."

In his early paintings an affinity with American Action Painting, above all with De Kooning, was just as evident as the influence of Auerbach's great idol, Soutine, his admiration for de Staël, and his involvement with Giacometti and, not lastly, with Francis Bacon. Auerbach's paintings are based on impassioned, thoroughly worked-out drawings, whose black lines, he says, signal the colors to be used in the ensuing painting.

In terms of attitude and attack, the work of Leon Kossoff (p. 379 above), the son of Russian emigrés living in London, bears similarities with that of Auerbach. Places in the British capital are among Kossoff's themes,

Miquel Barceló
El Paseillo, 1990
Mixed media on canvas,
203 x 303 cm
Private collection. Courtesy
Galerie Bruno Bischofberger,
Zurich

recollections, is not readily classifiable in stylistic or substantial terms.

This statement also holds, if in a different way, for the neo-expressionist painting of the younger generation of Spanish artists. The death of Franco occasioned a turn to a specifically Spanish version of international trends, but not to a denial of national traditions. The majority of younger Spanish painters share a tendency as are pictures of people which, at first glance, recall those of the Expressionists. Yet on closer scrutiny we realize that the figures, as David Sylvester notes, do not play a role assigned them by the artist. For instead of being characters, they are creatures that are there only to be looked at, painted in matte, opaque colors suffused, here and there, by an accent of illumination.

Aggression and Self-Exploration

Quite different sources from the subjective mythologies of the Italians and the process-oriented gestural approach of Scottish artist Bruce McLean (p. 380) are tapped by Maria Lassnig (ill. below). Devoted to an exploration of self, and the body which is its vessel, the Austrian artist's very original work has run counter to current tendencies and only recently been accorded the attention it deserves. Lassnig's specific form of "body art" has nothing in common with happening or Fluxus, performance, or Body Art per se. She has never been tempted to abandon painting for one or the other current trend or fad. (The relatively realistic phase she passed through during a stay in America was a temporary exception.) Lassnig's approach, long rather restrictively defined by her own term "body awareness," cannot be called egocentric in the popular meaning of the word, despite, or perhaps because of the fact that she makes herself an object of study. Lassnig's special ego trip is undergone by proxy, because her profound exploration of self is designed to communicate what she discovers to others. Her personal experiments are simultaneously investigations into the issues of painting, espe-

cially into the complex question of how mental and emotional experience can be conveyed in visual terms.

Lassnig's palette continually tends towards grey, the universal color that contains all others. Yet paradoxically, her figures appear not precarious and complex, but forceful and evocatively symbolic. The chain of tradition that extends from the self-confident self-portraits of Velázquez, Munch, and van Gogh, through van Gogh's

Hermann Nitsch
Orgy Mystery Theater, 1984
Dispersion on burlap, 290 x 190 cm
Italy, private collection

tormented self-portrait with severed ear, to Lassnig's own crouching, grotesquely distorted figure, is no imaginary ancestral gallery. It is an indication of spiritual affinities, and as such, gives ironic, hybrid evidence of the artist's own – female – self-confidence. Although long befriended with Arnulf Rainer and closely associated with the early Austrian avant-garde around the legendary Monsignore Mauer, Lassnig has inspired no school, though she has provided crucial stimulus to younger Austrian artists like Hubert Schmalix, Siegfried Anzinger, and Erwin Bohatsch. In Herbert Brandl's work, the spontaneous painting act and a detachment from his own activity blend in an intelligent way which is without direct predecessors.

The Dialectics of Life and Death

The work of Arnulf Rainer holds a special place not only within Austrian art but within European art as a whole. It has repeatedly been directly linked with L'art informel and Tachism, perhaps because of the "perspectives of destruction" which followed Rainer's beginnings in Fantastic Realism and which evinced a dissolution of

Bruce McLean
Yucca Gloriosa, 1980
Acrylic and wax crayon on photo
paper, 179 x 137 cm
Private collection

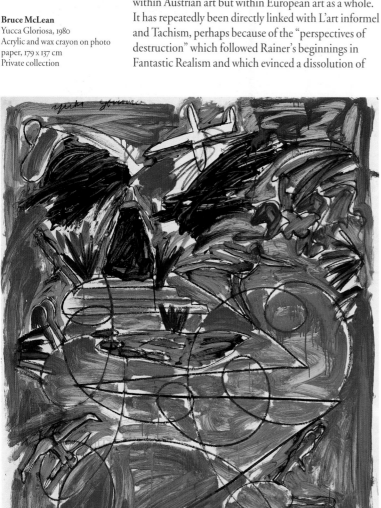

form and fine articulation of the picture plane reminiscent of these styles.

But there is a deeper layer in Rainer's work, represented by the gesturally expressive *Übermalungen*, or over-paintings, begun as early as the first years of the 1950s (p. 381 above). These set the thorough bass that runs through his œuvre: the dialectics of life and death. The image was obscured, destroyed, in order to bring to light something new. In the dark, sometimes jet black overpaintings, in which a deep blue occasionally seemed encaged, a narrow zone of light shone through – a source of illumination, or its last refuge? "Everything depends on this small remainder," the artist says.

The contained, masochistically restrained expressiveness of these formulations oscillates between a "burial" or "drowning" of painting (Rainer's words) and its rebirth in an awareness of death. The result is a mood of meditative calm, the complement of a deep-seated existential anxiety. Grünewald's *Isenheim Altarpiece* is the past work of art that has impressed Rainer most. The crucifix became one of his early basic forms, the cross understood as "an abbreviation for the human face," a theme that has fascinated 20th-century artists from Javlensky and Mondrian all the way down to Newman and Rothko. Faces, both his own and the grotesque heads of neoclassical sculptor Franz Xaver Messerschmidt, the demonic masks of Hieronymus Bosch, the distorted faces of Goya's victims and madmen, the merciless self-portrayals of Rembrandt and van Gogh, the grimaces of the mentally ill, even death masks, have followed Rainer throughout his career. His obsessive grimace paintings compellingly evoke a despairing expressiveness, an existential anxiety which has frequently, if mistakenly, been religiously over-interpreted in terms of a negative theology.

Rainer's expressiveness has little in common with gestural abstraction or Action Painting, for he never entirely reveals his inmost self. The over-paintings and *Zumalungen*, or total over-paintings, he says, "are not abstractions, but my disguises, or, as it were, a psychophysical reproduction." Rainer's œuvre spans the poles of resignation and aggression, sadness and anger, concealment and disclosure, ranges from the self-castigating control of a passionate temperament seen in the early monochrome imagery to the unleashed, explosive gesturalism of the brightly hued, if not always entirely convincing recent work. As Armin Zweite points out, this is an artist who articulates "the problem of the individual in contemporary society, his lack of ties, his helplessness and despair."

The Viennese movement known as "Actionism," especially the *Orgy Mystery Theater* of Hermann Nitsch (p. 380 above and p. 585), is ultimately rooted in Austrian Catholicism. Its celebration of black masses, with their suspenseful combination of heathen and Christian elements, perhaps represent Austria's most important contribution to contemporary art, second only to Rainer's work. It should be noted that Nitsch, author and director of his highly individual Gesamtkunstwerk, also considers himself a painter, and the relics of his activities to be paintings in their own right.

When we recall that Dionysus was not only the god of ecstasy and revelling, but the god of tragedy and death, we might be justified in calling Swiss artist Mar-

tin Disler a Dionysian painter (p. 382). Disler works at night, listening to music. His gestural approach owes much to Pollock and to European Tachism, "due to its structure, its frenzy, and perhaps also due to *one* of its roots, which lies in psychoanalytic symbolism," as Dieter Koepplin points out. In Disler's paintings and drawings love and death mingle. Despite the artist's reflective detachment, certain autobiographical references do appear. The frenzy of his brushwork is a painterly expression of deep existential unrest.

Like Rainer's work, the drawings and paintings of Walter Stöhrer (p. 382) have been associated with Tachism and L'art informel. At the most this holds only for his early style, which was inspired by the gesturalism of Schultze, Brüning, or Götz. What distinguishes Stöhrer from the majority of his contemporaries who work in an expressive, spontaneous vein is a combination of sweeping brushwork with graphic precision, explosiveness with control, temperament with a fine sense of form. This combination is the result of an unusual capacity for concentration, trained by the Grieshaber student's practice in the dry-point tech-

Arnulf Rainer
Michelangelo, 1967
Oil on synthetic sheet, 118 x 88 cm
Napa (CA), Hess Collection

Arnulf Rainer
Macrocosm, 1994/95
Oil and appliqués on textured cardboard, 102 x 73 cm
Courtesy Galerie Ulysses, Vienna

Martin Disler
Untitled, 1980
Acrylic on cotton, 172 x 256 cm
Private collection

Neil Jenney
Litter and Bin, 1970
Acrylic and pencil on canvas,
155.6 x 159.4 cm
USA, private collection

nique, which permits of no corrections or second thoughts. Stöhrer's work evinces a quite unique counterpoint between dynamic swaths of paint, graphic lineatures, and quotes from texts in which painting becomes calligraphy. Series and cycles of canvases are the underlying principle of his oeuvre, for, as the artist says, "I see paintings, too, in terms of sequences. I think that you cannot even view one painting independently of the next."

The gestural art of French painter Eugène Leroy (p. 383 above), which was only very belatedly discovered, reflects none of the obsession with self-exploration seen in the work of younger artists. Leroy, born in 1910, has spent most of his life in Lille. It was not until 1992, at

documenta 9, that the world became aware of the mastery of his apparently gestural abstractions. Though it is going too far to maintain, as Jan Hoet did, that Leroy's work is "painting in the sense of a Titian or Giorgione," his gestural expressionism is truly not an end in itself. Rather, it is always based on some real subject, be it figure or landscape. The real is mingled with the unreal frequently to the point of indistinguishability, with an emphasis on the paint material itself and its dynamic movement which has increased as Leroy's career has progressed. Still, the subject remains a concern even in his late work, which includes self-portraits admired by many younger artists such as Baselitz.

Walter Stöhrer
Untitled, 1984
Mixed media on paper,
78 x 54.5 cm
Germany, private collection

Susan Rothenberg
Untitled, 1979
Acrylic and glossy enamel on
paper, 107.3 x 76.8 cm
Private collection

Jonathan Borofsky
Canoe Painting at 2.491.537,
1978
Acrylic on composition board,
two parts, 235 x 150 cm
Formerly Saatchi Collection,
London

Eugène Leroy
Green, 1963
Oil on canvas, 161.5 x 129.5 cm
Private collection

Critique and Submission

There is more than one way to make art, more than one way to live and be happy, says American artist Jonathan Borofsky (ill. above left). Known for his early paintings, but even more for his monumental and ironic installations and figures, Borofsky's ideology is undogmatic openness. He takes ideas wherever they offer themselves, in Magritte or Fellini, Dalí or Disney, Pop or Conceptual Art, reality or dream, childhood experi-

Neil Jenney (p. 382 above) began, as one of the first representatives of American "New Image Painting," to translate real and Pop Art elements, and an as yet sparing figurative iconography, into a highly charged painterly approach. This set the stage for the expressively symbolic and metaphoric style of Louisa Chase, the pictorial signs of Susan Rothenberg, and the enigmatic picture-narratives of David Salle with their multifarious mixtures of styles and moods.

Nancy Spero
The Black and the Red III, 1994
Handprint and collage on paper,
panel 15 and 16 (of 22),
49.5 x 245 cm (each)
Munich, Barbara Gross Galerie

ences or adult confrontations with mass society. An intelligent, virtuoso eclectic, Borofsky believes that borrowing something from other people means learning something from them. His work, rich in figures and allusions and stories, has long since broken through the boundaries of painting and expanded into an effectively staged, as it were static theater, which the artist associates with a "magic circus." His sometimes surreal phantasmagorias are based as much on actual experience as on the projection of inner sensations outwards.

Rothenberg's paintings and drawings (p. 382 below) hold an ambiguous balance between personal expression and objectified form, between Cézanne, to whom she owes the spontaneity of her notations, and the Expressionists, whose concise, agitated lineatures she subjects to intellectual control – a woman artist exploring the potential of diverse styles and epochs.

The key theme of David Salle (p. 384 above), who is a few years younger than Rothenberg, is the human, especially the female, figure. In the footsteps of Picabia and

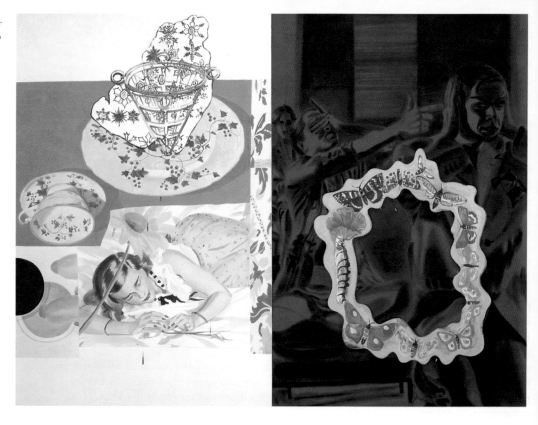

David Salle
Pink Teacup, 1995
Oil and acrylic on canvas,
183 x 245 cm
Zurich, Galerie Bruno
Bischofberger

Leon Golub
Mercenaries V, 1984
Acrylic on cotton, 305 x 437 cm
Formerly Saatchi Collection,
London

Polke, employing projections, black and white photos,
film, translucent paint layers, and many other techniques, Salle investigates the body as a vessel of human
existence. In terms of technique, content and form, his
work holds a strange and quite original balance between
history and contemporaneity, psychological and physiological reality, between high and trivial art, eroticism and
pornography, historicist pathos and banality. Salle's
imagery is suffused with the skepticism of a culture of
surfeit, as well as with a covert yearning to overcome it.

A belated but all the more radical turn to fundamental feminism was reflected in the mature work of Nancy
Spero (p. 383). Born in 1926, as late as the early 1970s
Spero could still devote two painting sequences to
Antonin Artaud, father of absurd theater and known
misogynist (*Artaud Paintings* and *Codex Artaud*). But for
over twenty years now, men have been entirely absent
from the panel-like series – paper bands with collaged
figures and text fragments – of the wife of artist Leon
Golub and mother of several children. The dominant
theme of Spero's recent work is the body of the self-
confident, active woman, independent and sexually
self-determined.

Men may not have vanished from Leon Golub's
work (ill. below), which combines pure painting with
script, usually inspired by graffiti and slogans scribbled
on city walls. But his male figures tend to be gross urban
characters of the type the artist says he observes with
growing dismay. The anonymous figures of Golub's
anti-war paintings of the 1970s have increasingly taken
on personal features. Instead of Vietnam, he now
addresses the brutality of surburban life, an issue most
of us are reluctant to face.

Eric Fischl (p. 385 above) was a co-student of Salle's
at the California Institute of the Arts, in Valencia near
Los Angeles, which is known for its experimental atmosphere. Fischl's theme is the deadly boredom endemic to
affluent Western societies, Baudelaire's *ennui* brought
up to date. In scenes of life on the beach, in front of a
television set, or in the midst of the monotony of the

American suburbs, Fischl shows how human beings come to treat themselves as objects. The relationship of the figures to the pictorial space signals isolation, lives lived in parallel to one another instead of with one another. Even in the orgiastic, obscene scenes, immobility prevails, recalling a movie still.

While Fischl unmasks the middle-class monotony he for a time attempted to escape as a hippie, most representatives of "Free Figuration" in France raise monotony to a principle (and thus inadvertently reveal the limits of their freedom). The statement of painter and performer Jürgen Klauke to the effect that now, for the first time in history, serious art is being sold and marketed like entertainment, applies to many of the young French artists.

Going beyond certain affirmative tendencies in the work of camp followers of the Neo-Expressionist scene, Free Figuration in part signals an uncritical submission to the laws of the entertainment industry. A defector from the avant-garde cause, Jean Clair, has made himself the prophet of this counter-movement. Hervé de Rosa announced his "total rejection of the intellectual and critical discourse," in favor of painting as "fun rock." François Boisrond says, "I have the impression that I learn more when I watch bad films or see bad painting," and is ostensibly proud of "accepting a stupid culture that is fascinating."

Not only comics and science-fiction but gruesome war movies have become the source of intelligent young people's technicolor dazes. Rejecting unrealistic dreams of a New Human in an earthly paradise, they have instead become fanatics of resignation. This represents, writes Marie-Luise Syring, "a trivialization of the so-called *modern myths.*"

The art of Jean-Charles Blais leaves the vulgar, programmatic infantilism of many of his generation behind (ill. below). His unconventional treatment of familiar commonplace material – Blais paints over torn posters –

avoids the cliché by being formally coherent and skilled in execution. The works were evidently stimulated by the figures of the early Malevich, and perhaps also by the later, post-Suprematist ones. Other possible influences are van Gogh, and, very likely, Léger and his "Proletarian Olympus," whose optimism about the future, however, is tempered by skepticism with Blais. Blais's heavily contoured, super-individual, monumental figures suggest a humanity made insecure by the complexity of the modern world.

Eric Fischl
The Old Man's Boat and the Old Man's Dog, 1982
Oil on canvas, 213.4 x 213.4 cm
Formerly Saatchi Collection, London

Jean-Charles Blais
Untitled, 1986
Paint on torn poster, 173 x 238 cm
Courtesy Galerie Yvon Lambert, Paris

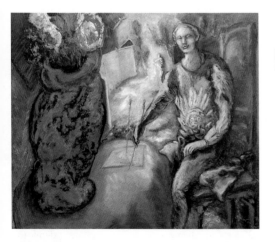

Gérard Garouste
Columbia, 1981
Oil on canvas, 250.8 x 294.6 cm
New York, Leo Castelli Gallery

Keith Haring
Toledo, 1987
Acrylic on canvas, 244 x 376 cm
Düsseldorf, Galerie Hans Mayer

Even more complex, allusive, and ambivalent is the work of Gérard Garouste (p. 385 below left). The French artist's approach to painting is characterized by a blend of unleashed temperament and skeptical intelligence, a blend very close to that of Romantic irony. Garouste's expressive paintings reflect the consciousness of a late epoch, a disillusioned, fragmented reality devoid of myths, as well as a certain nostalgic melancholy. This comes through despite the Baroque verve of the brushwork, for the imagery teems with figures and associations and barely concealed historical reminiscences. Anyone familiar with history knows that premonitions of the world's end were not foreign even to an epoch as vital as the Baroque.

Pictures from the Underground

One of the most salient contributions made to fine art by representatives of a sub-culture is that of grafitti. Dubuffet and others began at an early date to collect and adapt the figures and inscriptions in which outsiders and underdogs, children and the mentally ill, found a means of self-expression. But it was not until the 1970s that the attention of the public and the art trade was drawn to grafitti as an art form in its own right. The development was spearheaded by the "pieces" sprayed by young "writers" on New York subway cars, in which an untamed, under-class creativity found explosive expression. In the meantime, mass, puerile imitation in America and Europe has undermined the cre-

Hervé Télémaque
Port-au-Prince, the Rose, 1988
Acrylic on canvas, 200 x 310 cm
France, private collection

Keith Haring
Untitled, 1988
Acrylic on canvas,
152 x 152 cm
Private collection

ative potential of such work and reduced it to hollow gesturing.

A quite different impetus lay behind the pointed critique of civilization and culture mounted by the "Sprayer of Zurich," Harald Nägeli, a trained psychologist. Nägeli's stick-men raised the ire of the philistines, who immediately – and of course successfully – appealed to the authorities to do something about this desecration. After Nägeli was tracked down by Interpol and spent several terms in jail, his subversive activities were gradually legalized, which could not help but rob them of their force.

The work of New York artist Keith Haring, in contrast (p. 386 above and below right), raised grafitti to the status of fine art, without sacrificing its freshness and impact. Haring, who would later succumb to Aids, was honored by inclusion in the documenta, which immediately caused the prices of his paintings to skyrocket. This was in the mid-1980s, as, grotesquely, the city of New York was spending four million dollars to destroy the then still very original imagery of the "writers," from whose ranks Haring himself had so rapidly risen to prominence.

The Hispanic-American artist Jean-Michel Basquiat (ill. above) died in 1988 not of Aids, like Haring, but from an overdose of heroin. He too began as a grafitti painter in New York, but developed beyond it to transfer to canvas his critical, often macabre, graphic picture stories about the situation of underdogs and under-privileged minorities.

Haring also depicted himself in these narratives, in bizarrely expressive, near-portrait likenesses, playing the role of an acutely endangered wanderer along the thin line between life and death. Nor did he gloss over his adaptation and submission to the rituals of the elite who lionized him, the self-denying, prostituting strategies of survival which were nonetheless unable to prevent his premature death at the age of 27.

Explorations into High and Low Culture

Perhaps the most prolific, restless, humorous, and at the same time most enigmatic contemporary artist is – or at least was, for a considerable period of time – Sigmar Polke (pp. 387–389). The rational and the irrational, irony and magic, combine in his key works with an employment of highly original, experimental techniques, pointedly expressed ideas, and aesthetic concision.

In Polke's imagery, elements of the real are confronted with elements of fantasy and pure idea, and all take their place in a holistic pictorial reality which

Jean-Michel Basquiat
Zydeco, 1984
Acrylic and oil crayon on canvas,
three parts, 219 x 518 cm
Private collection. Courtesy
Galerie Bruno Bischofberger,
Zurich

"I wanted to be a star not a gallery mascot."
JEAN-MICHEL BASQUIAT

Sigmar Polke
Bunnies, 1966
Oil on canvas, 150 x 100 cm
Washington, Hirshhorn Museum
and Sculpture Garden

Sigmar Polke
The Raven, 1966
Dispersion on textile,
190 x 200 cm
Bad Münstereifel, Galerie Klein

encompasses both what can be experienced through the senses and what can only be mentally conceived. Polke's procedure is not analytic but synthetic in character. When he painted screen-dot pictures in the 1960s, instead of mechanically resolving a given image into a system of dots like Lichtenstein, Polke began with the dots themselves, consciously arranging them to form a vital, visually vibrating image based on intrinsic aesthetic laws.

Polke's explorations are devoted as much to the mass media and the trivialities of mass culture as they are to received artistic traditions and techniques. He also delves into physical and chemical processes, such as the changes caused in specially sensitized paint layers and the changes in their appearance due to the effects of light, heat, humidity – or even the viewers' reactions to the work. Thanks to these unpredictable changes in the materials and their fragile nature, the factor of time enters into Polke's open-ended imagery.

It is very much in character when the artist states that his untraditional and anti-traditional pictures were done under the supervision of a "higher being." Such are the risks he takes in exploring unexplored territory, so

innovative is his creative process, that they can lead to trance-like moments in which the sense of being a mere tool of the universal spirit can overcome even an ironic and skeptical mind. But masquerade or not, Polke's statement reveals the seriousness of his untiring attempts to pin down and capture both visible and invisible realities, in the frustrating knowledge of their ultimate elusiveness.

Encompassing both high and low culture, Polke's oeuvre paradigmatically illustrates that an uncompromising openness of artistic practice, beyond all conventions and ideologies, need not necessarily lead to conformity, affirmation, or an escape into arbitrariness. Polke stands as an example of the fact that an artist, even on today's scene, need not sacrifice his intelligence in order to be successful. Admittedly, in recent years some of the artist's work has shown a certain discrepancy between effort and result, between a huge format and relatively unexciting ideas and composition. In this regard the work of even this ingenious but inconsistent artist reflects the insecurity of a period of crisis in which everything has become *questionable* – in both the literal and figurative sense.

Sigmar Polke
Lovers II, 1965
Oil and lacquer on canvas,
200 x 140 cm
Private collection

14

At this Writing

Artistic Issues at the Turn of the Millennium
Painting in the Age of Electronic Media

Art always reacts to the period in which it is made, and to the problems and issues of that period. Hence, strictly speaking, there is no such thing as "timeless" art. There never was. Any artist who refuses to accept this insight and attempts to escape from the present day, risks artistic failure. This was recently illustrated by the short-lived phenomenon of post-modernism. In a period of upheaval and insecurity like our own, which has thrown overboard every universal scheme and system, art can no longer hope to proclaim indubitable truths. Even the border between "high and low" – the title of a 1990 exhibition at the Museum of Modern Art, New York – begins to blur.

Thus the painting of the final decade before the year 2000 has evinced no predominating tendency, no forward-looking avant-garde theory, no standard-setting group, not even a dominant artistic personality, comparable to a Pollock or a Bacon – not to mention a Picasso

Peter Halley
CUSeeMe, 1995
Acrylic, Day-Glo and Roll-a-Tex
on canvas, 274.5 x 280 cm
Munich, Goetz Collection

– around mid-century. Though Warhol's part cynical, part melancholy prognosis that everyone would be famous for at least a quarter of an hour has not been fulfilled, it no longer seems as as naive during our own increasingly fast-paced period as it did during the artist's lifetime.

All rules have gone out of force. Even the most ambitious theories of art have an individualistic tinge nowadays, and can hardly claim universal validity. Intellectual reflection, an essential component of contemporary artistic activity, is frequently indulged in at the cost of creativity. Sometimes the gap between the philosophical and theoretical ambitiousness of a work of art and the banality of its statement grows so large that it takes itself ad absurdum.

Among younger artists, apart from a few exceptions, the idea of "immediacy" is no longer a concern. Today's art no longer establishes guidelines, it seeks orientation; it no longer makes statements, it asks questions – questions about a reality growing ever more complex, and about the role of art itself within this reality. Wherever it sets its sights on that ominous "social relevance" so central to the generation of Vietnam and campus revolts, even in an honorable commitment to the marginal groups of society, art generally flips over into propaganda whose social effectiveness tends to be null.

An awareness of these problems is shared by serious artists everywhere, not only in the Western world but in Eastern Europe, Latin America, and China, countries where critical reflection was long present under the surface but only recently gained the opportunity for public expression. This basic, shared awareness could contribute to an overcoming of deep-seated prejudices, and to that "decolonialization of the mind" promoted by Edward W. Said. Yet in the course of such efforts, we must beware of succumbing to the old illusion of an all-encompassing "world art" or, indeed, "world culture." Because that would entail confusing a beneficial and stimulating cultural permeability with that sterile sameness which is just as fatal in the artistic and cultural domain as it is in the political. As Hans Belting says, "There is no universal conceptual scheme to cover the diversity of world cultures." The defects of large-scale projects such as "Magiciens de la Terre" at Centre Pompidou, Paris, in 1989, and documenta 9 in Kassel three

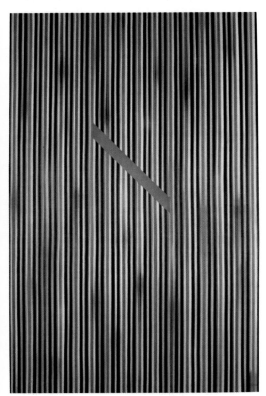

years later, resulted from just such misunderstandings, as reflected in the idealistic but diffuse conceptions on which they were based. In the case of documenta this idealism, paradoxically, was paired with a bias against the art of Eastern nations.

Yet these are not the only reasons for skepticism with regard to the question whether something in the nature of a global exhibition of the arts is possible in our time (or ever was). In view of the enormous variety of positions, a superhuman effort of coordination would be required to prevent such an exhibition from becoming a mere congeries of more or less unrelated works – unless one set out from the start to illustrate the "New Unmethodicalness."

In painting today, anything goes, from a rigorously conceptual or even "radical" painting all the way to elementary paint-for-paint's-sake. The issue of abstraction versus objectivity has become anachronistic. As Gerhard Finckh notes, the crux of the matter is "determining where one stands, making an analysis, and building a basis.... The 'Cry, Art, Cry' [of Lucas Moser, early 15th century] is something other media now lay claim to.... Bruce Nauman's documenta 9 video-audio installation 'Help Me' is one of the few successful examples of this."

Allan McCollum
Plaster Surrogates, 1982–1990
Plaster and email, 10 parts,
51 x 410 cm
Haigerloch, Sabine Schwenk
Collection

"I want my paintings to attempt a belief and sincerity which I, as an artist, don't necessarily feel, and certainly don't feel continuously. I want them to have a relationship to the world, to know how the world works and, nevertheless, to retain an optimism." ROSS BLECKNER

Ross Bleckner
Wreath, 1986
Oil on canvas, 274 x 183 cm
Private collection

Artistic investigations can lead to highly divagating results even within the œuvre of a single artist, as indicated by the paintings of Ross Bleckner (p. 391 below). The American artist produced, almost concurrently, compositions of abstract bands in vibrant colors (*The Arrangement of Things*, 1982–1985), and surreal, universalistic visions (*In Memory*, 1987). If such works have a common denominator, it is the Vanitas motif. Yet even a motif of this kind, says the painter, has the situation of the artist as its theme, and concerns itself with this self-reflection.

Bleckner's friend Peter Halley (p. 390) paints imagery whose great color sensibility and precise formal geometry recall both Albers and the Bauhaus and Barnett Newman. Though Halley accepts Bleckner's approach, he considers it to involve a critique of the "diverse idealisms of Plato, Descartes, and Mies [van der Rohe]." For his own part Halley attempts to reduce Constructivism, Minimalism, and Color Field Painting to their fundamental source, their "sociological basis" – the square as a symbol of the prison cell, the color red as an allusion to the dangers of technology. Luckily the pictures bear up well under the philosophical weight, derived from French savants Jean Baudrillard and Michel Foucault, they are made to carry.

In sharp contrast to Halley's approach stands that of Philip Taaffe (ill. above), as well as that of Christopher Wool (ill. below), with its employment of stencils and illegible sequences of letters. Taaffe, who lives in New York and on the Gulf of Naples, considers his paintings a contribution to mass culture, filtered through critical choice. In their continuation of the "New Ornamentation" on a higher twist of the spiral, Taaffe's works combine substantial and formal elements from two cultures, Arabian and European past and present, whereby the decorative merges with the aesthetic in an effective way.

Objective configurations floating free across the pictorial plane are the theme of Terry Winter's painting, which in the 1980s held an intermediate position between abstraction and figuration. His more recent work, with its graphic and calligraphic networks, tends to non-objectivity despite the suggestions of organic forms it contains (p. 393 above right).

A tension between spontaneously notated and planned, stringent, and dissolved forms, between color fields and linear sheaves, characterizes the compositions of Jonathan Lasker (p. 394 below left). They might be described as a late version of Mannerism, especially as the artist consciously employs historical quotations from a variety of periods and climes. David Reed's painting (p. 394 above) is inspired by the movies, and accordingly uses the wide-screen format. As in the case of Newman, whom Reed admires, his paintings cannot be taken in at a single glance. The viewer, Reed hopes, will make the effort to visually construct "a whole out of parts" – a statement that might have come from Newman. Yet Newman's theme was the sublime, whereas Reed addresses the fantastic, as illustrated by the agi-

Joseph Marioni
Blue Painting, 1994
Acrylic on cotton, 56 x 51 cm
Vienna, Rosemarie Schwarzwalder Collection

Terry Winters
Phase Plane Portrait, 1994
Oil on cotton, 274.3 x 365.8 cm
New York, collection of the artist

Left:
Frederic Thursz
Vixen, 1989
Oil on canvas, 146 x 73 x 5 cm
Private collection

tated shapes in which mundane things are monumentalized and surrealistically alienated, if not always entirely
convincingly.

Similarly, the long series of *Surrogates* produced by
Allan McCollum (p. 391), plaster casts of various sizes
painted black and framed in various colors, articulate a
critique of society and its institutions, as well as of the
"elitist," exclusive original work of art. Another instance,
that is, of art directed against art, against the "fiction" of
the autonomy of the arts and their authenticity, in the
footsteps of the ubiquitous Baudrillard. Whether and to
what extent the messages of McCollum's "contextual
painting" (Peter Weibel) reach the addressee are questions that, as so often in art, remain open.

A different case entirely is the theoretically founded
yet ideologically unburdened *Radical Painting* of American artist Joseph Marioni (ill. above left) or his compatriot Frederic Thursz (ill. left). Both share a conviction
that a painting should represent nothing other than
itself. A painting cannot resolve the internal contradiction of attempting to be something it is not, says Marioni. The result of his considerations are subtly nuanced
monochrome images in changing colors. Thursz, in
contrast, restricts himself to a black whose differentiated
texture becomes perceptible only on patient observation. Unlike Ad Reinhardt, the artist does not expunge
every last trace of the personal hand. Rather, as Hanne-
lore Kesting notes, the "physical texture" of his works
"becomes a substantial component," that is, serves to
convey content.

Much the same holds for the monochrome works of
Jürgen Meyer with their impasto paint application.
The formally disciplined, precisely executed painting
series and painting-sculpture combinations of Heinrich
Dunst are convincing enough in their own right to
do without the theories with which they are encumbered.

Page 392 above:
Philip Taaffe
Bad Seed, 1996
Mixed media on canvas,
262 x 282 cm
Germany, private collection

Page 392 below:
Christopher Wool
Untitled, 1993
Enamel paint and aluminum,
230 x 172 cm
Germany, private collection

David Reed
349, 1996
Oil and alkyd resin on canvas,
137 x 300 cm
Cologne, Galerie Rolf Ricke

As little as Ad Reinhardt brought to canvas the last painting anyone would ever be able to do, just as little has "art & language" exhausted the theme of image and language. Richard Prince (ill. below), who earlier worked in a surrealist style, used the media as ready-mades, and combined imagery with typography, now paints jokes in acrylic on canvas, precisely lettered and in carefully chosen color combinations. According to Prince, his intention is to make paintings in which there is nothing to interpret, nothing to speculate about – another method, if a rather obvious one, of reacting against visual pollution.

The intellectually more challenging paintings of French artist Bernard Frize (p. 395 below right), with their multifarious layerings, abrupt caesuras, and exchange of figure and ground, and the ambivalent, as it were diagnostic works of the Belgian artist Luc Tuymans (p. 395 below left) with their austere coloration, both illustrate in different ways the attempts of young artists to explore the potentials still available to painting in this late modernist age, without resorting to substantial or formal borrowings or making historical compromises.

Painting in Russia and China is likewise marked by a

Jonathan Lasker
Reasonable Painting, 1990
Oil on cotton, 162.5 x 203 cm
Private collection

Richard Prince
Untitled, 1996
Acrylic and silkscreen on canvas,
221 x 147.3 cm
Courtesy Jablonka Galerie, Cologne

Ilya Kabakov
Holidays No. 9, 1987
Oil and rosettes on canvas,
100 x 160 cm
Private collection

skepticism that takes nothing for granted. In the meantime, artists in these nations have begun to ask the same questions as their Western counterparts. But their questions have a stronger political and socio-critical thrust, and are concerned less with issues immanent to art. The

reasons for this are obvious. In the periods of dictatorship and isolation, inofficial art understood itself largely as a weapon in the battle against an unloved political system imposed upon the people from above. Its ammunition consisted above all in irony, as seen even in the

Below:
Bernard Frize
Spitz, 1991
Acrylic and resin on canvas,
254 x 361 cm
London, Tate Gallery. Courtesy
Frith Stret Gallery, London

still dictatorially governed China, whose economic opening to the West has started to bring sand into the totalitarian machinery.

Not only current Chinese but Russian art still shows evidence of the intellectual and emotional sources from which it arose, whether it be the persiflage of Socialist Realism conducted by "Soz Art" or the conceptual work

Left:
Luc Tuymans
Dildo, 1996
Oil on canvas, 69,5 x 43.7 cm
Munich, Goetz Collection

Dimitri Prigov
Nietzsche with Hitler
on His Hip, 1994
India ink and acrylic on paper,
130 x 190 cm
Aachen, Ludwig Forum für
Internationale Kunst

A quite different thrust is seen in the painterly and formal problems addressed by the twenty-year younger Nikolai Filatov (p. 397 above). His expressive paintings have a bold coloration and reveal a spiritual attitude that definitely recall the mythologically founded hopes for the future of the German Expressionists, Franz Marc foremost. The realistic imagery of Alexander Petrov, in contrast (ill. below right), takes affirmative Socialist Realism ad absurdum, in terms of both style and content. The suggestive force of Petrov's paintings occasionally recalls Hopper.

Erik Bulatov (ill. below left) mixes linguistic and painterly, realistic and symbolic, aesthetic and literary elements with ironic intentions, whether to show up the contradiction between private atmosphere and state deprivatization or to allude to the insecurity of a crumbling empire in an image of a simultaneously rising and setting sun, combined with Soviet emblems with hammer and sickle, hovering over a globe (*Sunrise or Sunset*, 1989; Aachen, Ludwig Forum für Internationale Kunst). Whether Georgi Pusenkoff (p. 397 below) paints large-format abstract stripe canvases with indeterminate upper and lower edges or quotes famous colleagues past and present – from Bronzino through Malevich and Kabakov to Lichtenstein – the focus of his imaginative variations is always the pictorial space. For as Bulatov says, "space is what counts."

The end of political and social illusions is even more compellingly evoked by the pictorial and calligraphic signs of Dimitri Prigov (ill. above) whose work provides evidence of the fact that the Russian Conceptualists extended their radically pessimistic critique to the period after the fall of the Soviet Empire. Also concep-

now being done in Moscow. This holds despite the fact that important Russian protagonists such as Vitali Komar and Alexander Melamit, or Ilya Kabakov, now live in the United States.

Kabakov's works (pp. 395 and 575), the earlier paintings as well as the later installations that brought him fame, have a narrative character. His style is accordingly realistic to naturalistic. Kabakov's subject is human loneliness in general, and that of the regimented Soviet citizen in particular. His more recent works demonstrate with dramatic pointedness the jeopardy in which culture, East and West, now finds itself, and the struggle for survival of humane values.

Erik Bulatov
Ne Prislonjazja, 1987
Oil on canvas, 240 x 170 cm
Basel, Öffentliche Kunstsamm-
lung Basel, Kunstmuseum

Alexander Petrov
The House by the Railway, 1981
Oil on canvas, 150 x 120 cm
Beijing, Ludwig Museum of
International Art

Grigori Bruskin
Alefbet No. 2, 1988
Oil on canvas, 116 x 88 cm
Emden, Kunsthalle in Emden

Nikolai Filatov
Crystalline Man, 1987
Oil on canvas, 200 x 150 cm
Emden, Kunsthalle in Emden

tually oriented in their ambiguity are the paintings and installations of Komar and Melamit. After being deprived of their work permits and even prohibited from visiting art exhibitions, the two went to Israel in 1977, and the year after to New York. Their dual experiences in East and West provide the basis for sarcastic and ironic works which point up the interchangeability of personalities and systems, and blithely employ a range of past and contemporary styles and techniques. Komar and Melamit's unmasking of phraseology, personality cult, and false myths is merciless, yet not embittered. A humorous detachment, with undertones of nostalgia, makes their work convincing.

Mention should be made of an outsider of great originality who was born in Russia and now makes his home in New York. Grigori Bruskin (ill. above left) creates cyclical depictions combining image with script in which Jewish spirituality and religiosity take on a compelling form for which there is no comparison in contemporary art.

No review of the art of our era would be complete without a reference to a critical style of painting in China which, as Dieter Ronte says, "does not conform to the Chinese cultural authorities' definition of art." Practiced largely by younger artists between 30 and 40 working in oils, this approach developed with extreme rapidity in a country where the oil medium was unknown just over a century ago.

Though Western influences are taken up, these are reformulated and blended with elements of the Chinese tradition to produce imagery of an amazing originality and great diversity. Abundant evidence of this was provided by the first comprehensive review shown in Germany, at the Kunstmuseum Bonn in 1996. The quality of

the work now going on in China corresponds to the growing number of Chinese collectors of contemporary art, a phenomenon long overlooked in the West. Several European and American galleries immediately drew their conclusions and opened branches in the Middle Kingdom.

Despite certain realistic and formalistic developments in Chinese art of the late 1970s and early 1980s,

hardly anyone would have predicted what has come about in the years following Mao's cultural revolution and the 1989 massacre on the Square of Heavenly Peace. There can be no doubt that the development is still in its beginnings. It is being carried forward not so much by the expatriates among Chinese artists as by those who live and work in their own country, despite the fact that

Georgi Pusenkoff
From Malevich to Kabakov, 1994
Acrylic on canvas, 220 x 350 cm
St. Petersburg, Russian State
Museum

Dai Guangyu
Wall Landscape, 1993
Oil on canvas, three parts,
105 x 125 cm (each)

they rely to a large extent on foreign customers, as the frequent employment of Latin characters as typographical elements in their paintings indicates.

Contemporary Chinese painting evinces an astonishing stylistic range, from realism to serial abstraction, from surrealism to approaches verging on strict monochromy. In terms of subject matter, amazingly frank or ironically tinged criticism of living conditions (and hence of the regime) is accompanied by a focus on the human body and sexuality which surpasses even that of American and European art. As an example of the former category let us take Zhang Xiaogang's three-part *Large Family* of 1995 (p. 399 above). Picture no. 1 represents a couple, no. 3 depicts two young men, and only picture no. 2 shows a wife and husband with a child – a boy, of course. True large families with several children

are just as undesired by the Chinese authorities as are girls.

Dai Guangyu uses different means to break taboos, because the obscene, as he says, is not permitted despite the ancient and wonderfully beautiful erotic depictions of Chinese art. This is precisely why Dai makes it his theme. In his *Wall Landscape* (ill. above) – the title itself is ambiguous – the artist inserts several overpainted portraits of Chairman Mao into a series of Marilyn Monroe photos. "Two great figures in history merged on a Chinese wall for the purpose of making a public-relations statement," explains the artist. No further comment necessary. A juxtaposition of a Chinese girl in a tanga and a copulating couple with an erotic scene in the traditional style is titled *Sensual Misunderstanding* by artist Wei Guangqing (ill. below left). Liu Wei's *Bathing*

Wei Guangqing
Sensual Misunderstanding,
Chapter 83, 1994
Oil on canvas, 160 x 120 cm

Liu Wei
Bathing Beauty, 1994
Oil on canvas, 200 x 150 cm

Beauty (p. 398 below right) is ogled by panting men in the water around her. As these examples indicate, despite official prudery, contemporary Chinese painting addresses the theme of sexuality with great frankness.

Such depictions stand in contrast to the painted collages of newspaper reports made by Wang Cheng, such as *Reports from the Insane Asylum* (ill. below), to the practically monochrome paintings of the older Qiu Shihua, who describes them as "soul landscapes," or – as an antithesis – to the musical portraits and landscapes of Chen Yifei, who divides his time between Shanghai and America, where his blend of Western influences with Chinese realism has proven especially successful. The list of examples could go on and and on. What they illustrate is that contemporary Chinese painting has found its own, unique language. It has digested Western influences and can hardly be called eclectic any longer, let alone derivative.

In sum, we can say that final, definitive answers can no longer be given, in no field of human affairs, neither in the West nor the East. In art, such answers never existed anyway. Doubt has always been a stimulus to creativity. An artist like Marcel Broodthaers provided an exemplary illustration of this, both in his art and his life. His colleagues of today are even more certain than he that there are no absolute certainties. To this extent the insistent questioning and inquiry of many young artists who no longer accept anything at face value, past or present, is an encouraging sign. Because their doubt is just as opposed to the misunderstanding of art as a status symbol and mere ornament to life, as it is to the superficiality of the art business, with its market leaders who are not always the right ones, its immoralism which, blind to quality, equates *world* rankings with *price* rankings, and its widespread, uncritical, conformist political correctness.

Nor does young artists' critique stop at the "bias and hypocrisy" involved in the organization of great exhibitions, and the lack of courage to risk "comparison with significant old artists" of which Baselitz, himself one of the great public stars in contemporary art, so bitterly complains. As long as young artists remain aware of the fact that it is one of the functions of art to engender knowledge and insight, as Friedrich von Schiller stated and Joseph Beuys demonstrated, there is no reason for skepticism or indeed pessimism about the future of art, all the prophets of doom to the contrary. Art, and not least painting, so frequently pronounced dead, have survived every ominous prediction until now, and will continue to survive even in the age of the electronic media. We should put our trust in the viability of art and, with Georg Christoph Lichtenberg, "leave the metaphysical cogitations to those who are incapable of doing anything better."

Zhang Xiaogang
Great Family, No. 2, 1995
Oil on canvas, 170 x 210 cm

Wang Cheng
Reports from the Insane
Asylum, 1995
Oil on canvas, 153 x 180 cm

Abakanovicz Abramovic Acconci Adams Adler Afro Agam Albers
Albright Alechinsky Almy Altenbourg Anderson Andre Anselmo Antes
Anuszkiewicz Appel Arakawa Arbus Arcangelo Archipenko Armagnac
Armajani Arman Armitage Arp Arroyo Artschwager Atget Atlan
Auerbach Aycock Bacon Baertling Baj Baldessari Balla Balthus
Baranov-Rossiné Barceló Barlach Baselitz Basquiat Bauchant Baumeister
Bazaine Baziotes Beaton Becher Beckmann Belling Bellmer Benton
Berghe Berlewi Bernard Beuys Bill Birnbaum Birolli Bissier Bissière
Blais Blake Bleckner Blossfeldt Blume Blumenfeld Boccioni Boeckl
Boltanski Bombois Bonnard Borofsky Botero Bourgeois Brancusi
Brandt Braque Brauner Brecht Brisley Broodthaers Bruch Brüning
Brus Bruskin Buchheister Buchholz Buffet Bulatow Burden Buren
Burri Bury Butler Byars Cage Calder Calderara Campendonk
Campigli Campus Capogrossi Caro Carrà Casorati Caulfield César
Cézanne Chadwick Chagall Chaissac Chaldei Chamberlain Charchoune
Charlton Chia Chillida Christo & Jeanne-Claude Ciurlionis Claasen
Clemente Close Coburn Colville Constant Corinth Corneille Cornell
Corpora Cottingham Cragg Crippa Crotti Cruz-Diez Csáky Cucchi
Dado Dai Guangyu Dalí Darboven Davie Davis D. Davis S. Davring-
hausen De Chirico Degas De Kooning Delaunay Delaunay-Terk Delvaux
De Maria Demuth Denis Depero Derain Dewasne Dexel Diebenkorn
Diller Dine Disler Di Suvero Dix Doesburg Doisneau Domela
Dominguez Dongen Dorazio Dove Drtikol Dubuffet Duchamp
Duchamp-Villon Dufy Duncan Eddy Eisenstaedt Emshwiller Ensor
Epstein Erfurth Ernst Erró Estes Estève Etienne-Martin Evans Export
Exter Fabro Fahlström Fautrier Feininger A. Feininger L. Felixmüller
Fetting Filatov Filliou Fischer Fischl Flanagan Flavin Fleischmann
Fontana Förg Francis Frankenthaler Freud Freund Freundlich Friesz
Frize Fruhtrunk Gabo Gargallo Garouste Garrin Gaudier-Brzeska
Gauguin Geiger Gertsch Gerz Giacometti Gidal Gilbert & George
Girke Glarner Gleizes Gnoli Gober Gogh Goings Goldin Goller
Golub Gontscharova Gonzáles Gorky Gormley Gottlieb Götz Graeser
Grandma Moses Graubner Graves Green Gris Gromaire Grossberg

Grosz Gruber Grützke Gundlach Günther Gursky Guston Gutfreund
Guttuso Haacke Haas Hains Hajek Halley Hamilton Hanson Hantaï
Haring Hartley Hartung H. Hartung K. Hausmann Hausner Heartfield
Heckel Heerich Hegedüs Heiliger Heisig Heizer Held Hélion
Helnwein Henri Hepworth Herbin Hérold Hesse Hill Hine Hirshfield
Hirst Höch Hockney Hödicke Hodler Hoehme Hoelzel Hoerle Hofer
Hofmann Holzer Hoover Hopper Horn Horst Hoyningen-Huene
Hubbuch Hundertwasser Huszár Ignatovich Immendorff Indiana Itten
Jacobsen Jacquet Janco Javlensky Jenney Jensen Jetelová Jochims Johns
Jonas Jones Jorn Judd Kabakov Kahlo Kandinsky Kanoldt Kanovitz
Kantor Kaprow Karavan Kassák Kawamata Kawara Keetman Kelley
Kelly Kemény Kertész Kiefer Kienholz King Kippenberger Kirchner
Kirkeby Kisling Kitaj Klapheck Klauke Klee Klein Klimt Kline Kljun
Knoebel Kobro Kokoschka Koons Kossoff Kosuth Kounellis Kramer
Kricke Krims Kruger Krull Kubota Kudo Kudojarov Kühn Kupka
Kushner La Fresnaye Lafontaine Lakner Lam Lang Lange Lanskoy
Lapicque Lardera Larionov Lasker Lassnig Laurencin Laurens Lavier
Lebeck Leck Le Corbusier Léger Lehmbruck Le Moal Lempicka Le
Parc Leroy Levine LeWitt Lhothe Lichtenstein Liebermann Lindner
Lipchitz Lissitzky Liu Wei Lohse Long Longo Louis Luginbühl
Lüpertz McBride McCollum Macdonald-Wright Maciunas Mack Macke
McLean Magnelli Magritte Maillol Malevich Manessier Manet
Mangold Manguin Mantz Manzoni Manzù Marc Marcks Marcoussis
Marden Marini Marioni Marquet Martens Martin Masson Mathieu
Matisse Matta Matta-Clark Mattheuer Meidner Meistermann Merz
Metzel Metzinger Meyer Michaels Michaux Miller Miotte Miró
Modersohn-Becker Modigliani Moholy Moholy-Nagy Mondrian Monet
Monory Moore Morandi Moreau Morellet Morgner Morley Morris
Mortensen Motherwell Muche Mueller Munch Munkacsi Münter
Nauman Nay Neusüss Nevelson Newman Newton Nicholson Nitsch
Nolan Noland Nolde Nothhelfer O'Keeffe Odenbach Oehlen Oelze
Oldenburg Olitski Opalka Oppenheim D. Oppenheim M. Orozco
Oursler Ozenfant Paik Paladino Palermo Panamarenko Paolini Paolozzi

Parks Pascin Pasmore Pearlstein Pechstein Pedersen Penalba Penck Penn Penone Permeke Petrov Petrussov Pevsner Pezold Phillips Picabia Picasso Piene Pistoletto Plessi Poirier Poliakoff Polke Pollock Pomodoro Poons Popova Prager Prampolini Prigov Prince Puni Purrmann Pusenkoff Räderscheidt Radziwill Rainer Ramos Rauschenberg Ray Raysse Redon Reed Reinhardt Renger-Patzsch Renoir Reusch Rheims Richier Richter G. Richter H. Rickey Riley Rinke Riopelle Rist Rivera Rivers Rodin Rodchenko Rohlfs Rosai Rosenbach Rosenquist Rosso Rotella Roth Rothenberg Rothko Rouault Rousseau Rozanova Rückriem Ruff Ruscha Russolo Ruthenbeck Ryman Saint Phalle Salle Salomon Samaras Sander Santomaso Saura Schad Schapiro Schiele Schlemmer Schlichter Schmidt-Rottluff Schnabel Schneider Schöffer Scholz Schoonhoven Schrimpf Schultze Schumacher Schütte Schwarzkogler Schwitters Seaman Segal A. Segal G. Segall Seiwert Sekine Séraphine Serra Sérusier Servranckx Seurat Severini Seymour Shahn Shaiket Shaw Sheeler Sherman Sieverding Signac Sima Simonds Singier Siqueiros Sironi Slevogt Smet Smith D. Smith K. Smith T. Smithson Snelson Solano Soldati Sonderborg Sonnier Soto Soulages Soutine Soutter Spencer Spero Spoerri Staël Stamos Stazewski Steichen Steinbach Steinert Stelarc Stella F. Stella J. Stepanova Stieglitz Still Stöhrer Strand Strelow Struth Strzeminski Sugaï Survage Sutherland Taaffe Taeuber-Arp Takis Tal-Coat Tamayo Tanguy Tàpies Tatlin Télémaque Thek Thiebaud Thieler Thorn-Prikker Thursz Tillmans Tilson Tinguely Tobey Tomlin Torres-García Toulouse-Lautrec Toyen Trakas Trier Trockel Tübke Tucker Tuttle Tuymans Twombly Tworkov Uecker Uhlmann Ullman Umbo Ursula Utrillo Vallotton Valmier Vantongerloo Vasarely Vasulka Vedova Velde Verefkin Vieira da Silva Villeglé Villon Viola Virnich Visser Vivin Vlaminck Vordemberge-Gildewart Vostell Vuillard Wagemaker Wall Walther Wang Cheng Warhol Weegee Wegman Wei Guangqing Weibel Wesselmann Weston Wilson Winter Winters Witkiewicz Wölfli Wols Wood Woodrow Wool Wotruba Wyeth Zadkine Zao Wou-ki Zeniuk Zhang Xiaogang Zorio

Ruhrberg · Schneckenburger · Fricke · Honnef

ART
of the 20th Century

Edited by Ingo F. Walther

Part II

SCULPTURE

by Manfred Schneckenburger

NEW MEDIA

by Christiane Fricke

PHOTOGRAPHY

by Klaus Honnef

Contents

Sculpture
by Manfred Schneckenburger

New Media

Non-Traditional Forms of Artistic Expression
by Christiane Fricke

Photography

by Klaus Honnef

Lexicon of Artists

by Ingo F. Walther

Metamorphoses of Modern Sculpture

When the 19th century German critic and philosopher Johann Gottfried von Herder described painting as illusory dream and sculpture as harsh reality, he coined a definition that still held true as the 19th century drew to a close. Yet within less than a hundred years, it had been swept aside so radically that it was no longer valid even as a guideline or general rule of thumb. Indeed, when Joseph Beuys described sculpture as thought, he actually placed three-dimensional art in a sphere of intellectual reflection closely related to the realm of the dream. In the course of those one hundred years, the very concept of sculpture was reconsidered, redefined and reworked more profoundly than it had ever been in all the millennia before. It was a century in which painting, in spite of all its new directions, still remained painting. It was also a century in which the classical distinctions between the sculpturality of hewn stone or wood and the plasticity of the composite object became blurred to the point where these very distinctions were themselves questioned. In fact, nothing less than the crisis of identity itself had become the true productive principle behind the extension of the term "sculpture".

Let us chart this path that leads in an endless circle from volume to space to object to situation to concept and back again – from the archaic block to what Julio González called the "marriage of volume and space", across ever more distant deserts, skies and spaces, using ever different materials and media in ever different combinations. In 1968, the American sculptor Carl Andre summed up this development with the extraordinarily bold assertion that, whereas sculptors were once interested in the sword sheath of the Statue of Liberty on Bedloes Island, they eventually took an interest in Eiffel's reinforcing framework structure, and finally came to be interested in Bedloes Island itself. In other words, it is but a hop, a skip and a jump from outer shell to inner structure to topographical situation.

The much-vaunted expansion of art was first and foremost an expansion of sculpture. Before exploding into tangible reality after 1960, this had taken place between 1906 and 1916 as an implosion in the minds of a few revolutionary artists. Roughly speaking, its most concentrated generative phases can be pin-pointed between 1906 and 1916 and between 1960 and 1970. Though there were certainly some important caesura and watersheds in the interim periods, it was during these phases that the fundamental paradigms were established. Bearing this in mind, we can adopt an approach that differs somewhat from previous linear examinations of the history of modern sculpture. After all, every generation re-invents the past and writes its own history. With the notable exception of Rosalind Krauss' brilliant case study, all the major historiographies to date were published before the fundamental

changes of the 60s. Carola Giedion-Welcker, Michel Seuphor, Eduard Trier and Ulrich Gertz saw 20th century sculpture moving along two tracks, the gap between them ever widening. The double-doored propylaeum from which they branched out was the work of Auguste Rodin and Aristide Maillol respectively: Rodin melted form in space, merging the two and furrowing them with light, while Maillol condensed volumes and rounded forms, consolidating them tectonically. From here, the path leads on the one side towards an analytically crystalline handling of space and on the other side towards a dense, closed block. Naum Gabo and Constantin Brancusi spring to mind.

Instead of examining these two directions of development, let us consider the history of 20th century sculpture in the light of two generative phases. Rodin, whose mature work spans the entire period of the first phase, may be regarded as a central figure in the beginnings of modern sculpture. He introduced an unruly element, and his unfettered extroversion of sculptural plasticity was countered in 1907 by the radically compressed and almost block-like introversion that informed the work of André Derain, Brancusi and Picasso in their quest to re-create sculpture out of the elemental form of the material. Yet, just two years later, Picasso's *Head of a Woman* and Matisse's series of *Jeannette* busts actually adopted Rodin's furrowed surfaces. Thus, both countering and emulating the omnipresent Rodin contributed to the development of modern sculpture. Seen from this angle, the line of descent from Maillol becomes secondary, while Rodin's artistic heritage is marked by the ascendance of a complex and experimental avant-garde.

Does the history of sculpture, and of art in general, reflect political and social history? Are world wars and economic slumps, the fall of empires and the rise of the nation state reflected in the art of the 20th century? Is art the expression of historic and social relations, just as it is, for Marxist theorists, the superstructure of class interests? Or does it develop along its own lines, with all the biographical breaks, distractions and asides that this entails? This essay does without the usual introductory sketch of the general historical and cultural climate of the day and, in doing so, isolates sculpture from its broader contemporary context.

Yet this certainly does not mean it is entrapped within some ivory tower. On the contrary; as an independent expression of the period in which it is created, a sculpture necessarily embodies the conflicts, caesura and hopes of its time. Wherever the contemporary context is specifically addressed in the work or where an explanation is necessary in order to understand the sculpture more clearly, this will be taken into account, as for example, in the case of the Russian Constructivists.

"Art has its tradition, but it is a visual heritage. The artist's language is the memory from sight. Art is made from dreams, and visions, and things not known, and least of all from things that can be said. It comes from the inside of who you are when you face yourself. It is an inner declaration of purpose, it is a factor which determines artist identity."
DAVID SMITH

Between Tradition and Modernity

Rodin: Perfection and Experiment

In the past, Rodin's modernity tended to be linked primarily to Impressionism. The sculptor Rodin was more or less the same age as the painters Claude Monet, Alfred Sisley, Pierre-Auguste Renoir and Paul Cézanne. His tendency to apply the principle of sketchiness, and the way he moulded and furrowed the surface of his works in a fluid and vibrant play of light and shadow, certainly marks him as a contemporary of the Impressionists. Yet the label does not suit him. For Rodin, though he adopted much of the Impressionist formal syntax, also clung to all that the true Impressionists were only too eager to jettison. He drew upon mythology and literature, invoking heroism and passion – in short, he represented the shadow of tragedy and pessimism that darkened the face of the century. Even the fleeting and transitory vitality of his sculptures is not impressionistically motivated. Nothing in them reflects the atmosphere, the sun, the passing of clouds, or the influence of the outer world. Instead, they visualise the inner forces of the soul seeking outward expression in a writhing, threshing, swelling flow of physical rhetoric.

Rodin, in other words, is more aptly regarded as the heir and executor of the fertile French Romantic movement. He was the only artist to channel the pathos and passion of Théodore Géricault and Eugène Delacroix, of Victor Hugo, Théophile Gautier, Charles Baudelaire and even the exuberant joie de vivre and detailed realism of Honoré de Balzac into a cosmos of physicality. As a portrayer of the human form, Rodin was a true apprentice of the sculptural tradition that embraces the art of Ancient Greece, the Gothic cathedral, Donatello, Michelangelo and Gianlorenzo Bernini. He transported this tradition, by his truly modern approach, into the realms of psychological subtlety, and he did so, like Thomas Mann, without contradicting the archetypal. In this respect, he was the last – and as a sculptor the only – exponent of the 19th century penchant for perfection with all the triumphs and failures that entails, and with a taste for the great, cyclical life work.

Rodin's *Gates of Hell*, the alpha and omega of his œuvre, ranks alongside the great cycles such as Balzac's *Comédie humaine*, Richard Wagner's *Ring der Nibelungen*, Edouard Manet's planned panorama of "modern life" and Emile Zola's *Les Rougon-Macquart*. It is a work

in which Rodin's romantic vision is condensed just as his keenly realistic powers of observation are condensed in his *Burghers of Calais*.

Nevertheless, Rodin's sculpture (pp. 408–411), for all its affinity to great literature from Dante to Baudelaire, has nothing of the consumptive pallor of Salon art's sickly love of literature. He is a sculptor through and through. The high-minded reformist efforts of Adolf von Hildebrand, who sought to impose neo-classicist forms in a bid to discipline the nascent neo-baroque and the naturalistic panopticum, are anathema to him. The terms he used – "modelé", "profile" or "drawing from all sides" – sum up what was important to him: the vitality of the swelling, furrowed bodies and limbs with their pools and trails of light and shadow, the significance of various "fertile" angles which alternate to create a fluid, organic movement, the inclusion of the surrounding space and intermediate spaces as an integral part of the sculpture. Rodin's *Burghers of Calais* are a masterpiece of this "mouvement en l'air".

Though his work may have represented the culmination of 19th century sculpture and the essence of 19th century thought, Rodin untiringly challenged the boundaries of his era at the same time, anticipating in many ways the art of the 20th century. In its dynamic diagonality, his *Balzac* (ill. below) soars like a vast and rocky reef, foreshadowing Brancusi. For the young revolutionaries of the new century who were to become the founding fathers of modern sculpture, Rodin was not only the hero of yesteryear, but also the omnipresent challenge.

It should be mentioned at this point that earlier histories of modern sculpture insisted upon the anticipatory role of certain painter-sculptors, most notably Géricault and Honoré Daumier, who created miniature, sketch-like studies modelled by hand, taking abstraction and expressive exaggeration to the point of caricature, and Edgar Degas, whose *Little Fourteen-Year-Old Dancer*, embellished with real horse-hair and tulle not

only points the way towards the readymade, but also prepares for the gestural inclusion of surrounding space. Most of their sculptures, however, were to remain in the studio or were destined, like the work of Degas, to shock the public simply because they failed to pander to clichéd contemporary notions of beauty. Only Paul Gauguin, who charged his work with complex borrowings from Breton folk art and from Indonesian and Polynesian imagery, regenerating sculpture in the spirit of *taille directe*, was to have a direct impact on Modernism. In 1906, Picasso and André Derain visited an exhibition of his work in Paris and drew their far-reaching conclusions. Yet it was Rodin alone who sparked the flame of modern sculpture. No later sculptor can ignore him.

Auguste Rodin
Head of Balzac (Study for the Monument to Balzac), 1897
Plaster. Paris, Musée Rodin

Auguste Rodin
Monument to Balzac, 1897
Plaster, 300 x 120 x 120 cm
Paris, Musée Rodin

The patriarch of Meudon knew this full well when he referred to himself as a bridge between the shores of the past and the present.

Fame came late in the day to the ever-controversial Rodin. What was it, then, that made him so important? It was certainly not the powerful influence he had on a number of sculptors who clung to the human image in the 20th century and thereby relegated themselves to the role of a nobly contemplative or expressive rearguard – Rodin's student and lover Camille Claudel, Charles Despiau and Antoine Bourdelle, the Germans Hans Albiker, Bernhard Hoetger and Georg Kolbe, the Norwegian Gustav Vigeland. There was no school of Rodin in the narrower sense, for this restless and obsessively experimental searcher never established a formal canon.

It was the "contradicatory filiations", as J. A. Schmoll alias Eisenwerth described them, that led to Modernism, and they did so by a far more direct route. These were artists who broke away from Rodin, yet continued to look back nonetheless, as though seeking the

Auguste Rodin
The Three Shades (detail from the
Gates of Hell), 1880
Bronze, 635 x 400 x 85 cm (total size)
Paris, Musée Rodin

reassuring safety of distance. The swelling curves and ruggedly gouged surfaces with their ridges and furrows drenched in pools of light and shadow, liberated younger sculptors to pursue abstraction. The break-down of traditional narrative patterns and accepted compositional hierarchies in Rodin's *Gates of Hell* sub-verted the hegemony of central perspective. Though his work did not go so far towards a new formal order as that of Cézanne, it nevertheless had important repercus-sions in terms of changing the ways of seeing that had prevailed for centuries. Above all, Rodin appears as the mediator between the Romantic aesthetic of the frag-mentary and the modern principle of montage. As a modeller who had his assistants transpose his plaster casts into larger and smaller formats, Rodin stood with both feet firmly in the 19th century. This sculptor, who kept a large collection of plaster arms, hands, legs, feet and torsi, arranged by size (like a "typecase of body parts", according to Werner Spies), actually lived to see the advent of the montage. His figural assemblages of plaster casts of various origins paved the way for Expres-sionist and Cubist fragmentation.

Rodin's modernism did not simply prepare the ground for the next generation, but led on deep into the 20th century. The very aspects of his work that met with incomprehension among his contemporaries are those in which we can discern this tremendous far-sighted-ness. Whether Frank Popper was right in claiming that excessive instability, fluidity, and the dissolution of firm sculptural forms already announced the advent of Futurism and kinetic art, is beside the point. Today, the *Burghers of Calais* would appear to herald the dawn of a new age more clearly. In an earlier design, Rodin had envisaged mounting them on a shallow plinth without a pedestal, almost level with the ground. It is precisely this fact that made them so controversial in Calais, until an inconspicuous place was found for them. Rodin had

undermined the classical monument, but by taking his bronze figures down from their pedestal and allowing them to intrude into the real space that they share with the observer, foreshadowed some of the fundamental changes in sculpture from the 1960s onwards. Alberto Giacometti's so-called space sculptures marked a fur-ther milestone on this road.

By the time Rodin died in 1917, the next generation had already begun to ring in changes and had achieved a breakthrough on many fronts – some by building on the achievements of Rodin, and some by turning against him. However logical it may seem to pass directly from here to the dramatically accelerated revolution of mod-ern sculpture, we would do well to take a look first at some of the less spectacular modifications that took place within the progress of tradition.

Maillol and the Vitality of Classicism

Aristide Maillol, born in 1861 in the south of France, updated the classical tradition, lending it a valid moder-nity. His masterpiece, the seated female figure, *The Mediterranean* (p. 412) echoes the eastern metopes of the Temple of Zeus at Olympia. The limbs seem to frame and structure the body, with supports and loads in har-monious balance, reinforced by only a few diagonals. The tectonic structure is in total harmony with the organic modelling and gentle undulations of the limbs. It is a work that combines the architectural with the anatomic. The fact that Maillol was capable of power-fully heightening his expressive portrayal of the human body is evident in his study for a monument to the social revolutionary Louis-Auguste Blanqui. It is a torso whose (fragmented) arms seem bound as they lift the entire twisting body. From the 1920s onwards, even in the work of Maillol, the heroic ideal, as opposed to a classically balanced one, tended to be reduced to a cult of the body beautiful, healthy and strong.

"When a good sculptor models human bodies, he not only portrays the muscles, but also the life that courses through them ... indeed, more than the life ... the force that formed them and gave them grace or strength, charm or unfettered joy."
AUGUSTE RODIN

and elegance on a grand scale, and to imbue them with a blossoming and erotic sensuality. Maillol was a sculptor through and through. He cast off the shadow of Rodin by returning to the classical origins of sculpture, and remained in Rodin's shadow for the same reason. He was a step ahead of Hildebrand, that other counterpoint to Rodin, in the sense that his sculptures did not radiate any noble, historically founded theory of relief nor any artificial order of foreground and background levels. They captured the vitality and strength of the female body through their stringency of form, lending it an anonymous and purely sculptural existence and linking it in elementary coordinates of space without robbing it of vitality and development.

Barlach: Expressive Robed Figures
Ernst Barlach and Wilhelm Lehmbruck are regarded as typically German sculptors, though both of them found their greatest inspiration outside Germany – Barlach on a visit to Russia in 1907 and Lehmbruck during his stay in Paris from 1910 onwards. As the sculptural revolution

Aristide Maillol
The Mediterranean, 1901
Bronze; height: 103 cm
Winterthur, Oskar Reinhart
Collection

"There is something to be learned from Rodin ... nevertheless I felt an inner need to return to more stable and closed forms. Freed from the small psychological details, forms can be shaped to the sculptural qualities of a work all the more."
ARISTIDE MAILLOL.

Maillol is often regarded as an artist diametrically opposed to Rodin. That is true to a certain extent. While Rodin's figures are centrifugally oriented and embrace the space in which they stand, the works of Maillol are bound to their corporeal volume and remain within a firm tectonic framework. Rodin tended to create groups and complex, eccentric interweavings, while Maillol limited his sculptures to a single monumental figure. Rodin scored the surface, breaking it open and bathing it in streams of light, while Maillol rounded the limbs to a firm and magnificently sensual organism, lending the body volume and gravity, paring forms down to compact entities with clearly contoured silhouettes. They were opposites indeed.

Whether or not this makes Maillol a second founder of modern sculpture, comparable to Rodin, remains a moot point. Can he be said to stand at the beginning of a path which, irrespective of all changes of direction and paradigm, eventually leads to Brancusi and from there to such sculptors as Fritz Wotruba and Ulrich Rückriem – sculptors who work with forms of solid plasticity?

In retrospect, it might be more appropriate to regard Maillol as the last great master in the classical tradition; as a sculptor of calm and potent images, who rejected Neo-classicist restrictions and turned his back on the 19th century tendency towards psychology, narrative, genre scenes and rhetorical kitsch. His strength and his historical contribution – following Rodin's intermittently crisis-ridden destruction of plasticity – lie in his capacity to endow his figures with structural simplicity

Aristide Maillol
Ile de France, 1925
Bronze; height: 166.5 cm
Cologne, Museum Ludwig

Barlach's work. His *Man Drawing a Sword* (ill. below) has a base that all but disappears under the great dome of the mantle: a taut and tensely strung outer shell that clenches with a solidly compacted inner form. The body of the *Old Woman with a Stick* (ill. left) is curved inwards, like a dent within the intractable surrounding space. The cloak lies like a shield around the figure. In this, Barlach moves among the avant-garde without sharing the mould-breaking radicalism or incisive analysis of Umberto Boccioni or Alexander Archipenko. His retreat to the provincial town of Güstrow was not a retreat from artistic urbanity.

It has been written of Barlach that he did not develop much further after visiting Russia. Yet the outer and inner energy of his figures did undergo a distinct transformation. His early beggars, peasants and herdsmen have an air of dullness and oppression, the elementary and laconic formal syntax reflecting their elementary and essential needs in the face of bourgeois conventions. After 1910, with war looming, an aggressive pathos broke out in the figures of the *Berserker*, the *Man Drawing a Sword* and *The Avenger*, the folds of their robes drawn into rushing lines charged with tension. The fury of war (based on drawings of the demise of Saul and the *Nibelungenlied*) is expressed in flashes of powerful mass dynamics. It was not until his later work, most notably his frieze for the Church of St. Katharinen in Lübeck

swept Paris, Milan and Moscow, both these artists continued to work in the figural mode. Both formulated an expressionistic contribution to this period of change, for both of them were "modernists", yet the touchstone of their modernism was and remains the human image as an image of humanity. In this respect, both Barlach and Lehmbruck continued to exert an influence on the figurative tendency in German sculpture well beyond mid-century. Indeed, in terms of emotive expression, the work of Lehmbruck was an essential benchmark for Beuys. Barlach's work has been all but obscured by its popularity. Because of this, he is all too easily associated with a certain rather dubious and very German sense of import, cosy clichés and arts and crafts stylisation. His distinctively dialetic handling of gravity and elevation can, at times, seem heavy-handed and hackneyed. Yet Barlach's wooden sculptures were very much part of a wider European context at the time, particularly in the formative years around 1910.

One of the foremost undertakings between 1906 and 1910 lay in a return to the elementary forms of stone and wood, and the block-like compression of the figure. Derain, Picasso and Brancusi made the greatest inroads in this respect. At the time, Barlach, too, was cutting and reducing seated figures to a cuboid form whose stereometric ideal is reminiscent of ancient Egyptian block statues. A highly charged relationship between outer form and inner core emerges from the exploration of concave and convex undulations of volume in the robed figure that forms the contours and boundaries of and in his *Fries of the Listeners,* originally planned for a Beethoven monument, that Barlach was to achieve the spiritual purity that is uncorporeal under flowing robes and which can be compared to High Gothic mystic figures.

Lehmbruck: Structure and Spirituality

Lehmbruck's mature sculptural œuvre (pp. 414 f) was created in less than a decade. The son of a miner from Duisburg, Lehmbruck initially took as his role model the worker hero Constantin Meunier and, from 1908 – by the time he moved to Paris, at the latest – he quickly found a footing among the international avant-garde. From then on, each step marked a clear and conscious development. In the revolutionary climate of the Paris art world during the second decade of the century, Lehmbruck, though fully aware of the many innovations, continued to treat the naked human body as a metaphor for existence and spirituality. He remained,

Wilhelm Lehmbruck
Kneeling Woman, 1911
Bronze, 178 x 71 x 141 cm
Duisburg, Wilhelm Lehmbruck Museum

Wilhelm Lehmbruck
Standing Youth, 1913
Bronze, 228 x 78 x 62 cm
Duisburg, Wilhelm Lehmbruck Museum

like Brancusi, unaffected by the new Cubist formal syntax, finding his own unconditional response to the progressive central problem of the decade. Unlike Henri Gaudier-Brzeska or Jacob Epstein, he brooked no compromise, seeking instead to render the structural perfection of the body as a sign of human suffering. As early as 1912, at the Sonderbund exhibition in Cologne, Hans Hildebrandt described his *Kneeling Woman* (ill. above) as a "symbol of expressionism". There is more to this than an ambivalent epithet – it defines the characteristic traits of a work that unites formal stringency with extreme psychological and spiritual intensity.

The tall and earthy *Standing Woman* with its sensually harmonious body rhythm marks the close of his early phase in 1910. It was Lehmbruck's magisterial response to Maillol. Created one year later, his *Kneeling Woman* marks a decisive break. Its extreme elongation echoes an imagined body build rather than a natural one, situated somewhere between the tectonic and the organic. In short, it is a masterpiece of what Werner Haftmann described as the "secret Gothic" to which the Expressionist generation subscribed, as did Amedeo Modigliani and Derain, albeit without the slightest outburst of emotion, full of grace, tenderness, sensibility and gestural contemplation.

The *Standing Youth* of 1913 (ill. left) is the first work to go beyond the architectural into the fragile and vulnerable. The torso and one leg form a pillar buttressed by the other slightly outstretched leg. This pose channels the surrounding space into a geometric inner contour with an emphasis on the vertical. Tormented hands lead over angular elbows to a stern and brooding physiognomy. The figure of this young man still guides the surrounding space along his slender body. By contrast, Lehm-

Abstraction and Cubism's Sound Shift

Spatial Dimension

The revolution in modern sculpture initially centred on the human image. Indeed, at first it was such traditional subjects as the bust, the head and the nude that were revolutionized in an almost uninterrupted chain of progression from 1906 to 1916. Brancusi, Picasso, Boccioni, Duchamp-Villon, Archipenko and Naum Gabo liberated the human figure from its traditional conventions, breaking down the organic context and charging it with a new and tension-laden syntax, and transforming anatomy into autonomy.

For decades, the approach to modern sculpture was dominated by the spatial dimension. However, before the surrounding space penetrated the sculpture, streaming through it and hollowing it, the genre returned once more to its original form, the block. As though seeking to secure its fundamental stance, the invasion of space was preceded by a return to the block-like archetype or the rough-hewn trunk. There was a tendency to include elements of "primitive" art in which European artists at that time were taking a keen interest.

For thousands of years, and in spite of all the exuberant sweeping and spiralling and hollowing of the Baroque and Mannerist periods, the plasticity of three-dimensional volume had remained. Every sculpture was, at core, a solid mass. Now it was worked by hands that modelled, sculpted and constructed. The hollow spaces that penetrated and permeated that solid mass were no longer mere areas of emptiness between tangible forms, but were themselves forms of equal validity. Concave hollows complemented convex swellings. There was no longer a clear-cut boundary between the epidermis and the surrounding space. Either the surrounding space itself encroached upon the sculpture with a vitality of its own that broke and distorted the continuum of the sculpture; or the sculpture opened out to embrace the surrounding space in which it was situated. The many ways in which sculpture and space merged, analytically systematic or expressively dynamic, was the great generative issue of the period. The spectrum ranges from Archipenko and Boccioni to Lehmbruck and Jacques Lipchitz.

There was a second and even more radical break with tradition that constituted nothing less than the emancipation of the still life as a subject in sculpture.

Relegated for centuries to the realm of painting alone, guitars, bottles and glasses now came under scrutiny in the aesthetic laboratory of the sculptor. Through the reconstruction of their spatiality they entered the third dimension. Tentatively at first, as though sounding out the dialogue with this particular art form, Picasso and Braque included elements of everyday reality in their pictures – a scrap of wallpaper or newspaper, a piece of imitation basketweave, became touchstones of aesthetic integration, conjuring up references to a wall, a table or a chair.

The consequences were far-reaching indeed. However closely Picasso may have linked such references to an aesthetic and formally determined artistic syntax, this seemingly minor development was the thin end of the wedge that opened the floodgates, sweeping such utterly different artists as Boccioni and Tatlin into the world of the *objets trouvés* and the culture of materials within the space of just two years – not to mention the more or less contemporary appearance of Marcel Duchamp's readymade. A new sculptural possibility – the object – was born.

All these developments, interactions and independent innovations between 1906 and 1916 were promoted by formal analysis or craftsmanship and underpinned by the latest scientific, philosophical or esoteric theories. The incision was deeper and the changes more far-reaching than ever before. It was more than just a question of a new form, new structures, proportions, expressive energies – in short, a new "style". By the end of the decade, sculpture was exploring hitherto unknown worlds of pre-historic, African and Oceanic art, and was looking to everyday life in search of new sources. From then on, sculpture could be a structure of metal, glass, plaster, cardboard, wire or an abstract gesture. It started being receptive, at first only in theory, to new media such as light, movement, sound and electricity. It expanded its concept (seen from today's vantage point) so far that an industrially manufactured bottle-rack could suddenly become a cornerstone in the history of sculpture. It also forged ahead in directions that were not to be accepted on a wider scale for decades, including, for example, kinetic art.

Important forces and catalysts tend to be concentrated within a few specific places and their repercus-

"The empty spaces must have as much significance as the volumes in a sculpture. Sculpture involves first and foremost taking possession of a space, a space bounded by forms. There are some who make sculptures without a sense of space, which is why their figures have no character at all."
HENRI LAURENS

Henri Laurens
Clown, 1915
Painted wood, 51.5 x 29.5 x 22.5 cm
Duisburg, Wilhelm Lehmbruck
Museum

sions spread out from there. This was true of Florence in the 15th century just as it was of Paris in the early 20th century. The emergence of modern sculpture between 1906 and 1913 took place almost entirely in Paris. It was in Paris that Picasso invented his collages and *papiers collés*. It was in Paris that Duchamp declared the first readymade. Paris was the city where Rodin was still working, the city to which the future pioneers of art flocked from as far afield as Barcelona, Tîrgu Jiu, Moscow, Smolensk and Kiev. Paris was the cradle of the Italian Futurist movement.

Yet from 1913 onwards, other forces began to emerge in resistance to the hegemony of Paris (though not necessarily that of France). From Rome and Milan, Boccioni added a distinctly Italian touch to progressive sculpture. The Russians in particular, already an important source of innovative ideas in Paris, made Moscow an eastern counterpoint. Wherever sculpture eschewed these centres of influence and sought its regeneration directly from purportedly "primitive" sources – as did the Expressionists of the German group Brücke – it ended up within the confines of a narrowly defined and barren modernism.

Paul Gauguin
"Soyez amoureuses, vous serez hereuses" (Be in Love, You Will Be Happy), 1889
Painted wood relief, 95 x 75 cm
Boston (MA), Museum of Fine Arts, Arthur Tracy Cabot Fund

Primitivism: a New Ideal

A key aspect of modern sculpture in its early stages was the discovery of tribal art. Shortly after the turn of the century, it was not, strictly speaking, a new discovery. After all, the ethnographic museums of Paris, London, Berlin and Dresden already possessed vast collections of masks, ancestral figures and totem poles from Africa, Oceania and Indoamerica. What was new was the way in which artists now regarded the aesthetic qualities of these objects. What was also new was the misplaced adulation of the primordial, natural and primitive qualities projected onto the highly conventionalised art of "indigenous peoples".

Admittedly, the allure of Roussean simplicity and Nietzschean barbarism and the appeal of the primordial and the instinctive, of vitality, youth and strength already informed the spirit of the time. It was only now, however, that these found an echo in the long-disparaged "fetishes" of an exotic art. Only now did "primitive" art come to be regarded as a fountain of youth at which a jaded European art might sup, having found in art nouveau, despite its charming embellishments, only the superficiality of stylisation. Only now was tribal art seen as the cure-all for an academically exhausted Graeco-Roman tradition. The rhythmic proportions of African wooden sculptures, their figures standing firmly on legs set parallel and slightly bent at the knee, offered an alternative to the classical contrapposto. Under the influence of the masks, a bold new formulation of the human face began to appear. Above all, however, the technique of *taille directe*, involving directly sculpting and carving out of the wood or stone, gained impetus against the surface effects of "smeared modelling" and the pointing machine, going even further than the over-intellectualised reforms posited by Hildebrand and Joseph Bernard.

The sculptor Henri Gaudier-Brzeska stated in 1914 that the sculpture he admired most was the work of master craftsmen, in which every inch of the surface had been chiselled, every blow of the hammer involved physical and intellectual effort, and in which there was no longer any arbitrary transposition of a design into some material or other. *Taille directe* and an appreciation of material properties that went beyond the choice of "appropriate material" called for by Gottfried Semper and the Jugendstil artists were the most advanced achievements of sculpture around 1910.

A reduction to block or pole was another innovation to be learned. Not that all such works were based on an African or Oceanic model. Brancusi's *Kiss* of 1908 (p. 425), for example, translates Rodin's extroversion of the fleeting moment into a solid Ur-form. On the other hand, not every source of inspiration meant reduction. Picasso, who in 1912 drew a parallel between the protruding cylindrical eyes of a West African Wobe mask and the resonator of a guitar, was taking a formal analytical approach rather than a primitivist one. Even Lipchitz, Henri Laurens and Ossip Zadkine, who modelled their cubist figures with short legs, long torsos and large heads according to African proportions, turned against the formal canon of classical antiquity without seeking regression. In this respect they differed fundamentally from the founding father of all primitivist movements – Paul Gauguin.

"The Greeks are the great mistake. We have to go back beyond the horses of the Parthenon to the rocking-horse of our childhood," wrote Gauguin, underlining the biogenetic theory of Ernst Haeckel, which was prevalent around the end of the 19th century. Haeckel maintained that the development of human civilisation from pre-history to modern times echoed the development of the individual from child to adult. "Indigenous peoples" were, accordingly, still at the "childhood" stage. How easy for the colonialists to declare such children incapable of reasoned thought and responsibilty. And what motivation for Gauguin to seek the paradise of his own childhood among the "savages"! In 1894 he finally travelled to the South Seas to capture images of Tahitian women by the most progressive symphonies of line and colour that European painting had to offer. His sculptures of clay and wood, on the other hand, possess that savage, barbarian edge that he associated with the primordial. Even the ceramics he produced in Brittany before his first voyage to Tahiti in 1891 recall his childhood in exotic Peru. His self-portrait in the form of a tobacco pot is reminiscent of the moulded portrait pots of the pre-Columbian Mochica civilization – a compressed block bearing the facial traits of Gauguin, thumb in mouth like an infant.

His wood relief *Soyez amoureuses et vous serez heureuses* (ill. left) shows the same infantile regression, with its elements of childhood and early civilization, Peru and the dreamed-of South Seas. Under the thumb-sucking self-portrait a Peruvian mummy from the Musée de l'Homme flows into an embryonic position. On Tahiti and Hiva Ova Gauguin carved Polynesian deities in relief on a solid, cylindrical form in the style of the Marquesan Tikis. He also portrayed idols in Buddha-like positions with oversized heads and inserted cannibalistic filed teeth and Marquesan tattoos (ill right). In adopting the idol he updated a sculptural archetype which, in Europe, had been relegated to the field of folk art for more than a thousand years. This marked the beginning of a long line of idols, totems and fetishes that were to be leitmotifs of surrealist art and of 1950s American sculpture.

In 1906, three years after Gauguin's death on the Marquesas islands, a major memorial exhibition was mounted in Paris. It marked a fulcrum point between Post-Impressionism and the young avant-garde that included Picasso, Brancusi and Matisse. The following year, Picasso carved a number of rough and simple pole figures, their limbs barely articulated and closely bound to their bodies. Following Gauguin, Picasso reduced the type of sign-covered and precisely structured Marquesa Tikis to a massive primary style whose most distinctive feature is its solidity and idol-like rigidity.

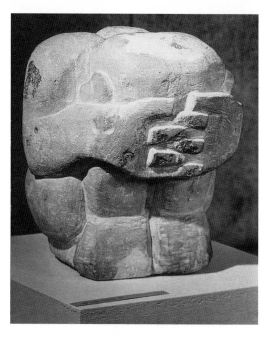

André Derain
Crouching Figure, 1907
Stone; height: 33 cm
Vienna, Museum moderner Kunst

That same year, André Derain created his *Crouching Figure* (ill. above) with only a few markings in the stone, knees drawn up, head in hands, hands clasped like angular brackets. Here, the block is a cuboid formal principle that integrates the human figure. Rigid concentration on the primordial form of the limestone and the tangible core is turned against the fluidity of Rodin's visual sensations and spans an arc to Aztec figures of divinity and Egyptian block statues. The extreme radicalisation and sublimation of this principle was achieved in the autumn of 1907 with Brancusi's *Kiss*, which was presumably created under the influence of Derain. It uses the block to portray the duality and oneness of man and woman, and may be regarded as the manifesto of Brancusi the sculptor as opposed to Rodin the modeller. It is a seminal work of modern sculpture and can be seen as the very foundation of its renewal on the basis of elementary forms and *taille directe*. Generation by generation, the early work of Henry Moore, Fritz Wotruba and Ulrich Rückriem firmly established this approach and translated it into the language of the 20th century.

Although, according to Epstein, Brancusi actually destroyed some of his sculptures which he felt were all too "African", his interest in this aspect was evident from 1913 onwards. Wherever the material used is wood and is cut along the grain, the work has a distinctly African feel. In 1913, Brancusi created his first wood sculpture, *The First Step*. The axial rounding of the body, the egg-shaped head, the triangular mouth drawn upwards, and the sharply undercut eyebrows would appear to be based on a Bambara figure in the Musée de l'Homme.

In 1914, Brancusi destroyed the body, leaving only the head intact with the title *The First Cry*. A bronze version translated the African influence into the harder medium of brightly polished metal and pared the form

Paul Gauguin
Idol with Mussels, 1892
Ironwood and other materials
Heigth: 27 cm, diameter: 14 cm
Paris, Musée d'Orsay

Amedeo Modigliani
Head, 1911/12
Limestone, 63.5 x 12.5 x 35 cm
London, Tate Gallery

Jacob Epstein
Rock Drill, 1913/14
Sculpted bronze,
70.5 x 44.5 x 58.4 cm
London, Tate Gallery

down to that of the primordial egg, which was to remain the symbolic basic figure of Brancusi's sculptural œuvre from then on. Haeckel's biogenetic theory of the correlation between the first step or first cry of a child and alleged early tribal history proved an invariably fruitful comparison in the field of sculpture.

From 1909 the Italian artist Amedeo Modigliani had a studio beside Brancusi's in the rue Montparnasse. An impassioned sculptor, ill health and lack of money had obliged him to turn to painting instead. Of his sculptures, 23 *Heads* and two *Caryatids* have survived. Their relationship to architectural works remains to be clarified. Were they intended, for example, to adorn the portals of an envisaged temple?

Modigliani, eight years younger than Brancusi, had very probably become aware of African sculptures before the two artists met and became friends. What fascinated him was not so much their crude and elementary aspects as their refined sophistication and even elegant stylisation. In his paintings he would combine this with individuality and psychological analysis. The limestone *Heads* (ill. right) he created between 1909–1914 show the same extreme elongation, smooth roundness, graphic scoring, narrow bridge-like nose and isolated round mouth of the masks of the West African Baule, Guro and neighbouring tribes. Modigliani pares down the traits of the masks into unpretentious, expressionless faces in which nothing has been left to chance, reducing

them to pure symmetrical axiality, strengthening their vertical rhythm and placing the head on a cuboid base to stabilise the sweeping curve. This marks a bold development towards the enigmatic in comparison to Brancusi's 1907 *Head of a Girl* which, together with the African masks, foreshadows Modigliani's *Heads*.

In the years running up to the first world war, there was hardly a single progressive sculptor in Paris who ignored "primitive" art, and few indeed who would admit to having been corrupted by the classicism of Rodin's modelling. Yet their motivations differed widely. Picasso and Brancusi made no attempt at the impossibility of identifying fully with it. Freundlich worked in a studio alongside Picasso's in the Bateau-Lavoir for a few months in 1908 and spent most of 1910–1914 in Paris. The rugged architectonic syntax of his *New Man* (1912) in all its monumentality is derived from the huge Easter Island heads and is his distinctive contribution to a primitivist concept of man with a cosmic dimension. In 1937 his sculpture was shown on the cover of the catalogue of the Nazi exhibition of "Entartete Kunst" to illustrate the epitome of "degenerate art".

Others used tribal art as a syncretic escape from their own era. Instead of addressing the conceptual principle, they used it as a source of form and exotic aura. Through their sculpture they sought a freer, wilder, more sensual intensity of life. Jacob Epstein, who visited Paris repeatedly from 1902 onwards, and who became a friend of

Modigliani and Brancusi, unerringly selected and interpreted the sexual aspects of African and Oceanic art in a short-lived, early phase between 1913 and 1915. Sex, pregnancy and birth were presented as phallic visual worlds, while a marble Venus of African proportions set on copulating pigeons demonstrated a new ideal of beauty. Yet even his brilliantly monstrous *Rock Drill* (ill. left) does have a distinct leaning towards Vorticism, which was then the specifically English variation of Futurism, Cubism, Expressionism and Machine Art. After the first world war, Epstein's rough, realistic colossal figures and his dramatic, tension-charged, Rodinesque portrait busts brought him fame and notoriety as a publicly commissioned artist in England.

It is said of his young French friend Henri Gaudier-Brzeska that he wanted to "go native" like Gauguin on a Pacific island and that he had even considered having a 10 cm rod pierced through his nose. He, too, sought new vitality and strong emotive expression in the art of indigenous peoples. It is for this reason that the dynamic Oceanic sculptures appealed to him more than the stringent tectonic approach of African art. From 1911–1914 he worked in England, and it was there, most

Ernst Ludwig Kirchner
Male Nude (Adam), before 1923
Poplar wood, stained brown and
burned, 169.6 x 40 x 31 cm
Stuttgart, Staatsgalereie Stuttgart

*"Sculptural energy is the mountain.
Sculptural feeling is the appreciation
of masses in relation. Sculptural
ability is the defining of these masses
by planes."*
HENRI GAUDIER-BRZESKA

notably in the British Museum, that this prodigious and highly talented young artist overcame the "conventional Rodin-Maillol mélange" of his early period. His œuvre as we know it was begun in 1913.

The *Red Stone Dancer* (ill. left) with its maelstrom of arms and hands whirling around a triangular face still has distinct Vorticist leanings, for all its solid force. In 1914, Gaudier-Brzeska created a *Hierarchical Head* of Ezra Pound, who greatly admired the *Dancer*. Its monumentality, forceful verticality and angularity reminiscent of the Easter Island heads merge with a contemporary tendency towards abstract planes and sharp angles. The sculptor fell in action in 1915, before he had quite abandoned the vibrant eclecticism of his youth. He left behind a small œuvre that is paradigmatic of primitivism.

In Dresden, too, the Expressionist artists of the Brücke group approached life through art. They "discovered" the carved wooden beams of the Palau islands and the figures from Cameroon around 1906 (and not, as Kirchner claimed, in 1903) in the ethnographic museum of Dresden. The impact on their work is evident by 1909. Painters and graphic artists, they also carved objects for their own studios. Their sculptures created an exotic atmosphere and homely echo of the paradisical summers spent working and relaxing on the Moritzburg Lakes.

From 1918 onwards, Ernst Ludwig Kirchner began furnishing his farmhouse in Davos with items he had

Henri Gaudier-Brzeska
Red Stone Dancer, 1913
Waxed stone, 43 x 23 x 23 cm
London, Tate Gallery

fashioned and carved in Swiss pine, including a bed, mirror frames, a fireplace, some of them borrowing from the iconography of Cameroon house posts and chieftains' chairs. European peasant art and African tribal art were meant to evoke a primordial and natural ambience for this nervous and highly-strung artist. In this respect, the carvings of the Brücke artists were intended for their own personal use and had little impact on the history of modern sculpture as such.

Nevertheless, Kirchner, Heckel and Schmidt-Rottluff did lend some weight to their sculptural œuvre. Kirchner, especially, who is known to have produced more than a hundred carved works (ill. left) repeatedly remarked on the significance of *taille directe* woodcarving for the creative process. In a letter to Gustav Schiefler in 1911, he wrote "... it is a sensual pleasure when, blow by blow, more of the sculpture grows out of the trunk. In every trunk there is a figure; it just has to be peeled out." This corresponds almost exactly with remarks made by Michelangelo on the way he related to the block of marble he was working. It is one of the most fundamental experiences of the sculptor, as opposed to the modeller, and one that influenced Kirchner's Swiss followers Hermann Scherer and Albert Müller. Half a century later the painters Georg Baselitz and Markus Lüppertz were to return to Kirchner's heavy figural style.

Of all the Brücke artists, it was Karl Schmidt-Rottluff in particular who looked to sculpture in his search for a means of expressing the spirit of his age. His *Heads*, all of which were produced during the first world war, found

their precursors in Carl Einstein's 1915 publication *Die Negerplastik* (Negro Sculpture). They heighten the concave structure of Fang reliquary figures from Gabon into an excited and ecstatic formal language. Whether or not the wooden figure of the *Worker Wearing a Cap* (ill. below left) is derived directly from a Congolese chieftain figure, the dignity of the crouching figure of authority is turned into its very opposite, and the cut edges of the amputated thighs emphasise the helpless isolation of the torso, while the open hand suggests, all the more poignantly in 1920, the begging of the war-wounded. The African seated figure is linked with a leading theme of Expressionist humanity. Karl Einstein's harsh verdict that "Exoticism intoxicated the Saxon primitives for their lack of visual imagination" certainly does not apply in this case.

Brancusi: Being and Form

For the Romanian artist Brancusi, primitivism was only one side of the coin. In his work, African influences merge with the heritage of Romanian folk art. It is a heritage that Brancusi, who arrived in Paris in 1904, having walked all the way from Bucharest via Vienna, was to carry with him always. African art, on the other hand, was a source he used sparingly. Between 1913 and 1923 he carved and sculpted wooden figures that were almost ungainly, additive, bizarre, bound and notched. They evoked a dissonant counterworld to the purity of form that predominates in his œuvre. Such titles as *Adam and Eve*, *The Prodigal Son* (p. 425), *Chimera* or *Witch* indicate that we are dealing here with an animalistic, grotesque,

Karl Schmidt-Rottluff
Worker Wearing a Cap, 1920
Wood; height: 66 cm
Berlin, Brücke-Museum

Constantin Brancusi
Mlle Pogany, 1912
Marble; height: 44.5 cm;
stone base: 15.4 cm
Philadelphia, Philadelphia
Museum of Art, Gift of Mrs.
Rodolphe Meyer de Schauensee

Werner Hofmann described as the "purism of modern sculpture" but set an example for the minimalist serial art of the 1960s.

Yet the art historian's eye does not fully capture the essence of Brancusi's work. Perhaps it would not even be going to far to say that his work is primarily the mystical experience of the world, sensual wisdom of form that is transformed into the spritual. He unerringly and painstakingly seeks an increasingly pure and perfect body of form that is transcendental in its immaculate finish. This has nothing to do with abstraction or even with stylisation, for, as Brancusi himself stated, "my work is aimed above all at realism. I seek the inner, hidden reality, the inner essence of things in their own unchanging nature." Revealing the essence – this is what Brancusi spent almost half a century trying to do. His way of thinking in this respect is close to Eastern philosophy. The architect Alvar Aalto saw Brancusi as the "hyphen linking Europe and Asia". For years, Brancusi

dark and even demonic world, from which Brancusi was to withdraw in 1922. With few exceptions, these works in wood were never cast in bronze, a material that would have dissolved their materiality through reflection. When Max Ernst gave the older artist a wooden arm of African origin, Brancusi threw it over the fence like some menacing fetish. There was no room left in his spiritual universe for the dangerous vitality of magically charged African sculpture.

Brancusi's star lit a different path. He began by making vivaciously academic busts and sensitively modelled children's heads in the manner of Rodin or Medardo Rosso. The turning point came in 1907. It was the year in which Picasso painted his epoch-making *Demoiselles d'Avignon* (pp. 68, 69) and the year in which Brancusi created his own incunabulae of modernism. The *Head of a Girl* (now lost) was his first sculpture directly hewn in stone. The extreme simplicity of the figure *Prayer* vindicated its own scuptural existence. The historical watershed can be identified most clearly between Brancusi's *The Kiss* (ill. above) and the romantically exalted *Kiss* created twenty years earlier by Rodin. Romanian-born Brancusi surmounted Graeco-Roman tradition with his programmatic return to the stone and the block, arriving almost directly at the emblematically abbreviated sculptural sign. At the same time, he established the only independent counter-position to the Cubist fragmentation of form. He thus founded not only what

Constantin Brancusi
Sleeping Muse, c. 1912 (?)
Marble, 27 x 30 x 17 cm. Paris, Musée National
d'Art Moderne, Centre Georges Pompidou

Constantin Brancusi
The Gate of the Kiss, 1937/38
Stone, 513 x 654 x 169 cm
Tîrgu Jiu (Romania)

kept the autobiography of the 11th-century Tibetan ascetic Jetsun Milaresa under his pillow. Yet, as a sculptor, he remained far removed from the esoteric mysticism of some of his interpreters.

The block, the cylinder and the pyramid make up Brancusi's elementary vocabulary. By 1909 at the latest, however, he had found his most important archetypal form, the elongated sphere. It was not the definitive and unchangeable ideal of the sphere, but the moving and changeable ovoid – Goethe's "vitally developing form", Ezra Pound's "general key to form, not only Brancusi's, but form as such".

Out of the conventional marble *Sleep* he developed his *Sleeping Muse* in 1909. It is the original image of the reclining head which he translated into a bronze version in 1910, culminating in the very zenith of formal clarity and purity in an alabaster version of 1917 (ill. left). In his *Beginning of the World* the ovoid form melts beyond all physiognomic connection with the cosmic egg of which the Upanishadi speak. The *First Cry* links it again with its "African" counterworld that is, after all, more than just diametrically opposed. By 1910 it had entered the body of the fairytale bird *Maestra* – the forerunner of all Brancuis birds, through to the metaphors of flight and boundless elevation in space. Head, bird, swan, fish and seal – all variations on the living Ur-form that is contained within the ovoid, or egg.

No other sculptor of the 20th century turned again and again to the same motifs the way Brancusi did, obsessively and patiently varying the same motif in polished bronze, in white, black, yellow or blue marble, or in alabaster. It was not, as he himself stated, a question of doing the same sculpture again, but of moving on. However clearly his reductive, essential style may have been distilled by 1909, and however obvious it may have remained with minor changes, Brancusi kept moving on. Moving on towards the ever more perfect form, until the well-groomed, large-eyed head of his 1912 *Mlle Pogany* became, in the bronze version of 1931, a sheer dome over a fan of soaring arches (p. 424 below right). Moving on until the *Maestra* bird of 1910 became an ever more slender spindle, flashing in its verticality like a soaring bird, the very essence of flight condensed within a single feather.

Constantin Brancusi once told Carola Giedion-Welcker that "All my life I have sought the essence of flight. Flight, pure joy!" Which explains the mirroring dematerialisation, first in the shimmer of marble, then in the lucid reflexes of polished bronze that refract the surrounding space like a vision. A photo by Brancusi of a "bird in space" dissolves the sculpture into kinetic variations. In the end, he places bronze sculptures on blank steel sheets so that their optical echo fluctuates reciprocally.

The Tîrgu-Jiu ensemble, a war memorial, monumentalises this tendency. The decisive factor is the order. It begins with the *Table of Silence* and its twelve

"In my opinion, a true form should suggest infinity. The surfaces should look as though the were ascending out of the mass into perfect and complete Being."

CONSTANTIN BRANCUSI

Constantin Brancusi
Blonde Negress, 1926
Polished bronze, 38.5 x 14 x 18 cm
San Francisco (CA), San Francisco
Museum of Modern Art

Constantin Brancusi
Bird in Space, 1928
Polished bronze; height: 137.2 cm,
circumference: 9.5 – 37.7 cm
New York, The Museum of
Modern Art

Left:
Constantin Brancusi
Endless Column, 1937
Cast iron; height: 29.35 m
Tîrgu Jiu (Romania)

massive stone seats as satellites forming a circle of calmly poised equilibrium. It continues with the *Gate of the Kiss* (ill. left) representing the rite of passage to a higher plane of reality and ends where there is no end – in the *Endless Column* (ill. above) of stacked pyramids which, for Brancusi, touch the heavens. Ira Klein was reminded of a stairway to heaven and recognised in it a transitory quality as meta-operator to an infinite cosmos. Other researchers see in it, more simply, a derivation from Rumanian balustrade pillars. American minimal artists adopted the principle of seriality pragmatically, without any cosmic ambition. Today, Brancusi stands for both – the mystic and the sculptor who inspired emotive faith and artistic strategy.

"Art must penetrate into the spirit of nature and, like nature, create beings whose forms and lives are independent."

CONSTANTIN BRANCUSI

"I have turned to sculpture when I was tired of painting. For a change of medium. But I approached sculpture as a painter, not as a sculptor. Sculpture does not say the same as painting. Painting does not say the same as music. These are parallel paths, but they should not be mixed."   HENRI MATISSE

Matisse: Modelled Space

The painter Henri Matisse, unlike the painters Gauguin and Picasso, played only a brief role in the historical development of sculpture. His bronze statuettes and heads after 1900 reflect the motifs and formal problems of the painter. In short, their bronze outer skin reflecting the contours of an inner dynamism had distinct leanings towards the work of Rodin. But then Matisse created a few sculptures of enormous spatial astuteness which placed him at the cutting edge of the artistic avant-garde for a number of years. By 1907, his sculpture had become Fauvist, as evidenced by the sheer force of his *Reclining Nude* with its twisted, distorted, ex-centric anatomy. From the strong upward and outward thrust of the pelvis, structured by the upper torso and limbs, the entire body writhes and stretches in a purely sculptural rhythm, going far beyond the photograph on which it is based (though the artist does adhere to it closely). Here, distortion becomes a means of expression and decoration alike, both of which are central concepts in the work of Matisse.

Two years later, he was to pare down the harmoniously curved statuette *La Serpentine* (ill. above right) with its Hellenistically influenced pose, to a torso and limbs of almost identical proportion. The volume is extended to a linear figure which underlines the inner space between support, body, bend of arm in much the same way that it draws out the arabesques of the contour. In this work, Matisse introduces what is to be the

major theme of the following decade: the permeation of the body with space.

In 1910/11 he then modelled the first of his four heads of *Jeanette* with a fifth, his boldest of all, following in 1913. They mark a departure from the Rodinesque true-to-life portrait, and a move towards the kind of free transformation and asymmetrical distortion of the physiognomic topography that does not even stop at rough incisions in the skull (ill. above left). Masses become sculptural energies which Matisse cloaks, shifts, merges or enhances. It is a freedom that echoes the spirit of Picasso's 1909 *Head of a Woman*, albeit without even seeking the latter's early Cubist systematic facetting. In the important series of heads by Picasso, Brancusi, Duchamp-Villon, Modigliani and Boccioni that mark the beginning of modern sculpture, Matisse's *Jeanette I-V* command a key position.

Picasso the Groundbreaker

It would undoubtedly be wrong to regard such sculptors as Maillol, Barlach or Lehmbruck merely as followers-on. Their sculptures possess a formal stringency that sets them apart clearly from the art of the 19th century, even without any radical process of abstraction. Nevertheless, the revolution of modern sculpture breaks through in other areas as well. The most far-reaching development set in before 1910, almost as a by-product of painting. Indeed, the major stimuli are to be found concentrated in the work of a painter who was to return to his easel in

1914 for another fifteen years, only to turn once more to sculpture around 1930 to take his art in a new direction yet again. That artist was Pablo Picasso.

The focal point was still the omnipresent Rodin. With his *Monument to Balzac* he had shown how a head can be forged out of hollows, mounds and furrows and how the artist's hand could model it until it took on on its own potent sculptural life. In 1909, Picasso created a *Head of a Woman* (ill. below), presumably his mistress Fernande Olivier. From a sinewy neck the furrowed physiognomy spirals upwards to the softly rounded pillows of her hair. A number of individual particles of form structure the head into concave and convex areas. The alternation of light and shadow thus takes on a rough regularity. The modelling follows neither bone structure nor epidermis, being built up instead of sharply angled sculptural curves and incisions. The same sweeping curve can indicate an eyebrow, a cheekbone or a nose. Convex areas – forehead cheeks, throat – seem concave. It is the position alone that leads the eye back time and time again from ambiguity to unequivocality. This is a tension that will later influence Cubist sculpture.

What had happened? Picasso subjected the head to an alternation of convex and concave forms. He did not stylise it or heighten it expressively, but consolidated form instead within its own early Cubist system. Instead

Pablo Picasso
Guitar, 1912
Cardboard, paper, canvas, string, oil and pencil, 33 x 18 x 9.5 cm
Paris, Musée Picasso

"Cubism is neither a mustard seed not a foetus, but an art in which the main issue is form, and once a form has been created it is there and it lives its own life." PABLO PICASSO

of imitating form, he recreated it. It is this freedom that explains the significance of the work, which Werner Spies has claimed to be as important to modern sculpture as the epoch-making *Demoiselles d'Avignon* (pp. 68, 69).

All things said and done, however, the *Head of a Woman* was still the product of traditional modelling techniques. Although it stands at the beginning of a new sculptural emancipation, it can also be seen as the conclusion of Picasso's early bronze-cast sculptures. Three years later, in 1912/13, following a phase of intensive painterly exploration, Picasso constructed a guitar out of layers of sheet metal, creating a *bricollage* rather than a picture. The resonator is not a depression, but a protrusion (originally a stovepipe) in the form of a cylinder. Seen from the front, it can be read as a resonator. The negative and positive forms are merely reversed. Other guitar reliefs vary the strings and the resonator board, have zigzag folds or play with the appeal of variously coloured cardboard (ill. above). The unified surface of the image is surmounted, as is the imitative or imaginative modelling of mass.

Rarely has such a seemingly marginal innovation had such a major impact. What was intended as a

Pablo Picasso
Head of a Woman (Fernande), 1909
Bronze, 40.5 x 23 x 26 cm
New York, The Museum of Modern Art

Pablo Picasso
Glass of Absinthe, 1914
Painted bronze after a wax
maquette with silver absinthe
spoon, 21.5 x 16.5 x 8.5 cm
New York, The Museum of
Modern Art, Gift of Mrs. Bertram
Smith

figures, standing and reclining, prior to 1906/07, with
their elongated, snaking limbs, remained demonstratively distinctive extremes of modelling that seemed to
be both a continuation and a correction of Rodin at one
and the same time. Even the older Medardo Rosso, who
made the wax surfaces of his scenes and heads receptive
to the oscillations of the surrounding space and the subtle dissolution of form, was to all intents and purposes a
modeller. The task of inextricably merging figure and
space was the issue of the day. Yet it was the Cubist fragmentation of form that first gave artists the tools with
which to do so.

Another seminal innovation by Picasso (and Braque)
has almost the intimacy of chamber music. With their
papiers collés and their implantation of real objects such
as oilcloth, basketweave or turned wood, they shattered
the material unity of the picture in 1912. Quotes from the
studio environment replaced pure depiction. It was a
cautious step towards the material world, for it still
remained within the scope of a formal artistic unit. It
was Duchamp who first opened the floodgates for the
century's deluge of object citations.

Picasso, however, had prepared the ground. In 1914,
he made six casts of his *Glass of Absinthe* in bronze from
wax models (ill. left) and painted each of them differently. He then placed a real absinthe spoon, an everyday
object, on each of them, as a pointer towards the world
beyond art. By his own admission, what Picasso was
interested in here was "the relationship between the real
spoon and the modelled glass". This interest is at the
basis of all assembled and combined sculptures, assemblages and collages that combine art with fragments of
reality. Picasso stands at the beginning of a rapidly
spreading line in which the artefact and the *factum bru-
tum* come together. He thus stands at the beginning of a
new and fundamental freedom in the field of sculpture.

The genius of Picasso thus condensed the most
advanced problems of sculpture within a period of just
four years. He made seemingly nonchalant contributions that were adopted, developed and expanded. Not
all sculptors took them up, however. Brancusi continued to pursue his own path, while Lehmbruck clung to
tradition. Yet most artists, even the strongest talents,
realised that sculpture was undergoing what Werner
Hofmann described as a "sound shift" from which a new
language would emerge. Picasso himself did not actually
use that language. Its most verbose and eloquent proponents, innovators and poets were others.

Archipenko: Emancipation of Empty Form
The Russian artist Alexander Archipenko arrived in Paris
in 1908 at the age of twenty. From 1910 onwards he
worked at developing his own style of stereometrically
simplified physical volumes, upwardly spiralling figures
incorporating the wedges, acute angles and crystalline
breaks out of the Cubist inventory and involving some
Mannerist borrowings. In 1912 Archipenko recognised
his true theme to be the interaction between volume and

critical correction of painting, as a studio experiment,
proved to be a new foundation for sculpture. At one fell
swoop, the centuries-old distinction between a sculpture created by adding clay or plaster and a work of plastic art created by removing stone had become redun-
dant. When space, volume and three-dimensionality are
made up of planes and surfaces, the modelling hand and
the chisel are no longer needed. Admittedly, this did not
mean that the organic swell of the corporeally rounded
or the cubically hewn volume disappeared completely.
From here on in, however, the new principle would continue to front developments time and time again, in the
work of such diverse artists as Gabo and González,
Anthony Caro and Richard Serra. Picasso himself was to
heighten his sheet-cut sculptures to the point of monumental silhouettes.

The intervention of painting did not end here.
Beginning in 1909/10, Picasso and Braque opened up the
unified surface of the painting, fragmenting it and splin-
tering it in their cubist works. What remained legible of
the subject matter in their portraits and still lifes was
spatially embedded in rhythmic layers and permeated by
space. When sculptors such as Archipenko and Boccioni began creating voids in their figures and integrating the surrounding space, activating it and charging it
with its own sculptural energy, they used the cubistically
broken surface of the picture as their magic formula.

The art historical aim of going beyond the compact
core figure had already been formulated by Henri
Matisse years before. Yet his sweepingly gestural female

Alexander Archipenko
Walking Woman, 1912
Bronze; height: 67.5 cm
New York, Perls Galleries

space. With that, he became one of the most important of European sculptors for a number of years, shifting the focus of Picasso's casual pointers from the no-man's land between painting and sculpture to the very centre of plastic art and systematically exploring individual aspects of it.

It would be unfair to regard Archipenko's later tendency towards decorative synthesis and his academic approach to his own innovations as in any way diluting the force of his contribution to modern sculpture. He forged ahead in his *recherche des formes* at a very early stage and with the utmost radicality. No other sculptor, with the possible exception of Boccioni, took such an absolutist approach to the question of space, which was the key issue of the decade. No other artist drove the interaction of volume and space so distinctively in the direction of the expressive, lyrical, dynamic and statuary. The fact that some of his work, even that produced at the height of his creative powers, appears almost didactic and schematic to us today, lies to some extent in the fact that it was rapidly emulated by a large following on a broad basis, even in the field of applied arts.

Nevertheless, some important sculptures remain. In his *Dance* (1912) a vibrantly soaring inner space is framed by the arabesque of the couple. In his famous *Boxing Match* (1914) the boxers are reduced to colliding, clenched wedges. Muscles are replaced by the flow of

Rudolf Belling
Triad, 1919
Bronze, 91 x 73 x 80 cm
Saarbrücken, Saarland-Museum
Saarbrücken

Alexander Archipenko
Marching Soldier, 1917
Bronze; height: 116.8 cm
Private collection

Alexander Archipenko
Médrano II, 1913
Painted sheet metal, wood, glass and painted oilcloth, 126.6 x 51.5 x 31.7 cm
New York, Solomon R. Guggenheim Museum

Boccioni and the Futurist Vision

Boccioni's sculptural œuvre is exceptional. It stands out even among the work of the many pioneering artists prior to 1914. As a thirty-year-old artist who had devoted his energies to the boundlessly ambitious Manifesto of Futurist Painters (p. 86), presenting one programmatic work after another within the space of just two years, he now turned his attention to the revolution of sculpture. In April 1912 his Manifesto of Futurist Sculpture was published. Between the summer of 1912 and the spring of 1914 he created no fewer than fourteen sculptures in a period of intensive and concentrated work. Five of them have survived, seven are known only from photographs. Each one directly addressed the issues of the day in the field of sculpture and each one offers some fundamental

rhythmic energies. The volumetric masses follow the lines of movement. In this, Archipenko takes an enormous step towards the kind of expressive plastic art that Rudolf Belling emancipated completely from its anthropomorphic context in 1919 with his *Triad* (p. 431 below).

Apart from these sculptures which heighten the stylistic means of Cubism to the point of the expressive and energetic, as of 1912 there was also a tendency towards the formation of concave and convex curves, an aesthetics of the void by which, according to Heinz Fuchs, "plasticity of form is rendered tangible through its matrix". Archipenko developed his own theory of complementary forms based on the maxim that each empty space produces its imaginary counter-image. His theory is boldly illustrated by his 1912 *Walking Woman* (p. 431) in which, for the first time, he simply presents the head as a negative form. Another far-reaching conclusion that Archipenko drew in 1912 from Picasso's *Constructions* (or perhaps it was a conclusion he reached entirely independently) can be found in his *Médranos* – puppet-like figures made of wood, glass metal, wire, spheres, cones, cylinders, discs, activated by polychromatic painting. Here, too, Archipenko was the first to fully exploit the possibilties of montage, uniting formal stringency with irresistible wit.

contribution towards clarifying the ongoing discourse in that field. Some of them articulated a new formal language for sculpture that was to have repercussions far into the future. Whereas Picasso, almost the same age, re-founded sculpture within painting, Boccioni set out systematically to explore a new route of his own.

From the autumn of 1911 he acknowledged the priority of Cubism. At the same time, he was aware of the extent to which the generation and permeation of Cubist form could serve his own purposes. His criticism was aimed at the studio as ivory tower, cloistered from the industrial, urban, exhilarating modern world that he felt should inform paintings and sculptures alike. In his manifesto he therefore announced that figure and ground should go together (the Cubists had shown the way) and that the entire environment should penetrate the sculpture. He was strengthened in his resolve by another Italian artist, the subtly Impressionistic Medardo Rosso, who had gone further than Rodin in imbuing his street scenes and garden scenes with an atmospheric setting that seemed like a fragile material in its own right, peopling them with chatting groups, bus passengers or readers. Described by Joris-Karl Huysmans as a "Sculpteur de la vie moderne", Rosso lived in Paris from 1889, where he captured fleeting moments of urban genre scenes, children's heads, movement and light. Boccioni admired the continuity of volume and space in his small-scale sculptures, and it certainly suited him to find his own endeavours reflected in the work of a fellow Italian. It was a spark of life in an ossified tradition.

Rosso's rapid and improvisational lightness was, however, an aspect that appealed rather less to this rigorous "engineer of light". In the autumn of 1912, in his first assemblage *Head + House + Light*, Boccioni combined a real balcony railing as a sign of the city with the convul-

sive half-figure of his mother. Soon afterwards, in *Fusion of Head and Window* (p. 434 above), he crowned the plaster head with elements of a real window-frame and inserted a piece of horsehair and a glass eye. These were precursors of the readymades that Duchamp was to introduce just one year later. Uwe Schneede is right in describing these assemblages – which survive today only in photographs – as modern art's first sculptures of

"The human face is no longer a shell, an immobile form, for nothing is immobile and everything is part of the hurried and manifold improvisations of the universe."
MEDARDO ROSSO

Umberto Boccioni
Fusion of Head and Window
Plaster (destroyed). Photograph
Milan, private collection

montaged material. In his manifesto, Boccioni (who was killed in action in 1916) took this bold approach one step further: "We reject the exclusive use of a single material. …We maintain that even twenty different materials can be used in a single work to achieve pictorial emotion … glass, wood, board, iron, cement, horsehair, leather, fabric, mirror, electric light etc."

Umberto Boccioni
Development of a Bottle in Space,
1912/13
Bronze, 38.1 x 60.3 x 32.7 cm
Milan, Civica Galleria d'Arte
Moderna

In a different way, the sculpture *Development of a Bottle in Space* (ill. below) bears the traits of a manifesto in practice. The still life was very much a Cubist domain. Boccioni's arrangement of table, plate, bottle and glass corrects them, as it were, on their own territory. Like all the Futurists, he rejected all that was static and harmoniously calm in favour of speed, movement and departure as metaphors for progress and modernity. In this *Weltbild* time becomes a visible dimension of space. This explains why the fragments rotate around the vertical core of a bottle, why the interior is sliced open, allowing us to see how concave and convex forms, hollows and shells curve within each other, gliding and interacting. This also explains why the frontally fixed bottle appears as an object in motion. The sculpture is the model of a world in which "absolute motion" – the frontal, upright, movement-triggering bottle – and "relative motion" – the circling fragments – are inextricably linked with one another.

Boccioni was not satisfied with this counter-design to the Cubist still life. The Italian in him still sought the great classical human form, even though this Futurist iconoclast considered a racing car more beautiful than the Nike of Samothrace. Is not the dynamically forward-rushing figure – *Unique Forms of Continuity in Space* (ill. right) – with its flame-like, wing-like, elongated muscles, ball-bearing joints, protruding and receding components – a synthesis of Nike, racing car and some future monster? Is this not a sculptural icon on the eve of the Great War whose pathos-laden faith in the machine era was soon to turn to horror?

Was this human whirlwind still too anatomical and not cosmic enough for the other great Futurist, Giacomo

Page 435:
Umberto Boccioni
Unique Forms of Continuity
in Space, 1913
Bronze, 112.2 x 88.5 x 40 cm
London, Tate Gallery

Balla? Is Balla's manifesto, *The Futurist Reconstruction of the Universe*, written in 1915 together with Fortunato Depero, actually addressing Boccioni in stating that "We shall find the abstract equivalent for all forms and elements of the universe. Then we shall combine them in sculptural constructions according to the moods of our inspiration"? Does his 1915 sculpture *Boccioni's Fist* (ill. right) in red-painted board, later cast in bronze, fulfil that statement of intent?

Preliminary drawings document step by step how the abstraction and reduction of the final version was developed out of a running figure with fist alternately extended and drawn back. Yet at the same time, the curves and glistening lines are entirely at one with Balla's *Line of Speed* sculptures derived from cars, aircraft, swallows in flight or stellar orbits. Whereas Boccioni anchors the feet of his figures in heavy blocks, Balla's *Fist* seems to leap up as though on a spring. It thus marks an early milestone on the path towards an abstract and sign-laden sculpture.

In contrast to such effusions, the colourful sculptures of Fortunato Depero (ill. below) seem calm without being static. They are, in contrast, coolly balanced

Giacomo Balla
Boccioni's Fist, 1915 – 1917
(Reconstruction 1956 – 1958)
Painted bronze, 80 x 76.2 x 25.5 cm

Fortunato Depero
Construction of a Girl, 1917
Varnished wood, 41 x 21 x 14 cm
Rovereto, Museo Fortunato Depero

Raymond Duchamp-Villon
Seated Female Figure, 1914/15
Bronze, gildes, 73 x 22 x 29 cm
Cologne, Museum Ludwig,
Ludwig Collection

"It is impossible to satisfy the demands of today's art with the means of the past alone. We want to include in sculpture the things that sculpture would never have accepted before. Will we fail or will sculpture fail in this?"

RAYMOND DUCHAMP-VILLON

Raymond Duchamp-Villon
Horse, 1914
Bronze, 150 x 97 x 153 cm
Antwerpen, Openluchtmuseum
voor Beeldhouwkunst Middelheim

and lead the additive structure, the colority and naive charm of children's toys into the world of modern sculpture.

Duchamp-Villon and the Mechanisation of Man

Cubism's sound shift had laced the figure into a rhythmic-geometric corset. Cuts, breaks and planes regulated the figure. Taken one step further, geometry became the expressive vocabulary that set the Cubist particles in motion or swept them along. The most frequently voiced criticism of Cubism was levelled at its static nature: it was the most modern form of perception, and yet it did not breathe the stormy spirit of modernity. It studied the world in the laboratory of art, while the world went on living beyond the confines of such still life studies. It undertook fundamental analysis, but applied its findings indiscriminately to man and form. Raymond Duchamp-Villon, brother of Marcel Duchamp, also started out leaning towards Rodin. In 1910 he discovered Cubism and, soon afterwards, the work of Archipenko. In the work of Duchamp-Villon, however, the compositional approach of these artists never tends towards rhythmic planarity, never pushes aside sculptural dynamics and invariably retains a tendency towards the psychological and physiognomical, which many sculptors at that time were abandoning. This is what makes him such a significant portraitist. The heads of *Baudelaire* (1910), *Maggy* (1911) and *Professor Gosset* (1918) not only illustrate a progressive increase in abstraction, stereometry and furrowing, but also a heightened intensity in the captivating gaze of eyes staring from deep hollows, graduating from the unemotive distance of *Baudelaire* to the idol-like drama of *Maggy* and the monumental division of the Gosset head into a convex forehead and nose and a concave lower face.

His Cubist analysis culminated in the various versions of *The Horse* which Duchamp-Villon created between 1914 and 1918 (ill. above), with obvious borrowings from Archipenko. The *Horse* is made up of straight lines, curves, spirals, hollows and arches. It is a demonic hybrid of gyrating mechanics and animal nature, pistons and organs thrown together in a synthesis of pure sculptural energy. Duchamp-Villon died in 1918 as a result of war-related physical exhaustion. He was arguably the most important sculptor to have become a victim of the first world war.

Vladimir Baranov-Rossiné
Symphony Number 1, 1913
Multi-coloured wood, painted
board and ground eggshell,
161.1 x 72.2 x 63.4 cm
New York, The Museum of
Modern Art, Katia Granoff Fonds

Vladimir Baranov-Rossiné
Counter-Relief, c. 1913
Assemblage; wood and other
materials, 131 x 46 cm
Private collection

*"This is the sinister armoured figure
of today and tomorrow. Nothing
human, only the terrible Frankenstein's monster into which we have
transformed ourselves."*
JACOB EPSTEIN

A New Human Image for the Machine Age

From 1912 the human image changed, above all in sculpture. In contrast to the Graeco-Latin tradition, it condensed visions of synthesis of man, machine and
mechanics. The spectrum ranges from Archipenko's
witty *Médranos* to the violent pathos and grotesque
deformation of organic contours in Boccioni's flaming
giants of steel who vie with the aircraft and the automobile. This was Filippo Tommaso Marinetti's vision
of the mechanical superman resisting the shock of
omnipresent speed.

In 1913 Jacob Epstein began his visored, robotic *Rock
Drill* (p. 422). It was originally mounted on a drill base
whose function was transferred in the final, more con-

densed, version to the machine-like right arm. On its
chest, between ribs of armoured steel, it retained its own
(more human?) heirs: armoured knight, miner and
demon of progress in one. In 1914, Raymond Duchamp-
Villon's *Horse* merged the anatomy of the horse (Boccioni's symbol of the emergent city) with the turning,
spiralling components of a machine. Without rider,
without legible movement, this is an independent creature in which the spiralling energy of a new and vital
creature is condensed. Albert Elsen pointed out correctly that these metaphors were created beyond the
scope of classical mythological convention and that they
euphorically glorify man and the extension of his powers
by mechanical means.

Rudolf Belling
Sculpture 23, 1923
Bronze, partly silvered,
41.5 x 21.5 x 23.5 cm
Kaiserslautern, Pfalzgalerie
Kaiserslautern

Raoul Hausmann
Mechanical Head (The Spirit of
our Times), 1919/20
Wood, leather, aluminium, brass,
and board, 32.5 x 21 x 20 cm
Paris, Musée National d'Art
Moderne, Centre Georges
Pompidou

Even Alexander Archipenko's *Médranos* (based on a Paris circus) of 1913 are light-hearted puppets somewhere between a child's plaything and a wooden robot, ideal figures of a mechanically controllable, eternally contented population of marionettes. Vladimir Baranov-Rossiné's famous *Symphony Number 1* (p. 438 left) of multi-coloured wood, painted board and crushed eggshells seems to provide an ironic response in a musical figure of abstract forms with the rhythm of broken melody lines and dissonant chords. In 1921, the Dadaist Raoul Hausmann codified the prevailing *Zeitgeist* in his *Mechanical Head* (ill. above right) with tape measure, clock, camera components, number-plate and typographic cylinder. The spirit of the day was metric. In 1923, the brass construction of Rudolf Belling's *Sculpture 23* (ill. above left) combined the rigidity of the mask with technical traits – note the skull as planetarium.

From Cubism to the Myth of Nature: Lipchitz, Laurens, Zadkine

The Eastern Europe contribution comes from Russia, Lithuania and the Danube monarchy. Oto Gutfreund, a Czech, works for a time in Paris and is one of the first to make use of Picasso's early Cubist example (ill. right). The Hungarian Joseph Csáky (p. 442 right) develops this in a geometric, stream-lined Synthetic Cubism. Jacques Lipchitz (pp. 440, 441) was the most impassioned and versatile of these pioneering artists. In 1913, at the age of twenty, he arrived in Paris from Vilnau (Lithuania) for the second time. The influence of Cubism tautened the serpentine curves of his unruly figures, adding an angu-

"The sculptor realises an imaginary portrayal within a real space and halts the flow of events by means of spatial materialisation."
Oto Gutfreund

Oto Gutfreund
Viky (Cubist Head),
c. 1911–1913
Bronze; height: 33 cm
Private collection

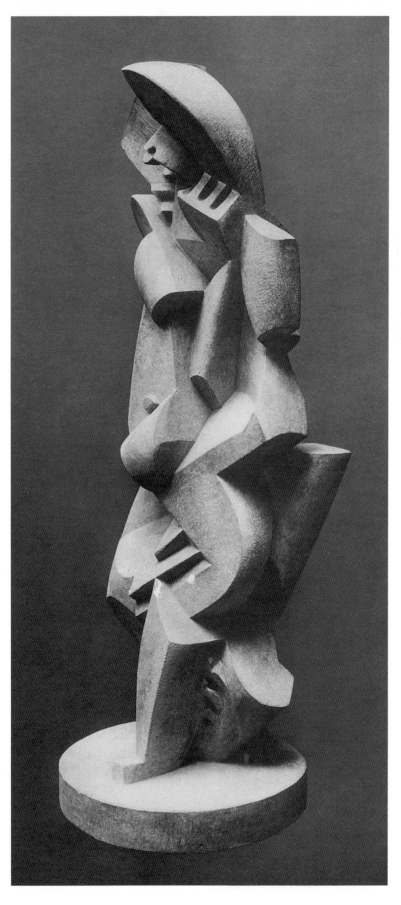

larity of structure to their axial symmetry. Interwoven, rhizomatic forms draw the surrounding space into the torsos and limbs of his sculptures. Yet just one year later, more radical solutions began to take hold. Picasso's step towards planar structure formed the basis for architectonically graduated and almost flat figures in which vertical lines predominate. Then Boccioni, Duchamp-Villon and Juan Gris presented a more nuanced grammar. From 1917 onwards the figures were fugue-like compositions of interactive straight and curved, concave and convex lines in which the axis zig-zigs angularly around a solid core.

Guitar players, dancers, bathers allowed the artist to explore the possibilities of rhythmic movement in harmony with organic and crystalline forms. In the 20s Lipchitz condensed this synthesis into emblematically reduced corporeal signs of concentrated energy. Abstract and later increasingly organic furrows converged in a broad and heavy flow. The rhythm slowed to one of fettered expression – the climax of a genuinely Cubist sculpture going far beyond any formalistic pattern.

After 1925 Lipchitz turned away from Cubism. The flow of organic growth processes took the place of analytic breakdown, just as it had before Cubist intervention. Formal structures took on a duality that gave them a symbolic force generated entirely from their own sculptural originality. The *Large Figure* with its magically staring cylinder eyes is more like an idol, a heavy-set progression of paired forms united beneath the sheltering horizontal oval of the head. Transitions between human, animal and plant forms in such subjects as *Mother and Child* or *The Couple* lead the motifs back to an archetypal foundation. Instead of the formal exercises with guitar-playing harlequins, he now began to address the existential themes that were to occupy him for half a century. These included such fundamental human issues as the polarities of gender, fertility and conflict, as reflected in Jewish and classical mythology.

In the 30s, Lipchitz created undulating figures of baroque exuberance. During the second world war, the harrowing awareness of Jewish persecution changed his figures into monstrous, torn creatures. Surreal cage-bars devoured the surrounding space with sharpened teeth. After the war, this latent pathos was heightened into a sweeping stylistic credo whose drama was sublimated in the pathos of form.

At the same time, of all the sculptors to have passed through Cubism, Lipchitz is the only one to have intervened a second time in the history of sculpture. His Cubist works had already been exceptional for the sheer audacity of their entirely abstract treatment of space. From 1928 onwards he repeatedly condensed the volume of his *Musicians* or *Heads* into narrow bands and serpentines that draw almost signature arabesques in space: scripturally dissolved corporeal signs whose sweeping eccentricity anticipated the metal sculptures of González. For the focal issue of the second decade,

Jacques Lipchitz
Figure, 1926–1930
Bronze, 210 x 100 x 100 cm
New York, The Museum of
Modern Art

Jacques Lipchitz
Woman with Guitar, 1927
Bronze; height: 35 cm
Private collection

*"I suddenly discovered that volume
in sculpture is created by light and
shadow. Volume is light. In a
smoothly rounded or curvilinear
sculpture the light washes over the
surface and may even diminish or
destroy the sense of volume, the sense
of the third dimension. When the
forms of the sculpture are angular,
when the surface is broken by deep
interpenetrations and contrasts,
light can work to bring out the truly
sculptural qualities."*
JACQUES LIPCHITZ

Henri Laurens
Guitar, 1914
Sheet iron, painted; height: 44 cm
Cologne, Museum Ludwig,
Ludwig Collection

namely the flow of space into volume, Lipchitz once again provided an essential solution.

The French sculptor Henri Laurens (pp. 418 and 443) had been a friend of Braque since 1911, yet he did not join the sculptural avant-garde until 1914 or 1915. His first constructions – two wooden clowns of 1915 (p. 418) – are derived from the conically worked and fragile *Médranos* of Archipenko. Yet the search for classical harmony and the sensual vitality of Laurens' work was soon to turn away from hybrid balancing acts and abstract symmetries. He did not radicalise formal elements so much as transpose them into balanced and gracefully bizarre compositions.

Up to 1919 he produced the most persuasive sculptural counterpart to Cubist painting in the form of his still lifes with musical instruments, bottles and fruits, as well as figures and heads resembling vertically elongated still lifes. Picasso's cylindrical, protruding guitar aperture became a leitmotif in what may be regarded as a late echo of the African Grebe mask that had such a remarkable impact on modern sculpture. During this phase, for all his contrasting planarity, crystalline angles, overlap-

ping planes, rhythmic modulations and tension-charged layering, Laurens remained heavily influenced by painting. His constructions, surely the purest contribution to the sculpture of Synthetic Cubism, remained reliefs to be viewed from one angle only.

Yet Laurens, a sculptor through and through, went still further, moving away from material contrasts, planarity and frontality. By 1917 he was working in stone, and exploring the block as an integral sculptural core that was structured, but not dissected, by cubes, angles, spheres or waves. These new sculptures possessed a compelling presence. The simplification of Cubist rhythms created a solid physicality (or vice versa) which, though still adhering to Cubist techniques, became increasingly rounded, mobile and ex-centric in the course of the 30s.

This new, post-Cubist Laurens was one of the greatest and most distinctive portrayers of the female form in modern art. The sheer vitality of his *Hommage à la femme* is surpassed only by Picasso. In the 1930s he transposed massive volumes and moving bodies into serene, playful, dance-like motion. From now on, Laurens pre-

Ossip Zadkine
Mother and Child (Forms and Light), 1918
Marble, 58.4 x 50 x 16.7 cm
Washington, Hirshhorn Museum and Sculpture Garden, Smithsonian Institution

Joseph Csáky
Head, 1914
Stone, 39 x 20 x 21.5 cm
Paris, Musée National d'Art Moderne, Centre Georges Pompidou

ferred to work in bronze, a material more versatile and
vibrant than solid stone. His stretching, writhing, gesticulating bathers and nymphs are swept and flooded by
space – voluptuous and graceful goddesses of fertility
awakened from the stony sleep of their ancient Mediterranean tradition and brought to life with melodiously
vibrant curves. They unite vitality and the immutability
of mythical being.

The young Russian Ossip Zadkine (p. 442 and ill.
below) arrived in Paris in 1909. He was, by nature, not so
much an analytical artist as a sculptor of the elementary,
a lyricist and expressionist. This approach brought him
at a very early stage to the block-like form and it also
explained why he returned time and time again to the
wooden trunk as the solid basis for his figures. With
hindsight, he would appear to be the only genuine wood
sculptor, apart from Barlach, that classical Modernism
produced. It is in this medium that we find his purest
and most forceful works. They are soaring, closely contoured figural poles in which the anatomy is carved and
notched as though from the outside, yet subtly modelled. His female figures are imbued with a quiet grace
and sensuality that bring the wood to life. Does this
make Zadkine a noble traditionalist emancipated from
the classical ideal?

Even the Cubist semi-figures created around 1920
retain their solid core. Even where Zadkine rigidly
encloses the body in a formal framework, geometrically

Henri Laurens
Siren, 1945
Bronze, 117 x 77 cm
Mannheim, Städtische Kunsthalle
Mannheim

angled and concavely hollowed, he is merely marking
the surface. Breaks, angles, corners, distortions, serve to
consolidate and heighten emotional expression. What
his externalised version of Cubism lacks in structural
depth, it gains in force of expression and emotion. It is
therefore only logical that Zadkine should have been
one of the first to move on after 1920 in the direction of a
more curvilinear, organic art. Yet in doing so, he took
with him the Cubist freedom of combining viewpoints,
and of offsetting the convex with the concave (the
Archipenko paradigm).

Around 1930, apart from his nudes, he began producing deeply furrowed, baroquely moving and staggered
groups with sculpted contours – an overstrained and
dichotomous eclecticism whose ambition dissolves in a
plethora of sweeping forms. The Rotterdam memorial
The Destroyed City (ill. left) is the outstanding work of his
mature œuvre. This fragmented, angular giant of pain is
one massive lament, and the encroaching space a yawn-
ing wound. A work that unites once more the experience
of Cubism and Expressionism, it is a rare example of
modernism meaningfully exploring war.

Ossip Zadkine
The Destroyed City. Monument
for Rotterdam, 1948–1953
Bronze; height: 6.5 m
Rotterdam, Schiedamse Dijk

3 Constructing the World

Russia: Monuments and the Culture of Materials

Until the mid 20s, the revolution in the plastic arts was concentrated predominantly in the melting-pot that was Paris. Boccioni, of course, was an exception. Even Lipchitz, Laurens, Zadkine, Gutfreund and Csáky were sons of Cubism rather than its founding fathers. The next seminal influence was to emerge in Mosow rather than Paris. It was here that developments in the field since 1914/15 (some of them passionately nationalistic) took on a dynamism of their own. It was here, especially given the fact that the first world war severed contacts with Paris, that new stategies and paradigms became established. It was here, too that the formal history of modern sculpture finally merged with the profound social and political changes wrought by the 1917 October Revolution.

The term Constructivism has become widely accepted in referring to broad areas of Russian art between 1915 and 1925. Strictly speaking, however, a rapid succession of diverse movements had mushroomed in Moscow under the *nom de guerre* of Futurism. They ranged from the craftsmanship of Tatlin's so-called culture of materials to the esoterically cosmic Suprematism of Malevich and the Productivism of industrially manufactured consumer goods. Tatlin's emphasis on "real materials in real space" contrasts starkly with the idealistic flights of Malevich, El Lissitzky and Gabo. The actual Constructivists in the historically correct sense of the term numbered no more than twenty young artists and theoreticians who created a "constructivist working group" at the Moscow Institute of Artistic Culture (Inkhuk) and who exhibited together in May 1922. They coined the term. For the sake of simplicity, we shall use this term.

This fertile artistic and intellectual scene of painters, architects and critics rushed from one "ism" to the next. Not one of their spokesmen had actually trained as a sculptor originally. For most of them, reliefs, sculptures and objects were merely an intermezzo between painting and sculpture, stage design and revolutionary design. This is what distinguishes their work from the continuity of the œuvre produced by the Russian emigré artists in Paris. And yet, in a broader sense, they created sculptures more radical than any other developments at the time. What they saw as fundamental research, as a preparation for more useful products – buildings, pro-

"My apparatus is built on the principle of utilizing living, organic forms. The observation of these forms led me to the conclusion that the most aesthetic forms are the most economic. Art is: work with the shaping of the material, in this respect." VLADIMIR TATLIN

Vladimir Tatlin
Model for the Monument to the Third International, 1919
Wood, steel and glass,
420 x 300 cm
Photo of original state. Formerly Moscow (destroyed)

paganda kiosks, versatile furnishings – are early highlights in an abstract and thoroughly structural, conceptually organised sculpture. The Russian artists of the period taught sculpture to float, like a weightless and yet painstakingly devised choreography in a space without gravity. It was the art of aviators with boundless faith in revolutionary progress and the ability to compensate a real technological deficit.

In 1920, Gabo stated in his *Realistic Manifesto*: "The plumbline in our hand, eyes precise as a ruler, a mind as finely tuned as a compass, we construct our work as the universe constructs its own, as the engineer builds his bridges, as the mathematician his formulae of orbits." Wherever the optics of mathematical and technically rational construction, linear structure and the precision of engineering appear to regulate modern sculpture, they can be traced back to Russia. Much was destroyed after the advent of Stalinism and restructured in the spirit of doctrinaire realism, and is known today only from photographs or in the form of reconstructions. Nevertheless, the surviving material is still enough to recapitulate an enormously influential moment in recent art history.

Vladimir Tatlin
Model for a Monument to the Third International, 1919
(Reconstruction 1979)
Wood, steel and glass, 420 x 300 cm
Paris, Musée National d'Art Moderne, Centre Georges Pompidou

Tatlin: Counter-Relief, Monument and Flying Machine

Vladimir Tatlin (pp. 444–447) stands at the very beginning of modern Russian sculpture, for the Russians in Paris followed the path of western art. He is a father figure, just as Malevich (pp. 160 f) is in painting. Of course, Tatlin visited Paris, but his legendary meeting with Picasso did not take place until February 1914, although it is often assumed to have been earlier. As a result, this progressive painter returned to Moscow as a constructor of reliefs. His critical response consists in a series of assemblages of metal, wood, plaster, board, asphalt and putty, created in a feverishly prolific output from 1914 onwards, soon to take the form of his freely suspended *Corner Reliefs*.

The superficial similarity of his early work to the still lifes of Picasso is deceptive. Tatlin did not seek to bridge a gap between portrayal and reality, and soon abandoned any associative references to a bottle, a newspaper or a guitar. He developed the reliefs directly from the *faktura* (a key word in Russian modernism) of the materials, their living language and specific characteristics such as colour, brilliance, structure, weight, firmness, elasticity. He called for the prerequisites of form to be sought in the material itself. Accordingly, Tatlin set about bending sheet metal, modelling plaster, breaking glass and tautening wire. He explored and staged, contrasted, composed and constructed every material according to its natural qualities.

The way this former seaman handled wood, tar, knots and bolts has more in common with the craft of the boatbuilder than with the traditional techniques of sculpture. He is as far removed from Picasso's border-crossing painting as he is from Boccioni's merging of man and city. His work rejects even the last vestige of quotation and illusion, positing sculpture as a perfect entity and as a structure complete within itself. These reliefs with their alternating elements of tension, curvature and anchoring, with their matt and reflecting surfaces, with their subtly elaborated haptic appeal and their traces of use challenge us, as El Lissitzky put it in a 1922 lecture on Tatlin, to "focus our eyes on the sense of touch".

Tatlin himself regarded his "culture of materials" as being in the tradition of the brightly coloured Russian icons, illustrated news sheets and shop signs, as opposed to the illusionist tradition of western art. His friend the poet Victor Chlebnikov had already explored the physical presence of words as opposed to their semantic meaning.

Tatlin was one of the first to unconditionally acknowledge the October Revolution after 1917 and to re-direct his creative powers accordingly. His model for a *Monument to the Third International* (competition entry) is a vast utopian vision located somewhere between architecture and apparatus, a cross between a government building, a social organism and an emphatic symbol of progress (pp. 444 f). If built, it would be a 300 metre high spiral framework of steel incorporating a cylinder, a cone and a cube. These three components were to house the parliament, the executive and the headqurters for information and propaganda respectively, reflecting the actual decision-making process in the young Soviet Republic. It was planned by Tatlin, that each component was to revolve on its own axis at different speeds: the parliament housed in the cylinder once a year, the executive housed in the cone once a month and, at the very top, the office of information and propaganda housed in the cube once a day, thus placing the political instances within a larger cosmic cycle. Unrealistic as this bold design may have appeared in 1920, it heralded art's claim to have a hand in shaping the new society.

Rodchenko and the Inkhuk Constructivists

The collaboration between artists and revolutionaries was not to be taken for granted at first. After the events

Vladimir Tatlin
Counter-Relief, 1914/15
Metal, wood, and wire, 118 x 71 cm
St. Petersburg, Russian State
Museum

Vladimir Tatlin
Complex Corner Relief, 1915
(Reconstruction 1979)
Iron, zink and aluminium,
78.8 x 152.4 x 76.2 cm
London, Annely Juda Fine Art

Even so, it would be rather one-sided to emphasise only the inherent expressive power of the material. Hubertus Gaßner quite rightly casts doubt upon the assumption that Tatlin regarded the properties of the material itself as absolute. The sweep of the arc and the elasticity of the curve oscillate with the rhythm of a living process of growth – the very opposite of that "great white god, the straight line" (Alexander Samayalin) worshipped by the younger, technology-loving Inkhuk Constructivists. Tatlin externalised the "inner constitution" of materials rather than reshaping it with ruler and compass. Even his *Letatlin* flying machine (p. 446 above) is based on an organically rhythmic concept of flying rather than a mechanical understanding of it. The notion of Tatlin as a "machine artist" is thus based on a misconception. His work demonstrates the bio-dynamic energies of the materials as well as their structural qualities.

Real materials are situated in real space. Herein lies an essential innovation, recognised by his Russian contemporaries. Picasso's *Guitar* and Boccioni's *Bottle* still function within their own restricted space. The bottle stands on a pedestal. Tatlin's *Corner Reliefs* (ill right and above), by contrast, are mounted on a taut wire across a corner like bizarre flying machines, and balanced around a gravitational core. They do not draw the space towards them, but depend on it instead. They do not link space to any ideal axis, but take it as it is. Their tensile strength corresponds with the corner. Thus, Tatlin distances himself more clearly than his contemporaries from the tradition of sculpture on a plinth.

Alexander Rodchenko
Hanging Construction No. 12, 1919
Painted plywood and wire,
83.5 x 58.5 x 43.3 cm
The George Costakis Collection
(Art Co. Ltd.)

cal" revolution. At first, painting was called into question. Influential theoreticians railed against the Suprematist works of Malevich, proclaiming that it was not idealism, but the "material object" produced by the worker that was the aim of art. This triggered a move towards the tangible, three-dimensional object in which technical and aesthetic polish were to be substituted for industry.

Tatlin, though he continued to have faith in art, provided a catalyst with his *Monument*. By 1920/21 an increasing number of avant-garde artists had begun to adopt the new line. In Moscow the Inkhuk group, from which Productivist Art was later to emerge, discussed and analysed the relationship between composition and construction. The die, once cast, fell in favour of Constructivism – a term we shall now examine more closely.

Alexander Rodchenko (ill. left) was their leading theoretician. Having demonstrated once more what Varvara Stepanova described as "nothing but painting" with his all-black paintings in 1919, he announced in an essay on *The Line* towards the end of that same year "Colour has died in black ... Let the brushstroke now die too!" The next step led from linear composition to the linearity of structure in real space. This took place at the end of 1919, when he joined the Association for the Synthesis of Painting, Sculpture and Architecture. Rodchenko now began designing ex-centrically balanced propaganda kiosks as his contribution to the Bolshevik revolution. Between late 1920 and early 1921, he created six hanging cardboard constructions comprising geometric figures such as the circle, triangle, hexagon, cut inwards concentrically. These were translations from the second dimension into the third dimension, anti-individual, reproducible entities which followed their immanent geometric logic entirely, allowing mass and materiality to dissolve into supple movement and light reflexes.

Here, Rodchenko intensified the sense of weightlessness that epitomised Russia's early contribution to modernism. Some may see in it the first mobiles. Other sculptures, asymmetrically suspended as in a tower building, explore the combinatory possibilities of geo-

of October 1917, the victorious Bolsheviks were just as suspicious of bourgeois relics of autonomy in art as the artistic avant-garde were of attacks on their autonomy. What would be the role of the artist under the future government of the proletariat? Would he be needed at all? The turn-around came as the result of a serious crisis of legitimation and dragged on until 1920. It was only then that a new understanding of the artist's role filtered through, reflecting the turnaround from political revolution to an emphatically propagated industrial "electri-

El Lissitzky
Proun-Room for the Great Berlin
Art Exhibition, 1923
(Reconstruction 1965)
Wood, colour-varnished,
320 x 365 x 365 cm
Eindhoven, Stedelijk Van Abbe
Museum

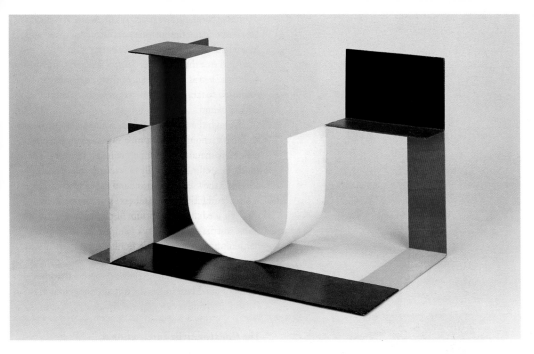

Katarzyna Kobro
Spatial Composition, 1929
Welded and painted steel,
40 x 40 x 64 cm
Lódz, Muzeum Sztuki

"Construction is the modern requirement for organization and utilitarian use of material."
ALEXANDER RODCHENKO

metric modules. Only Karl Ioganson, who was also a member of Inkhuk, achieved a similarly rigorous and absolutely logical systematic construction with his variable hybrids of steel bars and steel rope. His (no longer extant) *Studies in Equilibrium* are among the most radical experiments and most conclusive results in this laboratory phase of Productivist Art: ideal sculptures of power lines and study models for useful, versatile items in one.

Other Inkhuk members were less interested in a useable invention than in technical appearance. The brothers Vladimir and Georgi Stenberg, for example, when they were barely twenty years old, were creating mechanical, framelike structures reminiscent of elegantly propped apparatus, cranes or signal masts. Constantin Medunezki transposed Tatlin's aesthetics of materials into a technogically informed and gestural spatial context. For most of these young artists however, the exploration of sculpture was no more than a brief interlude before moving on to successful careers designing stage sets, trade-fair stands, industrial design and typography.

"Transit Stations Between Painting and Architecture"

Did this, for a time at least in Russia, spell the end of modern sculpture, whose history as we know it has so often been synonymous with a history of its autonomy? From 1922 onwards the concept of Constructivist sculpture was imported by emigré artists such as Katarzyna Kobro, Naum Gabo and Antoine Pevsner to Warsaw, Paris, London and America, where it continued to develop outside the Soviet Union. Nevertheless, even in Moscow, a number of remarkable developments continued to take place. The outstanding achievements were

almost invariably situated in the forcefield of painting, sculpture and architecture, an area El Lissitzky described as "transit stations between painting and architecture". Gabo, referring to his work up to 1924, spoke of an "endeavour to unite the sculptural and the architectural elements".

No wonder the bizarre agitatory propaganda kiosks, speakers' tribunes, trade-fair stands, Socialist parade decorations which are also of interest as sculptural works, were generally created by painters and graphic artists such as Rodchenko and Gustav Klucis or architects such as Natan Altmann and the Vasnin brothers. They created their own type of architectural sculpture which Siah Armajani was to adopt and develop some fifty years later.

Even the painter Malevich, at times a keen rival of Tatlin, had left one problem unanswered. If the non-figurative world of his Suprematist paintings consists of rectangles, triangles, squares, crosses and circles, what happens when their purely planar geometry is transposed into three dimensions? What happens when their abstract forms are adopted in keeping with the spirit and ideology of the times and applied to some practical purpose such as architecture? In 1919 Malevich confronted the painter, graphic designer and trained architect El Lissitzky with this problem.

That same year, Lissitzky started work on his *Proun* paintings (meaning, roughly, "project for confirmation of the new") which he continued until 1924 (p. 168). They are axiometrically designed views of imagined cities, floating, soaring urban situations, housing blocks, squares and streets, interacting levels in dynamic diagonality devoid of all earthbound qualities – as though Malevich's forms had become three-dimensional.

"Proun begins on the plane, proceeds to the spatial model and from there to the construction of all the objects of life in general. In this respect, the Proun goes beyond the painting and its artists on the one hand, and beyond the machine and the engineer on the other hand, and passes to structuring the space and breaking it down by the elements of all dimensions, and builds a new, versatile yet uniform figure of nature."
EL LISSITZKY

Antoine Pevsner
Portrait of Marcel Duchamp, 1926
Celluloid on copper, 94.3 x 65.1 cm
New Haven (CT), Yale University
Art Gallery

In 1923 Lissitzky installed a "demonstration room" at
the Große Berliner Kunstausstellung where his *Prouns*
invade the surrounding space in the form of spheres,
cubes and bars, providing the most conclusive example
of a Constructivist environment (p. 448). The famous
Cloud Hangars project he designed in 1924 as an urban
highrise development for eight Moscow sites is relatively
conventional by comparison and almost represents a
step backwards compared to the visionary complexity of
his *Proun* works.

The *Prouns* also forge a link with Malevich's own
three-dimensional studies. Although he was not actually
a sculptor, he considered the actual physical presence of
a work important enough to create at least seventy
Architectones between the years 1922 and 1929. These are
vertically or horizontally staggered, cubistically angled
dream buildings akin to cathedrals or broad-based,
boldly cantilevered office tracts. They can be understood as immaculate intellectual models of a "non-figurative" universe within a material world. Perhaps they
also represented a tentative step towards the ideology of
the day, which called for applied ideas. They were certainly never intended to be realised. Soon afterwards,
the leading Polish avant-garde artist and theoretician
Vladislav Strzemiński (ill. right) reduced the fugue-like
wealth "unistically" to a few massive, distinctly directed
blocks which he also called *Architectones*.

Strzemiński's Russian-born wife Katarzyna Kobro,
who settled in Poland in 1924, was one of the rare examples of a genuine sculptor among the many painters and
architects of the Constructivist movement. She devised

Vladislav Strzemiński
Suprematist Architecton, 1923
(Reconstruction 1979)
Painted wood, 39 x 36 x 36 cm
Paris, private collection

a concept for sculpture based on the work of Malevich.
Her suspended compositions in fibreglass, wood and
metal lend the Suprematist vocabulary a floating lyricism and transparency. Her *Spatial Sculptures* and *Spatial
Compositions* (p. 449) activate and modulate the surrounding space, lending it rhythm with its simple flat or
curved planes.

Though the notion that "sculpture penetrates space
and space penetrates sculpture" was no longer a new
insight by the 1920s, never before had it been realised so
fundamentally, so naturally or so harmoniously. By
adopting the Golden Section and the mathematical
sequence of Fibonacci numbers (3, 5, 8, 13 etc.) and
through the tense equilibrium of planar and linear relations, restricted to primary colours or black and white,
her sculptures – for all their architectural foundations –
are amongst the purest of autonomous works produced
by Constructivism. It is interesting to note that they
were not produced in Russia, but after her emigration to
Poland.

The Constructivist International

1921–1922 were years of fundamental change for Russian
Constructivism. The Productivist artists became organised and disappeared into production companies and
the New Economic Policy (NFC) opened up the Soviet
Union to the west, with the People's Commissariat
for Education holding a huge exhibition of some 600
works, including the work of all the major Constructivists, which went on tour to Berlin. The Productivist
idea became increasingly dogmatic. The brothers
Naum Gabo and Antoine Pevsner turned their backs
on Moscow's political pressure and emigrated.

In Berlin, El Lissitzky, who constantly sought to link up the various movements in Moscow, Berlin, Weimar, Hanover and Holland, published the magazine *Gegenstand* in collaboration with Ilya Ehrenburg. Responses and parallels became evident. In Holland in 1917, the De Stijl group was formed. In Weimar and Dessau, the Bauhaus had outgrown its early Expressionistic pathos and had begun to adopt a more Constructivist line. The experimental media artist Moholy-Nagy arrived in Germany from Hungary. From now on, Constructivism finally branched out from its specifically Russian beginnings to become an international movement with many different directions and variations.

What was it that made this movement so attractive in the interwar years? After the catastrophe of the nation states' turbulent catharsis, venting enormous emotional pressure in the apocalyptic scenes and anarchistic idylls of the Expressionists, and after the ecstatic confession of the Self, this new design for a rationally lucid, supranational, supraindividual art – and, for that matter, society as well – banished many fears and anxieties.

The Constructivism of the 20s was optimistic. It was a downpayment on a better future, the horizon of Utopia. It was not the aesthetic religion of simple, straight-forward reason, but was polarised between the industrial prototypes of the Bauhaus and the mystical spirituality of Malevich and Mondrian. In formal terms, it sought universally applicable principles, a general key that could be varied from image to sculpture, to design and building. For this reason, sculpture is just one facet of the spectrum and is frequently situated as an open genre between architecture, apparatus, scientific and mathematical model.

Gabo and Pevsner: Crystalline Development

Naum Gabo and his brother Antoine Pevsner are regarded as the fathers of Constructivist sculpture. They were the only artists of the founding generation to make the new sculptural design their life work. Both of them spent their youth in Paris and were of course subjected to the prevailing artistic climate of Cubism. Both of them worked on the *Realistic Manifesto* (though Gabo played a more active role) which was published, as the result of a misunderstanding (the authorities believing it to be in praise of "realism"), by the State Printing House in Moscow on August 5, 1920. It confidently relativises the significance of Cubism and Futurism, and addresses the problems involved. "Realistic" means "space and time are the only forms in which life is built and therefore art must also be constructed in these forms ... We know that everything has its own specific quality: chair, table, lamp, telephone, book, house, person ... they are all entire worlds with their own rhythms, their own orbits. This is why, we in creating remove ... all that is accidental and local, leaving only the reality of the constant rhythm of the forces in them."

Up to this point, Boccioni would have had no qualms about signing such a manifesto. It concludes, however, "We renounce volume as a pictorial and plastic form of space ... we take four planes and construct with them the same volume as of four tons of mass. Thus we bring back to sculpture the line as a direction and in it we affirm depth as the one form of space ... We affirm in these arts a new element, the kinetic rhythms, as the basic forms of our perception of real time."

The programme they posited may seem to us more idealistic than realistic, for what does idealism in art mean if not cleansing it of all that is "accidental" to the point of sheer transcendence of space and time. Pevsner worked on implementing this programme from 1915 onwards and, by 1920, in an act of elementary border-crossing, he had staked out the most extreme point of

Naum Gabo
Head of a Woman, c. 1917–1920
Celluloid and metal, 62 x 49 cm
New York, The Museum of
Modern Art

all: a steel spring set in motion with the aid of a motor, transforming its physical mass into traces of form in space. It is almost like a prototype of the concept that Gabo was to continue to explore for more than half a century. Pevsner, originally a painter, finally crossed over to sculpture in 1924. For both these brothers, the Manifesto was to remain the Magna Carta of their art.

In 1937, Gabo illustrated a sentence of the Manifesto in the form of a diagram. He drew a closed cube made of four planes, from which he constructed "the same volume as of four tons of mass". He then drew an open cube without side walls and showed it intersected by two diagonal planes: an inner framework whose point of intersection forms the heart of the structure. His *Head of a Woman* (ill. above) of 1917–1920 is based on the same principle. Strip-like segments of cardboard or plywood radiate from a central axis, creating rhythmically segmented hollow spaces. It is a cellular system related to Picasso's 1909 *Head of a Woman* and clearly illustrating the step from the externally facetted mass to the visible constructive skeleton. In the mid-20s, Pevsner also

Naum Gabo
Column, 1923
(Replica 1975)
Plexiglas, wood, metal, and glass,
105.3 x 73.6 x 73.6 cm
Humblebæk (Denmark), Louisiana
Museum of Modern Art

created his closely related *Portrait of Marcel Duchamp* (p. 450 above).

Gabo's early *Heads* and arched bodies demonstrate his approach with didactic clarity, like demonstration models of a new sculptural theory. Yet it was not long before he began to move away from the human figure. In keeping with the spirit of the times, his *Column* of 1923 (ill. right) and other works of the early 1920s are situated somewhere between architectural concept, monument, apparatus and sculpture. The development of this sculpture around a vertical core remains fully transparent. Herein lies its ideal reality, whereas Tatlin's *Tower* addresses a real social place, however remote, rotating within real time. The transparent material plexiglass corresponds to the transparent structure.

In the 30s, the angular, additive and apparative disappeared from his sculptures. The central axis became the fulcrum point for curved wings, and the spatial interaction became more complex and polyphanous. Nylon threads or slender wires were spanned over the rounded plexiglass planes or metal frames. Lines were bundled to create light energy, refracting and breaking on angles. At the same time, the entire volume remained transparent: a multi-dimensional harp of light as an oscillating spatial entity whose lyricsim is a far remove from Pevsner's more rugged tone.

In terms of process and external structure, the work of the two brothers bears an astonishing similarity. Both build up the volume increasingly freely and openly out of curvilinear planes. Both use points of intersection as focal points of energy. Yet whereas Gabo uses transparency, Pevsner seeks a harshly metallic contrast. And whereas Gabo works his sculpture in gentle visual torsions and rotations, Pevsner captures them in rigid frontality. Whereas Gabo captures the central axis and plays around it, Pevsner lifts it through symmetrical lines of radiation in which the magical enchantment of fetishes is evident. Whereas Gabo has the light glide softly over curves, Pevsner closes a nest of light and shadow impenetrably into the inner life of the structure. Is this a case of the lyrical temperament versus the dramatic temperament? At any rate, together with the confident fundamentalism of Katarzyna Kobro, they indicate the expressive range of the Constructivist approach.

Bauhaus and De Stijl: New Media and Experimentation

Remarkable as it may seem, the two most important European Constructivist movements – Bauhaus and De Stijl – produced few sculptors. They did not follow Russian art in turning away from painting towards the "object" around 1920. At the Bauhaus, initiated in 1919 with Expressionist pathos by the architect Walter Gropius, painting was very much to the fore. Admittedly, Gropius himself created a major early work of abstract monumental sculpture in his 1920 *Memorial to the Fallen of March* and even the painter Oskar

László Moholy-Nagy
Light-Space Modulator, 1930
(Replik 1970)
Metal and plastic, electric motor,
151 x 70 x 70 cm
Cambridge (MA), Busch-Reisinger
Museum

László Moholy-Nagy
Nickel Construction, 1921
Nickel-plated iron, welded,
35.6 x 17.5 x 23.8 cm
New York, The Museum of
Modern Art, Gift of Mrs. Sibyl
Moholy-Nagy

"Because light is a spatial-temporal problem, the mere accentuation of the question of light brings us into the field of a new spatial awareness that cannot yet be fully analysed. We can, however, find a word to describe it: floating."
LÁSLÓ MOHOLY-NAGY

Schlemmer gave his ideal human figure a sculptural profile.

On the whole, however, sculpture was very much a secondary concern at the Bauhaus, even though – or perhaps because – it played an important role as a fundamental part of the Basic Course. Exercises addressing the "nature of materials" focused on texture, structure, hardness, elasticity, transparency etc. were aimed at strengthening a sense of touch and spatial awareness. The titles of student papers occasionally read like a list of options on current or future developments in sculpture: material combintions, cuboid composition, haptic panels, floating sculpture, studies in equilibrium. Most, however, got no further than the experimental stage, serving merely to sensitise without actually resulting in any historic contribution to sculpture.

The great exceptiomn was the Hungarian artist László Moholy-Nagy. In 1923, at the age of 28, he took over from Johannes Itten as head of the Basic Course and was also put in charge of the metal workshop. Originally a painter (p. 178), he became the first modern multi-media artist, working in light sculpture, design, photography, film, typography, stage design and theory as component parts of a new social vision. His communicative spirit extended the concept of sculpture to include motion and openness, redefining the relationship between space, time, material and light, and emancipating mechanical apparatus to the point of art. He was the eternal forerunner, restless experimentor and enthusiastic researcher in the optical media of light and transparency whether he was developing photograms or,

in the early 1920s, creating his glittering sculptures out of combinations of wood, glass, steel, zinc and nickel alloys.

In 1930, after eight years of experimentation, he exhibited his *Light-Space Modulator* (ill. above left) in Paris. It was a 120 cm high apparatus of perforated and translucent discs, bars and glass spirals, which cast the brightness of 140 lightbulbs and five spotlights on the wall in an abstract theatrical display of shifting light and shadow, a drama in three acts with three tempi – calm, delayed, counter-movement.

It was the key to Moholy-Nagy's entire œuvre, his *Vision in Motion*, to quote the title of his subsequent publication. He not only referred to it in his scenarios

Georges Vantongerloo
Construction in the Sphere, 1918
Blue painted wood, 18 x 12 x 12 cm
Private collection

stringent rationalisation, whose *Construction in the Sphere* took modern sculpture to new heights of geometric ideality in 1917. The point of departure is still a seated female figure, systematically transposed onto a sphere, a cone, or a pyramid. Although Vantongerloo moved away from De Stijl after 1922, proportioning (and naming) his minimalist layered blocks according to mathematical formulae, he remained true to the orthogonal equilibrium of the De Stijl aesthetic.

In his later work after 1945 he drew sweeping curvilinear wires in the air and then moved towards undulating and organically intertwined entities of plexiglass, Medusas of light, transformations of colour. An œuvre that had remained within the strictest methodical bounds for a full two decades finally ended in lyrical abstraction. At the same time, Max Bill was taking Vantongerloo's methodical approach one step further in the direction of Concrete Art.

Georges Vantongerloo
Spatial Sculpture
($y = ax3–bx2 + cx$), 1935
Nickel silver; height: 38.5 cm
Basel, Öffentliche Kunstsammlung Basel, Kunstmuseum, Emanuel Hoffmann-Stiftung

for Alexander Korda's film *The City of the Future* in stage sets and trade-fair designs – on the horizon appeared fountains of light and electric motion, "entertainment at fairs and heightened tension in the theatre". Moholy-Nagy was not only a pioneer of light kinetics, but also anticipated, with delight, the blurring of borders between "high" and "low" art.

In 1928 the left-wing ideology of the new Bauhaus director prompted Moholy-Nagy to leave. In 1934 he emigrated via Amsterdam to London, where he created the first of his *Space Modulators* – curved sheets of plexiglass whose shifting points suggest changing spatial curvature. After 1940, by which time he was living in Chicago and running his own School of Design, he bent the plexiglass into floating, transparent, interconnected tubes with an aura of gliding light: a counterpole to the technoid world of his work twenty years before. The arch-Constructivist Gabo moved in a similar direction at the time.

Fundamental research of a different kind was undertaken by Georges Vantongerloo, the only sculptor of the Dutch De Stijl movement. Instead of trawling the visual media, he pursued a mathematical fundamentalism whose "objective truth" he saw as the basis of art. Although Gerrit Rietveld's famous chair and the axial architectural sections by Theo van Doesburg do focus on Constructivist three-dimensionality, Vantongerloo stands alone as a sculptor and as a rigorous adherent of

"Through their relationship to one another, volumes convey to us a sense of space and through their distance from one another they convey a sense of time."

GEORGES VANTONGERLOO

Georges Vantongerloo
Construction from an Oval, 1918
Mahogany, painted blue, yellow and red, 16.5 x 6.5 x 6.5 cm
Private collection

Max Bill
Endless Torsion, 1953–1956
Bronze, 125 x 125 x 80 cm
Antwerpen, Openluchtmuseum
voor Beeldhouwkunst Middelheim

"The mathematical approach in today's art is not actually mathematics. It is the design of rhythms and relationships, of laws with an individual origin, just as mathematics originates in the individual thinking of pioneering mathematicians." MAX BILL

Abstraction-Création and Concrete Art

Paris had been the undisputed centre of the avant-garde since the artistic demise of Russia and Germany under their totalitarian regimes. With the German occupation of Paris, that centre moved to London, and later to New York. In Paris, the painers Auguste Herbin (p. 220), Jean Hélion (p. 304) and František Kupka (pp. 81 f), and the sculptors Vantongerloo (as vice-president), Hans Arp (pp. 120, 480 f) and others founded the international Abstraction-Création group in 1931. They channeled a wide variety of non-figurative trends, especially the late Cubists, the De Stijl followers and Constructivist emigrés such as Gabo and Pevsner. Abstraction-Création thus stood primarily for an art of basic geometric forms and interactions. Although this meant that their stance was predominantly a counterpoint to Surrealism, there were still a number of personal and artistic links with that movement.

By 1934 the group had some 50 members and 410 loosely associated friends from England to Paris and from Zurich to Italy, Germany and Poland. Its six year-books, published between 1932 and 1936, contained illustrations of works by such diverse artists as Arp, Calder, Freundlich, Gabo and Moholy-Nagy, covering a broad spectrum of non-figurative art whose creative autonomy was a powerful counterblast to totalitarianism. In terms of art history, this collective movement can be quite easily broken down into its component parts.

Abstraction refers to the progressive reduction of the mimesis of nature. Création refers to an elementary geometric order that is not derived from nature. The concept of Création was taken furthest by the Swiss artist Max Bill (p. 222). Following the approach of Theo van Doesburg, Bill called for the pure expression of van Doesburg's concept of "concrete art" in every field. As a member of the Züricher Konkreten group, he created a bastion of consistently rational, mathematically grounded "cold" art that was to have international influence after 1945.

Sculpture was only one aspect of the work by this Bauhaus student, architect, painter, designer, exhibition organiser and theoretician (ill. above and below). In the mid-1930s he constructed lightweight frames within which the inner and outer contours of cubes permeate each other, or stacked triangles and rectangles into airy, gravity-defying towers. At the same time, his *Endless Loop* marked the beginning of a lifelong fascination with the principle of the Mœbius strip and its finite-infinite flow. His sculptures show that rational relationships and visual logic, including mathematical formulae, can harbour dynamic streams and topological mysteries. Bill was a master of such transformation.

In 1933, the English painter and sculptor Ben Nicholson and his wife Barbara Hepworth both became members. In a brief phase from the end of that year until 1936, Nicholson created white reliefs cut out of flat circles and rectangles of cardboard. In 1937, together with Gabo, he published his book *Cercle*. It was a swansong to the Constructivist idea that had made such an impact in Eastern Europe twenty years before, and which, at its zenith, had touched Germany and Holland, had been formalised in Paris on a broad front and was now fermenting once more at the very fringes of Europe in the fragile cardboard reliefs by Nicholson.

Max Bill
Units of Three Identical Volumes, 1961
Chromium-plated brass, 26 x 43 x 32 cm
Napa (CA), Hess Collection

From Readymade to Surrealist Object

Duchamp: Creation through Negation

In retracing the progress of art history, it is tempting to regard the step from Picasso or Boccioni to Duchamp as no more than the logical consequence of early object art. Picasso incorporates fragments of basketweave or newspaper into his pictures. Boccioni inserts half a window-frame. Duchamp mounts the front wheel of a bicycle on a kitchen stool. But that would be telling the story the wrong way.

After all, Duchamp neither based his readymades on the work of any precursors nor did he seek to set object art in motion. On the contrary, he was looking for a way out of art. Bicycle wheel, bottle-rack and urinal were all valedictions to accepted mores of aesthetics, style and taste – a negation that was to be transformed by subsequent generations into an fascinated and resounding Yes. And so Duchamp, with his readymades and kinetic objects, unwittingly made a seminal contribution to the historiography of modern sculpture by opening up a new dimension in aesthetic consciousness. This is why it is these that are of primary interest to us here, as opposed to his *Large Glass* (p. 458).

Over the years, there have been a number of explanations have been offered for the advent of the readymade in art. The interpretation offered here makes no claim to being the only valid one. In the brief period between 1906 and 1913 the face of art was changed as never before. Narrative symbolism, anatomical correctness, sculptural modelling, unity of material – all these givens were called into question. Surely a sceptic or even a cynic would feel compelled to ask "What is art?" "What makes it art?" "Who is an artist?" Duchamp answered these questions – not as a theoretician, but by means of tongue-in-cheek demonstration. He formulated his objections to painting and its "retinal" approach in an aphoristic object. The *Bicycle Wheel* on a stool (ill. above) that heralded a series of readymades in 1913 maintains that art is a question of definition, an agreed term. The artist himself, his autobiography, his feelings, have nothing to do with it. Art is what is placed on a plinth rather than on a department store shelf. In the end, art is in the eye of the beholder.

Of course, this effrontery against the aura of art contained more than a pinch of nihilism and amounted to a rejection of the Romantic notion of the creative artist, a

Marcel Duchamp
Bicycle Wheel, 1913
(Replica 1964)
Readymade; bicycle wheel
mounted on a stool; height: 132 cm,
diameter: 64.8 cm
Milan, Arturo Schwarz Collection

notion that was soon to be renounced by the Russian Constructivists as well. These objects are by no means mysterious things whose enigma is meant to torment us. Nor do they represent "life" as the art of the 60s did. They pose questions – critical and subversive questions about the condition of art itself.

Whether or not Duchamp saw things this way right from the start remains a moot point. The early readymades in his studio met with little response. The *Bottle-Rack* appeared for the first time at Charles Ratton's 1936 "Surréaliste d'objets" exhibition in Paris. The final definition was probably coined in retrospect when Dadaists and Surrealists took it up. It was now up to Duchamp to underpin the declaration. In doing so he occasionally over-stylised the abrupt break with his earlier art. Does not the wheel with its slender spokes recall the rollers of the *Chocolate Grinder* (p. 130) spanned as threads? Does not the round kitchen stool under the bicycle wheel recall the table on which the grinder stands? Is it really a radical break in protest against all older art, or is it the demonstrative replacement of painting by the principle of the readymade?

Marcel Duchamp
The Bride Stripped Bare by Her
Bachelors, Even (The Large Glass),
c. 1915–1923
Oil, varnish, lead foil, lead wire and
dust on two glass plates mounted
with aluminium, wood and steel
frames, 272.5 x 175.8 cm
Philadelphia, Philadelphia
Museum of Art, Bequest of
Katherine S. Dreier

Marcel Duchamp
Fountain, 1917
(Replica 1964)
Readymade; porcelain urinal,
61 x 48 x 36 cm
Milan, Galleria Schwarz

follow the other path, as did the Surrealists and, in other directions, Pop Art, Nouveau Réalisme, Kinetic Art, Process Art.

In 1921 Duchamp created an assemblage entitled *Why not Sneeze, Rrose Sélavy?* (p. 460) for the sister of a friend. It is what he calls an *objet assisté*: a birdcage painted white and filled with marble cubes in imitation of sugar-lumps or ice cubes, cuttle-bone (for the missing canary) and a thermometer. The nonchalant title, containing Duchamp's female pseudonym, is mirrored downwards. The relationship between the various items remains enigmatic. Lautréamont's famous phrase of 1864 "beautiful as the chance encounter of an umbrella and a sewing machine on a dissecting table" could well have motivated Duchamp long before André Breton discovered it for the Surrealists.

The cage evades any logical, narrative metaphorical interpretation. Even the pun *Rrose Sélavy* (Eros, c'est la vie?) is indicative of an underlying sexual promise that cannot be fulfilled. The marble imitations are a variation on the old illusionism of painting and recall Picasso's *Glass of Absinthe*. In Duchamp's work we recognise them by feeling and tasting them, by their weight and coolness (the thermometer?) rather than visually – a programmatic piece of non-retinal art. Here we find the object theatre of absurdity that was to be the starting point for so many Surrealist objects featuring cages, animal bones or measuring instruments which were to appear ten years later in the work of Giacometti and many Surrealist followers.

The Shock of Dada: Man Ray and Schwitters

Although Duchamp could not be classified as belonging to any particular movement, he did for a time have close links to the anarchist revolt known as Dada; that frenzied rebellion against the insanity of war and genocide, instrumental logic and arms production, nationalist policy and petty bourgeois narrow-mindedness that spread out from its beginnings in Zurich in 1916 to take hold quickly in Cologne, Berlin, Hanover and New York. The Dadaist contribution to sculpture went hand in hand with a wealth of nonsense poetry, shock readings, noise music, chaotic manifestos and typographies, satirical photo-montages. Nevertheless, there are two object artists who would have been unthinkable without the liberating blow of Dadaism which toppled the hierarchy of values. Man Ray followed directly in the footsteps of Duchamp. Kurt Schwitters sublimated Dada's shock therapy by aestheticising and lyricising the heritage of the Cubist *papiers collés* and constructions and the diversity of the "modern" materials proclaimed by Boccioni.

The American-born artist Man Ray was perhaps the only student Duchamp ever had. Originally a painter, he founded a branch of Dada in New York in 1919 together with Duchamp and Francis Picabia. His early *objets assistés* which languished for so long in the shadow of his work as an innovative Surrealist photographer have since

Even the famous *Fountain* (ill right), a urinal turned at an angle of ninety degrees, is not entirely devoid of associations with previous art. Are not these symmetrical, centred, concave-convex forms a parody or a perhaps even a rehabilitation of classical composition? Do not these soft curves and rounded forms evoke associations with the female body? The urinal is signed "R. Mutt, 1917": Is this pure cynicism or does it betray a more gentle irony that reaffirms the concept of art rather than trashing it?

Duchamp pursued this path to its logical conclusion, staking out its extremes. Within these boundaries there are only individual strategies, combinations or a new interpretation of the object. Duchamp points out the first path himself before withdrawing almost entirely from production to scepticism. The Dadaists chose to

Marcel Duchamp
Why not Sneeze, Rrose Sélavy?,
1921
Readymade; 152 marble cubes in
the form of sugar-cubes with
thermometer and cuttle-bone in a
birdcage, 10.5 x 16.5 x 21 cm
Philadelphia, Philadelphia
Museum of Art, Louise and Walter
Arensberg Collection

Marcel Duchamp
Rotary Glass Plates, 1920
Five painted glass plates that rotate
around a metal axis and appear to
be a single circle when viewed at a
distance of one meter,
120.6 x 184 cm and 99 x 14 cm
(glass plate). New Haven (CT),
Yale University Art Gallery

Man Ray
Emak Bakia, 1927
(Reconstruction 1970)
Wood and horsehair; height: 46 cm
Private collection

Page 461:
Kurt Schwitters
Hanover Merzbau, c. 1933
Hanover, Sprengel Museum
Hannover

become icons of object art. They reduce the laconic hermeticism of Duchamp's readymade to a legible common denominator, and loosen it into a visual enigma, expressive and proto-surrealist. Emotions and associations are provoked by contradiction.

Man Ray's 1921 *Gift* is an upended iron with 13 nails, rising like a Gothic-arched monument. The metal surface that normally glides warmly over soft fabric is presented here as an object of brute aggression. The Surrealists referred to such works as *objets desagréables*. By contrast, his *Emak Bakia* of 1927 (ill. right) features a blonde ponytail emerging from the convoluted arm of a double bass: silky, flowing hair, in which the anthropomorphous suggestion of strings blends with a visual, haptic metaphor for the softly flowing sound of the instrument.

In his 1923 *Self-Destructive Object* a cut-out photo of an eye swings to and fro, pinned to the end of a metronome needle by a paperclip. It is the eye of God before the triangle of the Trinity. The stringently regulated world of measured time, the eternal Father, in short, the rational and determined world of strict laws and obligations, the counterworld to that of improvisation, association or chance – is undermined by this absurd combination and thrown offbeat, out of time. It is a Dada polemic for the freedom of creativity and anarchism, something which has become firmly established in the optical consciousness of our century.

Man Ray anticipated much that was to shape Surrealist sculpture ten years later: approximations between apparatus and the anthropomorphous, the aggressive, menacing, dissecting cruelty of the anatomic cut, floating and oscillating. Indeed, in comparison to his controversially epigrammatic objects, much of Surrealist art seems pretentious in its shallow pursuit of banal eroticism.

Their work could hardly be more different. Yet Man Ray and Kurt Schwitters both developed their œuvre on the basis of the same starting point around 1920: the *objet trouvé*. The fact that these two artists took such very different paths indicates just how ambiguous the concept was in the first place.

Schwitters, however, did far more than preparing the ground for other artists. His early material reliefs possess their own distinctive chromatism, and their own atmosphere. His *MERZ* pictures (the title is derived from Com*merz*- und Darlehnsbank) update the Cubist *papiers collés* by adding a Futurist dynamism and by

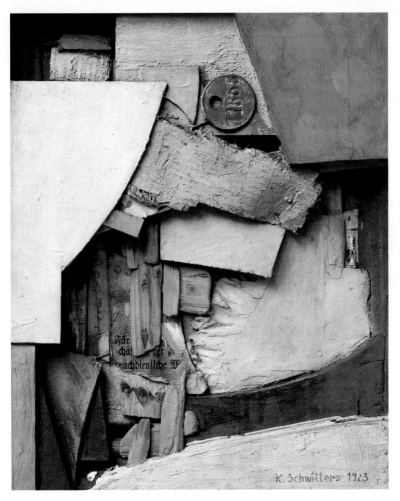

Kurt Schwitters
Relief, 1923
Collage of various materials on
wood, 35.5 x 30 cm
Cologne, Museum Ludwig

*"I nailed pictures so that, alongside
the painterly effect, there would also
be a sculptural relievo effect. This
was done to blur the borders of artistic genres."* KURT SCHWITTERS

plaster (p. 461). Behind the stalactite cladding are
posters bearing witness to political and social aspects,
relics of the everyday, garbage. The whole, according to
Harald Szeemann, is a monomanic "cross between
cathedral, cave, castle and ivory tower of its creator." For
decades, the *Merzbau* stood on the fringes of art history,
until, in the 60s, like El Lissitzky's *Proun-room* of 1923
or Duchamp's surreal staging of the 1938 Surrealist
exhibition, it became a milestone on the road towards a
new genre of art known as environment.

Russian artists like Ivan Puni (p. 163), Olga Rozanova
(p. 167) or Ivan Kliun (p. 164), who, like Schwitters, created provocative sculptural montages around 1920,
either produced very few such works or else these works
are barely documented. Much was lost or destroyed,
including the filigree wire constructions created in 1917
by Marcel Janco (p. 121) in Zurich, the cradle of
Dadaism. Johannes Baargeld's Cologne assemblages of
garbage that cocked a snook at bourgeois values are also
lost. Hans Arp, although he had been creating his biomorphic, curvilinear layered reliefs since 1916, assembled
rotting pieces of painted wood on boards for his 1920/21
Trousseaux. Here, we find decay, waste and shoddy material representing a rough and tongue-in-cheek objection
to the supposedly noble principles of art, using the
cheap, throwaway materials that were to be adopted
forty years later by the neo-Dadaists and Nouveaux
Réalistes. The strangest fancies of all, however, were
conjured up by the Surrealists in Paris.

The Surrealist Object

Although André Breton proposed producing dreamt-of
objects as early as 1924, it was not until 1930 that Salvador
Dalí actually did so. Surrealism, which calculatedly
explored the world of dream, chance, free association
and *écriture automatique*, was originally more a literary
movement than an artistic one. Sculpture was at first far
removed from it. How were the strategies of chance and
automatic writing, the messages of dreams and the dismantling of rational control to find expression in sculpture? Was not sculpture inextricably linked with a form
of conscious action and handling?

It was not until Surrealism itself underwent a change
around 1930, and precisely painted reality was laid over
the abyss of the psyche as a thin veil of illusion, with
painters such as Dalí (pp. 143–145) and René Magritte
(pp. 146 f) mirroring the surreal in the real and trawling
the depths of the subconscious to come up with iconographies as bizarre as they were precise, that Surrealism
became tangible enough for what Dalí called "surreal
objects with a symbolic function". The year 1931 marked
the turning point.

The "surrealist object" was Surrealism's specific contribution to sculpture. What distinguishes it from *objets
trouvés* and the *objets assistés*, apart from the fact that it
foreshadowed them? Duchamp's readymades deny the
emotion, the signature of the artist and the autobiography, eschewing his aesthetic intervention.

taking the step from the political Berlin Dada to the aesthetic (pp. 126 f). They have all the melancholy brightness of flowers growing on wasteland, romanticising
and darkening the painted-over realities of everyday life
– posters, tickets, brochures, newspaper clippings, wire
mesh, pieces of wood. Although these are, strictly speaking, reliefs, and although the no longer extant *Schwitters
Column* or *Merzbau* included actual sculptures, such as
the *Lust Gallows* and the *Culture Pump*, Schwitters' work
has, on the whole, a closer affinity to painting than to
sculpture. Even after he turned to the principles of Constructivism after 1923, and adopted more organic and
natural forms following his emigration in 1937, the laws
of planarity remained more important to Schwitters
than three-dimensionality.

There is, however, one exception. The *Merzbau*, or
Schwitters Column, which was his life's work, and which
he started anew three times: in Hanover in 1918
(destroyed in a bomb attack in 1943), then in Norway,
and finally in England. What began in the form of a column in his studio soon grew into a Dadaist votive
chapel, a labyrinth of grottoes in which found objects
and his own smaller sculptures were placed. On photographs dating from 1933 one can already see the developed constructive version of whitewashed wood and

Salvador Dalí
Telephone-Homard, c. 1936
Assemblage, 18 x 12.5 x 30.5 cm
Private collection

Breton, who was familiar with the writings of Freud, took a very different approach in probing the subconscious. While including chance or excluding reflection and calculation, he did not withdraw from the work itself. In his 1928 novel *Nadja*, Breton describes strolling aimlessly along the Boulevard Bonne-Nouvelle without knowing why, but in the firm conviction that "it will happen here". An inspiration? An encounter? A find – an *objet trouvé?* The chance encounter to which Breton refers makes no distinction between the author and his work. Instead, it is the principle of chance from which the work emerges in the first place, revealing the truth that lurks within our subconscious energies, drawing it from the depths of the libido. Chance, according to Breton, is the undercurrent beneath all rational planning and vision. It does not exclude the person, but drives the individual to the fore, in a profound sense, unveiling their clandestine imaginings and extreme wishes.

The Surrealists certainly mystified this "objective" chance in their choice of objects, adorning even the most astutely calculated found objects with the magical air of archaeological treasures from the very womb of the earth. Nevertheless, this sense of touching the environment with the divining rod of psychic inner worlds was to prove productive for sculpture. It psychologised, eroticised and charged Duchamp's readymade. Wherever these *objets* appeared, they adopted the full potency of Lautréamont's disparate metaphor.

Sigmund Freud paved the way for them. Given that they were generally exploring clandestine and suppressed desires, a tendency towards issues that are sexual or pathological, is almost to be expected. The forbidden, censored depths and taboos in which lust is linked to violence, pain and loathing, are brought to the fore. Giacometti's huge, penetrating, thorn-like *Disagreeable*

Object, and his *Caught Hand* enmeshed in some strange instrument of torture, are extreme expressions of this. Meret Oppenheim's famous *Fur-Lined Teacup Object* (ill. below) with its worldly-wise play on appeal, disgust, oral eroticism and refusal, evokes a typically ambivalent mood. Kurt Seligman offered a variation featuring a soup tureen covered in white hen feathers. Dalí (ill. above) worked drawers into a plaster cast of the *Venus de Milo*, following the curves of her body, adorned with furry handles. Even the lyrically narrative Joan Miró juggled evocativelly with female limbs and suspended spherical objects. The Surrealist sculpture of the 30s was imbued with a pan-sexual obsession involving every possible leitmotif – cage, concealment, doll – and was

Meret Oppenheim
The Fur-Lined Teacup Object
(Le Déjeuner en Fourrure), 1936
Fur-lined spoon, saucer and
teacup; cup 10.9, saucer 23.7,
spoon 20.2 cm; height: 7.3 cm
New York, The Museum of
Modern Art

Joseph Cornell
Hotel de l'Océan, 1959/60
Wooden box, clay pipe, children's
block, postage stamp, several paper
clippings from unknown sources,
four brass rings on metal rod,
metal sun, 21.5 x 36 x 10.2 cm
Cologne, Museum Ludwig

Joseph Cornell
Portrait. From the Series "Medici
Slot Machine", 1942
Various materials, 35.5 x 28 x 9.5 cm
Private collection

even evident in the occasional sculpture by Magritte,
Victor Brauner, Yves Tanguy, Marcel Jean, Oscar
Dominguez and William Freedie.

In 1936 Ratton provided an overview at his Paris
gallery. The exhibition "Surréaliste d'objets" added fuel
to the flames. Artists scoured the flea-markets and bric-
a-brac shops. Subsequent classics such as Duchamp's
Bottle-Rack and his *Why not Sneeze* ensemble stood in
showcases alongside sculptures by Max Ernst, Hopi
Indian ceremonial dolls and a motley assortment of
other objects. The exhibition was the intimate, small-
scale climax of Surrealist object art, just as, two years
later the "International Surrealist Exhibition" at the
Galerie des Beaux-Arts was to become the triumphant
swansong of the entire Parisian Surrealist scene. Once
again, on the eve of war, Breton and his followers pulled
out all the stops. Duchamp was the driving force behind
the staging of grand operas that were a milestone in the
development of environment art. As in the theatre, the
individual areas were divided up into technical, lighting,
props and sound, with each artist taking charge of one
such area. The central obsessions or fads of the Surrealist visual world were parades in a grotesque display of
mannequins covered in snails, spoon costumes, fantastic headgear, cages, body fragments.

Duchamp transformed the central hall into a uter-
ine grotto with 1200 sacks of coal on the ceiling, a carpet
of leaves on the floor, a pool with water-lilies, a coal-
fired brazier (Bohemians in winter!) and a huge love-
bed. To the aroma of Brazilian coffee, Prussian military
marches resounded from a female-shaped gramophone.
One year later, the Germans marched into Paris. The
Surrealists emigrated to New York.

Soon afterwards, an entire generation of sculptors
were caught in the wake of Surrealism. At times, it
blends with the edges of the Constructivist movement,
represented by Piet Mondrian (pp. 169–171) who had
been in New York since 1940. This explains why it is not
the Surrealist object that predominates, but the fully
modelled, and often bronze-cast, sculptures. Remarkably, it was not the emigrant artists who had the
strongest influence, but Giacometti, who lived far away
in France. David Hare, Seymour Lipton, Louise Bourgeois, Ibram Lassov, Theodore Roszak, the Brancusi
student Isamu Noguchi, and the early David Smith all
have in common, albeit with differing emphases, cage-
like grids and frames containing aggressively angular or
biomorphically vegetable inner forms. American Indian
influences added a vague totemism. In the end, like
so much in Paris, this remained an externalised and
second-hand Surrealism.

Only the American Joseph Cornell (ill. left), working
in self-imposed isolation, succeeded in creating an
authentic variation on Surrealist combination. His *Boxes*
eschew the histrionics of cruelty. On the contrary, as in a
Wunderkammer of disparate objects, they celebrate a
complex conglomeration of familiar and unfamiliar
things: bric-a-brac and nostalgic souvenirs of art, music,

theatre, literature, nature. They contain ballet photographs, star postcards, maps, bird-feathers. The viewer is invited to manipulate them in the manner of a board-game, creating an aleatory context. The past, the present, the now of the viewer, abstraction and objects all interweave, and forms correspond beyond any degree of reality. Each box is a pœtic metaphor of memory, in which submerged reminiscences meet current projections. This is one of the most charming, precise and complex enrichments of the *objet assisté*.

Giacometti: Staging Psychological Terror

The Surrealists pursued the production of *objets* like a cult on the verge of becoming a fashion. When Giacometti created his *Invisible Object* in 1934, presenting an idol-like female figure with hands embracing empty space like a vessel – did the title turn ironically, or even polemically, against the "object"-obsession of his friends? Giacometti himself was the only artist who actually continued to create truly Surrealist sculptures for half a decade. Although, in keeping with Breton's doctrine, he insisted upon the subconscious, medial emergence of these sculptures, mystification did not hinder their precise formal realisation. In this respect

Giacometti took the spatial breakthroughs, concave hollows and convex curves of late Cubist sculpture one step further and re-interpreted them. He used Cubist frameworks to give his sculptures a clear spatial definition. Even his "sculpture-as-board-game" works were to

have a direct influence on the emergence of horizontal, landscape-oriented rather than anthropomorphic sculpture in the 60s and 70s.

From 1925 onwards, as a result of the influence of Cubism and "primitive" art, Giacometti moved towards a more strongly abstractive syntax influenced by Laurens and Lipchitz. With his "flat sculptures", most of them radically simplified *Heads*, he left Cubism behind him in 1927/28. The transition to Surrealism was fluid. It was not Giacometti who discovered Surrealism, but the Surrealists who discovered Giacometti. Was this new horizon already evident in the hierarchically towering and radically abbreviated idol of the *Reclining Woman* of 1926? Or did it not emerge until the injurious, aggressive figural signs of 1929 in which the act of love escalates into the murderous thrust of a dagger?

From 1930 onwards the central motif of man and woman becomes one of deadly copulation, an animal-insectoid gender struggle in which spindle (body), sphere (head), hacked ovaries or leaves interact. On several occasions, the merciless struggle is gridded by the bars of a cage: taboo zones are opened voyeuristically. His *Woman with her Throat Cut* lies directly on the floor, as though disemboweled, dissected, boned; remains that recall the battle of the scorpions in Luis Buñuel's film *L'Age d'or*. Duchamp's erotic fantasies of bachelor images are echoed in the anatomic interweavings, and Picasso's 1930 designs for monuments in the frame-like structures.

Giacometti's famous *Suspended Ball* of 1939 (ill. left) originally modelled in plaster, then painstakingly carved in wood by a carpenter, is a flagship of Surrealist sculpture, with its ambivalent crossing of male and female

Alberto Giacometti
The Surrealistic Table, 1933
Bronze, 143 x 103 x 43 cm
Paris, Musée National d'Art
Moderne, Centre Georges
Pompidou

*"Whatever I look at, everything goes
beyond me and astonishes me and I
myself do not know exactly what I
see. It is too complex. One simply has
to try to copy the visible in order to
take stock of what one sees."*
ALBERTO GIACOMETTI

specifics: a segmented sphere is suspended over the comb of a curved spindle form, the ball and the edge are close, stimulating each other without actually touching or gliding into one another in a tantalizing sexual stimulation. The sculpture embodies at one and the same time the sexual act and injury, erogenous zones and wound, forced touch and fear of touch, libido and destructive drive. The framework and the interim level present this as though on a stage, in a theatre of cruelty, but also in a prison from which there is no escape. We ourselves provide the impulse for the act of failure and are thus included in it. The movement is also a physiological potential.

In his magisterial Giacometti monograph, Reinhold Hohl has shown that the work not only exploits ambivalent sexual projections, but that gender polarity, torture, and futility reveal the depths of a (pessimistic?) view of humankind. The ultimate pain, as in André Malraux' novel *La Voie Royale* of the same period, becomes the touchstone of ultimate human reality. Here, we find ourselves sailing dangerously close to the abyss of anti-

human excess. Giacometti's crass revelation of cruelty does not aim to shock, but to present existential images of a polarised totality. In his *Board-Games* (1931–1932) he abstracts this theme from all the lurid extroversion of the psychological and transposes them to tracks in the ground plane of the board. A ball that will never reach its destination, figure circles of man and woman flank a row of graves and bomb craters. These are conclusive, concrete variations on the old topos of "the game of life", just as other sculptures address the topos of "the theatre of life".

The most enigmatic image of all is the model-like framework entitled *The Palace at 4 A.M.* (p. 465 above) which merges elements from the stage at the Meyerhold Theatre, Giotto's *Annunciation* and autobiographical elements. The work of art becomes a "stage of ideas" (R. Hohl), on which the primordial drama of life, love and death are coded with dream. The programmatic sculpture *Surrealistic Table* (ill. left) presents the tabletop as a stage tableau above which the half-veiled bust of a woman presides over a crystalline tetrahedron and a realistic model of a hand. Her veil floats under the table, which stands on four differently styled legs. In place of tormenting excess we find a mysterious ensemble somewhere between portraiture and still life.

Was Giacometti thinking here of his own artistic path, with friendly reference to the works of Magritte, Léger and Brancusi? Does the tetrahedron – a head, perhaps – indicate a style of semiotic abstraction? Does the hand suggest more realistic possibilities? Does the half-veiled head refer to a break between familiar and older and unknown future work? Towards the end of 1934 Giacometti, filled with doubts about the potential of sculpture, said he wished that he could succeed in making just one head. Breton retorted that everyone knew what a head was. Giacometti was moving away from Surrealism. He returned to the study of models.

The Spectre of Surrealism

Giacometti was not the only one to place himself at a distance from the coquettishly provocative aspect of the *objets surréalistes*. Towards the end of the 40s, confidence in the projection of unaltered objects as quotations and the magic of the disparate had begun to wane. Too much had ended up in what amounted to little more than an artistic freakshow. Instead of Breton's literary-minded obsession with the object, the need for the author's shaping hand began to surface again. This does not mean that the Surrealist impulse ground to a halt, yet two of its leading painters turned to sculpture which concealed the object within the sculpture.

Max Ernst spent the summer of 1934 with Giacometti in the Italian mountain resort of Maiola near Stampa. In a riverbed, the two friends found large stones, weathered by the glacial flow, whose ovoid form inspired Max Ernst to make relief engravings like the scratching of newly hatched chicks. This was the first time he had transposed his ubiquitous bird motif into the three-dimensional mode of a sculpture based on nature. During the following winter, he plastered and modelled eight sculptures containing objects of everyday use (his *Moon Asparagus* for example uses stacked flowerpots, and his *Œdipus* features sand-buckets). In 1960 he went one step further and had them cast in bronze.

Wherever Max Ernst worked from 1944 onwards, he surrounded himself with mural reliefs and figures. There were phases (1934/1935, 1944, 1948, 1967) when he created hybrid creatures that were a cross between plants, animals and humans, adding a new and grotesque species to the surrealist world of metamorphic transitions. The largest and most complex of these composite sculptures is his cast concrete *Capricorne* (ill. right) which Ernst installed in front of his house in the bizarre Arizona landscape in 1948. It is a "family portrait" featuring his wife Dorothea Tanning and the two dogs, with the man as a ruler enthroned in the guise of Capricorn and the woman as a gracefully elongated nymph with a fish-like head-dress, blending many motifs from collages and pictures, evoking the archetypal, and recalling Hopi ceremonial dolls and other Indian art. A powerful synthesis of the found and the modelled, it is one of the most stunning transformations of the Surrealist visual imagination.

Max Ernst
Capricorne, 1948–1964
Bronze, 240 x 205 x 130 cm
Destroyed; fragments: USA,
private collection

"Sculpture is created in an embrace, by two hands, as in love. It is the simplest and most original art. I do not have to force myself or really push myself to it. It does not demand the same concentration or effort as painting." MAX ERNST

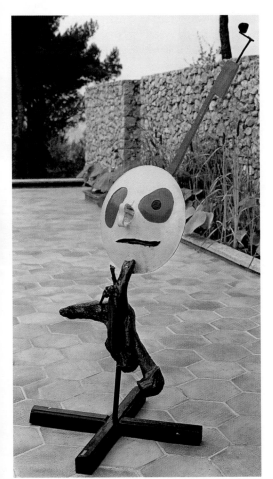

Joan Miró also found and invented his own world by drawing from the wellspring of his richly associative and thoroughly pictorial imagination (ill left). He, too, combined found objects, stones, flotsam, craftsmen's tools with modelled parts and then merged the whole in a bronze cast. Herein lies an essential difference to the direct appeal of the objets trouvés. Above all, however, from 1944 onwards, he created his works in a primarily intuitive act of modelling in plaster or clay, diametrically opposed to the detached formal syntax of Max Ernst. From 1953–1956 he worked increasingly closely with his friend, the potter Artigas. Out of the unusual terracotta mixtures, oxydations and firings, he created a major series of maternal, grotesque, monstrous women and birds of childlike intensity and formal decisiveness. From 1966 onwards the sculptures began to take on monumental dimensions, particularly in his work for the Fondation Maeght at St Paul de Vence. Miró created rounded and angular variations on body volumes with a sheer enjoyment of biomorphic growth reminiscent of Ancient Mediterranean goddesses. His sculptures as a whole constitute an important œuvre in their own right and, as such, go far beyond the mere exploratory forays of a painter working in another genre.

Joan Miró
Figure, 1968
Painted bronze, 165 x 60 x 100 cm
Private collection

5 New Materials: Iron and Steel

Around 1930, a new material entered the realms of sculpture: iron and its alloy, steel. Although sculptures and liturgical instruments had been made of cast iron in Classical Antiquity and the Middle Ages, iron came to be regarded during the industrial era of the 19th century as a cheap substitute for expensive bronze. As such, it was relegated to use in the field of decorative arts, and it was only in the world of civil engineering that it took on a new and functionally aesthetic character. Yet suddenly, around 1930, iron and steel became the preferred material of the avant-garde. Picasso (who had already experimented with sheet metal in his *Guitar* reliefs), González, Calder, and later David Smith, Anthony Caro and Eduardo Chillida, all placed this base metal at the forefront of progressive art. Iron, the more archaic of the two, tended to represent a timeless, pre-industrial view of the world, whereas steel was seen as a modern material redolent of the utopian spirit of a technologically advancing world.

Admittedly, most of these sculptures can also be regarded as representing the later stages of Expressionism, Constructivism or Surrealism, but the new material did create its own language, making a distinctive mark on the second third of the century. Used to express a number of styles, it may not have shaped a style of its own, but it did generate a new aesthetic approach that embraced a number of new developments.

Above all, iron and steel proved the perfect vehicle for two major themes in modern sculpture. Though neither of these themes was particularly new, they were channeled in different directions during this period. One involved the interaction of volume and space, positive and negative, which Lipchitz had been exploring in his *Transparencies* with their extreme spatial breakthroughs since 1926. The other was the principle of montage and collage involving the juxtaposition of found objects, garbage and commonplace utensils in a tradition that can be traced directly from Boccioni to Tatlin to Schwitters.

Picasso's Discovery of the Metal Montage

In 1928, Picasso began experimenting with small figures made of wire. These were extremely simplified abstractions, reduced to pure contours. Condensation and open space balance each other out. Daniel-Henry Kahnweiler described these wire constructions as "drawings in space". The larger versions, especially, also pose a technical challenge in terms of construction, joints and seams. For this reason, Picasso called upon his fellow Catalonian Julio González, who had lived in Paris since 1900 and who was an outstanding metalsmith and craftsman. González taught Picasso to handle an oxyacetylene welding torch and, in turn, learned from Picasso a new freedom and decisiveness in his artistic ambitions, which, for almost three decades, had been distributed vaguely between painting, sculpture and applied art. Picasso freed the artist within the craftsman and cured him of the notion that sculpture in iron was work, while painting was art.

Until 1932, these two friends worked closely together, mainly in Picasso's studio at Boisgeloup. It was a collaboration that was to crystallise into one of the most felicitous moments of modern sculpture. Whatever assemblages Picasso later created in diverse materials were based on that collaboration. On the other hand, Picasso also acted as a catalyst on the work of González, liberating the powers that were to make him, in the following twelve months, the founding father of modern iron sculpture, described by David Smith as "the master welder". Even the ornamentally decorative work of another Catalonian artist in Paris, Pablo Gargallo (p. 474), with its boldly sweeping concave and convex curves, paled by comparison.

Encouraged by González, Picasso made his mark a second time on the history of sculpture. His purist metal wire constructions developed in the course of 1929/30 into a series of bizarre and unprecedented life-sized figures and heads based entirely on sculptural concepts, as opposed to the principles of drawing or painting. Such assemblages as the white-painted *Woman in a Garden* (p. 470 above left) and the *Head of a Woman* (p. 470 above right) are works of extraordinary wit and new-found imaginative freedom, a far cry indeed from the tense and at times tormented associative eroticism of the contemporary Surrealist objects.

Scrap-yards, storerooms and kitchens served as a source of found objects which were adventurously welded, soldered and bolted together, cut out or driven in iron. According to Picasso, "We roared with laughter as we did that." Everything is disparate and is as close to

"A piece of iron is above all the idea that captivates; an idea and a force, immutable as a thing."
EDUARDO CHILLIDA

Alexander Calder
Le Hallebardier, 1971
Red painted iron; height: 800 cm
Hanover, Kurt-Schwitters-Platz
(Sprengel Museum Hannover)

Art Brut as it is to Surrealism. Fragments of iron form a body, a kitchen sieve a head, springs become hair, nails eyes, while two cast-iron rhododendron blossoms mark the transition to the world of plants, creating a semi-abstract figure.

The views are as diverse as the materials. All the components can be read, depending on the angle from which they are viewed, as head, body, or hair. Picasso deliberately used these transformations, playing with them and charging the object with ambivalence (as he had previously done in his Cubist collages) as both object and autonomous form. It is this double reading, in particular, that distinguishes his work from that of Boccioni and the early Russian assemblage artists such as Vladimir Baranov-Rossiné (p. 438). At the same time, he goes one step further in the interaction of volume and space. Panels, bars, kitchen utensils are not even extremely reduced volumes, but entities that rebuild, embrace and envelop space. And while Picasso was soon to turn again to sculptural mass and swelling volume, González was to continue in his consistent exploration of these themes.

González: Founding Father of Iron Sculpture

In 1900, González and his family moved from Barcelona to Paris. Apart from a few Cubist touches, and in spite of his friendship with Brancusi, the emergence of Modernism had little influence on his work until well into the 20s. In 1928, under the influence of African art, he caught up on some lost ground, creating Cubistically stylised masks and ornamentally cut sihouettes of copper or repoussé iron. He curved and bent sheet metal out of the plane, opening up interim spaces, creating layers and bridges. It was not until 1930, however, that

his œuvre as we know it was begun. Just how much he owed to the liberating influence of Picasso remains a matter of speculation.

For the groundbreaking sculptures of the *Little Dancer* and *Don Quixote* (both 1929/30), at any rate, no precursors can be found in the œuvre of Picasso. They are derived entirely from the tradition of wrought iron. The limbs still recall the metal ingots and bear the traces of hammer, pincers and welding torch. Even at this early stage, González went beyond the bounds of Cubism to handle space "like a newly acquired material" equal to iron, as he himself claimed. The upper body of the melancholy knight is curved entirely out of air. The Catalonian in Paris took the path towards iron sculpture entirely on his own initiative and by his own strength.

Occasionally, especially after 1935, he continued to use the solid density of form that characterised his earlier works. His famous *Montserrat* created in 1935/36 for the Spanish pavilion at the World Fair appears to be armour-plated. It stands full square against the surrounding space, epitomising the stance of the individual in resistance. Even the thirty-odd heads (mainly in stone) and the figures wrought out of metal sheets present their closed form and their hardness as though in resistance. They tear, they erode, but they do not open up. Their resistance against penetration by the surrounding space lends a sense of resistance as such. Resistance, perhaps, against the Falangist terror of the Civil War?

The main thrust of his work, however, addressed the problem of gesturally embracing space. This central challenge inspired sculptures which, together with Giacometti's surrealist objects, were among the most influential innovations of the 30s. It began almost without warning in 1930, with the *Harlequin* (p. 470 below), a sculpture that sweeps into its surroundings with broad curves and jutting triangle, and draws them back into its innermost parts. All in all, it is a sketchy abbreviation made up of soldered-together iron pieces. A protruding

rectangle is the stabilising element, replacing the upper body, while lozenge shapes recall the costume, and the face is a mere cut-out lying at an angle within the semi-transparent triangle that suggests the hat. A funnel forms the isolated head, and bow-like arcs suggest spindly arms. The precarious balance between transparent and non-transparent parts that meet and seem to fall apart, the abrupt discontinuity in the change of views, make this the perfect example of an open sculpture in the round. In 1932/33 the *Head* also known as the *Tunnel* (ill. left) interprets the inclusion of space as an exclusion of light. Not even in the work of Lipchitz and Picasso is there any parallel for such a complete turnaround of sculptural concepts.

From here on in, masterpiece was followed by masterpiece. The wild and fragmented conglomerate, *Woman Combing her Hair* of 1931 was followed two years later by a depiction of the same motif. This time the motif was taken up in a balanced and angular composition of verticals, arcs, protrusions and sweeping hair. In the mid 30s, González went a step further in his simplification of forms, in the spirit of Picasso's "drawings in space", by paring the complex equilibrium down to the dynamically stretched and dance-like movement of a single line. Picasso's geometric construction burst into vibrantly gesticulating eccentricity with verticals binding the body's framework, while curved lines contour and follow the upper bodies, heads, imaginary volumes.

González by now had mastered a wide range of rhythms and expressions within the scope of his actual

"Great art is not made by drawing perfect circles and squares with a compass and ruler; really new things are directly inspired by nature and executed with love and honesty."
JULIO GONZÁLEZ

Julio González
Cactus Man I, 1939
Wrought iron, 65.5 x 27.5 x 15.5 cm
Paris, private collection

metalsmithing background, from the statuary verticalism of the *Grande Maternité* to the floating ecstacies of the dancers and the accomplished blend of the structural and the biomorphic, cubes and curves, warrior and plant in his peasant-cum-mercenary *Cactus Man* (ill. left). His work covered a spectrum from the graphic linearity of bars to the frenzied gestural movement of welded wrought-iron components, to the solid structure into which complementary spaces are inserted. Any inspiration he may have taken from the pictures by Magnelli (p. 220) or Miró (pp. 150 ff) are subordinate to his own authentic language. While they may influence individual aspects, they have no bearing on the overall form.

Calder and the Poetry of the Mobile

Can Alexander Calder be properly added to a list of sculptors in metal, after González? Would it not be more appropriate to place him (almost) at the beginning of the Kinetic Art movement that emerged in the 1950s and 1960s. After all, the fragile choreography of his mobiles surely belongs within the context of moving and changeable art. Following the theoretical farsightedness of the Futurists, Rodchenko's suspended reliefs and Gabo's vibrating steel springs, Calder made mobility and mutability his aesthetic *leitbild* in which he recognised an inherent pœtry and universal symbolism. In this respect, he is very much a part of that complex of modern sculpture described by Rosalind Krauss as "mechanical ballets".

A different categorisation would thus be possible. Strictly historically, however, Calder is an artist of the same period and the same context as González, and both arrived at their own formal language at almost the same time. Both came into contact 1930 with the key Parisian influences of Surrealism and late Constructivism. Both go beyond the boundaries of these movements. Both were not originally sculptors and were therefore freer in their approach to a new medium. Calder soon restricted his work to steel, lending it the same lightness, malleability and compositional flexibility that González gave to iron.

A trained engineer, he came to Paris from Philadelphia in 1926. He began making witty and whimsical wire sculptures (p. 471), lines drawn in the air, unaware of the experiments being carried out in the same field by Jean Cocteau, Picasso and Arp – a parthenogenesis of three dimensionality out of drawing. Calder touched the pulse of art in his time. When he exhibited his miniature circus of wire, animals and weightless acrobats as linear sculptures of arabesque wit and stunning caricature, the doors of the avant-garde studios were open to him. However, it was his visit to Mondrian in 1931 that gave his sculpture the decisive boost, turning it into a series of moving, suspended Mondrians, their component parts balanced and turning in mutual dependency like the stars of the universe. The influence of Magnelli, Arp and above all Miró soon toned down

"Symmetry and order do not make a composition. It's the apparent accident to regularity which the artist contrls by which he makes or mars a work." ALEXANDER CALDER

Alexander Calder
Four Red Systems (Mobile), 1960
Painted metal and wire,
195 x 180 x 180 cm
Humblebæk (Denmark), Louisiana
Museum of Modern Art,
Ny Carlsbergfondet

his initial geometric stringency, adding a playful touch of energetic motion and organic curves far better suited to Calder's artistic temperament.

His most important contribution to modern sculpture was and has remained the mobile (ill. above). His achievement lies not least in the speed and determination with which he solved the aesthetic problems of this new genre, developing a valid, and for his followers dangerously accessible, lyricism. It makes all earlier kinetic art seem like some peripheral preparatory experiment. Soon, Calder was to abandon the motor drive as well as the geometric circles and rectangles he had derived from Mondrian. He adopted Magnelli's dynamic contours and Miró's leafy forms, threaded them onto slender iron wires and suspended them in counterweight against heavier, slower-moving slabs. The breath of air became the element of change. Outline, size, metal thickness, length and thickness of arms all affect the ponderation by which the mobile develops its full scope. The move-

ment describes virtual volumes – yet how much richer, more contemplative and more natural this seems than Gabo's whirring spindle of 1920.

Calder's stabiles (the term was coined by Hans Arp) are frequently regarded as being diametrically opposed to his mobiles, which Duchamp termed as such. Indeed, they soar with force and presence, in contrast to the mobiles, which gently cut the air, gliding through it smoothly. Elephants instead of floating fish, birds and blossoms. Yet these massive, humorously biomorphic, zoomorphic steel colossuses of brilliant red seem to push away from the ground, stretching out their slender arms, tentacles, crests and arcs, leading around and through the sculpture itself. Their monumentality goes hand in hand with dance-like lightness. It is for this reason that the large stabiles, which form the focal point of Calder's mature work, form a perfect contrast to urban architecture. They are among the few paradigmatic examples of urban art (p. 468).

With Hammer and Cutter

In the 19th century, iron and steel were the materials used by innovative engineers for their bold new projects. After 1950 their distinctive aesthetics spread throughout the world of sculpture in the form of free-standing, sweeping, asymmetrical sculptures, wire "drawings in space" and axially aligned metal slabs. The metal was wrought and hammered, cut and welded. Wherever the traces, notches and scars of the hammer, the cutter or the welding torch were to be found, wherever the tension of iron and steel made its mark on the conceptual, compositional and gestural aspect of the work, these sculptors were a group apart. Those who assembled sculptures, seeking their materials in scrap-yards and spare parts stores are also part of that group.

The ground was prepared by González, at times by Picasso and to some extent by Pablo Gargallo – three Spanish artists in Paris whose work married the ancient Spanish craft of the smith with the spirit of Modernism. Gargallo's masks of iron and copper sheeting marked the beginning around 1910. Yet even his large figures after 1930 still leaned heavily towards a theatrically elegant stylisation (ill. right). In 1930, González had already demonstrated with his *Don Quixote* how a figure can

consist fundamentally of a void embraced by iron. The void as opposed to volume was to become a key word for the Basque artist Eduardo Chillida (ill. left and right) who rejected stone and figurative sculpture in Paris, to start from scratch in 1951 as an apprentice to the village smith of Hernani. Like no other 20th century sculptor, he revealed the dynamism and malleable resistance of iron. From 1954 to 1966 he created seventeen versions of the *Dream Anvil* that is a *leitmotif* throughout his œuvre. The anvil seems to bite into the wood in a sculptural abstraction that pays homage to the mythical yet still contemporary craft of the metalsmith.

The steles that Chillida dedicated to Pablo Neruda, Manuel Millares, Salvador Allende and others from the 60s onwards were also derived from the anvil motif. At that time, the bars were more massively rounded and angled, and the negative form was modelled almost violently into many-fingered interweavings. Undulations seem to trap their inherent power. In 1977 Chillida developed his famous *Combs of the Wind* to gigantic proportions. The three sculptures defy the spray, waves and wind on a rocky outcrop by San Sebastián. After 1973 this Basque sculptor also worked in alabaster and terracotta. Outwardly, these works clench together in a block. The walls reflect the light and draw the mystery of the space into the interior.

Instead of working in raw iron, the Swiss artist Bernhard Luginbühl (p. 475 above right). has been assembling industrially manufactured structural elements and machine parts like components in a gigantic metal building block set since 1954. In the 60s, bolted girders, nuts, propellors and turbine fragments were mutated into animal silhouettes – a frog, a bulldog, a giraffe, an elephant – of grotesquely powerful expressiveness. The largest sculptures address the myths of work and futility, with spheres rolling up and down as though in some mechanised Sisyphean labour – an absurd technical procedure of the kind that Luginbühl's compatriot, friend and occasional collaborator Tinguely also stages.

Whether iron wires draw bold lines in the air, as in the work of the American artist Ibram Lassow or the Swiss artist Walter Bodmer, whether iron sheets can be shifted on an axis to work expressively against one another, as in the work of the Italian artist Berto Lardera (ill. above left) or whether, in the merging of Constructivist and Surreal roots, they aggressively besiege, dissect and spear the space as in the work of the Danish artist Robert Jacobsen (ill. below) the material itself invariably intervenes massively in the creative act.

Berto Lardera
Colloquio 8, 1959/60
Iron; height: 280 cm
Private collection

Bernhard Luginbühl
Small Cyclops, 1967
Iron, red painted, 292 x 485 x 300 cm
Hamburg, Hamburger Kunsthalle

Eduardo Chillida
Comb of the Wind XVII, 1990
Steel, 230 x 189 x 120 cm
Collection of the Artist

Robert Jacobsen
Sculpture, 1956
Iron, 74 x 57 x 40.5 cm
Clas Anshelm Collection

Biomorphic Sculptures – A Vitalistic Counterposition

"Like Nature"

The Constructivist world design shimmers on the horizon of modern technology with all the brilliance of a social utopia. Gabo and Pevsner wax lyrical in their manifestos on the plumbline, the rule and the compass, on the craft of the engineer, on mathematics, and on the linear structures and arcs upon which the universe is built. By the 1930s, this design had fallen prey to the histrionics of power and the philistine reactionary ideas of totalitarian regimes in Eastern and Central Europe. Almost simultaneously, an alternative design emerged – with neither manifesto nor programme, with cross-references to Surrealism, but without Surrealism's abysses and labyrinths of paranoia. It was an approach to art that did not seek to build and construct rationally, but to emulate the germinal forces of nature and be shaped by the erosive forces of the elements. "Like nature" became a fundamental aesthetic slogan of modernism, taking on its greatest resonance in the work of Paul Klee (pp. 119 ff).

Among sculptors it was adopted primarily by Hans Arp and Henry Moore. According to Arp, "We do not seek to imitate nature ... we want to create, as the plant creates its fruit, and not to imitate." According to Moore himself, "I am most deeply interested in the human figure, but I have discovered laws of form and rhythm in studying natural forms such as pebbles, rocks, bones, trees and plants." Sculpture became receptive to analogies of growth, its powers, structures and laws. This did not lead to the formation of any group or "style", but to a broad-based movement that was to spawn many others.

Its origins lay in Rodin's fluidity of form and in the organic morphology of Art Nouveau and Jugendstil. In 1914, the young sculptor Gaudier-Brzeska collected material for an essay on "The necessity of organic forms". Brancusi's ovoid form contains the essence of all life. Around 1930 the Constructivist founding father Tatlin actually based his *Letatlin* flying machine on the flight of birds, following an organically rhythmic, biodynamic principle rather than a mechanical one. The Surrealist influence came from Yves Tanguy (pp. 140, 142), whose fluid metamorphoses languish and melt on metaphysical beaches. Signs of a breakthrough became increasingly evident. At Boisgeloup, around 1930, Picasso created fertility idols of purely sculptural corporeality with

Karl Hartung
Composition VIII, 1948
Limewood; heigth: 33.5 cm
Private collection

ample, expansive limbs. Arp invented creatures of concentrated naturalness, in which stone, plants, animals and torsos are vividly united. Moore translated the inspiration of rocks, mountains, bones and branches into sculpture with dramatic effect.

From the 30s the tendency towards the organic spread rapidly. In Germany, under the influence of Brancusi and Arp, Karl Hartung (ill. above) opened up his abstract sculptures to include gouges, tears and surging protrusions. In France, Henri Etienne-Martin (p. 478 above left) evoked the chtonic origins of architecture with his formations of imaginary labyrinhtian habitations (*Demeures*). Alicia Penalba (p. 478 below) who was born in Buenos Aires, modelled lush, tropical plant symbols of eroticism out of clay.

It is quite remarkable that biomorphic sculpture – a term actually coined in 1936 by Alfred H. Barr – should have emerged so late. Goethe's *Theory of metamorphoses* had already prepared the ground after 1800. Novalis had linked art and poetry with the building plans of Nature. In 1907 Henri Bergson had published his credo *Creative development* and proclaimed *élan vital* to be an all-per-

Henry Moore
King and Queen, 1952/53
Bronze; height: 170 cm
Glenkiln, Shawhead, Dumfrieshire (Scotland), Collection
W. J. Keswick

Henri Etienne-Martin
Dwelling No. 3, 1960
Plaster, 250 x 500 x 225 cm
Private collection

Pablo Picasso
Figure (Maquette for a Monument
to Apollinaire), 1928
Iron wire and sheet metal,
50.5 x 18.5 x 40.8 cm
Paris, Musée Picasso

vading energy, tantamount to the flow of life and intuition against the rigid deformations of reason and the inflexible mimesis of the world. According to Bergson, evolutionary processes and artistic creativity, the forces of nature and creative impetus all rise from the same source. No wonder artists from the futurists to Paul Klee looked to the theories of Bergson, that lyrically inspired philosopher, to underpin their work.

In 1917 the biologist d'Arcy Wentworth Thompson published two volumes tracing the link between "growth and form" and explored the visible laws of growth governing bone structure, rhizomes, shells etc. – obvious reflections can be found two decdes later in the work of

Moore. In this way, a more conservative direction in biology and the philosophy of life fed a more vitalistic trend in sculpture, a third way alongside the constructivist idea and the surrealist object. The English art historian Herbert Read saw in this a "genetic principle" of Modernism in which natural forms merge with vitalistic abstraction.

Picasso's Work at Boisgeloup

Picasso, meanwhile, had once again set about transforming opposites into aesthetic extremes. In 1928 he bent and knotted his wire constructions in space (ill. above). At around the same time he modelled a *Head of*

Alicia Penalba
Grande Ailée (Winged Figure),
1960–1963
Bronze, patina, 105 x 195 x 95 cm
Private collection

Alicia Penalba
Field with Wings. Sculpture for
St. Gallen Business College
(detail), 1962/63. Concrete
St. Gallen, Handelshochschule

abundantly hypertrophic work paid homage to an archetype of sculptural design that was diametrically opposed to the Constructivist world design. In creating it, Picasso gave expression to a *Weltbild* that has its own horizon in modern sculpture.

Arp: Dada Heads and Organic Concretions

The work of Hans Arp (pp. 480 f) is the very epitome of biomorphic sculpture. He made his sculptures into metaphors of the demiurgic act in analogy to nature as no other artist had done before. And, like no other, he united sheer sculptural form with the very essence of organic growth. In doing so he played through the entire evolutionary hierarchy from mineral to flora, fauna and the human body in a bid to show that no hierarchy exists and the same powers work through everything. He dreamt the "cosmic dream of unity and transformation with burlesque undertones" (C. Giedion-Welcker). "Out of a swelling heavenly fleece a leaf rises. The leaf turns into a vase, a huge navel appears. The navel has become a sun, an immeasurable source, the original source of the world."

a Woman (ill. above) in plaster to be cast in bronze. The difference between the two could harldy be greater. While one involves the reduction of form to a framework of slender rods, the other is a massive arch of firm-footed, elephantine proportion with a hypertrophic corporeal superstructure from which a broad head protrudes. What appears as physical deformation holds the balance between mass and void, volume and interior space.

At his large studio in Boisgeloup to the north of Paris, Picasso continued in 1931 to work on these exuberant female bodies, reclining and standing, whose heavy and unwieldy components were joined to form an ungainly and yet arabsequely curving dancelike torsion. In modelling his Ancient Mediterranean fertility goddesses, he made plaster a material of growth and life. While such transformations do have certain affinities with Surrealism, Picasso approached them entirely from the stance of autonomous sculpture, applying a convulsive gravity and inversion of form that were not only entirely foreign to Surrealism, but also to Cubism. In doing so, he produced some of the greatest and most influential volumetric sculptures of the 20th century.

Important as the subsequent developments of the principles of material collage, *objet trouvé* and print might have been, no matter how consistent his variously angled views of Sylvette in sheet metal and no matter how impressive the step towards urbanity with huge planar sculptures of concrete, this exaggeratedly organic,

Hans Arp
Deposition of Birds and
Butterflies. Portrait of Tristan
Tzara, 1916/17
Painted wood relief,
40 x 32.5 x 9.5 cm
Zurich, Kunsthaus Zürich

Hans Arp
Head with Three Annoying
Objects, 1932
Plaster, 23 x 33 cm
Private collection

Page 481:
Hans Arp
Female Torso, 1953
(after a plaster model of 1930)
White marble, 88 x 34 x 27 cm
Cologne, Museum Ludwig,
Haubrich Collection

The Strasbourg artist began as a painter indebted to expressionism and the Blauer Reiter group. In 1916 the young, eloquent poet and artist joined the founders of Dada Zurich who met at the Cabaret Voltaire. At that time, he was sawing and cutting his first polychromatic wooden reliefs *(Portrait of Tristan Tzara;* ill. left) with overlapping contours – a pictorial alphabet that draws its own conclusions from Picasso's planar montages with hieroglyphs of moustache, gendarme's cap, fork, navel, mirror, fried egg etc., and whose witty juxtaposition echoes the punning of his poetry. In the course of the 20s his offbeat approach focused on fluidly amoebic ovals with sweeping outlines.

Arp repeatedly stressed the aleatory principle behind these early reliefs in which forms seem to swim against each other. Yet for Arp, the law of chance did not mean the same as it did for Duchamp in his strategy of indifference or his surrealist receptiveness to the projections of the self. Rather than a withdrawal from artistic design, it indicated complete devotion to the unconscious, anomymous process, a "gift of the muses" or (citing Novalis) "the touch of a higher being" – a kind of first cause that creates "pure life". Behind this is a romantic concept of art and the artist which, in the work of Arp, loses all that is shapeless and trailing, and "concretises" itself in firmly outlined entities.

By 1929, Arp was making the rounded sculptures in marble, plaster or bronze that he called "concretions" and wished to have installed in modest locations in forests, mountains, in the countryside (ill. below). Initially, around the same time as Giacometti's board-

Henry Moore
Reclining Figure, 1932
Carved reinforced concrete;
width: 110 cm
St. Louis (MO), City Art Musem
of St. Louis

games, he placed smaller forms like spores on the larger
fruit. In turn, his works became more torso-like, and he
subsequently developed a uniformly vibrant syntax of
condensed and inverted organic forms. The dense sculptural quality of these works was as far from the fragmented metamorphoses of the Surrealists as it was from
the geometric orders that prevailed in the work of the
Abstraction-Création group. In the mid-30s, Arp distanced from both these movements.

What extraordinary richness there is in simplicity.
Germination, budding and blossoming, growth and
fusion, hardening, coagulation, curvature, complexity;
anorganic stone and smooth bronze are vitalised as
though from within, the skin pulsates like a membrane
moved by inner forces, juices and rhythms, full and
round-fingered. Life is fruitfulness or cell division, all in
the sense of the vitalistic biology that Arp rendered visible once more as natural piety in a late triumph. With
the onset of war, his sculptures seemed to soar higher,
stretching upwards like laconic signs, rising out of the
broad still lifes of fruits and the earthbound stones to
address the animal and the human. Yet still they
retained their aspect of plant-like growth. After the war,
his work took on a smooth verticalism. Protrusions were
cropped as though pruned with a knife, without cutting
off the life force itself. The base also began to play a part

in the structural rhythm. In his late work, the semiotic
aspect was consolidated in his freestanding cut-out
reliefs. Growth became part of the picture. Is this a summing-up or a heraldic stylisation – even schematisation
– of his life's work?

Moore: the Landscape of the Body

The work of Henry Moore cannot be described as biomorphic sculpture with the same conclusiveness as that
of Arp. The human figure features far too prominently
in his work for that. The tectonic and constructive basis
is too powerful, the influences of non-European cultures – Sumerian, Egyptian, American, African, oceanic
– far too strong. What is more, though he adopted key
formal aspects of modern sculpture in a repertoire so
varied that he was occasionally accused of eclecticism,
he never actually touched upon its most important revolutionary breakthrough, the critical destruction of the
medium and the rejection of material unity. On the contrary, Moore carefully cultivated the notion of "appropriate material", probing the block of stone, gliding
along the annual rings and the grain of the wood, pursuing the lively, abrupt mobility of bronze.

Though most of his formal motifs were not his own
invention, he was the quickest to close the gap on what
had been missing in British sculpture since the prema-

ture death of Gaudier-Brzeska. He not only adopted and varied the repertoire of the modernists, but translated it into the language of the true sculptor. He reconciled modernism with classical sculpture and was strong enough, or uncomplicated enough, not to falter under this heavy burden in what W. Spies has described as his "sculptural conservatory".

The early work, before 1930, still heavily emphasised the solid block and the technique of *taille directe* in the tradition of Derain and Brancusi. In 1924, Moore merged Mother and Child to create a towering bastion of almost brutal intimacy. In 1929, the famous Toltec rain-god Chacmool inspired the Ur-form of his *Reclining Figures*. On the immobile basis of leg and arm rest a knee and an elbow level with the head. They do not break out of the block. In this way, the two essential archetypes in Moore's work – the Mother and Child and the reclining Earth Goddess (according to Erich Neumann) are already fully present in his early work. Neumann, a psychoanalyst, has explored the interaction between interior and exterior form, shell and core, and has traced the biomorphic trait of the sculptures and examined their symbolism. Later, the theme of the family was added. Individual, semi-abstract motifs such as surrealistically hermaphrodite idols or the cage-like instrumentalisation of a space with the aid of slender wires were to remain on the periphery of this central trinity.

In 1930, a new development began. The next *Reclining Figure* lost its massive frontality, offering views from several angles, allowing hollows to enter. This tendency

Henry Moore
Head, 1937
Hopston-woodstone; height: 54 cm
New York, private collection

continued throughout the 30s until, by the end of the decade, he was creating figures that were slender, hollowed and bounded by the positioning of the limbs. From here on, Moore's *Reclining Figures* rose and fell in a rhythm of hills and dales. Moore himself claimed that it was possible to express something non-human, such as landscape, through the human figure. And indeed, his many *Reclining Figures*, right up to the dual and tripartite

Henry Moore
Reclining Figure No. 5 (Seagram), 1963/64
Bronze, 240 x 360 x 180 cm
Humblebæk (Denmark), Louisiana Museum of Modern Art, Ny Carlsbergfondet

Henry Moore
Reclining Figure, 1959–1964
Elmwood; length: 229 cm
Much, Hadham, Estate of
Henry Moore

monumental sculptures of the 60s (p. 483), do suggest mountains, cliffs and precipices. A precise imagination reworks natural processes: "Pebbles show the grinding, scrubbing treatment of stone and possess fundamental aspects of asymmetry. Rocks show a hacking, hitting treatment of stone ... bones have a wonderful structural power and hard formal tension ... trees illustrate the principles of growth and the power of joints with smooth transitions ...". Such was the wellspring from which Moore drew his concepts of form. It was a (sculpturally consolidated) awareness of nature anchored in the English romantic tradition.

In the 30s, Moore adopted the innovations of the early pioneers. Archipenko had been the first to lend autonomy to breaks and apertures. Picasso and Arp had led the way in organically fluid deformation. Anatomy had been inverted into the plasma of inner and outer forms. Body and interior spaces oscillated in a melodious or dramatically heightened equilibrium. In the war years and the immediate postwar era, his figures took on a doughy roundness that gently embraced the motif of the family. Moore avoided the pitfalls of an all too obviously schematic approach in the early 50s by calling upon the expressive energies of the demonic, the menacing and the tragic. The cylinder-eyes of his *Helmet Head 2* stare out through a narrow slit, and the mythical majesty of his *King and Queen* (p. 476) is heightened to a tragicomic cross between Pan and Don Quixote. His *Warrior with a Shield* is a mutilated and dramatic torso evoking resistance, while his *Three Standing Figures* seem like gnarled skeletons of the Fates.

After 1959, Moore was to break down his *Reclining Figures* repeatedly into two or three pieces, not in order to fragment them, but in order to let the interruption – the interim space – breathe as part of the whole. In an architectural context (for example, in front of the New York Lincoln Center) the landscape metaphor is set against an urban background. From now on, Moore was master of the entire spectrum, and rose to become the leading sculptor of his generation, surpassed only by Giacometti.

Growth and Construction

The biomorphic and the constructive are not mutually exclusive. Indeed, they seem to attract each other constantly. Even in the post-cubist work of the pioneering artists, we can often find organic tendencies. Lipchitz created baroque metamorphic transitions as bi-polar symbols of fertility. Laurens' nereids possess an ample-bodied roundness in keeping with the new-found awareness of nature. For all the predominance of geometry, the links are clearest in the melting pot of Abstraction-Création. In 1933, Barbara Hepworth and her husband Ben Nicholson joined the group. Otto Freundlich was one of the first members. Different as their work may have been, both Hepworth and Freundlich helped to consolidate the biomorphic tendencies of the 1930s.

Hepworth (ill. right), a sculptor from Yorkshire, England, has often been compared with her compatriot Henry Moore. Like Moore, she began with solidly block-like heads, then went on to foreshadow Moore's *Leitmotif* of the hollow core, and passed through various phases influenced by Brancusi and Arp, though leaving aside the Surrealists, before arriving at the geometric clarity of her multi-faceted and asymmetrically vitalist forms. She used strings drawn taut over concave hollows to create classical solutions in an œuvre that echoes a spectrum from Gabo to Arp, from elementarily stereometric works to totem-like steles set in the landscape and, finally, sculptures that recall shells or weathered stones. The cool lyricism and finely tuned formalism of her œuvre sets it apart from the dramatic intensity of Moore.

By looking now at the work of the German painter and sculptor Otto Freundlich, we can appreciate the full scope of the polarity between growth and construction. Yet he does not really fit in here. Freundlich was always a maverick, somewhere between abstraction, architecture and mineral analogy. A contemporary of Picasso and the German Expressionists, he arrived in Paris in 1908, finally settling there in 1924. As a painter, he worked geometrically, with coloristic modulations (p. 221). As a sculptor, he began in an expressionistic, primitivistic style and went on to create a small but ambitious œuvre that anticipates social utopianism in the spirit of classical modernism.

Freundlich's masterwork, *Ascension* (ill. below) is the model of a "social process involving the coalition of independent individual forms into a living community."

A bronzecast of dynamically super-imposed chunks of stone in three phases: a pyramidal base on which a narrow angular link-piece rests, forming a bridge to a broad, top-heavy "head". It is an ascension against cyclopic resistance, against gravity itself. It is related to biomorphic sculpture in the way that its rock-like individual parts seem to have been smoothed by water, and in the way that the pieces of clay, applied with a knife, distill the light that falls on them. What seems biomorphic is above all the energy that courses through the entire sculpture, uniting all the component parts to a single, collective structure. Any associations of a fist or a head are purely coincidental. Instead of aiming, like Picasso, for an anthropomorphic approach, Freundlich aims at a universal approach, seeking the kind of "cosmic socialism" reflected in his sculpture.

Barbara Hepworth
Two forms, 1961
Bronze; height: 117 cm
Private collection

"A sculpture might, and sculptures do, reside in emptiness, but nothing happens until the living human encounters the image."
BARBARA HEPWORTH

Otto Freundlich
Ascension, 1929
Bronze, 200 x 104 x 104 cm
Cologne, Museum Ludwig

Post-War Positions:
The Existential and the Abstract

Aftershock or New Freedom?

The second world war made its mark on art. Picasso's *Man with Lamb* evokes the archaic image of the good shepherd, while his *Death's Head* with its harrowed face and vacant, staring eyes is a direct reference to war. Both these sculptures were created in 1942. At the same time, Lipchitz was modelling his ecstatically smouldering metamorphoses between machine, plant, animal and human in which the concept of the victim is tangible. Meanwhile, the Constructivist and Surrealist tendencies of prewar art were being further developed and expanded on the other side of the Atlantic.

Is it possible to speak of a specifically postwar art after 1945? If so, does it cover a spectrum ranging from the brutal dissolution of the human figure into flesh in the work of Germaine Richier to the faddishly misery-ridden posturing of the epigones? Does it include that frisson of angst and jeopardised identity we find in the twisted, tortured and amputated human fragments of the young British sculptors? Are not Marini's falling horsemen the fruit of a decade spent on the powder-keg of nuclear disaster? Is not the sprawling expansion of hollowed, gnawed, corroded surfaces and the bursting energy of Art Informel a sign of false security? Even Giacometti was interpreted in such a light at the time, his figures seen as representing the human figure devouring itself in the emptiness of space instead of asserting its independent existence. Was Giacometti's impassioned exploration of the fundamentally phenomenological problem of distance a reflection of the existentialist *Zeitgeist* after all?

Yet the self-same phenomena can also be interpreted in a very different way. Do we not find the expression of a new freedom in the sweeping and intensifying rhythms? Is this not a reflection of individuality returning at last after the strictly ordered structures of war and dictatorship? Does not the relaxation, scattering and labyrinthine interweaving of structures and gestures suggest a highly personal involvement with the materials into which the artists of the day poured their soul-searching dramas? The discourse of the day, with its emphasis on the essence of things, highlights above all the creative primary act in which a rapidly accessible strategy was quickly established in painting, and soon afterwards in sculpture.

Pessimistic interpretations do not apply by any means to the gestural Abstract Expressionism of the Americans in the work of David Smith, Tony Smith, Mark Di Suvero and John Chamberlain. In Germany, Hans Uhlmann and Norbert Kricke pursued a similar approach. Kricke, in particular, streamlined the contours of González to the point of racing linearity, infusing his work with the relaxed gliding of organic growth. Postwar sculpture drew its own highly original consequences from the classical modernism of Gabo, Picasso and González.

Giacometti and the Threat to Humanity

The outstanding sculptor of the era was Albert Giacometti. For a long time, his self-doubting struggle to grasp the appearance of reality – the sole visible reality, that is – was peppered with crises, in which the years 1935, 1950/51 and 1956 each mark a radical break. It is quite possible that Giacometti himself actually saw his life in that light and even styled his œuvre according to a pathos of failure. Today, in his œuvre, the artist's constant self-questioning also reflects the continuity that held sway in the second half of his life.

It began in 1935 with a return to the life study. In the long run, neither the exalted surrealist theatre of cruelty nor the cubistically abstracted *Heads* of 1934 could withstand Giacometti's relentless pursuit of a more definitive reality. The great discovery that took him ten full years to grasp was this: we perceive each other merely as an "apparition" surrounded by space, within a certain field of vision and perspectively reduced. This mode of perception, long an accepted component of painting, was one that Giacometti was determined to transpose into the field of sculpture. In 1945, the philosopher Maurice Merleau-Ponty published his famous study of the "phenomenology of perception" in which he examines how specific, concrete reality is altered by the situation in which it is perceived. Reinhold Hohl, in his monographic study of Giacometti, emphasised the connection, writing of the sculptor's "phenomenological realism". Giacometti himself said that "life-size does not exist", and reduced his figures to matchstick dimensions, making them almost disappear, to the point that they actually crumbled between his fingers by 1943.

Pablo Picasso
Woman with Baby Carriage, 1950
Bronze, 203 x 145 x 61 cm
Paris, Musée Picasso

*"The composition with seven figures
reminded me of a forest corner seen
for many years (thus was during my
childhood) and where trees – behind
which could be seen granite boul-
ders – with their naked and slender
trunks, limbless almost to the top,
had always appeared to me like personages immobilized in the course
of their wanderings and talking
among themselves."*
ALBERTO GIACOMETTI

Alberto Giacometti
Head of Diego, 1957
Bronze; height: 38.8 cm
Private collection

Alberto Giacometti
The Forest, 1950
Bronze, 57 x 61 x 49.5 cm
Zurich, Kunsthaus Zürich,
Alberto Giacometti Stiftung

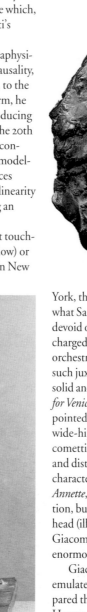

Why should a human being seem more real in the distance than in close-up? As soon as Giacometti realised that he was schematising the problem of distance, he found a distinctive artistic "style" for his archaic standing figures of life-embracing women and wiry, striding men. It was not distance, but encounter, its directness and intensity, that were the focal point. Which was why he began kneading the figures over a wire frame until they were slender as threads, paring them down linearly until they soar up before us vertically. It is the reason why he merges proximity and distance in a frontal rigidity "that summarises all the postures and glances of the world" (Albert Camus). These heads, busts and figures keep their distance. And yet, like idols, they also keep the observer at bay. The loss of corporeality becomes a stylistic figure which, paradoxically, lends visual stability to Giacometti's sculpture.

Though Giacometti illuminates, almost metaphysically, such Sartrean notions as the sublation of causality, sudden alienation and insurmountable solitude, to the point of losing sight of his obsessive quest for form, he clearly renounces the concept of "failure" by producing some of the most stunningly vital sculptures of the 20th century. Surrounding space gnaws at the ragged contours and blurred details of his works, while the modelling itself uses a classic means of rendering surfaces fluid, vibrant and potent. Slender, wiry, soaring linearity is created by the dissolution of distance, evoking an idolatric epiphany.

Where several figures are juxtaposed without touching, as in the 1948-49 *Place*, the 1950 *Forest* (ill. below) or the 1958 project for the Chase Manhattan Bank in New

York, this does not necessarily point to isolation or to what Sartre described as being thrust into an existence devoid of meaning. Instead, the effect is a highly-charged constellation of different scales and precisely orchestrated intermediate spaces. In his mature work, such juxtapositions become increasingly corporeal, solid and persuasive. In 1956 his series of *Seven Women for Venice* summed up the female types between the pointed, rod-like figure and the broad-shouldered, wide-hipped, ample earth-mother, indicating that Giacometti had by now developed a mastery of of proximity and distance. Instead of external distance, the expressive character came to the fore. The later busts (*Diego, Annette, Elie Lotar*) no longer rely on extreme contraction, but possess a balanced silhouette of base, neck and head (ill. above). The visionary gaze of the eyes mirrors Giacometti's own gaze, which grasps reality with an enormous final effort.

Giacometti was a loner who, though frequently emulated, never founded a school. Nevertheless, he prepared the ground for a new way of seeing in sculpture. He was the pioneer of that anti-Cartesian counterposion to Cubism that replaces rational systems with experienced perception, knowledge with specific experience.

Instead of the six sides of the cube, which I know to exist, I present only four sides, which I see. Minimal Art and post-Minimalist sculpture drew upon this basic premise for their artistic credo until well into the 70s. Giacometti was the first to radically posit this stance. Small wonder that his philosophical counterpart, Merleau-Ponty, was destined to become the theoretician of the next generation.

Germaine Richier (ill. above) overshadows all the other artists vaguely referred to as postwar sculptors,

creating weathered bronze shells and skeletons that weave humanity into a tapestry of survival teeming with harrowed, menaced and menacing creatures. Cracks, shards and rhizomes of bronze, handled with magisterial virtuosity, stress the unequivocality of the human condition. The *Migofs* by the painter Bernard Schultze (ill. above right) in paper, wire and plastic heighten morbidity and decay in a fantastic ghostly dance. The spikey, bush-like constructs by the Americans Theodore Roszak, Herbert Ferber and Seymour Lipton also draw upon the tormented Surrealist heritage in their aggressive displays of human existence as a symbolically heightened garden of thorns.

Herbert Read somewhat unfairly criticised the British sculptors after Moore, lambasting Kenneth Armitage (ill. left), Reg Butler (p. 491 below left) and Lynn Chadwick (p. 491 above) for the "excoriated flesh, frustrated sex, the geometry of fear" he saw reflected in their shrunken-headed, insect-limbed figures. Their early success owed much to the prevailing stylistic tastes of the day and a few bold methods of iron construction. Today, of all these sculptors, it is still Eduardo Paolozzi's robotic three-dimensional collages that have the greatest impact, transposing the Vorticist tradition of the machine-man into the realms of the fragmented, damaged and distressed.

Giacometti's complex phenomenology remains singular. An antipode may be found in the 40s and 50s in the work of the Austrian stone sculptor Fritz Wotruba (p. 491 below right). His œuvre is a bastion of humanity unscathed, hewn in stone, a rock of assertion in space. From the late 20s onwards his block-like figures upheld the tradition of early Derain and Brancusi, for the next generation. In the 40s he expanded the oscillating energy of concave joints into a cylindrical rounding of torso and limbs. In the 1950s he developed an exuberant dynamism with softer transitions towards standing, walking sitting, reclining figures in which, at strategic points, the pose shifts from the rigidly static to the distinctly vital without losing its stoney balance. Around 1960, the cubic rhythms of architectonic structures then began to re-emerge, with human figures layered into stele-like structures.

Informel: Process and Structure

Are there links between the torn and riven surfaces of Giacometti and Richier and the more abstract structures for which Michel Tapié coined the term "Informel" in 1952, referring to both painting and sculpture? Do the tangled evocations of the psyche in the paintings by Wols (pp. 249 ff) have direct analogies in sculpture? Or do sculptures, with their "higher material and temporal resistance" (in the words of Hans Uhlmann) hinder direct intellectual and emotional access to the material? Is there such a thing as Informel sculpture? Sculpture in which the formal impulse feels its way gently towards the material, as in a sketch? Sculpture that does not over-form its material between the raw state and the process, but allows it to grow and sprawl like cell

Lynn Chadwick
Seated Couple, 1986
Bronze; height: 23.5 cm
France, private collection

division, coral reefs or rust? Sculpture of malleable material such as clay, terracotta, plaster, bronze, wax, papier maché, wire but also in the more rugged and individualistic *cire perdu* technique, rather than sculpture with the purely reproductive approach of sand

"The choice of means by which a creative person expresses himself may be unimportant. But I firmly maintain that I see in stone the only true medium, because it is the real material of the sculptor."
Fritz Wotruba

Reg Butler
Working Model for the
Monument to the Unknown
Political Prisoner, 1952
Bronze wire, sheet metal and
plaster; height: 224 cm
London, Tate Gallery

Fritz Wotruba
Head, 1962
Marble; height: 47 cm
Private collection

Jean Dubuffet
Chair II, 1967
Painted polyester, 168 x 60 x 75 cm
Private collection

Lucio Fontana
Spatial Concept, Nature, 1959/60
Bronze, 74 x 80 cm
Cologne, Museum Ludwig,
Loan of Karsten Greve

casting? Sculpture that contradicts in many ways the classical concept as a firmly outlined volume and, by no coincidence, takes the painterly relievo, in particular, to its climax.

Such a sculpture does exist and it became widespread during the 50s. Its forefathers were Picasso, whose *Owl* spread its ragged wings in 1933, and Lipchitz, whose effusively undulating mature work forged a link with Baroque concepts. Its fathers, interesting enough, were painters one and all.

In his *Hostages* created in 1943/44, when France was under German occupation, Jean Fautrier had already applied oil paint, paper and clay to canvas in *haut-pate* relief (pp. 252 ff) and had cast bronze figures of irregularly fine and rough textures, described by André Malraux as "ideograms of suffering", shattered physiognomies whose fleetingly textured surface structure and anxiety-charged pose are a prelude to the art of the 50s. Jean Dubuffet's work (pp. 254 ff) is similarly harrowing, creating a new aesthetic with found objects. Although Schwitters and Arp had already revalued the worn, torn

waste of everyday life, only now did this combine with a deliberate renunciation of aestheticisation and an anticultural stance to create Art Brut.

In 1954, Dubuffet (ill. above) modelled forty *Statuettes of Endangered Life* out of newspaper, cellulose and iron slag in cement, lava, sponges, pieces of string, shards of glass, between a few centimetres and more than one metre in height. Their raw, expressively charged figuration can still be found reflected in Oldenburg's *Street* environment, Finally, Fontana's baroque, fluid ceramics, some of them as early as the 30s, and later the fruit-like expansions of his *Concetti spaziali – Natura* (ill. left) touch upon Informel sculpture, though Fontana, in particular, with his arabesque light-drawing of 1951 was to become a major source of inspiration for the Zero group of artists who railed against the Informel. He was, in other words, a borderline artist between the generations (cf p. 300).

For most young artists, the L'art informel of the 50s, especially in the field of sculpture, marked a transitional period. Its biomorphic, mineral tendencies and echoes of growth and decay reflected the artistic spirit of the era in which the new freedom of creativity merged with the evocations of the material. Thomas Lenk, Otto Herbert Hajek (ill. below), Erich Hauser, Ernst Hermanns, Jan Schoonhoven, as well as Paolozzi, César, Etienne-Martin and in America the syncretist Peter Grippen and the ceramic artists Peter Voulkos and John Masen all went through an Informel phase or touched upon the Informel to some degree.

François Stahly, Zoltán Kemény (ill. above right) the brothers Arnaldo (ill. above left) and Giò Pomodoro consolidated the amorphous flow to the point of rhythmic rapport before it became systematised around 1960 in patterns of grids and lines that eschew all authorial and subjective components. One of the most consistent of the Informel modellers was Emil Cimiotti, whose lyrical works addressing the fecund growth processes of nature are at the same time pictorial processes. He was perhaps the only one to adhere to the Informel throughout his entire œuvre while also adopting decorative and floral components, as in his later fountains.

Abstract Expressionism: Construction of the Gesture

The key words were blot, drip, structure, process, and there was talk of malleable materials. Other buzzwords were gesture, action, traces of movement, and the main materials were iron and steel. The umbrella concepts beneath which this 50s inventory was gathered were Informel and Abstract Expressionism. The leading figures in painting were, above all, Wols on the one hand and Jackson Pollock (pp. 269 ff) and Franz Kline (p. 279) on the other hand. Unlike the world of painting, it was Europe that led the field in sculpture. While the Americans were still touting a second-hand Surrealism, or, like David Smith and Louise Bourgeois, exploring totemistic variations, European sculptors were transforming the Constructivist heritage into works of dynamic force as early as 1950.

In America, such re-orientation did not begin until ten years later. In 1959, Tony Smith made the shift from architecture to tension-charged modular systems. That same year, John Chamberlain created his first compressed automobile parts and Mark Di Suvero mounted his first beams. America's sculpture of the Fifties actually happened, for the most part, in the 60s. In other words, art historical reality sometimes tacked wildly through the decades.

In Europe, the Constructivist tradition still had much of its powerful appeal despite its Cold War defamation. Hans Uhlmann, a trained engineer, had already mounted *Heads* of wire and sheet iron in the 30s. Since 1946 he had reduced them to linear, arabesque signs worked from a single metal wire, in vibrantly choreographed forms that pierced the surrounding space like flashes of lightning. In his work, lines act as pointers, just as planes act as spatial boundaries (p. 494). Uhlmann worked with both these elements. Protruding planes conglomerate to form energetic silhouettes, rising, folding and breaking, embracing a dense spatial core, and at times protruding from the conglomeration or projecting beyond it. In his three-metre high sculpture *Concerto* for the Berlin Conservatory, linear cantilenas rotate and planar rhythms oscillate in polyphonic harmony, creating a melodious textural effect in steel whose gestural movement merges with a clearly stereometric approach.

Around 1950, Norbert Kricke (ill. right) took up where Uhlmann's linearity had left off. His *Space Sculpture* marks a major step in the direction that begins with the light-pooled gouging of Rodin, leading on, through the work of the Russian Constructivists, to Calder, Picasso and González. Yet Kricke, in adopting a favourite idea of the 50s, namely movement, radicalised the approach to mass and statics. His sculptures have neither volume nor outline, circumscribe no space and have no vestige of corporeality. They shoot and stream beyond the actual course of the lines, creating visual runways in an eruptive countdown of velocity or in the life rhythm of the organic world, in swirling curves of unfettered energy or gentle gliding fluidity. They evoke the quest for the future or a positively biological sense of time. In his mature work, Kricke reduced his sculpture one step further, paring the directional plurality to a single curve and enhancing the archetype, the piece of wire bent by hand and placed on the floor, curving, writhing, grasping space, vast and urban, railing against the sterile grid patterns of concrete architecture.

Uhlmann and Kricke, who were then joined by Heiliger after his beginnings in biomorphic sculpture drove the Constructivist mode towards Abstract Expressionism. Kricke added a new dynamic paradigm and imbued it with the changing spirit of the 50s, 60s and 70s. It is this that makes him the most important German sculptor in the era between Lehmbruck and Beuys.

David Smith and Gestural Abstraction

The American sculptor David Smith could just as easily be discussed as the successor to the steel and iron sculpture of Picasso, González and Calder or as the precursor of Minimalism. Here, we intend to regard this constructor with a welding torch in the context of the 50s. At that time, his sculpture had a certain proximity to the Action painting of Kline and Willem De Kooning (pp. 274 ff) and in America (though only there) it made him a myth of modern art. He was the first truly American sculptor between modern industrial society and tribal mythology. The *Ziks* (since 1961, referring to Babylonian stepped pyramids) intersect vibrantly painted, cut-up concave and convex pipe components. The *Cubi* (ill. below) created between 1961 and 1965 pile up variously high blocks, cubes and cylinders in precarious balancing acts. Seen from the side, they seem tightly compressed. The surfaces of stainless steel sparkle with the swirling patterns of the steel brush.

Smith's simplification of forms and his use of mechanical production methods influenced Minimal Art. Nevertheless, one should not lose sight of the fact that, Smith remained a traditionalist, insisting on figurative verticality and never taking the step towards the horizontality of "landscape". He also retained the concept of compositional tension.

The architect Tony Smith (p. 497 below right) who constructed sculptures of enormous formal variabilty on the basis of crystalline octahedra from 1959 onwards came closer to the modular seriality that we find in the work of Donald Judd and Sol LeWitt. Yet here, too, linearity and contour tend to give a gestural dynamic to the architectural stability of the work.

Barnett Newman, the classicist of a metaphysically profound Color Field painting (pp. 289 f) also made a brief contribution to sculpture. In 1967, his steles culminated in the *Broken Obelisk* (p. 497 below left) whose brilliant simplicity succinctlly summarises a monumental tradition and at the same time breaks with it. Upward and downward movement collide at the points of the obelisk in a concentration of energy that is suspended in a perfect balancing act. Two years later, Newman left verticalism behind him to create two walk-through

David Smith
Blackburn–Song of an Irish
Blacksmith, 1949/50
Iron on marble base,
117 x 103.5 x 58 cm
Duisburg, Wilhelm Lehmbruck
Museum

"To the creative artist, in the making of art it is doubtful whether aesthetics have any value to him. The truly creative artist deals with vulgarity."   DAVID SMITH

David Smith
Cubi XVIII 2–4, 1964
Stainless steel; height: 294 cm
New York, Marlborough Gallery

whose work ranged from pre-war Surrealism to the fringes of Minimal Art.

It was not until around 1950, however, that Smith's work took on its distinctive independence with his (long prepared) *Drawings in Space* in the tradition established some twenty years before by the pioneers of iron sculpture. Surrealism gave his work its narrative, almost literary edge, and its rich lyricism. What is new is the sheer frontality, as in a painting, and the unexpected views from many sides. In *Blackburn–Song of an Irish Blacksmith* (ill. above) he rendered linear arabesques as one with the figure and bound all the details within a framework that allows the viewer's eye to penetrate the interior freely. It is an emblematic, silhouetted torso. Viewed from the side, it seems tangled and unstable, contrasting starkly with the serene equilibrium of the frontal view. Here, Smith radicalises the principle of discontinuity, which also informs his later works. These sculptures cannot be taken in at one glance, affording instead specific individual images which seem to click into place with each new angle.

The stilted *Tank Totems* (made of round tank lids and referring to Freud's essay *Totem and Taboo*) are anthropomorphically protruding signs that occupy a position sculptures that foreshadowed the architectonic sculptures of the 70s.

All things said and done, the true Abstract Expressionists in the world of sculpture are Mark Di Suvero and John Chamberlain. Di Suvero (p. 498 below) added a spatial aspect to the advances already made in painting when he created his powerful beam structures, initially made of construction beams, chains, ropes and later from double T-girders. Although he shared the compositional discontinuity of Smith, the lines of energy in his sculptures have their own physically tangible tension, equilibrium and pressure, grasping and embracing the surrounding space. Towards the end of the decade, this physicality was to become a key theme of new sculpture.

Chamberlain (p. 498 above) was even more direct in articulating the concepts and spontaneity of the Abstract Expressionists in sculpture. His compressed, bent, welded and painted car parts have distinct affinities with the work of the Assembage artists as well as with the compressions of the French sculptor César. Yet in the work of Chamberlain, compression and balance of mass, nests of shadow, maelstroms of line, sweeping curves all give the impression of controlled catastrophe – composed rather than compressed. In this respect he has more affinities with Di Suvero than with César.

At this point, the English sculptor Anthony Caro immediately springs to mind. Until 1959 this former assistant of Henry Moore concentrated primarily on heavy-bodied female nudes, only to take a radical change of direction following a visit to David Smith. Together with Di Suvero, he is the true heir of the American sculptor – and yet his sculpture is so far removed from all notions of totemism and verticalism that we tend to associate him with the (almost) contemporary Minimal Art movement.

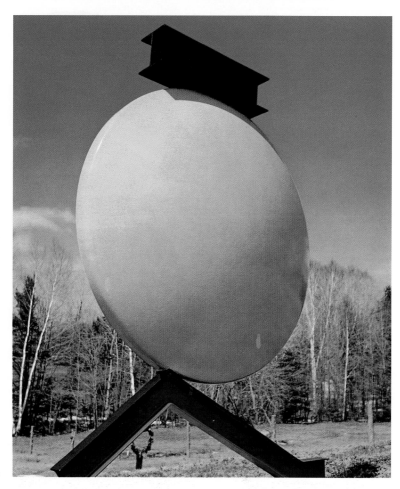

David Smith
Bec-Dida Day, 12 July 1963
Steel, polychromiert, 230 x 150 cm,
diameter: 47.5 cm
Bolton Landing, Estate of David Smith

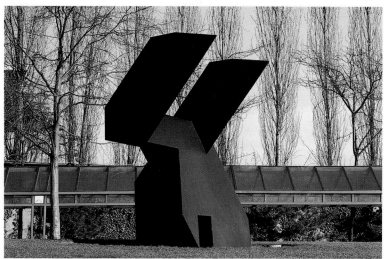

Barnett Newman
Broken Obelisk, 1963–1967
Steel, 775 x 306 x 306 cm. Houston (TX), Institute
of Religion and Human Development

Tony Smith
Moses, 1968–1974
Steel, 518 x 434 cm. Seattle (WA), Seattle City
Light, Courtesy of Seattle Arts Comission

John Chamberlain
Colonel Splendid, 1964
Sheet steel, painted, 63 x 67 x 57 cm
Frankfurt am Main, Museum
für moderne Kunst, Sammlung
Ströher

*"Wood has its own life, wants its
own way, has its grain, and it's
grown, suffered, and by the time you
get it it has already been killed, and
your're supposed to do something;
and they have done great things
with it, just incredible sculptures in
wood."* MARK DI SUVERO

Mark Di Suvero
Che Faro Senza Euridici, 1959/60
Wood, rope and nails,
213 x 264 x 231 cm
Private collection

Kinetic Expansion

8

Composition and Psychology Renounced

Around 1960, two fundamental forces of Modernism came under fire: composition and psychology. Criticism was aimed at the icons of universal harmony and at the kind of art that identifies the work in an almost mystical way with the author, his or her biography, signature and gesture. Around 1960, the groundswell of resistance to Mondrian's equilibrium and Pollock's eruptiveness spread from Düsseldorf to Paris and New York, sweeping in its wake more than just painting.

Donald Judd objected that the expressive sculptor Mark Di Suvero "uses beams as if they were brushstrokes, imitating movement, as Franz Kline did." Both the Constructivist and the Expressionist view of the world had run their course. To the young generation, both seemed to be dead-end roads to pure subjectivity. The belief that art represented the order of the world or expressed the inner life of the artist was no longer an accepted credo.

The new slogans, as in Russia forty years before, called for an end to easel painting and and for concentration on the object instead. The new aims were society, life, reality, technology, beauty of the elements and the sky, fascination with street life and the media world. An immense medial breadth and enormous lust for life entered art. Not since the formative years of modern sculpture around 1910 had art moved so quickly in so many new directions.

Three forces made their mark. First of all, under the generic name of "Nouvelle Tendance", groups in South America, Britain, France, the Netherlands, Germany and Italy explored, with varying focal points, the reconciliation of art, technology and nature. In Düsseldorf, the Zero group pursued its romantic vision of the Futurist dream, while in Paris the Groupe de Recherche d'Art Visuel (GRAV) socialised it, with vibrant structures of motion, light, air, glitter and immaterial energy. Kinetic sculptures moved from the periphery to the very centre of art.

Secondly, the all but forgotten tradition of Marcel Duchamp came to light again. This time around, what Duchamp had viewed with critical consciousness, scepticism and detachment was widely accepted. The ready-made had come of age. Nouveau Réalisme, Pop Art, the Assemblage artists (a term coined in 1962 on the occa-

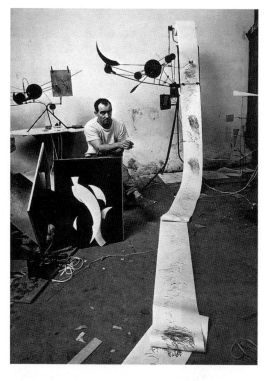

Jean Tinguely
Méta-matic No. 12
(Le Grand Charles), 1959
Iron, electric motor, paper
Private collection

sion of an exhibition organised by William Seitz) charged their objects with the everyday prose of social reality, urban folklore, cityscape, mass media, wear and tear or consumption. For a while, garbage tips and rubbish heaps became what the flea-market had once been for the Surrealists.

Thirdly, at the opposite end of the spectrum, Minimal Art fundamentally redefined the relationship between viewer, object and space. It more or less stripped bare our powers of perception, leaving no shelter, and forcing viewers to find their own response to what they saw. It was the most influential purism of the entire decade. Its consequences and the shift of emphasis it entailed were to reverberate for many years.

Many of the new directions in art were at first inextricably linked. A tactical front against the art of yesteryear formed a bond between otherwise heterogeneous approaches. Apart from a few important exceptions, there was a general rejection of composition and psychology, right across the board. Serial and modular sys-

Hans Haacke
Condensation Cube,
(first version), 1963
Acrylic glass, water, climatological
conditions of the environment,
60.3 x 60.3 x 60.3 cm
Private collection

*"A 'sculpture' that physically reacts to
its environment nd/or affects its surroundings is no longer to be regarded
as an object. The range of outsiede
factors influencing it, as well as its
own radius of action, reach beyond
the space it materially occupies. It
thus merges with the environment
in a relationship that is better
understood as a 'system' of interdependent processes. ... A system is
not imagined; it is real."*
HANS HAACKE

tems were accepted as instruments to combat aesthetic arbitrariness and the signs of individual authorship. Impersonal and mechanical production lost its stigma. It was the end of an understandable postwar phobia that had tended to push technology, industrial standarisa-tion and communications system into what Werner Haftmann described as the "processing world".

By the end of the 60s, the very face of sculpture had been transformed and sculpture had gone through metamorphoses as far-reaching as those half a century before, when the autonomy of Cubist rhythm had bro-ken the mould of the anatomically intact human figure. Duchamp planted the timebomb known as the ready-made. Tatlin placed real materials in a real space. The image of sculpture was fundamentally transformed and yet, at its core, it still remained bound to the figure, the sign, the object. After all, it was still a visible, tangible art, an art that could be touched.

Now sculpture began to turn to new materials, media, aggregates and spaces. Sculpture could be a wedge of lard, a cloud of gas, a piece of land, an action, an idea, a video arrangement. It took place in the gallery, on the street, in the desert, in the sky, on the body or simply in our minds. New terms and concepts followed one another at breakneck speed – from object to process to concept to attitude to situation to model – and labels such as Kinetic, Sky Art or Body Art were coined. Most of them came from America. Only Pierre Restany's Nouveau Réalisme at the beginning of the decade and Germano Celant's Arte Povera at the end of the decade survived as European models.

What emerged was not only a boundless opening and morphological promiscuity, not only an unparal-leled fireworks of new possibilities, but also, if we con-sider sculpture in the narrower sense of the term, a crisis of identity. Around 1970, it tended towards what Lucy Lippard has described as its dematerialisation into fleet-ing media images, notes or ideas. This gave all the more weight to attempts to redefine sculpture as such on the basis of these innovative new sources. Anthony Caro, Richard Serra, Ulrich Rückriem spring to mind.

Julio Le Parc
Perpetuum Mobile, 1964
Aluminium and painted wood,
119 x 119 cm
Private collection

The unadulterated patriotism of American artists and critics made the 60s the American decade. New York's hegemony was consolidated by the Assemblage artists in Chicago and California. The intensity with which each step was immediately considered, analysed and countered in practice and in theory alike was unpar-alleled elsewhere. Only in America was an uninter-rupted chain of artistic developments forged in sculp-ture as well, link by link. The ousting of the "figurative mode of sculpture" by the "landscape mode" (according to Robert Morris) began in New York. Instead of verti-cality, it was now horizontality that prevailed.

In Europe, too, a central force-field was emerging in the triangle between Paris, Düsseldorf and Milan. The Zero and Nouveau Réalisme groups, with Yves Klein and Tinguely as bridge-builders, formed something akin to an unequal common front. Piero Manzoni was the messenger between them, flitting to and fro like a weaver's shuttle linking the threads. From the early 60s onwards, Joseph Beuys came into the limelight and was increasingly recognised as a major figure. In spite of its formative role in Pop Art and despite the important con-tributions from Eduardo Paolozzi, Anthony Caro and Philip King, Britain was still isolated. The fact that experiments with light fire, water and action had also been going on in Japan since 1955 did not come to the attention of the western world until 1963. When it finally did, however, the parallels and priorities of the Gutai group provided inspirational for the nascent Fluxus movement and made a playfully ritualised contri-bution to Happenings and Concept Art.

Nature, Light, Movement, Technology
Whether or not the anecdote is true, or simply a good yarn, it highlights the art historical situation. Otto Piene told how Yves Klein suggested to him in 1958 that the world should be divided up: Klein himself would be responsible for the air, Norbert Kricke for the water and Piene for the fire (which would not prevent them poach-

ing on each others' territory). This demiurgic gesture
certainly suits Klein's aura as an enormously inspirational force and self-styled saviour too well to be entirely
fabricated. If anything, it might even sound a little too
self-effacing! Piene widened the spectrum by adding,
"Our artistic interest is aimed not only at movement and
light, but also at warmth, sound, optical illusion, magnetism, condensation and expansion of materials, water,
the movement of sand and foam, fire, wind, smoke and
many other natural and technical appearances."

This approach was by no means the sole preserve of
the Zero group (and its general attitudes) or its young
leader Yves Klein. As early as 1955, Kricke was designing
water sculptures as mirror surfaces, wave patterns, stream,
low tide, high tide and in 1957 he created his first *Water-
forest* of plexiglass columns. Werner Ruhnau worked on
an aerial architecture. Manzoni projected a *Pneumatic
Theatre*. Hans Haacke captured condensation in his 1963
Condensation Cube (p. 500 above). In London, David
Medella planted growing organic environments.
Around 1960, the staging and alienation of physical phenomena, as Piene put it, was quite literally in the air.

At the same time, the painters of the Ecole de Paris,
now in the third generation, still held sway in Paris.
Since 1948, however, Nicolas Schöffer, a Hungarian in
Paris, who, like his fellow countryman Victor Vasarely,
was a utopian thinker in search of total urban aestheticism, had been developing his *Space-dynamic Sculptures*
(p. 582). His long-term aim was the creation of a cybernetic city that reacted to times of day, temperatures and
weather with light and movement.

Since the early 50s, a few younger artists had also
been taking their creative experiments beyond the
bounds of painting and traditional sculpture for the first
time since the war. They came from Israel, Switzerland,
Belgium and South America. Their centre was the
recently opened Galerie Denise René. Their common
factor was movement as an artistic element, in contrast
to the immutability of beauty, and as a foray into the
fourth dimension of time, already promised by the Constructivists in 1920 and now opening up new horizons.
They saw movement as a creative principle that forges a
link between art and life.

Admittedly, there had already been moving sculptures. Their history can be traced back to Duchamp's
Rotary Glass Plates (p. 460 above left) and Naum
Gabo's vibrating steel spring (both 1920), to the Bauhaus
experiments with colour and light, and to Calder's
mobiles. The American artist George Rickey had been
constructing mobiles of glass since 1949 and was now
systematically exploring movement as a creative
medium. According to Rickey, even Calder, who had
influenced him, was still too profoundly inspired by
the abstract motifs of Magnelli, Arp and Miró. What
Rickey wanted instead was pure kinetic sculpture
based on highly qualified principles of engineering –
oscillating, floating, circling, dangling, rising, sinking,
vibrating.

"The catalogue of natural processes that have so far
been overlooked in painting and sculpture, is endless"
wrote Rickey in 1964 in his essay "The Morphology of
Movement". Their combination in widely radiating,
sharply pointed needles or cradling rectangular areas
marks the spectrum of kinetic art. The weightlessness
with which steel fingers dance around a point, graceful
and languid, penetrating the light, circumscribing the
radius of the trees, setting themselves apart with their
rigid linearity – all this makes the breath of air, with its
currents and strengths, subtly visible (ill. above). With
an unconcealed technical construction, this follows the
laws of nature. Rickey, along with Calder, is the master
of an authentic kinetic sculpture.

The Impetus of the Group: GRAV, ZERO, EAT, CAVS

In America Rickey remained a lone maverick for a long
time. It was in Paris, with his call to form a group, that
Kinetic Art moved into centre court. By 1955, the exhibition "Le Mouvement" at Denis René showed that the
trend was already in full swing. The exhibition included
works by Yaacov Agam, Pol Bury, Tinguely, Vasarely and
others. Three years later, François Morellet (p. 348), the
Argentinian artists Julio Le Parc, Francisco Sobrino and
others founded the Groupe de Recherche d'Art Visuel
which remained a cohesive group until 1968. Their
statutes called for teamwork to explore the technical and
physical problems of light movement, replacement of
the Romantic concept of the artist-as-genius by a
research team, and audience involvement.

In 1967, visitors to the "Lumière et mouvement"
exhibition had to move through dark passageways, feel
their way through mirrored labyrinths, trip over steps
with padded traps and bump into all manner of unexpected interactive components. In a *Perpetuum Mobile*
Le Parc (p. 500 below) threaded together a number of
polished metal discs which moved in the draught of air,

Otto Piene
Automatic Light Ballett, 1962
Perforated metal, light, electronics
Private collection

mirroring each other and the room in a fluctuating play of lines, angles, moving reflexes – a mobile that transformed the confusion of baroque mirrored cabinets and the shimmering light of Impressionist paintings into kinetic effects.

In Düsseldorf, too, ideas, manifestos and happenings were everywhere. In 1957, Otto Piene and Heinz Mack founded the Zero group and began corresponding with all the avant-garde movements in France, the Netherlands and Italy. In 1961, Günther Uecker joined them. Other artists such as Christian Megert, the young Hans Salentin, Hermann Goepfert, Jan Schoonhoven (of the Dutch group Nul) were loosely associated through exhibitions or cropped up in the three isues of the *ZERO* magazine. The hard core consisting of Piene, Mack and Uecker were at the vanguard of the breakthrough to the post-Informel, serial, monochrome picture. Their contribution to sculpture cannot easily be extricated from their contribution to painting. Pictures, reliefs and objects were all used as instruments to capture, rhythmicise and nuance light, with punched and perforated patterns or nail structures binding vibrations and optical energies.

Piene (ill. above) was an efficient organiser and enthusiastic theoretician. From projections of his perforated grid pictures, he developed his *Light Ballet* from 1959 onwards, initially using hand-held lamps and later by increasingly mechanical methods and electronic programming. The aim was to achieve an appearance of immateriality rather than presenting the apparatus itself. Later, Piene, as the founder of Sky Art, celebrated large-scale aerial projects. In 1972 his rainbow made of five 460 metre, helium-filled polyethylene tubes arched over the closing ceremony of the Olympic Games in Munich. Alternating with the silver water-cloud by Mack, 600 electric bulbs lit up in an arch. Was this a festive Zero zone in anticipation of a – perhaps purely decorative – preserve of art? In 1974, Piene became director of the Center of Advanced Visual Studies in Cambridge, MA, and a leading promoter of a techno-aesthetically oriented art.

Heinz Mack
The Time of the Stars, 1963
Plexiglass, Fresnel lense,
c. 325 x 35 x 9 cm
Ibiza, Spain

Heinz Mack's sculptural œuvre (p. 502 below) alternates between a utopian dream of beauty and its pragmatic payment by instalments in the form of art-to-order. Here is a lyricist in light who wants to sing (and can) and who sometimes finds himself bogged down in the elegant rhetoric of silver reflexes and granite surfaces. A pioneer of Land Art, his Sahara project teeming with great fountains of light, artificial suns, a mirror wall, sand reliefs, a stele of light (realised in 1967), was subsequently transposed into stunning sculptures for public galleries and urban sites. Nevertheless, Mack imbued his rotating discs and dynamos with a hitherto unknown vibrancy. He also developed differentiated strategies for an urban sculpture. In the steles which were Mack's preferred form, light became a material like stone or metal.

The Zero group disbanded in 1967. Uecker resisted Piene's attempts to proclaim a New Idealism along the lines of the Nouveau Réalisme in Paris. The break-up was not only due to a conceptual disagreement. Behind it lay a latent tension that had fuelled a productive force for many years, but now caused a split. To regard Uecker, the strongest and most dedicated sculptor in the Zero group, only within the context of that group, fails to do him justice.

For Uecker (ill. above and below) Zero was not some utopian horizon, but a rite of passage. For him, art was not a reserve of idealism inebriated by light, but "the space within which he acted out his existence", according to Dieter Honisch, and within which a number of influences are evident, from Rudolf Steiner to Taoism

Günther Uecker
Corner, 1968
Nails on canvas on wood,
200 x 200 x 200 cm
Collection of the artist

and Zen. In this respect, the Mecklenburg-born German artist bears more affinities with Yves Klein than with the euphoric dreamers with whom he came into contact in 1961.

When he drove in the first nails in 1957, bordering a monochrome picture, that still had nothing to do with the rhythms of light and shadow. It was only after 1959 that he also began using nails to set light in vibrant motion. He sprayed them white, overcoming their materiality in this way, and transposed them onto a floating white structure. His circle, spiral, field and wave movements, light boxes and "light plantations" were

Günther Uecker
Forest of one trunk, 1990
Nails, ashes, glue and wood; 7 parts,
170 x 600 cm, diameter: 80 cm
Private collection

among the most subtle expressions of Zeroist sensibilities. In this respect, Uecker's work fitted in with that of the Zero group for a while at least.

Nails, however, are also real utensils. They derive from a practical area and represent manual work. When Uecker aestheticises them, he shows that art is made in a simple and understandable way. At the same time, these nails clearly display their physicality and aggressiveness. Uecker's path runs from light structure to physical perception and tangibility, from optics to object. Apart from pure structure, by the early 60s there were already haptic objects, brushes, nailed everyday objects such as tables, stools, a piano. The oversized nail, an extroverted, brutal object that Uecker drove through the outside wall of the Kaufhof department store in Dortmund in 1968, marks his break with the meditative panel. From then on, Uecker also presented Happenings. His sculptures became objects the viewer could walk over or through, such as his architectonically conceived table of nails.

In the 70s he expanded his sensorium, softening his materials (in the course of what might be seen as a post-Minimalist anti-form tendency), hanging torn canvases, corrugated cardboard and ropes. When he returned to the nail-relief in the 80s, he began creating expressive whirling patterns daubed in white and black. Destruction and tranquility balance each other out. This side of Uecker's work shows him to be a European sculptor who goes far beyond Zeroist idealism.

Elsewhere, related groups formed. In Milan, the Gruppo T was founded in 1959 with Giovanni Colombo, followed in Padova a little later by the Gruppo N. In Cordoba, the Gruppo Espacio turned their attention to the kinetics of light. In Amsterdam, the Nul group was formed in direct response to Zero. In London, from 1964 onwards, the artists around David Medella's *Signals* magazine propagated collaboration with industry and

the inclusion of natural forces such as steam, water, fire and magnetism in art. Even in Moscow, Lev Nusberg's Dvishene group (meaning "movement") expanded its geometric vocabulary to include works dealing with the kinetics of light.

In the USA, there was no history of Constructivist and Dadaist machine art. Even the theoretical basis derived from the Bauhaus tradition took hold relatively late. Industrial resources and rapidly progressing mass media, however, were present at a very early stage. 1964 saw the publication of Marshal MacLuhan's *Understanding Media* which heralded the end of the Gutenberg era and the age of the printed word. Isolated, abstract information would be replaced in future by a more direct and sensory pictorial experience. The neural system of global communications would produce a new, sensorily more complex individual. In his 1968 book *Beyond Modern Sculpture* Jack Burnham posited his vision of 20th century sculpture becoming assimilated into cybernetic systems. From the mid-60s onwards such ideas found currency in art practice. Accordingly, US art was dominated by a more comprehensive multimedia and multi-sensory approach.

The composer John Cage was the first to exploit fully the possibilities of audio-visual media. Right from the start, his work included happenings, theatre and ballet. The "theatrical" element became the hallmark of an art that treated objects as actors. In 1966, Robert Rauschenberg and the Swedish engineer Billy Klüver brought these various approaches together. Their EAT (Experiments in Art and Technology, Inc.) constituted the American counterpart to GRAV, with the emphasis on the artist-engineer synthesis rather than on the anonymity of the creative collective.

In October 1966, in the building where the legendary Armory Show had been held in 1913, a series of "Nine Evenings" was held featuring nine artists, including Cage, Rauschenberg, Robert Whitman, Öyvind Fahlström and Yvonne Rainer. They involved "reactive environments" with electronic switch systems, control nets for light patterns, amplifiers for internal body sounds, infrared television, air cushions … "initiation rites for a new media: total theatre" according to Fahlström. One year later, the Moholy-Nagy student Gyorgy Kepes founded his Center for Advanced Visual Studies at the Massachussets Institute of Technology (MIT).

For the space of twenty years, the Center remained at the hub of a technically generated, though not technically determined art that was unafraid of popular sky decor and pneumatic starflowers. From laser artist Rokne Krebs to video pioneer Nam June Paik, almost every significant artist who helped to roll back the boundaries of what was acceptable was a fellow of the Center at some time or another. In 1977, the *Centerbeam* was presented at the documenta 6 exhibition in Kassel, Germany. It was a 61 metre long multimedia viaduct and action theatre featuring steam explosions, strobe flashes, water prisma, windwheel, neon, argon, laser, hologram, radio, video. The construct presented biological growth processes, the archaic powers of water and wind, the prototypical industrial energy of steam, various versions of artificial light, several information systems and relais switches. in short, it was a brief history of technical progress, translated to sensorily palpable effect. Was this art in the embryonic phase of its development from the mechanical to the cybernetic age?

Kinetic Art: Crisis and Complexity

By 1977 the artist-engineer honeymoon was over. The "Art and Technology" exhibition in Los Angeles in 1971 marked the turning-point. The enthusiasm for storms of light, chromatic rainbows, flashing mirror images and synaesthetics was on the wane. Had it all just been one big funfair, the "rusting ruins of Utopia" (according to Lászlö Glozer)? Or had the prejudice that art is by definition the opposite of technology rather than its creative partner won the upper hand again? At the height of the Vietnam war, America's art-and-technology movement was accused of moral blindness.

Yet the mistrust needed no political motivation. With their halting, wobbling constructions, such machine artists as Tinguely and Harry Kramer (ill. above) had undermined the technological enthusiasm of the GRAV kinetic artists even in the 60s. They countered the smooth standardised efficiency of the machine slaves with an anarchic freedom of chance and irregularity. In the 60s art moved away from optimistic alliance with technology and the media.

The Belgian artist-engineer Panamarenko went beyond the irony with which Tinguely and Luginbühl had addressed the machine. From 1967 onwards, his

response to anonymous perfection in the supersonic age was a series of alternative, individual flying machines (p. 504 above). Though painstakingly constructed, they do not leave the ground. This is Panamarenko's personal adventure in progress – a utopia of yester-year and a poetic vision.

The historical significance of kinetics and its multi-media expansion did not, however, lie in the spectacular participatory theatre of the apparatus. Nor did it lie in the firmly established artistic principle of motion as such. Even today, it still lies in the way in which motion is applied as a differentiated expressive language: dramatic, lyrical, contemplative or comical? The Italian

Harry Kramer
B. E. N., 1963
Wire and wood; height: 87 cm,
diameter: 142 cm
Germany, VEBA OEL A. G.

Pol Bury
Fifty Tons of Columns, 1972
Stainless steel; height: 200 cm each,
diameter: 30 cm each
Saint-Paul-de-Vence, Fondation
Maeght

Jean Tinguely
Carnival Fountain, 1977
Various materials, basin: 16 x 19 m
Basel, Theaterplatz

Jean Tinguely
Eureka 1963/64
Iron bars, steel wheels, metal pipes,
various 220 V motors, painted,
780 x 660 x 410 cm
Zollikon, Walther Bechtler
Foundation

Page 507:
Jean Tinguely
Prole Art No. 3, 1989
Assemblage, 90 x 96 x 68 cm
Zurich, Galerie Bruno
Bischofberger

artist Bruno Munari, who constructed "useless machines" set in motion by a breath of air as early as the 30s, calculated the breaking of light according to precise mathematical formulae. The Belgian artist Pol Bury (p. 505 below) uses the infinitely slow movement of spheres, discs or columns to recall the growth of nature or the orbit of the stars. The eye is geared to slow motion and meditation.

The Greek artist Takis (p. 504 below) calls upon invisible physical energy sources, especially magnetism, and translates them into visible action of almost inexplicable sudden movements and intervals. In his impressive audio spaces, magnetic effects, kinetics and a whirring, droning sound merge.

The Israeli artist Yaacov Agam (p. 346) goes through an almost limitless permutation of positions, translating the theme of variation and series into a process of virtual possibilities. Swedish artist Olof Utveldt sets objects in

motion in an ingenious way that illustrates the names by which we know them: brushes brush, flycatchers catch flies – here is motion as object art with a touch of wit.

Op Art has its own form of kinetics. It derives from the laziness of the human eye rather than from any real motion. The interference of radiating, moiré, shimmering effects confuses the retina and does allows the eye no rest. Naturally, this tends to stimulate strategies for two-dimensional rather than three-dimensional art. For this reason, the work of Victor Vasarely (pp. 345 f) is discussed in the section on painting. By contrast, the Venezuelan artist Jesús Rafael Soto, who worked in Paris from 1950, forged a link with sculpture (p. 347). In 1962, he hit upon his most effective constellation, involving thin white bars suspended on nylon threads of varying lengths in front of a striped ground. The tiniest movement by the spectator, the slightest change in viewpoint, even the blinking of an eye, fragments the bars and the threads into pieces that seek to reunite. Mistily shimmering millky ways emerge. The result is a vibration as subtle as it is intensive, and Soto later sought to transpose the same effect to architectural spaces.

Even if its heyday is clearly past, Kinetic Art is by no means relegated to history, but remains a continuing expansion of sculpture.

Tinguely: the Machine as Theatre

The Swiss artist Jean Tinguely is an outstanding figure. From his arrival in Paris in 1953 until his death in 1991, he explored the immense expressive possibilities and subtle animation of moving sculpture, revealing ever new images that were both whimsical and earnest, ironic and pathos-laden, constructive and auto-destructive, charming and monstrous. He robbed the machine of its specialist application, emancipating it into the uselessly ludic and making it the vehicle of his own emotions. He made the machine a global theatre in which, on the one hand, a vibrant lust for life and on the other hand a metaphysical fear are projected in the shaking and rattling of machine parts, scrap-yard finds and bric-a-brac. It is a spectacle that leads the practical efficiency of the machine ad absurdum while at the same time paying homage to the fascination of the mechanical universe. Yet machines with electric motors now belong to a dying age – a fact that has prompted Werner Spies to describe Tinguely's work as a "requiem to the movements and stereotypes of the homme-machine". One is reminded of Thomas Mann's description of parody "playing its game late in the day with the honoured vestiges of a longstanding tradition".

Because Tinguely was very much alone in his distinctive œuvre, he soon became a European figure of integration, like Yves Klein. Scrap-iron as readymade linked him to the Nouveaux Réalistes and the New York Assemblage artists, while his work with motion linked him to the Kineticists and his aerial "happenings" with the manifesto *Für Statik* (For Statics) over Düsseldorf to

Jean Tinguely
Eva Aeppli and the Burghers of
Calais, 1989
Sculpture, 7 parts; iron, found
objects, electric motors,
300 x 300 x 220
Zurich, Galerie Bruno
Bischofberger

*"Life is movement. Everything
transforms itelf, everything modifies
itself ceaselessy, and to try to stop it,
to try to check life in mid-flight and
recapture it in the form of a work of
art, a sculpture or a painting, seems
to me to be a mockery of the intensity of life."* JEAN TINGUELY

the Zero group. He touched upon the issues that moved
an entire generation of artists. Yet his early moving
reliefs were little more than astute comments on the static image. In 1958 he took the decisive step from hidden
motors mobilising otherwise traditional compositions
to machines as independent sculptures. In 1958/59 he
created his series of *Méta-Matics*. They do not merely
parody the automatism of the Tachiste gesture, but, like
many of his later sculptures, also call for the utopia of a
quasi-humane machine world reconciled with humanity, "full of joy and with joy".

After 1958 it was the visitor who triggered the movement and sound. In the early 60s, his *Balubas*, named
after an African tribe, performed their shaking dance
with feathers, fur, tin cans and cowbells. In *Paradise*,
now in Stockholm, seven complex machines attack
seven burlesque fertility dolls (*Nanas*), rendered by his
wife Niki de Saint Phalle (p. 520) with ribald jokes. In his
Carnival Fountain in Basel (p. 506 above) the useless
fountains engage each other in veritable spraying com-
petitions. It marks the climax of the lively, tongue-in-
cheek wit of which Tinguely was a master.

There was, however, another side to his work. In the
course of the 60s, his machines grew to monumental
proportions, solidly built, densely contoured, sculptural
and monumental. The black-outlined *Requiem for a
Falling Leaf* celebrates its movements in silhouette with
a solemn earnestness bordering on pomp. The "sculp-
ture-machine-géante-sonore-variable-extensible" bearing the title *Eureka* (p. 506 below) involves almost eight

metres of wheels, bars, pistons, girders, five discs, each
with a motor, presided over by a huge iron pan. Rolling
and stamping, pushing and shoving, lifting and pulling,
they have little in common with the more relaxed spirit
of the *Méta-Matics* and fountains. Heavy limbs repeat
the same movements time and time again, conveying
cogs and wheels to and fro, pushing bars back and forth
with Sisyphean effort. The parts, according to Pontus
Hulten, are "condemned to lead a prisoner's life". Here,
the demonstration of the senselessness of anonymous
mechanisms takes on a dramatic and almost tragic
dimension.

In the last ten years of his life, Tinguely expanded
into space or, to be more precise, into a kind of stage
space. Altar-like constructions bear heaps of civilisation's garbage – a monstrous jungle of machine parts,
consumer objects, wrecks, lightbulbs (ill. above and p.
507). In 1980, he began to add symbols of death, animal
skeletons, skulls. The shock effect became increasingly
lurid, the noise increasingly unbearable. These are apocalyptic scenarios in the form of monstrous assemblage
tableaux. According to Tinguely, "The artists still making art in future will either be fantastic artists or mere
decorators." Something of the aesthetics of terror is certainly evident in the pandemonium of his late mechanical Hells.

The Direct Language of Reality

The Ubiquitous Readymade

"I really begin to understand any society by going through its junk shops and fleamarkets. It is a form of education and historical orientation for me. I can see the results of ideas in what is thrown away by a culture," said the Californian artist Edward Kienholz in 1970, and he used his found objects to create mordantly critical social tableaux. Objects represent an entire culture. Could Duchamp have been saying something similar when he took the bottle-rack from the department store shelf or the urinal from the sanitary-fittings supplier? Could he have said that he understood French society the better for it? Had he not thrown down the gauntlet of the readymade to the Kienholz generation, only for them to discover its aesthetic beauty, as he noted, half flattered, half annoyed, in the early 60s? Was not the bottle-rack, for half a century, the question mark behind art?

The confidence Kienholz placed in the expressive power of things betrays a completely different attitude. Things no longer call art into question, nor do they present a gesture of refusal. A complex No has transformed itself into a resounding Yes. Duchamp's strategy of indifference towards art proved an immensely fertile principle. The readymade, and its derivative, the assemblage, exploded after 1960 into an unquestioningly accepted and broad-based approach. Behind that was not so much a renewal of Duchamp, as an almost insatiable hunger for reality and for immediate, commonplace, everyday reality at that. It marked the end of solemnly celebrated, excessively abstract prohibition. It marked the end of a moral attitude that disdained any attention to what Clement Greenberg termed mass culture and Theodor W. Adorno termed the *Kulturindustrie*, denouncing such trivial pursuits as tantamount to high treason against the noble realms of art.

Half a generation began delving through the rubbish tips and scrap-yards, through the junk-shops and toy stores, through the building sites and supermarkets, dismantling street signs or nailing dinner-plates to boards. In a television series that looked at different occupations, Kienholz, representing the craft of the artist, had himself filmed looking for material in a car-wreckers' yard. Arman and Dieter Roth filled wastepaper baskets

Piero Manzoni
The Base of the World (Hommage à Galileo), 1961
Corten steel, 82 x 100 x 100 cm
Herning, Herning Kunstmuseum

and trashcans, and the Prague artist Milan Knížák set up "sweeping environments" on the street. The way Rauschenberg, Kienholz, Tinguely, Arman or Spoerri handle the readymade has nothing to do, however, with Duchamp's negative gesture or with the projection of private wishes and drives onto the Surrealist object. The principle of the readymade had opened the floodgates through which everyday life came rushing. Here were things that retained their own life, they had own language, origins and history. Here were things that represented "life" itself – and this, of course, was modern art's most productive myth of all.

From here on in, life was linked to the commonplace, and to our urban environment with all its wear and tear and consumerism. For the readymade, this meant that the surrealist psychology of the object became a realistic sociology. The radical Dada equation of art as a way of life was turned on its head – life had become a way of art. In 1960, Manzoni placed the planet earth on an upturned base (ill. above).

In 1964, the English artist Mark Boyle began throwing nails onto maps, removing one square metre at the place they landed and preserving it. This was, in short, an aleatory fragmentation of Manzoni's globe. Manzoni, however, instead of painting them, had directly

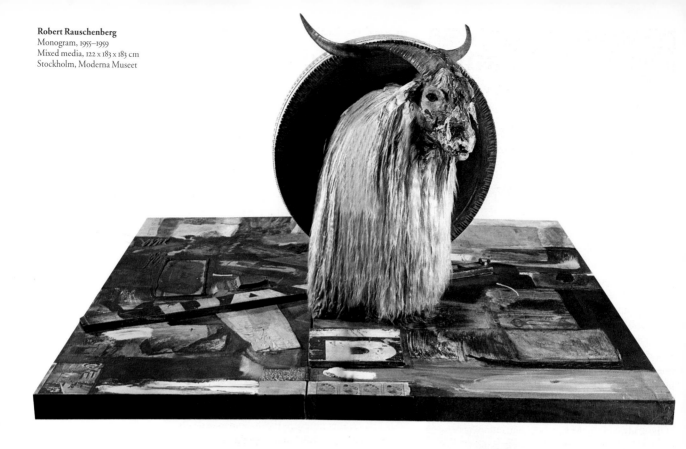

Robert Rauschenberg
Monogram, 1955–1959
Mixed media, 122 x 183 x 183 cm
Stockholm, Moderna Museet

signed models in 1961. That same year, Timm Ulrichs presented himself as a living work of art and went on to build up an entire catalogue and monologue of the Self as quantity and entity.

Rauschenberg and the Gap between Life and Art

The first artist to mirror America's mass-consumption society was Robert Rauschenberg. In 1949 he arrived in New York from Texas and discovered an inexhaustible reservoir in the streets of downtown Manhattan. Mostly, he only needed to walk around the block to get his

Jasper Johns
Painted Bronze II
(Ale Cans), 1964
Painted bronze, 13.7 x 20 x 11.2 cm
Collection of the Artist

material. No artist since Schwitters, whose *Merz* art Rauschenberg had studied in detail, had turned his attention so devotedly to trash.

From 1953, he produced his *Combine Paintings* – fragments of an expressive gestural painting combined with street signs, traffic signs, discarded furniture, animal skins and photos from magazines. A stuffed angora goat stands on roughly painted boards with a car tyre slung around its body. The combination certainly adds life to the title *Monogram* (ill. above). Or is Rauschenberg presenting some disguised symbolism of sexuality with the goat as a faun embraced? The heterogeneous context from which the parts have been wrested, opens up a complex wealth of associations. Definitions are avoided by Rauschenberg, who fears that they take the life out of things. Rauschenberg's much-cited claim that his work plays in the gap between life and art includes a distinct formal awareness. The *Combine Paintings* (p. 315) are by no means merely a vital, arbitrary conglomeration like the impression of a street scene, but a polyphonic fabric of formal, iconographic and political cross-references.

During this period, Rauschenberg was often seen in the company of Jasper Johns, who also had a studio in Pearl Street. Johns, however, was a genuine painter who rarely worked in three dimensions. If his *Flags* and his *Targets* (pp. 309 f) and his bronze cast, painted *Ale Cans* (ill. left) nevertheless had an impact on Minimal Art, then it was primarily because they proved that pictures can be objects and objects can be pictures. This 60s

Robert Rauschenberg
Odalisque, 1955–1958
Wood, fabric, wire, grass, paper,
photographs, metal, cushion,
stuffed rooster, four light bulbs,
205 x 58 x 58 cm
Cologne, Museum Ludwig,
Ludwig Donation

sation and emotional spontaneity linked him with the typically Californian Funk Art named after the relaxed, anarchic, funky jazz of the West Coast (as opposed to the cooler, more disciplined jazz of the East Coast). As early as 1951, Funk Artist Bruce Conner had created enormous horror-structures of raw materials which he left to rot in what Günter Metken has described as "horrifically brutal *vanitas* statements in the manner of Kienholz".

Around 1960 Kienholz arranged socially critical, satirical objects, followed shortly afterwards by scenic tableaux, in which junk and bric-a-brac were used to form a precisely reconstructed atmosphere clashing with lurid horror. An old woman awaits death as the ghost of her own memories. She is still sitting in the photographic pose, although the photographer has long since gone. A photograph of her in her youth on a glass ball (her awareness of self) and an animal skull replace the head. A chain of glass pots with the relics of childhood, marriage, births and deaths hang around her neck. Legs and arms are made of cow bones. The cosy idyll and the artificially mounted, dehumanised figure are steeped in halted time. It is an image of frozen decay, strictly formulated in circles, ovals and rectangles. *The Wait* (ill. below) possesses an almost tender touch, which is rare indeed in the work of Kienholz.

In other scenes he reveals the shabbiness of death more tormentingly: dolls bound together as in an atomic mushroom, the sevenfold pain of birth merging with the sevenfold thorn of violation, mask-faced racists castrating a black man. *The Portable War Memorial* (p. 512 above) which can be used for all wars, is also politically complex. On the left are the propaganda clichés – the barrel-body of the singing troop-entertainer Kate Smith endlessly trilling "God bless America", Uncle Sam on the enlistment letter, the famous scene of placing the flag on Suribachi mountain, soldiers in real uniforms, the gravestone with the names of 465 countries destroyed by war. On the right is a bar with tubular steel

"I really begin to understand any society by going through its junk stores and flea markets. It is a form of education and historical orientation for me. I can see the results of ideas in what is thrown away by a culture." EDWARD KIENHOLZ

Edward Kienholz
The Wait, 1964/65
Fibreglass, furniture, glasses,
photographs, stuffed cat and other
materials, c. 250 x 400 x 220 cm
New York, Whitney Museum of
American Art, Gift of the Howard
and Jean Lipman Foundation

paradigm, turned every which way since Frank Stella (pp. 351 f) and Donald Judd, has little bearing on Rauschenberg.

Kienholz and the American Way of Life

Edward Kienholz, on the other hand, seemed in many ways to be his Californian opposite, distorting the New Yorker's realism into shocking grimaces through Surrealist moments. He did not insert the dynamism of the street into his pictures, but staged instead monstrous counterworlds to the illusory beauty under the Pacific skies in a grotesque *memento mori* against the suppression of suffering and the Hollywood-style cosmetic camouflaging of death.

At about the same time as the first *Combine Paintings* he nailed fragments of furniture, appliances and garbage together to create wooden reliefs which he then painted with a broom. Cheap materials, do-it-yourself improvi-

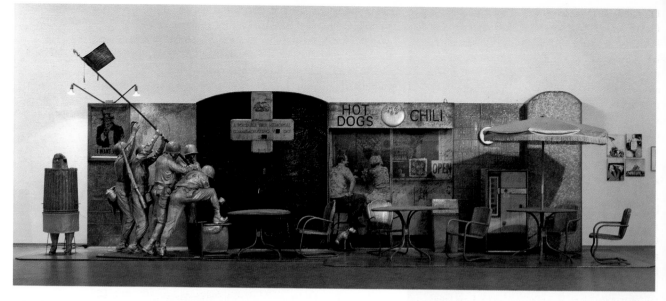

Edward Kienholz
The Portable War Memorial, 1968
Environment of various materials
and objects, tape recorder, Coca
Cola dispenser, 285 x 950 x 240 cm
Cologne, Museum Ludwig,
Ludwig Donation

furniture: Coca-Cola imperialism, business as usual. The fact that the two belong together is indicated by the soldiers, who are hoisting their flag over a fallen chair onto a coffee-house table. A multi-purpose war memorial as an anti-war memorial.

The closest we come to Kienholz' horror scenes of the 60s is in the work of Paul Thek (ill. below) whose assemblages attack the hypocrisy of bourgeois morality with glaring shock effects. From 1970 onwards his social satire fades into a world of symbolistic landscapes that weave the tapestry of their Surrealist heritage in overwhelmingly ritualised histrionics.

Like Kienholz, George Segal also whets our critical view of the American scene. Like Kienholz, he presents his tableaux as though the theatre curtain were rising. Yet the plays he stages could hardly be more different. Whereas the Californian Kienholz attacks specific out-

rages with grim, unreal allegories, the New Yorker Segal heightens situations of American solitude to the point of universality in an almost classicist mode. He fixes breakdowns in communication against a black ground: a two-man combo with a single dancer (p. 513 below), an evening meal at the counter, a woman at the cinema box-office. From 1961, the figures he used were actually plaster casts he had made of his own friends in everyday poses, removed by a bandage process and mounted externally with the skin of the cast. They contrast with real objects like white-plastered fossils. Segal creates an aura somewhere between silence, melancholy and depression.

Whereas the bizarre assemblages by Lucas Samaras (p. 513 above), often strewn with nails, seem more closely related to Surrealism and Neo-Dadaism, the documentary realism of Duane Hanson's work is influenced by Kienholz and Segal. In the mid-60s he began modelling his socially critical, warts-and-all figures of people on the margins of society, soldiers, the homeless, in polyester, fibreglass and resin. Later, he turned his attention to typical middle-class Americans, skilled workers, tourists, shoppers (p. 514), depicting them with an astonishing true-to-life realism that is by no means naturalistic. These figures are individuals and generic representations at one and the same time, caught in an almost autistic void.

Rauschenberg, Kienholz, Segal, the three assemblage artists of contemporary America are frequently linked to Pop Art. They explore the city in all its vitality, its wear and tear, its brutality and its breakdown of communication. Yet Pop Art, by contrast, sees urban life in the folklore of bright media images and an attractively packaged consumer world. Nothing is dirty, everything is ready to use. Although Jim Dine's mounted tools (p. 318), Rosenquist's cellophane foils and Warhol's Brillo packs may be typical of their era, the only truel sculptor at the hard core of Pop Art is Claes Oldenburg.

Paul Thek
Ark, Pyramid, 1971/72
Installation; various materials,
c. 250 x 830 cm
Kassel, documenta 5 (1972)

Oldenburg's Double Irony

Can Oldenburg be described as a Pop artist like Roy Lichtenstein, Andy Warhol and James Rosenquist? Or is he a realist who also builds on abstraction, volume, planes and colour? Or is this self-styled "everyday surrealist" an artist who leads sculpture into a new physicality, tactility, eroticism and that rare thing, irony? A sculptor who subjects form to gravity and the flexibility of the material and whose work beats a direct path to the "anti-form" of the late 60s.

In 1956, Oldenburg, the son of a Swedish diplomat, arrived in New York from Chicago. He, too, was fascinated by the street – not by the glamour of Fifth Avenue, but by the harsh and dirty life of the Lower East Side. In 1960 he put his first environment together in the Judson Gallery: traffic signs, grafitti with child-like spelling mistakes, ragged cardboard silhouettes of people and cars, found objects, echoing the power of the city as a formless, anarchic living process. In formal terms, Oldenburg followed in the footsteps of Dubuffet's Art Brut, children's art and the comic-book mythology of the ray-gun.

Whatever he drew, modelled, cut or tailored after that, he blew up into gigantic proportions, creating the same tension between intensity and irony. One year later, he presented his legendary "Store" in a former warehouse as a studio-cum-exhibition-cum-performance venue and piled shelves high with enamel-

Lucas Samaras
Shoe Box, 1965
Wooden construction, wool, shoe, steel nails, cotton, paint, 26.7 x 39.4 x 28 cm
Formerly Saatchi Collection, London

"I love to watch people. I'm interested in their gestures and I'm interested in their experiences and mine. In the early years I spent a lot of time trying to look as bluntly as I could at people in their environments. Very often I saw them against garish light, illuminated signs. I saw them against visually vivid objects that were considered low class, anti-art, un-art, kitsch, disreputable ..."
GEORGE SEGAL

George Segal
Rock and Roll Combo, 1964
Figures made of gauze dipped in liquid plaster and mounted on a wood-and-wire frame, electric guitar, drums, wooden stool, 186 x 190 x145 cm
Frankfurt am Main, Museum für Moderne Kunst

painted women's dresses roughly made of plaster and muslin strips, shoes, hot dogs and hamburgers – still lifes bursting with juicy puns from the male ice cream cone to the female sandwich. These were showcase exhibits whose wildly streaming paint undermined the existential pathos of Action Painting and translated it into a vibrant quiddity.

In his second "Store" exhibition, this time at the Green Gallery, in 1962, he showed his *Soft Sculptures* for the first time – huge, sewn items of food or clothing. From here on in, *Soft Sculpture* was to be Oldenburg's hallmark (ill. right). Its origins lie in the stuffed rags he had begun to use in performances in 1960. *Soft Sculpture* is based on a carefully considered aesthetic approach in which the transformation of an object into a soft, limp, drooping, oversized replica was preceded by hard, rigid cardboard models. In his third environment, *Bedroom Ensemble* (ill. above) in 1963, Oldenburg blended this cooler geometry of reconstructed perspectives and angular parallelograms (as in newspaper advertisements) with the deceptively sumptuous fabric imitations of the soft final version. Between cardboard models and these metallic black, porcelain white or garishly glossy final versions in vinyl, there is usually a more tempered interim version in natural-coloured canvas, which Oldenburg compares with "ghosts".

He has used this process of "softening" and magnifying telephones, typewriters, lipsticks, even toilet bowls. Although they are functional everyday objects, they feature universal forms such as the circle, the cube and the cylinder. The soft plastic materials and cushion-like, malleable curves heighten the ambiguous sensuality to the point of association with breasts or genitals. Domestic appliances are placed in a closer and almost loving relationship with people and take on anthropomorphic traits. They interact as in osmosis between one analogy and another, and in doing so almost succeed in achieving Oldenburg's utopian aim of ending the schism between humans and things.

His other strategy apart from "softening" involves magnifying objects into monumentality. The joke lies in the contrast between the monumental size and the banality of the object. In a world in which everything on the television screen is small and everything on the cinema screen is large, our sense of scale is confused anyway. At the same time, Oldenburg calculates geometries that work at a distance. Until 1969 he only drew them: house-high crispbread walls for Stockholm, a banana ventilator for Times Square, a scissor monument to replace the obelisk in Washington.

In 1969, the first of these was actually realised: at the height of the student protests against the war in Vietnam, he installed an eight-metre high lipstick on caterpillar tank tracks – a phallic cruise missile, war as a femininely undermined macho erection. The collapse of the (originally inflatable) bellicose-pacifist lipstick was only a question of time. In 1971, Oldenburg noticed the many building site holes and a pond with swans in the Sonsbeek exhibition park. He installed a 12-metre high trowel with its point stuck into the ground, the curve of its handle reminiscent of a swan's neck (ill. left). Since them, numerous monuments have been built. With their precise reference to their specific location, their iconographic wit and their formal stringency, they are among the rare examples of successfully innovative sculpture for public places.

British Pop Art and Paolozzi's Machine World Collages

In the course of the 50s, the sense of unease regarding art as noble form took hold in Britain as well. Were not Henry Moore and Barbara Hepworth already on the way towards aesthetic canonisation? Did not the influential critic Herbert Read play a role similar to that played in America by Clement Greenberg? Did not the omnipresent Institute of Contemporary Arts determine what was officially fine art? Since 1951 a small debating club of artists, architects and theoreticians known as the Independent Group had begun to rebel. Their lectures and discussions on mass media, science fiction, the visual worlds of optics, information theory and mechanisation shaped the *leitbild* of popular culture and sowed the seeds of British Pop Art.

However, this generation and the subsequent one, the true Pop generation, was influenced less by an expansion of sculpture and the metamorphoses of the readymade than was the case in America and France. In the foreground were the secondary visual worlds of photography, reproduction and unlimited editions. This meant that British Pop Art was founded primarily by young painters whose fascination for the American consumer paradise found its expression in subtle, considered images. Even Peter Blake's (p. 306) nostalgic *Toyshop* of 1962 and Joe Tilson's (p. 304) mixed media works, for all their encyclopaedic wealth of objects ordered in boxes like miniature museums are in fact a variation on painting. The pin-up dolls and shoe objects

Eduardo Paolozzi
The Last of the Idols, 1963
Aluminium, oil paint,
244 x 71 x 64 cm
Cologne, Museum Ludwig,
Ludwig Donation

"It is my opinion that to talk of Art or, to be specific, modern sculpture, requires a special language: Avoid using worn clichés, the words that can't even indicate or scratch at the hundred hidden meanings in objects and structures."
EDUARDO PAOLOZZI

Page 516:
Claes Oldenburg
Trowel, 1971
Steel tinted with spray-paint,
1170 x 365 cm
Otterlo, Rijksmuseum Kröller-
Müller, Sculpture Park

*"I didn't discover the principle of
'accumulation'; it discovered me. It
has always been obvious that society
feeds its sense of security with a pack-
rat instinct demonstrated in its window displays, its assembly lines, its
garbage piles. As a witness of my
society, I have always been very
much involved in the pseudo-biolog-
ical cycle of production, consumption, and destruction. And for a long
time, I have been anguished by the
fact that one of its most conspicuous
material results is the flooding of our
world with junk and rejected odd
objects."* ARMAN

presented by Allan Jones turn a Surrealist tradition into
a sexual fetish. In the end, the British Pop Art scene produced only one genuine sculptor: Eduardo Paolozzi
(p. 517).

Paolozzi, a Scot, had fallen in love with the America
of the glossy magazine and the Hollywood film as early
as 1947, in Paris of all places. His sketchbooks record neither the Eiffel tower nor the Louvre, but advertisements
for vacuum cleaners, Libby's canned peaches, starlets,
Mickey Mouse: collages that were pure Pop Art even in
1947. As he moved away from Pop motifs in the course
of the 50s, he held on to the collage principle with the
tenacity of Max Ernst. He tested ever new variations on
the cast, the copy and the objet trouvé. He adopted the
theme of man and machine from the discussions of the
Independent Group. Even before 1960 he was pressing
particles of scrap, cogs and bolts into the epidermis of
anthropomorphic figures. After 1960, he piled brightly
painted alumium casts of batteries, crankshafts and tur-
bines to create frontal mechanical idols.

Later, the static rigidity relaxed, blocks became
angled, and curved, and meandering pipelines emerged.
The man-machine became the mechanical-vegetative
mixed media image. Towards the end of the 60s, concave and convex profiles followed in polished steel,
which distort and collage our mirror image. Then came
multi-part wood reliefs, floor sculptures and fountains
brimming with signs and diagrams. The kaleidoscopic,
multivocative formal world of the computer had
replaced machine art.

Nouveau Réalisme: the Sociology of the Object

The most consistent and radical new interpretation of
the readymade occurred exactly where it had emerged
thirty-five years before–in Paris, which became a further
centre of the revolt against psychogenic drives and deco-

rative *peinture*. Here, in 1960, the thirst for direct, outward reality was felt just as keenly as it was in New York.
Here, too, Schwitters was to play an important inspirational role. Here, too, casts of objects or bodies conjured
up reality. In 1949, Rauschenberg had printed blueprints
of nude models, and, in 1951, he had had a Ford drive
over an ink-smeared road to create monotypes of the
tyre profile. In Paris in 1958, after experimenting with
stamp prints, Arman scattered coloured nails, radio
tubes and splinters of glass onto the canvas. In 1959, Yves
Klein used blue-painted women's bodies as "living
brushes" in creating his *Anthropometries* (p. 298).
Whether it was in 1949 that he signed the sky over Nice
or whether legend has back-dated that event, it is a
fitting gesture to mark art's quest to embrace reality.

In Paris, in 1960, the critic Pierre Restany founded
the Nouveaux Réalistes group together with such
unlikely Dioscuri as Yves Klein, Tinguely, Raymond
Hains and his Affichiste friends, Arman, Spoerri
and Martial Raysse. Soon they were joined by César and
Niki de Saint Phalle. Klein was the high priest who was
difficult to integrate, Tinguely the forceful artistic
authority, Restany the eloquently seductive lyricist and
patron. Right from the start, Klein fragmented the
group with his emphatic spirituality and his mystically
inspired insistence on the "immaterial" essence of reality. The focus, however, was not on Klein's assimilation
of the void but on Tinguely's, Arman's and Spoerri's
assimilation of city, factory, machine, mass media and
consumerism.

The paradigmatic guarantors of Restany's concept of
assimilation were Arman and Spoerri. Both system-
atized what Camille Bryen called the "adventure of the
object", and both developed it in countless experiments
and inventions. For Arman, a constructive path and a
destructive one opened up. From 1959 onwards, he col-

condense welded-together tools into a single battering ram of black hammer-heads. A comprehensive inventory of new possibilities in the wake of the readymade begins to emerge which, in the long term, cannot avoid seeming somewhat mannered.

Spoerri's approach is similarly systematic, though it has a strong touch of post-Surrealist unreality. It would be far too one-sided to pin his œuvre down to the *Tableaux-pièges* (variously known as "trap" or "snare" pictures; p. 328) in which he affixed the remains of a table after a meal in an equation of our sensual, vital, untidy, dirty world, and in a quest for evidence of what Spoerri has described as "one split second in an entire cycle of life and death, decay and rebirth". Yet the hotel table that he nailed to the wall in 1960 as an *objet trouvé* was merely the point of departure in the œuvre of this dancer, publisher, poet, author, cook (p. 580), restorer, Nouveaux Réalistes, inventor of Eat Art and founder of the Musées Sentimentaux.

In 1966 he noted no fewer than seventeen "developments of the trap picture" including the "square trap picture" in which the tools for affixing the picture are also affixed with it, and (together with Robert Filliou) the *Word Traps* or idioms reified in the form of object puzzles. These include, for example, illustrating the

Christo
Package in Shopping Cart, 1964
Packaging; shopping cart, film, string, 100 x 45 x 37.5 cm
USA, private collection
© Christo 1964

"But actually, what is a sculptor, a sculpture? Sculpture is something three-dimensional, that gives one the opportunity to move around it. But that is only the starting point, for the further one moves away from this sculpture, the broader is the spectrum of its possible meanings and the different ways that one can experience sculpture." CHRISTO

lected radio tubes, jugs, combs, dolls, cogwheels and dollar notes in plexiglass containers for his *Accumulations* (p. 518).

His first *Poubelles* – trashcans containing the discarded waste of friends, children, bourgeois homes or market halls – date from the same year. Arman began sealing organic waste in polyester. There is more to this than a cursory evasion of composition; it is the condensation of consumption into the signature of our everyday life, a patinaed still-life or portrait of our civilisation. A bridge built from the readymade to sociology and psychology, a collection of cog-wheels as the commando headquarters of a mechanical, anonymous power. Under the title *Grandmother's Village*, sliced-open coffee grinders make a tongue-in-cheek comment on the "good old days". The quotation of objects is heightened by sheer quantity into the expressive, the narrative and the representative.

Alongside this positive re-evaluation of objects, Arman destroyed objects in his prototypical *colères* or bursts of rage, smashing, sawing, cutting or burning musical instruments, household goods, clocks, exploding a sports car and then fixing the fragments as relics of destruction. Again, the issue at stake is one of liberating and magnifying the power of expression lost in mass production. From 1967 onwards, other serial works formalise new Renault parts into abstract compositions or

"I start out with an idea that is inside me, a nothing, and I venture out to the point where I find myself confronted with a thing that is alien to me. It is precisely this that makes it reality. It is detached from me, it exists in its matter, its content, its space. A sculpture has to possess its space." CÉSAR

César
Compression of a Car, Ricard, 1962
Compressed automobile parts, 153 x 73 x 65 cm
Paris, Musée National d'Art Moderne, Centre Georges Pompidou

Niki de Saint Phalle
Black Nana, 1968/69
Painted polyester, 293 x 200 x 120 cm
Cologne, Museum Ludwig,
Ludwig Donation

German word for flattery – "bauchpinseln" (literally belly-brushing) – by applying a red, green and yellow brush to the lilac belly of a shop window dummy. Spoerri's later assemblages transpose kitsch images, meat mincers, water taps, artificial limbs, animal skulls, knives and forks in lurid juxtaposition and syncretic analogy.

In the year the group was founded, the successful trash sculptor César joined the Nouveaux Réalistes. He had recently seen the latest American car-press and had immediately recognised the chance of using the automobile as a means of direct expression for technology and urban iconography. Unlike Chamberlain, César's *Compressions* involve no formal intervention (p. 519 below). From 1962, César began regulating the pressure and cutting process to one of *Compression dirigée*, or controlled compression. Though the proximity to the concept of reality propounded by the Nouveaux Réalistes was evident, it did not last long. In 1967 César began moulding polyurethene foam, initially as a street performance. Soon, he was using this process to create sculptures that placed him close to Pop-related process art.

The Bulgarian-born artist Christo had been wrapping bottles, shoes, furniture, a pram, and a motorbike in rough plastic or fabric (p. 519 above) since 1958. Was this a critical response to the commercial world of packaging? Or was it a demonstrative alternative to the consumer aesthetic of Pop Art? Christo's further development indicates that he was not only expressing his criticism of consumption, but also aiming to aestheticise the wrapped object, building or landmark. Ropes structure a wrapped motorcycle like nervously sketched lines, the images between the lines of power tauten to a relief in dialogue with the motocycle's contours. In the 60s, Christo and Jeanne-Claude blocked the view of entire displays of goods by curtaining and concealing shop window façades or shopping malls with fabric and wrapping paper. They turn their attention in 1961 to the great outdoors (*Dockside Packages* in Cologne), installing a curtain in a Colorado valley (1970–1972), surrounding islands in Miami in the years 1980–1983 (p. 549) and, in 1995, wrapping the Berlin Reichstag (pp. 330).

Whereas Christo and Jeanne-Claude wrap the world of consumer goods and (critically?) distort it, the montages of Martial Raysee present that same world in all its seductive appeal as a glossy cosmetic finish to an artificial world that generates wishful images. Niki de Saint Phalle's monstrous yet delightful *Nanas* also address wishful images. The huge, burlesque fertility dolls play somewhere between childhood imagination and male fantasy (ill. left). Her association with Nouveau Réalisme is based not so much on her *Nanas* as on her wreaths and hearts of toys, dolls, puppets and artificial flowers veiled by a white cover. Is she returning in search of something she missed out on in the far from childlike stringency of her upbringing in an aristocratic French family?

Intermedia, Fluxus: Object and Concept

Rauschenberg's approach, working in the gap between art and life, requires a firm footing based on specific values. These values came openly to the fore around 1960 in the work of several artists. Art was touched by life and occasionally flooded by it. The readymade, if it occurred at all, no longer merely represented reality, but became a vehicle that stimulated ideas and general creativity. Dick Higgins adapted Rauschenberg's approach, applying it to other situations and, in 1962, he coined the term Intermedia. Before moving on to Happenings he carved out a fairly unobtrusive niche for noise music, poetry readings and concrete poetry, artists' books, multiples, mail art, games without rules, and witty nonsense. This niche was dominated by the Fluxus movement from 1961.

Fluxus was not primarily concerned with objects. It tended to evoke the ephemeral. The name is as much a part of the history of Action Art and the artist's book as it is a part of the history of sculpture. Yet it also points to a productive crisis where the object is concerned. On 2 March 1961 the name graced an invitation to the New York A/G Gallery, later turning up as the title of a magazine issued by Lithuanian-born designer George Maciunas. It suggests fluidity, instability, change and chance. The imperial organisation with Maciunas as "president" and – in the manner of Breton – as Fluxus Pope, with coordinators and vice-coordinators for the zones of America and Eastern and Western Europe, was a semi-ironic, semi-utopian reference to revolutionary world changes wrought by the Fluxus concept. Anti-bourgeois, anti-commercial concepts of art, the merging of everyday reality and absurdity, musical scores and pure chance, western actionism and oriental philosophy, and anarchistically playful liberty were promoted to become articles of faith.

The spirited notion of a cultural revolution, however, initially went no further than a few fairly modest Fluxus concerts held in Wiesbaden, Copenhagen, Amsterdam and Düsseldorf, and their "unspecific creativity", as Maciunas put it, was devoted primarily to dismantling the bourgeois piano. John Cage, who had been experimenting in this vein since around 1937, paved the way with his first *Piece for prepared piano*.

Nam June Paik's *Piano Intégral* (ill. right) is the result of several concerts given beween 1958 and 1963. Eggshells, photos and glass were placed between the strings, and bicycle bells, sirens, a vacuum cleaner and a transistor radio were built in and set in motion at the touch of a key. A musical score programmed this acoustic anarchy. Though this is a process that could be continued at will, its acceptance by the established art scene marked its end, at least for a time.

Such was the more spectacular aspect of Fluxus. The typical Fluxus object, however, is a great deal less spectacular, often unaesthetic, usually small and generally boxed. The idea of the box was derived from Duchamp's *Boîte en valise*. Since 1962, Maciunas produced editions

Nam June Paik
Piano Intégral, 1958–1963
Assemblage; Ibach piano prepared with various items, 136 x 140 x 65 cm
Vienna, Museum moderner Kunst, formerly Hahn Collection

in specially made leather cases (p. 587), some of them containing more than thirty items by various artists: household articles, bric-a-brac, even invented games, puzzles, collages, multiples, evocative printed cards, records, stamps, miniature private messages ... all documenting "that the borders to art are further than previously assumed, or that art and certain barriers are no longer meaningful", according to George Brecht. The most faithful contributors were Brecht and Robert Watts. Objects were also supplied by Ay-O, Joe Jones, Per Kirkeby, Alison Knowles, Oldenburg, Saito and others.

The "old masters" of everyday Fluxus creativity were Robert Filliou and George Brecht (p. 522 above left). From 1965 to 1968 they worked together in a house at Villefranche-sur-mer. According to Brecht, "we made games, invented and de-invented objects, ... drank and chatted with our neighbours, produced flux poems ... and sold them by mail". Such were the activities of the *Institute for permanent creativity* projected by Filliou. His *Tool Box* of 1969 (p. 522 below) gave form to this attitude. On the lid, in neon letters, are the words *imagination*

"The piano is a taboo. It has to be broken. By the way, it isn't even that expensive ... it's just the transport costs that are expensive."
NAM JUNE PAIK

and *innocence*, the only tools we need in order to be creative. In the box there are wooden sticks with hooks and eyes.

There is virtually no end to the possible permutation of links and cross-links. All solutions are equally valid in Brecht's game, which has neither rules nor winners. The course of the universe is not affected by our decisions anyway. Filliou learned his laid-back attitude from Taoism. Brecht learned his simple, logic-defying paradoxes from Zen Buddhism. In practice, the utopia of the general accessibilty of art had failed even then. Yet the idea of Intermedia and Fluxus survived.

Artists' books and artists' magazines burgeoned. The Dutch artist Stanley Brouwn, the Czech Milan Knižák, the Dane Arthur Köpcke, the Germans Tomas Schmit and Wolf Vostell, the Romanian-born Spoerri, all found a medium here that oscillated between media, tending towards the object. Timm Ulrichs, the most imaginative Intermedia loner, is associated primarily with visual poetry and object art. The painter, typographer, poet and Intermedia artist Dieter Roth (p. 363) replaced

hierarchical qualification by quantification in his many-facetted work and manically produced arbitrary series of *Collected Works*, in keeping with the spirit of the times. He chopped up twenty volumes of Hegel and packed them into sausage skins with pork dripping and spices, thereby returning the history of human intellectual achievement to the realms of everyday life.

Happening: Object and Action

Put extremely simply, the move away from the picture led to the object, and the move away from the object led to the Happening. Though a creative idea cannot be reduced to its historical source alone, the sensual appeal of the material, commonplace things as actors and silent partners in a game were the notions behind the early Happenings.

Allan Kaprow (p. 583) who set the ball rolling in 1959, saw the Happening as an extension of the Assemblage. Vehicles were pushed to and fro, barrels rolled, chairs moved. In 1968, eye witness Michel Ragon described the destruction of cars during the Paris student uprising of

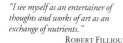

May not only as Happenings on a huge scale, but also as oversized versions of César's *Compressions* – the real readymade being the act itself.

Everywhere, the things featured in the Happenings were becoming the focal point. In Osaka, the painter Jiro Yoshihara founded the Gutai group in 1954, in which artists aimed to "make the naked materiality of things speak". In 1955, Kazuo Shiraga "painted" with his body in mud and made his footprints ecstatically on a canvas lying on the ground, years before Klein's *Anthropometries*. Tetsumi Kudo (p. 522 above right), who radicalised Japanese anti-art with his destructive, expressive energy, went to Paris in 1962 where, together with Jean-Jacques Lebel, he became a key figure on the Happening scene. The series of Happenings known as *Philosophy of Impotence* showed mankind (after the Day Zero of Hiroshima) as a creature caught between sexuality and collapse, metamorphosis and decay. Phallically bound cripples fragment the body.

The street also played a role. Vostell derived his *decollage* Happenings from the earlier tearing of billboard posters on the street (ill. above). In Prague, Milan Knižák piled the garbage of his "sweeping" Happenings on the street. In Poland, Tadeusz Kantor made the stage of his *Teatr Crico*, reactivated in 1955, "as concrete as the auditorium": Wheels were really dirty, old boards were really used, the gunbarrel really came from the scrapyard. The "poorer" and more "lowly" (Kantor's key terms) an object, the greater the chance of turning it into poetry. Kantor's *Emballages* were derived from the theatre. Both these Eastern European artists thus corresponded in some way with Nouveau Réalisme – Knizak corresponding with Arman's *Poubelles* and Kantor with Christo's packaging. They arrived at much the same conclusion from a totally different point of departure, confirming the close contact between readymade and action.

Strategies of Object Art

Our art historical memory tends to look for categories. This explains why generic terms such as Pop Art, groups like the Nouveaux Réalistes or movements such as Fluxus tend to be admitted more quickly to the pantheon. Loners often find it more difficult to take their place in art history. In the field of object art, in particular, there are nevertheless a number of solitary figures of considerable importance. The 60s are full of them. The present and the past are addressed by direct or aliented quotation. There is nothing that might not advance to the worthy echelons of art and succumb to an aesthetic label. Manzoni's can containing his own excrement not only cocks a snook at the romantic notion of artist-as-genius, but also comments on its development.

At around the same time as Rauschenberg, the Russian-born artist Louise Nevelson (ill. right) was combing the streets of New York, gathering wood from house conversions and demolitions, from the docks and the carpentry workshops and stockpiling huge quantities of it at her Spring Street home. From the late 50s onwards she piled crates on top of each other, filled them with table legs, fragments of balustrades, stairs, doors and boats, creating iconostases of memory, shrines, walls, pillars out of the wooden flotsam of our civilisation, a mixture of construction, composition, ornament and chance. Later the structure became more stringent, with pre-fabricated abstract forms reiterated in a geometric rapport. By colouring everything black, she created a sense of darkness and mystery – a self-styled "architect of shadows", but also of wan paleness when she used white, and of sacred brilliance when she used gold.

Wolf Vostell
Phenomenons, 1965
Décollage-Happening on a car dump, Berlin

Louise Nevelson
Royal Tide IV, 1959/60
Wood, spray-painted with gold-coloured solution, 35 parts, 323 x 445.5 x 55 cm
Cologne, Museum Ludwig, Ludwig Donation

American and European Minimalists

Minimal Art: Pure Perception

At the height of Object art in the early 60s, a new and radical movement emerged in New York. All that Rauschenberg, Kienholz and the Pop artists had piled into the world of art from the street, from rubbish tips and junk shops was exorcised. The term object repressed its derivation from *objet trouvé*. Donald Judd used it to stake his claim for a new fundamentalism of three-dimensionality. Machine-made cubes or boxes emerged. Floor tiles and mass produced neon lights were juxtaposed, modular grids and open spatial structures spread out. These things possessed a simplicity untrammeled by distracting details. They were simple enough to lead perception back to its own basic prerequisites such as viewpoint and lighting. They excluded any associative, symbolic or intellectual added value. Names like "ABC Art" and "Primary Structures" were short-lived. In 1965 the philosopher Richard Wollheim coined the term that was to take hold (though it originally covered a broader scope): Minimal Art.

The simpler the work, the more complex the commentary? Rarely has more been written about sculptures and objects that are expressly accessible without any verbal introductions and circumscriptions. Rarely have so many words been used to say what really needs no words at all. Even the artists themselves founded and fixed their positions in texts that are well worth reading. With that, it transpired that even the root of the matter is open to controversy. Judd and most American critics insisted on the validity of a direct American line of descent according to which Pollock's overall paintings prepared the ground for the non-relational, non-hierarchical, serial juxtaposition that was regarded as decidedly anti-European (pp. 268–274). Barnett Newman's huge, monochrome canvases make use of the pictorial field as an entity (pp. 289 f). With his elegantly curved aluminium sculptures, Ellsworth Kelly (p. 350) forged a link between Newman and Minimal Art from 1959 onwards. The late work of the sculptor David Smith and the crystalline, monumental forms of architect-turned-sculptor Tony Smith also forged a link between Abstract Expressionism and the younger generation.

This notion of a purely American line of descent has just one flaw—it plays down the explicit links with Bran-

"Actual space is intrinsically more powerful and specific than paint on a flat surface. Obviously, anything in three dimensions can be any shape, regular or irregular, and can have any relation to the wall, floor, ceiling, room, rooms or exterior or none at all. Any material can be used, as is or painted."

DONALD JUDD

Donald Judd
Untitled, 1984
Aluminium, spray-painted,
150 x 165 x 750 cm
Private collection

cusi, most notably his *Endless Column*, in the work of
Andre, Judd and Morris. Extreme formal reduction was
also very much a part of the Constructivism of Rodchenko and of Strzemiński's Unism. Sometimes the
debate about the end of easel painting actually sounded
like a replay of the Russian discourse forty years before.
As the influential art critic Patrick Ireland noted, "In the
60s we talked about Paris, but we looked to Moscow".
Gestalt psychology, which both Judd and Morris were
fond of citing, also provided some European arguments
for Minimal Art. So too did Maurice Merleau-Ponty's
Phenomenology of Perception which appeared in English
in 1961.

So why is it that Minimal Art nevertheless remains,
in the words of Gregor Stemmrich, the "first exclusively
American art movement". In what respect does it break
with Europe and the past? Not through its form, surely,
for Minimal Art, by rejecting content, cannot be a formal art. Its true *raison d'être* lies elsewhere, in the relationship of viewer to object, in the altered aesthetic
experience. Unlike Malevich's *Black Square* (p. 164) or
Mondrian's right angle (p. 169), the simplicity of these
cubes and structures is not based on a belief that the
sum of the figural world is contained within the non-
figural, or that a universal harmony is condensed within
the basic form. They do not herald any utopia. They
restrict themselves to the interaction of object, space
and spectator and thus to the experience of self. They
draw our attention to their structural framework and
thereby reinforce our powers of perception. In 1967, the
French philosopher Roland Barthes announced the
death of the author and the birth of the reader. Which is
why Duchamp, with his dictum that a work of art is
created as much by the viewer as by the artist, is a forerunner of Minimal Art.

All the Minimalists have in common their rejection
of compositional equilibrium and their concentration
on elementary geometry, seriality and progression.
However fully this may apply (and it even includes
musicians such as La Monte Young, Steve Reich, Phil
Glass and Terry Riley) each of them followed their own
individual idea and made it their hallmark. That is true
of the dynamic Robert Grosvenor and of Fred Sand-
back, whose spanned threads de-materialised sculpture
to the point of virtuality. It applies to the lighter, almost
carefree Californian version of Minimal Art with the
brightly-painted fibreglass planks by John McCracken
and the tinted plexiglass cubes by Larry Bell, which fracture light and space. It also applies to the inner core:
Donald Judd, Robert Morris, Carl Andre, Dan Flavin
and Sol LeWitt.

Judd's objects (ill. left and above) overcome what he
perceived as the inadequacy of painting. Only in the
third dimension does he see the last remnant of illusion
removed. The portrayal and the portrayed are meant to
coincide. To this end, Judd built "specific objects".
Boxes of stainless steel, galvanised aluminium or plexiglass are attached to a wall in a vertical alignment at

Donald Judd
Untitled, 1968
Stainless steel and anodized
aluminium; 10 parts,
23 x 101.6 x 78.7 cm
Formerly Saatchi Collection,
London

equal intervals. They present not only their front, but
also, depending on the distance of each box to the
viewer's eye level, their topside or underside as well. In
this way, the object plays through every possible permutation: frontal view, view from above, view from below,
through view, fractured light, reflection. This is what
makes Judd, for all his Minimalist orthodoxy, the most
richly contrasting and formally aware of the five. He
stimulates our awareness and perception by his judi-
cious use of scale, rhythm, angle and by his alternation
of materials, surfaces, colours, open and closed forms,
positive and negative, convex and concave. His economy of means disciplines our aesthetic pelasure, but
does not negate it.

.   Judd thus more or less programmed perception into
the object. He was obsessed with the object. Morris, on
the other hand explored perception itself. His sculptures
of this period were simpler and rougher, exemplary
works of Minimalism situated between art in practice

and theoretical discourse. In 1965, at the Castelli Gallery in New York, he placed three grey plywood L-beams of the same size and shape on the ground, but in different positions, e.g. forming an upright L or up-ended to form a triangle (cf ill. below). This demonstrated that, even when we know that they are identical, we are incapable of perceiving them as identical. In other words, our visual perception is not determined by the form alone, but also by such factors as distance and viewing angle – in short, by the situation. Other works by Morris involve fine wire mesh, permitting a prompt overview and, at the same time, demonstrating the endless optical multiplicity created by the countless overlaps.

This gap between knowledge and experience, described by Merleau-Ponty as "geometry and presence", is at the centre of Minimal Art. It is also the counter-pole to Cubism, or at least to Kahnweiler's neo-Kantian interpretation of Cubism, which posits "I know that this cube has six sides, therefore I paint them". As soon as perception became charged in the following decade with aspects of experience, confusion and idiosyncrasy, the wide field of "interesting", psychophysically intensive spaces that were to shape the post-Minimalist generation opened up. In this, too, Morris was a pioneer with his mirroring and his labyrinths.

Carl Andre (p. 527 below left) put himself at a distance from Judd's object-bound approach as well as from Morris' perceptual purism. He pared down volume in sculpture to the point of mere floor covering, without actually giving it up. In doing so, he imbued his work with a social and even socialist statement to the effect that mass-produced materials should be affordable, available and usable for all. Whether lining up metal plates, building bricks, concrete blocks, bars or

Robert Morris
Untitled (Tan Felt), 1968
Nine strips, 304.8 x 20.3 cm (each);
Installation: 172.7 x 182.8 x 66 cm
Formerly Saatchi Collection,
London

Robert Morris
Untitled, 1967
Playwood, painted,
244 x 244 x 61 cm
USA (CT), private collection

Carl Andre
Aluminium and zinc, 1970
18 aluminium squares, 18 zinc
squares, 183 x 183 cm
Formerly Saatchi Collection,
London

Below right:
Carl Andre
Secant, 1977
Pinewood, 30 x 30 x 90 cm (each)
Roslyn (NY), Nassau County
Museum of Fine Arts

Below:
Carl Andre
Timber Piece (Well), destroyed
1964. reconstructed 1970
Wood, 28 parts, 213 x 122 x 122 cm
Cologne, Museum Ludwig,
Ludwig Donation

wire (from a nearby scrapyard) on the floor – this former railyard worker sought in his materials their proximity to their production and social context.

His work developed from wooden sculptures influenced by Brancusi to complex layered beams inspired by his college friend Frank Stella in the mid-60s and from there to his first floor pieces: three squares of styrofoam planks measuring out and activating the exhibition space. One year later he placed a row of 137 bricks running from the wall into the room. The horizontal sculpture was born. Here was sculpture as "place" and as "path", as a field of operation that invited exploration.

Dan Flavin
Fluorescent light installation, 1974
Cologne, Kunsthalle

"Regard the light and you are fasci-
nated – inhibited from grasping its
limits at each end."   Dan Falvin

Since then, Andre has produced many variations in steel, lead, copper, magnesium, aluminium and zinc, in different colours, stages of oxydisation and weight, transforming them quite literally into resonators for our own corporeality and placing them in dialogue with a wide variety of settings. Here we find a new paradigm that has made its mark indelibly on the history of sculpture.

Dan Flavin (ill. above and p. 529 below) is the conjurer of light and the lyrical poet of Minimal Art. He is the classic Minimalist who left the exercises in perception propounded by Judd and Morris furthest behind. In 1963 he mounted a 244 cm long fluorescent tube directly onto his studio wall at an angle of 45 degrees and thereby abandoned the object. These standard, mass-

Sol LeWitt
Three-Part-Set 789 (B), 1968
Painted steel, tape strips,
80 x 208 x 50 cm
Cologne, Museum Ludwig,
Ludwig Donation

produced tubes became an elementary entelechy from which the medium of flurorescent light radiated into the distance and the realms of subtlety. Following his first installations of this kind, Flavin quickly developed a repertoire of lucid corner overlaps and dissolutions, light barriers and corridors. Since 1969 he has installed them in entire museum tracts and buildings. Few artists since the neo-Impressionists have so consistently included such phenomena as optical mix, simultaneous contrast and colour temperature and made them shine as light within a room. None has used white and coloured, cold and warm fluorescent light with such purity, stringency, precision and richness. The sparse strategies of Minimal Art are transcended here in masterpieces of precision-orchestrated light.

Sol LeWitt (p. 528 below and ill. right) takes the opposite approach. Where Flavin allows sensuality to triumph over an ascetic system, LeWitt approaches optical sensations with deliberate detachment, emphasising the intellectual concept instead. Primary forms, gener-

Sol LeWitt
Three Part Variations on Three Different Kinds of Cubes, 1967
Steel, lackiert, 123 x 250 x 40 cm

"Conceptual Artists are mystics rather than rationalists. They leap to conclusions that logic cannot reach."
SOL LEWITT

ally squares, are arranged serially in open or closed modules. The optical impression is confusingly irregular. It is only by reconstructing the underlying grammar that the system becomes recognisable. This is what distinguishes LeWitt from Judd and Morris with their emphasis on object and observation. The given that Judd and Morris seek to exclude returns in this way to Minimal Art – not as geometric idealism in the manner of Mondrian, but as a contrast to the confused visuality of the world as it appears. In this respect, LeWitt foreshadows certain aspects of Conceptual Art.

Europe: System, Composition and Caro's Strategy of Discontinuity

At the same time, sculptors in Europe set about abbreviating their geometric vocabulary. They were neither Constructivists nor Concrete Artists of the second generation, nor were they disciples of Minimal Art. They had turned away from the compositional ideals of Gabo and Pevsner to explore the inner structure of volumes and the de-central tensile forces of spatiality. However, they also placed more value on an awareness of form than did the American serialists and addressed fundamental issues of sculptural language rather than basic precepts of perception. They thus established their own distinctly European position situated between economy of form and complexity, between system and composition, between analysis and intuition.

The Dutch artist Carel Visser (p. 530 above left) built his œuvre more firmly than any other on the aesthetic foundations laid by de Stijl. However, without abandoning orthogonality and balance, he brought it considerably closer to the serial approach of Minimal Art. Erwin Heerich (p. 530 above right) moved much further away from the Constructivist tradition with his fragile card-

Dan Flavin
Monument for Tatlin, 1966
Seven neon tubes of various lengths, 365.8 x 71 x 11 cm
Formerly Saatchi Collection, London

Carel Visser
Multitude, 1964
Iron, 30 x 139 x 60 cm
Apeldoorn, Netherlands

Erwin Heerich
Cardboard Object, 1969
Cardboard, 60 x 60 x 60 cm
Cologne, Museum Ludwig,
Ludwig Donation

*"I can't imagine getting up in the
morning full of enthusiasm to make
something that I already made the
day before. I just couldn't do that to
myself. That's why it's good to question the things you're sure about and
to relativize your own work."*
CAREL VISSER

board objects. Any comparison between his œuvre and
the works of Minimal Art is flawed, for Heerich
explored real morphological variety in the logically
grounded formal richness of his sculptures made up of
regular shapes such as the cube, block, sphere, cylinder
etc. Though he shares with LeWitt the subordination of
practice to thought (consider, for instance, the transience of his cardboard objects), Heerich operates by
subtraction – dividing, halving, omitting – rather than
by the addition or multiplication of modules. Since the
70s he has also been applying his "sculptural way of
thinking" to more robust material such as steel and to
architecture.

Erich Reusch
Paving Stones, Bochum, 1980

Erich Reusch explored the possibilities of horizontal
sculpture (ill. below). In 1956/57, years before Andre,
this student of Uhlmann was designing de-centralised,
earthbound disc sculptures. He activated, intensified
and expanded the surrounding space by means of tem-
plate forms, panels, beams and cubes placed on the
ground. Even the interim spaces oscillate in what is, to
all intents and purposes, a thoroughly urban version of
Land Art or at least "landscaping" art. Ernst Hermanns,
on the other hand, concentrated all the tension of his
work within the tiny surface space of a plinth. From 1964
onwards he erected rods, split spheres and placed them
"with the sure touch of the magician" (according to
Gottfried Böhm) at precisely calculated distances,
abstracting the concept behind Giacometti's late spatial
sculptures. In the following generation of artists, Lutz
Fritsch used just one or two simple, coloured rods to
create a sense of spatial tension. The steel sculptor Alf
Lechner developed his elementary explorations of form
(predominantly cubes) from 1964 onwards on the highly
visible basis of the laws and reactions to which his chosen
material, steel, is subject: bending, cutting, sawing, and
later splitting the red-hot steel by means of sudden cooling. A purist and master of measurement, mass and material resistance, he influenced the following generation.

At around the same time, the English sculptor
Anthony Caro (p. 531) put forward an alternative to Minimal Art. In the autumn of 1959, Caro, a former assistant
of Moore, who had previously concentrated on heavy-
limbed female nudes, paid a visit to David Smith. His
discovery of Smith's work (and the sculptures of Kenneth Noland) was to become a fundamental catalyst
for his own sculpture. In 1960, he undertook a radical
change of course to ally himself with abstract steel sculpture, He welded open structures of steel plates and bars,
but avoided the American step towards seriality, progression and modular regularity. On the contrary, he
stressed individuality, syntax and composition, becoming the first English, and possibly even the first Euro-

Anthony Caro
Early One Morning, 1962
Painted steel, and aluminium,
289 x 620 x 335 cm
London, Tate Gallery

"I have been trying, I think, all the time to eliminate references, to make truly abstract sculpture. It is like using these things like notes in music. But the note must not remind you too much of the world of things ..."
ANTHONY CARO

pean, sculptor to find his artistic direction through American art without losing his European complexity.

He adopted Smith's strategy of discontinuity, his deliberately multi-facetted approach into which various viewpoints lock. His affinity with Minimal Art and the component that distinguishes him clearly from Smith is his earthbound contact, the inclusion of the surrounding space and the emphasis on the horizontal rather than the vertical. Rosalind Krauss has pointed out that there are two ways of relating to a sculpture such as *Early One Morning* (1962). Viewed from the side, it appears as a drawn-out horizontal sequence of beams, bars and rectangle. It casually dissolves a sense of mass, weight and centre, appearing like a piece of furniture we can walk around. Viewed from the front, it is totally different. It appears as a distinctly horizontal structure – a high

Anthony Caro
Early One Morning, 1962
Painted steel, and aluminium,
289 x 620 x 335 cm
London, Tate Gallery

Anthony Caro
Midday, 1960
Painted steel, 148 x 366 x 97 cm
London, Kasmin Ltd.

Phillip King
Open (Red-Blue) Bound, 1974/75
Wire mesh and steel panels,
painted, 366 x 366 x 213 cm
Private collection

rectangle with a broad cross in front of it and three fin-
ger-like protrusions jutting diagonally upwards. This
view emphasises the pictorial rather than the sculptural
aspect of the work and is reminiscent of an abstract
painting by, say, Kandinsky. Physical structure and
illusionistic composition, a sculptural aspect and a
painterly aspect, physical and optical experience, all
diverge. The appeal of Caro's work of the 60s lies
primarily in this artful alternation between the open
and the closed, the linear and the planar.

In his later work, the painterly, compositional aspect
becomes stronger. His *Table Sculptures* since 1967 offer
the spectator a single viewpoint again: abstract, decorative still lifes that overlap and thereby break the horizontality of the table. In Italy, Caro found a factory that could
supply entirely irregular steel cuts, which he lacquered
in their unfinished state. He all but abandoned the stringency of his early sculptures of standardised elements.

Caro's art historical position is one of principle. The
critic Clement Greenberg and his followers have celebrated Caro as the founder of a sculpture based purely
on relations, planes, lines, intervals and correspondences. Other critics have emphasised the fact that he
dispensed with the base, verticality and solid core. They
have pointed out his early move towards horizontal
sculpture, emphasizing Caro's work of the 60s rather
than the decorative work that followed.

As a teacher at St. Martin's School of Art, Caro also
became the leading influence in British sculpture after
Moore and made his mark on two generations of artists.
Clement Greenberg's theories added a theoretical

superstructure and even occasionally provided directives
for actual praxis. Caro's most distinctive student, apart
from William Tucker (ill. below), was Phillip King (ill.
above). Born in Tunisia, King's work with its vibrant
colours and its use of waved, domed and tented forms
often has an exotic touch tempered by strong influences
of American Minimal Art. Opposing positions, such as
the work of Richard Long, also emerged from St. Martin's School of Art.

William Tucker
Nine Poles, 1967
Iron, 224 x 91 cm
London, Kasmin Ltd.

Post-Minimal: Sensual Intensity and the Expansion of Art

The Sixties Revised

In 1968, at the Dawn Gallery in New York, Californian artist Walter De Maria (ill. right) showed his sculpture of five 2 x 2 metre steel plates covered in rows of needle-sharp spikes. At first glance, this *Bed of Spikes* is a perfect example of Minimal Art, its flawlessly geometric basic form paired with seriality and progression. On closer inspection, however, it triggers a sense of danger, with its menacingly protruding spikes which really do go under the skin, and not just figuratively. The potential for injury goes further than the formal alignment, for this sculpture is quite literally painfully sharp. In this respect, the work adds a new and immediate sensory dimension to the perceptual purism of Minimal Art, whetting perception in a very physical way.

Is this the context in which to regard the work of an artist such as Rebecca Horn (ill. right)? A winglike fan, a mask of feathers, intensify infinitely tender rituals of touch (p. 601). They are instruments meant to expand our powers of sensory perception and increase our contact with the self or with the outside world. In later works, the appliances take on a mechanical and artistic life of their own and are no longer mere props. Ladles splatter colour onto canvases jutting from the wall. A pointed pendulum hovers above a pile of pigment. In the ruins of a former prison in the northern German town of Münster, tiny steel hammers endeavour, in the words of Thomas Deecke, "to break the thick walls with their gentle yet irritatingly persistent beat" and recall at the same time the desperate communication attempts of prisoners knocking at their cell walls. The hectic irregularity of the myriad hammer-blows is countered by the languid sound of a drop of water splashing at regular intervals into a pool. Here, we find appliances imitating life and yet still remaining sculpture. They belong to a world of aesthetics that intensifies touch into energy and sublimates it at the same time.

Is sculpture responding in this way to secondary visual worlds which Pop Art would have sought to embrace, or is it a response to some deficit in direct experience? Does it render experience direct once more, and physical? Art is perceived here as a palpable flow of energy. De Maria and Horn saw in it a psychopathic force, while Beuys and the artists of Italian Arte Povera saw in it a spiritual and cultural energy.

Walter De Maria
Bed of Spikes, 1968/69
Stainless steel, 5 parts,
200 x 10.7 x 37.3 cm (each)
Plates, heigth: 6.5 cm
Spikes, heigth: 26.8 cm
Private collection

Rebecca Horn
The Moon, the Child,
the River of Anarchy, 1991
Installation, various materials
Kassel, documenta 9 (1992)

Is the trend towards an intellectualisation of art diametrically opposed to this kind of heightened sensuality? Does the conceptual approach represent a force whose impact goes far beyond the 70s and Conceptual Art as such? Language visualised and semantic questions permeate sculpture. The objects, installations and "museums" by the Belgian artist Marcel Broodthaers (ill. left and below) express a general criticism of cultural and perceptual mores based on the ambivalence of image and reality, concept and object. In the tradition of Duchamp and Magritte, they reflect a certain spirit and poetic irony, full of metaphors such as the winter garden for the 19th century or the pot of mussels suggesting *savoir vivre* (as opposed to the hamburger of Pop Art, perhaps), posing yet again the question as to the nature of art and life. Reflection is magnified by self-reflection, with art referring to art in a hermetically closed system.

The Italian artist Giulio Paolini, heir to a rich visual culture, refuses to indulge in the production of additional images, preferring instead to use his sophisticated arrangements of props to analyse the conditions of seeing and material visual elements such as frame, canvas, the myth of the artist, subjects. In one of his sculptures, entitled *Mimesis*, (p. 535 above) two casts of a Greek statue face one another. Art, this suggests, invariably has to do with art alone. American artist Joseph Kosuth (p. 535 below) also isolates art radically from non-art. Every work of art, according to Kosuth, is tautological. It describes only itself. On four glass panes of equal size leaning against the wall, we can read the words "glass", "leaning", "clear", "square". Each statement corre-

Marcel Broodthaers
Condemnation of Magritte, 1966
Woodpanel, painted and printed, board, 4 jars with cotton and blue paint, 78 x 62 x 32 cm
Brussels, Estate Broodthaers

"Since Duchamp, the artist is the author of a definition."
MARCEL BROODTHAERS

Marcel Broodthaers
Hexagon, 1966
Hexagonal shelf with 10 small caps and 7 large jars,
57 x 66,3 x 12,3 cm
Berlin, private collection

sponds to a fact. Anything beyond that is falsification of the hermetic model of art as aesthetics. Art is the epistemological criticism of art.

Towards the end of the decade, commentaries and correctives begin to address the immediate past. This does not mean that Pop Art and Minimal Art (and with them, the inclusion of everyday reality and viewer involvement) are lost. They are simply countered from various directions. Sculpture counters the design formalism of Minimal Art by using mutable materials such as glass fibre, felt, rubber, textiles, lead and even ashes, and by fluidity, processuality and sheer physicality. It is also reduced to pure physical experience and, defends corporeality as an integral part of the self. In the form of Land Art, it expands into vast uncharted territories. The traditional concept of sculpture is completely dissolved, only to restitute itself repeatedly in individual aspects.

Many artists now begin turning away from the obsession with civilisation, consumerism and media, looking instead to nature, mythology and ecology. They choose to use "poor" materials. For a while, Arte Povera even turns up as a generic name for this entire approach. In America, Robert Pincus-Witten coins the term Post-Minimal and Morris the term Anti-form. In Europe,

"Works of art are analytic propositions. That is, if viewed within their context – as art – they provide no information what so ever about any facts. A work of art is a tautology in that it is a presentation of the artist's intention, that is, he is saying that, that particular work of art 'is art', which means, is a 'definition' of art. Thus, that it is art is true a 'priori'…" JOSEPH KOSUTH

Giulio Paolini
Mimesi, 1976
Plastercasts after the Medici
Venus, 213 x 50 x 44 cm
Mönchengladbach, Städtisches
Museum Abteiberg

Joseph Kosuth
Leaning, Clear, Glass, Square, 1965
Four panes of glass, 100 x 100 cm (each)
Varese, Panza di Biumo Collection

Joseph Kosuth
Neon Electrical Light, English
Glass Letters, 1966
Milan, Panza di Biumo Collection

artists such as Beuys, Broodthaers, Mario Merz and Jannis Kounellis seek to set their own cultural tradition against what they see as the positivist materialism and behaviourism of the Americans, and play it off against America's perceived lack of historicity.

Minimal Processes and Physicality

Minimal Art imposed preconceived stereometrics and serial systems on sculpture. An early counter-movement was based on the materials used. Towards the end of the decade, flexibility, expansion, weight, gravitation, pressure and traction emerged as independent sculptural themes. Sculptures were no longer merely standing or reclining figures, but could lean, prop, hang, bend, be tautened, fluid or rigid. Masses of earth breaking through wooden props under the weight of tons, asphalt seeking its way, plates of lead supported by their own weight, weights balancing. The physical logic of stability, lability, freefall, processes of warming and cooling – all these were turned directly into an aethetics of material syntax. This went far beyond the old adage of choosing material appropriate to the intended form and subjected form instead to the specific properties of the material. Oldenburg's soft sculpture developed out of Pop Art.

Since 1965, British artist Barry Flanagan (ill. below) had been sewing sand and paper into flexible textile coverings, folding cloths or hanging them from a line. The concept of process art had begun to take hold. Depicting nothing and representing nothing "which it is not itself" (Max Imdahl) it was a paradigm for behavioural and learning processes that released new energies.

Artists such as Morris (whose felt works are amongst the most impressive demonstrations of this anti-form; p. 526), Bruce Nauman, Serra or Keith Sonnier (ill. left) touched only briefly on process art. For Italian Arte Povera it was only one aspect. Others, such as the German-born American artist Eva Hesse (ill. right) arrived

Keith Sonnier
Wrapped Neon Piece, 1969
Neon tubes, wiring, transformer,
248 x 187 x 151 cm
Cologne, Museum Ludwig,
Ludwig Foundation

Barry Flanagan
Four Rahsbs 4, 1967
Resin, hessian and sand,
127 x 152.4 x 152.4 cm
New York, Solomon R.
Guggenheim Museum

Right:
Richard Tuttle
Wheel, c. 1964
Wood, 79 x 20.5 x 76.5 cm
Cologne, Museum Ludwig,
Ludwig Collection

Page 537 below:
Eva Hesse
Accession III, 1968
Fibreglass and plastic tubing,
80 x 80 x 80 cm
Cologne, Museum Ludwig,
Ludwig Foundation

at psychological models through mutable and vulnerable materials – glass fibre, latex, string, wire – which seemed to freeze in a state of turmoil. According to Hesse, "I try out the most absurd, extreme opposites, I was always more interested in that than in something normal that has just the right heights and proportions." Her cuboid *Accession* reflects another form favoured by Minimal Art, but it has thousands of perforations, through which countless flexible plastic tubes run inwards like feelers, bristling and teeming, drawing the viewer's gaze into constant movement and touch. Her very last work, *Sieben Stäbe*, created while she was in hospital, heightens the effect of the upright gait of legs with milky fibreglass bandages to the point of individuality, subjectivity and even monstrosity. Hesse thus inscribed upon the anti-form her own deeply personal and sensitive physical gesture. In doing so, she led material processes towards a fragile and at times witty body language.

The Polish artist Magdalena Abakanovicz (p. 538 above) arrived at the material process entirely independently and with no contact to the western mainstream. From her beginnings in weaving and textile design, she developed monumental, biomorphic sculptures of coire, rope and jute from 1966 onwards. They are hung from the ceiling, stacked on the floor or set like bent shells of bodies. She describes them as "soft-life" sculpture. Her six-part *Embryology* of 1978-1981 is a gigantic ensemble of large, full ovoids of varying sizes, charged with the dramatic pathos that informs so much of Abakanovicz' work. In her œuvre, Process Art takes on an existential dimension paralleled only by the work of Eva Hesse.

Others have tended to concentrate more on the inherent sensibility of the material. Richard Tuttle (p. 536 below right) marks spaces with slats, scraps of fabric, thread or wire without actually defining them. A few centimetres of rope "balance a wall" (Gerhard Mack). Ephemeral materials are charged with light, fluid energies. Reiner Ruthenbeck (p. 538) translates the materiality of soft cloth and hard glass, elastic rubber and rigid steel into elementary geometric figures – such as a triangle or a cross – creating a wonderfully meditative and powerful equilibrium out of gravity and counterforce.

Ulrich Rückriem (p. 539) on the other hand employs his skills as a trained stonemason. In the 60s he sought inspiration in the work of Maurice Lipsi, Wotruba and Di Suvero. A turning point came in 1968 when he met Carl Andre. Rückriem, however, was not to become an adept of Minimal Art. He uses the American innovations as a source for a classical sculptural concept. He divides the unworked block with systematic logic and enormous economy of form. Simple interventions such as drilling, breaking, sawing and splitting do not overwork the stone, but simply reveal its underlying structure. The cuts are economical enough to avoid breaking the force of the mass when Rückriem layers the segments together again. Each step in the working process

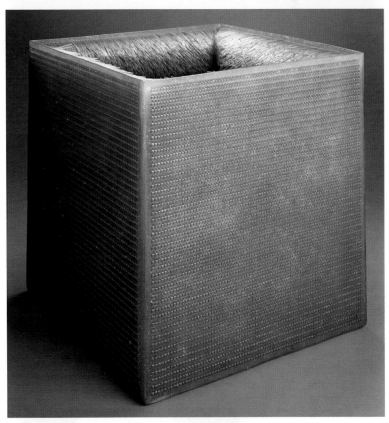

remains legible in the end result. The aim is not some kind of didactic unequivocality, but a sensual sculptural presence. The steel sculptor Alf Lechner may be seen as a counterpart to the stone sculptor, Rückriem. Lechner's "compressions" involve rolling liquid steel up against a barrier, throwing it up in loops, pressing it together or bursting the steel by means of sudden temperature changes.

Above:
Eva Hesse
Untitled, 1970
Fibreglass on wire, latex over fabric and wire, each element 103-128 x 70-103 x 5-15 cm
New York, private collection

Magdalena Abakanovicz
Crowd, 1986/87
Hessian and resin; 19 figures,
170 x 530 x 40 cm (each)
Napa (CA), Hess Collection

Reiner Ruthenbeck
Suspension IV, 1969/70
Dark red fabric, retangular metal
tubing, 350 x 300 cm
Collection of the artist

Reiner Ruthenbeck
Seven Black Barriers, 1977
Aluminium, iron, lead; total
length: 30 m; mast length: 11 m;
lower diameter: 17.5 cm;
upper diameter: 8 cm
Stuttgart, Bundesgartenschau

Page 539:
Ulrich Rückriem
Dolomite, 1972
Dolomite, cut with stone-cutter,
220 x 90 x 110 cm, 310 x 110 x 110 cm
Düren, Renker Collection

Ulrich Rückriem
Dolomite, cut, 1976
Dolomite, 3.3 x 7.2 x 1.2 m
Münster, an der Petrikirche

Around 1970 sculptors discovered the sensibility of physics. At the same time, the American psychologist James J. Gibson recognised our fundamental awareness of gravity and balance as our sixth sense. A number of sculptors sublimated this sixth sense with orderly precision, dramatising it to lend it greater reality, power or nuance than sculpture had ever possessed before.

Richard Serra stages the weight of heavy metal plates as a dramatic test of strength for iron, steel and lead. Kenneth Snelson (p. 540 above left) mounts short aluminium pipes with steel cables to create a powerfield of infinitely repeating crossovers. Wolfgang Nestler presents a fragile system of iron bars, metal bands and hinges in a sequence of sculptural processes that we not only perceive with the eye, but also weigh up and sublate through our physical sense of ponderation. Alf Schuler addresses the sculptural properties of filigree suspended beams. The Japanese sculptor Jiri Takamatsu, who became a co-founder of the Japanese Anti-Art group in 1962, balances the massive statics of iron blocks with tilted plates, suspended beams and lightly placed bars. Whereas Serra and Morris release the heavy gravitational force of the material, Takamatsu seems to cancel out weight and transform it into lightness. Nobuo Sekine (p. 540 below left) heightens this approach to create the drama of a twelve-ton rock on a polished pillar of steel. The mirror effect dissolves the surroundings, the rock seems to float weightlessly in the air, in a "state of nothingness" subject to no conditions. The creative play on perception becomes the metaphor for a philosophical maxim of "only nothingness is eternal" derived by Sekine from the Chinese Tao-te-ching and modified by a Japanese heritage.

The physical properties of water were also harnessed in sculpture. Apart from his physical *Primary Demonstrations*, Klaus Rinke (p. 540 above right) used the flow of water to portray the passing of time, and stretches of water or plumblines to translate gravity into a strict formal concept.

Serra: from Materialism to Urban Sculpture

Richard Serra (pp. 541–543) dominated American sculpture for three decades. He broke with its conventions like no other sculptor, yet retained the elementary language of plasticity in its strictest form. He is that rare being – a genuine sculptor who embraced entire landscapes and cityscapes in his work. In doing so, he took weight, mass, gravity, and their expression in direction, sequence and horizon, and transformed them into sculptural qualities.

Serra's first steps are directed against the firmly defined orders of Minimal Art. In 1967 he hung strips of rubber he had found on Canal Street on the wall as *Bridles*. In 1968 he flung liquid lead into the corners of a room and then placed the solid cooled masses on the floor in the order in which they had been thrown. The form reflects the acts of throwing, flowing, cooling and solidifying. He had plates of metal left over from this which he then used to create his famous *One Ton Prop*, consisting of four plates measuring 122 x 122 cm leaned against one another in a precarious balance. They stand and fall on the basis of their own physicality alone. In his later *Towers*, including the *Terminal* (p. 541) in Bochum, Germany, the sense of confusion and danger is caused by deviations from the vertical.

Since 1972 Serra has also intervened in the landscape and soon afterwards in the urban landscape. In *Shift*, to the north of Toronto, he marked out and developed an entire slope, as far as the eye can see, with six walls of equal length. The motoric exploration on walking through this work contrasts with the overall view, and it is this dialectical approach that forms the basis of the

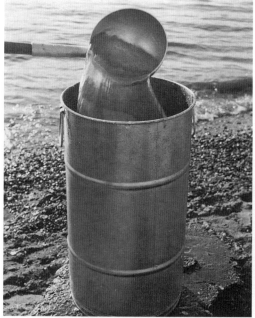

Kenneth Snelson
Fair Leda, 1968. Stainless steel tubes and cable,
387.5 x 561.5 x 331.5 cm. USA, private collection

Klaus Rinke
Change of Location in Intervals, 1972
Photograph on paper, 132 x 68 cm. Private collection

Nobuo Sekine
Phases of Nothingness, 1970
Stainless steel and rock,
625 x 216 x 435 cm
Humblebæk (Denmark), Louisiana
Museum of Modern Art,
The Japan Foundation

Klaus Rinke
12 casks of Rhine water, 1969
Scooped from the Rhine
at 12 points on 28 June 1969
Illustrated: Düsseldorf

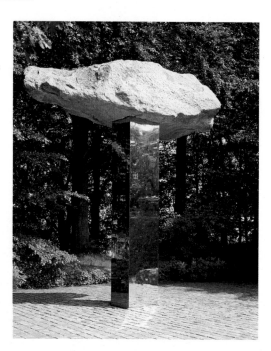

Page 541:
Richard Serra
Terminal, 1976/77
Cortensteel, 4 plates,
1230 x 360 x 274 cm (each 2),
1230 x 274 x 360 cm (each 2)
Kassel, documenta 6 (1977)
Current location: Bochum,
Bahnhofvorplatz

Richard Serra
St. John's Rotary Arc, 1980
Cortensteel, 61 x 366 x 6.5 cm
New York, Holland Tunnel

new experiences and open forcefields that have now become part of his sculpture. He thus establishes a new paradigm for public art in which, according to Serra himself, the experience of the sculptural construction by the viewer is decisive.

His large-scale sculptures of straight, bent, curved and tilted plates of Corten steel possess a sculptural soverignty, but they also embrace coordinates of street plans, buildings, horizon. The react subtly and critically to the spatial situation. They alter conditions of percep-

Richard Serra
Shift, 1970–1972
Concrete, 6 parts, height and thickness of each section: 152 x 20 cm
Installed at King City (Ontario),
Roger Davidson Collection,
Toronto

Richard Serra
Untitled, 1978
Steel, wrought, 2 blocks,
150 x 70 x 70 cm and 180 x 70 x 70 cm
Stadt Marl

Richard Serra
Splash, 1969
Lead, 268 x 272 x 47,5 cm
New York, Jasper Johns Collection

Richard Serra
House of Cards (One Ton Prop),
1968/69
Lead, each plate 139.7 qcm
Formerly Saatchi Collection,
London

tion, creating a place as sculpture, and sculpture as place. These works clarify the vague contexts of urban traffic hubs, countering them, charging them with tension, condensing them into sculptural energy in an offensive strategy of assertion at the heart of an urban need.

Land Art: Painting with Mountains

Towards the end of the 60s, a number of artists began operating outside the white-walled gallery spaces of Soho, creating works in the deserts and mountains of Nevada, Utah, Arizona and New Mexico. They used diggers and caterpillar trucks to create chasms in the earth or to construct huge ramps. The result was an enormous expansion of art, in which landscape, earth formation, horizon, weathering and erosion all became real materials. Is Land Art, as it quickly came to be known, simply a brutal intervention in the untouched expanses of the West? Or is it a protest against the alienation of nature with an escapist tendency towards ecological reparation?

Certainly, there are enormous regressive forces at work here. Circles and spirals in the earth are more than just a colossal extension of Minimal Art. The projection of a romantic atmosphere, association with cosmic orbits, cultic faith in the mythical power of place, dissemination in vast panorama images – all this touches in some way on the picturesque landscape painting of the 18th and 19th centuries. Land Art can be regarded within the Northern Romantic tradition traced by Robert Rosenblum from the work of such artists as Caspar David Friedrich and William Turner to the art of our

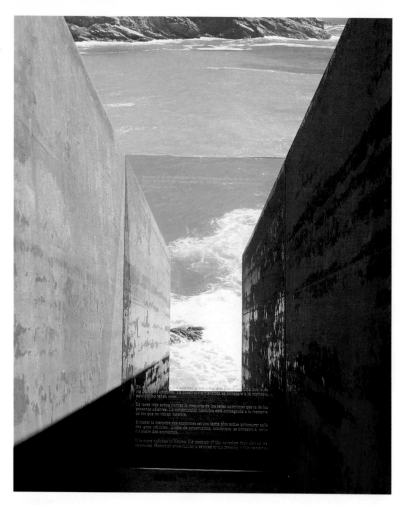

Dani Karavan
Hommage à Walter Benjamin,
1990–1994. Steel, glass and other
materials. Port Bou (Spain)

own times. In the paintings of John Constable pre-
historic ritual sites evoke a frisson of the primordial and
the cosmic. The American land artists, too, constantly
recall megalithic stone circles, Indian calendar structures or the huge pictograms of the Peruvian coastal
desert, distant vanishing points and Japanese Zen
gardens.

There are also some direct precursors. As early as
1940, Isamu Noguchi created landscaped *Playgrounds*
and *Playmountains*. The versatile Bauhaus emigré Herbert Bayer had explored the possibilities of the sculpted
landscape in drawings as early as 1947 and had created an
actual *Earth Mound* near Aspen, Colorado in 1966,
approximating in effect the work of Robert Smithson.
The Israeli artist Dani Karavan (ill. left) erected the
architectural structure of his *Peace Monument* in the
Negev Desert in 1963–1968. Dunes and chasms, water-
courses and windstreams in the surrounding area were
transformed into sculpture. All three artists approached
Land Art *ante festum*.

Michael Heizer, Smithson, Morris and James Turrell
moved vast quantities of earth. The primordial force of
the scenery, the denuding of geological layers, the exposure to erosion and weather, the corporeal involvement
of humans in artificial depths and heights monumen-
talised their work, placing it between natural history
and art. It was Heizer who made the start (p. 545) by
scraping his geometric patterns directly into the soil of
the Mojave Desert.

One year later he stepped up the level of intervention in the natural landscape when he created his *Double
Negative* on the Mormon Mesa in Nevada, excavating
some 220,000 tons of earth to cut two chasms facing
each other at right angles to the edge of the natural
plateau. His huge *Complex I* (1972–1974) leans more
towards pre-Columbian architecture. In 1986 Heizer,

Robert Smithson
Closed Mirror Square, 1969
Mineral salt, mirror and glass

Robert Smithson
Asphalt Rundown, Rome,
1969

commissioned to create a work on the site of a former coal-mine, formed four more such complexes featuring pictograms of a turtle, fish, water-beetle, snake and frog. Land Art as pre-historic landscape decor.

The path taken by Smithson (pp. 544 below and 546) leads from Abstract Expressionist paintings to the non-site theme: photos or maps document a place outside the gallery, often juxtaposed with pieces of ore, chunks of rock or minerals from the original site. From here, Smithson went on in 1970 to develop his concept of site sculpture, which defined sculpture as part of a certain place, rather than as an isolated and moveable object. The *Sleeping Cyclone under Leaden Water* on the Great Salt Lake in Utah found its response in the 1970 *Spiral Jetty* (p. 546) – a spiral of pebbles running far into the reddish water and now flooded over. The organic growth represented by the spiral counters perpetual barrenness and geological, entropic decay.

Smithson's last work, the *Amarillo Ramp* in Texas is not simply a monument in the wilderness, but a runover for the artificial Tecovas lake with its nearby subterranean cellars for helium gas. It is by no coincidence that Smithson's favourite projects are the artificial reactivation of abandoned mining sites: post-industrial spaces subject to natural forces. His version of Land Art also derived from a social strategy and was thus anything but escapist.

The light artist James Turrell takes a more formal approach. Since 1977 he has rounded the volcanic Roden Crater near Flagstaff, Arizona, to a perfect sphere. Built-in chambers and hollows allow observation of cosmic events. The *Observatory* by Robert Morris (p. 546 below) in Oostelijk-Flevoland, Netherlands, addresses the solstice with an archaic double ring recalling Stonehenge. Other artists work entirely with time. Dennis Oppenheim for example, cuts *Annual Rings* in the ice (p. 548 above) with his snowmobile or uses a combine harvester to cut patterns in ripe wheatfields, obstructing any sale of the work, comparing this to an embargo on raw pigment's development of illusionistic power on the canvas.

Walter De Maria (p. 547) sets different priorities. His laconic works of exemplary stringency are not only limited to Land Art. Whereas his works of the early 60s combined the hermetic approach of Duchamp with the serial forms of Minimal Art, De Maria's later works exemplify the most direct contemporary response to the concept of the sublime as posited by Edmund Burke in the 18th century. This explains the pronounced sense of

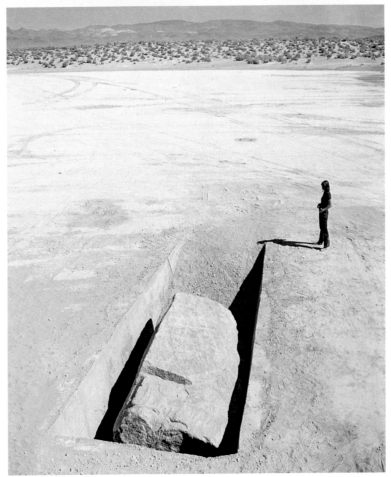

Above:
Michael Heizer
Double Negative, 1969
Sandstone, 240 000 tons excavated and shifted, 457 x 15 x 9 m
Virgin River, Mormon Mesa (NV)

Below:
Michael Heizer
Displaced/Replaced Mass, 1969
Silver Springs (NV)
New York, Robert C. Scull Collection

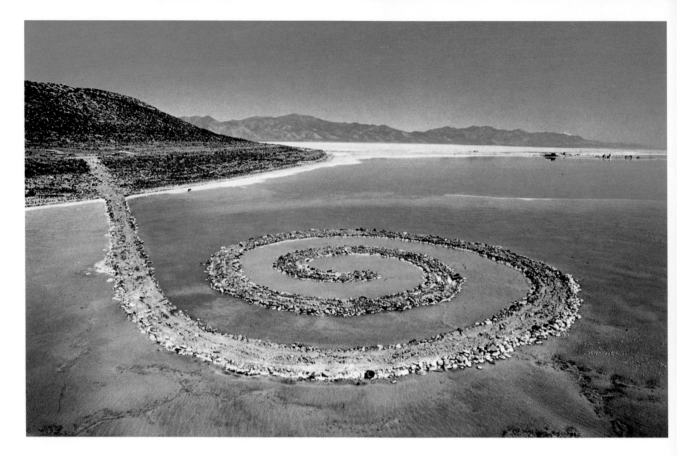

Robert Smithson
Spiral Jetty, 1970
Rock, Salt, Crystals, Earth and
Water; length: 475 m, width: 4.5 m
Utah, Great Salt Lake (destroyed)

Robert Morris
Observatory, 1977
Earth, grass, wood, steel, granite;
diameter: 91 m
Oostelijk Flevoland (Netherlands)

danger in his *Bed of Spikes* (p. 533). It also explains the 400 stainless steel lightning rods in his remote *Lightning Field* north of Quemedo, New Mexico, a major work of Land Art which dramatises nature, storms, sunshine in a precisely calculated geometric ritual. The desert as a metaphysical space, an extreme landscape as a place to experience the sublime.

At the same time, De Maria challenges our powers of imagination as few other artists do. His (unrealised) Munich earth sculpture (1970–1971) was planned as a 6-metre deep shaft drilled through a piled-up mound and the same distance into the earth. History and geology, war and peace as associations, with an invisible vanishing point for imagination and reflection. It is, like the *Vertical Earth Kilometer* in Kassel, an immaterial anti-monument. On the other hand, De Maria is also a master of *mis en scène*. His *Five Continents Sculpture* (1987) consisting of white lumps of rock from five continents set inside walls of glass and flooded with light radiates a cool aura of distance and vastness, as magical as a desert.

Compared to the scale on which American artists have intervened in the landscape, Richard Long (p. 548) seems like a lightfooted wanderer. What he does seems neither monumental nor heroic, but transitory and transient. As early as 1967, when he was still a student, he walked back and forth, trampling a line in the grass and documenting it in photographs (p. 591). The same sensitivity he showed in allowing traces to merge with the landscape also marks his later epic walks in the Himalayas, the Andes, Australia, Japan and Iceland. The only marks Long leaves in these solitary places are a circle of stones, a square of grass, or a spiral of seaweed, which he photographs. Soon, he also began placing his signs in museums and exhibitions in the form of geometric basic figures whose universality leave personal experience behind. With his walks Long not only continues a British tradition, from Celtic stone circles through to Wordsworth's famous walks in the Lake

District, but he also contributes towards shaping the paradigms of a new sculpture that defines itself in terms of journey and locus.

Little could be further removed from the romantic solitude of Long than the cosmopolitan work of Christo and Jeanne-Claude. Their temporary large-scale projects demand not only political assertiveness, organisational talent and independent financing through the sale of collages and preliminary sketches (p. 336), but they also play a role in society from the very moment of their inception to their media coverage in books and film. The socio-political and economic framework is an important part of the work – it is no coincidence that the major landscape projects from the *Wrapped Coast* north of Sydney (1969) to the *Running Fence* in the Californian hills (1976), the *Surrounded Islands* of Miami in 1983 (p. 549) and the *Umbrellas* (p. 560 below) on the west coast of America and the east coast of Japan (1991) have always gone hand in hand with projects that involved "wrapping" historic urban edifices such as the Pont Neuf in Paris in 1985 and the Berlin Reichstag in 1995 (p. 550 above).

In their work, Christo and Jeanne-Claude have epitomised the extension of art and its total integration into the landscape or cityscape. The *Running Fence* meandered for some 40 km through the hills of California. Seen close up, it looked like a sail blown in convex and concave curves by maritime breezes. From a distance, it looked like a sprawling sketch underlining the wave-like rhythm of the hills and structuring it in a sequence of perspectival foreshortenings. Obvious plasticity merged with a distant and vanishing linearity. Unparalleled as all these projects may be, they clearly fulfil a traditional aesthetic requirement in terms of the harmony between man and landscape, art and nature, as sculpture and drawing, rhythm and linear melody, even the changing mood and atmosphere of light. Two weeks later, the landscape or the urban location looks just as it did before and the materials are recycled.

Walter De Maria
Lightning Field, 1974–1977
Earthwork; 400 steelpoles, heigth:
470-830 cm, diameter: 5.1 cm;
area: 1.6 x 1 km
Quemado (New Mexico)

Walter De Maria
Munich Earth Room, 1968
Peat, c. 50 m³, 60 cm deep, spread
over 3 rooms
Munich, Galerie Heiner Friedrich
(Sept./Oct. 1968)

Nauman and the Body as a Medium

Proximity meets distance when Heizer and De Maria set the scale of the human body against the vast scale of nature. One of the most fundamental experiences of the late 60s and early 70s was the discovery of the body as a medium. Or, to put it more precisely, the interaction of physical and spatial perception. Even psychologists began to question the predominant role of the retinal image. According to psychologist Norbert Bischof in 1966, "The order of perceived space is founded on the systems of motoric spatial orientation and cannot be understood without it."

The artist Bruce Nauman (pp. 561 f) applies this to the experience of the self when he maintains that undertaking physical activities fosters certain forms of awareness. Consequently, since 1966, he has been using his own body as an instrument by which to explore art and the identity of the artist. Casts of knees, arms, hands, ears, sometimes distorted or elongated, illustrate given states or reiterate Duchamp's puns. A work consisting of a hand, arm and mouth is called *From Hand to Mouth* and may either be read as a literal visual portrayal of the idiomatic saying or as an ironic comment on the life of the artist. Nauman is radically consistent in his juxtaposition of physical and spatial experience. Since 1967 he has been recording videos of detailed self-observation in his studio – walking in a square, rhythmically bouncing a ball, grimacing. These are exercices in motion within a psycho-physical space, with the body as research subject.

In 1970, he began to treat space as an independent subject, filtering perception through chambers and corridors, and later through inverted pyramids and tunnels (p. 598). These spaces are stations of isolation in which the ego (as in the more relaxed and less tortured light installations by the Californian artists Turrell, Robert Irwin and Maria Nordman) is caught up entirely in its self-awareness and insecurity.

After 1976, following numerous experiments with neon lettering, film, video, photography and hologram (p. 515), Nauman turned again to sculptures in iron, wood and fibreglass, creating large, sweeping figures of interwoven rings and arcs whose vibrant interaction is undermined by bridging, open seams, out-of-sync joints and fragile superstructures with wedge-like cross-sections open to different sides. Each site or location poses its own challenges. Nauman remains true to himself by refusing to adopt any routine based on experience, be it that of the artist or that of the viewer.

In the past decade, he has taken this approach further, to the point of shocking the viewer. Social criticism has become increasingly evident. Cast iron chairs as instruments of torture suspended from beams, life-size casts of heads dangling on wires. Cloned wild animal

Above: **Dennis Oppenheim**
Annual Rings, 1968. Pattern of tree's annual rings, bisected by the United States / Canada border at Fort Kent, Maine, and Claire, New Brunswick

Middle: **Richard Long**
A Circle in Iceland, 1974
Dimensions unknown
(destroyed)

Below: **Richard Long**
Alpine Circle, 1990
Sculpture; diameter: 600 cm
Rochechouart, Château de Rochechouart

Page 549: **Christo & Jeanne-Claude**
Surrounded Islands, 1980–1983
Fabric, 603 850 m². Biscaye Bay Greater Miami (FL). © Christo 1980–1983

Christo & Jeanne-Claude
Wrapped Reichstag, Berlin,
1971–1995
Length: 135.7 m, width: 96 m, roof
heigh: 32.2 m, tower heigh: 42.5 m
Berlin, Deutscher Reichstag (1995)
© Christo 1995

*"Throughout the history of art, the
use of fabric has been a fascination
for artists. From the most ancient
times to the present, fabric – forming
folds, pleats and draperies – has
played a significant part in painting,
frescoes, reliefs and sculptures made
of wood, stone or bronze. The use of
fabric on the Reichstag follows that
classical tradition. Fabric, like clothing and skin, is fragile. It expresses
the unique quality of imperma-
nence."*
CHRISTO & JEANNE-CLAUDE

Christo & Jeanne-Claude
The Umbrellas
Japan – USA, 1984–1991
(Ibaraki, Japan Site)
© Christo 1984–1991

Christo & Jeanne-Claude
The Umbrellas
Japan – USA, 1984–1991
(California Site)
© Christo 1984–1991

Page 551:
Bruce Nauman
Animal Pyramid, 1989
Foam, iron, wood, and wire,
365.8 x 213.4 x 243.8 cm
Berlin, Marx Collection

Bruce Nauman
Model for Tunnel Made up of Parts
of Leftover Projects, 1979/80
Glass fibre, plaster and wood,
56 x 700 x 650 cm
Schaffhausen, Halle für Neue
Kunst

Bruce Nauman
From Hand to Mouth, 1967
Wax over cloth, 71.1 x 26.4 x 11.1 cm
Washington, Hirshhorn Museum
and Sculpture Garden

Right:
Franz Erhard Walther
Straight Line and Semi-Circle,
Same Length, 1975
Steel, 10 mm, 800 x 36 x 8 cm
(straight, 4 parts), 577 x 36 x 8 cm
(semicircle), 800 cm (track, 4 parts)
Stuttgart, Institut für Auslands-
beziehungen

Page 553:
Franz Erhard Walther
Work Demonstration 1,
Working aggregate, 1971
Darmstadt, Hessisches Landes-
museum, Ströher Collection

Joseph Beuys
Fat Chair, 1963
Wood, grease, metal 47 x 42 x 100 cm
Darmstadt, Hessisches Landes-
museum, Beuys Block,
Hessische Kulturstiftung

bodies of foam rubber are dismembered, abruptly remembered and rotate around themselves in a gruesome
nightmare of genetic engineering. Nauman's fury finds
its expression in the maltreated body, just as it is the
body that is the alpha and omega of his inexhaustible
artistic curiosity.

Such terms as Body Art hardly do justice to Nauman's probing questions. It may apply more aptly to

some of the 70s artists working on the borderline
between sculpture and performance: Stuart Brisley
(p. 602) and his social criticism, or Chris Burden
(p. 601) with his fascination with violence, Gilbert
George's self-projection as *Singing Sculpture* (p. 608) in
which the artists are synonymous with the art or Vito
Acconci (p. 607), Gina Pane or Marina Abramovic
(p. 608) whose self-inflicted injuries demonstrate bor-

derline experiences. In his *Trademark* performance in 1970, Acconci sank his teeth into his own body as deeply as possible and transposed the resulting coloured imprints onto other surfaces as a primordial, pre-linguistic articulation that translates the physical boundaries of emotion and pain directly into a visual language.

The most fundmantal, systematic approach to the use of the body in sculpture, without recourse to injury or aggression, was conceived by Franz Erhard Walther (ill. right and p. 562 below). The object becomes a *Werksatz* or "set of working components" and the viewer becomes the user. It is the experience of actually handling the material that constitutes the work of art. Textile books, sacks, bags, covers, strips and steel planes, bars, angles or box-like fabric niches, garments affixed to the wall, determine certain attitudes, movements, counter-movement, attraction, repulsion, contact and distance. Places are occupied and silent dialogues arise. Measurements and materials interlock with physical givens.

Working in the 60s, Walther made a very early inroad into the concept of sculpture as an instruction to act, in which physical awareness, and the sense of "being at one with oneself" or "with oneself" become states in which to experience a sense of inner calm. In this respect, he provides an alternative to Nauman's idiosyncratic curiosity, though Walther does have in common with Nauman the counter-position to a media world of second-hand impressions and passive visual consumption.

Beuys: Aura and Sculpture

In Europe, Beuys is a singular figure whose influence is wide: Fluxus, happenings, process art, environments. In the 60s and 70s, he was a maverick artist who had already prepared the ground for his life's work in the 50s and 60s. Yet as long as the Constructivist and Expressionist design for the world still seemed valid, Beuys remained an isolated figure. It was not until the mid 60s, when open processes and direct energies were starting to be explored that his extended concept of art began to make its presence felt on a broad basis without changing its course or compromising.

By then, Beuys had already created a highly distinctive œuvre ranging from infinitely subtle drawings that explore vital processes and structures to sculptures informed by an utterly untimely symbolism of material and energy. He soon added happenings, environments and, after lengthy preparation, his utopian vision of "social sculpture". From then on, Beuys the artist could barely be distinguished from Beuys the teacher, politician, theoretician and preacher. All these functions became integrated within an extended concept of art, with all forms of expression based upon the quest for the "whole person" in which nature, myth, science, intuition and reason become one again. All this is but a hair's breadth from the ideas of the Romantic movement, especially Novalis. The question of whether age, conduction and insulation as properties of grease, felt, copper, iron etc. in which reality and metaphor are one.

Nine piles of one hundred felt mats with copper covers – the basic idea of a battery with felt as aggregate and copper as conductor. The felt stores and insulates warmth and so, for Beuys, it creates "a kind of power station, a static action" – not as a superficial and decodable meaning, but with the "evocative capacity of the material ... possessing a compelling presence" (according to Georg Jappe). A radical realignment of aesthetic categories also permits language, thought and even social and political activities to be regarded as sculptural activities. This is the root of Beuys' frequently misconstrued maxim that "everyman is an artist".

From the year 1964 onwards Beuys began to direct his energies towards concentrating his holistic concepts in large-scale happenings. They differ from the Fluxus concerts in terms of their concentrated, lengthy and ritualised working approach. The photographs of them have served to shape our image of Beuys as messianic "medium" in his signature hat and angler's waistcoat (p. 555). The happenings that led to the foundation of a Student Party in 1968 and a Free University in 1973 have provided us with most of the objects, display cases and environments in the form of fragments or relics. The display cases in which Beuys collated his objects are authentic presentations in their own right, the Beuys Block in Darmstadt, Germany, (ill. left) being the most arresting and concentrated example. Only at first glance are the rooms hermetic. On closer inspection, they reveal a welter of correspondences, precisely ordered and painstakingly formulated.

Joseph Beuys
Queen-Bee 2, 1952
Queen-Bee 3, 1952
Beuys Block, showcase 6
Wood, wax
Darmstadt, Hessisches
Landesmuseum

Right:
Joseph Beuys
Place (Fatfelt Sculpture), 1967
Darmstadt, Hessisches
Landesmuseum

Page 555:
Joseph Beuys
Before Leaving Camp I, 1970–1980
Environment, c. 600 x 600 cm
Private collection

Beuys actually pandered to regressive needs in pursuing such a concept is of secondary importance – after all, regression and progression have always been closely linked in the history of European thought. Claims that Beuys allegorised his materials in a traditional aesthetic sense ignore the formal precision and auratic force of his work.

Yet even those who consider his charisma and sense of calling sectarian, pseudo-religious, irrational or even fascist (all of these accusations having been explicitly voiced) find themselves confronted with an œuvre of "auratic monumentality" (in the words of Georg Jappe). It all began, after his studies under Ewald Mataré and his beginnings in the field of decorative art, with his 1962 wax sculpture *Queen Bee* (ill. above). In the soft and malleable energy-store of wax on the one hand and in the crystalline honeycomb structure on the other hand, we can already discern the basic pattern of his sculptural theory (the polarities of which, incidentally, Beuys had derived from an essay on bees by Rudolf Steiner). Beuys saw sculpture as a fluid process between organic life and stability, between chaos and crystal, between warmth and hardness. On this basis, Beuys developed the material syntax of his sculpture in the 50s: mass, weight, stor-

Above: **Joseph Beuys**
Snowfall, 1965. Felt mats on 3 peeled
pine trunks, 120 x 375 cm. Basel,
Emanuel Hoffmann-Stiftung,
Depositum im Museum für
Gegenwartskunst

Below: **Joseph Beuys**
Honey-Pump at the Workplace, 1974–1977. Electronic motor,
2 marine engines with copper rollers, steel container, pewter pipe,
plastic tube, 2 tons of honey, 1000 kg of magerine. Kassel,
documenta 6. Current location: Humblebæk (Denmark),
Louisiana Museum of Modern Art

Nothing is pure coincidence or surrealistic chance.
His works stand up to stringent formal criteria and convey complex ideas in a structured way. *Show Your Wounds*
(1976) addresses the experience of death, while *Capital
Room 1970–1977* deals with revolution and the reactivation of all the senses. The 1977 *Honey-Pump at the Workplace* (ill. left) explores the circulation of cultural and
thermal energies between art and life, and the *Tram-Stop*
created in the same year addresses the artist's own childhood. In 1986, one year before his death, Beuys created
his *Palazzo Regale*, musing on the regal, fur-coated
artist-herald and the impoverished wanderer on the face
of the earth. Time and time again, Beuys explores the
fate of the earth. The rocks in his sculpture *At the End of
the 20th Century* lie before us like a field of ruins or a
cemetery, its petrification countered (perhaps in vain)
only by a tiny implantation of grease.

The planting of *7000 oaks* in Kassel between 1982 and
1987 reversed this ratio. Next to each tree stands a stone
stela. The trees, not all of them oaks, by the way, are
destined to grow higher than the accompanying stone.
According to Beuys, this represents "a complete transformation from the sick to the healthy." The 39-part
bronzecast sculpture *Lightning Flash with Light Striking
Stag* (1986) is an apocalyptic vision between icy death
and hope. The sculptor who had opened up sculpture
to new materials as no other had done before, returned
to the classical material bronze. This is a sculptor
whose magnetic appeal goes far beyond any cult-like
following.

Arte Povera: an Alphabet for Materials

Manzoni's canned *Artist's shit* (1961) trashed the romantic
notion of the artist-as-genius in no uncertain terms. In
the course of the 60s other Italian artists also sought
some legitimation beyond the painterly gesture and they
found it in the socio-political proclamation. The militant spirit of the Futurists reared its head once more,
with artists seeing themselves as cultural revolutionaries
in the struggle against sclerotic social structures, the
economic system and the art establishment.

In 1967, Michelangelo Pistoletto rolled bales of
newspaper across the street between Turin galleries,
illustrating how art absorbs the topical and the everyday.
The writer Umberto Eco propagated what he described
as the "open work of art": ambiguous, uncertain and
fragmented as life itself. The young critic Germano
Celant, who sought from 1967 onwards to bundle cul-
turally-critical, anti-institutional artistic forces ideologically under the name Arte Povera also belonged to the
circle around Umberto Eco's Grupa 63.

The term is derived from Jerzy Grotowski's *teatro
povero* and its reference to the use of "poor" materials
such as earth (Pino Pascali), coal (Kounellis), sticks
(Merz), newspaper (Fabro), eternit (Alighiero E. Boetti)
is misleading. Not only because these artists also use
gold, marble, silk and Murano glass, but more importantly because they dismantled the hierarchy of mater-

ials, turned their backs on consumerism and looked instead to the forces of nature, without excluding industrial modernism, and to the spiritual permeation of material without abandoning themselves to conceptualism.

Strictly speaking, no Arte Povera group as such ever actually existed. Does this mean that the term is merely the product of strategic mediation set loose by a single critic, and soon to take on a life of its own on the art scene? Though Mario Merz, Pistoletto, Kounellis, Luciano Fabro (ill. above right), Giovanni Anselmo (ill. above left), Giuseppe Penone and Gilberto Zorio (ill. below) did not ascribe themselves to a group, they all

used art as a base from which to address life (whatever that may have meant in the 60s), and clearly imbued their material with associations of Italo-European mythology and cultural history, reflecting on the present through the vehicle of the past.

Theirs was a poetic criticism of modern civilisation in which regressive and utopian traits often became inextricably interwoven. Influenced by Beuys, they contributed to the history of sculpture an interpretation of the world in metaphors, based on the symbolic power and sensual density of new, unorthodox and often clashing materials. The fact that their cultural revolution led almost immediately to art exhibitions, while the rest-

Giovanni Anselmo
Direzione, 1967
Granite with compass,
220 x 101 x 16 cm
New York, Sonnabend Collection

Luciano Fabro
Feet, 1968–1972
Installation; Murano glass and Shantung silk
Venice, Biennale 1992

Below left: **Gilberto Zorio**
Spears and Lamps Live, 1974
Installation; 4 spears, 12 lamps,
c. 250 x 250 cm
Duisburg, Wilhelm Lehmbruck Museum

Mario Merz
The House of the Gardener, 1983/84
Metal tubes, wire mesh, oil and acryl on canvas, wax, metal, mussels and pine cones, 200.6 x 401 cm. Courtesy Sperone Westwater, New York

Mario Merz
My Homes Wind and Fibonacci
Tables, 1969–1982
Various materials,
diameter: 200 cm
Humblebæk (Denmark), Louisiana
Museum of Modern Art

Mario Merz
Che fare?, 1968
Metal pan, wax, neon lettering,
15 x 45 x 18 cm
Private collection

Jannis Kounellis
Untitled, 1978
Plastercasts, stuffed crow, table,
chair, cello
Mönchengladbach, Städtisches
Museum Abteiberg

lessly wandering artist-as-nomad became a highly marketable master of metaphor, is something the Arte Povera artists have in common with the Futurists who preceded them by half a century.

Mario Merz and Jannis Kounellis are regarded as the paradigmatic artists of a movement that knew no paradigms. Merz (ill. above and p. 557) was originally a painter (p. 361), but in the mid-60s he turned his attentions to such materials as earth, sticks, glass and neon tubes. Their symbolic power is as palpable as it is striking: origins, growth, transparency, modern energy. In 1968, the year of the May demonstrations, he found the original cell of human and nomadic dwelling in the form of the *Igloo* and went on to create meaningful variations on it in the primordial material clay, applied over thin ribs of glass or sticks, sometimes coupled with panels of lead or leather. It formed a personal centre and world model as the expression of an alternative culture. The Fibonacci numbers are closely involved. The discovery of this mediaeval mathematician was to become, for Merz, the ubiquitous growth spiral of life, the "universal equation". The sequence 1,2,4,8,16,32... extends infinitely from the snail's shell to the galaxy. In whatever Merz staged in the course of three decades, he sought to counter the "emptiness of today's technical-mindedness ... a very distant non-void". This explains the evocation of his metaphors and materials, his igloos, tables, bundles of sticks, fruits, neon lances, number sequences, newspapers, pre-historic animals and the way they appeal to our imagination, opening up new areas of freedom. A regressive utopianism as harbinger of a counterworld of poetic enlightenment.

In comparison to Merz, who lived and worked in Turin, Kounellis (ill. left and p. 559), a Greek, who lived and worked in Rome is more strongly oriented towards the heritage of antiquity, Byzantium and the Renaissance. One issue addresses the origins of culture and the historic processes of alienation in mass civilisation.

With metaphors of fire, smoke, glass, coal, scree, steel plates and plaster fragments of ancient statues, he presents a precise and subtly calculated emblematic theatre between remembrance and presence, a stage of cultural levels that denies the linear progressiveness of classical modernism, tableaux of rugged, evocative presence that were not to petrify into self-citation until the 90s. The spectrum of art gathered beneath the makeshift umbrella of Arte Povera ranges from Paolini's staged explorations of visual perception to Fabro's opulent materials and culturally analytical metaphors. It reaches from Anselmo's conceptual demonstrations to Zorio's symbols of energy and purification featuring stars and glowing spears (p. 557) and from Pino Pascali's experimentations with scale and material to Pier Paolo Calzolari's emotive visual theatre (Marlies Grüterich) with its neon signs and thermal processes.

Pistoletto and Penone use the most varied vocabulary. Pistoletto (p. 346) has been encoding the interaction between image, spectator and reflection since 1962. In the upheavals of the 60s, he brought his revolutionary stimulus to bear in the *azione povera* of street performances and combined museum-style casts with commonplace junk and rags. This anti-aesthetic stance was to turn in 1980 to powerful sculptures of polyurethane or marble in which the canon of Michelango's œuvre is fragmented and barbarised.

Penone (ill. above) is already one of the younger generation. His Mediterranean homage to a "vegetative culture", his intervention in the natural process of growth, are accompanied by skinprints of his own body. He explores the magic of the imprint, as a zone of contact with the outside world, in subtle strategies between identity and alienation.

Above:
Giuseppe Penone
Untitled, 1974
Plaster, body hair, slide projection
Collection of the Artist

Below:
Jannis Kounellis
Untitled, 1975
Fragment of plaster head,
propan gas cylinder, steel base,
fragment: 28 x 18 x 12 cm;
base: 125 x 40 x 40 cm
Private collection

The Delta of the Contemporary

The End of the Avant-Garde

At what point do we define art as contemporary? When it is produced by artists who are still alive and continually developing? When it involves the latest new movement to differ from all previous movements? Or is it simply a chronological question, no matter in what era the style may have originated? Although Louise Bourgeois works in a mode that follows on directly from Giacometti's psychological extroversion of sexuality in the 30s, she did not really come into her own as an artist until thirty years later. Born in Paris in 1911, she settled in New York in 1938. Her fragile, totemic works of the 60s possessed a delicate equilibrium. In the 60s she created "unconscious landscapes" of swelling body fragments with gaping wounds like vulva or bulbous, phallic protrusions. In her later work she presented, as though in miniature theatres, the neuroses and hysteria she derived from childhood experience of her father. *Precious Liquids*

(1992) is a dimly lit barrel which the spectator can enter, containing two wooden spheres and dozens of glass phials (ill. below) Suspended from bars, they hover over a metal-framed bed. According to Barbara Catoir, this is "an alchemy of memory sealed in vessels, barrels and cages, in minds and skulls".

What if the linear thread is lost in the pluralistic confusion of rival designs? What if related approaches no longer achieve a superficial stylistic similarity, as they did in the 60s? Then we no longer examine the external appearances, but the concepts behind them. What has frequently been hailed as the end of the avant-garde or even as the end of art history refers primarily to the end of an all-embracing epochal style. Perhaps our contemporary era begins at the point where style as the hallmark of a period disappears. This began to happen in the 70s.

This does not mean that there is no key challenge. However, it does mean that there are a number of con-

Louise Bourgeois
Precious Liquids (detail), 1992
Installation. wood and various materials. Height and diameter: 426.7 cm
Kassel, documenta 9 (1992)

Alice Aycock
The Angels Continue Turning
the Wheels of the Universe,
Part II, 1978
Wood, 700 x 700 x 500 cm (tower)
Made for the Stedelijk Museum in
Amsterdam (dismantled)

*"The works are a synthesis. They
give me pleasure. They turn back on
history and back on themselves.
Like the example of Christianity
outrunning the sign of the cross, the
generative ideas/sources outrun the
actual structures."* ALICE AYCOCK

trasting responses. In the 70s, artists reacted critically to
the onslaught of secondary images and illusions in which
the Baudrillardian *simulacrum* came to replace primary,
tangible reality. Sculpture, on the other hand, offers
direct experience. Much can be heightened to focus on
things and their traces as a means of defining the body
and its basic orientation within a given space. It is here
that we can find the common denominator of such diverse
directions as architectonic sculpture and the ever-widen-
ing annual rings that lead us from object to readymade
to traces of evidence. Herein lies the core of a dialectic
counterposition set against the previous decade.

The media world, too, began to make its presence
felt. In the course of the 80s, new sculpture revoked the
approach that appealed to direct physical experience.
Instead, the principle of depiction became predominant. Portrayal, illustration and fiction became key
strategies of presentation. Theatre, architectural models, simulated museum situations and showcases set the
tone. Suddenly, it became acceptable for sculpture to be
whimsical, literary, symbolic, narrative or even anecdotal. What classical modernism had regarded as detrimental to sculptural autonomy now became an independent quality in sculpture. In the post-modern 90s
this tendency grew. In recycling readymades and found
objects, their presentation became the *raison d'être* that
imbued the objects with meaning, lending them aura
and significance.

Another question arose in this connection. Following the intensification of exercises in individual perception, did the art of the 80s backtrack in the face of historic social developments? After the era of Arte Povera,
did sculpture return once more to the arena of memory
and recollection? Did sculpture gain in social impact
following the myth of autonomy and the self-referential-
ity of the medium? Did it develop critical models for
social action? And, if so, were these models a part of the
critical social and philosophical discourse, albeit with a
certain ironical detachment? Or was it only such artists
as Hans Haacke, Ilya Kabakov, Haim Steinbach, Robert
Longo and Olaf Metzel who touched upon the political?

Architecture, Sculpture and Forms of Action
In 1978, Robert Morris pointed out that white gallery
spaces could be taken in at a single glance, that they
were, in this sense, the equivalent of Minimal Art, anti-
spatial or un-spatial in terms of behavioural experience.
He made a point of correcting this demonstratively in
his own installations. At the Louisiana Museum near
Copenhagen he positioned large beams in the gallery
with mirrors between them to create a space so complex
and that it became a confusingly labyrinthine, fragmented challenge to the spectator's powers of perception and orientation.

Morris demonstrated what the younger generation
no longer wanted. No pure stereometry, no anonymous
space, no absorption in the institution of Art as represented by the white cube. Instead, he presented places
charged with psychology and specific behavioural patterns or with the memory and traces of daily use. "Interesting" places that take Smithson's concept of site speci-
ficity one step further, creating a transition from landscape to architecture. The important point here is the
new approach to space. Space is no longer derived from
the dissolution and crystalline fragmentation of volume,

George Trakas
Transfer Station, 1978
Wood and steel
Toronto, Art Gallery of Toronto

heightens the psycho-physical properties of a space to the point at which it begins to seem threatening. Long's *Walks* take the principle of following a path quite literally, just as his stone circles are archetypal sites. In the 20th century precursors range from Giacometti's *Board-Game* and *City-Square* sculptures around 1930 to Noguchi's *Playgound* and *Playmountain*. Now, such diverse artists as Alice Aycock, Claus Bury, Richard Fleischner, Dani Karavan, Per Kirkeby, Mary Miss, Walter Pichler, George Trakas and Micha Ullman devise their sculptural constructions and spaces as places of psycho-physical shelter or unease. Their corridors tunnels, labyrinths, towers, shafts, bridges and piers influence our behaviour to the point of evoking the claustrophobia of a maze from which there is no escape.

In Europe, the Austrian artist Pichler set an early example with his concepts of subterranean buildings, his mythically charged excavations and ritual architecture in the village of St Martin in Burgenland. In America, there was a renaissance of spatial forms that link idiosyncratic effects with universal symbolism, such as the labyrinth. Fully aware of the literary analogies in the works of Jorge Luis Borges, Octavio Paz and Lawrence Durrell, Alice Aycock (p. 561) constructed mazes and labyrinthian architectural meta-apparatuses as metaphors for the disorientation of modern life.

George Trakas (ill. above) dramatised exterior spaces with his bridges, piers and contrasting materials, exploring physical perception and he experience of walking. Israeli artist Karavan's *Hommage à Walter Benjamin* (p. 544) combines a steel shaft in the cliff face with a view of the sea, whirling water and horizon. For Micha Ullman, a fellow Israeli, the *Earth Chair* (ill. below left) is a concise formula referring to the body, excavation, occu-

as in the work of the Constructivists. Nor is it the equally weighted counterpart to volume, as in Minimal Art. It is neither ideal nor abstract, but operates instead with fundamental concepts of our architectural and natural surroundings. It is, in short, what Christian Norberg-Schulz described as the "existential space" in which we live and move. From here on in, many sculptures can be defined in terms of such categories as path and direction, place and centre, field and era, inside and outside, rather than according to such traditional concepts as material, mass, volume, composition and rhythm.

Some influences from the late 60s and 70s are still evident. Nauman's *Corridors* explore perception between irritation and hesitant self-assurance. Serra

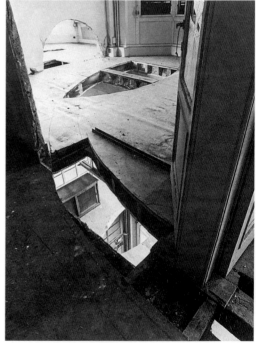

Micha Ullman
Earth Chair, 1983
Limestone, 280 x 280 x 400 cm
Tel Hai, Contemporary Art
Meeting

Gordon Matta-Clark
Office Baroque, 1977
Sections through a condemned
building
Amsterdam, I. C. C.

"Wood includes all the elements of origin, of growth and of time."
MAGDALENA JETELOVÁ

Magdalena Jetelová
Der Setzung andere Seite, 1987
Wood, c. 385 x 700 x 300 cm
Aachen, Ludwig Forum für
Internationale Kunst

pation, observation, shelter – a symbolic place whose instability also reflects the political situation.

The sculptures invite the viewer to become the user and, with that, to become a protagonist who, in the words of Merleau-Ponty, does not permit the space to affect him passively, but who absorbs and discovers its intrinsic significance. We have to experience this space at first hand, by walking it, climbing it, touching it. F. E. Walther realised this in the early 60s, summing up the concepts of "instructions for use" and "fields of use" without taking his fundamental phenomenology of the body to architectural or psycho-physical extremes.

Other artists posited their sculptures as architectural criticism. Gordon Matta-Clark (p. 562 below right) opened up condemned buildings by cutting sections representing a breakthrough in new forms of communication for a changing and more open society. Japanese artist Tadashi Kawamata (ill. right) uses outwardly spiralling welters of wooden planking to make a critical comment not only on architecture, art and the city, but also on categorisation, the ghettoisation of culture and the prevailing political power structures. Matta-Clark, would undubitably have approved.

Magdalena Jetelová (ill. above) who came to Germany from Prague in 1986, forces her huge wooden stairs, chairs and tables into tiny spaces. In Vienna, she cut a wall open with a chain saw and used computer control to bundle the light that flowed through it in the next room. At the opposite pole to the deconstructivist form of architectural criticism, are such artists as Gerhard Merz, who clarifies architectural sculpture into

ideal proportions and pure beauty, or the Danish sculptor Kirkeby, whose brick structures are variations on ancient temples and the Gothic traditions of his homeland.

The transition to the next generation is marked in 1980 by the Büro Berlin group centred around Raimund Kummer and Hermann Pitz. Other leading artists are also willing to cooperate. The connection between place and intervention becomes increasingly important. However, the intervention is now aimed at places not related to art, such as a factory or a railway station, to be infiltrated, interpreted and creatively developed. In Paris and Düsseldorf, Bogomir Ecker placed non-

Tadashi Kawamata
Destroyed Church Project, 1987
Wood, 10 x 12 x 20 m
Kassel, Garnisonskirche
(documenta 8, 1987)

doors was built on the grounds of the Auerpark in Kassel, illustrating a topographical view of a house between cellar and roof. Alongside it, a 60 cm wide steel pier by Trakas ran 200 m long into the park. At right angles to it was an unwieldy bridge of wood. Ascent and descent, a forward rush, a perspectival pull, the staccato of hurried footsteps, the subtle experience of one's own body in space – all these were typical of sculpture in the 70s.

In 1987, Thomas Schütte (ill. left) placed his bucket-like *Ice* pavilion at the edge of that same park. To the side of it, Heinrich Brummack placed his whimsical tent-like baldachins. In the middle was a circular ottoman by Scott Burtun, with plants growing in it. Near the Orangery was Klaus Kumrow's imaginative, perspectivally structured *Sedan-Chair*. Inside the Orangery was Armajani's decorative paraphrasing of doors, windows, stairs, a framework of plants. Everything was playful, narrative and either destined for actual use or ironically suggesting functionality. Ice cream and coffee were on sale in Schütte's pavilion. Instead of addressing the fundamental experience of self or orientation in space, sculpture was taking on an increasingly functional aspect. In this respect, it was narrowing the gap betwen sculpture and building, furniture or appliance. Whether this already heralded the beginnings of a social utopia, suggesting a return from the ivory tower of autonomy in society, remains a moot point.

Armajani and Burton see their buildings and model sculptures in this light. Armajani even cites the utopian visions of Russian revolutionary artists such as El Lissitzky and Klucis or the "enlightened" American architecture of the late 18th century. His *Dictionary of Building* isolates, in more than 200 models, such ele-

Thomas Schütte
Ice, 1987
Concrete, plaster and other
materials, max. diameter: 664 cm;
max. height: 526 cm
Kassel, documenta 8 (1987)

descript objects on the street, such as a dummy letterbox and a viewing apparatus in the late 70s. Norbert Rademacher develops this into subtle interventions between intimacy and the public sphere. Instead of exhibitions, we find stationary and temporary "situations" taking us into the next decade.

Furniture and Models

The shift in focus can be seen clearly in the difference between the documenta 6 art show of 1977 and the documenta 8 ten years later. In 1977, Aycock's wooden tower complex with its platforms, ladders and trap-

"My intention is to build open, available, useful, common, public, gathering places. Gathering places which are neighbourly. They are not conceived in terms of wood or steel but in terms of their nature as places at hand, ready to be used."
SIAH ARMAJANI

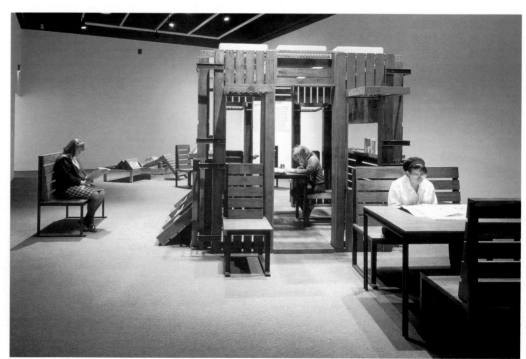

Siah Armajani
Sacco and Vanzetti Reading
Room #2, 1987/88
Steel, brick, aluminium, wood and
paint; various dimensions
Cambridge (MA), List Visual Arts
Center, M. I. T. (dismantled)

ments as wall, roof, window, stairway, cupboard, fireplace, "deconstructs" them and puts them together again according to formal rules. Since 1967 he has been designing bridges, reading-houses, reading-gardens, reading-rooms (p. 564 below) or picnic-gardens. In doing so, he has set new standards for a public art, which, for Armajani, means a useable and communicative art.

The pioneers of these furniture sculptures is Richard Artschwager (ill. above). In the 50s and 60s he even ran a professional carpentry workshop for individually designed items of furniture. Since 1962, each item of furniture is an independent sculpture. Tables, benches, mirrors and doors consist of cheap fibreboard and formica, in all manner of patterns and colours. They oscillate between reality and illusion–tangible ideas for reappraising established ways of seeing. In this way, Artschwager forges a link between Jasper Johns' critique of knowledge and the cool styling of post-modern Object art.

Not all the artists working within what Armin Zweite has described as the "broad frame of reference

between free object, architectural model, environment and furniture design" go for pure utility or exercise a critique of knowledge. Susana Solano (ill. below) mediates between the Catalonian traditions of iron sculpture and the younger generation. Compact planes and weight are set against grids, grilles and bars that render spaces permeable and full of correlations. The objects recall a bed, a table, steps or a doorway, but also a landscape, and thus keep our powers of association in suspense. Hers is the most important Spanish contribution to art since Chillida.

The winds of change swept through the world of German sculpture in the 60s too. Whereas the "hunger for images" led to enormously expressive wooden figures in the work of the painter-sculptors Baselitz and Lüpertz, a certain leaning towards the iconic led to rigidly simplified and narratively eloquent models by the generation that followed them. These artists either came straight from the Art Academy in Dusseldorf (Schütte, Reinhard Mucha, Katharina Fritsch, Ludger Gerdes, Wolfgang Luy, Ecker, Harald Klingelhöller, Thomas Virnich) or from Berlin (Hermann Pitz), Hamburg (Klaus Kumrow) or Munich (Stephan Huber and Albert Hien). The general designation "model" leaves room for misinterpretation, for these are not "models" intended to be constructed on a larger scale. Unlike archictecture, they do not designate a field of action, but a field of imagination. They stimulate our imagination in an interim zone in which attitudes, memories, associations and projections become fluid. They offer visual food for thought.

Armajani's perhaps somewhat naive belief in a return to social values by entering the world of utilisation is broken by the sceptical, ironical fictionality of their work. These artists use traditional rhetorical means in doing so. Stephan Schmidt-Wulfen has shown how the metonymic principle of *pars pro toto* exceeds other symbolic languages (metaphor, allegory). In Stephan Huber's work, a chandelier stands for luxury and

Richard Artschwager
Chair, 1966
Formica, 151 x 46 x 77 cm
Formerly Saatchi Collection, London

"I'm making objects for non-use: by use, I mean cups to drink out of, a spoon to stir with. By killing off the use part, non-use aspects are allowed living space, breathing space."
RICHARD ARTSCHWAGER

"The proportions of a sculpture, the material, the craftsmanship, have to correspond to the material: this is important. Nothing has priority, proportion, concept, material, craftsmanship have to be equal. The atmosphere exuded by an object interests me more than the object itself." SUSANA SOLANO

Susana Solano
Pervigiles Popinae, 1986
Iron, 303 x 342 x 105 cm
Kassel, documenta 8 (1987)

wealth, a barrow for labour and endeavour, both loosely associated with a feudal or capitalist society. Ecker's red megaphones and hearing appliances represent entire systems of communication and at the same time undermine them through their visibly simple construction. Hien uses miniature ships sinking in sand and aircraft sinking in water to demonstrate the Janus-headed nature of civilisation's progress. The first to present "models" with a critical content as opposed to those intended as preliminary studies, was Schütte, around 1980. His tongue-in-cheek scenographic installations, architectural designs and monuments marry potentially practical functionality with formal stringency and autonomy. Yet the "model" approach does not apply to all the sculptors of this generation.

Reinhard Mucha piles up pieces of furniture he find to create tipping, tumbling visual symbols for trains, aircraft or fun-fairs, in memory patterns that recall his childhood in the 50s. Felt (as a decorative material) and linoleum (for low-income housing) are pointers to his petty bourgeois youth. Yet he creates a balance that has all the artistry of a stage performance. Mucha reflects on the principle of presentation, museum and gallery like no other artist. A chair bears a base which bears a chair – the relationship between the base and the work could hardly be expressed and doubly inverted more elegantly. Unlike Mucha, Thomas Virnich destroys and mutilates his found objects: a doll's house, an instrument case, a rotting boat found on the banks of the Arno (ill. below left). He dimantles them, makes casts of voids, covers them, giving them a new and seemingly provisional order. This is an open, playful approach to the *object trouvé,* which Virnich certainly sees as an expression of human liberty in the spirit of Friedrich von Schiller.

Felix Droese and Olaf Metzel are moralists whose work is a far cry from such artistic speculation. Droese is primarily a painter, though his large-scale *House of Non-Armament* shown at the Venice Bienale in 1988 is a major work reflecting a profound sense of artistic responsibility: "Art, not as a question of style, but as a question of truth, as a question of humankind's future." In the more keenly critical atmosphere of Berlin, Metzel (ill. below right) shifts the focus from the existential to the specifically political: his themes address leisure culture, consumerism, racism, state violence and counterviolence, technology and media. Metzel is not driven by the passion that informs Droese's work, but by a rage against the injustice of the system. He channels this rage into a precise, destructive and formally sure-footed strategy.

Above:
Thomas Virnich
Amerigo Vespucci at the Scala,
1987/88
Wood, lead, aluminium, clay and
paint; 400 parts, c. 50 m²
Aachen, Ludwig Forum für
Internationale Kunst

Below:
Olaf Metzel
13.4.1981, 1987
Cordons, shopping carts and
stones; height: c. 900 cm
Berlin, Kurfürstendamm
(Sculpture Boulevard 1987)

His carefully targeted aggressive interventions in the public sphere are rare examples of a complex political art in Germany.

The fact that fundamental questions of sculptural language are being explored at the same time is evident in the work of two generations of steel sculptors: represented by Erich Hauser and Thomas Lenk, and the younger generation by Joachim Bandau, Ansgar Nierhoff, Heinz-Günther Prager, James Reineking, Edgar Gutbub, Wilfried Hagebölling. Hauser uses curved segments and pipe constructions, while Lenk uses spatial layering. Bandau's sculptures have a certain block-like reduction, exploring problems of shell and core, with expressive references to bunkers and fortifications. Nierhoff's folds and changing stereometries have affinities with certain aspects of Process art. Prager (ill. right) develops his square-and-cross sculptures from a formal system based on anthropometric modules of scale. Reineking, Gutbub and Hagebölling employ stringently syntactic planar sections. There is a plastic autonomy of form here, that has left its mark in particular in German cities.

Traces of Memory

In the 70s a different, "quieter" avant-garde had emerged. The extroversion of the 60s was followed by an introversion, a return to the private, memories of a personal or a different past. Reconstruction and documentation replaced art in the present tense. This had been foreshadowed by Beuys, Etienne-Martin, Nouveau Réalisme and Arte Povera. Yet the subtle experience of self filtered through the world outside was new. It set itself apart from Arman's sociology of the object and remained at a modest remove from the cultural-revolution claims of Arte Povera. On the other hand, parallels for self-questioning could be found in the medium of objects in the Nouveau Roman or in the poems of François Ponge.

The critic Günther Metken specified the line of observation. It was Metken, too, who coined the term "Spurensicherung" or "trace or clue-finding art" in this context. Accurate as the term may be, there was also a question of fictional traces and their reconstruction in the form of a model – a spectrum ranging from Nikolaus Lang to Christian Boltanski to Anne and Patrick Poirier. What may be regarded as evidence differs very widely indeed: objects, photographs, videos, drawings, texts. This accumulation of evidence thus overlaps with the history of sculpture and is not absorbed by it.

Here, too, presentation is an important artistic aspect. In this respect, we find a number of parallels between the 70s and the 90s. Collections and museums influence content. The seeming objectivity of inventory, archive or showcase is structured with pseudo-scientific mimicry and self-questioning. When Lang presents the relics of the dead Götte siblings – clothing, household goods, letters, animal bones, reports, maps, photos – in a grain chest (ill. right) he is, at the same time, examining his own childhood memories and himself within the context of place, time, past, present and imagination. When Boltanski (pp. 568 f), on the other hand, uses the school class photos of others, reconstructed toys, paper weapons and so on to recreate a fictitious childhood for himself, he still adheres to the same average childhood. He experiences it as a sociological model, or, to use the terminology of the 70s, as a sociological structure. Yet

Heinz-Günther Prager
Double Cross 14/89, 1989
Steel, burned; height: 130 cm,
diameter: 320 cm
Bonn, Foreign Office

Nikolaus Lang
Chest for the Götte Siblings, 1973/74
Grain chest, inserts, found objects, texts,
photographs, maps, 60 x 320 x 87 cm
Munich, Städtische Galerie im
Lenbachhaus

Christian Boltanski
Untitled, 1988
Three columns of 84 pewter boxes,
three framed black-and-white
photographs and three electric
lamps with cables, 235 x 50 x 23 cm
Private collection

Nancy Graves
Camels VII, VI, and VIII, 1968/69
Wood, steel, canvas, polyurethane,
animal skin, wax, oil paint,
244 x 274 x 121, 228 x 366 x 122,
and 228 x 305 x 122 cm. Ottawa,
National Gallery of Canada

class in Lyon, the Mickey Club–are rendered anonymous by the laws of statistical averages. The containers of the administratively ordered world extinguish the individual. A depressive silence merges archive, file and store, right through to the trauma of the Holocaust. The archives are also monuments to the dead.

Boltanski returns time and time again, with almost obsessive persistence, to the house of his childhood: French, non-religious, middle class. Lang draws sweeping arcs from his native Bavarian village near Oberammergau to Japan and the Australian aborigines. Just as Boltanski takes the approach of the sociologist, Lang takes the approach of the ethnologist among the collectors of traces of evidence. He delves deep into his childhood and, in his *Chest for the Götte Siblings* he collates a major work of early "Spurensicherung". He returns from a four-year expedition to Australia with a *Culture Heap* of real and fabricated stone weapons and other primitive paraphernalia, grids of nuanced sacred ochre earth and eerie wedge formations of hunting dingos and hunted kangaroos. Here, we have traces of evidence as a deliberate exploration of mythical thinking from the standpoint of Western consciousness.

Anne and Patrick Poirier (p. 569 above) began lyricising ancient archaeological sites in model situations in 1971. Eclecticism and imagination conjure up an urban repertoire from the Roman villa of Hadrian to the revolutionary architecture of Claude-Nicolas Ledoux. Dark night, glittering water, labyrinthine corridors conjure up the "myths, dreams and wishes of a collective subconscious". Freud's famous analogy of archaeology and the psyche, ruins and amnesia, takes on firm contours in imaginary architecture.

At the same time, the American artist Charles Simonds (p. 569 below) places the miniature villages of a fictitious "little people" in the niches of crumbling walls on the Lower Eastside, without any reference to Classical Antiquity, but as timeless, organic, spiraling or axial Ur-forms of architecture behind which there is a variety of different archaic social systems and matriarchal or

the search for the past is also the search for self. Museum-style presentation and encyclopaedic rationality are merely operative.

Boltanski is the paradigmatic producer of "traces of evidence". The showcases full of childhood documents are followed by huge, illuminated puppets, projections and shadows of marionetties in fleeting twilight, jerky movement or enchanting dance between vanitas and *varieté*. Later, he recorded his childhood in files, drawers, piled-up boxes, accessible through dimly lit corridors. Photos of the early years–the D. family, the school

Anne and **Patrick Poirier**
Ausée, the Black City, 1975/76
Charcoal, cork, water basin,
c. 1000 x 550 cm
Cologne, Museum Ludwig

patriarchal stages of development. Fictitious traces of evidence thus represent a regressive utopia against the New York skyline.

By contrast, Nancy Graves (p. 568 below) takes a more scientific approach to pre- and proto-history, though her reconstructions, including ice-age camels, still claim to be abstract sculptures, however true to life they may appear. "Spurensicherung" in the narrower sense of a quest to secure "traces of evidence" ranges from Dorothee von Windheim's auratic prints to Raffael Rheinsberg's history-laden series of found objects. More broadly defined, it also includes Anna Oppermann's hypertrophic chains of association in the form of sprawling ensembles of photographs and objects. Can we also include in this category the singular work of Christiane Möbus? Can her metaphoric juxtaposition of, say, fish and glass, or crow and stone, be seen as "associative ordering" in the spirit of Novalis? Can they be regarded as metaphors of flowing, swimming, flying that suggest departure and travel within a context of yearning for distant places and familiar home territory?

Others, such as the French artists Jean Le Gac, Didier Bay and Paul-Armand Gette, have moved away from the history of sculpture. Jochen Gerz, by contrast, the most radical sceptic of all, who casts doubt on concretion and communication much as Boltanski does, has moved ever closer to the field of discourse on monuments and memory – one of the most important sculptural tasks of the 80s and 90s. Precisely because he is a "conceptual" artist, a "writer" who writes books against the writing of books, he is able to open up a new view of a traumatically burdened past in his *Harburg Monument* (p. 570 above). The call for solidarity against "fascism, war and violence" which allows the stele to be submerged ever further into the ground, does not uphold the memory of the dead, but places the living under moral obligation instead. It adds a new paradigm to the discourse by addressing the way people deal with memory, rather than addressing memory itself. At the same

Christian Boltanski
Showcase II, 1972
Various materials, 20 x 122 x 71 cm
Private collection

Below:
Charles Simonds
Dwelling, 1975
Brick, wood, sand
New York, Queens, rooftop of
P. S. I. Building

Esther and **Jochen Gerz**
Harburg Monument Against
Fascism, 1986
Hamburg-Harburg, 1986

The Hamburg stela documented
at various stages of submersion
until it disappears completely in the
ground (far right)

Steinbach transform Duchamp's question. Bertrand
Lavier (ill. below) plays the established game of Object
art in which two quotations, when juxtaposed, produce
a new poetic sentence. A heater on an office cupboard –
a magically radiant sculpture, a fetish of commonplace
product, sculptural intensity and the bizarre. The
stronger the transformation, the more brilliant the irony.
Lavier's answer, then, is that art arises out of the physiognomic, expressive concentration inherent in the
object itself. Its forerunners are Duchamp's *Bottle-Rack*
and Picasso's *Head of a Bull* (p. 479) made of a bicycle
saddle and handlebars.

Haim Steinbach (p. 571 above) turns the founding
father upside down, as it were. He replaces Duchamp's
dispassionate approach by a strategy in which the object
is allowed to convey its full socio-cultural powers of
expression. Here, we find once more the important
principle of metonymics: an artificial limb or a necklace
on a velvet neck represent the entire body, while a child's
potty or school desk suggest forced cleanliness, obedi-
ence, repression. By placing the objects side by side on a
hand-made shelf, Steinbach gives the mass produced
item a firm position as art. By allowing the objects to
speak, he transforms the Duchampian readymade into
a wordless theatre of the object with a mordant social
critique.

The same is true of Mike Kelley's "socialist readymades", as Thomas Kellein has called them. They are
animals and dolls, presented in multi-media mode,
revealing the gender-specific games, the mythology of

time, it marks a departure from monuments and monumentality, and is, in this respect, an anti-monument that
sublates itself by disappearing. The invisible stele passes
the burden of memory back to us. This, too, secures
traces of evidence – within each individual.

Recycling and Readymade

In 1914, Marcel Duchamp placed a *Bottle-Rack* on a
pedestal. In doing so, he raised the question as to the
conditions under which art is created. He posed a critical question that seemed to bear within it the unequivo-
cal answer that art is the consensus regarding art. Yet
neither the question nor the answer have come to rest in
the course of the 20th century. Their intrinsic ambivalence is one of the most productive stimuli in modern
art. Attempts are still being made to somehow circcum-
vent Duchamp in order to imbue the readymade with a
new significance.

In the 60s, Assemblage and Accumulation expanded
the horizons of the objet trouvé, which thus entered a
new phase, that of the "adventure of the object". In the
words of Pierre Restany, the object became "entirely
dependent on the institutions of the museum and commentary". Because it was displayed in a museum the
mass-produced object was now elevated to the status of
a piece of art. Nevertheless, Object artists such as the
Frenchman Betrand Lavier and the American Haim

Bertrand Lavier
"5/9", 1986
Plaster and metal, 194 x 80 x 81 cm
Paris, Galerie Durand-Dessert

"I am conscious that in many ways today the distinctions between an elite as opposed to a more general audience are becoming blurred. There is an equalizing factor at work in the way things are produced now giving an illusion of a shared freedom, of one audience. This kind of dynamic interests me, and I attempt to deal with it in my work."
HAIM STEINBACH

Haim Steinbach
Untitled (Walking Canes, Fireplace Sets) # 1, 1987
Chrome and brass laminated wood shelf, aluminium, plastic and rubber walking canes; brass fireplace sets, 157.5 x 229 x 67 cm
FER Collection

everyday life in America and the mechanism of early childhood repression (p. 571 below right). They serve as an ideological model, soft and uncontradictory, just as parents hope their children will be, albeit at the price of repression.

Steinbach's American antipode is Jeff Koons (ill. below left). Opinions vary as to whether his work possesses the same critical clout and whether his bunnies, piglets and Cicciolinas (Ilona Staller), frozen as idols, in icy stainless steel, smooth porcelain or decroatve Venetian glass, represent an actual transcendence or merely a variation of that which they portray. Are they a double-coding of the simulacrum or a mere replica? Does the polished presentation of a cliché reveal the

"I believe that the taste is really unimportant. My work tries to present itself as the underdog. It takes a position that people must embrace everything."
JEFF KOONS

Jeff Koons
Pink Panther, 1988
Porcelain, 104.1 x 52.1 x 48.3 cm
Private collection

Mike Kelley
Estral Star No. 1, 1989
Fabric animals, 80 x 30 x 15.2 cm
USA, Collection of Mr. and Mrs. Melvin J. Estrin

machinations of the art market? All these issues are hotly debated. As a media star who introduced the iconography of kitsch to sculpture, with or without breaks and ambivalence, Koons is very much a figure of his time, an artist who rose with the art-boom that continued into the late 80s.

Young British Sculptors

An independent centre of gravity has emerged in the British Isles. Here, a keenly critical artistic consciousness has seen the emergence of a group of "young sculptors" to follow on from the "new generation" of the Caro school. Assisted by public funding and brought together in group exhibitions, they have in common with the German "model builders" a distinctly figurative tendency. Nevertheless, a thoroughly English preference for empiricism has led to direct inductive derivation of fiurations from the specific materials and objects in question. The result is a vibrant form of Assemblage, often witty and humorous.

It was Tony Cragg (ill. above) who led the way. As a teacher at the Düsseldorf Art Academy, he has also imported certain elements of this approach to Germany. Since 1976, he has sorted and arranged flotsam and jetsam, used, battered, thin-walled plastic articles and waste from rubbish tips, to create synthetically puzzle-like portrayals of the Union Jack, a submarine, a policeman – all of them totem figures of the consumer age. In the 80s he expanded his repertoire by adding commonplace wooden household items. He realigns the discarded objects so that they march off, ramp-like into their new existence. Later, Cragg was to turn to such traditional techniques as turning, welding and casting for oversized works situated somewhere between laboratory pistons and organic mutations, on the knife-edge between industry and nature.

Bill Woodrow (ill. middle), Richard Wentworth and Alison Wilding also use household items or office appliances, car parts or tools, to create effective metaphors, albeit in a rather different vein. Woodrow's visually stunning capriccios are full of references and associations, and their mordant wit belies their underlying moral stance.

The large-scale projects of younger artists beyond the established mainstream are based on the direct language of reality. In 1993, Rachel Whiteread cast in concrete the rooms of a condemned housed in the East End of London (where she had previously lived). The doors, windows and panelling form mouldings on the concrete block, which stands as a multi-facetted monument to the sum of all memories. Damien Hirst (p. 573 below right) takes quotation to the point of monstrosity, monumental as his works may be: a shark or half a cow swimming in huge glass tanks filled with formaldehyde. Does this mean that galleries and exhibition spaces are becoming fairgrounds and sideshows for today's notion of undecaying eternity?

Not all the young British sculptors work with found

Above: **Tony Cragg**
Middle Layer, 1984
Wood components;
length: c. 600 cm
Cologne, Kölnscher
Kunstverein

Middle: **Bill Woodrow**
Cello Chicken, 1983
Two car bonnets,
150 x 300 x 1300 cm
London, Saatchi Collection

Below: **Anthony Gormley**
Fathers & Sons, Gods & Artists,
Monuments & Toys, 1985/86
Lead, fibreglass, air, plaster;
258 x 68 x 48 cm, 103 x 35.5 x 25.4 cm
Private collection

objects and direct reality, however. Richard Deacon, for example, combines the sweeping curves of his cut, sawn, drilled and bonded sculptures with outer and inner convergences derived from the realms of linguistic theory. Anish Kapoor covers the sculptural form in pure pigment to draw the spectator's gaze into what seems like a void of infinite depth. Anthony Gormley (p. 572 below) also looks to Buddhism in emphasising the spirituality of the human body in the fluent transition from birth to life to death.

Intimacy and the Public Sphere

In 1974, in his widely debated book *The Fall of Public Man*, Richard Sennett diagnosed the end of public life and regretted the tyranny of intimacy. Surely such a tendency must have some bearing on sculpture, as the genre with the greatest public exposure. Do younger artists such as Kiki Smith and Robert Gober confirm Sennett's thesis of the prevailing *zeitgeist* by addressing the intimacy of the human body to the radical exclusion of everything else?

Kiki Smith casts bodies, male and female, in bronze, using wax, fabric, clay or glass, with protruding veins and arteries. They show signs of stress, give birth, withdraw in a foetal position, trailing traces of blood or urine or chains behind them like some ornamental floral frieze. Here are bodies that are biologically determined yet still capable of elevation to the status of biblical heroines (p. 574 above). Gober fragments the male

Kiki Smith
Untitled, 1990
Wax, pigments; life size
Courtesy Pace Wildenstein,
New York

body, positing it as the arena where the struggle between his own homosexuality and anti-gay social conventions is acted out. Body parts, such as a leg or lower torso, protrude through the wall, with plug-holes embedded in thighs or buttocks like some festering ulcer. These are dense, deep-rooted metaphors for isolation, exclusion, expulsion. Gober acts out the conflict quite literally on his own body (ill. below).

Yet that is only one side of the coin. On the other hand, we have been witness for a number of years now to a return of sculpture (in the broader sense) to the realms of public and political discourse and critique. Be it Jonathan Borofsky's *Hammering Man* – gigantic urban guardians whose huge black form is outlined against the sky at the entrance to Frankfurt's trade fair grounds, and other sites – (p. 573 below left), be it the ideological critique posited by Robert Longo, Hans

Haacke or Ilya Kabakov. In creating their anti-monument, Esther and Jochen Gerz have even developed a new paradigm of public art. The notion of the absolute autonomy of art, which is a modern hypothesis in any case, seems to be fading into uncertainty as the century comes to a close. At the same time, the various generations overlap. While Smith and Gober create their monument to the prevailing *zeitgeist*, other older artists continue to uphold the tradition of an emancipatory and critical modernism. This vibrant juxtaposition of contradictory approaches is very much a characteristic of the 90s. Longo (p. 573 above), like Kienholz, is a fascinated critic of the American way of life. He focuses on the ecstacies and horrors of the postmodern urban scene, its lawlessness, its corporate wars, the struggle for money and survival, the arms race, the illusion of the media. His direct and hard-hitting tableaux somewhere between photography and sculpture take the visual language of advertising, Hollywood, science fiction and computers and charge it with vehement criticsm. The work of Haacke, on the other hand, is still rooted very much in the elementarism of Zero art. From the anorganic to the organic, he moves on to social "real time systems". Originally geared to statistical polls of museum visitors, he later demonstrated the covert seizure of power in the cultural domain by corporations and the manipulation of the arts by the business world, and the connections with dictatorial and racist regimes.

Ilya Kabakov (p. 575) brought a touch of globalism to art following decades of East-West dualism. Not that his works do not convey a precise location. On the contrary, they refer specifically to their origins and the visual repertoire that entails. Kabakov, who came to the West from Moscow in 1987, has created a detailed monument to the last days of the Soviet system. His works chart the complete topography of a society, from the cramped

Robert Gober
Untitled (Leg), 1990
Wood, wax, cotton, leather,
human hair, 32 x 15 x 52 cm
Private collection

*"One of the most important protago-
nists in a gesamtkunstwerk is light.
Literally everything depends on light.
Its functions in the installation are
incredibly varied. Above all, it is
involved in creating the setting and
a distinctive, intensive atmosphere."*
ILYA KABAKOV

Ilya Kabakov
NOMA or Moscow Conceptual
Circle, 1993
Mixed media, round space;
diameter: 25 m, height: 3.5 m
Hamburg, Hamburger Kunsthalle

Communal Living Quarters to the permanently unfinished building site to the red propaganda pavilion. Realism and symbolism are united. He goes beyond Kienholz
in creating "installations" without surreal refractions,
which draw their own aesthetic laws and totality from
the visual impact, setting, mood, voices and memories.
It is, indeed, partly because of this consistent expansion
of the genre that Kabakov is so successful in his work.

As the 20th century draws to a close, everything
seems to remain open-ended. The delta becomes a
paddy-field in which we cannot even discern the various
directions. Not even the explanation that the present
invariably seems chaotic seems to hold true. Did we not
have a clearer view of things in the 60s and 70s, and even
in the 80s? The sign of the 90s is the lack of direction.
Some may choose to see in that the underlying pattern
for a post-avatgarde era. Is the avant-garde running out
of steam? Whether that triggers feelings of disorientation, resignation or freedom depends very much on
one's personal point of view. in the mid-90s, the artistic
design is no longer moving forward in sync with other
designs. The collective developments have either come
to a standstilll or have slowed to the point of invisibility.
Art – or perhaps just sculpture, or maybe only painting –
is no longer regenerating itself from the revolutionary
breaks and grand evolutionary lines of the past, but is
drawing instead on the wellspring of each individual work.

The fetish-word "new" is losing ground – perhaps
only temporarily – to the claim of "authenticity". Where
the driving force of a widespread movement is lacking,
the work must be sufficient unto itself. And so, the "stylistic unease" noted by Werner Schmalenbach does not
only represent a loss, but also a fresh opportunity.

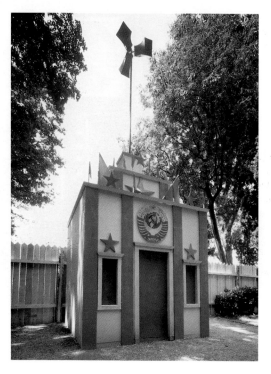

Ilya Kabakov
Red Pavilion, 1993
Installation; wood, loudspeakers,
music system, tapes,
500 x 920 x 460 cm
Cologne, Museum Ludwig,
Sammlung Ludwig

Activation of the Senses

"Everything disappears"

"You have to be quick if you want to see something. Everything disappears." If Paul Cézanne were alive today he would see his fears confirmed to an alarming degree. By the latter part of the last century it was becoming clear that the technical media developing in the wake of the industrial revolution could not fail to have a radical effect on traditional art production methods. Yet the majority of those interested in art remained unaware of these far-reaching changes. We are sitting on a mountain of artefacts that has piled up over thousands of years and are still busily trying to take stock of it, to order it and to understand it. In the meantime, ideas developed in our own era have been yellowing with age. So many experiments and innovations which have so enriched this century are just being forgotten. Others are simply stored in photographic or electronic archives or have entered the realm of myth, like the Actions of Joseph Beuys. Who was there when he explained the pictures to the dead hare (ill. right)?

Artists have been reacting to the extraordinary dynamics of this century with its wars and disputes, its major scientific and technological changes. They have turned hitherto accepted notions of aesthetic structures upside-down, tested them for their validity today and rejected them. They have adopted the new technical media of photography, film, video and computers as creative tools and as modes of communication. Today they are beating a path into electronic information systems in order to explore promising digital territory. Working with the limitations and potential of the new media, artists are searching for answers that are both creative and critical.

"Burn the Museums!"

The 20th century was barely ten years old when a determined handful of young artists set about dismantling high art in order to devote their energies to the changes in the real world. As Futurists, they were fascinated by racing cars "more beautiful than Nike of Samothrace," by "lurid electric moons," by "greedy stations" and by "broad-chested locomotives" – and "with compelling, inflammatory force" they hurled their 1st Manifesto out into the world. Their hope was to free the world from its cancerous proliferation of museums and libraries. The

Joseph Beuys
how You Explain Pictures to a
Dead Hare, 1965
Performance at the opening of the
exhibition '... irgend ein Strang ...'
in the Galerie Schmela, Düsseldorf, 26 November 1965

"A hare understands a lot more than many human beings with their stubborn rationalism ... I told him that he just had to look straight at the pictures to understand what was really important about them. Doubtless the hare knows better than human beings that directions are important." JOSEPH BEUYS

Futurists were the first to recognise how far the arts were lagging behind the reality of the fundamental scientific and technological changes that had affected contemporary life.

Neither traditional modes of artistic expression (media) nor their parameters seemed equal to the challenges of the present and the future. The Futurists used their Manifesto to put forward their provocative demands for an unlimited *tabula rasa* and a Futuristic "newly constructed universe." Even before the outbreak of the First World War, they were concentrating their efforts on finding themes and developing forms that were relevant to their era of heavy industry and accelerated communications.

In the initial Manifesto which came out on 20. February 1909, written by the Futurists' spiritual mentor, Filippo Tommaso Marinetti, the vitalist concept of art as propounded by Umberto Boccioni and Carlo Carrà was extended to include news technology as a model of a vital source of experience. In his manifesto, *Il Tattilismo*, (1921) Marinetti speaks out for the "devel-

Nam June Paik
Voltaire, 1989
Video sculpture, 300 x 200 x 55 cm
Courtesy Galerie Beaubourg, Paris

Jacques de la Villeglé tearing
down posters in Paris, 1961

opment and intensification of communications" and
wants to see "people linked into the network of the
media" with the ultimate aim of bringing human beings
back to humanistic values.

In 1933 Marinetti and Pino Masnata wrote in *LA
RADIA – Manifesto futurista* on the Futuristic use of the
new mass-medium of television. They viewed television
as the "perfect synthesis of synaesthetic dreams" with
radio simply being a transitional stage in the process.
"We now have at our disposal a television with more
than 50,000 dots for each large picture on the large
screen. In expectation of the invention of tele-touch,
tele-smell and tele-taste, we Futurists are perfecting
radiophony, which will multiply the creative genius of
the Italian race by hundreds and will put an end to the
time-honoured torment of distance and will establish
liberated words as its logical and natural mode of expression."

Demonstrative Gestures, Furious Protests and
Constructive Plans

Marcel Duchamp regarded the exhibiting of a signed
urinal (*Fountain,* p. 459) as a demonstrative gesture, taking radical issue with the principle of individual creativity and with art as an institution. All too aware of the
absurd horrors of the First World War and subsequent
socio-political developments, the Dadaists gave vent to
furious protest at the way the system was being propped
up by beautiful museum pieces and threadbare Philistinism. They transferred their artistic activities from the
studio to publishing houses and the stage. They entered
the public arena with provocative texts, ironic caricatures, aggressive slogans and pseudo-advertisements in
journals they published themselves. In a constant race
against the censor they sold these publications as part of
a Dadaist campaign. Radical left-wing artists and writers found a platform in publications by the Malik Verlag

Lucio Fontana perforating a canvas

*"The affected material reveals its
entire being, as it unfolds in time
and space and in the process of
changing goes through various stages
of existence. We ask that the primary
values of existence should be fully
understood."* LUCIO FONTANA

founded by John Heartfield in 1917 (p. 122). Hugo Ball,
striving for the Gesamtkunstwerk, included theatrical,
action-based and poetic elements in his exhibitions.
In 1921 Kurt Schwitters (pp. 130 ff, 461 f) set his sights
on a *Merzgesamtkunstwerk* that was to unite all art-forms
in one artistic entity in order to "blur the boundaries
of art."

During this same period, the Russian and East European avant-garde aims were constructive rather than
anarchic. They saw what they were doing as their part in
the construction of a new society, determinedly believing this society would be free from despotic power and
capitalist domination. Many artists gave up painting in
order to work in 'production art,' using photography,
typography and film to help build their new society.
People had to work for life, declared Alexander Rodchenko (p. 448), not just for palaces, churches, cemeteries and museums. "Down with art that is simply a means
of escaping from a life that is not worth living." Vladimir
Tatlin conceived his *Model for the Monument to the Third
International* (p. 444) as a political headquarters and as a
propagandistic communications centre.

In the Bauhaus, László Moholy-Nagy (p. 454), much
to the alarm of his colleagues, was energetically exploring the radically new materials, media and methods of
the time. "Nothing but optics, mechanics, the decom-
missioning of the static painting of the past," com-
plained Lyonel Feininger in a letter to his wife. There
was endless talk of cinema, optics, mechanics, projection and motion – even of machine-produced optical
slides, multi-coloured, in all the most beautiful colours
of the spectrum, that could be stored like gramophone
records.

Pioneering work in the field of abstract film was being carried out by figures such as Viking Eggeling, Hans Richter, Walther Ruttmann and Oskar Fischinger. With the ultimate aim of replacing the static character of painting with the dynamism of film, they addressed themselves to the practical and theoretical fundamentals of art in motion.

Forays into the Third and Fourth Dimensions

After the Second World War the prevalent negative mood meant that artists immediately "moved away from painting." The persecution and annihilation of recent years had put paid to the notion that art should relate as closely as possible to reality. On the contrary, the autonomy of art was now regarded as the guarantor for maximum personal freedom. This was seen at its most extreme in Action Painting which was often described as 'lyrical' rather than 'anarchic.'

When L'art informel was at its height, Lucio Fontana made some momentous forays into the third and the fourth dimensions and, in his *Manifesto blanco*, called for the rejection of traditional art forms. In his *Concetti spaziali – Spatial Concepts* (pp. 300, 301; 1949/50 onwards) Fontana introduced 'space' into the picture by perforating or slitting his canvases (ill. left). He determinedly opened up the picture surface to an encounter with a phenomenon that would soon be beyond the artistic capabilities of both painting and sculpture. "In our art the lines of the horizon multiply into infinity, into infinite dimensions. They derive from a striving for an aesthetic where the picture is no longer a picture, sculpture is no longer sculpture and the written page becomes independent of its typographical form": Fontana's words in his 1952 *Manifesto del movimento spaziale per la televisione*, where he was also speaking on behalf of his colleagues Alberto Burri (p. 260), Roberto Crippa (p. 260), Gianni Dova, Milena Milani and Benjamino Joppolo, expounded the notion of a form of spatial art that would be transmitted by television. After 1948, Jackson Pollock with his 'drip paintings' (pp. 268–274) developed the idea of 'walkable' pictures, which he created in a radically free manner – dripping, dribbling and even throwing liquid paint onto the canvases.

A low level of resistance and a lack of vision were to be the death of L'art informel. Rapidly and comprehensively commandeered by the new cultural establishment of the post-war years, this style of painting, with its inflationary, rigidly academic tendencies was heading for a crisis. The final blow was delivered by the so-called *affichistes* with their 'torn posters' and by the New Realists. 'Pure' painting was abandoned in favour of a new form of artistic activity centering on phenomena and objects from everyday life and using these for a whole number of different purposes: for tearing down – Raymond Hains (p. 329), Jacques de la Villeglé (p. 329), Wolf Vostell (p. 329); for movement – Jean Tinguely (pp. 499, 506–508), Otto Piene (p. 502), Heinz Mack (p. 502), Günther Uecker (p. 503); for collecting and accumulat-

Günther Uecker
Günther Uecker, Works 1960–1977
(Light Objects, Sculptures and Actions)
Still from a 16 mm video film by Karl Wiehn, 1977
Video tape, colour, sound, 45 mins
Cologne, Westdeutscher Rundfunk

"But tomorrow in our search for a new dimension in art, we will also have to search for new places where our art will be incomparable: places like the sky, the sea, the Antarctic, the deserts, with areas, like purpose-built islands, set aside for art."
HEINZ MACK

Heinz Mack
TELE MACK, TELE-MACK, TELEMACK, 1968/69
2 stills from a 16 mm video film
Video tape, colour, sound, 45 mins
Cologne and Saarbrücken, Westdeutscher and Saarländischer Rundfunk

in a quarry near Düsseldorf, where he exploded a white sports car belonging to the successful advertising photographer Charles Wilp, as well as a piano, a fridge and a television set. Afterwards, the remains of these dynamited status-symbols of civilisation were then fixed to panels of wood and exhibited in the Galerie Schmela in Düsseldorf.

Niki de Saint Phalle's *Shooting Pictures* (tirs/tableaux-surprises) were only finished when they had been shot with live ammunition and had, so to speak, yielded up their inner life, in the form of liquid paint. Spoerri's *Trap-Pictures* (tableaux pièges) were made from the left-overs from meals to which Spoerri would send out official invitations from time to time. The leftovers plus bowls, plates and ashtrays were then fixed on a base and hung up on the wall (p. 328).

Yves Klein's *Anthropométries* of the blue era, (p. 298) were created during a solemn ceremony in front of an invited audience and to orchestral accompaniment. The artist used 'live' paintbrushes in the form of three naked,

Georges Mathieu in Otto Piene's studio having just painted – in 70 mins – 'The Abduction of Henry IV by Archbishop Anno of Cologne when He was Taken from Kaiserpfalz to Kaiserswerth' for the opening of Mathieu's first solo exhibition in the Galerie Schmela, Düsseldorf, 11 January 1958

ing, dissecting, destroying and singeing – Arman (p. 518); for compressing – César (p. 519); for fixing – Daniel Spoerri; for wrapping – Christo (p. 519); for shooting (pictures) – Niki de Saint Phalle (p. 581 below); for playing, dismantling and reconstructing – Dieter Roth (p. 363).

By 1958, when Georges Mathieu (p. 258) took no more than 70 minutes to paint the picture *The Abduction of Henry IV by Archbishop Anno of Cologne when He was Taken from Kaiserpfalz to Kaiserswerth* in the Atelier Otto Piene (ill. above), *informel* was no more than a gimmick and Tinguely poked fun at it with his 'drawing and painting machines' (p. 499).

Restaurant in the Galerie J, Paris, März 1963. The Chef **Daniel Spoerri** talking to his guests

"In the exhibition 'Restaurant in the Galerie J' I showed some hundreds of kitchen utensils and turned the gallery into a restaurant.
a) The tables in the restaurant functioned as 'Trap-Pictures'
b) As in 'Krämerladen' items of food served as exhibits without being specially presented.
c) Each person was allowed, under license, to create 'their own 'Trap-Picture' form the remains of their meal ..."
DANIEL SPOERRI

Artistic Activity: a Splendid Spectacle

Whereas Pollock, in his own words, was using his canvas as an "arena," where painting functioned as part of his biography, Mathieu chose to perform feverish acts of painting on stage. Similarly Nicolas Schöffer (p. 582) organised a grand entrance for his kinetic, later cybernetic sculptures. He was the first artist to equip his works with photo-electric cells, sensors and microphones, and used electronic automatic control technology to construct systems that reacted to sounds and silence, to movement, light and darkness. In 1956 he installed his first cybernetic sculpture, *CSYP*, in the Théâtre Sarah Bernhardt on the occasion of the 'Nuit de la poésie,' and in the same year Mathieu painted his *Hommage aux poètes du monde entier* before an audience of 2000.

The farewell to 'pure' painting and the exploration of new artistic materials went hand in hand with experiments with gestural modes of expression. Under the gaze of the public, artists put on actions during which a work of art might be created. Some of the results have been preserved in museums as incunabula. Thus in 1963, Arman realised his most spectacular work, *White Orchid*,

RESTAURANT
DE LA
GALERIE J.
8, Rue de Montfaucon
PARIS (6ᵉ)   DAN. 30-65

A l'occasion de l'Exposition de Daniel SPOERRI
" 723 USTENSILES DE CUISINE "
la Galerie J. annonce l'ouverture d'un Service de Restaurant
du 2 au 13 Mars 1963
8. RUE DE MONTFAUCON — PARIS (6ᵉ)

La Galerie fermant ses portes sur l'Exposition chaque jour à 19 heures, le Restaurant ouvrira à 20 heures (fermeture hebdomadaire le Dimanche).

Aux Fourneaux le Chef SPOERRI "DANIEL"
Les Critiques d'Art assurent le Service

Attention : Le nombre des couverts étant limité à 10 par soirée (sauf le buffet exotique qui sera de 20 couverts) les amateurs éventuels sont priés d'indiquer le menu de leur choix, soit en téléphonant à DANton 30-65, soit en faisant parvenir le bon ci-joint sans délai au Service Restaurant de la Galerie J, le cachet de la poste faisant foi pour les priorités. (Les places retenues et non occupées demeureront à la charge de la personne ayant fait la réservation)

L'activité gastronomique du Chef SPOERRI "DANIEL" entraînant d'immédiates conséquences esthétiques (dans la plus pure orthodoxie du No veau Réalisme, le public est prié de venir juger sur pièces, le lendemain du jour de clôture du Restaurant : **le 14 Mars à partir de 17 h.**

VERNISSAGE DES MENUS-PIÈGES
COCKTAIL

Daniel Spoerri
Menu from the 'Restaurant in the Galerie J', Paris, 1963

female models (ill. right). Meanwhile Tinguely was making auto-destructive works that reversed the process of artistic creation. Between 1960 and 1962 he constructed elaborate machines, purely for the purposes of self-destruction.

Proto-Actions and Proto-Installations and the first Multiples

Despite their critical attitude to *informel*, the gestural works of the *affichistes* and the 'New Realists' were the apotheosis of the pictorial. A sense of a new beginning rather than of rejection characterised these artists' attitude in a time when the burgeoning economic miracle was marking both the end of the era of post-war reconstruction and the start of the adventure of space exploration. In this context their gestures, which were staged purely for their own sake, had more to do with liberation than explosive destruction.

In his 1959 manifesto *For Statics* Tinguely exhorted his fellow artists to "Stop 'painting' time. Cease building cathedrals and pyramids that crumble away like sugar decorations. Breathe deeply, live in the Now, live on and in time. For a beautiful and absolute reality!" He then abridged his manifesto, had 150,000 copies printed and dropped them from airplane over Düsseldorf. For his part, Yves Klein released blue balloons at an exhibition opening (Galerie Iris Clert, Paris 1957), 'sensitised' a room by his presence (Galerie Colette Allendy, Paris 1957) and followed a blue line (Galerie Schmela, Düsseldorf 1957). In 1961 and 1962, the ZERO artists, who had adopted Tinguely as their mentor, put on exuberant ZERO parties, namely light-demonstrations with ZERO soap-bubbles, ZERO girls, ZERO hot-air balloons, aluminium flags and sheets of metal with light shows, search lights and fireworks.

However, no artistic intervention on a limited time scale could have been more solemn or splendid than when Yves Klein put a guard in republican uniform at the entrance to *Le Vide* (The Void) when it was 'exhibited' at the Galerie Iris Clert in Paris in 1958. Arman provided something alien to a reply two years later with *Le Plein* (The Abundance). In its approach, this last work, which involved completely filling the gallery up with all sorts of objects until it was no longer possible to enter the space, was clearly light years away from Walter De Maria's 1968 room filled with earth. At the time De Maria was pointedly marking his withdrawal from the art business in the expectation of not needing it again. Christo and Jeanne-Claude made a more thought-provoking point in Paris 1962 when they reacted to the Berlin Wall with a street barricade made from piled up barrels. They called it *Iron Curtain* (Rideau de fer).

Still in the 50s Spoerri was making mobiles going back to Duchamp's notion of multiple reproductions. Confronted with the tactile serial objects that Spoerri produced under the name 'édition MAT' ('Multiplication d'Art Transformable,' 1959–1965), the hitherto passive viewer was now to become active, 'responding' to

art. Naturally enough, the artists who participated in the production of 'édition MAT' were above all those artists who were experimenting with light and movement, with investigations into seeing and perception. Amongst others these included Paul Talman, Yaacov Agam, Mack, Jesús Rafael Soto and Tinguely, but also the inventors of kinetic objects: Marcel Duchamp, Man Ray and Victor Vasarely.

Opposition to salon painting seems to have been the most important common denominator shared by a veritable concert of different artistic trends in the 50s – from Schöffer's somewhat totalitarian notion of art as all-embracing and with an aesthetic effect on both society and the environment, through Tinguely's confident

Yves Klein painting three nude female models blue: following this they imprinted their bodies on canvas according to his directions. Paris, Galerie Internationale d'Art Contemporain, 9 March 1960

Niki de Saint Phalle
Shooting Picture
(Shooting with a rifle), 1963
Munich, Neue Galerie im Künstlerhaus

sense of freedom that allowed him to create works that would self-destruct and disappear into nothing, to the miraculously radical work of an Yves Klein. The latter boldly exhibited the 'void,' sold shares in *Zones of Immaterial Pictorial Sensibility* (Zone de sensibilité picturale immatérielle, 1959) and even dared leap into the emptiness of the void of space itself (*The Leap into the Void,* 1960).

"It was an astonishing feeling, shooting at a picture and seeing how it changed into a new one. It was exciting and sexy but also tragic because we were witnessing simultaneous birth and death. It was a mysterious event, and everyone who shot found it utterly gripping."
NIKI DE SAINT PHALLE

Destruction and emptiness or silence – setting the tone for what was to follow, but the one too noisy and the other too quiet for the eyes and ears of the older generation, which was so busily involved with the economic miracle, firmly believing that it would last forever and that it could only improve our daily lives. What did they expect from art in a time when economic and political conditions had changed so rapidly and when peace could only exist in an awareness of the worst possible scenario?

Nicolas Schöffer
Space-Dynamic Sculptures, c. 1960
Mixed media, 107 x 90 x 75 cm
Paris, Musée National d'Art Moderne,
Centre Georges Pompidou

Intermedia: Happenings, Actions and Fluxus

John Cage and the Intermingling of Art Forms

In Europe in the 50s, the progressive mingling of individual art forms was an accepted part of 'conventional' art practice – but when it emerged in the USA around 1960 it took a much more radical form than anyone might have expected, and it was the composer John Cage (p. 583 above) who 'pushed open' this particular aesthetic door. In 1947 John Cage came into contact with Zen-Buddhism and he was as deeply affected by it, as was Yves Klein. Cage discovered the phenomenon of silence as the musical equivalent of pure nothingness; at the same time he became convinced of the equality of all aspects of Creation. Consequently he rejected any form of hierarchy, preferring to see all intentionally and unintentionally produced sounds and noises as equal. In addition, he was also guided by the Buddhist precept that everything should be able to develop freely. Finally, taking the principle of chance to its logical conclusion,

Cage freed himself from the obligation 'to want to seek out the best' by relying in all he did on the Chinese oracle book, the *I Ching*.

In a sound-proof room at Harvard, Cage discovered that there is no such thing as pure silence. A year later, in 1952, he premiered his legendary composition 4'33". It has three movements called 33", 2'40" and 1'20" and the performer David Tudor 'played' the piece by closing the piano lid at the beginning of the movement and opening it again at the end. The sounds that the audience had come for were not to be heard. However, as a result of this, the audience became aware that it was getting noisier and noisier in the auditorium and that they were the ones making the noise.

Cage's treatment of sound broke a whole number of taboos. Yet he was never destructive. On the contrary, Cage's work was about integration. He did not separate the auditory sense from the other senses. Instead of writ-

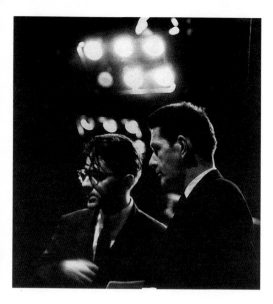

ing music he organised sounds and events. His scores –
for example, his *Water Music* for prepared piano, radio, 3
pipes, waterball, 2 water-containers, a deck of cards and
wooden stick (1952) – contain instructions beyond those
referring to the sounds, as to how they could be performed interestingly. Thus his performances took on
something of the character of multi-sensory theatrical
events.

Cage became a key figure at the interface of various
art forms. In the late 50s he was teaching at the New
York School for Social Research, where he communicated to his students a sensitivity towards complex situations, taught them about the principles of chance and
discussed ways of organising sounds and events. This
was to a large extent the source of the many very different 'action arts' that then went down in art history as
'Happenings' and 'Fluxus.'

Allan Kaprow's Happenings

Allan Kaprow, who was a student of John Cage's and the
inventor of the Happening, developed Cage's concept
of lived experience and the experience of perception,
taking it to the point where reality broke into art, as it
were, in a form that embraced the totality of life. His
first publicly performed piece, *18 Happenings in 6 Parts*
(1959) comprised film and slides, dance, music and language, a sculpture on wheels, concrete music and sound
constellations, the production of a painting and various
banal acts. In this piece, Kaprow mingled visual material
and events in the way that the Dadaists had once done,
when they had constructed their collages. Yet no single
person was in a position to take in the whole event.
Kaprow confronted and overwhelmed his public with
simultaneous events in three separate spaces.

As far as Kaprow's early Happenings were concerned, the public either had very little part in them or
none at all. In his 1961 *Spring Happening*, the public were
put into a narrow tunnel with peep-holes. They were

then subjected to the droning noise of a lawn-mower
and the entrance was blocked with an over-sized ventilator. There was the sound of car horns and drums. When
the noise had reached its peak the walls of the tunnel fell
away and the public could leave the room. Later Kaprow
developed a different type of Happening, where the
public and the artist participated to an equal degree. For
Yard (ill. below), the artist collected together a huge
number of tires in a yard, where the public could
actively move about or just be passive observers. In the
late 60s Kaprow devoted himself increasingly to the
question of interpersonal relationships. He developed a
form of 'activity' for a small number of participants
which had, if anything, an intimate and playful feel
about it, and which needed no public.

Wolf Vostell and the Therapeutic Disaster

Rather than creating tangible, material works, Happenings produced lasting effects and experiences in the
minds of the participants. According to the curator
Henry Geldzahler they also had group-therapeutic
effects. At any rate, he maintained that whenever he had
taken part in a Happening he was much easier to get on
with even ten days later.

As opposed to the 'loose structures' of Kaprow's
Happenings, Vostell's instructions for his Actions
seemed authoritarian and hampered any initiatives by
the participants. In fact, one is more likely to do his
activities justice if one views them from their destructive
side. Vostell always worked with shock tactics, generally
in a demonstrative form, more directed towards confrontation than real participation. When he looked
back, he felt that his childhood had been dominated by
the sight of dying people. He experienced his own first
'Happenings' at the age of eight or nine when individuals were thrown back on their own resources and had to
find shelter from horrendous air-raids as best they
could.

John Cage (right) in the Sixties
with his favourite interpreter,
David Tudor, 1960s

Allan Kaprow
Yard, 1961
Environment with car tires etc.
Remscheid, Feelisch Collection

Wolf Vostell
Neun-Nein-dé-collagen, 1963
Happening in nine locations in
the town of Wuppertal (Detail),
Wuppertal, 1963

Wolf Vostell
Neun-Nein-dé-collagen
(Partitur), 1963
Pencil and coloured crayon on
paper, 70 x 100 cm
Wuppertal, 1963

Vostell's art lives and breathes brute force. Traffic
accidents and the thought of a plane crash immediately
after take-off gave him the idea of using the term 'décollage' ('unsticking' or 'take-off'). Since that time he
would appear to have been working on destruction –
using décollage, blurring, distorting and manipulating
it. In the late 50s and early 60s Vostell started tearing
down posters in Paris.

Next he took to blurring images in illustrated journals, manipulated television sets (*Television Decollage*,
New York 1963), caused interference on a television
screen (*Sun in Your Head*, 1963), the burial of a television
(as part of the "Yam" Festival, 1963) and caused a loco-
motive travelling at 80 miles an hour to smash into a
Mercedes standing on the railway track. Finally, he shot
a television while it was turned on (Wuppertal 1963).

Viennese Actionism

From Vostell's traumatic disasters, which were generally
directed against inanimate objects, it is only a short step
to the 'abreaction-games' in the 'Orgies Mysteries
(O.M.) Theatre' devised by Hermann Nitsch (p. 585
below), or the 'material actions' put on by Otto Mühl,
the self-decorations and self-mutilations of Günter Brus
(p. 585 above), or the auto-destructive actions of Rudolf
Schwarzkogler (p. 586). There could be no stauncher
refusal to gloss over society's dark chasms, and artists
like Vostell and the Viennese Actionists showed us that
large tracts of Western society no longer have the necessary rites to deal with trauma and mental stress.

Of course Nitsch's Action Theatre derives from the
Action Painting of *informel*. And a similar connection
could reasonably be made between the use of dead
animals, the attacks on organic materials and Fontana's
attacks on the picture surface and the New Realists'
appropriation of reality. In order to understand the phenomenon of the Viennese Actionists it is essential to
bear in mind the extremely conservative social context
in which they were working.

Nitsch saw his 'abreaction-games' as relieving inner
drives during which pent-up energies would come to the
surface and become part of the subject's conscious
awareness. In its most disturbing manifestation, the
breaking of taboos turned from gestural painting and
self-decoration into the self-mutilations of Brus. It was
in the mid-60s that Brus – who has been called the
'Father of Body Art' – made the transition from fictive
to actual self-mutilation, while Schwarzkogler created
tableaux of bandaged bodies, demonstrating his hypersensitive ideas on colour, proportions and the spatial
relations between objects.

In contrast to Happening and Fluxus artists, the
Viennese Actionists were alive to the possibilities of
photography and film, and used them for their own purposes. Their interest, which was at its height in the 60s,
can partly be traced back to the fact that Austrian avant-
garde film was already well-established at the time. But
probably the main reason for their interest in transpos-

ing their work into film and photography was their distinctly pictorial, painterly approach.

The Phenomenon of Fluxus

"Fluxus-art-fun should just be simple, entertaining and undemanding, it should be about insignificant things, it shouldn't require special skills and countless rehearsals, it should have no commercial or institutional value" – the words of George Maciunas, who devoted himself to the phenomenon of Fluxus as its self-styled chief co-ordinator, having also given the movement its name. Fortunately Fluxus never could be reduced to some common denominator, due largely to the resilience and waywardness of its own protagonists, due also to its international dimensions and also to its indeterminate position amongst the other arts. Fluxus resisted definition: it was neither painting nor sculpture, neither theatre, literature, film nor music, even although it was born in the environs of the musical avant-garde and would have been unthinkable without John Cage. It was the first inter-medial art form since Dada that transcended and mingled individual genres.

While most Fluxus artists were part of the experimental avant-garde in literature and music, they had originally come from very different professional backgrounds. First the New Yorkers: Maciunas, an immigrant from Lithuania was a trained artist, art-historian, architect and musicologist. He served as a graphic designer in the US Army in Wiesbaden where he organised the Fluxus 'Internationale Festspiele Neuester Musik' in 1962. Benjamin Patterson was a classical double-bass player with the 7th US Army in Germany and with the Ottawa Philharmonic; George Brecht worked as a chemist and Robert Watts as an engineer. Yoko Ono arrived on the New York Fluxus scene having studied both literature and music; Alison Knowles came from painting; Dick Higgins from music and graphic design. Charlotte Moorman (Nam June Paik's partner for many years) was a cellist, Al Hansen studied social pedagogy, Joe Jones studied music. Takako Saito came to New York from Japan in 1963, uniquely able to arouse creative powers in others by his playing.

In Cologne there were Nam June Paik, a trained composer, and Wolf Vostell, a graphic artist in advertising; in Berlin there was Tomas Schmit, of no fixed occupation. In Paris were Robert Filliou, nomad, economist (by training) and poet (by vocation), and Emmett Williams, also a poet. Nice was and still is the home of the artist-shopowner, Ben Vautier. From Copenhagen came Arthur a.k.a. Addi Köpke, artist and avant-garde gallerist, and from Prague came Milan Knižák, who had trained as a painter.

Fluxus was not a movement, if one ignored the nomad-like wanderings of the artists who came into contact with it. It was a phenomenon that appeared on an international level. In some places it was more concentrated at certain times, perhaps because a certain person or institution was emerging there at the time

Günter Brus
Self-Decoration, 1964
Action. Vienna, Atelier Otto Mühl,
December 1964

Hermann Nitsch
Scene from a performance by the
Orgies Mysteries Theatre, 50th
action, 1975. Prinzendorf (Austria),
Schloß 1

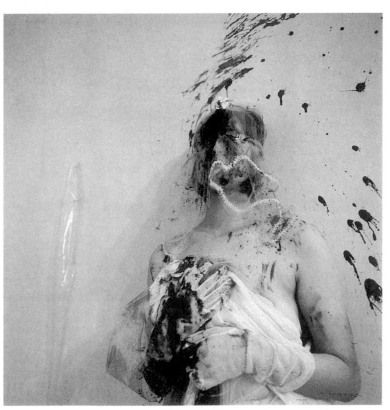

Rudolf Schwarzkogler
Wedding, 1965
Action, 6 February 1965 Vienna,
Heinz Cibulka's flat

(Proto-Fluxus involving Cage's students in New York from 1958–1960; Nam June Paik and Mary Bauermeister's studio and the studio for electronic music at the Westdeutscher Rundfunk in Cologne), which meant that Fluxus events would be taking place there (1962 in Wiesbaden, Copenhagen and Paris, 1963 in Düsseldorf, Amsterdam, Den Haag, London and Nice), or that Fluxus protagonists lived there.

What did Fluxus have to offer? No collages of events, time and materials as in Happenings, no group-dynamic processes, no therapeutic systems. Instead it offered concerts consisting of sequences of simple, self-contained acoustic and visual acts, and were called 'events' or sometimes even 'activities.' They could be performed with or without their originators, in front of an audience, occasionally with the audience, but very seldom completely without an audience. In addition, Fluxus sometimes offered apparently oddly constructed objects and 'instruments' such as Paik's *Ur-Musik*, a wooden packing chest strung with simple wire (strings) and with a removable box mounted on the front that could be rotated and that produced sounds (ill. below). From 1962 onwards George Maciunas produced countless little objects and editions which were extremely cheap and could be ordered by mail or bought in 'Flux-shops'. Amongst these were a number of games, so-called 'Flux Kits' (p. 587 above right) leatherette suitcases with a representative selection of Fluxus objects by various artists, special Fluxus postage stamps and rubber stamps (Mail Art), signs and anthologies, artists' books in low print-runs, pamphlets and posters, audio cassettes and films.

Nam June Paik
Ur-Musik, 1961
Object Instrument, 52 x 92 x 68 cm
Vienna, Museum moderner Kunst,
Stiftung Ludwig

George Brecht
Water Yam, 1963–1965
Multiple; Acrylic box with cards,
13 x 18.2 x 3.1 cm
Remscheid, Feelisch Collection

Variations for Butterflies and Double-Bass

Some Fluxus events were playful and high-spirited like La Monte Young's *Composition 1960 # 5* with butterflies that were supposed to be released from the room where the performance was taking place. Other Fluxus events could be facetiously shocking like Paik's 'peeing competition' called 'fluxus contest' or his piece, *One for Violin* where a violin was raised slowly upwards with the utmost concentration, the light went out and suddenly the violin was smashed (1962). Philip Corner's *Piano Activity* (ill. below) lasted for several performances during which a grand piano was painstakingly dismantled, little by little.

Fluxus events were spontaneous in so far as their execution depended on participants and materials, both present and absent. Furthermore, the scores that were used left the interpreters plenty of room for manoeuvre. In his *Variations for Double-Bass*, (1962), Patterson pulled a long rope made of old rags and bits of cable out of the body of the bass, drew it as quickly as possible through the strings and then stuffed it back in again. Paik interpreted La Monte Young's *Draw a Straight Line and Follow It* by dipping his tie and his hair into a chamber pot filled with ink and then drawing a line on strips of paper lying on the floor: *Zen for Head* (p. 588 above). Fluxus events could be succinct like George Brecht's word-event *Exit*, which ended the Fluxus concert on the first day in Düsseldorf in 1962. Some events 'performed themselves.' Williams, appointed by Maciunas as the Fluxus co-ordinator in Europe, created his concrete poetry by letting mice run around with fluorescent letters on their backs.

Brecht also originated events that anyone could put on for themselves. From 1962 onwards, Maciunas put his scores on little, square cards and offered these for sale in so-called 'Water Yam' boxes (ill. above). These also included instructions for building an 'instrument' that would make 'droplet music' or a 'droplet event.' In 1970 Wolfgang Feelisch realised his eponymous event with a water tap and water pipe mounted on a piece of wood with a bowl to catch the water (p. 589). Another card, entitled *Symphony*, has a hole in the middle that one can look through. Whatever one sees through it, that is now a "symphony" of the passing moment and is unquestionably a matter of perspective.

George Maciunas
Flux Kit, 1964
Suitcase with representative choice of multiples produced by George Maciunas
Stuttgart, Staatsgalerie Stuttgart, Archiv Sohm

"Fluxus-art-fun should just be simple, entertaining and undemanding, it should be about insignificant things, it shouldn't require special skills and countless rehearsals, it should have no commercial or institutional value."

GEORGE MACIUNAS

Philip Corner
Piano Activity, 1962
Action, Internationale Festspiele Neuester Musik
Wiesbaden, Städtisches Museum

Infected by the Fluxus Virus

Fluxus came into being with the 'concerts' and festivals that Maciunas organised in 1962/63. Yet opinion differs as to whether its origins and its end can be dated with any real certainty. Fluxus turned out to be too unwieldy and undefined to fit conveniently into any particular art-historical compartment. "Fluxus has not been invented yet," as Emmett Williams said. Perhaps it has not yet been invented because it is impossible to take out a patent on phenomena which are more a state of mind than anything else. "A long history with many knots" was the description used in the comprehensively documented exhibition in the Institut für Auslands-beziehungen in Stuttgart in 1994, dedicated to 32 years of Fluxus in Germany.

The immense influence of Fluxus is unquestionable, but there has been as yet little research into its detail. Joseph Beuys soon became a thorn in its flesh and sub-sequently established a position that was distinctly dif-ferent from Fluxus as propagated by Maciunas. As Uwe M. Schneede put it, Beuys was not the one for short,

focused events where materials and objects were employed for their own sake and freed of any other sig-nificance. On the contrary, he piled them high with autobiographical, historical and mythical meaning. Nor could Beuys do anything with the required anonymity of Fluxus. His Actions were imbued with his personal experience of life, suffering and happiness – coloured in every sense with his own range of expression, his biogra-phy and his body language.

Nam June Paik, the 'Father of Video Art,' was hugely influenced by Fluxus. Born in Korea, he had studied piano and composition in Freiburg, and moved into Fluxus with theatrically staged performances of com-positions and absurd acts of aggression that went far beyond Cage. Paik wanted to disturb and to shock and, at the same time, he was searching for his own mode of expression. This was perhaps what induced him to cut off his highly-respected teacher's necktie during the Action *Etude for Piano (forte)*, (1960). However, the trig-ger for his decision to work with television was not his destructive leaning, which in itself, sets him clearly apart from Vostell. The deciding factors were his technical skills in electronics (driven initially by sheer curiosity) and his knowledge of the experiments and theories relat-ing to the production of abstract, tele-visual images by the painter Karl Otto Götz.

Paik, unlike Vostell, was not concerned with the 'box' as an object. He was much more interested in the aesthetics of the images that he was creating and affect-ing by his own interventions, that is to say, he was inter-ested in the software. These then are the circumstances which meant that Paik could take his work beyond Fluxus and usefully extend it to video art. Thus it is hardly surprising that Paik was one of the first to buy the new portable video recorders that came on to the market in 1965, or that in 1970 he and Shuya Abe (p. 590

above right) carried out pioneering work on video-syn-
thesisers.

Fluxus has been a rich source of inspiration to young
artists. Sigmar Polke's (pp. 387 ff) *Potato Machine* of 1969
and Rosemarie Trockel's chewed and silvered *Mouth
Sculptures* of the early 90s positively exude the spirit of
Fluxus. Concept Art, Performance Art, Video Art and,
not least, the remarkable revival of Multiples are all
unthinkable without Fluxus. The only regret is perhaps
that the original Fluxus objects and Multiples, despite
their apparent waywardness, have nevertheless largely
fallen prey to museums and galleries. But does that
mean that Fluxus failed?

The Principle of "Permanent Creation"

Why is it that artists are held solely responsible when
their apparently promising endeavours in fact have no
real impact on everyday life? Artistic works are about
communication, whatever form this may take – as an
idea, transient or tangible – and are intrinsically dependent on an opposite number. This even applies to a
phenomenon like Fluxus which managed to tear down
the barriers between supposedly 'high art' and a much
broader public. Filliou went a step further when he said:
"Whatever I say is meaningless if it does not inspire you
to follow up my ideas with your own."

Filliou, whose motto was 'permanent creation,' saw
creation as a process that every human being could take
forwards. He viewed himself as providing the necessary
tools for this, namely 'imagination' and 'innocence.' In
1969 he stored these in the form of a neon sign in a *Permanent Creation Tool Shed* (ill. above). His message was
that there is no need for a technically complex array of

tools for creating the world: the most important thing
was that a person should use these two, intrinsically
childlike qualities – imagination and innocence.

As far as disseminating his ideas was concerned, Filliou was always restrained and relatively low-key. He was
the epitome of casual and wrote above his door: "Le
vagabond de l'art est *toujours* en voyage. Laissez nom et
('et' was then crossed out and replace with 'sans')
adresse, il vous touchera *un jour* sans doute. (*par télé-
pathie*)." Anyone trying to get in touch with the 'vagabond of art' was kindly requested to leave behind their
name without address and, no doubt, one day Filliou
would touch them, if only by telepathy.

The Message of Felt TV

In contrast to Filliou, Beuys devoted his entire life and
energy as an artist to propagating his own inner convictions. It would simply not have occurred to him to put
his message up on a sign above his front-door. He knew
of more effective tools and channels. Beuys capitalised
first and foremost on his own charismatic personality
(in Actions from 1963 onwards), then after 1965 he made
multiples and following this turned to the mass-media.
He carried out over thirty Actions in the period
1963–1985, mostly in the 60s. These were accompanied by
tireless appearances as a speaker, in interviews and discussions. He took part in documenta 5 in Kassel in 1972
with his "Büro der Organisation für direkte Demokratie
durch Volksabstimmung". For 100 days he sat there
with two colleagues and discussed issues with interested

Robert Filliou
Permanent Creation Tool Shed,
1969
Garden shed with neon installa-
tion, 250 x 300 x 300 cm
Remscheid, Feelisch Collection

*"I could never do the things that
people who have been to art school
do. I doubt whether they can do
what I can do. But my child can."*
ROBERT FILLIOU

George Brecht
Drip Music (Fountain), 1963–1970
Oak with brass and bronze
installation, 200 x 35 x 8 cm
Remscheid, Feelisch Collection

*"A source of dripping water and a
container are arranged so that the
water falls into the container."*
GEORGE BRECHT

Nam June Paik
Sonatine for Goldfish, 1975
Old television casing with
aquarium

Fred Barzyk, Shuya Abe and **Nam
June Paik** at the synthesizer in a
studio at the WGHB-TV station in
Boston, 1970

Joseph Beuys
Felt TV II, 1968
Television set made by Nordmende,
89 x 62.5 x 64.5 cm with felt-covered
screen, 37 x 47 cm; internal aerial,
felt-covered wooden panel on the
wall, 58 x 90 x 2 cm
Kassel, Staatliche Museen Kassel,
Neue Galerie

visitors: ranging from his attitude to what being human
means, through the creativity that results from individual freedom and the related notion of 'democracy
from below,' to the matter of pay for housewives and any
other questions that visitors might put. At 3 o'clock on
one of the 100 days, Dirk Schwarze from the *Hessisch
Niedersächsischen Allgemeine*, a local newspaper, noted
down: "560 visitors so far. A young girl comes up to
Beuys and says, 'This is art?' – Answer: 'A special kind
of art. You are allowed to think too."

Beuys made use of the mass-media just as he used
his multiples, namely as a vehicle for spreading his concept of 'social plastic.' In June 1977, when he had the
chance at the opening of documenta 6 to participate in a
live satellite broadcast and to make whatever use he
liked of television, he decided simply to deliver a speech.
Whatever form of address Beuys chose, his over-riding
concern was to spread his own 'extended concept of art'
which was to go beyond mere aestheticism and to
embrace all areas of life.

Consequently he also viewed his own artistic activity
as a 'far-reaching educative programme' for freedom.
This was effectively reflected in *Felt TV*: a television
Action first performed in 1966 and then again in 1970 for
Gerry Schum's television exhibition, *Identifications*.
"Turn the television away, look at yourselves!" With
these words the art historian Wulf Herzogenrath got to
the heart of the message of *Felt TV*. Sitting in front of a
television screen covered in felt (ill. left) and boxing
himself in the face, Beuys symbolically negated the one-
sided broadcaster-viewer relationship, so that something "could develop in radically new circumstances."

At the Interface of Art and the Media Industry

Land Art

Richard Long did not stop walking across the field until his footsteps had beaten a clearly visible track. *A Line Made by Walking* (ill. right) was his first 'walked' sculptural work. In order to present it to the public he had to photograph it. A year later, in 1968, he undertook *A Ten Mile Walk on November 1.* There were not even any footsteps left behind after this walk. Afterwards the only aesthetic experience offered to the viewer was a map in landscape format with the route of the walk marked as a straight, diagonal line crossing the whole area. The art historian Antje von Graevenitz has described the actual work as lying between the documents. It has to be "(re)-constructed" in the viewer's imagination.

The need to explore new 'work'-spaces outside of the studio presented artists with a problem. How should such expansive works be presented to the public? What form should these artistic works take in a time when the notion of the 'art-work' as a commercially viable product had been so seriously discredited? Different artists found different solutions, some taking a conventional path, others taking a more unusual route. But the results were seldom as brittle and conceptual as Long's ten mile walk. For example Dennis Oppenheim's *snow projects* (p. 548) are practically all presented as collages, consisting of coloured or black and white photographs, cartographic materials, aerial shots and a short typewritten description of the work itself.

Michael Heizer (p. 545) presented his at times extremely transient and inaccessible works partly on mural-sized coloured photographs which a contemporary critic mockingly described as "big, brightly coloured landscapes." Robert Smithson devised a possibly more elegant solution to the problem of how one should bring works created in inaccessible places to the public: he made the question of representation part of his own strategy as an artist. He used photographs, plans and sketches as intermediaries and transferred items, such as pebbles, from the 'site' of the work to the exhibition space ('non-site'). Thus he spared his public tedious pilgrimages to the sites where he had been working – that is, until he created his *Spiral Jetty* in 1970, the first of his stunning outdoor sculptures (p. 546).

When on-site artistic activities only produced perishable results, or wholly intangible results, conven-

tional modes of expression such as plans, sketches or work-descriptions and photographs came up against their natural limitations. A number of ambitious storyboards by Smithson (usually as drawings) have survived, although only one could ever be realised – a 30 minute 16 mm film called *Spiral Jetty* (1970). In 1967 he was thinking about using "the real land as a medium" and then to televise his work and broadcast it throughout the world.

Walter De Maria pursued a similar idea in the expectation that in the future he would be able to do without museums and art galleries altogether. In 1968 he made a dramatic exit from the 'art business' because he had bigger things in mind. But before he went into the desert to start work on his *Three Continents Project*, he planned to bury the Galerie Friedrich in Munich in earth (p. 547). Regrettably, De Maria was not able to find a sponsor for his project that was to have been photographed from a satellite and broadcast via television. It was never realised and thus shared the fate of so many similar projects which failed because of the conditions of production and distribution that prevail in the film and television industry.

Richard Long
A Line Made by Walking, 1967

By 1970 the numbers of artists using previously 'unusable' materials had grown to such an extent that the New York Museum of Modern Art felt justified in putting on a major exhibition presenting an overview of these activities. "Information" brought together numerous works from previous years that had left behind no tangible results and which were now only to be found as drawings. What a shock for the public whose perceptions had been trained in the luscious visual world of the Pop Artists and the gigantic canvases of the Abstract Expressionists! The works in "Information" were hiding behind mounds of stored audio, photographic and film records. Even their originators seemed to be disappearing behind banks of telex machines, telephones, radio equipment and screens. As one artist commented sarcastically at the time: "There weren't any artists in the show."

Laboratories for the Art of the Future

In 1965 in the USA, the Japanese firm of Sony brought out a piece of portable electronic equipment for semi-professional use, called 'Portapak.' With it the person-in-the-street could record and play back visual images. Until this point, only television stations had had this type of equipment. Of course these new gadgets were somewhat restricted in their use. By all accounts Paik bought one of the very first 'Portapaks' when they came onto the market. He shot his first tape during a taxi journey on 4 October 1965 when the Pope visited New York. Then he sent out flyers to announce the presentation of

Andy Warhol
John Giorno in 'Sleep,' 1963
16 mm film, black and white, silent,
6 hrs

"It started with someone sleeping and then it just went on and on. I did actually spend all those hours filming it, although I did somewhat tidy up the end-result in order to achieve a better line."
ANDY WARHOL

his tape in the Café "Au Go Go". On the flyer he prophesied a bright artistic future for the medium: "Just as collage has ousted oil painting, so the cathode ray tube will replace the canvas."

In the years that followed, three distinct groups began to use video. The first group consisted of engineers, film-makers and artists with a professional or non-professional interest in electronics. The second group consisted of artists with a background in music, the theatre, dance and the visual arts; they saw video as the logical extension of their creative work at the time. The third group consisted of collectives who, in a conscious rejection of television, were concerned to publicly document social and political reality.

In the USA in the late 60s and early 70s, numerous artists had the opportunity to apply their know-how in professional television studios. Hitherto television producers had been relatively conventional in their use of electronics. Now there was a need for new ideas. Financial assistance from specifically created foundations made it possible for WGBH in Boston, WNET in New York and KQED in San Francisco to accommodate 'guests' in the studios and to run workshops. Thus the first television program created by artists was made at WGBH and was transmitted in March 1969. Aldo Tambellini, Thomas Tadlock, Allan Kaprow, James Seawright, Otto Piene and Paik were all invited to test the creative potential of television and to explore it as a new art form.

Of the six participants in the workshop, the 'artist-technicians' Tadlock and Seawright proved to be most professional in the way they handled the possibilities of electronic image makingt that were given to them. Tambellini and Piene, on the other hand, were less interested in the possibilities provided by equipment and technology: they created a multi-media event in the ZERO-Action tradition and controlled it from the mixing desk. Kaprow and Paik also stayed true to their own backgrounds. As committed representatives of Fluxus and Happenings they included the viewers in their concept. Kaprow put on a live broadcast from four squares in Boston during which the public in the four locations could talk and wave amiably to each other. Paik emerged as an exuberant technician and Fluxus-man uncowed by the supposed humiliations of art and life. He humorously exhorted the viewers to join in: "This is participating TV. Please follow instructions!" Not only did he offer them a deformed Richard Nixon and a few Hippies, but also a naked go-go girl and decorative, electronically produced 'dancing patterns.'

Explorers of the Moving Picture

The technically adept artists, who were already working in the 60s in the USA at the interface of art and media-technology, only enjoyed the limelight in the art world for a short time. They had been thrown up in the general explosion of forces, tiny pieces in a kaleidoscope of political, artistic and technological ideas and experiments. And yet this was not a happy moment, for with the culmination of the events of 1968 and their imminent failure, the climate changed. Cracks were beginning to show in the belief in infinite economic growth – as its limitations and its detrimental effect on humankind and Nature were becoming increasingly obvious – and it seemed that the art business was no longer interested in innovation in visual technology.

In the 70s Larry Cuba was recognised worldwide as one of the few artists exclusively using digital computer techniques to explore the possibilities of abstract animation. His work followed in the tradition of abstract film going back to the 20s in the work of artists such as Oskar Fischinger, Len Lyes, Norman McLaren and the Whitney brothers. Cuba collaborated with the pioneer of computer-animation, John Whitney Sr., but also worked for Hollywood. However, he used 16 mm film which meant that his work was of not of primary interest to art-mediators. Significantly enough, this was the same fate that awaited Andy Warhol's films (p. 592) and also the less well-known, yet richly endowed, field of independent experimental and underground film.

Ed Emshwiller on the other hand received wider public recognition, as did the married couple Steina and Woody Vasulka, who – for reasons of their individual talents – oriented their work more strongly towards the artistic avant-garde. In the 60s and early 70s Emshwiller produced experimental films, cinema-dance projects, documentaries and low-budget feature films. He was employed for most of the 70s as permanent artist at WNET/13 in New York, which is also where he created a number of video tapes that are now regarded as classics in the genre (ill. above).

During the course of the 70s the Vasulkas built up their own laboratory. Having made their own equipment, they then devoted themselves to producing and working with sounds and video-images (ill. below). In 1970 Paik, in collaboration with Shuya Abe, was also constructing technical equipment (Paik/Abe Synthesisers) specifically to suit his own needs. However, Paik did not use this synthesiser to create images but to synthesise existing images. He was of the opinion that it was much harder to reverse information than to record it. And this attitude, plus his conviction that video art should be an intrinsic part of both art and everyday life, in effect prevented him from losing his way as an explorer in the lonely electronic image world. Paik's interest is in communication, not research. His sphere of operation is the world-wide culture of television and communication, including shows, rock music and advertising just as much as traditional Asian dance, Indian ritual and various other things particularly dear to his heart, such as when Cage talks about silence or when Charlotte Moorman, the cellist, uses her body as a string instrument (p. 594).

Ed Emshwiller
Sunstone, 1979
Video tape, colour, sound, 3 mins

"Now we are trying to visualise the space which only exists as an electromagnetic field."
WOODY & STEINA VASULKA

Woody & Steina Vasulka
Heraldic View, 1974
Video tape, colour, sound, 5 mins

'Black Gate Cologne'

Although German viewers are as prone to television-fatigue as any, and there is a constant search for innovation, financial support for artists in television studios was only short-lived. Even the legendary WDR production, *Black Gate Cologne*, by Tambellini and Piene was only made by chance. After the event, television producers were surprised at the art-historical success of this "brew of black and white pictures with humming noises and sirens" which is claimed to be the first artist-made television production.

The raw material was two performances of a joint multi-media production by Tambellini and Piene called *BLACK air*. It was filmed using a number of studio cameras and then finished at the mixing desk. In addition, Piene contributed two light sculptures and a pneumatic flower, while Tambellini contributed documentary slides and footage of the assassinations of Martin Luther King and Robert Kennedy, amongst other things. After this, all that was needed was eleven monitors, four screens and an audience. Originally consisting of two 45 minute programmes it was heavily cut both before and after its first broadcast in January 1969 because it was felt that the audience could not take more than 23 minutes of *Black Gate Cologne*. The final bill for those 23 minutes of broadcast material came to 45,000 DM, and was accompanied by the undisguised regret that instead of the brilliant masterpieces mediating art to an enthused audience, it is this 'meta-artwork' that seems to have entered the annals (ill. right).

If it was not possible to use television in Germany as a laboratory for artistic experiment – as was happening in the USA – then this was also because the technology and the personnel in German television studios were primarily geared towards handling pre-packed film material. Experimental, electronic productions, on the other hand, require a particular kind of cost and labour intensive professionalism – this was true of the audio-visual works that José Montes-Baquer directed between 1969 and 1980, composed by Jan W. Morthenson, Bernard Parmegiani, Jan Bark and himself. Morthenson's *Supersonics* of 1969 even had specially programmed computer and speaker software to create the visual and sound effects he wanted. The automatic mixing desk was capable of producing 35 images per second, cox-box fades and optical feedback effects.

The Gerry Schum Television Gallery

As a state institution with a public duty to disseminate culture and information to as wide a spectrum of the population as possible, German television barely demonstrated any interest whatsoever in testing the level of its own art coverage. Therefore it was hardly surprising when a young independent camera-man and film-maker dared to set up an alternative to the all-encompassing claims of professional television. In 1968 Gerry Schum, together with the art historian Hannah Weitemeier and the artist Bernhard Höke, came up with the idea of a television gallery.

Probably the television gallery would not have excited so much criticism and notice if it had only been about mediating art in a manner suited to the medium

"I have got a hangover from music. It looks as though I can handle a music-video better than someone coming from the visual arts. I think I understand time and sequences, kinetics, better than a video artist with a visual background."
NAM JUNE PAIK

Nam June Paik
Global Groove, 1973
Video tape, colour, sound,
28 mins

of television. But in 1968 it had to be about more. The aim was to rescue art from the "art-aura of the museum and the gallery" and to create a forum where discussion could focus on the notion of art serving society. However, when the first of a total of four programmes was transmitted in 1969, there was little left of the earlier high expectations. Schum, in his television gallery, used television as it ever had been, as a means of publication. He put on a vernissage-style 'opening' with invited guests and left no-one in any doubt that the transmitted 'exhibits' were of his own artistic making.

"Land Art" was the title of the first television exhibition to be transmitted nationwide. It presented an overview of a new, artistic phenomenon, namely Earth Art: in Europe it became known as "Land Art" following this programme. It consisted of eight, carefully constructed film reports without commentary and set in magnificent locations: the breathtaking mountain panorama of the Mohjave Desert in Walter De Maria's *Two Lines Three Circles in the Desert* – filmed from a camera as it rotated three times on its own axis, while the artist grew smaller and smaller, walking all alone between two white lines; Jan Dibbets's square marked out in the sand, parallel to the edge of the picture, which was then obliterated by the tide; *Hole in the Sea* by Barry Flanagan, and more. While these were impressive images, nevertheless they were open to criticism as smacking of 'blood and soil' mysticism and were scorned by some as a *Heimatfilm*. Even some of the more elevated critics felt that these artists had somehow succumbed to the age-old search for the blue flower (Jürgen Claus), or asked what was the difference between Richard Long and a rambler putting on a slide show in his sitting room. In an article for *Die Zeit*, Petra Kipphoff asked pointedly: "Is it possible to behave more aestheticisingly than this or to beat a hastier retreat from reality?"

What matters is the heated debate that Schum's productions aroused and how controversial they seemed, particularly when one bears in mind that today they are held in the picture stores and video-archives of a number of museums: now they are regarded as fine examples of a classic avant-garde movement, however precarious

it was at the time. They were never originally intended to end up in museums. Film-artworks were only supposed to exist for the duration of the transmission. They were never intended for the art market. As it turned out, it was Schum's persistent refusal to add any form of commentary to his films that ultimately meant an end to the television gallery.

Schum was then left with no alternative other than to retreat back into the art business. He therefore realigned his focus, turning to video, and in 1971 opened the first gallery in the world specialising in video art. However, in doing so he in effect fell between two stools. He had initially gone into television art in order to escape the commercial exploitation of art, but now that he had a new medium, namely video, at his disposal – that seemed like no other art form before it to hold out hope of the democratisation of access to art – he set about establishing it precisely where many people felt it did not belong: right inside the art market.

Otto Piene and **Aldo Tambellini**
Black Gate Cologne, 1968
A light-show, black and white, sound, 23 mins (abridged version)
Broadcast by the Westdeutscher Rundfunk, Cologne, 26 January 1969. Directed by Ferdi Roth

"We live in a reality with structures defined by the inventions of the mass media – printed and electronic images are the building blocks of our cultural evolution."
ALDO TAMBELLINI

Video-Software, Hardware and Performance

Pixel-Theatre on the Screen

In the art world, video most frequently appears in the form of video tapes, that is to say as an immaterial, screen-dependent artwork. Thus right from the outset – and seen from a conservative perspective – it has struggled for recognition as an artform in its own right. In his day, Schum sought a way out of this dilemma by bringing out not only unlimited video editions, but also certain video tapes in limited numbers like multiples. From a more progressive perspective, things look rather different. For example, Fred Forest, living and working in France as a media and communication artist, believes that what he sees as a broadly-based cultural evolution, beginning in 1970, means that eventually electronic image production will completely supersede the traditional variety.

The most serious and persistent problem facing video as a medium is that one cannot hold a tele-visual image in one's hands and one cannot hang it above one's sofa. It shatters our perception by the shock of its momentary transmission, but offers no bodily resistance. "Our problem," writes Forest, "is no longer that of Classical art – the beholding of an object – but rather the dynamics of the emergence of the object!"

Visual information is electronically stored on tape. One cannot take a tape between one's fingers and pour over it frame by frame like a film strip. The video camera codifies the received light rays as abstract values which are then transformed into individual pixels on the screen when the tape is played. Thus there is no sequence of images as in a film. It is much more a case of images that are in a constant process of transformation and nowadays each individual pixel can be edited electronically or digitally, eliminated, hidden, reversed, coloured and replaced.

Mishandled Objects, Sculptures and 'Short' Circuits

Video objects, video sculptures and video installations are, if anything, closest to traditional art forms. Even Vostell's prepared, shot and buried television sets and Paik's objects with their altered image-creation capability from the early 60s acquired the character of objects in that they had been 'prepared.' In a similar vein, Beuys covered over the screen of a television set with felt. Thus he alienated the set from its actual purpose and released it for a new function (*Felt TV*, p. 590).

Similarly traditional in approach are those works which are constituted as a closed form with integrated software. The deciding factor is whether or not the plastic object and the video image come together in such a way that the two are mutually dependent. For example, Shigeko Kubota's *Nude Descending a Staircase* (ill. left) without the software would be no more than a plywood box which could equally well be a prop in a shop-window display. Kubota, born in Japan, created this piece – by now a classic – in homage to Duchamp's 1912 picture of the same name (p. 129). The irony of this work lies in the total immovability of the plywood staircase which Kubota uses for her 'running' electronic animation of a nude going down some stairs.

Shigeko Kubota
Nude Descending a Staircase
(Duchampiana), 1975/76
Video sculpture; 4 monitors,
1 recorder, 1 video tape, plywood
structure, c. 170 x 79 x 170 cm
Kassel, documenta 6 (1977)

"The invasion of sculpture by video has finally dismissed persistent prejudices against video, namely that it is 'fragile,' 'superficial,' time-dependent' and 'transient.'"
SHIGEKO KUBOTA

The Belgian artist Marie Jo Lafontaine integrates a monitor into a larger sculptural form that the public can walk into. *Victoria* (ill. right) draws visitors into its spirally opened interior, where they are enveloped in a maelstrom of time-delayed images. Two young men circle round each other, watching each other, wooing each other? It is impossible to tell. It is about life and death on a highly erotic level, where hatred and lust, beauty and horror come together. Again and again the artist draws visitors out of their distanced attitude and involves them emotionally, despite themselves and the feeling of contradiction this induces. She seems unintimidated by taboos and is not frightened of pathos.

Video objects and sculptures are characterised by their flexibility and movability. By contrast, 'installations' generally have a much more intimate relationship with the location. Klaus vom Bruch's works require constructions much like 'installations.' *The Hardening of the Average Souls* (Die Verhärtung der Durchschnittsseelen), made in 1986, consists of two video recorders and metal structures, placed between the floor and the ceiling in two opposite parts of the room. These serve as carriers for transmitting and receiving equipment. Two antennae transmit visual material on video tapes to two monitors positioned opposite each other, sending a signal across the space between them. But of course this is not all. What intransigent technology does not allow – namely physical and bodily intervention – is demonstrated by the artist in video images. These show a rotating parabola antenna superimposed on a breathing thorax. What seems to be a puzzling object in interstellar space turns out to be a close-up of a bicycle pump. Is this perhaps the key that vom Bruch will use to unlock the 'hardening of the average souls'?

Other works involve an entire room and are clearly following in the tradition of environments. An example

Marie Jo Lafontaine
Victoria, 1987/88
Video sculpture made from 19 wooden sections in the form of a spiral; 19 monitors, 6 video tapes; width: c. 900 cm
Installation; Prato, Centro per l'Arte Contemporanea Luigi Preti

Marcel Odenbach
Tobacco College or I am itching to ..., 1994/95
Installation with video projection Bonn, Kunst- und Ausstellungshalle der Bundesrepublik Deutschland

"I don't evaluate what is more important and what is less important: instead I work with juxtapositions."
MARCEL ODENBACH

Fabrizio Plessi
Roma, 1987
Video installation; marble slab,
43 monitors, conveyor belt,
380 x 1000 x 700 cm
Kassel, documenta 8 (1987)

*"An awareness of one's own person
comes from a certain level of activity
and not just from thinking about
oneself. You have to practise it."*
BRUCE NAUMAN

Bruce Nauman
Live Taped Video Corridor,
1968–1970
Installation; 2 monitors, camera,
video tape, walls,
c. 533 x 1220 x 90 cm
Milan, Count Panza di Biumo
Collection

of these would be Paik's *TV Garden* (1974–1978) made from about thirty different television sets plus plants and trees, which can be viewed from a raised ramp. In 1977, Fabrizio Plessi (ill. above) designed an 'environment project' for an empty swimming pool, where a swimmer swims lengths on 24 monitors set up next to each other. The images were shot using 24 synchronised, fixed underwater-cameras. A huge effort but results are simply breathtaking. This particular project was realised by the artists of the Studio Azzurro who were working on the boundary between art and entertainment, and who repeatedly demonstrated their skill in making the best use of effects, as Edith Decker has pointed out. Perhaps one might just add a sentence here from Walter Benjamin's 1936 essay "The Work of Art in the Age of Mechanical Reproduction": "The history of every art form shows critical epochs in which a certain art form aspires to effects which could be fully obtained only with a changed technical standard, that is to say, in a new art form."

Things become more complicated for the viewer, when the environment consists of not only images but also sound. Marcel Odenbach's *Tobacco College or I am itching to …* (Tabakkollegium oder es brennt mir unter den Nägeln; p. 597) takes place in a darkened room. The viewer is faced with video images and sound projected simultaneously and in succession from different directions. On the two longer walls, facing each other, there is a counterpoint of images: on the one side there are images of hatred and violence from a society spinning out of control and on the other side is the artist looking stoically into the camera and smoking a cigarette. This is accompanied by live sound until suddenly Beethoven piano music wells out of one of the four

Wolf Vostell
Grashoppers, 1969/70
Collage; 20 TVs, camera, photo on
canvas overpainted and smeared
with acid, bones, hair, shoes, tennis
racquets, 280 x 800 x 200 cm
Vienna, Museum Moderner Kunst,
on loan from the Austrian Ludwig
Stiftung

speakers positioned in the corners of the room, distracts
the viewer's attention and completely changes the atmosphere.

Odenbach proves himself to be a virtuoso choreographer in this audio-visual event which only lasts a few
minutes. With a fine sense of timing he controls perception and the mood in a way that could almost be
described as totalitarian. But Odenbach is not only a
master of smoothly operating equipment: he also

throws a few monkey wrenches into the works, generating ambiguity and confusion. Taking on the role of the
viewer, he presents himself as a voyeur and perhaps even
as an observer somewhat out of his depths. He neither
takes sides nor pins the work he is presenting to any particular ideology. Doubtless this is the source of the challenge inherent in his work.

Yet other installations involve closed circuit television, where live video pictures are played on a monitor.

Below left:
Peter Campus
Interface, 1972
Closed circuit installation; 1 black
and white camera, 1 black and
white video projector, 1 spotlight,
1 sheet of glass, 180 x 250 cm
Cologne, Kölnischer Kunstverein

Below right:
Nan Hoover
Movement from Either Direction,
1995
Video installation
Bonn, Kunst- und Ausstellungs-
halle der Bundesrepublik Deutsch-
land

Nam June Paik
TV-Buddha, 1974
Monitor, camera, statue
Amsterdam, Stedelijk Museum

Frequently the viewer is caught up in the 'short' circuit between camera and monitor. Vostell integrates the viewer on twenty monitors into an eight metre wide scenario showing a collage of a lesbian couple and the violent end of the 'Prague Spring' (p. 599 above). Bruce Nauman creates a deep sense of unease in the visitor to his *Live Taped Video Corridor* (p. 598 below): having squeezed into a narrow passage, the visitor then walks down this, approaching an image of him or herself on one of two monitors (placed on top of each other) only to find, contrary to expectations, that the image is grow-

ing ever smaller. Instead of confronting visitors with themselves, as it were, Paik shows an antique statue of a meditating Buddha facing an image of itself on a television screen (ill. left).

Peter Campus, who first worked in experimental psychology, created spaces where a person could encounter his or her own image (pp. 599 and 608). His closed circuit installations, made between 1972 and 1978, are characterised by an immense stillness which results from a combination of darkened room, black and white images, and a strictly limited means of expression. Dan Graham's specialised in reflected time-delay spaces where the viewer is confronted with his or her own immediate past.

In works produced during the 80s, the pendulum swings towards interventions which have concrete aesthetic or optical consequences. The American artist Nan Hoover works in her closed circuit installations with coloured, video projections of light phenomena. The visitor can then enter into these and intervene in them (p. 599 below right). Klaus vom Bruch's 1988 *Radar Space (*Radarraum) in fact has nothing to do with video any more. It consists of a rotating radar dish with an ultra-sound sensor and a monitor mounted on it. Using a time-delay, it translates the presence of bodies and their movements into graphic curves. Members of the public produce the images.

Transformations in Live Art

The appropriation of the hitherto artistic phenomenon of the Happening by the revolutionaries of the Paris Spring marked both the highpoint and the end, for the time being, of modes of artistic expression that tried to

Klaus Rinke
Mutations I. Primary Demonstration, 1970
Photo sequence (112 parts in total), each 59.5 x 42 cm

"I have chosen the body and bodily gesture as a dematerialised, particularly clear medium and explained it with a text."

KLAUS RINKE

enter into 'real' life by means of explosion and provocation. It was also not possible to go on endlessly repeating acts intended to expand and heighten consciousness, if these were not so much performed as simply reliant on shock tactics, spontaneity and an element of therapy. Performable live art only developed into an independent art form when the energies formerly invested in proclamations and Actions were redirected towards art-immanent questions.

One way out was taken by certain artists working in the tradition of the Viennese Actionists who, although much more analytical than their predecessors, were now turning their attention to their own bodies. The Austrian artist Valie Export devoted herself in her feminist Actions to historical manifestations of female body language (ill. right). Gina Pane and Chris Burden set out on a voyage of self-discovery via their own bodies (ill. below left). Nauman and Klaus Rinke used their bodies as a sculptural medium (p. 600 below) and Arnulf Rainer also used his body as a telling means of expression.

In its essence a performance is intended to be a-medial, conveying information directly and without any other intermediary. It 'happens' in a particular place at a particular time, but also in the hearts and minds of those present. It is a unique poetic act with a potentially enduring effect if it then takes on a life of its own in the viewer's head. For this reason it is also quite impossible to document performances adequately. No photograph and no film could convey the ceremonial, highly aesthetic, atmospheric moments of a James Lee Byars performance with all its sights and sounds (p. 602 below

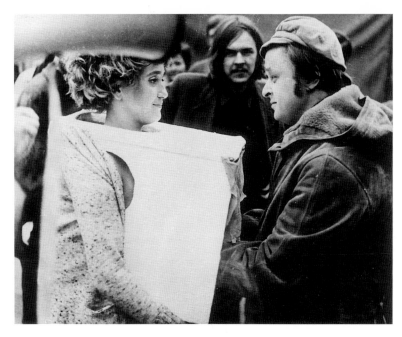

left); however sensitive, no documentation could convey the almost unbearable tension that was created between Beuys and his public.

Performance would not have acquired the significance that it has already commanded for some time, if it had *only* remained an a-medial medium. When performance reached the point that it began to embrace photography, film and video it also began to develop a wide spectrum of modes of expression. Rebecca Horn

Valie Export
Tap and Touch Cinema, Expanded
Movie, 1968. Action, Vienna

Chris Burden
Stills from 'Documentation of
Collected Works,' 1971-1975
Video tape, black and white and
colour, 36 mins
Cologne, 235 Media

Rebecca Horn
The Gentle Prisoner, 1978
Metal, peacock feathers and other
materials, 100 x 83 x 32 cm (closed)
Private collection

Jochen Gerz
Calling Out until the Point of
Exhaustion, 1972
Performance recorded on video,
black and white, sound, 25 mins

Gerz stands 60 metres away from a
video camera plus microphone and
shouts as long and as loudly as possible until his voice becomes hoarse
and then inaudible.

staged her puzzling acts with body objects purely for
film and the video camera (p. 601 below right). Jürgen
Klauke (p. 603 below) and Rainer, in intimate performances, poured existential psychograms into frozen, photographic images.

The use of video made it possible to undertake performances without the constraints of time and place or
even without an audience. Certain artists like Nauman
and Rinke working on body/space processes, conceived

performances for the camera alone. In the case of
Jochen Gerz the camera was the only viewer at his
Action *Calling Out until the Point of Exhaustion* (Rufen
bis zur Erschöpfung; ill. left). Sixty metres away from a
video camera plus microphone, he shouted as loudly as
he could until his voice began to go and finally went
completely. Vito Acconci also used the camera to witness his activities: however, unlike Gerz, there was an
audience, although either kept at a distance from the
performance or excluded altogether. In *Isolation is transparent* (1973), Ulrike Rosenbach performed behind a
transparent sheet, where she spun herself like a spider
into a net of thick, white rope. The public were able to
watch on a monitor which showed the proceedings from
a bird's eye view above the artist.

In the 70s, performance entered its 'monitor phase.'
This was when Gerhard Johann Lischka coined the
phrase "Taumel des Sehens" meaning something along
the lines of 'giddy vision.' And indeed, when an event is
simultaneously filmed or shown on a monitor the
demands on the viewer are at least doubled. In principle,
as in Cubism, the viewer is now confronted with several
perspectives at once. The difficulty here for the viewer,
however, is that the perspectives are not all shown in the
same medium: the multiple views in a Cubist picture or
sculpture are at least all contained within the same whole.
By contrast, the public in a video performance is confronted with an event that is both live and on film, invit-
ing comparison between the two modes of expression.

How differently real and camera-mediated events
can be weighted is demonstrated by Rosenbach in *Don't*

James Lee Byars
The Play of Death, 1976
Performance
Cologne, Dom Hotel

Stuart Brisley
Untitled, 1993
Performance. Hellerau

think I'm an Amazon (Glauben Sie nicht, daß ich eine Amazone bin; ill. right). In this live video action in 1975 she shot fifteen arrows at a reproduction of Stefan Lochner's famous *Madonna im Rosenhag* (1451, Wallraf Richartz Museum, Cologne). The crux of the performance lies in the superimposition and synthesis on the screen of images from two different cameras, which means that the arrow not only pierces the face of the Madonna, but also her own.

By the late 70s there was a clear move towards camera-led image production: there were economic reasons for this, but it was also connected with the fact that individual self-discovery became less important as a theme. Some artists turned back to painting which had recently been resurrected, as it were. Others turned their attention to the realm of installation which was now creating a higher level of interest in the art business. Some performance activists sought out new surroundings and a new, unprejudiced public. For years Tom Marioni attended a regulars' table in his local pub. Tehching Hsieh spent a year in a cage and another year outside in the open air. Res Ingold founded his own airline. And if performance art still has an effect today, then that may have something to do with the fact that we live in a time that is sadly in danger of choking on its own clutter.

Below: **Jürgen Klauke**
The eternally masculine – as eternally boring
(Das ewig männliche – als ewig langweiliges)
From 'Formalisierung der Langeweile' (Detail from plate IV), 1980/81
Photograph, silver gelatin, 7 of 15 parts, total size: 180 x 210 cm

Above: **Ulrike Rosenbach**
Don't think I'm an Amazon, 1975
Video-Life-Action on video tape, black and white, sound, 15 mins

Centre: **Ben d'Armagnac**
Untitled, 1977
Performance
Cologne, Kunstmarkt Köln

5 The Seventies: a Reservoir of Ideas

Actors in Time and Space

Many artists in the late 60s and early 70s made videos because what they wanted to do could be best expressed on video. This was also true of John Baldessari, whose *Folding Hat* (ill. below) is about the genesis of a plastic work. The video shows a half-hour, uncut close-up of the artist holding a hat which he proceeds to knead, form, manipulate and generally play with. The work is intrinsically bound up in video, although this may not at first sight be obvious. It is neither a documentation that could have been filmed nor do Baldessari's actions actually result in a plastic work: the point of the work is in fact the interaction between the artist and the video camera. The instant replay of the recorded images allowed him to re-adjust the appearance both of the object and of himself on the screen moment by moment. Baldessari's *Folding Hat* is therefore at one and the same time a plastic creation and a two-dimensional picture-surface composition.

In photography, film and video, 'interactivity' could well be the most fitting description of the relationship between artist and medium. In this dialogue with a cer-tain mode of visual expression, the action of the artist takes on a new aesthetic identity. And the work can be carried out unhampered by economic constraints (which dominate the work done in television studios) in the intimate atmosphere of the studio and with a mini-mum of equipment.

The video pioneer Bruce Nauman ended his train-ing at a time when many young artists were painting their last ever pictures, and he, too, rapidly turned his back on painting. In 1965/66 he began to address the question of "how objects relate to the space around them." He created abstract objects using flexible materi-als such as fibre glass and rubber. After 1968 he also used his own body as a sculpture and staged poses and sequences of movements for film and video.

In *Manipulating a Fluorescent Tube* (p. 605 above) which he made in 1969, he created a variety of poses involving a fluorescent tube and himself, and concern-ing the relationship between the two. Nauman's use of a neon tube is of course reminiscent of Dan Flavin's gleaming neon light zones creating walls of light and later entire rooms of light (p. 528f). However, while

"It should not be called: 'Now I am going to make a video piece' but: 'What I want to do is best expressed on video.'" JOHN BALDESSARI

John Baldessari
Folding Hat: Version 1, 1970
Video tape, black and white,
sound, 30 mins

Flavin – in accordance with the precepts of Minimal Art – was working with neutral, geometric and above all pre-existent basic forms, Nauman introduces his own body into the situation and, in doing so, re-introduces all those qualities into the artwork that the Minimalists had banned: namely the organic (with all its ambiguity and uncertainty), the mystic and the erotic. Nauman's exploration of the parameters of plastic forms is typical of a particular kind of basic research that was being carried out in the arts at the time by musicians, dancers, film-makers, theatre people and artists alike, sometimes even in collaboration. Interest centred on the principles and procedures of any artistic activity, be it music, movement or plastic, in a search for the intrinsic aesthetic of these principles. Richard Serra, inspired by the experimental motion studies carried out by the dancer Yvonne Rainer, made a series of 16 mm films in which hands perform particular, almost pictorial, actions (p. 606). The length of the films is dictated by the length of time required to perform the individual actions. Franz Erhard Walther used textiles in his Actions which were intended to induce an awareness in the 'user' of his own body and of his relationship to others (ill. below).

Bruce Nauman
Manipulating a Fluorescent Tube, 1969
Video tape, black and white,
sound, 60 mins
Zurich, Kunsthaus Zürich

Messages in the First Person

There is a commonly held view that in the 70s, after the failure of 1968, people withdrew back into their own private spheres in order to explore their own inner worlds. But this is blinkered at best. Self-discovery was indeed an essential element in the mood of the late 60s and the full emancipation of the individual leading to mental, physical and creative freedom was the aim of all the 're-volutions.' However, in actual fact, artists took up at the point the 68ers had vainly tried to reach, vainly in that their vision was clouded with ideological ballast. In Beuys's words: *La rivoluzione siamo Noi* (We are the re-volutions; ill. left). He located the creative source of freedom within the individual. The situation would only be changed through human creativity.

Franz Erhard Walther
Just Before Dark No. I/32 (Kurz vor der Dämmerung Nr. I/32), 1967
Action with cotton material,
c. 600 x 45 cm, 9 loops, 9 bolts
From "Walking as Sculpture"
(Gehen als Skulptur)
Frankfurt/Main, Museum für Moderne Kunst

Joseph Beuys
La rivoluzione siamo Noi, 1972
Photoprint on polyester sheet,
191 x 100 cm
Heidelberg, Edition Staeck

Richard Serra
Hand Catching Lead, 1968
16 mm film, black and white,
silent, 210 mins
Bochum, m Bochum, Galerie

Pieces of lead fall at short intervals and are visible as a grey blurred movement. The hand just has time to close and to open again. If Serra manages to catch the falling lead he immediately lets go again in order to have his hand ready for the next piece. The constant tension eventually tires the hand out. It becomes cramped and its reaction times slow down until it seizes up altogether. The effect is oppressive.

Vito Acconci
Recording Studio from Air Time,
1973
Monitor, camera, loudspeaker, 7
tape recorders, sound tape loops
Video performance
New York, Sonnabend Gallery

representation on the other. In *Vertical Roll* (ill. below) which she made in 1972, she increases the distance between the two (which she has established by means of video) by enveloping herself in material, hiding her face with a mask, or formalising her image to the point of unrecognisability by cropping it, showing it in extreme close-up, or hopping rhythmically.

Easily the most unusual form of self-representation is seen in the team of Gilbert & George, who have billed themselves as living sculpture since 1969. They set out neither to ask questions or to explore things nor to pursue any form of critical enquiry. The beginning of their work together was to be a 'tabula rasa.' In their words,

Looking back today, the 70s seem like a huge reservoir of ideas. It was a time of experiment focusing on the ego. Vito Acconci, with his background in literature, emerged in 1969 with performances and body works, where he exposed himself to highly volatile inter-personal situations. Later, he also used video and sound in order to communicate his experiences to the viewer, typically involving the viewer in his own personal feelings, by addressing him or her directly. In *Recording Studio from Air Time* (ill. above), he spent two weeks in a room in the Leo Castelli Gallery in New York. The room itself was closed to the public. There he then sat in front of a mirror and relentlessly tried to come to terms with an old, failed relationship. A video camera transmitted his at times dramatic attempts to understand what had happened and the blame he heaped on himself.

Nobody confronted their public more directly with fear, oppression, courage and aggression than Acconci. In performances by Marina Abramovic and Ulay there are echoes of the young Acconci's provocative manner and willingness to lay himself on the line. Characteristic of the work done by Abramovic and Ulay, who worked together after the mid-70s, is the fact of having to endure an oppressive or dangerous situation. In *Light/Dark* (p. 608 below left), lit by bright lamps, they knelt and hit each other in the face until one of them stopped. In the 80s Abramovic/Ulay dealt with intercultural experiences. In 1988 they set out from opposite ends of the 4,000 kilometre long Great Wall of China, only to part forever at the moment, weeks later, when they met up in the middle.

Peter Campus and Joan Jonas looked at the 'question-ability' of their own personas. *Three Transitions* (p. 608 above) was produced in 1973 by Campus at the WGBH television station in Boston and was to become a classic amongst early coloured videos. In this six-minute work, one sees Campus (by means of superimposition and two camera images) apparently slitting himself open and stepping through himself, creating a second face for himself and getting rid of it again by burning it.

Jonas's video works operate a fine balance of intimate self-reflection on the one hand and distanced self-

Joan Jonas
Vertical Roll, 1972
Video tape, black and white,
sound, 20 mins

Reiner Ruthenbeck
Object for Partially Hiding a Video
Scene, 1972–1974
Metal plate on a tripod, video tape,
black and white, c. 10 mins

Peter Campus
Three Transitions, 1973
Video tape, colour, sound, 6 mins
Bonn, Städtisches Kunstmuseum

they neither wanted nor were able to add anything more to art: they refused to be creative. They decided to declare themselves, their life and their partnership as the art work. Nowadays it is no longer possible quite to imagine how extraordinary this apparently utterly indifferent artistic partnership appeared against a background of heated debate in so many areas. These two young men simply enjoyed their own existence in a state of Epicurean pleasure. They performed as 'singing sculptures' and justified their role as 'living sculptures' in the most diverse of media – initially in letters, then in photography and video or in drawing and painting (ill. below right).

It is naturally no coincidence that it was specifically men who felt that everything had already been said in art. Contemporary female artists would not have dreamt of making a similar statement. They had other things to do at this late stage in a culture which, for the last however many thousands of years, had had its contents and standards almost entirely dictated by men. Now women were taking up an issue that had hitherto been an exclusively male preserve: the portrayal of their own sex. In order to achieve this they turned to the new, as yet impartial, medium of video. Between 1973 and 1977 Friederike Pezold created a staged video cycle called *The New Incarnate Sign Language of a Sex According to the Laws*

Marina Abramovic and **Ulay**
Light / Dark, 1977
Performance; duration: 20 mins
Cologne, International Art Fair

"We kneel opposite each other. Our faces are lit by two strong lights. We hit each other alternately in the face until one of us stops."

MARINA ABRAMOVIC / ULAY

Gilbert & George
Underneath the Arches - Singing Sculpture, 1970
Performance
Düsseldorf, Kunsthalle

"People thought it was very clever. But it was quite simple. We called it sculpture because we were studying sculpture."

GILBERT & GEORGE

Videos, Politics and the Media

In the 70s there was no shortage of attempts to rescue art from its ivory tower by means of video. Thus video in its simplest form – namely as a sound-synchronised recording of an event that takes place in time – was taken up above all by those who wanted their work to have an effect on the reality of everyday life. The New Zealander, Darcy Lange, set out in the 70s to depict the sheep-farmers of New Zealand and steel-workers in England exactly as he found them, in order to instigate discussion on the issues raised. Others set up as production groups with the aim of developing 'alternative' media work with ordinary citizens, minorities and those on the margins of society. However, the fact that other artists – such as Rosenbach, vom Bruch and Odenbach – who

Ulrike Rosenbach
Dance for a Woman, 1975
Video tape, black and white, sound, 12 mins
Bonn, Städtisches Kunstmuseum

Friederike Pezold
The New Incarnate Sign Language of a Sex According to the Laws of Anatomy, Geometry and Kinetics, 1973–1976
Video tape, 6 parts, black and white, silent, 10 mins (per section)
Bonn, Städtisches Kunstmuseum

of Anatomy, Geometry and Kinetics (Die neue leibhaftige Zeichensprache eines Geschlechts nach den Gesetzen der Anatomie, Geometrie und Kinetik; ill. right). This consisted of ten-minute motion sequences of body parts covered in black make-up. These were translated by a fixed camera into strongly abstracted symbols. In a sequence of unedited close-ups breasts, arms, eyes, thighs and pudenda took on a highly stylised life of their own, which in turn opened up a whole range of associations.

With the goals of the student movement in mind, in the early 70s Rosenbach set out in search of a strong, female ego. Her early videos are stylistically still broadly in line with the purism that held sway at the time. As far as content is concerned they are analytical and initially also autobiographical. In these works Rosenbach uncovers fixed roles and patterns of behaviour that women are subjected to in a male-dominated society.

Without doubt one of her most beguiling videos is her ten-minute *Dance for a Woman* (Tanz für eine Frau; ill. above). Wearing heavy, white, circular skirts she dances to the well-known waltz melody 'Ich tanze mit Dir in den Himmel hinein,' turning round and round until she becomes completely dizzy and sinks to the ground.

Vom Bruch and Odenbach also confront historical role-models and definitions. Vom Bruch uses video to examine historical documentary material and intimate self-portraits, which he then harshly juxtaposes. In his 1982 *Allied Band* (Alliiertenband; p. 610 above) he creates a collage of Gioacchino Rossini's *The Dance* and melodies from the film *Notte a Venezia*, archive footage of the advancing allied troops in the Second World War, aerial shots of the Rhineland devastated by bombing, and himself in a double role: as a voyeur who saves himself in a game of forgetting, and as a participant mimicking a bomber pilot. Narcissism, male eroticism, the pathos of the hero and the horror of annihilation are closely linked here. This video which won a number of awards owes its explosive impact not least to its finely balanced ambiguity.

Klaus vom Bruch
The Allied Band, 1982
Video tape, colour, sound, 10 mins
Bonn, Städtisches Kunstmuseum

were mainly producing 'art videos' – nevertheless also turned to a wider public with similar initiatives of their own, gives a significant insight into the deep sense of contradiction that must have accompanied their artistic work at the time.

Art that loses itself in everyday reality – as opposed to having formerly been totally isolated from it – forfeits any real distance to reality and with this, the capacity to take a critical stance vis-à-vis that reality. It was for precisely this reason that the American media artist Les Levine had to close his "Levine's Restaurant" – opened in New York in 1969 – after only one year. His "Museum of Mott Art Inc." which he founded as a service-oriented meeting place for interested amateurs and profes-

sionals turned out to be a more suitable venue for looking at the function of the artist: the artist's tasks and modes of expression as well as his or her role in society.

With Levine, Lange and the German group "Telewissen" as notable exceptions [translator's note: "Telewissen" is a German word-play which sounds like 'television' and means 'tele-knowledge'], few artists made any real effort to meet their untrained lay-public – a strenuous task and one for which they would receive few laurels from the art world. Artists were much more likely to adopt the position of critical analyst. There are numerous analyses of television, our 'Big Brother,' its forms of mediation and its aesthetic. Daniel Buren interrupted Schum's television exhibition, *Identifications* (1970), creating interference with a specially developed jamming signal. Serra served up harmless music plus a continuous text detailing critical facts and evaluations on the subject of television consumption and its effects (*TV delivers People*, 1973). Reiner Ruthenbeck retreated behind his *Object for Partially Hiding a Video Scene* (Objekt zur teilweisen Verdeckung einer Video-Szene; p. 607 below). Douglas David on the other hand sought actual contact with his viewers: in his *Austrian Tapes* (1974; ill. left) made for broadcast by Austrian Television, he incites viewers to go to the screen and make contact with the palms of their hands, their finger-tips, their cheeks and their lips.

Douglas Davis
The Austrian Tapes, 1974
Video tape, colour, sound, 15 mins

"Please come right up to the screen in front of you. Put your hands against my hands. Think about the fact that we are touching each other."
DOUGLAS DAVIS

The Eighties: "We're switching over!"

Accelerated Images

In the 80s the visual arts became socially acceptable. In 1982, at the opening of an exhibition of the Neue Wilden at the Folkwang Museum in Essen, hundreds of buyers, television shows and magazines fought to acquire the new figurative paintings by artists from Berlin and Cologne. Four months earlier, a mere 25 visitors had attended an opening for a joint-exhibition by Baldessari and Odenbach in the same venue. Odenbach recalls exhibitions with a social and political message "for a society that did perhaps exist but which was just not interested." In addition, he also recalled "empty galleries, pieces that were unsellable: exhibitions for colleagues." In the booming art business video found itself increasingly marginalised, and ultimately relegated altogether from the art league: "Down with video art!" ran the art-critic Alfred Nemeczek's cover for the March issue of the journal *Art* in 1983.

All those who were not painting in a 'young' enough style now had to embark on various survival strategies. However, the barque manned by the Neue Wilden then foundered more quickly than had been expected and the art market greedily set about launching new trends. Odenbach described the situation at the end of the decade: "first there was sculpture, then everything had to have a text and now it's photography." But who would refuse to go along with this when starvation was the only alternative? Odenbach began working with large format drawings again. In 1986 vom Bruch produced his last studio tape, before turning exclusively to sculpture and installations. Nan Hoover announced that she would not be making any more videos because she had started drawing again.

However, these moves back towards the traditional genres of art history were certainly not purely strategic on the part of these artists. A whole new 'clip industry'

Jenny Holzer
Protect Me from What I Want.
From the 'Survival Series,' 1987
Installation, San Francisco
Courtesy Barbara Gladstone
Gallery, New York

Les Levine
Sell Yourself, 1987
Screen prints on billboards,
c. 292 x 658 cm (each)
Kassel, documenta 8 (1987)

Barbara Kruger
Untitled, 1994/95
Spatial installation with photo-
graphic screen prints on paper;
various sizes
Cologne, Museum Ludwig,
Ludwig Collection

was beginning to change the customary modes of perception of broad swathes of the population, but in a
manner that some more critical observers felt to be
threatening. Technical progress provided the means.
The introduction of VHS standards, improved colour
systems for videos and new possibilities for electronic
post-production created a less expensive product, which
could nevertheless achieve a high technical standard. At
the same time improved systems of training and education smoothed the path for younger artists wanting to
work with electronic art. Was this the chance to make
use at last of those mass-media that had previously
always been rejected on the grounds of technical inadequacy?

Perhaps the 80s, blithely going to seed, were just the
foil needed by socially committed artists such as Levine,
Jenny Holzer and Barbara Kruger for their uncompromising and disturbing work. In 1979 Levine primarily

aroused attention with his billboard campaigns (p. 611
right). Holzer displayed her initially laconic, later
provocative, texts on posters and commercial advertising hoardings, LED signs, electronic message boards
and in magazines (p. 611 left). Kruger combined existing
black and white pictures with disconcerting texts, which
she then put on walls, hoardings, T-shirts, shopping
bags and postcards (ill. above).

Cross-Fertilisation: High and Low Art
In the 70s video art was caught somewhere between the
clip-world (with its clip-criticism) and other unrelated
areas. It was elaborate and optically sophisticated. Its
makers, a new generation of video artists, had grown up
with television, were at home with different media and
open-minded towards technology. "We're switching
over: 'Let's go for the real public!'" This was the title
given by the well-known video-joker, Herbert Went-

Bob Wilson
Stations, 1982
Video tape, colour, sound, 57 mins

Laurie Anderson
United States I–IV, 1979–1983
Performance

scher, to an article he wrote for the journal *Kunstforum* in early 1985. In it he brought to Europe the glad tidings of a new style of American video art.

The borders between different professions began to blur with astonishing speed. Freelance authors, directors and visual technicians all began to produce art videos, while artistic activity began to extend into the world of commercial film and television. The 80s celebrated the resurrection of a number of the ambitious pioneers who had already occupied the interface between research, commerce and art in the late 60s. Now personalities – such as the American couple working as video and TV artists, John Sanborn and Mary Perillo, or the performance artist Laurie Anderson (ill. p. 612 below left) – emerged into the light of the art world's attention, with careers that were centred as much in the media industry as in the art business.

Anderson, a trained violinist, art-historian and sculptor, became known in the 70s for her incisive, minimalist sound performances. Towards the end of the decade she then turned to multi-media music performances using synchronised instrumental, vocal, visual and text elements, which later became positively operatic performances. In the early 80s she moved into film and the electronic media. Anderson in fact managed to switch from audio-art actions into the popular media industry, while Brian Eno trod precisely the opposite path. In 1979 he stopped writing songs, brought his career as a pop musician in *Roxy Music* to a halt and

started to work on spatial, very meditative sound and video installations, which are at times reminiscent of the psychedelic light shows of the late 60s.

Clearly the cross-fertilisation of high and low art had something to do with the fact that video art, long thought to be dead and gone, was once again the subject of animated discussion. Max Almy made a name in the early 80s as the author of biting clips in which she

Pipilotti Rist
Pipilottis' Fault, 1988
Video tape, colour, sound, 12 mins
Collection of the artist

Upper row:
Paul Garrin
Free Society, 1988
Video tape, colour, sound,
c. 300 mins
Cologne, 235 Media

Lower row:
Max Almy
Perfect Leader, 1983
Video tape, colour, sound, 251 mins
Cologne, 235 Media

Gary Hill
Circular Breathing, 1994
Single channel video / sound
installation
5 video projectors, video disc and
video disc player, computer-controlled video-switcher, amplifier,
loudspeaker; various sizes
Basel, Öffentliche Kunstsammlung Basel, Museum für Gegenwartskunst

Bill Viola
Nantes Triptychon, 1992
Installation on three screens with
projection from behind
Nantes, Musées des Beaux-Arts de
Nantes

Tony Oursler
Broken, 1994
Video recorder, VCR, video tape,
wood, fabric; various sizes
Munich, Goetz Collection

directed acerbic asides towards the latest video and
computer based modes of expression (ill. p. 613 upper
row). Dara Birnbaum isolated stereotypical elements
from popular television series like *Kojak/Wang* (ill. p. 615
left). She then integrated these as 'readymades' into her
video collages, using repetition, time lapse and time
delay techniques to uncover their concealed codes. In
the compelling video clip, *Free Society* (ill. p. 613 lower
row), Paul Garrin 'sold' his criticisms to a society that
thought it could only secure its 'freedom' by employing
a "special unit of the God Squad" (Pat Robertson,
American television preacher).

The Video-Maker as Seer

The question is whether artists who put their 'artistry' at
the service of the media industry can, in the long run,
still produce independent works of a high artistic standard – that is to say, whether they can maintain any real
distance from the media industry. In 1987 the media
expert, Dieter Daniels, declared that "it is not the job of
video art to produce demo-clips for industrial products." Barely two years later it seemed to him that video
had been led into "an albeit comfortable" cul-de-sac by
the electronics industry that was marketing it. The position of the artist was now more insecure than ever. Now
it was entirely the artists' own decision as to where they

should concentrate their energies and where they might find a forum for their work. What precisely are those artists doing who are not using the visual potential of the media industry to create a form of commercial added-value, but who use the screen as an opportunity for creative, experimental interchange with another language? In the hands of those such as Bill Viola, Gary Hill and Nauman, video techniques are simply a transition into a different, inner reality. Hill uses video as a visual medium to explore the complex inter-relationships between language, image and our processes of comprehension and perception (ill. p. 614 above). The American Bill Viola, past master of video art, reveals phenomena that are otherwise hidden below the surface, by speeding up images, or stretching them until they come to a complete halt; expanding and dissolving them, superimposing and reversing them. His works are extraordinarily pictorial in the way that they are conceived.

Viola's images not only have the tendency to burrow right into the viewer's consciousness, they also touch an existential chord. As early as 1979 his desert portrait, *Chott-el-Djerid (A Portrait in Light and Heat)*, took the viewer right to the threshold between physically verifiable facts and figments of one's imagination. Viola's main interest is in the unfathomable macrocosm of consciousness, ideas and phantasmagoria. For him the door

into this world is to be found in archetypal conditions of existence, in the secrets of the new-born child (*Silent Life*, 1979), in the cry of fear (*Anthem*), in the mystery of sleep (*The Sleepers*, 1992), in the silence of death and in the expectation of life (*Nantes Triptychon*, p. 614).

In his more recent video works since 1985 – having made none for twelve years previously – Nauman has been addressing traumatic, scarcely bearable aspects of human existence. "No, No, No, No" a clown cries in the face of some invisible threat. Other participants in the installation *Clown Torture* (ill. above right) try to complete absurd, impossible tasks. One is even observed in the toilet "while shitting."

No other contemporary artist has come so movingly close to the pitiable and the wretched as this supreme master of all media. "The True Artist Helps the World by Revealing Mystic Truths" (Window or Wall Sign, Rijksmuseum Kröller-Müller, Otterlo): a neon sign by Bruce Nauman in 1967. The sentence was a test that was to be examined for its validity. Today Nauman would like to extend the word 'mystic' to include notions of the hidden and the real. He has said that most of his works are the product "of aggression and anger." Sometimes this was specifically in response to world politics but, whatever the case, it was always about "the inability of human beings to get on with each other."

Dara Birnbaum
Pop-Pop Video: Kojak / Wang,
1980
Video tape, colour, sound, 4 mins

Bruce Nauman
Clown Torture (Dark & Stormy
Night with Laughter), 1987
Installation; 2 colour monitors,
4 loudspeakers, 2 video projectors,
4 video tapes, colour und sound;
various sizes
Installation; Lannan Foundation,
Los Angeles

The Nineties: Interaction in Virtual Space

Stelarc
The Third Hand, 1995
Performance
Tokyo, Yokohama, Nagoya

Encounters on the User-Interface

Little by little the avant-garde movement in this century "moved away from painting" in order to meet the challenges of reality. Improving the world is no longer an option for artists working with technical media today. At best one might see oneself as helping to form the world. Media artists today benefit from the fact that interactive media available both on CD-ROM and on-line are competing increasingly effectively with the classical mass media. Meanwhile we are beginning to understand how radically digital technology is changing the reality of our everyday lives. Artists who concentrate their efforts on the interface between humans and technology show us what it means to live under these conditions.

In 1988 Jeffrey Shaw (Director of the Institute for Visual Media at the Centre for Art and Media Technology in Karlsruhe) and Dirk Groeneveld created an interactive, computer-graphics installation where the 'viewer' had to get on to a bicycle in order to simulate a journey through a virtual, three-dimensional space. This space was called *The Legible City* (ill. below). Its streets are formed from letters, that is, from words and sentences.

No-one could fail to be moved by a work like this: in contrast to our response to a painting or a video where

Jeffrey Shaw and
Dirk Groeneveld
The Legible City, 1988
Interactive computer installation
Karlsruhe, Museum für Neue
Kunst, ZKM

we can only ever be a viewer or an observer. Indeed the 'legible city' requires bodily activity even to get into the space itself. And what then emerges in that space depends entirely on the input and decisions of individual users. They can travel quickly or slowly, to the left or to the right, they can turn off or take a short cut. The walls are permeable. There is no dramatic action, no beginning and no end. Shaw and Groeneveld turn the readers into *flâneurs*, who create their own 'story' from the textual building blocks, making the best use they can of the possibilities open to them – change of speed, change of direction, short-cuts.

There is one thing, however, that the readers of the *Legible City* most certainly cannot do: they cannot look behind the 'facades' or into the 'cellars.' There are no doors that can be opened to reveal more information with the click of a 'mouse' like the 'hot spots' on a CD-ROM or on the Internet. Hypertext is the name given to a non-linear collage of information that users can create for themselves combining networked text or other materials (images, film, sound and video sequences). A specialist in this field, using hypertext data on several levels with text and video, is the American media artist Bill Seaman. The user navigating his or her way through his systems will find an infinite variety of combinations of text, language and images (ill. below). The user thus creates audio-visual poetry, or can have the computer create them.

The technology of virtual reality (VR) does not merely offer access to an artificial, computer generated landscape. It also offers the user the chance to personally – in the form of an artificial body – enter into that landscape and to interact bodily with other users in the system. One of the central challenges to the artists in the realm of tele-virtuality is to test and develop substitute body languages. With *Between the Words* (ill. above) the Hungarian artist Agnes Hegedüs has created equipment whereby two people can enter into a realm of virtual communication. The participants see each other as an outline through a semi-transparent opening in a wall, but they cannot talk to each other. They hold joysticks in their hands which they then use to steer computer generated substitute hands in the space between them. Each movement creates an algorithmic metamorphosis of the line of the hands which is then translated into a specific gesture.

The Australian performance artist, Stelarc, takes the basic genetic deficiency of the human body as the basis

Peter Weibel
Virtual Reality: Language World
(Virtuelle Welt: Sprach-Welt), 1992
Interactive computer installation
Video projector, projection screen,
carpets, sensors, dial box, silicone
graphics 4D / 320 vgx, computer,
silicone graphics video framer
Cologne, Klemens Gasser and
Tanja Grunert GmbH

*"I wouldn't like to limit myself to
individual media in my work. I
don't like that kind of professionalism where you say, that one's a
painter but the other one's a writer.
My slogan is: Everything is poetry."*
PETER WEIBEL

of his work. He is seeking to answer the question
whether a "two footed, breathing body with binocular
vision and a brain of 1400 cubic centimetres is a viable
biological structure." In order to bolster the functioning
and performance of this 'out-moded' body he develops
robots, medical and virtual systems. In his performances
he interacts with miniaturised technologies that link up
with his own body, in the form of a third hand, a virtual
arm or an implant (p. 616 above). For one of his most
recent projects he has developed a touch-screen interface whereby objects can be remotely controlled and
choreographed through muscular stimulation.

The Gesamtkunstwerk in the Public Arena

What became of William S. Burrough's dream of the
viruses that were to make many programmes out of
"one?" Bertolt Brecht had already made the visionary
suggestion that radio should be transformed from a
broadcasting service into a communicating service. As
early as 1932 he wrote in his theory of radio that then
"radio would be the most magnificent imaginable system of communication in public life." It could be a vast
"system of channels if it were only able not just to transmit but also to receive, that is, allowing the listener not
only to listen but also to speak and not to isolate the
listener but to establish contact." However, the history

of electronic media shows all too clearly that this potential means of democratisation has until now only achieved the opposite, namely state-controlled centralisation.

Despite unfulfilled visions and attempts that have
fallen by the wayside, artists have continued to search
for ways to open up official systems of communication
for the emancipation of the users. In 1977 the Australian
sound artist, Bill Fontana, called for all radio listeners in
the whole of Australia to record the sounds of their
everyday environment and to transmit them (by telephone) live to the studio where they were then mixed by
artists. In 1984 Ingo Günther (ill. right), in his study of
satellite images, discovered a hitherto unknown lake,
which then gave Iraq the decisive strategic advantage
over Iran in the war between them. Thus he showed that
even an isolated individual can gain access to apparently
closed computer systems and have a major impact on
events.

Since 1986 the teams 'Minus Delta t,' 'Van Gogh TV'
and 'PONTON, Fernseh- und Radiosender' have been
working on the development of multi-media communications systems. At the 1992 documenta Van Gogh TV
invited visitors to their *Piazza Virtuale* to take part in the
(inter)active production of a television programme
which in itself was part of a largely open-ended sched-
ule. For the virtual location the team created a computer-controlled tele-visual field where video images,
computer animations, text and sound could be combined. Visitors could actively participate in this project
in a number of ways. They could dial in by telephone,
make live contact with the screen via a modem or fax,
use the key-pad to access an 'interactive orchestra,' or try
out digital painting in a 'virtual studio (p. 617).'

"You don't throw a grand piano away just because you've got a synthesiser."

The question as to the effect electronic information and
communications systems are having on traditional art
production elicits a variety of responses from experts in
the field. Some see the electronic media as having
already stepped into the shoes of traditional art. However, many view the situation today with a certain degree
of scepticism. According to the media artist and theoretician Peter Weibel (ill. left), our culture is dominated
by an aesthetic which is both static and object-based,
while motion and time, despite their increasing importance, are either marginalised or banned altogether.
Heinrich Klotz, the founder and director of the Karlsruhe 'Zentrum für Kunst und Medientechnologie' is
convinced that traditional art forms will never in fact
become anachronistic. In his view, we now "simply have
a wider spectrum of medial forms at our disposal" and
conventional art remains a part of this spectrum. The
history of art over the last 180 years has shown that the
spectrum of media has been extended without resulting
in any single medium becoming obsolete. "You don't
throw a grand piano away just because you've got a synthesiser."

The American media specialist, Gene Youngblood, is prepared to risk some bold predictions. Taking an overall loss of meaning in art as his premise, he contends that this may only be reversed if we avail ourselves of the tools to match our current situation. Youngblood pleads for a genuine alliance of art and technology, which would both enliven art and humanise technology. He suggests that a new creative discipline should be developed: it would no longer be art in the familiar sense, but a kind of design. He envisions a "true renaissance, where art, science and social interaction grow inextricably together as one."

Will this form of design ever outstrip art as Youngblood would like to imagine? After all, many artists working today on the interface between humanity and technology are above all seeking to find new paths to images and virtual worlds. Of course the achievement of the arts may be defined in their capacity to criticise, to reflect and to search for aesthetic standards and how these may be operated. But perhaps some are beginning to weary of taking responsibility for the cultural deficiencies of our present-day media society. So far, attempts to open up new media for art have always foundered on the conservative structures of the art world. It is perfectly understandable that artists actively involved at the crossroads between art and the media are turning increasingly to software firms and television companies. On the other hand, the undisputed success of a figure such as Bruce Nauman demonstrates just how much our society needs a form of art that can step back and pose the basic questions of our existence which must be answered, helping us to understand better the meaning of our lives.

Thus we can only hope that the broad range of the arts, touching each and every one of our senses, may not fall victim to digitalisation. It might even be that one day it will seem a luxury to switch on a 'machine' after an exhausting day at the computer screen. And then it will be good to remind oneself of the message Beuys was transmitting with his *Felt TV* and to turn again to the tools that Filliou has stored in his tool-shed: "innocence" and "imagination."

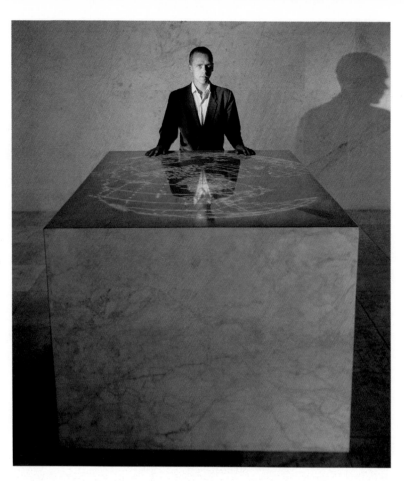

Ingo Günther
K4 (C31), 1987
Video installation; video projector,
video tape, sound, marble
Kassel, documenta 8 (1987)

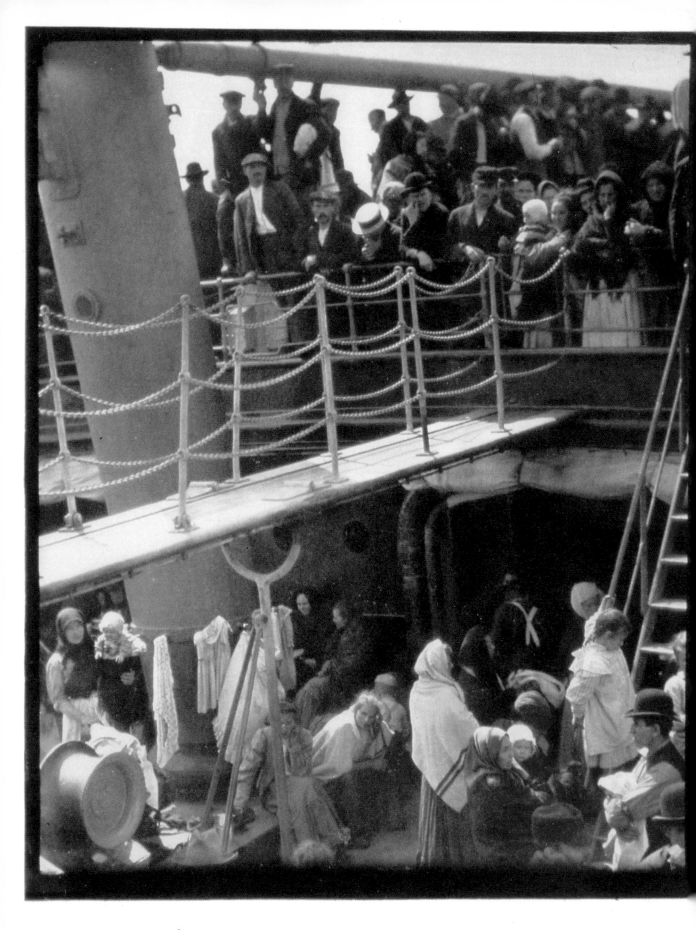

Photography between Art and Consumerism

Shortly before the turn of the century it seemed as though it was all over. On the one hand photography was becoming an industry in its own right and rapid technical advances had made taking photographs ever simpler but at the same time there was a strikingly obvious qualitative decline in photography. Yet the two factors were not directly connected – even although the siren sounds of commerce, reinforced by technical progress, had indeed largely undermined photography's artistic substance.

In June 1888 George Eastman brought out the first box camera and called it 'Kodak No. 1.' It contained his new, recently patented film-roll and the firm of Eastman, later to become the mighty Kodak empire, advertised it with the catchy slogan: "You press the button – we do the rest." All people had to do was send the camera with the film still in it to the factory: now they no longer needed to bother about the complicated business of developing and fixing.

And so it was that Eastman, inventive as well as a skilled organiser, ushered in the age of mass media. Photography now entered a period of major change. Thanks to the appeal of Eastman's idea, photography little by little persuaded almost everyone to see the world through its eyes at the same time as giving many of those same people the means to create their own images of the visible world. So the 'industrialisation' of photography also meant the 'democratisation' of the visual arts.

But it would be quite wrong to blame Eastman, the astute entrepreneur, for the pitiful aesthetic standards of the photography of the day. Its decline was due to a whole complex of reasons: for example technical innovation, that eased the lot of the professional photographer and brought the price of the end-product down, was combined with unimaginable demand, and this tempted some to neglect the finer details of the photographic process. In fact, the climate of economic competition was too much even for some respected, successful, important photographers such as Nadar in Paris and Mathew Brady in Washington, artist and entrepreneur in one. Although these photographers now rarely took a direct hand in the process in the studio, nevertheless they were still at pains to maintain professional standards in photography with the result that their pictures were beyond the means of most customers. "In the end,

though, businessmen invaded professional photography from every side, and when later on the retouched negative, which was the bad painter's revenge on photography, became ubiquitous, a sharp decline in taste set in. This was the time that photograph albums came into vogue."[1]

This situation was exacerbated by the deep-rooted economic crisis that followed the Franco-Prussian War in Europe (1870/71), in the wake of which there was a sharp downturn in interest in photography. And few small photographic businesses, still reliant on manual skills, were equal to this. Many had to give up. This in itself exemplifies one of the many paradoxes that have defined and determined the course of photography, in that it was pure coincidence that manual skills in the newest of the visual arts were to wither away at exactly the point when its commercial side was taking off.

Whereas on a social level it was only the economic basis of photography that changed, on an aesthetic level there was a real decline in standards. "This was the period of those studios, with their draperies and palm trees, their tapestries and easels, which occupied so ambiguous a place between execution and representation, between torture chamber and throne room, and to which an early portrait of Franz Kafka bears pathetic witness. There the boy stands, perhaps six years old, dressed up in a humiliatingly tight child's suit overloaded with trimming, in a sort of conservatory landscape. The background is thick with palm fronds. And as if to make these upholstered tropics even stuffier and more oppressive, the subject holds in his left hand an inordinately large broad-brimmed hat, such as Spaniards wear."[2]

Walter Benjamin's drastic assessment also applies equally to the portraits of the social elite – for example, the Crown Prince William, later to be Kaiser and King of Prussia (1888–1918), dressed as a member of a fraternity at Bonn University, sits forlornly like a lost holiday-maker against a truly kitsch Rhine backdrop: the photographer, Theo Schafgans, had simply copied the image of his illustrious client into a hideously romantic painting. More grotesque variations on the theme emanated from the famous studios of Hippolyte Lazergues and Adolphe-Jean François Maria Dallemagne in France. In addition to the usual visual props of grand

Alfred Stieglitz
The Steerage, 1907
Heliogravure, 19.7 x 15.8 cm
Cologne, Museum Ludwig

Stieglitz had exceptional skills of organisation and an incredible feel for the artistic mood of that restless time at the beginning of the 20th century. He was a gifted photographic artist and although by no means a theoretician he turned to art to underpin the aesthetic claims of photography – despite the fact that it was the leading artists of the time such as Jean Auguste Dominique Ingres and Eugène Delacroix or that incomparable critic and most sensitive of poets, Charles Baudelaire, who, along with other luminaries of the 'beaux arts,' had denied any claims that photography might have had to artistic viability. They were, in fact, perfectly happy to quietly profit from the benefits of photography at the same time as refusing to see any artistic value in "pictures from a machine," which they saw as automatic imprints of the visible and neither imbued with the artist's inspiration nor formed by the artist's hand.

Stieglitz retaliated in a piece for *Scribner's Monthly* (1889) with the bold proposition that "photographic equipment: the lens, the camera, the plate and so on

curtains, "pedestals and balustrades and little oval tables" (Benjamin), they also often provided their upper-class sitters with a kind of baroque surround which lent them a ridiculous air as though they were the last travellers from the disappearing age of the post-coach.

Let there be no misunderstanding: these pictures are not clouded by the slightest shimmer of irony, least of all self-irony. It was only in the USA that photography avoided the worst excesses, perhaps because social conflict and the contradictions of a fluid society in a young country prevented people exploring their land visually – and photography would have had an important hand in this – before they had come to terms with it on a physical level.

It was in the USA and in Great Britain, the most industrially advanced country in 'old' Europe, that the strongest forces amassed to prevent the demise of photography. It may surprise some to learn that the most powerful of these were the enthusiasts, the amateurs, artists, photographers and collectors who were immune to the lure of commerce. Alfred Stieglitz (ill. above and pp. 620 and 624) was one of the most influential spirits in this respect. After high school in New York he studied engineering at the Technische Hochschule in Berlin. In Germany he also encountered photography. There is still much work to be done on the inspiration that he found there as well as the inspiration that he later provided for others. At any rate, after his return to New York, Stieglitz became a member of the Society of Amateur Photographers and by 1892 he was already publishing the journal, *American Amateur Photographer.* Then he started taking his delicate shots of winter in New York followed by his first night-shots. In 1902, together with Alvin Langdon Coburn (ill. right) and Edward Steichen, he founded the 'Photo Secession' as well as the hugely influential journal, *Camera Work.*

constitute a flexible instrument and not a mere mechanical tyrant."[3] He was quite ready to admit that negative attitudes to photography were not without foundation and indeed wholly justifiable in most cases, but nevertheless the "skilled photographer" was able to extract a whole "variety of interpretations" from the photographic plate or negative without interfering manually in the process.

The negative itself, that "incomparably faithful" (Alexander von Humboldt) material basis of the automatic reproduction of the visible, was taboo. Stieglitz was insistent on a strict code of ethics for photographers: there was to be no unauthorised image manipu-

Alfred Stieglitz
End of the Line
("Camera Work" 36), 1911
Photogravure, 12.2 x 15.9 cm
Cologne, Museum Ludwig,
Gruber Donation

*"Photography being in the main a
process in monochrome, it is on
subtle gradations in tone and value
that its artistic beauty so frequently
depends."* ALFRED STIEGLITZ

lation! But at the same time, in mapping out the territory for artistic manoeuvre for the serious photographer,
he opened up the route into the laboratory. What
throngs of assistants had previously attended to for the
pioneers in the medium, namely the 'secondary' matter
of producing the prints themselves, was now viewed by
Stieglitz and his friends as a yardstick of artistic quality.
For Stieglitz, everything centred on the precision with
which individual shots were handled, which led him
quite simply to put the photographer's laboratory on a
par with the artist's studio.

Stieglitz & Co found their European kindred spirits
in Great Britain as well as in the Austro-Hungarian
Empire and Germany. In the United Kingdom the
secessionist photographers became known as the
"Linked Ring". Despite national differences the various
groups shared the same motivation and the arguments
they put forward for the aesthetic aspirations of photography are, bar a few nuances, wholly interchangeable.

Symptomatic of these arguments is, however, their
striking ambivalence. On the one hand, they looked to
art as the arbiter of the aesthetic value of photography.
There was, after all, the story of one artist's reaction to
his first sight of a photographic reproduction. This was
in the earliest days of the discovery of photography
(1839) and the artist, one now long forgotten Paul
Delaroche, a leading proponent of the still sacrosanct
traditions of academic art, is said to have cried out when
he saw the photograph that "now painting was dead."
On the other hand, Stieglitz and other like-minded spirits simply re-drew the battle lines in the conflict over
whether photography was an art form by freeing it from
the constraints of artistic considerations whose authority was in any case crumbling under the onslaught of the

avant-garde in the form of Edouard Manet, Edgar
Degas, Paul Cézanne and the Impressionists.

A strangely duplicitous situation – for the outraged
question facing the art-conscious bourgeoisie as to
whether 'this was art' was by no means directed at photographers alone. It was also familiar to the artists of the
avant-garde, namely Cézanne, Manet, Monet – in short,
the Impressionists. A reminder: 'Impressionist' had
been an insult on the part of an art critic. It was the great
photographer Nadar who had opened the doors of his
atelier on the boulevard des Capucines to the artists
under attack so that they could show their works free
from the dictates of a blinkered panel of selectors. The
real cause of the aesthetic hullabaloo was the widespread shift in artistic focus. And, as so often, this in
itself was the result of a shift in society as a whole,
spurred on not least by ground-breaking advances in
science along with all the practical consequences that
this implied.

In a word, if art up until this point had been primarily concerned with depicting the world, both tangible
and otherwise, now, since the middle of the 19th century,
art was becoming increasingly concerned with the problem of the individual perception of this same world. As
the art-historian Wolfgang Kemp puts it: "Now artists
were not so much concerned with the sight of something, as with sight itself."[4] Although Stieglitz cannily
restricted his comments to matters of manual technique, he was already, presumably subconsciously,
coupling the by-now free carriages of photography
behind the engine of advanced art as it hurtled into
the future.

Of course he turned a blind eye to the possibilities of
photography as a mass medium. These no doubt did not
particularly interest him. In any case it was only to the
sounds of battle across Europe that the technical conditions were created that would truly bring photography
to the masses: for example the epoch-making invention
of halftone printing was still far from technically perfect,
and although as early as 1880 the New York newspaper,
the *Daily Graphic,* had printed a photograph mechanically, transferring the image directly from the original to
the newsprint, the process was immensely complicated
and involved dividing the image up into infinitesimal
parts. 'Experiments' of this kind were thoroughly un-
satisfying to photographers. Nevertheless, Tim N. Gidal
(p. 636), one of the most successful photo-journalists
between the 20s and 40s, who later wrote on the history
of photography, rightly included Stieglitz amongst the
forerunners of his own profession, namely 'modern
photo-reportage.'

This is perfectly plausible in view of his early motifs.
Stieglitz's pictures deal with wholly unspectacular
events and occurrences. In fact, they are only remarkable
in the sense that the photographer has decided to capture them on film. Stieglitz probably took the legendary
picture *End of the Line* (ill. above) at the last stop of a
New York horse-drawn tram line. It shows the coach-

man attending to his steaming tram-horses on an icy winter's night. At the right-hand edge of the shot someone is shovelling snow, on the left a bowler-hatted man is stamping out of the picture and in the background there is the façade of a building with a grand entrance. Nothing that would really catch one's attention beyond, perhaps, its subtle composition. A picture like this would certainly have added immeasurably to any photo-reportage.

The choice here of an everyday subject links this masterpiece with the best of photo-reportage as the age of mass media was dawning in the early 30s. And yet the difference between the two is equally evident: not so much the fact that Stieglitz conceived this as an individual photograph, as the particular quality of the prints themselves, precious and exquisite. Collectors' items in the truest sense. One prerequisite of this was the use of pigment paper which allowed the photographer to intervene, treating each picture individually and subtly differently during the printing process. The picture was dependent for its very existence on direct manual intervention and was therefore subject to the whims of the photographer's will rather than to some iron natural law, as the critic Robert de la Sizeranne wrote: "The negative is the province of the equipment, the print is the province of the human being, and the style is the person."[5]

The aesthetic standards that were set by this form of art-centred photography defined the medium in the early decades of this century. But of course even this was a temporary state of affairs and was soon discredited, above all by the many who leapt on the bandwagon. Beyond this it was the First World War and its consequences that finally lifted the lid on that idyllic art-realm of bromine and gum bichromate prints with atmospheric landscapes and sunny portraits, exposing them as just as false as the grandiose platitudes about love of the Fatherland for which millions of young people were killed.

Yet not all serious photographers accepted the aesthetic maxims of art-photography. There were those who not only wanted to see its documentary nature preserved – but in fact viewed this as the real domain of the aesthetics of photography and took a dim view of those who were constantly looking over their shoulders towards art. The British photographer, Frederic H. Evans pleaded for pure, thoroughly "photographic" photography, which he called 'straight photography.' In his view the creative moment in photography was concentrated in what went on behind the camera and not in devising nifty tricks in the lab. If he was not happy with a shot he refused to rescue it in the laboratory – he would take it again even if that meant a long journey.

Evans' preferred motifs were Gothic cathedrals, both from outside and from inside. He also loved fine prints and perfected the use of expensive platinotypes. His friend and comrade-in-arms George Bernard Shaw, a passionate amateur photographer, supported him in

this, emphasised the "realistic representational power" of photography and, letting his love of paradox run riot, romped towards the conclusion that painting was the mechanical art form, and not photography, for all that it was a technical medium.

But for too long the images of Pictorialism were viewed through the spectacles of the later photographic avant-garde. In the meantime we have developed a more sober approach and, in addition, outstanding examples of art-photography have since become much sought-after collectors' items. Gradually, too, they are also being recognised for their aesthetic contribution to direct photography. Numerous elements in the matter of motif and pictorial composition as well as in the choice of apparently unremarkable details – significant features of art-photography – have passed more or less fluidly into the repertoire of avant-garde photography today.

Edward Steichen (ill. below and p. 623), one of the key figures in the history of photography, once virtually lost control when it seemed to him that the whole discussion – art photography as opposed to pure photogra-

Edward Steichen
The Flatiron Evening
("Camera Work" 14), 1906
Three-colour halftone
reproduction, 20.6 x 16 cm
Cologne, Museum Ludwig,
Gruber Donation

Heinrich Kühn
Alfred Stieglitz, 1907
Gum bichromate print,
29.6 x 23.2 cm
Cologne, Museum Ludwig

phy – was narrowing down the potential of the medium to an unacceptable extent, even before it had been properly explored. Steichen had been trained as a painter and, as a photographer, was extremely successful in all disciplines and areas of photography, an indescribably skilled operator in its cause, albeit perhaps not without a degree of self-interest. In his words: "We have experienced the astonishingly rapid unfolding of ideas in the area of photo-mechanics. Colour art-photography is at a problematic stage, in the cinematograph we have the completely unexploited possibility of creating a completely new art form all of its own. We still have to learn to master countless other technical possibilities – so how can we talk about technical limits, limitations on and the limitedness of a form of artistic expression? A whole world lies before us, we feel its heartbeat, it pulsates with life, beauty and strength – we can't have people simply telling us: this is as far as art goes."[6]

So it is not surprising that the critic Eugenia Perry Janis, looking back, should describe photographers such as Stieglitz, Steichen, Coburn, Karl Struss and others from that circle as the "young moderns." Indeed she even risks a direct comparison between the supposed opposing sides in the photographic dispute of the day, between the one side supporting photographic photography and the other who favoured artistic photography. In her view, at least in terms of the USA, both sides had portrayed the growing city metropolises with equal success, "documenting the physiognomies of America's new citizens, and while one side celebrated modern technology the other concentrated on the might of technical symbolism."[7]

Misconceptions of art-photography derive perhaps above all from its European exponents: these included Hans Watzek, who was actually more interested in the technical side of photography, and Heinrich Kühn (ill. left). Although they were both Austrians, they were in touch either in person or through letters with their American and British colleagues, their compatriot Hugo Henneberg, the German brothers Theodor and Oscar Hofmeister, Robert Demachy and Constant Puyo from France, and James Craig Annan whose father, Thomas, had used a naive reportage style for his photographs of the appalling conditions in the slums of Glasgow. They loved to indulge their taste for cosy landscapes and enchanting townscapes, preferably of Venice and created ardent portraits of prominent artists with a decided preference for their own friends. Delightful pictures – the ultimate in photographic skill. Against the backdrop of a society that was being driven by the fires of the industrial revolution towards World War and catastrophe these images do, however, seem like pure escapism.

In contrast to this, it was not through chance alone that the Flatiron Building in New York – reaching out into the junction of Fifth Avenue and Broadway, a bold structure and a stirring monument to the dawning technical age – should become the striking symbol of American art-photography and Pictorialism. Although American photographers, too, flooded their seductive images with iridescent light, nevertheless their more 'technical' approach set them apart from their kindred spirits in Europe. They breathed the air of the modern cities. And even the clear, identifiable structures of a picture like Kühn's *At the Coast* pointed towards the photographic avant-garde. Constantly looking towards art had put photography under somewhat negative pressure to legitimise itself but, as it turned out, photography simply emerged all the stronger from the crisis.

2 Art from a Machine: 'New Seeing'

No helpful hints here for the viewer's orientation. The author has even denied the picture a title. In the lower centre there is a circle surrounded by other circles; above this there is a diagonal section of scaffolding breaking off at a right angle at the right-hand edge. A few flowing lines, partly very dark grey, partly light grey, are as uninformative as the even lines around the circles. The picture has no real centre, somehow things have slipped out of the schema of traditional composition theory, although there is a certain, albeit uneasy, balance within the picture itself. And yet this picture is by no means an abstract composition.

In many respects this photograph, *Untitled,* taken in 1928 by László Moholy-Nagy is, in fact, more realistic than any of the images of art-photography. Nothing has been manipulated here: this is a product of direct photography par excellence. Yet there is one difference: normal perception is not equal to a picture of this sort. This is not some detail of reality that one can immediately assimilate visually. There is no focal point drawing together the lines of perspective, nor does there seem to be any particular object at their centre. And when viewers discovered what they were looking at, a sudden dizziness must surely have hit them – for Moholy-Nagy had taken his camera up the Berlin radio tower and photographed the view looking virtually vertically downwards.

The shock created by pictures of this sort is hard to reconstruct now; although a certain sense of irritation remains. The moment the supposedly abstract distorting image has revealed its true nature as an identifiable slice of reality, the viewer's gaze hits the ground with a thud, like the body of a suicide victim. Subliminal fears are aroused. In his masterpieces, Alfred Hitchcock, having perfected his skills as a film-maker in 20s Berlin played the same devilish game with people's fears and even today, shots from up above still signal acute danger in the better horror films.

In this sense the photographie image that Moholy-Nagy created also lent vivid expression to a feeling shared by many at the time. Nothing was any longer the way it used to be. The certainties and ideas that had shaped and steadied the world had been shattered in the battles of the First World War. In Russia the Bolsheviks had waged a bloody civil war and set up a new regime that held out hope to all those who had up until then been at the foot of the social pyramid in Europe, including the majority of intellectuals and artists. In Germany revolution had only been avoided by a hair's breadth. Uprisings on both sides of the political spectrum had shaken the country and reparations to the victorious powers were a huge burden to the economy, yet for a few short years before the Great Depression was to hit the world, the Weimar Republic basked in a wholly false sense of security. The forces of democracy were, however, too weak and too fragmented to prevent the disaster that was looming on the horizon and not even intellectuals and artists had much to say in the Republic's favour. For most it was no more than a form of camouflage.

While the First World War had wrought radical change in the world, many people could see only too clearly traits of the bad, old world in this new, changed world. No brave, new world here – with the exception of

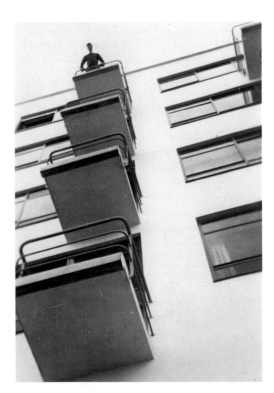

László Moholy-Nagy
Bauhaus Balconies, 1925
Gelatin silver print, 8.2 x 6.1 cm
Cologne, Museum Ludwig,
Gruber Donation

the Soviet Union, where war and art had been enlisted in the attempt to create a new kind of human being and a new kind of society. In the face of the might of Soviet 'revolutionary art' even the brand-new, refreshingly trivial culture of the USA blenched. However, it had ultimately been the power of American industrialism that had decided the outcome of the war. The furious attacks by the Dadaists in Germany were still making themselves felt and enlightened artists saw bourgeois art as synonymous with the false cultural face of a social system that was morally, economically and culturally bankrupt. In rejecting this, it seemed simplest to include Futurism and Cubism whilst one was about it.

The cry for a completely new form of art did the rounds and found a particular resonance above all in the defeated nations of Europe, in Germany and in the Soviet Union. And the collapse of the imperial Austro-Hungarian monarchy released a positive explosion of creative energy in middle and southern Europe. However, as the rise of nationalist and anti-Semitic sentiment suppressed this again, the more forward-looking artists of largely Jewish origin went on the move: many were drawn to the German metropolis of Berlin, with its electric atmosphere and myriad contradictions. For a short while Berlin, even Germany itself, became the citadel of contemporary art. But what should be the demands on a new art form?

"Viewed in terms of traditional means of visual expression the photographic process is incomparable. And the results are also incomparable, when it uses its own potential" – Moholy-Nagy (ill. right and p. 627), in a programmatic text in the first volume of the yearbook *Das deutsche Lichtbild.*[8] As an avant-garde artist, unlike the art-photographers, he stressed the autonomy of the medium very much in the spirit of direct photography. Naturally he was only interested in purely photographic matters as a side-issue, purely as a means to an end as it were. His attitude was one of principle.

He was interested in the perception of reality unclouded by any kind of cultural convention and this he felt could be had from the pictures that came from the camera: "The secret of their effect is that the photographic equipment reproduces a purely optical picture and thus shows optically true images, distortions, foreshortenings and so on whereas our eyes take up what is seen and, with the assistance of our intellectual experience, make associative connections and round it out formally and spatially into some imaginary image. Thus in photography we have the most reliable aid to achieving the first stages of objective seeing. The individual viewer will be forced to see the optical truth, which can be understood from within itself, before even beginning to come to some possible subjective attitude..."[9]

This enthusiasm for the 'machine' after the experience of the First World War, the first technological war, which itself had been decided on superior machine power, may seem surprising. Had it not been the supremacy of American technological resources that

had tipped the balance on the battlefield? Yet, on the other hand, at the time those with any kind of an open mind could see no alternative to technology. It seemed that the only hope of improving the human condition was going to be by exploiting technology to the full. Only a few dreamers nurtured their anxieties about technology, harked back to Nature myths and adopted an "anti-civilisation" stance.

Nevertheless, the first technological conflict of major proportions in world history engendered an awareness in Germany that "the technology that had produced bombs and tanks could equally well be used to produce goods for a new society. Machines were now being used to make simple yet elegant kitchen utensils, lighting equipment or vehicles. Industrial architecture emphasised the technical structures of its building design and artists and other creative minds became increasingly interested in the precision engineering needed for cog-wheels, conduits and aircraft made from sheet aluminium and in the structural composition of other materials. From this extended awareness of the aesthetic possibilities of geometric forms, be it in machinery or be it in architecture, a new avant-garde movement in photography evolved in Germany which was often referred to as 'New Seeing.'"[10]

'New Seeing', (Neues Sehen). The very term makes it clear that what is meant here is not the mode of perception – a mixture of physiological pre-conditions and sensual, mental and spiritual mechanisms – nor is the illusionism of academic art nor the disruptive view of the avant-garde meant. 'New Seeing' is instead the immediate image produced by the camera lens. No subjective impulse falsifies this picture of the world. The technical apparatus guarantees objectivity. In the optics of 'New Seeing' visible reality manifests itself as a construct. As Moholy-Nagy stated: "You could say that we see the world with completely different eyes."[11] In the light of his views all other types of representation become, at best, inadequate illustrations of reality or, at worst, wholly inept. The 'constructivist' photographs of 'New Seeing' reflect the notion that science and technology should now also provide the guidelines needed by art.

Progressive artists like Moholy-Nagy and before him the Dadaists, George Grosz and John Heartfield (p. 122), along with Hannah Höch and Raoul Hausmann (p. 122), saw the 'apparatus-made,' so to speak automatically produced images of photography (which was in itself the product of research in chemistry and physics) as the only suitable artistic means to construct the longed-for 'new' world and to create its 'new' people.[12] In 1923 Walter Gropius invited Moholy-Nagy to the Bauhaus in Weimar to take up a position as 'Master of Forms in the Metal Shop.' From October of that year the Hungarian, responsible for the teaching of basic principles to second semester students, offered the course 'Material and Space', along with Gropius himself. Through his teachings, photographic experiments

Andreas Feininger
New York, Midtown Manhattan,
42nd Street, 1947
Gelatin silver print, 25.3 x 34.2 cm
Cologne, Museum Ludwig,
Gruber Donation

Boris Kudoyarov
October Revolution Celebration,
c. 1935–1940
Gelatin silver print, 26 x 37 cm
Cologne, Museum Ludwig,
Ludwig Collection

(married for a time to Herbert Bayer) and the great Umbo (Otto Umbehr).

Without mentioning him by name, Walter Benjamin, in his *Small History of Photography*, quotes a forward-looking statement by Moholy-Nagy: "'The illiteracy of the future,' someone has said, 'will be ignorance not of reading or writing, but of photography.'" But he had misunderstood the artist Moholy-Nagy's aesthetic aims, for the latter was not particularly concerned with photography as a medium and not at all with 'photography' as a means of expression: instead he saw photography as a viable way of presenting the complex inter-connections of space and time in keeping with the latest advances in science. There can be no doubt as to the fascination that his aesthetic thinking had for advanced artists both in Germany and in the Soviet Union – in the latter as a country where determined attempts were being made to realise, through positive action, the hope of a world where freedom and justice would prevail.

Yet, in the early days of the Soviet Union photography did not enjoy a high status. Although the artists of the avant-garde did occasionally try out various photographic games such as montage and photograms, nevertheless these were generally applied rather than actually experimental. Alexander Rodchenko (p. 633) illustrated Vladimir Mayakovsky's *Pro Eto* (1923) and created a poster for the 'History of the Russian Communist Party' as part of a series that the Constructivist El Lissitzky (p. 631 above) also participated in. It is possible that they had been inspired by the German Dadaist 'Fotomonteurs.' Lissitzky and Kasimir Malevich made frequent trips to Germany – and were good communicators.

Half in undisguised anger, half out of a boisterous delight in contradiction, the Dadaists had broken all the prevailing cultural codes, dismissed works that had long been held dear, exploded familiar symbols and invoked a *tabula rasa* scenario. Like Grosz and Heartfield they cut up coherent pictorial elements and combined them with trenchant, sometimes totally incomprehensible texts. Or, like Höch, Hausmann and Heartfield again, they would construct confusing visual impromptus from a montage of a wide variety of photographic images. These photomontages could be read like a text, not that one could be certain of being much the wiser afterwards. "The revolutionary power of Dada was that it tested the authenticity of art."[13] It did not in fact have any particular political striking power.

In the Soviet Union, where the communists were fighting for survival in a horrendous civil war, and also in Germany, where conflict was germinating, film was luring the masses into the cinema and its brand new aesthetics did not fertilise photography alone. Sergei Eisenstein, Vladimir Pudovkin and the 'documentarist' Dsiga Vertov did much to refine the principles of montage and their inventions also affected both art and photography. In the realms of popular culture montage was already a commonplace tool.

and bold publications, including the legendary Bauhaus book *Painting, Photography, Film* (1925), Moholy-Nagy exercised a decisive influence on the self-image of advanced art.

Although photography was not studied as such at the Bauhaus and Moholy-Nagy never taught it as a subject, his ground-breaking ideas were enthusiastically received by numerous students at the institute. Playfully yet persistently, many acquired the essential skills of photography and some, such as the brothers Andreas (ill. above) and Lux T. Feininger made productive contact with the new genre of photo-journalism that was blossoming in Germany at the time; others found their own individual visual language in various realms of photography, independent of Moholy-Nagy, with the list including Werner Graeff, Florence Henri, Lucia Moholy (p. 631 below), Moshe Raviv-Vorobeichic (Moi Ver), Xanti Schavinsky, Ellen Auerbach, Irene Bayer

Heartfield and Grosz had first met it in American advertising while Moholy-Nagy had encountered it in the military propaganda of the imperial army; and popular postcards from seaside and mountain resorts had long used montage to create more or less entertaining effects. But it was film that was to set alight the creative hot-heads in Germany and the Soviet Union: less so in fact the American films by David Wark Griffith, who was the first to utilise the hugely effective potential of montage, than the 'Russian films' with their association-laden montage sequences structured around collision and contradiction.

In comparison to film, photography in the 1920s in the Soviet Union was seen as old hat. Most photographers continued to pay homage to art-photography. In addition the fact that there was a paucity of suitable paper and a shortage of supplies of the right chemicals made it difficult for photography to become a propaganda tool, directed at the masses. After the dust had settled somewhat and film had so dramatically shown empirical reality as a subject for aesthetic treatment, then in the Soviet Union, too, there was a rapid rise in interest in a new visual language for photography.

In 1923 a group of artists founded LEF (The Left Front of Art): "a society of Futurist and Constructivist artists – the first to focus on and reflect the theoretical problems of photography as a medium that both creates and alters awareness."[14] A leading newspaper published their aesthetic views under the same name. Writers, film-makers, typographers, painters and theoreticians all belonged to LEF. After various interruptions – from time to time disagreements, conflicts and normal wear and tear put a halt to the group's activities altogether – it then reformed in 1928 as 'Nowy LEF.' Boris Ignatovich (p. 632 above), his wife Jelisaveta and his sister Olga, Eliasar Langman, Dimitri Debakov, Boris Kudoyarov (p. 630) and Georgi Petrussov (p. 632 below right) all became involved. Moholy-Nagy's Bauhaus book, *Painting, Photography, Film,* lifted their spirits and his declaration that in the "extended field of vision ... now even today's lens was no longer bound by the narrow confines of the human eye" and that "no manual tool (paintbrush, pencil etc) could "capture details of the world seen in this manner"[15] was absolutely in keeping with Vertov's definition of the "cinema-eye" and its "point of departure," whereby the "filmic eye" was "better able than any human eye" to examine the "chaos of visual phenomena."[16] With the help of montage Vertov constructed a new world in his films. "I am a cinema eye. I am an edifier,"[17] he declared.

On 14 November 1928 Rodchenko held a slide lecture with the title "On New Photography or Photo-LEF" in the State Academy of Art in Moscow. During the course of this lecture he explained that the new movement in photography in the Soviet Union brought together two opposing positions: one took the view that photography was a form of documentation (the position of LEF and Nowy LEF) while the other subscribed to the notion that photography was a constituent part of contemporary art. Although Rodchenko did speak out against art itself, saying that it was possible "through photography and other documents ... to expose the falseness that was inherent in all art products"[18] his attack was directed mainly at traditional art and art-photography.

He and other like-minded spirits drove the process of photographic innovation forwards on two fronts at once: on the one hand concentrating on honing the individual picture to perfection and on the other hand, in apparent contradiction of the 'supremacy' of the individual image, looking at series and picture sequences. In

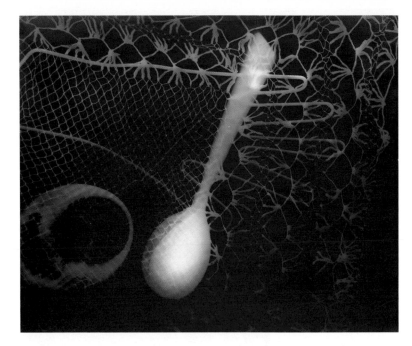

El Lissitzky
Composition with Spoon, c. 1924
Gelatin silver print, 23.4 x 29 cm
Cologne, Museum Ludwig,
Ludwig Collection

Lucia Moholy
Wassily and Nina Kandinsky in
their Dining Room, 1926
Gelatin silver print, 19.4 x 25.1 cm
Cologne, Museum Ludwig,
Gruber Donation

Boris Ignatovich
Factory Window, 1929
Gelatin silver print, 24 x 17.8 cm
Cologne, Museum Ludwig,
Ludwig Collection

his work he realised the artistic principles of 'New
Seeing' with his preference for extremely close close-
ups for portraits, his extensive use of steep angles from
above and monumentalising angles from below as well
as often arranging the pictorial motifs diagonally. The
fragmentary quality of the individual picture invites
viewers to complete it mentally, mobilises their powers
of imagination and accords them the status of co-
authors (p. 633).

In an essay with the revealing subtitle "Against the
synthetic portrait – for the monumental snapshot"
(1928) Rodchenko focused on the 'secular' figure of the
Soviet revolutionary Vladimir Ilich Lenin in order to
expound the problems surrounding any artistic attempt
to convey the full personality of one individual. "There
is no complete picture of Lenin," he wrote, "nor of anyone else ... yet, there is this: a representation based on
photography, books and notes. The fact is that since the
advent of photography there can be no more general,
immutable notions of what a picture is. And furthermore, a person is not a single entity, a person is many-
sided, dialectical."[19] In this Rodchenko was not only
drawing a parallel with film and its inspired use of montage but also with photo-journalism, which at the time
had its strongest foothold in Germany and the Soviet
Union – rather, significantly enough, than in the USA.

Nevertheless, within a relatively short time this tireless photo-artist – who always involved his intellect in
any practical steps he took – found himself buffeted by
storms of protest. These started with photographers
who had pinned their colours to reportage. They
denounced Rodchenko as a 'Formalist,' a reproach that
was potentially life-threatening during that period of
consolidation of the Soviet regime under the power politics of the feared figure of Stalin. He provoked criticism
for his sometimes daring visual constructions rather
than for his futuristic, serial working method which
points to the extent to which the supposedly leading
lights in the USSR were still entangled in out-dated
modes of seeing, even before the party instituted the
petit-bourgeois flavoured doctrine of Socialist Realism
in art.

The journal *Proletarske Foto*, the mouthpiece of the
Russian Society of Proletarian Photo-Reporters
(ROPF), started the most disgraceful attacks on Rod-

Arkadi Shaikhet
Strengthening the Body, 1927
Gelatin silver print, 31.5 x 41 cm
Cologne, Museum Ludwig,
Ludwig Collection

Georgi Petrussov
Soldiers with Helmets, 1935
Gelatin silver print, 30 x 25 cm
Cologne, Museum Ludwig,
Ludwig Collection

chenko and his followers. They accused him of pursuing
Western "decadence as purveyed by modern bourgeois
photographers,"[20] with Moholy-Nagy and his imitators
at their head, to the detriment of his commitment to the
proletariat. The fact that his staunchest critics, such as
the leading photographer, Arkadi Shaikhet (p. 632 below
left), were themselves infected by the 'bacillus' of 'New
Seeing' was obviously completely beside the point in
this confrontation fed by artistic jealousy.

However, Rodchenko continued to work as a photographer – although under considerably harder conditions than before – and still managed to have startling
reportages accepted by illustrated journals such as *Dai-
josch* and *Isogis,* reporting for example on the building of
the hydro-electric power station in Magnitogorsk on the
Dnieper or focusing on the Turkestan-Siberian Railway,
while an important piece on the building of the White
Sea Canal was published by *SSSR Na Stroike* (The
USSR under Construction). The precisely constructed
montages of individual pictures in the pages of these
journals as well as the fact that these pictures were
intended all along for mass-reproduction raises these
'documentations' far above the usual standard found in
illustrated journals at the time. "The different angles
from which an object is photographed set up ever new
tensions whose formal qualities modify the semantic
content."[20]

In the matter of form, some of Rodchenko's pictures, for example his *Woodcutters* (1932), seem strangely
inept as soon as they are extracted from their context –
in this case a photographic essay on a saw-mill. The
sense of unease only abates when they are restored to the
context of a whole spread of pictures on the same theme.
With supreme artistic intelligence Rodchenko was able
to integrate modern rotary printing processes and techniques of mass-distribution into his own aesthetic calculations. Amongst other advanced artists in the 20s
John Heartfield was the only one to pursue a similarly
radical course.

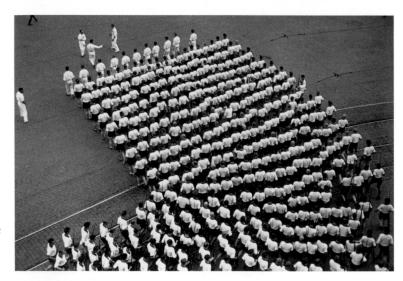

Alexander Rodchenko
Dynamo Club, 1930
Gelatin silver print, 26.5 x 40 cm
Cologne, Museum Ludwig,
Ludwig Collection

Alexander Rodchenko
Portrait of his Mother, 1924
Gelatin silver print, 39 x 29 cm
Cologne, Museum Ludwig,
Ludwig Collection

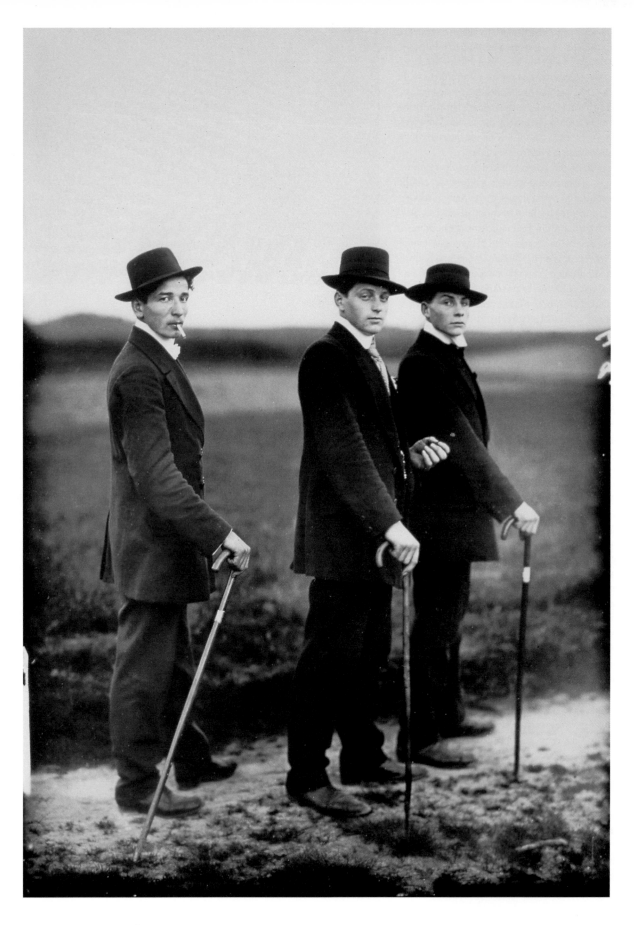

3 The Material World in Focus – 'Neue Sachlichkeit'

Photo-journalists in Germany came into the profession from all walks of life; most were new to the business. The impending world economic crisis had catapulted many out of their old jobs. On the other hand, the illustrated journals in the mid to late 20s were sorely in need of creative rejuvenation. Circulation numbers were stagnating and although the mechanisms for industrial plate printing from photographs were all in place, printed images only functioned as appendages to texts of varying quality. The publishers made money with serialisations of well-written novels such as Erich Maria Remarque's *All Quiet on the Western Front.* It seemed that even in the USA people had forgotten the committed reportages by photographers such as Jacob Riis, Lewis Hine (p. 636 above) or Francis Benjamin Johnston, although these admittedly could not yet be printed by the journals.

Under the Weimar Republic a particularly fortunate configuration of circumstances, not least an astonishing concentration of bright, daring spirits led to a positive blossoming of photo-journalism. Far-sighted publishers like Kurt Safranski, imaginative editors, gifted designers, including Richard Lindner for the *Münchner Illustrierte Presse,* who later achieved recognition as a painter and forerunner of Pop Art, as well as a number of inquisitive photographers all underpinned the huge contribution that photography made as a mass medium. The *Berliner Illustrirte Zeitschrift* had the highest circulation figures, at times swamping the market with over a million and a half copies; far behind it lay the *Münchner Illustrierte Presse* although in hot competition with its Berlin counterpart. Against a background of rising unemployment, spectacular business failures, increasingly brutal street fights and growing social misery and hunger, the insatiable thirst for 'authentic' images was fed amongst others by the *Arbeiter Illustrierte Zeitung* (AIZ, supported by the Communist Party and with Heartfield on its books), the *Kölnische Illustrierte Zeitung* and magazines such as *Uhu, Das Magazin* (which still exists), *Scherl's Magazin, Dame,* and the illustrated weekend supplements issued by the dailies.

A legendary figure amongst the photographers of the day was Dr Erich Salomon (p. 637) . With a doctorate in law and his shots of prominent contemporaries in 'unguarded moments' he was a star. Whether his subject

August Sander
Unemployed, 1928
Gelatin silver print, 22.5 x 14.2 cm
Cologne, Museum Ludwig

was the lighted windows of the presidential palace during a reception in honour of King Fuad, exhausted French and German ministers at one o'clock in the morning during an all-night sitting at the second Den Haag Conference, or the French Foreign Minister Aristide Briand at precisely the moment when he notices the photographer with his camera at the ready – thanks to their intelligent visual significance, Salomon's pictures always received a high degree of attention. He perfected the notion of 'snapshot photography.' His experience, his education, his pleasant demeanour along with his striking inventiveness and intrepid cleverness all marked him out as a specialist in the unusual.

Scarcely less successful was Martin Munkacsi (p. 650), born in a Hungarian enclave in Romania. He apparently managed to achieve the impossible: he com-

August Sander
Young Farmers in their Sunday Best, Westerwald, 1913
Gelatin silver print, 30.4 x 20.5 cm
Cologne, Museum Ludwig

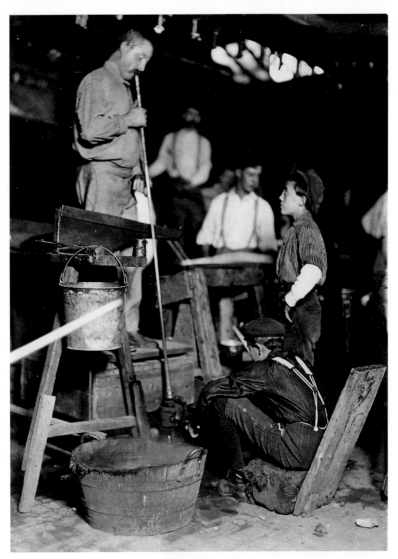

photographer; Hans Baumann, known as Felix H. Man who became one of the most interesting photographers in his field, also an art historian by training; Umbo (p. 640), a Bauhaus product and a real poet with the camera; the committed social critic Wolfgang Weber who had studied ethnography and musicology in Leipzig; and a physician with a doctorate, Dr Paul Wolff, who was the first to set the small Leicas on the road to success and was also soon producing Nazi propaganda.

Of course 'quick' cameras, the Leica and the Ermanox, one as handy as the other, in conjunction with the greater light sensitivity of the film that was now available had laid the technical basis for the blossoming of photo-journalism – but its massive success was due both to the individual achievements of the photographers themselves and to editorial ambitions to use images in the telling of remarkable stories. In the process, the structure of the reports became ever more filmic, ranging from the meaningful combining of individual pictures to an inspired montage of the wider context. "Nowadays, in the major journals we see behind the scenes, eavesdrop on politicians, gaze on distant lands: everything has become photographable. The photographers discover new angles on things and are expected to deliver new ways of looking at social and political life."[21]

Tim N. Gidal, one of the most prominent in the ranks of photo-journalists, once described the themes of everyday life as the main motif for the photo-reportages of the illustrated journals. "The real yardstick became the humanity of the photo-journalist, the honesty of the report on what was to be seen, whether beautiful or not,

Lewis Hine
Glass Factory, 1908
Gelatin silver print, 16.7 x 11.8 cm
Cologne, Museum Ludwig,
Jeane von Oppenheim Donation

bined the aesthetic principles of the artistic avant-garde with the demands of professional photography. Munkacsi was the aesthetic catalyst of artistic invention and electrifying visual effect. His particular way of seeing the world, his pronounced feel for original, accessible compositions, his extraordinary sensitivity towards the feverish dynamic of his own age, whose aura he both breathed and portrayed – all these marked his pictures out as unique records of the modern era.

Alongside Salomon and Munkacsi there was a whole troupe of excellent photographers, including Walter Bosshard from Switzerland, who had studied art history; Alfred Eisenstaedt (p. 643), originally a haberdashery salesman who took photographs in his spare time before becoming a legendary member of staff on the American magazine *Life* (from 1937 onwards); George Gidal (who died prematurely), brother of Tim N. Gidal (ill. right) who had studied history, art history and economics; Kurt Hübschmann (Kurt Hutton); André Kertész (pp. 638 f), a compatriot of Munkacsi's and one of the greatest photographers of all; Harald Lechenperg, the travel

Tim N. Gidal
Cheerful Self-Portrait, 1940
Gelatin silver print, 175 x 12 cm
Cologne, Museum Ludwig

whether positive or negative. The reader then experienced this immediate kind of reportage, observing hitherto unobserved spheres in the lives of his or her fellow human beings, a privilege brought to him or her by the modern photo-journalist, who nevertheless respected the actual boundaries of an individual's private life."[22]

This, then, is where the aims of the professional photographer meet the aesthetic intentions of the artistically ambitious photographer. Unlike the leading proponents of 'New Seeing' the photographers of Neue Sachlichkeit (New Objectivity) were keen to exploit the actual characteristics of photography and its very real possibilities, taking up where direct photography had left off in the 19th century. Among their number were Albert Renger-Patzsch, August Sander (pp. 634 f), Werner Mantz (p. 638) and Karl Blossfeldt (even if the latter qualified more on account of his photographic approach rather than his aesthetic intentions.)

As a result, they identified their sharpest aesthetic opposition as coming from the still tremendously successful art-photographers such as the sensitive portraitist Hugo Erfurth (ill. below). However, their work was not centred on perception and "seeing vision" (Max Imdahl) as was that of Moholy-Nagy and his followers. They were interested instead in the soberest, most factual representation of the photographic subject. Renger-Patzsch (p. 640) summed up the artistic aims of Neue Sachlichkeit: "The secret of a good photograph, which can have artistic value just like any work of art, lies in its realism. In photography we have a reliable means to communicate the impressions we might have at the sight of Nature, a plant, an animal, works by builders or sculptors, the creations of engineers and technicians."[23]

Furthermore, he appealed to his fellow photographers: "Let us therefore leave art to the artists and use the means of photography to create photographs that stand on their photographic quality alone – without having to borrow from art."[24]

His photographic works, prime examples of Neue Sachlichkeit, reveal a dry, engineer-like view, the precise representation of things, giving a clear over-view of their formal order, yet resisting any temptation into Formalism, in the same sense that the fine differentiation of their grey tones is achieved by even, wholly undramatic lighting. His impressive book, *Die Welt ist schön* (The World is Beautiful) – he himself would have preferred a more laconic title, namely *Die Dinge* (Things) – provoked scorn from Walter Benjamin, yet it became a kind of Bible to the photographers of Neue Sachlichkeit,

Erich Salomon
Round-Table Talks, 1930
Gelatin silver print, 27.8 x 36 cm
Cologne, Museum Ludwig

Erich Salomon
King Fuad of Egypt with Hindenburg, 1930
Gelatin silver print, 17.7 x 23.7 cm
Cologne, Museum Ludwig,
Gruber Donation

Hugo Erfurth
Käthe Kollwitz, 1929
Gelatin silver print, 24 x 18.5 cm
Bonn, Rheinisches Landesmuseum Bonn

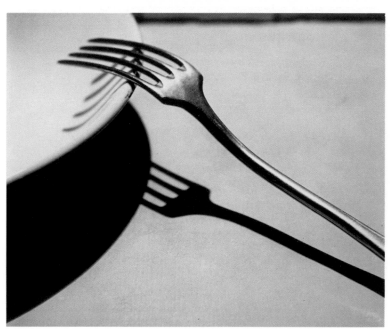

more influential even than Sander's *Antlitz der Zeit* (Face of the Times), a social panorama of the Weimar Republic embodied in its own social mask, and more influential too than Karl Blossfeldt's *Urformen der Kunst* (Art Forms in Nature; ill. below) with its monumental yet unpretentious depictions of flowers and plants against a neutral background.

Gustav F. Hartlaub, who invented the term 'Neue Sachlichkeit', described what this meant for painting as "the discovery of the thing after the crisis of the ego during Expressionism."[25] This description also exactly fits the photographic work of Renger-Patzsch, Sander and those of a similar leaning. Norbert M. Schmitz summed up the situation in film: "The films of 'Neue Sachlichkeit' ... practise an objective view of things, a distanced, distinctly scientific attitude which nevertheless presupposes an underlying acceptance of our industrial present."[26] Renger-Patzsch had just embarked on an ambitious project aiming at a photographic documentation of the Ruhr area, when the National Socialist government stripped him of his post at the Folkwang School in Essen. In response he abruptly called a halt to the project and withdrew into 'inner emigration' just as Sander, too, was also unable to pursue his ground-breaking chronicle of humanity under the Nazi dictatorship.

Advanced German photography celebrated its triumph in the Stuttgart exhibition "Film und Foto" in 1929. Yet by that time it was already past its artistic best. The future now belonged to American and French photography. The Americans included Berenice Abbott, Paul Outerbridge, Man Ray (although living in Paris), Charles Sheeler (also well-regarded as a painter), Steichen, Ralph Steiner and Edward Weston. Although this was a relatively small contingent, and without Stieglitz, nevertheless they manoeuvred more pragmatically and skilfully than the Europeans between the actual pitfalls of advanced photography, between the Scylla of formalist game-playing and the Charybdis of advertising. It was not only younger photographers like Margaret Bourke-White who had quietly, without any great ado, cut loose from the Pictorialism of the past: its leading proponents, Stieglitz and Steichen, had done exactly the same.

Albert Renger-Patzsch
At Oberhausen, 1932
Gelatin silver print, 21.7 x 16.4 cm
Bonn, Rheinisches Landes-
museum Bonn

Umbo
Sinister Street, 1928
Gelatin silver print, 29.8 x 22.8 cm
Cologne, Museum Ludwig

Albert Renger-Patzsch
Advertising Picture for the Jena
Works, c. 1935
Gelatin silver print, 38 x 28.2 cm
Cologne, Museum Ludwig

Although Stieglitz continued to handle photo-graphic prints with the utmost care, in his masterpiece – a series of portraits of his partner Georgia O'Keeffe – he in fact fulfilled, in an exemplary manner, all the aes-thetic demands of specifically photographic photogra-phy, absolutely in line with Rodchenko's thinking, which he had explained using the example of a portrait of Lenin. Using a whole number of different space and time angles the American created his breath-taking por-trait of the legendary artist, a project that has proved to be unique in its fragmented perfection, so suited to the medium.

Yet there was not such an abrupt rejection of art-photography in the USA as in Europe. Although the excellent Paul Strand (p. 641 below) pilloried the notion of mistaking the camera for a paintbrush, calling the whole discussion 'foolish,' he never became self-right-eous, but could not help being pleased that in the wake of this discussion, now nobody knew any more "what art is."[27] And the result of this was that "fortunately some photographers show in their work that the camera is a machine, indeed a truly wonderful machine. They prove that, used properly and sensibly, the camera can become the instrument of a new way of seeing, an instrument with undreamt of potential – admittedly related to painting and the other arts but in no way usurping their territory."[28] Strand's own sensitive works manage to maintain a balance between realistic-docu-mentary closeness and formal-aesthetic finesse and for him the camera was indeed, as the Italian philosopher Benedetto Croce had famously called it, an instrument of "intuitive recognition."

Given the two poles of sensitivity and analysis, Ger-man photography favoured an analytical attitude while Strand and Weston (p. 641 above) relied more on their sensitivity. "Dare to be irrational, steer clear of formulas, stay open to every fresh influence, stay flexible ... As soon as they are formed, theories lead straight to academism"[29] read a diary entry by Weston. Under the spiritual umbrella of American transcendentalism which saw things as "vital symbols" (Wolfgang Kemp), Weston sought to sink into the essence of things: not to mediate them empirically but, by means of empathetic assimilation, to experience them and to bring that experience to others too. He wanted to show the 'thing' in itself, not merely an object. As a result, the kaleidoscope of contrasting haptic qualities is virtually tangible in Weston's work: the lively fruitfulness of Nature and plants, the porcelain or metallic coldness of man-made artefacts, the finely-grained structure of the hot sands of the dunes, the tender skin of the naked human form.

Like Strand and Weston, Walker Evans (p. 642), the outstanding American photographer of the 30s, fought against what he despised as photography's "pretensions to art." Non-conformist and impressively cynical, although not without humour, Evans was a passionate photographer who scorned the work produced by his compatriots Stieglitz and Steichen whilst admiring Sander and – with certain reservations – Renger-Patzsch. He found his aesthetic legitimation in literature rather than in painting. His guiding lights were writers like Gustave Flaubert, Ernest Hemingway and James Joyce and his constant catch phrase was "I am a man of letters." Tangible reality was his terrain, the street was his route and the town was his world. "In the street I can train my sight and give it the nourishment it needs."[30]

He experimented tirelessly, with all kinds of cameras, with colour and even with instant photography. He

did not even disdain chance as an aesthetic tool, as for example in his candid shots in the subway; an undertone of Surrealism pervades his work. Evans became the definitive portraitist of the USA in the difficult years stretching from 1927 to 1974. His pictures say more than contemporary painting and sculpture. He was also one of the legendary troop of photographers who were commissioned by the Roosevelt Administration to realise an epoch-making project to create a photographic documentation of rural America (Farm Security Administration – FSA), covering the areas that had suffered worst in the world economic crisis. Other photographers involved in the project included Dorothea Lange (p. 642 below), Arthur Rothstein, the painter Ben Shahn, Russell Lee, Jack Delano, Carl Mydans, John Vacon, John Collier and Marion Post Wolcott – the elite of American photography; with the exception of Bourke-White, who with her husband, the writer Erskine Caldwell, was in any case working along the same lines.

American photography, which was already flourishing, then received another vigorous creative boost with the arrival of immigrants from Germany after Hitler came to power and the Nazis had begun their systematic policy of taking control of the country. And a few years

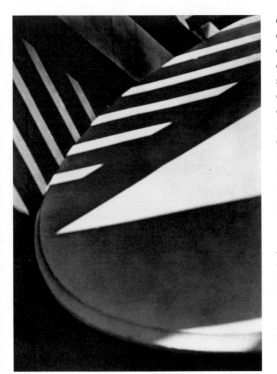

Edward Weston
Nude, 1934
Gelatin silver print, 24.5 x 19.3 cm
Cologne, Museum Ludwig

Paul Strand
Abstraction, Shadows of a
Veranda, Connecticut, 1916
Handgravure, provided by the
Aperture Foundation, 33.1 x 24.3 cm
Cologne, Museum Ludwig,
Gruber Donation

later, more were to come from Austria, Czechoslovakia, the Netherlands and France. The shadow of terror drove Munkacsi and Eisenstaedt to the USA, Gidal to Palestine and England, which also became the destination for Hübschmann and Man. Robert Capa, who had mainly only carried out lab work in Berlin and who was to become an unsurpassed chronicler of the war, first went to France and then, with the arrival of the German army of occupation, moved on to the USA along with Kertész,

George Hoyningen-Huene, the latter's pupil Horst P. Horst (p. 651) and the incomparable Erwin Blumenfeld (ill. below right). The young Helmut Newton fled via Asia to Australia. His teacher Yva was killed in Auschwitz, as was Salomon who had only found temporary refuge in Holland.

In England the newly founded *Weekly Illustrated* and the rather more successful *Picture Post* under the direction of Stefan Lorant, erstwhile chief editor of the

Münchner Illustrierte Presse, carried on the tradition of photo-journalism with Man, Hübschmann and Gidal and in 1963, *Life,* with the duo Bourke-White / Eisenstaedt, rang in the last and most brilliant phase of photo-reportage. Since then the USA has been the home of the mass media with New York as the centre of photography and Hollywood as the centre of the film industry.

Yet, in the first instance, France and its capital, Paris, were the first destinations for photographers leaving or fleeing from Germany, fearing for their lives because of their Jewish backgrounds. Some were swept temporarily towards Prague, such as Heartfield, where there was already a lively experimental photographic circle including František Drtikol (p. 645), Jaroslav Rössler, Jaromir Funke and Adolf Schneeberger. But most had already been attracted by the magnetic pull of the French capital. Now in Paris, Kertész (pp. 638 f) nevertheless continued to work for German publishers. Raviv-Vorobeichic, a convinced Zionist, drew inspiration from the art-soaked atmosphere of the city on the Seine, as did Germaine Krull from Poland (ill. below) and the American writers of the 'lost generation.' Surrealism was riding high, leading to heated debate in the ateliers and cafés and spicing the 'small talk' at luxurious parties. Paris was now the undisputed world centre of art and literature and second only to Hollywood in the film industry, now that Berlin had disappeared from sight in a brown haze.

Surrealist writers and painters harboured a distinct weakness for photographic images: what better parallel

to their own notion of écriture automatique than the 'automatic' process of photography? They could search photographic images unhindered for revelations from the subconscious. Eugène Atget (pp. 645 f), the tireless itinerant photographer, owes his reputation as an exceptional artist to the Surrealists. He had photographed a world on the verge of disappearing: old Paris, the customs of its long-term inhabitants, the palace at Versailles in decay. And this he did using out-dated techniques, yet utterly obsessively and stunningly systematically. The writer Camille Recht described his photographs in terms of shots taken at the 'scene of the crime,' and they do indeed convey a sense that here we are seeing the 'scenes of the crimes' of history.

Alfred Eisenstaedt
V-Day, 1945
Gelatin silver print, 24 x 15 cm
Cologne, Museum Ludwig

Germaine Krull
Pont Transbordeur, Marseille, 1926
Gelatin silver print, 19.8 x 14.4 cm
Cologne, Museum Ludwig

The Surrealist painter Man Ray (pp. 646 f), on the other hand, who much admired Atget's work, was a photographic magician by comparison. He earned his living with outstanding images and portraits from the world of fashion and high society, and no other artist extended the scope of the medium as he did. He embodied a completely new type of artist. He constantly moved between painting, photography and film as between 'free' and 'applied' art. A subversive magician with a tendency towards pragmatism. This may be why he was somewhat reluctant to agree with the painter Salvador Dalí's assertion that photography was a "pure creation of the spirit."[31]

While the night of terror gradually closed in on Germany and Adolf Hitler wrote the introduction to the 1934 edition of the periodical *Das Deutsche Lichtbild*, Paris was reaching new cultural heights. In the late 20s 'New Photography' had made a breakthrough in Paris too. Burgeoning consumerism leading to an increase in advertising plus a growing need for illustration was a fertile breeding ground for open-minded photographers who relished the risks involved. Kertész, his compatriot Ergy Landau, the Romanian Eli Lotar – all immigrants – and the Frenchman Jacques André Boiffard along with Man Ray and Krull forced French photography into self-renewal. The ball was kept in the air by Maurice Tabard, Emanuel Sougez, Roger Parry, the Hungarian-born Brassaï and Roger Schall along with the Bauhaus products Florence Henri (p. 646 below) and Raviv-Vorobeichic (Moi Ver) while artists such as Dora Maar, sometime companion of Pablo Picasso, Henri Cartier-Bresson and Raoul Ubac along with the photographers Nora Dumas and Emerique Feher played their part in creating a lively photographic scene.

They made their livings from illustrated journals such as *Vu,* under the committed leadership of Lucien Vogel, as well as from other magazines and the daily press. And while Kertész and Brassaï produced 'Poetic Realist' volumes of photographs putting a beguiling gloss on the myth of the French capital, Raviv-Vorobeichic portrayed the explosive vitality of the city and in his book – simply called Paris, with a foreword by none other than Fernand Léger – in keeping with 'New Seeing,' made the most of the possibilities of montage, double exposure and sandwich printing.

Thus the photographers who had fled, been driven out, or who had left Germany of their own accord, found themselves in an artists' paradise. Yet they were hardly welcomed with open arms and their work as photographers was not made any easier by their not having work permits. Ilse Bing, Hans Namuth, Georg Reisner, Josef Breitenbach, Gisèle Freund, Willy Maiwald, Robert Capa, Gerta Taro and more besides – they all had endless difficulties to overcome. Following a temporary relaxation of regulations, these were tightened again by later reactionary governments. For Namuth and Reisner and for Capa and Taro the Spanish Civil War marked the turning point in their professional careers.

Capa's disturbing images, epitomised by his *Death of a Spanish Loyalist* made him world famous. This cruel war cost his friend and sometime lover, Gerta Taro, her life. Although the real cause of her death was a terrible accident, Louis Aragon and the French Communist Party gave her an extravagant funeral and used this to portray her as a martyr to a 'just cause' – for a time her name was forgotten in the icy winds of the 'Cold War' until tenacious research by a German historian reawakened her memory in the early 90s.

Man Ray
Lips on Lips, 1930
Gelatin silver print, 22.9 x 17.5 cm
Cologne, Museum Ludwig

Florence Henri
Composition II, 1928
Gelatin silver print, 17.2 x 23.9 cm
Cologne, Museum Ludwig

Page 647:
Man Ray
Kiki, Violon d'Ingres, 1924
Gelatin silver print, 38.6 x 30 cm
Cologne, Museum Ludwig

A Meaningful Relationship: Fashion and Photography

Adolf de Meyer (ill. right), certainly no blue-blooded aristocrat but created a baron by his royal patron, was the product of that stratum of society that nurtured the rise of fashion. Social protection had allowed Meyer-Watson, as he was born, to enter the ranks of the fashion-conscious Prince of Wales's entourage even if, by the turn of the century, the latter's role as a leader of fashion in London already seemed to smack of an age that was slowly but surely fading away. In Donna Olga Alberta Caraciolo, supposedly an illegitimate daughter of King Edward VIII, de Meyer found a faithful wife and ideal partner. She planned his career and smoothed his path at court. According to his biographer Philippe Julian, the Jewish homosexual Meyer and his aristocratic wife Olga possessed all the right qualities for an ultra-modern version of a marriage à la mode.[32] Upstarts, parvenus, cocottes, actors and actresses, artists, in short: society's outsiders with their own looser social structures were always susceptible to fashion – exactly as they still are today.

Pictorialism lent character to the flamboyant baron's photographs while their light came from Whistler's painting. Stieglitz admired his photographs and exhibited them in his legendary gallery '291,' the 'entrée' for European avant-garde art into the USA, and published them in his journal *Camera Work*. Meyer's real breakthrough came at the beginning of the century when the American publisher Condé Nast engaged him for the magazine *Vogue* which he had recently acquired for his expanding empire. At the time *Vogue* had very low circulation figures but within a few years Nast, an imaginative and effective publisher and patron of modern fashion photography, had built it up into a force to be reckoned with in the world of fashion, into a publishing *arbiter elegantiarum*. Meyer's images with their gloss of extravagant glamour were the backbone of his campaign.

Vogue developed standards for society life and Baron Adolf, an entrepreneur of good taste – as the fashion historian Nancy Hall-Duncan was to call him – controlled the magazine's visual appearance until Steichen eventually took over. Meyer left when Nast had turned down his suggestion that the new British and French editions should be produced in Paris, at which point Nast's competitor, the newspaper tycoon Randolph

Hearst, who had achieved immortality in Orson Welles' *Citizen Kane,* snapped the celebrated fashion photographer up for his own illustrated magazine, *Harper's Bazaar.*

Vogue and the elite *Vanity Fair* were, along with *Harper's Bazaar,* the unchallenged leaders of opinion in matters of haute couture and high society, fulfilling the role of the royal courts in the early days of fashion magazines, even before the First World War broke out. These three magazines provided a suitable framework for socialites wearing the latest of fashions to see and be seen. Thus in Meyer's photos ladies of good breeding modelled the fashions, wearing what they had ordered

Adolf de Meyer
The Silver Cup, c. 1908
Gelatin silver print, 39.2 x 15.2 cm
Amsterdam, Heiting Collection

Page 649:
Irving Penn
Lisa with Roses, 1950
Gelatin silver print, 41.5 x 34.5 cm
Cologne, Museum Ludwig,
Gruber Donation

Martin Munkacsi
Torso, 1944
Gelatin silver print, 33.8 x 27.4 cm
Cologne, Museum Ludwig

Martin Munkacsi
Skier, 1930
Gelatin silver print, 29.7 x 21.6 cm
Private collection

and acquired. So, for a time there was no difference between mannequins, dummies and the owner of a new fashionable 'creation' – which means that the resulting fashion photography does have its own documentary authenticity.

However, the more fashions by new designers – led by the unforgettable Gabrielle 'Coco' Chanel – reflected women's aspirations towards a career outside the home, the more the world of fashion presented itself in a distinctly different manner. The war had swept aside numerous social barriers and young women no longer viewed themselves as the 'representatives' of their well-heeled, upper class husbands' 'conspicuous consumption.' Soon professional mannequins and specialist 'models' replaced the countesses, industrialists' wives, courtesans and actresses, rapidly establishing themselves as the new role-models of the time.

At the same time the popular theatre, born of operetta and vaudeville, was mutating into the mighty machinery of show business. Photography and film, the new medium of moving pictures, had a double role

in this. They drove the process speedily forwards, at the same time as producing the necessary publicity to make this happen. Film actors suddenly found themselves in the harsh light of public interest while stage actors were relegated to the margins of press attention.

And as 'show business' took off, leading serious artists, writers, musicians, painter and sculptors became promoters of fashion as had many of their forebears – including Baudelaire, Gioacchino Rossini, Jean-François Millet, Jules Champfleury, Giacomo Meyerbeer and Alexandre Dumas. Now Gertrude Stein, Aldous Huxley, Picasso, André Breton, even the shy James Joyce, the sensitive Virginia Woolf, the vitriolic Karl Kraus and the narcissistic poseur Jean Cocteau – more or less the entire serious avant-garde – were only too glad to oblige photographers because this was how to raise one's social profile. The artists in turn lent the relevant magazines and up-and-coming journals an air of legitimacy and respectability, propagated a life-style both exotic and enviable and held their own as permanent features in the roulette of the social elite in the years between the two World Wars.

Photography is the perfect means of visual expression for fashion. And the triumphant progress of this particular technical medium, hugely accelerated by the mass press with its circulation figures in the millions, greatly increased the sphere of influence of fashion. And beyond this there are other points of contact between fashion and photography: fashion is like the materialisation, as it were, of a fleeting moment in the continuum of time; a moment which is shown by photography to be irretrievably past. Fashion and photography complement one another. While fashion is utterly of the present, photography documents the passing of what it portrays. "There is a superimposition here: of reality and of the past" (Roland Barthes).[33] And there is another significant additional factor: fashion needs the wearer to pose, and in photography even a fraction of a second can be captured as a pose. Thus both photography and fashion are synonymous with artificiality and pure superficiality.

Nevertheless, it does seem at first sight as though the comparatively more recent genre of fashion photography, which does after all pre-date Meyer, still reflects a particularly antiquated notion of photography. Before Steichen nimbly came and cleared the stylistic clutter out of fashion photography, it was still wallowing in the out-dated precepts of art photography. The latest fashions were being shown in photographs which themselves seemed strangely old-fashioned. Not a trace of 'New Seeing' or 'Neue Sachlichkeit.' Is there perhaps a contradiction to be seen in this?

Clearly fashion photography had its own laws – as did its subject matter. It is an attempt to completely aestheticise visible and tangible reality and postulates an absolutely artificial universe. Even Steichen did not pilot fashion photography into the waters of cold sobriety. He chose instead a form of diluted Neo-Classicism with faintly absurd, occasionally even Surrealist overtones. Of course, fashion photography is not immune to impulses from external reality. Sometimes it even preempts these, but much more importantly, it creates a domain for collective dreams. And when it pointedly shuts out the complications of reality, this is at least indirectly a symptom of an underlying fear of the power of reality. Fashion photography is a web of expectation, ideas, wishes, dreams and anxieties.

One of the most radical innovators in the field of fashion photography was Martin Munkacsi. He was an outstanding photo-journalist, famous for his fine photographs, particularly for his sports and dance photographs (p. 650 above). Although he had virtually no experience of fashion photography, Carmel Snow of *Harper's Bazaar* and her art director, Alexei Brodovich, gave him a contract as soon as he arrived in the USA, having been driven out of Germany by the Nazis. Carmel Snow had come from *Vogue* to its competitor and within two years she had become the most influential fashion editor in the world. She had fired Meyer and completely revamped the magazine. Now she expected Munkacsi to blow a fresh breeze into the sails of fashion photography. He was not familiar with the old habits and well-worn clichés of fashion photography, which proved to be an advantage, because fashion trends in the 30s – replacing stiff elegance with a more relaxed style that drew heavily on sports clothing – perfectly suited his own ideas about photography.

At first sight the models in his shots could easily be taken for young women snapped by chance in the street, on the beach or at the sports ground. They seem to have passed before the camera apparently relaxed and wholly unintentionally, liberated from the corset of social strictures, and lending his pictures the spontaneity of 'snapshot photography.'

Of course, fashion as Munkacsi captured it was by no means 'natural,' having much more to do with attitude; in fashion everything is 'parure' – decoration (René König). And while Meyer was clothing his models in the glittering sheen of ostentatious luxury and Steichen was bathing his in the cool light of reserved elegance, Munkacsi was mobilising the dynamism of sport and of the hectic 'theatre' of street life. But even his Realism is stage-managed, if only for the reason that his subject was fashion. Fashion is the antithesis to Nature, even the nudist on the beach – as the sociologist René König mockingly pointed out – is as much a slave to fashion as ladies in the dim and distant past on holiday at the seaside with their elaborate clothes and hats as big as carriage wheels.[34]

Nevertheless, it seems that opposing positions in photography come together in Munkacsi's work, which combines a strictly authentic style of documentary photography with stage-managed fiction. And in the end, it in fact turns out that the two are interchangeable. For even the most undirected version of photographic praxis imposes a visual frame on the subject and, although this framework can take an immense variety of forms, it is still an ineradicable constituent of any photographic image. And fashion too rests on a paradox: its particular elixir of life is perpetual self-destruction. Each new fashion kills yesterday's fashion and it is only in photography that the fleeting appearance of fashion can find an apparent licence for permanence.

Munkacsi's aesthetic strategies wrought lasting changes in the stylistics of fashion photography and

Horst P. Horst
Mainbocher Corset, Paris, 1939
Gelatin silver print, 24.2 x 19.2 cm
Cologne, Museum Ludwig,
Gruber Donation

George Hoyningen-Huene
Bathing Suits by Izod, 1930
Gelatin silver print, 28.8 x 22.6 cm
Cologne, Museum Ludwig,
R. Wick Donation

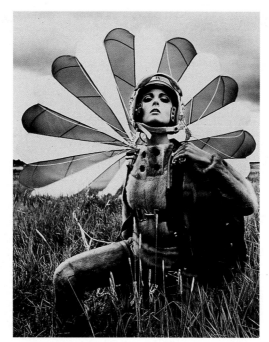

F. C. Gundlach
Jump Suit, Mirella, Oslo, 1963
Gelatin silver print, 40.8 x 30.5 cm
Bonn, Rheinisches Landes-
museum Bonn

inspired his contemporaries including Toni Frissell, Herman Landshoff, sometimes even leading figures such as Steichen and George Hoyningen-Huene as well as photographers from the next generation such as Richard Avedon, but this does not mean that they completely dominated fashion photography in the 30s and 40s. On the contrary, artificiality was also able to celebrate its own, bizarre triumph in the seductive photographs of Cecil Beaton (p. 654) with their double images, confusing reflections and formal poses. And at times Hoyningen-Huene and Horst P. Horst took Steichen's diluted Classicism to the point of involuntary parody.

Hoyningen-Huene (p. 651 below), in carefully constructed, evenly lit compositions with Classical Greek props lent his photographs the aura of some apparently timeless ideal of beauty, which he at the same time wholly consciously undermined with various Surrealist visual touches; meanwhile Horst P. Horst complicated the Classical moment by purposely ironically emphasising the *trompe l'œil* (deceiving the eye) of the Classical scenery, and thus destroying it in the process (p. 651).

Blumenfeld and Man Ray strove to synthesise the two poles; and in fact, with their unusual pictures, they succeeded in portraying – between the lines, as it were – the deep discrepancies of the era between the two World Wars, the tensions in Europe, dominated in large areas by National Socialism and Fascism, as well as the dormant anxieties just below the surface. High above Paris at the top of the Eiffel Tower, in one of Blumenfeld's most famous images, a model performs acrobatic feats above a deep abyss; the young woman spreads out her skirt like a bird spreading its wings, and yet her position is at least as precarious as that of the artiste in the circus tent. A distant echo of Moholy-Nagy's view from the

Berlin Radio Tower – but this time with a figure for the viewer to identify with.

The inferno that was the Second World War, with its unimaginable intensity and cruelty, brought with it the final demise of the old world and, against this backdrop, Louise Dahl-Wolfe's over-loaded fashion tableaux and Cecil Beaton's apparently contradictory photographs, that were shot amongst the ruins in London after the heavy bombing inflicted by the Germans, would seem to be a last desperate attempt to cling to the familiar ideas and habits of a 'golden' past. No documentary photographs betray the chasm between reality and what one wishes were true so movingly.

After the end of the Second World War, in the years marked by widespread deprivation, dreams flourished in fashion photography again. Fashion photographers portrayed an 'anti-world' in their images, contrasting with the reality of the ruined towns and cities of Europe as with the reality of the arduous struggle for daily survival. Although the shots are generally taken out of doors, the models behave exactly as though they are on a stage. In elegant dresses, suits and coats they re-awaken the ideal of the lady, far away from the grinding routine of professional life and far away from the ruins of destroyed cities. And of course in these constructs of fashion photography there is also a resonant sense of longing for a transfigured past. However, at the same time, there was a drive to get all those women – who had fought so 'manfully' while their men were away – back into their traditional place in the home. The men who had survived the war returned and were now demanding their old place in society back again. Yet, the impending gender-conflicts were only indirectly evident in European and American fashion photography – most notably, in fact, in the way that they were painfully avoided, with Avedon and Irving Penn providing the only real exceptions to the rule.

Following in Munkacsi's footsteps, whose intentionally lively style he much admired, Richard Avedon worked his way towards fashion. He had learnt his trade in the Marines taking photographs for identity cards. He then took up where Munkacsi left off. The Hungarian had freed fashion photography from the fetters of convention and literally got his models moving – and now Avedon allowed them to have souls, feelings, moods and weaknesses. His early pictures on the streets of Paris overflow with a zest for life after getting through the years of deprivation. The models positively spin through the pictures, seldom finding a moment's peace to smoke a cigarette or drink a glass of wine. The feverish intensity of their attitude to life translates directly into dynamic action.

In contrast to this, aesthetic discipline and a conscious economy of formal means characterise Penn's work (p. 649). Penn was a fashion photographer for *Vogue* – Avedon worked first for *Harper's Bazaar* before also going to *Vogue* – his rise to fame was as fast as Avedon's, and as a portraitist for the same magazine he also

Page 653:
Robert Lebeck
Jayne Mansfield, Berlin, 1961
Gelatin silver print, 61.4 x 50.7 cm
Köln, Museum Ludwig

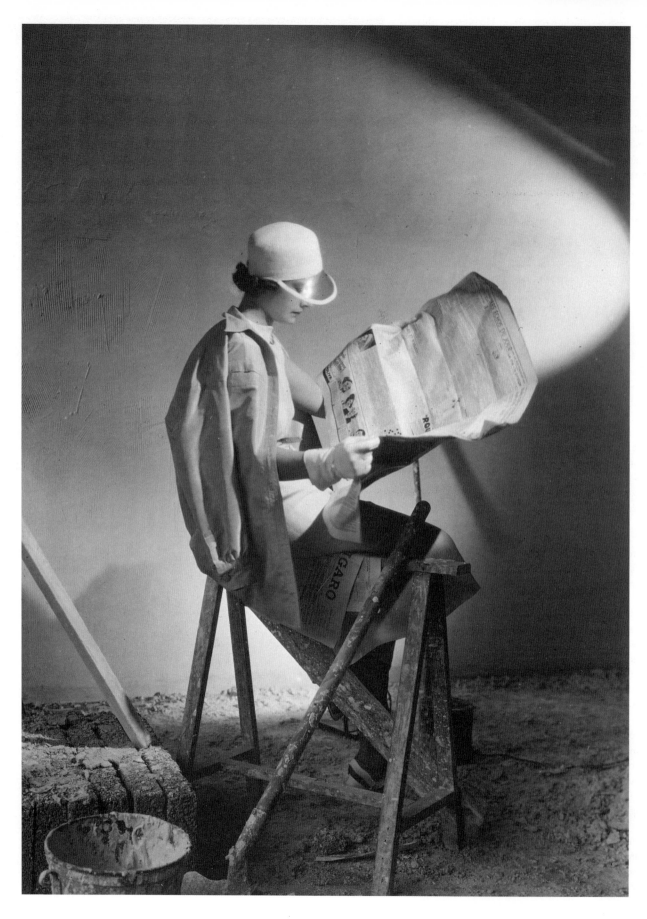

breathed new life into portraiture. His portraits, that seem to 'dissect' the subject, and his fashion shots which imperceptibly acquire the status of portraits of the models, portray the individual qualities and characteristics of the subject, as do also the majority of his pictures of American Indians, Arabs and people from other ethnic backgrounds. Many of his pictures are reminiscent of still lifes and later on he was to devote himself almost exclusively to this genre. But even his fashion photographs were often already imbued with a sense of momento mori.

In the 60s and 70s the aesthetics and the look of fashion photography underwent a radical change. This was due, on the one hand, to the shift from haute couture to *prêt-à-porter* and, on the other, to increasing prosperity which ensured a wide interest in cheaper fashion items – but most significant of all was the cult of youth that was now spreading like wildfire. And the cult of youth lost none of its impetus as the end of the century approached. On the second of two portraits of the renowned model Simone d'Aillecourt, taken twenty years apart by the German photographer F. C. Gundlach (p. 652), the model looks like her own daughter. Constant conflict between the generations became the prevalent social structure. In fashion photography the deep-seated external and internal changes in society were reflected more clearly in the aspect of the models than in the fashions they were presenting. Avedon and, even more so, David Bailey sensitively reflected impressions of the mood in Western society fixated on a youthful image of humanity. Little by little they blurred the boundaries between photo-journalism and fashion photography.

In this sense Helmut Newton's images (p. 657) also break the bonds of convention when it comes to his pictures of fashions by those such as Yves Saint-Laurent, Claude Montana and Karl Lagerfeld. In his hot-cold (Andreas Kilb) images, there are always undertones of the social and psychological discord which also pervade fashion. Although his work is characterised by an unsettlingly cool sense of distance, nevertheless it is as though there is something simmering just below the surface. Hidden aggressions break through, predominantly – but not only – sexual. Concealed desires come to the surface. Hidden anxieties. His work: a psychogram of *fin de siècle* society.

In Newton's photographic works one can see how deeply fashion is anchored in what drives humanity and how little it has to do with the need to protect oneself from the prevailing climate. And it is not surprising that, with time, Newton has switched his interest as a photographer from professional fashion photography to making portraits of the idols of our modern media society, that layer of society that has slipped into the erstwhile function of the 'upper crust.' In addition, Newton cultivates the language of the expressive German photographers and film makers of the 20s and 30s, as it was preserved in Hollywood's 'Black Series' which was entirely

Will McBride
Overpopulation, c. 1969
Gelatin silver print, 26.7 x 40.5 cm
Cologne, Museum Ludwig,
Uwe Scheid Donation

Robert Doisneau
Gate of Hell, Boulevard de Clichy,
Paris, 1952
Gelatin silver print, 30.4 x 24 cm
Cologne, Museum Ludwig

created by directors, camera men and musicians who had emigrated from Germany.

It may well be that fashion photography – along with journalistic photography – is the most suitable and convincing means of expression of this particular technical medium. And yet it is closer than any other photographic genre to questions of aesthetics, although art, submitting to the dictates of the avant-garde, rejects it as its supposedly opposite pole. In the 50s and 60s fashion photographers also examined photography's claims to authenticity by adopting various elements of photojournalism.

Amongst those who spring to mind in this connection are Avedon, William Klein, Will McBride (p. 655 above) and F. C. Gundlach (p. 652) as well as the obsessive 'scene of the crime' photographer Guy Bourdin,

Page 654:
Cecil Beaton
Fashion, c. 1935
Gelatin silver print, 24 x 18 cm
Cologne, Museum Ludwig

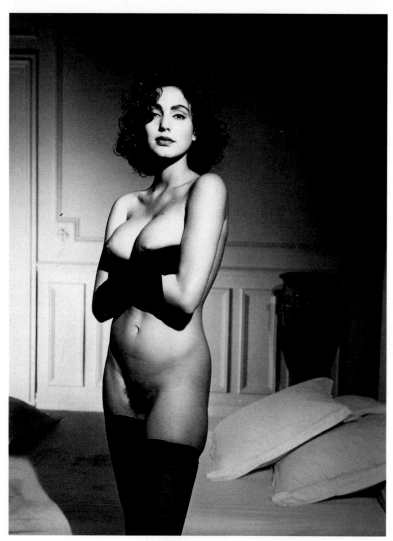

Bettina Rheims
Claudya with Gloves, Paris, 1987
Gelatin silver print, 57.3 x 42.8 cm
Cologne, Museum Ludwig,
Uwe Scheid Donation

realism of the image becomes a stage-managed representation. Therefore, in a certain sense, fashion photography, by never hiding its own stage-management, becomes the most authentic form of photographic representation.

Nick Knight and Olaf Martens (p. 675 below) – one a middle-class Englishman, the other an East-German – underline with their bold, brazen pictures the vitality of fashion photography in the late 20th century. It is neither infected by the boredom of contemporary art photography nor by the tribulations of new technologies such as digitisation and cyber space. Knight creates an utterly artificial world, a shrill reflection of that attitude to life that has surrendered unconditionally to the 'here and now.' Martens melds this attitude with the biting contrasts and grotesque distortions of reality. For this reason he generally chooses locations in Eastern Europe after the collapse of the Soviet government and the disappearance of 'truly existing Socialism' as settings for his photographic visions where fiction and real life collide with such force.

In the arc spanning Knight to Martens there are yet more outstanding talents such as Bruce Weber, Peter Lindbergh, Deborah Turbeville, Bettina Rheims (ill. above) and Herb Ritts; and while none of them is a specialist fashion photographer, they and many other talented and imaginative photographers have reached into people's hearts and minds with their unmistakable works.

whose radical treatment brought a new, sharper aestheticism to images of crime in New York of the kind that 'Weegee the Famous' had created two decades earlier. Sexuality and death were the essential backdrop to his images and, particularly in a widely acclaimed series for a Charles Jourdan advertising campaign, he often homed in on the trappings of fashion as fetishes pandering to the most dubious of desires.

As in fashion so, too, in photography everything is ultimately stage-managed; naturalness is no more than a fiction, or, at best, simply the least artificial moment. This means that in fact fashion photography is of greater documentary interest than a great deal of photography which is flagged as such. For the transience of existence is concentrated in fashion into laws with an immensely wide application but with a very short shelf-life, which is the reason that stage-management plays such an important part in this context.

And, vice versa, each picture grasps the fleeting moment like a model his or her clothes, as in war pictures by Capa, Cartier-Bresson's genre scenes and Robert Frank's visions of everyday political life. The

Page 657:
Helmut Newton
Violetta des Bains, 1979
Gelatin silver print, 40.3 x 30.3 cm
Cologne, Museum Ludwig,
Gruber Donation "

War – The Father of all Photographs

When Hermann Claasen (ill. below) climbed up to the top of the spire of Cologne Cathedral to turn his camera on the destroyed Hohenzollern Bridge across the river Rhine, he was confronted with an image of utter destruction. Not only had the bridge burst asunder, its mighty arches now lying in the water below – what Claasen saw was a scene of devastation of unimaginable dimensions.

The old town of Cologne was a heap of rubble, the writing on the wall had come true in the shape of ruined houses, churches and towers. This view out over the town and across the country to the horizon in the distance was like the symbolic end to what had begun on 26 April 1336 when the Italian poet Petrarch (1304–1374) had climbed Mont Ventoux in Provence: he wanted to feel the sense of liberation in a view of the whole landscape where he was living in self-imposed exile, and, with this gaze, set the ball of modern times rolling as it were. Petrarch raised himself up above perspective, that same perspective with which painting was soon to conquer symbolic space and humanity was to conquer real spaces, the world as it was known and as yet unknown.

Hermann Claasen
Neumarkt Cologne
First daylight bombing raid of
Cologne, October 1944, 1944
Gelatin silver print, 30.2 x 40.3 cm
Bonn, Rheinisches Landes-
museum Bonn

In photography the perspectives of spatial representation were confirmed on a technical level; but at the same time, by virtue of its capacity for infinite reproduction, photography also negated the apparently mandatory nature of this principle of spatial representation. Space in photography turned out to be a fiction, no more than a construct, in fact virtual space.

A few days before Claasen, the chronicler of the devastation of the Rheinland, two well-known photographers had also scaled the heights of the spire of Cologne Cathedral. Lee Miller (p. 659 below), a reporter with British *Vogue* and Margaret Bourke-White, the head photographer from *Life,* had come to Cologne in spring 1945 with the advance guard of the Ninth Army and had photographed conditions in Germany after its defeat, with the sober gaze of professional journalists and without sympathy for the losers. Writing not long afterwards about their experiences, Bourke-White gave a vivid account of her feelings as she looked out over the ruins on all sides: "The spire of Cologne Cathedral was a wonderful spot to take pictures from. After the steep climb I was a little out of breath when I looked through the gap in the stonework. But perhaps I would have felt that way anyway because far below me flowed the Rhine, splashing up against the edge of Pan-Germany. The river was still dangerous, the banks were swarming with German soldiers, hidden, lurking, ready to kill – the watch on the Rhine."[*]

It is not the motifs that distinguish these pictures from the airy peaks of the spires of Cologne Cathedral from other war pictures, but the perspective that was used in their creation. It is a perspective known familiarly as a 'bird's eye view.' And in contrast to the 'frog's eye view' where the low viewpoint makes even human beings seem larger than life, a bird's eye view affords the viewer a liberating overview and the edges of mountains and man-made constructions which usually halt the line of sight suddenly recede into the far distance where they dissolve in the haze so that the whole view opens up in a quite unaccustomed manner. Notions of escaping from gravity and dreams of flying have long been a persistent part of human mythology.

In photography Nadar was the first to put this into practice. He caused a sensation in Paris by having a huge balloon constructed for himself, which almost plunged him into commercial ruin and which gave him the nickname "Le Géant" (the Giant). A friend, the graphic artist and painter Honoré Daumier, teased him that he had elevated photography into an art form and portrayed Nadar with his camera in the basket of an ascending captive balloon. But in fact Nadar did open up a whole new dimension of photography and his deed resulted in nothing less than a dramatic change in the accepted view of perspective in the representation of visible objects. In his aerial images 'without perspective' the photographer was actually focusing on the dimension of time. Ever since then art critics refer to illusionistic perspective in painting as opposed to 'realistic/naturalistic' pictures.

If photography was already serving such utilitarian purposes as propaganda, Nadar then hammered it into an effective war weapon. It is probably fair to say that his aerial images saved the French capital from Prussian occupation in 1871. Examination of his aerial photographs revealed to the defenders of the French capital what the soldiers on the ground could not see: not only the exact positions of the troops laying siege to the capital but also their likely points of attack and tactical angles as well as the overall logistics that would have supported the Prussian army as they stormed the city. Nadar's images put the French in the position to react instantly and spared them unpleasant surprises. Nevertheless, short-sighted military leaders in the army at the time were quite unable to recognise or to capitalise on the value of Nadar's initiative.

It was to fall to another photographer to demonstrate the practical value of photography in the conduct of war. As a colonel in the United States expeditionary forces in France, Steichen was in charge of air-reconnaissance. Thanks to his particular organisational talents he made a major contribution in this field, and in the process also significantly affected accepted modes of perception. His war experiences radically changed his attitude to pho-

tography. On the one hand the images that were produced under his command documented the actual and symbolic superiority of the American forces and it is likely that the pilots of the British Royal Air Force used these same pictures to guide them on their 1000th raid on Cologne on 31 May 1942. On the other hand, Steichen ran his information delivery service like a small factory: "... it was the first time that pictures were produced on a production line. The photos lost their episodic quality, instead of individual pictures there was a flow of pictures, matching the tendency towards statistics of all kinds in this military/industrial war..."[36]

Steichen "was working towards a new concept of the image, which had a direct link with reconnaissance photography and the organised production processes involved. 'I decided to learn how to make photographs for newsprint because I was determined to reach a large public, rather than just the few I had reached as a painter.' In Steichen's hands war photography became the photography of the 'American dream.'"[37] After the war, around 1.3 million prints of war photographs found their way into Steichen's private collection. Then, having roundly renounced art photography, in his capacity as a fashion photographer he became one of the most successful magazine photographers of his day. In Robert Altman's ironic film on the fashion trade, *prêt-à-porter,* the actress Kim Basinger, playing a fashion editor, remarks, "Fashion is war."

The coda to the persistent interconnections between war and photography was orchestrated by Margaret Bourke-White with her ambitious project for *Life* magazine: a comprehensive series of pictures on the effects of the allied bombing of the towns and cities of the German Empire. "The pictures that she made for this purpose are amongst the most impressive

Lee Miller
Ludwigshafen, a bombed-out chemical plant, 1945
Gelatin silver print, 31.5 x 30.4 cm
Bonn, Rheinisches Landesmuseum Bonn

Yevgeni Chaldei
Russians Climb Atop the "Reichstag", Berlin, 1945
Gelantin silver print, 24.6 x 19.4 cm
Amsterdam, Heiting Collection

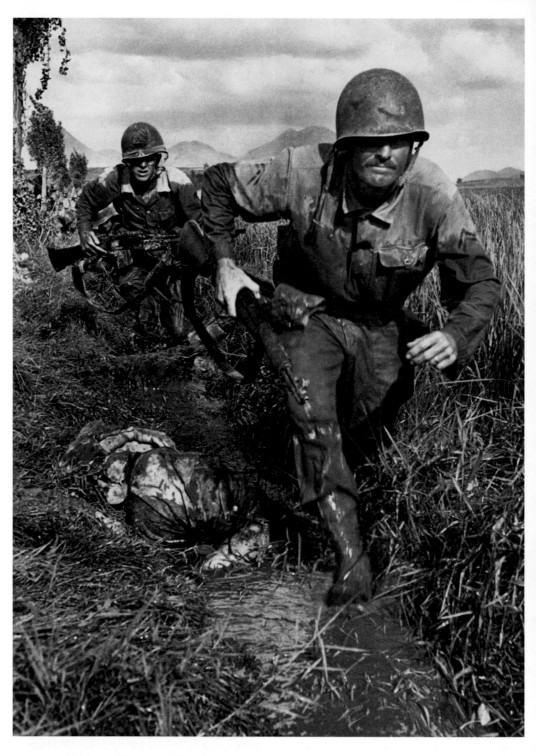

David Douglas Duncan
Corea, 1950
From "This was War", 1951
Gelatin silver print, 35.5 x 50.8 cm
Collection of the artist

documents of the time. They show with oppressive monotony how the allied aerial attacks had turned the towns of Germany into endless city deserts."[38] As a technical medium, photography registered from above with the neutral (objective) view of technical equipment the visible results of the final loss of human perspective.

The fact that photography repeatedly becomes entangled in modern warfare is due not least to the fact that photography is a 'machine art' and war in fact embodies the ultimate triumph of the machine over humanity. If the experience of war hastened Steichen's departure from art photography, then the contact with the mechanical/technological aesthetics of 'New Seeing' were crucial for Bourke-White. As the daughter of an engineer-inventor, she had no qualms about technological progress and an industrialised society, much like the artists of the avant-garde in Germany and the Soviet

Union. The smoothness and the coldness of the product was for her a synonym for authenticity and objectivity, as proof that here a purely photographic aesthetic was being applied.

The same aesthetic precepts also fired the leading Soviet war photographers: Georgi Selma, Arkadi Shaikhet, Georgi Petrussov, Max Alpert and others. Yevgeni Chaldei (p. 659 below), on the other hand, had formerly photographed workers and had been active since 1936 as a photojournalist. Soviet photographers portrayed the vast 'War for the Fatherland' as an affecting epic in black and white with many moving moments that came together as undeniably ambiguous ciphers: symbols of heroism and horror, of superhuman struggles and inhuman suffering. In the harshest of circumstances, occasionally having to resort to the most primitive of photographic techniques, they generally fought on the front with their weapons in one hand and a camera in the other. The Soviet photographers' coarse-grained, 'dirty' yet nonetheless theatrical war images bear all the hallmarks of authentic experience. Fear, horror, dirt and delirium transcend the pathos of the images themselves. Even before the outbreak of the Second World War, on 3 December 1938 the *Picture Post* had already hailed Capa as the greatest war photographer in the world; the pictures that he had taken during the Spanish Civil War and the Sino-Japanese War had established his reputation. This attentive and passionate promoter of the emergent media world was also one of its most fascinating protagonists. Incurably restless, a passionate drinker and loved by women, he hated war and yet it was war that determined his life and ultimately his death in Indo-China.

Not for him the cynicism of the credo that if a photograph was not quite satisfying then the photographer had not been close enough: instead, he followed his own instructions to the official photography unit of the US Army during a training course: "When you are under fire, don't go where the shooting is: go where there are good pictures to be had."

Capa worked for several North American and British magazines before he reported for *Life* on the invasion of Normandy in June 1944. The results were a handful of pictures that avoided any trace of heroic posturing. Yet somehow they got to the bottom of the truth of one aspect of that invasion: the sea itself was a much greater threat to the allied soldiers landing on Omaha Beach than the defending German soldiers. In Capa's images the brave attacking forces are in acute danger of drowning even before they have joined battle. Although Capa did admittedly jump with the paratroops before the last battle for the Rhine at Wesel, he was not fool-hardy. His pictures showed the victims of war, dead and wounded soldiers, helpless children in bombed-out cities, anxious boredom before battle, the misery of waiting, filth, madness. Because they showed the war from the point of view of the victims, from the point of view of the ordinary G.I.s and not from the command-

ing officers' vantage point, their success in the press was guaranteed.

Thanks to their renown as photographers, Capa and Bourke-White could seek out their own 'seats' in the theatre of war, as long as military considerations allowed. The extraordinarily wide distribution of their images helped them to overcome a certain degree of military resistance. In any case, most of the commanding officers recognised the propaganda value of the millions of reproductions of pictures by leading war photographers and Capa was positively 'adopted' by certain regiments.

He also reported on the struggle for independence in Palestine in 1948. Wherever he went, he only stayed for a relatively short time. Benno Rothenberg, himself once an Israeli war photographer and later a highly respected professor of architecture at a research institute in London, recalled Capa using vast quantities of film and, as a rule, producing by far the most impressive pictures of any event. It was, of course, not coincidence that war became the dominant subject in photography in Israel, which had to fight for its independence in the immense upheavals that followed the Second World War. Many immigrant photographers from Germany, committed to the cause, created a kind of visual myth of Israel in moving, powerful images comparable with pictures of Brady and his troops from the American Wars of secession, but also not unrelated to Soviet war photography particularly – sad to say – in their aesthetic standards.

Hans Chaïm Pinn made a sober, yet precise record of the daring landings of Jewish immigrants on the shores of Haifa, and also recorded the catastrophes, the street fights and the heavy fighting around the mosque between Tel Aviv and the old Arabian port of Jaffa. Rothenberg, who served in the army, as did the Soviet photographers, was generally able to use his military connections to beat the international press to the spot and produced the most up-to-the-minute pictures of the struggles for independence. A key photograph from that war was taken by Boris Carmi almost despite himself: he photographed a group of young Isreali soldiers without noticing that one of them had a concentration camp number tattooed on his arm.

Micha Bar-Am and David Rubinger produced their gripping images of the subsequent war with total commitment but also with a degree of distance in view of potential consequences. Bar-Am put together a photo-reportage on imprisoned Arab fighters and Rubinger created a symptomatic image of peace born of a mixture of exhaustion and reason during the meeting between President Sadat of Egypt with Minister President Begin of Israel, who for one moment in history looked just like old friends.

"War and photography now seem inseparable:"[39] the words of Susan Sontag, a moral critic of photography as a technical medium. And in photography she found evidence for what she saw as the sad state of a society that lived at more and more of a voyeuristic distance to first-hand reality. And, in accordance with this, photographers whose personal concern was apparently with finding out and understanding were doing no more than satisfying the human thirst for sensation and driving this to extremes by ever more sensational images – until ultimately all feeling was lost. And yet, after seeing pictures from Bergen-Belsen and Dachau by George Rodger and Miller, this same passionate critic did admit quite as a matter of course to dividing her life into two periods: "before I saw those photographs ... and after."[40] Nothing had ever cut her "as sharply, deeply, instantaneously"[41] as these image of unimaginable terror, nothing, neither photograph nor reality.

Bourke-White recorded some of the feelings of the allied photographers when they were confronted with the horror of the German death camps. She herself, travelling with the advance guard of the 3rd US Army, had gone to Weimar and the concentration camp at Buchenwald. "This April day in Weimar had something unreal about it. I could only feel one thing, and I clung to this. I kept saying to myself that I would only believe the indescribably abominable picture in the yard in front of me when I saw my own photos. It was almost a relief to operate my camera. It created a fragile barrier between me and the blank horror that was before me... I wanted it to disappear, for as long as it was there, I could not stop thinking that it really was human beings that had done this... and it made me ashamed to be a member of the human race."[42]

She photographed the charred remains of people who had got caught in the barbed wire trying to escape from the concentration camp at Erla near Leipzig-Mockau and she photographed a man mourning a dead friend who was so thin that he was no more than a skeleton. The formal precision of these pictures does not alleviate their awfulness, nor does it explain it. It remains incomprehensible. The instruments of reason fail in the face of such horror.

Miller sought refuge in bitter irony and acrid sarcasm, by remarking that her own 'Fine Baedecker Tour' of Germany with the American Army had included places such as Buchenwald and Dachau, which had received no mention in her 1930 edition of Baedecker. And then she added, that presumably editions after the war would not be recommending them to tourists either because apparently no-one in Germany knew anything about the camps.[43] In Buchenwald she photographed the 'unsuspecting' inhabitants (who had known nothing because they had wanted to know nothing) on their enforced visit to the concentration camp on the orders of General Patton, commander of the 3rd Army. Human beings had reduced other humans beings to soulless automata and after their ability to work had been utterly exhausted, reduced them yet further to their material value – the value of their hair and teeth – turning this into hard cash even before their tormented bodies were burnt.

The Second World War was also the first media war of global proportions. Words and images played a decisive role, with an immense task falling to photography and film with their 'mechanical' images. Their particular characteristic, the fact that "in the photograph, something 'has posed' in front of the tiny hole,"[44] endowed photographic and film images with an air of credibility and laid the foundations for people's trust in their authenticity. At the same time, however, this also meant that all kinds of potential had now been opened for deception, directed as much at the enemy as at one's own people. In fact the 'immutable' quality of a photograph is not only influenced by its surrounding context – the caption, its appearance in a newspaper with a particular leaning, the angle it has been taken from, editorial choice and layout: photography also 'documents' the sets which are created for no other purpose than to deceive the enemy and – from time to time – the home public as well.

In the 90s the French photographer Sophie Ristelhuber took shots of the deserted Gulf War battlefields from an angle that made them look like sandpits where children and generals fight their battles. She then created a provocative montage combining these images with close-ups of scarred skin-wounds. On the television screens of our media society the 'Gulf War' just seemed like a computer game. The bloody carnage in the Balkans, on the other hand, was a reminder to people that war means brutality, atrocities and endless suffering. There is no place any more for warlike heroes – and for 'conventional' war photography?

The Challenge from Television

Europe was largely destroyed. People were starving, and not only in defeated Germany. The Soviet Union extended its sphere of influence right to the river Elbe and forced eastern and south-eastern Europe to submit to the dictatorship of the Communist regime. The Western world set itself against this and East and West prepared for the Cold War. The vast Chinese empire was shaken by bloody civil war; in British, French and Dutch colonies independence fighters took to arms. The unconditional surrender of Germany and Italy with their allies, as well as of Japan on the other side of the globe, had radically altered the world and these changes would continue to determine the course of world history until the end of the century.

What the champions of international Communism had not managed to achieve was effected by two World Wars: namely world revolution; both political and social, economic and cultural – on a technological level and affecting individual and collective perceptions alike. But, for all that, change did not seem to go so deep as after the First World War. For various reasons. Perhaps there was a feeling that this had all happened once before. For a short time there was a sense of a new start, the benevolent influence of a supposed 'zero hour,' but then the shadow of the Cold War descended on the world and for nearly fifty years divided it into two rival halves. Restoration and rebellion marked its history, alternating with ever increasing speed.

At first photography, like film, prospered as never before. *Life* magazine reached its highest circulation figures and in the devastated continent of Europe there was a growing need for pictures from all four corners of the earth. War had speeded up transport routes immeasurably and had considerably telescoped the dimensions of time. Events in far away countries were no longer purely of exotic interest. In the age of atom bombs, hydrogen bombs and intercontinental rockets these could be the fuse to set off the proverbial powder keg. And the German word 'Angst' had become part of the English language. At the same time the experience of collective suffering in the war had greatly heightened the desire for individual freedom; and this desire was particularly pronounced amongst artists and photographers.

Many photographers were annoyed by the high-handedness with which the mighty illustrated maga-zines had used their pictures during the war. They felt they had been robbed of their rights. Capa realised a dream of his and founded the agency Magnum, together with Cartier-Bresson, the courageous war photographer David 'Chim' Seymour (p. 663) and two other kindred spirits – bringing together the most successful photographer-journalists in the world.

One of these was William Eugene Smith who many regarded as the best photographer who had ever worked for *Life*. Smith was the embodiment of a strongly individual, independent photographer, who consistently and unswervingly followed his own aesthetic aims, committed to the ethos of photographic truth and at the same time the visionary creator of an artistic universe in its own right. He had been severely wounded in the Pacific. His recovery took two years and he had to undergo over thirty operations on his mouth and nose. Smith has been hailed as a 'moralist' with a camera; he preferred to describe himself as a 'compassionate cynic.' His approach as an artist was defined by his understanding of the things he photographed, by his compassion for people living and working in harsh conditions, and by his deep sensitivity to human emotions and social strictures. And these were also reflected in his methods as a photographer.

Smith succumbed utterly to the object he was photographing, and his pictures were coloured with an intimate knowledge of the world in front of the camera lens. Before he put the finishing touches to his photo-essays, Smith would have spent a considerable amount of time with his subjects, sometimes even years – regardless of who these subject were: it could be a country doctor going about his daily business, he could be trying to track down a black midwife, it could be the fishermen of Haiti – "an underdeveloped, starving, wonderful land" (Smith) – he might be portraying a Spanish village during the dying years of Franco's reign, or it might be the people of Minamata – a Japanese town whose residents had been the victims of a terrible, hushed-up pollution scandal.

His human compassion was always in evidence, however open he was to the formal qualities of photography, contrasts of light and shade, the clarity of the overall composition, the occasional use of iconographic forerunners from art history, the effective choice of

Ernst Haas
Homecoming, 1947–1950
Gelatin silver prints, each
c. 18 x 12 cm
Cologne, Museum Ludwig,
Gruber Donation

detail. And Smith demanded the same level of commitment from those who viewed his pictures: "I try to lend my voice to those who have none," was how he explained his tremendous output.

Alongside Smith many photographers now laid a greater emphasis than before on the subjective nature of their work: these included his compatriots Walker Evans, Bourke-White and Strand (who moved to Europe) and in the next generation Avedon, Penn, the younger Diane Arbus and Turbeville. The same could also be said of Ansel Adams and, in France, of Cartier-Bresson, Robert Doisneau (p. 655) and Marc Riboud, in Great Britain Bill Brandt (p. 665), Philip Jones Griffiths and Donald McCullin, in Switzerland Werner Bischof and in Austria Ernst Haas (ill. above); and in Japan, too, little by little an independent photographic idiom was coming into being.

In Germany after its annihilating defeat, the physician, photographer and college lecturer Otto Steinert

Otto Steinert
Pedestrian's Foot, 1950
Gelatin silver print, 28.7 x 40 cm
Cologne, Museum Ludwig

(ill. below) referred to this current – with a fine sense of the prevalent mood – as 'subjective photography', although most of the photographers whom he counted as having a subjective view were really only adapting the aesthetic achievements of 'New Seeing' or of Neue Sachlichkeit and only a few, like Peter Keetman (p. 667 above), really developed a truly unmistakable pictorial style. While photographers in the United States, France and Great Britain were portraying visible reality in a variety of different, admittedly subjective ways, the 'subjective' photographers in Germany did their utmost to avoid this and were instead still trying to tap the flow of photographic experiment even although the source had long since run dry. They took up from before where the avant-garde had left off when it was stamped out by National Socialism and, like most Germans in the Bundesrepublik (founded in 1949), behaved as though the terror that the National Socialists had inflicted on the land had simply been a stroke of fate and certainly not of their doing.

The leading photo-journalist to have stayed in Germany, Wolfgang Weber, came back from his extensive travels and, as the chief photographer on the *Neue Illustrierte,* put together a series of critical reports from the four zones that Germany was now divided into. These reports were the only reflection of Italian Neo-Verismus in West German photography. Public opinion was ruled by a mixture of denial and self-pity, particularly in the West after it had been divided up, and these sentiments were faithfully reflected by the mass media even although the latter had actually been intended, on the initiative of the victorious allied powers, as a tool to re-educate the Germans into democracy. There was no shortage of films and illustrated journals. And, as in the USA, Great Britain and France, photo-journalism in Germany in the 50s found a huge response.

The 50s and 60s saw the end of the line for the German matadors of early photo-reportage and for the former propagandists from the Nazi era who had continued to work as though nothing had ever been: both groups were now replaced by photographers such as Robert Lebeck (pp. 653 and 669), Thomas Höpker, Will McBride, Heinz Mack, Werner Bockelberg and, in the field of fashion and society photography, Regi Relang, Hubs Flöter and Gundlach. And at the same time, the Folkwang School in Essen, where Steinert was a successful teacher, sent out important aesthetic impulses into professional photography in post-war Germany, much of which was, however, internationally underestimated.

And yet: their work was only rarely equal to that of Den Smith, Eliot Elisofon, David Douglas Duncan (p. 660), Dimitri Kessel, Arnold Newman, Philippe Halsman, Gjon Mili, Gordon Parks (p. 669) – already working for the FSA – Mydans, Ralph Crane, Bert Hardy and Larry Burrows, not to mention Bourke-White, Capa, Seymour, Cartier-Bresson and, originally from Germany – Eisenstaedt, Gisèle Freund and Eric and both photography and the way people see things underwent radical change.

Electronic images were not only faster than photography: they also implied on-the-spot immediacy and did away with the inherent distance of photography, which always contains an element of 'you've just missed it,' and were able to transport viewers instantly anywhere in the world. The eye-witness taking photographs became superfluous. Photographers could only survive in some niche in the television world if they were ingenious enough to find pictures that the electronic media had missed. But now, ever since it has been possible to use advanced computing equipment to generate the 'immediate' images that television transmits across the world about the world, the question of credibility has become a matter of opinion.

With the advent of the 'virtual reality' of digitised images that seem as real as any authentic representation of reality it becomes hard to tell the two apart. The end of photography? Probably not. But its particular aesthetic flavour is disappearing. Photography no longer embodies the certainty that something must have happened in front of the camera and which is now shown as a photographic image, something irretrievable and yet which nevertheless "was there" (Barthes). And the simple loss of this claim to 'reality' is enough to invalidate the debate as to whether photography is an art form or not. But one thing is for certain: photographic techniques have been adopted by art, as a medium for the imagination and for aesthetic manipulation. The camera had become a additional technological extra to the artist's traditional tools – brushes, drawing tools, hammer and chisel...

But even before the artificial world of digitised images had become a kind of reality, there had been changes in what was generally expected of photography and this had already affected the medium's own self-image. Even before the War the Museum of Modern Art in New York had set up a photography section which

Peter Keetman
Volkswagen Plant, 1953
Gelatin silver print, 30.2 x 23.1 cm
Cologne, Museum Ludwig

Schaal – who were, without exception, all employed on *Life* magazine.

In the Soviet-occupied section of Germany which, under the watchful eye of its 'big brother' in Moscow, held its own for over forty years as the German Democratic Republic, the German tradition of socially committed photography continued unbroken although with a quite distinctive viewpoint as in the *AIZ (Arbeiter Illustrierte Zeitschrift* – Workers' Illustrated Journal), and with the occasional intermezzo of Socialist pathos. Once the German Democratic Republic had established itself, photographers such as Richard Peter Snr, Erich Höhne, Arno Fischer (ill. right) and Evelyn Richter took a decidedly realistic approach in their work, clearly at pains not to be taken in by the way things appear to be but to discover the mechanisms that lie behind the exterior.

An undreamt of variety of reproduced images was flooding into the consciousness of those living in the western hemisphere, who now were no longer content to experience the world at one remove through photography, but – like early American settlers – were setting out to record their own presence in those places that photography had now opened up to them.

As yet no-one was paying much attention to the wooden box in the corner of the room with its wavery, grey, unfocused images, and it was hard to imagine that these electronic television pictures – which were to be perfected with stunning speed by the 80s – would mean the end for most branches of professional photography. Nevertheless it was ultimately television that dug the grave for photo-journalism and destroyed the foundations of its existence. Very few illustrated journals survived the spread of this particular electronic medium

Arno Fischer
Berlin, 1956
Gelatin silver print, 33.4 x 50.1 cm
Cologne, Museum Ludwig

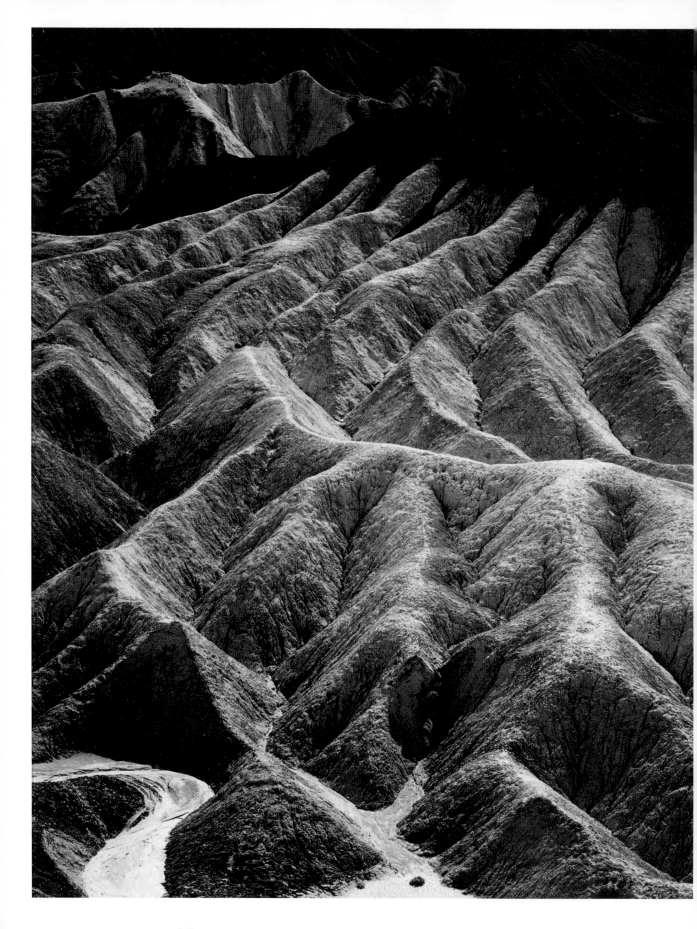

reaffirmed photography's claims to be an art form – claims which leading German museum directors such as Alfred Lichtwark and Carl Georg Heise had already lent credence to fifty years before. When the energetic Steichen took over the photography section of the Museum of Modern Art in 1947 the changes fermenting within photography were impelled effectively forwards. Steichen's legendary exhibition, "The Family of Man" (1955), was not only the most comprehensive photographic exhibition so far anywhere in the world, it also established photography as part of the museum and gallery world. At the same time, the anthropological basis of the show created an effective contrast to the success of abstraction in contemporary art, with the result that suddenly photography was seen as a convincing alternative. Indeed the very 'realism' of photography justified the movement towards abstraction in contemporary art.

Many photographers now turned to the walls of galleries and museums as a fitting place to publicise their work. Smith, Strand, Stieglitz, Steichen, Brassaï and Kertész now either only occasionally worked for illustrated journals or not at all. Most were unsatisfied with the quality of the images as printed in these journals and now discovered monographs in book form as a way of publishing their works which both suited the works and gave their makers editorial control.

The controversial project, *The Americans,* put on by the Swiss Robert Frank was also intended from the outset to be quite separate from the illustrated mass press. When it first came into the bookshops in 1958 with a French title, it was immensely shocking to Americans and some felt as though they were looking into a distorting mirror. The book's impact was huge. But it did not only provoke protest and rejection. It was also seen as a blow for liberation. In his unusual visual language Frank touched a nerve. Frank's pictures did not just capture the "crazy feeling" that you get "when the sun is burning on the streets and you can hear the sounds of music from a juke-box or from a funeral" as Jack Kerouac put it in the introduction to the American edition – he also did this in a style that directly communicated these feelings to the viewer.

The most notable aspect of Frank's work was not the shabby side of a country that had been the only symbol of hope to many people for so long, the important thing was the form that he adopted. Frank consciously ignored the conventional rules and laws of pictorial composition: falling lines structure his compositions; pictorial planes intersect; crude lighting sets the tone.

He consciously stage-managed his compositions – but not like Heartfield, the inspired creator of photocollages, or like Rodchenko with his disparate props – instead Frank would wait and simply not release the shutter until the reality before the lens had crystallised into its own montage: the picture with the American flag hiding the face of someone watching the Hoboken Parade, the view from a window looking down at a man

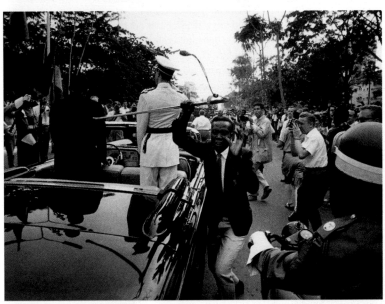

running along the street in the opposite direction to an arrow above him on the façade of a house. Smith called Frank the "Franz Kafka of photography." And he also said: "He maintains his own integrity at the expense of the object's." Frank's vision of the world is evident in his own particular language rather than in his choice of motifs.

The more photography lost ground to the mass media, the more it gained ground in the realms of art. Museums and galleries put on ever more exhibitions and built up their collections, while numerous American universities set up museums of photography, concerned to back up theoretical teaching with the best of visual material. Photographers such as Anselm Adams (p. 668) and Evans were successful teachers and, similarly in

Gisèle Freund
James Joyce behind Hortensias
with a Copy of *Transition,* Paris 1938
Gelatin silver print
Privat collection

Liselotte Strelow
Prof. Oskar Fritz Schuh, 1955
Gelatin silver print, 28.5 x 23.3 cm
Bonn, Rheinisches Landes-
museum Bonn

Duane Michals
Nude, 1972
Gelatin silver print, 12.1 x 17.8 cm
Cologne, Museum Ludwig

Germany, Steinert complemented the education of his students with exhibitions in the Folkwang Museum as well as donating a collection on the history of photography.

Step by step the medium of the fleeting moment became the subject of conservation and observation in galleries and museums. It is true that this process was not without complications and difficulties: nevertheless, by the 90s, photography, alongside the other 'new media' of virtual reality had reached a point where these now seemed to be the only really interesting modes of expression for contemporary art, particularly since traditional disciplines such as painting, drawing and sculpture were so obviously in decline.

In the second half of the 20th century photography took on a diverse, even confusing appearance. While it continued to extend its documentary role, photogra-

phers also were making increasing use not only of the book-market but also of galleries and museums, withdrawing of their own accord, as it were, from their established means of distribution. On the other hand, advanced art was slowly but surely assimilating the techniques of photography and, in the process, infecting photography with the germ of its own aesthetic. Photographers such as Garry Winogrand, Lee Friedlander and Duane Michals (ill. below) produced work exclusively for galleries and museums while vice versa the art business discovered and took on photographers such as Sander, Renger-Patzsch, Evans, Brassaï and Cartier-Bresson and outstanding portrait photographers such as Liselotte Strelow (ill. above right), Gisèle Freund (ill. above left), Milton H. Greene, Lisette Model and Lord Snowdon. And as it happened artistic photography was promoted by ephemeral phenomena like Happenings, Fluxus, Land Art, notably Conceptual Art, Performance Art and Action Art, although these movements' primary interest in photography was in order to record their own aesthetic aspirations.

Under these circumstances the work of the German photographic team of Hilla and Bernd Becher (p. 671) took on symptomatic significance. The range of responses it provoked reflects the changes that were occurring. Hilla Becher had trained as a photographer and her husband, Bernd, as a painter. Although they followed in the tradition of the industrial photography of Renger-Patzsch and Mantz with no less rigour than one such as Sander, at first they were simply greeted with laughter and scorn. 'Boring' was the kindest response to their vivid 'Anonymous Sculptures' as they called their photo objects. In images that were strikingly factual and avoided any form of dramatisation, with utterly neutral lighting and with the stereo-typical frame of the plate-back camera, they portrayed the architectonic face of

Bernd and Hilla Becher
Typology of Half-Timbered
Houses, 1959–1974
Gelatin silver prints, each
40 x 31 cm, arranged on 4 panels of
148.3 x 108 cm (2 panels shown)
Cologne, Museum Ludwig,
Ludwig Donation

industrialism photographed from exactly calculated distances and from fixed angles: winding gear and watertowers, blast furnaces and factory halls, industrially produced half-timbered houses and whole pubs.

In fact it was the art business that first provided them with a platform for their art. Their works began to emerge in exhibitions and catalogues of concept art. The Bechers ran the entire gamut of critical opinion without in the slightest altering their work as artists or their attitude to it; with documenta 5 in Kassel (1972) as the start of the process and documenta 6 (1977) as its conclusion. While the former ascribed a subordinate artistic role to photography, the latter elevated photography to an artistic medium in its own right.

This most important and influential of exhibitions of contemporary art anywhere was the first occasion that photography was not only shown as a vehicle for primarily artistic expression, but also the first time that the full range of its visual potential was accepted into the world of art. In addition to this, documenta 6 departed from the normal practice and, instead of concentrating exclusively on contemporary art, presented the whole of the history of photography by means of carefully selected examples. Furthermore it did away, once and for all, with the categoric difference between professional photography, responding to a commission from outside, and artistic photography which is purely an expression of the photographer's subjective drive. At the international art critics' conference (AICA) in 1977, Oto Bihalji-Merin declared this controversial mediadocumenta to be just as important as the Armory Show in 1913 which, at the time, had helped the avant-garde to make the breakthrough in the United States.

Thus the list of artists represented in Kassel in 1977 reads like a *Who's Who* of the history of photography:

alongside Stieglitz and Strand, Sheeler and Krull, Mantz and Renger-Patzsch, Sander and Erfurth, Freund and Halsman, Rodchenko and Steichen, Abbott and Evans, Capa and Duncan, Bourke-White and Cartier-Bresson, Salomon and Weegee (p. 672 below), Atget and Brassaï, Lange and Arbus, Blossfeldt and Friedlander there were also works by Robert Mapplethorpe (his European premiere), Gabriele and Helmut Nothhelfer (p. 672 above), Eve Sonneman, Bernhard Johannes Blume, Christian Boltanski, Ger van Elk, Gilbert & George, John Hilliard, Jürgen Klauke, Les Krims (p. 675), Jean Le Gac, Peter Roehr, Lucas Samaras and, last but not least, Katharina Sieverding.

Since then the corridor of photography in the world of art has continually broadened. This broadening has taken various forms: the traditional 'classical' genres of

Gottfried Helnwein
The Last Supper, 1987
Colour print, 40 x 59 cm (?)
Cologne, Museum Ludwig

photography – portrait, landscape and still life as well as the different genres of bourgeois art – have acquired a new artistic accent; specific photographic disciplines like social documentation, photo-reportages and systematic analysis in the form of rows, series and sequences have been developed further on aesthetic lines; artists have visibly turned their critical attention to photography as a mass phenomenon.

Klauke's (p. 673 below) often comprehensive photo sequences draw the viewer's attention to the monstrous sides of daily life and use conscious stage-management to open up a universe of hidden longings, fantasies, suppressed wishes and repressed fears. Klauke unites the aesthetic impulses of theatre, film, advertising photography, Surrealism and concept art. Along with Sieverding, Blume and Floris Neusüss (p. 674) Klauke was one of the first – in Germany and beyond – brave enough to use photography's striking ability to visibly portray those connections and resonances that are not in fact visible at all.

Anna and Bernhard Blume (p. 673 above), with their 'Transcendental Constructivism' (Blume) entered into the dangerous world of metaphysics and for years have been portraying things that do not exist, cannot exist, or at least which cannot be seen – although many sense the consequences of these things, some feel these consequences and others actively fear them. In their photo sequences, laden with the meaning, the world – to quote Bertolt Brecht – is distorted to the point of recognition. With their sardonic visual wit and sarcastic, cynical gestures, they provoke laughter that shocks. In their works things rebel against people, the system that claims to be running the world breaks apart – like the meanwhile outdated notion that the images of art could satisfy our Faustian search for knowledge.

But photography as practised by artists has not merely crossed beyond the bounds of the visible: it has also broken taboos that have hitherto obscured our vision. Robert Mapplethorpe tore the veil of lustful deceit and desiccated prudery that shrouded the premisses and abysses of sexuality, revealing with almost Classical restraint what had previously always been kept strictly behind closed doors; Andres Serrano attacked the Christian symbol of the Cross and pilloried the discrepancy between theory and practice in a society that claimed to follow the ideals of Christianity, and in increasingly aggressive images Cindy Sherman unrolled the shimmering sight of the woman in the modern world of consumerism and advertising; from filmic icon – a vessel for unfulfilled desires – through the cheap double spread in a girlie magazine to the repellent grimace of a male-chauvinist reflection. Nan Goldin (p. 677 above right) mercilessly dissected her own life with her camera.

In the hands of these artists photography often became a weapon in the conflict between the generations and the sexes, between the powerful and the oppressed. Is that why photography has found such favour amongst female artists? Although it has to be said that, in comparison to painting, women photographers have played a proportionately much greater role in this technological medium. While it would be unthinkable to conceive of a history of art without naming male artists, in the field of photography this could be done with very little loss to the quality of the result.

Many outstanding names spring to mind: Julia Margaret Cameron and Lady Hawardan in the 19th century, Johnston, Gertrude Kaesebier, Doris Ulman, Jelisaveta Ignatovicha, Abbott, Lucia Moholy, Imogen Cunningham, Lange and Bourke-White, Barbara Morgan, Frissell, Lilo Raymond, Helen Levitt, Arbus and Turbeville, Tina Modotti and Annie Leibowitz, Gina Lee Felber, Annette Frick, Barbara Klemm, Herlinde Koelbl, Angela Neuke, Freund, Henri, Karen Knorr, the formidable Mary Ellen Mark and many others – not even in the field of literature have so many excellent female artists carved out such a clear identity for themselves.

Did Stieglitz not once praise photography for its flexibility? It has to be said, that on the verge of a new millennium which humanity may or may not survive, photography as an independent medium would seem to represent a historic chapter in the history of the visual arts. Certainly more than a footnote and possibly as significant as the invention of printing with movable type. But in the sense that photography, as a means of artistic expression, cannot be defined as pursuing any particular direction or programme, it is still waiting to be properly discovered.

Old photographic techniques are currently inspiring artists again while others are experimenting with new techniques: amongst the latter are William Wegman (p. 676), Toto Frima, Bernard Faucon, Gottfried Helnwein (p. 671 below), Axel Hütte, Thomas Ruff, Anke Erlenhoff (with a smart combination of photography and painting) and Candida Höfer. Whatever the case, photography has in the meantime become a perfectly natural art medium.

Bernhard and **Anna Blume**
Meal, 1986
Gelatin silver print, 5 parts,
each 126.8 x 91.1 cm
Cologne, Museum Ludwig,
Hypo-Bank Donation

Jürgen Klauke
Self-Portrait (from: Pro Securitas),
1987
Gelatin silver print, 60.8 x 51.6 cm
Cologne, Museum Ludwig,
Gruber Donation

The Conquest of Art and the Loss of Character

At the Venice Biennale in 1993 the photographers Hilla and Bernd Becher were awarded the prize for sculpture. But a number of questions are raised by what at first sight may look like a witty or even inspired choice – par-

Floris Neusüss
Nudogram, 1966
Gelatin silver print on canvas,
231 x 104 cm
Cologne, Museum Ludwig,
Gruber Donation

ticularly if this choice was based on a regressive tendency on the part of the jury to regard photography as a representational medium, seeing the photographic images as no more than a vehicle to depict the subject matter and display technical skills instead of taking into account the artists' actual stage-management of the photographs in their own right. The use of aesthetic strategies and methods such as sequences, series and montage diverts the viewer's attention from the real photographed subject matter towards the artistic construction of these works.

By means of their particular form of construction, the Bechers had specifically abandoned crude representation in favour of a revelatory, open, even contradictory form of empiricism where the very appearance of the photography is affected by fault lines and ruptures. This approach by the Bechers marks a shift in the paradigms of photography which, with their assistance and that of other advanced artists, is now entering into a critical phase. And it is at this point that it suddenly becomes clear that the history of photography is now a whole chapter in its own right.

Although artists involved in photography came together from very different directions, nevertheless they always had one thought in common. They viewed photography as something which they could, by their own artistic intervention, transform into an autonomous aesthetic material. For them photography was no longer a means to appropriate and appropriately depict chunks of visible reality: instead they recognised photography as itself being part of that reality and, as such, open to question. Comparable moves were being made in painting, similarly critical, yet also with the ultimate aim of both laying bare the essence of the medium in question and taking advantage of its aesthetic potential.

Sigmar Polke experimented at length with the multifarious possibilities of photo-chemistry and destroyed the apparent oneness of photographic motif and chemical ingredients. The material substratum that under normal circumstances leads from the photographic shot to the image itself was suddenly accorded its own aesthetic value and now entered into competition with the representation of the visible subject. Besides this Polke also revealed the beguiling range of colours of the chemicals used in the process of photography and discovered a new colourfulness with many fascinating connections and 'poisonous' aesthetic effects. Numerous artists followed Polke down this path – particularly in Germany – including Johannes Brus, Achim Duchow (who worked with Polke from time to time) and Floris Neusüss. This led to striking "infringements" (Theodor W. Adorno) between photography and painting. Brus simultaneously did away with the smooth surface of the photographic image and the stasis of the world of photography by unhinging both the laws of probability and the laws of gravity. He presented photographic images that made nonsense of human experience. Polke (pp. 387 ff), inspired by Andy Warhol (pp. 323 ff), used technical procedures such as screen printing to transfer photographic Benday dots to large canvases and thus constructed a 'montage' of various elements – photography, painting, the physical world around us – creating pictures that operate in a kind of inter-media sphere and which are no longer subject to the perameters of conventional aesthetics.

These experiments led to a flood of imitative photopainting which, however, only succeeded in discrediting this entire route, until younger artists like Anke Erlenhoff began to systematise the process, which was possible partly thanks to the availability of digital techniques. This in itself again set up antagonistic yet informative correspondences between autonomous painting and photographic representation; although admittedly at the expense of the essence of photography which was gradually being stripped of its apparent claims to authenticity.

The Canadian artist Jeff Wall (p. 676) approached the problem from another side and undermined photography's claims to authenticity by doubling images. Using massive light boxes he created scenes of almost uncanny normality. But this very depiction of normality is disturbing and seems to open up some kind of an abyss although it would be impossible to say what is generating this latent feeling of anxiety. This confusing

Jeff Wall
Jell-O, 1985
Aluminium box, plexiglas, neon
tubes, cibachrome, 143 x 148 cm
Munich, Goetz Collection

William Wegman
Directional Shepard, 1987
Polacolour II print, 61 x 50.8 cm
Amsterdam, Heiting Collection

response is a result of the careful, sometimes even mannered, staging of the tableaux, where every nuance is deliberate – so that all life seems somehow petrified – and where carefully planned lighting lends the scene a touch of horror, realer than real. Photographic reality slips into the wholly calculated artificiality of the art of photography.

The result is an aesthetic heightening even of photorealist painting which nevertheless does not cast doubt on the 'noema' (Roland Barthes) of photography as a medium which claims that photographic slides show that that is 'how it was.' And yet what a camera captures is not in itself empirical but is the result of an intentional artistic act for the purposes of representation. Thus what began as authentic becomes fake, created solely for the purposes of illusion, to create the sense of 'as though.'

Wall's images are influenced both by painting and the commercial film industry. His varied works – some peopled with human protagonists, others strangely bereft of human beings – seem like condensed film

sequences. His works, whether describing a narrative or not, are in some way reminiscent of still lifes, and the oppressive stillness spreading over everything is reflected in the deathly rigidity of what is being shown. If the camera would only 'travel' slowly as it would in a similar situation in a film, then there might be some release, but Wall refuses his viewers this as long as they are caught up in the spell of his visual images.

Film was also an early source of inspiration to the American Cindy Sherman (p. 677 above left) who shot like a comet into the international scene in the 80s and at times even glittered like a megastar. Her early, small-format black and white photographs bring to mind nostalgic memories of scenes in certain films although one cannot immediately identify these: generally these consist of a figure without any particular distinguishing features alone in some rural, urban or domestic situation. The figure in them seems vaguely at home and yet oddly alien as though it does not really belong there. In fact, this figure in a variety of outfits turns out to be the artist herself. Allowing her imagination to run free in a

Andreas Gursky
Paris-Montparnasse, 1993
Colour print, mixed media,
180 x 350 cm
Cologne, Museum Ludwig,
Ludwig Collection

Nan Goldin
Cricket Putting a Wig on
Siobhan, Paris 1991
Cibachrome print, 61 x 50.8 cm
Hamburg, F. C. Gundlach Collection

whole series of roles, she nevertheless concealed her own identity behind the striking masks she adopted, revealing nothing of her own personality, other perhaps than to hint that she was doing all of this as an alien in an alien world. Her ego manifests itself as a multiple subject, ready to split on demand, the embodiment of multiplicity.

Her later photographic works, in increasingly lurid colours and also using larger formats extended the range of vision from commercial film to the whole panorama of culture. At the same time Sherman's works also became more critical reflecting, in predominantly aggressive scenarios and arrangements, the image of women in a male-dominated society where women were not in control of their own lives. For these she used anything from double spreads of female models in the relevant magazines – typically with the staple through the woman's navel – to parts of fetish dolls with monstrously inflated private parts. And she did not even shrink at using female figures from art history, different representations of the Madonna, finding even there a primarily male view plus the – at least underlying – intention to deny the female half of human society the chance to develop freely or to determine its own role.

Later, with a group of 'disgust pictures' Sherman moved out from the sphere of social issues and extended her artistic range to include anthropological questions of growing and dying, mostly focusing on the process of rotting and abandoning social issues. Ultimately she replaced visual horror with dreadful outsized masks clearly drawing on modern horror films with their dreadful organic growths.

Left:
Cindy Sherman
Untitled, 1982
Colour print
Private collection

Thomas Struth
Galleria dell'Accademia,
Venice, 1992
Colour print, 184.5 x 228.3 cm
Private collection

Thomas Ruff
Portrait (Sabine Weirauch), 1988
Colour print, 205 x 166 cm
Collection of the artist

Katharina Sieverding
Night-Owl (Double-Portrait), 1982
Colour print (unikum), 85 x 60 cm
Bad Münstereifel, Galerie Klein

Richard Prince
Untitled (Cowboy), 1980–1984
Colour print, 127 x 177.8 cm
Collection of the artist

Living and dying are also the main themes in Nan Goldin's (p. 677) photographic output, although her pictures neither have a sociological nor an anthropological backdrop: her perspective is directed much more towards her own biography. Unlike a written diary that she might consciously withhold from public scrutiny, Goldin sees her photographic records as a "public report." And although these deal with the most intimate moments of life and portray death as a long drawn out, tortuous process, although life and death are shown in some ways to be excessive, the images are not there to satisfy some voyeuristic cravings. And are any notions of voyeuristic titillation simply dispelled by Goldin's uncompromising honesty towards herself and others? Are they equally dispelled by the direct, apparently unforced objectivisation of private matters?

The boundaries between the public and the private are blurred – boundaries which bourgeois society had put in place and which Goldin's generation, once part of the 'hot' scene in New York in the 70s and 80s, had removed. Many of them have since died – artists, designers, stylists, mostly the victims of AIDS and drug misuse. Goldin's radically narrow view plus her subjective approach produces objectively quantifiable results. Thus she has created a disturbing portrait of a generation that had lost its way, thrown back on the most basic needs of existence, longing for a sense of security and yet at the same time obsessed with a disproportionate desire to break down the bounds of social convention. Goldin is not a trained photographer but her stunning work shows just how breath-taking photography can be – today as ever – even without trying to grind some particular artistic axe.

The 'Becher School,' apparently without artistic pretension, has produced photographers such as Candida Höfer, Thomas Struth and Thomas Ruff as well as Axel Hütte and Andreas Gursky (p. 676 below) who in their various ways have achieved international renown as artists. It is only on closer examination that their photographic works reveal their aesthetic refinement. They cut through conventional patterns of perception and with the subtlest of means draw out the dazzling complexity of the medium.

Many of their shots, often out-sized, focus on the act of seeing and on modes of perception. They capture the viewer's interest with the full rhetorical power of the photographic image, before gradually revealing their inner construction. And suddenly, faced with townscapes and landscapes by Hütte or with towns and museums photographed by Thomas Struth (p. 677 below), viewers find that they have become part of the visual equation and that they are no longer simply a beholder viewing a world outside of themselves with the proverbial 'disinterested pleasure.' In short, they have become protagonists in an aesthetic game that is apparently unfolding before their very eyes.

In addition to this, Ruff (p. 678 above left) explores as yet uncharted territory in photography, which it has acquired through technical developments – although these do at the same time radically change the character of photography. He became famous for his larger than life portraits of young people of no particular distinction, people whose names were not specially known. These images make an ironic point with regard to the personality cult found elsewhere in the medium: here normality itself is being lionised. Now, thanks to the Bechers and their students, as well as Neusüss, Klauke, Bernhard and Anna Blume, Astrid Klein and Katharina Sieverding (p. 678 above right), photography in Germany once again had the status that it had previously enjoyed during the era of 'New Seeing' in the 20s. In their ability to explore the aesthetics of photography, their willingness to take risks and their sensual intelligence, these artists put similar endeavours in Europe and the USA largely in the shade.

During the 80s and the 90s art photography in the USA indulged in more or less fruitless exercises which involved adopting intellectual property from elsewhere, as in 'Appropriation Art' which topped the artistic fashion charts for a short time. The artists concerned included Sherrie Levine – who followed this route with baffling stubbornness – Richard Prince (p. 678 below) – criticising the media – and Louise Lawler. At the same time the British performance artists Gilbert & George were also vastly overrated. They put together montages of vast dimensions showing images of socially unacceptable issues which they then sent circling around their own gleaming personalities (ill. above) like planets round the sun. The Frenchman Christian Boltanski, on the other hand, has maintained a high standard although his photographic installations do at times take on a rather too ghostly aspect – death watches! Photogra-

Above:
Gilbert & George
Hands up, 1984
Colour print, 241.3 x 401.3 cm
Private collection

Wolfgang Tillmans
Suzanne & Lutz,
Bournemouth, 1993
Colour print, 60 x 40 cm

phers with artistic ambitions, for example, Lewis Baltz and Robert Adams took forward the aesthetic precepts of those such as Walker Evans and W. Eugene Smith in their extensive documentations of social and ecological calamities.

Against the backdrop of the millennium which has lured cultural pessimists of every shade out of the woodwork, it is nevertheless clear that 'photographic photography' (Renger-Patzsch) can still achieve stunning results as in the work of Michael Ruetz and Angela Neuke in Germany, the Frenchman Gilles Peress with his 'revelatory' camera and Sebastião Ribeiro Salgado in Paris with his gripping, aggressive reportage essays on the lives of country labourers in Latin America, the famine in the Sahel region of Africa and the demise of craft skills through the introduction of industrial production processes in the world's most sensitive regions. And yet: for lack of suitable routes to publicise their work, they are forced to channel their work through the art market in order to present it to the public. This liaison has not been without certain consequences. On the one hand, photography has profited from adapting the aesthetic strategies and methods of contemporary art, but this has meant, on the other hand, that it has lost its specifically photographic character – at least according to the theories of media aesthetics as proposed by Siegfried Kracauer and Roland Barthes.

But for every loss there is a gain. After a visit to a private collection of photography with works by Sherman, Matthew Barey, Wolfgang Tillmans (p. 679 below) Mike Kelley and the obsessive Nobuyoshi Araki from Japan – a collection which included works by most of today's advanced photography-artists – the art critic Rudolf Schmitz expressed his amazement: "Far from being filled with a sense of imitative repetition going down a well-trodden visual path, one is overcome with astonishment at the fertility of the photographic notion of the constructiblity of images and of the world." A hopeful view of the future, even if he does add the proviso that this collection does not show "photographers as impassioned artists, but artists as impassioned photographers."

1 Walter Benjamin, 'A Small History of Photography', in *One Way Street,* transl. by Edmund Jephcott and Kingsley Shorter, London 1979, p. 246

2 Ibid., p. 247

3 Alfred Stieglitz, transl. from 'Bildmässige Fotografie', in: Wolfgang Kemp (ed.), *Theorie der Fotografie I* 1839-1912, Munich 1980, p. 221

4 Wolfgang Kemp, 'Fotografie als Kunst', in: Wolfgang Kemp (as note 3), p. 20

5 Robert de la Sizeranne, 'Ist die Fotografie eine Kunst?', in: Wolfgang Kemp (as note 3), p. 215

6 Eduard J. Steichen, 'Grenzen', in: Wolfgang Kemp (as note 3), p. 215

7 Eugenia Parry Janis, in: *At the Still Point. Photographs from the Manfred Heiting Collection,* Amsterdam 1995, p. 265

8 László Moholy-Nagy, 'Beispiellose Fotografie', in: Wolfgang Kemp, *Theorie der Fotografie II* 1912–1945, Munich 1979, p. 72

9 László Moholy-Nagy, *Malerei-Fotografie-Film,* ed. by H.M. Wingler. Facsimile reprint of the original 1927 edn, Mainz 1967, p. 26

10 Van deren Coke, *Avantgardefotografie in Deutschland* 1919–1939, Munich 1982, pp. 8f.

11 László Moholy-Nagy (as note 9), p. 27

12 Cf. Herbert Molderings, 'Lichtjahre eines Lebens', in: exh. cat. *László Moholy-Nagy, Fotogramme* 1922–1943, Essen 1996, pp. 8f.

13 Walter Benjamin in a lecture given in Paris on the opposing artists. Cited from Eckard Siepmann, *Montage: John Heartfield,* Berlin 1977, p. 166. Cf. also Klaus Honnef, 'Symbolische Form als anschauliches Erkenntnisprinzip', in: Peter Pachnicke and Klaus Honnef (eds), *John Heartfield,* Cologne 1991, pp. 38ff.

14 Rosalind Sartori, in: exh. cat. *Film und Foto der zwanziger Jahre,* Stuttgart 1979, p. 184

15 László Moholy-Nagy, (as note 9), p. 5

16 Cited from Alexander Lavrentiev, 'Die Photo-Träume der Avantgarde', in: exh. cat. *Russische Photographie,* Berlin and Bonn 1993, p. 61

17 Alexander Lavrentiev, ibid.

18 Alexander Rodchenko, 'Gegen das synthetische Porträt, für den Schnappschuß', in: Wolfgang Kemp (as note 8), p. 81

19 Alexander Rodchenko, ibid.

20 Hubertus Gaßner, 'Analytische Sequenzen', in: exh. cat. *Rodtschenko. Fotografien* 1920–1938, Cologne 1978, p. 32

21 Ute Eskildsen, in: exh. cat. Fotografie in deutschen Zeitschriften, Stuttgart 1982, p. 12

22 Tim N. Gidal, *Chronisten des Lebens,* Berlin 1993, p. 40

23 Albert Renger-Patzsch, 'Ziele', in: Wolfgang Kemp (as note 8), p. 74

24 Albert Renger-Patzsch, ibid.

25 Cited from Norbert M. Schmitz, 'Zwischen Neuem Sehen und Neuer Sachlichkeit', in: *Gleissende Schatten,* Berlin 1994, p. 86

26 Norbert M. Schmitz, ibid.

27 Paul Strand, 'Fotografie und der Neue Gott', in: Wolfgang Kemp (as note 8), p. 61

28 Paul Strand, ibid., pp. 61f.

29 Edward Weston, 'Präsentation statt Interpretation', in: Wolfgang Kemp (as note 8), p. 69

30 All quotations from Walker Evans in: John T. Hill, Gilles Mora, Walker Evans, *Der unstillbare Blick,* Munich 1993

31 Salvador Dalì, 'Die Fotografie, reine Schöpfung des Geistes!', cited from Wolfgang Kemp, (as note 8), p. 98

32 Cited from Nancy Hall-Duncan, *The History of Fashion Photography,* New York 1979, p. 32

33 Roland Barthes, *Camera Lucida,* transl. by Richard Howard, London 1982, p. 76

34 René König, *Menschheit auf dem Laufsteg. Die Mode im Zivilisationsprozeß,* Munich and Vienna 1985, p. 32

35 Margaret Bourke-White, transl. from *Deutschland, April 1945,* Munich 1979, p. 33

36 Paul Virilio, transl. from *Krieg und Kino – Logistik der Wahrnehmung,* Munich 1986, pp. 36ff.

37 Paul Virilio, ibid.

38 Klaus Schröder, transl. from introduction to German edn of Margaret Bourke-White (as note 35).

39 Susan Sontag, *On Photography,* London 1979, p. 167

40 Ibid., p. 20

41 Ibid.

42 As note 35, p. 90

43 *Lee Miller's War,* Boston, Toronto and London 1992, p. 161

44 As note 33, p. 78

Lexicon of artists

by Ingo F. Walther

The LEXICON OF ARTISTS is a 150 pages appendix providing biographical data and bibliographies on all 780 artists whose works are illustrated in this publication, including photographs of the artists wherever possible. The biographies are brief outlines of key facts such as place of birth, education or training, importants events, meetings with other artists, time spent abroad, awards and prizes, maior solo and group exhibitons etc. and generally forego or keep to a minimum any aesthetic or art historical classification.

The detailed bibliographies are intended as suggested further reading or specific themes or individual artists. The length of a bibliography or biography has no bearing whatsoever on the evaluation of an artist or his/her work. In the case of major publications translated into several languages, the original edition is frequently given alongside those of the translations. The bibliographies are divides into three groups:

WRITINGS
CATALOGUES RAISONNES
MONOGRAPHS, CATALOGUES

We have endeavoured to list CATALOGUE RAISONNES as complete as possible. These are often difficult to trace. The result is the most comprehensive listing of this kind in any available publication.

The individual titles are alphabetically ordered rather than chronologically. Exhibition catalogues (**cat.**) are ordered according to the name of the respective editor (**ed.**) or main author. In some cases, this may be an editor, organiser, author of preface or other individual involved in the organisation of the respective exhibition.

We have made every effort to list exhibition catalogues bibliographically by author, as the conventional listing of catalogues merely by the name of the artist and the venue is both strenuous to read and barely informative. The place specified in the case of catalogues may also be the exhibition venue and need not necessarily correspond with the place of publication, which was not always possible to determine. Martin De Mattia, Marc Weis, Ludger Derenthal, Antje Günther and Birgit Mersman (all based in Munich) assited in compiling the biographies and bibliographies (more than 1.5 million characters).

ABAKANOVICZ Magdalena
born **1930** Falenty (Warsaw)
Polish sculptress. **1950–1954** Studied at the Academy of Art in Warsaw. **1960–1969** Invented her own weaving technique. Made *Abakany*, large-scale sculptures out of soft materials. **1965** Grand Prix at the São Paulo Biennale. **1965–1990** Professorship at the Academy in Posen. **1970–1979** Series entitled *Alterations*, figurative und non-figurative groups of sculptures made of sacking and synthetic resin. Wrote metaphorical essays on the human brain, mythology and religion. In subsequent years worked in various materials such as wood, ceramics, stone and bronze. Produced numerous works for public places and museums. **1988** Ten bronze animal heads for the Olympic Park in Seoul. **1991/92** a 36-figure group *The Crowd* for the Walker Art Center, Minneapolis.
WRITINGS: M. A. and P. Restany: Katarsis. Florence 1987
MONOGRAPHS, CATALOGUES: M. A. Städtische Kunsthalle Mannheim. Mannheim 1969 (cat.).– M. A. Musée d'Art Moderne de la Ville de Paris. Paris 1982 / Museum of Contemporary Art, Chicago. New York 1982 (cat.).– M. A. Mücsarnok. Budapest 1988 (cat.).– Brenson, M. et al. (ed.): M. A. Sculpture. Institute for Contemporary Art P. S. 1. New York 1993 (cat.).– Gallwitz, K. (ed.): M. A. Skulpturen 1967-1989. Städtische Galerie im Städelschen Kunstinstitut. Frankfurt-on-Main 1989 (cat.).– Kato, K. L.: M. A. Tangible Eternity. Tokyo 1991.– Murray, P. (ed.): M. A. Bronze Sculpture. Llandudno 1996 (cat.).– Neray, K. et al.: M. A. Budapest 1988.– Rose, B.: M. A. New York 1994.– Rosenfeld, D. (ed.): M. A. Recent Sculpture. Museum of Art, Rhode Island School of Design, Providence et al. Providence 1993 (cat.).– Turske, I. (ed.): M. A. 2 vols. Galerie Turske & Turske. Zurich 1988 (cat.)

ABRAMOVIC Marina
born **1946** Belgrade
Serbian performance and video artist. **1965–1970** Studied at the Academy of Fine Arts in Belgrade. From **1973** put on performances with dangerous objects and medicines to explore the limits of physical and psychic endurance. **1975–1988** Worked with Ulay. Besides the juxtaposition of dualistic principles, the two artists focused on questions raised by archaic cultures they had encountered on their extensive travels. **1982–1992** Participation in documenta 7 – 9 in Kassel. **1988** End of collaboration with Ulay, after a 90-day exploration of the Great Wall of China, *The Great Wall Walk*. From **1989** tried to bring about the transition from individual to collective consciousness through meditative installations and object arrangements, using materials such as wood, crystals and stones. **1992–1995** Professorship at the Academy of Fine Arts in Hamburg.
WRITINGS: M. A.: The Architecture of M. A. Champaign and Urbana 1963.– M. A. and Ulay: Relation Work and Detour. Amsterdam 1980.– M. A. and Ulay: Performance – eine andere Dimension. Berlin 1983.– M. A.: Sur la voie. Ulay: Ode à l'urne. 2 vols. Centre Georges Pompidou. Paris 1990 (cat.)
MONOGRAPHS, CATALOGUES: Birnie Danzker, J.-A. and C. Iles (ed.): M. A. Museum Villa Stuck, Munich et al. Munich 1996 (cat.).– Drahten, D. v. (ed.): M. A. Galerie des Beaux-Arts. Paris 1992 (cat.).– Iles, C. (ed.): M. A. Objects, Performance, Video, Sound. Museum of Modern Art, Oxford et al. Oxford 1995 (cat.).– Iles, C. (ed.): Ulay & A. Perfomances 1976-1988. Stedelijk Van Abbe Museum. Eindhoven 1997 (cat.).– McEvilley, T. et al. (ed.): Ulay/ M. A. Modus Vivendi. Works 1980-1985. Stedelijk Van Abbe Museum, Eindhoven et al. Eindhoven 1985 (cat.).– Meschede, F. (ed.): M. A. Neue Nationalgalerie, Berlin. Stuttgart 1993 (cat.).– Mignot, D. (ed.): M. A./Ulay. The Lovers. Stedelijk Museum. Amsterdam 1989 (cat.).– Pijnappel, J. (ed.): M. A. Cleaning the House. London 1995.– Wulffen, T.: M. A. Biography. Stuttgart 1993

ACCONCI Vito
born **1940** New York
American sculptor and action artist. **1962–1964** Studied at the University of Iowa. **1964–1969** Freelance writer. **1968–1971** Lectureship at the School of Visual Arts, New York. From **1969**, through his performances and environments, became one of the main exponents of Concept and Body Art. **1971** *Centers*, a video-installation in which he films himself pointing at a television screen. **1969** Joint editor of the art magazine o to 9. **1972–1982** Took part in documenta 5 – 7 in Kassel. **1976** Lectured at California Institute of Art, Valencia, and took part in the Venice Biennale.
WRITINGS: V. A.: Four Book. New York 1968
MONOGRAPHS, CATALOGUES: Barzel, A. (ed.): V. A. Museo d'Arte Contemporanea Luigi Pecci. Prato 1992 (cat.).– Diacono, M.: V. A. Dal test-azione al corpo come testo. New York 1975.– Eigenheer, M. and M. Kunz (ed.): V. A. Cultural Space Pieces 1974-1978. Kunstmuseum. Lucerne 1978 (cat.).– Herzogenrath, W. (ed.): V. A. Arbeiten in Deutschland 1971-1981. Kölnischer Kunstverein et al. Cologne 1981 (cat.).–

ADAMS Ansel
1902 San Francisco–**1984** Monterrey (Mexico)
American photographer. **1916** First visit to Yosemite valley, to which he returned many times to photograph. **1914–1927** Studied Music. Developed a strong interest in landscape photography. **1916/17** Studied Photography with Frank Dittman in San Francisco. **1927** First book published with his *Parmelian Prints of the High Sierras*, elevating landscape photography to mythical realms. **1932** Founded the f/64 group together with Weston, Willard Van Dyke, Imogen Cunningham and others, to promote *straight photography*: exploring all technical possibilities to the full in order to prove that photography has an artistic character of its own. **1935** Publication of *Making of Photography*. **1936** Solo-exhibition at Stieglitz' gallery. **1940** Together with Beaumont Newhall, set up a department of photography in the Museum of Modern Art in New York; fighting for recognition of photography as art. **1946** Guggenheim stipendium. **1958** Brehm Award from the Rochester Institute of Technology. Numerous prizes and honours in later years. **1981** Hasselblad Award.
WRITINGS: R. A.: Why People Photograph. Selected Essays and Reviews. New York 1994
MONOGRAPHS, CATALOGUES: A. A. Classic Images. Kunstverein für die Rheinlande und Westfalen. Düsseldorf 1993 (cat.).– Alinder, A. (ed.): A. A. Classic Images. National Gallery of Art, Washington. Boston 1985 (cat.).– Callahan, H. M. (ed.): A. A. in Color. Boston 1993 / A. A. Farbfotografie. Munich 1993.– De Cock, L. (ed.): A. A. New York 1972.– Newhall, N.: A. A. The Eloquent Light. San Francisco 1963, New York 1980.– Wortz, M. (ed.): A. A. Fiat Lux. University of California. Irvine (CA) 1990 (cat.)

ADLER Jankel
1895 Tuszyn – **1949** Aldbourne (near London)
Polish painter. **1906** Began training as an engraver. **1912–1918** Studied with Wiethüchter at the School of Arts and Crafts in Barmen. From **1922** joined Max Ernst and Campendonk in Düsseldorf; Member of the Rhenish Secession. **1931–1933** Lectureship at the Düsseldorf Academy. Made contact with Klee. Works rescued from the Nazis and sent to Poland. **1935** First major

exhibition, followed by others in Italy, Czechoslovakia and Russia. Influenced by his Jewish background, his paintings develop a quasi-religious, quasi-mystical lyricism. **1937** Came to know Picasso in Cagnes-sur-Mer. His painting style became more monumental and his colours more intensive. **1940** Volunteered for the Polish army. **1941** Discharged from military service; settled in Kirkcudbright (Scotland). Lived in Aldbourne, near London, until his death in **1943**.
MONOGRAPHS, CATALOGUES: J. A. Städtisches Museum. Wuppertal 1955 (cat.).– J. A. Galerie Ketterer. Munich 1971 (cat.).– J. A. Galerie Hasenclever. Munich 1977 (cat.).– J. A. 100 Werke zum 100. Geburtstag. Düsseldorf 1995 (cat.).– Feldhaus, I. (ed.): J. A. Clemens-Sels-Museum. Neuss 1967 (cat.).– Fierens, P.: J. A. London 1948.– Guralnik, N. (ed.): J. A. Tel Aviv Museum. Tel Aviv 1985 (cat.).– Hayter, S. W.: J. A. London 1948.– Klapheck, A.: J. A. Recklinghausen 1966.– Krempel, U. and K. Thomas (ed.): J. A. 1895-1949. Städtische Kunsthalle Düsseldorf et al. Cologne 1985 (cat.).– Themerson, S.: J. A. London 1948

AFRO
(Afro Basaldella)
1912 Udine – **1976** Zurich
Italian painter. Studied art in Florence and Venice. **1933/34** and **1940–1944** military service. **1930–1933** lived in Milan. Had contact with Birolli and Ennio Morlotti. **1932** First solo-exhibition in the Galleria del Milione, Milan. Joint projects with the sculptor Arturo Martini. Lived **1936–1940** in Rome. **1952** Joined the abstract-gestural painters' association Gruppo degli otto Pittori italiani. Took part in the Venice Biennale. Became acquainted with Abstract Expressionism on a trip to the USA; especially impressed by Gorky's works. **1955** Awarded International Prize for Painting at the São Paulo Biennale and participation in documenta 1 in Kassel. **1956** Received special honours at the Venice Biennale. **1958** Guest-professor at Mills College, Oakland (CA). **1964** Participation in documenta 3 in Kassel.
CATALOGUES RAISONNES: Bettini, L. (ed.): A. Tutta l'opera grafica. Galleria d'Arte Moderna, Udine. Milan 1986 (cat.).– Brandi, C. et al. (ed.): A. Roma 1977

MONOGRAPHS, CATALOGUES: A. Kestner-Gesellschaft. Hanover 1953 (cat.).– A. Galleria del Milione. Milan 1974 (cat.).– A. L'itinerario astratto, opere 1948-1945. Milan 1989 (cat.).– Amico, F. d' (ed.): A. Il disegno. Galleria Civica, Modena. Florence 1992 (cat.).– Drudi, G.: Immagini di A. Roma 1986.– Feo, G. di (ed.): A. Galleria Nazionale d'Arte Moderna e Contemporanea. Roma 1978 (cat.).– Manturana, B. (ed.): A. fino al 1952. Palazzo Rosari-Spada. Spoleto 1987 (cat.).– Sweeney, J. J. (ed.): A. Roma 1961.– Venturi, L.: A. Florence 1954

AGAM Yaacov
(Jacob Gibstein)
born **1928** Rishon-le-Zion
Israeli painter and object artist. **1947/48** Studied at the Academy of Art in Bezalel, Jerusalem. **1949** Zurich School of Arts and Crafts. **1951** Moved to Paris; worked at the Atelier d'Art Abstrait. Built his first kinetic objects that change their appearance depending on the position of the viewer or when handled directly. **1953** Solo-exhibition in the Craven gallery, Paris. **1955** Experimental abstract films. From **1961** extended the sensual effect of his objects by incorporating sound effects and tactile stimuli. Produced large murals and playgrounds with variable colour components for architectural schemes. **1964** Participation in documenta 3 in Kassel. **1972** Retrospective in the Musée d'Art Moderne, Paris.
WRITINGS: Y. A. Textes de l'artiste / Texte des Künstlers. Neuchâtel 1962
MONOGRAPHS, CATALOGUES: Y. A. Stedelijk Museum, Amsterdam. Amsterdam 1973 / Y. A. Bilder und Skulpturen. Städtische Kunsthalle Düsseldorf. Düsseldorf 1973 (cat.).– Grambu, H. (ed.): Y. A. Pictures – Sculptures. Tel Aviv Museum. Tel Aviv 1973 (cat.).– Leymarie, J. et al. (ed.): Centre National d'Art Contemporain. Paris 1972 (cat.).– Metken, G.: Y. A. London and New York 1977.– Popper, F.: A. New York 1976, 1990.– Reichardt, J. (ed.): Y. A. Marlborough-Gerson Gallery. London 1966 (cat.)

ALBERS Josef
1888 Bottrop – **1976** New Haven (CT)
German-American painter and art teacher. Studied **1913-1915** at the Berlin Academy, **1916-1920** at Essen School of Arts and

---

Crafts with Thorn-Prikker and the Munich Academy with Franz von Stuck, and **1919/20** at the Bauhaus in Weimar. **1922** Qualified and then taught preliminary courses himself at the Bauhaus. Directed workshop for stained glass and later furniture design. **1925** Appointed Bauhausmeister. Married the artist Anneliese Fleischmann. **1933-1949** Emigrated to the USA and taught at Black Mountain College, North Carolina. His pupils included Motherwell, De Kooning und Rauschenberg. **1950-1960** Head of Department of Design at Yale University School of Art in New Haven. Visiting lecturer at numerous universities and institutes in America and at the Academy of Art and Design in Ulm, Germany. **1955** Participation in documenta 1 in Kassel. **1963** Wrote *Interaction of Colour*, research into the perception of colour. Albers became interested in geometric abstraction as early as **1920** and is best known for his series of paintings, begun in **1950**, entitled *Homage to the Square*. Can be regarded as a forerunner of Op Art and Minimal Art.
WRITINGS: J. A.: Structural Constellations. New York 1961.– J. A.: Hommage to the Square. New Haven (CT) 1962.– J. A.: Interaction of Color. New Haven (CT) 1940, 1975, London 1963 / J. A.: Interaction of Color. Grundlegung einer Didaktik des Sehens. Cologne 1970.– J. A.: Search versus Research. Hartford 1969.– J. A.: Formulation. Articulation. New Haven 1972
CATALOGUE RAISONNE: Miller, J. (ed.): J. A. Prints 1915-1970. Brooklyn 1973
MONOGRAPHS, CATALOGUES: Alviani, G. (ed.): J. A. Milan 1988.– Benezra, N: D. The Murals and Sculpture of J. A. New York 1985.– Bucher, F.: J. A. Trotz der Geraden. Eine Analyse seiner graphischen Konstruktionen. Bern 1961 / J. A. Despite Straight Lines. An Analysis of His Graphic Constructions. New Haven (CT) 1961, Cambridge (MA) 1977.– Fox-Weber, N. et al. (ed.): J. A. A Retrospective. Solomon R. Guggenheim Museum. New York 1988 (cat.).– Gomringer, E.: J. A. Starnberg 1968, 1971 / J. A. His Work as a Contribution to Visual Articulation in the 20th Century. New York 1968 / J. A. Son œuvre et sa contribution à la figuration visuelle au cours du XXe siècle. Paris 1972.– Licht, F. and N. F. Weber (ed.): J. A. Glass, Color and Light. Solomon R. Guggenheim Museum. New York 1994 (cat.).– Lück, M. and A. Schmidt: A. Bibliographie. Bottrop 1983.– Poetter, J. (ed.): J. A. 1888-1976. Staatliche Kunsthalle Baden-Baden. Baden-Baden 1988 (cat.).– Schell, M. (ed.): A. und J. A. Eine Retrospektive. Museum Villa Stuck, Munich et al. Munich 1989 (cat.).– Spies, W.: A. Stuttgart 1970, New York 1970.– Stockebrand, M. (ed.): J. A. Photographien 1928-1955. Kölnischer Kunstverein et al. Munich 1992 (cat.).– Thomas, K. (ed.): J. A. Eine Retrospektive. Staatliche Kunsthalle Baden-Baden et al. Cologne 1988 (cat.).– Weber, N. F.: The Drawings of J. A. New Haven (CT) and London 1984 / Die Zeichnungen von J. A. Bottrop 1988.– Wißmann, J.: J. A. Recklinghausen 1971

ALBRIGHT Ivan Le Lorraine
1897 Chicago – **1983** Woodstock (VT)
American painter. **1916/17** Studied architecture at the University of Illinois, Urbana. **1918/19** served as a medical draughtsman in World War I. **1920-1923** Studied at the Art Institute of Chicago and at the National Academy of Design, New York. **1926** Awarded special honours by the Art Institute of Chicago. **1930** First solo-exhibition in the Walden Bookshop in Chicago. His meticulous representations of processes of bodily growth and decay, often so exagger-

---

ated they become surreal, are closely related to Magical Realism. From **1938** Professorship at the Art Institute of Chicago. **1942** Special award for a painting in the exhibition "Artists for Victory" at the Metropolitan Museum of Art, New York. **1943** various commissions to paint film set details for Hollywood films such as *Dorian Gray*, *Bel Ami* and *The Temptation of Saint Anthony*. **1964** Retrospective at the Art Institute of Chicago.
CATALOGUE RAISONNE: Coryden, M. (ed.): Graven Image. The Prints of I. A. 1931-1977. Lake Forest 1978
MONOGRAPHS, CATALOGUES: Croyden, M.: I. A. New York 1978.– Donnell, C. et al. (ed.): I. A. The Art Institute of Chicago. New York 1997 (cat.).– Sweet, F. and J. Dubuffet (ed.): I. A. The Art Institute of Chicago. Chicago 1964 (cat.)

ALECHINSKY Pierre
born **1927** Brussels
Belgian painter. **1944-1948** Studied at the Ecole Nationale Supérieure d'Architecture et des Arts Décoratifs in Brussels. **1947** Travelled through Morocco and Yugoslavia; joined the group of painters known as the Jeune Peinture Belge. **1949-1951** With Appel, Jorn and Constant, formed the group Cobra. **1951** Moved to Paris; worked in Hayter's studio Atelier 17. **1955** Visited Japan. Strongly infuenced by calligraphic characters and Eastern painting techniques. **1957** Wall paintings for the Cinémathèque in Paris. **1964** and **1977** participation in documenta 3 and 6 in Kassel. Up to **1970** on the committee for the Salon de Mai. Alechinsky's form of Abstract Expressionism, his paintings peopled with grotesque and fantastic figures, are clearly influenced by Surrealism and techniques developed in American Action Painting.
WRITINGS: P. A.: La Vie comme elle tourne. Montrouge 1979.– P. A.: L'Autre main. Saint-Clément-de-Rivière 1988.– P. A.: Lettre suit. Paris 1992.– P. A.: Baluchon et ricochets. Paris 1994.– P. A.: Travaux à deux ou trois. Paris 1994.– Ionesco, E. and Y. Rivière (ed.): P. A. Peintures et écrits. Trois approches. Paris 1977 / P. A. Paintings and Writings. New York 1977
CATALOGUES RAISONNES: Butor, M. and M. Sicard (ed.): P. A. Travaux d'impres-

---

sion. Paris 1992.– Loo, O. v. d. (ed.): P. A. 20 Jahre Impressionen. Œuvre-Katalog Druckgraphik. Munich 1967.– Rivière, Y.: P. A. Les Estampes de 1946 à 1972. Paris 1973
MONOGRAPHS, CATALOGUES: Bonnefoy, Y.: A. Les Traversées. Saint-Clément 1992.– Bosquet, A.: P. A. Paris 1971.– Butor, M. and M. Sicard: A. dans le texte. Paris 1985.– Butor, M. and M. Sicard: A. Travaux d'impression. Paris 1992.– Güse, E.-E. (ed.): P. A. Zwischen den Zeilen. Saarland Museum, Saarbrücken. Stuttgart 1993 (cat.).– Haenlein, C. (ed.): P. A. Bilder, Aquarelle, Zeichnungen. Eine Retrospektive. Kestner-Gesellschaft. Hanover 1980 (cat.).– Heusch, L. d.: A. Copenhagen 1950.– Putman, J.: A. Milan 1967, Paris 1967.– Sello, K. and O. Paz (ed.): P. A. Margin and Center. Solomon R. Guggenheim Museum, New York et al. New York 1987 (cat.) / P. A. Margin and Center. Kunstverein Hanover et al. Hanover 1988 / P. A. Centres et marges. Musées Royaux des Beaux-Arts de Belgique et al. Brussels 1988 (cat.).– Sicard, M. (ed.): P. A. Extraits pour traits. Paris 1989.– Sicard, M. (ed.): P. A. Séquence 1980-1992. Paris 1994.– Sicard, M.: A. sur Rhône. Arles (n. d.).– Tardieu, J. et al. (ed.): A. Entre les lignes. Paris 1996.– Vree, F. d.: A. Schelderode 1976

ALMY Max
born **1948** Omaha (NE)
American video artist. **1970** Studied art and art history at the University of Nebraska, Lincoln and the University of Minnesota, Minneapolis. From **1974** worked as a video and media artist. Moved to Los Angeles. **1978** Graduated as a Master of Fine Arts in Film and Video from Californian College of Arts and Crafts in Oakland. **1984-1994** Taught at the UCLA School of Theatre, Film and Television. **1995** Awarded the International Prize for Video Art by ZKM in Karlsruhe.

ALTENBOURG Gerhard
(Gerhard Ströch)
1926 Roedichen-Schnepfenthal (Thuringia) –**1989** Altenburg
German painter and graphic artist. **1944** Active military service. **1945-1948** Worked as a journalist and writer. **1946-1948** Drawing lessons with Erich Dietz. **1948-1950** Studied at the Academy of Fine Arts in Weimar under Hans Hoffmann-Lederer. **1950** First engravings. **1957** Early sculptures. **1952** First one-man exhibition in the Springer gallery, Berlin. **1959** Took part in documenta 2, and **1977** in documenta 6 in Kassel. **1966** Burda Award for Graphic Art. **1968** Won the Will-Grohmann Award. From **1970** member of the Academy of Arts in West Berlin. **1988** Retrospectives in various German cities. Altenbourg's works are closely related to Fantastic Realism.
WRITINGS: G. A.: Ich-Gestein. Frankfurt-on-Main 1971.– Brusberg, D. (ed.): G. A. Das einschauende Anschauen. Köpfe und

Szenen 1949-1986. Berlin 1986 (cat.).– Brusberg, D. (ed.): Das dritte Auge. Ein Dialog der Freunde G. A. und Erhart Kästner. Frankfurt-on-Main 1992 CATALOGUES RAISONNES: Altenbourg, G. and A. Janda (ed.): G. A. Werk-Verzeichnis 1947-1969. Hanover 1969.– Thormann, O. and A. Janda (ed.): Sah ichs wie Feuer glänzen um und um. Werkverzeichnis der Metallarbeiten und zugehörigen Zeichnungen von G. A. Berlin and Leipzig 1994 MONOGRAPHS, CATALOGUES: G. A. Hamburger Kunstverein. Hamburg 1970 (cat.).– G. A. Staatliche Kunstsammlung Dresden. Dresden 1979 (cat.).– Brusberg, D. (ed.): G. A. "Schnepfenthaler Suite" und "Aus dem Hügelgau". Galerie Brusberg. Berlin 1989 (cat.).– Janda, A. (ed.): G. A. Arbeiten aus den Jahren 1947-1989. Institut für Auslandsbeziehungen. Stuttgart 1992 (cat.).– Roters, E. et al. (ed.): G. A. Das einsschauende Ausschauen. Köpfe und Szenen 1949-1986. Galerie Brusberg, Berlin. Hanover 1986 (cat.).– Salzmann, S. et al. (ed.): G. A. Arbeiten 1947-1987. Kunsthalle Bremen et al. Bremen 1988 (cat.).– Ströch, A. and G. Brusberg (ed.): G. A. Der Gärtner. Eine Monografie in Bildern. Frankfurt-on-Main 1996

ANDERSON Laurie
born **1947** Chicago
American musician and performance artist. **1954-1966** Studied violin. **1958-1965** Attended the Saturday School of the Art Institute of Chicago. **1966** Moved to New York. **1966-1969** Studied history of art. **1969** Became acquainted with Philip Glass. **1970** First objects and sound sculptures with taped sound effects. **1972/73** Studied sculpture at Columbia University, New York. Worked as a teacher and art critic. **1972** First *Automotive* performance. Used a variety of mediums of expression in her performances, such as music, dramatic and sculptural elements, gestures or off-stage voices or sounds. **1977** Participation in documenta 6 in Kassel. **1979** Release of the record *Big Ego*. **1981** Publication of the pop song *O Superman*. **1983** Guggenheim Fellowship. **1986** Took the show *Home of the Brave* on an international music and performance tour. A film-musical of the same name appeared in the cinemas. **1995** Toured with *Stories from the Nerve Bible*.
WRITINGS: L. A.: The Package. New York 1971.– L. A.: The Rose and the Stone. New York 1974.– L. A.: Typisch Frau. Regensburg 1981.– L. A.: United States. New York 1984 MONOGRAPHS, CATALOGUES: L. A. Solomon Gallery. New York 1977 (cat.).– Kardon, J. (ed.): L. A. Works from 1969 to 1983. Institute of Contemporary Arts, University of Pennsylvania. Philadelphia 1983 (cat.)

ANDRE Carl
born **1935** Quincy (MA)
American sculptor. **1951-1953** Studied at the Phillips Academy, Andover. **1954** Trav-

elled through England and France. **1958/59** Came to know Stella whose comic strips (*Black Series*), together with Brancusi's works, inspired him to create his first large wood sculptures. **1960-1964** Worked on the Pennsylvania railroad as a brakeman and conductor. **1964** Took part in "8 Young Americans", an exhibition of the works of sculptors using a formalised, minimalist language. Developed grounded sculptures (*Element Series*) based on identical wooden units arranged in horizontal configurations on the ground. **1965** First solo-exhibition in the Tibor de Nagy gallery, New York. From **1967** applied his module technique to metal sculptures: arrangements of iron, aluminium or copper plates laid out flat on the floor to be walked over. **1968** Participated in documenta 4 in Kassel and in the exhibition of Minimal Art at the Geementemuseum in The Hague, where he was presented as a leading exponent of this movement. Gave sculpture a new direction by redefining its spatial location. **1982** Participation in documenta 7 in Kassel.
WRITINGS: Buchloh, B. H. D. (ed.): C. A. and H. Frampton. 12 Dialogues 1962-1963. Halifax and New York 1980 MONOGRAPHS, CATALOGUES: C. A. Solomon R. Guggenheim Museum. New York 1971 (cat.).– C. A. The Museum of Modern Art. New York 1973 (cat.).– C. A. Die Milchstrasse, der Frieden von Münster und andere Skulpturen. Westfälischer Kunstverein Münster et al. Münster 1985 (cat.).– C. A. Haags Gemeentemuseum, The Hague et al. The Hague 1987 (cat.).– Battcock, G.: C. A. New York 1968.– Bourdon, D. (ed.): C. A. Sculpture 1959-1977. Laguna Gloria Art Museum. Austin 1978 (cat.).– Brouwer, M. and D. Zacharopoulos (ed.): C. A. Sculptor 1997. Musée Cantini. Marseille 1997 (cat.).– Develing, E. (ed.): C. A. Haags Gemeentemuseum. The Hague 1969 (cat.).– Develing, E.: C. A. The Hague 1974.– Jonge, P. d. (ed.): C. A. Haags Gemeentemuseum et al. The Hague 1987 (cat.).– Lauter, R. (ed.): C. A. Extraneous Roots. Museum für Moderne Kunst. Frankfurt-on-Main 1991 (cat.).– Meyer-Hermann, E. (ed.): C. A. Sculptor. Krefelder Kunstmuseum und Kunstmuseum Wolfsburg. Stuttgart 1996 (cat.).– Serota, N. (ed.): C. A. Sculpture 1959-1978. Whitechapel Art Gallery. London 1978 (cat.).– Waldman, D. (ed.): C. A. Solomon R. Guggenheim Museum. New York 1970 (cat.).– Westwater, A. (ed.): C. A. Sculpture 1958-1974. Kunsthalle Bern. Bern 1975 (cat.)

ANSELMO Giovanni
born **1934** Borgofranco d'Ivrea
Italian object and concept artist. Self-taught. **1967** Exhibited two works as part of an exhibition in the Sperone gallery in Turin. **1965-1968** Constructed a series of untitled, three-dimensional objects representing basic physical concepts such as *energy* and *power*. After **1969** focused on more abstract concepts such as *infinity* and *invisibility*. **1972** and **1982** participation in

documenta 5 and 7 in Kassel. From **1974** installations involving projected images, drawings or granite rocks, as in *particolare*, a work requiring 20 slide projectors. Anselmo could be said to stand somewhere between Italian Arte Povera and Concept Art. **1992** Received special honours at the Venice Biennale.
WRITINGS: G. A.: Leggere. Torino 1972.– G. A.: 116 Particolari visible e misurabli di INFINITO. Torino 1975 MONOGRAPHS, CATALOGUES: Ammann, J.-C. (ed.): G. A. Kunstmuseum. Lucerne 1973 (cat.).– Ammann, J.-C. and R. Fuchs (ed.): G. A. Kunsthalle Basel. Basel 1979 / G. A. Stedelijk Van Abbe Museum. Eindhoven 1979 (cat.).– G. A. Musée de Peinture et de Sculpture. Grenoble 1980 (cat.).– Merz, B. and W. Guadagnini (ed.): G. A. Palazzo de Giardini Publici. Modena 1989 (cat.).– G. A. Musée d'Art Moderne et d'Art Contemporain. Nice 1996 (cat.).– Pagé, S. and D. Soutif (ed.): G. A. Musée d'Art Moderne de la Ville de Paris. Paris 1985 (cat.)

ANTES Horst
born **1936** Heppenheim
German painter. **1957-1959** Studied at the Karlsruhe Academy under HAP Grieshaber. **1960** Received a grant from the arts society of the national association of German industries. First solo-exhibition in Der Spiegel gallery in Cologne. One of the first exponents of a new figurative style of painting in Germany, taking over from the L'art informel of the 50s. A central feature in his paintings is the *cephalopod*, an archaic figure with an oversized head in boxed-in spaces. **1962/63** Study visit to the Villa Romana in Florence, and scholarship from the Villa Massimo in Rome. **1964-1977** Participation in documenta 3, 4 and 6 in Kassel. **1966** UNESCO Award at the 33rd Venice Biennale. **1967-1973** Professorship at the Karlsruhe Academy. Since **1984** teaching again in Karlsruhe.
WRITINGS: H. A.: Poggibonsi 1979-1980. Frankfurt-on-Main 1980 CATALOGUES RAISONNES: Fehlemann, S. et al. (ed.): H. A. Auflagen von flachen dreidimensionalen Gegenständen. Ein Werkverzeichnis. Museum Moderner Kunst, Passau et al. Passau 1997 (cat.).– Franzke, A. (ed.): H. A. Metallplastik.

Vollständiges Werkverzeichnis. Munich 1976.– Gercken, G. (ed.): Werkverzeichnis der Radierungen H. A. 1962-1966. Munich 1968.– Lutze, B. (ed.): H. A. Werkverzeichnis der Lithographien, Offsets, Siebdrucke, Holzschnitte und verwandten Techniken. Stuttgart 1976 MONOGRAPHS, CATALOGUES: H. A. Kunstmuseum Hannover. Hanover 1983 (cat.).– H. A. Votives. Solomon R. Guggenheim Museum. New York 1984 (cat.).– H. A. Bilder von 1959-1993. Von der Heydt-Museum. Wuppertal 1994 (cat.).– Bischoff, U. (ed.): A. Bilder von 1959-1993. Bayerische Staatsgemäldesammlungen im Haus der Kunst, Munich et al. Munich 1993 (cat.).– Gallwitz, K. (ed.): A. Bilder 1965-1971. Staatliche Kunsthalle Baden-Baden. Baden-Baden 1971 (cat.).– Gallwitz, K. (ed.): H. A. 25 Votive. Städtische Galerie im Städelschen Kunstinstitut. Frankfurt-on-Main 1983 (cat.).– Lehmann, U. and N. Nobis (ed.): H. A. Druckgraphik, Farbige Blätter, Zeichnungen, Collagen und Skulpturen. Verzeichnis der Bestände Sammlung Wolf und Ursula Hermann. Sprengel Museum. Hanover 1989 (cat.).– Lutze, B.: H. A. Lithographien. Stuttgart 1976.– Schwarz, M. (ed.): H. A. Der Kopf. Badischer Kunstverein, Karlsruhe et al. Karlsruhe 1978 (cat.)

ANUSZKIEWICZ Richard
born **1930** Erie (PA)
American painter and graphic artist. **1948-1953** Studied at Cleveland Institute of Art, Ohio. **1953-1955** studied at Yale University of Art in New Haven under Albers and **1955/56** at the University of Ohio. **1957** Moved to New York. **1963-1965** Taught at the Cooper Union School of Art in New York. **1968** Participation in documenta 4 in Kassel. Since **1983** teaching at the School of Visual Arts in New York. Influenced by Alber's theories, Anuszkiewicz is one of the leading exponents of Op Art in America. His work is typically concerned with radiating expanses of lines, and visual perceptual phenomena.
CATALOGUE RAISONNE: Brooke, D. and G. Baro (ed.): R. A. Prints and Multiples. Brooklyn Museum. New York 1979 (cat.) MONOGRAPHS, CATALOGUES: R. A. Retrospektive. Josef Albers Museum. Bottrop 1997 (cat.).– Lunde, K.: A. New York 1976

APPEL Karel
born **1921** Amsterdam
Dutch painter. **1940-1943** Studied painting at the Rijksakademie in Amsterdam. **1948** Co-founder of the Experimental Group that later became Cobra. Other members of the group included Alechinsky, Jorn, Constant and Corneille. They put on joint-exhibitions and published a magazine. **1948** Unveiling of a large wooden relief, commissioned for the city hall in Amsterdam, caused a scandal. **1950** Moved to Paris. **1951** Cobra disbanded. Produced oil paintings,

ceramics, church windows, reliefs and sculptures in wood and polyester. **1956** Murals for the Stedelijk Museum in Amsterdam and **1958** for UNESCO in Paris, as well as the 100 metre long *Energy Wall* in Rotterdam. **1959** and **1964** participation in documenta 2 and 3 in Kassel. Paris 1987.– K. A. **1964/65** large multicoloured reliefs and figures in wood and polyester. **1971** First monumental sculptures out of aluminium in the USA. **1989** large retrospectives in five Japanese museums.
WRITINGS: K. A. over K. A. Amsterdam 1971
CATALOGUES RAISONNES: Kuspit, D. (ed.): K. A. Sculpture. Catalogue Raisonné. New York 1994.– Ragon, M. (ed.): C. A. Catalogue raisonné des peintures de 1937-1957. Paris 1988
MONOGRAPHS, CATALOGUES: Alvard, J. et al. (ed.): K. A. 40 ans de peinture, sculpture et dessins. Paris 1987.– K. A. Stedelijk Museum. Amsterdam 1965 (cat.).– Bellew, P.: K. A. Paris and Milan 1968.– Berger, P.: K. A. Venlo 1977.– Berger, P. et al. (ed.): Ecrits sur K. A. Paris 1982.– Claus, H.: K. A. Painter. Amsterdam 1962.– Frankenstein, A.: K. A. The Art of Style and Styles of Art. New York 1980.– Frankenstein, A.: K. A. Amsterdam 1989.– Fuchs, R. et al. (ed.): K. A. Dipinti, sculture e collages. Castello di Rivoli, Museo d'Arte Contemporanea. Milan 1987 (cat.).– Fuchs, R. (ed.): K. A. Ik wou dat ik een vogel was. Berichten uit het atelier/Ich wollte ich wäre ein Vogel. Berichte aus dem Atelier. Haags Gemeentemuseum et al. The Hague 1991 (cat.).– Hagenberg, R. (ed.): K. A. Dupe of Being. Paris 1989.– Lambert, J.-C.: K. A. Works on Paper/Œuvres sur papier. New York 1980, Paris 1988.– Ragon, M.: K. A. Peintures 1937-1957. Paris 1988.– Ragon, M.: K. A. De Cobra à un art autre. Paris 1988.– Restany, P.: Street Art: le second souffle de K. A. Paris 1982.– Restany, P. and A. Ginsberg: K. A. Street Art, Ceramics, Sculpture, Wood Reliefs, Tapestries, Murals. Villa El Salvador. New York 1985 (cat.).– Schmidt, K.: K. A. Arbeiten auf Papier. Staatliche Kunsthalle Baden-Baden. Baden-Baden 1982 (cat.).– Vrijman, J.: De werkelijkheid van K. A. Amsterdam 1962

ARAKAWA Shusaku
born **1936** Nagoya
Japanese painter and graphic artist. **1954**-

1958 Studied medicine and mathematics at the University of Tokyo. **1958-1961** Took part in neo-dadaist exhibitions and happenings. **1960** Founded his own Dada movement in Japan. **1961** First solo-exhibition in the Mudo gallery in Tokyo. **1961** Moved to the USA. Joint projects with his wife, the American writer Madeline Gris. Began large-scale drawings, paintings and diagrams. **1968** and **1977** participation in documenta 4 and 6 in Kassel. **1970** Took part in the Venice Biennale. **1972** DAAD scholarship to Berlin. **1978** Retrospectives in the Stedelijk Museum, Amsterdam, and **1979** at the Minneapolis Institute of Art.
WRITINGS: A.: For Example (A Critique of Never). Milan 1974.– A. and M. H. Gins: Mechanismus der Bedeutung. Munich 1971 / The Mechanism of Meaning. Work in Progress. New York 1979, 1988.– A. and M. H. Gins: Pour ne pas mourir. To not to die. Paris 1987
MONOGRAPHS, CATALOGUES: A. Editions Maeght. Montrouge 1977 (cat.).– A. Editions Maeght. Montrouge 1982 (cat.).– A. Bilder und Zeichnungen 1962-1981. Kestner-Gesellschaft. Hanover 1981 (cat.).– Gins, M. H. (ed.): S. A. Seibu Museum of Art. Tokyo 1979 (cat.).– Govan, M. and J.-F. Lyotard (ed.): S. A. & Madeline Gins. Reversible Destiny. Guggenheim Foundation, SoHo. New York 1997 (cat.).– Iwasaki, Y. (ed.): Constructing the Perceiver. A. Experimental Works. National Museum of Modern Art, Tokyo et al. Tokyo 1991 (cat.).– Partenheimer, J. (ed.): S. A. Städtische Kunsthalle Düsseldorf 1977 (cat.).– Zweite, A. (ed.): A. Bilder und Zeichnungen 1962-1981. Städtische Galerie im Lenbachhaus. Munich 1981 (cat.)

ARBUS Diane
(Diane Nemerov)
1923 New York–**1971** New York
American photographer. **1941** Married the fashion photographer Allan Arbus. Worked in advertising. **1955-1957** Studied under Lisette Model. From **1960** became a freelance photographer. Took fashion photos for *Harper's Bazaar*, *Esquire* and *New York Times Magazine*. Photographs of marginalised groups: drug addicts, the destitute and disabled people, as well as numerous pictures of "typical American citizens" in absurd or grotesque poses and sterile surroundings. **1965/66** Taught at Parsons School of Design in New York. **1968/69** Taught at the Cooper Union in New York. **1971** Solo-exhibition at the Museum of Modern Art, New York. Commited suicide. In the same year, a book was published of her photographs taken in the last eight years of her life.
MONOGRAPHS, CATALOGUES: D. A. and M. Israel (ed.): D. A. An Aperture Monograph. Millerton (NY) 1972.– D. A. Stedelijk van Abbe Museum. Eindhoven 1977 (cat.).– D. A. (ed.): D. A. Magazine Work. Helen Foresman Spencer Museum of Art et al. Millerton (NY) 1984 (cat.).– Bosworth, P.: D. A. A Biography. New York

1984/D. A. Eine Biographie. Munich 1984.– Roegiers, P.: D. A. ou le rêve du naufrage. Paris 1985

ARCANGELO Allan d'
born **1930** Buffalo (NY)
American painter. **1948-1953** Studied art history at Buffalo University, New York. **1953/54** Studied at City College and at the New School for Social Research, New York, and **1957-1959** at Mexico City College. From **1959** taught at the School of Visual Arts in New York. His early pictures of film stars and everyday subjects foreshadowed American Pop Art. Used abstract style of Hard-Edge painting in his pictures of highways, roadblocks and fences, representing landscape as seen from a car driver's seat. **1965** Artist-in-residence at Aspen Institute, Colorado. **1973** Professorship at Brooklyn College in New York. In **1982**, after a long pause, started painting again, focusing primarily on clearly delineated, geometric paintings of aspects of modern civilization.
MONOGRAPHS, CATALOGUES: A. d'A. Paintings of the Early Sixties. Neuburger Museum, State University of New York. New York 1978 (cat.).– Ashton, D. (ed.): The American Landscape. Paintings by A. d'A. Burchfield Center, Western New York Forum for American Art. Buffalo 1979 (cat.).– Towle, T. (ed.): A. d'A. Institute of Contemporary Art, University of Pennsylvania, Philadelphia et al. Philadelphia 1971 (cat.)

ARCHIPENKO Alexander
1887 Kiev–**1964** New York
Russian sculptor. **1902-1905** Studied painting and sculpture at Kiev School of Arts. **1906** Moved to Moscow, and in **1908** on to Paris. Made contact with Léger, and Apollinaire and the Cubists. **1910-1919** Exhibited regularly at the Salon des Indépendants and Salon d'Automne. Applied the cubist style of painting to sculpture, thereby creating Sculpto-painting: objects made of various materials such as wood, glass, metal and steel wire. **1912** Founded his own art school and the Section d'Or in Paris, exhibiting works by Picasso, Braque and Gris among others. **1913** Took part in the Armory Show in New York. **1921-1923** Taught at his own art school in Berlin. **1923** Emigrated to

America. **1924** Produced a series of movable paintings, including *Peinture Changeante* and *Archipentura*, seen as forerunners of Kinetic art. Opened further art colleges in New York and other cities in America. Lectured frequently at universities on the definition of sculpture.
WRITINGS: A. A. et al.: Fifty Creative Years 1908-1958. New York 1960
CATALOGUES RAISONNES: Karshan, D. (ed.): A. The Sculpture and Graphic Art. Including a Print Catalogue Raisonné. Tübingen 1974, Boulder (CO) 1975.– Karshan, D. (ed.): A. Sculpture, Drawings and Prints 1908-1963. Centre College, Danville (KY). Bloomington (IN) 1985 (cat.)
MONOGRAPHS, CATALOGUES: A. Fifty Creative Years 1908-1958. New York 1960.– Jánszky Michaelsen, K. and N. Guralnik (ed.): A. A. Centennial Tribute. National Gallery of Art, Washington et al. Washington 1986 (cat.).– Karshan, D. H.: A. Content and Continuity 1908-1963. Chicago 1968.– Karshan, D. H. (ed.): A. Visionnaire international. Musée Rodin. Paris 1969 (cat.).– Karshan, D. (ed.): A. Themes and Variations 1908-1963. Museum of Arts and Sciences. Daytona Beach (FL) 1989 (cat.).– Michaelsen, K. J.: A A Study of the Early Works 1908-1920. New York and London 1977.– Michaelsen, K. J. and N. Guralnik (ed.): A. A. A Centennial Tribute. National Gallery of Art, Washington et al. New York 1986 (cat.).– Pontiggia, E. (ed.): A. A. L'arte e l'universo. Montebelluna 1988.– Schmoll gen. Eisenwerth, H. and G.-W. Költzsch (ed.): A. A. 2 vols. Vol. 1: A. A.'s Erbe. Werke von 1908-1936 aus dem testamentarischen Vermächtnis. Vol. 2: Aufsätze, Archipenko-Symposion in Saarbrücken. Moderne Galerie des Saarland-Museums. Saarbrücken 1986 (cat.)

ARMAGNAC Ben d'
1940 Amsterdam–**1978** Amsterdam
Belgian painter and multimedia artist. **1959** -**1963** Studied painting at the Antwerp Academy. **1965** Worked together with Gerrit Dekker. Moved out of the city to Süd-Beverland. Concentrated on meditative environments and performances. **1976** Moved to Maastricht. **1977** Took part in documenta 6 in Kassel. **1981** Retrospective in the Stedelijk Museum, Amsterdam.
MONOGRAPHS, CATALOGUES: Brand, J. et al. (ed.): B. d'A. Stedelijk Museum, Amsterdam et al. Amsterdam 1981 (cat.).– Gachnang, J. and A. Hubschmidt (ed.): Armanac/Dekker 1968-1973. Stichting De Appel. Amsterdam 1974 (cat.)

ARMAJANI Siah
born **1939** Teheran
American environment artist, architect and philosopher of Iranian origin. **1960** Moved to the USA. **1960-1963** Studied at Macalester College, St. Paul. Began concept art projects involving computers. Since **1967** has worked as an architect, focusing on the design of reading gardens, common-rooms

and parks. **1974–1976** Published a *Dictionary of Buildings*, a complex of 2000 architects' models. Since **1986** developing so-called *Elements*, objects raising questions about architectural situations and their significance. **1987** Exhibitions at the Stedelijk Museum, Amsterdam, and the Kunsthalle Basel.
MONOGRAPHS, CATALOGUES: Ammann, J.-C. (ed.): S. A. Kunsthalle Basel et al. Basel 1987 (cat.).– S. A. List Visual Arts Center, Massachusetts Institute of Technology, Cambridge (MA) 1988 (cat.).– Brown, J. (ed.): S. A. Hudson River Museum. Yonkers (NY) 1981 (cat.).– Bußmann, K. et al. (ed.): S. A. Westfälisches Landesmuseum, Münster et al. Münster 1987 (cat.).– Kardon, J. and K. Linker (ed.): S. A. Bridges, Houses, Communal Spaces. Dictionary for Buildings. Institute for Contemporary Art, University of Philadelphia. Philadelphia 1985 (cat.).– Princethal, N. and J.-P. Vienne (ed.): Anarchistics Controbutions 1962-1994. Nice 1994 (cat.).– Reck, H.-U.: S. A. Nicht Stil: Konstruktion. S. A.'s Abneigung der Moderne. Frankfurt-on-Main 1991 (cat.)

ARMAN
(Armand Fernandez)
born **1928** Nice
French-born object artist who became an American citizen. **1946–1949** Studied at the Ecole Nationale des Art Décoratifs in Nice, and **1949–1951** at the Parisian Ecole du Louvre. Became acquainted with Yves Klein, with whom he organised joint happenings and events from **1953** onwards. **1955** Influenced by the works of Schwitters, produced neo-dadaist *Cachets*, pictures covered with ink stamps. **1958** Adopted the name Arman as a result of a printer's error on the cover of a catalogue. **1959/60** Produced *Poubelles* – domestic rubbish poured into plexiglas containers – and Accumulations – assemblages of similar junk material in showcases. **1961** First *Coupes* (sliced objects) and *Colères* (smashed up objects). **1963** Began work on *Combustiones* (incinerations) during his stay in New York. **1964** and **1977** participation in documenta 3 and 6 in Kassel. **1967/68** Taught at the University of California, Los Angeles. **1972** Became an American citizen. **1975–1982** Worked on *Long Term Parking*, a tower of 60 crushed automobiles. Together with Klein, Tinguely, Raysse and César, considered one of the main exponents of Nouveau Réalisme.
CATALOGUES RAISONNES: Durand-Ruel, D. (ed.): A. Catalogue raisonné. 4 vols. Paris 1991ff.– Kuspit, D. (ed.): A. Monochrome Accumulations 1986-1989. Catalogue Raisonné. Stockholm 1990.– Otmezguine, J. and M. Moreau (ed.): A. Estampes. Catalogue raisonné. Paris 1991.– Otmezguine, J. and M. Moreau (ed.): A. Multiples. Catalogue raisonné. Paris 1992
MONOGRAPHS, CATALOGUES: A. Ol'oggetto come alfabeto: retrospettiva 1955-1984. Museo Civico di Belle Arti, Villa

Ciani. Lugano 1984 (cat.).– A. Objets armés 1971-1974. Musée d'Art Moderne de la Ville de Paris. Paris 1985 (cat.).– Bréhammar, M. et al. (ed.): A. Lunds Konsthall. Malmö 1989 (cat.).– Cabanne, P.: A. Paris 1993.– Hahn, O.: A. Paris 1972.– Hahn, A. and O: A. Mémoires accumulés, entretiens. Paris 1992.– Holeczek, B. (ed.): A. Parade der Objekte. Retrospektive 1955-1982. Kunstmuseum Hannover mit Sammlung Sprengel, Hanover et al. Hanover 1982 (cat.).– Jouffroy, A.: A. Milan 1963.– Lamarche-Vadel, B.: A. Paris 1987, New York 1990.– Marck, J. v. der: A. New York 1984.– Martin, H.: A. New York 1968, Paris 1973.– Martin, H.: A. Or Four or Twenty Blackbirds Baked in a Pie. Or Why Settle for Less When You Can Settle for More. New York 1973.– Restany, P. et al. (ed.): A. 1955-1991. A Retrospective. Houston Museum of Fine Arts. Houston 1992 (cat.).– Scheps, M. (ed.): A. Parade of the Objects. Retrospective 1955-1983. Tel Aviv Museum. Tel Aviv 1983 (cat.)

ARMITAGE Kenneth
born **1916** Leeds
English sculptor. **1934–1937** Studied at Leeds College of Art and **1937–1939** at the Slade School. His early work was influenced by Egyptian and Cycladic sculpture, and the works of Moore. **1946–1956** Director of the department of sculpture at Bath Academy of Art in Corsham. Destroyed almost all the wooden sculptures from his early phase and began to make models in plaster, later in clay, as casts for his bronze figures and groups. **1952** First one-man exhibition at Gimpel Fils in London and participation in the Venice Biennale. **1955** and **1959** participation in documenta 1 and 2 in Kassel. **1958** Won first prize in an international competition for a war memorial in Krefeld. **1964** Visited Caracas. Used materials such as wax, resin and aluminium in stark, abstract figures. **1970** Guest-professor at Boston University.
CATALOGUE RAISONNE: Woollcombe, T. (ed.): K. A. Life and Work. London 1997
MONOGRAPHS, CATALOGUES: K. A. Marlborough Fine Art Limited. London 1962 (cat.).– K. A. The Arts Council of Great Britain. London 1972 (cat.).– Bowness, A. (ed.): K. A. Whitechapel Art Gallery. London 1959 (cat.).– Lynton, N.: K. A. London 1962.– Penrose, R.: K. A. Amriswil 1960.– Schmalenbach, W. (ed.): K. A./Lynn Chadwick. Kestner-Gesellschaft. Hanover 1960 (cat.).– Spencer, C.: K. A. London 1973.– Woollcombe, T.: The Sculpture of K. A. New York 1996

ARP Hans (Jean)
1886 Strasbourg – **1966** Basel
German-French sculptor, painter and poet. **1904–1908** Studied at the Academy of Fine Arts in Weimar and at the Académie Julian in Paris. **1910** Founded the Moderner Bund with Lüthy and Helbi in Lucerne. Came in contact with the Blauer Reiter group. **1914** Beginning of a long friendship with Max

Ernst. **1915** Met Sophie Taeuber; they collaborated closely on artistic projects and married in **1922**. **1916** Together with Hugo Ball, Tristan Tzara and Richard Huelsenbeck, started the Cabaret Voltaire in Zurich. **1917** First abstract wood reliefs; simultaneous poems and automatic writing. Worked on Dada publications. **1920** Joined the Dadaists in Cologne, centred around Johannes Theodor Baargeld and Max Ernst; after the summer, active in the Parisian Dada movement. **1923** Collaborated with Schwitters on various publications. From **1924** took part in Surrealist exhibitions and activities and contributed to their publications. **1930** First round sculptures in plaster. From **1931** member of Abstraction-Création. **1954** Received special honours at the Venice Biennale. **1958** Large bronze relief for the UNESCO building in Paris. In the poetic, pictorial worlds he created, Arp succeeded in uniting two seemingly incompatible styles: Surrealism and Abstraction.
WRITINGS: A. on A. Poems, Essays, Memories. New York 1971.– Arp-Hagenbach, M. and P. Schifferli (ed.): H. A.: Gesammelte Gedichte. 3 vols. Zurich and Wiesbaden 1963, 1984.– H. A.: Unsern täglichen Traum … Erinnerungen und Dichtungen aus den Jahren 1914-1954. Zurich 1955.– H. A.: On My Way. Poetry and Essays 1912-1947. New York 1948, 1967.– H. A. and E. Lissitzky: Die Kunst-Ismen. Zurich et al. 1924.– Jean, M. (ed.): J. A. Jours effeuillés. Poèmes, essais, souvenirs 1920-1965. Paris 1966, 1986
CATALOGUES RAISONNES: Arntz, W. F. (ed.): H. A. Das graphische Werk. Haag 1980.– H. A. Skulpturen. Œuvre-Katalog. Frankfurt-on-Main 1957-1969.– H. A. Minneapolis Institute of Arts. Minneapolis 1986 (cat.).– J. A. Musée National d'Art Moderne de la Ville de Paris 1986 (cat.).– Giedion-Welcker, C. (ed.): H. A. Stuttgart 1957/H. A. 2 vols. London and New York 1957-1968.– Rau, B.: H. A. Die Reliefs. Œuvre-Katalog. Stuttgart 1981/H. A. The Reliefs. Catalogue of Complete Works. New York 1981.– Trier, E.: H. A. Skulpturen 1957-1966. Stuttgart 1968/H. A. Sculpture 1957-1966. New York 1968
MONOGRAPHS, CATALOGUES: Andreotti, M.: The Early Sculpture of H. A. London and Ann Arbor (MI) 1989.– H. A. The Arts Council of Great Britain. Tate Gallery. London 1962.– H. A. Centre Georges Pompidou. Paris 1987/H. A. San Francisco Museum of Modern Art. San Francisco 1988 (cat.).– H. A. Museum Würth, Künzelsau. Sigmaringen 1994 (cat.).– Bleikasten, A.: A. Bibliographie. 2 vols. London 1981, 1983.– Bolliger, H. et al. (ed.): H. A. zum 100. Geburtstag (1886-1966). Ein Bilder- und Lesebuch. Bahnhof Rolandseck et al. Rolandseck 1986 (cat.).– Buffet-Picabia, G.: J. A. Paris 1952.– Cathelin, J.: A. Paris 1959.– Derouet, C. et al. (ed.): Sophie Taeuber – H. A. Künstlerpaare – Künstlerfreunde. Kunstmuseum Bern et al. Bern 1988 (cat.).– Döhl, R.: Das literarische Werk H. A.'s 1903-1930. Zur poetischen Vorstellungswelt des Dadaismus. Stuttgart 1967.– Fauchereau, S.: A. Paris 1989.– Gohr, S.

(ed.): H. A. Die Metamorphose der Figur. Museum Ludwig, Cologne. Bonn 1991 (cat.).– Hancock, J.: Form and Content in the Early Work of H. A. Harvard 1980.– Hancock, J. et al. (ed.): A. 1886-1966. Württembergischer Kunstverein, Stuttgart et al. Stuttgart 1986 (cat.).– Hopfengart, C. (ed.): H. A. Kunsthalle Nürnberg. Stuttgart 1994 (cat.).– Jianou, I.: H. A. Paris 1973.– Larsen, S. C. (ed.): J. A. Centenary Exhibition: Sculpture, Reliefs and Graphic Work. Fort Lauderdale Museum of Art 1987 (cat.).– Last, R. W.: H. A. The Poet of Dadaism. Chester Springs (PA) 1969.– Marchiori, G.: A. Cinquante ans d'activité. Paris 1954.– Marchiori, G.: H. A. Milan 1963.– Poley, S.: H. A. Die Formensprache im plastischen Werk. Stuttgart 1978.– Poley, S. (ed.): H. A. Stuttgart et al. Stuttgart 1986 (cat.).– Read, H.: The Art of J. A. London and New York 1968.– Schramm, U.: Der Raumbegriff bei H. A. Münster 1995.– Seuphor, M.: H. A. Cologne and Berlin 1961, Paris 1961, New York 1961.– Soby, J. T. (ed.): A. The Museum of Modern Art. New York 1958 (cat.).– Wasmuth, J. (ed.): H. A. und Sophie Taeuber-Arp. Ein Künstlerpaar der Moderne. Stuttgart 1996 (cat.).– Weber, S. (ed.): A. Museum Würth. Sigmaringen 1994 (cat.).– Zutter, J. (ed.): H. A. "nach dem Gesetz des Zufalls geordnet". Kunstmuseum Basel. Basel 1982 (cat.)

ARROYO Eduardo
born **1937** Madrid
Spanish painter. Self-taught. Educated at the Lycée Français in Madrid. **1958** After working for a short time as a journalist, moved to Paris. **1961** First solo-exhibition at the Claude Lévin gallery. As an exhibition of his paintings in Madrid had been closed owing to their provocative political message and realism, he decided not to return to Spain under the Franco regime. From **1970** used Spanish painters such as Velázquez and Miró as well as Magritte's works, which he parodied, as source material for his allusive paintings. **1975–1978** Took movie gangsters from the 30s as models for his series *Among the Painters*. Since **1980** has used sandpaper and other materials in large-scale collages.
WRITINGS: E. A.: España il poi prima. Milan 1973.– E. A.: Trente-cinq ans après. Paris 1974.– E. A.: Panama Al Brown 1902-1951. Paris 1983.– E. A.: Sardines à l'huile. Paris 1989/Sardinen in Öl. Frankfurt-on-Main 1991.– E. A.: Saturne ou le Banquet perpétuel. Paris 1994
CATALOGUE RAISONNE: Rocco, F. di (ed.): E. A. Obra gráfica. IVAM Centro Julio González, Valencia 1989 (cat.)
MONOGRAPHS, CATALOGUES: E. A. 30 Jahre danach – 30 ans après, Frankfurter Kunstverein und Musée d'Art Moderne de la Ville de Paris. Frankfurt u. Paris 1971 (cat.).– E. A. Knock-out 1969-1996. Musée Olympique. Lausanne 1997 (cat.).– E. A. Museo Nacional Centro de Arte Reina Sofía. Madrid 1998 (cat.).– Aillaud, G. et al. (ed.): A. Centre Georges Pompidou. Paris

1982 (cat.).– Astier, P.: A. Paris 1982.– Bozo, D. et al. (ed.): A. Leonard Hutton Gallerie. New York 1983 (cat.).– Dahan-Constant, B. and S. Hiekisch-Picard (ed.): E. A. Theater, Boxen, Figuration, Entwürfe, Bilder und Skulpturen. Museum für Kunst und Kulturgeschichte der Stadt Dortmund. Munich 1987 (cat.).– Serraller, F. C.: Diccionario de ideas recibidas del pintor E. A. Madrid 1991.– Soriano, J. (ed.): E. A. Sala Parpalló Provincial de Valencia. Valencia 1986 (cat.).– Spies, W. et al. (ed.): E. A. Theater – Boxen – Figuration. Museum für Kunst und Kulturgeschichte der Stadt Dortmund. Dortmund 1987 (cat.).– Zweite, A. (ed.): E. A. Blinde Maler und Exil. Bilder aus den Jahren 1970-1979. Städtische Galerie im Lenbachhaus. Munich 1980 (cat.)

ARTSCHWAGER Richard
born **1924** Washington
American object artist and painter. **1941-1948** Studied science at Cornell University, Ithaca. Attended the Amédée Ozenfant School in New York. **1953** Manufactured furniture. From **1961** produced his first *Pseudo paintings*, influenced by Johns, Rauschenberg and Di Suvero. Used mainly plastic coatings and fibreboard products for his furniture-like pieces. **1965** First solo-exhibition at Leo Castelli, New York. Prepared painted designs from photographs of interior decorations. From **1968** regular participation in documenta in Kassel (except for documenta 6). A recurring theme in Artschwager's œuvre is the perception of space in sculpture and painting.
CATALOGUE RAISONNE: Brooke, A. (ed.): R. A. Complete Multiples. New York 1991
MONOGRAPHS, CATALOGUES: Ammann, J.-C. (ed.): R. A. Kunsthalle Basel et al. Basel 1985 (cat.).– Armstrong, R. et al. (ed.): R. A. Themes. Albright-Knox Art Gallery, Buffalo et al. Buffalo 1979 (cat.).– Armstrong, R. (ed.): R. A. Whitney Museum of American Art, New York et al. New York 1988 (cat.).– R. A. Kunsthalle Basel. Basel 1988 (cat.).– Danto, A. C. et al. (ed.): R. A. Fondation Cartier pour l'Art Contemporain. Paris 1994 (cat.).– Blistène, B. (ed.): R. A. Centre Georges Pompidou. Paris 1989 (cat.).– Hentschel, M. (ed.): R. A. Archipelago. Portikus. Frankfurt-on-Main 1993 (cat.).– Kord, C. (ed.): R. A. Beschreibungen, Definitionen, Auslassungen. Hamburger Kunstverein. Hamburg 1978 (cat.)

ATGET Eugène
1856 Libourne – **1927** Paris
French photographer. **1875-1877** Sailor. **1879-1881** Studied at the Academy of Drama in Paris. **1881-1896** Toured with a theatre company throughout France. **1896** Began to draw, paint and photograph. In the years **1898-1914** he photographed in the Saint-Séverin district of Paris. **1899** Opened his own studio in Paris und began a long series of photographs of shopkeepers, shop-windows, houses and streets. **1920**

Sold a large portion of his Paris pictures to the Musée des Beaux-Arts. **1924** Continued the Paris series. **1926** Met Berenice Abbott, who later catalogued and published Atget's entire photographic legacy.
CATALOGUE RAISONNE: Szarkowski, J. and M. Morris Hambourg (ed.): The Work of A. 4 vols. New York 1981-1985
MONOGRAPHS, CATALOGUES: Abbott, B.: E. A. Prague 1963.– Abbott, B.: The World of A. New York 1964, 1979.– E. A. Centre National de la Photographie. Paris 1984 (cat.).– Barbin, P. (ed.): Colloque A. Paris 1986.– Borcoman, J. (ed.): E. A. 1857-1927. National Gallery of Canada. Ottawa 1984 (cat.).– Buisine, A.: E. A. ou la mélancholie en photographie. Nîmes 1994.– Christ, Y.: Le Paris d'A. Paris 1971.– Honnef, K. (ed.): E. A. Das alte Paris. Rheinisches Landesmuseum, Bonn. Cologne 1978 (cat.).– Leroy, J.: A. Magicien du vieux Paris et son époque. Paris 1976.– MacOrlan, P. (ed.): A. photographie Paris. Paris 1930.– Neal, D. L.: The Sequential Photographs of E. A. Photographer of Paris. Ann Arbor (MI) 1979.– Nesbit, M. (ed.): A.'s Seven Albums. New Haven (CT) 1992.– Nesbit, M. and F. Reynaud: E. A. Intérieurs parisiens. Un album du Musée Carnavalet. Paris 1992.– Recht, C. et al.: E. A. Lichtbilder. Munich 1975.– Reynaud, F.: E. A. Paris 1984

ATLAN Jean
1913 Constantine – **1960** Paris
Algerian painter. **1930** Moved to Paris. **1930-1934** Studied philosophy at the Sorbonne. **1941** First poems and drawings. **1942-1944** Imprisoned for his involvement in the Resistance. **1944** First exhibition at the gallery L'Arc-en-Ciel. Began abstract painting. **1945** First abstract paintings. Participation at the Salon des Surindépendants. His entire exhibited works purchased by Gertrude Stein. His symbolic style, with elements of pre-Columbian and African primitive art, made Atlan an important representative of the Ecole de Paris.
WRITINGS: A.: Le Sang profond. Paris 1944.– A.: Le Sommeil dans l'art. Paris 1959
CATALOGUES RAISONNES: Atlan, D. et al. (ed.): J.-M. A. Catalogue raisonné de l'œuvre complet. Paris 1996.– Woimant, F. (ed.): A. Catalogue raisonné de l'œuvre gravé. Paris 1980

MONOGRAPHS, CATALOGUES: Cousseau, H. C. et al. (ed.): A. Premières periodes 1940-1954. Paris 1989.– Dorival, B.: A. Essai et biographie artistique. Paris 1962.– Fricker, J. (ed.): Rétrospective A. Musée National d'Art Moderne. Paris 1963 (cat.).– Le Breton, G.: A. Paris 1947.– Ragon, M.: L'Architecte et le magicien. Paris 1951.– Ragon, M. and A. Verdet: J. A. Geneva 1960.– Ragon, M.: A. mon ami 1948-1960. Paris 1989.– Verdet, A.: A. Paris 1956.– Woimant, F. (ed.): A. Œuvres des collections publiques françaises. Centre Georges Pompidou. Paris 1980 (cat.)

AUERBACH Frank
born **1931** Berlin
English painter. **1939** Brought to England to escape the Nazi regime in Germany. **1947** Adopted British nationality. **1948-1952** Studied at St. Martin's School of Art, London and **1952-1955** at the Royal College of Art. **1956** First solo-exhibition at the Beaux-Arts Gallery, London. **1956-1968** Taught at various art schools. **1978** Large retrospective put on by the Arts Council in London. **1986** Received special honours at the Venice Biennale. Recurrent themes in his paintings are rows of houses and parks. He often uses an extreme impasto of dark, earthy colours.
WRITINGS: R. A.: An Autobiography. Munich 1993
CATALOGUE RAISONNE: F. A. The Complete Etchings 1954-1990. Marlborough Graphics. London 1990 (cat.)
MONOGRAPHS, CATALOGUES: Gooding, M. (ed.): F. A. Rijksmuseum Vincent van Gogh. Amsterdam 1989 (cat.).– Hughes, R.: F. A. London 1990, 1992.– Kossoff, L. et al. (ed.): F. A. Retrospective Exhibition. Hayward Gallery, London et al. 1978 (cat.).– Krempel, U. and K.-E. Vester (ed.): F. A. Kunstverein in Hamburg et al. Hamburg 1987 (cat.).– Lampert, C. (ed.): F. A. Paintings and Drawings 1977-1985. British Pavilion XLII. Venice Biennale. London 1986 (cat.).– Mathis, F. J.: F. A.'s Œuvre. Untersuchungen zur Farbgestaltung im kontextuellen Umfeld. Frankfurt-on-Main et al. 1993.– Shanahan, M. (ed.): Evidence 1944-1994, R. A. Whitney Museum of American Art, New York. Munich 1994 (cat.).– Spender, S. (ed.): F. A. Marlborough Gallery. New York 1982 (cat.)

AYCOCK Alice
born **1946** Harrisburg (PA)
American sculptress. **1964-1968** Studied at Douglas College in New Brunswick, New Jersey, and **1968-1971** at Hunter College in New York under Morris. **1972/73** Taught at Hunter College and **1977-1982** at the School of Visual Arts, New York. **1977** and **1987** participation in documenta 6 and 8 in Kassel. **1980** National Endowment for the Arts Fellowship. **1983** Retrospective of *Projects and Ideas 1972-1983* at the Cologne Kunstverein. **1987** Exhibition at Lenbachhaus, Munich, and participation in docu-

menta 7 in Kassel. Aycock builds huge architectonic pieces of apparatus and machine-like constructions. Her fantastic, nonsensical installations are a parody on modern technology.
WRITINGS: A. A. Labyrinth, Symbol and Meaning in Contemporary Art. Norton (MA) 1975
MONOGRAPHS, CATALOGUES: A. A. Kölnischer Kunstverein. Cologne 1984 (cat.).– Denton, M. (ed.): A. A. After Years of Ruminating on the Events that Led up to this Misfortune. Projects and Proposals 1971-1978. Allentown Art Museum. Allentown (PA) 1978 (cat.).– Friedel, H. (ed.): A. A. Munich Installation the Six of Pentacles. To Know All Manners of Things, Past and Future. Städtische Galerie im Lenbachhaus. Munich 1987 (cat.).– Fry, E. (ed.): A. Y. Projects 1979-1981. Tampa (FL) 1981 (cat.).– Osterwald, T. (ed.): A. A. Retrospektive der Projekte und Ideen 1972-1983. Württembergischer Kunstverein. Stuttgart 1983 (cat.)

BACON Francis
1909 Dublin – **1992** Madrid
English painter. **1925** Moved to London. **1926** Spent a year in Berlin. **1927/28** Worked as a decorator in Paris. First drawings and watercolours, inspired by Picasso's paintings. **1928** Returned to London. **1929** Began to paint in oils. **1944** Destroyed almost all his early work and developed a new painting style, independent of contemporary trends in art. **1946** Close friendship with Sutherland. **1946-1950** Spent summer in Monaco. **1952** Trip to North Africa. **1954** British representative (along with Nicholson and Freud) at the Venice Biennale. **1955** First retrospective at the London Institute for Contemporary Arts. **1957** First one-man exhibition in Paris at the Rive Droite Gallery. **1959-1992** Participation in documenta 2, 3, 6 and 9 in Kassel. **1962** Painted his first large triptychon *Three Studies for Figures at the Base of a Crucifixion* and **1964** the triptychon *Three Figures in a Room.* **1967** Refuse the Carnegie Institute Award for Painting at the World Fair in Pittsburgh, and won the Rubens Award in Siegen. **1971** First large American retrospective at the Grand Palais in Paris and **1990** first major retrospective in the Hirshhorn Museum in Washington. Bacon's 'existential' paintings are characterised by an

unusual blend of realism and surrealism, of the figurative and the abstract, subjective experience and universal, supra-personal forms of expression.
WRITINGS: F. B. Entretiens avec M. Archimbaud. Paris 1992 / Conversation with M. Archimbaud. London 1993.– Sylvester, D. (ed.): Interviews with F. B. London and New York 1975, 1980 / Gespräche mit F. B. Munich 1982, 1997 / L'Art de l'impossible. Entretiens avec David Sylvester. Geneva 1976, Paris 1995
CATALOGUE RAISONNE: Alley, R. and J. Rothenstein (ed.): F. B. Catalogue Raisonné. London and New York 1964
MONOGRAPHS, CATALOGUES: Alley, R. (ed.): F. B. Hamburger Kunstverein et al. Hamburg 1965 (cat.).– Ades, D. et al. (ed.): F. B. Tate Gallery, London et al. London and New York 1985 / F. B. Staatsgalerie Stuttgart 1985 (cat.).– Alloway, L. (ed.): F. B. Solomon R. Guggenheim Museum, New York et al. New York 1963 (cat.).– Alphen, E. v.: F. B. and the Loss of Self. London 1992, Cambridge (MA) 1993.– Carlucci, L. (ed.): F. B. Galleria Civica d'Arte Moderna, Torino et al. Torino 1962 (cat.).– Chiappini, R. (ed.): F. B. Museo d'Arte Moderna della Città di Lugano. Milan 1993 (cat.).– Davies, H. M.: F. B. The Early and Middle Years 1928-1958. New York and London 1978.– Davies, H. and S. Yard: F. B. New York 1986, Munich and Lucerne 1986.– Deleuze, G.: F. B. Logique de la sensation. 2 vols. Paris 1981 / F. B. Logik der Sensation. 2 vols. Munich 1995.– Farson, D.: The Gilded Gutter Life of F. B. London 1993 / F. B. Aspects d'une vie. Paris 1994.– Gowing, L. and S. Hunter (ed.): F. B. Hirshhorn Museum and Sculpture Garden, Washington et al. London 1989 (cat.).– Jardine, L.: F. B. Discovery and the Art of Discourse. Cambridge (MA) 1974.– Kundera, M. and F. Borel: B. Portraits and Self-Portraits. London and New York 1997.– Leiris, M. (ed.): F. B. Grand Palais, Paris et al. Paris 1971 (cat.).– Leiris, M.: F. B. Face et profil. Paris 1983 / Full Face and Profile. Oxford and New York 1983 / F. B. Munich 1983.– Leiris, M.: F. B. London and New York 1988.– Monsel, P.: B. 1909-1992. Paris 1994.– Oliva, A. B. (ed.): F. B. Figurabile. Museo Correr, Venice. Milan 1993 (cat.).– Peppiatt, M.: F. B. Anatomy of an Enigma. New York 1996.– Peyré, Y.: L'Espace de l'immédiat, F. B. Paris 1991.– Rothenstein, J. and R. Alley: F. B. London 1964, Paris 1967.– Russell, J.: F. B. London 1971, Paris 1971, Berlin 1971.– Schmied, W.: F. B. Vier Studien zu einem Porträt. Frankfurt-on-Main 1985, Munich 1996.– Sinclair, A.: F. B. His Life and Violent Times. London 1993.– Sylvester, D. et al. (ed.): F. B. 1909-1992. Retrospektive. Centre Georges Pomidou. Paris 1996 / F. B. 1909-1992. Retrospektive. Haus der Kunst, Munich. Stuttgart 1996 (cat.).– Trucchi, L.: F. B. Milan 1975, New York 1975, London 1976.– Whitney, C.: F. B. and Modernity. New Haven (CT) 1986.– Zimmermann, J.: F. B. Kreuzigung. Versuch, eine gewalttätige Wirklichkeit neu zu sehen. Frankfurt-on-Main 1986

BAERTLING Olle
1911 Halmstad – **1981** Stockholm
Swedish painter. **1948** Pupil of Lhote and later Léger. **1949** First solo-exhibition in Stockholm. **1950** Friendship with Herbin. **1950-1956** Member of Réalistes Nouvelles. **1952** Co-founder of the group Espace. **1963** São Paulo Biennale. **1964** *Compositions for Television* for Swedish television; national awards. **1981** Major retrospectives in the Konsthall, Malmö, and in the Moderna Museet, Stockholm. Strongly impressed by the works of Mondrian, Baertling set out to extend the theory of Neo-Plasticism,

without limiting himself to straight lines and rectangles.
CATALOGUE RAISONNE: Joosten J. M. and R. P. Welsh (ed.): P. M. Catalogue raisonné. Antwerp 1997
MONOGRAPHS, CATALOGUES: Brunius, T.: B. Discoverer of Open Form. Uppsala and New York 1965 / B. Précurseur de la forme ouverte. Paris 1968.– Brunius, T.: B. Mannen, verket. Uddevalla 1990.– Claeson, I. and E. Högestätt (ed.): O. B. 1911-1981. Den öppna formens skapare. Malmö Konsthall. Stockholm 1981 (cat.).– Reutersvärd, O.: B. Formelements dramaturg. Stockholm 1976.– Reutersvärd, O. et al. (ed.): O. B. Bilder und Skulpturen. Moderne Galerie Quadrat, Bottrop. Das bildhauerische Werk. Skulpturenmuseum Glaskasten, Marl et al. Bottrop 1983 (cat.).– Rickey, G. et al. (ed.): O. B. Creator of Open Form. Stockholm 1969

BAJ Enrico
born **1924** Milan
Italian painter. Studied at the Brera in Milan. **1951** Together with Sergio Dangelo founded the movement Movimento Nucleare, who saw themselves as the successors of Cobra, and developed a style of painting close to L'art informel. **1952** Publication of the *Manifesto della Pittura Nucleare*. **1953** With Jorn, sparked off Le Mouvement International pour une Bauhaus Imaginiste, by proposing ideas for a fantasy-orientated Bauhaus. **1959-1966** Contact with various Surrealist painters. Strongly influenced by Picasso. **1981** Set up his own exhibition centre in Milan. Created a grotesque, naive figures in collages incorporating string, wood and wallpaper.
WRITINGS: E. B.: Baj par Baj. Paris 1980.– E. B.: Automitobiografia. Milan 1983.– E. B.: Cose, fatti, persone. Milan 1988.– Eco, U. (ed.): E. B. Apocalisse. Milan 1979.– Fréchuret, M. (ed.): B., Jorn. Lettres 1953-1961. Saint-Etienne 1989
CATALOGUES RAISONNES: Crispolti, E. and H. Lust (ed.): Catalogo generale Bolaffi dell' opera di E. B. Torino 1973.– Petit, J. (ed.): B. Catalogue de l'œuvre graphique et des multiples. 2 vols. Geneva 1973.– Petit, J. (ed.): B. Catalogo generale delle stampe originali. Milan 1986.– Sanesi, R. (ed.): B. Catalogo generale delle stampe. Milan 1986
MONOGRAPHS, CATALOGUES: Bau-

BALDESSARI John
born **1931** National City (CA)
American photographer and multimedia artist. **1949-1953** Studied painting at San Diego State College. **1953/54** Director of the Fine Arts Gallery in San Diego. **1955-1968** Taught at various art schools and universities in San Diego, Berkeley, Los Angeles. **1960** First one-man exhibition at the Art Center in La Jolla, California. **1962-1970** Taught at the University of California, San Diego, and at Hunter College, New York. **1972** and **1982** Participation in documenta 5 and 7 in Kassel. From **1980** focused on photography, arranging pictures in multipartite compositions. **1990** Exhibition at the Musée d'Art Contemporain in Lyon and **1992** in Montréal. His alteration of his own photographs, posters and advertising bills, usually by painting over them with simple coloured dots, was meant as a comment on the role of art and artists in society. Regarded as an early exponent of Concept Art in America.
WRITINGS: J. B.: Ingres and Other Parables. London 1972.– J. B.: Four Events and Reactions. Florence 1975.– J. B.: Close Cropped Tales. Buffalo 1981
MONOGRAPHS, CATALOGUES: J. B. Works 1966-1981. Stedelijk Van Abbe Museum, Eindhoven et al. Eindhoven 1981 (cat.).– J. B. Centre National d'Art Contemporain de Grenoble. Grenoble 1988 (cat.).– Bruggen, C. v. (ed.): J. B. Museum of Contemporary Art, Los Angeles et al. New York 1990 (cat.).– Davies, H. M. and A. Hales (ed.): J. B. National City. Museum of Contemporary Art. San Diego 1997 (cat.).– Drohojowska, H. (ed.): J. B. Santa Barbara Museum of Art. Santa Barbara 1986 (cat.).– Echevarria, G. et al. (ed.): Ni por ésas – J. B. Musée d'Art Contemporain, Bordeaux et al. Bordeaux 1989 (cat.).– Gilbert-Rolfe, J. (ed.): J. B. RMS W VU. Wallpaper, Lampsand Plants. Zurich 1998 (cat.).– Haenlein, C. (ed.): J. B. Photoarbeiten. Kestner-Gesellschaft. Hanover 1988 (cat.).– Melo, A. et al. (ed.): J. B. This Not That. Manchester et al. 1995 (cat.).– Tucker, M. and R. Pincus-Witten (ed.): J. B. New Museum. New York 1981 (cat.)

drillant, J.: E. B. Paris 1980.– Baudrillard, J. et al. (ed.): B. I grandi quadri. Palazzo della Ragione, Mantua. Milan 1982 (cat.).– Baudrillard, J. et al.: E. B. Il giardino delle delizie / The Garden of Delights. Milan 1991.– Bellasi, P. et al. (ed.): E. B. 2 vols. Pinacoteca Communale, Casa Rusca, Locarno. Milan 1993 (cat.).– Jaguer, E.: B. Milan 1956.– John-Willeke, B. (ed.): E. B. "Das Begräbnis des Anarchisten Pinelli" und andere Werke aus vier Jahrzehnten. Mathildenhöhe. Darmstadt 1995 (cat.).– Jouffroy, A.: B. Paris 1972.– Lemaire, G.-G. (ed.): B. Du général au particulier. Centro attività artistiche Perrière, Bard. Milan 1985 (cat.).– Marck, J. v. d.: B. Milan 1969.– Mussini, M. (ed.): I libri di B. Teatro Municipale Romolo Valli, Reggio Emilia. Milan 1990 (cat.).– Sanesi, R.: A proposito B. Lonato 1987

BALLA Giacomo
1871 Turin – **1958** Rom
Italian painter and interior architect. Attended preparatory courses at the Accademia Albertina di Belle Arti in Turin, otherwise a self-taught painter. **1895** Moved to Rome. Worked as an illustrator, caricaturist and portraitist. **1900** Stayed seven months in Paris for the World Fair, where he encountered Pointillism. Returned to Rome. Met Boccioni, Severini und Sironi, and showed them new painting techniques he had learnt in Paris. **1910** Together with Boccioni, Carrà, Russolo and Severini signed Marinetti's *Manifesto of Futurist Painting* and shortly afterwards the *Technical Manifesto of Futurist Painting*. **1912** Several trips to Düsseldorf to decorate and furnish Haus Löwenstein. **1914/15** Together with Fortunato Depero, drew up the *Manifesto of Futurist Reconstruction of the Universe*. **1916** *Manifesto of Futurist Cinematography* (with Marinetti). **1912-1930** Applied himself intensively to decorative art. Designed furniture and futuristic objects. **1929** One of the initiators of futuristic *Aeropittura*. After **1933** turned away from Futurism and took up figurative painting again. **1935** Elected to the Accademia di San Luca in Rom. Applied Pointillist painting techniques in renderings of dynamism and speed – a favourite subject of the Futurists.
WRITINGS: Balla, E.: Con B. 3 vols. Milan 1984-1986
CATALOGUES RAISONNES: Battaglia, G. and A. M. Gambuzzi (ed.): B. Modena 1982.– Lista, G. (ed.): B. 1871-1958. Catalogo ragionato dell'opere. Modena 1982
MONOGRAPHS, CATALOGUES: G. B. Galleria Civica d'Arte Moderna. Torino 1963 (cat.).– G. B. Galleria Nazionale d'Arte Moderna. Roma 1971 (cat.).– G. B. Musée d'Art Moderne de la Ville de Paris. Paris 1972 (cat.).– Barricelli, A.: B. Roma 1966.– Crispolti, E. (ed.): Casa B. e il futurismo a Roma. Accademia di Francia a Roma. Roma 1989 (cat.).– Crispolti, E. and M. Sczdiero: B. Depero. Ricostruzione futurista dell'universo. Modena and Milan 1989.– Dorazio, V. D.: G. B. An Album of His Life and Work. New York 1970.– Fagiolo dell'Arco, M.: B. pre-futurista. Roma 1968.– Fagiolo dell'Arco, M. (ed.): Futur-Balla. Un profeta dell'avanguardia. A Prophet of the Avant-Garde. Basel et al. 1982.– Fagiolo dell'Arco, M. (ed.): B. The Futurist. Scottish National Gallery of Modern Art, Edinburgh et al. Milan 1987, New York 1988 (cat.).– Lista, G.: B. Futurista. Modena 1982, Lausanne 1984.– Magagnato, L. and E. Balla (ed.): G. B. Studi, ricerche, oggetti. Museo di Castelvecchio. Verona 1976 (cat.).– Marchis, G. d.: G. B. L'aura futurista. Torino 1977.– Robinson, S. B.: G. B. Divisionism and Futurism 1871-1912. Ann Arbor (MI) 1981

BALTHUS
(Balthazar Klossowski de Rola)
born **1908** Paris
Polish-born French painter. Spent his youth

in Paris, Berlin and Switzerland. **1920** Met Rainer Maria Rilke, who discovered and promoted his talent. **1921** Rilke published a portfolio entitled *Mitsou* with forty of the boy's engravings and his own preface. **1924** Studied in Paris. **1925** Study trip to Italy with André Gide. After military service in **1933**, made friends with Surrealists, Giacometti and Antonin Artaud. First artistic successes. **1935** Designed sets and costumes for Artaud's "Theatre of Cruelty". **1939–1945** Lived in Switzerland. **1961–1976** Director of the French Academy at the Villa Medici in Rome. **1977** Settled in Switzerland. **1956** Exhibitions at the New York Museum of Modern Art and **1968** at the Tate Gallery, London. **1980** Participated in the Venice Biennale. **1983** Exhibition at the Pompidou Centre in Paris. Since **1981** honorary member of the Royal Academy in London. Through Surrealism, came to adopt a figurative style of painting, which melds poetic and erotic accents with cryptic subjects. CATALOGUE RAISONNE: Roy, C. and J. Leymarie (ed.): B. Catalogue raisonnée. Paris 1991
MONOGRAPHS, CATALOGUES: Caradente, G. (ed.): B. Disegni e acquarelli. Palazzo Racani-Arroni, Spoleto. Milan 1982 /B. Drawings and Watercolors. Boston 1982.– Clair, J.: Metamorphosen des Eros. Essays über B. Munich 1984.– Clair, J. et al. (ed.): B. Peintures, aquarelles, dessins. Roma 1990 (cat.).– Davenport, G.: A B. Notebook. New York 1989.– Klossowski de Rola, S.: B. New York 1996, Paris 1996.– Leymarie, J.: B. Geneva and New York 1978, 1982, Leipzig 1993.– Leymarie, J. and J. Helfenstein (ed.): B. Zeichnungen. Kunstmuseum Bern. Bern 1993 (cat.).– Leymarie, J. et al. (ed.): Omaggio a B. Accademia Valentino, Roma. Geneva 1997 (cat.).– Mentha, H. (ed.): B. Zeichnungen. Kunstmuseum Bern. Bern 1994 (cat.).– Regnier, G. (ed.): B. Centre Georges Pompidou. Paris 1983 (cat.).– Rewald, S. (ed.): B. Metropolitan Museum of Art, New York et al. New York 1984 (cat.).– Roy, C.: B. New York and Boston 1996, Paris 1996, Munich 1996.– Zutter, J. (ed.): B. Musée Cantonal des Beaux-Arts de Lausanne. Geneva 1993 (cat.)

BAR-AM Micha
born **1930** Berlin
Israeli photographer. **1945–1948** Active member of the Haganah underground movement. **1948/49** Fought in the infantry in the Israeli war of independence. **1949–1957** Metalworker and youth leader on a kibbutz in West Galilee. **1957–1966** Worked as a photojournalist for the magazine *Bamahane* in Israel, and freelanced for various Israeli newspapers for a year. Since **1968** photographic correspondent in the Middle East for the *New York Times* and member of *Magnum Photos* in Paris and New York. Bar-Am is credited with having increased worldwide public awareness of Israel's political conflicts and cultural inconsistencies through his photography.

BARANOV-ROSSINE Vladimir
1888 Cherson (Ukraine) – **1942** (during deportation)
Russian sculptor and painter. **1903–1907** Studied painting at the Academy of Art in St. Petersburg. Contact with Larionov and the Burliuk brothers. **1910–1914** Went to Paris. Met Delaunay and the Cubists. First sculptural works. From **1913** participated regularly in the Salon des Indépendants. **1915** Inspired by Futurism to produce *Piano Optophonique*, an attempt to fuse colours, musical notes and sculptural elements so they could be experienced simultaneously. **1917** Returned to Russia. Professorship at the Academy of Art in Moscow. **1925** Settled in Paris and founded an institute of painting and audiovisual sychronisation. Transition from painting to object art, of which he became a leading exponent. CATALOGUE RAISONNE: Breuillaud-Limondin, P. and M. J. Mausset (ed.): B.-R. Diss. Paris 1980
MONOGRAPHS, CATALOGUES: V. B.-R. Galerie Jean Chauvelin. Paris 1970 (cat.).– V. B.-R. Musée National d'Art Moderne. Paris 1973 (cat.).– Marcadé, J.-C. (ed.): V. B.-R. Galerie Brusberg. Berlin 1983 (cat.)

BARCELO Miquel
born **1957** Felanitx (Mallorca)
Spanish painter and material artist. **1972** Studied at the Escuela de Artes y Oficios in Palma. Encountered Art brut in Paris. **1975** Studied at the Escuela de Bellas Artes in Barcelona. Designed wooden boxes and laid various objects inside them. **1976** First one-man exhibition at the Museo de Mallorca. Joined a group of concept artists known as Taller Lunàtic. **1980** Produced abstract drip-paintings, later painted over in white. Painted books and telephone directories with thick coats of paint, made iron books, and did some figurative animal drawings. Moved to Barcelona. **1982** Took part in documenta 7 in Kassel. Met Beuys and Lucio Amelio. **1983** First sculptures. **1988–1991** Trips to Africa. Explored the river Niger in his self-constructed 'painter's boat'. **1994** Stayed in Mali. Presentation of naturally produced reliefs, such as strips of paper devoured by termites. MONOGRAPHS, CATALOGUES: M. B. Pinturas 1984. Galerie Juana de Aizpuru. Madrid 1984 (cat.).– M. B. Galeria Soledad

Lorenzo. Madrid 1989 (cat.).– M. B. Musée de Nîmes. Nîmes 1991 (cat.).– Froment, J.-L. (ed.): M. B. Peintures 1983-1985. Musée d'Art Contemporain de Bordeaux. Bordeaux 1985 (cat.).– Lampert, C. (ed.): M. B. Whitechappel Art Gallery. London 1994 (cat.)

BARLACH Ernst
1970 Wedel – **1938** Rostock
German sculptor, graphic artist and poet. **1888–1891** Studied at the School of Arts and Crafts in Hamburg. **1891–1895** Attended the Academy in Dresden as a pupil of Robert Diez. **1895–1897** Lived in Paris, working at the Académie Julian. **1904/05** Professorship at the School of Ceramics in Höhr. **1907/08** First major wooden sculpture. **1909** Trip to Russia. Inspired by the wholesome earthiness of the farming communities and by Russian folk art, developed a form of sculpture with powerful folkloristic elements. Also produced several sets of engravings to illustrate plays he had written. After **1910** settled in Güstrow, Mecklenburg. **1917** First exhibition put on by Paul Cassirer in Berlin. **1919** Member of the Academy of Arts in Berlin. **1933** Awarded the order of merit *Pour le mérite*. Discredited by the Nazis. Systematic removal of his works from museums, churches and public places. Alongside Zadkine, the most important wood sculptor of the classical Modernist period. WRITINGS: E. B. Ein selbsterzähltes Leben. Berlin 1928 / A Selftold Life. Toronto 1990.– E. B.: Briefe. 2 vols. Ed. by F. Droß. Munich 1968-1969.– E. B.: Dramen. 8 vols. Ed. by H. H. Fischer. Munich and Zurich 1987-1998.– Droß, F. (ed.): E. B das dichterische Werk. 3 vols. Munich 1956-1959 CATALOGUE RAISONNE: Schult, F. (ed.): E. B. Werkverzeichnis. 3 vols. Hamburg 1958-1971
MONOGRAPHS, CATALOGUES: E. B. 1870-1938. Koninklijk Museum voor Schone Kunsten, Antwerp. Leipzig 1995 (cat.).– Carls, C. D.: E. B. Das plastische, graphische und dichterische Werk. Berlin 1968.– Carls, C. D.: E. B. New York 1968.– Chick, E.: E. B. New York 1967.– Crepon, T.: Leben und Leiden des E. B. Rostock 1988.– Doppelstein, J. (ed.): E. B. Bildhauer, Zeichner, Graphiker, Schriftsteller 1870-1938. Antwerp 1994 (cat.).– Doppelstein, J.: B. und Goethe. Leipzig 1997.– Flemming, W.: E. B. Wesen und Werk. Bern 1959.– Franck, H.: E. B. Leben und Werk. Stuttgart 1961.– Groves, N. J.: E. B. Life in Work. Toronto 1982.– Hooper, K.: E. B.'s Literary and Visual Art. The Issue of Multiple Talent.– Hupp, K.: Der Kieler Geistkämpfer von E. B. Kiel 1989.– Jansen, E. (ed.): E. B. Werk und Wirkung. Frankfurt-on-Main 1972.– Jansen, E. (ed.): E. B. Werke und Werkentwürfe aus drei Jahrzehnten. 3 vols. Altes Museum. Berlin 1981 (cat.).– Jansen, E. (ed.): E. B. Werke, Meinungen. Wiener Künstlerhaus. Vienna 1984 (cat.).– Jentsch, R. (ed.): E. B. Museum Villa Stuck. Munich 1981 (cat.).– Kleberger,

I.: E. B. Der Wanderer im Wind. Munich 1986.– Knobling, H.: Studien zum zeichnerischen Werk Ernst Barlachs 1892-1912. Worms 1989.– Krahmer, C.: E. B. in Selbstzeugnissen und Bilddokumenten. Reinbek 1984.– Krahmer, C. (ed.): E. B. Un sculpteur-écrivain. Musée d'Orsay. Paris 1988 (cat.).– Kurth, W.: E. B. Berlin 1989.– Lautz-Oppermann, G.: E. B. der Illustrator. Wolfshagen-Scharbeutz 1952.– Piper, E. R.: E. B. und die nationalsozialistische Kunstpolitik. Munich 1983.– Schilling, J. (ed.): E. B. Plastik, Zeichnung, Druckgraphik 1906-1937. Schloß Cappenberg. Unna 1988 (cat.).– Schulz, I. (ed.): E. B. Denkzeichen. Kulturhistorisches Museum, Rostock et al. Rostock 1988 (cat.).– Schurek, P.: B. Eine Bildbiographie. Munich 1961.– Stubbe, W.: E. B. Plastik. Munich 1959, 1985.– Werner, A.: E. B. New York 1966

BASELITZ Georg
(Georg Kern)
born **1938** Deutschbaselitz (Saxony)
German painter and sculptor. From **1956** studied at the School of Fine and Applied Arts in East Berlin under Walter Womacka. Met Peter Graf und Ralf Winkler (A. R. Penck). **1957–1962** Further classes in painting under Hann Trier at the School of Arts in West Berlin. **1961** Adopted the pseudonym Baselitz. Inspired by Breton's Surrealist manifestos, wrote his own manifestos to accompany his action pictures: *The Night of Pandemonium* (**1962**) and *Why the Picture 'Great Friends' is a Good Picture* (**1966**). First strictly representational pictures directed against Tachisme and abstract art. **1966** Moved to Osthofen near Worms. First woodcuts. **1969** Began painting upside-down portraits and landscapes. **1965** Scholarship to the Villa Romana in Florence. **1978** Took a studio in Imparia. **1978** Professorship at the Academy of Arts in Karlsruhe. **1979** First roughly hewn wood sculptures. **1980** Together with Kiefer, represented Germany at the Venice Biennale. Taught from **1983–1988** and again from **1992** at the Berlin Academy. **1995** Major retrospective at the Guggenheim Museum, New York. WRITINGS: G. B. im Gespräch mit H. P. Schwerfel. Cologne 1989.– G. B.: Ballsaison in Schweden. Briefe zwischen Strindberg und Hill. Derneburg 1992.– G. B. Manifeste 1961-1985. Paris 1989.– Werner, M. (ed.): G. B. Malelade. Cologne 1990 CATALOGUES RAISONNES: Gallwitz, K. (ed.): G. B. Der Weg der Erfindungen. Werkverzeichnis der frühen Zeichnungen, Bilder und der Skulpturen 1979-1988. Städtische Galerie im Städel. Frankfurt-on-Main 1988 (cat.).– Gohr, S. et al. (ed.): Pastelle 1985-1990. Bern 1990.– Haenlein, C. (ed.): G. B. Skulpturen und Zeichnungen 1979-1987. Werkverzeichnis der Skulpturen und der Zeichnungen zu den Skulpturen. Kestner-Gesellschaft. Hanover 1987 (cat.).– Jahn, F. and J. Gachnang (ed.): B. Peintre-Graveur. Werkverzeichnis der Druckgraphik 1963-1982. 2 vols. Bern and

Berlin 1983-1987.– Salzmann, S. (ed.): G. B. Das Motiv. Bilder und Zeichnungen 1987-1988. Werkverzeichnis der Aquarelle. Kunsthalle Bremen. Bremen 1988 (cat.).– Weisner, U. (ed.): B. Holzschnitte 1966-1989. Stuttgart 1991
MONOGRAPHS, CATALOGUES: G. B. Grabados, Gravures, Prints. Musée d'Art et d'Histoire, Geneva 1991 (cat.).– Laffon, J. et al. (ed.): G. B. Musée d'Art Moderne de la Ville de Paris. Paris 1996 (cat.).– Franzke, A.: G. B. Munich 1988.– Gallwitz, K. (ed.): G. B. Der Weg der Erfindung. Städtische Galerie im Städel. Frankfurt-on-Main 1988 (cat.).– Gercken, G. et al. (ed.): G. B. Skulpturen. Hamburger Kunsthalle. Stuttgart 1994 (cat.).– Gohr, S.: G. B. Retrospektive 1964-1991. Kunsthalle der Hypo-Kulturstiftung, Munich et al. Munich 1992 (cat.).– Gohr, S.: Über B. Aufsätze und Gespräche 1976-1996. Cologne 1996.– Grigoteit, A. et al. (ed.): G. B. aus der Sammlung der Deutschen Bank. Moscow et al. Frankfurt-on-Main 1997 (cat.).– Güse, E.-E. (ed.): B. Werke 1981-1993. Saarland Museum, Saarbrücken. Stuttgart 1994 (cat.).– Haenlein, C. (ed.): G. B. Skulpturen und Zeichnungen 1979-1987. Kestner-Gesellschaft. Hanover 1987 (cat.).– Hofmann, W. (ed.): G. B. Bilder 1965-1987. Hamburger Kunsthalle. Hamburg 1988 (cat.).– Honisch, D. et al. (ed.): G. B. Staatliche Museen zu Berlin. Stuttgart 1996 (cat.).– Jablonka, R.: Ruins. Strategies of Destruction in the Fracture of G. B. 1966-1969. London 1982.– Koepplin, D. and R. Fuchs (ed.): G. B. Zeichnungen 1958-1983. Kunstmuseum Basel et al. Basel 1984 (cat.).– Meyer zu Eissen, A. et al. (ed.): G. B. Das Motiv. Kunsthalle Bremen. Bremen 1988 (cat.).– Muthesius, A. (ed.): G. B. Cologne 1990.– Quinn, E.: G. B. Eine fotografische Studie. Bern 1993.– Serrota, N. and M. Francis (ed.): G. B. Paintings 1960-1983. Whitechapel Art Gallery, London et al. London 1983 (cat.).– Szeemann, H. et al. (ed.): G. B. Kunsthaus Zurich et al. Zurich 1990 (cat.).– Waldman, D. (ed.): G. B. Solomon R. Guggenheim Museum, New York et al. New York 1995 (cat.).– Wedewer, R. and F. Jahn (ed.): G. B. Radierungen 1963-1974, Holzschnitte 1966-1967. Schloß Morsbroich, Städtisches Museum. Leverkusen 1974 (cat.).– Weisner, U. (ed.): G. B. Vier Wände. Kunsthalle Bielefeld. Bielefeld 1985 (cat.)

BASQUIAT Jean-Michel
1960 Brooklyn (NY) – **1988** New York
Graffiti artist. His father was a Haitian book keeper and his mother Puerto Rican. Had a difficult childhood. Aged 17, joined his friend Al Diaz painting graffiti in subway stations and on house-fronts under the assumed name of Samo. Jobbed and played guitar and synthesizer in a band. Became a media star after taking part in the documenta 7 in Kassel **1982** and the Whitney Biennale in New York **1983**. Worked with Warhol, even painting each other's portraits. Basquiat turned graffiti

into a respected art form without denying his Brooklyn ghetto origins. Constructed assemblages from bits of rubbish. Painted on surfaces ranging from torn pieces of paper to a fridge door. Died from an overdose of drugs.
WRITINGS: J.-M. B.: Amateur Bout. New York 1989.– Warsh, L. (ed.): J.-M. B. The Notebook. New York 1993
MONOGRAPHS, CATALOGUES: Adès, M. C. (ed.): J.-M. B. Peinture, dessins, écriture. Paris 1993 (cat.).– Baghoomian, V.: J.-M. B. New York 1989.– J.-M. B. Drawings. Robert Miller Gallery. New York 1990 (cat.).– J.-M. B. Fondation Dina Vierny. Musée Maillol. Paris 1997 (cat.).– J.-M. B. King for a Decade. New York 1997.– Chemin, J. (ed.): J.-M. B. Drawings. New York 1990.– Enrici, M.: J.-M. B. Paris 1989.– Haenlein (ed.): J.-M. B. Kestner-Gesellschaft. Hanover 1986 (cat.).– Haenlein, C. (ed.): J.-M. B. Das zeichnerische Werk. Kestner-Gesellschaft. Hanover 1989 (cat.).– Hebdige, D.: J.-M. B. New York 1992.– Marshall, R. (ed.): J.-M. B. Whitney Museum of American Art, New York et al. New York 1992 (cat.).– Marshall, R. (ed.): J.-M. B. Museo de Bellas Artes. Malaga 1996 (cat.).– Michetti-Prod'hom, C. and A. B. Edelman (ed.): J.-M. B. Musée d'Art Contemporain. Lausanne 1993 (cat.).– Millet, B. et al. (ed.): J.-M. B. Une rétrospective. Musée Cantini. Marseille 1992 (cat.).– Navarra, E. et al. (ed.): J.-M. B. 2 vols. Galerie Enrico Navarra. Paris 1996 (cat.).– Vierny, D. et al. (ed.): J.-M. B. Works on Paper. Galerie Enrico Navarra. Paris 1997

BAUCHANT André
1873 Chateaurenault (near Tours) –
1958 Montoire (Loir-et-Cher)
French painter. Apprenticed to a gardener. **1917** Worked as a surveyor. Did not turn to painting until the age of 46. Painted numerous landscapes with historical features and scenes from nature, such as gardens and birds, in a naive, poetic style. **1920** Discovered and promoted by Ozenfant and Le Corbusier. **1921** Exhibited 16 works in the Salon d'Automne. From **1927** exhibitions in the Jeanne Bucher gallery in Paris. **1928** Designed the stage set for Sergei Diaghilev's production of Igor Stravinsky's ballet *Apollon Musagète*. **1937** Exhibited together with Henri Rousseau, Camille Bombois and Louis Vivin in "Popular Masters of Reality" in Paris, Munich and New York. Alongside his painting, continued to work as a professional gardener and builder.
MONOGRAPHS, CATALOGUES: A. B. 1873-1958 Rétrospective. Musée des Beaux-Arts. Tours 1960 (cat.).– A. B. G. A. Musée d'Art Moderne et d'Art Contemporain. Nice 1987 (cat.).– A. B. Peintures, Dessins 1915-1958. Musée des Beaux-Arts. Tours 1991 (cat.).– Gauthier, A.: A. B. Paris 1942.– Killer, P.: A. B. Zurich 1991.– Zander, L.: A. B. Retrospektive. Galerie Charlotte. Munich 1993 (cat.)

BAUMEISTER Willi
1889 Stuttgart – **1955** Stuttgart
German painter. **1905-1907** Apprenticeship in his uncle's decorating business. From **1908** attended the Stuttgart Academy and from **1909** studied composition with Schlemmer under Hoelzl. **1914** Travelled to Holland and France with Schlemmer. **1914-1918** Military service. **1919** Returned to Stuttgart. Co-founder of Üecht, a group of Stuttgart artists. Early figurative works influenced by the Cubists were superseded by his wall pictures. **1924** Met Ozenfant, Le Corbusier and Léger in Paris. **1927** Became a member of the Circle of New Promotional Designers. **1928** Taught commercial art, typography and textile printing at the Städel Art School in Frankfurt am Main. **1930** Joined Cercle et Carré and, in **1932** Abstraction-Création. **1933** Denounced, professionally banned as a "degenerate" artist and dismissed from his post. Works painted secretly in Stuttgart became increasingly removed from the representational. **1939-1944** Worked as a painting instructor for the paint manufacturer Kurt Herbert in Wuppertal. **1941** Exhibition of his works forbidden. **1943-1947** Wrote the theoretical work *The Unknown in Art*. **1946-1955** Appointed Professor of Painting at the Stuttgart Academy. **1948** First German artist to exhibit at the Salon des Réalistes Nouvelles. **1951** Won major award at the São Paulo Biennale. After **1951** participated three times at the Venice Biennale.
WRITINGS: W. B.: Das Unbekannte in der Kunst. Stuttgart 1947, Cologne 1968.– W. B.: Magie der Form. Baden-Baden 1954
CATALOGUES RAISONNES: Gauss, U. et al. (ed.): W. B. Gemälde, Serigraphien, Zeichnungen, Gouachen, Collagen. 3 vols. Staatsgalerie Stuttgart. Stuttgart 1989.– Grohmann, W.: W. B. Leben und Werk. Cologne 1963 / W. B. Life and Work New York 1966, London 1985.– Ponert, D. J. (ed.): W. B. Werkverzeichnis der Zeichnungen, Gouachen und Collagen. Cologne 1988.– Spielmann, H.: W. B. Das graphische Werk. 2 vols. Hamburg 1972
MONOGRAPHS, CATALOGUES: Adriani, G. (ed.): B. Dokumente, Texte, Gemälde. Kunsthalle Tübingen. Cologne 1971 (cat.).– Boehm, G. et al.: W. B. Der Maler. Stuttgart 1995.– Bott, G.: Figuration und Bildformat. Zur Auflösung des Bildbegriffs in der Malerei W. B.'s. Frankfurt-on-Main et al. 1990.– Chametzky, P.: Autonomy and Authority in German Twentieth-Century Art. The Art and Career of W. B. New York 1991.– Hirner-Schüssele, R.: Von der Anschauung zur Formerfindung. Studien zu W. B.'s Theorie moderner Kunst. Worms 1990.– Kermer, W. (ed.): W. B. Typographie und Reklamegestaltung. Staatliche Akademie der Bildenden Künste. Stuttgart 1989 (cat.).– Kermer, W.: Der schöpferische Winkel. W. B.'s pädagogische Tätigkeit. Stuttgart 1992.– Roh, F.: W. B. Magie der Form. Baden-Baden 1954.– Schneider, A. (ed.): W. B. Gemälde. Nationalgalerie Berlin. Stuttgart 1989 (cat.).– Semff, M. (ed.): W. B. Zeichnungen. Kupferstichkabinett Dresden et al. Dresden 1996 (cat.)

BAZAINE Jean
1904 Paris – **1995** Paris
French painter. **1922-1925** Studied sculpture and literature at the Ecole des Beaux-Arts in Paris. **1924** Studied painting at the Lanskoy Academy. Exhibited regularly at the Tuileries from **1930** and at the Salon d'Automne from **1931** onwards. **1941** Organised the exhibition "Young Painters of the French Tradition" at the Braun gallery in Paris. Designed windows for churches at Assy **1944-1946** and Audincourt **1948-1951**, and later in his years. **1953/54** Trip to Spain. **1955-1964** Participation in documenta 1 – 3 in Kassel. **1959** One-man exhibitions in Bern, Eindhoven and Amsterdam, and **1965** at the Musée d'Art Moderne de la Ville de Paris. His non-figurative painting made him one of the most important representatives of the Ecole de Paris. His abstract representations of nature are made up of rhythmically composed colour patterns with intense lighting effects.
WRITINGS: J. B.: Notes sur la peinture d'aujourd'hui. Paris 1947 / Notizen zur Malerei der Gegenwart. Frankfurt-on-Main 1959.– J. B.: Exercice de la peinture. Paris 1973.– J. B.: Le Temps de la peinture. Paris 1990
MONOGRAPHS, CATALOGUES: J. B. and J.-C. Schneider: Habiter la lumière. Regards sur la peinture de J. B. Montolieu 1994.– Begny, J. d. and J.-Luc Daval (ed.): B. Grand Palais, Paris. Geneva 1990 (cat.).– Cabanne, P. et al.: J. B. Geneva and Paris 1990.– Chessex, J. et al. (ed.): B. Fribourg. Geneva 1996 (cat.).– Greff, J.-P. and J.-C. Schneider (ed.): B. Galerie Adrien Maeght. Paris 1987 (cat.).– Greff, J.-P. (ed.): B. Dessins 1931-1988. Musée Matisse. Le Cateau-Cambrésis 1988 (cat.).– Prat, J.-L. et al. (ed.): B. Rétrospective. Fondation Maeght. Saint-Paul 1987 (cat.).– Tardieu, J. et al.: B. Paris 1975

BAZIOTES William
1912 Pittsburgh (PA) – **1963** New York
American painter. **1933-1936** Studied at the National Academy of Design, New York. Painted in a naturalistic style. **1938-1941** Involved, as a teacher, in the Works Progress Administration Federal Art Project. Began abstract painting. **1942** Took part in an exhibition of leading Surrealists in New York. **1944** First solo-exhibition in Peggy

Guggenheim's gallery entitled "Art of this Century". **1948** Together with Rothko, Motherwell and Newman founded the school of painting *Subjects of the Artist*, which laid the cornerstone for Abstract Expressionism in America. **1949–1952** Taught at the Museum Art School in Brooklyn and at the People's Art Center of the Museum of Modern Art, New York. From **1952** professorship at Hunter College, New York. **1955/56** Took part in the exhibition "The New American Painting" organized by the Museum of Modern Art that was taken to Europe in **1958/59**. **1959** Participation in documenta 2 in Kassel. In his paintings, displaying Surrealist influences, Baziotes attempts to portray the diversity and ambiguity of the unconscious in an extremely sparse pictorial language.
MONOGRAPHS, CATALOGUES: Alloway, I. (ed.): W. B. A Memorial Exhibition. Solomon R. Guggenheim Museum. New York 1965 (cat.).– W. B. Late Works 1946-1962. Marlborough Gallery. New York 1971 (cat.).– Cavaliere, B. and M. Hadler (ed.): B. A Retrospective Exhibition. Newport Harbor Art Museum. Newport Beach 1978 (cat.)

BEATON Cecil
1904 London – **1980** Broadchalke
English photographer. **1922** Developed his skills as a photographer and painter. **1922–1925** Studied history and architecture at St. John's College, Cambridge. **1925** Numerous self-portraits. **1926–1930** Fashion photographs and portraits of the Royal Family, Winston Churchill and Marlene Dietrich, among others; **1928–1950** for *Vogue* and later for *Harper's Bazaar*. From **1938** Court Photographer to the British Royal Family. **1939–1944** Worked for the British Ministry of Information. From **1951** worked in Hollywood and London as a film designer. Designed stage sets and costumes for the theatre. **1957** and **1965** Awarded Oscars. **1957** Wrote a version of *My Fair Lady*. **1974** Suffered a stroke. From **1978** took up portrait and fashion photography again.
MONOGRAPHS, CATALOGUES: Danzinger, J.: B. New York 1980.– Mellor, D. (ed.): C. B. London 1986, Torino et al. Florence 1986.– Mellor, D. and P. Garner (ed.): C. B. Boston 1975.– Mellor, D. and P. Garner (ed.): C. B. Photographien 1920-1970. Munich 1994.– Sagne, J.: C. B. Paris 1984.– Spencer, C.: C. B. Stage and Film Designs. London 1977.– Vickers, H.: C. B. A Biography. Boston 1985

BECHER Bernd and Hilla
born **1931** Siegen (Bernd Becher)
born **1934** Potsdam (Hilla Becher)
German photographers. Bernd Becher studied painting at the Stuttgart Academy. Since **1956** has worked as a photographer. **1957** First photographs of industrial buildings. Hilla Becher trained as a photographer and first worked in advertising. **1958–1961** Studied together at the Düsseldorf

Academy. Set up a department of photography. From **1959** worked together on a systematic photographic register of industrial buildings of the 19th and 20th centuries, applying strict structural criteria. **1959–1963** Photographic inventories of industrial plants around Siegen. **1961** Married. **1963** Photographs of mines and cement and lime works. Photographic projects throughout Europe (Belgium, France, Wales and England). **1966** British Council grant. **1968** Took a series of photographs in the USA. **1972/73** Both taught at the Hamburg Academy. **1972–1982** Participation in documenta 5 and 7 in Kassel. **1976** Professorship for Bernd Becher at the Düsseldorf Academy. **1992** Sculpture prize at the Venice Biennale.
WRITINGS: B. and H. B.: Anonyme Skulpturen. Eine Typologie technischer Bauten. Düsseldorf 1969
MONOGRAPHS, CATALOGUES: Adriani, G. (ed.): B. und H. B. Typologien industrieller Bauten 1963-1975. XXIV. Bienal internacional de São Paulo 1977. Stuttgart 1977 (cat.).– Banham, R. (ed.): B. und H. B. Wassertürme. Munich 1988.– B. and H. B. Chevalements. Centre Georges Pompidou. Paris 1985 (cat.).– Bußmann, K. (ed.): B. & H. B. Tipologie. XLIV Esposizione Internazionale d'Arte, La Biennale di Venezia 1990. Munich 1990 (cat.).– Fabrikhallen: B. und H. B. Typologien. Westfälisches Landesmuseum, Münster. Munich 1994 (cat.).– Felix, Z. (ed.): B. und H. B. Fördertürme. Museum Folkwang, Essen et al. Munich 1985 (cat.).– Finkeldey, B. and M. Müller (ed.): Aus der Distanz. Photographien von B. und H. B. Kunstsammlung Nordrhein-Westfalen. Düsseldorf 1991 (cat.).– Fuchs, R. and B. Kerber (ed.): B. and H. B. Stedelijk Van Abbe Museum. Eindhoven 1981 (cat.).– Honnef, K. (ed.): B. und H. B. Fotografien 1957-1975. Rheinisches Landesmuseum, Bonn et al. Cologne 1975 (cat.).– Lange, S. (ed.): B. und H. B. Häuser und Hallen. Frankfurt-on-Main 1992.– Morris, L. (ed.): B. and H. B. Institute of Contemporary Arts, London et al. London 1974 (cat.).– Steinhauser, M. and K.-U. Hemken (ed.): B. und H. B. Industriephotographie im Spiegel der Tradtion. Bochum 1994 (cat.)

BECKMANN Max
1884 Leipzig – **1950** New York
German painter, graphic artist and sculptor. **1894** Death of his father. Family moved to Braunschweig. **1899–1903** Studied at the Weimar Academy. **1903** Long stay in Paris. **1904** Settled in Berlin. **1906** Took part in exhibition of the Berlin Secession. Awarded a six-month scholarship to the Villa Romana in Florence. Married Minna Tube. **1907** Returned to Berlin. **1907–1913** Joined the Berlin Secession, becoming a leading member in **1910**. **1911** Resigned from the Secession. **1914** Military service. **1915** Discharged after a nervous breakdown. Moved to Frankfurt am Main. **1925** Taught at the Städel Art School. Took part in the exhibi-

tion "Neue Sachlichkeit" (New Objectivity) at the Kunsthalle, Mannheim. **1929** Professor of Painting at the Städel School. **1929–1932** Lived for months at a time in Paris in a rented apartment. **1933** Dismissal. Moved back to Berlin. **1937** Ten paintings included in the exhibition of "Degenerate Art", and 590 works confiscated from German museums. Emigrated to Holland, living in Amsterdam. **1947** Moved to the United States. Taught at Washington University Art School in St. Louis. **1949** Professorship at Brooklyn Museum Art School in New York. **1950** Conte-Volpi Award at the Venice Biennale. Honorary doctorate from Washington University, St. Louis. Beckmann is important as a figurative painter working within the framework of classical Modernism.
WRITINGS: Göpel, E. (ed.): M. B. Tagebücher 1940-1950. Munich and Zurich 1984.– Kinkel, H. (ed.): M. B. Leben in Berlin. Tagebuch 1908-1909. Munich and Zurich 1984.– Schmidt, D. (ed.): M. B. Frühe Tagebücher 1903/04 und 1912/13. Munich and Zurich 1985.– Schneede, U. M. et al. (ed.): Max Beckmann. Briefe. 3 vols. Munich and Zurich 1993-1996
CATALOGUES RAISONNES: Göpel, E. and B. (ed.): M. B. Katalog der Gemälde. 2 vols. Bern 1976.– Hofmaier, J.: M. B. Catalogue Raisonné of His Prints. 2 vols. Bern 1990.– Weisner, U. and K. Gallwitz: M. B. Aquarelle und Zeichnungen. Bielefeld 1977.– Wiese, S. v.: M. B.'s zeichnerisches Werk 1903-1925. Düsseldorf 1978
MONOGRAPHS, CATALOGUES: Beckmann, M. Q.: Mein Leben mit M. B. Munich 1983.– Beckmann, P. and J. Schaffer (ed.): Die Bibliothek M. B.'s. Unterstreichungen, Kommentare, Notizen und Skizzen in seinen Büchern. Worms 1992.– Belting, H.: M. B. die Tradition als Problem in der Kunst der Moderne. Munich 1984.– Billeter, F. et al.): M. B. Bibliographie 1971-1993. Munich 1994.– Buchheim, L.-G.: M. B. Feldafing 1959.– Busch, G.: M. B. Eine Einführung. Munich 1989.– Erpel, F.: M. B. Leben im Werk. Munich 1985.– Fischer, F. W.: Der Maler M. B. Cologne 1990.– Gallwitz, K. (ed.): M. B. Frankfurt 1915-1933. Städtische Galerie im Städel. Frankfurt-on-Main 1983 (cat.).– Gallwitz, K. (ed.): M. B. Gemälde 1905-1950. Museum der Bildenden Künste, Leipzig et al. Stuttgart 1990 (cat.).– Gärtner, P. J.: M. B. Der Traum von der Imagination des Raumes. Weimar 1996.– Gerkens, G. (ed.): M. B. Seine Themen, seine Zeit. Kunsthalle Bremen. Bremen 1984 (cat.).– Göpel, B. and E. (ed.): M. B. Berichte eines Augenzeugen. Frankfurt-on-Main 1984.– Hüneke, A. (ed.): M.-B.-Colloquium 1984. Berlin 1985.– Joachim, H. and P. T. Rathbone (ed.): M. B. Museum of Fine Arts, Boston et al. New York 1980.– Lackner, S.: M. B. Cologne 1979, 1991.– Nobis, N. (ed.): M. B. Kunstmuseum Hannover. Hanover 1983 (cat.).– Peter, N.: M. B. Landschaften der Zwanziger Jahre. Frankfurt-on-Main et al. 1993.– Pillep, R.: M. B. Leben und Werk. Neue Forschungen. Halle 1993.– Reinartz,

S.: M. B. Reinbek 1995.– Rother, S.: M. B. als Landschaftsmaler. Munich 1990.– Schneede, U. M. (ed.): Stadtnächte: Der Zeichner und Grafiker M. B. Hamburger Kunstverein. Berlin 1980 (cat.).– Schneede, U. M. (ed.): M. B. Selbstbildnisse. Hamburger Kunsthalle et al. Stuttgart 1993 (cat.).– Schulz-Hoffmann, C. and J. C. Weis (ed.): M. B. Retrospektive. Haus der Kunst, Munich et al. Munich 1984 (cat.).– Schulz-Hoffmann, C. and J. C. Weis (ed.): M. B. Retrospective. Saint Louis Art Museum. Saint Louis 1984 (cat.).– Schulz-Hoffmann, C.: M. B. Der Maler. Munich 1991.– Schütz, H. G.: Sphinx B. Exemplarische Annäherung an M. B. Munich 1997.– Selz, P.: M. B. The Self-Portraits. New York 1992.– Spieler, R.: M. B. 1884-1950. The Path to Myth. Cologne 1995

BELLING Rudolf
1886 Berlin – **1972** Krailling (near Munich)
German sculptor. **1905–1907** Apprenticeship as modeller in industrial arts. **1908** Opened a workshop for small sculptures with Emil Kasalov. Commissions from the Max-Reinhardt Theatre. **1911** Attended Peter Breuer's class at the Berlin Academy. Strong Cubist influence. **1918** Founded the Novembergruppe with Mies van der Rohe and Pechstein. Held joint-exhibitions. Worked on the sculpture *Dreiklang*. **1920** First one-man exhibition at the Gurlitt gallery in Berlin. In later years, numerous commissions for public buildings and spaces. **1924** Solo-exhibition at the Nationalgalerie, Berlin. Sold *Dreiklang*. **1937** Denounced by the Nazis. Emigrated to Turkey and taught at the Art Academy and University of Technology in Istanbul. **1966** Returned to Germany.
CATALOGUES RAISONNES: Hoffmann, D. (ed.): R. B. Plastiken, Zeichnungen, Lithographien. Mit einem Werkverzeichnis des plastischen Werkes. Munich 1967 (cat.).– Nerdinger, W. (ed.): R. B. und die Kunstströmungen in Berlin 1918-1923. Mit einem Katalog der plastischen Werke. Berlin 1981
MONOGRAPHS, CATALOGUES: Killy, H. E. (ed.): R. B. Akademie der Künste. Berlin 1962 (cat.).– Schmoll gen. Eisenwerth, J. A.: R. B. St. Gallen 1971

BELLMER Hans
1902 Kattowitz – **1975** Paris
German painter, graphic artist and sculptor. **1924** Worked as graphic artist. Made contact with Surrealists in Paris. **1931–1933** Travelled to Tunisia, Italy and France. **1933** Worked on *Puppe* (Doll) reminiscent of surrealist painting. **1935** Drawings of his dolls in the magazine *Minotaure* made him famous in France. **1935/36** Took part in the Surrealist exhibition at the Museum of Modern Art in New York. **1938** Moved to Paris. Close contact with Surrealists. **1939** Imprisoned, along with Ernst and Wols, in the French camp *Les Milles*. Returned to Paris after the war. **1943** Worked on

Cephalopods. **1953/54** Stayed in Berlin. **1966** Took part in documenta 3 in Kassel. In his anarchistic and traumatic representations of eroticism and sexuality, Bellmer built on the basic tenets of Surrealism.
WRITINGS: H. B.: Die Puppe. Karlsruhe 1934, Berlin 1962 / La Poupée. Paris 1949.– H. B.: Les Jeux de la poupée. Paris 1949.– H. B.: L'Anatomie de l'image. Paris 1957.– H. B.: Petite anatomie de l'inconscient physique ou l'anatomie de l'image. Paris 1957
CATALOGUE RAISONNE: Pieyre d. Mandiargues, A. (ed.): H. B. L'œuvre gravé. Paris 1969, 1976 / H. B. Das grafische Werk. Frankfurt-on-Main et al. 1973
MONOGRAPHS, CATALOGUES: H. B. photographe. Centre Georges Pompidou. Paris 1983 (cat.).– Crété, M. (ed.): H. B. Centre National d'Art Contemporain. Paris 1971 (cat.).– Eluard, P. et al. (ed.): H. B. Centre National d'Art Contemporain. Paris 1971 (cat.).– Grall, A.: Les Dessins de H. B. Paris 1966.– Grall, A. (ed.): H. B. London and New York 1973.– Haenlein, C. (ed.): H. B. Photographien. Kestner-Gesellschaft. Hanover 1984 (cat.).– Jelenski, C.: Les Dessins de H. B. 1966 / Die Zeichnungen von H. B. Berlin 1969.– Lattes, J.-C. (ed.): H. B. Musée Goya. Castres. Albi 1992 (cat.).– Lust, H.: H. B. New York 1990.– Pieyre d. Mandiarques, A.: Le Trésor cruel de H. B. Paris 1979.– Orgeix, C. (ed.): H. B. Paris 1950.– Prokopoff, S. S. and M. v. d. Guchte (ed.): H. B. Photographs. Kranert Art Museum, University of Illinois at Urbana-Champaign 1991 (cat.).– Revol, J.: B.: Peintures, gouaches, collages. Paris 1983.– Sayag, A.: H. B. Photographien. Munich 1984.– Schmied, W. (ed.): H. B. Kestner-Gesellschaft. Hanover 1967 (cat.).– Seuphor, M.: J. A. Cologne and Berlin 1961.– Webb, P. and R. Short: H. B. London 1985

BENTON Thomas Hart
1889 Neosho (MO) – **1975** Kansas City (MO)
American painter. **1907/08** Studied at the Art Insitute in Chicago. **1908–1911** Lived in Paris. Attended the Académie Julian and Académie Colarossi. Studied Old Masters and contemporary styles of painting exemplified by Cézanne, Picasso and Matisse. **1912** Returned to New York. Continued to paint in an abstract style. **1917** First one-man exhibition at the Daniel Gallery in New York. **1918** Began representational paintings of subjects taken from American history and everyday life. **1923** Worked on the mural *American Historical Epic.* **1926– 1935** Taught at the Art Students League in New York; pupils included Pollock. **1935** Moved to Kansas City and taught at the art academy there. **1949** Travelled to France and Italy. Honorary member of the Accademia Fiorentina delle Arti del Disegno. One of the best-known exponents of American Regionalism.
WRITINGS: T. B.'s America. An Artist in America. New York 1937
CATALOGUE RAISONNE: Fath, C. (ed.): The Lithographs of T. H. B. Austin and London 1990
MONOGRAPHS, CATALOGUES: Adams, H. (ed.): T. H. B. An American Original. The Nelson-Atkins-Museum of Art, Kansas City et al. New York 1989 (cat.).– Adams, H. (ed.): T. H. B. Drawing from Life. Henry Art Gallery, University of Washington, Seattle et al. Seattle 1990 (cat.).– T. H. B. Whitney Museum of American Art. New York 1989 (cat.).– Baigell, M.: T. H. B. New York 1973.– Chiappini, R. (ed.): T. H. B. Museo d'Arte Moderna della Città di Lugano. Milan 1992 (cat.).– Coe, R. T. et al. (ed.): T. H. B. An Artist's Selection 1908-1974. William Rockhill Nelson Gallery of Art, Mary Atkins Museum of Fine Arts, Kansas City et al. Kansas City 1974 (cat.).– Doss, E.: B., Pollock and the Politics of Modernism. From Regionalism to Abstract Expressionism. Chicago 1991.– Douglas Hurt, R. and M. K. Dains: T. H. B. Artist, Writer and Intellectual. Columbia 1989.– Marling, K. A.: T. B. and His Drawings. Columbia 1985 (cat.).– Weintraub, L. (ed.): T. H. B. Chronicler of America's Folk Heritage. Edith C. Blum Art Institute, Bard College, Annandale-on-Hudson (NY) et al. Annandale 1984 (cat.)

BERGHE Frits van den
1883 Ghent – **1939** Ghent
Belgian painter. **1897–1904** Attended the Académie Royale des Beaux-Arts in Ghent. First painted portraits, landscapes and interiors in the Impressionist style. **1907–1911** Professorship at the Ghent Academy of Art. Murals for the Community Centre in Ghent. **1914** Six-month visit to the USA. Returned to Amsterdam at the outbreak of World War I. Confrontation with Fauvism, Expressionism and Cubism. **1922** Set up house, near Laethem-Saint Martin, with his artist friend Smet. After his dark Dutch period, he chose brighter colours and painted larger pictures. **1927** Returned to Ghent. Joined the group L'Epoque and took up Surrealism. Painted fantastic visionary landscapes with eerie figures, in the spirit of Bosch and Ensor. **1938** Member of the Académie Picard in Brussels.
CATALOGUE RAISONNE: Langui, E. (ed.): F. v. d. B. 1883-1939. Catalogue raisonné de son œuvre peint. Brussels 1966

MONOGRAPHS, CATALOGUES: F. v. d. B. Museum voor Schone Kunsten, Ghent. Brussels 1983 (cat.).– Hecke, P.-G. v.: F. v. d. B. Antwerp 1948.– Langui, E.: F. v. d. B. 1883-1939. Brussels 1966.– Langui, E.: F. v. d. B. De mens en zijn werk. Antwerp 1968

BERLEVI Henryk
1894 Warsaw – **1967** Paris
Polish painter. **1904–1909** Studied at the Warsaw Academy, **1909–1912** at the Académie des Beaux-Arts in Antwerp and later in Paris. **1913** Returned to Warsaw. **1921** Met Lissitzky, Richter and van Doesburg. His work became clearly influenced by Constructivism. Took part in exhibitions of the Novembergruppe. Interest in mechanical processes leads to publication of a manifesto entitled *Mechano-Faktura* in **1924.** Started a business promoting mechanical advertising. One-man exhibition in Herwarth Walden's gallery Der Sturm, in Berlin. **1926** Took up figurative art again. **1927** Moved to Paris. Met Malevich. **1957** Renewed experiments with *Mechano-Faktura.*
MONOGRAPHS, CATALOGUES: Destré, J. (ed.): H. B. portraits et masques. Antwerp 1937.– Colley, H.: H. B. peintre polonais. Antwerp 1937.– Grohmann, W. and M. Besset (ed.): Retrospektive Ausstellung H. B. Gemälde, Zeichnungen, Grafik, Mechano-Fakturen, Plastik von 1908 bis heute. Maison de France. Berlin 1964 (cat.).– Olszewski, A. K.: H. B. Warsaw 1968

BERNARD Emile
1868 Lille – **1941** Paris
French painter. From **1878** lived in Paris. Began artistic training at the Ecole des Arts Décoratifs and, after **1884**, entered the studio of Cormon where he met Louis Anquetin, Toulouse-Lautrec and van Gogh. **1885** Travelled through Normandy and Brittany. **1886** Van Gogh introduced him to Gauguin, whom he greatly admired. **1888– 1891** Worked with Anquetin and Gauguin, leading exponents of Cloisonnism. **1891** Broke with Gauguin after an argument over a definition of the new style. Exhibition in the Salon des Indépendants. **1892** Organized the first major Van Gogh retrospective. **1893** Left Paris and travelled to Italy and the Orient. Settled in Cairo. **1896** Visited Spain. **1900** and **1903** Trips to Venice. Solo-exhibitions **1901** in Paris, **1905** at Cassirer, in Berlin and **1908** at the Munich Art Society. **1904** Returned to Paris. Important correspondence with Cézanne on theories of art. **1905** Brought out the famous magazine *La Rénovation Esthétique.* An important representative of Symbolism.
CATALOGUE RAISONNE: Luthi, J.-J. (ed.): E. B. Catalogue raisonné de l'œuvre peint. Paris 1982
MONOGRAPHS, CATALOGUES: Cailler, P.: E. B. Geneva 1959.– Cheyron, J. and Z. El Hakim: E. B. 1868-1941. Geneva 1966.– Luthi, J.-J.: E. B. Chef de l'école de Pont-Aven. Paris 1976.– Luthi, J.-J.: E. B. en Orient et chez Paul Cézanne 1893-1904. Paris 1979.– Mornard, P.: E. B. et ses amis. Geneva 1957.– Stevens, M. A. et al. (ed.): E. B. 1868-1941. Ein Wegbereiter der Moderne. Städtische Kunsthalle Mannheim et al. Mannheim 1990 (cat.)

BEUYS Joseph
1921 Kleve – **1986** Düsseldorf
German performance and environment artist, draughtsman and sculptor. **1941– 1945** Military service as fighter pilot. When his plane crashed, Tartars saved his life by wrapping him in felt and fat, materials that came to figure prominently in his later work. **1947–1951** Studied sculpture at the Düsseldorf Academy, where from **1949** he was the principal pupil of Ewald Mataré, and from **1961–1972** Professor of Monumental Sculpture. **1964–1982** Participation in documenta 3–7 in Kassel. By combining several artistic media and merging them with his own life story, he attempted to achieve a unity of art and life. Clear influence of anthroposophy, mythology and religion in his works. **1962** Met Paik and Maciunas, artists of the Fluxus movement. **1963** Staged his own Fluxus happenings; including his first *Aktion* with fat in the Rudolf Zwirner gallery in Cologne. Through a vast output of drawings, sculptures, objects, environments and performances, developed a symbolism based on mythological themes, mystical rites and archetypes. **1967** Became politically active, founding various associations and parties with the aim of promoting creativity in all areas of life. **1973** Dismissed from the Düsseldorf Academy. Founded the Free International School of Creativity and Interdisciplinary Research. As an artist, teacher and thinker, had a profound influence on subsequent generations of artists.
WRITINGS: J. B.: Kunst = Kapital. Achberger Vorträge. Ed. by R. E. Rappmann. Wangen 1992.– J. B. et E. Devolder: Conversation avec J. B. Gerpinnes 1991.– Beuys, E. and W. (ed.): J. B. Das Geheimnis der Knospe zarter Hülle. Schriften des Bildhauers aus seinem Nachlaß 1942-1986. Munich 1994.– Harlan, V. (ed.): Was ist Kunst. Werkstattgespräch mit J. B. Stuttgart 1986.– Kuoni, C. (ed.): J. B. Energy Plan for the Western Man. J. B. in America. Writ-

ings by and Interviews with the Artist. New York 1990.– Wijers, L. (ed.): J. B. Schreiben als Plastik 1978-1987. Berlin 1992
CATALOGUES RAISONNES: Grigoleit, A. (ed.): J. B. Wasserfarbe auf Papier 1936-1984/85). 2 vols. Frankfurt-on-Main 1992.– Grinten, J. J. and H. (ed.): J. B. Wasserfarben/Watercolors 1936-1963. Frankfurt-on-Main et al. 1975.– Grinten, J. J. and H. (ed.): J. B. Ölfarben/Oilcolors 1936-1965. Frankfurt-on-Main et al. 1975.– Schellmann, J. et al. (ed.): J. B. Die Multiples 1965-1989. Werkverzeichnis der Auflagenobjekte und Druckgraphik 1965-1986. Munich 1992, 1997/The Multiples: Catalogue Raisonné of Multiples and Prints. New York 1997.– Schneede, U. M. (ed.): J. B. Die Aktionen. Kommentiertes Werkverzeichnis mit fotografischen Dokumentationen. Stuttgart 1994.– Theewen, G. (ed.): J. B. Die Vitrinen. Ein Verzeichnis. Cologne 1993.– Temkin, A. and B. Rose (ed.): Thinking is Form. The Drawings of J. B. London 1992.– Weiss, P. and F. Britsch (ed.): J. B. Plakate. Werbung für die Kunst. Munich 1991
MONOGRAPHS, CATALOGUES: Adriani, G. et al.: J. B. Leben und Werk. Cologne 1973, 1994/J. B. Life and Works. Woodbury (NY) 1979.– Angerbauer-Rau, M.: B.-Kompaß. Ein Lexikon zu den Gesprächen mit J. B. Cologne 1998.– Barré, A. et al. (ed.): J. B. Centre Georges Pompidou. Paris 1994 (cat.).– Bastian, H. (ed.): J. B. Skulpturen und Objekte und Zeichnungen. 2 vols. Martin-Gropius-Bau, Berlin et al. Munich 1988 (cat.).– Beuys, E. et al. (ed.): J. B. Block B. Munich 1990.– Boijiscul, W.: Zum Kunstbegriff des J. B. Essen 1985.– Borer, A. et al. (ed.): J. B. Kunsthaus Zurich et al. Zurich 1993 (cat.).– Borer, A.: The Essential J. B. Cambridge 1997.– Cooke, L. and K. Kelly (ed.): J. B. Arena – wo wäre ich hingekommen, wenn ich intelligent gewesen wäre. New York and Stuttgart 1994 /J. B. Arena – Where Would I Have Got if I Had Been Intelligent. New York 1994.– De Domizio, L. et al.: Incontro con Beuys. Pescara 1984.– De Domizio, L.: The Felt Hat. J. B. a Life Told. New York 1997.– Fabo, S.: Joyce and B. Ein intermedialer Dialog. Heidelberg 1997.– Haenlein, C. (ed.): J. B. Eine Innere Mongolei. Dschingis Khan. Schamanen. Aktricen. Ölfarben, Wasserfarben und Bleistiftzeichnungen aus der Sammlung van der Grinten. Kestner-Gesellschaft. Hanover 1990 (cat.).– Harlan, V. et al.: Soziale Plastik. Materialien zu J. B. Achberg 1976.– Harlan, V.: Was ist Kunst? Werkstattgespräche mit J. B. Stuttgart 1986.– Harlan, V. et al. (ed.): J.-B.-Tagung Basel 1.-4. Mai 1991. Basel 1991.– Hergott, F. (ed.): J. B. Kunsthaus Zurich et al. Paris 1995 (cat.).– Jappe, G.: B. packen. Dokumente 1968-1996. Regensburg 1997.– Kramer, M.: J. B. Das Kapital Raum 1970-1977. Heidelberg 1991.– Loers, V. and P. Witzmann (ed.): J. B. Documenta-Arbeit. Museum Fridericianum. Kassel 1993 (cat.).– Müller, M.: Wie man dem toten Hasen die Bilder erklärt. Schamanismus und Erkenntnis im Werk von J. B. Alfter 1993.– Olt-mann, A.: "Der Weltstoff letztendlich ist ... neu zu bilden". J. B. für und wider die Moderne. Stuttgart 1994.– Raussmüller-Sauer, C. (ed.): J. B. Schaffhausen 1988.– Röder, S. and G. Storck (ed.): Transit. J. B. 3 vols. Kaiser Wilhelm Museum. Krefeld 1991 (cat.).– Rosenthal, M.: J. B. Blitzschlag mit Lichtschein auf Hirsch. Frankfurt-on-Main 1991.– Schade, W. (ed.): J. B. Early Watercolors. New York 1991.– Schade, W. (ed.): J. B. Early Drawings. New York 1993.– Schirmer, L. (ed.): J. B. Eine Werkübersicht. Munich 1996.– Schneede, U. M.: J. B. Die Aktionen. Stuttgart 1993.– Szemann, H. (ed.): J. B. Kunsthaus Zürich. Zurich 1993 (cat.).– Szeemann, H.: Beuys-

nobiscum. Eine kleine Enzyklopädie. Dresden 1997.– Temkin, A. and B. Rose (ed.): Thinking is Form. The Drawings of J. B. The Museum of Modern Art, New York et al. New York and London 1993 (cat.).– Tisdall, C. (ed.): J. B. Coyote. Paris 1988.– Verspohl, F.-J.: J. B. Das Kapital Raum 1979-1977. Frankfurt-on-Main 1984.– Vierneisel, K. (ed.): Hauptstrom Jupiter. B. und die Antike. Glyptothek. Munich 1993 (cat.).– Vischer, T.: J. B. und die Romantik. Cologne 1983.– Vischer, T.: J. B. Die Einheit des Werkes. Zeichnungen, Aktionen, plastische Arbeiten, soziale Skulptur. Cologne 1991.– Zimmermann, R.: Kunst und Ökologie im Christentum "700 Eichen" von J. B. Wiesbaden 1994.– Zweite, A. (ed.): B. zu Ehren. Städtische Galerie im Lenbachhaus. Munich 1986 (cat.).– Zweite, A. (ed.): J. B. Natur, Materie, Form. Kunstsammlung Nordrhein-Westfalen, Düsseldorf. Munich 1991 (cat.)

BILL Max
1908 Winterthur – **1994** Berlin
Swiss architect, painter, sculptor and designer. **1924-1927** Attended Zurich School of Art and Crafts. **1927-1929** Studied at the Bauhaus in Dessau under Albers, Kandinsky und Klee, then returned to Zurich. **1932-1936** Joined Abstraction-Création. Met Arp and Mondrian. From **1944** worked as a designer. **1949** Kandinsky Award. **1951** Inspirational force behind the Ulm School of Design. Tried to direct it in the tradition of the Dessau Bauhaus. Resigned after five years. **1956/57** Retrospectives in Ulm and Munich. **1959** and **1964** participation in documenta 2 and 4 in Kassel. **1967** Professorship at the Hamburg Academy. An important pioneer of abstract art, Bill coined the term "Concrete Art" for non-figurative modes of representation.
WRITINGS: M. B.: Robert Maillard. Zurich 1949.– M. B.: Moderne Schweizer Architektur. Basel 1950.– M. B.: Wassily Kandinsky. Paris 1951.– M. B.: Form. Eine Bilanz über die Formentwicklung um die Mitte des XX. Jahrhunderts. Basel 1952.– M. B.: Mies van der Rohe. Milan 1955.– M. B.: Le Corbusier und P. Jeanneret. Zurich 1965.– M. B.: System mit fünf vierfarbigen Zentren. Anleitung zum Betrachten eines Bildes. St. Gallen 1972
CATALOGUE RAISONNE: Felix, Z. and M. Bill (ed.): M. B. Das druckgraphische Werk bis 1968. Kunsthalle Nürnberg. Nuremberg 1968 (cat.)
MONOGRAPHS, CATALOGUES: Alloway, L. (ed.): M. B. Albright-Knox Art Gallery. Buffalo 1974 (cat.).– Anker, V.: M. B. ou la recherche d'un art logique. Essai d'une analyse structurale de l'œuvre d'art. Lausanne 1979.– M. B. Hamburger Kunsthalle, Hamburg et al. Zurich 1976 (cat.).– Caramel, L. and A. Thomas (ed.): M. B. Pinacoteca communale, Casa Rusca. Locarno. Lugano 1991 (cat.).– Frei, H.: Konkrete Architektur? Über M. B. als

Architekt. Baden 1991.– Gomringer, E. et al. (ed.): M. B. Teufen 1958.– Holeczek, B. (ed.): M. B. Wilhelm-Hack-Museum. Ludwigshafen 1990 (cat.).– Hüttinger, E.: M. B. Zurich 1977.– Hüttinger, E. et al. (ed.): M. B. Retrospektive. Skulpturen, Gemälde, Graphik. Schirn Kunsthalle, Frankfurt-on-Main et al. Frankfurt-on-Main and Zurich 1987 (cat.).– Maldonado, T.: M. B. Buenos Aires 1955.– Quintavalle, A. C. et al.: M. B. Parma 1977.– Rotzler, W.: M. B. Stuttgart 1977.– Schmidt, G.: M. B. Neuchâtel 1959.– Spies, W. (ed.): Kontinuität. Granith-Monolith von M. B. Frankfurt-on-Main 1987.– Staber, M.: M. B. London 1964, St. Gallen 1971

BIRNBAUM Dara
born **1946** New York
American video and multimedia artist. Up to **1968** studied architecture at the Carnegie Mellon University, Pittsburgh, and then studied art for five years at the San Francisco Art Institute and the New School of Social Research, New York. **1982** and **1987** took part in documenta 7 and 8 in Kassel. **1983-1986** Taught at the School of Visual Arts in New York. **1988** Commission to set up a video-installation in a public place in Atlanta. **1989** Took part in the exhibition "Video-Skulptur" in Köln. **1991** Visual Arts Fellowship and National Endowment for the Arts. **1992** German video-art award from the ZKM in Karlsruhe. Participated in documenta 9. With her video-tapes and installations, Birnbaum highlights the confrontation between new communication technologies and individual consciousness in modern society.
MONOGRAPHS, CATALOGUES: D. B.: Every TV Needs Revolution. Imschoot 1992.– Celant, G. (ed.): D. B. IVAM Centro del Carme. Valencia 1991 (cat.).– D. B. Musée d'Art Contemporain. Bordeaux 1993 (cat.)

BIROLLI Renato
1906 Verona – **1959** Milan
Italian painter and art critic. Studied at the Accademia Cignarolli in Verona. **1927** Moved to Milan. Met Futurist Carrà. His early portraits show the influence of van Gogh and Ensor. **1936** Encountered Impressionism in Paris. Greatly impressed by Matisse. **1937** Returned to Milan and founded Corrente, an association of young artists. Detained for anti-fascist activities. After his release, went underground. **1947-1952** Travelled to France and Germany to study Gothic churches and Cubism. Contact with the French avant-garde led to development of a concrete-abstract style. **1955** and **1958** participation in documenta 1 and 2 in Kassel. **1957** Moved to Antwerp. Affinities with L'art informel without any personal connections.
WRITINGS: R. B.: Metamorfosi. Milan 1937.– R. B.: D'Arena. Galleria Schettini. Milan 1956.– Emanuelli, E. (ed.): R. B. Taccuini 1936-1939. Torino 1960

CATALOGUE RAISONNE: Mussini, M. et al. (ed.): R. B. Parma 1976
MONOGRAPHS, CATALOGUES: Birolli, Z. et al.: R. B. Milan 1978.– Emanuelli, E. (ed.): R. B. Taccuini 1936-1959. Torino 1960.– Marx, E. (ed.): R. B. Mannheim 1959 (cat.).– Tullier, A.: R. B. Milan 1951.– Valsecchi, M.: R. B. Milan 1966.– Vivarelli, P. (ed.): R. B. Palazzo Reale, Milan et al. 1989 (cat.)

BISSIER Julius
1893 Freiburg i. Br. – **1965** Ascona
German painter. **1913/14** Studied history of art in Freiburg and attended the Karlsruhe Academy. **1914-1918** Military service. **1918** Took further courses in painting in Munich. **1919** Made friends with the sinologist Ernst Grosser. **1929-1933** Chair at Freiburg University where, in **1934**, a fire destroyed all his works. Met Schlemmer und Baumeister. In the 30s, his paintings became increasingly abstract. **1935-1938** Several trips to Italy. **1939** Moved to Hagnau on Lake Constance. From **1945** developed an individual calligraphic sign language, reminiscent of Far Eastern ink painting. which had a great influence on the first generation of German Informel artists. **1955/56** Began series of miniatures. **1959** and **1964** took part in documenta 2 and 3 in Kassel. **1960** Special honours at the 30th Venice Biennale.
WRITINGS: Bärmann, M. (ed.): J. B. – Oskar Schlemmer: Briefwechsel. St. Gallen 1988
MONOGRAPHS, CATALOGUES: Büchner, J. et al. (ed.): J. B. Kunstsammlung Nordrhein-Westfalen. Düsseldorf 1970 (cat.).– Essers, V. (ed.): J. B. Kunstsammlung Nordrhein-Westfalen, Düsseldorf. Stuttgart-Ruit 1993 (cat.).– Gianadda, L. et al. (ed.): J. B. Opere 1930-1965. Museo d'Arte Mendrisio et al. Mendrisio 1988 (cat.).– J. B. 1893-1965. A Retrospective Exhibition. San Francisco Museum of Art. San Francisco 1968 (cat.).– Kettelsen, A. D.: J. B. Der Mensch und der Künstler. Stuttgart 1986.– Kuenzi, A. (ed.): J. B. Fondation Pierre Gianadda. Martigny 1989 (cat.).– Leonhard, K.: J. B. Stuttgart 1963.– Ludwig, J. and D. Weißenberger (ed.): J. B. Vom Anfang der Bilder. Städtische Museen, Museum für Neue Kunst. Freiburg 1994 (cat.).– Schiff, G.: J. B. Tuschen. Stuttgart 1989.– Schilling, J. (ed.): J. B. 1893-1965. Kunstverein Braunschweig. Brunswick 1980 (cat.).– Schmalenbach, W.: J. B. Stuttgart 1963, New York 1963, Cologne 1974.– Schmalenbach, W. (ed.): J. B. Tuschen und Aquarelle. Frankfurt-on-Main et al. Frankfurt-on-Main 1978

BISSIERE Roger
1888 Villeréal (Lot-et-Garonne) – **1964** Marminiac (Lot)
French painter. **1905-1910** Studied painting at the Académie des Beaux-Arts in Bordeaux. **1910-1914** Journalist in Paris. **1920** Made friends with Lhote and Braque. Solo-exhibition at the Paul Rosenberg gallery and

participation at the Salon d'Automne in Paris. **1925–1938** Professorship at the Académie Ranson in Paris. Forced to give up painting owing to an eye ailment. **1948** Saved from blindness by a successful operation. Resumed painting with a renewed intensity and a highly colourful, poetic style that made him internationally famous. **1952** Grand Prix National des Arts. **1964** Participated at the Venice Biennale.
WRITINGS: Baptiste-Marrey (ed.): B. T'en fais pas Marie … Ecrits sur la peinture 1954-1964. Cognac 1994
CATALOGUE RAISONNE: Bissière, L. (ed.): R. B. Catalogue raisonné (in preparation)
MONOGRAPHS, CATALOGUES: Abadie, D.: B. Neuchâtel 1986.– Fouchet, M.-P.: R. B. Paris 1955.– Weelen, G. et al. (ed.): B. 1886-1964. Musée d'Art Moderne de la Ville de Paris et al. Paris 1986 (cat.)

BLAIS Jean-Charles
born **1956** Nantes
French painter. **1974–1979** Studied at the Ecole des Beaux-Arts in Rennes. **1979–1981** shared a studio with the sculptor Peter Briggs in Rennes. **1981** Presented blown-up reproductions of the smaller works of Malevich and Kandinsky in the exhibitions "Sans titre ou les figures du vide" (No Title or Figures from Emptiness) in Rennes and "Finir en beauté" (To End in Beauty). Affinity to Figuration Libre. Began painting on torn posters. Painted sheets of newspaper. Took capital letters as a starting point for his compositions, and often for the title too. Designed clothing for the fashion designer Jean Charles de Castelbajac. **1984** Moved into a new studio where he could paint larger canvases. The faces of the figures are lost in the vast expanse of the picture and the bodies amalgamate with the painting. In the late 80s, turned to colour drawings and graphic reproductions.
MONOGRAPHS, CATALOGUES: J.-C. B. Kestner-Gesellschaft. Hanover 1986 (cat.).– J.-C. B. Musée d'Art et d'Histoire de Fribourg. Fribourg 1984 (cat.).– J.-C. B. Galerie Buchmann. Basel 1984.– J.-C. B. Centre Georges Pompidou. Paris 1987 (cat.).– J.-C. B. Dessins. Basel 1988 (cat.).– J.-C. B. Suites lithographies, monotypes et variations. Paris 1995.– Haenlein, C. (ed.): J.-C. B. Kestner-Gesellschaft. Hanover

---

1986 (cat.).– Marin, L.: J.-C. B. Du figurable en peinture. Paris 1988

BLAKE Peter
born **1932** Dartford (Kent)
English painter. **1946–1951** Trained as a technical draughtsman at Gravesend School of Art in London. **1953–1956** Studied at the Royal College of Art in London. **1956/57** Studied folk art. Extended travels through Europe. **1964** Started teaching at St. Martin's School of Art in London. From **1959** painted collages with captivating irony and vibrant colours. **1967** Cover design for the Beatles LP *Sergeant Pepper*. **1969–1979** Member of the Brotherhood of Ruralists, based near Bath. **1980** Returned to London. **1981** Member of the Royal Academy, London. **1983** Major retrospective at the Tate Gallery, London. After his early period of Realism, Blake joined Hamilton in becoming a key figure of English Pop Art. Frequently took trivial pictorial clichées and worked them over in 30s style.
WRITINGS: P. B.: No Place Like Utopia. Modern Architecture and the Company We Kept. New York 1993
MONOGRAPHS, CATALOGUES: P. B. Souvenirs and Samples. Waddington Galleries and Tooth Gallery. London 1977 (cat.).– Coleman, R. (ed.): P. B. City Art Gallery. Bristol 1969 (cat.).– Compton, M. et al. (ed.): R. B. Tate Gallery. London 1983 (cat.)/P. B. Retrospektive. Kestner-Gesellschaft. Hanover 1983 (cat.).– Schneede, U. M. (ed.): P. B. Hamburger Kunstverein. Hamburg 1973 (cat.).– Vaizey, M.: P. B. London 1986

BLECKNER Ross
born **1949** New York
American painter. **1971–1973** Studied at New York University and California Institute of the Arts, Valencia; graduated as Master of Fine Arts. **1975** First one-man exhibition put on by Mary Boone in New York. Famous for his striped pictures, related to Op Art. The strict geometry of the stripes is broken up by flecks of colour and ornamental elements giving the pictures an atmospheric, shimmering character. Further exhibitions in London, Cologne and Tokyo. **1988** Took part in the BiNationale in Boston and Düsseldorf. Bleckner

---

uses fire, wax, varnish and other materials to produce hallucinatory colour effects. Expansion and contraction are the fundamental creative forces underlying his art.
MONOGRAPHS, CATALOGUES: Bürgi, B. (ed.): R. B. Kunsthalle Zürich et al. Zurich 1990 (cat.).– Crone, R. (ed.): R. B. Mary Boone Gallery. New York 1987 (cat.).– Dennison, L. et al. (ed.): R. B. Solomon R. Guggenheim Museum. New York 1995 (cat.).– Schjedahl, P. (ed.): R. B. Waddington Galleries. London 1987 (cat.).– Sobel, D. (ed.): R. B. Milwaukee Art Museum. Milwaukee 1989 (cat.)

BLOSSFELDT Karl
1865 Schielo (Harz) – **1932** Berlin
German photographer. **1881–1884** Apprenticeship as sculptor and modeller at the art foundry in Mägdesprung. **1886–1890** Studied at the School of Art and Crafts and the Academy in Berlin. **1891** Grant for tours of Italy, Greece and North Africa; first photographic projects. **1896** Assistant to Prof. Ernst Ewald at the Royal School of Art in Berlin. **1898** Professor of botanical modelling in the education department of the Museum of Arts and Crafts, Berlin. **1900** Took a series of photographs of plants with a home-made view camera. **1928** Publication of book *Urformen der Kunst* (Art Forms in Nature), followed by *Wundergarten der Natur* (Nature's Garden of Wonders) in **1932**.
MONOGRAPHS, CATALOGUES: Honnef, K. (ed.): K. B. Fotografien 1900-1932. Rheinisches Landesmuseum Bonn. Cologne 1976 (cat.).– Hüneke, A. and G. Ihrke (ed.): K. B. Fotografien zwischen Natur und Kunst. Leipzig 1990.– Mattenklott, G.: K. B. 1895-1932. Das fotografische Werk. Munich 1981.– Sachsse, R.: K. B. Photographien 1895-1932. Cologne 1993.– Schreier, C. (ed.): K. B. Fotografie. Kunstmuseum Bonn et al. Bonn 1994 (cat.).– Wilde, A. (ed.): K. B. Photographien. Munich 1991.– Wilde A. and J. Wilde (ed.): K. B. Fotografie. Kunstmuseum Bonn et al. Stuttgart 1994 (cat.)

BLUME Anna and **Bernhard Johannes**
born **1937** Bork (Anna)
born **1937** Dortmund (Bernhard Johannes)
German photographers. Bernhard trained as a cinema and decorative painter and graphic artist, while Anna had a technical training. **1960–1965** Studied together at the Düsseldorf Academy. From **1964** Anna worked as an art teacher in a number of high schools. **1966** They married. **1967–1971** Bernhard completed his philosophy degree and taught for 15 years in Cologne. Since **1980** intensive team-work on large-scale photographic projects centering on the theme of absurd and alienating encounters with the world of objects.
WRITINGS: A. and B. B.: Ideoplastie. Cologne 1970.– A. and B. B.: Paraphrase zur Psychopathologie künstlerischer Produktion. Cologne 1973.– A. and B. B.:

Malerei als Medienreflexion. Bergisch-Gladbach 1976.– A. and B. B.: heilig, heilig, heilig. Munich 1986.– A. and B. B.: Vasen Exstasen. Frankfurt-on-Main 1991
CATALOGUE RAISONNE: Honnef, K. et al. (ed.): A. and B. B. 3 vols. Cologne 1992-1995
MONOGRAPHS, CATALOGUES: Ammann, J. C. et al. (ed.): A. and B. B. Kunsthalle Basel. Basel 1987 (cat.).– Ammann, J. C. (ed.): Das Ich und die Dinge: Kommentare zu einem philosophischen Text von A. and B. B. in Form inszenierter Fotografien. Frankfurt-on-Main 1991.– A. and B. B.: Trautes Heim. Fotos aus dem wirklichen Leben. Kunsthalle Basel. Basel 1989 (cat.).– A. and B. B. Photo-Work. Milwaukee Art Museum, Milwaukee et al. Stuttgart 1996 (cat.).– Brock, B. and N. Smolik (ed.): A. B. Die reine Empfindung. Stuttgart 1994.– Hamburger, K.: Zu den Ideografien B. J. B. Cologne 1977.– Schulte, G.: Zur Ästhetik der Fotografie, insbesondere der transzendentalen Fotografie B. J. B.'s. Bonn 1976.– Wieland, A. (ed.): A. & B. B.: Grossfotoserien 1985-1990. Rheinisches Landesmuseum, Bonn. Cologne 1992 (cat.)

BLUMENFELD Erwin
1897 Berlin – **1969** Rome
German photographer. **1913–1916** Apprenticeship as a fashion designer. Contact with Else Lasker-Schüler, Grosz and the Dadaists. **1916–1918** Military service. **1919** Moved to the Netherlands. **1919–1923** Opened a Dada centre in Amsterdam with Paul Citroën. Began to paint, write and photograph. **1922–1935** Sold photographs in his own leather shop. **1936** Moved to Paris, working as a professional photographer. First publications of portraits and advertising photographs. From **1938** worked for *Vogue* and *Harper's Bazaar*. **1940/41** Held as prisoner of war in the USA, where he then emigrated. **1941–1943** Worked for numerous American magazines. **1943** Set up his own studio in New York. Used various distancing effects such as solarisation, double exposure and positive/negative combinations in his fashion photography. **1955** Began writing his autobiography. **1962** Lived in Berlin for a year. **1976** Autobiography published.
MONOGRAPHS, CATALOGUES: Ewing, W. A. and M. Schinz (ed.): B. Photographs, a Passion for Beauty. New York and Kilchberg 1996.– Gundlach, F. C. and P. Weiermair (ed.): E. B. Museum Folkwang, Essen et al. Essen 1987 (cat.)

BOCCIONI Umberto
1882 Reggio di Calabria – **1916** Verona
Italian painter and sculptor. **1898–1902** Studied painting in Rome. Met Severini and Balla. **1902** Travelled to Paris. Strongly influenced by Neo-Impressionism, especially by the works of Seurat. **1907** Settled in Milan. **1910** Met Marinetti and, along with Carrà, Russolo, Balla and Severini,

signed the *Manifesto of Futurist Painters*.
1911 Returned to Paris and made contact
with the Cubist circle centred around Apollinaire, Picasso, Braque and Dufy. Fused
elements of Cubism with Futurist concepts
of dynamism and speed. **1912** Took part in
the first international Futurist exhibition at
the Bernheim-Jeune gallery in Paris and
drew up the *Manifesto of Futurist Sculpture*. **1913** Exhibition of his Futurist sculptures at the Galerie de la Boètie. **1914** Critical analysis of the basic tenets of Futurism
in an article entitled *Pittura, scultura futurista, dinamismo plastico* (Painting, Futurist
Sculpture, Plastic Dynamism). One of the
leaders of the Futurist movement.
WRITINGS: Birolli, Z. (ed.): U. B. Gli
scritti editi e inediti. Milan 1971.– Birolli, Z.
(ed.): U. B. Altri inedite e apparati critici.
Milan 1972
CATALOGUES RAISONNES: Bellini, P.
(ed.): Catalogo completo dell'opera grafica
di U. B. Milan 1972.– Bruno, G. and A.
Palazzeschi (ed.): L'opera completa di B.
Milan 1969.– L'opera completa di B. Milan 1983.–
Marinetti, F. T. (ed.): U. B. Opera com-
pleta. Florence 1927.– Palzzeschi, A. and G.
Bruno (ed.): L'opera completa di B. Milan
1969.– Taylor, J. (ed.): The Graphic Work of
U. B. The Museum of Modern Art. New
York 1961 (cat.).– Verzotti, G. (ed.): B. Cat-
alogo completo dei dipinti. Florence 1989
MONOGRAPHS, CATALOGUES: Argan,
G. C. and M. Calvesi: U. B. Roma 1953.–
B. prefuturista. Museo Nazionale, Reggio
Calabria. Milan 1983 (cat.).– Ballo, G.: B.
La vita e l'opera. Milan 1964, 1982.– Ballo,
G. et al. (ed.): B. e Milano. Palazzo Reale,
Milan et al. Milan 1982 (cat.)/B. und Mai-
land. Kunstmuseum Hannover. Hanover
1983 (cat.).– Birolli, Z.: U. B. Racconto
critico. Torino 1983.– Calvesi, M.: U. B.
Incisioni e disegni. Florence 1973.– Cam-
poresi, F.: L'architettura e il dinamismo.
Studio sulla poetica di U. B. Bologna 1982.–
Coen, E. et al. (ed.): B. a Venezia. Chiesa
di S. Stae, Venice. Milan 1985 (cat.).– Coen,
E. (ed.): U. B. Metropolitan Museum of
Art. New York 1988 (cat.).– Golding, J.: B.
Unique Forms of Continuity in Space.
London 1985.– Grada, R. d.: B. Il mito del
moderno. Florence 1962.– Lista, G.: U. B.
Dynamisme plastique. Lausanne 1975.–
Marchiori, G.: U. B. scultore. Milan 1969.–
Rossi, L. M. (ed.): B., 1912, Materia. Galle-
ria dello Scudo, Verona. Milan 1991 (cat.)/
B. 1912, Materia. Fondazione Antonio Maz-
zotta. Milan 1995 (cat.).– Schneede, U. M.:
U. B. Stuttgart 1993.– Schulz-Hoffmann,
C.: U. B. Volumi orizzontali. Munich
1981.– Tallarico, L.: B. cento anni.
Roma 1982

BOECKL Herbert

1894 Klagenfurt – **1966** Vienna
Austrian painter. Self taught. Studied architecture at the Technical College in Vienna.
1913 Joined the Austrian Artists' Association. Became friends with Adolf Loos. **1921
-1924** Travelled to Berlin, Palermo and

Paris; leanings towards French art. **1928**
First important religious work, the fresco
*Rescue of the Apostle Peter from the Sea of
Galilee* in the pilgrims church at Maria Saal.
1931 Studied anatomy at the Franz-Joseph
Hospital in Vienna in preparation for an
extensive series of drawings and sketches
in oils for his treatise *Anatomy*. **1935–1939**
Professor of Painting at the Vienna
Academy. **1941** Joined the NSDAP but
continued to criticize the cultural policies
of the Nazis. **1945–1950** Withdrawal of
charges of collaboration with the Nazis.
Superintendent of art colleges around
Vienna. **1962–1965** Director of the Vienna
Academy.
CATALOGUE RAISONNE: Frodl, G.: H.
B. Mit einem Werkverzeichnis der Ölge-
mälde von Leonore Boeckl. Salzburg 1976
MONOGRAPHS, CATALOGUES: H. B.
Malerei, Zeichnungen und Aquarelle.
Städtische Galerie im Lenbachhaus.
Munich 1954 (cat.).– H. B. Museum des
20. Jahrhunderts. Vienna 1964 (cat.).– H. B.
Aquarelle und Zeichnungen. Graphische
Sammlung Albertina. Vienna 1969 (cat.).–
H. B. Gemälde und Collagen. Akademie
der bildenden Künste. Vienna 1976 (cat.).–
H. B. Werke nach 1945. Salzburger Land-
essammlungen Rupertinum et al. Graz
1988 (cat.).– H. B. Körper und Räume. 1915-
1931. Graphische Sammlung Albertina,
Vienna et al. 1989 (cat.).– H. B. Kunstforum
der Bank Austria. Vienna 1994 (cat.).–
Diehl, G.: H. B. Salzburg 1978.– Frodl, G.:
H. B. Salzburg 1976.– Skreiner, W.: H. B.
Gemälde. Graz 1979.– Stary, O. and W.
Kallen: Die Seckauer Apokalypse von H. B.
Graz 1989

BOLTANSKI Christian
born **1944** Paris
French object artist. Self-taught. **1958–1967**
Series of large-scale works representing historical events combined with personal experiences. After **1968** produced works (mostly
photographic) reconstructing his childhood
or tracing the life history of other people.
From **1970** collaborated with Jean Le Gac.
1971 Started to use videos. Publication of
photographs in book form. Since **1972**
regular participation at the documenta in
Kassel. Boltanski is a leading representative
of the so-called "trace- and clue-finding
artists" (Spurensicherer).

WRITINGS: C. B.: Livres. Paris 1991,
Cologne 1991.– C. B.: Zeit. Munich 1996
CATALOGUE RAISONNE: Flay, J. (ed.): C.
B. Books, Printed Matter, Ephemera 1966-
1991. Cologne 1991
MONOGRAPHS, CATALOGUES: C. B.
Württembergischer Kunstverein, Stuttgart.
Münster 1974 (cat.).– C. B. Modellbilder.
Rheinisches Landesmuseum. Bonn 1977
(cat.).– C. B. Reconstitution. Badischer
Kunstverein. Karlsruhe 1978 (cat.).– C. B.
Musée de Calais. Calais 1980 (cat.).– C. B.
Lessons of Darkness. Museum of Contem-
porary Art. Chicago 1988 (cat.).– C. B.
Réserves: La Fête de Pourim. Museum für
Gegenwartskunst. Basel 1989 (cat.).– C. B.
Reconstitution. Whitechapel ArtGallery,
London 1990 (cat.)/Reconstitution. Musée
de Grenoble 1990 (cat.).– C. B. Städtisches
Museum Abteiberg. Mönchengladbach 1993
(cat.).– C. B. Menschlich. Cologne 1994.–
Bozo, D. et al. (ed.): C. B. Centre Georges
Pompidou. Paris 1984 (cat.)/C. B. Staatliche
Kunsthalle Baden-Baden et al. Baden-
Baden 1984 (cat.).– Eccher, D. (ed.): C. B.
Bologna 1997 (cat.).– Franzke, A. and M.
Schwarz (ed.): C. B. Reconstitution. Badi-
scher Kunstverein. Karlsruhe 1978 (cat.).–
Gumpert, L.: C. B. Paris and New York
1994.– Holsten, S. (ed.): C. B. Staatliche
Kunsthalle Baden-Baden. Baden-Baden
1984 (cat.).– Jacob, M. J. and L. Gumpert
(ed.): C. B. Lessons of Darkness. Museum
of Contemporary Art, Chicago et al.
Chicago 1989 (cat.).– Metken, G.: C. B.
Memento mori und Schattenspiel. Frank-
furt-on-Main 1991.– Moure, G. (ed.): C. B.
Advent and Other Times. Santiago de
Compostela 1996 (cat.).– Schneede, U. M.
et al. (ed.): C. B. Inventar. Hamburger
Kunsthalle. Hamburg 1991 (cat.).– Schra-
nen, G. (ed.): C. B. Neues Museum Weser-
burg. Bremen 1996 (cat.).– Semin, D.: C. B.
Paris 1988.– Semin, D. et al.: C. B. London
1997.– Theewen, G. (ed.): Confusion –
Selection: Gespräche und Texte über Biblio-
theken, Archive, Depots von und mit C. B.
Cologne 1996.– Viéville, D. (ed.): C. B.
Compositions. Musée d'Art Moderne de la
Ville de Paris. Paris 1981

BOMBOIS Camille
1882 Venerey-les-Laumes – **1970** Paris
French painter. Self-taught. Earned his
living as a farm labourer, circus wrestler and
weightlifter. **1914–1918** Military service.
1922 His artistic talent was discovered
through a roadside exhibition in Montmartre, Paris. Promoted by Wilhelm Uhde
and Florent Fels. Increasing public recognition encouraged him to take up painting
full-time. **1964** Took part in the exhibition
"Le Monde des Naïfs" in Paris. His simple,
powerful scenes of the circus, and town and
country life put him alongside Rousseau
and Bauchant, as a key representative of
French naïve art.
MONOGRAPHS, CATALOGUES:
Bodmer, H. B.: C. B. Paris 1951.– Vallier, D.
et al. (ed.): C. B. Galerie Vierny. Paris 1981
(cat.)

BONNARD Pierre
1876 Fontenay-aux-Roses – **1947** Le Cannet
French painter. **1886–1889** Studied law in
Paris. **1888/89** Trained as a painter at the
Académie des Beaux-Arts and the Académie
Julian. Made friends with Denis, Vuillard
und Sérusier, who introduced him to
Gauguin's concept of art. **1889** Sold a stylistically novel poster design *France-Cham-
pagne*. After short military service, set up
studio in **1890** with Denis and Vuillard and
founded the artists' group Nabis, promoting
Symbolist and anti-naturalistic ideals.
Strongly attracted to Japanese art. **1891–
1905** Exhibitions in the Salon des Indépendants. Publication of his first poster.
Became acquainted with Toulouse-Lautrec.
1893 First lithographs printed in *La Revue
Blanche*. From **1895** onwards, Vollard published Bonnard's lithographs and book illustrations, partly influenced by Redon. **1896**
First solo-exhibition put on by Durand-
Ruel. **1903** Exhibition at the new Salon
d'Automne. **1906** Taught at the Académie
Ranson. **1905** Travelled to Spain with Vuillard. Numerous trips to neighbouring countries and to North Africa over the next few
years. **1909** Long visits to the South of
France, where he settled permanently after
1925. In a late-impressionist style and delicate colours, he painted porcelain-like
domestic scenes, portraits, female nudes,
landscapes and aspects of city life.
WRITINGS: Clair, J. and A. Terrasse (ed.):
B. – Matisse. Correspondance. 1925-1946.
Paris 1991
CATALOGUES RAISONNES: Bouvet, F.
(ed.): P. B. L'œuvre gravé. Catalogue
complet. Paris 1981. The Complete Graphic
Work. London and New York 1981.– Bou-
venne, A. (ed.): Catalogue de l'œuvre gravé
et lithographié de R. P. B. Paris 1873.–
Curtis, A. (ed.): Catalogue de l'œuvre litho-
graphié et gravé de R. P. B. London and
Paris 1939.– Dauberville, J. and H. (ed.): B.
Catalogue raisonné de l'œuvre peint. 4 vols.
Paris 1965-1974, 1993.– Dauberville, J. and
H. (ed.): B. Catalogue raisonné de l'œuvre
peint révisé et augmenté. Vol. 1. Paris 1992.–
Heilbrunn, F. and P. Néagu (ed.): P. B.
photographe. Musée d'Orsay. Paris 1987,
Munich 1988 (cat.).– Roger-Marx, C. (ed.):
B. Lithographe. Monte Carlo 1952, 1981.–
Terrasse, A. (ed.): B. Illustrateur. Catalogue
raisonné. Paris 1988/B. Illustrator. New
York 1989
MONOGRAPHS, CATALOGUES: Beer, F.
J.: P. B. Marseille 1947.– P. B. Kunstmu-
seum Basel. Basel 1955 (cat.).– P. B. The
Late Paintings. The Phillips Collection,
Washington et al. New York 1984 (cat.).– P.
B. Das Glück zu malen. Kunstsammlung
Nordrhein-Westfalen. Düsseldorf 1993
(cat.).– Clair, J. (ed.): P. B. Palazzo Reale.
Milan 1988 (cat.).– Cogeval, G.: B. Paris
1993.– Cogniat, R.: B. Paris 1989.– Ives, C.
et al. (ed.): P. B. The Graphic Art. New
York 1989 (cat.).– Gobin, M.: R. P. B. Paris
1950.– Hagen, M. v. (ed.): B. Kunsthalle der
Hypo-Kulturstiftung. Munich 1994 (cat.).–
Ives, C. et al. (ed.): P. B. The Graphic Art.
Metropolitan Museum of Art, New York et

al. New York 1989 (cat.).– Jedlicka, G.: P. B. Ein Besuch. Zurich 1949.– Mann, S.: B. Drawings. London 1991.– Matta, M. and T. Stoos (ed.): B. Kunsthaus Zurich et al. Zurich 1985 (cat.).– Natanson, T.: Le B. que je propose. Geneva 1951.– Raynal, M.: Histoire de la peinture moderne. De Baudelaire à Bonnard. Geneva 1949.– Rewald, J. (ed.): P. B. New York 1948 (cat.).– Russell, J. et al. (ed.): B. Centre Georges Pompidou, Paris et al. Paris 1984 (cat.).– Shirley, A.: B. London 1940.– Terrasse, A.: P. B. Paris 1967 / P. B. Leben und Werk. Cologne 1989.– Terrasse, A. (ed.): P. B. Haus der Kunst, Munich 1967 (cat.) / Musée National du Louvre, Paris 1967 (cat.).– Terrasse, A.: P. B. Paris 1988, Cologne 1989.– Terrasse, M.: B. Du dessin au tableau. Paris 1996.– Thomson, B. and S. Mann (ed.): B. at Le Bosquet. Hayward Gallery, London et al. London 1994 (cat.).– Vaillant, A.: B. ou le bonheur de voir. Neuchâtel 1965.– Vaillant, A.: B. Munich 1966.– Watkins, N.: B. London 1994, 1996

BOROFSKY Jonathan
born **1942** Boston
American concept and multimedia artist. **1960–1964** Studied at the Carnegie Mellon University in Pittsburgh. **1964** Travelled to Paris. **1964–1966** Studied at Yale School of Art and Architecture in New Haven. **1969–1977** Taught at the School of Visual Arts in New York. After **1972** numbered his drawings, painting and sculptures consistently. Some recurring motifs: the hammering man, silhouettes riddled with hole and the flying figure. **1975** First one-man exhibition at the Paula Cooper Gallery, New York. Spatial arrangement of single objects into combination art works. Numerous commissions for schlptures in public places. **1977–1980** Taught at the California Institute of Art in Los Angeles. **1982–1992** Took part in documenta 7 – 9 in Kassel. **1984** Start of a major touring retrospective at the Philadelphia Museum of Art.
MONOGRAPHS, CATALOGUES: Ammann, J.-C. et al. (ed.): J. B. Träume 1972-1981. Kunsthalle Basel et al. Basel 1981 (cat.).– J. B. The Museum of Modern Art. New York 1978 (cat.).– J. B. Philadelphia Museum of Art. Philadelphia 1984 (cat.).– J. B. Tokyo Metropolitan Art Museum. Tokyo 1987.– J. B. Counting 3287718-3311003. Portikus, Frankfurt-on-Main. Cologne 1991 (cat.).– Cuno, J. (ed.): Subject(s). Prints and Multiples by J. B. 1982-1991. Hood Museum of Art, Dartmouth College et al. Hanover 1992 (cat.).– Geelhaar, C. (ed.): J. B. Zeichnungen. 1960-1983. Kunstmuseum Basel et al. Basel 1983 (cat.).– Kittelmann, U.: J. B. Dem Publikum gewidmet. Stuttgart 1993.– Rosenthal, M. and R. Marshall (ed.): Philadelphia Museum of Art, Philadelphia et al. New York 1984 (cat.).– Simon, J. (ed.): J. B. Dreams 1973-1981. Institute of Contemporary Arts, London et al. London 1981 (cat.).– Springfeldt, B. (ed.): J. B. Moderna Museet. Stockholm 1984 (cat.)

BOTERO Fernando
born **1932** Medellín
Columbian painter, sculptor and draughtsman. **1944–1946** Trained as a torero. **1951** Moved to Bogotá, where his first exhibition was held at the Galerías de Arte-Foto Estudio Leo Matiz. **1952** Studied painting at the Real Academia de Bellas Artes de San Fernando in Madrid and, from **1953**, at the Academia die San Marco in Florence. Studied Renaissance painting and the Old Masters, Dürer, Rubens and Velázquez. **1958** Taught at the Art Academy in Bogotá. **1959** Took part in the São Paulo Biennale. **1960** Moved to New York. Became acquainted with Franz Kline, Willem De Kooning, Mark Rothko. **1966** First European solo-exhibition in the Kunsthalle Baden-Baden. **1973** Moved to Paris. From **1976** did still lifes and animal sculptures in bronze, marble and cast synthetic resin. **1977** Participation in documenta 6 in Kassel. **1979** Retrospective in the Hirshhorn Museum, Washington. **1992** Exhibition of 32 monumental bronzes at the Champs-Elysées in Paris. Combined painting styles of the Old Masters with modern pictorial language in portraits and naive-narrative paintings displaying a grotesque sense of humour and luxuriant sensuality.
MONOGRAPHS, CATALOGUES: Arciniegas, G.: F. B. New York 1977.– Atkinson, T.: B. Munich 1970.– Auzias de Turenne, S. (ed.): B. en Avignon: le gai savoir de F. B. Palais des Papes. Avignon 1993 (cat.).– Bode, U.: B. The Sculpture. San Francisco 1978.– F. B. Fondation Pierre Gianadda. Martigny 1990 (cat.).– F. B. Antologica 1949-1991. Palazzo delle Esposizioni. Roma 1991 (cat.).– F. B. New Works on Canvas. New York 1997.– Brusberg, D. (ed.): F. B. Das plastische Werk. Galerie Brusberg, Hanover et al. Hanover 1978 (cat.).– Caballero Bonald, J. M.: B., la corrida. Un réalisme énigmatique. Paris 1990.– Daix, P. et al. (ed.): B. aux Champs-Elysées. Exposition. 3 vols. Galerie Didier Imbert, Mairie de Paris. Paris 1992 (cat.).– Durozoi, G.: F. B. Paris 1992.– Escallom: B. New York 1997.– Jouvet, J. (ed.): F. B. Gemälde, Aquarelle, Pastelle. Zurich 1983.– Lascault, G.: B. Eloges des sphères, de la chair, de la peinture. Paris 1992.– McCabe, C. J. (ed.): F. B. Hirshhorn Museum and Sculpture Garden. Washington 1979 (cat.).– Paquet, M.: B. peintures. Paris 1983.– Paquet, M.: B. Philosophie de la création. Tielt 1985.– Ratcliff, C.: B. New York 1980.– Restany, P.: B. New York 1984.– Rivero, M.: B. Bogotá 1973.– Soavi, G.: F. B. Milan 1988.– Spies, W. (ed.): F. B. Bilder, Zeichnungen, Skulpturen. Kunsthalle der Hypo-Kulturstiftung, Munich et al. Munich 1986 (cat.).– Spies, W. (ed.): B. Retrospektive. Zeichnungen, Bilder, Skulpturen. Kunsthaus Wien. Vienna 1992 (cat.).– Spies, W.: B. New York 1997.– Sullivan, E. J.: B. Sculpture. New York 1986.– Sullivan, E. J.: F. B. Dessins et aquarelles. Paris 1992 / F. B. Drawings and Watercolors. New York 1993

BOURGEOIS Louise
born **1911** Paris
French-American sculptress, graphic artist and painter. **1936–1938** Studied painting at the École des Beaux-Arts and in the studios of Bissière and Léger. **1938** Moved to the USA. **1945** First solo-exhibition at the Bertha Schaefer Gallery, New York. Subsequently taught at the Pratt Institute, the School of Visual Art and New York University. **1949** Gave up painting and turned to sculpture. Tried various methods in combination with different materials. Published numerous essays in American art journals. **1977** Received an honorary doctorate from Yale University and other public honours. **1992** Designed the American pavilion at the Venice Biennale and took part in documenta 9 in Kassel. Her symbolic and psychologizing sculptural language revolves around topics such as sexuality, feminism and repression.
WRITINGS: Bernadac, M.-L. and H.-U. Obrist (ed.): L. B. Destruction of the Father. Writings and Interviews 1923-1997. London 1998.– Kuspit, D.: B. Interview. New York 1988
CATALOGUE RAISONNE: Wye, D. and C. Smith (ed.): The Prints of L. B. The Museum of Modern Art. New York 1995 (cat.)
MONOGRAPHS, CATALOGUES: Bernadac, M.-L. and D. Wye (ed.): L. B. Paris 1995, New York 1996.– Bernadac, M.-L. et al. (ed.): L. B. Recent Works. Bordeaux et al. Bordeaux 1998 (cat.).– L. B. Retrospective 1947-1994. Galerie Maeght-Lelong. Paris 1985 (cat.).– L. B. Fundació Antoni Tàpies. Barcelona 1990 (cat.).– L. B. Rijksmuseum Kröller-Müller. Otterlo 1991 (cat.).– Felix, Z. et al. (ed.): L. B. Der Ort des Gedächtnisses. Deichtorhallen. Hamburg 1995 (cat.).– Gardner, P.: L. B. New York 1994.– Gorovoy, J. and J. Cheim (ed.): L. B. Drawings. Robert Miller Gallery. New York 1988 (cat.).– Gorovoy, J. et al. (ed.): L. B. Blue Days and Pink Days. Palazzo Reale. Milan 1997 (cat.).– Haenlein, C. (ed.): L. B. Skulpturen und Installationen. Kestner-Gesellschaft. Hanover 1994 (cat.).– Kotik, C. et al. (ed.): L. B. The Locus of Memory. Works 1982-1993. The Brooklyn Museum, New York et al. New York 1994 (cat.).– Lippard, L. R.: L. B. From the Inside Out. New York 1978.– Meyer-Thoss, C.: L. B. Konstruktionen für den freien Fall. Designing for Free Fall. Zurich 1992.– Parent, B. (ed.): L. B. Sculptures, environnements, dessins 1938-1995. Musée d'Art Moderne de la Ville de Paris. Paris 1995 (cat.).– Strick, J. (ed.): L. B. The Personages. Saint Louis Art Museum. Saint Louis 1994 (cat.).– Weiermair, P. et al. (ed.): L. B. Frankfurter Kunstverein. Zurich 1989 (cat.) / L. B. Städtische Galerie im Lenbachhaus, Munich. Schaffhausen 1989 (cat.).– Weiermair, R. et al. (ed.): L. B. New York 1995.– Wye, D. (ed.): L. B. The Museum of Modern Art, New York et al. New York 1982 (cat.).– Xenakis, M.: L. B. Lieux de mémoire. Paris 1996

BOURKE-WHITE Margaret
1904 New York – **1971** Stamford (CT)
American photographer. Studied at the Clarence H. White School of Photography. **1929–1933** Worked for the magazine *Fortune* and took numerous industrial photographs in Germany. From **1930–1932** made three trips to the Soviet Union, photographing machines and people. **1939** Worked working on his first version of the documentary of the life of tenant farmers in the southern states of America entitled *You Have Seen Their Faces*. From **1936** photographed for *Life* magazine. **1941** War correspondent in the Soviet Union and elsewhere. Took photographs of the concentration camp Buchenwald and the devastation left at the end of the war in Germany. **1956** Forced to stop working for health reasons.
MONOGRAPHS, CATALOGUES: Ayer, E. H.: M. B.-W. Photographing the World. Parsippany 1992.– M. B.-W. Amerika-Haus. Berlin 1984 (cat.).– Brown, T. M.: M. B.-W. Photojournalist. Ithaca (NY) 1972.– Callahan, S. (ed.): The Photographs of M. B.-W. New York 1972, London 1973.– Goldberg, V.: M. B.-W. A Biography. New York 1986.– Silverman, J.: The Life of M. B.-W. New York 1983

BRANCUSI Constantin
1876 Pestisani (Gorj) – **1957** Paris
French-Romanian sculptor. **1894–1902** Attended the School of Arts and Crafts in Craiova and the Art Academy in Bucharest. **1904** Moved to Paris. **1907** Met Rodin, already working on his first version of the sculpture *The Kiss*. Simplified his shapes to elementary abstract forms. Made friends with Modigliani, Rousseau and Léger and had contact with the Cubists. **1913** Took part in the Armory Show in New York. **1914** First solo exhibtion in Alfred Stieglitz' gallery. **1914–1918** Produced his most important wood sculptures. **1918** Beginning with his series *Endless Column*, attempted to break down the barriers between sculpture and architecture. **1937/38** Travelled to India and designed a temple. Carried out a huge sculptural project in the small Romanian town of Tîrgu-Jiu, including *Endless Column, Gate of Kisses and Table of Silence*. **1938/39** Visited Egypt, Holland, Romania and the USA. **1952** Took French

citizenship. His pure, symbolic forms strongly influenced future generations of sculptors.

CATALOGUES RAISONNES: Geist, S.: B. The Sculpture and Drawings. New York 1975.– Jianou, I.: B. Paris 1963, 1982, New York 1963

MONOGRAPHS, CATALOGUES: Aillagon J.-J. et al.: Album B. Paris 1997.– Bach, F. T.: C. B. Metamorphosen plastischer Form. Cologne 1987.– Bach, F. T.: B. Photoreflexion. Paris 1991.– Bach, F. T. et al. (ed.): C. B. Centre Georges Pompidou, Paris et al. Paris 1995 (cat.).– Balas, E.: The Sculpture of B. in the Light of His Rumanian Heritage. Ann Arbor (MI) 1982.– Balas, E.: B. and the Romanian Folk Tradition. New York 1987.– Brezianu, B.: B. in Romania. Bucharest 1976.– Bush, F. T. (ed.): C. B. 1876-1957. Philadelphia Museum of Art. Philadelphia 1995 (cat.).– Chave, A. C.: C. B. Shifting the Bases of Art. New Haven (CT) and London 1993.– Geist, S.: B. A Study of His Sculpture. New York 1968.– Geist, S. (ed.): C. B. Solomon R. Guggenheim Museum. New York 1969.– Giedion-Welcker, C.: C. B. 1876-1957. Neuchâtel 1958, New York 1959.– Hetzler, F. M.: B. The Courage to Love. New York 1992.– Hulten, P. et al. (ed.): B. Paris 1986, New York 1987, Stuttgart 1987.– Jianou, I.: B. Paris 1963, New York 1963.– Klein, I.: C. B. Natur, Struktur, Skulptur, Architektur. 2 vols. Cologne 1995.– L'Atelier de B. Centre Georges Pompidou. Paris 1997 (cat.).– Lewis, D.: C. B. Chicago 1957, 1975, Teufen 1958.– Miclea, I.: B. at Targu Jiu. Bucharest 1973.– Miller, S.: C. B. A Survey of His Work. Oxford 1995.– Partenheimer, J. (ed.): C. B. Der Künstler als Fotograf seiner Skulptur. Eine Auswahl 1902-1943. Kunsthaus Zürich. Zurich 1976 (cat.).– Salzmann, S.: C. B. Plastiken, Zeichnungen. Wilhelm Lehmbruck Museum. Duisburg 1976 (cat.).– Shanes, E.: C. B. New York 1989.– Spear, A. T.: B.'s Birds. New York 1969.– Tabart, M. and I. Monod-Fontaine (ed.): B. photographe. Centre Georges Pompidou. Paris 1977 (cat.).– Tabart, M. and I. Monod-Fontaine (ed.): B. Photographer. Centre Georges Pompidou, Paris. New York 1980 (cat.).– Varia, R.: B. New York 1986.– Viatte, G. et al. (ed.): C. B. Centre Georges Pompidou, Paris et al. Paris 1995 (cat.).– Zervos, C.: C. B. Sculptures, peintures, fresques, dessins. Paris 1957

BRANDT Bill
1904 London – **1983** London
English photographer. **1929/30** Assistant to Man Ray in Paris. Interested in Surrealism. Made friends with Brassaï. **1931** Returned to England. Photo-documentary of the misery of the English people during the recession. Worked for *Verve*, *Picture Post* and *Lilliput*. **1940-1945** Began series of portraits of artists and writers. Commissioned by the British Home Office to document life in bunkers and air-raid shelters during German bombardments. From **1945** focused on nude photography, often comic, combined with

landscapes and surrealist city scenes. **1959** Stayed in Provence. **1961** Publication of *Perspective of Nudes*. **1977** Honorary doctorate from the Royal College of Art in London. **1980** Honorary member of the Royal Photographic Society of Great Britain.
WRITINGS: Warburton, N. (ed.): B. B. Selected Texts and Bibliography. Oxford and New York 1993
MONOGRAPHS, CATALOGUES: Haworth-Booth, M. (ed.): Literary Britain – Photographed by B. B. Victoria and Albert Museum. London 1984 (cat.).– Jeffrey, I. (ed.): B. B. Photographs 1929-1983. London 1994.– Mellor, D. (ed.): B. B. Behind the Camera. Philadelphia Museum of Art. Oxford and New York 1985 (cat.).– Roegiers, P.: B. B. Paris 1990.– Scharf, A. (ed.): B. B. Photographs. Hayward Gallery, London et al. London 1970 (cat.).– Turner, P. (ed.): B. B. Early Photographs 1930-1942. Hayward Gallery. London 1975 (cat.)

BRAQUE Georges
1882 Argenteuil-sur-Seine – **1963** Paris
French painter. Apprenticed to a decorator in Le Havre. **1902-1904** Attended the Académie Humbert and the Ecole des Beaux-Arts in Paris. **1905** Links with the Fauves. **1907** The Cézanne memorial exhibition, a meeting with Picasso, and seeing *Les Demoiselles d'Avignon* in his studio had a powerful influence on Braque's painting. **1908** His intersecting shapes and curving planes forming structural blocks, described by the critic Louis Vauxcelles as cubes. **1909 -1912** Period of Analytical Cubism in which objects were broken down into a multitude of facets and presented as flat, almost unrecognisable structures. **1912** Birth of Synthetic Cubism: a bringing together of the fragmented, multi-facetted view of the subject in a compositional unit. Worked closely with Picasso until the outbreak of World War I. **1917** Resumed painting and produced monumental figure paintings, mantelpiece and table pictures and numerous landscapes. Worked with Gris. **1920** First sculptures. **1948** Received special honours at the Venice Biennale. **1952/53** Painted ceilings in the Louvre. **1956** Retrospective in the Tate Gallery, London. Beside Picasso, the most important representative of Cubist painting.
WRITINGS: G. B.: Le Jour et la nuit. Paris 1952, 1988 / Der Tag und die Nacht. Zurich 1953
CATALOGUES RAISONNES: Engelberts, E. and W. Hofmann (ed.): G. B. L'œuvre graphique de G. B. Lausanne 1960. Das graphische Werk. Stuttgart 1961.– Mangin, N. S. (ed.): Catalogue de l'œuvre de G. B. 7 vols. Paris 1959-1973.– Mourlot, F. (ed.): B. lithographe. Monte Carlo 1963.– Vallier, D. (ed.): B. Catalogue raisonné de l'œuvre gravé. Paris 1982 / B. Das graphische Gesamtwerk. Stuttgart 1982 / B. The Complete Graphics. New York 1988.– Worms de Romilly, N. and J. Laude (ed.): B. Cubisme 1907-1917. Paris 1987.– Wünsche, H. (ed.): G. B. Das lithographische Werk. Bonn 1971

MONOGRAPHS, CATALOGUES: B. The Late Works. Royal Academy of Arts, London. New Haven (CT) 1997 (cat.).– Brunet, C.: B. et l'espace. Langage et peinture. Paris 1971.– Chipp, H. B. (ed.): G. B. The Late Paintings 1940-1963. Phillips Collection, Washington et al. Washington 1982 (cat.).– Clement, R. T.: G. B. A Bio-Bibliography. Westport (CT) 1994.– Cogniat, R. G. B. New York 1980.– Heinrichs, H.-J. (ed.): Raumgestaltungen: der Beginn der modernen Kunst im Kubismus und Werk von G. B. Frankfurt-on-Main 1986.– Hope, H. R. (ed.): G. B. The Museum of Modern Art. New York 1949 (cat.).– Leymarie, J. (ed.): G. B. Solomon R. Gugenheim Museum, New York 1988 (cat.) / G. B. Kunsthalle der Hypo-Kulturstiftung, Munich 1988 (cat.).– Leymarie, J.: B. Les Ateliers. Aix-en-Provence 1995.– Martin-Méry, G. (ed.): G. B. en Europe. Galerie des Beaux-Arts, Bordeaux et al. Bordeaux 1982 (cat.).– Monod-Fontaine, I. and E. A. Carmean (ed.): G. B. Les Papiers collés. Centre Georges Pompidou, Paris et al. Paris 1982 (cat.) / G. B. The Papiers Collés. National Gallery of Art, Washington et al. Washington 1982 (cat.).– Mullins, E.: B. London 1968.– Paulhan, J.: B. Le Patron. Paris 1987.– Ponge, F. et al.: G. B. New York 1971, Stuttgart 1972.– Pouillon, N. et al. (ed.): B. 1882-1963. Centre Georges Pompidou. Paris 1982 (cat.).– Prat, J.-L. et al. (ed.): G. B. Fondation Pierre Gianadda. Martigny 1992 (cat.).– Prat, J.-L. et al. (ed.): G. B. Retrospective. Fondation Maeght. Saint-Paul 1994 (cat.).– Rubin, W. (ed.): Picasso and B. Pionering Cubism. The Museum of Modern Art, New York. Boston 1989 (cat.).– Rubin, W. (ed.): Picasso and B. Die Geburt des Kubismus. The Museum of Modern Art, New York. Munich 1990 (cat.).– Zurcher, B.: B. Vie et œuvre. Paris 1988 / B. Leben und Werk. Munich 1988 / B. Life and Work. New York 1988

BRAUNER Victor
1903 Piatra Neamtz – **1966** Paris
Romanian painter. **1921** Studied briefly at the Academy of Fine Arts in Bucharest. **1924** Founded a Dada magazine *75 HP*. Exhibition of Dadaist paintings in the Mozart gallery in Bucharest. Publication of the manifesto Pictopoesie. **1930** Moved to Paris. Met Brancusi, Giacometti and Tanguy. **1933** Joined the Surrealists. **1935** and **1937** in Bucharest. **1938** Returned to Paris again. Lost one eye in a fight, having painted a one-eyed self-portrait seven years earlier. **1940** Fled to the Pyrenees and later to the Alps. Experimented with wax painting. Developed his own mythology through his paintings and poetry. **1945** Returned to Paris. **1948** Broke away from the Surrealists. From **1953** spent three years on the Côte d'Azur for his health. Worked with the ceramic artists at Vallauris. **1959** Participation in documenta 2 in Kassel. In the 50s, inspired by Heidegger's existentialist philosophy, produced many paintings on the theme of premonitions of death.

MONOGRAPHS, CATALOGUES: Alexandria, S.: V. B. l'illuminateur. Paris 1954.– Bozo, D. and J. Leymarie (ed.): V. B. Musée National d'Art Moderne. Paris 1972 (cat.).– Carrein, C. (ed.): V. B. Musée d'Art Moderne, Saint-Etienne et al. Saint-Etienne 1992 (cat.).– Ceysson, B. (ed.): V. B. 1903-1966. Graphik aus der Sammlung des Musée d'Art Moderne de Saint-Etienne. Villa Merkel, Galerie der Stadt Esslingen. Lyon 1991 (cat.).– Fagiolo dell'Arco, M. (ed.): V. B. L'enigma del veggente. Galleria del Sogno. Lugano 1993 (cat.).– George, P. and D. Bozo (ed.): V. B. Les Dessins de V. B. au Musée National d'Art Moderne, Centre Georges Pompidou. Paris 1975 (cat.).– Jouffroy, A.: V. B. Paris 1959.– Kuni, V.: V. B. Der Künstler als Seher, Magier und Alchimist. Untersuchungen zum malerischen und plastischen Werk 1940-1947. Frankfurt-on-Main et al. 1995.– Ottinger, D. (ed.): Les V. B. de la collection de l'Abbaye Sainte-Croix des Sables d'Olonne. Paris 1991 (cat.).– Semin, D.: V. B. Musée d'Art Moderne. Paris 1990 (cat.)

BRECHT George
born **1924** Halfway (OR)
American action artist and theoretician. **1943-1945** Military service. **1946-1950** Studied natural sciences in Philadelphia. **1950-1965** Worked as a chemist and engineer. **1958/59** Studied at the New School for Social Research in New York; some courses with Cage. **1959** First solo-exhibition "Towards Events" at the Reuben Gallery in New York. Involved in key international Fluxus events and happenings. **1962** Took part in "Festum Fluxorum" in Copenhagen. From **1962** worked together with Paik, La Monte Young and Cage. **1966** Founded the Non-Ecole de Villefranche together with Filliou. **1972** Moved to Germany. Took part in documenta 5 in Kassel and later in documenta 6 and 8. **1978** Joint publication of the book *Die Scheinwelt des Paradoxons* (The Illusory World of the Paradox) with Patrick Hughes. **1983** Won the Will-Grohmann Award presented by the Berlin Academy. Brecht took part in international Fluxus events and concerts, and wrote many theoretical analyses of the relationship between aspects of new music and specific environments.
WRITINGS: G. B.: Change Imagery. New York 1966.– G. B. and R. Filliou: Games at the Cedilla, or the Cedilla Takes Off. New York 1967.– G. B. and P. Hughes: Vicious Circles and Infinity. New York 1975.– Daniels, D. et al. (ed.): G. B. Notebooks 3 vols. Cologne 1991
MONOGRAPHS, CATALOGUES: Frank, P. et al. (ed.): G. B. Works 1957-1973. Onnasch Galerie. New York 1973 (cat.).– Martin, H.: An Introduction to G. B.'s "Book of the Tumbler on Fire". Milan 1978.– Schmidt-Miescher, M. et al. (ed.): Jenseits von Ereignissen. Texte zu einer Retrospektive von G. B. Kunsthalle Bern. Bern 1978 (cat.)

BRISLEY Stuart
born **1933** Haslemere
English performance artist. Studied painting at the Munich Academy. **1960–1964** Lived in America. **1966** First performances. Since **1971** member of the Performance Art Cooperative of the British Artists Union. Presently working with other artists on performances extending over several days and representing a temporal dimension linked with a sense of human alienation. **1973–1974** Scholarship from the DAAD (German academic exchange programme) to Berlin. Since **1974** taught at the Slade School, London. **1977** Participation in documenta 6 in Kassel. Brisley belongs to the Artist Placement Group, who incorporate the passage of time into their works.
MONOGRAPHS, CATALOGUES: S. B. Tate Gallery. London 1982 (cat.).– S. B. Georgiana Collection. Third Eye Centre. Glasgow 1986 (cat.).– Nairne, S. (ed.): S. B. Institute of Contemporary Arts. London 1981 (cat.).

BROODTHAERS Marcel
1924 Brussels – **1976** Cologne
Belgian artist. Began his career as a lyrical abstractionist. **1940** Had contact with Magritte. From **1945** connected to Groupe Surréaliste-révolutionnaire (The Surrealist Revolutionaries). **1957** Publication of first volume of poetry *Mon livre d'Ogre* and his first film *La clef de l'Horloge*. From **1964** wrote critiques of exhibitions of contemporary American art. First objects and pictorial works. **1968** Founded the fictitious Musée d'Art Moderne, Department des Aigles with sections on the 17th and 19th centuries, Cinéma and Des Figures, by means of which he referred in disparaging quotes and ironic descriptions of art institutions and theories of art. **1969** Became acquainted with Byars. **1970** Moved to Düsseldorf and in **1972** to London. **1973–1975** Scholarship from the DAAD (German academic exchange programme) to Berlin. **1972–1975** Series of exhibitions in which he took recourse to 19th century techniques to illustrate his new concept of art. **1977** and **1982** participation in documenta 6 and 7 in Kassel.
WRITINGS: M. B. Correspondances, Korrespondenzen. Ed. by Galerie Hauser & Wirth, Zurich, and Gallery David Zwirner,

New York. Stuttgart 1995.– Buchloh, B. H. D. (ed.): M. B. Writings, Interviews, Photographs. Cambridge 1988.– Dickhoff, W. (ed.): M. B. Interviews und Dialoge 1946-1976. Cologne 1994
CATALOGUES RAISONNES: Borja-Villel, M. et al. (ed.): M. B. Cinema. Barcelona 1997 (cat.).– Brachot, I. (ed.): M. B. Œuvres 1963-1975. Brussels 1990 (cat.).– M. B. Katalog der Bücher 1957-1975. Galerie Werner. Cologne 1982 (cat.).– M. B. The Complete Prints. Gallery Werner. New York 1991 (cat.).– Lubbers, F. (ed.): M. B. Projections. Stedelijk Museum. Eindhoven 1994 (cat.).– Nobis, N. and W. Meyer (ed.): M. B. Katalog der Editionen, Graphik und Bücher. Hanover et al. 1996.– Nuyens, M.-C. (ed.): M. B. Het volledig grafisch werk en de boeken/Komplettes graphisches Werk und Bücher. Knokke-Duinbergen 1989
MONOGRAPHS, CATALOGUES: Borgemeister, R. and P. Viaccoz (ed.): M. B. L'œuvre graphique. Centre Genevois de gravure contemporaine. Geneva 1991 (cat.).– M. B. L'Angelus de Daumier. 2 vols. Centre Georges Pompidou. Paris 1975 (cat.).– M. B. Œuvres 1963-1975. Galerie Isy Brachot. Brussels 1990 (cat.).– Compton, M. and B. Reise (ed.): M. B. Tate Gallery. London 1980 (cat.).– Compton, M. et al. (ed.): M. B. Museum of Contemporary Art, Los Angeles et al. Los Angeles 1990.– Cuenat, P. (ed.): M. B. Autour de la Lorelei/En lisant la Lorelei. 2 vols. Musée d'Art Moderne et Contemporain, Geneva 1997 (cat.).– David, C. (ed.): M. B. Galerie Nationale du Jeu de Paume, Paris et al. Paris 1991 (cat.).– De Vree, F.: M. B. Œuvres 1963-1970. Brussels 1990.– Gevaert, Y. (ed.): M. B. Catalogue. Palais des Beaux-Arts. Brussels 1974 (cat.).– Gilissen, M. (ed.): M. B. in Zuid-Limburg. Fotos 1961-1970. Bonnefantenmuseum. Maastricht 1987 (cat.).– Gilissen, M. (ed.): M. B. La salle blanche, l'emsemble des plaques et l'entrée de l'exposition. Bienal Internacional de São Paulo. São Paulo 1994 (cat.).– Gilissen, M. and B. H. D. Buchloh (ed.): M. B. Musée d'Art Moderne. Marian Goodman Gallery. New York 1995 (cat.).– Goldwater, M. and M. Compton (ed.): M. B. Walker Art Center, Minneapolis et al. New York 1989 (cat.).– Marí, B. (ed.): M. B. L'Architecte est absent. Le Maçon. Fondation pour l'architecture, Brussels. Ghent 1991 (cat.).– Weiss, E. et al. (ed.): M. B. Museum Ludwig. Cologne 1980 (cat.).– Zwirner, D. (ed.): M. B. Korrespondenzen. Galerie Hauser & Wirth, Zurich et al. Zurich and New York 1995 (cat.).– Zwirner, D.: M. B. Die Bilder die Worte die Dinge. Cologne 1997

BRUCH Klaus vom
born **1952** Cologne
German video artist. **1975/76** Studied at the California Institute of the Arts in Valencia. **1976–1979** Studied philosophy at Cologne University. Put together videotapes like collages of film sequences on sociological and political themes. **1984** Took part in the

Venice Biennale. **1986** Stopped producing videotapes and focused on video-installations. **1987** Took part in documenta 8 in Kassel. Since **1991** Professorship at the Karlsruhe School of Design. **1996** Stage sets for the opera house in Frankfurt am Main.
MONOGRAPHS, CATALOGUES: Andersson, P. (ed.): K. v. B. Surface to Surface. Installation 1989. Moderna Museet, Stockholm et al. Stockholm 1989 (cat.).– K. v. B. Radarraum. Städtisches Museum Abteiberg. Cologne 1988 (cat.).– K. v. B. Arbeiten 1987-1989. Städtische Kunsthalle Düsseldorf. Düsseldorf 1989 (cat.).– Haenlein, C. (ed.): K. v. B. Video-Iinstallationen. Kestner-Gesellschaft. Hanover 1990 (cat.).– Mecky, A. et al. (ed.): K. v. B. Jam-Jam-Projekt. Kölnischer Kunstverein. Cologne 1993 (cat.)

BRÜNING Peter
1929 Düsseldorf – **1970** Ratingen
German painter. **1950** Studied at the Stuttgart Academy under Baumeister. **1952–1954** Travelled to Spain, Italy and France. Through Cubism developed his own abstract and autonomous pictorial language. **1955** Cornelius scholarship from the City of Düsseldorf. First experiments in Tachisme. Affinity to L'art informel. **1961** Selected for the Villa Romana Award. **1964** Received special honours at the III. International Biennale for young artists in Tokyo. **1969** Professor of Painting at the Academy in Düsseldorf. Constructed objects outside in the open-air. Brüning is one of the main exponents of Lyrical Abstraction in Germany.
CATALOGUES RAISONNES: Otten, M.-L.: P. B. Studien zur Entwicklung und Werk. Werkverzeichnis der Bilder und Objekte. Cologne 1988.– Otten, M.-L.: P. B. das zeichnerische Werk. Mit dem Werkverzeichnis der Zeichnungen. Cologne 1977
MONOGRAPHS, CATALOGUES: P. B. Städtische Kunsthalle Mannheim et al. Mannheim 1962 (cat.).– Dienst, R. G.: P. B. Recklinghausen 1973.– Dienst, R.-G. et al. (ed.): P. B. Superländer und Signale. Kunstverein für die Rheinlande und Westfalen. Düsseldorf 1970 (cat.).– Dienst, R.-G. et al. (ed.): P. B. Retrospektive. Moderne Galerie des Saarland Museums, Saarbrücken et al. Cologne 1988 (cat.).– Motte, M. d. la and M.-L. Otten: P. B. Berlin 1989.– Nobis, N. et al. (ed.): P. B. Arbeiten auf Papier 1952-1970. Sprengel Museum, Hanover et al. Cologne 1997 (cat.)

BRUS Günter
born **1938** Ardning (Steiermark)
Austrian action artist and writer. **1950–1956** Studied at the School of Arts and Crafts in Graz and at the Vienna Academy of Applied Arts. **1963** First solo-exhibition "Malerei-Selbstbemalung-Selbstverstümmelung" (Painting-Self-decoration-Self-mutilation) **1964** Together with Otto Muehl, Nitsch and Schwarzkogler founded Wiener Aktionismus. **1968** Sentenced to six months

imprisonment for degrading the Austrian national symbol and offending public morals and modesty through his Action painting *Art + Revolution* at the University of Vienna. **1969–1976** Editor of the magazine *Die Schastrommel*. **1970** Last Action painting *Zerreißprobe* in Munich. **1971** Publication of his novel *Irrwisch*. **1972–1982** Took part in documenta 5–7 in Kassel. **1974** Together with Arnulf Meifert founded the *I. Deutsches Trivialeum*. **1980** Participation in the Venice Biennale. Touring exhibition "Bild-Dichtungen" (Picture Poems).
WRITINGS: Amannshauser, H. and D. Ronte (ed.): G. B. Der Überblick. Salzburg and Vienna 1986.– G. B.: Irrwisch. Frankfurt-on-Main 1971.– G. B.: Der Geheimnisträger. Roman. Salzburg and Vienna 1984.– G. B.: Morgen des Gehirns, Mittag des Mundes, Abend der Sprache. Schriften 1984-1988. Salzburg 1993
MONOGRAPHS, CATALOGUES: Fuchs, R. (ed.): G. B. Augensternstunden. Stedelijk Van Abbe Museum, Eindhoven 1984 (cat.).– Grenier, C. (ed.): G. B. Limite du visible. Centre Georges Pompidou. Paris 1993 (cat.).– Meifert, A.: G. B. Zeichnungen und Schriften. Kunsthalle Bern. Bern 1976.– Meifert, A. (ed.): G. B. Blitzartige Einfälle in vorgegebenen Ideen. Neue Galerie im Landesmuseum Graz. Graz 1996 (cat.).– Serota, Nicholas et al. (ed.): G. B. Bild-Dichtungen. Whitechapel Art Gallery, London 1980 (cat.)

BRUSKIN Grigori
born **1945** Moscow
Russian painter. **1963–1968** Studied in the Faculty of Applied and Decorative Art at the Textile Institute in Moscow. **1966** First exhibition of his works with other young artists in Moscow. From **1969** member of the Artists' Association of the USSR. After **1980** in contact with Moscow intellectuals and artists propounding alternative lifestyles, including Dimitri Prigov. **1983** Forced closure of a one-man exhibition in Wilna. Ordered to explain his paintings to the Moscow Artists' Association. From **1983** worked on the series *Alefbet and Lexika*. **1984** Another exhibition cancelled by the Cultural Department of the Moscow City Soviets. **1988** One of Bruskin's works fetched a record price for contemporary Russian art at a Sotheby's auction in Moscow.

BUCHHEISTER Carl

1890 Hanover – **1964** Hanover
German painter. Studied art in Hanover
and Berlin. **1921** Friendship with Kurt
Schwitters. From **1923** his painting became
more abstract. **1925** Contact with van
Doesburg and De Stijl. **1926** First solo-
exhibition at the gallery Der Sturm, in
Berlin. **1928** President of the artists' group
Die Abstrakten Hannover (The Hanoverian
Abstractionists), also joined by Schwitters
and Vordemberge-Gildewart. **1932–1936**
Member of Abstraction-Création. **1933**
Denounced by the Nazis and forbidden
to paint. **1945** Resumed painting and
founded the artists' association for north-
west Germany. Since **1954** professor at the
Meisterschule in Hanover.
WRITINGS: Rump, G. C. (ed.): B.
Schriften und Briefe in Auswahl.
Hildesheim 1980
CATALOGUES RAISONNES: Buchheister,
E. and W. Kemp (ed.): C. B. Werkverzeich-
nis der abstrakten Arbeiten. 2 vols. Cologne
1998.– Buchheister, E. and W. Kemp (ed.):
C. B. 1890-1964. Werkverzeichnis der
gegenständlichen Arbeiten, Gemälde,
Gouachen, Aquarelle, Zeichnungen, typo-
grafische Arbeiten, Druckgraphik. Nurem-
berg 1986
MONOGRAPHS, CATALOGUES:
Büchner, J. and P. Lottner (ed.): C. B.
Sprengel Museum. Hanover 1990 (cat.).–
Fath, M. (ed.): C. B. Städtische Kunst-
sammlungen, Ludwigshafen et al. Ludwig-
wigshafen 1975 (cat.).– Holeczek, B. et al.
(ed.): C. B. Gemälde und Zeichnungen.
Verzeichnis der Bestände. Ausstellung zum
90. Geburtstag. Kunstmuseum mit Sammlung Sprengel. Hanover 1980 (cat.).– Lange,
R.: C. B. Göttingen 1964.– Lange, R. (ed.):
C. B. Kunstverein Hannover. Hanover
1964 (cat.).– Schönewald, U. (ed.): C. B.
Altes Rathaus. Göttingen 1994 (cat.)

BUCHHOLZ Erich

1891 Bromberg – **1972** Berlin
German painter. **1911–1915** Taught at an
elementary school. From **1915** lived in
Berlin. **1917** Engaged as artistic director at
the theatre in Bamberg. Member of the
Novembergruppe. **1919** First abstract, geo-
metric works. **1921** Exhibition at Herwarth
Walden's gallery Der Sturm, in Berlin.
Contact with Lissitzky, the Dadaists led by

Richard Huelsenbeck in Berlin and Haus-
mann, Mies van der Rohe and Moholy-
Nagy. **1925** Left Berlin to live in the country.
From **1926** involved in the "Große Berliner
Kunstausstellung". **1933** Banned from
exhibiting by the Nazis. Resumed painting
after World War II. Retrospectives at the
Rose Fried Gallery in New York **1956**,
Munich and Ludwigshafen **1979**, and
Tübingen **1996**.
WRITINGS: E. B.: Rotes Heft 1. Berlin
1927.– E. B.: Die große Zäsur. Berlin 1953.–
E. B.: Grundelemente. (n. p.) 1970
MONOGRAPHS, CATALOGUES: E. B.
Galerie Teufel. Cologne 1978 (cat.).– Buch-
holz, M. and E. Roters (ed.): E. B. Berlin
1993.– Heckmanns, F. W. (ed.): E. B.
Städtisches Kunstmuseum Düsseldorf et
al. Cologne 1978 (cat.).– Wiesenmayer, I.:
E. B. (1891-1972). Tübingen 1996

BUFFET Bernard

1928 Paris – **1999** Tourtour
French painter and graphic artist. **1944**
Studied at the Ecole des Beaux-Arts in
Paris. **1946** Exhibited at the Salon des
Indépendants. **1948** Critics Award. Member
of the anti-abstract artists' group L'homme
témoin. From **1950** worked on the series
Christ's Passion (1952), *The Circus* (1956)
and *Bullfight* (1967) as well as on book illus-
trations. Buffet's ascetic and realistic paint-
ings portray fear, suffering, poverty and the
experience of war.
WRITINGS: B. B.: Les Oiseaux. Paris 1960
CATALOGUES RAISONNES: Pichon, J.
Le (ed.): B. B. 1943-1981. 2 vols. Paris 1986.–
Mourlot, F. (ed.): B. B. Lithographies 1952-
1966. Paris 1967.– Reinz, G. F. (ed.): B. B.
Gravures 1948-1967. Nice 1968, Cologne
1968, New York 1968.– Rheims, M. (ed.): B.
B. Graveur. Catalogue raisonné de l'œuvre
gravé de 1948-1980. Paris 1984.– Simenon,
G. (ed.): B. B. Lithographs 1952-1966. New
York 1968.– Sorlier, C. (ed.): B. B. Lito-
graphe. 2 vols. Monte Carlo 1975-1979, San
Francisco 1987
MONOGRAPHS, CATALOGUES: Avila,
A. A.: B. B. Paris 1989.– Bergé, P.: B. B.
Geneva 1958.– B. B. Geneva 1964.–
Cabanne, P.: B. B. Paris 1966.– Descargue,
P.: B. B. Paris 1952.– Druon, M.: B. B.
Paris 1964.– Giono, J.: B. B. Paris 1956.–
Le Pichon, Y.: B. B. 1943-1981. Paris 1986.–
Letze, O. and T. Buchsteiner (ed.): B. B.
Retrospektive. Documenta-Halle, Kassel.
Stuttgart 1994 (cat.).– Mourlot, F.: B. B.
œuvre gravé. Paris 1967

BULATOV Erik

born **1933** Sverdlovsk
Russian painter. **1947–1952** Participate in a
drawing group in the Pioneers' House.
Studied at the Technical College of Art in
Moscow. **1952–1958** Studied painting at the
Surikov Art Institute. **1957** Exhibited *At the
Source* in the Soviet pavilion at the World
Youth Festival in Moscow. From **1959** illus-
trated children's books. **1965** Tried to put
on his first exhibition at the Kurtshatov

Institute for Nuclear Physics. Forced to
remove his paintings one hour after the
opening. **1967** Admitted to the Moscow
Association of Book Illustrators. **1968–1986**
Joint-exhibition with Kabakov in the young
people's café Der blaue Vogel. Further exhibitions in Moscow and at the museum in
the city of Tartu, Estonia. **1986** One of his
most important works, the painting *The
Poet Vsevolod Nekrassov*, shown at the Art
Fair in Chicago.
MONOGRAPHS, CATALOGUES: E. B.
Kunsthalle Zürich et al. Zurich 1988 (cat.).–
E. B. Centre Georges Pompidou. Paris 1989
(cat.).– Jolles, C. et al. (ed.): E. B. Moscow.
Institute of Contemporary Arts, London et
al. London 1989 (cat.)

BURDEN Chris

born **1946** Boston
American performance artist. **1969–1971**
Studied sculpture at the University of California, Irvine, graduating with a Master's
degree in Fine Arts. The extreme dimensions of his sculptures, reaching heights of
60 m, rendered his objects inaccessible and
awakened a desire for a return to human
dimensions. He then took up Body Art.
From **1971** events, performances and videos
exploring the limits of physical and psychic
tolerance to enable the viewer to experience
extreme physical situations. **1974** Built
vehicles and gave lectures about them. **1977**
Participation in documenta 6 in Kassel.
WRITINGS: Perrin, F. (ed.): C. B. Un livre
de survie. Paris 1995
MONOGRAPHS, CATALOGUES: C. B.
Musée d'Art Contemporain. Marseille 1996
(cat.).– C. B. Born in the USA. Österrei-
chisches Museum für angewandte Kunst.
Vienna 1996 (cat.).– Hsayre, M.: C. B. The
Object of Performance. Chicago 1989.–
Kuspit, D. et al. (ed.): C. B. A Twenty-Year
Siurvey. Newport Harbor Art Museum et al.
Newport Beach 1988 (cat.).– Mourne, G. et
al. (ed.): C. B. Barcelona 1996 (cat.)

BUREN Daniel

born **1938** Boulogne-sur-Seine
French artist. **1965** Together with Olivier
Mosset, Michel Parmentier and Niele
Toroni founded the group BMPT whose
aim was to reduce painting to a few basic
elements. **1969** Worked around Paris. **1971**

Installation in the Guggenheim Museum,
New York. **1972–1982** Participation in
documenta 5–7 in Kassel. **1976** DAAD
scholarship to Berlin. Buren's backgrounds
were always alternating white and coloured
stripes painted onto various grounds or prefabricated as in awning canvas. Through
their definite spacing, striped paintings
create a tight interweaving of space and
form.
WRITINGS: D. B.: Limites critiques. Paris
1970.– D. B.: Rebondissements. Brussels
1977.– D. B.: Entrevue. Conversations avec
A. Baldassari. Paris 1987.– D. B.: Les Ecrits
1965-1990. 3 vols. Musée d'Art Contemporain de Bordeaux. Bordeaux 1991 (cat.).–
Celant, G. (ed.): D. B. Scritti 1967-1979.
Milan 1979.– Fietzek, G. and G. Inboden:
D. B. Achtung! Texte 1969-1994. Dresden
1995.– Poinsot, J.-M. (ed.): D. B. Les écrits
1965-1990. 3 vols. Bordeaux 1991
MONOGRAPHS, CATALOGUES:
Baldessari, A.: D. B. Entrevue. Paris 1987.–
Buchloh, B. H. D. (ed.): D. B. Les
Couleurs: sculptures. Les Formes: pein-
tures. Centre Georges Pompidou, Paris et
al. Paris 1981.– D. B. Ponctuations. Statue/
Sculpture. Lyn 1980.– D. B. Photos Sou-
venirs 1965-1985. Le Nouveau Musée.
Villeurbanne 1987 (cat.).– Couderc, S. et al.
(ed.): D. B. Arguments topiques, CAPC
Musée d'Art Contemporain de Bordeaux.
Bordeaux 1991 (cat.).– Francklin, C.: D. B.
Paris 1987.– Granath, O. (ed.): D. B. Coin-
cidences. Arbeten in situ. Moderna Museet.
Stockholm 1984 (cat.).– Inboden, G. and J.
Meinhardt (ed.): D. B. Staatsgalerie Stutt-
gart. Stuttgart 1990 (cat.).– Krystof, D. et
al. (ed.): D. B. Erscheinen. Scheinen. Ver-
schwinden. Kunstsammlung Nordrhein-
Westfalen. Düsseldorf 1996 (cat.).– Lyotard,
J.-F.: Über D. B. Stuttgart 1987.– Mahr, B.
and H. Merten (ed.): D. B. Voile/Toile,
Toile/Voile. Akademie der Künste. Berlin
1975 (cat.).– Maubant, J.-L. (ed.): D. B.
Erinnerungsphotos 1965-1988. Basel 1989.–
Martin, J.-H. and R. Fuchs (ed.): D. B. So
ist es und anders. Kunsthalle Bern. Bern
1983 (cat.).– Nuridsany, M. (ed.): D. B. au
Palais-Royal. "Les deux plateaux". Le
Nouveau Musée. Villeurbanne 1993 (cat.).–
Parmentier, M. (ed.): D. B. Propos
délibérés. Le Nouveau Musée. Villeurbanne
1991 (cat.)

BURRI Alberto

1915 Città di Castello (Perugia) – **1995** Nice
Italian painter. **1934–1939** Studied medicine in Perugia. Served four years as a military doctor in North Africa. **1945** On
returning from prisoner of war camp in
America, gave up his medical career and
started to paint full-time. **1949** First abstract
paintings, the *Catrame*, in tar and oil on
canvas. **1950** Together with Capogrossi,
Ettore Colla and others, founded Gruppo
Origine in Rome. **1952** First sack pictures
and experiments with materials such as
wood, metal and plastic. **1953–1960**
Worked as an art teacher in the USA. **1959–
1982** Participation in documenta 2, 3 and 7

in Kassel. **1960** Returned to Rome. **1973** First *Cretto*, a clay picture the aesthetic attraction of which lies in the cracks formed when the kaolin surface cracks open on firing. **1976** Created a monumental *Grande Cretto Nero* for the sculpture garden at the University of California in Los Angeles. **1981** Plans to transform the ruins of the town of Gibellina in Sicily, destroyed by an earthquake, into a huge Cretto. Work began in **1985** but the project was abandoned in **1989**. Burri was a pioneer of monochrome reduction and the transformation of pictures into 3-dimensional objects. In his works he developed an individual polymaterialistic style, combining elements of Neo-Dadaism, material Informel, Constructivism and Arte Povera.
CATALOGUE RAISONNE: Zamboni, G. P. et al. (ed.): A. B. Contributi al catalogo sistematico. Città di Castello 1990 MONOGRAPHS, CATALOGUES: Christov-Bakargiev, C. et al. (ed.): A. B. Palazzo delle Esposizioni, Romaa et al. Milan 1997 (cat.).– Christov-Bakargiev, C. and M. G. Tolomeo (ed.): A. B. Opere 1944-1995. Palazzo delle Esposizioni, Roma et al. Milan 1996 (cat.).– Brandi, C.: A. B. Roma 1955, 1963.– Brandi, C.: Collezione Burri. Città di Castello 1982.– Calvesi, M.: A. B. Milan 1971.– Caroli, F.: A. B. La forma e l'informe. Milan 1979.– Collezione B. Citta di Castello. Perugia 1986 (cat.).– Engelke, I. S.: A. B. Betrachtungen, Analysen, Materialien zum Werkabschnitt 1944-1990. Hamburg 1991.– Mantura, B. and G. De Feo (ed.): A. B. Galleria Nazionale d'Arte Moderna. Roma 1976 (cat.).– Nordland, G. (ed.): A. B. A Retrospective View 1948-1977. The Frederick S. Whight Art Gallery, University of California. Los Angeles 1977 (cat.).– Pirovano, C. (ed.): B. Pinacoteca di Brera. Milan 1984 (cat.).– Pirovano, C. (ed.): A. B. Palazzo Pepoli Campogrande, Bologna. Florence 1991 (cat.).– Rubio, V.: A. B. Torino 1975.– Steingräber, E. (ed.): A. B. Il viaggio. Staatsgalerie moderner Kunst. Munich 1980 (cat.)

BURY Pol
born **1922** Haine-Saint-Pierre
Belgian painter and sculptor. **1938** Studied at the Académie des Beaux-Arts in Mons. **1943** Member of the surrealist group Jeune Peinture Belge (Young Belgian Painters).

1949 Co-founder of the artists' association Cobra. **1952** Joined the group Abstrakte Kunst (Abstract Art). Developed an interest in displacement of space and time, which led in **1953** to his first kinetic objects *Plans mobiles*. **1955** Participated in the exhibition "Mouvement" at the Denise René gallery in Paris. **1964** Travelled to New York. Took part in the Venice Biennale and documenta 3 in Kassel. From **1970** taught at the University of California, Berkeley. **1979** Work on monumental sculptures. Designed large public fountains in Paris and Brussels, and for the Guggenheim Museum in New York. **1983** Professor of Sculpture at the Ecole Nationale Supérieure des Beaux-Arts in Paris.
WRITINGS: P. B.: La Boule et le trou. Brussels 1961.– P. B.: L'Art à bicyclette et la révolution à cheval. Paris 1972.– P. B.: Les Gaietés de l'esthétique. Paris 1984.– P. B.: Le Monochrome bariolé. Paris 1991 MONOGRAPHS, CATALOGUES: Abadie, D. (ed.): P. B. CNAC. Paris 1972 (cat.).– Ashton, D.: P. B. Paris 1970.– Balthazar, A.: P. B. Milan 1967.– Balthazar, A. and W. Schmied (ed.): P. B. Kestner-Gesellschaft. Hanover 1971 (cat.) / P. B. Städtische Kunsthalle Düsseldorf. Düsseldorf 1972 (cat.).– P. B. Solomon R. Guggenheim Museum. New York 1971 (cat.).– P. B. Musée d'Art Moderne de la Ville de Paris, Paris 1982 (cat.).– Pahlke, R. E. (ed.): P. B. Museum am Ostwall, Dortmund et al. Dortmund 1994 (cat.).– P. B. Miroirs et fontaines. Galerie A. Maeght. Paris 1995 (cat.).– P. B. and P. Alechinsky: Le Dérisoire absolu. La Louvière 1980.– Dorchy, H.: P. B. et le temps dilaté. Brussels 1976.– Ionesco, E. and A. Balthazar: P. B. Brussels 1976.– Langui, E. (ed.): P. B. 25 tonnes de colonnes. Fondation Maeght, Saint-Paul. Paris 1974 (cat.).– Selz, P. (ed.): P. B. University Art Museum, Berkeley et al. Berkeley 1970 (cat.)

BUTLER Reg
1913 Buntingford (Hertfordshire) –
1981 Berkhamstead (Hertfordshire)
English sculptor. **1937** Studied architecture and became a member of the Royal Institute of British Architects. **1941** Conscientious objector. Worked as a smith in Sussex. **1944** First sculptures inspired by Giacometti. **1950**–**1953** Taught at the Slade School in London and at the University of Leeds. **1953** Won an international competition for a *Monument to the Unknown Political Prisoner*. **1955** Participation in documenta 1 in Kassel. Together with Chadwick and Armitage, the first of the post-war generation of abstract metal sculptors in England.
WRITINGS: R. B.: Creative Development. Five Lectures to Art Students. London 1962 MONOGRAPHS, CATALOGUES: Bowness, A. et al. (ed.): R. B. Tate Gallery. London 1983 (cat.).– R. B. Pierre Matisse Gallery. New York 1973 (cat.).– Calvocoressi, R. (ed.): R. B. Tate Gallery. London 1983 (cat.)

BYARS James Lee
1932 Detroit – **1997** Cairo
American performance and concept artist. Studied at the Merill Palmer School and at Wayne State University. **1958** One-year visit to Japan. Later lived mainly in Kyoto, being intensely interested in Japanese culture and philosophy. **1960** William Copley Award. **1965** Staged the performance *A Mile Long Paper Walk*. Numerous works over the following years were characterised by a concentrated stillness, in the spirit of Japanese tradition. **1969** Travelled to Europe. Met Broodthaers and Beuys. Participated regularly in subsequent documenta and the Venice Biennale. **1974** DAAD scholarship to Berlin. After **1975** reduction of sculptures to basic forms such as circles or spheres, and increasing use of granite, marble, glass and *objets trouvés* (found objects). **1977**–**1987** Participation in documenta 6 – 8 in Kassel.
WRITINGS: J. L. B. im Gespräch mit J. Sartorius. Cologne 1990
CATALOGUE RAISONNE: Deecke, T. and G. Schraenen (ed.): J. L. B. Perfect is My Death Word. Bücher, Editionenen, Ephemera. Bremen 1995
MONOGRAPHS, CATALOGUES: J. L. B. Golddust is My Wxlibris. Musée d'Art Moderne de la Ville de Paris. Paris 1983 (cat.).– Deecke, T. (ed.): J. L. B. im Westfälischen Kunstverein. Münster 1982 (cat.).– Elliott, J. (ed.): The Perfect Thought. Works by J. L. B. University Art Museum, University of California. Berkely 1990 (cat.).– Gachnang, J. (ed.): J. L. B. Kunsthalle Bern. Bern 1978 (cat.).– Harten, J. (ed.): J. L. B. The Philosophical Palace / Palast der Philosophie. Städtische Kunsthalle Düsseldorf. Düsseldorf 1986 (cat.).– Heil, H. et al. (ed.): J. L. B. The Perfect Moment. IVAM Centro Julio González, Valencia 1995 (cat.).– Todoli, V. (ed.): J. L. B. The Palace of the Perfect. Villa Serralves. Porto 1997 (cat.).– Winkler, R.: J. L. B. Cologne 1985

Taught at Mills College, California, where he became acquainted with László Moholy-Nagy. **1941** Lectured in experimental music at Chicago Institute of Design. **1942** Moved to New York, where he met Mondrian, Breton and Duchamp. From **1946** Musical Director of the Merce Cunningham Dance Company. **1948** Taught at Black Mountain College, North Carolina. From **1950** aleatoric compositions and experiments with unusual purpose-built instruments, computers and audiotapes. Incorporation of theatrical elements into his musical compositions. **1952** Performance of the composition 4'33, inspired by Rauschenberg's *White Paintings*. Together with Merce Cunningham and Rauschenberg, organised early forms of happenings. **1956**–**1958** Taught at the New School of Social Research, New York. By incorporating aleatoric elements and everyday sounds into his works, Cage contributed significantly to a broadening of the definitions of classical music and art. WRITINGS: J. C.: Silence. Lectures and Writings. Middletown (CT) 1963, London 1968, Frankfurt-on-Main 1995.– J. C.: A Year from Monday. New Lectures and Writings. Middletown (CT) 1967.– J. C.: Notations. New York 1969.– J. C.: Writing Through Finnegans Wake. New York 1978.– J. C. I-IV. The Charles Eliot Norton Lectures 1988/89. Cambridge (MA) 1990.– Kostelantz, R. (ed.): J. C. Writer. New York 1993.– Nattiez, J.-J. (ed.): J. C. & Pierre Boulez. Der Briefwechsel. Hamburg 1997 MONOGRAPHS, CATALOGUES: Amiot, A.-M. et al. (ed.): J. C. Toulouse 1988.– Bischoff, U. (ed.): J. C. als Grenzbeschreibung J. C. und die Moderne. Neue Pinakothek. Munich 1992 (cat.).– J. C. An Anthology. New York 1991.– Campana, D. A.: Form and Structure in the Music of J. C. Ann Arbor (MI) 1985.– Charles, D.: J. C. oder Die Musik ist los. Berlin 1979.– Charles, D.: J. C. Pour les oiseaux. Entretiens avec D. Charles. Paris 1976 / Für die Vögel. J. C. im Gespräch mit D. Charles. Berlin 1984.– Erdmann, M.: Untersuchungen zum Gesamtwerk von J. C. Bonn 1993.– Fürst-Heidtmann, M.: Das präparierte Klavier des J. C. Regensburg 1979.– Gena, P. (ed.): A. J. C. Reader. New York 1982.– Kostelantz, R. (ed.): J. C. New York 1970, London 1971.– Kostelanetz, R. (ed.): J. C. im Gespräch. Cologne 1989.– Kostelanitz, R. (ed.): J. C. An Anthology. New York 1991.– Kostelanitz, R. (ed.): Writings about C. Ann Arbor (MI) 1994.– Lazar, J. et al. (ed.): J. C. Rolywholyover. New York 1993.– Metzger, H.-K. and R. Riehn (ed.): J. C. I. Munich 1978.– Pritchett, J. W.: The Development of Chance Techiques in the Music of J. C. New York 1988.– Pritchett, J. W.: The Music of J. C. Cambridge 1993.– Revill, D.: The Roaring Silence. J. C. a Life. New York 1992 / Tosende Stille. Eine J. C. Biographie. Munich 1995

CAGE John
1912 Los Angeles – **1992** Los Angeles
American composer. **1930** Studied architecture and took music lessons in France. **1931**–**1937** Studied composition at the New School of Social Research in New York and at the University of California in Los Angeles, under Arnold Schönberg. Intensely interested in Far-Eastern philosophy. **1938**

CALDER Alexander
1898 Philadelphia – **1976** New York
American sculptor. **1916**–**1919** Studied

engineering in New Jersey. **1923-1925** Attended the Art Students League in New York. **1926** Lived in Paris where his acquaintance with Miró inspired him to create animal and plant figures out of steel wire that were exhibited in the New York Salon des Indépendants in **1928**. **1929** Met Mondrian, van Doesburg and Léger. Experiments with mobile wire constructions. **1931** Joined the group Abstraction-Création. From **1932** made mechanical and later airborne sculptures, termed *Mobiles* by Duchamp. **1936** Works shown at the exhibition "Cubism and Abstract Art" at the Museum of Modern Art, New York make him famous throughout the USA. **1935/36** Various stage designs for the choreographer Martha Graham. **1941** Constructed large mobile sculptures, termed *Stabiles* by Arp. **1943** Retrospective in New York. **1955-1964** Participation in documenta 1-3 in Kassel. **1968** Produced the largest stabile *Red Sun* (24 m high) and the largest mobile *Red, Black and Blue* (14 m wide). In Calder's sculptures elements of Abstract Surrealism are combined with a severe Constructivism. In the 60s and 70s, his monumental steel constructions gave a new impetus to sculpture in public places.
WRITINGS: A. C.: An Autobiography with Pictures. New York 1966/Autobiographie. Paris 1972
CATALOGUE RAISONNE: Caradente, G. (ed.): C. Palazzo a Vela, Torino. Milan 1983 (cat.)
MONOGRAPHS, CATALOGUES: Abadie, D. and P. Hulten (ed.): A. C. Die großen Skulpturen. Der andere C. Kunst- und Ausstellungshalle der Bundesrepublik Deutschland, Bonn. Stuttgart 1993 (cat.).– Arnason, H. H.: C. Princeton (NJ) 1966.– Arnason, H. H. and U. Mulas: C. New York 1971, Paris 1971, Munich 1971.– Besset, M. (ed.): C. Haus der Kunst, Munich et al. Munich 1975 (cat.).– Bourdon, D.: A. C. Mobilist/Ringmaster/Innovator. New York 1980.– Bruzeau, M. and J. Masson: C. New York 1979.– A. C. Stedelijk Museum, Amsterdam et al. Amsterdam 1959 (cat.).– A. C. Fondation Maeght. Saint-Paul 1969 (cat.).– A. C. Whitney Museum of American Art. New York 1976 (cat.).– A. C. 1898-1976. Musée National d'Art Moderne. Paris 1996 (cat.).– A. C. The Major Sculptures. New York (n. d.).– Elsen, A. E. (ed.): A. C. A Retrospective Exhibition. Works from 1925 to 1974. Museum of Contemporary Art. Chicago 1974 (cat.).– Gibson, M.: C. Paris 1988.– Lipman, J. (ed.): C.'s Circus. Whitney Museum of American Art. New York 1972 (cat.).– Lipman, J. and R. Wolfe (ed.): C.'s Universe. Whitney Museum of American Art, New York et al. New York 1976, Philadelphia 1989 (cat.).– Lipman, J. and M. Aspinwall: A. C. and His Magical Mobiles. New York 1981.– Marcadé, J.-C.: C. Paris 1996.– Marchesseau, D.: C. intime. Musée des Arts Décoratifs. Paris 1989 (cat.)/The Intimate World of A. C. Musée des Arts Décoratifs. Paris. New York 1989 (cat.).– Marter, J. M.: A. C. Cambridge and New York 1991, Cambridge 1997.– Prévert, J.: C. Montrouge 1966.– Sweeney, J. J.: A. C. New York 1951, 1964.– Sweeney, J. J.: A. C. The Artist, the Work. Boston 1971/A. C. L'Artiste et l'œuvre. Montrouge 1971

CALDERARA Antonio
1903 Abbiategrasso (near Milan) – **1978** Vacciago
Italian painter. Self-taught. First studied engineering then took up painting in **1924**. For a long time preferred to paint landscapes and portraits. **1959** Influenced by Mondrian and Albers, changed his style to a

geometric Constructivism with subdued translucent colouring. He applied many layers of colours, with about 40 coats of glazes, which he then abraded. **1960** First solo-exhibition in Ulm. **1968** Participated in documenta 6 in Kassel.
WRITINGS: Jochims, R. (ed.): A. C. in Briefen und Gesprächen. Kiel 1982
MONOGRAPHS, CATALOGUES: Agnetti, V.: 12 opere di A. C. Milan 1970.– Eco, U.: Novi serigrafie di A. C. con una piccola antologia di scritti pitagorici. Milan 1964.– Giolli, R.: A. C. Domodossola 1944.– Haldemann, M. (ed.): C. Kunsthaus Zug. Zug 1993 (cat.).– Heckmanns, F. W.: A. C. Aquarelle. Cologne 1974.– Heckmanns, F. W.: A. C. 1903-1978. Kunstverein für die Rheinlande und Westfalen und Kunstmuseum Düsseldorf. Cologne 1981 (cat.).– Holeczek, B. (ed.): A. C. 39 Ölbilder von 1957-1975. 27 Aquarelle von 1959-1976. Kunstverein Freiburg. Freiburg 1976 (cat.).– Jensen, J. C. (ed.): Der Maler A. C. Freunde, Einflüsse, Anregungen. Kunsthalle zu Kiel der Christian-Albrechts-Universität. Kiel 1982 (cat.).– Jochims, R.: Der Maler A. C. Starnberg 1972.– La Penna, G. (ed.): A. C. Pittura dal 1936 al 1974. Termoli 1974.– Lipman, J.: C.'s Universe. New York 1977.– Lipman, J.: C. Creatures. Great and Small. New York 1985.– Mendes, M.: A. C. Pitture dal 1925 al 1965. Milan 1965.– Saba Sardi, A. (ed.): F. C. Milan 1965

CAMPENDONK Heinrich
1889 Krefeld – **1957** Amsterdam
German painter. **1905 – 1909** Studied art at the Krefeld School of Arts and Crafts with Thorn-Prikker. **1911** Became acquainted with Marc, Macke and Kandinsky. Participated in an exhibition of the Blauer Reiter group at the Thannhauser Gallery. **1913** Participation in the First german Autumn Salon in Berlin and the exhibition of the Rhenish Expressionists in Bonn. In **1916**, after military service, moved to Seeshaupt on lake Starnberg in Bavaria. Inspired by traditional Bavarian folk art, he worked on glass-paintings. **1920** Travelled to Italy. **1922** Returned to Krefeld and taught at the School of Arts and Crafts there. **1926** Professor of Monumental Painting at the Düsseldorf Academy. **1933** Emigration to Belgium. **1935** Nomination to the Rijksakademie in Amsterdam. **1937** Eighty seven

of his works in German museums confiscated and classified as "degenerate art". **1955** Participation in documenta 1 in Kassel. **1989** Retrospective at the Kaiser Wilhelm Museum in Krefeld.
CATALOGUES RAISONNES: Engels, M. T. (ed.): H. C. Holzschnitte. Werkverzeichnis. Stuttgart 1959.– Engels, M. T. (ed.): H. C. als Glasmaler. Mit einem Werkverzeichnis. Krefeld 1966.– Engels, M. T. and G. Söhn (ed.): H. C. Das Graphische Werk. Düsseldorf 1996.– Firmenich, A. (ed.): H. C. 1889-1957. Leben und expressionistisches Werk. Mit Werkkatalog des malerischen Œuvres. Recklinghausen 1989.– Wember, P.: H. C. (mit Werkverzeichnis der Gemälde). Krefeld 1960
MONOGRAPHS, CATALOGUES: H. C. Städtische Galerie. Munich 1960 (cat.).– H. C. Städtische Kunsthalle Düsseldorf. Düsseldorf 1972 (cat.).– H. C. Städtisches Museum. Bonn 1973 (cat.).– Engels, M. T.: H. C. Recklinghausen 1958.– Fiedler-Bender, G. and H. Campendonk (ed.): H. C. 1889-1957. Pfalzgalerie. Kaiserslautern 1982 (cat.).– Röder, S. (ed.): H. C. Ein Maler des Blauen Reiter. Kaiser Wilhelm Museum, Krefeld et al. Krefeld 1989 (cat.).– Wember, P.: H. C. Krefeld 1889-1957 Amsterdam. Krefeld 1960

CAMPIGLI Massimo
1895 Florence – **1971** Saint-Tropez
Italian painter. Self-taught. **1914** Military service. Taken prisoner in Russia in **1916**. From **1919**, newspaper correspondent in Paris. His interest in modern French art led him to painting. Through the study of Egyptian art at the Louvre, he developed an archaic style of painting. While travelling to Rome in **1928** he became familiar with Etruscan art. **1929** Solo-exhibition at the Jeanne Bucher Gallery in Paris. Further presentations of his work in Milan, New York, Amsterdam, London and elsewhere. **1933** Signing of the *Manifesto of Wall Painting*. Collaboration with Sironi, Funi and De Chirico on murals for the Triennale in Milan. **1959** Participation in documenta 2 in Kassel.
WRITINGS: M. C.: Prefazione dello stesso. Milan 1931
MONOGRAPHS, CATALOGUES: Apollonio, U. (ed.): M. C. Galleria Civica d'Arte Moderna. Ferrara 1979 (cat.).– Carrieri, R.: M. C. Milan 1941.– Cassou, J.: C. Paris u. Zurich 1957.– Chastell, A.: Les Idoles de C. Paris 1961.– Mantura, B. and P. Rosazza Ferraris (ed.): M. C. Palazzo della Ragione, Padua. Milan 1994 (cat.).– Mele, G. L. (ed.): Mostra di M. C. Palazzo Reale. Milan 1967 (cat.).– Ruggeri, G.: Lo specchio di Giuditta. La favola senza fine di M. C. Bologna 1981.– Russoli, F.: C. pittore. Milan 1965.– Serafini, F. (ed.): Omaggio a C. Roma 1968, 1972

CAMPUS Peter
born **1937** New York
American video artist. **1955-1962** Studied

psychology at Ohio State Universitiy, Columbus and at the City College Film Institute in New York. **1960-1962** Also worked as producer's assistant in film and television. **1970-1972** Video adviser at the Metropolitan Museum of Art in New York. First video tapes. **1972** Video installation with black and white projectors dealing with man's experience of himself through technical media. First solo-exhibition at the Bykert Gallery in New York. **1973** Research grant at the television stations WGBH in Boston and WNET in New York. **1975** Guggenheim grant. **1976-1980** Lecturer at the Massachusetts Institute of Technology, Cambridge. **1977** Participation in documenta 6 in Kassel. **1979** Focused again on photography, employing digital techniques. **1980** Solo-exhibition at the Pompidou Centre in Paris. **1982/83** Lectureship at Rhode Island School of Design.
MONOGRAPHS, CATALOGUES: P. C. Everson Museum of Art. Syracuse (NY) 1974 (cat.).– Herzogenrath, W. et al. (ed.): P. C. Video-Installationen, Foto-Installationen, Fotos, Videobänder. Kölnischer Kunstverein. Cologne 1979 (cat.).– Kersting, H. (ed.): P. C. Dia-Projektionen. Städtisches Museum Abteiberg. Mönchengladbach 1990 (cat.).– Niemczyk, T. (ed.): P. C. Selected Works 1973-1987. Freedman Gallery Albright College. Reading (PA) 1987

CAPA Robert
(André Friedmann)
1913 Budapest – **1954** Thai-Binh (Indochina)
Hungarian photographer. **1930** Started to photograph. **1931-1933** Studied politics at the University of Berlin. **1931** Published his first photographs in the *Berliner Illustrirte Zeitung*. **1933** Moved to Paris. Changed his name to Capa. **1933-1939** Photographed for the magazines Life, Time and the *Illustrated London News*. In **1936** his photographs of the Spanish Civil War for *Vu* and *Regard* made him internationally renowned. **1939** Emigrated to America. **1941-1945** War correspondent, covering Europe and North Africa for *Life* magazine. **1947** Founded the photo agency *Magnum* with Cartier-Bresson, Seymour and Roger and acted as president from **1948-1954**.
MONOGRAPHS, CATALOGUES: Capa, C. (ed.): R. C. 1913-1954. New York 1974.– Capa. C. and R. Whelan (ed.): R. C. Pho-

tograps. New York 1985.– Capa, C. (ed.): Children of War, Children of Peace. Photographs by R. C. Boston 1991.– R. C. 1913-1954. London 1974.– R. C. Photographs. New York 1985.– Fárová, A. (ed.): R. C. New York 1968.– Karinthy, F.: Vége a világnak: R. C. képeivel. Budapest 1988.– Lacouture, J. (ed.): C. Centre National de la Photographie. Paris 1993 (cat.).– Martinez, R.: R. C. Milan 1979.– Whelan, R.: R. C. A Biography. New York 1985.– Whelan, R.: Die Wahrheit ist das beste Bild. R. C. Photograph. Cologne 1989.– Whelan, R. et al. (ed.): R. C. Photographies. Paris 1996

CAPOGROSSI Giuseppe
1900 Rome – 1972 Rome
Italian painter. **1919-1923** Studied law in Rome. **1926** Started painting. **1927-1933** Lived in Paris. Influenced by the Cubists. **1928** Participation at the Venice Biennale. **1946 – 1965** Lecturer at a school of art (Liceo Artistica) in Rome. **1951** Founded the Gruppo Origine together with Ettore Colla and Burri. Developed his own abstract, ornamental picture-writing consisting of curved comb-like signs with which he produced strong rhythmical compositions. **1952** Member of Gruppo Spaziale in Milan. **1955** and **1959** Participation in documenta 1 and 2 in Kassel. Lectureship at the Academy of Arts in Naples. **1974** Retrospective at the Galleria Nazionale d'Arte Moderna, Rome.
CATALOGUE RAISONNE: Hase-Schmundt, U. v. (ed.): C. Das graphische Werk. St. Gallen 1982
MONOGRAPHS, CATALOGUES: Apa, M. (ed.): C. Opere dal 1947 al 1972. Urbino 1987 (cat.).– Argan, G. C.: C. Roma 1967.– C. Staatliche Kunsthalle Baden-Baden et al. Baden-Baden 1967 (cat.).– Mantura, B. et al. (ed.): G. C. Galleria Nazionale d'Arte Moderna. Roma 1974 (cat.).– Mantura, B. (ed.): C. Fino al 1948. Palazzo Rosari Spada, Spoleto. Roma 1986 (cat.).– Porzio, F. (ed.): C. Gouaches, collages, disegni. Milan 1981.– Seuphor, M.: C. Venice 1954.– Tapié, M.: C. Venice 1962

CARO Anthony
born 1924 London
English sculptor. **1942-1944** Studied engineering in Cambridge and **1946-1952** art at

the Royal Academy Schools. **1951-1953** Assisted Moore who, together with Picasso, Bacon and De Kooning had a strong influence on his early bronzes. From **1953** lectureship at St. Martin's School of Art. **1959/60** Travelling grant from the Ford Foundation to New York where he met Noland and David Smith. Gave up figurative sculpture and started to make densely painted, abstract steel constructions. **1964** and **1968** participation in documenta 3 and 4 in Kassel. **1969** Retrospective at the Hayward Gallery, London. From **1984** bronze sculptures related to his earlier works from the 50s. As a reformer of his own teaching methods, Caro had a great influence on subsequent generations of artists in England.
CATALOGUE RAISONNE: Blume, D. et al. (ed.): The Sculpture of A. C. Catalogue Raisonné. 9 vols. Cologne 1981-1991
MONOGRAPHS, CATALOGUES: Blume, D. (ed.): A. C. Table and Related Sculptures 1976-1978. Städtische Galerie im Lenbachhaus, Munich et al. Munich 1979 (cat.).– Caradente, G.: C. at the Trajan Markets, Romae. New York 1994.– A. C. Städtische Galerie im Städelschen Kunstinstitut. Frankfurt-on-Main 1981 (cat.).– A. C. Sculpture 1969-1984. Serpentine Gallery, London et al. London 1984.– A. C. Œuvres 1961-1989. Musée de Calais. Calais 1990 (cat.).– Fauchereau, S.: A. C. The Marker Series. Paris 1996.– Fenton, T.: A. C. London 1986.– Fried, M. (ed.): A. C. The Arts Council of Great Britain. Hayward Gallery. London 1969 (cat.).– Fried, M. (ed.): A. C. Tisch-Skulpturen. 1966-1977. Städtische Kunsthalle Mannheim. Mannheim 1979 (cat.).– Hilton, T. (ed.): A. C. Sculptor 1969-1984. The Arts Council of Great Britain. London 1984.– Moorhouse, P. (ed.): A. C. Sculpture Towards Architecture. Tate Gallery. London 1991 (cat.).– Rubin, W. (ed.): A. C. The Museum of Modern Art. New York 1975 (cat.).– Spurling, J. et al. (ed.): The Trojan War. Sculptures by Sir A. C. English Heritage and Yorkshire Sculpture Park. London 1994 (cat.).– Sylvester, D.: A. C. Sculptures. Munich 1991.– Waldman, D.: A. C. New York and Oxford 1982.– Whelan, R. et al.: A. C. Harmandsworth 1974, New York 1975.– Wilkin, K.: C. Munich 1991

CARRA Carlo
1881 Quargneto – 1966 Milan
Italian painter. After attending classes at the Milan Brera School, worked as a freelance painter. Joined the Futurists in **1909** and signed their manifesto. **1911** Acquaintanceship with Modigliani, Picasso and Apollinaire in Paris. In **1915** he split with the Futurists. **1917** During military service in Ferrara became acquainted with De Chirico who was developing his ideas on *Pittura Metafisica* (Metaphysical Painting). As a result, Carrà's paintings became calmer, with a structured objectivity and subdued coloration. **1919-1922** Intensive collaboration with the journal *Valori Plastici*. **1924**

Wrote a monograph on Giotto and numerous critical and therotical essays on art. In **1926** and **1929** participated in the exhibitions of the group Novecento calling for a return to traditional values. Development of a stylized and archaic realism of melancholy solemnity. Carrà lived and worked in Milan until he died.
WRITINGS: C. C.: Pittura metafisica. Florence 1918, Milan 1945.– C. C.: Giotto. Roma 1924, London 1925.– Carrà, M. and V. Fagone (ed.): C. C. e Ardegno Soffici. Lettere 1913-1929. Milan 1983.– Carrà, M. (ed.): C. C. Tutti gli scritti. Milan 1978.– Caruso, L. (ed.): C. C. Guerra pittura, Futurismo politico, dinamismo plastico. 12 disegni guerreschi, parole in libertà. Florence 1978
CATALOGUES RAISONNES: Bigongiari, P.: L'opera completa di C. Dal futurismo alla metafisica e al realismo mitico 1910-1930. Milan 1970.– Carrà, M.: C. C. Tutta l'opera pittorica 1900-1963. 3 vols. Milan 1967-1969.– Carrà, M. and M. Valsecchi (ed.): C. C. Opera grafica 1922-1964. Vicenza 1976.– Carrà, M. (ed.): C. C. Disegni, acquaforti, litografi. Florence 1980
MONOGRAPHS, CATALOGUES: Ballo, G.: L'opera grafica di C. Milan 1967.– Carile, L. (ed.): C. C. Disegni 1908-1923. Palazzo Rosso. Genoa 1983 (cat.).– Carrà, M. (ed.): C. C. Mostra antologica. Palazzo Reale. Milan 1987 (cat.).– C. C. The Primitive Period 1915-1919. Kouros Gallery. New York 1987 (cat.).– C. Mostra Antologica. Palazzo Braschi, Roma. Roma 1987 (cat.).– Dell'Acqua, G. A. et al. (ed.): C. Palazzo Reale. Milan 1987 (cat.).– Fagiolo dell'Arco, M. (ed.): C. C. Il primitivismo 1915-1919. Chiesa di S. Bartolomeo, Venice. Milan 1988 (cat.).– Haenlein, C. (ed.): C. C. Zeichnungen. Kestner-Gesellschaft. Hanover 1981 (cat.).– Longhi, R.: C. C. Milan 1945.– Pacchioni, G.: C. C. Milan 1959.– Poetter, J. (ed.): C. C. Staatliche Kunsthalle Baden-Baden. Milan 1987 (cat.).– Riccio, L. and F. Riccio (ed.): C. C. Disegni 1918-1965. Torino 1987.– Russoli, F. and M. Carrà: C. Disegni. Bologna 1977.– Sprovieri, P. (ed.): C. C. Zeichnungen 1908-1920. Berlin 1987 (cat.)

CARTIER-BRESSON Henri
born 1908 Chanteloup
French photographer and film-maker. **1928-1930** Studied painting in the studio of Lhote in Paris. **1930** Took up photography. **1936-1939** Assistant to director Jean Renoir. In **1937** he shot the documentary film *Return to Life*. During World War II he was taken prisoner but escaped. Joined the Resistance and became a war correspondent after the liberation of France. **1945** Shot the documentary film *Le Retour* and photographed for *Harper's Bazaar*. **1946** Visited New York. **1947** Founded the photographic agency *Magnum* together with Capa and Seymour. Exhibition of his photographs at the Museum of Modern Art in New York. **1955** Publication of several photographs taken in the Soviet Union the pre-

vious year in the book *People in Moscow*.
MONOGRAPHS, CATALOGUES: Bonnefoy, Y. (ed.): H. C.-B. Photographer. London 1981, New York 1979, 1992 / H. C.-B. Die Photographien. Munich 1992.– Clair, J.: Line by Line. The Drawings of H. C.-B. New York 1989.– Contensou, B. et al. (ed.): H. C.-B. Dessins 1973-1981. Musée d'Art Moderne de la Ville de Paris. Paris 1981 (cat.).– Elliott, D. et al. (ed.): H. C.-B. Drawings and Paintings. Museum of Modern Art. Oxford 1984 (cat.).– Fárová, A.: H. C.-B. Prague 1958.– Galassi, P. (ed.): H. C.-B. The Early Work. The Museum of Modern Art, New York et al. Boston 1987 (cat.).– Gombrich, E. H.: H. C.-B. Fruit Market Gallery. Edinburgh 1978 (cat.).– Kirstein, L. and B. Newhall: The Photographs of H. C.-B. New York 1947, 1963.– Montier, J.-P.: H. C.-B. L'art sans l'art. Paris 1995 / H. C.-B. Seine Kunst, sein Leben. Munich 1997.– Palazzoli, D.: H. C.-B. Milan 1978.– Roy, C.: H. C.-B. Paris 1976

CASORATI Felice
1886 Novara – 1963 Turin
Italian painter. **1907** Qualified as a lawyer. Until **1915** attended art academies of Padua, Naples and Verona. In **1913** exhibition at the Ca' Pesaro in Venice. Absorbed strong Symbolist and Pre-Raphaelite tendencies into his painting. **1914-1918** After military service, settled in Turin. **1920** Influenced by the ideas of *Pittura Metafisica*, as expounded in the journal *Valori Plastici*, his style moved towards a poetic realism. A large room was dedicated to him at the **1924** Venice Biennale. **1928/29** Lectureship at the Accademia Albertina in Turin. **1938** Awards at the Venice Biennale and the International Exhibition of Art in Paris. **1941** Professor at the Accademia Albertina, and from **1954** its president.
CATALOGUE RAISONNE: F. C. Opera grafica. Milan 1966
MONOGRAPHS, CATALOGUES: Carluccio, L.: F. C. Le Sculpture. Milan c. 1980.– Carluccio, L. (ed.): F. C. Galleria Civica d'Arte Moderna. Ferrara 1981 (cat.).– Carluccio, L. and M. Rosci (ed.): F. C. Incisioni, sculture e disegni. Academia Albertina di Belle Arti, Torino. Padua 1985 (cat.).– Galvani, A.: F. C. Milan 1947.– Lamberti, M. M. (ed.): F. C. 1883-1963. Accademia Albertina di Belle Arti di Torino. Milan 1985 (cat.).– Lamberti, M. M. (ed.): C. Palazzo Reale. Milan 1989 (cat.).– Lamberti, M. M. and P. Fossati (ed.): F. C. 1883-1963. Academia Albertina di belle arti, Torino. Milan 1985 (cat.).– Marinelli, S. (ed.): F. C. a Verona. Milan 1986.– Valsecchi, M.: F. C. Roma 1977

CAULFIELD Patrick
born 1936 London
English painter. **1956-1960** Studied at the Chelsea School of Art, and **1960-1963** at the Royal College of Art. **1961** Participation in the exhibition Young Contemporaries in

London. **1963–1971** Lectureship at the Chelsea School of Art. Early still life and landscape paintings mainly influenced by Gris, Léger and Magritte. Caulfield painted till the mid-60s with brilliant domestic gloss paints on hard fibreboard. **1965** Participation at the Biennale des Jeunes in Paris. Applied silk-screen printing to his paintings. **1979** Developed a *trompe-l'œil* realism. **1981** Major retrospective at the Tate Gallery, London. Caulfield was inspired by Pop Art, particularly by Lichtenstein. Many of his works are representations of commonplace objects as shining colour fields framed by uniform black lines.
MONOGRAPHS, CATALOGUES: Finch, C.: P. C. Harmondsworth 1971.– Livingstone, M. (ed.): P. C. Paintings 1963-1981. Tate Gallery, London et al. London 1981 (cat.).– Livingstone, M. (ed.): P. C. Paintings 1963-1992. Serpentine Gallery. London 1992 (cat.).– Robertson, B. (ed.): P. C. Prints 1964-1981. Waddington Galleries. London 1981 (cat.)

CESAR
(César Baldaccini)
1921 Marseille – **1998** Paris
French sculptor and object artist. **1935–1942** Studied at the Ecole des Beaux-Arts in Marseille and in **1943-1948** at the Ecole Nationale Supérieure des Beaux-Arts in Paris. From **1950** made metal sculptures from collected pieces of industrial waste and scrap metal. **1954** First solo-exhibition "Animaux en ferraille" at the Lucien Durand Gallery in Paris. **1959-1968** Participation in documenta 2-4 in Kassel. From **1960** started to produce *Compressions Dirigées*, car bodies or other metal objects compressed into rectangular cuboids with a hydraulic press. He took part in Nouveau Réalisme events. **1961** During a visit to America he became acquainted with Duchamp and various Pop Art artists. Created sculptures which represent enlarged parts of the body such as thumbs or parts of the chest. **1967** First *Expansions*: happening-like events involving the pouring of liquid plastics. **1970** Professorship at the Ecole Nationale des Beaux-Arts in Paris. **1972** Mask series with the cast of his own face. **1985/86** Flat compressions of Peugeot cars. **1997** Major retrospective at the Galerie du Jeu de Paume in Paris.

CATALOGUE RAISONNE: Durand-Ruel, D. (ed.): C. Catalogue raisonné. Vol. 1: 1947-1964. Paris 1994
MONOGRAPHS, CATALOGUES: Cabanne, P. (ed.): C. par C. Paris 1971.– C. Musée d'Art Moderne de la Ville de Paris. Paris 1976 (cat.).– C. Œuvres de 1947 à 1993. Musée de Marseille 1993 (cat.).– Cooper, D.: C. Amriswil 1960.– Franzke, A. et al. (ed.): C. Galerie Nationale du Jeu de Paume. Paris 1997 (cat.).– Hahn, O.: Les sept vie de C. Lausanne 1988.– Hahn, O. (ed.): C. Compressions 1959-1989. Galerie Beaubourg. Paris 1990 (cat.).– Legrand, V. et al. (ed.): C. Œuvres de 1947 à 1993. Centre de la vieille Charité. Marseille 1993 (cat.).– Mason, R. M. (ed.): C. Rétrospective des sculptures. Musée d'Art et d'Histoire. Geneva 1976 (cat.).– Mathey, F. and P. Restany (ed.): C. Centre National d'Art Contemporain. Paris 1970 (cat.).– Restany, P.: C. Paris and Monte Carlo 1975, New York 1976.– Restany, P. and D. Durand-Ruel: C. Paris 1988

CEZANNE Paul
1839 Aix-en-Provence – **1906** Aix-en-Provence
French painter. Came to Paris in **1861** to study law and attend classes at the Académie Suisse. Rejected by the Ecole des Beaux-Arts in Paris for lack of talent, he returned to Aix-en Provence to join his father's bank. **1862–1864** Second stay in Paris. Made friends with Renoir, Monet, Sisley and Bazille. Met Manet in **1865**. **1872–1874** Joined Pissarro and Guillaumin in Anvers. **1874** Participation in the first Impressionist exhibition. **1879** Returned to Aix-en-Provence. **1882** Broke away from the Impressionists and developed a new style of painting: clear tectonic compositions in which he tried to reveal the underlying structure of nature rather than capturing the fleeting effects of light. **1895** Important solo-exhibition at Vollard with 150 paintings. **1900–1905** Geometrical compositions culminate in his painting *The Bathers*. **1907** Retrospective at the Salon d'Automne. Working parallel to the first generation of Impressionists and periodically also belonging to that circle, Cézanne nevertheless followed his own artistic creed. His art had a great influence on subsequent generations of painters and laid the foundations for modern painting.
WRITINGS: Doran, M. (ed.): Conversations avec C. Paris 1978, Zurich 1982.– Kendall, R.: C. by Himself. Drawings, Paintings, Writings. London 1988.– Rewald, J. (ed.): P. C. Correspondance. Paris 1937, 1978 / P. C. Correspondance. New York 1984 / P. C. Briefe. Zurich 1962, 1988
CATALOGUES RAISONNES: Chappuis, A. (ed.): Die Zeichnungen von P. C. 2 vols. Olten and Lausanne 1962 / The Drawings of P. C. A Catalogue Raisonné. 2 vols. London and Greenwich (CT) 1973.– Dunlop, J. (ed.): The Complete Paintings of C. London 1972.– Gatto, A. (ed.): L'opera completa di C. Milan 1970.– Orienti, S.

(ed.): The Complete Paintings of C. London 1972, New York 1972.– Picon, G. and S. Orienti: Tout l'œuvre peint de C. Paris 1975.– Rewald, J. (ed.): P. C. The Watercolours. A Catalogue Raisonné. Boston and London 1984 / Les Aquarelles de C. Catalogue raisonné. Paris 1984.– Rewald, J. and W. Feilchenfeldt): The Paintings of P. C. A Catalogue Raisonné. 2 vols. New York 1997.– Venturi, L. (ed.): C. Son art, son œuvre. 2 vols. Paris 1936, San Francisco 1989
MONOGRAPHS, CATALOGUES: Adriani, G. (ed.): P. C. Zeichnungen. Cologne 1978.– Adriani, G.: P. C. "Der Liebeskampf" Aspekte zum Frühwerk C. Munich 1980.– Adriani, G. (ed.): P. C. Die Aquarelle 1866-1906. Kunsthalle Tübingen. Cologne 1981 (cat.).– Adriani, G. (ed.): C. Gemälde. Meisterwerke aus vier Jahrzehnten. Kunsthalle Tübingen. Cologne 1993 (cat.) / C. Paintings. Kunsthalle Tübingen. New York 1993 (cat.).– Barnes, A. C. and V. d. Mazia: The Art of C. Merion (PA) 1986.– Boehm, G.: P. C. Montagne Sainte-Victoire. Eine Kunst-Monographie. Frankfurt-on-Main 1988.– Cachin, F. and J. J. Rishel (ed.): C. Grand Palais, Paris et al. Paris 1995 (cat.).– C. les années de jeunesse 1859-1872. Musée d'Orsay. Paris 1988 (cat.).– Coutagne, D. et al. (ed.): Sainte-Victoire. C. Musée Granet, Aix-en-Provence. Paris 1990 (cat.).– Düchting, H.: P. C. 1839-1906. Nature into Art. Cologne 1989.– Geist, S.: Interpreting C. Cambridge (MA) 1988.– Gowing, L. et al. (ed.): C. The Early Years 1859-1872. Royal Academy of Arts, London et al. London and New York 1988 (cat.).– Kendall, R.: C. by Himself. Drawings, Paintings, Writings. New York 1988 / P. C. Leben und Werk in Bildern und Briefen. Munich 1989.– Krumrine, M. L. (ed.): P. C. Die Badenden. Kunstmuseum Basel. Basel 1989 / The Bathers. Kunstmuseum Basel. New York 1990 (cat.).– Lévêque, J.-J. (ed.): La Vie et l'œuvre de P. C. Paris 1988.– Lévêque, J. J.: P. C. Le Précurseur de la modernité. Courbevoie 1995.– Lewis, M. T.: C.'s Early Imagery. Berkeley 1989.– Loran, E.: C.'s Composition. Analysis of His Forms with Diagrams and Photographs of His Motifs. Berkeley 1943.– Perruchot, H.: C. Paris 1956, London 1961.– Plazy, G.: C. ou la peinture absolue. Paris 1988.– Reff. T. and I. H. Shoemaker. P. C. Two Scetchbooks. Philadelphia Museum of Art. Philadelphia 1989 (cat.).– Rewald, J.: C. A Biography. New York 1939, 1996.– Rewald, J. et al. (ed.): C. The Early Years 1859-1872. Royal Academy of Art, London et al. London 1988 (cat.).– Rewald, J.: C. and America. Dealers, Collectors, Artists and Critics. Princeton 1989.– Rubin, W. (ed.): C. The Late Work. The Museum of Modern Art. New York 1977 (cat.).– Vallès-Bled, M.: C. Biographie 1839-1906. Paris 1995.– Venturi, L.: C. New York 1978

CHADWICK Lynn
born **1914** London
English sculptor. Trained as an architect. **1941-1944** Military service. **1945** First

sculptural works. **1950** Influenced by Calder and González, created movable abstract metal sculptures. First solo-exhibition at Gimpel Fils in London. **1953** Participation in the international competition for the unknown political imprisoner. Incorporated more and more semi-figurative motifs, such as centaur-like creatures, into his formal idiom. **1956** International award for sculpture at the Venice Biennale. **1959** and **1964** participation in documenta 2 and 3 in Kassel. Beside Butler and Armitage, Chadwick is one of Britain's leading metal sculptors.
CATALOGUE RAISONNE: Farr, D. and E. Chadwick (ed.): L. C. Sculptor. With a Complete Illustrated Catalogue 1947-1988. Oxford 1990
MONOGRAPHS, CATALOGUES: Bowness, A.: L. C. London 1962.– Causey, A. (ed.): L. C. Sculpture 1951-1991. Yorkshire Sculpture Park. Wakefield 1991 (cat.).– L. C. Musée National d'Art Moderne. Paris 1957 (cat.).– Hodin, J. P.: C. Amsterdam, London and New York 1961.– Koster, N. and P. Levine: L. C. The Sculptor and His World. Leyden 1988.– Levine, P.: L. C. London 1988.– Read, H.: L. C. Amriswil 1958

CHAGALL Marc
1887 Liosno (near Vitebsk) – **1985** Saint-Paul-de-Vence
Russian painter and graphic artist. **1907** Studied painting at St. Petersburg. **1910–1913** Lived in Paris. Met Modigliani, Delaunay, Gleizes and other artists. Encountered the contemporary art movements Cubism and Fauvism. **1914** First solo-exhibition at Herwarth Walden's gallery Der Sturm in Berlin. **1915** Returned to Russia. During World War I, developed an intensely personal style in which he combined Jewish-folkloristic ideas with forms of Western avant-garde. **1917** Founder and director of the School of Art in Vitebsk. Appointed, among others, Lissitzky, Pougny and Malevich as teachers. After interim periods in Moscow and Berlin, went to Paris in **1923** where he started doing book illustrations. From **1925** the circus became a recurrent theme in his works. His figures, painted in bright colours, are often suspended in pictorial space. **1941** Emigration to the United States, where he met Léger, Masson, Mondrian and Breton. **1946** Major retrospective exhibition at the Museum of Modern Art in New York. In **1947** he moved back to France, settling in Vence in **1950**. Public commissions for church windows, ceiling-paintings, tapestries and murals. Important representative of classical Modernism, combining elements of Fauvism and Surrealism with his own formal language and brilliant coloration.
WRITINGS: M. C.: Ma Vie. Paris 1931, 1957 / M. C. Mein Leben. Stuttgart 1959 / M. C.: My Life. New York 1960, London 1967.– Sorlier, E. (ed.): C. by C. New York 1979
CATALOGUES RAISONNES: Forestier, S. and L. Sigalas (ed.): M. C. L'œuvre gravé.

Musée National Message Biblique, Nice. Paris 1987.– Forestier, S. and M. Meyer (ed.): Les Céramiques de C. Catalogue raisonné du travail de C. céramiste. Paris 1990. C. Keramik. Munich 1990.– Kornfeld, E. W. (ed.): Verzeichnis der Kupferstiche, Radierungen und Holzschnitte von M. C. Vol. 1: Werke 1922-1966. Bern 1970.– Leymarie, J. (ed.): M. C. Monotypes 1966-1975. 2 vols. Geneva 1966-1977.– Maier-Preusker, W. (ed.): M. C. Kritischer Werkkatalog der originallithographischen Künstlerplakate und Varianten. Bonn 1996.– Meyer, F.: M. C. Leben und Werk. Cologne 1961/M. C. Life and Work. New York 1963/M. C. Paris 1964, 1995.– Mourlot, F. and C. Sorlier (ed.): C. Lithographe. 6 vols. Monte Carlo et al. 1960-1986/The Lithographs of C. 6 vols. New York et al. 1960-1986.– Sorlier, C. (ed.): Les Céramiques et sculptures de M. C. Monte Carlo 1972/The Ceramics and Sculptures of C. Monte Carlo 1972/Die Keramiken und Skulpturen von C. Monaco 1972.– Sorlier, C. (ed.): Les Affiches de M. C. Paris 1975/C.'s Poster. A Catalogue Raisonné. New York 1975/Die Plakate von M. C. Geneva 1976.– Sorlier, C. (ed.): M. C. The Illustrated Books. Paris 1990/C. Le Livre des livres. Catalogue raisonné des livres, albums, revues … illustrés par C. Paris 1990
MONOGRAPHS, CATALOGUES: Alexander, S.: M. C. A Biography. New York 1978.– Anatova, I.: C. Discovered. From Russian and Private Collections. Moscow 1988.– M. C. Œuvres sur papier. Centre Georges Pompidou. Paris 1984 (cat.).– M. C. Musée National Message Biblique. Nice 1990 (cat.).– M. C. Die russischen Jahre 1906-1922. Schirn Kunsthalle, Frankfurt-on-Main. Bern 1991 (cat.).– Chatelain, J. (ed.): Le Message biblique. M. C. Paris 1972.– Compton, S. (ed.): M. C. Royal Academy of Arts, London et al. London 1985 (cat.).– Compton, S. (ed.): M. C. Mein Leben, mein Traum. Berlin and Paris 1922-1940. Wilhelm-Hack-Museum, Ludwigshafen. Munich 1990 (cat.).– Crespelle, J.-P.: M. C. Liebe, Traum und Leben. Hamburg 1970.– Forestier, S. et al. (ed.): M. C. 1908-1985. Palazzo dei Diamanti, Ferrara. Roma 1992 (cat.).– Forestier, S.: M. C. Seine Farbfenster aus aller Welt. Stuttgart, Zurich 1995/C. Les Vitraux. Paris 1996.– Güse, E.-E. (ed.): M. C. Druckgraphik. Saarland Museum, Saarbrücken. Stuttgart 1994 (cat.).– Haftmann, W.: M. C. Stuttgart 1975, New York 1984.– Kamenski, A.: C. Période russe et soviétique 1907-1922. Paris 1988. The Russian Years 1907-1922. New York 1988. Die russischen Jahre 1907-1922. Stuttgart 1989.– Keller, H.: M. C. Leben und Werk. Cologne 1978.– Krens, T. and J. Blessing (ed.): M. C. and the Jewish Theatre. Solomon R. Guggenheim Museum. New York 1992 (cat.).– Leymarie, J. (ed.): M. C. Grand Palais. Paris 1969 (cat.).– McMullen, R.: The World of M. C. Garden City 1968.– Mathey, F. (ed.): M. C. Musée des Arts Décoratifs. Paris 1959 (cat.).– Meyer, F.: M. C. His Graphic Work. New York 1957.– Rakitin, W. et al. (ed.): C. Bilder, Träume, Theater. 1908-1920. Jüdisches Museum der Stadt Wien. Vienna 1994 (cat.).– Schmalenbach, W. (ed.): M. C. Frankfurt-on-Main 1979.– Schneider, P.: M. C. Fast ein Jahrhundert. Stuttgart 1995.– Sidney, A.: M. C. eine Biographie. Munich 1984.– Sorlier, C.: M C.: Traum, Vision und Wirklichkeit. Munich 1991, 1995.– Vitali, C. (ed.): M. C. Die russischen Jahre 1906-1922. Schirn Kunsthalle. Frankfurt-on-Main 1991 (cat.).– Vogt, P. (ed.): M. C. Kunsthalle der Hypo-Kulturstiftung. Munich 1991 (cat.).– Walther, I. F. and R. Metzger: M. C. 1887-1985. Painting as Poetry. Cologne 1987

CHAISSAC Gaston
1910 Avallon (Bourgundy) – **1964** La Roche-sur-Yon
French painter and graffiti artist. Encouraged to paint by the German sculptor and painter Freundlich. **1938** Produced gouaches, watercolours and animal drawings. **1940** Participation at the Salon des Indépendants. **1942-1945** First graffiti works and painted stones. **1944** Started to paint with oils. Correspondence with Jean Paulhan and Dubuffet who remained close friends for life. **1947/48** Acquaintance with André Breton. Continued stone painting and graffiti on buildings. Made sculptures from pieces of rubbish and roots. Utilization of *empreintes*, object outlines for oil and gouache paintings. **1953-1955** Series of collages and *objets*, painted and pasted objects. **1959-1963** Worked on a series of totem poles, monumental oil paintings on wrapping paper, and collages of patterned wallpaper.
WRITINGS: G. C.: Hippobosque au Bocage. Paris 1951
CATALOGUE RAISONNE: Cousseau, H.-C. (ed.): L'Œuvre graphique de G. C. 1910-1964. Paris 1981
MONOGRAPHS, CATALOGUES: Affentranger-Kirchrath, A. (ed.): G. C. Galerie Nathan. Zurich 1994 (cat.).– Affentranger-Kirchrath, A. et al. (ed.): G. C. 1919-1964. Neue Galerie, Linz et al. Linz 1996 (cat.).– Brütsch, F.: G. C. Berlin 1994.– G. C. Musée National d'Art Moderne. Paris 1973 (cat.).– G. C. Kunsthalle Tübingen et al. Tübingen 1996 (cat.).– Cousseau, H.-C.: G. C. Paris 1986.– Fauchereau, S. (ed.): G. C. Paris et al. Paris 1989 (cat.).– Gachnang, J. and F. Brütsch (ed.): G. C. Neuchâtel 1988.– Jakovsky, A.: G. C. L'Hommeorchestre. Paris 1952.– Michaud, D. A.: G. C. Puzzle pour un homme seul. Paris 1974, 1992.– Nathan-Nehler, B.: C. Stuttgart 1987

CHALDEI Yevgeni
born **1917** Moscow
Russian photographer. First trained as a steel worker. **1930** Apprenticeship at the photographic agency TASS in Moscow. From **1941-1945** war photographs, including front-line pictures, taken with a portable Leica, of the first day of Hitler's invasion of the Soviet Union. Documented the retreat of German troops through Romania, Bul-

garia, Hungary and Austria, right back to Berlin. **1945/46** Photojournalist at the Potsdam Conference and at the Nuremberg Trials. **1946-1949** Commissioned by TASS to photograph crisis points along the Chinese border and in Yugoslavia. **1950** Dismissal from Pravda-editorial staff due to his Jewish origins. **1956** Reemployment. Worked until the 70s as a photojournalist for TASS and *Pravda*.
MONOGRAPHS, CATALOGUES: Volland, E. (ed.): Von Moskau nach Berlin: Bilder des russischen Fotografe J. C. Berlin 1994, 1995

CHAMBERLAIN John
born **1927** Rochester (IN)
American sculptor. **1951/52** Studied at the Art Institute in Chicago and in **1955/56** at Black Mountain College, North Carolina. **1957** Impressed by Abstract Expressionism and the tendencies of Nouveau Réalisme, he made his first works out of old metal and compressed car elements of particular shapes, combined with other pieces of industrial waste, like flexible tubes and iron bars. From **1966** on produced *Instant Sculptures* made from urethane-plastic foam and experimented with various materials such as acrylic glass, aluminium foil, electroplated metal and car finish on plastic material. **1974** Resumed his car-parts series of sculptures. **1977** Started to use a panoramic camera with a wide-angle lens of 26 mm and a fixed focus. **1982** Participation in documenta 7 in Kassel. **1986** Retrospective at the Museum of Contemporary Art in Los Angeles.
WRITINGS: Thomson, E. M. (ed.): The C. Letters. London 1965
CATALOGUE RAISONNE: Sylvester, J. (ed.): J. C. A Catalogue Raisonné of the Sculpture 1954-1985. New York and Los Angeles 1986
MONOGRAPHS, CATALOGUES: Auping, M. (ed.): J. C. Reliefs 1960-1982. The John and Mable Ringling Museum of Art. Sarasota (FL) 1983 (cat.).– J. C. Cleveland Museum of Art. Cleveland 1967 (cat.).– J. C. Stedelijk Van Abbe Museum. Eindhoven 1980 (cat.).– Fuchs, R. et al. (ed.): J. C. Current Works and Fond Memories. Amsterdam 1996 (cat.).– Gachnang, J. and R. Fuchs (ed.): J. C. Kunsthalle Bern et al. Bern 1979 (cat.).– Gachnang, J. (ed.): J. C. Oils. Galerie Fred Jahn. Munich 1986 (cat.).– Poetter, J. and D. Judd (ed.): J. C. Staatliche Kunsthalle Baden-Baden et al. Stuttgart 1991 (cat.).– Waldman, D. (ed.): J. C. Solomon R. Guggenheim Museum. New York 1971 (cat.)

CHARCHOUNE Sergei
1888 Buguruslan (Ukraine) – **1975** Paris
Russian painter. Attended classes at various academies in Moscow. Moved to Paris in **1912**. **1913** Exhibited with the Cubists Le Fauconnier and Metzinger at the Salon des Indépendants. **1914-1917** Lived in Spain. Participation in some Dada events in Barcelona and Zurich. Settled in Berlin in

1922 and exhibited his abstract paintings in Herwarth Walden's gallery Der Sturm. Collaboration with Schwitters, Lissitzky, Tzara and Arp. International exhibitions in Barcelona, Stockholm, Brussels and New York. **1923** Returned to Paris. **1947-1956** Repeated exhibitions at the Creuze gallery.
CATALOGUES RAISONNES: Creuze, R. (ed.): C. 2 vols. Paris 1975-1976.– Delettre, P. (ed.): Catalogue raisonné de l'œuvre peint de S. C. 1888-1975 (in preparation)
MONOGRAPHS, CATALOGUES: Brisset, P.: C. le solitaire. Paris 1970.– S. C. Musée National d'Art Moderne. Paris 1967 (cat.).– Creuze, R.: Charchouiana. Paris 1989.– Delettre, P. (ed.): C. Galerie Fanny Guillon-Laffaille. Paris 1988 (cat.).– Delettre, P. (ed.): C. 1888-1975. Centre Culturel de la Somme, Amiens et al. Amiens 1989 (cat.).– Waldberg, P. (ed.): C. Centre National d'Art Contemporain, Musée National d'Art Moderne. Paris 1971 (cat.)

CHARLTON Alan
born **1948** Sheffield (Yorkshire)
English painter and sculptor. **1965/66** Studied at Sheffield School of Art, **1966-1969** at Camberwell School of Art and **1969-1972** at the Royal Academy in London. As a student, painted his first monochrome paintings in grey. **1972** First solo-exhibition at the Konrad Fischer Gallery in Düsseldorf. **1982** Participation in documenta 7 in Kassel. **1991** Solo-exhibition at Haus Esters and Haus Lange in Krefeld. In ever-changing variations Charlton arranges his monochrome-grey canvases in strict geometrical order to form integrated compositions.
MONOGRAPHS, CATALOGUES: A. C. Stedelijk Van Abbe Museum. Eindhoven 1982 (cat.).– A. C. Institute of Contemporary Arts. London 1991 (cat.).– A. C. Museum Haus Esters. Krefeld 1992 (cat.).– Fuchs, R. (ed.): A. C. Castello di Rivoli, Museo d'Arte Contemporanea. Milan 1989 (cat.).– Raussmüller, U. and C. Sauer (ed.): A. C. Hallen für Neue Kunst. Schaffhausen 1991 (cat.).– Tosatto, G. (ed.): A. C. Musée d'Art Contemporain. Nîmes 1997 (cat.)

CHIA Sandro
born **1946** Florence
Italian painter. **1965-1969** Studied at the Accademia di Belli Arti in Florence. First

solo-exhibition at the La Salita Gallery in Rome. **1979** Solo-exhibition at the Paul Maenz Gallery in Cologne. **1980/81** Lived in Germany. From **1981** temporary jobs in Ronciglione and New York. **1982** Participation in documenta 7 in Kassel. **1984** Solo-exhibition at the Metropolitan Museum of Art in New York. **1993** Retrospective at the Nationalgalerie in Berlin. Numerous solo and group shows in America, Japan and Europe. Together with Clemente, Cucchi and Paladino, Chia belongs to the young generation of Italian artists named by Achille Bonito Oliva the Transavanguardia. In his predominantly mythological paintings he developed a free gestural style which repeatedly refers back to elements of painterly tradition.
WRITINGS: S. C.: Intorno a Se. Roma 1978
MONOGRAPHS, CATALOGUES: Celaya, G.: Die Räume bei C. Barcelona 1974.– S. C. Desert Museum. Palm Springs 1992 (cat.).– S. C. Novanta spine al vento. Museum Moderner Kunst. Vienna 1989 (cat.).– Esteban, C.: C. Paris 1972.– Frisa, M. L. (ed.): S. C. Dipinti, e titoli recenti. Palazzo Medici Riccardi, Museo Mediceo, Florence. Milan 1991.– Geldzahler, H. (ed.): S. C. Prints 1973-1984. Metropolitan Museum of Art. New York 1984 (cat.).– Haenlein, C. et al. (ed.): S. C. Bilder 1976-1983. Kestner-Gesellschaft. Hanover 1983 (cat.).– Honisch, D. et al. (ed.): S. C. Nationalgalerie. Berlin 1992 (cat.).– Weisner, U. (ed.): S. C. Passione per l'arte. Kunsthalle Bielefeld. Bielefeld 1986 (cat.).– Wilde, E. d. and A. v. Grevenstein (ed.): S. C. Stedelijk Museum. Amsterdam 1983 (cat.)

CHILLIDA Eduardo
born **1924** San Sebastián
Spanish sculptor. **1943-1946** Studied architecture at Madrid University. **1947** Artistic training at a private school in Madrid. **1948** Moved to Paris. Made his first figurative sculptures from plaster and clay. **1951** Returned to Spain. First abstract iron sculptures. **1958** Received special honours at the Venice Biennale. Started to use other materials like steel, wood, marble or alabaster for his sculptures. Over the following years, awarded numerous prizes and honours. **1964-1977** Participation in documenta 3, 4 and 6 in Kassel. **1966** Wilhelm Lehmbruck award in Duisburg. **1971** Guest-professorship at the Carpenter Centre, Cambridge. **1974** First retrospective in Chateau de Ratilly, Burgundy. Chillida's abstract-monumental sculptures combine expressive intensity with stylistic elements of Constructivism.
CATALOGUES RAISONNES: Aresti, G. (ed.): C. Obra gráfica completa. Madrid 1977.– Esteban, C. (ed.): C. (mit Werkverzeichnis der Skulpturen). Paris 1971.– E. C. A Retrospective. Carnegie Institute, Pittsburgh et al. Pittsburgh 1979 (cat.).– Clay, J. (ed.): C. L'œuvre graphique. Paris 1978.– Koelen, M. v. de (ed.): E. C. Catalogue Raisonné of the Prints 1973-1996. 2 vols.

Mainz 1996-1997.– Michelin, G. (ed.): E. C. Das graphische Werk 1959-1972. Ulm 1973.– Michelin, G. (ed.): C. 2 vols. Paris 1979.– Paz, O.: C. Paris 1979
MONOGRAPHS, CATALOGUES:
Barañano, K. M. d. (ed.): La obra artistica de E. C. Bilbao 1988.– Barañano, K. M. d. (ed.): Symposium C. San Sebastián 1993.– Barañano, K. M. d. et al. (ed.): E. C. Palacio de Miramar. San Sebastián 1992 (cat.).– Bußmann, K. et al. (ed.): E. C. Zeichnungen als Skulptur. Städtisches Kunstmuseum Bonn et al. Münster 1989 (cat.).– Celaya, G.: Les Espaces de C. Paris 1974. C.'s Räume. Geneva 1974.– Dempsey, A. et al (ed.): E. C. Neuer Berliner Kunstverein. Stuttgart 1991 (cat.).– C. en San Sebastián. Palacio de Miramar, San Sebastián. Madrid 1992 (cat.).– E. C. Hayward Gallery. London 1990 (cat.).– Esteban, C.: C. Paris 1971.– Gervasoni, M.-G. (ed.): E. C. Galleria Internazionale d'Arte Moderna Ca' Pesaro. Venice 1990 (cat.).– Haenlein, C. (ed.): E. C. Kestner-Gesellschaft. Hanover 1981.– Jabès, E. et al (ed.): C. Musée d'Art Moderne. Brussels 1985 (cat.).– Lichtenstern, C. (ed.): C. und die Musik. Baumeister von Zeit und Klang. Bad Homburg 1997 (cat.).– Messer, T. M. et al. (ed.): E. C. Eine Retrospektive. Schirn Kunsthalle. Frankfurt-on-Main 1993 (cat.).– Paz, O. et al. (ed.): C. Martin-Gropius-Bau. Berlin 1991 (cat.).– Ragon, M.: C. Paris 1968.– Schmalenbach, W. (ed.): E. C. Zeichnungen. 3 vols. Frankfurt-on-Main 1977.– Schmidt, K. and M.-A. v. Lüttichau (ed.): E. C. Zeichnung als Skulptur 1948-1989. Städtisches Kunstmuseum Bonn et al. Bonn 1989 (cat.).– Selz, P. and J. J. Sweeney: C. New York 1986.– Volboudt, P.: C. Paris 1967, Stuttgart 1967

CHRISTO & JEANNE-CLAUDE
born **1935** Gabrovo (Christo)
born **1935** Casablanca (Jeanne-Claude)
Christo: born Christo Javacheff, June 13, Gabrovo, of a Bulgarian industrialist family. Jeanne-Claude: born Jeanne-Claude de Guillebon, June 13, Casablanca, of a French military family, educated in France and Switzerland. **1953-1956** Christo: Studied at Fine Arts Academy, Sofia. **1956** Arrival in Prague. **1957** One semester's study at the Vienna Fine Arts Academy. **1958** Christo: Arrival in Paris. Packages and "Wrapped Objects". **1960** Birth of their son, Cyril, May 11. **1961** Project for the "Wrapping of a Public Building". "Stacked Oil Barrels" and "Dockside Packages" in Cologne Harbor (their first collaboration). **1962** "Iron Curtain-Wall of Oil Barrels" blocking the Rue Visconti, Paris. **1963** "Showcases". **1964** "Stor Fronts". Establishment of permanent residence in New York City. **1966** "Air Package" and "Wrapped Tree", Stedelijk van Abbe Museum, Eindhoven. "42,390 cubic feet Package" at the Walker Art Center, Minneapolis School of Art. **1968** "Wrapped Fountain" and "Wrapped Medieval Tower", Spoleto. Wrapping of a public building "Wrapped Kunsthalle Berne, Switzerland".

"5,600 Cubicmeter Package" documenta 4, Kassel, an Air Package 280 feet high. **1969** "Wrapped Museum of Contemporary Art" Chicago. "Wrapped Floor and Stairway" Museum of Contemporary Art, Chicago. "Wrapped Coast, Little Bay, One Million Square Feet, Sydney, Australia." **1970** Wrapped Monuments, Milano: Monument to Vittorio Emanuele, Piazza Duomo; Monument to Leonardo da Vinci, Piazza Scala. **1971** "Wrapped Floors and Covered Windows and Wrapped Walk Way", Museum Haus Lange, Krefeld, Germany. **1972** "Valley Curtain, Grand Hogback, Rifle, Colorado, 1970 – 1972." **1974** "The Wall, Wrapped Roman Wall", Via V. Veneto and Villa Borghese, Rome. "Ocean Front, Newport, Rhode Island. **1976** "Running Fence, Sonoma and Marin Counties, California, 1972 – 1976". 18 feet high, 24-1/2 miles long. **1978** "Wrapped Walk Ways, Loose Park, Kansas City, Missouri, 1977-1978. **1979** "The Mastaba of Abu Dhabi, Project for the United Arab Emirates," (in progress). **1979** "The Gates, Project for Central Park New York City", (in progress). **1983** "Surrounded Islands, Biscayne Bay, Greater Miami, Florida, 1980 – 1983." **1985** "The Pont Neuf Wrapped, Paris, 1975 – 1985." **1991** "The Umbrellas, Japan-U.S.A., 1984 – 1991." 3100 umbrellas. **1992** "Over The River, Project for the Arkansas River, Colorado", (in progress). **1995** "Wrapped Floors and Stairways and Covered Windows" Museum Würth, Künzelsau, Germany. "Wrapped Reichstag, Berlin, 1971 – 1995" 100,000 sq. meters (1,076,000 sq. ft.) of fabric, 15,600 m. (51,181 feet) of rope and 200 tons of steel. **1997** "Wrapped Trees, Project for Foundation Beyeler and Berower Park, Riehen-Basel, Switzerland", (in progress).
CATALOGUES RAISONNES: Hovdenakk, P. (ed.): C. Complete Editions 1964-1982. New York and Munich 1982.– Schellmann, J. and J. Benecke (ed.): C. Prints and Objects. Munich and New York 1988, 1996.– Varenne, D. (ed.): C. Catalogue raisonné (in preparation)
MONOGRAPHS, CATALOGUES: Alloway, L.: C. New York and London 1969, C. Stuttgart 1969.– Baal-Teshuva, J. (ed.): C. The Reichstag and Urbane Projects. Kunst-Haus, Vienna et al. Munich 1993 (cat.).– Baal-Teshuva, J. and W. Volz: C. & J.-C. Berlin 1995, New York 1995.– Bourdon, D.: C. New York 1970.– Bourdon, D. (ed.): C. Running Fence. New York 1978.– Bourdon, D. (ed.): C. Surrounded Islands. New York 1986.– Bourdon, D. (ed.): C. The Pont-Neuf Wrapped. New York 1990.– Bourdon, D. et al.: C. Milan 1965.– Bourdon, D.: C. The Pont Neuf, Wrapped. Cologne 1990.– C. John Kaldor Projekt 1990. Art Gallery of New South Wales. Sydney 1990 (cat.).– C. & J.-C. et al.: C. Le Pont-Neuf empaqueté. Paris 1990.– C. & J.-C.: Wrapped Reichstag. Berlin 1971-1995. Photographs: W. Volz, Picture notes: D. Bourdon. Cologne 1996.– Cullen, M. S. (ed.): C. Der Reichstag. Frankfurt-on-Main 1984.– Kellein, T.: Montage der Abstraktion. C.'s Kölner Anfänge zu Großprojekten. Cologne 1986.– Laporte, D. G.: C. New York 1985, Paris 1985.– Sommer, A. (ed.): C. The Pont Neuf, Wrapped, Paris 1974-1985. Städtisches Kunstmuseum Bonn. Bonn 1993 (cat.).– Spies, W.: C. The Running Fence. New York and Paris 1977, Stuttgart 1977.– Spies, W.: C. Surrounded Islands. Cologne 1984.– Vaizey, M.: C. New York 1990, Recklinghausen 1990.– Volz, W. (ed.): C. Surrounded Islands. Cologne 1985.– Weiss, E. et al. (ed.): C. Projekte in der Stadt. 1961-1981. Museum Ludwig. Cologne 1981 (cat.).– Yard, S. (ed.): C. Oceanfront. The Art Museum, Princeton (NJ) et al. Princeton 1975 (cat.)

ČIURLIONIS Mikolajus Konstantinas
1875 Varéna (Lithuania) – **1911** Pustelnik (near Warsaw)
Lithuanian musician and painter. **1884-1889** Studied at the Warsaw Institute of Music and **1901/02** at the Imperial Conservatory in Leipzig. **1904-1906** Attended the Warsaw School of Art. **1903-1905** First Symbolist works such as *The Flood* and the *Creation of the World*. **1906** Gave up traditional composition to develop a dynamic formal language of lines and circles creating an abstract pictorial space. **1907-1909** Exhibition curator and choir director in Vilnius. Author of therotical essays on art. **1908/09** Worked in St. Petersburg, painting the symbolic, abstract series *Sonata of the Stars* and *Sonata of the Pyramids* and landscapes of his homeland. **1909** Nervous breakdown. **1910** Admitted to a sanatorium near Warsaw. **1911/12** First posthumous solo-exhibitions in St. Petersburg and Moscow. Regarded as one of the founding fathers of abstract painting.
CATALOGUE RAISONNE: Landsbergis, V. (ed.): M. K. C. Vilnius 1992
MONOGRAPHS, CATALOGUES: Brockhaus, C. et al. (ed.): C. und die litauische Malerei 1900-1940. Wilhelm Lehmbruck Museum. Duisburg 1989 (cat.).– Landsbergis, V.: Tvorchestro Churlyonisa. Leningrad 1975.– Landsbergis, V. et al. (ed.): M. K. C. Vilnius 1997.– Rannit, A.: M. K. C. 1875-1911, Pionnier de l'art abstrait. Paris 1949.– Rannit, A.: M. K. C. Lithinian Visionary Painter. Chicago 1984.– Senn, A. et al. (ed.): M. K. C. Music of the Speres. Newtonville 1986.– Vaitkunas, C.: M. K. C. Dresden 1975.– Venclova, A.: M. K. C. Vilnius 1961.– Verkelyte-Federaviciene, B. et al. (ed.): M. K. C. Paintings, Sketches, Thoughts. Vilnius 1997.– Worobiow, N.: M. K. C. Der litauische Maler und Musiker. Leipzig 1938

CLAASEN Hermann
1899 Cologne – **1987** Cologne
German photographer. Before World War I experimented with photography using a camera constructed out of a cigar box and spectacle lense. **1914** Suspected of spying and arrested for photographing with his home-made camera. Gave up working in his parents' textile business in order to become a professional photographer. **1927/28** Pho-

tographed skaters on the frozen Rhine. **1930** Worked as a portrait and advertising photographer. Took colour photographs of paintings in Cologne museums and churches. **1942** Lost nearly all his early works in the bombardment of May 31. Despite strict prohibition, photographed war damage in the city of Cologne from **1943-1945**. In **1947** met Konrad Adenauer. Took portrait-photos of the chancellor. Further portraits of VIPs from political and cultural circles. **1950** Participation in the first photokina. In the 60s, focused on industrial and portrait photography.

CLEMENTE Francesco
born **1952** Naples
Italian painter. **1968** Acquaintance with Twombly in Rome, whose work made a great impression on him. **1970** Began studying architecture in Rome. **1971** Exhibited first collages at the Valle Giulia Gallery in Rome. Travels to India and Afghanistan, which he later revisited many times for longer periods. Elements of these foreign cultures appear in his paintings. **1980** Visited New York. First solo-exhibition at the Sperone Westwater Gallery. **1982** Installation of a studio in New York. Participation in documenta 7 in Kassel. Clemente's pictures combine abstract forms with figurative elements. Together with Chia and Cucchi, is one of the main representatives of the Italian Transavanguardia.
WRITINGS: F. C.: Chi pinge figura, si non puo esser lei non la puo porre. Adyar 1980.– Crone, R. and G. Marsh (ed.): An Interview with F. C. New York 1987 / Interview mit F. C. Cologne 1990
MONOGRAPHS, CATALOGUES:
Ammann, J.-C.: F. C. Bestiarium. Frankfurt-on-Main 1991.– Auping, M. (ed.): F. C. The John and Marble Ringling Museum of Art, Sarasota (FL) et al. New York 1985 (cat.).– Cortez, D. et al. (ed.): F. C. Fundación Caja de Pensiones. Madrid 1987 (cat.).– Crone, R. (ed.): F. C. Pastelle 1973-1983. Nationalgalerie, Berlin et al. Munich 1984 (cat.).– Francis, M. (ed.): F. C. Whitechapel Art Gallery, London et al. London 1983 (cat.).– Geldzahler, H. et al. (ed.): F. C. Affreschi. Pinturas al fresco. Fundación Caja de Pensiones. Madrid 1987 (cat.).– Haenlein, C. (ed.): F. C. Bilder und Skulpturen. Kestner-Gesellschaft. Hanover 1984 (cat.).– Koepplin, D. (ed.): F. C. Museum für Gegenwartskunst, Basel et al. Zurich 1987 (cat.).– McClure, M.: F. C. Testa coda. New York 1985.– Maenz, P. (ed.): F. C. "Il Viaggiatore Napoletano". Cologne 1982.– Percy, A. and R. Foye (ed.): F. C. Three Worlds. Philadelphia Museum of Art et al. New York 1990 (cat.)

CLOSE Chuck
born **1940** Monroe (WA)
American painter. **1958-1962** Studied at the University of Washington, **1962-1964** at Yale University in New Haven and **1964/65** at the Academy of Fine Arts in Vienna. **1967**

Lectureships at the School of Visual Arts in New York and at New York University. From **1970** did colour as well as black and white paintings, superimposing layers of primary colours to imitate commercial printing techniques. **1972** and **1977** participation in documenta 5 and 6 in Kassel. From **1979** painted over and manipulated enlarged polaroid photographs, and later used pâpier-maché collages to produce screen images. **1980** Retrospective in Minneapolis. Close is one of the most important representatives of American Superrealism and Photorealism. As demonstration material for his full size portraits, he uses self-made passport photos.
CATALOGUE RAISONE: C. C. Editions: A Catalogue Raisonné. The Butler Institute of American Art. Youngstown (OH) 1989.– Lyons, L. and R. Storr: C. C. Paintings and Drawings. New York 1987
MONOGRAPHS, CATALOGUES: Brehm, M. et al. (ed.): C. C. Werke 1967-1992. Stuttgart 1994.– C. C. Works on Paper. Contemporary Arts Museum. Houston 1985.– Danto, A. C. (ed.): C. C. Recent Paintings. The Pace Gallery. New York 1993 (cat.).– Kern, H. (ed.): C. C. Kunstraum. Munich 1979 (cat.).– Lyons, L. and M. Friedman (ed.): C. Portraits. Walker Art Center. Minneapolis 1980 (cat.).– Poetter, J. and H. Friedel (ed.): C. C. Retrospektive. Staatliche Kunsthalle Baden-Baden et al. Stuttgart 1994 (cat.).– Storr, R. (ed.): C. C. The Museum of Modern Art, New York et al. New York 1998 (cat.).– Westerbeck, C. (ed.): C. C. The Art Institute of Chicago. Chicago 1989 (cat.)

COBURN Alvin Langdon
1882 Boston – **1966** Colwyn Bay
American-English photographer. **1898** First photos. **1899-1900** Together with F. Holland Day, organized the exhibition "American Pictorial Photography". As an exponent of Pictorialism, he was convinced that photography could be as expressive a medium as painting. **1900** Travelled to Europe. **1902** Founding member of the Photo-secession. Specialized in portrait photography. Photographed numerous famous artists, authors and actors including Rodin, Henry James and Mark Twain. **1910** Published 20 photos in Stieglitz' Camera Work. **1912-1928** Worked as a photo-

grapher in London. **1916** Together with Gertrude Kaesebier and Clarence H. White, set up the group Pictorial Photographers of America **1917** Inspired by Cubism, produced his first abstract photos. **1917/18** Joined the Vorticists. **1931** Gave up photography.
WRITINGS: Gernsheim H. and A. (ed.): A. L. C. An Autobiography. London and New York 1966, 1978
MONOGRAPHS, CATALOGUES: Blatchford, P. (ed.): A. L. C. 1882-1966. Camden Arts Centre. London 1966 (cat.).– Weaver, M.: A. L. C.: Symbolist Photographer 1882-1966. New York 1986

COLVILLE Alex
born **1920** Toronto
Canadian painter. **1938-1942** Studied painting at Mount Allison University in Sackville, New Jersey. **1942-1946** Military service. From **1963** lived and worked as a freelance painter in Nova Scotia. **1967** Commissioned by the Canadian government to design various gold coins. **1946-1963** Lectureship at Mount Allison University and **1967/68** at the University of California in Santa Cruz. **1971** DAAD scholarship to Berlin. Numerous prizes and honorary awards from various universities and institutions in the United States and Canada. In his detailed and intensely atmospheric portrayals of man and nature, Colville displays a close affinity to the school of Magic Realism.
WRITINGS: Meston, G. and C. Maclean (ed.): A. C. Diary of a War Artist. Halifax 1981
CATALOGUE RAISONE: Dow, H. J. (ed.): The Art of A. C. Toronto 1972
MONOGRAPHS, CATALOGUES: Burnett, D. and M. Schiff (ed.): Art Gallery of Ontario. Toronto 1983 (cat.).– Burnett, D. and M. Schiff (ed.): A. C. Gemälde und Zeichnungen. Munich 1983.– A. C. Gemälde und Zeichnungen (1970-1977). Städtische Kunsthalle Düsseldorf. Düsseldorf 1977 (cat.).– C. Staatliche Kunsthalle Berlin et al. Berlin 1983 (cat.).– Cheetham, M. A.: A. C. Toronto 1994.– Dow, H.: The Art of A. C. Toronto 1972.– Fry, P. (ed.): A. C. Embarquement. Musée des Beaux-Arts. Montreal 1994 (cat.).– Schmied, W. and R. Melville (ed.): A. C. Kestner-Gesellschaft. Hanover 1969 (cat.)

CONSTANT
(Constant A. Nieuwenhuys)
born **1920** Amsterdam
Dutch painter, sculptor and architect. **1938/40** Attended the School of Applied Arts and **1940-1942** the Rijksakademie in Amsterdam. **1945** Abstract iron sculptures and expressive paintings. Together with Jorn, Corneille and Appel, founded the group Cobra. From **1952** focused on architecture, especially problems of regional and town planning. **1956** Participation at the Venice Biennale. **1959** and **1964** participation in documenta 2 and 3 in Kassel. **1958** His futuristic architectural ideas developed

into a visionary model of a "New Babylon" combining politics, architecture and aesthetics. **1965** Retrospective in the Gemeentemuseum in The Hague. **1991** Resistance Prize for artists.
WRITINGS: C.: New Babylon. The Hague 1974.– C.: A propos Cézanne. Amsterdam 1980
MONOGRAPHS, CATALOGUES: C. Schilderijen 1969-1977. Stedelijk Museum. Amsterdam 1978 (cat.).– Haaren, H. v.: C. Amsterdam 1967.– Honnef, K. (ed.): C. 1945-1983. Rheinisches Landesmuseum, Bonn. Cologne 1986 (cat.).– Jitta, M. J. et al. (ed.): C. Schilderijen 1940-1980. Haags Gemeentemuseum. The Hague 1980 (cat.).– Lambert, J.-C.: C. Les trois espaces. Paris 1992.– Lambert, J.-C.: C. Les Aquarelles. Paris 1994.– Locher, J. L. (ed.): C. Schilderijen 1940-1980. Gemeentemuseum. The Hague 1980 (cat.).– Vree, F. De: C. Schelderode 1972

CORINTH Lovis
1858 Tapiau – **1925** Zandvoort
German painter and graphic artist. **1876-1880** Attended the Königsberg Academy. **1880-1884** Studied with Franz von Defregger at the Munich Academy. **1884** Travelled to Antwerp where he became familiar with the works of Rubens. From **1884-1886** studied at the Académie Julian in Paris under Adolphe William Bougereau and Joseph Nicolas Robert-Fleury. Strongly impressed by works of Gustave Courbet. **1887-1891** Lived in Berlin. **1891** Moved to Munich for 8 years; first successes with landscapes, religious paintings and portraits. **1901** Returned to Berlin. Joined the Berlin Secession and, together with Walter Leistikow, founded a painting school for women. Inspired by Slevogt and Liebermann, developed an impressionist style. **1911** Chairman of the Berlin Secession. A stroke forced him to interrupt his creative work but then induced a change of style: violent brush strokes, strong colour and a sombre mood mark his later work, bringing it closer to Expressionism. From **1918** onwards lived in his country house at Urfeld on the Walchensee.
WRITINGS: Englert, K. (ed.): L. C. Gesammelte Schriften. Berlin 1920, 1995.– Hartleb, R. (ed.): L. C. Selbstbiographie. Leipzig 1993

CATALOGUES RAISONNES: Berend-Corinth, C. and B. Hernad (ed.): L. C. Die Gemälde. Werkverzeichnis. Munich 1992.– Müller, H. (ed.): Die späte Graphik von L. C. Hamburg 1960/The Late Graphic Work. San Francisco 1994.– Schwarz, K. (ed.): Das graphische Werk von L. C. 2 vols. Berlin 1917-1922. The Graphic Work. San Francisco 1985
MONOGRAPHS, CATALOGUES: Bussmann, G.: L. C. Carmencita. Malerei auf der Kante. Frankfurt-on-Main 1985.– Corinth, T.: L. C. Eine Dokumentation. Tübingen 1979.– Deecke, T.: Die Zeichnungen von L. C. Studien zur Stilentwicklung. Diss. Berlin 1973.– Felix, Z. (ed.): L. C. 1858-1925. Museum Folkwang, Essen et al. Cologne 1985 (cat.).– Hahn, P.: Das literarische Figurenbild bei L. C. Tübingen 1970.– Heise, C. G.: L. C. Bildnisse der Frau des Künstlers. Stuttgart 1958.– Keller, H.: L. C. Walchensee. Munich and Zurich 1976.– Müller, H.: Die späte Graphik von L. C. Hamburg 1960, San Francisco 1994.– Netzer, R.: L. C. Graphik. Munich 1958.– Osten, G. v. d.: L. C. Munich 1955.– Schröder, K. A. (ed.): L. C. 1858-1925. Landesmuseum Hanover et al. Munich 1992 (cat.).– Schuster, P.-K. et al. (ed.): L. C. Haus der Kunst, Munich et al. Munich 1996 (cat.).– Timm, W. et al. (ed.): L. C. Die Bilder vom Walchensee. Vision und Realität. Ostdeutsche Galerie, Regensburg et al. Regensburg 1986 (cat.).– Uhr, H.: L. C. Berkeley 1990

CORNEILLE
(Cornelis Guillaume van Beverloo)
born **1922** Liège
Belgian painter with Dutch parents. **1940-1943** Attended drawing classes at the Art Academy in Amsterdam. **1946** First solo-exhibition in Groningen. **1948** Together with Appel, Constant and Alechinsky, founded the group Cobra. **1948** and **1949** visits to Tunisia. Solo-exhibition in Paris followed by others in Amsterdam, Budapest, Copenhagen and Antwerp. **1950** Moved to Paris. Participated regularly in the Salon de Mai. Took part in the São Paulo Biennale in **1953** and was represented at the Venice Biennale in **1954**. Worked on ceramics with Jorn. **1956** Guggenheim Award for the Netherlands. **1957/58** Toured Africa visiting the Sudan, Nigeria, Ethiopia and Kenya, and gathering many strong impressions later incorporated into his work. **1958** Visited South America, Mexico and New York. **1959** and **1964** participation in documenta 2 and 3 in Kassel. Corneille's fine style of drawing and economic, delicate use of colour have close affinities to French Informel.
CATALOGUES RAISONNES: Birtwistle, G. et al. (ed.): C. L'Œuvre gravé 1948-1975. 1993.– Donkersloot-v. d. Berghe, P. (ed.): C. Het complete grafische werk 1948-1975. Amsterdam 1992.– Maurizzi, E. (ed.): L'Opera grafica di C. 1948-1974. Pollenza 1975
MONOGRAPHS, CATALOGUES: Bierman, M. den (ed.): C. An Early Bird.

Amsterdam 1997 (cat.).– Claus, H. Over het werk vamn C. Amsterdam 1951.– Cluny, C.-M.: C. Paris 1992.– C. Stedelijk Museum. Amsterdam 1966 (cat.).– Dupen, L. and E. Slagter (ed.): C.'s weergaloze werkelijkheid. Amsterdam 1997.– Gribling, F. T.: C. Amsterdam 1972.– Kerkhoven, T. A. T.: Het Afrikaanse gericht van C. The Hague 1992.– Lambert, J. C.: C. Paris 1960.– Lambert, J.-C.: C. L'Œil de l'été. Paris 1989.– Lambert, J.-C. (ed.): C. Het oog van de zomer. Jaski Art Gallery, Amsterdam. Venlo 1992 (cat.).– Laude, A.: C. Le Roi-image. Paris 1973.– Paquet, M.: C. La Sensualité du sensible. Paris 1988.– Paquet, M.: C. Peintures et gouaches. Paris 1989.– Slagter, E.: C. Schelderode 1976

CORNELL Joseph
1903 Nyack (NY) – **1972** New York
American sculptor. Originally a self-taught painter. **1932** Inspired by works of Max Ernst and other Surrealists, produced his first assemblages, collages and boxes. Participation in the exhibition "Surrealist Group Show" at the Julien Levy Gallery in New York. **1939-1945** Close contact with the Surrealists living in New York. First film projects. **1967** Retrospectives at the Pasadena Art Museum and at the Solomon R. Guggenheim Museum, New York. **1968** and **1972** Participation in documenta 4 and 5 in Kassel. Cornell's poetic, farcical assemblies of commonplace objects, usually displayed in glass boxes, anticipate various neo-dadaist techniques and Pop Art trends.
WRITINGS: Caws, M. A. (ed.): J. C.'s Theater of the Mind. Selected Diaries, Lettersand Files. New York 1993
MONOGRAPHS, CATALOGUES: Ashton, D.: A J. C. Album. New York 1974, 1989.– J. C. Musée d'Art Moderne de la Ville de Paris. Paris 1981 (cat.).– Hartigan, L. R. (ed.): J. C. An Exploration of Sources. National Museum of American Art. Washington 1983.– Huici, F. (ed.): J. C. Fundación Juan March. Madrid 1984 (cat.).– Jaguer, E.: J. C. Jeux, jouets et mirages. Paris 1989.– McShine, K. (ed.): J. C. The Museum of Modern Art, New York et al. New York 1980, Munich 1990 (cat.).– Porter, F. (ed.): J. C. Pasadena Art Museum. Pasadena 1966 (cat.).– Simic, C.: Dimestore Alchemy. The Art of J. C. Hopewell (NJ) 1992.– Solomon, D.: Utopia Parkway: The Life and Work of J. C. New York 1997.– Starr, S. L.: J. C. Art and Metaphysics, New York 1982.– Starr, S. L. and M. Kobayashi (ed.): J. C. Museum of Modern Art, Kamakura. New York 1994 (cat.).– Tashjian, D.: J. C. Gifts of Desire. Miami Beach 1992.– Waldman, D.: J. C. New York 1977

CORPORA Antonio
born **1909** Tunis
Italian painter. Studied art in Tunis. Moved to Florence in **1929** where he copied Old Masters in the Uffizi. **1930** Continued to study in Paris, encouraged and supported by

the art dealer Léopold Zborowski, a friend of Modigliani. Up to **1937** lived alternately in Paris and Tunis. Influenced by French painting, developed a neo-cubist style and rejected the traditional ideas of the Novecento group. **1947** Joined Fronte Nuovo delle Arti whose members, such as Vedova, Birolli and Giulio Turcato, represented a variety of abstract styles. After some changes in membership and under the name Gruppo degli otto Pittori italiani this group made its first public appearance at the **1952** Venice Biennale exhibiting gestural abstract paintings. **1955** and **1959** Participation in documenta 1 and 2 in Kassel. Corpora has been represented in numerous exhibitions throughout Italy, Tunisia and France.
CATALOGUE RAISONNE: Steingräber, E. and H. Friedel (ed.): A. C. Druckgraphik. Werkkatalog. Bayerische Staatsgemäldesammlungen in der BMW-Galerie. Munich 1976 (cat)
MONOGRAPHS, CATALOGUES: Ballo, G.: C. Roma 1956.– Frazzetto, G. (ed.): A. C. Opere 1945-1988. Monastero dei Benedettini. Catania 1990 (cat.).– Monferini, A. (ed.): C. Galleria Nazionale d'Arte Moderna, Roma. Segrate 1988 (cat.).– Restany, P. et al. (ed.): C. Gallerie dell'Accademia, Venice. Roma 1988 (cat.).– Schulz-Hoffmann, C. (ed.): C. Bayerische Staatsgemäldesammlungen, Munich. Baierbrunn 1981 (cat.).– Steingräber, E. et al. (ed.): A. C. Die Grenze des Unendlichen. Galerie Günther Franke. Munich 1973 (cat.).– Viviani, C.: A. C. Roma 1971

COTTINGHAM Robert
born **1935** Brooklyn (NY)
American painter. **1959-1964** Studied at the Pratt Institute in Brooklyn. **1962** Supplementary studies in design. **1955-1958** Military service. **1959-1964** Art Director for advertising in New York and in **1964-1968** in Los Angeles. **1968** First solo-exhibition at the Molly Barnes Gallery in Los Angeles. As a freelance painter he specialized in hyperrealistic representations of neon-advertising and store fronts for which he used sections of enlarged photographs. **1969/70** Lectureship at the Art Centre of Design, Los Angeles. **1972** Participation in documenta 5 in Kassel. Received the National Endowment for the Arts Grant in **1974** and, in **1988**, the Artist of the Year Award from the Fairfield

Chamber of Commerce, Connecticut.
MONOGRAPHS, CATALOGUES: R. C. Wichita Art Museum. Wichita (KS) 1983 (cat.).– R. C. The Museum of Art, Science and Industry. Bridgeport (CT) 1986 (cat.)

CRAGG Tony
born **1949** Liverpool
English sculptor. **1966-1968** Worked as a laboratory technician in the chemical industry. **1970-1973** Studied painting at Wimbledon School of Art. **1973** Studied sculpture at the Royal College of Art in London. **1976** Lectureship at the Art Academy in Metz. **1977** Moved to Germany. **1979** First solo-exhibition at the Lisson Gallery, London. Ambiguous, farcical sculptures made of materials such as synthetic plastics, consumer waste, metal and gum. **1982** and **1987** participation in documenta 7 and 8 in Kassel. **1988** Received the Turner Prize in London. Represented Great Britain at the Venice Biennale. **1989** Professorship for sculpture at the Düsseldorf Academy. With his murals of plastic debris and object arrangements made from stone, glass, silicates and other materials, Cragg highlights the material wealth of this world, as manifest in nature, science, technology and industry, and draws attention to the prefabricated nature of everyday objects and modern life.
WRITINGS: T. C. Schriften 1981-1972. Brussels 1992 (cat)
MONOGRAPHS, CATALOGUES: Barnes, L. et al. (ed.): T. C. Sculpture 1975-1990. Newport Harbor Art Museum et al. London 1990 (cat.).– Castro Flórez, F. C. et al. (ed.): T. C. Museo Nacional Centro de Arte Reina Sofía. Madrid 1995 (cat.).– Celant, G. and D. Eccher (ed.): T. C. Galleria Civica d'Arte Contemporanea, Trento. Milan 1994 (cat.).– Celant, G.: T. C. London 1996.– Cooke, L. (ed.): T. C. Hayward Gallery. London 1987 (cat.).– T. C. Openluchtmuseum voor Beeldhouwerkunst. Middelheim 1997 (cat.).– Grenier, C. et al. (ed.): T. C. Paris 1995 (cat.).– Haenlein, C. (ed.): T. C. Skulpturen. Kestner-Gesellschaft. Hanover 1985 (cat.).– Martin, J.-H. (ed.): T. C. Kunsthalle Bern. Bern 1983 (cat.).– Mittringer, M. (ed.): T. C. Silikate. Holbein-Haus. Augsburg 1994 (cat.).– Müller, M. (ed.): T. C. Kunstsammlung Nordrhein-Westfalen. Düsseldorf 1989 (cat.).– Pohlen, A. (ed.): T. C. Palais des Beaux-Arts. Brussels 1985.– Schimmel, P. (ed.): T. C. Sculpture 1975-1990. Newport Harbor Art Museum. London 1991 (cat.).– Schwarz, M. (ed.): T. C. Skulpturen. Badischer Kunstverein. Karlsruhe 1982 (cat.).– Wildermuth, A.: T. C. Zwei Landschaften. Basel 1983.– Wildermuth, A.: T. C. Eine Werkauswahl. Stuttgart 1990.– Wildermuth, A. (ed.): T. C. Dessins, Zeichnungen. Stuttgart 1994 (cat.)

CRIPPA Roberto
1921 Monza – **1972** Milan
Italian painter. Studied at the Milan Brera

for the house of Pierre Cocteau in the Touraine, through which he developed a naturalistic formal language. **1973** First retrospective at the Dépot 15 gallery in Paris.
MONOGRAPHS, CATALOGUES: J. C. Musée d'Art Moderne. Troyes 1986 (cat.).– Karshan, D.: C. Paris 1973.– Reichard, R.: J. C. 1888-1971. Einführung in das plastische Werk. 2 vols. Frankfurt-on-Main 1983.– Reichard, R. (ed.): J. C. Kubistische und nachkubistische Skulpturen 1913-1950. Galerie Reichard. Frankfurt-on-Main 1988 (cat.)

School with Achille Funi and Carrà till **1940**. Influenced by Matta, he developed an abstract-expressionistic style. With his free, expansive calligraphy, he ranks with Fontana and Emilio Scanavino as one of the most important protagonists of the Movimento Spaziale in Italy. He participated regularly in the Venice Biennale. From **1951** his works were also exhibited in the United States. **1955** Participation in documenta 1 in Kassel. In **1972** he died in an airplane crash near Milan.
MONOGRAPHS, CATALOGUES: Ballo, G. (ed.): R. C. Palazzo Reale. Milan 1971 (cat.).– Giani, G. (ed.): R. C. Venice 1954.– R. C. Galleria Cortina. Milan 1971 (cat.).– Tapié, M.: C. Milan 1969

CROTTI Jean
1878 Bulle (near Fribourg) – **1958** Paris
Swiss painter. **1896** Studied applied art in Munich and then worked for four years as a stage designer in Marseille. From **1901** studied in Paris. Travelled to Italy in **1905** and **1912**. Was influenced by Cubism and after **1923** incorporated Orphist ideas into his paintings. **1915/16** Lived in New York where he made friends with Duchamp. First paintings on glass and mechanical constructions. **1919** Married the artist Suzanne Duchamp, sister of Marcel Duchamp, in Paris, and exhibited with her in **1921** and **1923**. Bought a house in Mougins in **1925**, where he was a neighbour of Picabia. **1937** Gave an abstract, coloured light performance at the Paris World Fair. **1947** Exhibited his *Gémeaux* (Gemini) at the cultural centre of the French Embassy in New York, demonstrating a new technique of painting on glass.
MONOGRAPHS, CATALOGUES: Camfield, W. A. and J.-H. Martin (ed.): Tabu Dada. J. C. & Suzanne Duchamp 1915-1922. Kunsthalle Bern et al. Bern 1983 (cat.).– Cartier, J. A.: J. C. (n. p.) 1956.– J. C. 1878-1958. Gimpel Fils Gallery, London et al. London 1974 (cat.).– J. C. Centre Georges Pompidou. Paris 1983 (cat.).– George, W.: J. C. Paris 1930.– George, W.: J. C. et la primauté du spirituel. Geneva 1959

CRUZ-DIEZ Carlos
born **1923** Caracas
Venezuelan painter and kinetic artist. **1940**-

1945 Studied at the Escuela de Artes Plásticas in Caracas. **1944–1955** Graphic designer for the Creole Petrolium Corporation. **1946**–**1951** Art director for the advertising company McCann-Erickson. **1957** Set up his own graphic and industrial design company. **1958–1960** Second chancellor of the Escuela de Artes Plásticas in Caracas. **1959** Started his series *Psychochromatics* and *Chromatic-Interferences*. **1960** Took part in the exhibition "Mouvement" at the Stedelijk Museum in Amsterdam and at the Moderna Museet in Stockholm. **1962** Participation at the Venice Biennale and in **1963** in the exhibition "Nouvelle Tendance" in Zagreb. **1965** First solo-exhibition in London and Paris. **1967** Received special honours at the São Paulo Biennale. Published the book *Refléxion sobre el color* in **1989**. Cruz-Diez experiments in his pictures and objects with optical phenomena set up by overlapping colour fields and stripes. His works, in which objects can be manipulated by the spectator, are closely linked to kinetic art.
WRITINGS: C.-D.: Reflexión sobre el color. Caracas 1989
MONOGRAPHS, CATALOGUES: Bordier, R.: C.-D. ou la couleur comme événement. Paris 1972.– Boulton, A.: C.-D. Caracas 1975.– Clay, J.: C.-D. et les trois étapes de la couleur moderne. Paris 1969.– C. C.-D. Musée des Beaux-Arts. Caracas 1960 (cat.).– C. C.-D. Didattica e polemica del colore. Centro iniziative culturali. Pordenone 1981 (cat.).– Guevara, R. (ed.): C. C.-D. Museo de Arte Contemporánea. Caracas 1974 (cat.)

CSAKY Joseph
1888 Szeged (Hungary) – **1971** Paris
Hungarian-French sculptor. **1908** Moved to Paris after attending a few classes at the Academy of Applied Arts in Budapest. Acquaintance with Léger and Archipenko, later with the Cubists centred around Picasso and Braque. **1911** Exhibition at the Salon d'Automne in Paris. **1912** Some works exhibited at the Salon de la Section d'Or and in **1913/14** at the Salon des Indépendants. **1921–1923** Participation in the permanent exhibition "Maître du Cubisme". **1922** Acquired French citizenship. **1922** Member of the Hungarian artists' group KUT. **1927–1930** Created fish sculptures

CUCCHI Enzo
born **1950** Morro d'Alba
Italian painter, sculptor and draughtsman. Apprenticed to a restorer. **1966–1968** Worked as a surveyor before becoming a freelance artist. **1977** First solo-exhibition in Milan. **1979** Together with Chia, Clemente, Paladino and others, formed the group Transavanguardia. **1982** and **1987** participation in documenta 7 and 8 in Kassel. **1984** Designed a sculpture for the Bruglinger-Park in Basel, followed by a series of works for public places. **1986** Retrospective at the Pompidou Centre, Paris and solo-exhibition at the Guggenheim Museum, New York. Numerous stage and costume designs for the theatre, among others for operas by Gioacchino Rossini and dramas by Heinrich von Kleist. Absorbed elements of painterly tradition in his pictures and sculptures, combining them in his own individual pictorial and sign language.
WRITINGS: E. C.: Disegno finito. Roma 1978
MONOGRAPHS, CATALOGUES: Ammann, J.-C. et al.: E. C. Giulio Cesare Rom. Stedelijk Museum, Amsterdam et al. Amsterdam 1983 (cat.).– Barzel, A. (ed.): E. C. Centro per l'Arte Contemporanea Luigi Pecci. Prato 1989 (cat.).– Blistène, B. et al. (ed.): E. C. Centre Georges Pompidou. Paris 1986 (cat.).– E. C. Sparire. 2 vols. New York 1987.– Delgado, G. (ed.): E. C. Musée d'Art Contemporain de Bordeaux. Bordeaux 1986 (cat.).– Eccher, D.: E. C. Roma. Paris 1992.– Felix, Z. (ed.): E. C. Museum Folkwang. Essen 1982 (cat.).– Friedel, H. (ed.): E. C. Testa. 2 vols. Städtische Galerie im Lenbachhaus, Munich et al. Munich 1987 (cat.).– Gianelli, I. (ed.): C. Castello di Rivoli, Museo d'Arte Contemporanea. Milan 1993 (cat.).– Hohl, H. et al. (ed.): E. C. Roma. Hamburger Kunsthalle. Stuttgart 1992 (cat.).– Perucchi, U. (ed.): E. C. Zeichnungen 1975-1989 / La disegna 1975-1988 / Drawings 1975-1989. Kunsthaus Zurich et al. unich 1988, New York 1990 (cat.).– Schneider, U. (ed.): E. C. Näher zum Licht. Aachen 1997 (cat.).– Schulz-Hoffmann, C. and U. Weisner (ed.): E. C. Guida al disegno. Kunsthalle Bielefeld et al. Munich 1987 (cat.).– Schwander, M. and D. Davvetas: E. C. L'ombra vede. 1987.– Waldman, D. (ed.): E. C. Solomon R. Guggenheim Museum. New York 1986 (cat.)

DADO
(Miodrag Djuric)
born **1933** Cetinje (Montenegro)
Montenegran painter. **1947–1952** Studied at the Academy of Arts in Hercegnovi, Montenegro and in **1947–1952** at the Belgrade Academy. **1956–1958** Worked as a lithographer in Paris. Discovered by Dubuffet, he worked as a freelance painter in Paris and Courcelle from **1958** and had his first solo-exhibition at the Daniel Cordier gallery in the same year. **1964** and **1977** participation in documenta 3 and 6 in Kassel. **1982** Retrospective at the Pompidou Centre in Paris. Dado's paintings, which are a blend of veristic Realism and magic Surrealism, are animated by illusory figures.
MONOGRAPHS, CATALOGUES: Barousse, P.: D. Un signe des temps. Musée Ingres, Montabon. Paris 1984 (cat.).– Bosquet, A.: D. Un univers sans repos. Paris 1991.– D. Centre National d'Art Contemporain. Paris 1970 (cat.).– Derouet, C. (ed.): D. Dessins, tekeningen. Galerie Isy Brachot. Brussels 1982 (cat.).– Louis-Combet, C.: Dadomorphes et dadopathes. Montolieu 1992.– Picon, G.: D. Galerie J. Bucher. Paris 1971 (cat.)

DAI Guangyu
born **1955** Cchengdu (Province of Sichuan)
Chinese painter. **1986** Founded the Red-Yellow-Blue Group. **1994** Invited by the US information office to spend two months in the USA as a guest researcher.

DALI Salvador
1904 Figueras (near Gerone) –
1989 Figueras
Spanish artist. Even as a student Dalí was a trouble-maker: after three years of studying at the Madrid Academy, he was expelled in **1924**. **1925** Became interested in the psychoanalytical theories of Sigmund Freud. **1929** Moved to Paris, the centre of Surrealism. Developed "critical paranoia", a positive form of automatism, whereby he aimed to portray not visible objects but their associated images and subconscious meanings. Stay in Cadaqués together with Magritte, Luis Buñuel, Paul Eluard and his wife Gala. Gala, the Muse of the Surrealists, was to become Dalí's lover. Collaboration on Buñuel's film *Un Chien andalou* and in

1931 on the film *L'Age d'or*. **1937** Despite being officially excluded by Breton, he participated in the activities of the Surrealist Circle. Travelling through Italy in **1937–1939**, he studied Palladian architecture and Renaissance and Baroque painting. **1940** Went to America where he proclaimed his return to classical art. **1949** Returned to Port Lligat in Spain and converted to Catholicism. **1951** Published his *Mystical Manifesto*. **1971** Opening of a Dalí Museum which was later transferred to St. Petersburg, Florida in **1982**. In **1979**, the largest-ever Dalí retrospective at the Pompidou Centre in Paris, and the Tate Gallery in London.
WRITINGS: S. D.: Diary of a Genius. Garden City 1965.– S. D.: La conquête de l'irrationnel. Paris 1935, 1971.– S. D. and F. G. Lorca: Correspondance 1925-1936. Paris 1987.– Mathes, A. and T. D. Stegmann (ed.): S. D. Unabhängigkeitserklärung der Phantasie und Erklärung der Rechte des Menschen auf seine Verrücktheit. Gesammelte Schriften. Munich 1974
CATALOGUES RAISONNES: Descharnes, R. and G. Néret (ed.): S. D. The Paintings. 2 vols. Cologne 1994.– Löpsinger L. and R. Michler (ed.): S. D. Das druckgraphische Werk 1924-1980. 2 vols. Munich 1994. S. D. Catalogue Raisonné of Etchings and Mixed-Media Prints 1924-1980. 2 vols. Munich 1995
MONOGRAPHS, CATALOGUES: Abadie, D. (ed.): S. D. Rétrospective 1920-1980. Centre Georges Pompidou. Paris 1979 (cat.)/S. D. Retrospektive 1920-1980. Centre Georges Pompidou, Paris. Munich 1980 (cat.).– Abadie, D. (ed.): La Vie publique de S. D. Paris 1979.– Ajame, P.: La double vie de S. D. Paris 1984.– Bosquet, A.: Entretiens avec S. D. Paris 1983.– Cowles, F.: Der Fall S. D. Munich 1981.– S. D. Museum Boymans-van Beuningen. Rotterdam 1974 (cat.).– S. D. 400 Obras de S. D. del 1914 al 1983. Palau Reial de Pedralbes, Barcelona et al. Madrid 1983 (cat.).– Descharnes, R.: S. D. Stuttgart and Munich 1985.– Descharnes, R. and G. Néret: S. D. Cologne 1990.– Descharnes, R.: D. The Work, the Man. New York 1989, 1997.– Etcherington-Smith, M.: D. une vie. Paris 1994.– Finkelstein, H.: S. D.'s Art and Writing 1927-1942. The Metamorphoses of Narcissus. New York 1996.– Gallwitz, K. (ed.): D. Staatliche Kunsthalle Baden-Baden. Baden-Baden 1971 (cat.).– Gibson, I. et al. (ed.): S. D. The Early Years. Hayward Gallery, London et al. London 1994 (cat.).– Gibson, I.: The Shameful Life of S. D. London 1997.– Gomez de la Serna, R.: D. Paris 1989.– Gorsen, P.: S. D. Der kritische Paranoiker. Frankfurt-on-Main 1983.– Lubar, R. S. (ed.): The S. D. Museum Collection. Boston 1991.– Maur, K. v. (ed.): S. D. 1904-1989. Staatsgalerie Stuttgart et al. Stuttgart 1989 (cat.).– Musidlak-Schlott, G.: S. D. und die Bildtradition. Tübingen 1982.– Parinaud, A. (ed.): The Unspeakable Confessions of S. D. New York 1981.– Passoni, F. et al.: D. nella terza dimensione. Milan 1986.– Radford, R.: S. D. London 1997.– Raeburn, M.: S. D. The Early Years. Hayward Gallery, London et al. London and New York 1994 (cat.).– Rey, H.-F.: D. dans son labyrinthe. Paris 1974.– Rogerson, M.: The D. Scandal. An Investigation. London 1987.– Rojas, C.: El mundo mitico y magico de S. D. Barcelona 1985.– Romero, L.: D. Barcelona 1975.– Santos Torroella, R.: La miel es más dulce que la sangre: las épocas lorquiana y freudiana de S. D. Barcelona 1984.– Schiebler, R.: Das geheime Leben des S. D. Munich 1984.– Schiebler, R. (ed.): D., Lorca, Buñuel. Aufbruch in Madrid. Stuttgart 1993.– Secrest, M.: S. D. The Surrealist Jester. London and New York 1986/S. D. Bern and Munich

1987/S. D. L'extravagant surréaliste. Paris 1988.– Toroella, R. S.: S. D. Richford 1997

DARBOVEN Hanne
born **1941** Munich
German artist. Studied at the Hamburg School of Fine Arts. **1966–1968** Lived in New York, where she established contact with minimal artists such as Sol LeWitt and Carl Andre. Serial drawings with numbers on graph paper with millimetre squares. **1967** First solo-exhibition at the Konrad Fischer gallery in Düsseldorf. From **1968** created registers of calendar dates, set out in columns and strictly organised squares. **1969** Return to Hamburg. **1972–1982** Participation in documenta 5–7 in Kassel. After **1973** worked on the subject of re-writing literature (among others Homer's *Odyssey* and Heinrich Heine's *Atta Troll*). Her pages entitled *Writing Time* of **1975–1980** are concerned with historical and political events. **1978** Integrated photographic material in her writing-drawings. **1982** Participation at the Venice Biennale. **1986** Won the Edwin Scharff Award in Hamburg. **1989** Retrospective at the Musée d'Art Moderne de la Ville de Paris.
WRITINGS: H. D.: Das Sehen ist nämlich auch eine Kunst. Brussels and Hamburg 1974.– H. D.: El Lissitzky. Hamburg and Brussels 1974.– H. D.: New York Diary. New York 1976.– H. D. Briefe. Stuttgart 1995
CATALOGUE RAISONNE: H. D. Kinder dieser Welt. Stuttgart 1996 (cat.)
MONOGRAPHS, CATALOGUES: Bischoff, U. (ed.): H. D. Evolution "86". Staatsgalerie moderner Kunst. Munich 1991 (cat.).– Burgbacher-Krupka, I.: Konstruiert, Literarisch, Musikalisch/Constructed, Literary, Musical. H. D. The Sculpting of Time. Stuttgart 1994.– Cladders, J. and H. Honnef (ed.): H. D. Ein Monat, ein Jahr, ein Jahrhundert. Kunstmuseum Basel. Basel 1974 (cat.).– Cladders, J. (ed.): H. D. Pavillon der Bundesrepublik Deutschland. Venice 1982 (cat.).– H. D. Westfälischer Kunstverein. Münster 1971 (cat.).– H. D. Een maand, een jaar, een eeuw. Werken von 1968 en met 1974. Stedelijk Museum. Amsterdam 1975 (cat.).– H. D. Musée d'Art Moderne de la Ville de Paris. Paris 1986 (cat.).– H. D. Quartett "88". University of Chicago. Cologne 1990 (cat.).– H. D. Evolution Leibniz 1986. Sprengel Museum, Hanover. Stuttgart 1997.– Honnef, K. et al. (ed.): H. D. Bismarckzeit. Rheinisches Landesmuseum. Bonn 1979 (cat.).– Jochimsen, M. (ed.): H. D. Wende "80". Bonner Kunstverein. Bonn 1982 (cat.).– Meyer, F. (ed.): H. D. Stedelijk Museum. Amsterdam 1975 (cat.).– Tacke, C. (ed.): H. D. Für Rainer Werner Fassbinder. Kunstraum. Munich 1988 (cat.).– Vries, G. d. (ed.): ART RANDOM. H. D. Kyoto Shoin. Kyoto 1990 (cat.).– Vries, G. d. (ed.): H. D. Die geflügelte Erde, Requiem. Deichtorhallen, Hamburg. Stuttgart 1991 (cat.).– Weiss, E. (ed.): H. D. XII. Bienal. São Paulo 1973 (cat.)

DAVIE Alan
born **1920** Grangemouth
Scottish painter. **1937–1940** Studied at Edinburgh College of Art and at the Royal Scottish Academy. **1941–1946** Military service. **1945** First abstract colour compositions, influenced by Klee and the formal language of Picasso. **1946** First exhibition in Edinburgh. **1947/48** Public performances as jazz musician. **1948** Extended travels to France, Spain and Italy. Intensive study of Pollock's paintings. Settled in London in **1949**. From **1953** trained goldsmiths at the Central School of Arts and Crafts in London. **1956** Visited New York. Won Prix Guggenheim at the Musée d'Art Moderne, Paris. From **1959** taught at the Central School in London. **1959–1977** Participation in documenta 2, 3 and 6 in Kassel. **1963** Received special honours at the São Paulo Biennale. Graphic award in Krakow. **1973–1975** Travelled around the central American archipelago.
CATALOGUE RAISONNE: Bowness, A. (ed.): A. D. London 1967
MONOGRAPHS, CATALOGUES: A. D. Kunsthalle Bern et al. Bern 1963 (cat.).– A. D. Kunstverein für die Rheinlande und Westfalen. Düsseldorf 1968 (cat.).– A. D. Royal Scottish Academy, Edinburgh 1972 (cat.).– Hall, D. and M. Tucher (ed.): A. D. London 1992.– Horowitz, M.: A. D. London 1963.– Robertson, B. (ed.): A. D. Whitechappel Art Gallery. London 1958 (cat.).– Tucker, M. (ed.): A. D. Quest for the Miraculous. New York 1992

DAVIS Douglas
born **1933** Washington
American performance and video artist. **1948–1950** Studied at Abbott Art School, Washington, **1952–1958** at the American University, Washington, and at Rutgers State University in New Brunswick (NJ). From **1960** worked as an art critic and editor for *Art in America*, *Newsweek* and other magazines. **1967** First events and performances. From **1970** video series and actions. **1972** First solo-exhibition at Everson Museum of Art, Syracuse (NY). From **1976** taught at many art colleges and universities. **1977** DAAD scholarship to Berlin and participation in documenta 6 in Kassel. **1981** Grant from the National Endowment for the Arts, Washington. **1988**

Retrospective at the Solomon R. Guggenheim Museum, New York and **1995** at the Muzeum Sztuki, Lódz. Davis has written several books on art and art theory.
WRITINGS: D. D.: Art and the Future. New Yok 1973.– D. D.: Vom Experiment zur Idee. Die Kunst des 20. Jahrhunderts im Zeichen von Wissenschaft und Technologie. Cologne 1975.– D. D.: Artculture: Essays on the Post-Modern. New York 1977.– D. D.: Photography as Fine Art. Tokyo 1993, New York 1984.– D. D.: The Museum Transformed. New York 1990.– D. D.: The Five Myths of TV Power. New York 1993
MONOGRAPHS, CATALOGUES: Czartoryska, U. (ed.): D. D. Redness. Muzeum Sztuki. Lodz 1995 (cat.).– D. D. Arbeiten 1970-1977. Neuer Berliner Kunstverein und Berliner Künstlerprogramm des DAAD. Berlin 1978 (cat.).– Kuspit, D.: D. D. Solomon R. Guggenheim Museum. New York 1988 (cat.).– Stanislawski, R. (ed.): D. D. Video Objekty Grafika. Muzeum Sztuki. Lódz 1982 (cat.)

DAVIS Stuart
1894 Philadelphia – **1964** New York
American painter. **1909–1912** Private instruction from Robert Henri in New York. **1913** Participation in the Armory Show. **1913–1916** Illustrator and cartoonist for *The Masses* and *Harper's Weekly*. **1917** First solo-exhibition at the Sheridan Square Gallery in New York. About **1919** took up non-figurative painting. **1927/28** First abstract paintings, including the series Eggbeater. **1928** Travelled to Paris. **1933–1940** Held numerous public offices as a politician and trade unionist. Publisher of the journal *Art Front*. **1949–1950** Lectureship at the New York School for Social Research, New York and in **1951** at Yale University. **1956** Member of the National Institute of Arts and Letters. **1957** Retrospective in Minneapolis and **1966** in Paris. Outlined his attitude towards modern art in numerous essays and in his autobiography.
CATALOGUES RAISONNES: Agee, W. C. (ed.): S. D. A Catalogue Raisonné. New Haven (CT) 1989.– J. Myers and D. Kelder (ed.): S. D. Graphic Works and Related Paintings. With a Catalogue Raisonné of His Prints. Amon Carter Museum, Fort Worth. Austin 1986 (cat.)
MONOGRAPHS, CATALOGUES: Arnason, H. H. (ed.): S. D. Memorial Exhibition 1894-1964. Smithsonian Institution, Washington et al. Washington 1965 (cat.).– Blesh, R.: S. D. New York 1960.– S. D. The Drawings of S. D. American Federation of Fine Arts, New York et al. New York 1992 (cat.).– S. D. Peggy Guggenheim Collection. Venice 1997 (cat.).– Goosen, E. C.: S. D. New York 1959.– Hills, P.: S. D. New York 1996.– Kelder, D.: S. D. New York 1971.– Lane, J. R. (ed.): S. D. Art and Theory. The Brooklyn Museum. New York 1978 (cat.).– Rylands, P. (ed.): S. D. Venice et al. 1997 (cat.).– Sims, L. S. (ed.): S. D. American Painter. Metropolitan Museum of

Art, New York et al. New York 1991 (cat.).– Sims, P. (ed.): S. D. Whitney Museum of American Art. New York 1980 (cat.).– Wilkin, K.: S. D. New York 1987

DAVRINGHAUSEN Heinrich Maria
1894 Aachen – **1970** Cagnes-sur-Mer
German painter. **1913/14** Studied at the Düsseldorf Academy and took private lessons from Wilhelm Eckstein. **1914** Exhibition at Alfred Flechtheim's gallery in Düsseldorf. Visited Carlo Mense in Ascona. **1915–1918** Lived in Berlin. In **1918** moved to Munich. Participation in the exhibition "New Religious Art" at the Kunsthalle Mannheim. **1919** Solo-exhibition in Hans Goltz' gallery Neue Kunst in Munich. Participation in the first exhibition of the Junges Rheinland (Young Rhineland), later known as the Rhenish Expressionists, at the Düsseldorf Kunsthalle. **1922** Returned to Berlin. **1924/25** Travelled to Spain. Participated in the exhibition "Neue Sachlichkeit" (New Objectivity) at the Kunsthalle Mannheim. In **1927** he moved to Cologne and made friends with Räderscheidt. **1928** Participation in the exhibition "Raum und Wand" (Space and Wall) in Cologne. **1933** Fled to France. **1939/40** Internment in Cagnes-sur-Mer and escape from the Germans. **1945** Returned to Cagnes-sur-Mer.
CATALOGUES RAISONNES: Eimert, D. (ed.): H. M. D. Leben und Werk. Cologne 1995.– Heusinger v. Waldegg, J. (ed.): H. M. D. 1894-1970. Monographie mit Werkkatalog 1912-1932. Cologne and Bonn 1977.– Tekampe, H. (ed.): H. M. D. 1894-1970. Monographie und Werkverzeichnis. Leopold-Hoesch-Museum Düren. Cologne 1995 (cat.)
MONOGRAPHS, CATALOGUES: Eimert, D. (ed.): H. M. D. Emigration 1933-1945. Leopold-Hoesch-Museum. Düren 1988 (cat.).– Eimert, D. (ed.): H. M. D. Spätwerk. Leopold-Hoesch-Museum. Düren 1991 (cat.).– Heusinger v. Waldegg, J. (ed.): H. M. D. Der General. Aspekte eines Bildes. Rheinisches Landesmuseum. Bonn 1975 (cat.)

DE CHIRICO Giorgio
1888 Volos (Greece) – **1978** Rome
Italian painter. **1906–1908** Studied painting under Max Klinger at the Munich Academy. Moved to Florence in **1910**. From **1911–1915**

lived in Paris, where he had contact with the Cubists centred around Apollinaire, and painted the series *Italian Squares*, combining his impressions of piazzas in Turin and Florence with classic architecture. **1915** Military service in Italy. **1917** Together with Carrà, Alberto Savinio and Morandi, developed *Pittura Metafisica* and became the most important representative of that style. **1918/19** Lived in Rome and had contact with artists and writers contributing to the journal *Valori Plastici*. Tended towards classical composition in his paintings. **1924–1931** Joined the Surrealists led by Breton in Paris and participated in the exhibition "La Peinture Surréaliste" in **1925**. **1926** Exhibited with the group Novecento in Milan. **1929** Designed stage sets for Diaghilev. **1936** Visited America. After World War II he lived alternately in Milan, Florence and Rome. **1949** and **1955** major retrospectives in London and New York. In De Chirico's *Pittura Metafisica*, objects, figures and scenes are brought together in strange combinations. This method of free association and combination creates an alienating and enigmatic stillness in his pictures.
WRITINGS: Carrà, M. (ed.): G. De C. Metafisica. Milan 1968.– Carrà, M. et al. (ed.): G. De C. Metaphysical Art. New York and London 1971.– G. De C.: Piccolo trattato di technica pittorica. Milan 1929, 1962.– G. De C.: Hebdomeros. Paris 1929, 1983.– G. De C.: Memorie della mia vita. Roma 1945.– G. De C.: Wir Metaphysiker. Gesammelte Schriften. Berlin 1973.– G. De C.: De C. par De C. Paris 1978.– G. De C.: Penso alla pittura, solo scopo della vita mia. 51 lettere ad Ardengo Soffici 1914-1942. Ed. by L. Cavallo. Milan 1987.– G. De C.: L'Art métaphysique. Ed. by G. Lista. Paris 1994.– Fagiolo dell'Arco, M. (ed.): G. De C.: Il meccanismo del pensiero. Critica, polemica, autobiografia 1911-1943. Torino 1985
CATALOGUES RAISONNES: Brandani, E. (ed.): G. De C. Catalogo dell'opera grafica 1969-1977. Bologna 1990.– Brandani, E. (ed.): G. De C.: Catalogue Raisonné of the Graphic Work 1969-1977. San Francisco 1990.– Bruni, C. and I. Far (ed.): Catalogo generale dell'opera di G. De C. 8 vols. Milan 1971-1983.– Ciranna, A. (ed.): G. De C. Catalogo delle opere grafiche. Incisioni e litografie 1921-1969. Roma and Milan 1969.– Fagiolo dell'Arco, M. and P. Baldacci: G. De C. Parigi 1924-1929. Dalla nascita del Surrealismo al crollo di Wall Street. Milan 1982.– Fagiolo dell'Arco, M. (ed.): L'opera completa di De C. 1908-1924. Milan 1984.– Fagiolo dell'Arco, M. (ed.): I Bagni Misteriosi. De C. negli anni trenta. Milan 1991.– Sakraischik, C. B. (ed.): Catalogo Generale De C. 3 vols. Milan 1971-1987.– Vastani, A. (ed.): G. De C. Catalogo dell'opera grafica 1921-1969. Bologna 1997
MONOGRAPHS, CATALOGUES: Baldacci, P. G. De C. La metafisica 1888-1919. Milan 1997.– Benzi, F. and M. G. T. Speranza (ed.): G. De C. Pictor optimus. Palazzo delle Esposizioni. Roma 1992 (cat.).– Calvesi, M. and M. Ursino: G. De C. The New Metaphysics. Roma 1996.– Carlino, M.: Una penna per il pennello. G. De C. scrittore. Roma 1989.– Dalla Chiesa, G. et al. (ed.): G. De C. Gallerie Civiche d'Arte Moderna, Ferrara. Roma 1985 (cat.).– Dalla Chiesa, G.: De C. scultore. Milan 1988.– Duca, L: G. De C. Milan 1945.– Fagiolo dell'Arco, M.: G. De C. Le Rêve de Tobie. Un interno ferrarese. 1917 e le origini del Surrealismo. Roma 1980.– Fagiolo dell'Arco, M. (ed.): G. De C. The Museum of Modern Art, New York et al. London 1982 (cat.).– Fagiolo dell'Arco, M.: G. De C. Il tempo di "Valori plastici" 1918-1922. Roma 1980.– Fagiolo dell'Arco, M.: G. De C. Il tempo di Apollinaire. Paris 1911-1915. Roma 1981.– Fagiolo dell'Arco, M. (ed.): De C. Gli

anni venti. Palazzo Reale. Milan 1987, 1995 (cat.).– Fagiolo dell'Arco, M.: La vita di G. De C. Torino 1988.– Fagiolo dell'Arco, M. (ed.): De C. Anni trenta. Milan 1991 (cat.).– Far, I.: G. De C. Roma 1953, 1979. New York 1970. Herrsching 1979.– Far, I. and D. Porzio (ed.): Conoscere De C. La vita e l'opera dell'inventore della pittura metafisica. Milan 1979.– Gribaudo, E.: 194 disegni di G. De C. Torino 1967.– Hüttinger, E.: Zeichnungen von G. De C. Zurich 1969.– Jouffroy, A. et al.: De C.: La vita e l'opera. Milan 1979/De C.: Leben und Werk. Munich 1980.– Rubin, W. et al. (ed.): G. De C. The Museum of Modern Art. New York 1982 (cat.)/G. De C. der Metapysiker. Haus der Kunst. Munich 1982 (cat.)/G. De C. Musée Georges Pompidou, Paris. Paris 1983 (cat.).– Schmied, W. et al.: G. De C.: Leben und Werk. Munich 1980.– Schmied, W.: De C. und sein Schatten. Munich 1989.– Schmied, W.: G. De C. Die beunruhigenden Musen. Frankfurt-on-Main 1993.– Soby, J. T.: G. De C. New York 1954, 1966.– Soby, J. T. (ed.): The Early De C. The Museum of Modern Art. New York 1941, 1969 (cat.).– Vivarelli, P. et al. (ed.): G. De C. 1888-1978. Galleria Nazionale d'Arte Moderna. Roma 1981 (cat.)

DEGAS Edgar
(Hilaire Germain Edgar de Gas)
1834 Paris – **1917** Paris
French painter and sculptor. After briefly studying law, attended the Ecole des Beaux-Arts in Paris from **1855/56**, and entered the studio of Louis Lamothe. **1856–1859** Lived in Italy, then returned to Paris where he joined the Impressionists and made friends with Manet. **1870** Developed an eye disease which had almost blinded him by **1900**. In **1872/73**, he travelled to New Orleans. **1874–1881** and **1886** participated in seven Impressionist exhibitions despite being a critic and opponent of Impressionism. From **1880** many paintings of ballet dancers from unusual viewpoints and in various unconstrained attitudes. After **1909**, owing to his failing eyesight, he created only wax models of dancers, horses and female nudes which were cast in bronze after his death. His work was suffused with a very personal kind of psychological observation that sought to capture fleeting scenes and fragments, as did the new technique of instantaneous photography. He was less interested in nature than in modern city life and people.
WRITINGS: Guérin, M. (ed.): E. D. Lettres. Paris 1931, 1945/E. D. Letters. Oxford 1945.– Halévy, D. (ed.): E. D. Lettres. Paris 1997.– Halévy, D. (ed.): D. parle … Paris 1996.– Reff, T.: The Notebooks of E. D. 2 vols. London 1976, New York 1984
CATALOGUES RAISONNES: Adhémar, J. and F. Cachin (ed.): D. Gravures et monotypes. Paris 1973/D. Radierungen und Monotypien. Munich 1973/D. The Complete Etchings, Lithographs and Monotypes. New York 1973.– Brame, P. et al. (ed.): D. et son Œuvre. A Supplement.

New York 1984.– Janis, E. P. (ed.): D. Monotypes. Catalogue Raisonné. Cambridge (MA) 1968.– Lassaigne, J. (ed.): Tout l'œuvre peint de D. Paris 1974.– Lemoisne, P. A. (ed.): D. et son œuvre. 4 vols. Paris 1946-1949, London and New York 1984.– Matt, L. v. and J. Rewald: D. Das plastische Werk. Zurich 1957.– Millard, C. W.: The Sculpture of D. Princeton (NJ) 1976.– Minervino, F. (ed.): Tout l'œuvre peint de D. Paris 1988.– Minervino, F. (ed.): Das Gesamtwerk von D. Lucerne (n. d.).– Parry Janis, E. (ed.): D. Monotypes. Cambridge 1968.– Pingeot, A. and F. Horvat (ed.): D. Sculptures. Paris.– Reed, S. W. and B. S. Shapiro (ed.): E. D. The Painter as Printmaker. The Complete Prints of E. D. Museum of Fine Arts. Boston 1984 (cat.).– Rewald, J. (ed.): D.'s Complete Sculpture. A Catalogue Raisonné. New York 1944, San Francisco 1990
MONOGRAPHS, CATALOGUES: Adriani, G. (ed.): E. D. Pastelle, Ölskizzen, Zeichnungen. Kunsthalle Tübingen et al. Cologne 1984 (cat.).– Armstrong, C. M.: Odd Man Out. Readings on the Work and Reputation of E. D. Chicago 1991.– Boggs, J. S.: Portraits by D. Berkeley 1962.– Boggs, J. S. et al. (ed.): D. Grand Palais, Paris 1988/D. Metropolitan Museum, New York 1988 (cat.).– Cabanne, P.: E. D. Paris 1957, Munich 1960.– Champigneulle: D. Dessins. Paris 1952.– Dunlop, I.: D. London and New York 1979, Neuchâtel 1979.– Fosca, F.: D. Etude biographique et critique. Geneva 1954.– Gordon, R. and A. Forge: D. Cologne 1985, Paris 1988.– Growe, B.: Zur Bildkonzeption E. D.'s. Frankfurt-on-Main 1981.– Guillaud, M. et al.: D. Form and Space. Paris 1984.– Kendall, R. (ed.): E. D. Leben und Werk in Bildern und Briefen. Munich 1988.– Kendall, R. (ed.): D. Beyond Impressionism. New Haven (CT) 1996.– Keyser, E. d.: D. Réalité et métaphore. Louvain 1981.– Lefèbvre, A.: D. Paris 1981.– Lipton, E.: Looking into D. Los Angeles 1986.– Loyrette, H.: D. Paris 1990.– McMullen, R.: D. His Life, Time and Work. Boston 1984, London 1985.– Pool, P.: D. New York 1963.– Reff, T.: D. The Artist's Mind. New York 1976.– Rewald, J.: D. Sculpture. New York 1956.– Rich, D. C.: D. Cologne 1959, New York 1985.– Roberts, K.: D. Oxford and New York 1976.– Rouart, D.: D. à la recherche de sa technique. Paris 1945.– Rouart, D.: D. monotypes. Paris 1948.– Sérullaz, M.: L'univers de D. Paris 1979.– Sutton, D.: E. D. Life and Work. New York 1986/Leben und Werk. Munich 1986.– Terrasse, A.: D. et la photographie. Paris 1983.– Terrasse, A.: E. D. Paris 1987.– Thomson, R.: The Private D. London 1987.– Thomson, R.: D. The Nudes. London 1988.– Vitali, L.: E. D. Milan 1966.– Werner, A.: D. Pastels. New York 1968

DE KOONING Willem
1904 Rotterdam – **1997** New York
American-Dutch painter. **1916-1920** worked for an art dealer in Rotterdam while

attending evening classes at the Academy. **1926** Emigrated illegally to the US. **1927-1935** Worked as a graphic artist. **1930** Shared a studio with Gorky. **1934** Member of the newly founded Artists' Union. **1937** Commission for a 27 m long mural for the Pharmacy Pavilion at the New York World Fair. **1938-1944** First pictures of women. From **1940** commissions for stage designs. **1942** Met Pollock. **1948** Taught at Black Mountain College in North Carolina and **1950** at the School of Fine Arts in Yale. **1950** Continued *Women* series and worked on abstract compositions with great colour intensity. **1957** First graphic prints. **1958** Rauchenberg did an etching from one of De Kooning's drawings. **1959-1977** Participation in documenta 2, 3 and 6 in Kassel. **1963** New studio in Springs on Long Island. **1970** Life-size sculpted figures. **1975** Founded the Rainbow Foundation, supporting the work of young artists. **1989** In spite of his serious illness, he went on working until his death. Beside Pollock, De Kooning is one of the most important Abstract Expressionist painters.

WRITINGS: W. De K.: Écrits et propos. Paris 1993

CATALOGUE RAISONNE: Graham, L. (ed.): L'Œuvre gravé de W. De K. 1957-1971. Paris 1991

MONOGRAPHS, CATALOGUES: Abadie, D.: De K. ou le corps dispersé. Paris 1994.– Cummings, P. et al. (ed.): W. De K. Drawings, Paintings, Sculptures. Whitney Museum of American Art, New York et al. New York 1984/Zeichnungen, Gemälde, Skulpturen. Akademie der Künste, Berlin et al. Munich 1984 (cat.).– W. De K. Stedelijk Museum, Amsterdam et al. Amsterdam 1969 (cat.).– W. De K. Museum of Art, Carnegie Institute. Pittsburgh, Pennsylvania 1979 (cat.).– W. De K. The North Atlantic Light 1960-1983. Stedelijk Museum. Amsterdam 1983 (cat.).– W. De K. Centre Georges Pompidou. Paris 1984 (cat.).– Denby, E. W.: W. De K. Paris 1994.– Drudi, E.: W. De K. Milan 1972.– Gaugh, H. F.: W. De K. New York 1983, Munich and Lucerne 1984.– Gohr, S. (ed.): W. De K. Skulpturen. Josef-Haubrich-Kunsthalle. Cologne 1983 (cat.).– Hess, T. B. (ed.): W. De K. Stedelijk Museum, Amsterdam et al. Amsterdam 1968 (cat.).– Hess, T. B. (ed.): W. De K. Drawings. London and Greenwich (CT) 1972.– Kertess, K. (ed.): W. De K. Guild Hall Museum. East Hampton 1994 (cat.).– Prather, M. et al. (ed.): W. De K. Paintings. National Gallery of Art, Washington et al. Washington and London 1994 (cat.).– Rosenberg, H.: W. De K. New York 1974, 1978.– Sollers, P.: De K., vite. Paris 1988.– Storr, R. and G. Garells (ed.): W. De K. The Late Paintings. San Francisco Museum of Modern Art et al. San Francisco 1995 (cat.)/W. De K. Das Spätwerk. Kunstmuseum Bonn et al. Bonn 1996 (cat.).– Waldman, D.: W. De K. New York 1988.– Wilde, E. d. et al. (ed.): W. De K. Het Noordatlant. licht. 1960-1983. Stedelijk Museum, Amsterdam et al. Amsterdam 1983 (cat.).– Yard, S.: W. De K. The First Twenty-Six Years in New York. New York 1980.– Yard, S.: W. De K. New York 1997.– Zilcer, J.: W. De K. From the Hirshhorn Museum Collection. Hirshhorn Museum, Washington et al. New York 1993 (cat.)

DELAUNAY Robert
1885 Paris – **1941** Montpellier
French painter. **1902** Apprenticed to a decorator. **1904** Visited Brittany. Influenced by the Pont-Aven group. Studied Neo-Impressionist colour theories and philosophical works in depth. **1910** Participated in the Salon des Indépendants and revealed Cubist tendencies in his Eiffel Tower series. **1911**

Participation in the first exhibition of the Blauer Reiter group. **1912/13** With his *Formes Circulaires* developed an individual, coloristic and formal language related to Cubism and described by Apollinaire as "Orphism" emphasizing the relation of colour to sound and musical resonance. **1913** Travelled to Berlin and exhibited in Herwarth Walden's gallery Der Sturm. **1914-1920** Lived in Spain. **1921** Returned to Paris where his painting became more abstract. **1937** Designed decorations for the Palais des Chemins de Fer at the Paris World Fair. **1939** Co-founder of the Salon des Réalités Nouvelles.

WRITINGS: Cohen, A. A.: The New Art of Colour. The Writings of R. and S. D. New York 1978.– Düchting, H. (ed.): R. D. Zur Malerei der reinen Farbe. Schriften von 1912-1940. Munich 1983.– Francastel, P. (ed.): R. D. Du cubisme à l'art abstrait. Documents inedits. Paris 1957

CATALOGUE RAISONNE: Loyer, J. and C. Péruseau (ed.): Catalogue de l'œuvre lithographique. Paris 1974

MONOGRAPHS, CATALOGUES: Buckberrough, S. A.: R. D. The Early Years. Ann Arbor (MI) 1981.– Buckberrough, S. A.: R. D. The Discovery of Simultaneity. Ann Arbor (MI) 1982.– Cassou, J.: R. D. Première époque 1903-1910. Paris 1961.– Chadwick, W.: Significant Others. S. and R. D. London 1993.– Dorival, B.: R. D. 1885-1941. Paris 1975.– Düchting, H.: R. D.'s "Fenêtres". Peinture pure et simultané. Paradigma einer modernen Wahrnehmungsform. Diss. Munich 1982.– Hoog, M. et al. (ed.): R. D. Orangerie des Tuileries. Paris 1976/Staatliche Kunsthalle Baden-Baden. Baden-Baden 1976 (cat.).– Hoog, M.: R. D. Munich 1983.– Jenderko, I. (ed.): R. D. Staatliche Kunsthalle Baden-Baden. Baden-Baden 1976 (cat.).– Kuthy, S. and K. Satonobu (ed.): Künstlerpaare, Künstlerfreunde. Sonia und R. D. Kunstmuseum Bern. Stuttgart 1991 (cat.).– Molinari, D. (ed.): R. et Sonia D. Musée d'Art Moderne de la Ville de Paris. Paris 1985 (cat.).– Molinari, D. le: R. et Sonia D. Paris 1987.– Schuster, P.-K. (ed.): D. und Deutschland. Staatsgalerie moderner Kunst, Munich. Cologne 1985 (cat.).– Tourette, F. G. d.: R. D. Paris 1950.– Vriesen, G. and M. Imdahl: R. D. Licht und Farbe des Orphismus. Cologne 1967, 1992/R. D. Light and Color. New York 1967

DELAUNAY-TERK Sonia
1885 Gradisk (Ukraine) – **1979** Paris
Russian-French painter. **1903** Studied in Karlsruhe, Germany. In **1905** she moved to Paris and studied at the Académie de la Palette; contact with Ozenfant and André Dunoyer de Segonzac. Married Robert Delaunay in **1910**. **1911** First simultaneous compositions of circular forms, combining the ideas of the Fauves and Cubists in intensely expressive abstract paintings. From **1913** onwards, she used her own rhythmical colour-orchestrations for book illustrations, book covers, textile designs and decorations.

1914-1920 Lived in Spain and Portugal. **1918** Costume designs for Diaghilev's ballet *Cleopatra*. **1920** Returned to Paris and came in contact with the Surrealists gathered around Aragon and Breton. Applied her style of painting to fashion and textile designs. **1924** Opened her own fashion studio. From **1935-1937**, together with Robert Delaunay, worked on a large mural for the Paris World Fair. **1939** Co-founder of the Salon des Réalités Nouvelles.

WRITINGS: Cohen, A. A. (ed.): The New Art of Colour. The Writings of R. and S. D. New York 1978.– S. D.-T.: Compositions, couleurs, idées. Paris 1930.– S. D.-T.: Nous irons jusqu'au soleil. Paris 1978

MONOGRAPHS, CATALOGUES: Baron, S. and J. Damase: S. D. The Life of an Artist. New York 1995/S. D. Ihre Kunst, ihr Leben. Munich 1995.– Buckberrough, S. A. et al. (ed.): S. D. A Retrospective. Albright-Knox Art Gallery, Buffalo et al. Buffalo 1980 (cat.).– Callu, F. et al.: S. et R. D. Paris 1977.– Chadwick, W.: Significant Others: S. and R. D. London 1993.– Cohen, A. A.: S. D. New York 1975, 1988.– Damase, J.: S. D. Notes biographiques. Paris 1971.– Damase, J.: S. D. Rythms and Colors. London and Greenwich (CT) 1972.– Damase, J. (ed.): S. D. Mode et tissus imprimés. Paris 1991/S. D. Fashion and Fabrics. New York 1991/S. D. Mode und Design. Zurich 1991.– Desanti, D.: S. D., magique magicienne. Paris 1988.– Dorival, B.: S. D. Sa Vie, son œuvre 1885-1979. Paris 1980/S. D. Leben und Werk 1885-1979. Munich 1985.– Dupuits, P. (ed.): S. D. Metz est venu. Stedelijk Museum. Amsterdam 1992 (cat.).– Hoog, M. et al.: S. D. Rythmes et couleurs. Paris 1971.– Kuthy, S. and K. Satonobu (ed.): Künstlerpaare, Künstlerfreunde. S. und Robert D. Kunstmuseum Bern. Stuttgart 1991 (cat.).– Madsen, A.: S. D. Artist of the Lost Generation. New York 1989.– Molinari, D. le (ed.): Robert et S. D. Musée d'Art Moderne de la Ville de Paris. Paris 1985 (cat.).– Morano, E.: S. D. Art into Fashion. New York 1986.– Viatte, G.: S. D. Dessins: Noirs et blancs. Paris 1978

DELVAUX Paul
1897 Antheit – **1994** Furnes
Belgian painter. **1917-1924** Studied architecture and painting at the Académie des Beaux-Arts in Brussels. Influenced by

Belgian Expressionism and Ensor. **1932** Strongly impressed by the waxwork figures of the Musée Spitzner which became a recurrent theme in his pictures. Seeing the works of Magritte, De Chirico and Max Ernst at the Surrealist exhibition "Minotaure" in Paris in **1934** inspired paintings remarkable for their veristic detail and subued coloration. **1938** Participation in the international exhibition of the Surrealists organized by Breton. After discovering the Italian Renaissance on travels through Italy, he tended to paint classical landscapes as backgrounds for his somewhat theatrical compositions. **1944/45** First retrospective at the Palais des Beaux-Arts in Brussels. **1950-1962** Professor of Monumental Painting at the Ecole Nationale d'Art et d'Architecture. Stage decorations and murals. **1965/66** President of the Académie des Beaux-Arts of Belgium. Numerous retrospectives in Paris, Rotterdam, Tokyo and elsewhere. Beside Magritte, the most important representative of Belgian Surrealsim.

CATALOGUES RAISONNES: Butor, M. et al. (ed.): D. Catalogue de l'œuvre peint. Brussels 1975, Lausanne and Paris 1987.– Jacob, M. (ed.): P. D. L'œuvre graphique. Monte Carlo 1976

MONOGRAPHS, CATALOGUES: Bock, P.-A. d.: P. D. Der Mensch, der Maler. Hamburg 1965/P. D. L'homme, le peintre, psychologie d'un art. Brussels 1967.– Butor, M. et al.: D. Bruxelles 1975.– P. D. Museum Boymans-van Beuningen. Rotterdam 1973 (cat.).– P. D. Rétrospective. Musée d'Art Moderne. Brussels 1997 (cat.).– Debra, M.: Promenades et entretiens avec P. D. Paris 1991.– Devillers, V.: P. D. Le Théâtre des figures. Brussels 1993.– Dypéreau, J. et al. (ed.): P. D. Gallerie Civiche d'Arte Moderna. Ferrara 1986 (cat.).– Emerson, B.: P. D. Antwerp 1985, San Francisco 1996.– Engen, L. and C. van Deun (ed.): Le Pays Mosan de P. D. Musée Communal, Huy et al. Liège 1997 (cat.).– Meure, J. and M. v. Jole (ed.): P. D. Fondation Pierre Gianadda. Martigny 1987 (cat.).– Grall, A. (ed.): Die Zeichnungen von P. D. Berlin 1968.– Hammacher-v. d. Brande, R. (ed.): P. D. Kunsthalle der Hypo-Kulturstiftung. Munich 1989 (cat.).– Langui, E.: P. D. Venice 1949.– Meuris, J.: 7 dialogues avec P. D. Accompagnés de 7 lettres imaginaires. Paris 1971.– Nadeau, M.: Les Dessins de P. D. Paris 1967.– Paquet, M.: P. D. et l'essence de la peinture. 2 vols. Paris 1982.– Rombaut, M.: P. D. Paris 1990, London 1991.– Scheurmann, K.: P. D. Gießen 1976.– Scott, D.: P. D. Surrealizing the Nude. London 1992.– Sojcher, J.: P. D. ou la passion puérile. Paris 1991.– Spaak, C.: P. D. Brussels 1948.– Vignon, D. and C. (ed.): P. D. Galleria Civica d'Arte Moderna. Ferrara 1986 (cat.)

DE MARIA Walter
born **1935** Albany (CA)
American artist. **1953-1959** Studied at the University of California in Berkeley. **1959** Staged first happenings and decided, in **1960**, to move to New York. Exhibited

plywood boxes, for example his *Box for Meaningless Work* and *Invisible Drawings*, words pencilled extremely lightly onto paper. **1963** First solo-exhibition in Nine Great Jones Street, New York. **1965** Played drums in Velvet Underground. **1968** Presented his *Earth Room* (1,600 cubic feet of earth spread over the gallery floor) at the Heiner Friedrich gallery in Munich, and carried out his Land Art action *Mile Long Drawing* (two lines, 360 cm apart running parallel for a mile) in the Mogave desert in California. **1968** Participation in documenta 4 in Kassel. **1969** Participation in documenta 4 in Kassel. **1970** Participated in the exhibition "Land Art, Conceptual Art, Arte Povera" in Turin. **1977** His earth sculpture (a one-kilometre long brass pole pointing down towards the centre of the earth), planned in **1972** for the Olympiade in Munich, presented with slight modifications at documenta 6 in Kassel and entitled *The Vertical Earth Kilometer*. **1984** Took part in the exhibition of 20th century sculpture in the Merian Park in Basel. De Maria's Land Art, developed against a background of art trends and movements such as happenings, Concept Art and Minimal Art, has symbolic, mythological roots.
WRITINGS: Mac Low, J. et al. (ed.): W. De M. An Anthology. New York 1963
MONOGRAPHS, CATALOGUES: Kellein, T. (ed.): W. De M. 5 Kontinente Skulptur. Staatsgalerie Stuttgart. Stuttgart 1987 (cat.).– W. De M. Skulpturen. Kunsthalle Basel. Basel 1972 (cat.).– W. De M. Der große Erdraum. Hessisches Landesmuseum. Darmstadt 1974 (cat.).– W. De M. Museum Boymans-van Beuningen. Rotterdam 1984.– Meyer, F.: W. De M. Frankfurt-on-Main 1991.– Nittve, L. (ed.): W. De M. 2 Very Large Presentations. Moderna Museet. Stockholm 1989 (cat.).– Schoon, T. (ed.): W. De M. Museum Boymans-van Beuningen. Rotterdam 1984 (cat.).– Szeemann, H. (ed.): W. De M. The 2000 Sculpture. Kunsthaus Zürich. Zurich 1992 (cat.)

DEMUTH Charles
1883 Lancaster (PA) – **1935** Lancaster American painter. **1903–1905** Studied at the School of Industrial Art in Philadelphia, and in **1905/06** at the Pennsylvania Academy of Fine Arts. **1907** Travelled to Paris but returned to America to continue his studies. From **1912–1914**, lived in Paris again, attending classes at various academies. Close relations with Picasso, Delaunay and Picabia; became friends with Duchamp. **1915** First solo-exhibition at the Daniel Gallery in New York. Contact with Alfred Stieglitz and the collector-couple Arensberg. Painted watercolours for book illustrations, displaying elements of Cubism and Realism. **1916/17** Travelled to the Bermudas. Over the following years, worked intensively on representations of architecture. **1925** First joint projects with the Stieglitz gallery. **1929** Participation in the exhibition "Paintings by 19 Living Americans" at the Museum of Modern Art, New York.

MONOGRAPHS, CATALOGUES:
Eiseman, A. L.: C. D. New York 1982.– Fahlman, B.: Pennsylvania Modern. C. D. of Lancaster. Philadelphia Museum of Art et al. Philadelphia 1983 (cat.).– Farnham, E.: C. D. His Life, Psychology and Works. Diss. Columbus (OH) 1959.– Farnham, E.: C. D. Behind a Laughing Mask. Norman (OK) 1971.– Frank, R. J. (ed.): C. D. Poster Portraits 1923-1929. Yale University Art Gallery. New Haven (CT) 1994 (cat.).– Haskell, B. (ed.): C. D. Whitney Museum of American Art, New York et al. New York 1987 (cat.).– Ritchie, A. C. (ed.): C. D. The Museum of Modern Art. New York 1950 (cat.).

DENIS Maurice
1870 Granville – **1943** St.-Germain-en-Laye French painter. **1888** Studied at the Paris School of Art and at the Académie Julian. Met Bernard, Bonnard and Sérusier, who introduced him to the ideas of Gauguin and painters of the Pont-Naven school. **1890** Co-founder of the symbolist group, the Nabis. He shared a studio with Bonnard and Vuillard. **1892/93** Stage designs for the Théatre de l'Œuvre. In **1895** and **1898** he travelled to Italy to study Early Renaissance painting, particularly Piero della Francesca and Fra Angelico. **1901** Group portrait of the Nabis and *Hommage à Cézanne*. Worked as a book illustrator and lithographer. **1903** Travelled to Germany. **1906** Went with Bernard and Roussel to visit Cézanne in Aix-en-Provence. Besides Impressionist portrait studies and garden scenes, produced mainly Art-Nouveau-style and Symbolist paintings on religious themes. In **1914** and **1917** Decorations in St. Paul, and glass paintings for Notre-Dame in Geneva. **1909** Joined Rouault in founding workshops for religious art.
WRITINGS: Collet, G.-P.: Correspondance Jacques-Emile Blanche-M. D. 1901-1939. Geneva 1989.– M. D.: Théories 1890-1910. Paris 1920.– M. D.: Paul Sérusier, sa vie, son œuvre. Paris 1942.– M. D.: Journal 1884-1943. 3 vols. Paris 1957-1959.– M. D.: Du symbolisme au classicisme. Théories. Paris 1964.– M. D.: Le Ciel et l'arcadie. Ed. by J.-P. Bouillon. Paris 1993
CATALOGUE RAISONNE: Cailler, P. (ed.): Catalogue de l'œuvre gravé et lithographié de M. D. Geneva 1968
MONOGRAPHS, CATALOGUES:
Barazzetti-Demoulin, S.: M. D. Paris 1945.– Barruel, T. et al. (ed.): Un nouveau regard sur M. D. Paris 1996.– Bouillon, J.-P.: M. D. 1870-1943. Geneva 1993.– Bouillon, J.-P. (ed.): M. D. 1870-1943. Musée des Beaux-Arts, Lyon et al. Lyon 1994 (cat.).– Dellanoy, a. (ed.): Symbolistes et Nabis. M. D. et son temps. Saint-Germain-en-Laye 1996 (cat.).– M. D. Musée de l'Orangerie. Paris 1970 (cat.).– M. D. 1870-1943. Musée des Beaux-Arts, Lyon et al. Lyon 1994, Merseyside 1995 (cat.).– Gerkens, G. et al. (ed.): M. D. Gemälde, Handzeichnungen, Druckgraphik. Kunsthalle Bremen. Bremen 1971 (cat.).– Janin-Juvigny, S. (ed.): M. D.

DEPERO Fortunato
1892 Fondo (Trentino) – **1960** Rovereto Italian painter and sculptor. Self-taught. From **1913** belonged to the inner circle of the Futurists. Wrote several manifestos of which *La ricostruzione futurista dell' universo* was published. **1916** Costume and stage designs for a Diaghilev ballet. **1919** Opened the Casa d'arte in Rovereto, a workshop in which numerous *objets d'art*, vases, textiles and wallpapers were made. Influenced by the post-Cubist works of Léger, entered a second Futurist phase, in which his paintings had a stronger narrative content and his figures more plasticity. **1924** Staging of the ballet *Anihccam*. **1927** Signed the manifesto of the *Aeropittura*. **1928–1930** Stay in America.
WRITINGS: F. D.: Spezzatura-Impressioni. Segni e ritmi. Rovereto 1913.– F. D.: So I Think so I paint. Trento 1947
MONOGRAPHS, CATALOGUES: Belli, G. et al. (ed.): F. D. La Casa del Mago: le arti applicate nell'opera di F. D. 1920-1942. Archivio del '900, Rovereto. Milan 1992 (cat.).– Belli, G. (ed.): F. D. Dal Futurismo alla Casa d'Arte. Roma 1994 (cat.).– D. Futurista. Milan 1927, Florence 1978.– F. D. Museum am Ostwall. Dortmund 1994 (cat.).– Fagiolo dell'Arco, M. et al.: D. Milan 1988.– Passamani, B. (ed.): D. e la scena da colori alla scena mobile 1916-1930. Torino 1970.– Passamani, B. (ed.): F. D. Museo Depero. Rovereto 1981 (cat.).– Passamani, B. (ed.): La sala del Consiglio Provinciale di Trento di F. D. Trento 1990.– Scudiero, M. et al. (ed.): D. Futurista + New York. Futurism and the Art of Advertising. Museo Depero. Rovereto 1986 (cat.).– Scudiero, M. F. D. Opere. Trento 1987.– Scudieo, M. (ed.): D. per Campari. Milan 1989.– Universo, M. (ed.): F. D. Fiero di Padova. Padua 1990 (cat.)

DERAIN André
1880 Chatou (near Paris) – **1954** near Garches
French painter. **1898–1900** Studied at the Académie Carrière in Paris. **1901** Met Matisse and Vlaminck who were to become important companions. **1901–1904** Painting studies interrupted but taken up again briefly at the Académie Julian. During summer **1905** he painted together with Matisse in Collioure on the Mediterranean and exhibited his Fauvist paintings at the Paris Salon d'Automne in the same year. **1908** Spent several months with Picasso in Avignon and was strongly influenced by Cubism. **1912** Beginning of the *période gothique*. **1913** Participation in the First

100 ans après à Alençon. Musée des Beaux-Arts et de la Dentelle. Alençon 1985 (cat.).– Lacambre, G. and D. Delouche (ed.): M. D. et la Bretagne. Musée de Morlaix. Morlaix 1985 (cat.).– Salmon, M.-J. (ed.): L'âge d'or de M. D. Musée Départemental de l'Oise. Beauvais 1982 (cat.).– Terrasse, A.: D. Intimités. Lausanne 1970

Autumn Salon in Berlin. **1920–1930** Visits to the South of France. Produced *Pierrot* and *Harlequin* paintings. **1935** Retrospective at the Kunsthalle Bern. Numerous commissions for costumes and sets at the Paris Opera. **1944** Worked on illustrations and stage set designs. **1994** Important retrospective at the Musée d'Art Moderne de la Ville de Paris.
WRITINGS: A. D. Lettres à Vlaminck. Paris 1955, 1994
CATALOGUES RAISONNES: Cailler, P. (ed.): Catalogue raisonné de l'œuvre sculpté de A. D. L'œuvre édité. Lausanne 1965.– Kellermann, M. (ed.): A. D. Catalogue de l'œuvre peint. 1895-1934. 2 vols. Paris 1992-1996
MONOGRAPHS, CATALOGUES:
Adhémar, J.: D. peintre-graveur. Paris 1955.– Bachelard, P.: D. Un fauve pas ordinaire. Paris 1994.– Cabanne, P.: A. D. Paris 1990.– D. The Late Work. Scottish National Gallery of Modern Art. Edinburgh 1991 (cat.).– Flam, J. et al. (ed.): A. D. Paris 1994 (cat.).– George, W. A. D. Das plastische Werk. 37 Bronzen. Düsseldorf 1961.– Goray, P. (ed.): A. D. Bildhauer. Galleria Pierre Goray, Lugano et al. Milan 1994 (cat.).– Hilaire, G.: D. Geneva 1959.– Hoog, M. (ed.): Un certain D. Musée de l'Orangerie. Paris 1991 (cat.).– Kalitina, N. N.: A. D. Leningrad 1976.– Lee, J. (ed.): D. Museum of Modern Art, Oxford et al. London 1990 (cat.).– Leymarie, J. (ed.): A. D. Grand Palais. Paris 1977 (cat.).– Marquet, F.: D. et la photographie. Neuchâtel 1997.– Pagé, S. (ed.): A. D. Musée d'Art Moderne de la Ville de Paris. Paris 1994 (cat.).– Parke-Taylor, M. (ed.): A. D. in North American Collections. Norman Mackenzie Art Gallery, University of Regina et al. Regina 1982 (cat.).– Sutton, D.: A. D. London 1959, Cologne 1960

DEWASNE Jean
1921 Lille – **1999** Paris
French painter. Studied music and architecture at the Ecole des Beaux-Arts in Paris. **1943** First abstract paintings. Influenced by Mondrian, he painted in a geometric constructivist style. **1946** Kandinsky Award, Paris. Close contact with artists of the Denise René Gallery, like Hartung, Schneider and Poliakoff. Together with Arp, Pevsner and Sonia Delaunay-Terk he was a

committee-member of the Salon des Réalités Nouvelles. **1950–1952** Founder and co-director, with Edgar Pillet, of the Académie d'Art Abstrait. Experiments with varnish paint and use of prefabricated objects for his *Antisculptures*. **1968** Solo-exhibition at the Venice Biennale.
WRITINGS: J. D.: Robert Jacobsen, sculpteur danois. Copenhagen 1951
MONOGRAPHS, CATALOGUES: Cordier, D. (ed.): D. Lefebre Gallery. New York 1972 (cat.).– Descargues, P.: J. D. Paris 1952.– J. D. Kunsthalle Bern. Bern 1966 (cat.).– J. D. Musée de Grenoble. Grenoble 1970 (cat.).– J. D. Tenue de rigueur. Paris 1995

DEXEL Walter
1890 Munich – **1973** Brunswick (Germany) German painter and designer. **1910–1914** Studied history of art in Munich. Took private drawing lessons with Hermann Gröber. **1912/13** Travelled to Italy. **1914** Studied in Paris. First solo-exhibition at the Dietzel Gallery in Munich. **1916** Doctorate under Botho Gräf in Jena. **1916–1928** Director of the Jena Arts Association. **1917** First abstract paintings, influenced by Constructivism. **1918** Exhibition at Herwarth Walden's gallery Der Sturm in Berlin. **1919** Friendship with Schwitters. Close contact to the Bauhausmeister (Bauhaus Masters) in Weimar whose works he exhibited in Jena. **1921/22** Developed a concrete-abstract style of painting. From **1923** member of the Novembergruppe, and from **1928** joined Schwitters in the Ring Neuer Werbegestalter (Association of New Advertisers). **1928–1935** Lecturership at the Magdeburg School of Applied Arts and Crafts. **1933** Denounced by the Nazis, stopped painting. **1942–1955** Set up the Collection of Historic Forms in Brunswick and published numerous books on design. **1961** Took up painting again.
WRITINGS: W. D.: Unbekanntes Handwerksgut. Berlin 1935.– W. D.: Holzgerät und Holzform. Berlin 1943.– W. D.: Glas, Werkstoff und Form. Ravensburg 1950.– W. D.: Keramik, Stoff und Form. Berlin and Brunswick 1958.– W. D.: Das Hausgerät Mitteleuropas. Brunswick and Berlin 1962.– W. D.: Der Bauhausstil. Ein Mythos. Texte 1921-1965. Mit 4 Aufsätzen von G. Dexel. Ed. by W. Vitt. Starnberg 1976.– W. D.: Köpfe. 1930-1933. Starnberg 1979
CATALOGUES RAISONNES: Vitt, W. (ed.): W. D. Werkverzeichnis der Druckgraphik 1915-1971. Cologne 1971.– Vitt, W. et al. (ed.): W. D. 1890-1973. Werkverzeichnis. Heidelberg 1995.– Wöbkemeier, R. (ed.): W. D. Werkverzeichnis. Heidelberg 1995
MONOGRAPHS, CATALOGUES: Friedl, F.: W. D. Neue Reklame. Düsseldorf 1987.– Güse, E.-G. and W. Vitt (ed.): W. D. Bilder, Aquarelle, Collagen. Westfälisches Landesmuseum. Münster 1979 (cat.).– Hofmann, W.: Der Maler W. D. Starnberg 1972.– Vitt, W. (ed.): Hommage à W. D. 1890-1973. Starnberg 1980.– Vitt, W. and R. Stolz (ed.): Schöne Tage im Hause Dexel.

Das Gästebuch. W. D. zum 100. Geburtstag. Galerie Stolz. Cologne 1990 (cat.).– Wöbkemeier, R. et al. (ed.): W. D. Bild, Zeichen, Raum. Kunsthalle Bremen. Bremen 1990 (cat.)

DIEBENKORN Richard
1921 Portland (OR) – **1993** Berkeley (CA) American painter. **1940–1943** Studied in Stanford and Berkeley. **1946/47** Continued his studies in San Francisco and **1950–1952** at the University of New Mexico. His first paintings, influenced by Motherwell and Hoffmann, display elements of Abstract Expressionism. **1954** Participation in the exhibition "Younger American Painters" at the Guggenheim Museum, New York. Influenced by Hopper, his paintings became more figurative. From **1967** on he returned to abstraction. **1966–1973** Professorship at the University of California, Los Angeles. **1968** Took part in the Venice Biennale. **1972** Solo-exhibition at the San Francisco Museum of Art. One of the main representatives of Abstract Expressionism in California.
CATALOGUES RAISONNES: Guillemin, C.: R. D. Catalogue raisonné. Eaux-fortes de 1949 à 1980. Houston 1981.– Newlin, R. (ed.): R. D. Works on Paper. Houston 1987.– Stevens, M. (ed.): R. D. Etchings and Drypoints 1949-1980. The Minneapolis Institute of Arts et al. Houston 1981 (cat.)
MONOGRAPHS, CATALOGUES: Buck, R. T. et al. (ed.): R. D. Paintings and Drawings 1943-1976. Albright-Knox Art Gallery, Buffalo et al. Buffalo 1976 (cat.).– Cathcart, L. L. (ed.): R. D. 38th Venice Biennal 1978, United States Pavilion. New York 1978 (cat.).– R. D. Pasadena Art Museum, Pasadena et al. Pasadena 1960 (cat.).– R. D. Washington Gallery of Modern Art et al. Washington 1965 (cat.).– R. D. Paintings from the Ocean Park Series. San Francisco Art Museum. San Francisco 1973 (cat.).– Elderfield, J. (ed.): The Drawings of R. D. The Museum of Modern Art, New York et al. Houston 1989 (cat.).– Elderfield, J. et al. (ed.): R. D. Whitechappel Art Gallery, London et al. London 1991 (cat.)/R. D. Frankfurter Kunstverein et al. Frankfurt-on-Main 1992 (cat.).– Flam, J.: R. D. Ocean Park. New York 1992.– Livingstone, J. (ed.): The Art of R. D. Whitney Museum of American Art, New York et al. New York 1997 (cat.).– Newlin, R. (ed.): R. D. Works on Paper. Houston 1987.– Nordland, G.: R. D. New York 1987

DILLER Burgoyne
1906 Battle Creek (MI) – **1965** New York American painter. **1928–1933** Studied art at the Art Students League in New York and took private lessons from Hoffmann. Influenced by Mondrian, he developed his own abstract, geometric style, based on three primary colours and black. **1933** First solo exhibition at the Contemporary Art Gallery in New York. **1935–1941** Directed the department of mural painting within the Federal Arts Project. Worked with Pollock,

Rothko and Reinhardt. **1936** Together with Fritz Glarner and Albers, founded the artists' association American Abstract Artists. **1945–1964** Professorship at Brooklyn Art College. **1966** Retrospective at the New Jersey State Museum, Trenton. **1968** Participation in documenta 4 in Kassel. **1972** Retrospective at Walker Art Gallery, Minneapolis. Regarded as one of the founding fathers of Neo-Plasticism in America.
MONOGRAPHS, CATALOGUES: B. D. Trenton State Museum. Trenton (NJ) 1966 (cat.).– Haskell, B. (ed.): B. D. Whitney Museum of American Art. New York 1990 (cat.).– Larsen, P. and P. Dchjeldahl (ed.): B. D. Paintings, Sculptures, Drawings. Walker Art Center. Minneapolis 1971 (cat.).– Rand, H. (ed.): B. D. Meredith Long Contemporary Art. New York 1980 (cat.).– Schlégl, I. (ed.): B. D. 1906 New York City – 1965 New York City. Galerie und Edition Schlégl. Zurich 1991 (cat.)

DINE Jim
born **1935** Cincinnati (OH)
American painter and sculptor. **1953–1957** Studied at the University of Cincinnati, at Boston Museum School and finally at Ohio University, Athens. From **1958** he lived in New York, where, with his installations, environments and happenings, he set up a counter-movement to the predominant Abstract Expressionism. **1960–1965** various guest-professorships, among others at Yale University, New Haven and at Oberlin College, Ohio. **1964** Participated in the Venice Biennale. From **1967** he taught at the College for Architecture, Cornell University, Ithaca and lived temporarily in London in order to experience the English Pop Art scene directly. **1968** and **1977** participation in documenta 4 and 7 in Kassel. Since **1980** member of the American Academy of Arts and Letters. Created large murals for public places in Boston and San Francisco. Dine's paintings are usually combined with collages, assemblages and three-dimensional objects and have a homemade, personal character, distinguishing them from the mechanical style of picture production emphasized in Pop Art.
WRITINGS: J. D.: Welcome Home Lovebirds. London 1969.– J. D.: Letters to Nancy. New York 1970.– J. D.: Gedichte und Zeichnungen. Frankfurt-on-Main 1971

CATALOGUES RAISONNES: Bonin, W. v. and M. S. Cullen (ed.): J. D. Complete Graphics 1960-1970. Galerie Mikro. Berlin, Hanover and London 1970.– J. D. Prints 1970-1977. Williams College Museum, Williamstown. New York 1977.– D'Oench, E. G. and J. E. Feinberg (ed.): J. D. Prints. 1977-1985. Davison Art Center, Wesleyan University, Middletown et al. New York 1986 (cat.)
MONOGRAPHS, CATALOGUES: Ackley, C. (ed.): Etchings by J. D. New York 1983.– Beal, G. W. J. (ed.): J. D. Five Themes. Walker Art Center, Minneapolis et al. Minneapolis 1984 (cat.).– Codognato, A. (ed.): J. D. Galleria d'Arte Moderna Ca' Pesaro, Venice. Milan 1988 (cat.).– Dagbert, A.: J. D. Une exposition pour Paris. Paris 1986.– J. D. in der Glyptothek. Glyptothek. Munich 1990 (cat.).– J. D. et al. (ed.): J. D. Drawing from the Glyptothek. New York 1993.– J. D. Venus. Revoltella Museum. Triest 1996 (cat.).– Glenn, C. W.: J. D. Drawings. New York 1985.– Gordon, J. (ed.): J. D. Figure Drawings. Whitney Museum of American Art. New York 1970.– Livingston, M.: J. D. Flowers and Plants. New York 1994.– Livingstone, M.: J. D. The Alchemy of Images. New York 1997.– Rogers-Lafferty, S. (ed.): Drawings J. D. 1973-1987. The Contemporary Arts Center, Cincinnati et al. Cincinnati 1988 (cat.).– Shapiro, D.: J. D. Painting What One Is. New York 1981/J. D. Malen, was man ist. Stuttgart 1984.– Shapiro, D. et al.: J. D. Milan 1988

DISLER Martin
1949 Seewen (Solothurn) – **1996** Geneva Swiss painter and graphic artist. Self-taught. **1969** Worked as an auxiliary nurse in the psychiatric clinic in Rosegg, Solothurn. **1970** Stage director and theatre critic in Olten. Solothurn Award for graphics. **1971** First solo-exhibitions at the Kunstzone (Art Zone) Munich and Delphin Gallery, Olten. **1973** Studied in Bologna and Paris. **1976/77** Kiefer-Hablitzel Grant. Continued studies in America. **1978** Moved to Zurich. **1980** Solo-exhibition at the Kunsthalle, Basel. After **1981** travelled to America. Worked in various places, including Zurich, New York, Lugano and Harlingen. **1982** Participation in documenta 7 in Kassel. **1983** Solo-exhibitions at the Stedelijk Museum Amsterdam and at the Museum für Gegenwartskunst in Basel. **1985** Bremen Art Award, exhibition at the Folkwang Museum, Essen. **1987** Award from Zurich Art Society. **1997** Exhibition of last series of watercolours at the Kunstmuseum Basel and Museum Ludwig, Cologne.
WRITINGS: M. D.: Reise nach Pisa. Zurich 1975.– M. D.: Das Lebenjacket. Olten 1977.– M. D.: Bilder vom Maler. Dudweiler 1980.– M. D.: Der Zungenkuss. Biel 1980.– M. D.: Schwarzweisse Novelle. Zurich 1983
CATALOGUE RAISONNE: Davvetas, D. (ed.): M. D. Werke 1982-1986. Bern 1996.– Willi-Cosandier, J. and R. M. Mason (ed.): M. D. L'œuvre gravé 1978-1988. Musée d'Art et d'Histoire. Geneva 1989 (cat.)

MONOGRAPHS, CATALOGUES:
Ammann, J. C. et al. (ed.): M. D. Invasion durch eine falsche Spur. Kunsthalle Basel. Basel 1980 (cat.).– Cornips, M. H. et al. (ed.): M. D. Zeichnungen 1968-1983. Museum für Gegenwartskunst, Basel et al. Basel 1983 (cat.).– M. D. et al. (ed.): M. D. Dossier: Arbeiten der 70er Jahre und Bilderzyklus "Februar '91". Kunstmuseum. Solothurn 1991 (cat.).– Felix, Z. (ed.): M. D. Folkwang Museum, Essen et al. Essen 1985 (cat.).– Firmenich, A. and A. Sommer (ed.): M. D. Skulpturen 1985-1994. Kunsthalle Emden. Cologne 1995 (cat.).– Jenny, C. (ed.): M. D. Zeichnungen. Zurich 1989.– Kellein, T. (ed.): M. D. Häutung und Tanz. London, Basel and Munich 1991 (cat.).– Koepplin, D. (ed.): M. D. Die letzten Aquarelle. Kunstmuseum Basel et al. Stuttgart 1997 (cat.).– Osterwold, T. and D. Hall (ed.): M. D. Die Umgebung der Liebe. Württembergischer Kunstverein. Stuttgart 1981 (cat.)

DI SUVERO Mark

born **1933** Shanghai
American sculptor. **1941** Left China, emigrating to the USA. Studied **1953/54** at City College, San Francisco and **1954/55** at the University of California in Santa Barbara and in Berkeley, before settling in New York. **1960** First solo-exhibition at the Green Gallery, New York. **1968** Took part in documenta 4 in Kassel. **1969** Taught at the University of California, Berkeley. **1971** Moved to Holland. **1972** Solo-exhibition at the Stedelijk Van Abbe Museum, Eindhoven. **1973** Professorship at the Academy of Arts in Venice. **1975** Exhibited at the Whitney Museum, New York and participated at the Venice Biennale. **1988** Retrospective at the Württembergischer Kunstverein, Stuttgart. **1991** Retrospective at the Musée d'Art Moderne in Nice. Di Suvero's public sculptures articulate space but have no recognisable formal logic of their own; in essence, they are almost deconstructivist. After working in wood, the artist began to use steel, especially industrially manufactured double-T-beams, for his sculptures.
MONOGRAPHS, CATALOGUES: M. Di S. Open Secret: Sculpture 1990-1992. Gagosian Gallery. New York 1993 (cat.).– M. Di S. Storm King Center. New York 1985 (cat.).– M. Di S. Museo de Bellas Artes. Valencia 1994 (cat.).– Evrard, M. and B. Roge: M. Di S. Chalons-sur-Saône 1975.– Monte, J. K. (ed.): M. Di S. Whitney Museum of American Art. New York 1975 (cat.).– Osterwald, T. (ed.): M. Di S. Württembergischer Kunstverein. Stuttgart 1988 (cat.).– Perlein, G. (ed.): M. Di S. Retrospective 1959-1991. Musée d'Art Moderne et d'Art Contemporain. Nice 1991 (cat.)

DIX Otto

1891 Untermhaus (near Gera) – **1969** Singen
German painter and graphic artist. **1905-1909** Apprenticeship as a decorative painter in Gera. **1910-1914** Studied at Dresden School of Arts and Crafts School. **1914-1918** Military service. **1919-1922** Studied at the Dresden Academy. Founding member of Gruppe 1919 attached to the New Dresden Secession. **1922-1924** Contact with the Junges Rheinland, young artists gathered around the gallerist Johanna Ey in Düsseldorf and later known as the Rhenish Expressionists. **1925** Participation in the exhibition "Neue Sachlichkeit" (New Objectivity) at the Kunsthalle Mannheim. **1927-1933** Professorship at the Dresden Art Academy. **1933** Forbidden to exhibit his works and dismissed from the Prussian Art Academy for political reasons. **1937** More than 200 paintings confiscated as "degenerate art". **1939** Arrested for suspected participation in the Munich assassination attempt on Hitler. Burning of paintings classified as "degenerate". **1943** Started *Primamalerei*, a painting technique. **1945** Called up and taken prisoner in France. **1950** Professorship at Düsseldorf Academy. **1959** Cornelius Award from the City of Düsseldorf and Großes Bundesverdienstkreuz (National Service Cross). **1962** Guest-residency at the Villa Massimo, Rome. **1964** Honorary member of the Accademia delle Arte del disegno in Florence. Awarded the Carl-von-Ossietzky medal. **1966** Lichtwark Award from the City of Hamburg and Martin-Andersen-Nexö Prize from the City of Dresden. **1967** Ernst-Thoma Award from the federal state of Baden-Württemberg. **1968** Honorary member of Karlsruhe Art Academy.
WRITINGS: O. D.: Kinderalbum. Ed. by D. Gleisberg. Leipzig 1991
CATALOGUES RAISONNES: Karsch, F. (ed.): O. D. Das graphische Werk 1913-1960. Hanover 1970.– Löffler, F. (ed.): O. D. Werkverzeichnis der Gemälde 1891-1969. Recklinghausen 1981.– Pfäffle, S. (ed.): O. D. Werkverzeichnis der Aquarelle und Gouachen. Stuttgart 1991.– Rüdiger, U. (ed.): O. D. Werkverzeichnis der Zeichnungen und Pastelle. 4 vols. Weimar 1998
MONOGRAPHS, CATALOGUES: Beck, R. (ed.): O. D. 1891-1969. Museum Villa Stuck. Munich 1985 (cat.).– Beck, R.: O. D. 1891-1969. Zeit, Leben und Werk. Constance 1993.– Conzelmann, O.: Der andere D. Sein Bild vom Menschen und vom Krieg. Stuttgart 1983.– Fischer, L.: O. D. Ein Malerleben in Deutschland. Berlin 1981.– Hagenlocher, A. (ed.): O. D. Bestandskatalog. Zeichnungen, Pastelle, Aquarelle, Kartons und Druckgraphik der Jahre 1912-1969 aus der Stiftung Walther Groz. Albstadt 1985.– Hartmann, C.: Untersuchungen zum Kinderbild bei O. D. Münster 1989.– Hollmann, A. and U. Zeller (ed.): O. D. Zum 100. Geburtstag. Galerie der Stadt Stuttgart et al. Stuttgart 1991 (cat.).– Hollmann, A. and U. Zeller (ed.): D. Tate Gallery, London et al. London 1992 (cat.).– Karcher, E.: Eros und Tod im Werk von O. D. Studien zur Ikonografie des Körpers in den zwanziger Jahren. Münster 1984.– Karcher, E.: O. D. Life and Work.
Cologne 1989.– Kim, J.-H.: Frauenbilder von O. D. Münster 1994.– Kinkel, H.: Die Toten und die Nackten. Beiträge zu D. Berlin 1991.– Lehmann, H.-U. (ed.): O. D. Die Zeichnungen im Dresdner Kupferstichkabinett. Kupferstichkabinett Dresden et al. Dresden 1991 (cat.).– Löffler, F.: O. D. Leben und Werk. Dresden 1960, Wiesbaden 1982/O. D. Life and Work. New York 1982.– Rüdiger, U.: Grüße aus dem Krieg. Die Feldpostkarten der O.-D.-Sammlung in der Kunstgalerie Gera. Gera 1991.– Sabarsky, S. (ed.): O. D. Staatliche Kunsthalle Berlin et al. Berlin 1987 (cat.).– Schmidt, D.: O. D. im Selbstbildnis. Berlin 1978.– Schmidt, J.-K. (ed.): O. D. Bestandskatalog: Gemälde, Aquarelle, Pastelle, Zeichnungen, Holzschnitte, Radierungen, Lithographien. Galerie der Stadt Stuttgart. Stuttgart 1989 (cat.).– Schneede, U. (ed.): O. D. Zeichnungen, Aquarelle, Graphiken, Kartons. Kunstverein in Hamburg. Hamburg 1977 (cat.).– Scholz, D.: O. D. Bestandskatalog. Galerie der Stadt Stuttgart. Stuttgart 1989.– Schubert, D.: O. D. In Selbstzeugnissen und Bilddokumenten. Reinbek 1991.– Schwarz, B.: O. D. Großstadt. Frankfurt-on-Main and Leipzig 1993.– Strobl, A.: O. D. Eine Malerkarriere der zwanziger Jahre. Berlin 1996.– Tittel, L.: O. D. Die Friedrichshafener Sammlung. Bestandskatalog. Friedrichshafen 1992

DOESBURG Theo van

1891 Utrecht – **1931** Davos
Dutch painter, architect and theoretician. **1908** Exhibited Impressionist paintings for the first time in The Hague. From **1912** published criticisms and articles on art. After **1916** developed an austere geometrical style and collaborated on architectural projects with the architects Jacobus Oud and Jan Wils. **1917** Together with Mondrian, founded the association of artists De Stijl and periodical of the same name. Developed the style of painting known as Neo-Plasticism. **1922** Collaborated briefly with the Dada movement, introducing it to Holland, and published the magazine *Mecano*. **1923** Moved to Paris. **1924** Published the Bauhaus book *Principles of the New Art*. First contra-compositions laid the foundations for Elementarism and introduce the dynamic diagonal. **1926-1928** Wall paintings for a restaurant in Strasbourg. **1929** Founded the magazine *L'Art Concret* and built his house and studio in Meudon.
WRITINGS: T. v. D.: De nieuwe beweging in de schilderkunst. Delft 1917, Amsterdam 1983.– T. v. D.: Drie voordrachten over de nieuwe beeldende kunst. Amsterdam 1919.– T. v. D.: Grundbegriffe der neuen gestaltenden Kunst. Munich 1925/Principles of Neo-plastic Art. Greenwich (CT) 1968.– T. v. D.: Naar een beeldende architectuur. Nijmwegen 1983.– T. v. D.: Das andere Gesicht. Gedichte, Prosa, Manifeste, Romaan 1913-1928. Ed. by H. Bulkowski. Munich 1983.– T. v. D.: De Stijl en de Europese architectur. De architecturop-
stellen in het Boubedrijf 1924-1931. Nijmwegen 1986.– Polano, S. (ed.): T. v. D. Scritti di arte e di architettura. Roma 1979
MONOGRAPHS, CATALOGUES: Baljieu, J.: T. v. D. London and New York 1974.– Boekraad, C. (ed.): T. v. D. De Stijl en de europese architectur. Nijmwegen 1986.– Doig, A.: T. v. D. Painting into Architecture, Theory into Practice. Cambridge (MA) 1986.– Georgel, P. and E. d. Lillers (ed.): T. v. D. Projets pour l'Aubette. Centre Georges Pompidou. Paris 1977 (cat.).– Hedrick, H. L.: T. v. D. Propagandist and Practitioner of the Avant-Garde 1909-1923. Ann Arbor (MI) 1980.– Jaffé, H. L. C.: T. v. D. Amsterdam 1983.– Leering, J. et al.: T. v. D. 1883-1931. Eindhoven 1968.– Lemoine, S. (ed.): T. v. D. Peinture, architecture, théorie. Paris 1990.– Straaten, E. v. (ed.): T. v. D. Een documentataire op basis van materiaal uit de schenking Van Moorsel. The Hague 1983.– Straaten, E. v. (ed.): T. v. D. Schilder en architect. Museum Boymans-van Beuningen, Rotterdam. The Hague 1988 (cat.).– Weyergraf, C.: Piet Mondrian und T. v. D. Deutung von Werk und Theorie. Munich 1979

DOISNEAU Robert

1912 Gentilly – **1994** Paris
French photographer. **1925-1931** Apprenticeship as a lithographer and photographer. **1931** Assistant to the stage director André Vigneau. **1932** First photojournalism for *Excelsior*. **1934-1939** Photographer for Renault. After **1940** became a freelance photographer. From **1945** worked for the photographic agency *Agence Alliance Photo* and from **1946** for the agency *Rapho*. Collaboration on a book project with the author Blaise Cendrars. **1947** Kodak Award. From **1949** contracted to work for *Vogue* as a fashion photographer. **1960** Travelled to the United States. **1968** Reported on the 50th anniversary of the Soviet Union. **1973** Together with F. Porcile, made the short film *Le Paris de R. Doisneau*. **1983** Broadcasting of the film *5 photographes* on TV France 3. One of the leading French photographers of the 40s and 50s. Apart from his innumerable fashion photographs he became famous for his reportages, his advertising work and for his satirical portraits.
WRITINGS: R. D.: A l'imparfait de l'objectif. Souvenirs et portraits. Paris 1989.– R. D.: J'attends toujours le printemps. Lettres à M. Baquet. Arles 1996
MONOGRAPHS, CATALOGUES: Chevrier, J.-F. R. D. Paris 1982.– R. D. Musée des Arts Décoratifs. Nantes 1975 (cat.).– R. D. Centre national de la photographie. Paris 1983 (cat.).– R. D.: Un certain R. D. Paris 1986.– R. D.: R. D. London 1991.– R. D. and P. Ory: R. D. Paris 1994.– R. D. Musée Carnavalet. Paris 1996 (cat.).– Hamilton, P.: R. D. A Photographer's Life. New York 1995/R. D. La Vie d'un photographe. Paris 1995.– Roumette, S.: R. D. Paris 1983, London 1991.– Vautrin, J.: R. D. Paris 1996

DOMELA César
(César Domela-Nieuwenhuis)
1900 Amsterdam – **1992** Paris
Dutch painter. Self-taught. **1922/23** Brief
stays in Ascona and Berne. First Constructivist works. Participation in an exhibition
of the Novembergruppe in Berlin. **1924**
Moved to Paris. Met Mondrian and van
Doesburg and joined De Stijl. **1927–1933**
Lived in Berlin. Member of Die Abstrakten
Hannover (The Hanoverian Abstract
Artists). Contact with the Bauhaus. Made
relief-like assemblages out of various materi-
als. **1933** Went back to Paris. Joined Abstrac-
tion-Création. **1937** Founded the journal
Plastique with Taeuber-Arp and Arp. **1947–
1956** Participated in the Salon des Réalités
Nouvelles. **1955–1960** Wall paintings in
various Dutch cities. **1987** Exhibition at the
Musée d'Art Moderne de la Ville de Paris.
WRITINGS: C. D.: L'Art en écrit. Paris 1982
CATALOGUE RAISONNE: Clairet, A.
(ed.): D. Catalogue raisonné de l'œuvre de
C. D.-Nieuwenhuis. Peintures, reliefs,
sculptures. Paris 1978
MONOGRAPHS, CATALOGUES: Brion,
M.: D. Paris 1961.– Briot, M.-O. (ed.): D.
65 ans d'abstraction. Musée d'Art Moderne
de la Ville de Paris et al. Paris 1987 (cat.).–
Cless, F. (ed.): D. Schilderijen, reliefs,
grafisch œuvre. Van Reekum Museum,
Apeldoorn et al. Apeldoorn 1990 (cat.).–
Derouet, C. (ed.): D. Gouaches de la
période parisienne. Utrecht 1984.– C. D.
Schilderijen, reliefs, beelden, grafiek,
typografie, fotos. Gemeentemuseum. The
Hague 1980 (cat.).– C. D. Stedelijk
Museum. Amsterdam 1987 (cat.).– Hering,
K.-H. (ed.): C. D.: Werke 1922-1972. Retro-
spektive. Kunstverein für die Rheinlande
und Westfalen. Düsseldorf 1972 (cat.).–
Jaffé, H. L. C.: D. Paris 1980.– Martini, G.
B. and A. Ronchetti (ed.): C. D. Fotografie,
fotomontaggi, disegni. Galleria Martini &
Ronchetti. Genoa 1981 (cat.).– Pobé, M.:
D. Hilversum 1965.– Zervos, C.: D.
Amsterdam 1966

DOMINGUEZ Oscar
1906 La Laguna (Canary Islands) –
1957 Paris
Spanish-French painter. Self-taught. **1927**
Moved to Paris where he had contact with
the Surrealists. **1929** First Surrealist works.
1930 Founded an artists' centre on Tenerife

where he organised an exhibition of Surrealist paintings in **1933**. **1934** Returned to Paris
where he invented *Décalcomanie*, a blotting
technique used to generate images and
later adopted by Max Ernst. **1937** First abstract
works. **1938** Participation in the "International Surrealist Exhibition" in Paris. **1948**
Became a French citizen. **1957** Suicide.
MONOGRAPHS, CATALOGUES: Castro,
F. (ed.): O. D. y el surrealismo. Madrid 1978
(cat.).– O. D. Schloß Morsbroich, Städtisches Museum. Leverkusen 1967 (cat.).–
Vazquez de Parga, A. et al.: O. D. Antologica 1926-1957. Las Palmas 1996.– Walberg,
P.: Black Irises for O. D. London 1961.–
Westerdahl, E.: O. D. Barcelona 1968.–
Xuriguera, G.: O. D. Paris 1973, Berlin 1973

DONGEN Kees van
(Cornelis Theodorus Maria van Dongen)
1877 Delfshaven (near Rotterdam) –
1986 Monte Carlo
Dutch painter. Studied at an arts and crafts
school and trained as a technical draughtsman. **1897** Broke off his apprenticeship and
left home. Settled in Montmartre, Paris,
doing odd jobs to earn a living. **1906** Joined
the Fauves and shortly after became a guest-
member of the Dresden Brücke group. **1907**
He lived at Bateau-Lavoir in Rue Ravignan,
where he met Picasso. **1908** Contract with
the Bernheim-Jeune Gallery. Van Dongen's
paintings display intense, voluptuous colour
effects and emotive contrasts. After World
War I he became a successful portraitist,
mainly of prominent figures in high society,
although his style became increasingly trivial
and decorative.
CATALOGUE RAISONNE: Wildenstein
Institute (ed.): K. van D. Catalogue
raisonné (in preparation)
MONOGRAPHS, CATALOGUES:
Adrichen, J. v. et al. (ed.): K. v. D. Museum
Boymans-van Beuningen, Rotterdam.
Amsterdam 1989 (cat.).– Chaumeil, L.: V.
D. L'homme et l'artiste. La vie et l'œuvre.
Geneva 1967.– Diehl, G.: K. v. D. Paris
1968.– Hopmans, A. (ed.): K. v. D. Early
and Fauvist Drawings 1895-1912. Museum
Boymans-van Beuningen, Rotterdam et al.
Rotterdam 1997 (cat.).– K. v. D. Retrouvé.
L'œuvre sur papier 1895-1917. Musée des
Beaux-Arts. Lyon 1997 (cat.).– Hild, E.
(ed.): K. v. D. 1877-1968. Musée de l'Annon-
ciade. Saint-Tropez 1985 (cat.).– Kyriazi, J.
M.: V. D. et le fauvisme. Lausanne and
Paris 1971.– Kyriazi, J. M.: V. D. après le
fauvisme. Lausanne 1976.– Pagé, S. et al.
(ed.): V. D. le peintre 1877-1968. Musée
d'Art Moderne de la Ville de Paris. Paris
1989 (cat.).– Wentinck, C.: V. D. Amsterdam 1962

DORAZIO Piero
born **1927** Rome
Italian painter. Studied architecture in
Rome. **1942** Started to paint. **1947** Co-
founder of the artists' group Forma 1 which
opposed expressionist and traditional tendencies in painting and tended towards

abstraction. **1947/48** Studied painting in
Paris. Contact with avant-garde artist
circles. Over the following years worked
full-time as an exhibition curator and art
publisher. **1949** Travelled to Austria and
Germany where he met Baumeister, Geiger
and Winter. **1953** Moved to America. **1961–
1970** Lectureship at the Graduated School
of Fine Arts in Pennsylvania. **1963** Together
with Angelo Savelli, founded the Institute of
Contemporary Art at Pennsylvania University. **1964** Participation in documenta 3 in
Kassel.
WRITINGS: P. D.: La fantasia dell'arte nella
vita Moderna. Roma 1955
CATALOGUE RAISONNE: Volpi Orlan-
dini, M. et al. (ed.): D. Venice 1977, Stutt-
gart 1978
MONOGRAPHS, CATALOGUES: Boehm,
G. et al.: P. D. Arbeiten auf Papier. Saulgau
1992.– Durbé, D. and M. Faggio dell'Arco
(ed.): D. Galleria Nazionale d'Arte Moderna,
Roma. Milan 1983 (cat.).– Fry, E. E. et al.
(ed.): D. Bayerische Staatsgemäldesamm-
lungen, Munich et al. Munich 1981 (cat.).–
Schultz, D. G. (ed.): P. D. A Retrospective.
Albright-Knox Art Gallery, Buffalo et al.
Buffalo 1979 (cat.).– Ungaretti, G.: P. D.
St. Gallen 1976.– Vernizzi, N. (ed.): P. D.
Musée de Grenoble et al. Milan 1990
(cat.).– Zevi, A. (ed.): P. D. Pinacoteca
communale di Ravenna. Ravenna 1985 (cat.)

DOVE Arthur
1880 Canandaigua (NY) – **1946** Centerport
(NY)
American painter. **1898–1903** Studied
painting and law at Cornell University in
Ithaca, New York. **1906** Worked as a freelance advertising draughtsman in New
York. **1907/08** Lived in Paris. While in the
South of France, moved away from Impressionism and closer to Fauvism. **1909** After
his return to America, he ran a farm in Connecticut and continued to do illustrations.
Became friends with the art dealer Stieglitz.
1912 First solo-exhibition with ten abstract
pastel-crayon works at Stieglitz' Gallery 291
in New York. **1924–1930** Lived on a house-
boat on Long Island. Made assemblages
from *objets trouvés* and, influenced by
Kandinsky's musical approach to art, developed a more abstract style. **1930–1934** Produced abstractions that were somewhat
surreal but based on natural forms. **1935**

Gave up organic-abstractionism to experi-
ment with geometrical compositions.
CATALOGUE RAISONNE: Morgan, A. L.
(ed.): A. D. Life and Work, with a Cata-
logue Raisonné. London, Newark and
Toronto 1984
MONOGRAPHS, CATALOGUES: Balken,
D. B. et al. (ed.): A. D. A Retrospective.
Cambridge (MA) 1997 (cat.).– Cohn, S.: A.
D. Nature as Symbol. Ann Arbor (MI)
1985.– Haskell, B. (ed.): A. D. San Francisco
Museum of Art et al. San Francisco and
Boston 1974 (cat.).– Johnson, D. R. (ed.):
A. D. The Years of Collage. College Park,
University of Maryland Art Gallery. 1967
(cat.).– Newman, S. M. (ed.): A. D. and
Duncan Phillips. Artist and Patron. The
Phillips Collection, Washington et al.
Washington 1981 (cat.).– Wight, F. S. A. D.
Berkeley and Los Angeles 1958

DRTIKOL František
1883 Pribram (CSSR) – **1961** Prague
Czech photographer. **1895–1901** Apprenticeship in the photographic studio of
Antonin Matta. **1901–1903** Attended
classes at the Lehr- und Versuchsanstalt für
Fotografie (College of Experimental Photography) in Munich. **1903/04** Worked in
various studios. **1910** Set up his own business in Prague, receiving numerous commissions for portraits. Representations of
female nudes in highly abstract compositions. **1915–1918** Military service. Numerous publications of his work in magazines.
1925–1935 Designed Art Deco requisites
and started painting. Exhibitions all over
the world. **1929** Publication of a collection
of photographs in the book *Les Nus de
Drtikol*. From **1935** gave up photography in
order to concentrate on the study of theosophy. One of the main representatives of Art
Deco photography. In their formalised flatness, his frequently retouched photographs
resemble Art Nouveau paintings.
MONOGRAPHS, CATALOGUES: Birgus,
V. and A. Brandy: F. D. Prague 1988.–
Birgus, V. (ed.): Fotograf F. D. Prague
1994.– Fárová, A. (ed.): F. D. SICOF. Milan
1973 (cat.).– Fárová, A. (ed.): F. D. Photographie des Art Déco. Munich 1986, 1993.–
Klaricová, K.: F. D. Prague 1989

DUBUFFET Jean
1901 Le Havre – **1985** Paris
French painter. **1918** After a two-year course
in painting at the academy in Le Havre,
went to Paris to study at the Académie
Julian. Met Suzanne Valadon, Max Jacob,
Léger and Dufy. **1924** Worked as a technical
draughtsman in Buenos Aires. **1925–1932**
Gave up his artistic ambitions to work in his
father's wine business. **1933** Took up painting again. **1944** First solo-exhibition at the
René Drouin Gallery in Paris. **1945** Started
to collect Art Brut, paintings by children
and mental patients. **1947** Founded the
Société de L'Art Brut and painted the
humorous and ironical series of portraits
entitled *More beautiful than you think*.

1955 Moved to Vence. From **1956** he constructed large sculptures from small, jigsaw-like pieces. These structures, resembling mountain ranges, could be expanded into architectural forms. **1959–1968** Participation in documenta 2–4 in Kassel. **1960** Musical experiments with Asger Jorn. **1967** First architectural environments. **1973** Retrospective at Guggenheim Museum in New York, where his surrealist play *Coucou Bazar* was performed. **1976** Presented his Art Brut collection to the city of Lausanne.
WRITINGS: Damisch, H. (ed.): J. D. Prospectus et tous écrits suivants. 2 vols. Paris 1967.– J. D.: L'homme du commun à l'ouvrage. Paris 1973.– J. D.: La Botte à nique. Geneva and Paris 1973.– J. D.: Bâtons rompus. Paris 1986.– J. D.: Asphyxiante culture. Paris 1986.– J. D.: Lettres à Jacques Berne. 1946-1985. Paris 1991.– Franzke, A. (ed.): J. D. Schriften. 4 vols. Bern and Berlin 1991-1994.– Glimcher, M. (ed.): J. D. Towards an Alternative Reality. New York 1987
CATALOGUES RAISONNES: Arnaud, N. (ed.): J. D. Gravures et lithographies. 2 vols. Paris 1961-1966.– Bonnefoi, G. (ed.): J. D. L'œuvre lithographique 1944-1984. Paris 1992.– Franzke, A. (ed.): J. D. Petites statues de la vie précaire. Bern and Berlin 1988.– Graham, L. (ed.): L'œuvre gravé et les livres illustrés de J. D. Catalogue raisonné. 2 vols. Paris 1992.– Loreau, M. and A. d. Trentinian (ed.): Catalogue intégral des travaux de J. D. 38 vols. Paris 1964-1991
MONOGRAPHS, CATALOGUES: Armengaud, J.-P.: La Musique chauve de J. D. Paris 1991.– Barilli, R.: D. materiologo. Bologna 1962.– Berne, J. (ed.): L'Herne. J. D. Paris 1973.– Cordier, D.: Les Dessins de J. D. Paris 1960/ The Drawings of J. D. New York 1960.– Chalumeau, J.-L.: J. D. Paris 1996.– Damisch, H. (ed.): J. D. Del paisaje fisico al paisje mental. Fundación La Caixa, Madrid 1992 (cat.).– Danchin, L.: J. D. Peintre-philosophe. Lyon 1988.– Demetrion, J. T. (ed.): J. D. 1943-1963. Paintings, Sculptures, Assemblages. Hirshhorn Museum and Sculpture Garden. Washington 1993 (cat.).– J. D. 1942-1960. Musée des Arts Décoratifs. Paris 1960 (cat.).– J. D. Lithographies. Série des phénomènes. Paris 1960.– J. D. Livres et estampes. Bibliothèque nationale de France. Paris 1982 (cat.).– J. D. Hauts lieux, paysages 1944-1984. Palais des Papes. Avignon 1994 (cat.).– J. D. Les dernières années. Galerie Nationale du Jeu de Paume. Paris 1991 (cat.).– Franzke, A.: J. D. Basel 1975.– Franzke, A.: J. D. Zeichnungen. Munich 1980.– Franzke, A.: J. D. New York 1981, Cologne 1990.– Glimcher, M.: J. D. Towards an Alternative Reality. New York 1987.– Haas, M.: J. D. Materialien für eine "andere Kunst" nach 1945. Berlin 1988.– Lhote J.-M.: J. D. Dessins-peintures 1942-1983. Paris 1984.– Limbourg, G.: Tableau bon levain à vous de cuire la pâte. L'art brut de J. D. Paris 1953.– Loreau, M.: D. et le voyage au centre de la perception. Paris 1966.– Loreau, M.: J. D. Delits, deportements, lieux de haut jeu. Geneva 1971.–

Loreau, M.: J. D. Stratégie de la création. Paris 1973.– Marchesseau, D. (ed.): D. Fondation Gianadda. Martigny 1993 (cat.).– Merkert, J. et al. (ed.): D. Retrospektive. Akademie der Künste, Berlin et al. Berlin 1980 (cat.).– Messer, T. M. (ed.): J. D. 1901-1985. Schirn Kunsthalle, Frankfurt-on-Main et al. Stuttgart 1990 (cat.).– Monferini, A. and L. Trucchi (ed.): J. D. 1901-1985. Galleria Nazionale d'Arte Moderna, Roma. Milan 1989 (cat.).– Pacquement, A. and F. Bonnefoy (ed.): J. D. Les dernières années. Galerie Nationale du Jeu de Paume. Paris 1991 (cat.).– Pacquet, M.: D. Paris 1993.– Picon, G.: Le Travail de J. D. Geneva 1973.– Prat, J.-L. (ed.): J. D. Rétrospective. Peintures, sculptures, dessins. Fondation Maeght. Saint-Paul 1985 (cat.).– Ragon, M.: J. D. Paysage du mental. Paris and Geneva 1989.– Rowell, M.: J. D. A Retrospective. New York 1973.– Selz, P.: The Work of J. D. The Museum of Modern Art. New York 1962 (cat.).– Thévoz, M.: J. D. Mires, structures dissipatives. Paris 1984.– Thévoz, M.: D. Geneva 1986.– Trucchi, L.: J. D. Milan 1965.– Vialatte, A.: J. D. et le grand magma. Paris 1988

DUCHAMP Marcel
1887 Blainville Crevon – **1968** Neuilly-sur-Seine
French artist. Studied at the Académie Julian in Paris and was first influenced by Cézanne, then by the Fauves, the Cubists and Futurists. **1913** With his *Bicycle Wheel* on a stool he coined the term "readymade" for mass-produced articles. He held the view that the choosing of subject matter is an integral part of the creative process. **1915** Went to New York and, together with Man Ray, Picabia, Crotti and Marius de Zayas, founded the pre-Dada group around Arensberg and Stieglitz, the Society of Independent Artists and in **1920**, with Katherine Dreyer and Man Ray, the Sociéte anonyme, Museum of Modern Art 20. **1921** Published *New York Dada* with Man Ray. **1925** Construction of the optical machines *Rotating Hemispheres*. **1936** Participation in the exhibitions "International Surrealist Exhibition" in London and "Fantastic Art, Dada, Surrealism" at the Museum of Modern Art, New York. **1938** Project for the portable museum *Boîtes-en-Valise* which contained most of the artist's works reproduced on a smaller scale. **1951** Member of the Collège de Pataphysique. **1957** Exhibition "Les Frères Duchamp" at Solomon R. Guggenheim Museum, New York. **1967** Published *Boîte blanche* (Notes on the *Large Glass*) at Cordier & Ekstroem in New York. **1968** Participation in the exhibition "Dada, Surrealism and their Heritage" at the Museum of Modern Art, New York. Since Duchamp's anti-art radically challenged traditional concepts of art and anticipated numerous later developments, he is regarded as one of the most important avant-garde artists and a central figure in 20th century art.
WRITINGS: M. D.: D. du signe. Ecrits. Ed. by M. Sanouillet. Paris 1975.– M. D.: Inter-

views and Statements. Ed. by S. Stauffer. Stuttgart 1991.– Hill, A. (ed.): D. Passim. A M. D. Anthology. Roadtown 1994.– Sanouillet, M. and E. Peterson (ed.): M. D. Marchand de sel. Paris 1958/ Salt Seller. The Writings of M. D. New York and Oxford 1973.– Stauffer, S. (ed.): M. D. Die Schriften. 2 vols. Zurich 1981-1993
CATALOGUES RAISONNES: Clair, J. and P. Hulten (ed.): M. D. 4 vols. Centre Georges Pompidou. Paris 1977 (cat.).– M. D. Graphics. Kyoto 1991.– Schwarz, A. (ed.): The Complete Works of M. D. London 1969, New York 1970, Florence 1974, New York 1997
MONOGRAPHS, CATALOGUES: Adcock, C. E.: M. D.'s Notes from the Large Glass. An N-Dimensional Analysis. Ann Arbor (MI) 1983.– Bailly, J.-C.: M. D. Paris 1984.– Berswordt-Wallrabe, K. v. (ed.): M. D. Respirateur. Staatliches Museum, Schwerin. Stuttgart 1995 (cat.).– Bonk, E.: M. D. La Boite en Valise. Die Schachtel im Koffer. De ou par M. D. ou Rose Sélavy. Inventar einer Edition. New York 1989/ M. D. Box in a valise. New York 1989.– Cabanne, P.: Gespräche mit M. D. Cologne 1972.– Cabanne, P.: Les Trois Duchamp. Neuchâtel 1975/ The Brothers D. New York 1975/ Duchamp & Cie. Paris 1997.– Camfield, W. A. (ed.): M. D. Fountain. The Menil Foundation. Houston 1989 (cat.).– Clair, J.: M. D. ou le Grand Fictif. Essai de mythanalyse du Grand Verre. Paris 1975.– Daniels, D.: D. und die anderen. Der Modellfall einer künstlerischen Wirkungsgeschichte in der Moderne. Cologne 1992.– Dörstel, W.: Augenpunkt, Lichtquelle und Scheidewand. Die symbolische Form im Werk M. D.'s. Gespräche mit M. D. Cologne 1972.– Cabanne, P.: Pikturaler Nominalismus. M. D. – Die Malerei der Moderne. Munich 1987.– Duve, T. d.: Résonances du Readymade. D. entre avant-garde et tradition. Nîmes 1989.– Duve, T. d. (ed.): The Definitively Unfinished M. D. Halifax and Cambridge (MA) 1992.– Erfurth, E. (ed.): M. D. Flaschentrockner. Doxographie. Oldenburg 1997.– Fischer, A. M. and D. Daniels (ed.): Übrigens sterben immer die anderen. M. D. und die Avantgarde seit 1950. Museum Ludwig. Cologne 1988 (cat.).– Gibson, M.: Duchamp Dada. Paris 1991.– Hamilton, R. (ed.): The Almost Complete Work of M. D. Tate Gallery. London 1966 (cat.).– Harnoncourt, A. d' and K. McShine (ed.): M. D. The Museum of Modern Art, New York et al. New York 1973, Munich 1989 (cat.).– Hopps, W. (ed.): M. D. A Retrospective Exhibition. Pasadena Art Museum 1963 (cat.).– Hulten, P. et al. (ed.): M. D. Opera. Palazzo Grassi. Venice 1993 (cat.)/ M. D. Work and Life. Palazzo Grassi, Venice. Cambridge (MA) 1993 (cat.).– Jones, A.: Postmodernism and the En-gendering of M. D. Cambridge 1994.– Kuenzli, R. E. and F. M. Naumann (ed.): M. D. Artist of the Century. Cambridge (MA) 1989.– Lebel, R.: Sur M. D. Paris 1959, 1985, New York 1959.– Lebel, R.: D. Von der Erscheinung zur Konzeption. Cologne 1972.– Lebel, R.: M. D. Paris 1985.– Masheck, J. (ed.): M. D. in Perspective. Englewood Cliffs (NJ) 1975.– Molderings, H.: M. D. Parawissenschaft, das Ephemere und der Skeptizismus. Frankfurt-on-Main 1983, Düsseldorf 1997.– Moure, G. (ed.): D. Museum Ludwig. Cologne 1984 (cat.).– Partouche, M.: M. D. J'ai une vie absolument merveilleuse … Biographie 1887-1968. Une Vie d'artiste. Marseille 1991.– Paz, O.: M. D. Appearance Stripped Bare. New York 1978/ Nackte Erscheinung: Das Werk von M. D. Berlin 1987.– Schwarz, A.: M. D. The Large Glass and Related Works. 2 vols. Milan 1967.– Seigel, J.: The Private World of M. D.

Berkeley 1997.– Suquet, J.: Le grand verre rêvé. Paris 1991.– Tomkins, C.: D. A Biography. New York 1996.– Zaumschirn, T. et al. (ed.): 100 Jahre M. D. 3 vols. Klagenfurt 1986

DUCHAMP-VILLON Raymond
1876 Damville (Eure) – **1918** Cannes
French sculptor. Brother of Marcel Duchamp and Jacques Villon. **1898** Dropped his medical studies to take up sculpture. First influenced by Rodin. **1902** he participated regularly in the Salon de la Sociéte Nationale des Beaux-Arts and later in the Salon d'Automne in Paris. **1912** Had contact with the Cubists and applied their principles to his sculptures. Cofounder of the Section d'Or. Regular meetings with artists, writers and critics including Albert Gleizes, Jean Metzinger, Guillaume Apollinaire, Alexander Archipenko and his brothers. **1913** Participated in the Armory Show in New York. Together with Gleizes, organized the First German Autumn Salon in Berlin. **1914** Produced his most celebrated work *The Horse*.
MONOGRAPHS, CATALOGUES: Cabanne, P.: Les Trois Duchamp. Neuchâtel 1975/ The Brothers D. New York 1975/ Duchamp & Cie. Paris 1997.– Cassou, J. and R. V. Gindertael (ed.): R. D.-V. Le Cheval majeur. Galerie Louis Carré & Cie. Paris 1966 (cat.).– Hamilton, G. H. and W. C. Agee: R. D.-V. 1876-1918. New York 1967.– Pach, W.: R. D.-V. Sculpteur 1876-1918. Paris 1924.– Popovitch, O. and M.-N. Pradel: R. D.-V. 1876-1918. Musée des Beaux-Arts. Rouen 1976 (cat.).– Pradel, M. N.: R. D.-V. La Vie et l'œuvre. Diss. Paris 1960.– Sweeney, J. (ed.): J. V.-D. Solomon R. Guggenheim Museum. New York 1957

DUFY Raoul
1877 Le Havre – **1953** Forcalquier
French painter. Began work aged 14 in a coffee import business and attended evening classes at an art school. **1900** Awarded a scholarship at the Ecole des Beaux-Arts in Paris. From **1904** had contact with the group the Fauves and was greatly influenced by Matisse. When staying with Braque in L'Estaque, he adopted elements of Cubism and his palette became almost monochrome. **1912** Impressions from his

travels led to a brightening of the coloration of his landscapes. **1920** Moved to Vence. Paintings of racecourses, sandy bays and concerts. **1937** Designed a mural for the Palais d'Electricité at the World Fair in Paris with several panels, covering a surface ten metres high and sixty metres wide. **1950/51** Went to the United States. Numerous designs for textiles, stage decorations and carpets. CATALOGUES RAISONNES: Guillon-Laffaile, F. (ed.): R. D. Catalogue raisonné des aquarelles, gouaches et pastels. 2 vols. Paris 1981-1982.– Guillon-Laffaile, F. (ed.): Catalogue raisonné des dessins. Vol. 1. Paris 1991.– Laffaile, M. and F. Guillon-Laffaille (ed.): R. D. Catalogue raisonné de l'œuvre peint. 5 vols. Geneva and Paris 1972-1985 MONOGRAPHS, CATALOGUES: Cogniat, R.: D. décorateur. Geneva 1957.– Cogniat, R.: R. D. Paris and New York 1962.– Courthion, P.: R. D. Geneva 1951.– Dorival, B.: La Belle histoire de la fée électricité de R. D. Paris 1953.– R. D. Créateur d'étoffes. 1910-1930. Musée d'Art Moderne de la Ville de Paris. Paris 1977 (cat.).– Forneris, J. (ed.): R. D. 1877-1953. KunstHaus. Vienna 1996 (cat.).– Girard, X. and D. Perez-Tibi: D. Le Peintre décorateur. Paris 1993.– Guillon-Laffaille, F. (ed.): R. D. Kunsthaus Bühler. Stuttgart 1995 (cat.).– Hunter, S.: R. D. New York 1954.– Laffaile, M. (ed.): R. D. 1877-1953. Haus der Kunst. Munich 1973 (cat.).– Lassaigne, J.: R. D. Geneva 1954, 1970.– Pérez-Tibi, D.: D. Paris 1989, New York 1989.– Robertson, B. and S. Wilson (ed.): R. D. Paintings, Drawings, Illustrated Books. Hayward Gallery. London 1983 (cat.).– Sussan, R. B.: R. D. Paintings and Watercolours. London 1958.– Valaison, M.-C. et al. (ed.): R. D. et le Midi. Palais des Rois de Majorque. Perpignan 1990 (cat.).– Werner, A.: R. D. New York 1953, 1970, 1985

DUNCAN David Douglas
born **1916** Kansas City (MI)
American photographer. **1935** Studied archaeology at the University of Arizona, Tuscon, and **1935-1938** marine biology at the University of Miami. Through deep-sea diving developed an interest in underwater photography. **1938** Expeditions to Chile and Peru in his capacity as a photographer and art historian working for the American Museum of Natural History, New York. Short-term employment as a boxer and deep-sea diver. During World War II, photographed the capitulation of the Japanese on a battleship in the Bay of Tokyo. **1946-1956** Worked as a photojournalist for *Life* magazine, covering Korea, Indochina and Palestine. From **1957** took many photographs of Picasso, and became close friends with him. **1966** Awarded the Gold Medal by U. S. Camera. **1972** Retrospective at the Whitney Museum of American Art, New York. **1977** Participated in documenta 6 in Kassel. **1981** Exhibition of "250 Photographs of Picasso" at the Sidney Janis Gallery, New York. MONOGRAPHS, CATALOGUES: D. D. D. William Rockhill Nelson Gallery. Kansas City 1971 (cat.).– D. D. D. Whitney

Museum. New York 1981 (cat.).– D. D. D. 250 Photographs of Picasso. Sidney Janis Gallery. New York 1981 (cat.)

EDDY Don
born **1944** Long Beach (CA)
American painter. **1965-1970** Studied at the University of Hawaii, Honolulu and at the University of California, Santa Barbara. **1968** First solo-exhibition at Kranin Gallery Honolulu. Since **1972** professorship at the New York University. **1972** and **1977** participation in documenta 5 and 6 in Kassel. Painted in a hyper-realistic style mainly from photographs of chromium-plated car parts such as bumpers, engine bonnets or hub caps reflecting surroundings. From the early 70s, window-paintings in which the theme of consumerism is related to urban environments. MONOGRAPHS, CATALOGUES: D. E. University of Hawaii. Manoa 1982 (cat.).– D. E. Nancy Hoffman Gallery. New York 1986 (cat.).– Faison, S. L. and J. Hallmark (ed.): D. E. Williams College Museum. Williamstown (MA) 1975 (cat.)

EISENSTAEDT Alfred
1898 Dierschau – **1995** Oaks Bluffs Martha's Vineyard (MA)
German-American photographer. **1913-1916** Studied at the University of Berlin. **1916-1918** Military service. **1926** First photographs. **1928** Worked as a freelance photojournalist for the *Berliner Tagblatt* and the *Weltspiegel*. **1929** First reportage of Thomas Mann receiving the Nobel prize in Stockholm. **1929-1935** Worked for the agency Pacific & Atlantic. **1933-1935** Portraits of leading Nazis. **1935** Emigration to the USA. **1935/36** Worked for *Vogue* and *Harper's Bazaar*. **1936** Chief photographer at *Life*. Over the following years he illustrated more than 90 front pages. **1966** Publication of first book *Witness to Our Time*. **1979** Returned to Germany and took numerous photographs which were published in the picture book *Eisenstaedt: Deutschland*. It is thanks to Eisenstaedt that photojournalism became an independent discipline. WRITINGS: Adam, P. (ed.): E. on E. A Self-portrait. New York 1985/E. über E. Munich 1985.– A. E.: E.'s Guide to photography. New York 1978

MONOGRAPHS, CATALOGUES: A. E. Deutschland. Rheinisches Landesmuseum. Bonn 1980 (cat.).– O'Neil, D. C. (ed.): E. Remembrances. Boston 1990

EMSHWILLER Ed
born **1925** Lansing (MI)
American video artist and film-maker. After finishing his degree in design at the University of Michigan, Ann Arbor he moved to Paris in **1949** to study graphic arts at the Ecole des Beaux-Arts. **1951** Continued his graphic studies in New York. Besides working as a science-fiction illustrator he started to work with film in **1956** and in **1971** with video. **1971** First solo-exhibition at the Whitney Museum of American Art, New York. **1973** Artist in residence at WNET-TV station in New York. **1977** and **1987** participation in documenta 6 and 8 in Kassel. Through his video tapes Emshwiller experiments with the possibilities of electronic image manipulation, for example the graphical breakdown of the image into outlines.

ENSOR James
1860 Ostend – **1949** Ostend
Belgian painter and graphic artist. Ensor received his first drawing lessons as a child in Ostend. **1877-1880** Studied at the Academies of Ostend and Brussels. His darkly dramatic interiors, landscapes and portraits were a renunciation of traditional conventions of art as taught by the academies. **1883** Founder member of the group Les XX in Brussels where, from **1885**, he regularly exhibited works rejected by the Brussels Salon. **1886** Visited England and experienced the ephemeral, airy quality of Turner's paintings. Developed a more impressionist painting technique. **1888** Painted *Entry of Christ into Brussels*, later to become his most famous work. After **1900** his creativity waned. **1901** Co-founder of the Libre Académie de Belgique (Independent Academy of Belgium). **1926** Participation in the Venice Biennale. **1929** Raised to the peerage. **1929** Exhibition at the Palais des Beaux-Arts in Brussels. **1939** Important retrospective in Paris. Ensor's subject-matter tended towards the fantastic, macabre and other-wordly. In his carnavalesque, expressive and colourful paintings and grotesque, bizarre etchings he portrayed the world of human fears and nightmares in the form of frightening creatures and mask-like faces. WRITINGS: Hellens, F. (ed.): J. E. Mes écrits. Liège 1974 CATALOGUES RAISONNES: Croquez, A. (ed.): L'œuvre gravé de J. E. Geneva 1947.– Elesh, J. N. (ed.): J. E. The Complete Graphic Work. 2 vols. New York 1982.– Geyer, M.-J. et al. (ed.): J. E. Das druckgraphische Werk. Strasbourg 1995 (cat.).– Taevernier, A. (ed.): J. E. Catalogue illustré de ses gravures. Ghent and Brussels 1973.– Tricot, X. (ed.): J. E. Catalogue raisonné des peintures. 2 vols. Antwerp 1992 / J. E. Cata-

logue Raisonné of the Oil Paintings. 2 vols. London 1992, Cologne 1992, New York 1993 MONOGRAPHS, CATALOGUES: Avermaete, R.: J. E. Antwerp 1947.– Brown, C. (ed.): J. E. Theatre of Masks. London 1997 (cat.).– Croquez, A.: L'œuvre gravé de J. E. Geneva 1947.– Croquez, R.: E. en son temps. Oostende 1970.– Daguerre de Hureaux, A. and D. Morel (ed.): J. E. Musée du Petit Palais. Paris 1990 (cat.).– Damase, J.: L'œuvre gravé de J. E. Geneva 1967.– Delevoy, R. L.: E. Antwerp 1981.– Ik, J. E. Museum voor Schone Kunsten. Ghent 1987 (cat.).– Florizoone, P.: J. E. over dierenbescherming en vivisektie. Nieuwpoort 1994.– Florizoone, P.: J. E. Les Bains à Oostende. Antwerp 1996.– Gindertael, Roger van: E. Boston 1975.– Hassaerts, P.: J. E. Bruxelles 1957, Stuttgart 1959, New York 1959.– Heusinger v. Waldegg, J.: J. E. Legende vom Ich. Cologne 1991.– Hoozee, R. et al.: J. E. Dessins et estampes. Antwerp 1987.– Hostyn, N. and X. Tricot (ed.): J. E. in Oostendse verzamelingen. Museum voor Schone Kunsten. Oostende 1985 (cat.).– Hostyn, N.: J. E. Vie et œuvre. Bruges 1996.– Janssens, J.: E. Paris 1978, 1984.– Kiefer, T.: J. E. Recklinghausen 1976.– Lebeer, L.: J. E. aquafortiste. Antwerp 1952.– Legrand, F.-C.: E. cet inconnu. Brussels 1971.– Legrand, F.-C.: E., la mort et le charme. Un autre E. Antwerp 1993.– Lesko, D.: J. E. The Creative Years. Princeton (NJ) 1985.– McGough, S.: J. E.'s "The Entry of Christ into Brussels in 1889". New York 1985.– Magnaguagno, G. and M. Matta (ed.): J. E. Kunsthaus Zurich et al. Zurich 1983 (cat.).– Ollinger-Zinque, G.: E. par lui-même. Brussels 1976 / E. by Himself. Brussels 1976.– Ridder, A. d.: J. E. Herdacht. Brussels 1950.– Szeemann, H. et al. (ed.): J. E. Kunsthaus Zurich et al. Zurich 1983 (cat.).– Tannenbaum, L. (ed.): J. E. The Museum of Modern Art. New York 1951 (cat.).– Tavernier, S. (ed.): J. E. Gallerie Civiche d'Arte Moderna, Ferrara. Roma 1986 (cat.).– Tricot, X.: Ensoriana. Oostende 1985.– Verhaeren, E.: J. E. Brussels 1980

EPSTEIN Jacob
1880 New York – **1959** London
American-English sculptor of Russian descent. **1988-1900** Studied at the Art Students League and worked in a bronze foundry. **1902/03** Attended classes at the Ecole des Beaux-Arts and the Académie Julian in Paris. **1905** Moved to England. First commissions for portrait busts. **1907** First public commissions for building sculptures. **1911** Made a sculpture for the grave of Oscar Wilde. **1912/13** Contact with Picasso, Brancusi, and Modigliani in Paris. **1913** First solo-exhibition at Twenty One Gallery, Adelphi. Up to **1916** follower of Vorticism. Made numerous bronze busts of public figures and several sculptures on Christian themes. WRITINGS: J. E.: Let There Be a Sculpture. An Autobiography. London 1940, 1963.– Haskell, A. L. (ed.): J. E. The Sculptor Speaks. London 1931

CATALOGUE RAISONNE: Silber, E. (ed.): The Sculpture of E. With a Complete Catalogue. Lewisburg 1987
MONOGRAPHS, CATALOGUES: Black, R.: The Art of J. E. Cleveland and New York 1942.– Buckle, R. u. K. Epstein (ed.): E. Drawings. London 1962.– Buckle, R.: E. Sculptor. London and New York 1963.– Cork, R. (ed.): J. E. The Rock Drill Period. Anthony d'Offay Gallery. London 1973.– J. E. Sculpture. Corcoran Gallery of Art. Washington 1973 (cat.).– J. E. Centenary. Tate Gallery. London 1980 (cat.).– Friedman, T.: "The Hydepark Atrocity". E.'s Rima. Creation and Controversy. Leeds 1988.– Gardiner, S.: E. Artist Against the Establishment. London 1992.– Silber, E.: The Sculpture of J. E. Oxford 1986.– Silber, E. et al. (ed.): J. E. Sculpture and Drawings. City Art Galleries, Leeds et al. Leeds 1987 (cat.).

ERFURTH Hugo

1874 Halle – **1948** Gaienhofen (Lake Constance)

German photographer. **1892 – 1896** Apprenticed to the Dresden court photographer Höffert. Afterwards studied painting and photography at Dresden Art Academy. From **1896** on, set up his own studio in Dresden which became a meeting point for artists in **1906**. Co-founder of the Gesellschaft Deutscher Lichtbildner (Society of German Photographers). Moved to Cologne in **1933** and then to Lake Constance. Regarded as one of the most important portrait photographers of the 20s. His portrayals are remarkable for their psychological perception and avoidance of any characterization through choice of background or surroundings.

MONOGRAPHS, CATALOGUES: Dewitz, B. v.: H. E. Menschenbild und Prominentenporträt 1902-1936. Cologne 1989.– Dewitz, B. v. and K. Schuller-Procopovici (ed.): H. E. 1874-1948. Photograph zwischen Tradition und Moderne. Agfa Foto-Historama im Museum für angewandte Kunst, Cologne et al. Cologne 1992 (cat.).– H. E. Bildnisse. Museum Folkwang. Essen 1961 (cat.).– Grohmann, W. (ed.): H. E. Wesenberg Galerie. Constance 1947 (cat.).– Gruber, F. (ed.): Über H. E. Städtische Galerie Siegen. Siegen 1964 (cat.).– Lohse, B. (ed.): H. E. 1874-1948. Der Fotograf der Goldenen Zwanziger Jahre. Seebruck 1977.– Steinert, O. (ed.): Bildnisse H. E. Museum Folkwang. Essen 1961 (cat.)

ERNST Max

1891 Brühl (near Cologne) – **1976** Paris

German painter, graphic artist and sculptor. Studied classical philology at Bonn University and painted on the side. After military service, returned to Cologne and founded a Dada group with Arp in **1918**. **1919** First overpaintings, cliché-prints and collages which were exhibited, at the invitation of Breton, in Paris in **1921**. **1922** Moved to Paris and was a co-founder of the Surrealist

group led by Breton. **1925** Introduced and developed several new art techniques, such as *frottage, grattage* and *décalcomanie*, which were to introduce the stimulus of the coincidental into the creative process. His works from the late 20s had poetic, surreal titles such as *Windsbraut, Vogelmonument, Muschelblumen* (Bride of the Winds, Bird Monument, Shell Flowers). **1929 – 1934** Made collage novels. **1930** Collaborated with Luis Buñuel and Dalí on the film *L'Age d'Or*. **1938** Broke away from the Surrealists. **1939** Was interned in France. **1941** Emigrated to the USA. **1946** Settled in Sedona, Arizona, where he concentrated mainly on sculptural works. Despite the widespread recognition he received in America, he returned to Paris in **1953** and, in **1963**, settled in the South of France. **1961** First important retrospective at the Museum of Modern Art, New York.

WRITINGS: Bertelé, R. (ed.): M. E. Ecritures. Paris 1970.– Gallissaires, P. (ed.): M. E. Schnabelwax und Nachtigall. Texte und Bilder. Hamburg 1994.– Motherwell, R. et al. (ed.): M. E. Beyond Painting and Other Writings by the Artist and His Friends. New York 1948
CATALOGUES RAISONNES: Spies W. et al. (ed.): M. E. Œuvrekatalog. 6 vols. Cologne and Houston 1975-1997.– Spies, W. (ed.): M. E. Das plastische Werk. Düsseldorf and Hanover 1998
MONOGRAPHS, CATALOGUES: Alexandrian: M. E. Paris 1986.– Bousquet, A.: M. E. Œuvre sculpté 1913-1961. Paris 1961.– Camfield, W. A. (ed.): M. E. Dada and the Dawn of Surrealism. The Museum of Modern Art, New York et al. Munich 1993 (cat.).– Derenthal, L. and J. Pech: M. E. Paris 1992.– Ernst, J.: A Not-So-Still Life. A Memoir. New York 1984 / Nicht gerade ein Stilleben. Erinnerungen an meinen Vater M. E. Cologne 1985.– Herzogenrath, W. (ed.): M. E. in Köln. Die rheinische Kunstszene bis 1922. Kölnischer Kunstverein. Cologne 1980 (cat.).– Hofmann, W. et al. (ed.): M. E. Inside the Sight. Rice University Institute of Arts. Houston 1973 (cat.).– Lake, J.: Skulpturen von M. E.: aesthetische Theorie und Praxis. Frankfurt-on-Main 1986.– Legge, E. M.: M. E. The Psychanalytic Sources. Ann Arbor (MI) 1989.– Leffin, G.: Bildtitel und Bildlegenden bei M. E. Frankfurt-on-Main 1988.– McLeod, F. and J. Findlasy (ed.): M. E. The Sculpture. Newport Harbor Art Museum. Newport Beach and Edinburgh 1992 (cat.).– Pech, J. (ed.): M. E. Fotografische Porträts und Dokumente. Max-Ernst-Kabinett, Brühl. Cologne 1991 (cat.).– Pech, J. (ed.): M. E. Skulpturer. Malmö Konsthall. Malmö 1995 (cat.).– Quinn, E.: M. E. Boston 1976, Zurich and Freiburg 1977.– Rainwater, R. (ed.): M. E. Beyond Surrealism. New York 1986.– Russell, J.: M. E. Leben und Werk. Cologne 1966 / M. E. His Life and Work. New York 1967.– Schneede, U. M.: M. E. Stuttgart 1972 / The Essential M. E. London 1972.– Spies, W. (ed.): M. E. Retrospektive 1979. Haus der Kunst, Munich et al. Munich 1979 (cat.).– Spies, W.: M. E.

Frottagen. Stuttgart 1986.– Spies, W.: M. E. Loplop. Die Selbstdarstellung des Künstlers. Munich 1986.– Spies, W.: M. E. 1950-1970. Die Rückkehr der schönen Gärtnerin Cologne 1971, 1988 / The Return of La Belle Jardinière. M. E. 1950-1970. New York 1971.– Spies, W.: M. E. Collagen. Inventar und Widerspruch. Cologne 1974, 1988 / M. E. Les Collages. Inventaire et contradictions. Paris 1984 / M. E. Collages. The Invention of the Surrealist Universe. New York 1991.– Spies, W. et al. (ed.): M. E. A Retrospective. Tate Gallery, London et al. Munich 1991 (cat.) / M. E. Retrospektive. Staatsgalerie Stuttgart et al. Munich 1991 (cat.).– Spies, W. (ed.): M. E. Sculptures. Centre Georges Pompidou, Paris et al. Paris 1998 / M. E. Skulpturen. Kunstsammlung Nordrhein-Westfalen, Düsseldorf et al. Cologne 1998 (cat.).– Trier, E.: Schriften zu M. E. Cologne 1993.– Waldberg, P.: M. E. Paris 1958.– Waldman, D. (ed.): M. E. A Retrospective. Solomon R. Guggenheim Museum. New York 1975 (cat.)

ERRO

(Gudmundur Gudmundsson)

born **1932** Olafsvik (Iceland)

Icelandic painter. **1949 – 1951** Studied at the Art Academy in Reykjavik. **1952 – 1954** Studied mural painting at Oslo Academy. **1953/54** Visited France, Italy, Spain and Germany. **1955 – 1958** Studied at the Art Academy in Florence. Apprenticeship in mosaic techniques in Ravenna. **1957** Visited Israel. **1958** Moved to Paris. **1962** Published the first *Mécanifeste* in Venice. **1963** Visited the United States where he directed happenings. **1971** For nine months he travelled round the world, stopping in Thailand among other places. Erro's paintings combine styles and quotes from various eras and genres into amusing satires on modern society.

WRITINGS: E.: Easy is interesting. Paris 1993
CATALOGUES RAISONNES: Lebel, J.-J. (ed.): E. 1974-1986. Catalogo generale. Bergamo 1986 / Catalogue raisonné. E. 1974-1986. Paris 1986
MONOGRAPHS, CATALOGUES: Ammann, J.-C. (ed.): E. Tableaux chinois. Kunstmuseum Luzern. Lucerne 1975 (cat.).– Ammann, J.-C. (ed.): E. Art History, Politics, Science Fiction. Copenhagen et al. Copenhagen 1993 (cat.).– Augé, M. (ed.): E. peintre mythique. Paris 1995.– Brownstone: E. Paris 1972.– A. Museum Moderner Kunst. Vienna 1996 (cat.).– Kvaran, G. and H. J. Neyer: E. Politische Bilder 1966-1996. Stuttgart 1996.– Moreau, X: E. New York 1983, Paris 1983.– Sergeant, P.: E. ou le langage infini. Paris 1979.– Tilman, P.: E. Paris 1976

ESTES Richard

born **1936** Kewanee (IL)

American painter. **1952 – 1956** Studied at the Art Institute of Chicago and moved to New York in **1959**. Originally earned his

living by doing illustrations and lay-outs. From **1966** devoted himself to painting. **1968** First solo-exhibition at Alan Stone Gallery in New York. **1972** Participation in documenta 5 in Kassel. **1979** Retrospective in Washington and in **1983** at the Museum of Fine Arts in Boston. He is one of the American Hyper- or Photorealists who represent real situations but exagerrate them through minute attention to detail. As in Pop Art, his subject-matter is taken from everyday life, but he uses photos and postcards as starting material. To intensify the brilliancy and glamour in his paintings, he occasionally uses fluorescent colours.

CATALOGUE RAISONNE: Meisel, L. K. (ed.): R. E. The Complete Paintings 1966-1985. New York 1986
MONOGRAPHS, CATALOGUES: Arthur, J.: R. E. Paintings and Prints. San Francisco 1993.– Canaday, J. and J. Arthur (ed.): R. E. The Urban Landscape. Museum of Fine Arts, Boston et al. Boston 1978 (cat.)

ESTEVE Maurice

born **1904** Culan (Cher)

French painter. Studied at various Parisian Art Schools, including the Académie Colarossi, but was mainly self-taught. **1923** Went to Spain. Managed the design department of a textile factory in Barcelona. From **1924** worked as a freelance artist. **1930** First solo-exhibition at Yvangot Gallery in Paris. From **1931** exhibition at the Salon des Surindépendants and from **1941** at the Salon d'Automne. Participated in the group exhibition "Jeunes peintres de la tradition française". **1937** Joint projects with Delaunay at the Paris World Fair. **1939/40** Military service. **1953** Participation in the São Paulo Biennale and in the **1954** Venice Biennale. **1959** Participation in documenta 2 in Kassel. Estève, who combines Cubist forms with Fauvist coloration, is regarded as one of the main representatives of Lyrical Abstraction in the Ecole de Paris.

CATALOGUE RAISONNE: Prudhomme-Estève, M. and H. Moestrup (ed.): M. E. L'œuvre gravé. Catalogue raisonné. Skorping 1986
MONOGRAPHS, CATALOGUES: Elgar, F.: E. Dessins. Paris 1960.– Ferrier, J. L. (ed.): M. E. Städtisches Kunstmuseum Düsseldorf. Düsseldorf 1961 (cat.).– Francastel, P.: E. Paris 1956.– Francastel, P. (ed.):

E. Collagen. Neue Galerie. Zurich 1969 (cat.).– LeBot, M. (ed.): E. Œuvres de 1950 à 1980. Musée Cantini, Marseille et al. Marseille 1981 (cat.).– Leymarie, J. (ed.): E. Oelbilder. Galerie Nathan. Zurich 1982 (cat.).– Leymarie, J. (ed.): E. Grand Palais, Paris et al. Paris 1986 (cat.).– Müller, J. E.: E. Paris 1974.– Prudhomme-Estève, M. (ed.): Collection du Musée de la Ville. Bourges 1990 (cat.).– Vallier, D. et al. (ed.): Hommage à M. E. Paris 1975

ETIENNE-MARTIN Henri
(Martin Etienne)
1913 Loriol (Drôme) – **1995** Paris
French sculptor. **1929 – 1933** Studied sculpture at the École des Beaux-Arts in Lyon. **1933 – 1939** Studied at the Académie Ranson in Paris, attending classes given by Malfray. **1935** Acquaintance with Duchamp, later with Brancusi, Michaux and Dubuffet. **1939 – 1942** Military service and imprisonment. **1949** Prix de la Jeune Sculpture. Exhibited regularly at the Salon de Mai and at the Salon des Réalités Nouvelles. **1958 – 1960** Lectureship at the School for Applied Arts and from **1958** at the Art Academy in Paris. **1960** First solo-exhibition at the Breteau Gallery in Paris. **1964** and **1972** participation in documenta 3 and 5 in Kassel. **1966** Major Award at the Venice Biennale. **1972** Solo-exhibition at the Musée Rodin and at the Grand Palais in Paris. His enigmatic wood, wire and textile constructions have a symbolic quality and fascinate through their subtle expression of things hidden, unseen and untouchable.
CATALOGUE RAISONNE: Szeemann, H. et al. (ed.): E.-M. Paris 1991
MONOGRAPHS, CATALOGUES: Allemand, E.-D. (ed.): E.-M. Sculptures/passementeries. Musée des Beaux-Arts. Calais 1984 (cat.).– Ammann, J.-C. et al. (ed.): E. M. Paris 1991.– Bozo, D. et al. (ed.): E.-M. Les Demeures. Centre Georges Pompidou. Paris 1972 (cat.).– Dypréau, J. (ed.): E.-M. Musée d'Art et d'Industrie de Saint-Etienne. Saint Etienne 1966 (cat.).– Lassaigne, J. (ed.): E.-M. Musée Rodin. Paris 1971 (cat.).– E.-M. Les Demeures. Centre Georges Pompidou. Paris 1984 (cat.).– E.-M. 1913-1995. Fondation de Coubertin. Saint-Rémy-les-Chevreuse 1996 (cat.).– Le Buhan, D.: Les Demeures-mémoires d'E.-M. Paris 1982.– Ragon, M.: E.-M. Büssel 1970.– Szeemann, H. et al. (ed.): E.-M. Les Demeures. Centre Georges Pompidou. Paris 1984 (cat.)

EVANS Walker
1903 St. Louis (MO) – **1975** New Haven (CT)
American photographer. Studied literature and languages in Andover, at Loomis and Williams. **1926 – 1927** Studied at the Sorbonne in Paris. Returned to New York and started his career as a photographer. Beside reportage, he treated various themes such as African art. **1933** First solo-exhibition with architectural photos at the Museum of

Modern Art, New York. **1935 – 1937** Photoreportage on rural poverty commissioned by the Resettlement Administration and the FSA. Further reportages on social topics. **1945–1965** Editor and photographer for the magazine *Fortune*. From **1965** professorship at Yale University, New Haven. **1997** Posthumous participation in documenta 10 in Kassel.
WRITINGS: W. E.: Let Us Now Praise Famous Men. New York 1966
MONOGRAPHS, CATALOGUES: Baier, L. K. (ed.): W. E. at Fortune 1945-1965. Wellesley College. Wellesley (MA) 1978 (cat.).– W. E. American Photographs. Modern Museum of Art. New York 1939, 1988.– Farmer, D. and W. Scott (ed.): W. E. Austin 1974.– Greenough, S. (ed.): W. E. Subways and Treets. National Gallery of Art. Washington 1991 (cat.).– Hill, J. T. and G. Mora (ed.): W. E. The Hungry Eye. The Museum of Modern Art. New York 1993, London 1994/W. E. La Soif du regard. Paris 1993/W. E. Der unstillbare Blick. Die endgültige Monographie. The Museum of Modern Art, New York. Munich 1993 (cat.).– Keller, J. (ed.): W. E. The Getty Museum Collection. Los Angeles 1995 (cat.).– Papageorge, T. (ed.): W. E. and Robert Frank. New Haven (CT) 1981 (cat.).– Rathbone, B.: W. E. A Biography. Boston and London 1995.– Szarkowski, J.: W. E. New York 1971, London 1972.– Thompson, Jerry L. (ed.): W. E. at Work. New York 1982.– Trachtenberg, A.: The Presence of W. E. Boston 1978

EXPORT Valie
(Waltraud Höllinger)
born **1940** Linz
Austrian multimedia artist. Studied design at the School for Applied Arts in Linz and at HTL in Vienna. **1955 – 1958** First self-portraits in the photo-series *Metamorphosen der Identität* (Metamorphoses of Identity). **1968** Cofounder of Austrian Filmmakers' Cooperative. **1975** Participation in the 9th Paris Biennale. **1978** Recorded the record *Wahre Freundschaft* (Real Friendship) with Monsti Wiener. **1980** Together with Maria Lassnig, represented Austria at the Venice Biennale. From **1985** foreign member of the American Cinematheque in Los Angeles. **1987** Retrospective of her features and experimental films at the National Film Theatre in London and at San Francisco

Cinematheque. **1990** Prize of the city of Vienna. **1991** Austrian cultural award for film. Export's extended cinema-events, designed to intensify sensual aspects of psychophysical experience, are related to Viennese Aktionismus.
MONOGRAPHS, CATALOGUES: Braun, C. v. et al. (ed.): V. E. Oberösterreichische Landesgalerie. Linz 1992 (cat.).– Braun, C. (ed.): Split: Reality V. E. Vienna 1997 (cat.).– Breitwieser, S. (ed.): White Cube/ Black Box. Vienna 1996.– V. E. Projektstudie Alpha. Linz 1997.– Mueller, R.: V. E. Fragments of the Imagination. Bloomingtom (IN) 1994.– Prammer, A.: V. E. Eine multimediale Künstlerin. Vienna 1988

EXTER Alexandra
1882 Belostok – **1949** Fontenay-aux-Roses
Russian painter and stage designer. **1901 – 1903** Studied at Kiev Art Academy. **1906 – 1908** Attended classes at the Academie Grande Chaumière in Paris. **1908** First works exhibited in public. Book designs and illustrations. **1909 – 1914** Lived in Paris, in close contact with the Cubists centred around Picasso and the Futurists led by Marinetti. **1912** Travelled to Italy. **1915** Returned to Russia. Influenced by Tatlin and Malevich, turned to non-objective painting. **1916** Designed a mural for a studio theatre in Moscow. Started to work intensively as a costume and stage set designer. **1919** Artistic advisor to the Ukraine ministry of information. **1920** Moved to Moscow. **1925** Joined the Constructivist group 5×5 = 25 led by Rodchenko. **1922/23** Designed uniforms for the army. **1924** Helped to organize the Russian pavilion at the Venice Biennale. Moved to Paris. **1925 – 1930** Taught at the private academy of Léger. **1927** First solo-exhibition at Der Sturm gallery in Berlin.
MONOGRAPHS, CATALOGUES: Ciofi degli Atti, F. (ed.): A. E. e il teatro da Camera. Archivio del' 900, Rovereto. Milan 1991 (cat.).– A. E. Artist of the Theatre. New York Public Library. New York 1974 (cat.).– Nakow, A. B.: A. E. Galerie Jean Chauvelin. Paris 1972 (cat.).– Thompson, J. L.: A. E. at Work. New York 1982.– Tugendkhold, J.: A. E. Berlin 1922

FABRO Luciano
born **1936** Turin
Italian painter and object artist. Self-taught. **1954–1958** Experiments with kinetic objects. **1965** First solo-exhibition in the Galleria Vismara in Milan. **1968–1975** Series of representations of Italy, using materials such as metals, glass and textiles in outline entitled *Itàlia*. **1972** Participated in documenta 5 in Kassel. From **1980** created installations with an enigmatic, poetic atmosphere. **1981** Major one-man exhibition in Essen and Rotterdam. **1982** and **1992** Participation in documenta 7 and 9 in Kassel. **1996** Retrospective at the Centre Georges Pompidou, Paris. With his minimal object arrangements, made with simple

materials, Fabro is one of the most important exponents of Italian Arte Povera.
WRITINGS: L. F.: Apologhi 1969-1978. Attaccapanni. Torino 1978.– L. F.: Lavori 1963-1986. Torino 1987/Travaux, Entretiens. Paris 1987.– L. F.: Regole d'arte. Milan 1980.– L. F.: Aufhänger. Cologne 1983.– L. F.: Arte torna arte. Milan 1987/Kunst wird wieder Kunst. Arte torna arte. Bern and Berlin 1990
MONOGRAPHS, CATALOGUES: Caldwell, J. (ed.): L. F. San Francisco Museum of Modern Art. San Francisco 1992 (cat.).– L. F. Lavori 1963-1986. Torino 1987.– Felix, Z. and W. A. L. Beeren (ed.): L. F. Sehnsucht. Museum Folkwang, Essen et al. Essen 1981 (cat.).– L. F. Works 1963-1986. Fruitmarket Gallery, Edinburgh et al. Edinburgh 1986 (cat.).– Gachnang, J. et al. (ed.): L. F. Castello di Rivoli, Museo d'Arte Contemporanea. Torino 1989 (cat.).– Grenier, C. et al. (ed.): L. F. Centre Georges Pompidou. Paris 1996 (cat.).– Mauban, J. L. (ed.): L. F. Musée d'Art Moderne de la Ville de Paris et al. Paris 1987 (cat.).– Morris, F. (ed.): L. F. Tate Gallery. London 1997 (cat.).– Mundici, C. (ed.): L. F. Castello di Rivoli, Museo d'Arte Contemporanea. Milan 1989 (cat.).– Risso, B. L. F. Torino 1980.– Rowell, M. (ed.): L. F. Fundació Joan Miró. Barcelona 1990 (cat.).– Sanna, J. d. (ed.): F. Logetta Lombardesca. Ravenna 1983 (cat.).– Schwander, M. (ed.): L. F. Die Zeit. Werke 1963-1991. Kunstmuseum Luzern. Basel 1991

FAHLSTRÖM Öyvind
1928 São Paulo – **1976** Stockholm
Swedish painter, collage and object artist. **1949–1952** Studied history of art and archaeology at Stockholm University. **1950–1955** Began to draw and paint while working as a journalist, dramatist and lyricist. **1953** Influenced by Bill's Concrete Art, he brought out the *Manifesto of Concrete Poetry*. **1955** Exhibition with the artists' group Phase. From **1961** lived alternately in New York and Stockholm, and worked on *Variable Paintings*, pictures with component parts that can be rearranged by means of magnetic attachments. **1967** Designed the Swedish pavilion at the Venice Biennale.
MONOGRAPHS, CATALOGUES: Avery-Fahlström, S. et al. (ed.): Ö. F. Die Installationen, the Installations. Gesellschaft für

Aktuelle Kunst, Bremen et al. Stuttgart 1995 (cat.).– Ö. F. IVAM Centro Julio González. Valencia 1992 (cat.).– Hulten, P. (ed.): Ö. F. La Biennale di Venezia. Venice 1966 (cat.).– Hulten, P.: Ö. F. Milan 1976.– Hulten, P. and B. Springfeldt (ed.): Ö. F. Centre Georges Pompidou. Paris 1980 (cat.).– Springfeldt, B. et al. (ed.): Ö. F. Moderna Museet. Stockholm 1979 (cat.).– Springfeldt, B. (ed.): Ö. F. Solomon R. Guggenheim Museum. New York 1982 (cat.).– Springfeldt, D. and F. Feuk (ed.): Ö. F. IVAM Centro Julio González, Valencia 1992 (cat.)

gen. Josef-Haubrich-Kunsthalle. Cologne 1980 (cat.).– Lafargue, J. and R. M. Mason (ed.): F. 1898-1964. Musée d'Art Moderne de la Ville de Paris. Paris 1989 (cat.).– Paulhan, J. and A. Berne Joffroy (ed.): J. F. Rétrospective. Musée d'Art Moderne de la Ville de Paris. Paris 1964 (cat.).– Paulhan, J.: F. l'enragé. Paris 1989.– Peyré, Y.: F. ou les outrages de J. F. de leurs commencements a 1940. Diss. Paris 1982.– Tuchel, H. G. (ed.): J. F. Kunstverein in Hamburg. Hamburg 1973 (cat.)

FAUTRIER Jean
1898 Paris – **1964** Châtenay-Malabry
French painter. Lived from **1908** in London, where he studied at the Royal Academy and the Slade School of Art. **1917** Returned to France. At first enjoyed little success as a painter, but received important backing from André Malraux and Jean Paulhan. From **1934-1939** worked in the French Alps as an hotelier and ski instructor, neglecting his painting to a certain extent. **1945** First major artistic success with the series *Hostages*. **1950** Invented a process for printing reproductions, the *Originaux multiples*, with the aim of rendering the one-off original obsolete. **1955/56** Turned away from L'art informel, portraying *Objects* and *Nudes* in his former naturalistic style. Further development of *Multiples* for a wider distribution of works of art. **1959** Participated in documenta 2 in Kassel. **1960** Grand Prix at the Venice Biennale. **1963** Retrospectives in Scandinavia. **1976** Solo-exhibitions in the Stedelijk Museum, Amsterdam, and the Kunsthaus Zurich. **1979** Major retrospective in the Musée d'Art Moderne de la Ville de Paris. Fautrier is considered one of the main exponents of L'art informel, although he himself objected to this label.
WRITINGS: J. F.: Sur la virtuosité. Lettre à Jean Paulhan. Caen 1987
CATALOGUES RAISONNES: Bucarelli, P. (ed.): J. F pittura e materia. Milan 1960.– Engelberts, E. (ed.): J. F. Œuvre gravé. Œuvre sculpté. Essai d'un catalogue raisonné. Geneva 1969.– Galansino, G. (ed.): J. F. A Chronology of His Early Paintings (1921-1942). Chicago 1973.– Lefort, M.-J. (ed.): J. F. Catalogue raisonné (in preparation).– Mason, R. M. (ed.): J. F. Les Estampes. Geneva 1986 / J. F.'s Prints. San Francisco 1986 / J. F. Die Druckgraphik: neuer Versuch eines Werkverzeichnisses. Stuttgart 1987
MONOGRAPHS, CATALOGUES: Argan, G. C.: F. Matière et mémoire. Milan 1960.– Bucarelli, P.: F. Pittura e materia. Milan 1960.– Cabanne, P.: J. F. Paris 1988.– Dickhoff, W. (ed.): J. F. Bilder 1926-1956. Galerie Sprüth, Cologne. Düsseldorf 1989 (cat.).– J. F. Gemälde, Skulpturen, Radierungen. Insel Hombroich. Neuss 1987 (cat.).– J. F. Musée National Fernand Léger, Biot et al. Paris 1996 (cat.).– Gohr, S. et al. (ed.): J. F. Gemälde, Skulpturen und Handzeichnun-

FEININGER Andreas
1906 Paris – **1999** New York
American photographer and photojournalist. Studied **1925-1927** at the Weimar Bauhaus where his father Lyonel, was teaching. **1929-1931** worked as an architect in Dessau and Hamburg and **1932-1933** with Le Corbusier in France. From **1939** lived in Sweden, working as an architectural photographer. **1939-1962** Photojournalist for *Life* magazine in New York, and thereafter freelance photographer. **1997/98** Several large retrospectives. **1998** Cultural Prize of the German Photographic Society. Feininger wrote many books on photography.
WRITINGS: A. F.: F. on Photography. Chicago and New York 1949.– A. F.: Advanced Photography. New York 1952.– A. F.: Successful Color Photography. Englewood Cliffs (NJ) 1957.– A. F.: Das Buch der Farbfotografie. Düsseldorf 1959.– A. F.: Der Schlüssel zur Fotografie von heute. Düsseldorf 1960.– A. F.: Die Hohe Schule der Fotografie. Düsseldorf 1961, Munich 1977 / A Manuel of Advanced Photography. London 1962.– A. F.: The Complete Photographer. London 1966.– A. F.: Quellen der Fotografie. Düsseldorf 1975 / Roots of Art. New York and London 1975
MONOGRAPHS, CATALOGUES: Hattersley, R.: A. F. New York 1973

FEININGER Lyonel
1871 New York – **1956** New York
American painter and graphic artist. **1887** Moved with his family to Germany. **1887-1891** Attended the Hamburg School of Arts and Crafts and the Berlin Academy of Arts.

1890 First caricatures. **1892/93** Studied at the Académie Cola Rossi in Paris. **1893** Returned to Berlin where he worked as a caricaturist for German and American magazines until **1906**. **1906/07** Went to Paris and met the German artists gathered around Matisse, and also made contact with the Cubists and Delaunay, leading to a prismatic structuring of his paintings. **1909** Joined the Berlin Secession. **1913** Invited by members of the Blauer Reiter to take part in the First German Autumn Salon. **1918** Member of the Novembergruppe. **1919-1933** Taught graphic art and painting at the Bauhaus in Weimar and Dessau. **1924** Together with Jawlensky, Kandinsky and Klee, founded the group Die Blauen Vier. **1933** Moved to Berlin. **1936** Emigrated to the United States and taught at Mills College in Oakland, California. **1937** Moved to New York. **1945** Taught at Black Mountain College, North Carolina.
WRITINGS: Schreyer, L. (ed.): L. F. Dokumente und Visionen. Munich 1957
CATALOGUES RAISONNES: Hess, H. and J. Feininger (ed.): L. F. Mit Werkverzeichnis der Gemälde. Stuttgart 1959, 1989 / L. F. New York 1961.– Prasse, L. E. (ed.): L. F. Das graphische Werk. Radierungen, Lithographien, Holzschnitte. Berlin 1972 / L. F. A Definite Catalogue of His Graphic Work. Etchings, Lithographs, Woodcuts. Cleveland Museum of Art. Cleveland 1972 (cat.)
MONOGRAPHS, CATALOGUES: Büche, W. et al. (ed.): L. F. Die Halle-Bilder. Staatliche Galerie Moritzburg, Halle. Munich 1991 (cat.).– Deuchler, F. (ed.): F. in Paris. L. F.: Die Pariser Zeichnungen von 1892-1911. Germanisches Nationalmuseum. Nuremberg 1992 (cat.).– Deuchler, F.: L. F. Sein Weg zum Bauhaus-Meister. Leipzig 1996.– Dorfles, G.: L. F. Milan 1958.– L. F. Kunsthaus Zürich / Haus der Kunst, Munich. Munich and Zurich 1973 (cat.).– L. F. Zeichnungen und Aquarelle. Hamburger Kunsthalle et al. Hamburg 1998 (cat.).– Feininger, T. L.: Die Stadt am Ende der Welt. L. F. Munich 1965 / L. F. City at the Edge of the World. New York 1965.– Firmenich, A. and U. Luckhardt (ed.): L. F. Natur-Notizen. Skizzen und Zeichnungen aus dem Busch-Reisinger-Museum, Harvard University. Kunsthalle Emden et al. Cologne 1993 (cat.).– Hentzen, A.: L. F. Aquarelle. Munich 1958.– Hess, H. (ed.): L. F. Haus der Kunst. Munich 1973 (cat.).– Jensen, J. C. (ed.): L. F. Gemälde, Aquarelle und Zeichnungen, Druckgraphik. Kunsthalle zu Kiel. Kiel 1982 (cat.).– Kahn-Rossi, M. and M. Franciolli (ed.): L. F. Museo Cantonale d'Arte, Lugano 1991 (cat.).– Luckhardt, U.: L. F. Die Karikaturen und das zeichnerische Frühwerk. Munich 1987.– Luckhardt, U.: L. F. Munich 1989, New York 1995.– Luckhardt, U. (ed.): L. F. Karikaturen. Hamburg 1998 (cat.).– Luckhardt, U. (ed.): L. F. Die Zeichnungen und Aquarelle. Hamburger Kunsthalle et al. Hamburg 1998 (cat.).– März, R.: L. F. Berlin 1981.– Ness, J. L. (ed.): L. F. London and New York 1975.– Romanus, P. (ed.): L. F. Die Halle-Bilder. Munich 1991.– Sabarsky, S.: L. F. Zeichnungen und Aquarelle. (n. p.) 1991.– Schmied, W.: L. F. Frankfurt-on-Main 1961.– Schreyer, E.: L. F. Caricature and Fantasy. Detroit 1964.– Timm, W. (ed.): L. F. Erlebnis und Vision. Die Reisen an die Ostsee 1892-1935. Museum Ostdeutsche Galerie. Regensburg 1992 (cat.)

FELIXMÜLLER Conrad
1897 Dresden – **1977** Berlin
German painter and graphic artist. **1911** School of Arts and Crafts in Dresden. **1912-1915** Attended the Art Academy in Dresden.

1915 Contributed to the journals *Der Sturm* and *Aktion*. Contact with the Berlin avantgarde. **1918** Joined the German Communist Party. **1919** Founded the New Secession in Dresden and Gruppe **1911** and joined the Novembergruppe. **1920** Major national painting award. **1934** Moved to Berlin. **1937/38** Confiscation and destruction of 151 works by the Nazis. Forty works hung in the exhibition of "degenerate art" in Munich. **1944-1964** Lived in Tautenhain near Leipzig. **1945** Prisoner of war in Russia. **1949-1962** Professorship at the University of Halle. **1964-1977** Lived in East Berlin, then moved to West Berlin. **1973** First retrospective in the *Verein Bildender Künstler* in Berlin. **1974** Received special honours at the IV International Biennale for Graphic Art in Florence.
WRITINGS: Söhn, G. (ed.): C. F. Von ihm, über ihn. Texte von und über C. F. Düsseldorf 1977.– Herzog, G. H. (ed.): C. F.: Legenden 1912-1976. Tübingen 1977
CATALOGUES RAISONNES: Heckmanns, F. W. (ed.): Das druckgraphische Werk von C. F. Düsseldorf 1986.– Söhn, G.: C. F. Das graphische Werk 1912-1977. 2 vols. Düsseldorf 1975-1980, 1987.– Spielmann, H. (ed.): C. F. Monographie und Werkverzeichnis der Gemälde. Cologne 1996
MONOGRAPHS, CATALOGUES: C. F. 1897-1977. Museum am Ostwall. Dortmund 1978 (cat.).– C. F. Retrospektive. Städtisches Kunstmuseum Düsseldorf. Düsseldorf 1990 (cat.).– Gleisberg, D. et al. (ed.): C. F. Gemäldegalerie Neue Meister, Dresden. Berlin 1975 (cat.).– Gleisberg, D.: C. F. Leben und Werk. Dresden 1982.– Heckmanns, F. W.: F. Buch der Holzschnitte. Düsseldorf 1985.– Heckmanns, F. W. (ed.): C. F. Das druckgraphische Werk 1912-1976 im Kunstmuseum Düsseldorf. Düsseldorf 1986.– Herzog, G. H.: C. F. Legenden 1912-1976. Tübingen 1977.– Krempel, U. (Hg.): C. F. Die Dresdner Jahre 1914-1934. Gemäldegalerie Neue Meister, Dresden et al. Köln 1997 (cat.).– Pese, C. (ed.): C. F. Werke und Dokumente. Germanisches Nationalmuseum. Nuremberg 1981 (cat.).– Rathke, C. (ed.): C. F. Gemälde, Aquarelle, Zeichnungen, Druckgraphik, Skulpturen. Schleswig-Holsteinisches Landesmuseum, Schloß Gottorf. Schleswig 1990 (cat.).– Söhn, G. (ed.): C. F. Von ihm – über ihn. Düsseldorf 1977

FETTING Rainer
born **1949** Wilhelmshaven
German painter. **1972-1978** Studied painting at the Berlin School of Arts. **1975-1981** Made various films including *Birthday* and *Brooklyn 11238*. **1977** Together with Helmut Middendorf, Salomé and Bernd Zimmer, founded Galerie am Moritzplatz. **1977/78** DAAD overseas grant for New York. **1980** First group exhibition entitled "Vehement Painting" with members of the Galerie am Moritzplatz at Haus am Waldensee, Berlin. **1980-1983** Serial repetitions of specific themes in series of works. **1984** Worked with found materials, attached to the canvas

and then painted over. Fetting is one of the main representatives of the Junge Wilde.
MONOGRAPHS, CATALOGUES: Felix, Z. (ed.): R. F. Folkwang Museum, Essen et al. Essen 1986 (cat.).– R. F. Studio d'Arte Cannaviello, Milan et al. Berlin 1983 (cat.).– R. F. Berlin, New York. Gemälde und Skulpturen. Staatliche Museen, Nationalgalerie, Berlin et al. Berlin 1990 (cat.).– Georg, B. and U. E. Huse (ed.): R. F. Gemälde und Zeichnungen. Harenberg City-Center. Dortmund 1994 (cat.)

FILATOV Nikolai
born **1952** Lemberg
Russian painter. **1969–1971** Studied architecture at Lemberg Polytechnic. **1971–1977** Continued architectural studies at the Institute of Applied and Decorative Arts in Lemberg where from **1978–1982** he taught composition, colour theory and painting. **1982** Moved to Moscow. **1984** Joined the Youth Section of the Moscow Department of the Soviet Artists' Association. Since **1983** has taken part in exhibitions in the USSR and abroad.

FILLIOU Robert
1926 Sauve – **1987** Les Eyzies (Dordogne) French action and object artist. **1943** Fought with the Communist partisans. **1948–1951** Studied economics in Los Angeles. **1951–1954** Extensive travels in the Far East. Greatly interested in Zen-Buddhism. **1960** Returned to France where from **1961** he produced neo-dadaist action poetry and plays. From **1962** took part in numerous Fluxus events. **1965–1968** Together with

George Brecht, managed the business enterprise "La Cédille qui Sourit", marketing jewellery, games and Fluxus items, and **1966** founded the Non-Ecole de Villefranche, also with Brecht. From **1968** lived alternately in France and Germany. **1972** Participated in documenta 5 in Kassel. **1980** Guest-Professor at the Academy of Arts in Hamburg. **1982** Kurt Schwitters Award from the City of Hanover. **1984–1987** Retired to a monastery in the Dordogne. Filliou's performances and happenings revolve around the theme *Permanent Creation*, defining *Work as Play* or *Work as Thought*.
WRITINGS: R. F.: Ample Food for Stupid Thought. New York 1965.– R. F. and G. Brecht: Games at the Cedilla, or the Cedilla Takes Off. New York 1967.– R. F. et al.: Lehren und Lernen als Aufführungskünste. Cologne 1970
MONOGRAPHS, CATALOGUES: Erlhoff, M. et al. (ed.): R. F. Das immerwährende Ereignis zeigt. Sprengel Museum Hanover et al. Hanover 1984 (cat.)/La Fête permanente présente: R. F. Musée d'Art Moderne de la Ville de Paris, Paris et al. Paris 1984 (cat.).– Kellein, T. et al. (ed.): R. F. Kunsthalle Basel et al. Basel et al. 1990 (cat.).– Mirotchnikoff, F. (ed.): R. F. Centre Georges Pompidou. Paris 1991 (cat.).– Parsy, P.-H. et al. (ed.): R. F. Paris 1991 (cat.).– Schmidt, H.-W. (ed.): R. F. zum Gedächtnis. 1926-1987. Städtische Kunsthalle Düsseldorf. Düsseldorf 1988 (cat.)

FISCHER Arno
born **1927** Berlin
German photographer. **1947–1953** Studied sculpture at the Käthe Kollwitz School of Art in East Berlin and at the School of Art in Weissensee, near Berlin, where he worked as an assistant and teacher from **1956–1971**. Thereafter worked as a freelance photographer and journalist. **1985–1992** Guest-professorship at the Leipzig School of Graphic Art and Book Design, and full professorship from **1985–1993**. From **1990** taught at the Technical College in Dortmund. **1997** Nominated "Fotopersönlichkeit des Jahres" (Photo-personality of the Year). Fischer specializes in fashion photography, portraits and live photography. One of his photoseries documents life in Berlin when still divided into East and West.
MONOGRAPHS, CATALOGUES: Immisch, T. O. and K. E. Göltz (ed.): A. F. Photographien. Staatliche Galerie Moritzburg. Halle 1997 (cat.)

FISCHL Eric
born **1948** New York
American painter. **1968/69** Studied at Arizona State University in Phoenix and **1970–1973** at California Institute of the Arts in Valencia. Became acquainted with Salle and Bleckner. **1974** Continued studies at Nova Scotia College of Art and Design in Halifax, Canada. **1975** First solo-exhibition

at the Dalhousie Gallery, Halifax. **1976/77** After an early abstract phase, turned to figurative painting. Created the Fisher Family, whose members became principal figures in many of his paintings. **1978** Sojourn in New York. **1979/80** *Sleepwalker*, his painting of a boy masturbating in a swimming pool, made him famous throughout America and Europe. **1987** Took part in documenta 8 in Kassel. **1991** Exhibition at the Louisiana Museum for Modern Art, Humblebæk. Fischl's portrayals of everyday life and leisure activities highlight the ambiguity underlying American politics and society and the American way of life
WRITINGS: Kuspit, D.: An Interview with E. F. New York 1987
MONOGRAPHS, CATALOGUES: Billeter, E. (ed.): E. F. Bilder und Zeichnungen. Akademie der Bildenden Künste, Vienna et al. Bern 1990 (cat.).– Billeter, E. et al.: E. F. Aarhus Kunstmuseum et al. Aarhus 1991 (cat.).– Doctorow, E. L. et al. (ed.): E. F. Scenes and Sequences. Hood Museum of Art, Dartmouth College. Dartmouth 1990 (cat.).– E. F. Kunsthalle Basel et al. Basel 1985 (cat.).– Glenn, C. W. and L. Barbnes (ed.): E. F. Scenes before the Eye. Long Beach Museum of Art et al. Long Beach 1986 (cat.).– Schjeldahl, P.: E. F. New York 1988.– Whitney, D. (ed.): E. F. New York 1988

FLANAGAN Barry
born **1941** Prestatyn (Wales)
English sculptor. **1964–1966** Studied sculpture under Phillip King at St. Martin's School of Art in London. **1966** First solo-exhibition, at the Rowan Gallery London, of small sculptures, purposefully contrasted with the monumental works of Moore and Caro. Experiments with new materials such as textiles, brushwood, rope and sand. **1969** Lived in New York. **1972** Grant from the Gulbenkian Foundation. Collaborated with Carolyn Carlson on a ballet. From **1973** worked mainly in stone. **1979** In creating the sculpture *Leaping Hare*, he found an attractive motif that he developed in further variations and other materials such as bronze and plaster. **1982** Represented Great Britain at the Venice Biennale and participated in documenta 7 in Kassel. **1983** Retrospective at the Centre Georges Pompidou, Paris.

MONOGRAPHS, CATALOGUES: Compton, M. et al. (ed.): B. F. Sculpture. British Pavillion. Biennale Venice et al. London 1982 (cat.).– B. F. Sculptures. Centre Georges Pompidou. Paris 1983 (cat.).– B. F. Prints 1970-1983. Tate Gallery. London 1986 (cat.).– B. F. Musée de Nantes. Nantes 1993 (cat.).– Fuchs, R. and C. Lampert (ed.): B. F. Stedelijk Van Abbe Museum, Eindhoven 1977 (cat.).– Jourbert, C. and E. Pernoud (ed.): B. F. Estampes. Paris 1996 (cat.).– Juncosa, E. (ed.): B. F. Fundación La Caixa, Madrid et al. Madrid 1993 (cat.)

FLAVIN Dan
1933 New York – **1996** Riverhead (NY) American object artist. Self-taught. **1953** Trained as a meteorologist with the US Air Force. Served as a weather monitor during the Korean war. **1956–1959** Studied at the New School of Social Research and at Columbia University in New York. **1961** Exhibited watercolours and abstract constructions at the Judson Gallery in New York, and used light as an artistic medium. **1963** First light installations, incorporating standard, commercial fluorescent strip lighting. **1966** Took part in the exhibition of Minimal Art, entitled "Primary Structures" at the Jewish Museum, New York. **1967** Taught at the University of North Carolina. **1968** and **1977** Participation in documenta 4 and 6 in Kassel. **1973** Guest-professorship at the University of Bridgeport, Connecticut. **1992** Neon installations at the Guggenheim Museum, New York. **1996** Decorated the front of the Berlin Museum of Modern Art with green and blue fluorescent tubes. Flavin dedicated many of his light objects to well-known art historians, gallery-owners and artists such as Robert Rosenblum, Heiner Friedrich, Tatlin, Barnett Newman and Roy Lichtenstein.
MONOGRAPHS, CATALOGUES: Belloli, J. and E. S. Rauh (ed.): D. F. Drawings, Diagramms and Prints 1972-1975. The Fort Worth Art Museum et al. Fort Worth 1977 (cat.).– D. F. Fluorescent Light. National Gallery of Canada. Ottawa 1969 (cat.).– D. F. Fünf Installationen in fluoreszierendem Licht. Kunsthalle Basel. Basel 1975 (cat.).– D. F. Solomon R. Guggenheim Museum. New York 1982 (cat.).– Koshalek, R. and K. Brougher (ed.): D. F. Monuments for Tatlin 1964-1982. Museum of Contemporary Art. Los Angeles 1989 (cat.).– D. F. Städtisches Museum Abteiberg. Mönchengladbach 1990 (cat.).– Friedel, H. (ed.): D. F. Kunstbau Lenbachhaus München. Munich 1994 (cat.).– Gallwitz, K. et al. (ed.): D. F. Installationen in fluoreszierendem Licht 1989-1993. Städtische Galerie im Städel, Frankfurt-on-Main. Stuttgart 1993 (cat.).– Meyer, F. et al. (ed.): D. F. Drawings, Diagrams and Prints 1972-1975. The Fort Worth Art Museum et al. Fort Worth 1976 (cat.).– Poetter, J. and M. Deschamps (ed.): Neue Anwendungen fluoreszierenden Lichts mit Diagrammen, Zeichnungen und Drucken von D. F. Staatliche Kunsthalle Baden-

Baden. Stuttgart 1989 (cat.).– Schneckenburger, M. et al. (ed.): D. F. Drei Installationen in fluoreszierendem Licht. Kunsthalle Köln. Cologne 1973 (cat.)

FLEISCHMANN Adolf Richard
1892 Esslingen – 1968 Stuttgart
German painter. 1908–1913 Studied at the
Royal School of Arts and Crafts and at the
Stuttgart Academy. 1922 Exhibited in the
New Secession in Munich. 1925 First
abstract works in cubist style. 1930–1938
Long visits to Spain, Italy and Switzerland.
1938 Moved to Paris, and was active in the
underground movement during the war.
1946 Member of the group Réalités Nouvelles. 1950 Began the series *equérres*, taking
up and developing Mondrian's theories of
Neo-plasticism. 1952 Moved to the USA.
1962 Taught at Columbia University, New
York. Member of the group American
Abstract Artists. 1965 Returned to Germany.
With his geometrically structured, rhythmically vibrating colour compositions, Fleischmann anticipated Op Art.
CATALOGUE RAISONNE: Fischer, A. M.
(ed.): A. F. Tübingen 1976
MONOGRAPHS, CATALOGUES:
Damsch-Wiehager, R. (ed.): A. F. Retro-
spektive zum 100. Geburtstag. Galerie der
Stadt Esslingen, Villa Merkel. Esslingen
1992 (cat.).– Fischer, A. M.: A. Fleischmann
1892-1968. Tübingen 1976.– Gomringer,
E. (ed.): A. F. Bilder, Relief, Collagen,
Gouaches. Moderne Galerie. Bottrop 1979
(cat.).– Költzsch, G.-W. et al. (ed.): A. F.
Retrospektive. Moderne Galerie des Saar-
land Museums. Saarbrücken 1987 (cat.).–
Schneckenburger, M. et al. (ed.): A. F. Villa
Merkel. Esslingen 1975 (cat.).– Schulze-
Vellinghausen, A.: A. F. Stuttgart 1966.–
Wedewer, R.: A. F. Stuttgart 1977

FONTANA Lucio
1899 Rosario (Argentina) – 1968 Comabbio
(Varese)
Italian painter and sculptor. 1914/15 Studied
at the Istituto Tecnico Carlo Cattaneo and
1920–1922 at the Accademia di Brera in
Milan. 1922 Returned to Buenos Aires,
working as an assistant sculptor for four
years in his father's studio. 1926–1930 Continued his training as a sculptor at the Brera
in Milan. 1934 Founded an association of

Italian abstract artists and in 1935 joined the
Parisian group Abstraction-Création.
Despite his leanings to abstract art, he continued to produce some figurative works up
to 1947. 1936 Manifesto on Italian abstract
art. 1940–1947 Settled in Buenos Aires
again where, in 1946, he helped to issue the
White Manifesto, followed by four *Spatial-
ist Manifestos* and *The Technical Manifesto
of Spatialism*. 1949 Slit and perforated
monochrome canvases, creating his first
Ambienti Spaziali and *Buchi*, entitled *Concetti Spaziali*. 1951 Light installations with
neon tubes in the main entrance hall of the
Palazzo dell'Arte at the Milan Triennale.
1952–1957 Experiments with stone (*Pietri*),
pastels (*Barocchi*), gypsum (*Gessi*) and ink
(*Inchiostri*). 1958 First *Concetti Spaziali*,
with slit canvases creating special effect.
1959 and 1968 participation in documenta 2
and 4 in Kassel. 1966 Major retrospective at
the Walker Art Center in Minneapolis.
WRITINGS: L. F.: Primo manifesto dello
spazialismo. Milan 1947.– L. F.: Secondo
manifesto dello spazialismo. Milan 1948.–
L. F.: Manifesto tecnico dello spazialismo.
Milan 1951
CATALOGUES RAISONNES: Crispolti, E.
and J. v. d. Marck (ed.): L. F. 2 vols. Brussels 1974, Milan 1976.– Crispolti, E. (ed.):
F. Catalogo generale. 2 vols. Milan 1986,
1996
MONOGRAPHS, CATALOGUES: Ballo,
G.: F. Idea per un ritrastto. Torino 1970/B.
Cologne 1971/B. New York 1971.– Ballo, G.
(ed.): L. F. Mostra antologica. Sala Comunale d'Arte Contemporanea. Rimini 1982
(cat.).– Bartolomeis, F. d.: Segno Antidis-
egno di L. F. Torino 1967.– Billeter, E. et
al. (ed.): L. F. 1899-1968. A Retrospective.
Solomon R. Guggenheim Museum. New
York 1977 (cat.).– Blistène, B. (ed.): L. F.
Centre Georges Pompidou, Paris et al. Paris
1987 (cat.).– Cirlot, J. E.: F. Barcelona
1966.– Cispolito, E.: Ommaggio a F. Roma
1971.– Crispolti, E. et al. (ed.): F. e lo
Spazialismo. Villa Malpensata. Lugano 1987
(cat.).– L. F. 1899-1968. Fundació Caixa de
Pensiones. Barcelona 1988 (cat.).– Fuchs, R.
(ed.): L. F. La cultura dell'occhio. Castello
di Rivoli, Museo d'Arte Contemporanea.
Milan 1986 (cat.).– Giani, G. P.: L. F.
Venice 1958.– Gualdoni, F. (ed.): L. F. Il
disegno. Galleria Civica, Modena. Bologna
1990 (cat.).– Joppolo, G.: Une Vie d'artiste:
L. F. Marseille 1992.– Loers, V. (ed.): L. F.
Il disegno – Zeichnungen und Skizzen.
Mönchengladbach 1997 (cat.).– Manganelli,
G.: L'ironia teologica di F. Milan 1978.–
Messer, T. M. (ed.): L. F. Retrospektive.
Schirn Kunsthalle, Frankfurt-on-Main.
Stuttgart 1996 (cat.).– Pica, A.: F. e lo
spazialismo. Venice 1953.– Sanesi, R.: L. F.
Milan 1980.– Sanna, J. d.: L. F. Materia,
spazio, concetto. Milan 1993/L. F. Materie,
Raum, Konzept. Klagenfurt 1995.– Schulz-
Hoffmann, C. and C. Syre (ed.): L. F.
Staatsgalerie moderner Kunst, Munich et
al. Munich 1983 (cat.).– Tapié, M.: Devenir
de F. Torino 1961

FÖRG Günther
born 1952 Füssen
German painter, sculptor and photographer.
1973–1979 Studied painting under K. F.
Dahmen at the Munich Academy. 1980
Solo-exhibition at the Rüdiger Schöttle
gallery in Munich. 1984 Participation in the
exhibition "von hier aus" in Düsseldorf.
1992 Took part in documenta 9 in Kassel.
1993 Professorship at the ZKM in Karlsruhe. 1995 Solo-exhibition at the Stedelijk
Museum, Amsterdam. Förg combines
materials and media in painting, sculpture
and photography. The themes of his large-
scale architectural photographs are Bauhaus
aesthetic and Fascism, while his mono-

chrome wall paintings and lead paintings
and sculptures are reflexions on art.
WRITINGS: G. F. im Gespräch mit S.
Gohr. Cologne 1997
CATALOGUES RAISONNES: Buck, M.
and C. Nagel (ed.): G. F. Verzeichnis der
Arbeiten seit 1973. Munich 1987.– Capitain,
G. and J. Hofmaier (ed.): G. F. Gesamte
Editionen 1988-1991. Stuttgart 1991.– G. F.
Gesammelte Editionen 1974-1988. Museum
Boymans-van Beuningen, Rotterdam. Stutt-
gart 1989 (cat.)
MONOGRAPHS, CATALOGUES: Aupeti-
tallot, Y. and F. Migayrou (ed.): G. F.
Maison de la Culture et de la Communauté
de Saint-Etienne. Saint-Etienne 1987
(cat.).– Boerma, S. and K. Heymer (ed.): G.
F. Kunstverein Hannover. Düsseldorf 1996
(cat.).– Bool, F. and R. Fuchs (ed.): G. F.
1988. Haags Gemeentemuseum. The Hague
1988 (cat.).– Buhlmann, B. and M. Wechs-
ler (ed.): G. F. Museum Haus Lange,
Krefeld et al. Krefeld 1987 (cat.).– G. F.
Bilder, Skulpturen, Fotografien. Orangerie
Herrenhausen und Kunstverein Hannover.
Düsseldorf 1995 (cat.).– G. F. Große Zeich-
nungen. Galerie Gisela Capitain. Cologne
1990 (cat.).– Fuchs, R. (ed.): G. F. Stedelijk
Museum. Amsterdam 1995 (cat.).– Groot,
P. (ed.): G. F. Westfälischer Kunstverein.
Münster 1986 (cat.).– Henger, S. (ed.): G. F.
Painting, Sculpture, Installation. Newport
Harbour Art Museum et al. Newport Beach
1989 (cat.).– Horn, L. et al. (ed.): G. F.
Kunstraum. Munich 1984 (cat.).– Loers, V.
and I. Rein (ed.): G. F. Museum Frideri-
cianum, Kassel et al. Stuttgart 1990 (cat.).–
Loock, U. (ed.): G. F. Kunsthalle Bern.
Bern 1986 (cat.).– Parent, B. et al. (ed.): G.
F. Musée d'Art Moderne de la Ville de Paris.
Stuttgart 1991 (cat.).– Preiss, A. (ed.): G. F.
Fotografien 1982-1992. Werkbund, Frank-
furt-on-Main et al. Stuttgart 1993 (cat.).–
Sommer, A. and C. Schreier (ed.): G. F.
Druckgraphische Serien. Städtisches Kunst-
museum Bonn. Bonn 1994 (cat.).– Speck,
R. and G. Theewen (ed.): G. F. Munchs
Bettdecke. Cologne 1996.– Ungers, S.: G.
F. Brussels 1986.– Wechsler, M. and B. E.
Buhlmann (ed.): G. F. Museum Haus
Lange Krefeld et al. Krefeld 1987 (cat.)

FRANCIS Sam
(Samuel Lewis Francis)
1923 San Mateo (CA) – 1994 Santa Monica
(CA)
American painter. 1941–1943 Studied
botany and medicine at Berkeley. Military
service in the US Army Air Corps. 1944
Spinal injury in a plane crash. Taught
himself to paint while bedridden. 1948–
1950 Studied painting and history of art,
among other teachers, under Rothko and
Still. Travelled around the world, stopping
in Mexico, India, Japan and Thailand. Early
paintings influenced by Abstract Expressionism. Up to 1949 he painted irregular,
cell-like patches of colour with thinned oil
or acrylic paints, while after 1950 his characteristic patches and blot patterns flowed
into one another, forming monochromes.

1956 Wall paintings for the Kunsthalle,
Basel. 1958 Took part in the exhibition
"New American Painting" that was shown
in eight European cities. 1959 and 1964 participation in documenta 2 and 3 in Kassel.
1963 Moved to Santa Monica, California.
1969 Honorary doctorate from the University of Berkeley. 1973 Visited Japan. 1974
Returned to California. 1977–1983 Exhibi-
tions in Copenhagen, Paris, Boston and St.
Paul. Besides being one of the chief expo-
nents of Action Painting in America, Sam
Francis worked in other materials such as
clay and ceramics and also used techniques
such as lithographs and monotypes.
WRITINGS: S. F.: Aphorisms. Santa
Monica 1984
CATALOGUES RAISONNES: Hulten, P.
and G. Tullis (ed.): The Monotypes of S. F.
Die Monotypien von S. F. Stuttgart 1994.–
Lembark, C. W. (ed.): The Prints of S. F. A
Catalogue Raisonné. 1960-1990. 2 vols.
New York 1992
MONOGRAPHS, CATALOGUES: Buck,
R. T. et al. (ed.): S. F. Paintings 1947-1972.
Albright-Knox Art Gallery, Buffalo et al.
Buffalo 1972 (cat.).– Butterfield, J. (ed.): S.
F. Los Angeles County Museum of Art. Los
Angeles 1980 (cat.).– S. F. Pasadena Box.
Bern 1968.– S. F. Werke 1945-1900. Kunst-
halle Bern. Bern 1991 (cat.).– S. F. The Edge
Paintings. James Corcoran Gallery. Los
Angeles 1992 (cat.).– S. F. Les Années
parisiennes 1950-1961. Galerie du Jeu de
Paume. Paris 1995 (cat.).– Hulten, P. (ed.):
S. F. Kunst- und Ausstellungshalle der Bun-
desrepublik Deutschland, Bonn. Stuttgart
1993 (cat.).– Lytard, J. F.: S. F. Lessons on
Darkness Like the Paintings of a Blind
Mand. Venice (CA) 1993.– Michaud, Y.: S.
F. Paris 1992.– Paquement, A. (ed.): S. F.
Peintures récentes 1976-1978. Centre
Georges Pompidou. Paris 1978 (cat.).–
Schneider, P. et al. (ed.): S. F. 1968/69.
CAPC. Paris 1969 (cat.).– Schneider, P. et
al. (ed.): S. F. Les années parisiennes 1950-
1961. Paris 1995 (cat.).– Selz, P.: S. F. New
York 1975, 1982.– Sweeny, J. J. (ed.): S. F.
Houston Museum of Fine Arts et al.
Houston 1967 (cat.).– Tono, Y.: S. F. Tokyo
1964.– Waldberg, M.: S. F. Métaphysique
du vide. Paris 1987

FRANK Robert
born 1924 Zurich
Swiss photographer. 1941/42 Trained as a
photographer and graphic designer in
Zurich. 1946 Visited Milan and Paris. 1947
Fashion photographs for *Harper's Bazaar*.
1949 Documented his travels in Peru in
spiral-bound photo-books. 1950 Returned
to New York where he did freelance work
for *Fortune, Life, Look, McCall's* and the
New York Times. 1955 First European to
receive a Guggenheim grant. Worked with
Walker Evans on photo-essays. 1957 Photographed Eisenhower and Nixon's inauguration ceremony in Washington. 1958 Publication of the volume of photographs *The
Americans in France*. 1959–1971 Branched
into film as cameraman and producer. 1972

-1977 Began to use a Polaroid pack film camera for his photographic art work and experimented with prints from Polaroid negatives on photographic paper. **1985** Won the Erich Salomon Award from the German Photographic Society in Berlin.
MONOGRAPHS, CATALOGUES: Brookman, P. (ed.): R. F. Photographer / Filmmaker. Works from 1945-1979. Long Beach Museum of Art. Long Beach 1979 (cat.).– Di Piero, W. S. et al. (ed.): R. F. Moving out. Washington et al. Washington 1995 (cat.).– R. F. Centre National de la Photographie. Paris 1996 (cat.).– Greenough, S.: R. F. Moving Out. National Gallery of Art, Washington et al. Washington 1994 (cat.).– Katz, P. (ed.): R. F. Sidney Janis Gallery. New York 1979 (cat.).– Papageorge, T.: Walker Evans and R. F. An Essay on Influence. New Haven (CT) 1981.– Tucker, A. W. (ed.): R. F. New York to Nova Scotia. Museum of Fine Arts. Houston 1986 (cat.)

FRANKENTHALER Helen
born **1928** New York
American painter. **1945–1950** Studied at Bennington College in Vermont, at the Art Students League and with H. Hofmann in New York. From **1951** developed her own technique related to Pollock's drip paintings. **1958** Married Robert Motherwell. Taught at various universities including Yale and Princeton. **1959** Participation in documenta 2 in Kassel and special honours at the Paris Biennale. **1965** Took part in the Venice Biennale. With her technique of saturating raw, untreated canvas with thinned paint, Frankenthaler created free, lyrical improvisations which had a decisive influence on the works of Kenneth Noland and Morris Louis.
CATALOGUES RAISONNES: Harrison, P. (ed.): F. Catalogue Raisonné. Prints 1961-1994. New York 1996.– Krens, T. et al. (ed.): H. F. Prints 1961-1979. Sterling and Francine Clark Art Institute Williamstown (MA) et al. New York 1980 (cat.)
MONOGRAPHS, CATALOGUES: Belz, C. (ed.): F. The 1950s. Rose Art Museum, Brandeis University. Waltham (MA) 1981 (cat.).– Carmean, E. A. (ed.): H. F. A Paintings Retrospective. The Museum of Modern Art, New York et al. New York 1989 (cat.).– Elderfield, J.: F. New York 1989.– Fine, R. E. (ed.): H. F. Prints. National

Gallery of Art, Washington et al. New York 1993 (cat.).– H. F. Paintings 1969-1974. Corcoran Gallery of Art. Washington 1975 (cat.).– H. F. Solomon R. Guggenheim Museum, New York et al. New York 1998 (cat.).– Goosen, E. C. (ed.): H. F. Solomon R. Guggenheim Museum. New York 1969 (cat.).– O'Hara, F. (ed.): H. F. Paintings. The Jewish Museum. New York 1960 (cat.).– Rose, B.: F. New York 1971.– Wilkin, K. (ed.): H. F. Works on Paper 1949-1984. Solomon R. Guggenheim Museum, New York et al. New York 1984, 1995 (cat.)

FREUD Lucian
born **1922** Berlin
German-born English painter. Grandson of Sigmund Freud. **1933** Emigrated to England. **1938–1939** Attended the Central School of Arts and Crafts in London. **1939–1942** Studied at the East Anglian School of Painting and Drawing in Dedham. **1942/43** Part-time studies at Goldsmith's College in London. **1944** First exhibition in the Lefèvre Gallery in London. **1946/47** Trips to Paris and Greece. **1949–1954** Guest-lecturer at the Slade School of Fine Arts in London. **1951** Arts Council Prize at the Festival of Britain. **1954** Exhibited with Ben Nicholson and Francis Bacon in the British Pavilion at the Venice Biennale. **1958–1968** Series of exhibitions at the Marlborough Gallery, London. **1987–1993** Touring exhibitions organised wordwide by the British Council. With psychological acuity and analytical skill, Freud dissected subjects familiar to him, above all acquaintances and friends. Towards the end of the 50s, Freud's precise, veristic painting style became more expressive and he applied the paint more thickly as an impasto. By adding Kremnitz white Freud gave his paint the appearance of flesh.
CATALOGUES RAISONNES: L. F. The Complete Etchings 1946-1991. Thomas Gibson Fine Art Ltd. London 1991 (cat.).– Hartley, C. (ed.): The Etchings of L. F. A Catalogue Raisonné 1946-1995. London and New York 1995
MONOGRAPHS, CATALOGUES: Bernard, B. and D. Birdsall: L. F. New York 1996.– Calvocoressi, R. (ed.): L. F. Early Works. Edinburgh 1997 (cat.).– L. F. Gemälde. Neue Nationalgalerie. Berlin 1989 (cat.).– L. F. Dipinti e opere su carta 1940-1991. Palazzo Ruspoli. Roma 1991 (cat.).– L. F. Art Gallery of New South Wales, Sydney et al. Sydney 1992 (cat.).– Gowing, L.: L. F. London 1982.– Hughes, R. (ed.): L. F. Paintings. Hirshhorn Museum and Sculpture Garden, Smithsonian Institution, Washington et al. London 1987 (cat.).– Hughes, R.: L. F. Paintings. New York 1993, 1997.– Lampert, C. (ed.): L. F. Recent Works. Whitechapel Art Gallery, London et al. New York 1993 (cat.).– Mantura, B. et al. (ed.): L. F. Paintings and Works on Paper 1940-1991. Castello Sforzesco, Milan et al. Milan and London 1991.– Penny, N. and R. F. Johnson (ed.): L. F. Works on Paper. Ashmolean Museum of Art, Oxford

et al. London and New York 1988 (cat.).– Russel, J. (ed.): L. F. Hayward Gallery. London 1974

FREUND Gisèle
1912 Berlin – **2000** Paris
German photographer. **1931–1933** Studied history of art and social sciences in Freiburg and Frankfurt am Main. **1932** Met Walter Benjamin. **1933** Emigrated to France and studied at the Sorbonne in Paris until **1936**. Wrote a doctoral thesis on Photography in France in the 19th century. Thereafter published portraits of writers and artists, including James Joyce, Virginia Woolf, Jean-Paul Sartre, Simone de Beauvoir and Henri Matisse in *Life* magazine, *The Weekly Illustrated* and *Paris-Match*. **1940** Fled, via the South of France, to Argentinia and then Chile where, from **1943/44**, she worked with the theatre company of L. Jouvet. **1947–1954** Joined the photographic agency *Magnum*. **1950–1952** Lived in Mexico. From **1963** numerous exhibitions. **1977** Participated in documenta 6 in Kassel. **1978** Won a cultural award from the German Photographic Society and, in **1980**, the Grand Prix National des Arts in France. Pioneered the use of three-layer colour reversal film in art photography.
WRITINGS: G. F.: La Photographie en France au dix-neuvième siècle. Paris 1936.– G. F.: Photographie und bürgerliche Gesellschaft. Munich 1968, 1976 / Photographie et Société. Paris 1974 / Photography and Society. London and Boston 1980
MONOGRAPHS, CATALOGUES: G. F. and R. Jamis: G. F. Portrait. Paris 1991.– Honnef, K. (ed.): G. F. Fotografien 1932-1974. Rheinisches Landesmuseum. Bonn 1977 (cat.).– Puttni, H.: G. F. Paris 1991

FREUNDLICH Otto
1878 Stolp (Pomerania) – **1943** Lublin-Maidanek (Poland)
German painter and sculptor. Training business. **1903–1906** Studied history of art in Berlin, Munich and Florence. **1907** Studied sculpture with Arthur Levin-Funcke. **1909** Moved to Paris. First paintings and sculptures, inspired by Picasso and the Cubists. **1910** First exhibition at the Galerie Saguet, Paris. **1913** Exhibits at the First German Autumn Salon and the gallery

Der Sturm in Berlin. **1914–1924** Lived mostly in Cologne where he made friends with Siewert and joined the November-gruppe. From **1930** member of the group Cercle et Carré and from **1931** of Abstraction-Création. Worked for a Cologne workers' newspaper, the *Arbeiter-Zeitung*. **1934** First architectonic plastic works and architectonic relief. Founded the Académie de Peinture, Dessin, Sculpture, Gravure. **1937** The sculpture *L'homme nouveau* appeared on the cover of the catalogue of the exhibition of "degenerate art" in Munich. The same year, his works were confiscated from all German museums. **1939** Interned. **1940** Escaped to the Pyrenees. **1943** Deported to the concentration camp Maidanek and murdered. **1954** Retrospective in the gallery Rive Droite in Paris.
WRITINGS: Bohnen, U. (ed.): O. F. Schriften. Ein Wegbereiter der gegenstandslosen Kunst. Cologne 1982
CATALOGUE RAISONNE: Heusinger v. Waldegg, J. (ed.): O. F. Monographie mit Dokumentation und Werkverzeichnis. Rheinisches Landesmuseum, Bonn. Cologne 1978 (cat.)
MONOGRAPHS, CATALOGUES: Aust, G.: O. F. 1878-1943. Cologne 1960.– Bonfand, A. et al. (ed.): O. F. Musée Départemental de Rochechouart. Paris 1988. Paris 1988 (cat.).– Duvivier and E. Maillet (ed.): O. F et ses amis. Musée de Pontoise. Pontoise 1993 (cat.).– Fischer, Y. (ed.): O. F. Israel Museum. Jerusalem 1978 (cat.).– Heusinger v. Waldegg, J.: O. F. Ascension. Anweisung zur Utopie. Frankfurt-on-Main 1987.– Leistner, G. and T. Rodiek (ed.): O. F. Ein Wegbereiter der abstrakten Kunst. Museum Ostdeutsche Galerie, Regensburg et al. Regensburg und Osnabrück 1994 (cat.)

FRIESZ Othon
1879 Le Havre – **1949** Paris
French painter. Took lessons under Charles-Marie Lhuillier at the School of Drawing in Le Havre. **1899–1904** Studied at the Ecole Nationale Supérieure des Beaux-Arts in Paris. Met Dufy, Rouault, Marquet and Matisse, and was strongly influenced by their Fauvist style of painting. **1903/04** Exhibitions at the Salon d'Automne and the Salon des Indépendants. **1905** Participation in the exhibition "Fauves" at the Salon d'Automne. **1906** Stayed with Braque in La Ciotat. **1911** Travelled to Portugal. Explored the pictorial limits of Cubism. **1912** Opened an art school in Paris and taught there until **1914**. During this teaching period, his Fauvist approach lost some of its intensity and his paintings gradually became more harmonious and calm. From **1914** professorship at the Académie Moderne, from **1929** at the Académie Scandinave and from **1944** at the Académie de la Grande Chaumière. **1925** Won the Carnegie Foundation Award. **1937** Commissioned to decorate the Palais de Chaillot, together with Raoul Dufy.
MONOGRAPHS, CATALOGUES: Brielle, R.: O. F. Paris 1930.– Fleuret, F. et al.: F.

Œuvres 1901-1927. Paris 1928.– O. F. Exposition rétrospective 1879-1949. Musée des Beaux-Arts André Malraux. Le Havre 1979 (cat.).– Gauthier, M. and P. Cailler: O. F. Geneva and Paris 1957.– Giry, M.: La Jeunesse d'O. F. Diss. Lyon 1951.– Salmon: O. F. Paris 1920

FRIZE Bernard

born **1954** Saint Mandé
French painter who achieved fame in **1977** with his series *All over*, in which multicolored trails of paint, produced with a specially fine brush, form arabesques all over the canvas. **1979** First solo-exhibition at the Galerie Lucien Durand in Paris. **1986** Further exhibitions at the Maison de la Culture in St. Etienne and in the Villa Medici in Rome. Frize can be seen as a representative of aleatoric art. He used new subversive methods and unusual materials in his attempts to let painting produce itself through the medium of chance.
MONOGRAPHS, CATALOGUES: Meschede, F. (ed.): Malerei ohne Sprache. B. F. Kunstverein Arnsberg. Arnsberg 1995 (cat.).– Pagé, S.: B. F. Musée d'Art Moderne de la Ville. Paris 1988 (cat.).– Tosatto, G.: A l'image de la peinture. B. F. Musée Départemental d'Art Contemporain. Rochechouart 1991 (cat.)

FRUHTRUNK Günter

1923 Munich – **1982** Munich
German painter. **1940/41** Studied architecture. **1945–1950** Studied painting under William Straube, among other teachers, at a private school. **1954** Grant from the state of Baden-Württemberg and the French government. Moved to Paris and worked in the studios of Léger and Arp. **1961** Won the Jean Arp Award in Cologne. **1963** Retrospective at the Museum am Ostwall, Dortmund. **1966** Awarded a silver medal at the Prix d'Europe in Ostend. From **1967** Professor of Painting at the Art Academy in Munich. Impressed by the Concrete painting of Auguste Herbin, Fruhtrunk developed a dynamic formal language, of intensely coloured, diagonal stripes, like vectors, arranged in alternating colours to set up powerful rhythms. He thereby consciously distanced himself from Constructivism

CATALOGUE RAISONNE: Gomringer, E. et al. (ed.): F. Starnberg 1978
MONOGRAPHS, CATALOGUES: Besset, M. (ed.): F. Musée d'Art Moderne de la Ville de Paris. Paris 1970 (cat.).– G. F. Kunstverein Braunschweig. Brunswick 1983 (cat.).– Imdahl, M. et al. (ed.): F. Bilder 1952-1972. Städtische Galerie im Lenbachhaus. Munich 1973 (cat.).– Ludwig, J. and U. Spranger-Hauschild (ed.): G. F. Frühe Bilder 1950-1954. Museum für Neue Kunst, Freiburg. Waldkirch 1993 (cat.).– Schuster, P.-K. (ed.): G. F. Neue Nationalgalerie, Berlin et al. Munich 1993 (cat.)

GABO Naum

(Neemia Borissovich Pevsner)
1890 Brjansk (Russia) – **1977** Waterbury (CT)
Russian sculptor, painter and architect. **1909–1914** Studied medicine and natural sciences in Munich and attended H. Wölfflin lectures in art history on the side. **1912** Contact with Kandinsky and the Blauer Reiter. Trip to Italy. **1913/14** Stayed with his brother Antoine Pevsner in Paris. **1914–1917** Lived in Copenhagen and Oslo, where he produced his first sculptural constructions under the name of Gabo. **1917** Moved to Moscow and made contact with the group of artists around Tatlin, Malevich and Rodchenko. **1920** Together with his brother, published the *Realistic Manifesto*, in which they oppose the ideas of Cubism and Futurism and the bringing together of politics and art in the new Socialist Realism. First kinetic sculptures. **1922** Moved to Berlin. **1925** Became a director of the Novembergruppe. **1927** Together with his brother Antoine, designed sets and costumes for Diaghilev's ballet *La Chatte*. Guest-lecturer at the Bauhaus in Dessau. **1932** Joined Abstraction-Création, and from **1935** lived alternately in Paris and Berlin. **1935–1946** Lived in London and South England. **1946** Emigrated to the USA, settling in Middlebury, (CT). **1948** Exhibition in the Museum of Modern Art, New York. **1953/54** Professorship at Harvard University. Gabo contributed significantly to the development of Kinetic Art, as represented by artists such as George Rickey, Alexander Calder and Jean Tinguely.
WRITINGS: N. G.: Of Divers Arts. New York 1962
CATALOGUES RAISONNES: Nash, S. A. and J. Merkert (ed.): N. G. Sixty Years of Constructivism. Including a Catalogue Raisonné of the Constructions and Sculptures. Dallas Museum of Art et al. Munich 1985 (cat.)/N. G. Sechzig Jahre Konstruktivismus (mit dem Œuvre-Katalog der Konstruktionen und Skulpturen). Akademie der Künste, Berlin et al. Munich 1986 (cat.).– Williams, G. (ed.): N. G. Monoprints. Cambridge (MA) 1987, New York 1992
MONOGRAPHS, CATALOGUES: Beaud, M.-C. (ed.): N. G. G. A. Musée de Peinture et de Sculpture, Grenoble et al. Paris 1971 (cat.).– El-Danasouri, A.: Kunststoff und Müll. Das Material bei N. G. und Kurt

Schwitters. Munich 1992.– Forge, C.: Appreciation of N. G New York 1990.– N. G. Musée National d'Art Moderne. Paris 1971 (cat.).– Merkert, J. (ed.): N. G. Ein russischer Konstruktivist in Berlin 1922-1932. Skulpturen, Zeichnungen und Architekturentwürfe. Berlinsche Galerie. Berlin 1989 (cat.).– Moser, B. (ed.): N. G. und der Wettbewerb zum Palast der Sowjets, Moscow 1931-1933. Berlinische Galerie. Berlin 1992 (cat.).– Newman, T. (ed.): N. G. The Constructive Process. Tate Gallery. London 1976 (cat.).– Pevsner, A.: A Biographical Sketch of My Brothers N. G. and Antoine Pevsner. Amsterdam 1964.– Read, H. and L. Martin (ed.): N. G. Constructions, Sculpture, Paintings, Drawings, Engravings. Cambridge (MA) 1957.– Read, H. and L. Martin: N. G. Neuchâtel 1957.– Williams, L.: N. G. Monoprints. New York 1990

GARGALLO Pablo

1881 Maella (Zaragoza) – **1934** Reus (Tarragona)
Spanish sculptor. **1900** Attended the art school *La Lonja* in Barcelona. Grant to study in Paris. **1907–1911** First metal works in copper foil and wire. Contact with Picasso, Gris and Modigliani. **1912** First works in iron (*Napolitain*). **1915** Gave up sculpting in stone owing to a lung disorder and instead made small plastic works and jewellery. **1920–1923** Professorship at the Belli Officis in Barcelona. Returned to Paris and started to produce large-scale sculptures agian. **1934** Solo-exhibition at the Brummer Gallery in New York.
CATALOGUE RAISONNE: Courthion, P. (ed.): L'Œuvre complète de. P. G. Paris 1973
MONOGRAPHS, CATALOGUES: Anguera, J.: G. Paris 1979.– Borra, M. L. et al. (ed.): G. Exposició del centenari. Barcelona 1981.– Catalogo del Museo P. G. Saragossa 1988.– Cirici, A.: G. i B. Barcelona 1975.– Courthion, P.: P. G. Paris 1937.– Dagen, P. and R. Ordóñez Fernández (ed.): G. La nueva edad de los metales. Fundación Mapfre Vida. Madrid 1991 (cat.).– Fernández, R. O.: G. Madrid 1991.– Fernández, R. O. (ed.): Museo P. G. Madrid 1994.– P. G. 1881-1934. Musée d'Art Moderne de la Ville de Paris. Paris 1980 (cat.).– P. G. 1881-1934. Musées de Pontoise. Pontoise 1992 (cat.).– Ordóñez Fernández, R. (ed.): Catálogo del Museo P. G. Saragossa 1988

GAROUSTE Gérard

born **1946** Paris
French painter. **1965–1972** Studied at the Ecole Nationale des Beaux-Arts in Paris. **1979–1982** Designed scenery for the miniature Italian theatre at the theatre Le Palace in Paris and experimented with various stage set techniques. **1980** Performance of his play *La règle du Jeu* at the Museum of Contemporary Art in Ghent. **1984** Moved to Marcilly-sur-Eure. **1987** Painted his first *Indienne*, a free-hanging canvas, 7.60 m wide and 4.10 m long. Up to **1988** produced

further *Indiennes*, based on the theme of Dante's *Divine Comedy*. **1990** Helped in the setting up of a graphic studio at the French cultural centre in Tetouan, Morocco. Created mega-sculptures out of iron.
MONOGRAPHS, CATALOGUES: Blistène, B. et al. (ed.): G. G. Centre Georges Pompidou, Paris et al. Paris 1988 (cat.).– Dagbert, A.: G. G. Paris 1996.– Froment, J.-L. et al. (ed.): G. G. Peintures de 1985-1987. C. A. P. C. Musée d'Art Contemporain de Bordeaux. Bordeaux 1987 (cat.).– Giudiera, R. and B. Blistène (ed.): G. G. Centre Georges Pompdou, Paris et al. Paris 1988.– Giudiera, R. and B. Blistène (ed.): G. G. Städtische Kunsthalle Düsseldorf et al. Düsseldorf 1989 (cat.).– Lebeer-Hossmann (ed.): G. G. Palais des Beaux-Arts. Chaleroi and Brussels 1988 (cat.).– Risset, J. et al. (ed.): G. G. Peintures de 1985-1987. Musée d'Art Contemporain de Bordeaux. Bordeaux 1987 (cat.)

GARRIN Paul

born **1957** Philadelphia
American video and multimedia artist. **1978–1982** Studied at Cooper Union School of Arts in New York. From **1983** produced installation video tapes for Paik. From **1985** put together his own video tapes using original footage of street fighting and race riots as a critical documentary of race relations in America. Worked from **1981** for Paik, as one of his chief assistants. **1988** Prize at the Videonnale in Bonn. **1989** Retrospective at the Museum Folkwang, Essen. New York Foundation for the Arts Fellowship. **1991** Participation in Multimediale 2 in Karlsruhe. **1992** Featured at the Mediale in Hamburg with his computer-controlled, interactive video-installation *White Devil*. Won the Karlsruhe ZKM award for video art.

GAUDIER-BRZESKA Henri

1891 Saint-Jean-de-Braye (near Orléans) – **1915** Neuville-Saint-Vaast (Pas-de-Calais) French sculptor, painter and draughtsman. **1909** After a visit to England, began to study art while working as a textile designer in Paris. **1910** First sculptures. Met Sophie Brzeska from Poland. **1911** Returned to London. **1912** First published drawing in the

magazine Rhythm. Began to sign his works with the double-barrelled surname Gaudier-Brzeska. **1913** Friendship with Ezra Pound. Aligned himself with the Vorticist artists and writers, including Wyndham Lewis, Edward Wadsworth and Jacob Epstein, whose short-lived movement was strongly influenced by Futurism and Cubism. Devoted himself more intensively to sculpture. **1913/14** Participated in the Allied Artists' Association Exhibition. **1915** Exhibited various works in the Vorticist Exhibition. Signed up to fight on the French front and was killed at Neuville-Saint-Vaast. His sculptures had a strong influence on subsequent generations of English sculptors, including Henry Moore.
CATALOGUE RAISONNE: Silber, E. and D. Finn (ed.): H. G.-B. Life and Art. London 1996
MONOGRAPHS, CATALOGUES: Brodzky, H.: H. G.-B. 1891-1915. London 1933.– Cassat, B.: La Caritas. Une œuvre de G.-B. De Rodin à l'abstraction. Orléans 1992.– Cole, R.: Burning to Speak. The Life and Art of H. G.-B. Oxford 1978.– Ede, H. S.: Savage Messiah. A Life of G.-B. London and New York 1931.– H. G.-B. 1891-1915. Skulpturen, Zeichnungen, Briefe. Kunsthalle Bielefeld 1969 (cat.).– H. G.-B. Scottish National Gallery of Modern Art. Edingburgh 1972 (cat.).– H. G.-B. Musée des Beaux-Arts, Orléans et al. Orléans 1993 (cat.).– Koslow, F.: The Graphic Work of H. G.-B. Diss. Boston 1981.– Lewison, J. (ed.): H. G.-B. Sculptor 1891-1915. Cambridge et al. Cambridge 1983 (cat.).– Levy, M.: G.-B. Drawings and Sculpture. New York 1965.– Pound, E.: H. G.-B. London 1960, Paris 1992.– Secrétain, R.: Un sculpteur "maudit". G.-B. 1891-1915. Paris 1980

GAUGUIN Paul
1848 Paris – **1903** Atuona Hiva-Oa (Marquesas Islands)
French painter. **1849-1855** Grew up in Lima (Peru), thereafter living in Orléans and Paris. **1865-1871** Joined the merchant marine and went to sea. **1871-1883** Worked as a stockbroker in Paris. **1873** Married Dane Mette Gad and had five children. **1874** Studied at the Académie Colarossi. **1876** First work accepted by the Salon. Up to **1886** took part in the IV–VIII Impres-

sionist exhibitions. **1881** Worked with Pissarro und Cézanne. **1882** Moved to Rouen and later Copenhagen. Financial difficulties. **1885** Returned to Paris. **1886** Met Bernard while staying in Pont-Aven. Became acquainted with the van Gogh brothers in Paris. **1887** Travelled with the painter Laval to Panama and Martinique. **1888** Returned to Pont-Aven. Developed Synthetism in his paintings of Breton life and customs. Exhibition organised by Theo van Gogh. A disastrous quarrel with Vincent van Gogh in Arles severed relations between the two artists. **1889** Exhibited with the group Les XX in Brussels and in the Café Volpini at the Paris World Fair. **1891** Emigrated to Tahiti, where he painted symbolic pictures from life, in a flat decorative style with large areas of strong, glowing colours, that today are seen as incunabula of Exotic and Primitive Art. Contracted syphilis. **1893-1895** Lived alternately in Paris, Copenhagen and Brittany. **1895-1901** Returned to Tahiti. First sculptural works. **1897** Published his autobiographical work *Noa, Noa.* **1898** Attempted suicide. **1901** Settled on Dominica, one of the Marquesas Islands where, in **1902**, he had a political battle with the colonial authorities and was prosecuted. **1903** Died, weakened by illness and poverty, at the age of 54.
WRITINGS: P. G.: The Intimate Journals of P. G. Repr. London 1985.– Merlhès, V. (ed.): Correspondance de P. G. Documents, témoignages. Paris 1984.– Monfreid, G. D. d. (ed.): Lettres de P. G. Paris 1930.– Thomson, B.: G. par lui-même. Evreux 1993
CATALOGUES RAISONNES: Agustino, F. and G. Lari (ed.): G. Catalogo completo dell' opera grafica. Milan 1972.– Field, R. (ed.): P. G. Monotypes. Philadelphia Museum of Art. Philadelphia 1973 (cat.).– Gray, C. (ed.): Sculpture and Ceramics of P. G. Baltimore 1963, New York 1980.– Guérin, M. (ed.): Catalogue raisonné de l'œuvre gravé de G. Paris 1927, San Francisco 1980.– Joachim, H. et al. (ed.): P. G. A Catalogue Raisonné of His Prints. Bern 1988.– Morgan, E. et al. (ed.): P. G. Catalogue Raisonné of His Prints. Bern 1988.– Sugana, G. M. (ed.): Tout l'œuvre peint de G. Paris 1981.– Wildenstein, G. (ed.): G. Catalogue critique des peintures. Paris 1964
MONOGRAPHS, CATALOGUES: Beaute, G.: P. G. vu par les photographes. Lausanne 1988.– Brettell, R. (ed.): The Art of P. G. National Gallery of Art. Washington 1988 (cat.).– Burnett, R.: P. G. Munich 1948.– Clement, R. T.: P. G. A Bio-Bibliography. New York 1991.– Daix, P.: P. G. Paris 1989.– Gibson, M.: P. G. Recklinghausen 1991, New York 1993.– Goldwater, R.: P. G. Cologne 1957, 1989.– Hoog, M.: G. Vie et œuvre. Paris 1987/P. G. Life and Work. New York 1987/P. G. Leben und Werk. Munich 1987.– Jaworska, W.: P. G. et l'école de Pont-Aven. Neuchâtel 1971.– Lewandowski, H.: P. G. Die Flucht vor der Zivilisation. Frankfurt-on-Main 1991.– Prather, M. (ed.): P. G. 1848-1903. Cologne 1994.– Rohde, P.-A.: P. G. auf Tahiti. Rheinfelden 1988.– Sweetman, D.: P. G. A Complete Life. London 1995

GEIGER Rupprecht
born **1908** Munich
German painter. **1926-1935** Studied architecture at the School of Arts and Crafts and the College of Civil Engineering in Munich. Worked as an architect up to World War II when he began painting. **1948** First abstract painting exhibited in the Salon des Réalités Nouvelles in Paris. **1949** Together with Baumeister, Meier-Denninghoff and Winter, founded the group Zen 49. **1951** Received the Domnick Prize. Between **1959** and **1977** participation in documenta 2–4

and 6 in Kassel. **1962** Stopped working as an architect and devoted himself to radical abstraction and the visualisation of colours. **1965-1976** Professorship at the Düsseldorf Academy. From the mid-70s tended to use synthetic red tones that he condensed, by a spraying technique, into rectangular or oval colour fields. **1982/83** Member of the Academy of Fine Arts in Munich. **1987** Large sculpture *Gerundetes Blau* (Rounded Blue) for the cultural centre Gasteig in Munich. With his abstract colour compositions, Geiger is one of the main exponents of Color Field Painting in Germany.
WRITINGS: R. G.: Farbe ist Element. Düsseldorf 1972
CATALOGUES RAISONNES: Geiger, M. (ed.): R. G. Werkverzeichnis Druckgraphik 1948-1972. Düsseldorf 1972.– Honnef. K. and H. Read: R. G. Werkverzeichnis 1948-1972. Düsseldorf 1972
MONOGRAPHS, CATALOGUES: R. G. Gemälde und Zeichnungen. Städtische Galerie im Lenbachhaus. Munich 1978 (cat.).– Giloy-Hirtz, P. (ed.): R. G. Russian State Museum, St. Petersburg et al. Stuttgart 1994 (cat.).– Güse, E.-E. (ed.): G. Zeichnung als Licht. Saarland Museum, Saarbrücken. Munich 1990 (cat.).– Heißenbüttel, H.: G. Stuttgart 1972.– Riese, H.-P. et al. (ed.): R. G. Retrospektive. Akademie der Künste, Berlin et al. Berlin 1985 (cat.).– Schuster, P.-K. (ed.): R. G. Staatsgalerie moderner Kunst im Haus der Kunst. Munich 1988 (cat.).– Volkmann, B. and R.-F. Raddatz (ed.): R. G. Retrospektive. Akademie der Künste, Berlin et al. Berlin 1985 (cat.)

GERTSCH Franz
born **1930** Möringen
Swiss painter. Studied **1947-1950** at the Max von Mühlenen School of Painting in Bern. First woodcuts. **1950-1952** Learnt painting techniques from Hans Schwarzenbach in Bern. From **1969** produced monumental canvases with enormously enlarged motifs, using transparencies as models. Subsequent intensification, through painting over the images projected onto the canvas, produced a hyper-realistic effect that appeared to dematerialise the objects portrayed. **1972** Participated in documenta 5 in Kassel. **1974/75** DAAD scholarship to Berlin. Family and group scenes became a

favourite theme throughout the 70s. **1986** Last oil painting, entitled *Johanna II.* Thereafter produced large-scale, hyper-realistic woodcuts. Gertsch is one of the main exponents of Photo Realism in Europe.
CATALOGUE RAISONNE: Castleman, R. et al. (ed.): F. G. Large-scale Woodcuts/ Xilografias monumentales. Geneva 1990 (cat.).– Ronte, D. (ed.): F. G. (with catalogue raisonné). Bern 1986
MONOGRAPHS, CATALOGUES: Billeter, E. et al. (ed.): F. G. Kunsthaus Zurich et al. Zurich 1980 (cat.).– F. G. Holzschnitte. Kunstmuseum Bern et al. Baden-Baden 1994 (cat.).– Mason, R. M. et al. (ed.): F. G. Holzschnitte. Städtische Galerie im Lenbachhaus. Munich 1991 (cat.).– Ruhrberg, K. et al. (ed.): F. G. Deutscher Akademischer Austauschdienst, Berlin et al. Berlin 1975 (cat.).– Stuffmann, M. and P. Tanner (ed.): F. G. Landschaften. Graphische Sammlung der ETH Zurich et al. Stuttgart 1993 (cat.)

GERZ Jochen
born **1940** Berlin
German writer, installation and action artist. **1958-1962** Studied German and English literature and Chinese at Cologne University, and archaeology in Basel. **1960** First literary texts – in the style of Concrete Poetry. **1967** Moved to Paris. Founded the authors' self-publishing company "Agentzia". **1968** Published first book entitled *Footing.* First happenings and environments. From **1969** put together pictures from photographs and texts on the theme of the limitations of language and communication. **1970** First video works. **1972** Founded the Gesellschaft zum Studium des praktischen Lebens, (Society for the Study of Practical Life). **1975-1979** Series entitled *Griechische Stücke* (Greek Pieces). **1976** Presented the performance *Die Schwierigkeit des Zentauren beim vom Pferd steigen* (The Centaur having difficulty getting of his horse) at the Venice Biennale, for which the artist spent four days inside a wooden horse. As part of the happening *Transsib-Prospekt* at documenta 6 in **1977** he travelled from Moscow to Vladvostok behind blacked-out windows. **1978-1984** Series *Kulchur-Pieces.* **1981** Trips to Canada. **1984** Joint art projects with Esther Shalev-Gerz. Since **1987** coloration of used photographs and texts. Participated in documenta 8 in Kassel.
WRITINGS: Franz, E. (ed.): J. G. Texte. Bielefeld 1985.– J. G.: Von der Kunst. Dudweiler 1985.– J. G. Gegenwart der Kunst. Interviews 1970-1995. Regensburg 1995
MONOGRAPHS, CATALOGUES: Friese, P. (ed.): J. G. Life After Humanism. Photo, Text 1988-1992. Neues Museum Weserburg, Bremen et al. Stuttgart 1992 (cat.).– J. G. 2146 Steine. Mahnmal gegen Rassismus, Saarbrücken. Stuttgart 1993.– J. G. Les Images. Musée d'Art Contemporain. Strasbourg 1994.– J. G. Ancienne douane. Strasbourg 1994 (cat.).– J. G. The French Wall. Germanisches Nationalmuseum. Nuremberg 1996 (cat.).– Jussen, B. (ed.): J. G.

Von der künstlerischen Produktion der Geschichte I. Göttingen 1997.– Könneke, A. (ed.): J. G. Das Hamburger Mahnmal gegen Faschismus. Stuttgart 1994.– Rattemeyer, V. (ed.): J. G. Get Out of My lies. Wiesbaden 1997.– Schwarz, M. (ed.): J. G. Foto, Texte, The French Wall & Stücke. Badischer Kunstverein. Karlsruhe 1975 (cat.).– Shalev-Gerz, E. (ed.): J. G. Griechische Stücke, Kulchur pieces. Wilhelm-Hack-Museum. Ludwigshafen am Rhein 1984 (cat.).– Shalev-Gerz, E. (ed.): J. G. Kunstsammlung Nordrhein-Westfalen, Düsseldorf. Cologne 1988 (cat.).– Wolf, E.: J. G. Die Arbeit am Mythos. Diss. Brunswick 1992

GIACOMETTI Alberto

1901 Borgonovo (near Stampa) – **1966** Chur Swiss sculptor and painter. Studied sculpture at the Ecole des Arts et Metiers in Geneva. **1920/21** Travelled to Italy, staying in Rome. From **1922** pupil of the sculptor Emile Bourdelle at the Académie de la Grande Chaumière in Paris. **1927** Intense confrontation with Cubism. **1928** Exhibition of *Scheibenplastiken* (discs) at the Galerie Jeanne Bucher, Paris. Became friends with Masson, Leiris and Tériade. **1930** Met Aragon, Dalí and Breton. First Cage sculptures shown by Pierre Loeb in the exhibition "Miró – Arp – Giacometti". **1932** Joined the Surrealists. Encountered literary existentialism. First solo-exhibition at the Galerie Pierre Colle in Paris. **1935** Abandoned Surrealism and began to work again from natural models. **1940** Became acquainted with Picasso, Jean-Paul Sartre and Simone de Beauvoir. **1942–1945** Lived in Geneva. **1948** Returned to Paris and started portrait painting. Applied the principles of his later sculptures to paintings to develop his highly original conception of the human head. **1951** Friendship with Samuel Beckett. **1954/55** Painted portraits of Matisse. **1955** Retrospective at the Arts Council Gallery, London and the Solomon R. Guggenheim Museum, New York. **1962** Won a major award for sculpture at the Venice Biennale. **1965** Retrospective at the Tate Gallery, London and the Museum of Modern Art, New York. Setting-up of the Giacometti Foundation in Zurich. WRITINGS: Dupin, J. and Leiris, M. (ed.): A. G. Ecrits. Paris 1990.– Scheidegger, E. (ed.): A. G. Schriften, Fotos, Zeichnungen. Zurich 1958 CATALOGUE RAISONNE: Lust, H. C. (ed.): G. The Complete Graphics. New York 1970, San Francisco 1991 MONOGRAPHS, CATALOGUES: Aragon, L. et al. (ed.): Wege zu G. Munich 1987.– Barañano, K. M. d. (ed.): A. G. 2 vols. Museo Nacional Centro de Arte Reina Sofía, Madrid. Barcelona 1990 (cat.).– Beye, P. (ed.): A. G. Nationalgalerie, Staatliche Museen Preussischer Kulturbesitz, Berlin. Munich 1987 (cat.).– Bonnefoy, Y.: A. G. Biographie d'une œuvre. Paris 1991 / G. A Biography of His Work. New York 1991 / A. G. Eine Biographie seines Werkes. Bern

1992.– Bovi, A.: A. G. Florence 1974 / A. G. Lucerne 1974.– Brenson, M.: The Early Works of A. G. 1925-1935. Diss. Baltimore 1974.– Bucarelli, P.: A. G. Roma 1962.– Crescenzo, C. di: A. G. Early Works in Paris. 1922-1930. New York 1994.– Crescenzo, C. di (ed.): A. G. Sculture-dipinti-disegni. Palazzo Reale. Milan 1995 (cat.).– Derouet, C. et al. (ed.): A. G. Le Retour à la figuration. Musée Rath, Geneva et al. Geneva 1986 (cat.).– Didi-Hubermann, G.: Le Cube et le visage. Autour d'une sculpture d'A. G. Paris 1993.– Dufrêne, T.: G. Les Dimensions de la réalité. Geneva 1994.– Dupin, J.: A. G. Paris 1963, 1978.– Fletcher, V. J. (ed.): A. G. 1901-1966. Hirshhorn Museum and Sculpture Garden. Washington 1988 (cat.).– Fletcher, V.: A. G. The Paintings. Diss. Columbia University. New York 1994.– Genet, J.: A. G. Zurich 1962.– A. G. The Museum of Modern Art, New York et al. New York 1965 (cat.).– A. G. Royal Academy, London et al. London 1996 (cat.).– A. G. Kunsthalle Wien. Vienna 1996 (cat.).– Hohl, R.: A. G. Stuttgart 1971, 1987, New York 1972.– Juliet, C.: G. Paris 1985.– Klemm, C.: Die Sammlung der A.-G.-Stiftung, Kunsthaus Zürich. Zurich 1990.– Koella, R. (ed.): A. G. Munich 1997.– Kuenzi, A. (ed.): A. G. Fondation Pierre Gianadda. Martigny 1986 (cat.).– Lamarche-Vadel, B.: A. G. Paris 1984, New York 1989, 1995.– Lord, J.: A. G. Drawings. Greewich 1971.– Lord, J.: G. A Biography. New York 1983, London 1986 / A. G. Der Mensch und sein Lebenswerk. Bern 1987, Munich 1991.– Matter, H. and M.: A. G. Bern 1987, New York 1987.– Pagé, S. (ed.): A. G. Sculptures, peintures, dessins. Musée d'Art Moderne de la Ville de Paris. Paris 1991 (cat.).– Rotzler, W.: Die Geschichte der A.-G.-Stiftung Bern 1985.– Scheidegger, E.: Spuren einer Freundschaft. A. G. Zurich 1990 / A. G. Traces d'une amitié. Paris 1992.– Schneider, A. (ed.): A. G. Nationalgalerie, Berlin et al. Berlin 1987 (cat.).– Schneider, A. (ed.): A. G. Skulpturen, Gemälde, Zeichnungen. Nationalgalerie, Berlin et al. Munich 1994 (cat.) / A. G. Sculptures, Paintings, Drawings. Nationalgalerie, Berlin et al. New York 1994 (cat.).– Soavi, G.: G. Paris 1991.– Soldini, J.: Il colossale, la madre, il "sacro". L'opera di A. G. Bergamo 1991.– Stooss, T. et al. (ed.): A. G. 1901-1966. Kunsthalle Vienna et al. Stuttgart 1996 (cat.).– Sylvester, D. (ed.): A. G. Paintings, Drawings. Tate Gallery. London 1965 (cat.).– Sylvester, D.: Looking at G. London 1994, New York 1996

GIDAL Tim N.

(Nachum Ignaz Gidalevich) **1909** Munich – **1996** Jerusalem German-born Israeli photographer. One of the first photojournalists. Studied history. **1929** While still a student, published his first reportages in the *Münchner Illustrierte Presse*. **1936** Received his doctorate in Basel and emigrated to Palestine. Worked as chief photojournalist for *Picture Post* in London. **1947** Lectured in visual communications in

New York. **1975** Returned to Israel. Member of the German Photographic Society and the Royal Society of Photographers in England. **1983** Won the Erich Salomon Award together with Lotte Jacobi. WRITINGS: T. N. G.: Deutschland. Beginn des Modernen Photojournalismus. Frankfurt-on-Main 1972.– T. N. G.: Modern Photojournalism. Origin and Evolution 1910-1933. New York 1973 MONOGRAPHS, CATALOGUES: T. G. In the 30's. Israel Museum, Jerusalem et al. Jerusalem 1975 (cat.).– T. G. In the 40's. Israel Museum, Jerusalem et al. Jerusalem 1975 (cat.)

GILBERT & GEORGE

born **1943** St. Martin (South Tyrol): Gilbert Proersch born **1942** Devon (England): George Passmore English performance, photo and object artists. After attending various other art schools, Gilbert & George met at St. Martin's School of Art in London. **1968** First joint-exhibition of *Object-Sculptures* at Frank's Sandwich Bar. Radically extended the definition of sculpture in that they posed themselves as *Living Sculptures* and stylised everyday activities such as smoking, drinking and taking walks into exact, ritualised actions. **1969** Presented themselves as *Singing Sculptures* in *Underneath the Arches*. **1971** First photographic works on the themes of alcohol, grief and degeneration. **1972–1982** Participation in documenta 5 – 7 in Kassel. From **1974** photo-pieces, heavily screened by grouping of the photographs in black frames. **1977** Gilbert & George gave up living sculpture performances but continued with a media-oriented dramatisation of their lifestyle. Since **1980** large-format photographic self-portraits, mounted and framed. Supplemented with pictographs, everday scenes, graffiti and drawings, these photographs are ironic and diverse commentaries on sexuality, politics and aggression. **1981** Autobiographical film *Gilbert & George*. **1986** Retrospective in Bordeaux. WRITINGS: Obrist, H.-U. and R. Violette (ed.): The Words of G. & G. London 1997 CATALOGUE RAISONNE: Ratcliff, C. (ed.): G. and G. The Complete Pictures 1971-1985. CAPC Musée d'Art Contemporain, Bordeaux et al. Munich, New York and London 1986 (cat.) MONOGRAPHS, CATALOGUES: Farson, D.: With G. & G. in Moscow. London 1991.– G. & G. Musée d'Art Contemporain de Bordeaux. Bordeaux 1986 (cat.).– G. & G. Museo d'Arte Moderna della Città di Lugano. Milan 1994 (cat.).– Grosenick, U. (ed.): G. & G. Shitty Naked Human World 1994 und andere Bilder. Kunstmuseum Wolfsburg. Stuttgart 1994 (cat.).– Jahn, W.: The Art of G. & G. Or an Aesthetic of Existence. London 1987 / Die Kunst von G. & G. oder eine Ästhetik der Existenz. Munich 1989.– Ratcliff, C. et al. (ed.): G. & G. 1968-1980. Stedelijk Van Abbe Museum.

Eindhoven 1980 (cat.).– Ratcliff, C. and R. Rosenblum: G. & G. The Singing Sculpture. London 1993.– Richardson, B. (ed.): G. & G. Baltimore Museum of Art et al. Baltimore 1984 (cat.).– Rosenblum, R. (ed.): Worlds and Windows. London and New York 1990.– Rosenblum, R. (ed.): G. & G. The Fundamental Pictures. New York 1997

GIRKE Raimund

born **1930** Heinzendorf (now Jasienica near Kattowitz) German painter. **1951/52** Studied at the School of Arts and Crafts in Hanover and **1952–1956** at the Düsseldorf Academy. **1959** Won an award for painting from the City of Wolfsburg. From **1961** most paintings monochrome and predominantly white. **1962** Youth Art Prize, Stuttgart. In numerous series of works after **1970** experimented with the structure of his brush stroke and the effect of overlapping layers of colour. **1964–1966** Produced the series *Fluctuations*, followed in **1967/68** by *Progressions*. **1973** Series of large-scale gestural paintings of white structures on a dark background. **1966–1971** Taught at the School of Arts and Crafts in Hanover. **1971–1996** Professorship at the Berlin Academy. **1977** Took part in documenta 6 in Kassel. **1995** Retrospective at the Sprengel Museum, Hanover. WRITINGS: R. G.: Texte 1960-1995. Kunsthaus Zug. Zug 1995 MONOGRAPHS, CATALOGUES: Bischof, U. (ed.): R. G. zu Gast in der Gemäldegalerie Neue Meister. Dresden 1996 (cat.).– Boehm, G. (ed.): R. G. Malerei 1956-1986. Neuer Berliner Kunstverein et al. Berlin 1986 (cat.).– Elger, D. (ed.): R. G. Arbeiten auf Papier. Museum am Ostwall, Dortmund et al. Dortmund 1988 (cat.).– Elger, D. (ed.): R. G. Malerei. Sprengel Museum, Hanover et al. Stuttgart 1995 (cat.).– Heckmanns, F. W. (ed.): R. G. Arbeiten auf Papier. Daadgalerie, Berlin et al. Berlin 1981 (cat.).– Honnef, K. et al. (ed.): R. G. Westfälischer Kunstverein. Münster 1974 (cat.).– Schilling, J. (ed.): R. G. Arbeiten auf Leinwand und Papier. Kunstverein Hannover. Hanover 1979 (cat.).– Schmied, W. (ed.): R. G. Arbeiten 1953-1989. Kunstverein Ludwigshafen. Ludwigshafen am Rhein 1989 (cat.)

GLARNER Fritz

1899 Zurich – **1972** Locarno Swiss-American painter. **1914–1920** Studied at the Accademia di Belle Arti in Naples. **1923–1935** Lived in Paris. Attended the Académie Colarossi and became acquainted with Sonja and Robert Delaunay. **1929** First geometric, abstract paintings inspired by his meeting with Mondrian. **1931–1936** Joined Abstraction-Création. **1936** Moved to the USA and took American citizenship. **1938–1944** Member of the group American Abstract Artists. **1945** Began *Relational Paintings*, in which he experimented with alternating and contrast effects between figure and background, thereby extending

Mondrian's theory of Neo-Plasticism. **1955** Took part in documenta 1 in Kassel. **1958–1960** Wall painting for the Time-Life building in New York. **1964** Exhibited at the Venice Biennale.
WRITINGS: F. G.: What Abstract Art Means to Me. The Museum of Modern Art. New York 1951
MONOGRAPHS, CATALOGUES: Arici, L.: Der Tondo im Werk von F. G. Zurich 1987.– Bill, M. and C. Huber (ed.): F. G. Kunsthalle Bern. Bern 1972 (cat.).– Edgar, N. (ed.): F. G. 1944-1970. San Francisco Museum of Modern Art. San Francisco 1970 (cat.).– Frigerio, S.: F. G. Peintures 1949-1962. Paris 1966.– Hrikova, D. (ed.): F. G. im Kunsthaus Zürich. Zurich 1982 (cat.).– Kahn-Rossi, M. (ed.): F. G. Museo Cantonale d'Arte, Lugano et al. Lugano 1993 (cat.).– Mason, R. M. and D. Abadie (ed.): F. G. Dessins, peintures 1940-1969. Cabinet des estampes, Musée d'Art et d'Histoire. Geneva 1979 (cat.).– Staber, M.: F. G. Zurich 1976.– Staber, M. et al. (ed.): F. G. Museo Cantonale d'Arte. Lugano 1993 (cat.).– Wißmann, J. et al. (ed.): F. G. Quadrat, Moderne Galerie Bottrop 1978 (cat.)

GLEIZES Albert
1881 Paris – **1953** St.-Remy-de-Provence
French painter and writer. Trained as a technical draughtsman. **1903** Co-founder of the Salon d'Automne. **1910** Exhibited with leading Cubists, including Delaunay, Le Fauconnier, Metzinger and Picasso at the Salon des Indépendants. **1912** Joined the Section d'Or and, together with Metzinger, published the first theoretical treatise on Cubism: Du Cubisme. **1913** Exhibited at the Armory Show in New York. **1914/15** Military service. **1914** Extended trips to America, Spain and Cuba. **1919** Returned to Paris. **1923** Publication of the work La Peinture et ses lois, a study of religious art in the Middle Ages. **1927** Founded the craftsmen's association Moly-Sabata in Sablons. **1937** Wall paintings for the World Fair in Paris. **1941** Converted to Catholicism, which strongly influenced his attitude to art and also his painting. **1951** Grand Prix at the French Biennale in Menton. **1947** Retrospective in Lyon. **1952** Frescoes on religious themes for the chapel of Les Fontaines in Chantilly. As one of the Cubists around Metzinger,

Gleizes set out the theoretical principles of the style introduced by Braque and Picasso as well as developing them in his own paintings.
WRITINGS: A. G.: La Peinture et ses lois. Paris 1923, Aix-en-Provence 1961.– A. G.: Vers une conscience plastique: La Forme et l'histoire. Paris 1932.– A. G.: Homocentrisme. Sablons 1937.– A. G.: Souvenirs: Le Cubisme 1908-1914. Extraits. Lyon 1957.– A. G.: Puissances du cubisme. Chambéry 1969.– A. G.: Art et religion. Art et science. Art et production. Chambéry 1970.– A. G. and J. Metzinger: Du cubisme. Paris 1912, Sisteron 1980 / Kubismus. Munich 1928, Mainz and Berlin 1980
CATALOGUE RAISONNE: Fondation Gleizes (ed.): A. G. Catalogue raisonné (in preparation)
MONOGRAPHS, CATALOGUES: Alibert, P.: A. G. Naissance et avenir du cubisme. Saint-Etienne 1982.– Alibert, P.: G. Biographie. Paris 1990.– Chevalier, J.: A. G. et le cubisme. Basel 1962.– Dorival, B. and P. Alibert (ed.): A. G. 1881-1953. Legs de Madame Juliette Roche Gleizes. Fondation nationale des arts graphiques et plastiques, Paris. Saint-Etienne 1982 (cat.).– Georgel, P. (ed.): Dessins d'A. G. Musée National d'Art Moderne. Paris 1976 (cat.).– A. G. L'œuvre graphique. Musée de l'Imprimerie et de la Banque. Lyon 1990 (cat.).– Henry, A.: A. G. 1881-1953. Musée des Beaux-Arts et d'Archéologie de Besançon. Besançon 1993 (cat.).– Indlefofer Robbins, D. (ed.): A. G. Solomon R. Guggenheim Museum. New York 1964 (cat.).– Robbins, D.: The Formation and Maturity of A. G. Ann Arbor (MI) 1981.– Tapié, A. and P. Alibert (ed.): L'Art sacré d'A. G. Musée des Beaux-Arts de Caen. Caen 1985 (cat.)

GNOLI Domenico
1933 Rome – **1970** Rome
Italian painter. Self-taught. **1953/54** Lived temporarily in London and Paris. **1955** Visited the USA. Worked as a stage-set and costumer designer for various theatres in Italy. **1960** First major solo-exhibition at the Bianchini Gallery in New York, with paintings of domestic items. Illustrated literary publications and magazines such as Fortune, Holiday and Horizon. **1965** Influenced by American Pop Art and Surrealist Painting, painted enormously enlarged parts of the body and items of clothing. His pictures appeared regularly in the journal of the Society of Illustrators. **1966** Nominated American Illustrator of the Year and awarded a gold medal. In later years, he abandoned his fresco-type painting technique, in which he used a mixture of oil and sand, to work on bronze sculptures. **1968** Took part in documenta 4 in Kassel. **1970** Exhibition at the Krugier Gallery in Genoa. **1987** Retrospective in the Galleria Nazionale d'Arte Moderna in Rome. Gnoli's œuvre combines the commonplace directness of Pop Art with a form of magical, symbolic realism.

CATALOGUES RAISONNES: Calvino, I. et al. (ed.): G. Milan 1985.– Sgarbi, V. (ed.): L'opera grafica di D. G. Milan 1985
MONOGRAPHS, CATALOGUES: Carluccio, L.: D. G. Lausanne 1974, New York 1975.– Corral, M. and R. Barilli (ed.): D. G. Ultimas obras 1963-1969. Fundación Caja de Pensiones. Madrid 1990 (cat.).– Cortenova, G. et al. (ed.): D. G. Antologia. Galleria d'Arte Moderna e Contemporanea, Palazzo Forti. Verona 1982 (cat.).– D. G. Palazzo Forti, Verona. Milan 1982 (cat.).– Mantura, B. and M. Quesada (ed.): D. G. Padiglione d'Arte Contemporanea. Milan 1985 (cat.).– Mantura, B. (ed.): D. G. 1933-1970. Galleria Nazionale d'Arte Moderna, Roma. Milan 1987 (cat.).– Meyer zu Eissen, A. (ed.): D. G. 1933-1970. Gemälde, Skulpturen, Zeichnungen, Druckgraphik. Kunsthalle Bremen. Bremen 1981 (cat.).– Prat, J.-L. (ed.): D. G. Fondation Maeght. Saint-Paul 1987 (cat.).– Quesada, M. (ed.): D. G. Palazzo Racani-Arroni, Spoleto. Milan 1985 (cat.).– Quesada, M. (ed.): D. G. Disegno e pittura. Padiglione d'Arte Contemporanea. Milan 1985 (cat.).– Sgarbi, V.: G. Milan 1983

GOBER Robert
born **1954** Wallingford (CT)
American object artist. **1972–1976** Studied at Middleburg College in Vermont. **1973/74** Attended the Tyler School of Art in Philadelphia. Moved to New York, where he worked as a carpenter and joined the Johanna Boyce dance company. Influenced by minimal artists such as Donald Judd and Carl Andre, he took up sculpture. **1979** Took part in the exhibition "Amore Store" at 112 Greene Street, New York. **1984** First solo-exhibition at the Paula Cooper Gallery. **1986** Worked with the painter Kevin Larmon. Began joint projects with artists such as Christopher Wool, Sherrie Levine and Meg Webster. **1989** Designed the book Heat, written by Joyce Carol Oates, and printed the designs from the book onto wallpaper. **1990** Exhibition at the Boymans-van-Beuningen Museum in Rotterdam. **1992** Took part in documenta 9. Gober manually manipulated simple everyday items such as washbasins or playpens, to create installations full of poetic, erotic and ironic allusions.
MONOGRAPHS, CATALOGUES: David, C. and J. Simon (ed.): R. G. Galerie Nationale du Jeu de Paume, Paris et al. Paris 1991 (cat.).– R. G. The Art Institute of Chicago. Chicago 1988 (cat.).– R. G. Museum Boymans-van Beuningen, Rotterdam et al. Rotterdam and Bern 1990 (cat.).– R. G. Galerie Nationale du Jeu de Paume. Paris 1991 (cat.).– R. G. Museo Nacional Centro de Arte Reina Sofia. Madrid 1991 (cat.).– Hickey, D. (ed.): R. G. Dia Center for the Arts. New York 1994 (cat.).– Nesbit, J. et al. (ed.): R. G. Serpentine Gallery, London et al. London 1993 (cat.).– Rouse, Y.: R. G. Museo Nacional Centro de Arte Reina Sofia. Madrid 1991 (cat.).– Schimmel, P. (ed.):

R. G. Museum of Contemporary Art. Los Angeles 1997 (cat.).– Vischer, T. (ed.): R. G. Museum für Gegenwartskunst, Basel. Cologne 1995 (cat.)

GOGH Vincent van
1853 Groot-Zundert (North Brabant) – **1890** Auvers-sur-Oise (near Paris)
Dutch painter and draughtsman. First employed by a firm of art dealers with branches in The Hague, London and Paris. Worked as an unpaid assistant at an English school, and later as a Methodist preacher in the poor mining community of Borinage in Belgium. When dismissed from this post, he devoted himself to painting. His first paintings were of dismal scenes of poverty, painted in sombre colours. He often returned to his parents' house in Nuenen where, between **1883** and **1885**, he painted his best-known Dutch works. Up to **1886** he lived in Antwerp and tried to study at the Academy there. His discovery of Japanese coloured woodblock prints had a profound and lasting influence on his work. Spent two years in Paris from **1886–1888**, where he met the Impressionists and Gauguin, as well as the Symbolists and Pointillists. **1888** His longing for southern sunlight brought him to Arles, where Gauguin visited him. Between **1889** and **1890** he continued to paint in the asylum at St.-Rémy, after which he turned for help to the patron and friend of many painters, Dr. Paul Gachet, who lived in Auvers-sur-Oise. The doctor could not cure him, and in a severe fit of depression, van Gogh shot himself. In thirty months of frenzied creative activity, between **1888** and his death, van Gogh produced 463 paintings; paintings that became famous all over the world and were fundamental to the development of 20th century art, especially Fauvism and Expressionism.
WRITINGS: V. v. G.: The Complete Letters. 3 vols. London and Greenwich (CT) 1958, 1979 / Correspondance complète de V. v. g. 3 vols. Paris 1960 / V. v. G. Sämtliche Briefe. 6 vols. Berlin 1965-1968
CATALOGUES RAISONNES: Faille, J. B. d. la (ed.): L'œuvre de V. v. G. Catalogue raisonné. 4 vols. Paris and Brussels 1928.– Faille, J. B. d. la (ed.): The Works of V. v. G. His Paintings and Drawings. Amsterdam and New York 1970.– Heutgen, S. van et al. (ed.): V. v. G. Complete Paintings and Drawings. Vol. 1 and 2. London 1996-1997.– Hulsker, J. (ed.): V. G. en zijn weg. Het complete werk. Amsterdam 1977 / The Complete V. G. Paintings, Drawings, Sketches. New York 1977.– Hulsker, J. (ed.): The New Complete V. G. Paintings, Drawings, Sketches. Amsterdam and Philadelphia 1996.– Lecaldano, P. (ed.): Tout l'œuvre peint de v. G. 2 vols. Paris 1971.– Testori, G. and L. Arrigoni (ed.): V. v. G. Catalogo completo dei dipinti. Florence 1990.– Walther, I. F. and R. Metzger: V. v. G. Sämtliche Gemälde. 2 vols. Cologne 1989 / V. v. G. L'œuvre complète. 2 vols. Cologne 1990 / V. v. G. The Complete Paintings. 2 vols. Cologne 1990

GOINGS Ralph
born **1928** Corning (CA)
American painter. **1950–1953** Studied at the California School of Arts, Oakland and **1965/66** at Sacramento State College, California. **1955–1970** Taught at various schools and universities in California, including the State University of Sacramento and the University of California in Davis. **1972**, in documenta 5 in Kassel and, in **1974** Took part in the Tokyo Biennale. Goings is one of the main exponents of Hyperrealism in the USA. Status symbols of bourgeois society, such as houses, swimming pools, neat front-gardens and the car are recurring themes in his satirical paintings modelled on photographs.
MONOGRAPHS, CATALOGUES: Chase, L.: R. G. New York 1988.– R. G. Tampa Museum of Art. Tampa (FL) 1987 (cat.)

GOLDIN Nan
born **1953** Washington
American photographer. Photographed full-time from the age of 16. **1973** First solo-exhibition in Cambridge (MA). **1978** Moved to New York. Her slide show *The Ballad of Sexual Dependency* brought her instant fame in the 80s. This series of about 700 slides, with musical accompaniment, was shown in galleries, cinemas, museums and film festivals throughout Europe and America. The artist received numerous awards and a DAAD scholarship to Berlin **1991/92**. From the start, Goldin's photography has focused on the theme of human sexuality. For years she has photographed both men and women on the borderline of sexual norms.

GOLLER Bruno
1901 Gummersbach – **1998** Düsseldorf
German painter. Took private lessons from the landscape painter Julius Jungheim. **1920** Moved to Düsseldorf. Joined the young artists' association Das Junge Rheinland (Young Rhineland) and The Rhenish Secession. Contact with artists gathered around the gallery owner Mutter Ey. **1939–1945** Military service. **1943** All his early works destroyed in a fire in his Düsseldorf studio. In his new creative period, his early narrative formal language is replaced by a symbolic, magic realism in which commonplace

objects such as hats, umbrellas and ties are presented in an exaggerated and puzzling manner. **1949–1964** Professor at the Düsseldorf Academy, where his pupils included K. Klapheck. **1950** Cornelius Award from the City of Düsseldorf. **1958** Retrospective at the Kestner Society in Hanover. **1959** Took part in documenta 2 in Kassel. **1965** Major art award from the state of Nordrhein Westphalen. **1967** Member of the Berlin Academy of Arts. **1980** Lichtwark Award, Hamburg. **1981** Retrospective in the arts centre at the railway station Rolandseck near Bonn.
MONOGRAPHS, CATALOGUES: B. G. Städtische Kunsthalle Düsseldorf. Düsseldorf 1969 (cat.).– Kahmen, V.: B. G. zum 95. Geburtstag. Rolandseck et al. Bonn 1981.– Klapheck, A.: B. G. Recklinghausen 1958.– Krupp, W. et al. (ed.): B. G. Bilder, Zeichnungen. Bahnhof Rolandseck et al. Bonn 1991 (cat.).– Merkert, J. and W. Schmalenbach (ed.): B. G. Werke aus sechs Jahrzehnten. Kunstsammlung Nordrhein-Westfalen. Düsseldorf 1986 (cat.).– Ruhrberg, K. (ed.): B. G. Städtische Kunsthalle Düsseldorf. Düsseldorf 1969 (cat.)

GOLUB Leon
born **1922** Chicago
American painter. **1940–1942** Studied history of art at the University of Chicago. **1946–1950** Studied painting at the Art Institute of Chicago. **1943–1946** Military service. **1950** First solo-exhibition at the Contemporary Gallery, Chicago. **1951** Married Nancy Spero. **1956/57** Spent a year in Italy. **1959–1964** Lived in Paris. **1964** and **1987** participation in documenta 3 and 8 in Kassel. **1968** Awarded a Guggenheim grant. Since **1970** Professor at Rutgers University, New Brunswick. Golub is an opponent of Abstract Expressionism, preferring to follow the representational approach of the Chicago School of painting. A recurrent motif in his œuvre is the figure of an isolated, introverted person.
WRITINGS: Obrist, H.-U. (ed.): L. G. Do Painting Bite? Selected Texts. Stuttgart 1997
MONOGRAPHS, CATALOGUES: Alloway, L. (ed.): Museum of Contemporary Art, Chicago 1974 (cat.).– Bird, J. and M. Newman (ed.): L. G. Mercenaries and Interrogations. Institute of Contemporary Arts. London 1982 (cat.).– Fehlemann, S.

(ed.): L. G. Violence Report. Von der Heydt-Museum, Wuppertal et al. Wuppertal 1993 (cat.).– L. G. Kunstverein München. Munich 1993 (cat.).– Gumpert, L. and N. Rifkin (ed.): L. G. New Museum of Contemporary Art, New York et al. New York 1984 (cat.).– Kuspit, D. B.: The Existential/Activist Painter. The Example of L. G. New Brunswick (NJ) 1985.– Kuspit, D. (ed.): L. G. Kunstmuseum Luzern et al. Lucerne 1987 (cat.).– Marzorati, G.: A Painter of Darkness. L. G. and Our Times. New York 1990.– Murphy, P. T. (ed.): L. G. Paintings 1987-1992. Institute of Contemporary Art, University of Pennsylvania. Philadelphia 1992 (cat.).– Nordgren, S. (ed.): L. G. Malmö Konsthall et al. Malmö 1992 (cat.).– Robbins, C. (ed.): L. G. National Gallery of Victoria. Melbourne 1970 (cat.).– Schjeldahl, P. (ed.): G. Barbara Gladstone Gallery. New York 1986 (cat.)

GONCHAROVA Natalia
1881 Ladyshkino (near Tula) – **1962** Paris
Russian painter and stage designer. **1898** Studied sculpture at the Moscow Art Academy. Extensive travels through Europe. **1904** Took up painting. Met Mikhail Larionov, with whom she exhibited at the Salon d'Automne in Paris in **1906**. Together they developed the abstract style Rayonism, an attempted synthesis of the observed action of light rays with the Futurist idea of 'lines of force' and the Cubist fragmentation of the subject into bundles of slanting lines. **1913** Along with ten other artists signed a joint Rayonist and Futurist manifesto. **1914** Participation in an exhibition at the Galerie Guillaume in Paris. Painted less and began to design sets and costumes for the theatre and ballet. **1915** Moved to Paris. Met Diaghilev and designed sets for his ballets *Le Coq d'Or*, *Les Noces* and *The Firebird*. From **1917** illustrated numerous books and worked all over the world as a stage and costume designer for theatre and opera. **1948** Retrospective in Paris. **1956** Took up painting again.
MONOGRAPHS, CATALOGUES: Boissel, J. and G. Viatte (ed.): N. G. & Michael Larionov. Centre Georges Pompidou. Paris 1995 (cat.).– Boissel, J. (ed.): Larionov et G. Centre Georges Pompidou. Paris 1995 (cat.).– Chamot, M.: G. Paris 1972.– Chamot, M.: G. Stage Designs and Paintings. London 1979.– Cvetaeva, M. I.: N. G. Sa Vie, son œuvre. Paris 1990.– M. G. Musée des Beaux-Arts. Lyon 1969 (cat.).– Gray, C.: Larionov and G. London 1961.– Loguine, T.: G. et Larionov. Cinquante ans à Saint Germain-des-Prés. Paris 1971

GONZALEZ Julio
1876 Barcelona – **1942** Arcueil (near Paris)
Spanish sculptor. Taught metal working by his father, a goldsmith and sculptor, and studied painting at the Art Academy in Barcelona. **1900** Moved to Paris. Friendship

with Picasso, Braque and Brancusi. From **1908** numerous iron sculptures, inspired by Cubism. **1927** First forged and cut-out sculptures *Masques découpés et natures mortes*. **1929–1932** Intensive collaboration with Picasso. **1931** Contact with the Surrealists and joint-exhibitions at the Salon des Sur-Indépendants. **1932** Joined the artists' group Cercle et Carré in Paris. **1937** First large sculpture *La Montserrat* displayed in the Spanish pavilion at the World Fair in Paris. **1939/40** Started with the series *Cactus Man*. González' basic, constructive formal language had a profound influence on later generations of American and English sculptors.
WRITINGS: J. G.: Les Matériaux de son expression. 2 vols. Paris 1970
CATALOGUES RAISONNES: Cerni, V. A. (ed.): Julio, Joan, Roberta G. Itinerario de una dinastia. Barcelona 1973.– Gibert, J. (ed.): J. G. Catalogue raisonné des dessins de J. G. 9 vols. Paris 1975.– Merkert, J. et al. (ed.): J. G. Catalogue raisonné. Milan 1987.– Withers, J. (ed.): J. G. Sculpture in Iron. New York 1978
MONOGRAPHS, CATALOGUES: Cerni, V. A.: J. G. Roma 1962.– Cerni, V. A.: J. G. Madrid 1971.– Curtis, P. (ed.): J. G. Sculptures and Drawings. Art Gallery and Museum, Glasgow. London 1990 (cat.).– Degand, L.: G. Cologne 1956, London 1958.– Descargues, P.: J. G. Paris 1971.– Gibert, J.: J. G. Dessins. 9 vols. Paris 1975.– J. G. Tate Gallery. London 1970 (cat.).– J. G. Sculptures and Drawings. Whitechappel Art Gallery, London et al. London 1990.– Llorens, T. (ed.): J. G. Las colecciones del IVAM. Museo Nacional Centro de Arte Reina Sofia. Madrid 1986 (cat.).– Ritchie, A. (ed.): J. G. The Museum of Modern Art. New York 1956 (cat.).– Rowell, M. (ed.): J. G. 1876-1942. A Retrospective. Solomon R. Guggenheim Museum, New York et al. New York 1983 (cat.)/J. G. 1876-1942. Akademie der Künste, Berlin et al. Berlin 1983 (cat.).– Stooss, T. and T. Bhattacharya-Stettler (ed.): J. G. Zeichnen im Raum. Bern 1997 (cat.).– Vidal, C. et al. (ed.): J. G. Dibujos. Salas Pablo Ruiz Picasso. Madrid 1982 (cat.).– Withers, J. (ed.): J. G. Les matériaux de son expression. 2 vols. Galerie de France. Paris 1970 (cat.).– Withers, J.: J. G. Sculpture in Iron. New York 1978

GORKY Arshile
(Vosdanig Manoog Adoian)
1950 Hayotz-Dzore (Turkish Armenia) – **1948** Sherman (CT)
Armenian-born American painter. **1920** Emigrated to the USA. First auto-didactic attempts at painting clearly influenced by Cézanne's works. **1920–1922** Studied at Rhode Island School of Design. **1923/24** Taught at the New School of Design in Boston. Exhibitions of Surrealist Art in New York in the 30s introduced him to the works of Picasso, Miró, and Masson, and inspired experiments with biomorphic forms. From **1941** worked with luminous grounds and calligraphic lines. **1947** Abandoned Surreal-

ism and spoke out against Abstract Expressionism, although he had a fundamental influence on painters in this movement. After paralysing his right hand in a car accident, he commited suicide. With his Color Fields and *hybrid forms*, Gorky played a key role in the development of Abstract Expressionism in America.
CATALOGUE RAISONNE: Goldwater, R. and J. M. Jordan (ed.): The Paintings of A. G. A Critical Catalogue. New York and London 1982
MONOGRAPHS, CATALOGUES: Auping, M. (ed.): A. G. The Breakthrough Years. Modern Art Museum of Fort Worth et al. New York 1995 (cat.).– Billeter, E. (ed.): A. G. Œuvres sur papier 1929-1947/A. G. Arbeiten auf Papier. Musée Cantonal des Beaux-Arts de Lausanne et al. Bern et al. 1990 (cat.).– Golding, J. et al. (ed.): A. G. 1904-1948. Fundación Caja de Pensiones, Madrid et al. Madrid 1989 (cat.).– Goodrich, L.: A. G. New York 1957.– A. G. Drawings. New York 1970.– A. G. 1904-1948. Fundación Caja de Pensiones, Madrid et al. Madrid and London 1990 (cat.).– Lader, M. P.: A. G. New York 1985.– Levy, J.: A. G. New York 1966.– Melville, R. (ed.): A. G. Paintings and Drawings. Tate Gallery. London 1965 (cat.).– Mooradian, K.: A. G. Chicago 1978, 1980.– Mooradian, K.: The Many Worlds of A. G. Chicago 1980.– Rand, H.: A. G. The Implications of Symbols. Montclair (NJ) and London 1980, Berkeley 1991.– Reiff, R. F.: A Stylistic Analysis of A. G.'s Art from 1943-1948. New York 1977.– Rosenberg, H.: A. G. The Man, the Time, the Idea. New York 1962.– Schwabacher, E. (ed.): A. G. Memorial Exhibition. Whitney Museum of American Art, New York et al. New York 1951 (cat.).– Schwabacher, E. K.: A. G. New York 1957.– Seitz, C. (ed.): A. G. Paintings, Drawings, Studies. The Museum of Modern Art, New York et al. New York 1962 (cat.).– Spende, M. and B. Rose (ed.): A. G. and the Genesis of Abstraction. Drawings from the Early 1930's. Princeton (NJ) et al. Princeton 1994 (cat.).– Waldman, D. and D. Tabak (ed.): A. G. 1904-1948. A Retrospective. Solomon R. Guggenheim Museum. New York 1981 (cat.)

GORMLEY Anthony
born **1950** London
English sculptor. **1968–1970** Studied at Trinity College, Cambridge, **1973/74** at the Central School of Art and Design in London, and **1975–1977** at Goldsmith's College. **1981** First solo-exhibition at the Serpentine Gallery and Whitechapel Gallery, London. **1987** Participated in documenta 8 in Kassel. **1991** Designed an installation, entitled *Field*, consisting of 35,000 small terracotta figures, which was shown that year at the Galerie Salvatore Ala in New York. **1996** Guest-professor at the Munich Academy. Gormley's works are references to urban architecture. His stylised human figures are mostly made of lead, covered with fibreglass and terracotta, with

dimensions based on his own body measurements.
MONOGRAPHS, CATALOGUES: Briggs, L. et al. (ed.): A. G. Malmö Konsthall et al. Malmö 1993 (cat.).– Champ: A. G. Musée des Beaux Arts, Montreal. Stuttgart 1993 (cat.).– A. G. Malmö Konsthall et al. Malmö 1993 (cat.).– A. G. Body and Light and Other Drawings. 1990-1996. London 1996 (cat.).– A. G. Still Moving. Works 197-1996. Kamakura et al. Kamakura 1996 (cat.).– Hutchinson, J. and L. B. Njatin (ed.): A. G. London 1995.– Loers, V. et al. (ed.): A. G. Städtische Galerie, Regensburg et al. Regensburg 1985 (cat.).– Lomax, J. (ed.): A. G. Sculpture. Whitechapel Art Gallery. London 1981 (cat.)

GOTTLIEB Adolph
1903 New York – **1974** New York
American painter. **1920–1924** Studied under Robert Henri and John Sloan at the Art Students League in New York. **1921** Studied in Paris. **1935** Founder-member of the Expressionist group The Ten. **1939** Wall paintings for the post office in Yerington, Nevada. From **1941** produced *Pictographs*, symbolic drawings in a magic realist style. **1944/45** Director of the Federation of Modern Painters and Sculptors in New York. After **1951** numerous paintings for synagogues in Millburn, Springfield and New York. From **1957** reduced his pictorial language to a few minimal elements such as orbs and blotches hovering in suspended tension. **1959** Participated in documenta 2 in Kassel. **1963** Major prize at the São Paulo Biennale. **1974** Member of the New York Art Commission. Gottlieb's condensed pictorial language aligns him with Abstract Expressionists such as Marc Rothko and Franz Kline.
MONOGRAPHS, CATALOGUES: Alloway, L. and M. D. MacNaughton (ed.): A. G. 1903-1974. A Retrospective. Corcoran Gallery of Art, Washington et al. New York 1981 (cat.).– Burns O'Connor, L. (ed.): The Pictographs of A. G. The Phillips Collection, Washington DC. New York 1994 (cat.).– Doty, R. and D. Waldman (ed.): A. G. Solomon R. Guggenheim Museum. New York et al. New York 1968 (cat.).– Friedman, M.: A. G. Minneapolis 1963.– Hirsch, S. et al. (ed.): The Pictographs of A. G. Phillips Collection, Washington. New York 1994 (cat.).–

Wilkin, K. (ed.): A. G. Pictographs. Edmonton Art Gallery et al. Edmonton 1977 (cat.)

GÖTZ Karl Otto
born **1914** Aachen
German painter. **1932–1934** Attended the School of Arts and Crafts in Aachen. **1935/36** Travelled throughout Switzerland and Italy. **1936** Made abstract films and experimented with photographic painting and photograms. **1945** Joined Baumeister, Hartung and Nay in the group Rosen-Kreis. **1948–1953** Editor of the journal *Meta*. **1949** Contact with the Cobra artists. Contributed to their magazine. **1952** Together with O. Greis, H. Kreutz and Schultze, founded the group Quadriga in Frankfurt. First Informel paintings inspired by Wols and Tachisme. **1958** Participated in the Venice Biennale and **1959** in documenta 2 in Kassel. **1959–1979** Taught painting at the Düsseldorf Academy. Götz' calligraphic improvisations make him one of the main exponents of Lyrical Abstraction in Germany.
WRITINGS: K. O. G.: Bildende Kunst und Kommunikation. Düsseldorf 1965.– K. O. G.: Erinnerungen und Werk 1914-1959. 2 vols. Neuss 1983.– K. O. G.: Erinnerungen 1959-1975. Aachen 1996
CATALOGUES RAISONNES: Geiger, U. und Manfred Hügelow (ed.): K. O. G. Werkverzeichnis der Original-Lithographien 1946-1994. Offenbach 1995
MONOGRAPHS, CATALOGUES: Bojescul, W. (ed.): K. O. G. Bilder und Arbeiten auf Papier 1935-1988. Kunstverein Braunschweig. Brunswick 1988 (cat.).– Grohmann, W.: K. O. G. Malerei 1940-1943. Witten 1948.– Grohmann, W. et al. (ed.): K. O. G. Roma 1962.– Harten, J. and M. Heinz (ed.): K. O. G. Monotypien, Gemälde, Gouachen 1935-1983. Städtische Kunsthalle Düsseldorf et al. Düsseldorf 1984 (cat.).– K. O. G. Gemäldegalerie Neuer Meister. Dresden 1994 (cat.).– Motte, M. d. la (ed.): K. O. G. Eine Dokumentation. Galerie Hennemann. Bonn 1978

GRAESER Camille
1892 Carouge (Canton Geneva) – **1980** Zurich
Swiss painter and interior designer. **1913–1915** Studied interior- and product design

at the School of Arts and Crafts in Stuttgart. Member of the Werkbund in Germany. Contact with Herwarth Walden's Sturm gallery in Berlin. **1918/19** Private painting lessons with Adolf Hoelzel. **1929** Worked for Mies van der Rohe at Weissenhof in Stuttgart. **1933** Destroyed a large portion of his œuvre and Bill and Richard Paul Lohse in the Zürcher Konkrete began developing a new, abstract-constructivist style. **1938** Became a member of the group *Allianz*. **1964** Retrospective at the Kunsthaus Zurich. **1975** Art award from the City of Zurich. **1977** Took part in documenta 6 in Kassel. In Graeser's paintings basic, geometric forms are built into *Dynamic Constructions, Rotations* and *Loxodromic Compositions*.
CATALOGUES RAISONNES: Paradowski, S. (ed.): C. G. Druckgraphik und Multiples. Zurich 1990.– Schwarz, D. (ed.): C. G. Zeichnungen. Zurich 1986
MONOGRAPHS, CATALOGUES: Billeter, E. et al. (ed.): C. G. Kunsthaus Zurich et al. Zurich 1979 (cat.).– Heckmanns, F. W. et al. (ed.): C. G. Retrospektive. Westfälisches Landesmuseum, Münster et al. Münster 1976 (cat.).– Koella, R. (ed.): C. G. 1892-1980. Kunstmuseum Winterthur et al. Zurich, Munich and Stuttgart 1992 (cat.).– Ludwig, J. and D. Zinke (ed.): C. G. Museum für Neue Kunst, Freiburg et al. Freiburg and Zurich 1988 (cat.).– Müller, F. and E. Gomringer: C. G. Eine Monographie. Teufen 1968.– Rotzler, W.: C. G. Lebenswerk und Lebensweg eines konstruktiven Malers. Zurich 1979

GRANDMA MOSES
(Anna Mary Robertson)
1860 Eagle Bridge (NY) – **1961** Hoosick Falls (NY)
American naive painter. Married to a farmer, she first began to paint in **1930** at the advanced age of 70. **1938** First exhibition in a drugstore. **1939** Became widely known for her paintings of the seasons, shown at the exhibition "Unknown American Painters". **1952** Publication of her autobiography *My Life's History*. **1962** Solo-exhibition at the Galerie St. Etienne, New York. Grandma Moses is one of the main representatives of naive painting in America. Her portrayals of the landscapes of her homeland and childhood memories are not painted on canvas, but on plywood covered with three coats of white paint, so as to capture and enhance the magic of light.
WRITINGS: Kallir, O. (ed.): G. M. My Life's History. New York 1948, 1952
CATALOGUES RAISONNES: Kallir, O. (ed.): G. M. New York 1973/G. M. Ihre Kunst und ihre Persönlichkeit. Cologne 1979
MONOGRAPHS, CATALOGUES: Brown, C. (ed.): A. M. R. M. 1860-1961. National Gallery of Art. Washington 1979 (cat.).– G. M. The Artist Behind the Myth. New York State Museum. Albany 1981 (cat.).– Johansson, E.: R. M. Copenhagen 1962.– Kallir, J.: G. M. The Artist Behind the

Myth. New York 1982.– Ketchum, W.: G. M. An American Original. New York 1996.– Nirenstein, O.: Grandma Moses. New York 1973

GRAUBNER Gotthard

born **1930** Erlbach

German painter. **1947/48** Studied at the Berlin School of Fine Arts, **1948–1952** at the Dresden Art Academy and **1954–1959** at the Düsseldorf Academy. **1965** Taught at the Berlin School of Fine Arts. During his professorship at this school (**1969–1972**) he soaked cushions with synthetic covers in thinned paints, in an attempt to embody colour and make out of it a spatial entity. **1968** and **1977** participated in documenta 4 and 6 in Kassel. Created environments entitled *Nebelräume* (Fog Rooms). **1971** Extended his cushion series, creating *Farbraumkörpern* (Spatial colour bodies), enormous painted pillows. Extended trips to Central and South America. **1973** Study trip to Asia. **1976** Professor of Painting at the Düsseldorf Academy. **1988** Interior decoration of the official residence of the Bundespräsident in Schloss Bellevue, Berlin.

MONOGRAPHS, CATALOGUES: Bleyl, M.: G. G. Farbraumkörper der XL. Biennale Venice 1982. Frankfurt-on-Main 1991.– Güse, E. (ed.): G. G. Malerei. Saarland Museum, Saarbrücken et al. Saarbrücken and Cologne 1995 (cat.).– Harten, J. et al. (ed.): G. G. Farbräume, Farbraumkörper, Arbeiten auf Papier. Städtische Kunsthalle Düsseldorf. Düsseldorf 1977 (cat.).– Helms, D. et al. (ed.): G. G. Werke 1959–1969. Kunstverein für die Rheinlande und Westfalen. Düsseldorf 1969 (cat.).– Helms, D.: G. G. Recklinghausen 1974.– Hofmann, W. (ed.): G. G. Hamburger Kunsthalle. Hamburg 1975 (cat.).– Imdahl, M. et al. (ed.): G. G. Staatliche Kunsthalle Baden-Baden et al. Baden-Baden 1980 (cat.).– Merkert, J. and M. Imdahl (ed.): G. G. Malerei aus den Jahren 1984-1986. Kunstsammlung Nordrhein-Westfalen. Düsseldorf 1987 (cat.).– Peters, H. A. (ed.): G. G. Kunstmuseum. Düsseldorf 1982 (cat.).– Salzmann, S. et al. (ed.): G. G. Malerei auf Papier. Kunsthalle Bremen et al. Bremen 1990 (cat.).– Schmidt, K. (ed.): G. G. Farbräume, Farbraumkörper. Arbeiten auf Papier. Städtische Kunsthalle Düsseldorf. Düsseldorf 1977 (cat.).– Schmidt, K. and B. Growe (ed.): G. G. Zeichnung, Aquarell. Städtisches Kunstmuseum Bonn. Bonn 1986 (cat.).– Schmied, W. and V. Kahmen (ed.): G. G. Kestner-Gesellschaft. Hanover 1969 (cat.)

GRAVES Nancy

1940 Pittsfield (MA) – **1995** New York
American painter and object artist. **1957–1961** Studied literature at Vassar College in New York. **1961–1964** Studied art at Yale University, New Haven (CT). **1964/65** Trips to Paris and Italy. Developed the theme of the camel in drawings, sculptures and films. **1968** First solo-exhibition in the Graham Gallery, New York. **1969** First woman to

have a solo-exhibition in the Whitney Museum of American Art in New York. **1970** Made her first five documentary films. **1972** Focused once again on painting, producing expressive abstract paintings inspired by photographs of the surface of the moon. **1972** and **1977** participation in documenta 5 and 6 in Kassel. From **1976** experimented with old bronze casting techniques. Incorporated various materials, collected on her extensive travels, into her sculptures and objects. **1985** Received the Yale Arts Award. **1986** Created an outdoor sculpture for the United Missouri Bank, Kansas City. **1987** Retrospective at the Hirshhorn Museum, Washington.

CATALOGUE RAISONNE: Carmean, E. A. et al. (ed.): The Sculpture of N. G. A Catalogue Raisonné. Fort Worth Art Museum et al. New York 1987 (cat.).– Pardon, T. (ed.): N. G. Excavations in Print. New York 1996
MONOGRAPHS, CATALOGUES: Bricker Balken, D. (ed.): N. G. Painting, Sculpture, Drawing 1980-1985. Vasar College, Poughkeepsie et al. Poughkeepsie (NY) 1986 (cat.).– Cassidy, M. (ed.): N. G. Institute of Contemporary Art. Philadelphia 1972 (cat.).– Cathcart, L. L. (ed.): N. G. A Survey 1969-1980. Albright-Knox Art Gallery, Buffalo et al. Buffalo 1980 (cat.).– Tuchman, P. (ed.): N. G. Sculpture, Drawings, Films 1969-1971. Neue Galerie der Stadt Aachen. Aachen 1971 (cat.)

GREEN Alan

born **1932** London

English painter and graphic artist. **1949–1953** Studied at the Beckenham School of Art in Kent, and **1955–1958** at the Royal College of Art in London. **1953–1955** Military service. **1961–1966** Taught at Leeds College of Fine Arts. **1963** First solo-exhibition at the A1A Gallery in London. **1972/73** Produced *Block Paintings* and *Column Paintings*, in which several layers of paint document the process of picture production. From **1974** combined single panels into larger polyptychs. Started to work on graphic reproductions. **1977** Participated in documenta 6 in Kassel. **1979** Received special honours at the International Graphic Biennale in Tokyo. Green is famous for his structured grid-like paintings which are a schematic representation of the interaction of a limited number of colours.

GRIS Juan

(José Victoriano Gonzáles)

1887 Madrid – **1927** Boulogne-sur-Seine
Spanish painter. **1902–1904** Studied at the School of Arts and Crafts in Madrid while working as an illustrator on satirical periodicals. **1906** Went to Paris, where he rented a room in the same studio-apartment house as Picasso. Encouraged by the art dealer Daniel-Henry Kahnweiler to join the Cubists Picasso and Braque and develop their artistic ideas. **1912** Exhibition at the Salon des Indépendants. First *papiers collés*. **1914** Visited Collioure and became friends with Matisse. **1916–1919** Tectonic period. Subordination of form and colour to compositional structure. **1919** First major solo-exhibition organised by the art dealer Rosenberg. Participated in the last joint Cubist exhibition at the Salon des Indépendants. **1922/23** Designed stage sets and costumes for Diaghilev's ballets. **1924** Gave a lecture at the Sorbonne entitled *Sur les possibilités de la peinture* (The Possibilities of Painting). In his last years, Gris worked mostly as an illustrator. His goal was to combine the separate phases of Cubism and all the directions the movement had taken into one approach: Synthetic Cubism.

WRITINGS: Cooper, D. (ed.): The Letters of J. G. London 1956.– J. G.: Des possibilités de la peinture. Caen 1989/Über die Möglichkeit der Malerei. Hamburg 1997
CATALOGUE RAISONNE: Cooper, D. and M. Potter (ed.): J. G. Catalogue raisonné de l'œuvre peint. 2 vols. Paris 1977
MONOGRAPHS, CATALOGUES: Bréon, E.: J. G. à Boulogne. Paris 1992.– Cooper, D. (ed.): J. G. Staatliche Kunsthalle Baden-Baden. Stuttgart 1974 (cat.).– Derouet, C. (ed.): J. G. Correspondance. Dessins 1915-1921. IVAM Centro Julio González, Valencia/Centre Georges Pompidou. Valencia 1990, Paris 1991 (cat.).– Gaya-Nuño, J. A.: J. G. Geneva and Paris 1974, Boston 1975, New York 1986.– Green, C. et al. (ed.): J. G. Whitechapel Art Gallery, London et al. London and Stuttgart 1992 (cat.).– Kahnweiler, D. H.: J. G. Sa Vie, son œuvre, ses écrits. Paris 1946, 1990/J. G. His Life and Work. London and New York 1947, 1969/J. G. Leben und Werk. Berlin 1929, Stuttgart 1968.– Leymarie, J. (ed.): J. G. Orangerie des Tuileries. Paris 1974 (cat.).– Overy, P.: K. The Language of the Eye. New York 1969.– Richardson, J. (ed.): J. G. Museum am Ostwall. Dortmund 1965 (cat.).– Rosenthal, M. (ed.): J. G. National Gallery of Art, Washington et al. Berkeley and New York 1983 (cat.).– Schmidt, G.: J. G. und die Geschichte des Kubismus. Baden-Baden 1957.– Soby, J. T. (ed.): J. G. The Museum of Modern Art. New York 1958 (cat.).– Tinterow, G. (ed.): J. G. Salas Pablo Ruiz Picasso. Madrid 1985 (cat.).– Waldemar, G.: J. G. Paris 1931

MONOGRAPHS, CATALOGUES: Franz, E. (ed.): A. G. Paintings 1969-1979. Kunsthalle Bielefeld. Bielefeld 1979 (cat.)

GROMAIRE Marcel

1892 Noyelles-sur-Sambre – **1971** Paris
French painter and graphic artist. Attended various private schools in Montparnasse, including the Académie de la Palette and the Académie Colarossi. Acquainted with pupils of Matisse. **1911** Exhibited at the Salon des Indépendants. **1914** Military service. **1916** Wounded. After the First World War he developed a monumental, expressive style, influenced by the works of Léger. **1918** Woodcuts as illustrations for the book *Homme de Troupe*. **1922** First etchings. **1925** Illustrations for *Ruptures*. **1937** Member of the Société des Peintres-Graveurs français. Designed the Sèvres pavilion at the World Fair in Paris. **1939** Worked with Jean Lurçat as a designer at the Gobelin manufacturers in Aubusson. His tapestries had powerful structural elements with less emphasis on colour. **1952** Carnegie award. **1977** Retrospectives in Chicago and **1980** at the Musée d'Art Moderne de la Ville de Paris.

WRITINGS: M. G.: L'Art moderne. Paris 1919.– M. G.: Notes sur l'art d'aujourd'hui. Paris 1919
CATALOGUES RAISONNES: Gromaire, F. (ed.): L'œuvre gravé de M. G. 2 vols. Lausanne and Paris 1976.– Gromaire, F. and F. Chibret-Plaussus (ed.): M. G. La Vie et l'œuvre. Catalogue raisonné des peintures. Paris 1993
MONOGRAPHS, CATALOGUES: Besson, G.: M. G. Paris 1950.– Briot, M.-O. (ed.): M. G. 1892-1971. Musée d'Art Moderne de la Ville de Paris. Paris 1980 (cat.).– Briot, M.-O. (ed.): M. G. Peinture 1921-1939. Paris 1980.– Cassou, J.: M. G. Paris 1925.– Cassou, J. (ed.): M. G. Musée d'Art Moderne de la Ville de Paris. Paris 1963 (cat.).– George, W.: G. Paris 1928.– M. G. L'œuvre gravé 1892-1971. Musée du Dessin. Gravelines 1980 (cat.).– Johnson, R. S. (ed.): M. G. 1892-1971. R. S. Johnson Fine Art. Chicago 1987 (cat.).– Zahar, M.: G. Geneva 1961

GROSSBERG Carl

1894 Wuppertal-Elberfeld – **1940** Laon
German painter. **1913/14** Studied architecture in Aachen and Darmstadt. **1914–1918** Military service. **1919–1921** Studied at the Weimar Academy of Arts and the Bauhaus, where his teachers included Feininger. **1921**

Moved to Sommerhausen near Würzburg. **1925** Visited the Netherlands. Drawings and watercolours of industrial landscapes. **1926** First solo-exhibition at the Neumann-Nierendorf gallery and Kunsthaus Schaller in Stuttgart. **1929** Took part in the exhibition "Neue Sachlichkeit" (New Objectivity) at the Stedelijk Museum in Amsterdam. **1931** Won the Rome Award from the Prussian Academy of Arts, a scholarship to Villa Massimo in Rome. **1934** Retrospective at the Kestner Society in Hanover. Commission for a propagandist mural *Deutsches Volk, deutsche Arbeit* (German people, German work). **1935** Retrospective at the Folkwang Museum, Essen. **1939/40** Military service in Poland and France, where he died after a car crash.
CATALOGUE RAISONNE: Fehlemann, S. (ed.): C. G. Retrospektive zum 100. Geburtstag. Von der Heydt-Museum, Wuppertal et al. Cologne 1994 (cat.).
MONOGRAPHS, CATALOGUES: Hamburger, D.: C. G. Industrie und Imagination in der Malerei der Neuen Sachlichkeit. Kassel 1990.– Schmidt, H.-M. C. G. Gemälde, Aquarelle, Zeichnungen und Druckgraphik. Hessisches Landesmuseum, Darmstadt et al. Darmstadt 1976 (cat.)

GROSZ George
1893 Berlin – **1959** Berlin
German painter and graphic artist. **1909–1912** Studied at the Dresden Art Academy and **1912–1916** at the School of Arts and Crafts in Berlin, under Emil Orlik. **1914–1916** and **1917/18** military service. Courtmarshalled for anti-war protests. **1918** Co-founder of the Berlin Dada group. Joined the German Communist Party. **1919/20** Co-editor of the publications *Der blutige Ernst, Die Pleite* and *Der DADA.* **1920** First solo-exhibition at the Hans Goltz gallery in Munich. Prosecuted for attacking the military in his portfolio *Gott mit uns* (God with us). Helped to set up the first international DADA-Messe (Dada trade fair) in Berlin. **1922** Went to Russia. **1923** Charged with obscenity for his collection of drawings *Ecce Homo*. One-man exhibition at Alfred Flechtheim's gallery. **1924** Director of the Rote Gruppe (Red Group), Berlin: Contributed to the magazines *Der Knüppel* and *Der Querschnitt*. **1925** Took part in the exhibition "Neue Sachlichkeit" (New Objectivity) in the Kunsthalle Mannheim. Publication of *Spießer-Spiegel*. **1926** Co-publication, with Herzfelde, of the pamphlet *Die Kunst ist in Gefahr* (Art is in Danger). **1929** Took part in the exhibition "Neue Sachlichkeit" at the Stedelijk Museum in Amsterdam. **1931** Guest-lecturer at the Art Students League in New York. **1933** Emigrated to the USA. Opened his own art institute, the Sterne-Grosz School. **1937** Included in the exhibition of "degenerate art" in Munich. Confiscation of 285 works. **1940** Awarded the Carol H. Beck Medal. **1954** Major retrospective at the Whitney Museum of American Art, New York. Elected member of the American

Academy of Arts and Letters. **1958** Member of the Academy of Arts in Berlin. **1959** Awarded a Gold Medal by the United States National Institute of Arts and Letters.
WRITINGS: G. G.: Die Kunst ist in Gefahr. Berlin 1925.– G. G.: A Little Yes and a Big No. New York 1946/Ein kleines Ja und ein großes Nein. Sein Leben von ihm selbst erzählt. Reinbek 1974.– G. G.: Briefe 1913-1939. Ed. by H. Knust. Reinbek 1979.– G. G.: An Autobiography. New York 1983.– G. G.: Ach knallige Welt, du Lunapark. Gesammelte Gedichte. Munich 1986.– Knust, H. (ed.): G. G. Briefe 1913-1959. Reinbek 1979
CATALOGUE RAISONNE: Dückers, A. (ed.): G. G. Das druckgraphische Werk. Frankfurt-on-Main et al. 1979, San Francisco 1996
MONOGRAPHS, CATALOGUES: Anders, G.: G. G. Zurich 1961.– Baur, J. I. H.: G. G. New York 1954.– Bittner, H. (ed.): G. G. New York 1960.– Fischer, L.: G. G. in Selbstzeugnissen und Bilddokumenten. Reinbek 1976.– Flavell, K. M.: G. G. A Biography. New Haven (CT) 1988.– Hess, H.: G. G. London 1974, New Haven (CT) 1985, Dresden 1982.– Kane, M.: Weimar Germany and the Limits of Political Art: A Study of Work of G. G. and Ernst Troller. Tayport 1987.– Kranzfelder, I.: G. G. 1893-1959. Cologne 1994.– Lang, L. (ed.): G. G. Berlin 1979.– Lewis, B. I.: G. G. Art and Politics in the Weimar Republic. Princeton (NJ) 1991.– McCloskey, B.: G. G. and the Communist Party. Princeton (NJ) 1997.– Neugebauer v. d. Schulenburg, R.: G. G. Macht und Ohnmacht satirischer Kunst. Berlin 1993.– Sabarsky, S. (ed.): G. G. Gli anni di Berlino. Palazzo Reale. Milan 1985 (cat.)/G. G. Die Berliner Jahre. Museum Villa Stuck. Munich 1986 (cat.)/G. G. The Berlin Years. New York 1985.– Schneede, U. M. et al. (ed.): G. G. Leben und Werk. Hamburger Kunstverein. Stuttgart 1975 (cat.)/G. G. His Life and Work., London 1979.– Schneede, U. M.: G. G. Der Künstler in seiner Gesellschaft. Cologne 1977, 1984.– Schuster, P. K. (ed.): G. G. Berlin – New York. Nationalgalerie Berlin et al. Berlin 1995 (cat.).– Whitford, F. (ed.): The Berlin of G. G. Drawings, Watercolors and Prints 1912-1930. Royal Academy. London 1997 (cat.)

GRUBER Francis
1912 Nancy – **1948** Paris
French painter. **1929–1932** Studied at the Académie Scandinave under H. Dufresne, Friesz and Waroquier. Visited the studios of Braque and Bissière. Studied old German painting. **1939** Participated in the Salon d'Automne and the Salon des Tuileries. **1936** Designed a wall painting for the Lycée de Lakanel in Sceaux. **1937** Took part in the group exhibitions "Salon des jeunes artistes" and "L'Art cruel" at the Billiet-Worms gallery. **1942** His painting *Hommage à Jacques Callot*, exhibited at the Friedland gallery earned him widespread recognition. **1947** Prix National de la peinture. **1949** Retro-

spective at the 60th Salon des Indépendants.
1959 Retrospective at the Tate Gallery, London. Gruber's compositions, which can be taken as examples of Fantastic Realism, had a decisive influence on the recognition of the works of Bernard Buffet and Alberto Giacometti.
MONOGRAPHS, CATALOGUES: Bernad-Gruber, C. and A. Vanazzi: F. G. Neuchâtel 1989.– Dorival, B.: F. G. Musée National d'Art Moderne. Paris 1950 (cat.).– F. G. Musée d'Art Moderne de la Ville de Paris. Paris 1976 (cat.).– Huyghe, R.: F. G. 1912-1948. Tate Gallery. London 1959 (cat.).– Schmidt, M. and J. Gachnang (ed.): F. G. 1912-1948. Kunsthalle Bern et al. Bern 1976 (cat.).– Testori, G. et al. (ed.): F. G. 1912-1948. Compagnia del disegno. Milan 1991 (cat.)

GRÜTZKE Johannes
born **1937** Berlin
German painter. **1957–1964** Studied at Berlin School of Fine Arts. Prize pupil of Peter Janssen. **1973** Together with Manfred Bluth, Mathias Koeppel and Karlheinz Ziegler founded the Schule der neuen Prächtigkeit (School of New Magnificence). **1978/79** Published three plays, *Pantalon Ouvert, Im Watt* and *Die Schaukel*, and devoted his time to stage design. From **1985** artistic advisor to Peter Zadek in Hamburg. **1987/88** Monumental wall paintings portraying German parliamentarians in St. Paul's church in Frankfurt. Grützke uses critical realism and a traditional painting style modelled on the Old Masters to expose empty demonstrations of pathos and to parody certain forms of behaviour.
CATALOGUE RAISONNE: Holeczek, B. (ed.): J. G. Werkverzeichnis der Druckgraphik 1964-1975. Freiburg 1975
MONOGRAPHS, CATALOGUES: Bacher, J. (ed.): J. G. Theater der Menschheit. Aachen et al. Aachen 1997 (cat.).– Grisebach, L. et al. (ed.): "Unser Fortschritt ist unaufhörlich". J. G. Skizzen zu Bildern. Nationalgalerie. Berlin 1984 (cat.).– Hoffmann, K. and K. Beck (ed.): J. G. Kunstpreisträger der Stadt Wolfsburg. Städtische Galerie und Kunstverein Wolfsburg. Wolfsburg 1992 (cat.).– Holeczek, B. and E. Schenk zu Schweinsberg (ed.): J. G. Gemälde 1964-1977. Kunstverein Braunschweig. Brunswick 1977 (cat.).– Jensen, J. C. (ed.): J. G. Neue Bilder 1988-1990. Gemälde und Pastelle. Kunsthalle zu Kiel. Kiel 1990 (cat.)

GUNDLACH F. C.
born **1926** Heinebach (Hesse)
German photographer. **1947–1949** Studied at the Institute of Photography in Kassel. **1954** Set up his own photographic studio in Stuttgart. **1956** Moved his business to Hamburg and began working as a fashion photographer for women's magazines such as *Film und Frau, Elegante Welt* and *Annabelle*. Up to **1968** put together photoreportages on *haute couture* in Paris. Also specialised in taking portraits of filmstars.

1975 Founded the PPS-Galerie in Hamburg, with the aim of promoting photography and the recognition of photographs as art works and collector's items.
MONOGRAPHS, CATALOGUES: F. C. G. and U. Richter (ed.): Berlin en Vogue. Geschichte der Modephotographie in Berlin. Berlin 1993.– Honnef, K. (ed.): F. C. G. Modewelten. Photographien 1950 bis heute. Rheinisches Landesmuseum, Bonn et al. Berlin 1986 (cat.)

GÜNTHER Ingo
born **1957** Bad Eilsen (near Hanover)
German video and multimedia artist. **1978–1983** Studied at the Düsseldorf Art Academy under Uecker and Paik. **1979** First video sculptures and installations. **1982** Worked with the American Peter Fend on the project *Ocean Earth Corp.*, questioning the extent of man's capacity to process the huge amounts of data obtainable through computerised satellite photography. **1984** Participation at the Venice Biennale, and **1987** in documenta 8 in Kassel. **1990** Set up an independent TV broadcasting station *Kanal X* in Leipzig. Professorship at the Media Arts Academy in Cologne. Günther, one of the third-generation video artists, explores the technical possibilities of information manipulation in his sculptural video works.
MONOGRAPHS, CATALOGUES: Dehara, H. (ed.): I. G. After Hiroshima. Hiroshima City Museum of Contemporary Art. Hiroshima 1995.– Diwo, M. D.: Gesellschaftskritische Aspekte bei Joseph Beuys, Lothar Baumgarten und I. G. Bonn 1993.– I. G. World Processor. Produzentengalerie Hamburg. Hamburg 1989 (cat.)

GURSKY Andreas
born **1955** Leipzig
German photographer. **1978–1981** Attended the Folkwangschule in Essen. **1981–1987** Studied at Art Academy in Düsseldorf under Prof. Bernd Becher, among other teachers. From **1981–1984** produced serial works, while after **1984** he tended to take single pictures, each with a different motif. **1987** First solo-exhibition at Düsseldorf airport. **1989** Won the "Erster Deutscher Photopreis" (First German Photographic Award) and took part in the first

international Photo-Triennale in Esslingen. **1990** Participated in the Venice Biennale. **1991** Won the "Bremer Kunstpreis" (Bremen Art Award) and the Renta Prize awarded by the Kunsthalle Nuremberg. **1994** Solo-exhibition at the Deichtorhallen in Hamburg. Gursky's photographs are inspired by various motifs and genres from the history of art and photography. For him, pictorial language is more important than experiments with phototechnical processes. MONOGRAPHS, CATALOGUES: Bradley, F. (ed.): A. G. Bilder. Tate Gallery Liverpool. Stuttgart 1995.– Bürgi, B. (ed.): A. G. Kunsthalle Zürich. Cologne 1992 (cat.).– Felix, Z. (ed.): A. G. Fotografien 1984-1993. Deichtorhallen, Hamburg et al. Munich 1994.– A. G. Kunsthalle Zürich. Zurich 1992 (cat.).– Irrek, H. (ed.): A. G. Montparnasse. Portikus, Frankfurt-on-Main. Stuttgart 1995 (cat.).– Heynen, J. (ed.): A. G. Krefelder Kunstmuseum. Krefeld 1989 (cat.).– Tuyl, G. v. (ed.): A. G. Photographien 1994-1997. Kunstmuseum Wolfsburg. Wolfsburg 1998 (cat.)

GUSTON Philip
1913 Montreal – **1980** Montreal
Canadian-born American painter. Short training at the Arts High School and the Otis Art Institute in Los Angeles. Friendships with Pollock, De Kooning, Arshile Gorky and James Brooks. **1934/35** Extended trip to Mexiko. Mexican wall paintings and his study of the works of Picasso and de Chirico pushed him towards realism and social criticism in his art. Moved to New York. **1940** Involved in the WPA Federal Art Project. **1941-1947** Taught at the University of Iowa, Ames and later at Washington University in St. Louis. **1945** First solo-exhibition at the Midtown Galleries in New York. **1947** Guggenheim grant. **1949** Tours of Spain, Italy and France. Abandoned figurative paintings for lyrical, abstract improvisations. **1959** Participation in documenta 2 in Kassel. **1960** Participation at the Venice Biennale. **1962** Retrospective at the Guggenheim Museum, New York. **1968** Took up figurative painting again, but with parodistic elements. Though Guston's paintings from the 50s are representative of Abstract Impressionism, his works from the 80s anticipate New Image Painting.
MONOGRAPHS, CATALOGUES: Arnason, H. H. (ed.): P. G. Solomon R. Guggenheim Museum. New York 1962 (cat.).– Ashton, D.: A Critical Study of P. G. New York 1976, Berkeley 1990.– Corbett, W.: P. G.'s Late Work. A Memoir. Cambridge (MA) 1994.– Dabrowski, M. (ed.): The Drawings of P. G. The Museum of Modern Art, New York et al. New York 1988, London 1992 (cat.).– Dabrowski, M. (ed.): P. G. Opere su carta 1933-1980. Roma 1989 (cat.).– Feld, R. and H. Hopkins (ed.): P. G. San Francisco Museum of Modern Art et al. New York 1980 (cat.).– Feldman, M. (ed.): P. G. 1980. The Last Works. Phillips Collection. Washington 1981 (cat.).– P. G. Das Spätwerk. Kunsthalle Basel. Basel

1983 (cat.).– P. G. La raiz del dibujo. Sala de Exposiciones Rekalde. Bilbau 1993 (cat.).– Hunter, S. (ed.): P. G. Recent Paintings and Drawings. Jewish Museum. New York 1966 (cat.).– Lynton, N. (ed.): P. G. Paintings 1969-1980. Whitechapel Art Gallery, London et al. London 1982 (cat.).– Mayer, M.: Night Studio. A Memoir of P. G. by His Daughter. New York 1988.– Storr, R.: P. G. New York 1986

GUTFREUND Oto
1889 Dvur Králové (Königinhof) – **1927** Prague
Czech sculptor. **1903-1906** Trained at Bechin School of Ceramics. **1906-1909** Studied at Prague School of Arts and Crafts and **1909/10** at the private school Grande Chaumière in Paris. Encountered Cubism for the first time. **1910** Returned to Prague. **1911-1914** Joined a group of avant-garde artists attempting to fuse Cubism with Expressionism. **1914** Went with his friend Emil Filla to Paris, and signed up to serve in the Foreign Legion. **1916** Interned in the prison camp Saint Michel de Frigolet for subversive activities. **1920** Returned to Prague where, in **1921**, he became a member of the association of sculptors S.V.U. Mánes. From **1926** Professor of Sculpture at the School of Arts and Crafts in Prague. In addition to his small representational works of the 20s, in the style of Neue Sachlichkeit and contemporary realism, Gutfreund created numerous public monuments.
WRITINGS: O. G.: Zázemí tvorby. Ed. by Jirí Setlík. Prague 1989
CATALOGUE RAISONNE: Císarovský, J. (ed.): O. G. Prague 1962.– Setlik, J. (ed.): O. G. Prague 1995 (cat.)
MONOGRAPHS, CATALOGUES: Gaßner, H. (ed.): O. G. Haus der Kunst. Munich 1997 (cat.).– O. G. Internationales Kulturzentrum Egon Schiele. Krumau 1996 (cat.).– Kotalík, J. (ed.): O. G. Museum des 20. Jahrhunderts. Vienna 1969 (cat.).– Pecírka, J.: O. G. Prague 1948.– Setlík, J. (ed.): O. G. Prague 1989.– Weidemann, F. (ed.): O. G. 1889-1927. Plastiken und Zeichnungen. Staatliche Museen zu Berlin, Otto-Nagel-Haus. Berlin 1987 (cat.)

GUTTUSO Renato
1912 Bagheria (near Palermo) – **1987** Rome
Italian painter. Trained as a picture restorer. **1930** Began studying law in Rome. **1935/36** Military service in Milan. Became friends with Birolli, Manzù and Fontana. **1937** Moved to Rome. **1938** First still lifes and portraits. **1940** Became a member of the Communist party and the anti-Fascist artists' group Corrente. **1943** Joined the Resistance. **1947** Founded the group Fronte Nuovo delle Arti in Rome. **1948-1960** Regular participation at the Venice Biennale. **1952** and **1972** won the Soviet Lenin Award. **1963** Elected to the USSR Academy. **1968** Professorship at the Hamburg Academy of Arts. **1973** Deeply shaken by the death of Picasso, he produced the series

Omaggio a Picasso. His political career reached its peak in **1975** with his nomination as Senator of the Italian Republic. **1977** Participation in documenta 6 in Kassel. **1982** Major solo-exhibition at the Palazzo Grassi in Venice. Guttuso is one of the leading exponents of Socialist Realism in Italy.
WRITINGS: R. G.: Contadini di Sicilia. Roma 1951.– R. G.: Mestiere di pittore. Scritti sull'arte e la società. Bari 1972.– R. G.: Negli scritti. Milan 1976
CATALOGUE RAISONNE: Crispolti, E. (ed.): Catalogo ragionato generale dei dipinti di R. G. 4 vols. Milan 1983-1991
MONOGRAPHS, CATALOGUES: Brandi, C. and V. Rubiu (ed.): G. Opere dal 1931 al 1981. Palazzo Grassi, Venice. Milan 1982 (cat.).– Brandi, C.: G. Antologia crittica. Milan 1983.– Calvesi, M. et al. (ed.): R. G. Gemälde und Zeichnungen. Kunsthalle Tübingen et al. Stuttgart 1991 (cat.).– Calvesi, M. and D. Favatella Lo Cascio (ed.): R. G. Museo G. Palermo 1987 (cat.).– Constantini, E.: Ritratto di R. G. Milan 1985.– Cortenova, G. and E. Mascelloni (ed.): G. 50 anni di pittura. Palazzo Forti, Verona. Milan 1987 (cat.).– Crispolti, E. (ed.): G. nel disegno. Anni venti/ottanta. Roma 1983.– Crispolti, E.: Leggere G. Milan 1987.– Grasso, F.: R. G. Pittore di Bagheria. Catania 1982.– R. G. Whitechappel Art Gallery. London 1996 (cat.).– Haftmann, W.: G. Autobiographische Bilder. Frankfurt-on-Main et al. 1973.– Hiepe, R.: R. G. Dresden 1961.– Longhi, R. et al.: Hommage à G. Paris 1981.– Monferini, A. (ed.): La Donazione R. G. Galleria Nazionale d'Arte Moderna. Roma 1987 (cat.).– Moravia, A. and F. Grasso: R. G. La vita e l'opera. Palermo 1962.– Rubiu, V. (ed.): G. Opere dal 1931 al 1981. Centro di cultura di Palazzo Grassi, Venice. Florence 1982 (cat.).– Rubiu, V. et al. (ed.): G. Grandi opere. Palazzo Reale, Milan 1984 (cat.).– Vittorini, E.: Storia di R. G. e nota congiunta sulla pittura contemporanea. Milan 1960

HAACKE Hans
born **1936** Cologne
German concept and object artist. **1956-1960** Studied at the Academy of Arts and Crafts in Kassel. **1960/61** DAAD scholarship for Paris, where he worked in Hayter's

graphic studio Atelier 17. Contact with the Zero group in Düsseldorf. Interested in the representation of scientific phenomena. **1961** Fulbright scholarship to Philadelphia. **1962** Moved to New York. His fascination with natural physical laws led, in **1963**, to the construction of so-called *Condensation Cubes* which he used to demonstrate processes whose full timecourse can be observed. **1963-1965** Lived in Germany. **1966/67** Taught at various American universities. From **1967** taught at the Cooper Union in New York. **1972-1997** Participation in documenta 5, 8 and 10 in Kassel. **1973** Guest-professor at the Hamburg Academy of Arts. **1973/74** Guggenheim Fellowship Award. **1993** Represented Germany at the Venice Biennale. With his physical, meteorological, biological and sociological works, extended the traditional definition of sculpture and the plastic arts to include the representation of systems.
WRITINGS: Bourdieu, P. and H. H. Libreéchange. Paris 1994/Freier Austausch. Frankfurt-on-Main 1995
MONOGRAPHS, CATALOGUES: Aue, W.: P. C. A. Projekte, Konzepte, Aktionen. Cologne 1971.– Brown, T. and W. Grasskamp (ed.): H. H. Works 1978-1983. Tate Gallery. London 1984 (cat.).– Bußmann, K. (ed.): H. H. Bodenlos. Biennale Venice 1993, Deutscher Pavillon. Stuttgart 1993.– Fry, E. F.: H. H. Werkmonographie. Mit Texten des Künstlers. Cologne 1972.– Grasskamp, W. et al. (ed.): H. H. Obra Social. Barcelona 1995 (cat.).– H. H. Volume I. Museum of Modern Art. Oxford 1978 (cat.).– H. H. Volume II. Tate Gallery. London 1983 (cat.).– H. H. et al.: H. H. Bodenlos/Bottomless. Stuttgart 1993.– Martin, J.-H. (ed.): H. H. Artfairismes. Centre Georges Pompidou. Paris 1989 (cat.).– Straka, B. et al. (ed.): H. H. Nach allen Regeln der Kunst. Neue Gesellschaft für bildende Kunst. Berlin 1984 (cat.).– Wallis, B. (ed.): H. H. Unfinished Business. New Museum of Contemporary Art. New York 1987 (cat.)

HAAS Ernst
1921 Vienna – **1986** Vienna
Austrian photographer. **1939** Studied medicine and philosophy. **1943** Worked part-time in a photographic studio in Vienna. Photojournalist for the journals *Der Film* and *Heute*. **1945** Photographed soldiers returning home, at the railway station, and street scenes in Vienna after the war. **1948** Member of the photographic agency Magnum in Paris. **1951** Emigrated to the USA and began to use colour as a means of shaping his photographs. From **1953** photoseries and reportages for *Life*, *Look* and *Vogue*. **1959** Elected president of *Magnum*. **1960** Covered the Olympic Games for *Life* magazine. **1964** First film projects with John Houston. **1972** Commissioned to photograph Marlboro cowboys. **1972-1987** Participation in documenta 5, 7 and 8 in Kassel. **1980** Publication of the audiovisual work *To Dream with Open*

Eyes. **1986** First showing of the audiovisual work *Abstracts*.
WRITINGS: E. H.: The Joy of Photography. Rochester (NY) 1979.– E. H.: The Joy of Photography II. Rochester (NY) 1981

HAINS Raymond
born **1926** Saint-Brieuc (Côtes-du-Nord) French artist. **1945** Studied sculpture at the Ecole des Beaux-Arts in Rennes. Worked in the photographic department of *France Illustration*. **1948** Exhibited first abstract works (*Photographies hypnogogiques*) in Paris. **1950** Invented the idea of the *Ultra-lettre* and worked with *lettres éclatées* (fragmented letters). **1957** Exhibition of *Affiches déchirées* (torn posters) in Paris, followed by exhibitions at the first Paris Biennale, the Stedelijk Museum in Amsterdam and the Museum of Modern Art in New York. **1960** Founder member of the group Nouveaux Réalistes. **1963** Distanced himself from Nouveau Réalisme. **1964** Took part in the Venice Biennale. **1968** Exhibited three giant books of matches at documenta 4 in Kassel. **1968–1971** Lived and worked in Venice. **1971** Returned to Paris. **1990** Retrospective at the Centre Georges Pompidou in Paris. **1997** Participation in documenta 10 in Kassel.
MONOGRAPHS, CATALOGUES: Abadie, D. et al. (ed.): R. H. et la photographie. Centre Georges Pompidou. Paris 1976 (cat.).– Bompuis, C. (ed.): R. H. Centre Georges Pompidou. Paris 1990 (cat.).– David, C. et al. (ed.): Guide des collections ou mises en plis: R. H. Centre Georges Pompidou. Paris 1990 (cat.).– Fleck, R. et al. (ed.): R. H. Akzente 1949-1995. Vienna 1995 (cat.).– R. H. Fondation Cartier. Jouy-en-Josas 1986 (cat.).– R. H. Poitou-Charentes. PS 1. New York 1989 (cat.).– R. H. Musée de Poitiers. Poitiers 1989 (cat.)

HAJEK Otto Herbert
born **1927** Kaltenbach (Bohemia) German sculptor. **1947–1954** Studied sculpture at the Stuttgart Art Academy. From **1955** worked with *Raumknoten* (spatial knots), *Raumschichtungen* (spatial layers) and sculptures that can be walked on. **1959** Participation in documenta 2 in Kassel. **1960** Guest-lecturer at the University of California. **1963** Covered objects

with colour trails to create links with their surroundings. **1970** Director of the Deutsche Künstlerbund (German Artists' Association). From **1973** produced single sculptural works entitled *Raumzeichen* (spatial signs). **1977** Designed an artificial landscape which could be walked on, in Adelaide, southern Australia. **1979** Visited Japan and India. **1980–1992** Professor of Sculpture at the Karlsruhe Academy. With the colour combinations and spatial tensions he creates in his town-planning concepts and geometric designs for interiors and public spaces, Hajek is concerned with the integration of sculpture and architecture.
WRITINGS: O. H. H.: Darlegung zur Naturbetrachtung. Über die Voraussetzung, daß Kunst entstehen kann. Stuttgart 1982
MONOGRAPHS, CATALOGUES: Gomringer, E. (ed.): Kunst stiftet Gemeinschaft. O. H. H. Das Werk und seine Wirkung. Stuttgart and Berlin 1993.– O. H. H. Ikonographien, Zeichen, Plätze, Stadtbilder. Staatsgalerie Stuttgart. Stuttgart 1978 (cat.).– Pese, C. (ed.): O. H. H. Die Durchdringung des Lebens mit Kunst. Germanisches Nationalmuseum, Nuremberg. Stuttgart and Zurich 1987 (cat.).– Stulle, J. (ed.): O. H. H. Sculture, pitture e opere urbanistiche. Museo Nazionale di Castel Sant'angelo. Roma 1981 (cat.).– Stulle, J. (ed.): O. H. H. Plastiken, Bilder, Stadtikonographien. Stuttgart 1981 (cat.).– Weisner, U. (ed.): O. H. H. Farbwege 1952-1974. Kunsthalle Bielefeld. Stuttgart 1974 (cat.)

HALLEY Peter
born **1953** New York
American painter. Studied until **1975** at Yale University, New Haven, Connecticut, and up to **1978** at the University of New Orleans. **1977** Trip to Europe. **1978** First solo-exhibition at the Contemporary Art Center, New Orleans. **1980** Returned to New York. Abandoned traditional artists' materials in favour of industrial substitutes. Developed a Minimalist style. **1981/82** Joined a New York artists' group through which he met Rosalind Krauss, Renée Santos, Peter Fend and Jeff Koons. **1983** Artistic director of the exhibition "Science Fiction" in the John Weber Gallery. **1983–1988** Production of the series *Kodalithes basés*, an attempted synthesis of painting and writing. Besides painting, Halley has published numerous essays on art and aesthetics. His most important work, *The Crisis of Geometry*, is the fruit of intensive research into the works of Michel Foucault and Jean Baudrillard.
WRITINGS: P. H.: Collected Essays 1981-1987. Zurich 1988
MONOGRAPHS, CATALOGUES: P. H. Institute of Contemporary Art. London 1989 (cat.).– P. H. Museum Haus Esters. Krefeld 1989 (cat.).– P. H. Musée d'Art Contemporain, Pully. Lausanne 1992 (cat.).– P. H. Paintings 1989-1992. Art Center. Des Moines 1993 (cat.).– Hixson, K. (ed.): P. H. Madrid et al. Madrid 1991 (cat.).– Michetti-Prod'hon, C. (ed.): P. H. Œuvres de 1982 à

1991. Musée d'Art Contemporain, Bordeaux et al. Bordeaux 1993 (cat.)

HALSMAN Philippe
1906 Riga – **1979** New York
Latvian-born American photographer. **1924–1928** Studied electrical engineering in Dresden. Freelance photographer for the publishers Ullstein in Berlin. **1931** Studied at the Sorbonne in Paris. Opened a portrait studio. Became acquainted with Man Ray and Maurice Tabard through his work as a fashion photographer. **1940** Emigrated to the USA. **1941** Won the Art Directors Club Award. Photographed for magazines and newspapers including *Look* and the *Saturday Evening Post*. 103 of his photographs appeared on front covers of *Life* magazine. **1944** Nominated first President of the American Society of Magazine Photographers in New York. **1958** Photographed Robert Oppenheimer. **1967** Award from the American Academy of Achievement. **1969–1979** Taught at the Photographers School in Westport, Connecticut. **1971** Lectured at the New York School for Social Research. **1979** First solo-exhibition at the International Center of Photography in New York. Halsman took portrait photographs of numerous public figures including Albert Einstein, Winston Churchill, John F. Kennedy and Marilyn Monroe.

HAMILTON Richard
born **1922** London
English painter. **1938** Studied painting at the Royal Academy Schools in London. **1941–1945** Worked as a technical draughtsman. **1948–1951** Continued his studies at the Royal Academy Schools and the Slade School of Art. **1950** First solo-exhibition of etchings organised by Gimpel Fils. **1952** Taught silverwork, typography and industrial design at the Central School of Arts and Crafts. Together with Paolozzi, founded the Independent Group. **1953** Lecturer at the University of Durham. **1956** Created the first Pop collage as a catalogue and poster design for the exhibition "This is Tomorrow" in the Whitechapel Gallery. **1957–1961** Taught interior design at the Royal College of Art. **1965** Reconstruction of Marcel Duchamp's work *The Large Glass*. **1966** Organised a major Marcel Duchamp

retrospective at the Tate Gallery. **1968** and **1977** participation in documenta 4 and 6 in Kassel. **1970** Awarded the Talens International Prize. **1979** Retrospective at the Tate Gallery in London and the Kunsthalle Bern. After **1980** focused on computer art. Hamilton is a leading exponent of English Pop Art. His paintings are a biting critique of consumerism and mass culture. **1997** Took part in documenta 10 in Kassel.
WRITINGS: R. H.: Collected Words 1953-1982. London 1982
CATALOGUES RAISONNES: R. H. Prints 1939-1983. A Complete Catalogue of Graphic Works. Stuttgart 1984.– R. H. Prints. Graphic Works Continued 1984-1991. Waddington Graphics Gallery, London. Stuttgart 1992 (cat.)
MONOGRAPHS, CATALOGUES: Field, R. S. (ed.): R. H. Image and Process. 2 vols. Tate Gallery, London et al. Stuttgart 1983 (cat.).– R. H. Tate Gallery, London et al. London 1992 (cat.).– Leach-Ruhl, D.: Studien zu R. H. Das Frühwerk. Diss. Bochum 1986.– Leach, D.: R. H. The Beginnings of His Art. Frankfurt-on-Main et al. 1993.– Maharaj, S. (ed.): R. H. XLV Biennale di Venezia, British Pavilion. London 1993 (cat.).– Morphet, R. (ed.): R. H. Tate Gallery, London et al. London 1970 (cat.).– Nilson, B. (ed.): R. H. Teknologi, idé, konstverk. Moderna Museet. Stockholm 1989 (cat.).– Pauseback, M. and E. Kroppenstedt (ed.): R. H. Studies – Studien 1937-1977. Kunsthalle Bielefeld et al. Bielefeld 1978 (cat.).– Schwarz, D. et al. (ed.): R. H. Exteriors, Interiors, Objects, People. Kunstmuseum Winterthur et al. Hanover 1990 (cat.)

HANSON Duane
1925 Alexandria (MN) – **1995** Davie (Florida)
American sculptor. **1943–1951** Studied at art institutes in Washington, Minnesota and Bloomfield Hills. From **1951** taught at various schools. **1953** Tour of Europe. Taught in Munich and Bremen at American army schools. **1959** Kontact with George Grygo, who was experimenting with synthetic materials. **1961** Returned to America. **1965** Settled in Miami, Florida. **1967** Began to construct realistic life-size models of people out of polyester resin and fibreglass. **1972** Participation in documenta 5 in Kassel. **1974** DAAD scholarship to Berlin. **1979** Professorship at the University of Miami. **1985** Awarded first Florida prize for sculpture. **1992** Selected for the Florida Artists Hall of Fame. His precise, veristic representations of normal American people, e.g. housewives, cleaning ladies, workers or drug addicts, make Hanson one of the leading exponents of Hyper Realist sculpture.
CATALOGUE RAISONNE: Bush, M. H. and T. Buchsteiner (ed.): D. H. Skulpturen. Kunsthalle Tübingen et al. Stuttgart 1990 (cat.)
MONOGRAPHS, CATALOGUES: Bush, M. H. (ed.): D. H. Edwin A. Ulrich

Museum of Art, Wichita State University, Wichita et al. Wichita (KS) 1976 (cat.).– Bush, M. H.: Sculptures by D. H. McKnight Art Center. Wichita (KS) 1985 (cat.).– Hobbs, R. (ed.): D. H. The New Objectivity. Florida State University Art Gallery, Talahassee. Seattle 1991 (cat.).– Livingstone, M. (ed.): D. H. Montreal Museum of Fine Arts et al. Montreal 1994 (cat.).– Osterwold, T. (ed.): D. H. Württembergischer Kunstverein. Stuttgart 1974 (cat.).– Ruhrberg, K.: D. H. Skulpturen. Stuttgart 1992.– Varnedoe, K.: D. H. New York 1985

HANTAI Simon
born 1922 Bia (Hungary)
Hungarian-born French painter. 1941–1947 Attended the Budapest Art Academy. 1949 Moved to Paris. 1952 Contact with the Surrealists. Experiments with techniques such as frottage, automatism and collage leading to gestural lyrical abstraction. 1953 First solo-exhibition at the Galerie L'Etoile Scellée in Paris, for which Breton wrote a preface to the catalogue. 1954 Split away from the Surrealists and became interested in Pollock's drip painting technique. Inspired by contact with Georges Mathieu and J. Degottex to develop a new painting style. Adopted a radically different approach to subject matter, painting materials and painting surfaces, and ventured towards free canvas works, via folding techniques. 1957 Together with Mathieu, organised the exhibition "Cérémonies de la seconde condamnation de Siger de Brabant" at the Galerie Kléber in Paris. 1959 Artistic decoration of liturgical texts; participation in documenta 2 in Kassel. 1966 Took French citizenship. 1968 Won the Foundation Maeght Award. 1973/74 Series of white paintings. 1974 Began the *Tabula* series. 1976 Retrospective at the Musée National d'Art Moderne, Paris. 1982 Took part in the Venice Biennale.
MONOGRAPHS, CATALOGUES: Baldeassari, A.: S. H. Paris 1992.– Bozo, D. and Y. Michaud (ed.): S. H. La Biennale di Venezia. Venice 1982 (cat.).– Froment, J.-L. et al. (ed.): Musée d'Art Contemporain de Bordeaux. Bordeaux. 1981 (cat.).– Hulten, P. et al. (ed.): S. H. Musée National d'Art Moderne. Paris 1976 (cat.).– Mathey, F. (ed.): S. H. Peintures 1958-1968. Fondation Maeght. Saint-Paul 1968 (cat.)

HARING Keith
1958 Kutztown (PA) – 1990 New York
American painter. Began to draw comic figures at an early age. After attending the Ivy School of Art in Pittsburgh, studied from 1978 at the School of Visual Arts in New York, under Sonnier and Kosuth. 1979 First chalk drawings on New York subway billboards covered with black paper. 1981 Acquainted with Warhol, Basquiat, Clemente, Hopper, Borroughs, Madonna and Grace Jones. 1982 Distributed 20,000 posters, printed and designed by himself, at an anti-nuclear demonstration in Central

Park. First solo-exhibition at the Tony Shafrazi Gallery and participation in documenta 7 in Kassel. 1983 First body painting. Murals in Milwaukee, New York and Tokyo. 1984 Painted the body of Grace Jones in New York. 1985 Stage designs for Brooklyn Academy of Music in New York and the Ballet National de Marseille. 1986 Opened a *Pop Shop*, selling multiples and commonplace objects painted by the artist. 1987/88 Further stage set and costume designs. 1989 Involved 300 school children in a wall painting project in Chicago. Set up the Keith Haring Foundation supporting social projects. Haring's simple, symbolic statements, painted onto T-shirts, buttons and plaster casts of sculptures, helped to blur the distinctions between high art and trivial Pop culture.
WRITINGS: K. H.: Journals. New York 1996/Tagebücher. Frankfurt-on-Main 1997 CATALOGUE RAISONNE: Littmann, K. (ed.): K. H. Editions on Paper 1982-1990. Das druckgraphische Werk. Stuttgart 1993 MONOGRAPHS, CATALOGUES: Blinderman, B. (ed.): K. H. Future Primeval. Queens Museum, New York et al. New York 1990 (cat.).– Celant, G. et al. (ed.): K. H. Munich 1992.– Celant, G. and I. Gianelli (ed.): K. H. Castello di Rivoli, Museo d'Arte Contemporanea, Torino et al. Milan 1994 (cat.).– Gruen, J.: K. H. The Authorized Biography. Englewood Cliffs (NJ) and London 1991/K. H. Die autorisierte Biographie. Munich 1991.– Gysin, B. and S. Couderc (ed.): K. H. Musée d'Art Contemporain de Bordeaux. Bordeaux. 1985 (cat.).– K. H. Peintures, sculptures et dessins. Musée d'Art Contemporain de Bordeaux. Bordeaux 1985 (cat.).– K. H. A Retrospective. Whitney Museum of American Art, New York. Boston 1997 (cat.).– Littmann, K. (ed.): K. H. Editions on Paper 1982-1900. Galerie der Stadt. Stuttgart 1993 (cat.).– Sussman, E. (ed.): K. H. Whitney Museum of American Art. New York 1997 (cat.)

HARTLEY Marsden
1877 Lewiston (ME) – 1943 Ellsworth (ME)
American painter. 1899–1904 Studied at the Chase School and the National Academy of Art, New York. 1909 Exhibited post-impressionist landscapes at Alfred Stieglitz' Galerie 291. 1912/13 Lived in

Germany. Collaborated and held joint-exhibitions with artists of the Blauer Reiter movement, and took part in the First German Autumn Salon. 1913 Exhibited in the Armory Show in New York. 1921–1936 Lived alternately in France, Italy, Germany and Mexico. Abandoned abstract painting and devoted his time to landscapes and portraits. 1935 Unable to cover storage costs, destroyed more than a hundred of his own works, and went to live with a poor farming family in the Canadian province of Nova Scotia. 1937 Returned to the USA. Series of pantheistic coastal and mountain landscapes shown in a joint-exhibition with Stuart Davis at the Cincinnati Art Museum. Hartley, whose art is clearly influenced by Cézanne, Picasso and Matisse and whose intuitive abstractions successfully combine elements of Expressionism, Fauvism and Cubism, is considered one of the first American painters of the modernist.
WRITINGS: M. H.: Adventures in the Arts. New York 1921, 1972.– M. H.: Androscogging. Portland 1940.– Wells, H. W. (ed.): M. H. Selected Poems. New York 1945.– Scott, G. R. (ed.): On Art by M. H. New York 1982.– Scott, G. R. (ed.): The Collected Poems of M. H. Santa Rosa 1987 MONOGRAPHS, CATALOGUES: Burlingame, R.: M. H. A Study of His Life and Creative Achievement. Diss. Providence 1953.– Ferguson, G. (ed.): M. H. and Nova Scotia. Art Gallery Mont Saint Vincent University, Halifax et al. Halifax 1987 (cat.).– M. H. Somehow a Past. The Autobiography of M. H. Cambridge (MA) 1996.– Haskell, B. (ed.): M. H. Whitney Museum of American Art, New York et al. New York 1980 (cat.).– Hokin, J.: Pinnacles and Pyramids. The Art of M. H. Albuquerque 1993.– King, L. (ed.): M. H. 1908-1942. The Ione and Hudson D. Walker Collection. Visual Arts Gallery, Florida International University, Miami et al. Minneapolis 1984 (cat.).– Ludington, T.: M. H. The Biography of an American Artist. New York 1992.– McCausland, E.: M. H. Minneapolis 1952.– McCausland, E. (ed.): M. H. Stedelijk Museum. Amsterdam 1961 (cat.).– Scott, G. R.: M. H. New York 1988.– Scribner, A.: M. H. in Maine. Orono (ME) 1972

HARTUNG Hans
1904 Leipzig – 1989 Antibes
German-French painter. 1924/25 Studied philosophy and history of art at Leipzig University and then attended the Art Academies in Leipzig and Dresden. 1932 After living for a time on the island of Menorca, he settled in Paris. 1935 Contact with Domela, Kandinsky, Magnelli, Mondrian, Miró and Calder. Participated in exhibitions at the Salon des Surindépendants and Galerie Pierre in Paris. Joined the Foreign Legion. 1944 Severely wounded at the front. 1945 Returned to Paris and obtained French citizenship. From 1949 exhibitions in Paris, Brussels, Munich and Basel. 1955–1964 Participation in documenta 1–3 in Kassel. 1956 Received the Guggenheim Award and

was nominated a special member of the Berlin Academy. 1960 Major international award for painting at the Venice Biennale. 1964 National decoration for service to the German community. 1976 Publication in Paris of his autobiography *Autoportrait*. 1977 Member of the Institut de France and Académie des Beaux-Arts, Paris. 1981 Oskar Kokoschka Award from the Republic of Austria. Beside Fautrier, Wols and Riopelle, Hartung was one of the most important representatives of the Ecole de Paris. His works broke away from Abstract Expressionism and anticipated L'art informel.
WRITINGS: Lefebre, M. (ed.): H. H. Autoportrait. Paris 1976. Berlin 1981 CATALOGUE RAISONNE: Schmücking, R. (ed.): Werkverzeichnis der Graphik 1921-1965. Brunswick 1965, Basel 1990 MONOGRAPHS, CATALOGUES: Abadie, D. and M. Georget (ed.): H. et la musique. Centre d'arts plastiques. Royan 1993 (cat.).– Apollonio, U.: H. H. New York 1972.– Contensou, B. et al. (ed.): H. Œuvres de 1922 à 1939. Musée d'Art Moderne de la Ville de Paris. Paris 1980 (cat.).– Corray, L. et al. H. H. Milan 1992 (cat.).– Daix, P.: H. H. Paris 1991.– Descargues, P.: H. Paris 1977, New York 1977.– Gindertaël, R. V.: H. H. Paris 1960, Berlin 1962.– Giraudy, D. (ed.): H. H. Premières peintures 1922-1949. Musée Picasso, Château Grimaldi. Antibes 1987 (cat.).– Grohmann, W.: H. H. Aquarelle. St. Gallen 1966.– Haftmann, W. (ed.): H. H. Retrospektive 1921-1973. Staatliche Museen Preussischer Kulturbesitz, Nationalgalerie. Berlin 1975 (cat.).– H. H. Musée National d'Art Moderne. Paris 1969 (cat.).– H. H. Galleria Civica d'Arte Moderna, Palazzo dei diamanti. Ferrara 1988 (cat.).– H. Peintre moderne. Centre d'Art Contemporain, Paris et al. Milan 1996 (cat.).– Merkert, J. et al. (ed.): H. H. Malerei, Zeichnung, Photographie. Städtische Kunsthalle Düsseldorf et al. Berlin 1981 (cat.).– Rousseau, M. et al.: H. H. Stuttgart 1949.– Vergara, J.: H. Madrid 1961

HARTUNG Karl
1908 Hamburg – 1967 Berlin
German sculptor. 1923 Apprenticeship as a wood sculptor. 1925–1929 Studied at the Hamburg School of Applied Arts. 1929–1932 Lived in Paris. Most strongly influenced by Maillol. 1932 Visited Florence. Studied Etruscan art. 1935 First abstract sculptural works. 1936 Moved to Berlin. 1939 Met Brancusi, Arp and Laurens again in Paris. 1946 First solo-exhibition at the Gerd Rosen gallery, Berlin. 1950 First monumental sculpture. 1951 Professor of Sculpture in Berlin. 1953 Retrospective at the Kestner Society in Hanover. 1955–1964 Participation in documenta 1–3 in Kassel. 1961 Major prize for sculpture from the State of Nordrhein-Westphalen.
CATALOGUE RAISONNE: Krause, M. (ed.): K. H. 1908-1967. Metamorphosen von Mensch und Natur. Monographie und Werkverzeichnis. Germanisches Nationalmuseum, Nuremberg et al. Munich 1998 (cat.)
MONOGRAPHS, CATALOGUES: K. H. Haus Waldsee. Berlin 1952 (cat.).– K. H. Kestner-Gesellschaft. Hanover 1953 (cat.)

HAUSMANN Raoul
1886 Vienna – 1971 Limoges
German-Austrian painter, photographer and writer. 1901 Moved to Berlin. 1905 First contact with Johannes Baader. From 1912 wroted critiques and literary articles for the journals *Der Sturm, Die Aktion* and *Die Freie Straße*. Became acquainted with Hans Richter and Emmy Hennings. 1918 Close collaboration with the Zurich Dada move-

ment. Together with Baader, Grosz, Tzara and Huelsenbeck set up the Berlin Dada movement and signed the Berlin Dada Manifesto. Invented photomontage and exhibited his assemblage *Holzkopf*. **1919** Together with Baader, issued the journal *Der Dada*. Participated in the first Dada exhibition in Berlin at the Graphisches Kabinett Neumann. Publication of further manifestos. **1920** Organised the Erste Internationale Dada Messe. **1921** Contact, leading to joint happenings, with Kurt Schwitters in Hanover. **1922** Took part in the constructivist Dada congress in Weimar. **1927** Construction of the Optophone. **1931** Took part in an exhibition of photomontages organised by Domela, in Berlin. **1933** Fled from the Nazi regime to Ibiza. **1936** Fled from the Spanish Fascists to France where he lived illegally from **1939–1944** in Peyrat-le-Château. **1944** Moved back to Limoges where, from **1959** to **1964**, he produced impulsive gestural paintings. **1971** Finished writing *Am Anfang war Dada*, a retrospective account of Dadaism in Berlin. WRITINGS: R. H.: Hyle. Ein Traumsein in Spanien. Frankfurt-on-Main 1969.– R. H.: Am Anfang war Dada. Ed. by K. Riha and G. Kämpf. Gießen 1972, 1992.– R. H.: Texte bis 1933. Ed. by M. Erlhoff. 2 vols. Munich 1982.– R. H.: La Sensorialité excentrique. Die exzentrische Empfindung. Ed. by Adelheid Koch. Linz 1994.– Züchner, E. (ed.): Fort mit allen Stühlen. R. H. in Berlin 1900-1933. Unveröffentlichte Texte. Stuttgart 1995.– Züchner, E. (ed.): R. H. Scharfrichter der bürgerlichen Seele. Stuttgart 1998
MONOGRAPHS, CATALOGUES: Benson, T. O.: R. H. and Berlin Dada. Ann Arbor (MI) 1987.– Bory, J.-F.: Prolegomènes à une monographie de R. H. Paris 1972.– Erlhoff, M.: R. H. Dadasoph. Versuch einer Politisierung der Ästhetik. Hanover 1982.– Giroud, M.: R. H. Je ne suis pas une photographe. Paris 1975.– Haus, A. (ed.): R. H. Kamerafotografien 1927-1957. Munich 1979.– R. H. autour de l'esprit de notre temps. Assemblages, collages, photomontages. Musée National d'Art Moderne. Paris 1974 (cat.).– R. H. Retrospektive. Kestner-Gesellschaft. Hanover 1981 (cat.).– R. H. 1886-1971. Musée Départemental de Rochechouart. Rochechouart 1986 (cat.).– R. H. Musée d'Art Moderne. Saint-Etienne 1994 (cat.)/ R. H. IVAM Centro Julio Gonzáles. Valencia 1994 (cat.).– Hulten, K. G. (ed.): R. H. Moderna Museet. Stockholm 1967.– Koch, A.: Ich bin immerhin der größte Experimentator Österreichs. R. H., Dada und Neodada. Innsbruck 1994.– Züchner, E. et al. (ed.): Der deutsche Spießer ärgert sich. R. H. 1886-1971. Berlinische Galerie, Berlin et al. Stuttgart 1994 (cat.)

HAUSNER Rudolf
1914 Vienna – **1994** Mödling (near Vienna) Austrian painter. **1931–1936** Studied painting at the Vienna Academy. **1936** Toured as a jazz musician. **1941–1943** Military service. **1946** Together with Edgar Jené, Ernst

Fuchs, Wolfgang Hutter and others, founded a Surrealist art group. **1956** Completed his painting *Arche des Odysseus*. Created the mythical figure of Adam Jedermann. **1957** Produced the first *Adam* paintings. **1959** First joint-exhibition at Oberen Belvedere in Vienna and participation in documenta 2 in Kassel. **1966** Guest-professor at the Hamburg School of Fine Arts. From **1968** professorship at the Vienna Academy. **1970** Austrian national award. **1984** Retrospectives at the Neue Galerie in Linz and Künstlerhaus in Vienna. Hausner's paintings, which are closely related to Fantastic Realism, are portrayals of visionary, alienating Surrealist dreams. Together with Ernst Fuchs, he is one of the main representatives of the Vienna School.
WRITINGS: R. H.: Vom Bewußtsein des Unbewußten. Munich 1982
CATALOGUES RAISONNES: Holländer, H.: R. H. Werkmonographie. Offenbach 1985.– Huber, V. (ed.): R. H. Werkverzeichnis der Druckgraphik 1966-1975. Offenbach 1977.– Schmied, W.: R. H. Salzburg 1970
MONOGRAPHS, CATALOGUES: Flemming, H. T.: R. H. Stuttgart 1976.– R. H. 1914-1995. Museum Würth. Künzelsau 1996 (cat.).– Schurian, W. (ed.): R. H. Munich 1987

HEARTFIELD John
(Helmut Herzfelde)
1891 Berlin – **1968** Berlin
German painter, photographer, typographer and writer. **1907–1910** Studied at the School of Applied Arts in Munich and **1912 –1914** at the School of Arts and Crafts in Berlin. **1914/15** Military service. **1916** Publication and typographical design of the magazine *Neue Jugend*. **1917** Together with his brother Wieland, set up the Malik Verlag. Became friends with Grosz, Jung and Huelsenbeck. Made films at the UFA. **1918** Joined the German Communist Party. **1919** Together with Grosz, Huelsenbeck, Hausmann and others, took part in various Dada activities in Berlin. Published magazines such as *Jedermann sein eigener Fußball* and *Der Kunstlump*. **1920** First photomontages for book covers. **1921** Prosecuted for denigration of German Nationalism with his sculpture *Preussischer Erzengel* (Prussian Archangel). **1921–1923** Stage designs for

Max Reinhardt. **1929** Photographs and photomontages for Kurt Tucholsky's book *Deutschland über alles*. Up to **1933** contributed to various Communist and anti-nationalist publications. After ransacking of his house by the SA, he fled to Prague to escape the Nazi regime. **1938** Moved to London. From **1950** lived in East Berlin and Leipzig, and began working with Bert Brecht.
WRITINGS: März, R. (ed.): J. H. Der Schnitt entlang der Zeit. Selbstzeugnisse, Erinnerungen, Interpretationen. Dresden 1981
MONOGRAPHS, CATALOGUES: Evans, D. (ed.): J. H. AIZ/VI 1930-1938. Catalogue Raisonné of the Photomantages Published in AIZ and VI. New York 1992.– Frederiksson, I.: Konsten spränger ramarna. J. H. och det politiska fotomontaget. Stockholm 1979.– J. H. Krieg im Frieden. Fotomantagen zur Zeit 1930-1938. Munich 1972.– J. H. The Museum of Modern Art. New York 1993 (cat.).– Herzfelde, W.: J. H. Leben und Werk, dargestellt von seinem Bruder. Berlin 1962.– Honnef, K. and H.-J. v. Osterhausen (ed.): J. H. Dokumentation. Reaktionen auf eine ungewöhnliche Ausstellung. Cologne 1994.– Kahn, D.: J. H. Art and Mass Media. New York 1985.– März, R.: H. montiert. 1930-1938. Leipzig 1993.– Pachnicke, P. and K. Honnef (ed.): J. H. Akademie der Künste zu Berlin et al. Cologne 1991 (cat.)/J. H. New York 1993.– Siepmann, E.: Montage. J. H. Vom Club Dada zur Arbeiter-Illustrierten-Zeitung. Dokumente, Analysen, Berichte. Berlin 1977.– Thomas, et al. K. (ed.): J. H. Berlin, Bonn et al. Cologne 1991 (cat.).– Töteberg, M.: J. H. in Selbstzeugnissen und Bilddokumenten. Reinbek 1978

HECKEL Erich
1883 Döbeln (Saxony) – **1970** Hemmenhofen (near Radolfzell)
German painter and graphic artist. **1901** Friendship with Schmidt-Rottluff. **1904** Studied architecture at the Technical College in Dresden. On 7 July **1905** together with Bleyl, Kirchner and Schmidt-Rottluff, founded the artists' group Brücke. Rented a former butcher's premises as the Brücke studio. **1907** Visited Dangaster Moor for the first time. From May to October **1908** stayed with Schmidt-Rottluff in Dangast. **1909** Tour of Italy (Verona, Padua, Venice, Rome). Spent the summer with Kirchner at the Moritzburger lakes. **1910** Changed his early Brücke style replacing the flowing lines and rounded contours and somewhat decorative rhythmic elements being replaced with a reduced pictorial language in woodcut-style. **1911** Moved to Berlin. **1912** Made friends with Marc and Feininger. **1913** Break-up of the Brücke. First solo-exhibition at the Galerie Gurlitt, Berlin. **1914** Participated in the exhibition of the Werkbund in Cologne. Signed up as a medical orderly. **1915** Met Beckmann and Ensor. November **1918** settled in Berlin. **1919–1944** Spent summers in Osterholz.

1929 Tour of Provence, the Pyrenees, northern Spain and Aquitaine. **1937** Confiscation of 729 of his works from German museums. **1944** Destruction of his Berlin studio in a bombing raid. Moved to Hemmenhofen on Lake Constance. **1949–1955** Professorship at the Karlsruhe School of Fine Arts.
CATALOGUES RAISONNES: Dube, A. and W. (ed.): E. H. Das graphische Werk. 3 vols. New York and Berlin 1964-1974.– Vogt, P. (ed.): E. H. (mit Werkverzeichnis der Gemälde, Wandmalereien und Plastik). Recklinghausen 1965
MONOGRAPHS, CATALOGUES: Bojescul, W. (ed.): E. H. Kunstverein Braunschweig. Brunswick 1985 (cat.).– Borries, J. E. v.: E. H. Gemälde, Aquarelle und Zeichnungen im Besitz der staatlichen Kunsthalle. Karlsruhe 1968.– Felix, Z.: E. H. 1883-1970. Gemälde, Aquarelle, Zeichnungen und Graphik. Museum Folkwang, Essen et al. Munich 1983 (cat.).– Gabler, K. (ed.): E. H. 2 vols. Städtische Galerie im Prinz-Max-Palais, Karlsruhe et al. Stuttgart and Zurich 1983 (cat.).– Geissler, H.: E. H. Aquarelle vom Bodensee. Munich and Zurich 1981.– Henze, A.: E. H. Leben und Werk. Stuttgart and Zurich 1983.– Hofmann, A.: E. H. Die Jahre am Bodensee 1944-1970. Friedrichshafen 1992.– Lucke, A. and A. Hüneke: E. H. Lebensstufen. Die Wandbilder im Angermuseum zu Erfurt. Dresden 1992.– Moeller, M. M. (ed.): E. H. Aquarelle, Zeichnungen, Druckgraphik aus dem Brücke-Museum Berlin. Munich 1991.– Rathenau, E.: E. H. Handzeichnungen. New York 1993.– Rathke, C. (ed.): E. H. im Schleswig-Holsteinischen Landesmuseum. Gemälde, Aquarelle, Zeichnungen. Schloß Gottorf in Schleswig 1980 (cat.).– Stabenow, C. (ed.): E. H. Ein Farbmusterbuch für Walter Gramatté. Munich 1989.– Tormaehlen, L.: E. H. Karlsruhe 1953.– Vogt, P.: E. H. Recklinghausen 1965

HEERICH Erwin
born **1922** Kassel
German sculptor. **1945–1954** Studied sculpture under Ewald Mataré at the Düsseldorf Academy. **1950** First cardboard works and isometric drawings. **1961–1969** Taught in courses for workers in Düsseldorf. **1964** First solo-exhibition at Haus van der Grinten in Kranenberg. **1968** and **1977** participation in documenta 4 and 6 in Kassel. From **1969** Professor at the Düsseldorf Academy. **1974** Member of the Berlin Academy. From **1978** public commissions for large sculptures. Although Heerich's formal language developed out of Neo-Plasticism and the Bauhaus, his cardboard works, drawings, prints and graphic works are free stereometric constructions.
CATALOGUES RAISONNES: E. H. Kartonskulpturen. 5 vols. Düsseldorf 1979-1987.– Grinten, F. j. v. d. (ed.): E. H. Œuvrekatalog, Folge I (Kartenobjekte). Düsseldorf 1979.– Storck, G. (ed.): E. H. Œuvrekatalog, Folge II (Arbeiten aus Karton). Düsseldorf 1979

MONOGRAPHS, CATALOGUES: Brockhaus, C. (ed.): E. H. Plastische Prozesse. Wilhelm Lehmbruck Museum. Duisburg 1992 (cat.).– Claddders, J.: E. H. Arbeiten im Raum. Essen 1981.– Grinten, H. v. d. (ed.): E. H. und Hildegard Heerich. Cologne 1995.– E. H. Kunstverein Freiburg. Freiburg 1976 (cat.).– E. H. Städtische Kunsthalle Düsseldorf. Düsseldorf 1979 (cat.).– E. H. Städtisches Museum Schloß Morsbroich. Leverkusen 1980 (cat.).– E. H. Wilhelm Lehmbruck Museum. Duisburg 1992 (cat.).– E. H. Skulptur und der architektonische Raum. Cologne 1998.– Kastner, J. P.: E. H. Cologne 1991.– Kastner, P. and W. Zschokke: E. H. Museum Insel Hombroich. Stuttgart 1996

HEGEDÜS Agnes
born **1964** Budapest
Hungarian video artist. **1985–1988** Studied photography and video art at the Academy of Applied Arts in Budapest, **1988** at the Minerva Academy in Groningen and **1988–1990** at the Academy of Arts, Enschede. **1990** Postgraduate work under Weibel at the Städelschule and Institute of New Media in Frankfurt am Main. **1992** Guest-artist at the ZKM in Karlsruhe. **1993** Placed in the category of Interactive Art at Ars Electronica, Linz. **1995** Solo-exhibition at the Federal Art and Exhibition Centre in Bonn. Subsequently to her early video works in the early 90s, Hegedüs created interactive installations designed to encourage dialogue and games.

HEILIGER Bernhard
1915 Stettin – 1995 Berlin
German sculptor. **1934–1941** Studied at the Stettin School of Arts and Crafts and at the Berlin School of Fine Arts. **1938** Went to Paris. **1945** First busts and small sculptures inspired by Maillol and Despiau. **1950–1984** Professor at the Berlin School of Fine Arts. From **1951** his works became increasingly abstract. Produced a 28 m long mural relief for the Schiller Theater, Berlin. **1954** Member of the Deutscher Kunstrat (German Arts Council). **1955–1964** Participation in documenta 1 – 3 in Kassel. **1956** Took up organic abstraction. **1961** Tour of the USA. **1966** Stage designs for Ernst Schröder's production of *Faust II* in the

Schiller Theater, Berlin. **1978** Elected to the Accademia Fiorentina delle Arte del Disegno. **1980** Produced a series of monumental metal sculptures with notched and smooth surfaces setting up an interplay of the static and the dynamic. **1985/86** Retired from his professorship in Berlin. Heiliger's abstract sculptures are representations of time, speed and events. Beside his works in bronze, steel and aluminium, Heiliger also experimented with synthetic materials such as plexiglas and polyester.
WRITINGS: B. H.: Skizzen – Figuren – Entwürfe. Berlin 1957
CATALOGUE RAISONNE: Salzmann, S. and L. Romain (ed.): B. H. Frankfurt-on-Main and Berlin 1989
MONOGRAPHS, CATALOGUES: Brockhaus, C. and B. Lepper (ed.): B. H. Retrospektive. Wilhelm Lehmbruck Museum, Duisburg et al. Duisburg 1985 (cat.).– Flemming, H. T.: B. H. Berlin 1962.– Flemming, H. T. and W. Schmied (ed.): B. H. Kunstverein und Akademie der Künste, Berlin et al. Berlin 1975 (cat.).– Hammacher, A. M.: B. H. St. Gallen 1978.– Romain. L. (ed.): B. H. Retrospektive 1945 bis 1995. Kunst- und Ausstellungshalle der Bundesrepublik Deutschland, Bonn. Bonn 1995 (cat.).– Papies, H. J. (ed.): B. H. Staatliche Museen zu Berlin. Berlin 1991 (cat.).– Salzmann, S. (ed.). B. H. Skulpturen, Reliefobjekte, Collagen. Galerie Pels-Leusden. Berlin 1987 (cat.).– Volkmann, B. (ed.): B. H. Skulpturen und Zeichnungen 1960-1975. Akademie der Künste. Berlin 1975 (cat.)

HEISIG Bernhard
born **1925** Breslau
German painter and graphic artist. **1941/42** Attended the School of Arts and Crafts in Breslau but was forced by the war to interrupt his studies and enlist for military service. **1946/47** Worked as a graphic artist in Breslau. **1948** Resumed his training at the Leipzig School of Applied Arts, followed by a course at the School of Graphics and Book Design until **1951**. **1961** Appointed director of the Leipzig School of Arts. **1964** Dismissed from his post for his championing of artists' rights and provocative article *Kritik an seiner Zeit*. **1965/66** Publication of a series of lithographs, *Der faschistische Alptraum* (The Fascist Nightmare), in which he attempts to come to terms with his own history. **1968–1976** Worked as a freelance painter and graphic artists. **1975** Completed the monumental wall painting *Ikarus* for the Palast der Republik in East Berlin. **1976** Resumed directorship of the Leipzig School of Arts until his retirement in **1987**. **1977** Participation in documenta 6 in Kassel. **1989** Returned two national awards, received in **1972** and **1978**, in protest against abuse of power and corruption in the former GDR. Heisig is one of the most important painters of the former GDR. His expressive and aggressive painting style, showing the influence of Lovis Corinth and Oskar Kokoschka, consciously opposes Socialist Realism.

MONOGRAPHS, CATALOGUES: Hartleb, R.: B. H. Dresden 1975.– B. H. Gemäldegalerie Neue Meister. Leipzig 1973 (cat.).– B. H. Retrospektive. Gaphik und Illustration. Sprengel Museum, Hanover et al. Hanover 1990 (cat.).– B. H. Mönchehaus-Museum. Goslar 1996 (cat.).– Helmert-Corvey, T. (ed.): B. H. Zeiten zu leben. Daniel-Pöppelmann-Haus. Herford 1994 (cat.).– Merkert, J. and P. Pachnicke (ed.): B. H. Retrospektive. Berlinische Galerie, Berlin et al. Munich 1989 (cat.).– Kober, K. M. (ed.): B. H. Kulturhistorisches Museum. Magdeburg 1978 (cat.).– Kober, K. M.: B. H. Dresden 1981.– Pachnicke, P. (ed.): B. H. Malerei, Graphik, Zeichnungen. Museum der bildenden Künste. Leipzig 1985 (cat.)

HEIZER Michael
born **1944** Berkeley (CA)
American painter and land artist. **1963/64** Studied at San Francisco Art Institute. **1965/66** Abstract Expressionist style. **1966** Moved to New York. **1966–1968** Encounters and experiments with Minimal Art. From **1967** first Land Art projects: alteration of natural grassy areas, hills and river courses to give a vivid representation of temporal processes such as weathering and sedimentation. These projects were documented through film and photography. **1969** Two massive cuts made into rocks in the California desert, entitled *Double Negative*. **1969/70** *Displaced/Replaced Mass*, in which granite blocks were sunk into rectangular pits dug into the Nevada desert. Digging of a deep pit at a building site in Neuperlach near Munich (*Munich Depression*). **1971** First drawings on zinc plates. From **1973** grey monochrome paintings with minimal step-like geometric forms. **1977** Participation in documenta 6 in Kassel.
MONOGRAPHS, CATALOGUES: Brown, J. (ed.): M. H. Sculpture in Reverse. Museum of Contemporary Art. Los Angeles 1984 (cat.).– Celant, G. (ed.): M. H. Milan 1996 (cat.).– Felix, Z. and E. Joosten (ed.): M. H. Museum Folkwang, Essen et al. Essen 1979 (cat.).– M. H. Sculpture in Reverse. Museum of Contemporary Art. Los Angeles 1984 (cat.).– M. H. Waddington Galleries. London 1990 (cat.).– M. H. Effigy Tumuli. The Reemergence of Ancient Mount Building. New York 1990.– M. H. Double Negative. New York 1992.– McGill, D. C. (ed.): M. H. Effigy Tumuli. The Reemergence of Ancient Mound Building. New York 1990

HELD Al
born **1928** New York
American painter. **1948/49** Studied at the Art Students League in New York. **1949** Moved to Paris. Contact with Rivers, Kelly, Francis and Noland. **1950–1952** Studied under Ossip Zadkine at the Académie de la Grande Chaumière. **1952** First solo-exhibition at Galerie 8 in Paris. **1953** Returned to New York. **1960** Abandoned Abstract

Expressionism and experimented with simple, spatially related geometric forms, superimposed on each other. From **1962** taught at Yale University. Took part in the exhibition "Geometric Abstraction in America" at the Whitney Museum of American Art, New York. **1966** Guggenheim grant. **1968** and **1977** Participation in documenta 4 and 6 in Kassel. Eliminated colour and produced a series of black-and-white paintings, later broadening his palette again. In the politically active early phase of his career there were parallels between Held's works and Social Realism; later, however, he disengaged himself from the prevailing Abstract Expressionism and took up Hard-Edge painting.
MONOGRAPHS, CATALOGUES: Armstrong, T.: A. H. New York 1991.– Green, H. (G.): A. H. San Francisco Museum of Art. San Francisco 1968 (cat.).– A. H. Stedelijk Museum. Amsterdam 1966 (cat.).– A. H. Museum of Art. San Francisco 1968 (cat.).– A. H. Recent Paintings. Institute of Contemporary Art, Philadelphia et al. Philadelphia 1969 (cat.).– A. H. Paintings and Drawings 1973-1978. Institute of Contemporary Art. Boston 1978 (cat.).– Rotzler, W. and A. Forge (ed.): A. H. Quadrat, Moderne Galerie. Bottrop 1980 (cat.).– Sandler, I.: A. H. New York 1984, London 1987.– Tucker, M. (ed.): A. H. Whitney Museum of American Art. New York 1974 (cat.)

HELION Jean
1904 Couterne (Orne) – 1987 Paris
French painter. Studied architecture and engineering. **1922** Began painting. **1928** Exhibited at the Salon des Indépendants. **1929** First abstract paintings, inspired by Mondrian's Neo-Plasticism. Co-founder of the group and journal *Art Concret*. **1931/32** Travelled through Europe, Russia and the USA. **1932–1934** Joined Abstraction-Création. Went to America. **1933** Solo-exhibition at the John Becker Gallery, New York. **1936** Moved to the USA. **1937** Painted large abstract figures. **1939** Last abstract compositions. Return to figurative painting. **1944–1945** Solo-exhibitions at the Paul Rosenberg Gallery, New York. **1946** Returned to France. **1964** Sets and costumes for TV adaptation of *King Lear*. **1971** Retrospective "Cent tableaux, 1928–1979" at the Grand

Palais, Paris. In the 80s, further retrospectives at the Musée d'Art Moderne in Strasbourg, at Lenbachhaus in Munich, at the Guggenheim Museum in Venice and finally **1995** at the Musée d' Unterlinden in Colmar.
WRITINGS: J. H.: They Shall Not Have Me. New York 1943.– J. H.: Journal d'un peintre. 2 vols. Ed. by A. Moeglin-Delacroix. Paris 1992.– J. H.: Mémoire de la chambre jaune. Paris 1994.– J. H.: A perte de vue. Paris 1997.– J. H.: Lettres d'Amérique. Correspondance avec Raymond Queneau 1934-1967. Paris 1997
CATALOGUE RAISONNE: Cousseau, H.-C. and I. d'Hauteville: H. Paris 1992
MONOGRAPHS, CATALOGUES: Abadie, D.: Hélion ou la force des choses. Brussels 1975.– Alloway, L. (ed.): J. H. Paintings and Drawings from 1939-1960. Robert Miller Gallery. New York 1981 (cat.).– Cousseau, H.-C. et al. (ed.): J. H. IVAM Centro Julio González, Valencia et al. Valencia 1990 (cat.).– Micha, R.: H. Paris 1979.– Ottinger, D.: J. H. Paris 1992.– Zweite, A. et al. (ed.): J. H. Abstraktion und Mythen des Alltags. Bilder, Zeichnungen, Gouachen 1925-1983. Städtische Galerie im Lenbachhaus, Munich et al. Munich 1984 (cat.)

HELNWEIN Gottfried
born **1948** Vienna
Austrian painter and graphic artist. **1965-1969** Studied at the College of Education and Research in Vienna. **1966** First autoaggressive actions and bandagings. While studying at the Academy of Arts in Vienna (**1969-1973**), produced hyper-realistic paintings of injured and maltreated children. From **1971** used offset printing as an artistic medium in itself. **1973** First etchings. **1977** Lived in the USA. From **1981** works incorporating trivial-culture figures such as Donald Duck and celebrities such as Niki Lauda and The Rolling Stones. Numerous poster designs, cover pictures for magazines and record sleeves. **1983/84** Copies of his self-portrait with bandaged head and clamps on front covers throughout the international press. **1985** Moved to Germany and produced abstract gestural paintings as well as some monochrome canvases. Worked increasingly from enlarged photographs. **1986** Solo-exhibition at the Mittelrhein-Museum in Koblenz and **1992** at the Pfalzgalerie, Kaiserslautern and **1996** at the Fine Arts Museum, Otaru (Japan). **1997** Major retrospective at the Russian State Museum, St. Petersburg.
MONOGRAPHS, CATALOGUES: Borovsky, A. et al. (ed.): G. H. St. Petersburg 1997 (cat.).– Feierabend, P. (ed.): H. Cologne 1992.– Gorsen, P. (ed.): G. H. Autoportraits 1970-1987. Heidelberg 1988.– G. H. Neunter November Nacht. Museum Ludwig. Cologne 1988 (cat.).– G. H. Arbeiten auf Papier 1969-1989. Museum Folkwang, Essen et al. Essen 1984 (cat.).– G. H. Faces. Stadtmusem München. Schaffhausen 1992 (cat.).– G. H. Retrospektive. Petersburg Museum. St. Petersburg 1996.–

Koschatzky, W. et al. (ed.): G. H. Arbeiten von 1970-1985. Graphische Sammlung Albertina. Vienna 1985 (cat.).– Roschitz, K. (ed.): H. Vienna 1981

HENRI Florence
1893 New York – **1982** Bellival
Swiss photographer and painter. **1911-1914** Studied music at the Conservatoire in Paris. **1914** Studied painting at the Berlin Academy and **1915-1919** at the private academy of H. Hofmann in Munich. **1924** Attended Léger and Ozenfant's Académie Moderne. **1927** Studied painting and photography at the Bauhaus in Dessau under László Moholy-Nagy and Albers. From **1929** devoted herself exclusively to photography. Portraits of artists and advertising and fashion photographs published in leading periodicals and magazines such as Art et Décoration, Vogue and The New York Herald. Also took numerous self-portraits. **1930-1935** worked on the photoseries Vitrines. **1931** Took part in photographic exhibitions in Paris, Basel and Essen. **1933** Travelled to Spain and Greece. **1935/36** Extended stay in Italy. Took up painting again. **1937** Participation in the exhibition "Foto 37" in Amsterdam. Photographic work interrupted by the outbreak of war. **1962** Settled in Bellival near Paris, producing collages.
MONOGRAPHS, CATALOGUES: Du Pont, D. (ed.): F. H. Artist-Photographer of the Avant-Garde. San Francisco Museum of Modern Art. San Francisco 1990 (cat.).– Fagiolo, M.: F. H. Torino 1975.– F. H. Westfälischer Kunstverein. Münster 1976 (cat.).– F. H. 70 Photographies 1928-1938. Musée d'Art d'Histoire. Geneva 1981.– Marcenaro, G. et al. (ed.): F. H. Aspetti di un percorso. Banco di Chiavarie. Genoa 1979 (cat.).– Miro, E. de (ed.): F. H. Galleria Martini & Ronchetti. Genoa 1974 (cat.).– Molderings, H.: F. H. Aspekte der Photographie der 20er Jahre. Münster 1976.– Pagé, S. and H. Molderings: F. H. Paris 1978

HEPWORTH Barbara
1903 Wakefield (Yorkshire) – **1975** Saint Ives (Cornwall)
English sculptress. **1920** Attended Leeds School of Art. Friendship with Henry

Moore. **1921-1924** Studied at the Royal College of Art, London. **1924-1926** Extended visits to Florence, Carrara and Rome. **1926** Returned to London, later taking a studio in Hampstead, close to Moore and Nicholson. **1932/33** Travelled through France. Contact with Brancusi, Braque, Picasso and Arp. Joined Abstraction-Création and published Unit One, a compilation of the writings of that group of abstract artists. First pierced sculptures. **1934** Moved to St. Ives, Cornwall. Together with Nicholson and then Gabo, set up the nucleus of an artists' colony, later joined for a while by Gropius, Moholy-Nagy and Breuer. From **1939** used threaded string as a sculptural element. **1949** Bought the Trewyn Studio in St. Ives and settled there. **1951** and **1955** Stage sets and costume designs. **1952** First group sculptures (People waiting). **1955** and **1959** participation in documenta 1 and 2 in Kassel. **1956** Inspired by a trip to Greece, she made a series of sculptures out of African wood with Greek titles. **1962/63** Exhibition at the Whitechapel Gallery, London. Public commissions including a memorial to Dag Hammerskjöld (Single Form) in New York. **1968** Retrospective at the Tate Gallery, London. Hepworth was one of the leading English abstract sculptors. She died in **1975** in a fire at her studio in St. Ives.
CATALOGUES RAISONNES: Bowness, A. (ed.): The Sculpture of B. H. 1960-1969. London and New York 1971 (cat.).– Hodin, J. P.: B. H. Life and Work. London and New York 1961/B. H. Neuchâtel 1961
MONOGRAPHS, CATALOGUES: Adams, A. (ed.): B. H. A Pictorial Autobiography. Bath 1970, New York 1970.– Alley, R. et al. (ed.): B. H. Tate Gallery. London 1968 (cat.).– Baxandall, D. (ed.): B. H. Retrospective Exhibition. Whitechappel Art Gallery. London 1954 (cat.).– Bowness, A. (ed.): B. H. Late Carvings, Early Life. Elizabethan Exhibition Gallery. Wakefield 1985 (cat.).– Curtis, P. and A. G. Wilkinson: B. H. A Retrospective. Tate Gallery, Liverpool et al. London 1994, Seattle 1995.– Festing, S.: B. H. A Life of Forms. London 1995.– Gardiner, M.: B. H. Edinburgh 1982.– Gibson, W.: B. H. London 1946.– Hammacher, A. M.: B. H. Cologne 1958, London 1959, 1987, New York 1968.– B. H. Tate Gallery. London 1968 (cat.).– Read, H. (ed.): B. H. Carvings and Drawings. London 1952.– Sheperd, M.: B. H. London 1963.– Wilkinson, A. G. (ed.): B. H. The Art Gallery of Ontario Collection, Toronto et al. Toronto 1991 (cat.)

HERBIN Auguste
1882 Quiévy (near Cambrai) – **1960** Paris
French painter. **1900/01** Attended the Ecole des Beaux-Arts in Lille. Moved to Paris, where he joined the Impressionists and then the Fauves. **1913** First Cubist-inspired paintings. **1917-1921** Geometric abstract phase. Designs for Objets monumentaux. Wood sculptures and reliefs. **1920** Joined the Communist party. **1922** Brief return to a fig-

urative style. **1926-1939** Two geometric abstract periods. **1929** Co-founder of the Salon des Surindépendants. **1931** Together with Vantongerloo, founded the group Abstraction-Création. **1946** Invented the alphabet plastique as a compositional framework. **1947** Co-founder and vice-president of the Salon des Réalités Nouvelles. Protested against Socialist Realism by leaving the Communist party. **1949** Published his own theoretical treatise L'art non-figuratif non-objectif. **1953** Partially paralysed, he learned to paint with his left hand. **1955** President of the Salon des Réalités Nouvelles.
WRITINGS: A. H.: L'Art non figuratif, non objectif. Paris 1946
CATALOGUE RAISONNE: Claisse, G. (ed.): H. Catalogue raisonné de l'œuvre peint. Lausanne and Paris 1993
MONOGRAPHS, CATALOGUES: A. H. 1882-1960. Stedelijk Museum. Amsterdam 1963 (cat.).– A. H. Musée d'Art Moderne de la Ville de Paris. Paris 1984 (cat.)/A. H. Städtische Galerie im Lenbachhaus. Munich 1984 (cat.).– A. H. Musée de Céret /Musée Matisse. Cateau-Cambrésis 1994 (cat.).– A. H. Retrospektive. Wilhelm-Hack-Museum. Ludwigshafen 1997 (cat.).– Jakovski, A.: A. H. Paris 1933.– Massat, A.: A. H. Paris 1953.– Schmied, W. (ed.): A. H. Kestner-Gesellschaft. Hanover 1967 (cat.)

HEROLD Jacques
1910 Piatra – **1987** Paris
Romanian-born French painter. **1925-1927** Attended art school in Bucharest. **1927-1929** Studied at the Art Academy in Bucharest. **1930** Moved to Paris. Met Tanguy and joined the Surrealists, but dissociated himself from the movement in **1938**. When France capitulated, he first went to Marseille but later returned to Provence. **1947** Organised the Surrealist exhibition in Paris, in which his own sculpture Large Banner was displayed. **1951** Abandoned Surrealism and developed a lyrical abstract style. **1952-1954** Lived in Frankfurt am Main and Brussels. **1958** Awarded the Foundation Copley Prize. Exhibitions at the Salon de Mai and the Salon des Surindépendants.
MONOGRAPHS, CATALOGUES: Butor, M.: J. H. Paris 1964

HESSE Eva
1936 Hamburg – **1970** New York
German-born American sculptress. **1954** Studied drawing at the Art Students League, **1954-1957** at the Cooper Union, New York, and **1957-1959** at Yale University, New Haven. From **1961** gestural drawings in Abstract Expressionist tradition. **1964/65** Took up sculpture while living in Germany. **1965** Solo-exhibition at the Kunsthalle Düsseldorf. **1968** Solo-exhibition at the Fischbach Gallery in New York and participation in the exhibition "Antiform". Taught at the School of Visual Arts. **1969** Exhibited with Nauman, Serra

and Sonnier at the Whitney Museum of American Art in "Anti-Illusion: Procedures/Materials", an exhibition presenting new material concepts in sculpture. **1972** and **1977** participation in documenta 5 and 6 in Kassel. Hesse, who died at the age of 34 from a brain tumour, used a variety of materials including rubber, fibreglass, synthetic textiles and artificial resin in her amorphous arrangements and mural reliefs. Her obsessive, allusive surrealism had a profound influence on American sculpture in the 70s. CATALOGUE RAISONNE: Barrette, B. (ed.): E. H. Sculpture. Catalogue Raisonné. New York 1989, 1992 MONOGRAPHS, CATALOGUES: Cooper, H. A. et al. (ed.): E. H. A Retrospective. Yale University Art Gallery, New Haven et al. New Haven (CT) 1992 (cat.).– David, C. and C. Diserens (ed.): E. H. Galerie Nationale du Jeu de Paume, Paris et al. Paris 1993 (cat.).– Haenlein, C.-A. et al. (ed.): E. H. 1936-1970. Skulpturen und Zeichnungen. Kestner-Gesellschaft. Hanover 1979 (cat.).– Johnson, E. H. (ed.): E. H. A Retrospective of the Drawings. Allen Memorial Art Museum. Oberlin 1982 (cat.).– Lippard, L. R.: E. H. New York 1976, 1992.– Pincus-Witten, R. (ed.): E. H. A Memorial Exhibition. Solomon R. Guggenheim Museum. New York 1972 (cat.).– Reinhardt, B. (ed.): E. H. Drawings in Space. Bilder und Reliefs. Ulmer Museum. Ulm and Stuttgart 1994 (cat.).– Serota, N. et al. (ed.): E. H. Sculpture. Whitechappel Art Gallery, London et al. London 1979 (cat.)

HILL Gary
born **1951** Santa Monica (CA)
American multimedia artist. **1969** Attended the Art Students League in Woodstock. Created sculptural works out of wire netting. **1971** First solo-exhibition at the Polaris Gallery in Woodstock. Began to experiment with audiovisual media and took videos of performances and environments. **1973** First video-installation *The Fall*. **1974-1976** Employed by Woodstock Community Video. **1977** Set up the Open Studio Video Project in Barrytown. First use of digital technology in the work Bathing. **1979-1980** Lectured at the State University of New York in Buffalo. **1983** Installation *Primarily Speaking*, in which two "speaking" walls of screens hold a dialogue, exhibited at the Whitney Museum of American Art. **1985-1991** Taught at Cornish College of the Arts in Seattle. **1987** and **1992** took part in documenta 8 and 9 in Kassel. **1995** Received special honours at the Venice Biennale. Grants from the National Endowments for the Arts, the Guggenheim and the Rockefeller Foundation. Hill's video works, shown at the Anthology Film Archives, the Museum of Modern Art in New York and the Pompidou Centre in Paris, focus on the the role of the counterplay of projected image and speech in perception and communication.
MONOGRAPHS, CATALOGUES: Assche, C. v. et al. (ed.): G. H. IVAM Centre del

Carme, Valencia et al. Valencia 1993 (cat.).– Boehm, G. and T. Vischer (ed.): G. H. Museum für Gegenwartskunst, Basel. Stuttgart 1995.– Devrient, C.: L'œuvre vidéo de G. H. Rennes 1990.– G. H. And Sat Down Beside Her. Galerie des Archives. Paris 1990 (cat.).– G. H. Video Installations. Stedelijk Van Abbe Museum. Eindhoven 1992 (cat.)/ G. H. Centre Georges Pompidou. Paris 1992 (cat.).– G. H. Hirshhorn Museum. Washington 1994 (cat.).– Liesbrock, H. (ed.): G. H. Midnight Crossing. Westfälischer Kunstverein. Münster 1997 (cat.).– Mignot, D. et al. (ed.): G. H. Stedelijk Museum, Amsterdam et al. Amsterdam 1993 (cat.).– Quasha, G. and C. Stein: G. H. Heard Liminal Objects/Tall Ships/Viewer. G. H.'s Projective Installations. 3 vols. Barrytown 1996-1997.– Sarrazin, S.: G. H. Centre International de Création Vidéo. Montbéliard Belfort 1992

HINE Lewis
1874 Oshkosh (WI) – **1940** New York
American photographer. **1892-1900** Studied painting and drawing in Oshkosh. **1900-1902** Studied sociology and education theory at the University of Chicago. **1901-1908** Taught natural history and geography at the Ethical Culture School in New York. **1905** Photographed immigrants on Ellis Island. **1906-1918** Photographic director of the National Child Labor Committee in New York. **1908** First publication in *Charities and Common*, documenting the life of American miners. **1909** Photoseries on child labour in the USA. **1910-1914** Worked as a photographer for the Red Cross in America and later in Europe. **1922-1929** Photographed for Survey, the *Milbank Foundation* and the *National Consumers' League*. **1930/31** Documented the building of the Empire State Building in New York. **1936/37** Director of the "National Research Project". From **1938** until he died, worked as a freelance photographer. Hine's social documentations set new directions for FSA photography.
WRITINGS: Kaplan, D. (ed.): Photo Story. Selected Letters and Photographs of L. W. H. Washington and London 1992
MONOGRAPHS, CATALOGUES: Gutman, J. M.: L. W. H. and the American Social Conscience. New York 1967.– Gutman, J. M.: L. W. H. 1874-1940. Two Perspectives. New York 1974.– L. H. Musée Carnavalet. Paris 1990 (cat.).– L. H. Centre National de la Photographie. Paris 1992 (cat.).– Kaplan, D.: L. H. in Europe. New York 1988.– Rosenblum, W. and A. Trachtenberg: America and L. H. New York 1977.– Steinorth, K. (ed.): L. H. Passionate Journey. Photographs 1905-1937. Zurich 1997.– Trachtenberg, A. and N. Rosenblum (ed.): America and L. H. New York 1976, 1997

HIRSHFIELD Morris
1872 Poland – **1946** Brooklyn (NY)
Polish-born American painter. As a boy, carved figures for the temple in his home-

town. **1890** Emigrated to the USA and worked for twelve years as a tailor for a manufacturer of ladies' wear before setting up his own business, producing slippers. **1936** After a protracted illness, gave up his business and began to paint. **1937** First painting, *Beach Girl*. The main subjects of subsequent paintings were female nudes and animals. **1939** His exotic, oriental paintings were discovered by the American art dealer and critic Sidney Janis, who then promoted him as a modern primitive artist. In **1946**, the year in which the artist died, an extensive retrospective was held in the Museum of Modern Art in New York.
MONOGRAPHS, CATALOGUES: M. H. 1872-1946. American Primitive Painter. Sidney Janis Gallery. New York 1965 (cat.).– Saroyan, W.: M. H. Parma 1975

HIRST Damien
born **1965** Bristol
English sculptor and installation artist. **1986-1989** Studied at Goldsmith's College in London. Began to explore the theme of death in his works. **1991** Completion of the work *The Physical Impossibility of Death in the Mind of Someone Living*, showing a 4.5 metre long tiger-shark in an aquarium filled with formalin. **1993** Exhibited the carcass of a cow, also preserved in formalin, at the Venice Biennale. This style of work, which he continued, provoked much controversy. **1995** Awarded the Prix Eliette von Karajan and the Turner Prize for his Biennale project. **1997** Opening of *Pharmacy*, a bar designed by the artist in London.
MONOGRAPHS; CATALOGUES: Blazwik, I.: D. H. Internal Affairs. Institute of Contemporary Arts. London 1991 (cat.).– D. H. Galerie Jablonka. Cologne 1994 (cat.).– D. H. A Bad Environment for White Monochrome Paintings. Mattress Factory. Pittsburgh 1994 (cat.).– D. H. A Good Environment for White Monochrome Painting. Daadgalerie et al. Berlin 1994 (cat.).– D. H. Institute of Contemporary Arts. London 1991 (cat.).– D. H. Making Beautiful Drawings. Bruno Brunnet Fine Arts. Berlin 1994 (cat.).– D. H. Prix Eliette v. Karajan '95. Max Gandolph Bibliothek. Salzburg 1995 (cat.).– D. H. No Sense of Absolute Corruption. Gargosian Gallery. New York 1996 (cat.).– Shone, R. (ed.): D. H. Third International Istanbul Biennial. British Council. Istanbul 1992 (cat.).– Violette, R.: D. H. I Want to Spend the Rest of My Life Everywhere. London 1997

HÖCH Hannah
1889 Gotha – **1978** Berlin
German painter, photographer and collage artist. **1912** Attended the Modern School of Arts and Crafts. From **1915** studied at the college attached to the Berlin Museum of Arts and Crafts. Friendship with Raoul Hausmann. **1918** Participated in various events organised by the Berlin Dada movement. Made dadaesque dolls and worked

with Hausmann on a series of photomontages. **1919** Took part in the Dada exhibition at the Graphische Kabinett Neumann. Joined the Novembergruppe and exhibited with them regularly. Contact with Schwitters, van Doesburg, Arp and Moholy-Nagy. **1920** Participated in the First International Dada Trade Fair. **1921/22** Dada tour with Schwitters to Prague. Worked on the *Merzbau* project. **1924** Went to Paris, where she met Mondrian. **1926-1929** Lived in Holland. **1929** Several photomontages displayed in the exhibition "Film and Foto" in Stuttgart. **1933-1945** Denounced by the Nazis and forbidden to exhibit. After World War II experimented with printing techniques.
MONOGRAPHS, CATALOGUES: Adriani, G. (ed.): H. H. Fotomontagen, Gemälde, Aquarelle. Kunsthalle Tübingen et al. Cologne 1980 (cat.).– Boswell, P. et al. (ed.): The Photomontages of H. H. Walker Art Center. Minneapolis 1996 (cat.).– Dech, J.: Schnitt mit dem Küchenmesser DADA durch die letzte Bierbauchkulturepoche Deutschlands. Untersuchungen zur Fotomontage bei H. H. Münster 1981.– Dech, J. and E. Maurer (ed.): Da-da-zwischen-Reden zu H. H. Berlin 1990.– H. H. Kunst, Wissenschaft. Internationales Symposium. Berlin 1989.– H. H. Musée d'Art Moderne de la Ville de Paris et al. Paris 1985 (cat.).– Lavin, M.: H. H. Photomontage and the Representation of the New Woman in Weimar Germany 1918-1933. New York 1991.– Lavin, M.: Cut with the Kitchen Knife. The Weimar Photomontages of H. H. New Haven (CT) and London 1993.– Maurer, E.: H. H. Jenseits fester Grenzen. Das malerische Werk bis 1945. Berlin 1995.– Moortgat, E. and C. Thater-Schulz (ed.): H. H. 1889-1978. Ihr Werk, ihr Leben, ihre Freunde. Berlinische Galerie. Berlin 1989 (cat.).– Ohff, H.: H. H. Berlin 1968.– Pawlow, K. (ed.): H. H. Gotha 1889-1978 Berlin. Museen der Stadt Gotha. Gotha 1993 (cat.).– Remmert, H.: H. H. Werke und Worte. Berlin 1982.– Thater-Schulz, C. (ed.): H. H. Eine Lebenscollage. 2 vols. Berlin 1989

HOCKNEY David
born **1937** Bradford (Yorkshire)
English painter, graphic artist and photographer. **1953-1957** Studied at Bradford College of Art, and **1959-1962** at the Royal College of Art in London. Won his first art award before leaving the Royal College. **1961/62** Travelled to New York and Berlin and set off for Egypt to collect ideas for illustrations. Encouraged by Henry Geldzahler, custodian of the Metropolitan Museum of Art in New York, to move to Los Angeles. **1963-1967** Taught at the University of Iowa, the University of Colorado, in Los Angeles and in Berkeley. **1966** First stage designs. **1968** and **1977** participation in documenta 4 and 6 in Kassel. **1969** Guest-professor at the Hamburg School of Arts. **1975-1992** Designed numerous sets for ballets and the operas by Mozart,

Stravinsky, Wagner and Strauss. From **1982** made Polaroid collages, combining the Cubist principle of simultaneity with chronophotographic sequences. In the late 80s, produced four-colour prints, abstract computer graphics and fax-drawings. Hockney's penchant for harsh, cold acrylic paints led to the categorization of his works as Pop Art, a label he disliked. In paintings, based on his own photographs, he developed a stylised realism.
WRITINGS: H. on Photography. Conversations with Paul Joyce. London 1988.– Stangos, N. (ed.): D. H. by D. H. My Early Years. London 1976 New York 1988.– Stangos, N. (ed.): D. H. That's the Way I See It. London and New York 1993 / D. H. Die Welt in meinen Augen. Autobiographie. Cologne 1994
CATALOGUE RAISONNE: The Scottish Arts Council, The Midland Group and Petersburg Press (ed.): D. H. Prints 1954-1977. London 1979, Paris 1987
MONOGRAPHS, CATALOGUES: Friedman, M. (ed.): D. H. Paints the Stage. Walker Art Center, Minneapolis et al. New York 1983 (cat.).– Livingstone, M.: D. H. London and New York 1981, 1987, Paris 1991.– Luckhardt, U. and P. Melia (ed.): D. H. A Drawing Retrospective. Royal Academy. London 1995 (cat.) / D. H. Zeichnungen 1954-1995. Hamburg 1995.– Luckhardt, U. and P. Melia (ed.): D. H. Zeichnungen. Stuttgart 1995.– Mißelbeck, R. (ed.): D. H. Photoworks. Museum Ludwig. Cologne 1998 (cat.).– Melia, P. and U. Luckhardt: D. H. Gemälde. Munich 1994 / D. H. Paintings. New York 1994.– Sayag, A. (ed.): D. H. photographe. Centre Georges Pompidou. Paris 1982 (cat.).– Stangos, N. (ed.): D. H. by D. H. London 1976.– Stangos, N. (ed.): Bilder von D. H. Zurich 1980.– Stangos, N. (ed.): D. H. London 1981.– Tuchman, M. and S. Barron (ed.): D. H. A Retrospective. Los Angeles County Museum of Art et al. Los Angeles and London 1988, Cologne 1988 (cat.).– Webb, P.: A Portrait of D. H. London 1988 / D. H. Paris 1991.– Weschler, L. (ed.): D. H. Camera Works. London and New York 1984

HÖDICKE Karl Horst
born **1938** Nuremberg
German painter and object artist. **1959–1964** Studied under Fred Thieler at the Berlin School of Fine Arts. **1961** Joined the artists' group *Vision*. **1964** Founder member of the artists' cooperative gallery Großgörschen 35, where he held his first soloexhibition. City street-scenes with neon signs. **1966/67** Experimental film work in New York. **1968** Scholarship to the Villa Massimo in Rome. Developed the ideas of Duchamp and Magritte in his works combining sculpture and paintings. **1969** Created the work *Kalter Fluß*, in which fluid tar poured slowly out of a bin, attached to the wall, onto the floor. From **1974** professor at the Berlin School of Fine Arts. The main themes of Hödicke's

gestural paintings are Berlin cityscapes and human figures. **1977** Retrospective at the Badischer Kunstverein, Karlsruhe and **1986** at the Kunstsammlung Nordrhein-Westfalen, Düsseldorf.
WRITINGS: K. H. H.: Anatomie – Autonomie – Anomalie. Berlin 1976.– K. H. H.: Kalenderblätter. Aufzeichnungen. Berlin 1980
MONOGRAPHS, CATALOGUES: Billeter, E. et al. (ed.): K. H. H. Gemälde, Skulpturen, Objekte, Filme. Kunstsammlung Nordrhein-Westfalen, Düsseldorf et al. Düsseldorf 1986 (cat.).– Block, R. and M. Schwarz (ed.): K. H. H. Badischer Kunstverein. Karlsruhe 1977 (cat.).– K. H. H. Berliner Ring. Bilder und Skulpturen 1975-1992. Neuer Berliner Kunstverein et al. Stuttgart 1992 (cat.).– Schneede, U. (ed.): K. H. H. Hamburger Kunstverein. Hamburg 1984 (cat.).– Wiesler, H.: K. H. Hödicke. Bonn 1989

HODLER Ferdinand
1853 Bern – **1918** Geneva
Swiss painter. **1871–1876** Studied at the Geneva School of Arts under B. Menn, who promoted him and brought him into contact with Ingres, Delacroix, Corot, Courbet and Manet. Studied the works of Corot and the French Impressionists. **1878/79** Spent nine months studying paintings in Madrid. Developed his own monumental style characterised by flat areas of colour, firm contours and symmetric/rhythmic, repetitive patterns of lines. Produced portraits, history paintings and works with a symbolist flavour. **1891** Went to Paris and joined the Rosicrucians. **1892** Exhibited at the first Salon de la Rose + Croix in Paris. His tendency towards the monumental brought him many commissions for wallpaintings. **1897** Won first prize for his mural design for the armoury at the Landesmuseum in Zurich. **1901–1905** Took part in the Vienna Secession and also exhibited at the Munich and Berlin Secessions. In **1905** and **1911** made trips to Italy. **1907** Wallpaintings for Jena University. **1913** Made an officer of the French Legion of Honour. **1917** Major retrospective in Zurich. Hodler attempted to achieve a synthesis of Impressionism, Realism and Symbolism in his painting. He is one of the few Swiss painters with a worldwide reputation.
CATALOGUE RAISONNE: Loosli, C. A. (ed.): F. H. Leben, Werke und Nachlass. 4 vols. Bern 1921-1923
MONOGRAPHS, CATALOGUES: Bätschmann, O. et al. (ed.): F. H. (ed.): Sammlung Max Schmidheiny. Kunstmuseum des Kantons Thurgau. Frauenfeld 1989 (cat.).– Bender, E. and W. Y. Müller: Die Kunst F. H.'s. Reife und Spätwerk 1895-1918. Zurich 1941.– Brüschweiler, J. (ed.): Ein Maler vor Liebe und Tod. F. H. und Valentine Godé-Darel. Ein Werkzyklus 1908-1915. Kunsthaus Zurich et al. Zurich 1976 (cat.).– Brüschweiler, J. and G. Magnaguagno (ed.): F. H. Neue Nationalgalerie, Berlin et al. Berlin 1983 (cat.).– Brüsch-

weiler, J. (ed.): F. H. Fondation Pierre Gianadda. Martigny 1989 (cat.).– Der frühe H. Das Werk 1870-1890. Kunstmuseum Bern. Bern 1981 (cat.).– Eisenmann, S. F. and O. Bätschman (ed.): F. H. Landscapes. Los Angeles, New York and Chicago 1987 (cat.).– Grabner, S. et al. (ed.): F. H. und Wien. Vienna 1992 (cat.).– Guerzoni, S.: F. H. als Mensch, Maler und Lehrer. Zurich 1952 / F. H. Sa Vie, son œuvre, son enseignement, souvenirs personnels. Geneva 1957.– Hirsh, S. L.: F. H. Munich 1981, London and New York 1982.– F. H. Die Mission des Künstlers. Bern 1982.– F. H. Kunstmuseum Solothurn et al. Solothurn 1996 (cat.).– Hugelshofer, W.: F. H. Eine Monographie. Zurich 1952.– Magnaguagno, G. et al. (ed.): F. H. Kunsthaus Zürich et al. Zurich 1983 (cat.).– Perucchi, U. (ed.): F. H. Zeichnungen der Reifezeit 1900-1918. Kunsthaus Zürich. Zurich 1992 (cat.).– Selz, P. (ed.): F. H. University Art Museum, Berkeley et al. Berkeley 1972 (cat.).– Steinberg, S. D.: F. H. Ein Platoniker der Kunst. Zurich 1947.– Überwasser, W.: H. Köpfe und Gestalten. Zurich 1947

HOEHME Gerhard
1920 Greppin (near Dessau) – **1989** Neuss
German painter. **1948–1951** Studied under H. Post in Burg Giebichstein, near Halle. **1951** Moved to Düsseldorf. From **1952** studied at the Düsseldorf Art Academy. Painted in a style close to Tachisme. **1954–1957** Leading member of the Düsseldorf artists' association Gruppe 53. From **1955** took up Lyrical Abstraction. From **1957** painted on shaped canvases and mixed his paints with other materials to experiment with spatial structures. **1959** Participation in documenta 2 in Kassel. **1963** Extension of the painting into 3-dimensional space: the linear framework of the picture was broken up or actually replaced by concrete elements such as pieces of string. **1960** Villa Massimo Award in Rome. **1960–1984** Professorship at the Düsseldorf Academy. In the 70s, Hoehme produced his *Damastbilder*, which constituted a further step towards the *offenes Bild* (open picture) and the idea that paintings are not on canvas but in the mind of the viewer.
WRITINGS: G. H.: Wegzeichen im Unbekannten. Heidelberg 1962
MONOGRAPHS, CATALOGUES: Argan, G. C. and M. d. la Motte (ed.): G. H. Roma 1969.– Argan, G. C. and H. P. Thurn: G. H. Werk und Zeit 1948-1983. Stuttgart 1983.– Bartsch, I.: G. H. Wir haben den Kosmos in uns. Museum am Ostwall, Dortmund. Cologne 1992 (cat.).– Bojescul, W. (ed.): G. H. Das offene Bild. Kunstverein Braunschweig. Braunschweig 1984 (cat.).– Güse, E.-G. (ed.): G. H. L'Etna. Mythos und Wirklichkeit. Saarland Museum. Saarbrücken 1990 (cat.).– G. H. Kunstverein Bielefeld et al. Bielefeld 1996 (cat.).– Jensen, J. C.: In memoriam G. H. Kunsthalle Kiel. Kiel 1989 (cat.).– Partenheimer, J.: G. H. Städtische Kunsthalle Düsseldorf et al. Düsseldorf 1979 (cat.)

HOELZEL Adolf
1853 Olmütz – **1934** Stuttgart
German painter, art teacher and colour theoretician. **1876–1879** Studied at the Vienna Art Academy. **1880/81** Attended the Munich Academy. **1882** Encountered Impressionism on a visit to Paris. **1888** Founded a school of painting in Dachau near Munich. **1904** Published his first theoretical essays in *Die Kunst für Alle*. From **1906** professor at the Stuttgart Academy, where his pupils included Baumeister, Itten and Schlemmer. First abstract compositions. **1914** Stained-glass windows and decorative paintings for the factories of Wagner and Bahlsen in Hanover. **1923** Began a series of works in pastels. Hoelzel succeeded in extending the six-colour circle to a twelve-part chromatic circle. His theory of colour, based on the researches of J. W. v. Goethe and M. E. Chevreul, was developed by Itten and incorporated into Bauhaus theory and teaching.
WRITINGS: A. H.: Gedanken und Lehren. Stuttgart 1933
CATALOGUE RAISONNE: Venzmer, W. (ed.): A. H. Leben und Werk. Monographie mit Verzeichnis der Ölbilder, Glasfenster und ausgewählter Pastelle. Stuttgart 1982
MONOGRAPHS, CATALOGUES: Beck, R. (ed.): A. H. Aufbruch zur Moderne. Museum Villa Stuck. Munich 1980 (cat.).– Haenlein, C. (ed.): A. H. Bilder, Pastelle, Zeichnungen, Collagen. Kestner-Gesellschaft. Hanover 1982 (cat.).– Hildebrandt, H.: A. H. Zeichnungen, Farbe, Abstraktion. Darmstadt 1969.– Venzmer, W. et al. (ed.): A. H. Galerie der Stadt Sindelfingen et al. Sindelfingen 1987 (cat.)

HOERLE Heinrich
1875 Cologne – **1936** Cologne
German painter. Walking tours through Belgium and Holland. Joined various artists' groups. **1912** Sporadic attendance at the Cologne School of Arts and Crafts. **1913** Friendship with Max Ernst and contact with the Lunists. **1917** Military service. **1919** Worked with Baargeld and Ernst on the Dada magazine *Der Ventilator* and helped to found the group stupid. **1923** Produced a series of prints with a subversive political slant. **1924** Founded the Gruppe progressiver Künstler (Group of Progressive Artists) with Seiwert in Cologne. Returned to a sur-

realist style of painting. **1928** Produced some of his most famous works, including *Grüßende Jungfrau, Fabriklandschaft* and *Melancholie*. **1929** Issued the magazine *a bis z*. **1930** Joint-exhibitions with the Group of Progressive Artists in Cologne, Nuremberg, Berlin, Amsterdam, Paris and Chicago. Period of purist, constructivist compositions. **1932** Retrospective at the Cologne Kunstverein. **1933** Travelled to Mallorca. Paintings on religious themes.
CATALOGUE RAISONNE: Backes, D. (ed.): H. H. Leben und Werk. 1895-1936. Kölnischer Kunstverein. Cologne 1981 (cat.)
MONOGRAPHS, CATALOGUES: Schmidt-Rost, H.: H. H. Recklinghausen 1965

HOFER Karl
1878 Karlsruhe – **1955** Berlin
German painter and graphic artist. **1898** Studied at the Karlsruhe Academy. **1900–1902** Pupil of Hans Thoma. **1902** Went to the Stuttgart Academy. **1903–1908** Lived in Rome. **1908** Went to Paris where he was deeply impressed by the works of Cézanne. **1914–1917** Military service. Taken prisoner in France. **1917** Lived in Zurich. From **1919** taught at the Berlin Academy. **1923** Member of the Prussian Academy of Arts. **1933** Dismissed. **1934** First prize from the Carnegie Institute of Arts. **1937** Confiscation of many of his works. **1940** Moved to Konstanz. **1943** Destruction of his Berlin studio and numerous works in a bombing raid. **1948** Honorary doctorate from the Humboldt University in Berlin and honorary membership of the Karlsruhe Academy. **1950** Elected first president of the German Artists' Association. Hofer's combination of Expressionist subjectivity with a strict classical objectivity aligns him with Neue Sachlichkeit.
WRITINGS: Feist, U. and G. (ed.): K. H. und T. Reinhart. Maler und Mäzen. Ein Briefwechsel. Berlin 1989.– K. H.: Aus Leben und Kunst. Berlin 1952.– K. H.: Erinnerungen eines Malers. Berlin 1953.– K. H.: Über das Gesetzliche in der bildenden Kunst. Berlin 1956.– Hünecke, A. (ed.): K. H. Malerei hat eine Zukunft. Briefe, Aufsätze, Reden. Leipzig 1991.– Kupper, D. (ed.): K. H. Schriften. Berlin 1996
CATALOGUE RAISONNE: Rathenau, E. (ed.): K. H. Das graphische Werk. Berlin and New York 1969, 1991
MONOGRAPHS, CATALOGUES: Feist, U.: K. H. Berlin 1977.– Feist, U.: K. H. Bilder im Schlossmuseum Ettlingen. Berlin 1983.– Furler, E. (ed.): K. H. Leben und Werk in Daten und Bildern. Frankfurt-on-Main 1978.– Hartleb, R.: K. H. Leipzig 1987.– Hartleb, R. and K.-H. Mehnert (ed.). K. H. Tischgesellschaft. Museum der Bildenden Künste. Leipzig. Berlin and Leipzig 1992 (cat.).– Jannasch, A. C. H. Potsdam 1946.– Martin, K.: K. H. Karlsruhe 1957.– Raum, H. and S. Hartmann (ed.): K. H. Malerei, Grafik, Zeichnung. Staatliche Galerie Moritzburg. Halle 1978 (cat.).– Rigby, I. K.: K. H. New York 1976.–

Ruckhaberle, D. et al. (ed.): K. H. Staatliche Kunsthalle Berlin et al. Berlin 1978 (cat.).– Schilling, J. (ed.): K. H. Schloß Cappenberg. Unna 1991 (cat.)

HOFMANN Hans
1880 Weißenberg (Bavaria) – **1966** New York
German-born American painter. Grew up in Munich. **1904–1906** Studied at the Académie de la Grande Chaumière in Paris. Worked with Matisse in the Atelier Colarossi. Came to know Delaunay, Braque, Pascin, Gris and Picasso. **1910** First solo-exhibition at Paul Cassirer's gallery in Berlin. **1915** Returned to Munich and opened his own school of modern art with a strong emphasis on Cubism. **1930–1932** Taught at the University of California, Berkeley and at the Art Students League in New York. **1933** Settled in New York. His teaching at his own school in New York from **1934** to **1958** influenced a whole generation of American abstract artists. **1949** Met Braque, Brancusi and Picasso in Paris. **1959** Participated in documenta 2 in Kassel. **1960** Took part in the Venice Biennale. In the early 40s, Hofmann developed a form of Abstract Expressionism out of the traditions of Cubism and Fauvism, in which dynamic tension is set up through a counterplay of unbroken colour and free gestural elements.
WRITINGS: H. H.: Search for the Real and Other Essays. Andover (MA) 1948.– H. H.: Selected Writings on Art. New Hampshire 1962.– Seitz, W. C.: H. H. with Selected Writings by the Artist. New York 1963
MONOGRAPHS, CATALOGUES: Banard, W. D. (ed.): H. H. A Retrospective Exhibition. Hirshhorn Museum and Sculpture Garden Washington et al. Washington and Houston 1976 (cat.).– Friedel, H. (ed.): H. H. Wunder des Rhythmus und dr Schönheit des Raumes. Städtische Galerie im Lenbachhaus, Munich et al. Munich 1997 (cat.).– Goodman, C.: H. H. New York 1986.– Goodman, C. et al. (ed.): H. H. Whitney Museum, New York et al. New York and Munich 1990 (cat.).– Greenberg, C.: H. H. Paris 1961.– H. H. Das Spätwerk. Städtische Galerie im Lenbachhaus, Munich et al. Stuttgart 1997 (cat.).– Hoyland, J. (ed.): H. H. Late Paintings, Tate Gallery. London 1988 (cat.).– Hunter, S.: H. H. New York 1963, Paris 1963.– Seitz, W. C. (ed.): H. H. The Museum of Modern Art. New York 1963 (cat.).– Wight, F. S.: H. H. Berkeley and Los Angeles 1957

HOLZER Jenny
born **1950** Gallipolis (OH)
American multimedia artist. **1968–1970** Studied art at Duke University in North Carolina and at Ohio University in Athens. **1970/71** Transferred to the University of Chicago. **1973** Graduated in painting and graphic art from Ohio University. **1974–1977** Attended Rhode Island School of Design in New York, where she taught some undergraduate classes. From **1976**

incorporated words in her paintings. **1977** Collection of writings *Truism*, in which texts are circulated through media such as posters, audio-tapes, photos and printed T-shirts. **1979/80** Worked as a typesetter. **1980–1982** Together with Peter Nadin, drew up the texts for her *Living Series*. **1981** Participation in the exhibition "Westkunst" in Cologne. **1982** First presentation of *Truism* via neon signs in Time Square, New York. Experiments with electronic scripts. Took part in documenta 7 and **1987** in documenta 8 in Kassel. **1985/86** Chiselled her texts into granite benches. **1986** Texts from the *Survival Series* broadcast on American television. **1990** Retrospective at the Guggenheim Museum, New York. First woman to represent America at the Venice Biennale.
WRITINGS: J. H.: Abuse of Power Comes as no Surprise. Truisms and Essays. Halifax and New York 1983.– J. H. im Gespräch mit N. Smolik. Cologne 1993.– Smolik, N. (ed.): J. H. Schriften. Stuttgart 1996.– Smolik, N. (ed.): J. H. Gesammelte Schriften. Stuttgart 1996
MONOGRAPHS, CATALOGUES: Auping, M.: J. H. New York 1992.– J. H. Kunsthalle Basel et al. Basel 1984 (cat.).– J. H. Signs. Institute of Contemporary Arts. London 1988 (cat.).– J. H. The Venice Installation. Albright-Knox Art Gallery. Buffalo 1991 (cat.).– J. H. Signs. Art Center. Des Moines 1993 (cat.).– J. H. Lustmord. New York 1997.– J. H. Rosebud. New York (n. d.).– Waldman, D. (ed.): J. H. Solomon R. Guggenheim Museum. New York 1989, 1992 (cat.).– Waldman, D.: J. H. Stuttgart 1997

HOOVER Nan
born **1931** New York
American installation and performance artist. **1949–1954** Studied painting at the Corcoran Gallery School in Washington. From **1957** exhibitions of paintings and drawings in New York, Washington and Amsterdam. **1969** Moved to Amsterdam. **1972–1974** Worked alternately in France and Amsterdam. **1974** First videos and performances. **1975** Video exhibition with the painter Richard Hefti at the Jurka Gallery, Amsterdam. **1977** and **1987** took part in documenta 6 and 8 in Kassel. **1978/79** First film project entitled *Lapses*. Participated in

Videowochen at the Museum Folkwang in Essen. **1980/81** DAAD scholarship to Berlin. Since **1989** professorship at the Düsseldorf Academy.
MONOGRAPHS, CATALOGUES: Dabniels, D. et al. (ed.): N. H. Movements in Light. Amsterdam 1991 (cat.).– Gosselin, C. (ed.): N. H. Photo, Video, Performance 1980-1982. Musée d'Art Contemporain. Montreal 1982 (cat.).– N. H. Kunstverein Heilbronn et al. Heilbronn 1996 (cat.).– Mignot, D. et al. (ed.): N. H. Stedelijk Museum. Amsterdam 1979 (cat.).– Perée, R. (ed.): N. H. Kunstmuseum Bern. Bern 1988 (cat.).– Stoos, T. (ed.): N. H. Photowork, Video, Performance. Daadgalerie. Berlin 1981 (cat.)

HOPPER Edward
1882 Nyack (NY) – **1967** New York
American painter. **1900–1906** Studied commercial art and painting at the New York School of Art. **1906–1910** Extended trips to Europe, mainly to Paris, where he painted impressionist-style street scenes. **1908** Settled in New York. Worked as an illustrator and poster painter. Exhibited **1913** at the Armory Show and **1917** at the "First Annual Exhibition" of the American Society of Independent Artists. **1924** Exhibition of watercolours at the Frank K. M. Rehn Gallery. **1933** Retrospective at the Museum of Modern Art, New York. **1945** Made a member of the National Institute of Arts and Letters. **1950** Received an honorary doctorate from the Art Institute of Chicago. **1952** Participated at the Venice Biennale. **1964** and **1980** major retrospectives at the Whitney Museum of American Art. **1968** His entire œuvre donated to the Foundation of the Whitney Museum of American Art in New York. Hopper' distinctive style was uninfluenced by any of the avant-garde movements in Europe and America. The central themes of his work were modern civilization, particularly urbanization, loneliness in the city, the expansion of industry and the eccentricities of American architecture.
CATALOGUES RAISONNES: Levin, G. (ed.): E. H. The Complete Prints. New York 1979 / E. H. Die Druckgraphik. Munich 1986.– Levin, G. (ed.): E. H. A Catalogue Raisonné. 3 vols. New York and Munich 1995
MONOGRAPHS, CATALOGUES: Beck, H.: Der melancholische Blick. Die Großstadt im Werk des amerikanischen Malers E. H. Frankfurt-on-Main et al. 1988.– Beck, H.: E. H. Hamburg 1992.– Goodrich, L.: E. H. London 1949, New York 1964.– Güse, E.-G. and Borge-Keweloh, N. (ed.): D. H. Das Frühwerk. Westfälisches Landesmuseum. Münster 1981 (cat.).– Hobbs, R.: E. H. New York 1987.– Költzsch, G. W. and H. Liesbrock (ed.): E. H. und die Fotografie. Die Wahrheit des Sichtbaren. Museum Folkwang, Essen. Cologne 1992 (cat.).– Kranzfelder, I.: E. H. 1882-1967. Vision of Reality. Cologne 1995.– Levin, G. (ed.): E. H. as Illustrator. Whitney Museum

of American Art. New York 1979.– Levin, G. (ed.): E. H. The Art and the Artist. Whitney Museum of American Art, New York et al. New York 1980 (cat.).– Levin, G.: E. H. New York 1984.– Levin, G. (ed.): E. H. Gemälde und Zeichnungen. Folkwang Museum, Essen. Munich 1992 (cat.).– Liesbrock, H.: E. H. Die Wahrheit des Lichts. Duisburg 1985.– Liesbrock, H.: E. H. Das Sichtbare und das Unsichtbare. Stuttgart 1992.– Lyons, D. and A. D. Weinberg: E. H. and The American Imagination. New York 1995.– Renner, R. G.: E. H. 1882-1967. Transformation of the Real. Cologne 1992.– Schultze, S. (ed.): E. H. 1882-1967. Schirn Kunsthalle. Frankfurt-on-Main 1992 (cat.)

HORN Rebecca
born **1944** Michelstadt
German object artist and film-maker. **1964
–1969** Studied at the Hamburg School of Fine Arts. **1968** First body sculptures in which peacock feathers and other items are worn like clothes. **1971/72** DAAD scholarship to London. **1972** Moved to New York. **1972-1992** Participation in documenta 5 – 9 in Kassel. **1972/73** *Performances I + II* highlighting the interaction of people and objects. **1974** Guest-lecturer at the University of San Diego. **1978** and **1981** Made the films *Der Eintänzer* and *La Ferdinanda – Sonate für eine Medici-Villa*, later using objects and props from these films for arrangements and installations such as the work *Körper-Raum-Reflexe*. **1986** Won the Arnold Bode Award in Kassel. **1989** Production of the cinema film *Buster's Bedroom*. **1992** Prize for media art from the ZKM in Karlsruhe and Kaiserring, Goslar. **1994/95** Retrospective at the Guggenheim Museum in New York and the Gropius Bau in Berlin. Horn's videos and perfomances are choreographic rituals revolving around extensions of the body and the mythical identification of man with nature.
WRITINGS: R. H.: Dialogo della Vedova Paradisaca. Genoa 1975.– R. H. Buster's Bedroom. A Filmbook. Zurich, New York and Frankfurt-on-Main 1991.– R. H.: The Glance of Infinity. New York (n. d.) MONOGRAPHS, CATALOGUES: Baum, T.: Rebeccabook I. New Yok 1975.– Baum, T. et al. (ed.): R. H. Objekte, Video, Filme. Kölnischer Kunstverein et al. Cologne 1977 (cat.).– Celant, G. and K. Schmidt (ed.): R. H. Staatliche Kunsthalle Baden-Baden et al. Baden-Baden 1981 (cat.).– Celant, G. et al. (ed.): R. H.: Diving through Buster's Bedroom. Museum of Contemporary Art. Los Angeles 1990 (cat.).– Celant, G. et al. (ed.): R. H.: Filme 1978-1990. Kestner-Gesellschaft. Hanover 1991 (cat.).– Celant, G. et al. (ed.): R. H. Solomon R. Guggenheim Museum, New York et al. New York 1993 (cat.).– Celant, G. et al. (ed.): G. H. Kunsthalle Vienna et al. Vienna 1994 (cat.).– Curiger, B. et al. (ed.): R. H. Museum of Contemporary Art, Chicago et al. Chicago 1984 (cat.).– Haenlein, C.-A. et al. (ed.): R. H. Der Eintänzer. Kestner-Gesellschaft, Hanover et al. Hanover 1978 (cat.).– Haen-

lein, C. (ed.): R. H. The Glance of Infinity. Kestner-Gesellschaft. Hanover 1997 (cat.).– R. H.: La Lune rebelle. Stuttgart 1993.– Mosebach, M. et al. (ed.): R. H. Nuit et jour sur le dos du serpent à deux têtes. Musée d'Art Moderne de la Ville de Paris. Paris 1986 (cat.).– Stoss, T. et al. (ed.): R. H. Kunsthaus Zurich et al. Zurich 1983 (cat.)

HORST Horst P.
born **1906** Weißenfels (Saale)
German-born American photographer. **1926–1928** Studied art and architecture under Walter Gropius at the Hamburg School of Arts and Crafts. From **1931** photographed for numerous journals. Besides fashion photographs did mainly portraits of famous artists, writers and politicians, including Dalí and Cocteau. **1931–1935** Photographed for *Vogue* in Paris with Hoyningen-Huene. **1935–1943** Photographed fashion shows in New York and Paris. **1943–1945** Military service. Portraits of high-ranking officers. **1950** First advertising photographs for Cadillac. **1950–1968** Directed his own photographic studio in New York. **1974–1980** Regular exhibitions at the Ileana Sonnabend Gallery in New York. **1977** Participation in documenta 6 in Kassel. Horst often uses classical props in his photographs, and works with dramatic lighting effects.
MONOGRAPHS, CATALOGUES: Kazmair, M. (ed.): H. Sixty Years of Photography. New York 1996.– Lawford, V.: H. His Work and His World. Harmondsworth 1985

HOYNINGEN-HUENE George
1900 St. Petersburg – **1968** Los Angeles
Russian-born American photographer. **1912** Lived in Italy. **1917** Fled to England to escape the Russian revolution. **1921–1924** Lived in Paris, earning his living as a translator. Worked with Man Ray on a fashion portfolio. **1925** Drew fashion designs for *Harper's Bazaar*. Began working as a professional photographer. **1926** Head photographer for *Vogue* in France. **1927** Worked with Paul Outerbridge. Produced fashion films for *Vogue*. **1929** Sent by *Vogue* to Paris. Built up a portfolio of portraits of film celebrities in Hollywood. **1931** Took portraits for Condé Nast in Berlin. **1935–1945**

Worked for *Harper's Bazaar*. **1937** Trip to Greece. **1938** First book publication. From **1946** taught at the Art Center School in Los Angeles and worked as a portraitist for several leading film companies. **1955–1968** Made documentary films in Hollywood. MONOGRAPHS, CATALOGUES: Ewing, W. (ed.): Eye for Elegance. G. H.-H. National Center of Photography. New York 1980.– Ewing, W.: The Photographic Art of H.-H. New York 1986.– H. P. H. CCD-Galerie. Düsseldorf 1982 (cat.).– Pucciani, O. (ed.): H.-H. and the Fashion Image. Los Angeles County Museum of Art. Los Angeles 1970 (cat.)

HUBBUCH Karl
1891 Karlsruhe – **1979** Karlsruhe
German painter and graphic artist. **1908– 1914** Studied at the Karlsruhe Academy and under Emil Orlik at the institute attached to the Museum of Arts and Crafts in Berlin. **1914–1918** Military service. **1920–1922** Continued studies under Walter Conz at the Karlsruhe Academy, where from **1924/25** he himself taught drawing. Participated in the exhibition "Neue Sachlichkeit" at the Kunsthalle Mannheim. **1928** Appointed Professor at Karlsruhe. Member of the Vereinigung revolutionärer Künstler (ASSO), an association of revolutionary artists. **1929** Took part in the exhibition "Neue Sachlichkeit" at the Stedelijk Museum, Amsterdam. **1930** Co-founder of the journal *Monatsschrift für Zeitkunst, Zeitbetrachtung, Satire und Karikatur*. **1932/33** Publication of a collection of drawings entitled *Deutsche Belange* (German Interests). Dismissed from his post and forbidden to paint or exhibit. **1933** Painted flowers at the Majolika factory in Karlsruhe and at Schmid-Schlenkers, a firm in Schwenningen making cuckoo clocks. **1945–1947** Active in anti-fascist organisations. **1947** Taught architecture at Karlsruhe Technical College. **1948–1957** Professor of Painting at the Karlsruhe Academy.
CATALOGUE RAISONNE: Riester, R. (ed.): K. H. Das graphische Werk. Freiburg 1969
MONOGRAPHS, CATALOGUES: Goettl, H. et al. (ed.): K. H. 1891-1979. Badischer Kunstverein, Karlsruhe. Munich 1981 (cat.).– Hartmann, W. (ed.): K. H. Der Zeichner. Wilhelm-Busch-Museum, Hanover et al. Stuttgart 1991 (cat.).– Kinkel, H. (ed.): Der frühe H. Zeichnungen und Druckgraphik 1911-1925. Kunsthalle Bremen et al. Bremen 1973.– Rödiger, D. (ed.): K. H. Retrospektive. Städtische Galerie im Prinz Max Palais, Karlsruhe. Stuttgart 1993 (cat.).– Schmidt, D.: K. H. Munich 1976

HUNDERTWASSER Friedensreich
(Friedrich Stowasser)
1928 Vienna – **2000** on sea
Austrian painter and graphic artist. Attended the Montessori School Vienna, and studied for one year at the Vienna Art Academy. **1949** Travelled throughout

Europe and North Africa. On his return, he took the name Hundertwasser and produced his first art works, categorising them as "half Klee – half Rousseau". **1953** First solo-exhibition in Vienna, and further exhibitions in Cologne, Paris and Milan. **1956** Publication of his article *La visibilité de la création transautomatique*. **1958** Issued the *Verschimmelungsmanifest gegen den Rationalismus in der Architektur* (Mould Manifesto Against Rationalism in Architecture). **1959** Together with Bazon Brock staged the happening *Endlose Linie* in Hamburg. **1961** Worked with Japanese wood-engravers, and printed his graphic works in Japan. **1964** Participation in documenta 3 in Kassel. In the 70s, decorated buildings with murals inlaid with ceramic pieces. **1982** Promoted and designed ecological architecture. **1983– 1985** Building of Hundertwasser houses in Vienna and further architectural commissions. Hundertwasser's brilliantly coloured paintings are influenced by Viennese Jugendstil and the works of Klee. His spectacular public appearances and speeches, his commitment to nature and his highly individual lifestyle have made him well-known to a wide public.
WRITINGS: F. H.: Der Transautomatismus. Eine allgemeine Mobilmachung des Auges. Roma and Paris 1956.– F. H.: Verschimmelungsmanifest gegen den Rationalismus in der Architektur. Seckau 1958.– F. H.: Das H.-Haus. Vienna 1985.– Schurian, W. (ed.): F. H. Schöne Wege. Gedanken über Kunst und Leben. Munich 1983
CATALOGUES RAISONNES: Koschatzky, W. (ed.): F. H. Das vollständige druckgraphische Werk 1951-1986. Zurich and Schwäbisch Hall 1986.– Koschatzky, W. (ed.): Catalogue raisonné de l'œuvre gravé 1951-1986. Paris 1986.– Schmied, W. (ed.): H. Vollständiger Œuvre-Katalog. Hanover 1964
MONOGRAPHS, CATALOGUES: Chipp, H. B. and B. Richardson (ed.): H. University Art Museum, Berkeley. New York 1968 (cat.).– Hofmann, W.: H. Salzburg 1965, New York 1976.– Schmied, W. (ed.): F. H. Stedelijk Museum. Amsterdam 1964 (cat.).– Hulten, K. G. and K. Bergquist (ed.): F. H. Moderna Museet. Stockholm 1965 (cat.).– F. H. Regentag. Museum Ludwig. Cologne 1980 (cat.).– H. Tapisserien. Museum für Angewandte Kunst. Vienna 1978 (cat.).– Mathey, J. F.: H. Munich 1985.– Rand, H.: F. H. Der Maler. Munich 1986.– Rand, H.: F. H. Cologne 1993.– Restany, P.: H. Paris 1957.– Schmied, W.: H. Frankfurt-on-Main 1968.– Schmied, W.: H. Salzburg 1974

HUSZAR Vilmos
1884 Budapest – **1960** Hierden
Hungarian painter. Trained as a wall decorator at the Budapest School of Arts and Crafts. From **1904** studied at the Munich Academy of Arts. **1909** Moved to Holland. **1915–1916** First Cubist works and designs for stained-glass windows. **1917** Co-founder of De Stijl. First abstract compositions. Interior and colour designs, partly in collab-

oration with Jan Wils, Piet Zwart and van der Kloot Meyburg. **1921** Took part in the Constructivist convention in Düsseldorf, where he met El Lissitzky. **1922** Designed a room in the house of T. Brugman in The Hague, for which van Doesburg and Schwitters had also designed interiors. Stage designs. From **1925** graphic sketches for advertising, industry and exhibitions posters. **1930** Continued painting, but also designed furniture. Huszár was one of the theoreticians whose ideas contributed to Neo-Plasticism. He also tried to apply the principles of De Stijl to theatre design. MONOGRAPHS, CATALOGUES: Ey, S. and E. Hock: De mechanisch dansende Figur van V. H. Utrecht 1984.– Ex, S. and E. Hock: V. H. Schilder en ontwerper 1884-1960. Utrecht 1985

IGNATOVICH Boris
1899 Loutzk (Ukraine) – **1976** Moscow
Ukranian photographer. **1918–1921** Worked for various newspapers in Kharkov. **1919** Editor of the journal *Krasnaia Bachkria*. **1923** Studied photographic techniques with Rodchenko. **1926** Head of the Photoreporters' Association in Moscow. **1926–1930** Photographed for various newspapers and journals, including *Ogonyok*, and published the magazine *Bednota*. **1932–1939** Worked on a number of documentary films. **1941–1943** War correspondent. **1945** Worked as a photographer with the *Soyuzfoto* Agency. Experimented with colour photography. **1969** Publication of *The National Collection of Weapons in the Kremlin*. Ignatovich's photographs document many historical events and personalities.
MONOGRAPHS, CATALOGUES: Volkov-Lannit, L.: B. I. Moscow 1973

IMMENDORFF Jörg
born **1945** Bleckede
German painter. **1963/64** Studied theatrical set design at the Düsseldorf Academy. Joined Beuys' class. **1965/66** Happenings with social and political content at the Academy. **1968/69** Appeared under the name of *Lidl* in political rallies in Düsseldorf and other cities. Later began to produce pictures and posters heavily influenced by social realism. **1972** and **1982** took part in documenta 5 and 7 in Kassel. **1976**

Organised happenings in East Berlin with A. R. Penck. **1978** Started work on *Café Deutschland*, a series of paintings, rich in allusive symbolism, on the theme of divided Germany. **1979** Took part in "Initiative für eine bunte Liste". **1981** Guest-professor at the Academy in Stockholm. **1982/83** Taught at the College of Plastic Arts, Hamburg. **1997** Received the world's most lucrative award, the Marco Prize from the Museo de arte contemporáneo in Monterrey (Mexico). Immendorff stands for politically active art. WRITINGS: J. I.: Lidlstadt. Düsseldorf 1968.– J. I.: Den Eisbären mal reinhalten. Düsseldorf 1968.– J. I.: Hier und jetzt: Das tun, was zu tun ist. Cologne and New York 1973 Cologne 1990.– J. I. and A. R. Penck: Deutschland mal Deutschland. Munich 1979.– J. I. im Gespräch mit P. Kort. Cologne 1993
MONOGRAPHS, CATALOGUES: Boetzkes, M. and D. Nguy (ed.): I. Zeichnungen 1959-1989. 4 vols. Roemer-Museum, Hildesheim 1989.– Bojescul, W. (ed.): J. I. Kunstverein Braunschweig. Brunswick 1985 (cat.).– Fuchs, R. et al. (ed.): I. Langer Marsch auf Adeler. Museum Boymans-van Beuningen, Rotterdam et al. Rotterdam 1992 (cat.).– Gachnang, J. et al. (ed.): I. Kunsthaus Zurich et al. Düsseldorf 1983 (cat.).– Gohr, S. (ed.): J. I. The Rake's Progress. Stuttgart 1994.– Harten, J. and U. Krempel (ed.): J. I. Café Deutschland. Adlerhälfte. Städtische Kunsthalle Düsseldorf. Düsseldorf 1982 (cat.).– Harten, J. et al. (ed.): J. I. Kunstmuseum Wolfsburg. Stuttgart 1997.– I.'s Handbuch der Akademie für Adler. Portikus. Frankfurt-on-Main 1990 (cat.).– Koepplin, D. (ed.): J. I, Café Deutschland. Kunstmuseum Basel. Basel 1985 (cat.).– Kort, P.: J. I. Zeichnungen 1964-1993. Bern and Berlin 1994.– Schmidt, M. and J. Gachnang (ed.): J. I. Malermut rundum. Kunsthalle Bern. Bern 1980 (cat.).– Tolnay, A. (ed.): I. Malerei 1883-1990. Galerie der Stadt Esslingen, Villa Merkel. Esslingen et al. Esslingen 1991 (cat.)

INDIANA Robert
(Robert Clark)
born **1928** Newcastle (IN)
American painter. Studied at the John Herron School of Art in Indianapolis, at the Art Institute of Chicago and, while staying in Scotland **1953/54** at the Edinburgh College of Art. **1960–1962** Produced a group of Hermes figures with enormous phalli, made out of wood and metal. Made *objets trouvés*. From **1966** the word "Love" became one of his favourite motifs. **1968** Participation in documenta 4 in Kassel. **1973** Designed a postage stamp for the United States Post Office using the word and later transformed it into huge aluminium and steel sculptures. Friendship with Ellsworth Kelly in New York had an important influence on his formal language. Indiana's pictures and serigraphs are often categorized as Pop Art. He developed an individual style of Hard-Edge painting out of words, letters, and symbols.

CATALOGUE RAISONNE: Sheehan, S. (ed.): R. I. Prints. A Catalogue Raisonné 1951-1991. New York 1991
MONOGRAPHS, CATALOGUES: R. I. University Art Museum. Austin 1977 (cat.).– Katz, W. (ed.): R. I. Druckgraphik und Plakate 1961-1971/ The Prints and Posters. Stuttgart and New York 1971.– Katz, W. (ed.): R. I. Early Sculpture 1960-1962. Salma-Caro Gallery. London 1991.– McCoubrey, J. W. (ed.): R. I. Institute of Contemporary Art, Philadelphia et al. Philadelphia 1969 (cat.).– Mecklenburg, V. M. (ed.): Wood Works. Constructions by R. I. National Museum of American Art, Smithsonian Institution, Washington et al. Washington 1984 (cat.).– Weinhardt, C. J.: R. I. New York 1990

ITTEN Johannes
1888 Südern-Linden (near Thun) – **1967** Zurich
Swiss painter and art teacher. **1909–1913** Studied mathematics and attended the Ecole des Beaux-Arts in Geneva. **1913–1916** Studied under Hoelzel at the Stuttgart Academy. **1915** First abstract pictures, based on Delaunays *Formes Circulaires*. **1916** First solo-exhibition in the gallery Der Sturm in Berlin. Opening of the Itten Art School in Vienna. **1919–1923** Set up the preliminary course, teaching the general principles of form and colour, at the Weimar Bauhaus. **1926** Founded another art school in Berlin. **1931–1938** Director of Krefeld School of Textile Design. **1938** Emigration to Switzerland. Appointed director of the School and Museum of Arts and Crafts in Zurich. Director of the Museum until **1953** and of the Zurich College of Textile Design **1943–1960**. From **1949** helped to set up the Rietberg Museum, which he directed from **1952–1955**. **1961** Publication of the book *Kunst der Farbe*. Itten became known as an art teacher and colour theorist. His paintings, which run the gamut from Expressionism through Orphism to Constructivism, are a practical realisation of his theoretical research into colour.
WRITINGS: Badura-Triaska, E. (ed.): J. I. Tagebücher 1913-1919. 2 vols. Vienna 1990.– Itten, A. (ed.): J. I. Mein Vorkurs am Bauhaus. Gestaltungs- und Formenlehre. Ravensburg 1975/Design and Form. London 1964.– Itten, A. (ed.): J. I. Tagebuch. Beiträge zu einem Kontrapunkt der bildenden Kunst. Ravensburg 1980.– J. I.: Kunst der Farbe. Subjektives Erleben und objektives Erkennen als Wege zur Kunst. Ravensburg 1961/The Art of Colour. London and New York 1961, 1970.– J. I.: Elemente der bildenden Kunst. Ravensburg 1980.– Itten, A. and W. Rotzler (ed.): Werke und Schriften. Zurich 1972.– Wick, R. (ed.): J. I. Bildanalysen. Ravensburg 1988
CATALOGUES RAISONNES: Helfenstein, J. and H. Mentha (ed.): J. I. Das Frühwerk 1907-1919. Kunstmuseum Bern. Bern 1992 (cat.).– Itten, A. and W. Rotzler (ed.): J. I. Werke und Schriften. Zurich 1972 and 1978

MONOGRAPHS, CATALOGUES:
Baumhoff, A. et al. (ed.): Das frühe Bauhaus und J. I. Kunstsammlungen zu Weimar et al. Stuttgart 1994 (cat.).– Bogner, D. (ed.): J. I. Museum Moderner Kunst, Vienna et al. Vienna 1980 (cat.).– Bothe, R. et al. (ed.): Das frühe Bauhaus und J. I. Kunstsammlungen zu Weimar et al. Stuttgart 1994 (cat.).– Güse, E.-E. and N. Borger-Keweloh (ed.): J. I. Gemälde, Gouachen, Aquarelle, Tuschen, Zeichnungen. Westfälisches Landesmuseum. Münster 1980 (cat.).– Poot, J. (ed.): J. I. Het Velum. Stedelijk Museum. Amsterdam 1991 (cat.).– Tavel, H.-C. v. and J. Helfenstein (ed.): J. I. Künstler und Lehrer. Kunstmuseum Bern et al. Bern 1984 (cat.).– Thönissen, K. (ed.): J. I. und die Höhere Fachschule für textile Flächenkunst in Krefeld. Deutsches Textilmuseum. Krefeld 1992 (cat.)

JACOBSEN Robert
1912 Copenhagen – **1993** Egtved
Self-taught Danish sculptor. **1930** first wood sculptures. From **1936** began to use metal. **1940** First exhibition in the Copenhagen Autumn Salon. Friendship with Jorn and Mortensen. **1941** Stone sculptures influenced by Arp. **1947** Scholarship to Paris. Contact with the artists associated with the Salon des Réalités Nouvelles. **1949** Experimental film *Reality A*, with background music in the concrete style, in which his own iron sculptures play a key role. In the 50s, regular participation in exhibitions at the Salon de Mai, Salon de la Jeune Sculpture and the Salon des Réalités Nouvelles. After **1955** curving iron installation – sculptures bearing clear toolmarks. **1959** Participation in documenta 2 in Kassel. **1962–1981** Professor at the Munich Academy of Arts. **1966** Sculpture Prize at the Venice Biennale. **1967** Set design for the ballet *Don Juan*. Since **1970** strongly rhythmical constructions with a weightless appearance. **1984** Major retrospective at the Musée Rodin in Paris and the Musée des Beaux-Arts in Rennes.
MONOGRAPHS, CATALOGUES: Der Bildhauer R. J. und seine Welt. Kunsthalle Kiel et al. Kiel 1984 (cat.).– Descargues, P.: R. J. Passeport. Paris 1993.– Dewasne, J.: R. J. Sculpteur danois. Copenhagen 1951.– R. J. Parcours. Musées de Toulon et al. Paris 1984 (cat.).– Jespersen, G.: R. J. Oslo 1978.– Kronjäger, J. (ed.): Raum und Zeichen. Werke des Bildhauers R. J. Städtische Kunsthalle Mannheim et al. Mannheim 1987 (cat.).– Romain, L. and C. S. Weber (ed.): R. J. 2 vols. Museum Würth, Künzelsau. Sigmaringen 1992 (cat.)

JACQUET Alain
born **1939** Neuilly-sur-Seine (near Paris)
French painter. **1959/60** Studied architecture at the Ecole Nationale des Beaux-Arts in Paris. Was an actor before he became an artist. **1961** Appearance of the work *Jeu de Jacquet*, which presents the last name of the artist in the form of a backgammon board.

1962/63 Camouflage series, which also included a large-scale "camouflage" painting of a hot-dog picture by Lichtenstein; this was later cut up and sold in pieces. **1964** Started the picture series *Déjeuner sur l'Herbe*: a photographic reenactment of Manet's famous painting, using his friends as models. Preferred techniques: silkscreen and painting on plexiglas. In the late 60s he produced sculptures using apparently real but actually false materials. Since **1980** use of new media techniques, from satellite photographs to laser printing.
MONOGRAPHS, CATALOGUES: Hahn, O. (ed.): A. J. City-Galerie. Zurich 1965.– Pagé, S. and P. Restany (ed.): A. J. Donut Flight 6078. Musée d'Art Moderne de la Ville de Paris. Paris 1978 (cat.).– Restany, P.: A. J. Le Déjeuner sur l'herbe 1964-1989, 25e anniversaire. Paris 1989.– Smith, D.: A. J. Paris 1990

JANCO Marcel
(Marcel Iancu)
1895 Bucharest – **1984** Tel Aviv
Romanian painter and architect. **1910–1914** Studied painting under Josef Istler. **1912** Publication with Tristan Tzara and Ion Vinea of the journal *Simbolul*. **1915** Studied architecture in Zurich. **1916** Together with Hugo Ball, Richard Huelsenbeck, Tristan Tzara, Hans Arp and others, started up the *Cabaret Voltaire* and produced masks and decorations for its dadaist productions. Began abstract painting. **1917–1919** Work on abstract plaster reliefs. **1919** Founding of the Artists Radicaux group together with Arp, Richter, Eggeling, Giacometti and others. **1921** Moved to Romania, where he published the magazine *Contimporanul*. From **1926** architectural commissions. **1941** Emigration to Israel. **1953** Founding of the El Hod artists' colony. **1959** Retrospective at the Tel Aviv Museum. Participation in numerous retrospectives of the Dada Movement. **1982** Opening of the Marcel Janco Museum in the El Hod artists' colony. Janco, who combined the expressive power of folk art with Dadaism, can be considered the forerunner of modern art in Romania.
MONOGRAPHS, CATALOGUES: Enache, V. M.: M. J. in Romania. Diss. Bucharest 1976.– M. J. Tel Aviv Museum. Tel Aviv 1972 (cat.).– M. J. Tel Aviv Museum. Tel

Aviv 1982 (cat.).– Mendelson, M. L.: M. J. Tel Aviv 1962.– Seiwert, H.: M. J. Dadaist, Zeitgenosse, wohltemperierter morgenländischer Konstruktivist. Frankfurt-on-Main 1993.– Seuphor, M.: M. J. St. Gallen 1963

JAVLENSKY Alexei von
1864 Torschok (Russia) – **1941** Wiesbaden
Russian painter. **1882–1896** Military service as an officer, while continuing (from **1889**) his art studies at the Academy in St. Petersburg. **1896** Moved, together with Marianne von Verefkin, to Munich, where he attended Azbè's private art school and became friends with Kandinsky. **1903** Participation in the exhibition of the Berlin Secession. **1907** Acquainted with Matisse in Paris. **1909** Co-founder of the Neue Künstlervereinigung (New Artists' Association) in Munich. Resignation from the NKVM and participation in the exhibition of the Blauer Reiter. **1912** Takes part in the Sonderbund Exhibition in Cologne and the first show of the Blauer Reiter in Berlin, in Walden's gallery Der Sturm. Acquaintance with Nolde. Lived from **1914–1921** in exile in Switzerland. Separated in **1921** from Verefkin and moved to Wiesbaden. **1929** Founded the group Die Blauen Vier with Kandinsky, Klee and Feininger. First signs of paralysis. **1933** Forbidden to exhibit. **1937** 72 of his works classified as "degenerate art" and confiscated. **1938** Became totally paralysed. An increasing emphasis on religion in his late works reached a climax in his *Meditations*, in which the human face becomes an icon to be regarded with spiritual fervour.
CATALOGUES RAISONNES: Jawlensky, M. et al. (ed.): A. J. Catalogue Raisonné of the Oil Paintings, Watercolours and Drawings. 4 vols. London and Munich 1991-1998.– Rosenbach, D. (ed.): A. v. J. Leben und druckgraphisches Werk. Hanover 1985
MONOGRAPHS, CATALOGUES: Chiappini, R. (ed.): A. J. Pinacoteca Communale, Casa Rusca, Locarno. Milan 1989 (cat.).– Demetrion, J. T. (ed.): A. J. A Centennial Exhibition. Pasadena Art Museum. Pasadena 1964 (cat.).– Eichhorn, H. (ed.): A. v. J. Gemälde, Aquarelle, Zeichnungen. Städtische Galerie. Bietigheim-Bissingen 1994 (cat.).– Fäthke, B. (ed.): A. J. Zeichnungen, Graphik, Dokumente. Landesmuseum Wiesbaden. Wiesbaden 1983 (cat.).– Mochon, A. (ed.): A. J. From Appearance to Essence. Long Beach Museum of Art. Long Beach 1991 (cat.).– Moutashar, M. and A. Charron (ed.): A. v. J. Espace Van Gogh. Arles 1993 (cat.).– Rathke, E.: A. J. Hanau 1968.– Rattemeyer, V. (ed.): A. v. J. zum 50. Todesjahr. Gemälde und graphische Arbeiten. Landesmuseum Wiesbaden. Wiesbaden 1991 (cat.).– Rattemeyer, V. et al. (ed.): A. v. J. Museum Boymans-van Beuningen, Rotterdam 1994 (cat.).– Schampers, K.: A. v. J. Washington 1995.– Schultze, J.: A. J. Cologne 1970.– Weiler, C.: A. v. J. Der Maler und Mensch. Wiesbaden 1955.– Weiler, C.: A. J. Cologne

1959.– Weiler, C.: A. J. Köpfe, Gesichter, Meditationen. Hanau 1970.– Zweite, A. (ed.): A. J. 1894-1941. Städtische Galerie im Lenbachhaus, Munich et al. Munich 1983 (cat.)

JENNEY Neil
born **1945** Torrington (CT)
American painter. **1964–1966** Studied at the Massachusetts College of Art in Boston. Moved to New York. After an early minimalist phase in the early 60s, Jenney developed a more strongly substantive painting style, eclectically mixing styles and eras, which culminated in his so-called *Bad Paintings* of **1969–1971**. **1972** Participation in documenta 5 in Kassel. As a form of Concept Art, created simple narrative pictures often involving a play on words and set in severe frames. After these attempts to connect art and language, Jenney put more emphasis on the picture frame: picture fragments and cropped close-ups are set in massive black frames, like an architrave. **1980** Participation at the Venice Biennale. At the beginning of the 80s, the artist chose a narrow horizontal format, like a viewing slit, for his socially critical pictures, which document the destruction of the natural habitat.
MONOGRAPHS, CATALOGUES: N. J. The Museum of Modern Art. New York 1991 (cat.).– Rosenthal, M. (ed.): N. J. University Art Museum. Berkleley 1981 (cat.).– Yonkers, N. Y. (ed.): N. J. Hudson River Museum 1985 (cat.)

JENSEN Alfred
1903 Guatemala – **1981** Livingston (NJ)
Danish-American painter and concept artist. **1924–1925** Studied at the San Diego Fine Arts School, **1926–1928** at the Hofmann School in Munich, and from **1930** at the Académie Scandinave in Paris. **1938** Developed J. W. v. Goethe's *Theory of Colour* in diagrams through which he investigated light and colour values. **1951** Moved to New York. **1952** First solo-exhibition in the John Heller Gallery, New York. **1957** First murals. **1958** Taught at the Maryland Institute in Baltimore. **1961** Exhibition at the Guggenheim Museum in New York. **1964** and **1972** participation in documenta 3 and 5 in Kassel. **1974–1976** Works based on numerical systems and phenomena based on cyclical patterns, incorporating the theories of Michael Faraday. **1977** Participant at the São Paulo Biennale. **1978** Retrospective at the Albright-Knox Art Gallery, Buffalo. After an early phase of gestural abstraction, Jensen developed a geometric, abstract painting style combining colour analysis with numerical mysticism.
MONOGRAPHS, CATALOGUES: Cathcart, L. and M. Tucker (ed.): A. J. Paintings and Diagrams from the Years 1957-1977. Albright-Knox Art Gallery. Buffalo 1978 (cat.).– Schjeldahl, P. and M. Reidelbach (ed.): A. J. Solomon R. Guggenheim Museum. New York 1985 (cat.).– Schmied,

W. et al. (ed.): A. J. Kestner-Gesellschaft, Hanover et al. Hanover 1973 (cat.)

JETELOVA Magdalena
born **1946** Semil
Czech sculptress. **1965–1971** Attended the Academy of Art in Prague. **1967/68** Studied under Marini at the Accademia di Brera in Milan. **1984** Scholarship awarded by the city of Munich to the Villa Waldberta. **1986** Prizewinner in the *dimension V* competition. Grant from the city of Munich. First laser projection projects for removing existing space boundaries and creating new spacial orientation points. Exploration of the opposites Rationality and Irrationality, Stability and Instability in room-oriented sculptures, like *Steps, Chairs, Doors, and Houses.* **1987** Participant in documenta 8 in Kassel. **1988** Visiting professor at the Art Academy in Munich. Solo-exhibition in the Hamburg Kunsthalle. **1989** Professor at the summer academy in Salzburg. From **1990** professor at the National Art Academy in Düsseldorf. Multi-layered and associative installations in Plymouth, Halifax, Vienna, and Prague between **1990** and **1993** which incorporate architecture and landscape. Jetelová's complex artistic philosophy combines elements of Constructivism with features of Arte Povera and Land Art.
MONOGRAPHS, CATALOGUES: Guthbrod, H. (ed.): M. J. Multi Purposes – Zwischen den Stühlen. Karlsruhe 1997 (cat.).– M. J. Sculpture. Riverside Studios. London 1986 (cat.).– M. J. Staatliche Kunsthalle Baden-Baden. Baden-Baden 1987 (cat.).– M. J. Skulpturen. Städtische Galerie. Göppingen 1990 (cat.).– M. J. The Henry Moore Sculpture Trust Studio. Manchester 1991 (cat.).– M. J. Belveder, Royal Garden of the Prague Castle, Prague. Munich 1993 (cat.).– M. J. Kunstverein Hannover. Hanover 1994 (cat.).– Wolbert, K. (ed.): M. J. Orte und Räume. Mathildenhöhe, Darmstadt. Stuttgart 1996

JOCHIMS Raimer
born **1935** Kiel
German painter and art theoretician. During his philosophy and art history studies, he began as of **1955** to study painting as well. Developed his own conceptual identity after **1961** through work on his

chromatic pictures and fading pictures, which portray fluctuations between colour and surface. **1967** Taught at the Art Colleges in Karlsruhe and Munich. After **1971** professor for painting and art theory at the Art College in Frankfurt. **1973/74** Production of single and series works using plywood and torn paper, focusing on forms of colour. After **1979** production of painting books. **1986–1988** Exploration of the interplay of colour and form.
WRITINGS: R. J.: Visuelle Identität. Frankfurt-on-Main 1975
MONOGRAPHS, CATALOGUES: Bauermeister, V. et al. (ed.): R. J. Klagenfurt 1987 (cat.).– Boehm, G. et al. (ed.): R. J. Bilder/Paintings 1961-1993. Kunstmuseum Bonn. Stuttgart 1994 (cat.).– R. J. Arbeiten 1961-1975. Kunstmuseum Bonn et al. Bonn 1975 (cat.).– R. J. Bilder, Papierarbeiten R. J. Zueignung. Dichtung und Malerei, Zyklen von Papierarbeiten 1982-1988. Goethe-Museum. Frankfurt-on-Main 1990 (cat.)

JOHNS Jasper
born **1930** Augusta (GA)
American painter. **1947/48** Studied at the University of South Carolina. **1949** Attended art school in New York, followed by two years in the army including a posting to Japan. **1952** Returned to New York, where he earned his living selling books. **1954** Worked with Rauschenberg as a window decorator for department stores. **1956/57** Began to integrate objects into his paintings. Contact with Leo Castelli. First solo-exhibition in **1958** in the Leo Castelli Gallery in New York, generally heralded as the beginning of Pop Art. **1959** Carnegie Prize at the Pittsburgh Biennale. Participated in a happening with Kaprow. **1960** First lithographs; later, further graphic works for ULAE (Universal Limited Art Edition). **1961** Set designs and costumes for the Merce Cunningham Dance Company. Collaboration with the composer John Cage. **1963** Set up a foundation for contemporary performance art. Between **1964** and **1977** participation in documenta 3 – 6 in Kassel. **1967** Prize at the São Paulo Biennale. **1975** Illustrations for Beckett's *Fizzles/Foirades*. **1988** Important prize for painting at the Venice Biennale. Together with Rauschenberg, Johns is considered one of the artists who brought key innovations to modern art after Abstract Expressionism. His paintings draw on a relatively narrow repertoire of images, for example the American flag, letters, numbers or targets. He also produced assemblages of real objects as well as commonplace objects which he encased in molten metal (sculpmetals).
WRITINGS: Hollevoet, C. and K. Varnedoe (ed.): J. J. Writings, Sketchbooks, Notes, Interviews. New York 1996.– Stemmrich, G. (ed.): J. J. Interviews, Statements, Skizzenbuchnotizen. Dresden 1997
CATALOGUES RAISONNES: Field, R. S. et al. (ed.): The Prints of J. J. 1960-1993. A Catalogue Raisonné. 3 vols. West Islip

(NY) 1994.– Huber, C. (ed.): J. J. Graphik. Bern 1970
MONOGRAPHS, CATALOGUES: Bernstein, R.: J. J. Paintings and Sculptures 1954-1974. Ann Arbor (MI) 1985.– Boudaille, G.: J. J. Paris 1991, Recklinghausen 1991.– Cage, J. et al. (ed.): Echo and Allusion in the Art of J. J. Grunwald Center at the University of California. Los Angeles 1987.– Castelli, L.: J. J. Paris 1997.– Castleman, R. (ed.): J. J. A Print Retrospective. The Museum of Modern Art. New York 1986 (cat.)/J. J. Die Druckgraphik. Munich 1986 (cat.).– Chalumeau, J.-L. (ed.): J. J. Paris 1995.– Crichton, M. (ed.): J. J. Whitney Museum of American Art, New York et al. New York 1977 (cat.)/J. J. Museum Ludwig in der Joseph-Haubrich-Kunsthalle. Cologne 1978 (cat.).– Crichton, M.: J. J. London and New York 1977, 1994.– Francis, R.: J. J. New York 1984, Munich 1985.– Field, R.: J. J. Prints 1960-1981. San Francisco 1981.– Geelhaar, C. (ed.): J. J. Working Proofs. Kunstmuseum Basel. Basel 1979 (cat.).– Hulten, P. et al. (ed.): J. J. Centre Georges Pompidou. Paris 1978 (cat.).– J. J. Museum Ludwig. Cologne 1984 (cat.).– Johnston, J.: J. J. Privileged Information. London 1996.– Kozloff, M.: J. J. New York 1967.– Orton, F.: Figuring J. J. London 1994, Cambridge (MA) 1996.– Rosenthal, M. (ed.): J. J. Work Since 1974. Philadelphia Museum of Art. New York 1988 (cat.).– Rosenthal, N. and R. E. Fine (ed.): The Drawings of J. J. National Gallery of Art, Washington et al. London 1990 (cat.).– Shapiro, D.: J. J. Drawings 1954-1984. New York 1984.– Steinberg, L.: J. J. New York 1963.– Varnedoe, K. et al. (ed.): J. J. A Retrospective. The Museum of Modern Art, New York et al. New York 1996 (cat.)/J. J. Eine Retrospektive. Museum Ludwig, Cologne et al. Munich 1997 (cat.)

JONAS Joan
born **1936** New York
American performance and video artist. Until **1972** studied at various institutes, including the Boston Museum School, Columbia University and the Video School of Visual Arts in New York. First performances during her student days. Production of the film *Wind* in collaboration with Peter Camput. **1971** First video works together with Serra. **1964–1987** Participation in documenta 5 – 8 in Kassel. **1974** Taught at Princeton University, New Jersey, and at Yale University, New Haven. **1975** Teacher at the Otis Art Institute, Los Angeles. **1982** DAAD scholarship to Berlin. **1982/83** Branched out into video, film, dance, and environment-like stage sets in the performance *He Saw Her Burning*. **1987** Performance *Volcano Saga*, produced after a trip to Iceland. Jonas, who attempts to explode our stereotype perception through her video works, deals in her later performances with female roles and the female body.
MONOGRAPHS, CATALOGUES: Block, R. (ed.): J. J. He Saw Her Burning. Video-

installation, Videobänder, Zeichnungen. Daadgalerie. Berlin 1984 (cat.).– Crimp, D. (ed.): J. J. Scripts and Descriptions 1968-1982. University Art Museum, Berkeley et al. Berkeley 1983 (cat.).– Mignot, D. (ed.): J. J. Works 1968-1994. Stedelijk Museum. Amsterdam 1994 (cat.)

JONES Allen
born **1937** Southampton
English painter. Studied **1955–1959** at the Hornsey College of Art in London and then for a year with Kitaj and Hockney at the Royal College of Art. **1961–1964** Taught lithography at Croydon College of Art and drawing at the Chelsea School of Art. **1964** and **1968** participation in documenta 3 and 4 in Kassel. **1968–1983** Visiting professorships at the Hamburg Academy of the Arts, at the University of South Florida in Tampa, at the University of Los Angeles and at the Berlin Art Academy. **1984/85** Commission to do a sculpture for the Frederick R. Weisman Foundation in Los Angeles. **1986–1990** Further public commissions for steel sculptures. **1991** Design for a telephone card for the Pop Art exhibition at the Royal Academy in London. **1992/93** Large steel sculpture for the Chelsea and Westminster Hospital theatre and health project. Jones is one of the best-known exponents of English Pop Art. He used sex magazines and underground pornographic literature as models for his lascivious female figures in the form of furniture.
CATALOGUE RAISONNE: Lloyd, R. (ed.): A. J. Prints. London 1995
MONOGRAPHS, CATALOGUES: Jencks, C. et al. (ed.): A. J. London 1993.– A. J. Waddington Art Galleries. London 1993 (cat.).– A. J. Kunsthalle. Darmstadt 1996 (cat.).– Livingstone, M.: Sheer Magic by A. J. London and New York 1979.– Livingstone, M.: A. J. Retrospective of Paintings 1957-1978. Walker Art Gallery, Liverpool et al. London 1979 (cat.).– Peters, H.-A. et al. (ed.): A. J. A Retrospective of Paintings 1957-1978. An Exhibition. Walker Art Gallery, Liverpool et al. Liverpool and Baden-Baden 1979 (cat.).– Stünke, H.: A. J. Das graphische Werk. Cologne 1969

JORN Asger
(Asger Oluf Jorgensen)
1914 Vejrum (Jutland) – **1973** Århus
Danish painter. Moved in **1929** to Silkeborg, where he began to paint. Designed large decorations, in collaboration with Léger, for Le Corbusier's Pavillon des Temps Nouveaux at the **1937** Paris World Fair. **1938** First solo-exhibiton in Copenhagen of paintings full of imagery and fantastic figures inspired by Ernst and Klee. **1941** Co-founder of the magazine *Helhesten*. **1947** Participated at the Conference of the Surréalistes Révolutionnaires in Brussels. **1948** Founded the Cobra group, along with Appel, Constant, Corneille, Dotremont and Noiret. **1949** First large Cobra exhibition at the Stedelijk Museum, Amsterdam. **1959**

and **1964** participation in documenta 2 and 3 in Kassel. Up until **1961** he wrote manifestos for the Situationistische Internationale, a group of anarchistic artists who were against capitalist functionalism. **1963** Founding of the Institute for Comparative Vandalism, whose sole purpose was to collect graffiti and assess their artistic worth. **1964** Rejection of the Guggenheim Prize. Worked with décollage and torn paper. **1970–1972** Resumed painting and began bronze and marble sculptures. **1973** Major retrospective at the Kestner Society in Hanover. Jorn's expressive gestural pictures, full of demonic, mythical creatures, constitute a northern variety of Abstract Expressionism.
WRITINGS: Hofman Hansen, P.: Bibliografi over A. J.'s skrifter. Silkeborg 1988.– A. J.: Guldhorn og lykkehjul. Copenhagen 1957.– A. J.: Pour la forme. Paris 1958/Plädoyer für die Form. Entwurf einer Methodologie der Kunst. Munich 1990, 1997.– A. J.: Gedanken eines Künstlers. Munich 1966, 1997.– A. J.: La Langue verte et la cuite. Etude gastrophonique sur la marmythologie musiculinaire. Paris 1968.– A. J.: Folke kunstens Didrek. Copenhagen 1978.– A. J.: Fin de Copenhague. Paris 1995
CATALOGUES RAISONNES: Atkins, G. (ed.): A. J. Catalogue Raisonné. 4 vols. London and New York 1986.– Loo, O. v. de (ed.): A. J. Werkverzeichnis Druckgrafik. Munich 1976.– Rasmussen, M. (ed.): A. J.'s tegninger. Silkeborg 1983
MONOGRAPHS, CATALOGUES: Andersen, T.: A. J. 1914-1973. A Catalogue of Works in the Silkeborg Kunstmuseum. Silkeborg 1974.– Andersen, T.: A. J. Solomon R. Guggenheim Museum. New York 1982 (cat.).– Andersen, T.: A. J. En biografi. Copenhagen 1994.– Andersen, T. et al. (ed.): A. J. 1914-1973. A. J. Stedelijk Museum. Amsterdam 1994 (cat.).– Atkins, G. and E. Schmidt (ed.): A Bibliography of A. J.'s Writings to 1963. Copenhagen 1964.– Atkins, G. and T. Andersen: J. in Scandinavia 1930-1953. London 1968.– Atkins, G.: A. J. The Crucial Years 1954-1964. London 1976.– Atkins, G.: A. J. The Final Years 1965-1973. London 1980.– Birtwistle, G.: Living Art. A. J.'s Comprehensive Theory of Art Between Helhesten and Cobra. Utrecht 1986.– Caprile, L. et al. (ed.): A. J. 2 vols. Milan 1996.– De Micheli, M.: J. scultore. Torino 1974.– Jansen, P. H.: Bibliografi over A. J.'s skrifter. Silkeborg 1988.– A. J. Stedelijk Museum. Amsterdam 1964 (cat.).– A. J. Musée des Beaux-Arts. Nîmes. 1987 (cat.).– A. J. Pinacoteca Casa Rusca, Locarno. Milan 1996 (cat.).– Lehmann, H.-U.: A. J. 1914-1973. Das graphische Werk. Die Schenkung Otto van de Loo. Kupferstich-Kabinett der Staatlichen Kunstsammlungen Dresden im Albertinum et al. Dresden 1994 (cat.).– Loo, O. v. d. (ed.): A. J. in München. Dokumentation seines malerischen Werks. Munich 1997.– Messer, T. M. (ed.): A. J. Retrospektive. Schirn Kunsthalle. Frankfurt-on-Main 1994 (cat.).– Schade, V.: A. J. Copenhagen 1968.– Schmied, W.: J. St. Gallen 1973.–

Schmied, W. (ed.): A. J. Kestner-Gesellschaft, Hanover et al. Berlin 1973 (cat.).– Zweite, A. (ed.): A. J. 1914-1973. Gemälde, Zeichnungen, Aquarelle, Gouachen, Skulpturen. Städtische Galerie im Lenbachhaus. Munich 1987 (cat.)

JUDD Donald
1928 Excelsior Springs (MO) – **1994** New York

American sculptor. **1948–1953** Studied art at the Art Students League, New York. **1957–1962** Studied philosophy and art history under Rudolf Wittkower and Meyer Schapiro at Columbia University, New York. **1959–1965** Worked as art critic for various magazines. **1961** Gave up painting to make relief pictures and free-standing wood and metal objects. **1962–1964** Teacher at the Brooklyn Institute of Arts and Sciences, New York. **1967** Teaching fellowship at Yale University. Between **1968** and **1987** participation in documenta 4, 6 and 7 in Kassel. From **1970** his sculptures were more and more influenced by their architectural environment and began to take on the form and function of furniture. From **1973** worked on the construction and design of a large building complex in Marfa, Texas in conjunction with other artists, including Oldenburg and Kabakov. **1976** Appointed Baldwin Professor at Oberlin College, Ohio. **1986** Permanent installation, consisting of variations on an aluminium box module, to mark the opening of the Chinati Foundation in Marfa. **1987** Awarded the Skowhegan and the Brandeis University medals for sculpture. **1988** Retrospective at the Whitney Museum, New York. His minimal, factory-made and serially arranged sculptural works have established Judd as a leading exponent of Minimal Art.
WRITINGS: D. J.: Complete Writings 1959-1975. New York and Halifax 1976.– D. J.: Complete Writings 1975-1986. Eindhoven 1987.– D. J.: Ecrits 1963-1990. Paris 1991
CATALOGUES RAISONNES: Cowel, W. and J.-A. Birnie Danzker (ed.): D. J. Furniture. Museum Boymans-van Beuningen, Rotterdam et al. New York 1993 (cat.).– Schellmann, J. and M. J. Jitta (ed.): D. J. Prints and Works in Editions. A Catalogue Raisonné. Cologne and Munich 1993, 1997.– Smith, B. and D. d. Balso (ed.): D. J. Catalogue Raisonné of Paintings, Objects and Wood-Blocks 1960-1974. National Gallery of Canada. Ottawa 1975 (cat.)
MONOGRAPHS, CATALOGUES: Bois, Y.-A.: D. J. Paris 1991.– Foster, H. (ed.): D. J. Sculpture, Prints, Furniture. Lisbon 1997 (cat.).– Fuchs, R. and R. Crone (ed.): D. J. Stedelijk Van Abbe Museum, Eindhoven et al. Eindhoven 1987 (cat.).– Fuchs, R. et al. (ed.): D. J. Spaces. Stankowski Foundation. Stuttgart 1994.– Haskell, B. (ed.): D. J. Whitney Museum of American Art, New York et al. New York 1988 (cat.).– D. J. Pasadena Art Museum. Pasadena 1971 (cat.).– D. J. Skulpturen. Kunsthalle Bern. Bern 1976 (cat.).– D. J. Retrospective. Museum Boymans-van Beuningen, Rotter-

dam et al. Rotterdam 1993 (cat.).– D. J. Räume – Spaces. Kunst + Design. Landesmuseum Wiesbaden. Stuttgart 1994 (cat.).– Koepplin, D. (ed.): D. J. Zeichnungen/Drawings 1956-1976. Kunstmuseum Basel et al. Basel 1976.– Petzinger, R. and H. Dannenberger (ed.): Kunst und Design. D. J. Landesmuseum Wiesbaden et al. Stuttgart 1993 (cat.).– Poetter, J. (ed.): D. J. Staatliche Kunsthalle Baden-Baden. Stuttgart 1989 (cat.).– Smith, B. (ed.): D. J. The National Gallery of Canada. Ottawa 1975 (cat.).– Stockebrand, M. (ed.): D. J. Architektur. Westfälischer Kunstverein. Münster 1989, Stuttgart 1992 (cat.)

KABAKOV Ilya
born **1933** Dnjepropetrovsk (Ukraine)
Russian environment and installation artist. **1951–1957** Studied graphics at the Surikov Art Institute in Moscow. From **1956** worked as a book illustrator, illustrating over 100 books. **1955** Began to work as an independent artist. **1965** Joined the Artists Union of the USSR. **1970–1978** Put together albums of his drawings. Kabakov invented Expo Art with his environment-type spaces in which he placed souvenirs from his youth together with commonplace objects from everyday life in Russia in ironic and suggestive arrangements. **1978–1982** Large murals entitled *Schek Art*, in Socialist Realist style. **1982/83** Fictitious exhibition at the Pushkin Museum, Moscow ("Fly With Wings"). **1988** Took part in the Venice Biennale and, **1992**, in documenta 9 in Kassel. Moved to New York. **1993** Represented Russia at the Venice Biennale. Guest-professor in Frankfurt am Main.
WRITINGS: I. K. and B. Groys: Die Kunst des Fliehens. Dialoge über Angst, das heilige Weiß und den sowjetischen Müll. Munich and Vienna 1991.– I. K. and B. Groys: Die Kunst der Installation. Munich 1996.– I. K.: Les Souvenirs de la cuisine communautaire. Galerie Dina Vierny. Paris 1992 (cat.).– I. K.: SHEK 8, Bauman Bezirk, Stadt Moskau. Ed. by G. Hirt and Sascha Wonders. Leipzig 1994.– I. K.: Über die "totale" Installation. On the "Total" Installation. Stuttgart 1995
MONOGRAPHS, CATALOGUES: Groys, B. (ed.): I. K. Das Leben der Fliegen. Kölnischer Kunstverein. Stuttgart 1992 (cat.).– Groys, B. et al. (ed.): I. K. The Garbage Man. Oslo 1996 (cat.).– Jaukkuri, M. et al. (ed.): I. K. 5 albumia Installaatio Leikkaussali. Nykytaiteen Museo. Helsinki 1994 (cat.).– I. K. Vor dem Abendessen. Grazer Kunstverein. Graz 1988 (cat.).– I. K. Que sont ces petits hommes? Galerie de France, Paris et al. Paris 1989 (cat.).– I. K. Fliege mit Flügeln. Installation. Kunstverein Hannover. Hanover 1991 (cat.).– I. K. Night Lines. Centraal Museum. Utrecht 1991 (cat.).– I. K. We are Leaving Here Forever. Installation. Carnegie Museum. Pittsburgh 1991 (cat.).– I. K. Het grote archief. Stedelijk Museum. Amsterdam 1993 (cat.).– I. K. Incident in the Museum or Water Music. Museum of Contemporary Art,

Chicago et al. Chicago 1993 (cat.)/Zwischenfall im Museum oder Wassermusik. Hessisches Landesmuseum, Darmstadt et al. Darmstadt 1994 (cat.).– I. K. Lesesaal. The Reading Room. Deichtorhallen. Hamburg 1996 (cat.).– I. K. On the Roof. Palais des Beaux-Arts, Brussels et al. Düsseldorf 1997 (cat.).– Lingwood, J. (ed.): I. K. Ten Charakters. Institute of Contemporary Arts, London et al. London 1989 (cat.).– Martin, J.-H. and C. Jolles (ed.): I. K. Kunsthalle Bern et al. Bern 1985 (cat.).– Martin, J.-H. et al. (ed.): I. K. Installations 1983-1995. Centre Georges Pompidou. Paris 1995 (cat.).– Vischer, T. (ed.): I. K. Ein Meer von Stimmen. Museum für Gegenwartskunst, Basel. Stuttgart 1995 (cat.).– Wallach, A.: I. K. The Man Who Never Threw Anything Away. New York 1996

KAHLO Frida
(Magdalena Carmen Frieda Kahlo Calderón)
1907 Coyoacán (Mexico City) –
1954 Coyoacán
Mexican painter. **1925** Suffered serious back injuries at the age of 17 as a result of a car accident, necessitating repeated operations throughout her life. **1928** Joined the Mexican Communist Party and met her future husband, the painter Rivera. **1932** Moved to the USA for two years, where Rivera executed several murals. **1938** First solo-exhibition in New York. Acquaintanceship with Breton, who was travelling in Mexico and wanted to meet Leon Trotsky, who was living in Kahlo's house. **1939** During a trip to Paris, she met several of the important surrealist painters and poets. From **1943** taught drawing at the La Esmeralda school of painting and sculpture; along with her favorite students she started the Los Fridos group. **1946** Awarded the National Prize for Painting. In the late 40s, her health deteriorated rapidly; she had to wear a steel corset and could only get around in a wheelchair. **1953** First solo-exhibition in Mexico City at the Lola Alvarez Bravo gallery. A year later she died after a leg amputation. In her highly personal pictures, close to folk art, Kahlo, the incarnation of the surrealist woman, expresses the convulsive beauty of the injured body and suffering soul.
WRITINGS: Fuentes, C. (ed.): The Diary of F. K. An Intimate Self-Portrait. New York 1995.– F. K.: Le Journal de F. K. Paris 1995/Gemaltes Tagebuch. Munich 1995
CATALOGUES RAISONNES: Herrera, H. (ed.): F. K. The Paintings. London 1991/F. K. Die Gemälde 1926-1954. Munich 1992.– Prignitz-Poda, H. et al. (ed.): F. K. Das Gesamtwerk. Frankfurt-on-Main 1988
MONOGRAPHS, CATALOGUES: Billeter, E. (ed.): Das Blaue Haus. Die Welt der F. K. Schirn Kunsthalle, Frankfurt-on-Main et al. Bern 1993 (cat.).– Billeter, E. (ed.): The World of F. K. The Blue House. Museum of Fine Arts, Houston. Washington 1994 (cat.).– Conde, T. Del: Vida de F. K. Mexico City 1976.– Drucker, M.: F. K. Torment and Triumph in Her Life and Art. New York 1991.– García, R.: F. K. A Bibli-

ography. Berkely 1983.– Herrera, H.: Frida. A Biography of F. K. New York 1983.– Jamis, R.: F. K. Un portrait d' une femme. 1985.– Ketchum, W. C.: F. K. New York 1997.– Lowe, S. M.: F. K. New York 1991.– Salber, L.: F. K. Reinbek 1997.– Tibol, R.: F. K. Crónica, testimonios y aproximaciones. Mexico City 1977.– Tibol, R. F. K. Frankfurt-on-Main 1980/F. K. Una vida abierta. Mexico City 1983/F. K. An Open Life. Albuquerque (NM) 1993.– Ullán, J.-M. (ed.): F. K. Salas Pablo Ruiz Picasso. Madrid 1985 (cat.).– Zamora, M.: F. K. The Brush of Anguish. San Francisco 1990/F. K. Paris 1992

KANDINSKY Wassily
1866 Moscow – **1944** Neuilly-sur-Seine (near Paris)
Russian painter and art theoretician. **1886–1892** Studied law in Moscow. **1893** Taught at Moscow University. **1896** Moved to Munich. **1897** Attended the private school run by Anton Azbè. Transferred in **1900** to the Munich Academy to study under Franz von Stuck. **1901** Co-founder of the artists' group Phalanx. **1902** Meeting with Münter. **1903–1908** Trips with Münter to Italy, France, Switzerland, Tunisia and Russia. **1908** Returned to Munich, acquaintance with Werefkin and Javlensky; first study trip to Murnau. **1909** Chairman of the Neue Künstlervereinigung (New Artists' Association) in Munich. Moved with Münter to Murnau. Influenced by the Fauves and discovered Bavarian glass painting. **1910** Friendship with Marc. **1911** Resigned from the Neue Künstlervereinigung and set up, with Marc, the editorial committee of the Blauer Reiter. **1912** Published the book *Concerning the Spiritual in Art* and the Blauer Reiter almanac. **1913** First abstract watercolour painting, later predated to **1910**. Participated in the First German Autumn Salon in Berlin. **1914** Returned to Russia on the outbreak of war. **1916** Final separation from Münter. **1918** Professor at the State Art Workshops in Moscow. **1921** Co-founder of the Academy of Artistic Sciences in Moscow. **1822-1933** Teacher at the Bauhaus in Weimar and Dessau. **1924** Co-founder of the group Die Blauen Vier, with Feininger, Klee and Javlensky. **1926** Publication of his book *Point and Line to Plane*. **1928** Took German citizenship. **1933** Moved to Paris. **1939** Became a French citizen. In his last years, he came closer to Arp and Miró and began to favour organic forms and a brighter palette.
WRITINGS: W. K.: Über das Geistige in der Kunst. Munich 1911/W. K.: Du spirituel dans l'art et dans la peinture en particulier. Paris 1988/W. K. Concerning the Spiritual in Art. New York 1972.– W. K. and F. Marc (ed.): Der Blaue Reiter. Munich 1912/The Blaue Reiter Almanac. New York 1974.– W. K.: Klänge. Munich 1912.– W. K.: Punkt und Linie zur Fläche. Munich 1926/Point and Line to Plane. New York 1947/Point et ligne sur plan. Contribution à l'analyse des éléments de la peinture.

Paris 1991.– W. K.: Essays über Kunst und Künstler. Ed. by M. Bill. Stuttgart 1955.– W. K.: Regards sur le passé et autres textes 1912-1921. Paris 1974.– W. K.: Correspondances avec Zervos et Kojève. Ed. by C. Derouet. Paris 1992.– W. K. and A. Schöneberg: Der Briefwechsel. Ed. by J. Hahl-Koch. Stuttgart 1993.– Lankheit, K. (ed.): W. K. und F. Marc. Briefwechsel. Munich 1983.– Lindsay, K. C. and P. Vergo (ed.): K. Complete Writings on Art. 2 vols. Boston 1982.– Roethel, K. and J. Hahl-Koch (ed.): K. Die gesammelten Schriften. Bern 1980.– Sers, P. (ed.): W. K.: Ecrits complets. 3 vols. Paris 1970
CATALOGUES RAISONNES: Barnett, V. E. (ed.): K. Watercolors. Catalogue Raisonné. 2 vols. London and New York 1992-1993/K. Werkverzeichnis der Aquarelle 1900-1944. 2 vols. Munich 1992-1993. Catalogue raisonné des aquarelles. 2 vols. Paris 1992-1993.– Roethel, H. K. (ed.): K. Das graphische Werk. Cologne 1970.– Roethel, H. K. and J. K. Benjamin (ed.): K. Werkverzeichnis der Ölgemälde. 2 vols. Munich 1982-1984/K. Catalogue raisonné de l'œuvre de K. 2 vols. Paris 1982-1984/K. Catalogue Raisonné of the Oil Paintings. 2 vols. London 1984-1987
MONOGRAPHS, CATALOGUES: Barnett, V. and A. Zweite (ed.): K. Aquarelle und Zeichnungen. Kunstsammlung Nordrhein-Westfalen. Munich 1992 (cat.).– Barnett, V. E. and H. Friedel (ed.): K. im Lenbachhaus. Städtische Galerie im Lenbachhaus. Munich 1995 (cat.)/W. K A Colorful Fife: The Collection of the Lenbachhaus, Munich. New York 1996 (cat.).– Bill, M.: W. K. Paris 1951.– Becks-Malorny, U.: W. K. The journey to abstraction. Cologne 1994.– Boissel, J. and C. Derouet (ed.): K. Centre Georges Pompidou. Paris 1985 (cat.).– Brisch, K.: W. K. Untersuchungen zur Entstehung der gegenstandslosen Malerei an seinem Werk von 1900-1921. Diss. Bonn 1955.– Bowlt, J. E. and R.-C. Washton Long (ed.): The Life of V. K. in Russian Art. Newtonville 1980.– Cortenova, G. (ed.): W. K. Palazzo Forti, Verona. Milan 1993 (cat.).– Dabrowski, M.: K. Compositions. New Yok 1995.– Derouet, C. and V. E. Barnett (ed.): K. in Paris 1934-1944. Solomon R. Guggenheim Museum. New York 1985 (cat.).– Eichner, J.: K. und Gabriele Münter. Vom Ursprung moderner Kunst. Munich 1957.– Grohmann, W.: K. Leben und Werk. Cologne 1958, 1981/K. Life and Work. London and New York 1958 /K. Paris 1958.– Hahl-Koch, J.: K. Stuttgart 1992, New York 1993.– Halm, P. (ed.): W. K. Russian and Bauhaus Years 1915-1933. Solomon R. Guggenheim Museum. New York 1983 (cat.)/K. Russische Zeit und Baushausjahre 1915-1933. Bauhaus-Archiv. Berlin 1984 (cat.).– Hoberg, A. (ed.): W. K. und Gabriele Münter in Murnau und Kochel 1902-1914. Briefe und Erinnerungen. Munich 1994.– Kandinsky, N.: K. und ich. Munich 1976.– W. K. Die erste sowjetische Retrospektive. Schirn Kunsthalle. Frankfurt-on-Main 1989 (cat.).– Kleine, G.: Gabriele Münter und W. K. Biographie eines Paares. Frankfurt-on-Main 1990.– Lindsay, K. C.: An Examination of the Fundamental Theories of W. K. Diss. Madison (WI) 1951.– Long, R.-C.: The Development of an Abstract Style. Oxford 1980.– Moeller, M. M. (ed.): Der frühe K. 1900-1910. Brücke-Museum, Berlin et al. Munich 1994 (cat.).– Overy, P.: K. The Language of the Eye. New York 1969.– Poling, C. V.: K.'s Teaching at the Bauhaus. New York 1986.– Roethel, H. and K. Benjamin: K. New York 1979, Munich 1979.– Sers, P.: K. Philosophie de l'abstraction, l'image métaphysique. Geneva 1995.– Thürlemann, F.: K. über K. Der Künstler als Interpret eigener Werke. Bern 1986.– Washton-Long, R.-C.: K. The Development of an Abstract

Style. Oxford 1980.– Weis, P.: K. in Munich. The Formative Jugendstil Years. Princeton (NJ) 1979, 1985.– Weis, P. (ed.): K. in Munich 1896-1914. Solomon R. Guggenheim Museum. New York 1982 (cat.).– Weis, P.: K. and Old Russia. The Artist as Ethnographer and Shaman. New Haven (CT) 1995.– Zweite, A. (ed.): K. und München. Begegnungen und Wandlungen 1896-1914. Städtische Galerie im Lenbachhaus. Munich 1982 (cat.)

KANOLDT Alexander
1881 Karlsruhe – **1939** Berlin
German painter and graphic artist. **1899-1900** Studied at the Karlsruhe School of Arts and Crafts. **1901-1904** Continued his studies at the Karlsruhe Academy. **1908** Transferred to Munich. Travels to England, France, Italy, and Switzerland. **1909** Co-founder of the Neue Künstlervereinigung (New Artists' Association) in Munich, together with Javlensky, Kandinsky and Münter. **1913** Co-founder of the New Secession in Munich. **1914-1918** War service as an officer. **1924** While staying in Italy, he painted bleak suburban landscapes with multiple perspectives. **1925** Participated in the "Neue Sachlichkeit" exhibition in the Mannheim Art Museum. Appointed professor at the Breslau Academy. **1927** Participated in the "Neue Sachlichkeit" exhibition in the Neumann-Nierendorf gallery in Berlin. **1931** Resignation from his position in Breslau; opened a private painting school in Garmisch. **1932** Member of the Munich artists' group Die Sieben and participation in their exhibition. **1933** Appointed professor at the Art Academy in Berlin. **1937** Confiscation of several works classified as "degenerate art". Kanoldt painted mostly still lifes and Italian landscapes, whose sober, frozen aspects align them clearly with Neue Sachlichkeit.
CATALOGUES RAISONNES: Ammann, E. (ed.): Das druckgraphische Werk von A. K. Karlsruhe 1963.– Fischer-Hollweg, B. (ed.): A. K. und die Kunstrichtungen seiner Zeit. Diss. Bochum 1971
MONOGRAPHS, CATALOGUES: Dürr, H. (ed.): A. K. Städtische Wesenberg-Gemäldegalerie. Constance 1973 (cat.).– A. K. Stadthalle. Freiburg 1966 (cat.).– A. K. Graphik. Der Bestand des Graphischen Kabinetts an Handzeichnungen und Lithographien. Museum Folkwang. Essen 1977 (cat.).– A. K. 1881-1939. Gemälde, Zeichnungen, Lithographien. Museum für Neue Kunst. Freiburg 1987 (cat.)

KANOVITZ Howard
born **1929** Fall River (MA)
American painter. **1945-1951** Studied at the Rhode Island School of Design in Providence. **1951** Moved to New York, where he worked as a shop window dresser for Franz Kline. **1956-1958** Lived in Florence. **1962** First solo-exhibition in the Stable Gallery in New York. In developing his hyperrealist style, he began in **1963** to paint

from photographs and snapshots, limiting himself to narrow spatial fields seen from unusual angles. **1966** Important solo-exhibition at the Jewish Museum, New York. From **1967** painted with a spray-gun. **1972** and **1977** participation in documenta 5 and 6 in Kassel. **1979** DAAD scholarship to Berlin. **1979** Retrospective in the Berlin Art Academy. Kanovitz's hyperrealist pictures portray realistic scenes in new spatial constellations which deliberately subvert conventional perception.
MONOGRAPHS, CATALOGUES: Hunter, S. (ed.): H. K. Jewish Museum. New York 1966 (cat.).– Kotte, W. (ed.): H. K. Museum van Hedendaagse Kunst, Ghent. Utrecht 1974 (cat.).– Kultermann, U. (ed.): H. K. Wilhelm Lehmbruck Museum. Duisburg 1974 (cat.).– Merkert, J. (ed.): H. K. Akademie der Künste, Berlin et al. Berlin 1979 (cat.).– Volkmann, B. (ed.): H. K. Arbeiten 1951-1978. Akademie der Künste, Berlin et al. Berlin 1979 (cat.)

KANTOR Tadeusz
1915 Wielopole Skrzynskie (near Rzeszóv) – **1990** Cracow
Polish painter, set designer, and theatre director. **1936-1939** Studied at the Academy in Cracow. **1942-1944** Director of an underground theatre during German occupation. **1944-1955** Set design for various theatres in Cracow and Warsaw. **1945** Took up painting. **1947** Lived in Paris. **1948** Organized the first exhibition of contemporary Polish art after the war in Cracow. Withdrew from the art world **1949-1954** in protest against the imposed Socialist Realism. **1955** Returned to Paris and founded the Cricot 2 Theatres. Extension of paintings into three-dimensional objects. **1959** Informel paintings exhibited at documenta 2 in Kassel. **1965** Staged *Cricotage*, the first theatrical happening. **1967** Prize for painting at the São Paulo Biennale. Staged many pieces with his own Informel theatre group and other ensembles. **1987** Presented the performance *The Death and Love Machine* at documenta 8. **1992** Major retrospective in the Cracow National Museum. After an early Surrealist phase, Kantor extended his painting style, which was influenced by L'art informel, to develop an Informel-assemblage concept on the theme of the artist under threat.

WRITINGS: T. K.: Emballages. Chexbres 1963.– T. K.: Multipart. Warsaw 1970.– T. K.: Le Théâtre de la mort. Lausanne 1977.– T. K.: Metamorphoses. Paris 1982.– T. K. Ein Reisender. Seine Texte und Manifeste. Institut für moderne Kunst. Nuremberg 1988 (cat.)/Ma création, mon voyage. Commentaires intimes. Paris 1991
MONOGRAPHS, CATALOGUES: Borowski, W. and R. Stanislawski (ed.): T. K. Emballages. Muzeum Sztuki. Lodz 1975 (cat.)/T. K. Emballages 1960-1976. Whitechappel Art Gallery. London 1976 (cat.)/T. K. Emballages 1960-1976. Galerie R, Johanna Ricard. Nuremberg 1976 (cat.).– Borowski, W.: T. K. Warsaw 1982.– T. K. Métamorphoses. Galerie de France. Paris 1982 (cat.).– T. K. Muzeum Narodowe. Kraków 1991 (cat.).– T. K. Germanisches Nationalmuseum. Nuremberg 1996 (cat.).– Klossowicz, J.: T. K. Warsaw 1991.– Nowaczyk, W.: Dziela Tadeusza Kantora w kolekcji Muzeum Narodowego w Pozniu. Muzeum Narodowe, Poznaniu 1993 (cat.)

KAPROW Allan
born **1927** Atlantic City (NJ)
American artist. **1945-1949** Studied architecture. **1947/48** Painting classes under Hans Hofmann in New York. **1950-1952** Studied art history at Columbia University, New York. **1953** First solo-exhibition at the Hansa Gallery, New York. Encountered Abstract Expressionism, mainly through the works of Pollock. **1957-1959** Studied at the New School for Social Research under Cage, whose work inspired him to transform his environments into happenings. **1959** Staged *18 Happenings in Six Parts* in the Reuben Gallery in New York. **1961** Presented the environment *Yard*, which was a collection of old car tyres, in the M. Jackson Gallery in New York. **1961-1969** Lectureship at the State University in New York. From **1965** staging of actions and happenings. **1969-1972** Professorship in Princeton, New Jersey. **1974** Director of the Visual Arts Department at the University of San Diego. **1975** DAAD scholarship to Berlin. **1977** and **1987** participation in documenta 6 and 8 in Kassel. As an artist and director, Kaprow is one of the central figures on the action and happening scene.
WRITINGS: A. K.: Assemblage, Environments and Happenings. New York 1966.– A. K.: Untitled Essay and Other Works. New York 1967.– A. K.: Warm-ups. Cambridge (MA) 1975
MONOGRAPHS, CATALOGUES: Berman, B. (ed.): A. K. Pasadena Art Museum. Pasadena 1967 (cat.).– Diederichs, J.: A. K. Diss. Bochum 1971.– Diederichs, J. (ed.): A. K. Kunsthalle Bremen. Bremen 1976 (cat.).– A. K. Chicago 1981.– Schnackenburg, B. (ed.): A. K. Activity-Dokumente 1968-1976. Kunsthalle Bremen. Bremen 1976 (cat.).– Thiemann, E. et al. (ed.): A. K. Collagen, Environments, Videos 1956-1986. Museum am Ostwall. Dortmund 1986 (cat.).–

Williams, T. D. und Sanford Sivitz: Standards by A. K. Gallery of Art, University of Northern Iowa. Iowa 1979 (cat.)

KARAVAN Dani
born **1930** Tel Aviv
Israeli sculptor and environment artist. Studied art in Tel Aviv and at the Art Academy in Jerusalem. Until **1955** lived on a kibbutz, then continued his studies at the Accademia delle Belle Arti in Florence and at the Académie de la Grande Chaumière in Paris. **1960–1973** Worked as a stage designer for ballet and theatre. **1962** Worked on a wall relief for the Weizmann Institute in Rehovot, Israel. Over the following years received a large number of commissions for public sculptures and monuments. Produced numerous local environments using diverse media and materials such as lasers, glass, sand and water. **1976** Styled the Israeli Pavilion at the Venice Biennale. **1977** and **1987** participation in the documenta 6 and 8 in Kassel. **1978** Awarded the Israeli Prize for Culture and Art. **1984** Guest-professorship at the Ecole Nationale Supérieure des Beaux-Arts in Paris. **1996** Awarded the "Kaiserring" in Goslar. **1997** Received the Order of Merit in Germany and in **1998** the "Praemium Imperiale" in Japan.
MONOGRAPHS, CATALOGUES: Bott, G. and P. Laub (ed.): Straße der Menschenrechte. D. K. Germanisches Nationalmuseum. Nuremberg 1995 (cat.).– Brockhaus, C.: D. K. Ma'alot. Museumsplatz Cologne 1979-1986. Museen der Stadt. Cologne 1986 (cat.).– Finkeldey, B. (ed.): D. K. Dialog Düsseldorf – Duisburg. Kunstsammlung Nordrhein-Westfalen, Düsseldorf et al. Düsseldorf 1989 (cat.).– D. K. Due ambienti per la pace. Forte di Belvedere, Florenz et al. Milan 1978 (cat.).– D. K. Makom. Staatliche Kunsthalle Baden-Baden. Baden-Baden 1982 (cat.).– D. K. L'Axe majeur de Cergy-Pontoise. Paris 1987.– D. K. Dialogue with the Environment. Resonance with the Earth. Asahi Shimbun 1997 (cat.).– Restany, P. (ed.): D. K. Projekte im urbanen Raum. Museum Ludwig, Cologne. Munich 1992 (cat.).– Restany, P. (ed.): D. K. Tel Aviv Museum of Art. Tel Aviv 1990 (cat.).– Scheurmann, I. and K. (ed.): D. K. Hommage à Walter Benjamin. Mainz 1995

KASSAK Lajos
1887 Ersekújvár – **1967** Budapest
Hungarian painter and writer. **1909** Travels through Austria, Germany, and France. **1915** First poems published. Founded the magazine and movement *The Act.* **1919** During the Hungarian soviet republic era, he worked as an editor for socialist newspapers. **1920** Emigrated to Austria, settling in Vienna. Connections with Archipenko, Schwitters, Richter, Moholy-Nagy. **1922** Published the volume *Book of New Artists* together with Moholy-Nagy. **1924** First solo-exhibition at the Würthle Gallery in

Vienna. Exhibition in the gallery Der Sturm in Berlin. **1926** Returned to Budapest. Founding of *Document* magazine. Wrote various theoretical articles on Constructivism. **1945–1948** Held a cultural political post in Hungary. From **1957** dedicated himself again to painting and poetry writing. **1965** Received the Kosuth Prize. **1966** Participant in the Dada exhibition at the Zurich Art Museum. Kassák's constructivist pictures have much in common with Russian and Dutch abstraction.
WRITINGS: L. K. and L. Moholy-Nagy: Buch neuer Künstler. Vienna 1922, Baden 1991.– L. K.: Eljünk a mi időnkében. Irások a képzömüvészetröl. Budapest 1978.– L. K.: Als Vagabund unterwegs. Erinnerungen. Berlin 1979.– Vadas, J. (ed.): L. K. Laßt uns leben in unserer Zeit. Gedichte, Bilder und Schriften zur Kunst. Budapest 1989
MONOGRAPHS, CATALOGUES: Aradi, N.: L. K. Konstruktive Kunst. Nürnberg 1969.– Bori, I. and E. Körner (ed.): K. Irodalma és festészete. Budapest 1967.– Czaplár, F. and T. Frank (ed.): L. K. 1887-1967. Akademie der Künste der DDR. Berlin 1987 (cat.).– Körner, E. and T. Gergely (ed.): L. K. 1887-1967. Magyar Nemzeti Galéria. Budapest 1987 (cat.).– Kruse, J. A. (ed.): L. K. 1887-1967. Heinrich-Heine-Institut. Düsseldorf 1989 (cat.).– Laszlo, C.: L. K. Basel 1968.– L. K. 1887-1967. Neue Galerie am Landesmuseum Joanneum. Graz 1971 (cat.).– L. K. 1887-1967. Museum Bochum. Bochum 1973 (cat.).– L. K. Retrospective Exhibition. Matignon Gallery. New York 1984 (cat.).– L. K. 1887-1967. Magyar Nemzeti Galéria. Budapest 1987 (cat.).– L. K. 1887-1967. Budapest 1988 (cat.).– L. K. az európai avantgárd mozgalmakban. 1916-1929. Kassák Múzeum és Archívum. Budapest 1994 (cat.).– Rónay, G.: L. K. Budapest 1971.– Schmidt, L. E. (ed.): L. K. Ein Protagonist der ungarischen Avantgarde. Berlin 1991.– Straus, T. (ed.): K. Ein ungarischer Beitrag zum Konstruktivismus. Galerie Gmurzynska. Cologne 1975 (cat.).– Vadas, J.: K. a konstruktőr. Budapest 1979

KAWAMATA Tadashi
born **1953** Hokkaido
Japanese sculptor and installation artist. **1972** Went to Tokyo. Studied painting at Tokyo College of Art, graduating as a Bach-

elor of Fine Arts. From **1975** constructed unwieldy installations out of wood, that were displayed in public places from **1976** onwards. He favours deserted places such as ruins for his architectonic installations. **1981** Obtained his Master's degree in Fine Arts. **1984** Taught at Tokyo College of Art, and began to travel a great deal. **1987** Exhibited *Destroyed Church* at documenta 8 and *People's Garden* at documenta 9 in Kassel in **1992**.
MONOGRAPHS, CATALOGUES: Bekaert, G. et al. (ed.): T. K. Begijnhof Kortrijk. Gendaikikakushitsu Publishing and Kanaal Art Foundation. Tokyo and Kortrijk 1991 (cat.).– Bois, Y.-A. et al. (ed.): T. K. Project on Roosevelt Island. Gendaikikakushitsu Publishers and On the Table. Tokyo and New York 1993 (cat.).– Brayer, M.-A. et al. (ed.): T. K. Centre de Création Contemporain & Atelier Calder. Tours and Saché 1994 (cat.).– Finkenpearl, T. (ed.): T. K. Project. On the Table. Tokyo 1986 (cat.).– Gould, C. F. (ed.): T. K. Project in Roosevelt Island 1990. Kodama Gallery. Osaka 1989 (cat.).– Jurejewicz, V. et al. (ed.): T. K. Tram Passage. StadtRaum Remise. Vienna 1995 (cat.).– T. K. PH Studio. Tokyo 1979 and 1980 (cat.).– T. K. Projects 1980-1990. Annely Juda Fine Art. London 1990 (cat.).– T. K. Field Work. On the Table. Tokyo 1991 (cat.).– T. K. Gallery Kobayashi. Tokyo 1992 (cat.).– T. K. Prefabrication. Gallery Kobayashi. Tokyo 1993 (cat.).– Lienhard, M.-L. (ed.): T. K. in Zürich. Helmhaus. Zurich 1993 (cat.).– Obigane, A. (ed.): T. K. Maquettes. Kodama Gallery. Osaka 1992 (cat.).– Okouchi, K. (ed.): T. K. Archives 1984-1994. Izami City Museum of Art. Itami 1994 (cat.).– Orchard, K. (ed.): T. K. Field Work. Stuttgart 1997.– Ullrich, F. (ed.): T. K. Städtische Kunsthalle Recklinghausen. Cologne 1996 (cat.)

KAWARA On
born **1933** Aichi-ken
Japanese concept artist. Left Japan in **1955** to study architecture in Mexico. **1961** Moved to New York. From **1966** first of the *Date Paintings* in which he painted the date the work was created. **1968** Start of the series *I went:* street maps showing where the artist had been on a single day, and *I met:* lists of the people he met on one day. **1969** Creation of the ten-volume work *One Million Years,* a hand-drawn list of a million years. From **1970** he sent telegrams to certain people with the text, "I am still alive." **1972** Participated in the exhibition "Conceptual Art" at the Kunstmuseum, Basel, **1977** and **1982** in documenta 6 and 7 in Kassel, and **1989** in the exhibition "Bilderstreit" in Cologne. Kawara's systematic works, defining time and place in artistic terms, place him among the foremost proponents of Concept Art. Kawara's autobiography reads: 23,975 days on the day this book is published.
WRITINGS: O. K. 1952-1956. Tokyo 1991.– O. K.: I Went, I Met, I Read, Journal 1969. 4 vols. Cologne 1992
MONOGRAPHS, CATALOGUES: Block R. (ed.): O. K. 1976-1986. Daadgalerie. Berlin 1987 (cat.).– Denizot, R. and K. König (ed.): O. K. 1973. Produktion eines Jahres. Kunsthalle Bern. Bern 1974 (cat.).– Denizot, R.: Les Images quotidiennes du pouvoir. O. K. au jour le jour. Paris 1979.– Denizot, R.: O. K. Frankfurt-on-Main 1991.– Douroux, X. and F. Gautherot (ed.): O. K. Whole and Parts 1964-1995. Le Nouveau Musée. Villeurbanne 1996 (cat.).– Granath, O. and P. Nilson (ed.): O. K. Continuity/Discontinuity 1963-1979. Moderna Museet, Stockholm et al. Stockholm 1980 (cat.).– Hulten, P. (ed.): O. K. 97 Date-paintings consécutives et journaux. de 1966-1975. Centre

Georges Pompidou. Paris 1977 (cat.).– O. K. 1967. Otis Art Institute Gallery. Los Angeles 1977 (cat.).– O. K. Museum für Moderne Kunst. Frankfurt-on-Main 1994 (cat.).– Kittelmann, U. (ed.): O. K. Erscheinen – Verschwinden. Kölnischer Kunstverein. Cologne 1995 (cat.).– Schampers, K. (ed.): O. K. Date Paintings in 89 Cities. Museum Boymans-van Beuningen, Rotterdam et al. Rotterdam 1991 (cat.).– Wäspe, R. (ed.): O. K. 1964 – Paris – New York. St. Gallen 1997 (cat.)

KEETMAN Peter
born **1916** Wuppertal
German photographer. Studied at the Bavarian Photographic College in Munich from **1925**. After this training, he was employed in Gertrud Hesse's photographic studio in Duisburg and worked as an industrial photographer for the C. H. Schmeck company in Aachen. **1948** Continued his studies in Stuttgart under Adolf Lazi. **1949** Together with Otto Steinert, founded the Photo-Form Group. **1950** Participated in the first Photokina exhibition in Cologne. Since **1980** he has worked as a freelance commercial and industrial photographer in Thiersee, Austria. Keetman is considered one of the best representatives of subjective photography. He became well-known through his experimental photographs of water droplets as well as his abstract documentary photographs of the Volkswagen factory.

KELLEY Mike
born **1954** Detroit
American artist. Studied at the University of Michigan, Ann Arbor. **1976–1978** Studied under Baldessari at the California Institute of the Arts in Valencia. **1978** First public performance (*Poetry in Motion*) at the Los Angeles Contemporary Exhibitions. **1985** Grant from the National Endowment for the Arts. **1986** Began to make sculptures and installations out of found objects like teddy bears or rag dolls. **1988** In the installation *Pay for your pleasure*, he placed 42 poster-portraits of poets, philosophers, and other famous personalities facing paintings by a murderer. **1992** Participation in documenta 9 in Kassel with an installation combining instructive narrative texts with

schematic drawings of bodily functions. Exhibited *Riddle of the Sphinx*, an Afghan carpet which filled the entire gallery space. **1995** Retrospective at the Haus der Kunst in Munich. **1997** Participation in documenta 10 in Kassel. Kelley, whose works delight in juxtaposing "low" and "high" art to the point of caricature, is one of the most important American performance artists. WRITINGS: M. K. im Gespräch mit T. Kellein. Stuttgart 1993
MONOGRAPHS, CATALOGUES: Bartman, W. S. and M. Barosh (ed.): M. K. Art Resources Transfer. New York 1992.– Haenlein, C. (ed.): M. K. Missing Time. Works on Paper 1974-1976, Reconsidered. Kestner-Gesellschaft. Hanover 1995 (cat.).– Kellein, T. (ed.): M. K. Kunsthalle Basel et al. Stuttgart 1992 (cat.).– M. K. Three Projects. Renaissance Society at the University of Chicago. Chicago 1988 (cat.).– M. K. Jablonka Galerie. Cologne 1989 (cat.).– Lebrero Stals, J. (ed.): M. K. 1985-1996. Barcelona et al. Barcelona 1997 (cat.).– Sussman, E. et al. (ed.): M. K. Catholic Tastes. Whitney Museum of American Art, New York et al. New York 1993 (cat.)

KELLY Ellsworth
born **1923** Newburgh (near New York) American painter and sculptor. **1941/42** Art studies at the Pratt Institute, New York. **1944** Took part in the invasion of Normandy as a soldier. First visit to Paris. **1946-1948** Drawing and painting studies at the School of the Museum of Fine Arts, Boston. **1948** Studied at the Ecole des Beaux-Arts in Paris. **1950/51** Lectureship at the American School in Paris. Inspired by visits to the studios of Brancusi, Vantongerloo, Picabia, Arp and Taeuber-Arp, he produced his first abstract pictures, in which geometric areas in varying colour strengths are set against each other. **1954** Returned to the USA. **1957** Commission for a mural in Philadelphia. Between **1964** and **1992** participation in documenta 3, 4, 6 and 9 in Kassel. **1966** Participation in the Venice Biennale. **1969** Commissioned to design a mural for the UNESCO building in Paris. **1974** Prize for painting from the Art Institute of Chicago. Member of the National Insitute of Arts and Letters. **1980** First wood and metal sculptures with Peter Carlson. After the installation of a sculpture in Lincoln Park in Chicago, further commissions for public sculptures. **1989/90** Organized his own exhibition at the request of the Art Institute of Chicago and the Museum of Modern Art, New York. **1998** Major retrospectives in New York, Los Angeles and Munich. Kelly, who began by working in minimal and hard-edge styles, developed through his mathematically precise sculptures a new picture form, in which the classical 2-dimensional panel painting is replaced by a 3-dimensional pictorial object.
CATALOGUES RAISONNES: Axsom, R. H. (ed.): The Prints of E. K. A Catalogue Raisonné 1949-1985. New York 1987.– Bois, Y.-A. et al. (ed.): E. K. Die Jahre in Frank-

reich 1948-1954. Westfälisches Landesmuseum, Münster et al. Munich 1992 (cat.)/ E. K. Les années françaises 1948-1954. Paris 1992 (cat.).– Sims, P. and E. Rauh Pulitzer (ed.): E. K. Sculpture. Whitney Museum of American Art, New York et al. New York 1982 (cat.).– Waldman, D. (ed.): E. K. Drawings, Collages, Prints. Greenwich (CT) 1971
MONOGRAPHS, CATALOGUES: Baker, E. C. (ed.): E. K. Recent Paintings and Sculptures. Metropolitan Museum of Art. New York 1979 (cat.).– Boehm, G.: E. K. Yellow Curve. Stuttgart 1992.– Coplans, J.: E. K. New York 1973.– Goosen, E. C. (ed.): E. K. The Museum of Modern Art. New York 1973 (cat.).– Hentschel, M. (ed.): E. K. Yellow Curve. Portikus, Frankfurt-on-Main. Stuttgart 1992 (cat.).– Offay, A. d' and M. Marks (ed.): Spencertown. Recent Paintings by E. K. New York 1994.– Rose, B. (ed.): E. K. Paintings and Sculptures 1963-1979. Stedelijk Museum. Amsterdam 1979 (cat.).– Rose, B. et al. (ed.): E. K. Gemälde und Skulpturen 1966-1979. Staatliche Kunsthalle Baden-Baden. Baden-Baden 1980 (cat.).– Upright, D. et al. (ed.): E. K. Works on Paper. The Fort Worth Museum et al. New York 1987 (cat.).– Waldman, D. (ed.): E. K. Solomon R. Guggenheim Museum, New York et al. New York and London 1996 (cat.)/ E. K. Haus der Kunst. Munich 1997 (cat.).– Yakush, M. (ed.): E. K. The Years in France 1948-1954. National Gallery of Art, Washington et al. Munich 1992 (cat.)

KEMENY Zoltán
1907 Banica (Transylvania) – **1965** Zurich Hungarian-born Swiss sculptor and painter. Worked **1923-1930** as a cabinet maker in Budapest. **1927-1930** Studied architecture at the Ecole des Arts Décoratifs and painting at the Ecole des Beaux-Arts in Budapest. **1931** Moved to Paris, where he worked as an architect and fashion designer. **1942** Moved to Zurich. **1947** Began to incorporate materials like sand, stone, scrap iron and dried plants into his pictures. From **1951** he glued various materials onto illuminated reinforced glass to transform the picture into a lighted space. **1954** First metal reliefs. **1957** Became a Swiss citizen. Received numerous commissions from public institutions, including the University of St. Gallen and the Frankfurt Municipal Theatre. **1959** Took part in documenta 2 in Kassel. **1963** First architectural sculptures and three-dimensional brass constructions. **1964** Participation in documenta 3 in Kassel. Awarded first prize for sculpture at the Venice Biennale. **1967** Retrospective in the Musée National d'Art Moderne in Paris. Kemény became well-known at the beginning of the 50s for his metal reliefs, constructed from ready-made and handmade metal parts, assembled and welded together in a special process producing colour changes.
MONOGRAPHS, CATALOGUES: Bownes, A. (ed.): Z. K. 1907-1965. Tate Gallery. London 1967 (cat.).– Durrer, J. (ed.): Z. K.

Kunstmuseum Bern. Bern 1982 (cat.).– Giedion-Welcker, C.: Z. K. St. Gallen 1968.– Heusser, H.-J.: Z. K. Das Frühwerk. 1943-1953. Katalog der Peintures, Sculpture and Reliefs-Collages. Basel 1993.– Z. K. Kestner-Gesellschaft. Hanover 1963 (cat.).– Z. K. Musée National d'Art Moderne. Paris 1966 (cat.).– Z. K. Wallraf-Richartz-Museum. Cologne 1967 (cat.).– Z. K. Fondation Maeght, Saint-Paul 1974 (cat.).– Lauter, R.: Z. K. Galleria Peccolo. Livorno 1986 (cat.).– Picon, G. and F. Rathke: Z. K. Reliefs in métal. Paris 1974 (cat.).– Z. K. Neuchâtel 1960.– Ragon, M.: Z. K. Fondation Maeght. Saint-Paul 1974 (cat.).– Schwarz, D. (ed.): Z. K. Die Werke im Kunstmuseum Winterthur. Kunstmuseum. Winterthur 1993 (cat.).– Tavel, H. C. v. and H.-J. Heusser (ed.): Z. K. Kunstmuseum Bern. Bern 1982 (cat.)

KERTESZ André
1894 Budapest – **1985** New York Hungarian-American photographer. **1910-1912** Attended the School of Economics in Budapest. **1915** First documentary war photographs. **1922** Honorary diploma from the Hungarian Photographic Association. **1925-1935** Worked as a photographer in Paris for the *Berliner Illustrirte* magazine and the *London Times*. Acquaintanceship with Mondrian, Prampolini, Brancusi; contacts with P. Outerbridge, Man Ray and the Surrealist circle around André Breton. **1927** First solo-exhibition in Paris. **1936** Emigration to New York. **1937-1949** Photographed for various fashion magazines, such as *Harper's Bazaar*, *Vogue* and *Look*. Worked from **1949-1962** exclusively for Condé-Nast. **1963** Gold Medal at the Venice Biennale. **1974** Grant from the Guggenheim Museum in New York. **1977** Participation in documenta 6 in Kassel. **1982** Honorary doctorate from the Royal Photographic Society, London. **1983** Elected Knight of the Legion of Honour in France.
WRITINGS: A. K.: Kertesz on Kertesz. London 1985, New York 1996
MONOGRAPHS, CATALOGUES: Borhan, P. et al. (ed.): A. K. La Biographie d'une œuvre. Paris 1994 / A. K. His Life and Work. Boston and New York 1994.– Ducrot, N. (ed.): A. K. Sixty Years of Photography 1912-1972. New York 1972.– Fárová, A.: A. K. Prague and New York 1964.– Gaillard, A.: A. K. Paris 1980.– Harder, S. and H. Kubota: A. K. Diary of Light 1912-1975. New York 1987.– Harris, J. and M. Holtman (ed.): In Focus A. K. Photographs from the J. Paul Getty Museum. Malibu 1994 (cat.).– Hinson, H. and A. Gaillard: A. K. 70 années de photographie. Neuilly 1987.– Johnson, B.: A. K. Master of Photography. The Chrysler Museum. Norfolk 1982 (cat.).– A. K. Bibliothèque Nationale. Paris 1963 (cat.).– A. K. Fotografier 1913-1971. Moderna Museet. Stockholm 1971 (cat.).– A. K. Centre Georges Pompidou. Paris 1977 (cat.).– A. K. An Exhibition of Photographs from the Centre Georges Pompidou, Paris. London 1979 (cat.).–

A. K. Ma France. Palais de Tokyo. Paris 1990 (cat.).– Kincses, K. (ed.): A. K. 1894-1985-1994. Musée Hongrois de la Photographie. Budapest 1994 (cat.).– Kismaric, C.: A. K. Millerton 1977.– Omaggio ad A. K. 1894-1985. Budapest, Paris, New York, Romaa. Roma 1986.– Phillips, S. S. et al. (ed.): A. K. Of Paris and New York. Metropolitan Museum of Modern Art. New York 1985 (cat.).– Phillips, S. S. et al. (ed.): A. K. in Paris. Photographien 1925-1936. Munich 1995.– Szarkowski, J.: A. K. Photographer. New York 1964.– Wedewer, R. (ed.): A. K. Fotografien. 1914-1972. Städtisches Museum Leverkusen, Schloß Morsbroich. Leverkusen 1977 (cat.)

KIEFER Anselm
born **1945** Donaueschingen German painter. **1965** Studied law and romance languages at the University of Freiburg. **1966-1968** Attended painting courses under Peter Dreher in Freiburg and studied **1969** at Karlsruhe Academy under Antes. In the same year, he achieved notoriety with his photoseries *Besetzungen* (Occupations), in which he himself gives a Nazi salute at symbolic locations in France, Italy, and Switzerland. **1970-1972** Studied under Beuys at the Düsseldorf Academy and developed an individual painting style, in which paint is applied thickly in layers and often mixed with materials like earth, sand, straw, and hair. The impasto is often so thick that it is necessary to chop it away with an axe, or burn it off. The painting process reflects the theme of the picture, as in *Malerei der verbrannten Erde*, a confrontation with Germany's national (-socialist) history. **1976** Series of paintings entitled *Hermannsschlacht im Teutoburger Wald* (Hermann's victory over the Romans in the Teutoburger Forest). **1977** and **1987** participation in documenta 6 and 8 in Kassel. **1981-1983** Painted over photographs and books. Tackled the theme of the Jewish genocide in the picture series *Margarete* and *Sulamith*, which refer to Paul Celan's poem *Todesfuge*. **1987** Major retrospective at the Art Institute of Chicago and **1991** at the Nationalgalerie in Berlin. In the 90s numerous book objects, sculptures (for example, jet fighters constructed out of lead plates), and installations. Kiefer is the principal proponent of the so-called "Neue Deutsche Malerei" (New German Painting).
WRITINGS: A. K.: Die Donauquelle. Cologne 1978.– A. K.: Hoffmann von Fallersleben auf Helgoland. Groningen 1980.– A. K.: Nothung, ein Schwert verhieß mir der Vater. Baden-Baden 1983.– A. K.: A Book by A. K. New York 1988 / Ein Buch von A. K. Erotik im Fernen Osten oder: Transition from Cool to Warm. Stuttgart 1988.– A. K.: Zweistromland. Cologne 1989.– A. K. Über 5 Räume und Völker. Nachwort von K. Gallwitz. Frankfurt-on-Main 1990
CATALOGUES RAISONNES: Adriani, G. (ed.): A. K. Bücher 1969-1990. Kunsthalle Tübingen et al. Stuttgart 1990 (cat.) / The

Books of A. K. 1969-1990. Kunsthalle Tübingen et al. New York 1991 (cat.) MONOGRAPHS, CATALOGUES: Beeren, W. (ed.): A. K. Bilder 1980-1986. Stedelijk Museum. Amsterdam 1986 (cat.).– Cacciari, M. and G. Celant (ed.): A. K. Venice 1997 (cat.).– Esser, W.: A. K. Glaube, Hoffnung, Liebe 1973. Stuttgart 1992.– Felix, Z. and N. Serota (ed.): A. K. Museum Folkwang, Essen et al. Essen 1981 (cat.)/A. K. Whitechapel Art Gallery. London 1981 (cat.).– Fuchs, R. (ed.): A. K. Stedelijk Van Abbe Museum. Eindhoven 1979 (cat.).– Fuchs, R. (ed.): A. K. Verbrennen, verholzen, versenken. Biennale Venice, Deutscher Pavillon. Venice 1980 (cat.).– Gachnang, J. and M. Schmidt-Miescher (ed.): A. K. Kunsthalle Bern. Bern 1978 (cat.).– Gilmour, J. C.: Fire on the Earth: A. K. and the Postmodern World. Philadelphia 1990.– Harten J. and M. Heinz (ed.): A. K. Städtische Kunsthalle Düsseldorf et al. Düsseldorf 1984 (cat.).– Lopez-Pedraza, R.: A. K. The Psychology of "After the Catastrophe". New York 1996.– Meier, C.: A. K. Die Rückkehr des Mythos in der Kunst. Essen 1992.– Osterwold, T. (ed.): A. K. Württembergischer Kunstverein. Stuttgart 1980 (cat.).– Rosenthal, M. (ed.): A. K. The Art Institute of Chicago, Chicago et al. Munich 1987 (cat.).– Schmidt-Miescher, M. (ed.): A. K. Bilder und Bücher. Kunsthalle Bern. Bern 1978 (cat.).– Schneider, A. et al. (ed.): A. K. Neue Nationalgalerie. Berlin 1991 (cat.).

KIENHOLZ Edward
1927 Fairfield (WA) – **1994** Hope (ID) American sculptor. Self-taught. Studied at various colleges in the American west, and worked as a car dealer, male nurse, and restaurateur. **1953** Moved to Los Angeles, where he produced his first wood reliefs. **1956** Opening of the first avant-garde gallery in Los Angeles. **1957** Founding of the Ferus Gallery. Relief assemblages made of discarded objects, the waste products of consumerism. **1961** His environment *Roxy's* depicts in an obsessive, surrealist scenario a brothel from the 40s. **1966** First retrospective in the County Museum of Art in Los Angeles. **1968** Participation in documenta 4 in Kassel. **1972** Delivered a critical commentary on race discrimination in his environment *Five Car Stud* at documenta 5 in Kassel. **1973** DAAD scholarship to Berlin. Confrontation with German history in works such as *Volksempfänger*. **1977** Opening of a gallery in Hope, Idaho, with his wife Nancy. **1984** Important exhibition in the San Francisco Museum of Modern Art with works by Edward and Nancy Kienholz. **1996** Retrospective at the Whitney Museum of American Art, New York, and **1997** in the Berlinische Galerie. Kienholz, who started as a painter and went on to assemblages and environments via wooden reliefs, revealed with his deformed bodies and dehumanized figures the moral decline and alienation of the individual in our mass culture.

MONOGRAPHS, CATALOGUES: Baur, K. F. (ed.): Medien, Macht Manipulation. E. K., N. R. K. Stuttgart 1987 (cat.).– Conner, G. H. and J. Bernhardt: E. K. New York 1986.– Harten, J. et al. (ed.): E. and Nancy K. 1980's. Städtische Kunsthalle Düsseldorf et al. Düsseldorf and Vienna 1989 (cat.).– Hopps, W. et al. (ed.): E. K. Whitney Museum of American Art. New York 1996 (cat.)/E. K. Berlinische Galerie, Berlin. Munich 1997 (cat.).– E. and N. R. K.: Human Scale. San Francisco Museum of Modern Art et al. Houston 1984 (cat.).– Merkert, J. (ed.): E. K. Volksempfänger. Nationalgalerie. Berlin 1977 (cat.).– Pincus, R. L.: On a Scale that Competes with the World. The Art of E. and Nancy Reddin K. Berkeley 1990.– Reddin, N. et al. (ed.): E. K. Roxys and Other Works. GK-Gesellschaft für aktuelle Kunst, Bremen 1982 (cat.).– Schmidt, H.-W.: E. K. The Portable War Memorial. Moralischer Appell und politische Kritik. Frankfurt-on-Main 1988.– Tuchman, M. (ed.): E. K. Los Angeles County Museum of Art. Los Angeles 1966 (cat.).– Weschler, L. (ed.): E. K. 2 vols. Los Angeles 1977

KING Phillip
born **1934** Carthage (Tunisia) English sculptor. **1954–1957** Studied languages at Cambridge University. Studied art from **1957/58** at the St. Martin's School of Art in London, where he also taught between **1959–1978**. **1959/60** Assistant to Henry Moore. **1964** and **1968** participation in documenta 3 and 4 in Kassel. **1967–1969** Member of the board of the Tate Gallery. **1977** Elected member of the Royal Academy. **1979–1981** Guest-professorship at the Berlin Academy. **1980–1990** Professor of sculpture at the Royal College of Art and at the Royal Academy Schools in London. **1987** Participant at the International Sculpture Symposium in Yawata, Japan. **1990** Emeritus Professor at the Royal College of Art. King's cheerfully coloured, expansive sculptures out of moulded plastic and fibreglass combine abstract composition with real objects, and had an important influence on English sculpture in the 60s.

MONOGRAPHS, CATALOGUES: Hilton, T.: The Sculptures of P. K. London 1992.– P. K. Sculptures 1970-1975. Palais Galliera. Paris 1975 (cat.).– P. K. Skulpturen. Städtische Kunsthalle Mannheim 1992 (cat.).– Lampert, C. and R. Cass (ed.): P. K. Hayward Gallery. London 1981 (cat.).– Oxenaar, R. et al. (ed.): P. K. Hayward Gallery, London et al. London 1981 (cat.).– Thompson, D. (ed.): P. K. Kröller-Müller National Museum. Otterlo 1974 (cat.)

KIPPENBERGER Martin
1953 Dortmund – **1997** Vienna German painter. **1972** Studied at the Hamburg School of Fine Arts. Moved in **1978** to Berlin, where he founded Kippenberger's Office and organized exhibitions

with Walter Dahn, Werner Büttner, Oehlen, etc. **1984** Group exhibition "Arbeit ist Wahrheit" (Work is Truth) with Büttner and Oehlen in the Museum Folkwang, Essen. **1986** Extended study trip to Brazil. **1988** Move to Los Angeles. **1990** Guest-professor at the Städel Art School, Frankfurt am Main. **1991** Solo-exhibition at the San Francisco Museum of Modern Art. **1992** Took part in documenta 9 in Kassel. **1993** Founding of the Museum of Modern Art on the island of Syros as well as solo-exhibitions in the Pompidou Centre, Paris. **1994** Exhibition "The Happy End of Franz Kafka's Amerika" in the Boymans-van Beuningen Museum, Rotterdam. **1995** Unveiling of *Exit of the Underground Station Dawson City West*, a public sculpture in Dawson City, Canada. **1997** Participation in documenta 10 in Kassel. Kippenberger, whose anti-art polemic is related to Dada and Fluxus, works with mixed media. Drawing material from photos and text quotations from the mass media, commonplace objects, paintings, and photographs, he builds a kaleidoscopic, often contradictory pictorial world, centred around his own biography.

WRITINGS: Capitain, G. (ed.): Gespräche mit M. K. Stuttgart 1994
CATALOGUE RAISONNE: M. K.: Kippenbergerweg 25-2-53. (Œuvrekatalog der Plakate). Cologne 1989
MONOGRAPHS, CATALOGUES: Baumann, D. et al. (ed.): K. leicht gemacht/K. sans peine. Geneva 1997 (cat.).– Gretenkort, D. and J.-K. Schmidt (ed.): M. K. Miete, Strom, Gas. Hessisches Landesmuseum. Darmstadt 1986 (cat.).– M. K. Villa Arson. Nice 1989 (cat.).– M. K.: Tiefes Kehlchen. Topographie I: Festraum. Vienna 1991 (cat.).– M. K. Musée des Beaux-Arts. Le Havre 1993 (cat.).– M. K. Villa Merkel, Esslingen. Stuttgart 1997 (cat.).– M. K. Musée d'Art Moderne et Contemporain. Geneva 1997 (cat.).– Loers, V. (ed.): M. K. Der Eiermann und seine Ausleger. Cologne 1997.– Muthesius, A. (ed.): M. K. Ten Years After. Cologne 1991.– Ohrt, R. (ed.): M. K. Cologne 1997.– Schappert, R.: M. K. Die Organisation des Scheiterns. Cologne 1998.– Schmidt, J.-K. et al. (ed.): M. K. Miete Strom Gas. Hessisches Landesmuseum. Darmstadt 1986 (cat.)

KIRCHNER Ernst Ludwig
1880 Aschaffenburg – **1938** Frauenkirch (near Davos), Switzerland German painter and graphic artist. **1901–1903** Studied architecture in Dresden; acquaintanceship with Fritz Bleyl. **1903/04** Studied at the von Debschitz Art School, and continued architecture studies in Dresden. **1905** Founding of the artists' group Brücke together with Bleyl, Heckel, and Schmitt-Rottluff. **1906** Drew up the group's programme. Spent the summer of **1907** with Pechstein in Goppeln near Dresden. **1908** First stay on the island of Fehmarn. **1909–1911** Trips to Moritzburger lakes. **1910/11** Member of the New Secession. In October **1911** moved to Berlin, where he and Pechstein founded the MUIM Institute (Moderner Unterricht in Malerei). Painted numerous city scenes. His *Chronik der Brücke* led in **1913** to the disbanding of the group. **1914** Participation in the Werkbund exhibition in Cologne. Nervous breakdown after volunteering for military service. **1923** Large solo-exhibition in Basel. **1925/26** Travelled around Germany, visiting Frankfurt am Main, Chemnitz, Dresden and Berlin. **1929** Trips to Essen, Berlin and Frankfurt am Main. **1933** Extensive exhibition in Bern. **1937** His works classified as "degenerate art" and 639 confiscated from public collections. **1938** Suicide. Kirchner is probably the most important painter and graphic artist among the German Expressionists.

WRITINGS: Grisebach, L. (ed.): E. L. K.'s Davoser Tagebuch. Stuttgart 1996.– Henze, W. (ed.): E. L. K. und G. Schiefler. Briefwechsel 1910-1935/38. Stuttgart and Zurich 1990
CATALOGUES RAISONNES: Dube, A. and W.-D. (ed.): E. L. K. Das graphische Werk. 2 vols. Munich 1967, 1980, 1991.– Gordon, D. E. (ed.): E. L. K. Mit einem kritischen Katalog seiner Gemälde. Munich and Cambridge (MA) 1968.– Presler, G. (ed.): E. L. K. Die Skizzenbücher. Weingarten 1996.– Schiefler, G. (ed.): Das graphische Werk von E. L. K. 2 vols. Berlin 1926-1931
MONOGRAPHS, CATALOGUES: Ehrmann, A.-M. and V. Wahl (ed.): E. L. K. Von Jena nach Davos. Stadtmuseum Göhre in Jena. Leipzig 1993 (cat.).– Froning, H.: E. L. K. und die Wandmalerei. Entwürfe zur Wandmalerei im Museum Folkwang. Recklinghausen 1991.– Gabler, K.: E. L. K. Dokumente, Zeichnungen, Pastelle, Aquarelle. 2 vols. Aschaffenburg 1980.– Grisebach, L. and A. Meyer zu Eissen (ed.): E. L. K. 1880-1938. Nationalgalerie, Berlin et al. Munich 1979 (cat.).– Grisebach, L. and W. Henze (ed.): E. L. K. Zeichnungen, Aquarelle, Pastelle. Kunsthalle. Nuremberg 1991 (cat.).– Grisebach, L.: E. L. K. 1880-1938. Cologne 1996.– Grisebach, L.: K. New York 1996.– Grohmann, W.: E. L. K. Stuttgart 1958, London and New York 1961.– Henze, A.: E. L. K. Leben und Werk. Stuttgart 1980.– Henze, W. (ed.): E. L. K. Kirchner Museum Davos. Katalog. 2 vols. Davos 1992-1994.– Ketterer, R. N. (ed.): E. L. K. Zeichnungen und Pastelle. Stuttgart 1979/E. L. K. Drawings and Pastells. New York 1995.– E. L. K. Aquarelle, Pastelle, Zeichnungen. Museum am Ostwall. Dortmund 1986 (cat.).– Kornfeld, E. W.: E. L. K. Nachzeichnung seines Lebens. Bern 1979.– Lohberg, G. (ed.): E. L. K. Kunst und Technik der Radierung. Kirchner Museum, Davos 1994.– Moeller, M. M. (ed.): E. L. K. Meisterwerke der Druckgraphik. Stuttgart 1990.– Moeller, M. M. (ed.): E. L. K. Zeichnungen und Aquarelle. Brücke-Museum, Berlin et al. Munich 1993 (cat.).– Moeller, M. M.: E. L. K. Die Straßenszenen 1913-1915. Munich 1993

KIRKEBY Per
born **1938** Copenhagen
Danish painter and sculptor. **1957–1964**
Studied biology at the University of Copenhagen. **1958** and **1960** made expeditions to
Greenland. In later years numerous expeditions to various parts of the globe. **1962–
1964** Attended the Experimental Art School
in Copenhagen. **1964** First solo-exhibition
at the Hoved Library, Copenhagen. **1966/67**
Lived in New York, where he put together
his first brick sculptures. Performances in
collaboration with Beuys, Paik, Immendorff, and others. **1968** Published poetry
and essays on art. **1978** Lecturer at the
Karlsruhe Academy. **1980** Participant at the
Venice Biennale. **1982** Awarded a DAAD
scholarship to Berlin. Member of the
Danish Academy of Literature. Participation in documenta 7 in Kassel. **1986**
Journey to Australia. **1990** Awarded the art
prize of the Nord/Landesbank. **1992** Participation in documenta 9 in Kassel.
WRITINGS: P. K.: Selected Essays from
Bravura. Eindhoven 1982.– P. K.: Fort-
gesetzter Text – Hinweise. Bern and Berlin
1985.– P. K.: Rodin, la porte de l'enfer. Bern
and Berlin 1985.– P. K.: Kristallgesicht.
Ausgew. Essays aus Naturhistorie und
Udviklingen. Bern and Berlin 1990.– P. K.:
Nachbilder. Bern, Berlin 1991.– P. K.:
Natural History and Evolution. The Hague
1991.– P. K.: Handbuch. Texte zu Architektur und Kunst. Berlin and Bern 1993.– P. K.
im Gespräch mit S. Gohr. Cologne 1994.–
P. K.: Manuel. Musée d'Art Moderne de la
Ville de Paris. Paris 1998 (cat.).– P. K. –
Lars Morell. Gespräche. Cologne 1998
CATALOGUES RAISONNES: Andersen,
T. (ed.): P. K. Werkverzeichnis der Radierungen 1977-1983. Bern and Berlin 1986,
1992.– Gachnang, J. et al. (ed.): P. K. Bach-
steinskulptur und Architektur. Werkverzeichnis. Cologne 1997.– Honov, J. (ed.): P.
K. Œuvre Katalog 1958-1977. Copenhagen
1979
MONOGRAPHS, CATALOGUES: Anderson, T. et al. (ed.): P. K. Städtisches
Museum Abteiberg. Mönchengladbach
1986 (cat.)/ P. K. Museum Ludwig, Cologne
et al. Cologne 1987 (cat.).– Crouwel, W. et
al. (ed.): P. K. Museum Boymans-van
Beuningen. Rotterdam 1987.– Felix, Z.
and T. Andersen (ed.): P. K. Museum Folkwang. Essen 1977.– Fuchs, R. et al. (ed.): P.
K. Stedelijk Van Abbe Museum. Eindhoven 1982 (cat.).– Gallwitz, K. (ed.): P. K.
Gemälde, Arbeiten auf Papier, Skulpturen
1977-1990. Städtische Galerie im Städelschen Kunstinstitut. Frankfurt-on-Main
1990 (cat.).– Geyer, M.-J. (ed.): P. K. Musée
d'Art Moderne de Strasbourg. Strasbourg
1984 (cat.).– Godfrey, T. et al. (ed.): P. K.
Whitechapel Art Gallery. London 1986
(cat.).– Gohr, S. et al. (ed.): P. K. Retrospektive. Museum Ludwig. Cologne 1987
(cat.).– Haenlein, C. A. (ed.): P. K. Bilder.
Kestner-Gesellschaft. Hanover 1992 (cat.).–
Horn, L. and C. Tacke (ed.): P. K. 1964-
1984. Kunstraum Munich et al. Munich
1984 (cat.).– Jorgensen, T. and A. Schnack:
P. K. Stein, Papier, Schere. Münster 1991.–

P. K. Kunstverein Braunschweig. Brunswick
1985 (cat.).– P. K. Recent Painting and
Sculpture. Whitechapel Art Gallery.
London 1985 (cat.).– P. K. Ville de Lyon.
Lyon 1987 (cat.).– P. K. Pinturas, esculturas,
grabados y escritos. IVAM Centre del
Carme. Valencia 1989 (cat.).– P. K. Excur-
sions et expéditions. Grenoble 1992 (cat.).–
P. K. Großformatige Zeichnungen 1977-
1994. Portikus, Frankfurt-on-Main et al.
Münster 1994 (cat.).– P. K. Museum of
Modern Art. Ishoj 1996 (cat.).– P. K. and
L. Morell: Svanesoen. Copenhagen 1997.–
Koella, R. (ed.): P. K. Werke 1983-1988.
Kunstmuseum Winterthur 1989 (cat.).–
Lamarche-Vadel, B. (ed.): P. K. Centre de
Création Contemporain de Tours. Tours
1987 (cat.).– Morell, L.: P. K. Baukunst.
Copenhagen 1996.– Nilsson, B. and E.
Lidman (ed.): P. K. Malerei, skulptur, teck-
ningar, böcker, film. 1964-1990/ P. K. Paint-
ings, Sculptures, Drawings, Books, Films
1964-1990. Moderna Museet. Stockholm
1990 (cat.).– Schjeldahl, P. (ed.): P. K. Mary
Boone Gallery. New York 1986 (cat.).–
Schmidt-Miescher, M. and J. Gachnang
(ed.): P. K. Kunsthalle Bern. Bern 1979
(cat.).– Ullrich, F. (ed.): P. K. Städtische
Kunsthalle Recklinghausen. Recklinghausen
1994 (cat.)

KISLING Moïse
1891 Cracow – **1953** Sanary-sur-Mer (Var)
Polish painter. **1906** Studied at the Art
Academy in Cracow under J. Pankiewicz.
Influenced by Impressionism. **1910** Moved
to Paris. Contact with the artists around
Picasso. **1914/15** Fought with the French
Foreign Legion. **1915** Founded the artists'
group Morbidezza in Paris with Modigliani
and Soutine. **1919** First solo-exhibition at
the Galerie Drouet with melancholy pic-
tures in a realist style. **1940** Fled from the
Nazi regime to America via Portugal. **1947**
Returned to France and settled in Sanary-
sur-Mer. The focus of Kisling's work was
the human figure, particularly the female
body, preferably in dramatic, melancholic
settings.
CATALOGUE RAISONNE: Kessel, J. et al.
(ed.): K. 1891-1953. 3 vols. New York and
Lanshut 1971-1985
MONOGRAPHS, CATALOGUES: Kessel,
J.: K. 1891-1953. Torino 1971.– M. K. Petit
Palais Genève. Geneva 1972 (cat.).– M. K.
Rétrospective. Grand Palais. Paris 1984
(cat.).– M. K. Retrospective K. Grande
Galerie Odákyu. Tokyo 1984 (cat.).– M. K.
Centenaire K. Galerie Daniel Malingue.
Paris 1991 (cat.).– Rey-Pieferd, A. and P.
Ebéli (ed.): Montparnasse. Atelier du
Monde, ses artistes venus d'ailleurs.
Hommage à K. 1891-1953. Palais de la
Bource. Marseille 1992 (cat.)

KITAJ Ronald B.
born **1932** Cleveland (OH)
American painter. **1950** Studied at the
Cooper Union for the Advancement of
Science and Art in New York. **1951/52**

Studied at the Vienna Academy under
Albert Paris von Gütersloh and Fritz
Wotruba. **1953–1957** Worked as a merchant
seaman. **1958** Continued studies at the
Ruskin School of Drawing in Oxford and
from **1959–1961** at the Royal College of Art
in London. **1961–1967** Teacher at various
colleges and art schools in London. **1970**
Guest-professor at the University of California in Berkeley. **1964** and **1968** participation
in documenta 3 and 4 in Kassel. **1971**
Returned to London, where he taught at
various universities; in **1976** organized an
exhibition of figurative painting under the
title "The Human Clay". **1980** The Tate
Gallery bought his painting *The Rise of
Fascism*. **1995** Received the Painting Prize at
the Venice Biennale. In London, Kitaj's
figurative painting had a great influence on
his fellow-students Jones and Hockney; all
three later becoming well known as British
Pop artists. Kitaj himself, however, dis-
claimed belonging to the Pop Art movement, using the argument that his themes
came not from popular culture but from
philosophy, literature and politics.
WRITINGS: R. B. K. Erstes Manifest des
Diasporismus. Zurich 1988/ First Diasporit
Manifesto. London 1989.– R. B. K. Szét-
szórva a világban. Egy zsidó fető vallomása
az életröl, a művészetröl ... A diaszporizmus
elsö kiáltványa. Budapest 1994
CATALOGUES RAISONNES: Ashbery, J.
et al. (ed.): K. Paintings, Drawings, Pastels.
London 1986.– Kinsman, J. (ed.): The Prints
of R. B. K. Brookfield 1994
MONOGRAPHS, CATALOGUES: Ashbery,
J.: R. B. K. Städtische Kunsthalle Düssel-
dorf. Düsseldorf 1982 (cat.).– Deppner, M.
R.: R. B. K. Mahler Becomes Politics,
Beisbol. Hamburger Kunsthalle. Hamburg
1990 (cat.).– Deppner, M. R.: Zeichen und
Bildwanderung. Zum Ausdruck des "Nicht-
Seßhaften" im Werk R. B. K. Münster and
Hamburg 1992.– R. B. K. Kestner-Gesell-
schaft. Hanover 1970 (cat.).– R. B. K.
Museum Boymans-van Beuningen. Rotter-
dam 1970 (cat.).– R. B. K. Marlborough
Fine Art, London, Marlborough Gallery,
New York. London 1985 (cat.).– R. B. K.
Astrup Fearnley Museet, Oslo et al. Oslo
1998 (cat.).– Livingstone, M.: R. B. K.
Oxford and New York 1985, Oxford 1992.–
Morphet, R. et al. (ed.): R. B. K. Tate
Gallery, London et al. London and New
York 1994 (cat.).– Ríos, J. K.: Pictures and
Conversations. London 1994.– Shannon, J.
et al. (ed.): R. B. K. Hirshhorn Museum,
Washington et al. Washington 1982 (cat.).–
Spender, S. (ed.): R. B. K. Pastels and
Drawings. Marlborough Fine Art. London
1980 (cat.)

KLAPHECK Konrad
born **1935** Düsseldorf
German painter. Studied **1954–1958** under
Goller at the Düsseldorf Academy. Already
in his student days, he discovered the
central theme of all his works: figurative
portrayals of machinery in what he called
prosaic super-objectivity. First picture of a

typewriter. **1956/57** Study trip to Paris;
became acquainted with the work of
Duchamp. **1959** First solo-exhibition at the
Schmela Gallery in Düsseldorf. **1960** Met
Oelze. **1961–1966** Contact with the Surrealist circle around Breton. Between **1964**
and **1977** participation in documenta 3, 4
and 6 in Kassel. **1968** Participation in the
"Dada, Surrealism and Their Heritage"
exhibition in the Museum of Modern Art,
New York. **1974/75** Important retrospective
in the Boymans van Beuningen Museum,
Rotterdam. **1976–1980** Worked intensively
on etching techniques. **1979** Professor at the
Düsseldorf Academy. **1985/86** Retrospective
in Hamburg, Tübingen and Munich. Klapheck's painting, which soberly portrays
home appliances such as typewriters, sewing
machines, telephones and irons in stark
objectivity, is a reaction to lyrical Tachisme.
CATALOGUES RAISONNES: Pierre, J.
(ed.): K. K. Œuvre-Verzeichnis der
Gemälde. Cologne 1970.– Zwirner, R. (ed.):
K. K. Werkverzeichnis der Druckgraphik.
1960-1977. Cologne 1977.– Zwirner, R.
(ed.): K. K. Werkverzeichnis der Druck-
graphik. 1977-1980. Düsseldorf and
Cologne 1980
MONOGRAPHS, CATALOGUES: Breton,
A. and W. Schmied (ed.): K. K. Kestner-
Gesellschaft. Hanover 1966 (cat.).–
Chapon, F.: K. Montrouge 1980.–
Hofmann, W. (ed.): K. K. Retrospektive
1955-1985. Hamburger Kunsthalle et al.
Munich 1985 (cat.).– K. K. Neuen
Boymans-van Beuningen. Rotterdam 1974
(cat.).– K. K. Entwürfe und Bilder 1971-
1982. Kunstverein für die Rheinlande und
Westfalen. Düsseldorf 1983 (cat.).– K. K.
Peintures et dessins. Galerie Lelong. Paris
1990 (cat.)

KLAUKE Jürgen
born **1943** Kliding (near Cochem)
German artist. **1964–1970** Studied graphic
art at the Cologne School of Art and Design
and taught there from **1970** until **1975**.
Began in **1970** to make daily entries in a
kind of diary, with drawings and photographs describing his momentary surroundings. **1972** In performances such as *Transformer* or *Made in Germany (Hinsetzen-
Aufstehen)* of **1979**, used symbolic, rituali-
stic repetition to exaggerate and portray
gender roles and everyday conflicts. **1977**

Took part in documenta 6 in Kassel. Between **1980** and **1986** guest-professorships at the Hamburg and Munich Art Academies and Kassel Comprehensive Art College. **1980** Large-format picture series with posed photographs, such as the multipartite photoseries *Formalisierung der Langweile* (The Shape of Boredom). **1987** Professor of photography at the University of Essen. Participation in documenta 8 in Kassel. From **1993** professor at Cologne Media Academy. **1997** Retrospective in Tokyo. Klauke developed a mannered and theatrical style of performance art, which ritualized ordinary everyday situations. WRITINGS: J. K. im Gespräch mit H.-M. Herzog und G. J. Lischka. Cologne 1997 MONOGRAPHS, CATALOGUES: Herzog, H. M. (ed.): J. K. Prosecuritas. Kunsthalle Bielefeld. Stuttgart 1994 (cat.).– Honnef, K. (ed.): J. K. Formalisierung der Langeweile. Kunstmuseum Luzern et al. Cologne 1981 (cat.).– Honnef, K. et al. (ed.): J. K. Phantomempfindungen – Phantom Sensation. The Museum of Modern Art, Saitama et al. Saitama 1997 (cat.).– Poetter, J. (ed.): J. K. Sonntagsneurosen. Staatliche Kunsthalle Baden-Baden. Baden-Baden 1992 (cat.).– Vowinckel, A. and E. Weiss (ed.): J. K. Eine Ewigkeit ein Lächeln. Zeichnungen, Fotoarbeiten, Performances 1970-1986. Badischer Kunstverein, Karlsruhe et al. Cologne 1986 (cat.)

KLEE Paul
1879 Münchenbuchsee (near Bern) –
1940 Muralto (near Locarno)
German painter, graphic artist, and art theoritician. **1898** Art instruction at a private painting school in Munich under Heinrich Knirr. **1900** Attended Franz von Stuck's painting class at the Munich Academy. **1901** Trip to Italy. **1905** Lived in Paris. In the years from **1902-1906**, when he was living in Bern, he produced etchings inspired by Francisco de Goya, James Ensor and Aubrey Beardsley. **1911** Returned to Munich, where he became acquainted with Macke, Marc, Javlensky, Münter, Verefkin and Kandinsky. **1912** Participation in the second exhibition of the Blauer Reiter group. Trip to Paris, where he met Delaunay and saw pictures by Braque and Picasso **1914** Co-founder of the Munich New Secession. Travelled to Tunis with Louis Moilliet and Macke. **1916** Military service. **1919** Began painting in oils, taking abstract forms as objects. **1920** Appointed to the Bauhaus in Weimar. Published the essay *Creative Confessions*, begun in **1918**. **1931-1933** Professor at the Düsseldorf Academy. Period of divisionist painting. **1933** Returned to Bern owing to National Socialist pressure. **1937** Confiscation of 102 of his works by the Nazis, of which 17 were exhibited in the exhibition of "degenerate art" in Munich. Klee's hieroglyphic picture language, which works with an abstract vocabulary of forms but never completely loses its inner connection to the real world, is often ambiguous and slightly ironic.

WRITINGS: Geelhaar, C. (ed.): P. K. Schriften, Rezensionen und Aufsätze. Cologne 1976.– Klee, F. (ed.): P. K. Briefe an die Familie. 1893-1940. 2 vols. Cologne 1979.– P. K.: Tagebücher. 1898-1918. Textkritische Neuedition. Stuttgart 1988 / The Diaries of P. K. 1898-1918. Berkeley and Los Angeles 1964.– Regel, G. (ed.): P. K. Kunst-Lehre. Aufsätze, Vorträge, Rezensionen und Beiträge zur bildnerischen Formlehre. Leipzig 1991.– Spiller, J. (ed.): The P. K. Notebook. 2 vols. London and Woodstock (NY) 1992 CATALOGUES RAISONNES: Frey, S. and J. Helfenstein (ed.): P. K. Verzeichnis der Werke des Jahres 1940. Stuttgart 1991.– Glaesemer, J. (ed.): P. K. Handzeichnungen. 3 vols. Bern 1973-1984.– Kornfeld, E. W. (ed.): Verzeichnis des graphischen Werkes von P. K. Bern 1963.– Paul-Klee-Stiftung (ed.): Catalogue Raisonné P. K. Vol. 1: 1883-1912. Bern 1998 MONOGRAPHS, CATALOGUES: Bischoff, U.: P. K. Munich 1992.– Bonfand, A.: P. K. L'œil en trop. 2 vols. Paris 1988.– Boulez, P.: Le Pays fertile. P. K. Paris 1989.– Buderer, H.-J.: P. K. Konstruktion, Intuition. Städtische Kunsthalle Mannheim. Stuttgart 1990 (cat.).– Chapeaurouge, D. d.: P. K. und der christliche Himmel. Stuttgart 1990.– Compte, O.: K. Paris 1991, Woodstock (NY) 1991.– Cortenova, G. (ed.): P. K. Palazzo Forti, Verona. Milan 1992 (cat.).– Crone, R. and J. L. Koerner: P. K. Legends of the Sign. New York 1991.– Dennison, L. (ed.): P. K. at the Guggenheim Museum. Guggenheim Museum. New York 1993 (cat.).– Franciscono, M.: P. K. His Work and Thought. Chicago 1991.– Franz, E. (ed.): P. K. Späte Zeichnungen von 1939. Museum Folkwang. Essen 1989 (cat.).– Frontisi, C.: K. Anatomie d'Aphrodite. Le polyptyque démembré. Paris 1990.– Geelhaar, C.: P. K. und das Bauhaus. Cologne 1972 / P. K. and the Bauhaus. Grennwich 1972 / P. K. et le Bauhaus. Neuchâtel 1972.– Geelhaar, P.: P. K. Leben und Werk. Cologne 1974 / P. K. Life and Work. New York 1982.– Glaesemer, J. (ed.): P. K. Die farbigen Werke im Kunstmuseum Bern. Bern 1976 / P. K. The Colored Works in the Kunstmuseum Bern. Bern 1979.– Glaesemer, J. (ed.): P. K. Beiträge zur bildnerischen Formlehre. Basel 1979.– Glaesemer, J. et al. (ed.): P. K. Leben und Werk. Kunstmuseum Bern et al. Stuttgart 1988, 1996 (cat.) / P. K. Life and Work. The Museum of Modern Art, New York et al. New York 1988 (cat.).– Gohr, S. et al. (ed.): P. K. Das Werk der Jahre 1919-1933. Josef-Haubrich-Kunsthalle. Cologne 1979 (cat.).– Grohmann, W.: P. K. Stuttgart 1954, Paris 1954, New York 1954.– Güse, E.-G. (ed.): P. K. Wachstum regt sich. K. Zwiesprache mit der Natur. Saarland Museum, Saarbrücken et al. Munich 1990.– Güse, E. G. (ed.): P. K. Dialogue with Nature. New York 1995.– Haftmann, W.: P. K. Wege bildnerischen Denkens. Frankfurt-on-Main 1961.– Haxthausen, C. W.: P. K. The Formative Years. New York 1981.– Helfenstein, J. (ed.): P. K. Das Schaffen im Todesjahr. Kunstmuseum Bern. Stuttgart 1990 (cat.).– Hofmann, W. (ed.): P. K. 50 Werke aus 50 Jahren. 1890-1940. Hamburger Kunsthalle. Hamburg 1990 (cat.).– Hoppe-Sailer, R.: P. K. Ad Parnassum. Frankfurt a. M. 1993.– Huggler, M.: P. K. Die Malerei als Blick in den Kosmos. Frauenfeld et al. 1969.– Jordan, J. M.: P. K. and Cubism. Princeton (N J) 1984.– Kagan, A.: P. K. Art and Music. Ithaca (NY) et al. 1983.– Kagan, A. (ed.): P. K. At the Guggenheim Museum. Solomon R. Guggenheim Museum. New York 1993 (cat.).– Kersten, W.: P. K. Übermut. Allegorie der künstlerischen Existenz. Frankfurt a. m. 1990.– Kersten, W. and O. Okuda (ed.): P. K. Im Zeichen der Teilung. Die Geschichte zerschnittener Kunst Paul Klees

1883-1940. Kunstsammlung Nordrhein-Westfalen, Düsseldorf et al. Stuttgart 1995 (cat.).– Klee, F. (ed.): P. K. Leben und Werk in Dokumenten. Zurich 1960 / P. K. His Life and Work in Documents. New York 1962.– P. K. Œuvres de 1933 à 1940. Musées des Beaux-Arts. Nîmes 1984 (cat.).– Kornfeld, E. W.: Verzeichnis des graphischen Werkes von P. K. Bern 1963.– Kruszynski, A. (ed.): P. K. Im Zeichen der Teilung: die Geschichte zerschnittener Kunst P. K. 1883-1940. Kunstsammlung Nordrhein-Westfalen, Düsseldorf et al. Düsseldorf and Stuttgart 1995 (cat.).– Kuenzi, A. (ed.): K. Fondation Pierre Gianadda. Martigny 1985 (cat.).– Lanchner, C. (ed.): P. K. The Museum of Modern Art, New York et al. New York 1987 (cat.).– Moe, O. H. et al. (ed.): K. et la musique. Centre Georges Pompidou. Paris 1985 (cat.).– Nauber-Riser, C.: K. Paris 1997.– Osterwold, T. (ed.): P. K. Spätwerk. Württembergischer Kunstverein. Stuttgart 1990 (cat.).– Plant, M.: P. K. Figures and Faces. London 1978.– Rathke-Köhl, S. (ed.): P. K. nelle collezioni private. Museo d'Arte Moderna Ca' Pesaro. Venice 1986 (cat.).– Rewald, S. (ed.): P. K. The Berggruen Klee Collection in the Metropolitan Museum of Art. New York 1988.– Schulz-Hoffmann, C. et al. (ed.): P. K. Wachstum der Nachtpflanzen, Vogelgarten. Staatsgalerie moderner Kunst. Munich 1992 (cat.).– Verdi, R.: K. and Nature. New York 1985.– Vitali, C.: P. K. und die Musik. Schirn Kunsthalle. Frankfurt-on-Main 1986 (cat.).– Vogel, M.: Zwischen Wort und Bild. Das schriftliche Werk Paul Klees und die Rolle der Sprache in seinem Denken und in seiner Kunst. Munich 1992.– Werckmeister, O. K.: Versuche über P. K. Frankfurt-on-Main 1981 / The Making of P. K.'s Career 1914-1920. Chicago 1989.– Zweite, A. (ed.): P. K. Das Frühwerk 1883-1922. Städtische Galerie im Lenbachhaus. Munich 1979 (cat.)

KLEIN William
born **1928** New York
American photographer and film-maker. **1943-1947** Studied social sciences at the City College, New York and at the Sorbonne in Paris. **1948** Assistant in Léger's studio. **1952** First photographic work. **1954** Returned to New York. **1956** Published his book of photographs *New York*, in which he portrays life in the city in apparently random and often unfocused pictures. He was artistic advisor to Louis Malle during the filming of *Zazie in the Metro*. **1955-1965** Staff member at *Vogue*. In addition to fashion pictures, he did numerous portraits of celebrities. **1957** Received the Prix Nadar. **1958** Shot his first film, *Broadway by Light*, followed by 20 further films and documentaries. **1964** Published two photograph books on Tokyo and Moscow. **1965** Gave up photography and dedicated himself to film. **1966** Release of the film *Qui êtes-vous, Polly Maggoo?* In the 50s, Klein worked mostly as a photographer, experimenting with photographic manipulation to produce abstract effects. From the beginning of the 60s, he became increasingly interested in film production.
MONOGRAPHS, CATALOGUES: Caujolle, C. (ed.): W. K. Centre de la Photographie. Paris 1992 (cat.).– Heilpern, J. W. K. Photographs. New York 1981.– W. K. Schilderijen, foto's, films. Stedelijk Museum. Amsterdam 1967 (cat.).– Tweedie, K. (ed.): W. K. Photographer, Filmmaker. New York 1982

KLEIN Yves
1928 Nice – **1962** Paris
French artist. **1944-1946** Studied at the

Ecole Nationale de la Marine marchande. **1946/47** Friendship with Claude Pascal and Arman. Developed first theories on monochromism and composed his *Symphonie monoton*, a work consisting of one single note, which was performed in **1949** for the first time with Klein conducting. **1952/53** Lived in Japan, where he won a black belt in judo. **1955** Returned to Paris and ran a judo school. From **1956** worked exclusively in International Klein Blue (IKB), a luminous ultramarine blue whose mixture Klein himself developed. **1957** Showed his *Période bleue* in the Galleria Apollinaire in Milan. **1958** First *Anthropométries*: Body prints of female models, who were dipped in Yves Klein Blue. Presentations of empty rooms. **1960** Exhibition of his first *Monochrome gold* paintings at the Salon Antagonismes and of his *Anthropométries de l'Epoque* in the Galerie Internationale d'Art Contemporain in Paris. Founder member of the Nouveaux Réalistes. First *Cosmogonies*, images created by the action of natural elements (e.g. rain, wind, plant imprints). **1961** First planetary relief and first fire pictures. **1962** Composition of the *Symphonie Monoton No. 2*. Created complete body casts of his friends Arman, Martial Raysse and Claude Pascal. **1964** and **1968** participation in documenta 3 and 4 in Kassel. **1983** Major retrospective at the Pompidou Centre in Paris, and **1994** at the Ludwig Museum, Cologne. With his use of unusual materials and unconventional techniques, and the involvement of the elements fire, water and air in the creative process, Klein did much to extend the boundaries of what is considered "art".
WRITINGS: Caumont, J. and J. Gough-Cooper (ed.): Y. K. 1928-1962. Selected Writings. Tate Gallery. London 1974 (cat.).– Y. K.: Les Fondements du judo. Paris 1954.– Y. K.: Le Dépassement de la problématique de l'art. La Louvière 1959 CATALOGUES RAISONNES: Wember, P.: Y. K. Cologne 1969.– Klein-Moquay, R. et al. (ed.): Y. K. Catalogue raisonné (in preparation)
MONOGRAPHS, CATALOGUES: Heynen, J. (ed.): Y. K. Monochrome und Feuer, Krefeld 1961. Ein Dokument der Avantgarde. Krefeld 1994.– Krahmer, C.: Der Fall Y. K. Zur Krise der Kunst. Munich 1974.– Martano, G.: Y. K. Il mistero ostentato. Torino 1970.– Millet, C.: Y. K. Paris 1983.– Mock, J.-Y. et al. (ed.): Y. K. Centre Georges Pompidou. Paris 1983 (cat.).– Prats Okuyama, C. and K. Okuyama: K. L'Arbre, grande éponge bleue. Paris 1994.– Restany, P.: Y. K. Paris 1982, New York 1982, Munich 1983.– Restany, P. et al. (ed.): Y. K. 1928-1962. Retrospective. Rice University Museum, Houston et al. Houston 1982 (cat.).– Restany, P.: Y. K. Le feu au cœur du vide. Paris 1990 / Y. K. Fire at the Heart of the Void. New York 1992.– Restany, P. et al. (ed.): Y. K. Oslo et al. Oslo 1997 (cat.).– Rosenthal, N.: The Blue World of Y. K. Cambridge 1976.– Schneider, A. and H. Weitermeier (ed.): Y. K. Nationalgalerie Berlin et al. Berlin 1976 (cat.).– Stich, S.

(ed.): Y. K. Museum Ludwig, Cologne et al. Stuttgart 1994 (cat.).– Stöhr, J.: Y. K. und die ästhetische Erfahrung. Bochum 1992.– Weitemeier, H.: Y. K. 1928-1962. International Klein Blue. Cologne 1995.– Wember, P.: Y. K. Cologne 1969, 1972

KLIMT Gustav
1862 Baumgarten – 1918 Vienna
Austrian painter. 1876–1882 Attended the Vienna School of Arts and Crafts. 1886–1888 Along with his brother Ernst and Franz Matsche, painted a ceiling at the Burgtheater in Vienna. 1890–1892 Spandrel and intercolumnation paintings for the staircase of the Art History Museum in Vienna. 1897 Founder member of the Vienna Secession and its president until he resigned from the movement in 1905. 1898 Participation in the first exhibition of the Secession. Worked for *Ver Sacrum* magazine. 1890 Participation in the Paris World Fair. Mural decorations for the Banqueting Hall of the University of Vienna on the themes of Philosophy, Jurisprudence and Medicine. 1902 Creation of the *Beethoven Frieze* in the room of the left of the Vienna Secession. 1905 Designs for a mosaic in the Stoclet Palace in Brussels. 1906–1909 Travelled to Belgium England, Florence, Paris, and Madrid. 1910 Enthusiastic reception of his work at the Venice Biennale. 1917 Made an honorary member of the Vienna Academy after he had been refused a professorship. Klimt, with his preference for decorative motifs and symbolic images, had a formative influence on Viennese Jugendstil, especially on the work of the artists and craftsmen at the Wiener Werkstätte (Vienna Workshops).
CATALOGUES RAISONNES: Coradeschi, S. (ed.): Tout l'œuvre peint de K. Paris 1983.– Dobai, G. and F. Novotny (ed.): G. K. Catalogue Raisonné. Salzburg 1967, 1975 / G. K. With a Catalogue Raisonné of His Paintings. London 1968, Boston 1975.– Strobl, A. (ed.): G. K. Die Zeichnungen. 4 vols. Salzburg 1980-1989
MONOGRAPHS, CATALOGUES: Bisanz-Prakken, M.: G. K. Der Beethovenfries. Geschichte, Funktion und Bedeutung. Munich 1980.– Brandstätter, C.: G. K. und die Frauen. Vienna 1994.– Breicha, O.: G. K. Die goldene Pforte. Werk, Wesen, Wirkung. Bilder und Schriften zu Leben und Werk. Salzburg 1978.– Breicha, O.: G. K. Die Bilder und Zeichnungen der Sammlung Leopold. Salzburg 1990.– Comini, A.: G. K. London and New York 1975.– Dobai, J. and S. Coradeschi: L'opera completa di Klimt. Milan 1979.– Dobai, J.: G. K. Die Landschaften. Salzburg 1981/ G. K. Landscapes. London 1988.– Ducros, F.: K. Paris 1992.– Fliedl, G.: G. K. 1862-1918. The World in Female Form. Cologne 1990.– Fliedl, G.: K. The Definite Monograph on the Viennese Artist. New York 1997.– Frodl, G.: K. et l'école de Vienne. Paris 1990.– Frodl, G.: K. Cologne 1992, London 1992.– Hofmann, W.: G. K. und die Wiener Jahrhundertwende. Salzburg 1970/ G. K. New York 1971.– Hofstätter, H. H. (ed.)

G. K. Erotische Zeichnungen. Cologne 1979.– G. K. 1862 – Wien – 1918. Zeichnungen aus Privatbesitz. Düsseldorf 1987 (cat.).– Melloni, C.: G. K. Il sigillo della contraddizione. Venice 1989.– Nebehay, C. M.: G. K. Eine Dokumentation. Vienna 1969.– Nebehay, C. M.: G. K. Sein Leben nach zeitgenössischen Berichten und Quellen. Munich 1976, 1984.– Nebehay, C. M.: G. K. Das Skizzenbuch aus dem Besitz von Sonja Knips. Vienna 1987.– Nebehay, C. M.: G. K. Von der Zeichnung zum Bild. Vienna 1992/G. K. From Drawing to Painting. New York 1994/G. K. Paris 1993.– Néret, G.: G. K. Cologne 1993.– Partsch, S.: G. K. Maler der Frauen. Munich 1994.– Sabarsky, S. (ed.): G. K. Musées Royaux des Beaux-Arts de Belgique. Brussels 1987 (cat.).– Sabarsky, S. (ed.): G. K. Palazzo Strozzi. Florence 1992 (cat.).– Sármány, I.: G. K. Budapest 1989.– Stooss, T. and C. Doswald (ed.): G. K. Kunsthaus Zürich. Stuttgart 1992 (cat.).– Welz, F. (ed.): G. K. Salzburg 1975.– Whitford, F.: K. London 1990

KLINE Franz
1910 Wilkes-Barre (PA) – 1962 New York
American painter. 1931–1935 Studied in Boston and from 1936 at the Heatherley School of Fine Art in London. 1938 Moved to New York. 1943 Became friends with de Kooning, who kindled his interest in abstraction. At first he painted portraits, seated figures in rocking chairs, railway bridges, and Pennsylvania landscapes. By the end of the 40s, he had developed his own personal style of gestural painting requiring ever larger canvases. Finally limited himself to black and white. From 1950 produced powerful tectonic constructions, whose origin he attributed to Mondrian. 1954 Participation in the Symposium "Abstract Art Around the World Today" at the Museum of Modern Art, New York. 1958/59 Colour experiments with the goal of being able to use colours structurally, like the non-colours black and white. 1959 and 1964 participation in documenta 2 and 3 in Kassel. Kline, who died of a heart attack in 1962, developed an individual form of action painting language reminiscent of Far Eastern calligraphy.
MONOGRAPHS, CATALOGUES: Dawson, F.: An Emotional Memoir of F. K. New York 1967.– Foster, S. C. et al. (ed.): F. K. Art and Structure. Fundació Antoni Tàpies, Barcelona et al. Barcelona 1994 (cat.).– Gaugh, H. F. (ed.): F. K. The Color Abstractions. The Phillips Collection. Washington 1979 (cat.).– Gaugh, H. F. (ed.): F. K. The Vital Gesture. Cincinnati Art Museum et al. New York 1985, 1994 (cat.).– Gordon, J. (ed.): F. K. 1910-1962. Whitney Museum of American Art, New York et al. New York 1968 (cat.).– F. K. Stedelijk Museum. Amsterdam 1963 (cat.).– F. K. Museum des 20. Jahrhunderts. Vienna 1964 (cat.).– F. K. Kunsthalle Basel. Basel 1964 (cat.).– F. K. The Color Abstractions. Phillips Collection. Washington 1979

(cat.).– F. K. Whitechappel Art Gallery. London 1994 (cat.).– Whitney, D. and D. Anfam (ed.): F. K. Black & White 1950-1961. The Menil Collection, Houston et al. Houston 1994 (cat.).– Zevi, A.: F. K. Milan 1987

KLIUN Ivan
1873 Kiev – 1942 Moscow
Russian painter and sculptor. Art studies in Warsaw and Kiev. From 1900 private lessons in Moscow under Rerberg and Mashkov. 1907 Acquaintance with Malevich. 1910 One of the founders of the Moscow Salon. 1913 First relief sculptures. 1915 In depth study of Suprematism, the painting style invented by Malevich. Participation in the first Futurist exhibition "Tramway V" in St. Petersburg. Exhibited 1916 at the "Last Futurist Exhibition: 0,10" in St. Petersburg. From 1917 held various cultural posts; for example, director of the central exhibition office Narkompros. 1918–1921 Taught at the Vhumtemas art institute in Moscow. 1922 Participation in the "First Russian Art Exhibition" at the van Diemen gallery in Berlin. 1923 Worked on the production of various futurist book publications. 1925 Joined the Company of the Four Arts. Kliun experimented in his still lifes with geometric forms and investigated their colour relationships. With the advent of the politically motivated shift from abstract art to Socialist Realism in the 20s, Kliun gave up his geometric colour and form experiments and resumed figurative painting.
MONOGRAPHS, CATALOGUES: I. K. Matignon Gallery. New York 1983 (cat.).– Kliunkova-Soloveichnik, S.: I. K. New York 1993

KNOEBEL Imi
born 1940 Dessau
German painter and object artist. 1964–1971 Studied at the Düsseldorf Art Academy under Beuys. Close contact to Imi Giese and Palermo. Worked with light projections. 1968 First solo-exhibition together with Imi Giese in Copenhagen. First room installations out of fibre board. 1969–1975 Experiments with a single line in over 250,000 drawings. 1972 Production of the videotape *X* for the video gallery run by Gerry Schum. 1972–1987 Participation in

documenta 5 – 8 in Kassel. 1975/76 Multipartite picture constellations, entitled *White Pictures*. 1976–1981 Period of the *Mennige Pictures* with designs and construction sketches cut out of white paper. 1980 Large environment with coloured cut-out plywood rectangles, which are layered, stacked, and hung (*Genter Raum*). 1982 Environment *Radio Beirut*. 1984 Room construction using fibre board, outlining the measurements of the studio kitchen (*Heerstraße*). Influenced by Malevich's Suprematism and Russian Constructivism, Knoebel's geometric abstract works address the fundamental problems of painting and form.
MONOGRAPHS, CATALOGUES: Bloem, M. and H. Gaßner (ed.): I. K. Retrospektive 1966-1996. Haus der Kunst, Munich et al. Stuttgart 1996 (cat.).– I. K. Kunstmuseum. Winterthur 1983 (cat.).– I. K. Städtisches Museum Abteiberg. Mönchengladbach 1984 (cat.).– I. K. Rijksmuseum Kröller-Müller. Otterlo 1985 (cat.).– I. K. Staatliche Kunsthalle Baden-Baden. Baden-Baden 1986 (cat.).– I. K. Werken uit de verzameling Ingrid en Hugo Jung. Museum van Hedendaagse Kunst. Antwerp 1988 (cat.).– I. K. Tentoonstellingsinstallaties 1968-1988 / Austellungsinstallationen 1968-1988. Bonnefantenmuseum. Maastricht 1989 (cat.).– I. K. Hessischens Landesmuseum. Darmstadt 1992 (cat.).– I. K. Kunstverein St. Gallen. St. Gallen 1996 (cat.).– I. K. Rot Gelb Weiß Blau. Ludwig Forum für Internationale Kunst. Aachen 1996 (cat.).– Loers, V. (ed.): Shapes and Positions. Kunsthalle Ritter et al. Klagenfurt 1992 (cat.).– Stüttgen, J.: Der Keilrahmen des I. K. 1968/89. Cologne 1991

KOBRO Katarzyna
1898 Moscow – 1951 Lódz
Polish sculptress. 1917–1920 Studied painting in Moscow. 1920 Married Strzemiński and moved to Smolensk. Member of the Unowis artist's group. 1920–1921 Maintained contacts with the OBMOChU group. 1922 Moved to Poland. From 1924 member of the Blok artists' group. Taught in industrial schools in Szczekociny and Koluszki. 1925–1933 *Spatial Compositions* in sheet metal. 1929 Co-founder of the a. R. group. 1931 Taught at the Industrial School for Women in Lódz. 1933 Joined Abstraction-Création. 1936–1947 Due to the difficult wartime circumstances, she gave up her artistic activities. 1948 Last cubist-style nude sculptures. Kobro's floating metal compositions are similar to Tatlin's constructions.
WRITINGS: K. K. and W. Strzeminski: L'Espace uniste. Ecrits du constructivisme polonais. Lausanne 1977
MONOGRAPHS, CATALOGUES: Grzecha-Mohr, U.: K. und die konstruktivistische Bewegung. Diss. Münster 1986.– Jedlinski, J. (ed.): K. K. 1898-1951. Städtisches Museum Abteiberg, Mönchengladbach. Cologne 1991 (cat.).– K. K. Muzeum Sztuki, Lodz / Städtisches Museum

Abteiberg, Mönchengladbach. Mönchengladbach 1991 (cat.).– Zagrodzki, J.: K. K. i Kompozycja przestrzeni. Warsaw 1984 (cat.)

KOKOSCHKA Oskar
1886 Pöchlarn (on the Danube) – **1980** Villeneuve (on Lake Geneva)
Austrian painter, graphic artist and poet. **1905–1909** Studied at the Vienna School of Arts and Crafts. **1907–1909** Worked in the Wiener Werkstätte (Vienna Workshops). **1909/10** Period of portraits: dissecting the human psyche on canvas. **1910** Moved to Berlin and worked on *Der Sturm* magazine. **1911** Returned to Vienna, where he worked as an assistant at the School of Arts and Crafts, and began his fatal love affair with Alma Mahler. **1914** Separated from Alma Mahler. The male-female conflict, which he had already treated in his drama *Mörder, Hoffnung der Frauen* (Murderer: Women's Hope), became an allegory of unbridled love in his painting *Die Windsbraut* (Kunstmuseum, Basel). **1915** Taken to a military hospital soon after signing up for military service. **1917** Moved to Dresden, where he was appointed professor at the Art Academy in **1919**. In addition to portraiture painted pictures of towns. **1924** Resigned his professorship and travelled extensively through Europe, North Africa, and the Near East. **1933** Returned to Vienna. **1934** Moved to Prague. **1937** Confiscation of 417 works classified as "degenerate art". **1938** Emigrated to England and settled in London. **1947** Became a British citizen. **1953** Moved to Villeneuve on Lake Geneva. Found the School of Seeing at the summer school in Salzburg. **1975** Became an Austrian citizen again. Kokoschka, an artist who was responsible for introducing psychology into Expressionism, worked in many art forms. His œuvre includes not only paintings, but graphic works and stage designs, as well as poems, which he illustrated himself. WRITINGS: Breicha, O. (ed.): O. K. Vom Erlebnis im Leben. Schriften und Bilder. Salzburg 1977.– O. K.: Mein Leben. Munich 1971/My Life. London 1974.– Marnau, A. (ed.): O. K. Berichte aus einer eingebildeten Welt. Vienna, Graz and Cologne 1996.– Marnau, A. and O. Kokoschka (ed.): O. K. Letters 1905-1976. London and New York 1992.– Spielmann, H. (ed.): O. K. Das schriftliche Werk. 4 vols. Hamburg 1973-1976.– Spielmann, H. and Oda Kokoschka (ed.): O. K. Briefe. 4 vols. Düsseldorf 1984-1988.– Wingler, H. M. (ed.): O. K. Schriften. Munich 1956 CATALOGUES RAISONNES: Rathenau, E. (ed.): O. K. Handzeichnungen. 5 vols. Berlin 1935-1977.– Spielmann, H. (ed.): O. K. 1886-1980. Welt-Theater, Bühnenbilder und Illustrationen 1907-1975. Museum für Kunst und Gewerbe, Hamburg et al. Hamburg 1986.– Wingler, H. M. (ed.): O. K. Das Werk des Malers (mit Werkverzeichnis der Gemälde, Plastik und anderer Arbeiten). Salzburg 1956/O. K. The Work of the Painter. Catalogue Raisonné. London 1958.– Wingler, H. M. and F. Welz (ed.):

O. K. Das druckgraphische Werk. 2 vols. Salzburg 1975-1981.– Winkler, J. and K. Erling (ed.): O. K. Œuvrekatalog der Gemälde. Band I: Die Gemälde (1906-1929). Salzburg 1995
MONOGRAPHS, CATALOGUES: Borchert, B. K. Berlin 1959.– Bultmann, B.: O. K. Salzburg 1959, London 1961.– Borchert, B. K. London 1960.– Calvocoressi, R. et al. (ed.): O. K. 1886-1980. Tate Gallery. London 1986 (cat.)/O. K. 1886-1980. Kunsthaus Zürich. Zurich 1986 (cat.)/ O. K. 1886-1980. Solomon R. Guggenheim Museum. New York 1986 (cat.).– Calvocoressi, R.: K. Recklinghausen 1992, New York 1992.– Gallwitz, K. (ed.): O. K. Das Porträt. Badischer Kunstverein. Karlsruhe 1966 (cat.).– Gatt, G. : O. K. London 1971, Lucerne 1972.– Hodin, J. P.: O. K. The Artist and His Time. London and Greenwich (CT) 1966/O. K. Sein Leben, seine Zeit. Frankfurt-on-Main 1968.– Hodin, J. P.: O. K. Eine Psychographie. Vienna 1971.– Hoffmann, E.: K. Life and Work. London and Boston 1943, 1947.– Hofmann, W. (ed.): O. K. Tate Gallery. London et al. London 1986 (cat.).– Hülsewig-Johnen, J. (ed.): O. K. Emigrantenleben, Prag und London 1934-1953. Kunsthalle Bielefeld. Bielefeld 1995 (cat.).– O. K. Die frühen Jahre. Aquarelle und Zeichnungen 1906-1924. Kestner-Gesellschaft. Hanover 1983 (cat.).– O. K. 1886-1980. The Late Work 1953-1980. Marlborough Fine Art, London et al. London 1990 (cat.).– O. K. und Dresden. Gemäldegalerie Neue Meister, Dresden et al. Dresden 1996 (cat.).– Koller, G. and O. Oberhuber (ed.): O. K. Städteporträts. Österreichisches Museum für angewandte Kunst. Vienna 1986 (cat.).– Leshko, J.: O. K. Paintings 1907-1915. Ann Arbor (MI) 1981.– Lischka, G. J. O. K. Maler und Dichter. Bern und Frankfurt-on-Main 1972.– Mauron, V.: Werke der O. K.-Stiftung. Mainz 1994.– Mauron, V. (ed.): O. K. Viaggi e figure. Civica Galleria d'Arte Villa dei Cedri. Bellinzona 1995 (cat.).– Patka, E. (ed.): O. K. Symposium. Salzburg et al. 1986.– Plaut, J.: O. K. New York 1945.– Schmalenbach, F.: O. K. Königstein i. T. 1967.– Schröder, A. and J. Winkler (ed.): O. K. Kunstforum Länderbank Wien. Munich 1991 (cat.).– Schvey, H.: O. K. The Painter as Playwriter. Detroit 1982.– Schweiger, W. J.: Der junge K. Leben und Werk 1904-1914. Vienna and Munich 1983.– Schweiger, W. J.: O. K. Der Sturm. Die Berliner Jahre. 1910-1916. Eine Dokumentation. Munich 1986.– Spielmann, H.: O. K. Lebensspuren. Schleswig-Holsteinisches Landesmuseum. Schleswig 1992 (cat.).– Strobl, A. and A. Weidinger (ed.): O. K. Das Frühwerk 1897-1917. Albertina. Vienna 1994 (cat.).– Strobl, A. and A. Weidinger (ed.): O. K. Works on Paper. The Early Years 1897-1917. Solomon R. Guggenheim Museum. New York 1995 (cat.).– Werner, N.: K. Leben und Werk in Daten und Bildern. Frankfurt-on-Main 1991.– Whitford, F. O. K. A Life. London 1986

KOONS Jeff
born **1955** York (PA)
American object and concept artist. **1972–1975** Studied at the Maryland Institute of Art, Baltimore. **1975/76** Attended the Art Institute of Chicago. For many years he worked as a stockbroker on Wall Street in New York. In **1979**, he presented his first toys in plexiglas boxes. **1980** First solo-exhibition at the New Museum of Contemporary Art in New York with his series *The New*, which showed household appliances in illuminated display windows. **1985** Exhibition at the International With Monument Gallery in New York with the series *Equilibrium*, which consisted of aquariums with

floating basketballs and bronze castings of swimming and diving accessories. **1986** In the series *Statuary*, he dealt with artistic symbols and commonplace and kitsch objects manufactured either in precious metals (e.g. *Rabbit*, a inflatable plastic rabbit cast in stainless steel) or made by woodcarvers, such as the **1987** sculpture *String of Puppies*. The life-size sculpture *Made in Heaven*, produced for the **1990** Venice Biennale, depicted the artist and his wife, the Italian pornographic actress Cicciolina, making love. Koons' ironic presentations of consumer goods and his erotic-pornographic tableaux are his way of exposing the psychological manipulation and financial profiteering in the art market.
MONOGRAPHS, CATALOGUES: Beeren, W. and G. Inboden (ed.): J. K. Stedelijk Museum, Amsterdam et al. Amsterdam and Stuttgart 1992 (cat.).– Caldwell, J. et al. (ed.): J. K. Museum of Modern Art. San Farncisco 1992 (cat.).– Danoff, M. (ed.): J. K. The Art Institute of Chicago. Chicago 1988 (cat.).– J. K. Museum of Contemporary Art. Chicago 1988 (cat.).– Muthesius, A. (ed.): J. K. Cologne 1992.– Rosenblum, R. (ed.): The J. K. Handbook. New York 1992/Das J. K. Handbuch. Munich 1992.– Rosenblum, R. et al. (ed.): J. K. Celebration. Solomon R. Guggenheim Museum. New York 1996 (cat.).– Simpson, F. W. (ed.): J. K. San Francisco Museum of Modern Art 1992 (cat.)

KOSSOFF Leon
born **1926** London
English painter. **1945–1948** Military service in France, Belgium, Holland and Germany. Studied from **1949–1953** at St. Martin's School of Art and under David Bomberg at Borough Polytechnic in London. **1953–1956** Continuation of his art studies at the Royal College of Art. **1959–1964** Taught at the Regent Street Polytechnic and at Chelsea School of Art. **1966–1969** Teacher at St. Martin's School of Art. **1972** Solo-exhibition at the Whitechapel Art Gallery, London. **1981** Exhibition of his early drawings at Riverside Studios in London and his paintings from the 70s in the Museum of Modern Art in Oxford.
MONOGRAPHS, CATALOGUES: Elliott, D. (ed.): L. K. Paintings from a Decade 1970-1980. Museum of Modern Art. Oxford

1981 (cat.).– Gowing, L. (ed.): L. K. Anthony d'Offay Gallery. London 1988 (cat.).– L. K. Kunstverein für die Rheinlande und Westfalen. Düsseldorf 1995 (cat.).– Mercer, D. (ed.): L. K. Recent Paintings and Drawings. Whitechappel Art Gallery. London 1972 (cat.).– Moorhouse, P. (ed.): L. K. London 1996 (cat.)

KOSUTH Joseph
born **1945** Toledo (OH)
American concept artist and photographer. **1955–1962** Studied at the Toledo School of Design, **1963/64** at the Cleveland Art Institute and **1965–1967** at the School of Visual Arts in New York. **1965** Appearance of his first conceptual work, *One and three chairs* – a three-fold presentation of a chair as the actual object, a photograph, and an enlarged photograph of its dictionary entry. **1967** First one-man exhibition at the Museum of Normal Art, New York. From **1968** lecturer at the School of Visual Arts, New York. **1969–1970** As editor of the magazine *Art-Language*, wrote numerous theoretical texts on the subject of Concept Art. **1971/72** Studied philosophy. **1972–1982** Participation in documenta 5–7 in Kassel. **1975** Founded *The Fox* magazine. **1992** Installation *Documenta-Flânerie* at documenta 9 in Kassel. Kosuth is a principal proponent of analytical Concept Art. WRITINGS: Inboden, G. (ed.): J. K. Bedeutung von Bedeutung. Texte und Dokumentation der Investigationen über Kunst seit 1965 in Auswahl/The Making of Meaning. Selected Writings and Documentation of Investigations on Art Since 1965. Staatsgalerie Stuttgart. Stuttgart 1981 (cat.).– Guercio, G. (ed.): J. K. Art After Philosophy. Collected Writings 1966-1990. Cambridge (MA) and London 1991.– J. K.: J. K. Interviews 1969-1989. Stuttgart 1989.– Meyer, E. and S. Schmidt-Wulffen (ed.): J. K. A Grammatical Remark/Eine Grammatische Bemerkung. Stuttgart 1993
MONOGRAPHS, CATALOGUES: Ammann, J.-C. and M. Eigenheer (ed.): J. K. Investigationen über Kunst und Problemkreise seit 1965. Kunstmuseum Luzern. Lucerne 1973 (cat.).– Damsch-Wiehager, R. (ed.): J. K. Kein Ding, kein Ich, keine Form, kein Grundsatz "sich sicher". Villa Merkel, Esslingen. Stuttgart 1993/J. K. No Thing, No Form, No Principle (Was Certain). Stuttgart 1993 (cat.).– Freedberg, D. (ed.): J. K. The Play of the Unmentionable. An Installation by J. K. at the Brooklyn Museum. London 1992 (cat.).– Kaiser, W. M. H.: J. L. Artworks and Theories. Amsterdam 1991.– J. K. Bedeutung von Bedeutung. Staatsgalerie Stuttgart. Stuttgart 1981 (cat.).– J. K. Exchange of Meaning, Translation in the Work of J. K. Museum van Hedendaagse Kunst. Antwerp 1989 (cat.)

KOUNELLIS Jannis
born **1936** Piräus
Greek-Italian painter and object artist. **1956** Moved to Rome, where he attended the Art

Academy for a short time. **1958/59** Painted a series of text and alphabet pictures. **1960** First solo-exhibition with painting actions and songs at the Galleria la Tartaruga in Rome. From **1967** used materials and elements such as coal, soot, fire, wood, or flowers for his highly symbolic installations and performances. **1969** Exhibition of twelve live horses in the Galleria l'Attico in Rome. Began a series of room installations, for which he closed up doors and windows with pieces of furniture, plaster figures, bits of wood and other objects. **1972-1982** Participation in documenta 5-7 in Kassel. **1978** Short theatrical works with Carlo Quartucci. Numerous exhibitions, **1990** at the Stedelijk Museum, Amsterdam and **1995** at the Hamburg Kunsthalle. Kounellis, one of the most important practitioners of Arte Povera in Italy, often includes remnants of ancient culture in his installations.
WRITINGS: Fuchs, R. (ed.): J. K. Ein Magnet im Freien. Schriften und Gespräche 1966-1991. Bern and Berlin 1992.– J. K. Odyssée lagunaire. Ecrits et entretiens 1966-1989. Paris 1990.– J. K.: Fragmente der Erinnerung. Berlin 1991
CATALOGUES RAISONNES: Galleria Sprovieri, Roma (ed.): J. K. Catalogue raisonné (in preparation).– Schellmann, J. (ed.): J. K. Verzeichnis der druckgraphischen Arbeiten von 1972-1990 / J. K. Editions 1972-1990. Munich 1992
MONOGRAPHS, CATALOGUES: Celant, G. (ed.): J. K. Musei Comunali. Rimini 1983 (cat.).– Celant, G. (ed.): J. K. Padiglione d'Arte Contemporanea. Milan 1992 (cat.).– Codognato, M. (ed.): J. K. Odissea lagunare. Associazione Culturale d'Arte Contemporanea e Moderna. Palermo 1993 (cat.).– Corà, B. (ed.): J. K. Esposizione di paesaggi invernali. Palazzo Fabroni, Pistoia. Milan 1993 (cat.).– Corà, B. (ed.): J. K. Mistral. Bergamo 1996.– Danoff, I. M. et al. (ed.): J. K. Museum of Contemporary Art, Chicago et al. Chicago 1986 (cat.).– Felix, Z. and B. Corà (ed.): J. K. Museum Folkwang. Essen 1979 (cat.).– Friedel, H. (ed.): J. K. Städtische Galerie im Lenbachhaus. Munich 1985 (cat.).– Froment, J.-L. and R. Fuchs (ed.): J. K. Musée d'Art Contemporain de Bordeaux. Bordeaux 1985 (cat.).– Fuchs, R. (ed.): J. K. Stedelijk Van Abbe Museum, Eindhoven et al. Eindhoven 1981 (cat.).– Fuchs, R. (ed.): J. K. Castello di Rivoli, Museo d'Arte Contemporanea, Torino. Milan 1989 (cat.).– Haenlein, C.-A. (ed.): J. K. Frammenti di memoria. Kestner-Gesellschaft, Hanover et al. Hanover 1991 (cat.).– Jacob, M. J. (ed.): J. K. Museum of Contemporary Art. Chicago 1986 (cat.).– Mignot, D. (ed.): J. K. Via del Mare. Stedelijk Museum. Amsterdam 1990 (cat.).– Moure, G. (ed.): K. New York 1990.– Pagé, S. (ed.): J. K. Musée d'Art Moderne de la Ville de Paris. Paris 1980 (cat.).– Ullrich, F. and H. H. Schwalm (ed.): J. K. Lineare Notturno. Städtische Kunsthalle Recklinghausen. Recklinghausen 1993 (cat.).– Westheider, O. and H. R. Leppien (ed.): J. K. Die eiserne Runde. Hamburger Kunsthalle. Hamburg 1995 (cat.)

KRAMER Harry
1925 Lingen – **1997** Kassel
German sculptor and film-maker. Trained as a dancer and choreographer. From **1952** design of moveable figures out of wood and wire for his Mechanical Theatre. **1956** Moved to Paris. **1957** Collaborated with Wolfgang Ramsbott on the short films *Die Stadt* (The Town) and *Defense – 5.824*. **1958** First *Automobile Sculptures*. From **1961** exhibited wire sculptures set in motion by small electric motors. **1964** Participation in documenta 3 in Kassel. **1965/66** Lived in the USA, where he produced *Schiebeplastiken* (Sliding Sculptures), *Bauelemente* (Constructional Elements) and *Puzzles* out of industrially prefabricated materials. **1971** Lectureship at the Kassel Comprehensive Art College. Kramer's kinetic wire constructions show the influence of Tinguely's machine art.
CATALOGUE RAISONNE: Willhardt, M. (ed.): H. K. Ein Frisör aus Lingen. Stuttgart et al. Stuttgart 1990 (cat.)
MONOGRAPHS, CATALOGUES: H. K. Automobile Skulpturen. Atelierhaus Halfmannshof. Gelsenkirchen 1964 (cat.).– H. K. Plastik, Objekte, Filme. Städtische Kunsthalle Mannheim. Mannheim 1969 (cat.).– H. K. Objekte, Plastiken. Karl-Ernst-Osthaus-Museum. Hagen 1970 (cat.).– H. K. Retrospektive. Württembergischer Kunstverein. Stuttgart 1990 (cat.)

KRICKE Norbert
1922 Düsseldorf – **1984** Düsseldorf
German sculptor. **1946/47** Studied at the Berlin School of Fine Arts. **1947** Moved to Düsseldorf. **1949** First steel sculptures. **1953** First solo-exhibition at the Ophir Gallery in Munich. **1955/56** Commission for the Opera House in Münster. From **1955** sculptural designs for fountains. **1959** Designed water sculptures for the University of Bagdad with Walter Gropius. **1959** and **1964** participation in documenta 2 and 3 in Kassel. **1961** Exhibition at the Museum of Modern Art in New York. **1964** Professorship at the Düsseldorf Academy where, from **1972-1981**, he was director. The main elements in Kricke's abstract sculptures are usually metal rods welded together in various configurations, forming flat surfaces, moving in circles or at angles, and thrusting out into the surrounding space.

MONOGRAPHS, CATALOGUES: Adolphs, V. (ed.): Adolphs, A. u.a. (Hg.): N. K. Zeichnungen. Kunstmuseum Bonn et al. Cologne 1995 (cat.).– Kersting-Bleyl, H. and J. Morschel (ed.): N. K. Raumplastiken und Zeichnungen. Städtische Galerie im Städelschen Kunstinstitut. Frankfurt-on-Main 1980 (cat.).– Harten, J. and S. Salzmann (ed.): N. K. Wilhelm Lehmbruck Museum, Duisburg et al. Düsseldorf 1975 (cat.).– Morschel, J. (ed.): N. K. Staatsgalerie Stuttgart et al. Stuttgart 1976 (cat.).– Morschel, J. (ed.): N. K. Raumplastiken und Zeichnungen. Städelsches Kunstinstitut und Städtische Galerie. Frankfurt-on-Main 1980 (cat.).– N. K. The Museum of Modern Art. New York 1961 (cat.).– Thwaites, J. A.: N. K. Stuttgart 1964, New York 1964.– Trier, E.: N. K. Recklinghausen 1963

KRIMS Les
(Leslie Robert Krims)
born **1942** New York
American photographer. **1960-1964** Attended sculpture classes at the Cooper Union School in New York. **1964-1967** Continued his studies at the Pratt Institute in Brooklyn. **1966** First solo-exhibition at the Pratt Institute. **1967-1969** Photographer at the Rochester Institute of Technology. From **1969** professor at the State University of New York, Buffalo. **1971/72** Under the influence of the medium of film and produced a number of photoseries including *Little People of America* and *The Deer Slayers*: dramatic and provocative portrayals of everyday scenes and characters in America. **1975** Development of a process which he called Fictcrytokrimsography, for manipulating Polaroid photographs. **1977** Participation in documenta 6 in Kassel. **1980** Experiments with large format colour prints

KRUGER Barbara
born **1945** Newark (NJ)
American photographer and concept artist. Attended the Parsons School of Design in Syracuse, New York. Her teachers included the photographer Diane Arbus and the graphic designer and art director of *Harper's Bazaar*, Marvin Israel. Moved to New York in the mid-70s and became chief designer for *Mademoiselle* magazine. Also produced book covers for political texts and, from the early 70s, began writing her own texts. **1976** Taught photography and graphic design for one year at the University of California. Until **1980** lived and worked in Berkeley. *Pictures and Promises*, a video work that was shown in **1981** in New York in the alternative gallery The Kitchen documented the shifting boundaries between art and advertising. Kruger's photographic images, based on the iconography of cinema and TV, visually and verbally expose and breakdown the stereotypes of the mass media. **1982** and **1987** participation in documenta 7 and 8 in Kassel.
WRITINGS: B. K.: Picture/Readings. New York 1978.– B. K.: Beauty and Critic. New York 1983.– B. K.: Remote Control. Cambridge (MA) 1994
MONOGRAPHS, CATALOGUES: Fuchs, R. (ed.): B. K. Castello di Rivoli, Museo d'Arte Contemporanea. Milan 1989 (cat.).– King, S.: B. K. "My Pretty Pony". New York 1988.– Linker, K. and C. Miers (ed.): Love for Sale. The Words and Pictures of B. K. New York 1990, 1996.– Thomas, G. (ed.): B. K. National Art Gallery. Wellington 1988 (cat.)

KRULL Germaine
1897 Wilda (Poland) – **1985** Wetzlar
Polish photographer. **1916-1918** Attended the Munich School of Photography. **1919** Opened a portrait studio in Munich. **1921-1924** Worked as a free-lance photographer in Holland. **1924-1931** In Paris, fashion, advertising, and portrait photographs for magazines and companies such as Peugeot, Citroën and Columbia Records. She was fascinated by monumental engineering works such as the Eiffel Tower. **1925** Group exhibition with Abbott, Kertész, Lotar and Man Ray in Paris. **1931-1939** Numerous trips through Europe. **1940** Took over the photographic agency France Libre in Africa. **1943-1946** One of the first woman photographers to cover the war in Germany, Italy, and Indochina. **1965** Moved to India; friendship with the Dalai Lama. **1967** Major retrospective in Paris, opened by André Malraux. **1977** Retrospective at the Rheinisches Landesmuseum, Bonn and participation in documenta 6 in Kassel.
MONOGRAPHS, CATALOGUES: Bouqueret, C. (ed.): G. K. Photographie 1924-1936. Musée Réattu, Rencontres Internationales de la Photographie. Arles 1988 (cat.).– Fels, F. (ed.): 100 x Paris (G. K.). Berlin 1929.– Honnef, K. et al. (ed.): G. K. Fotografien 1922-1966. Rheinisches Landesmuseum, Bonn. Cologne and Bonn 1977 (cat.).– Langlois, H. (ed.): G. K. 1927-1967. Musée du Cinéma. Paris 1967 (cat.)

KUBOTA Shigeko
born **1937** Niigata (Japan)
Japanese video and multimedia artist. Studied at teacher training college in Tokyo. **1963** Acquaintance with Paik. **1964** First solo-exhibition in the Naigua Gallery in Tokyo. **1965-1968** Moved to New York,

where she attended the New School for Social Research and Art School of the Brooklyn Museum in New York and participated in happenings and Fluxus festivals. Since **1968** fascination with the figure of Duchamp, who appears in numerous works. **1972** First video sculpture *Marcel Duchamp's Grave.* **1974** Participation on the Projekt '74 in the Kunsthalle Cologne. **1977** and **1987** participation in documenta 6 and 8 in Kassel. Lectured at the School of Visual Arts in New York. Marriage to Paik. **1978** Teacher at the Düsseldorf Academy. **1979** DAAD scholarship to Berlin. **1985** Creation of the video installation *Niagara Falls,* exploring the theme of the American landscape.
MONOGRAPHS, CATALOGUES: Felix, Z. (ed.): S. K. Video Sculptures. Museum Folkwang, Essen et al. Essen 1981 (cat.).– Jacob, M. J. (ed.): S. K. Video Sculpture. American Museum of the Moving Image. Seattle 1991 (cat.).– S. K. Kodama Gallery. Tokyo 1989 (cat.)

KUDO Tetsumi
1935 Osaka – **1990** Tokyo
Japanese happening and object artist. **1954–1958** Studied at the University of Tokyo. **1955–1958** Taught at a private art school in Tokyo. From **1958** worked as a free-lance artist, exhibited objects and staged performances. **1962** Won the Young Asian Artists Exhibition prize in Tokyo. Moved to Paris, where he was involved in sadomasochistic happenings such as *Philosophy of Impotence* and in **1963** *Harakiri of Humanism* which dealt with the theme of the male body and male sexuality. **1965** First solo-exhibition in the Galerie J in Paris entitled "Rien n'est laissé au hasard". **1977** Award at the São Paulo Biennale.
WRITINGS: T. K.: Pollution, cultivation, nouvelle écologie. Amsterdam 1970.– T. K.: Sartori. Tokyo 1981
MONOGRAPHS, CATALOGUES: Hering, K.-H. (ed.): T. K. Cultivation by Radioactivity. Kunstverein für die Rheinlande und Westfalen. Düsseldorf 1970 (cat.).– T. K. Stedeljik Museum. Amsterdam 1972 (cat.)

KUDOYAROV Boris
1898 Taschkent – **1974** Moscow
Russian photographer. **1917–1920** Served in the Red Army, then worked for several years

as an amateur photographer. From **1926** photojournalist for *Russfoto* (later *Union-foto*). From **1931** overseas photographic correspondent for the magazine Sojusfoto. **1930–1932** Member of the avant-garde artists' group Oktober. Influenced by Rodchenko and Ignatovich. Became famous for his photographs of the siege of Leningrad, taken while working as a war correspondent in World War II. After the war, worked as a photojournalist for *TASS.* Kudoyarow's compositions adhere to the traditional tenets of Constructivism.
MONOGRAPHS, CATALOGUES: Dyko, L.: B. K. Moscow 1975

KÜHN Heinrich
1866 Dresden – **1944** Birgitz
German photographer. **1885–1887** Studied medicine in Leipzig, Berlin and Innsbruck. **1888** Began taking photographs. **1896** Member of the Vienna Kamera Klub. Founded the Kleeblatt group along with Hugo Henneberg and Hans Watzek; collaborated on experiments in photographic technique, including development of the autochrome process invented by Lumière. **1907** Acquaintance with Stieglitz and Steichen. **1909** Organised an international photo exhibition in Dresden. **1912–1916** Directed a school for artistic photography in Innsbruck. **1920** Move to Birgitz. **1923–1935** Photographed portraits, still lifes, architecture and landscapes for numerous magazines. Developed photographic processes for companies in Austria and Germany. **1937** Honorary doctorate from the University of Innsbruck. In numerous essays and books, Kühn discussed the aesthetics of photography from a technical point of view.
WRITINGS: H. K.: Technik der Lichtbildnerei. Halle 1921.– H. K.: Zur photographischen Technik. Halle 1926
MONOGRAPHS, CATALOGUES: Appel, M. O. and U. Eskildsen (ed.): H. K. 1866-1944. 110 Bilder aus der Fotografischen Sammlung, Museum Folkwang, Essen. Essen 1978 (cat.).– Kaufhold, E.: H. K. und die Kunstfotografie um 1900. Berlin 1988.– Kicken, R. (ed.): Eine Ausstellung von hundert Photographien von H. K. Stefan Lennert, Munich. Cologne 1981 (cat.).– Knapp, U.: H. K. Photographien. Salzburg and Vienna 1988.– Speer, H. (ed.): H. K. 1866-1944. Galerie im Taxispalais. Innsbruck 1976 (cat.).– Weiermair, P. (ed.): H. K. 1866-1944. Innsbruck 1978.– Weiermair, P. (ed.): H. K. 1866-1944. Photographien. Frankfurter Kunstverein. Frankfurt-on-Main 1981 (cat.)

KUPKA František
1871 Opocno (Bohemia) – **1957** Puteaux (near Paris)
Czech painter. After studying at the Prague Art Academy from **1888–1891** he transferred to the Vienna Academy for two years. **1895** Moved to Paris. From **1904** lived in Puteaux and joined the group of artists

around Jacques Villon, including Léger, Gris, Duchamp, Metzinger and Archipenko. Began to involve himself intensely with theosophy, eastern philosophy, and spiritualism. His neo-impressionist pictures were exhibited regularly at the Salon d'Automne. Around **1910** turned to abstraction; he is considered one of its founders, along with Kandinsky and Delaunay. In his pictures, he tried to portray movement and light as independent colour effects. **1912** His first fully abstract paintings (*Amorpha: Fugue à deux couleurs* and *Chromatique chaude*) exhibited at the Salon d'Automne and categorized as orphist on account of their close relationship to music. **1914** Volunteered for military service. **1918–1920** Guest-professor in Prague. **1931–1934** Member of the Abstraction-Création group. **1955** Participation in documenta 1 in Kassel. **1957** Retrospective at the Guggenheim Museum in New York. In the 40s and 50s Kupka was finally recognized as one of the pioneers of abstract art and his works were displayed in international exhibitions and purchased by important museums.
WRITINGS: F. K.: La Création dans les arts plastiques. Paris 1989
CATALOGUE RAISONNE: Vachtová, L.: F. K. Pioneer of Abstract Art. London and New York 1968
MONOGRAPHS, CATALOGUES: Andel, J. et al. (ed.): F. K. Painting the Universe. Kunstmuseum Wolfsburg. Stuttgart 1997 (cat.).– Arnoud-Grémilly, L.: F. K. Paris 1922.– Cassou, J. and D. Fédit: K. Paris 1964, Stuttgart 1964, London 1965.– Fauchereau, S.: F. K. Paris 1988, New York 1989.– Fedit, D. (ed.): L'Œuvre de K. Musée du Louvre. Paris 1966 (cat.).– Kotalik, J. (ed.): F. K. Palazzo Massari. Ferrara 1987 (cat.).– F. K. Kestner-Gesellschaft. Hanover 1966 (cat.).– F. K. Museum des 20. Jahrhunderts. Vienna 1967 (cat.).– F. K. Stedelijk Museum. Amsterdam 1968 (cat.).– Lamac, M.: F. K. Prague 1984.– Leroy, B. and A. Linthal (ed.): F. K. 1871-1957. Ou l'invention d'une abstraction. Musée d'Art Moderne. Paris 1989 (cat.).– Mladek, M. and M. Rowell (ed.): F. K. 1871-1957. Solomon R. Guggenheim Museum, New York et al. New York 1975, Zurich 1976.– Nasi, V. and C. Polcina: F. K. Carte e dipinti. Roma 1980 (cat.).– Pagé, S. et al. (ed.): F. K. 1871-1957 ou l'invention d'une abstraction. Musée d'Art Moderne de la Ville de Paris. Paris 1989 (cat.).– Rubinger, K. and H. Jordan (ed.): F. K. Galerie Gmurzynska. Cologne 1981 (cat.).– Vachtová, L. et al. (ed.): F. K. Die andere Qualität. Cologne 1995 (cat.)

KUSHNER Robert
born **1949** Pasadena (CA)
American artist. **1967–1971** Studied at the University of California in San Diego. **1971/72** Lived in Boston. First collages and performances with costumes he made himself. **1972** Moved to New York, where he designed costumes and sets for numerous theatre and ballet productions, and

staged performances dressed in his own costumes. From **1974** very interested in Siddha Meditation. **1976** First solo-exhibition in New York at the Holly Solomon Gallery. **1979** First lithographs. From **1981** occupied with painters of the early modern era such as Léger, Bonnard, Picasso and Gris. **1987** First retrospective at the Institute of Contemporary Art in Philadelphia. In addition to costumes, which are based on oriental models, Kushner also employed decorative elements from other cultures – Chinese, Japanese, and European – in his productions and performances.
WRITINGS: R. K.: The Persian Poems. New York 1980
MONOGRAPHS, CATALOGUES: Armstrong, R. (ed.): R. K. Dreams and Visions. Holly Solomon Gallery. New York 1981 (cat.).– Kardon, J. (ed.): R. K. Institute of Contemporary Art, University of Pennsylvania. Philadelphia 1987 (cat.).– Marshall, R. (ed.): R. K. Paintings on Paper. Whitney Museum of American Art. New York 1984 (cat.)

LAFONTAINE Marie Jo
born **1950** Antwerp
Belgian video artist. **1975–1979** Studied at the Ecole Nationale Supérieure d'Architecture et des Arts Visuels in Brussels. **1977** Awarded Prix de la Jeune Peinture Belge in Brussels. Produced monochrome textile murals and paintings. **1979** Prix de la Critique, Antwerp. First video work *La batteuse de palplanches.* **1982** Video-Prize Meatball, Amsterdam. **1985** Grant from the Institute of Arts and Humanities. **1987** Showed the video-installation *Les larmes d'acier* at documenta 8 in Kassel. Later created environments with multimonitor installations: *Victoria* **1987/88**, *Passio* **1989/90**, *Jeder Engel ist schrecklich* (Every angel is terrible) **1993**. **1990** Guest-professor at the Salzburg Summer Academy. Since **1992** professor at the Karlsruhe School of Design.
MONOGRAPHS, CATALOGUES: M. J. L. Immaculata. Ric Urmel Gallery, Ghent. Stuttgart 1992.– M. J. L. Himmel und Hölle. Dewer Art Gallery. Otegem 1993 (cat.).– MacLeon, F. et al. (ed.): M. J. L. The Fruitmarket Gallery, Edinburgh et al. Edinburgh 1989 (cat.).– Meyer, W. (ed.): M. J. L. Städtische Galerie. Göppingen

1990 (cat.).– Neumaier, O. et al. (ed.): M. J. L. Stuttgart 1998.– Foncé, J. (ed.): M. J. L. Videoskulpturen. Sculptures-Video. Video Skulpturen. Zedelgem 1987.– Bussmann, G. and L. Malle (ed.): M. J. L. Passio. Städtisches Museum Abteiberg. Mönchengladbach 1990 (cat.).– Pühringer, A. et al. (ed.): M.-J. L. La Vie – une hésitation. Salzburg 1991

LA FRESNAYE Roger de
1885 Le Mans – **1925** Grasse
French painter. **1903** Began studies at the Académie Julian, then transferred to the Ecole des Beaux-Arts and Académie Ranson in Paris where, in **1908** he attended the classes of Paul Sérusier and Maurice Denis. **1909/10** Exhibitions at the Salon de Indépendants and Salon d'Automne. **1913** Joined the Cubist movement. Contributed to the journal *Montjoie*. **1917** Worked on newspapers for soldiers at the front. Went to a sanatoruim in Grasse for his tuberculosis. Did several portraits there of his painter friend J.-L. Gampert as well as drawings and gouaches of the other patients. Works from around **1920** are closely related to Synthetic Cubism. Exhibition at the Salon des Tuileries. La Fresnaye painted in the tradition of the Nabis. Since he never gave up portraying people, he is classified as a humanist Cubist.
CATALOGUES RAISONNES: Cogniat, R. and W. George (ed.): Œuvre complète de R. d. L. F. Paris 1950.– Seligman, G. (ed.): R. d. L. F. Avec le catalogue raisonné de l'œuvre. Neuchâtel 1969, London and Greenwich (CT) 1969
MONOGRAPHS, CATALOGUES: Chabert, P. (ed.): R. de L. F. Musée de l'Annonciade, Saint-Tropez et al. Saint-Tropez 1983 (cat.).– Gaffé, R.: R. d. L. F. Brussels 1956.– R. de L. F. Musée National d'Art Moderne. Paris 1950 (cat.).– R. de L. F. aurait 100 ans. Abbaye de L'Epau. Le Mans 1985 (cat.).– Nebelthan, E.: R. d. L. F. Paris 1935.– Seligman, G.: R. d. L. F. Greewich (CT) 1945, 1969

LAKNER László
born **1936** Budapest
Hungarian artist. **1954–1960** Studied painting at the Budapest Academy of Arts. From **1968** made frequent visits to Germany.

Began to incorporate documentary materials such as press cuttings, photographs and letters into his paintings. From **1970** produced the book-object *Georg-Lukácz-Buch*, worked over and tied up with string. **1974** DAAD scholarship to Berlin. Participation in documenta 6 in Kassel. **1979/80** Lectured in history of art at the School of Art in Essen and the Freie Universität in Berlin. Experimented in so-called *Duchamp paintings* with writing scratched into thick layers of paint. **1981/82** Scholarship to New York. **1982** Professorship at the University of Essen. In the 70s, Lakner was occupied as a painter and object artist with written and printed texts, while in the 80s he resumed free-style gesural painting.
MONOGRAPHS, CATALOGUES: Becker, W. (ed.): L. L. Gesammelte Dokumente. 1960-1974. Neue Galerie – Sammlung Ludwig. Aachen 1974 (cat.).– Deecke, T. (ed.): L. L. Bilder, Bücher, Filme, Zettel. Neuer Berliner Kunstverein und Berliner Künstlerprogramm des DAAD. Berlin 1975 (cat.).– Index L. L. 1968-1993. 4 vols. Goethe Institut. Budapest 1994.– L. L. Malerei 1974-1979. Westfälischer Kunstverein. Münster 1979 (cat.).– Motte, M. d. la (ed.): L. L. Galerie Nothelfer. Berlin 1985 (cat.).– Motte, M. d.la and J. Sartorius (ed.): L. L. Papierarbeiten, Objekte und 3 Skulpturen. Daadgalerie. Berlin 1991 (cat.)

LAM Wifredo
(Wifredo Oscar de la Conception Lam y Castilla)
1902 Sagua la Grande (Kuba) – **1982** Paris
Cuban painter. **1920–1923** Studied at the Academy San Alejandro in Havanna. **1924** Continued studies in Madrid and Barcelona. **1928** Saw African sculptures from New Guinea and the Congo for the first time, which were to influenc his work as much as his meeting with Picasso in **1937** in Paris. **1940** Fled, along with other Surrealist artists to Marseille. **1941** Set sail with Breton, Masson and Lévi-Strauss for Martinique, finally disembarking in Cuba. **1945** Returned to Paris, met Gorky and Duchamp and from then on moved restlessly to and fro' between the continents. **1964** Set up house in Albisola Mare in Italy. **1959** and **1964** Participation in documenta 2 and 3 in Kassel. Lam's paintings are an excellent example of Surrealist attempts to incorporate African and Caribbean mythology into western art. Cuban gods and legends, the Voodoo cult and the dangerous, wild jungle are the main themes of his work.
CATALOGUES RAISONNES: Fouchet, M.-P.: W. L. Paris 1989.– Laurin-Lam, L. (ed.): W. L. Catalogue Raisonné of the Painted Work. Vol. 1: 1932-1960. Lausanne 1996.– Tonneau-Ryckelynck, D.: W. L. Œuvre gravé et lithographié. Catalogue raisonné. Gravelines 1994
MONOGRAPHS, CATALOGUES: Ayllón, J. and L. L. Lam (ed.): Homenaje a W. L. 1902-1982. Museo Nacional de Arte Contemporáneo, Madrid et al. Madrid 1982 (cat.).– Benitez, H. H.: W. L. Interlude

Marseille. Copenhagen 1993.– Blanc, G. (ed.): W. L. and His Contemporaries 1938-1952. Studio Museum of Harlem. New York 1992 (cat.).– Curzi, L.: W. L. Bologna 1978.– Daniel, S. G.: The Early Works of W. L. 1941-1945. Diss. College Park, University of Maryland 1983.– David, C.: W. L. Paris 1991.– David, C. et al. (ed.): W. L. Obra sobre papel. Fundació Caixa de Pensiones. Barcelona 1993 (cat.).– Fouchet, M.-P.: W. L. Paris 1976, 1984.– Gaudiberti, P. et al. (ed.): W. L. Kunstsammlung Nordrhein-Westfalen, Düsseldorf et al. Düsseldorf 1988 (cat.).– Jouffroy, A.: L. Paris 1972.– W. L. Les Années cubaines. Maison de l'Amérique latine. Paris 1989 (cat.).– W. L. ou "L'éloge du métissage". Académie de France à Rome. Roma 1992 (cat.).– W. L. Fundació Joan Miró. Barcelona 1992 (cat.).– W. L. Museo Nacional Centro de Arte Reina Sofía, Madrid et al. Madrid 1992 (cat.).– Leiris, M.: W. L. Paris 1970, New York 1970.– Merewether, C. (ed.): W. L. A Retrospective of Works on Paper. Americas Society Art Gallery. New York 1992 (cat.).– Nuñez Jiménez, A.: W. L. Havanna 1982.– Ortiz, F.: W. L. y su obra vista a través de significados criticos. Havanna 1950.– Soupault, P.: W. L. Dessins. Paris 1975.– Taillander, I.: W. L. Paris 1970.– Vidal, A. (ed.): W. L. 1902-1982. Musée d'Art Moderne. Paris 1983 (cat.).– Xuriguéra, G.: W. L. Paris 1974

LANG Nikolaus
born **1941** Oberammergau
German sculptor and object artist. **1956–1960** Trained as a wood-carver in Oberammergau. **1960–1966** Attended the Munich Academy. **1966/67** DAAD scholarship to London. **1967–1969** Taught sculpture at Camberwell School of Arts and Crafts in London. Worked with various synthetic objects. **1971/72** DAAD scholarship to Tokyo. Documented his own travels and excursions in photoseries, drawings, catalogue-type indexes and boxes of *objets trouvés*. **1973/74** Put together his work *Chest for the Götte Siblings*, a reconstruction of the life of a loner, incorporating collected objects and other biographical relics. **1976** Villa-Romana scholarship to Florence. **1977** and **1987** took part in documenta 6 and 8 in Kassel. **1979** First of numerous working trips to Australia and other countries including Sweden and Italy. **1984** Together with the architect Jürgen Wenzel won a competition for the design of a monument to victims of National Socialism, which however, was never realised. **1987** Overseas grant to work at the South Australian College of Art, Adelaide. Since **1989** member of the Bavarian Academy of Fine Arts in Munich. **1996** Another sojourn in Australia.
MONOGRAPHS, CATALOGUES: Haenlein, K. A. (ed.): N. L. Kestner-Gesellschaft. Hanover 1975 (cat.).– N. L. Japanische Landschaften. Städtische Galerie im Lenbachhaus. Munich 1973 (cat.).– N. L. Württembergischer Kunstverein. Stuttgart 1976 (cat.).– N. L. Farben, Zeichen, Steine. Westfälischer Kunstverein. Münster

1978 (cat.).– N. L. Australisches Tagebuch. Aargauer Kunstmuseum. Aarau 1979 (cat.).– Liebelt, U. (ed.): N. L. Druckstock I, 1980. Installation. Sprengel Museum. Hanover 1995 (cat.).– Schulz, I.: N. L. "Für die Geschwister Götte". Museum anonymer Persönlichkeiten. Hamburg 1985.– Tacke, C. et al. (ed.): N. L. Nunga und Goonya. Städtische Galerie im Lenbachhaus. Munich 1991 (cat.)

LANGE Dorothea
1895 Hoboken (NJ) – **1965** San Francisco
American photographer. **1914–1917** Teacher training. **1917/18** Studied at the Clarence H. White School of Photography at Columbia University in San Francisco. **1919** Opened her own portrait studio in San Francisco. **1935** Expanded her area of interest and did more documentary work. **1935–1942** Photographed for the Farm Security Administration. **1941** Grant from the Guggenheim Foundation. **1941** Solo-exhibition at the Guggenheim Museum of Modern Art. **1942** Documented the internment of the Japanese in concentration camps on the West Coast. **1943–1945** Photographic correspondent for the Office of War Information in Washington. **1954** Reportages on Asia, the Middle East and South America for *Life* and other magazines. Extensive travels abroad throughout the 70s. **1958–1962** Taught at the San Francisco Art Institute. **1966** Major retrospective at the Museum of Modern Art in New York.
MONOGRAPHS, CATALOGUES: Becker Ohrn, K.: D. L. and the Documentary Tradition. Baton Rouge and London 1980.– Davis, K. F.: The Photographs of D. L. New York 1996.– Elliott, G. P. (ed.): D. L. The Museum of Modern Art, New York et al. New York 1966 (cat.).– Meltzer, M.: D. L. A Photographer's Life. New York 1978.– Newhall, B. (ed.): D. L. Looks at the American Woman. Fort Worth et al. 1967.– Ohrn, K. B.: D. L. and the Documentary Tradition. Baton Rouge 1980.– Partridge, E.: D. L. A Visual Life. Washington 1994.– Thau Heyman, T. et al. (ed.): D. L. American Photographs. San Francisco Museum of Modern Art. San Francisco 1994 (cat.).– Wollenberg, C. (ed.): Photographing the Second Gold Rush. D. L. and the Bay Area at War 1941-1945. Berkeley 1995

LANSKOY André
1902 Moscow – **1976** Paris
Russian-born French painter. **1919** Fled to Kiev to join the White Army. **1921** Moved to Paris, where he studied painting at the Académie de la Grande Chaumière. **1925** First solo-exhibition in Paris of portraits, landscapes and still lifes, works clearly influenced by Matisse and van Gogh. **1939** First abstract gouaches. **1944** Abstract compositions with dynamic colour components. In his works from the 40s he focused on the handling of paint: crushing, squeezing or letting it flow freely. **1950** Took part in the exhibition "Advancing French Art", at the

galleries of Louis Carré in Paris and New York. **1959** and **1964** Participation in documenta 2 and 3 in Kassel. **1966** Tapestry designs on cardboard. **1974** Exhibition of mosaics in Caujours. Designed a monumental mosaic for the Faculté des Sciences in Rennes. With his brightly coloured abstract paintings, Lanskoy is representative of the Ecole de Paris.
CATALOGUES RAISONNES: Bernard, C. and M. Guinle (ed.): L. Catalogue raisonné des mosaïques. Lyon 1990
MONOGRAPHS, CATALOGUES: Allemand, M. (ed.): Exposition L. Galerie de la Société industrielle de la Bourse. Mulhouse 1970 (cat.).– Dron, P. and A. Pittiglio: A. L. Moscou, 1902 – Paris, 1976. Paris 1990.– Gindertael, R.-V.: L. Paris 1957.– Grenier, J.: A. L. Paris 1960.– A. L. Le Journal d'un fou, de Gogol. Collages, tapisseries et autres livres. Musée d'Art et d'Industrie de Saint-Etienne. Saint-Etienne 1968 (cat.).– A. L. Dernières œuvres. Galerie Cyrus. Paris 1977 (cat.).– A. L. Peintures de 1944 à 1961. Galerie Louis Carré & Cie. Paris 1990 (cat.)

LAPICQUE Charles
1898 Theizé (Rhône) – **1988** Orsay
French painter. Self-taught. **1919-1922** Studied natural sciences in Paris. **1922-1924** Worked as an engineer. **1929** First solo-exhibition at the Galerie Jeanne Bucher in Paris. Caused a sensation with his painting *Palestrina*, which has marked Cubist features. **1931-1943** Technical assistant at the Sorbonne. **1938** Completed a doctoral thesis on the perception of colour. **1937** Interior designs for the Palais de la Découverte. Contact with Manessier, Bazaine, Villon. **1940** Developed his Blue Grid style of painting combining figurative and abstract elements set against a blue grid, culminating in his masterpiece *Joan of Arc crossing the Loire*. **1954-1956** Scenes of Venice, inspired by the Venetian paintings of Tintoretto and Tiepolo. **1967** Retrospective at the Musée National d'Art Moderne, Paris.
WRITINGS: C. L.: Essais sur l'espace, l'art et la destinée. Paris 1958
CATALOGUES RAISONNES: Auger, E. and B. Balanci (ed.): C. L. Catalogue raisonné de l'œuvre peint et de la sculpture. Paris 1972.– Balanci, B. and G. Blanche (ed.): Catalogue raisonné de l'œuvre complet des lithographies, eaux-fortes et gravures. Paris 1981
MONOGRAPHS, CATALOGUES: Cousseau, C. (ed.): L. Oelbilder 1939-1978. Galerie Nathan. Zurich 1983 (cat.).– Dorival, B. (ed.): L. Musée National d'Art Moderne. Paris 1967 (cat.).– Dorival, B. (ed.): L. Galerie Nathan. Zurich 1978 (cat.).– C. L. Gemälde, Aquarelle, Zeichnungen. Folkwang Museum, Essen et al. Essen 1964 (cat.).– C. L. Musée Toulouse-Lautrec. Albi 1970 (cat.).– C. L. Peintures de 1940 à 1973. Galerie Louis Carré & Cie. Paris 1989 (cat.).– Lescure, J.: L. Paris 1956.– Nathan, P. and A. Affentranger (ed.): L. Nachtbilder. Galerie Nathan. Zurich 1986

(cat.).– Perregaux, A.: Espace et présence dans la peinture de L. Neuchâtel 1981.– Perregaux, A.: L. Neuchâtel 1983.– Perregaux, A.: L. et sa démarche créative. Paris 1983.– Uhlig, H. (ed.): C. L. Ölbilder, Aquarelle, Zeichnungen. Kunstamt Berlin-Tempelhof. Berlin 1967 (cat.).– Wilson, S. (ed.): L. ASB Gallery. London 1987 (cat.)

LARDERA Berto
1911 La Spezia – **1989** Paris
Italian sculptor. Self-taught. **1942** First 3-dimensional object, an assembly of metal plates. First solo-exhibition at the Milione gallery in Milan. **1946/47** Font relief in the Church of St. Piero ai Prati in Florence. **1948** Moved to Paris. Solo-exhibition at the Galerie Denise René. **1949/50** Large sculpture for Haus Lange in Krefeld, a house designed by Mies van der Rohe, leading to further commissions. His sculptures from the 50s are prime examples of Abstract Expressionism. **1954** Designed the sculpture *Colloquio terzo* for a town square in Marl. **1955-1964** Took part in documenta 1-3 in Kassel. **1958** His work *Alla I* erected near the Alvar Aalto and O. Niemeyer building in the Hansa district of Berlin. **1960** Exclusive presentation of his sculptures at the Venice Biennale. **1969** Invented a new technique for reproducing pictures with polygraphs on plexiglas and stainless steel.
WRITINGS: B. L.: Témoignage pour la sculpture abstraite. Paris 1956
CATALOGUE RAISONNE: Jianou, I.: L. Paris 1968
MONOGRAPHS, CATALOGUES: Brion, M.: L. Paris 1968.– Güse, E.-G. and S. Salzmann (ed.): B. L. Plastiken. Collagen. Graphiken. Wilhelm-Lehmbruck-Museum, Duisburg et al. Duisburg 1976 (cat.).– Haftmann, W.: L., la rose des vents. New York 1969.– Jianou, I.: L. Paris 1968.– B. L. Skulpturen. Museum Haus Lange. Krefeld 1956 (cat.).– B. L. Plastik, Gouachen, Collagen. Hamburger Kunstverein. Hamburg 1961 (cat.).– B. L. Kunstverein Hannover. Hanover 1971 (cat.).– Seuphor, M. B. L. Neuchâtel 1960

LARIONOV Mikhail
1881 Tiraspo – **1964** Fontenay-aux-Roses
Russian painter. **1898-1908** Studied at the Moscow Art Academy. **1906** Helped Diaghilev to organise an exhibition of Russian paintings in the Salon d'Automne in Paris. From **1907** member of the Society of Free Aesthetics. Organised numerous exhibitions of avant-garde art in Russia. While still painting in an Impressionist style, he showed strong tendencies towards abstraction. **1912** Together with Goncharova, launched Rayonism, the Russian counterpart of Futurism. **1913** Rayonist manifesto. **1914** Military service. Invalided out and settled in Paris. Worked almost exclusively for Diaghilev's Ballets Russes. **1915** Stage designs for L. Massine's *Soleil de nuit* and **1922** for Stravinsky's *Le Renard*. Larionov developed the theory of Rayon-

ism. Based on French Cubist theory and the ideas of the Futurists in Italy, it was an attempt to create a new form of pictorial space from the dynamic force of light alone.
WRITINGS: Hoog, M. and S. de Vigneral (ed.): M. L. Une avant-garde explosive. Lausanne 1978.– M. L.: Diaghilev et les Ballets Russes. Dessins et textes de M. L. Paris. 1970.– M. L.: Manifestes. Paris 1995
MONOGRAPHS, CATALOGUES: Boissel, J. and G. Viatte (ed.): Nathalie Gontcharova & M. L. Centre Georges Pompdou. Paris 1995 (cat.).– Bowlt, J. E. and A. Parton (ed.): M. L. Pasteller, gouacher, teckningar. Galerie Aronowitsch. Stockholm 1987 (cat.).– George, W.: L. Paris 1966, Lucerne and Frankfurt-on-Main 1968.– Kovtun, E.: M. L. London 1997.– M. L. Rétrospective. Maison de la Culture de Nevers et la Nièvre. Nevers 1972 (cat.).– M. L. et son temps. Musée Toulouse-Lautrec. Albi 1973 (cat.).– Nakov, A. B. (ed.). M. L. Der Weg in die Abstraktion. Werke auf Papier 1908-1915. Schirn Kunsthalle, Frankfurt-on-Main et al. Stuttgart 1987 (cat.).– Parton, A.: M. F. L. 1881-1964. A Study of Chronology and Sources of His Art. Diss. Newcastle upon Tyne 1985.– Parton, A.: M. L. and the Russian Avant-Garde. London and Princeton (NJ) 1993.– Rusza, G.: L. Budapest 1977

LASKER Jonathan
born **1948** Jersey City (New Jersey)
American painter. **1975-1977** Attended the School of Visual Arts in New York. From **1977** studied at the California Institute of the Arts in Valencia. **1981** First solo-exhibition at the Landmark Gallery, New York. In **1987** and **1989** received the National Endowment for the Arts Fellowship. **1989** Grant from the New York Foundation for the Arts Fellowship. Lasker is one of the great American abstract painters. He combines Color Field Painting with a minimalist gestural style. **1992** Participation in documenta 9 in Kassel.
WRITINGS: J. L.: Complete Essays 1984-1998. New York 1998
MONOGRAPHS, CATALOGUES: Crone, R. and D. Moos: J. L. Telling the Tales of a Painting. Stuttgart 1993.– Feldman, M. (ed.): J. L. Institute of Contemporry Art. Philadelphia 1992 (cat.).– Gooking, K. et al. (ed.): J. L. Sperone Westwater Gallery. New York 1991 (cat.).–

Herzog, H.-M. and K. Bitterli (ed.): J. L. Gemälde 1977-1997. Kunsthalle Bielefeld et al. Stuttgart 1997 (cat.).– Ostrow, S. (ed.): J. L. Paintings 1978-1982. Bravin Post Lee Gallery. New York 1994 (cat.).– Schjeldahl, P. (ed.): J. L. Soledad Lorenzo Galería. Madrid 1995 (cat.)

LASSNIG Maria
born **1925** Kappel am Krappfeld (Carinthia)
Austrian painter. **1941-1943** Studied painting at Klagenfurt Academy of Art. **1948** Met Arnulf Rainer. First compositions with surreal figures. **1951** Moved to Vienna. Grant to work in Paris, where she met Paul Celan and André Breton. **1961** Returned to Vienna. Painted large-scale *Körpergefühls-Figurationen* (Body awareness figurations). **1968** Emigrated to America, settling in New York. Experimented with large silk-screen prints. **1970** Attended an animation course at the School of Visual Arts in New York. **1973** Realist portraits, self-portraits and still lifes. **1978** DAAD scholarship to Berlin. **1980** Represented Austria at the Venice Biennale. Professor of Painting at the Vienna School of Applied Arts where, in **1981**, she set up an animation studio. **1982** Took part in documenta 7 in Kassel. **1988** Awarded the Großen Österreichischen Staatspreis. **1989/90** Retrospective at the Kunstmuseum in Lucerne and the Vienna Secession.
CATALOGUE RAISONNE: Gross, B. (ed.): M. L. Werkverzeichnis der Druckgraphik 1949-1987. Munich 1988.– Weskott, H. and J. Helfenstein (ed.): M. L. Zeichnungen und Aquarelle 1946-1995. Kunstmuseum Bern et al. Bern 1995 (cat.)
MONOGRAPHS, CATALOGUES: Breicha, O. (ed.): M. L. Aquarelle. Kärtner Landesgalerie, Klagenfurt et al. Klagenfurt 1988 (cat.).– Das Innere nach Aussen. M. L. Bilder. Stedelijk Museum, Amsterdam et al. Amsterdam 1994 (cat.).– Drechsler, W. et al. (ed.): M. L. Museum des 20. Jahrhunderts, Vienna et al. Klagenfurt 1985 (cat.).– Kunz, M. (ed.): M. L. Mit dem Kopf durch die Wand. Neue Bilder. Kunstmuseum Luzern et al. Klagenfurt 1989 (cat.).– M. L. La mostra Austriaca nell' quadro della Biennale de Venezia. Venice 1980 (cat.).– M. L. Von Innen nach Außen. Frankfurter Kunstverein. Frankfurt-on-Main 1985.– M. L. Ulmer Museum et al. Munich 1996 (cat.).– Murken, C.: M. L. Ihr Leben und ihr malerisches Werk. Ihre kunstgeschichtliche Stellung in der Malerei des 20. Jahrhunderts. Aachen 1990.– Peters, H. A. and W. Skreiner (ed.): M. L. Zeichnungen, Aquarelle, Gouachen 1949-1982. Mannheimer Kunstverein et al. Düsseldorf 1982 (cat.).– Tolnay. A. et al. (ed.): M. L. Neue Bilder und Zeichnungen. Berlinische Galerie, Berlin et al. Berlin 1997

LAURENCIN Marie
1883 Paris – **1956** Paris
French painter. Studied at the Ecole des Beaux-Arts in Paris. **1905** First works shown

at the Salon des Indépendants. **1907** Met Guillaume Apollinaire, who promoted her and introduced her to Picasso. Joined Bateau-Lavoir a group of artists and writers. Published her first poems under the pseudonym Louise Lalanne. **1908** Her painting *Apollinaire et ses amis* bought by Gertrude Stein. **1912** Exhibition at the Section d'Or. **1913** Exhibited at the Armory Show in New York. **1924** Stage design for Diaghilev's Ballet *Les Biches* with music by Poulenc. **1928** Worked for the Comédie Française. Numerous book illustrations including ones for André Gide's *La Tentative amoureuse* and Lewis Carroll's *Alice in Wonderland*. Despite her close contact with the Cubists, there are no traces of Cubism in Laurencin's paintings. She developed her own ornamental, figurative style, and favoured simple schematic compositions.
WRITINGS: M. L.: Le Carnet des nuits. Geneva 1956
CATALOGUES RAISONNES: Marchesseau, D. (ed.): M. L. Catalogue raisonné de l'œuvre gravé. Tokyo 1981.– Marchesseau, D. (ed.): M. L. 1885-1956. Catalogue raisonné de l'œuvre peint. Tokyo 1986
MONOGRAPHS, CATALOGUES: Day, G.: M. L. Paris 1947.– Gere, C.: M. L. London and New York 1977.– Groult, F.: M. L. Paris 1987/M. L. Ein Leben für die Kunst. Munich 1992.– Hyland, D. K. S. and H. McPherson (ed.): M. L. Artist and Muse. Birmingham Museum of Art et al. Birmingham et al. 1989 (cat.).– Marchesseau, D.: M. L. Paris 1981.– Marchesseau, D. (ed.): M. L. Cent œuvres des collections du Musée Martigny. Martigny 1993 (cat.).– M. L. 1885-1956. Städtische Kunsthalle Düsseldorf. Düsseldorf 1957 (cat.).– Pierre, J.: M. L. Paris 1988

LAURENS Henri
1885 Paris – 1954 Paris
French sculptor. Trained at a school of arts and crafts and in a workshop for ornamental stonemasonry. **1911** Introduced by Braque to leading Cubist artists and subsequently inspired to apply Cubist principles of form to sculptural works. **1913** Exhibited at the Salon des Indépendants. **1915-1919** Pasted paper works. **1916** First solo-exhibition at the Galerie de l'Effort moderne in Paris. **1917** *Papiers collés* and book illustrations.

1919 First real sculptures out of stereometric, angular and interlinked. From **1925** stage designs for Diaghilev's Ballets Russes. Sculptures of human figures with short, stubby limbs, curled up into a compact form. **1936/37** Numerous works displayed at the Paris World Fair, some in Le Corbusier's pavilion. **1948** Represented France at the Venice Biennale. **1953** Received special honours at the São Paulo Biennale. Along with Jacques Lipchitz, Laurens was one of the leading Cubist sculptors.
CATALOGUES RAISONNES: Brusberg, D. et al. (ed.): H. L. Werkverzeichnis der Druckgraphik. Berlin and Hanover 1985.– Goldscheider, G.: L. Cologne 1956, New York 1959.– Hofmann, W. and D.-H. Kahnweiler (ed.): H. L. Das plastische Werk. Stuttgart 1970/The Sculpture of H. L. New York 1970.– Nobis, N. et al. (ed.): H. L. Skulpturen, Collagen, Zeichnungen, Aquarelle, Druckgraphik. Œuvreverzeichnis der Druckgraphik. Sprengel Museum. Hanover 1985 (cat.).– Völker, B. (ed.): H. L. Werkverzeichnis der Druckgraphik. Berlin 1985/H. L. The Graphic Work. San Francisco 1985
MONOGRAPHS, CATALOGUES: Beloubek-Hammer, A. (ed.): H. L. 1885-1954. Bronzen, Steine und Arbeiten auf Papier. Staatliche Museen, Nationalgalerie. Berlin 1991 (cat.).– Falcidia, G.: H. L. Milan 1966.– Goldscheider, C.: H. L. New York 1959, Munich 1964.– Hohl, R. (ed.): L. cubista. Galleria Pieter Coray, Lugano. Milan 1986 (cat.).– Kuthy, S. (ed.): H. L. 1885-1954. Kunstmuseum Bern. Fribourg 1985 (cat.)/H. L. 1885-1954. Paris 1985.– H. L. Exposition de la donation aux Musées Nationaux. Grand Palais. Paris 1967 (cat.).– H. L. 1885-1954. Musée de Metz. Metz 1971 (cat.).– H. L. Plastiken, Grafiken, Zeichnungen. Kunsthalle Bielefeld. Bielefeld 1972 (cat.).– H. L. 1885-1954. 60 œuvres 1915-1954. Galerie Louise Leiris. Paris 1985 (cat.).– H. L. Rétrospective. Musée d'Art Moderne de la Communauté Urbaine de Lille, Villeneuve d'Ascq. Paris 1992 (cat.).– Laurens, M.: H. L. Sculpteur 1885-1954. Paris 1955.– Leymarie, J. (ed.): H. L. Accademia di Francia a Roma. Roma 1980 (cat.).– Monod-Fontaine, I. et al. (ed.): H. L. Le cubisme. Constructions et papiers collés 1915-1919. Centre Georges Pompidou. Paris 1985 (cat.).– Nardin, A. and J. Pijaudier (ed.): H. L. Rétrospective. Musée d'Art Moderne de la Commune Urbaine de Lille, Villeneuve d'Ascq. Paris 1992 (cat.).– Waldberg, P.: H. L. ou la femme placée en abîme. Paris 1980

LAVIER Bertrand
born 1949 Châtillon-sur-Seine
French painter and object artist. **1968-1972** Studied horticulture at the Ecole Nationale Supérieure d'Horticulture in Versailles. **1972** Gave up his studies to become an artist. Experimented with reproduction techniques and theories of perception using photography, painting and language. Since the 80s he has worked on modifications of

ready-made articles, covering commonplace objects with thick layers of paint in colours related to the object's original colouring. In **1982** and **1987** took part in documenta 7 and 8 in Kassel. **1984** First important solo-exhibition at the Kunsthalle Bern. **1984** Works drawing attention to the sculptural aspects of objects by placing two objects (e.g. a refrigerator and an armchair) one on top of the other. In his object art, Lavier not only weakens the distinctions between sculpture, painting, photography and language but also blurs the dividing line between the real object and its artistic image.
MONOGRAPHS, CATALOGUES: Celant, G. (ed.): B. L. Atheneum, Le Consortium, Musée des Beaux-Arts, Dijon et al. Dijon 1986 (cat.).– Douroux, X. and F. Gautherot (ed.): B. L. Le Nouveau Musée, Villeurbanne et al. Villeurbanne 1983/B. L. Kunsthalle Bern et al. Bern 1983 (cat.).– Duve, T. d. (ed.): B. L. Centre Georges Pompidou. Paris 1987 (cat.).– Gianelli, I. and G. Verzotti (ed.): B. L. Castello di Rivoli, Museo d'Arte Contemporanea. Milan 1996 (cat.).– Hegyi, L. and P. Restany (ed.): B. L. Museum Moderner Kunst Stiftung Ludwig. Vienna 1992 (cat.).– Millet, C. et al. (ed.): B. L. Centre Georges Pompidou. Paris 1991 (cat.)

LEBECK Robert
born 1929 Berlin
German photographer. Self-taught. **1944/45** Stationed with the German Army in Berlin and Stettin. **1948/49** Studied ethnology at Zurich University and **1949-1951** at Columbia University in New York. **1952-1955** Photojournalist for the *Heidelberger Tageblatt*, **1960-1965** for the magazine Kristall in Hamburg and **1969-1977** and since **1979** for *Stern Magazine* in Hamburg and New York. **1977/78** Editor of the journal *GEO* in Hamburg. **1980** Exhibited in the Photokina in Cologne. Lebeck, who has travelled and photographed in almost every country of the world, is considered one of the leading German photographers of the 20th century.
MONOGRAPHS, CATALOGUES: Nannen, H.: Augenzeuge R. L. 30 Jahre Zeitgeschichte. Munich 1984.– Steinorth, K. and M. M. Grewenig: R. L. Fotoreportagen. Stuttgart 1993.– Troeller, G. S. (ed.): R. L. Der Abenteurer. Gütersloh 1968

LECK Bart van der
1876 Utrecht – 1958 Blaricum (near Hilversum)
Dutch painter. **1891-1899** Worked in stained-glass workshops. **1900-1904** Attended a school of arts and crafts as well as evening classes at the Rijksakademie in Amsterdam. Designed furniture with Piet Klaarhamer and did book illustrations. From **1914** designs for stained-glass windows for the company Kröller-Müller. His early paintings are scenes of everyday life, especially factory work. From **1916**

close contact with Mondrian; the two artists influenced each other's work considerably, Leck's paintings becoming increasingly abstract. **1917** As a founder member of De Stijl, he contributed to the first edition of the journal published under that name. **1918** Broke away from De Stijl owing to disagreements over the function of architecture, and reverted to representational painting. Interior and textile designs and, from **1935**, ceramics. Despite their naturalistic motifs, Leck's later works, such as T*he Drinker* from **1955**, still betray a strong affinity to Neo-Plasticism, the formal language of De Stijl.
MONOGRAPHS, CATALOGUES: Feltkamp, W. C.: B. v. d. L. Leven en werken. Leyden 1950.– Hefting, P. and A. v. d. Woud (ed.): B. v. d. L. 1876-1958. Rijksmuseum Kröller-Müller, Otterlo et al. Hilversum 1976 (cat.).– Kooten, T. v. (ed.): B. v. d. L. 1876-1958. Rijksmuseum Kröller-Müller. Otterlo 1994 (cat.).– B. v. d. L. Stedelijk Museum. Amsterdam 1959 (cat.).– B. v. d. L. Städtische Kunsthalle Recklinghausen. Recklinghausen 1959 (cat.).– Müller-Haas, M. (ed.): B. v. d. L. Maler der Moderne. Kunstmuseum. Wolfsburg 1994 (cat.).– Oxenaar, W. D.: B. v. d. L. tot 1920: een primitief van de nieuwe tijd. Utrecht 1976.– Oxenaar, W. D. (ed.): B. v. d. L. 1876-1958. A la recherche de l'image des temps modernes. Institut néerlandais. Paris 1980 (cat.)

LE CORBUSIER
(Charles-Edouard Jeanneret)
1887 La-Chaux-de-Fonds (Switzerland) – 1965 Cap Martin
Swiss-French architect, sculptor and painter. **1900** Trained as an engraver. **1901-1905** Studied architecture at La-Chaux-de-Fonds School of Arts. **1917** Moved to Paris. Began to paint, concentrating mainly on still lifes. **1918** Became acquainted with Ozenfant with whom he drew up the manifesto *Après le Cubisme, le purisme*, rejecting Cubist painting and propounding an objective approach to art based on clear architectonic principles. **1920-1925** Published the journal *L'Esprit Nouveau* and began to sign his articles with the pseudonym Le Corbusier. **1924** Set up a professional architects' office with his brother Pierre in Paris, undertaking projects all over the world.

From **1929** designed metal furniture. In his painting, he gradually moved away from his own Purist theories, developing a freer, expressive style, with the human figure as his central theme. **1939** Joined the group Cercle et Carré. Zurich. **1953** Retrospective of his paintings at the Musée d'Art Moderne in Paris. **1959** Participation in documenta 2 in Kassel.
WRITINGS: Giedion-Welcker, C. (ed.): L. C. Schriften 1926-1971. Stationen zu einem Zeitbild. Cologne 1973.– L. C. and A. Ozenfant: Après le cubisme. Paris 1918.– L. C.: L'Atelier de la recherche patiente. Paris 1960.– L. C.: Mein Werk. Stuttgart 1960
CATALOGUES RAISONNÉS: Boesinger, W. (ed.): L. C. et P. Jeanneret. Œuvre complète 1910-1965. 7 vols. Zurich 1930-1971.– Weber, H. (ed.): L. C. L'œuvre lithographique. Zurich 1967
MONOGRAPHS, CATALOGUES: Baker, G.: L. C. An Analysis of Form. London 1984, New York 1991.– Besset, M.: L. C. Geneva et al. 1987.– Biadene, S. (ed.): L. C. Pittore e scultore. Museo Correr. Venice 1986 (cat.).– Billeter, E. (ed.): L. C. secret. Musée Cantonal des Beaux-Arts. Lausanne 1987 (cat.).– Bolle-Reddat, R.: Un évangile selon L. C. Paris 1987.– Brady, D.: L. C. An Annot. Bibliography. New York 1985.– Brooks, A. (ed.): L. C. The Garland Essays. New York 1987.– Cresti, C.: L. C. Lucerne 1973.– Curtis, W. J.: L. C. Ideas and Forms. New York 1986 / L. C. Ideen und Formen. Stuttgart 1987.– Ducret, A. et al. (ed.): L. C. Le peintre derrière l'architecte. Grenoble 1988.– Fondation L. C. (ed.): L. C. Sketchbooks. 4 vols. Cambridge 1981-1982.– Graves, M. E.: L. C. Selected Drawings. New York 1981.– Gresleri, G.: L. C. Il viaggio in Toscana. Palazzo Pitti. Florence 1987 (cat.).– Hervé, L. (ed.): L. C. Der Künstler und der Schriftsteller. Neuchâtel 1970.– Hohl, R.: L. C. Thesen und Werke. Stuttgart 1972.– Huse, N.: L. C. In Selbstzeugnissen und Bilddokumenten. Reinbek 1976.– Klopmann, A.: L. C. L'homme. Geneva 1995.– L. C. Architektur, Malerei, Plastik, Wandteppiche. Kunsthaus Zürich. Zurich 1957 (cat.).– Lucan, J. et al. (ed.): L. C. Une encyclopédie. Centre Georges Pompidou. Paris 1987 (cat.).– Monnier, G.: L. C. Lyon 1986.– Petit, J.: L. C. lui-même. Geneva 1970.– Sekler, M. P.: The Early Drawings of Charles-Edouard Jeanneret. Diss. Cambridge (MA), Harvard University. New York 1977.– Tentori, F.: Vita e opere di L. C. Roma 1983.– Weber, H. (ed.): L. C. Maler, Zeichner, Plastiker, Poet. Zurich 1988

LEGER Fernand
1881 Argentan (Orne) – **1955** Gif-sur-Yvette
French painter. Began his career as an architectural draughtsman and continued this work in Paris until **1903**. From **1908** mixed with artists from the artists' colony Zone, including Delaunay, Archipenko, Laurens, Lipchitz. From **1910** works exhibited by the dealer D.-H. Kahnweiler, who also represented Picasso and Braque. Léger was

drawn towards Cubism. **1914–1916** His experiences during World War I led him to the central theme of his œuvre, the technological face of the 20th century, and he did a series of paintings of a silent mechanized world populated solely by workers. **1917** The tubular appearance of his gigantic figures led one critic to suggest mockingly that the man's art be referred to not as Cubism but as Tubism. **1920** His friendship with the architect Le Corbusier inspired him to branch out into monumental murals, mosaics and stained-glass windows. This led to his so-called monumental period, in which he portrayed monstrous stereotyped figures with heavily outlined limbs. From **1927** his figures became increasingly realistic. **1932** Taught at the Académie de la Grande Chaumière in Paris. **1952** Decorations for the assembly hall of the UNESCO in New York. Despite his close connection to Cubism, Léger was not so much concerned with an analytical breakdown of the pictorial field but rather with an unfolding of art through a celebration of pure colours and rhythms, as shown in his work Form Contrasts.
WRITINGS: F. L.: Propos et présence. Paris 1959.– F. L.: Mes voyages. Paris 1960.– F. L.: Fonctions de la peinture. Paris 1965 / Functions of Painting. New York 1965.– F. L.: Lettres à Simone. Correspondance établie et annotée par C. Derouet. Paris 1987.– F. L.: Une correspondance de guerre à Louis Poughon 1914-1918. Texte présenté, établi et annoté par C. Derouet. Paris 1990.– F. L. Une correspondance d'affaires. F. L.- L. Rosenberg. Paris 1996
CATALOGUES RAISONNÉS: Bauquier, G. and N. Maillard (ed.): F. L. Catalogue raisonné de l'œuvre peint 1903-1931. 4 vols. Paris 1990-1995.– Cassou, J. and J. Leymarie (ed.): F. L. Dessins et gouaches. Paris 1972 / F. L. Drawings and Gouaches. London 1973, Greenwich (CT) 1973 / F. L. Das graphische Werk. Tübingen 1973.– Saphire, L. (ed.): F. L. The Complete Graphic Work. New York 1978, Yorktown 1992
MONOGRAPHS, CATALOGUES: Aragon, L.: F. L. Contrastes. Paris 1959.– Bauquier, G.: F. L. Vivre dans le vrai. Paris 1987.– Briot, M.-O. et al. (ed.): L. et l'esprit moderne. Une alternative d'avant-garde à l'art non-objectif (1918-1931). Musée d'Art Moderne de la Ville de Paris et al. Paris 1982 (cat.).– Buck, R. T. et al. (ed.): F. L. Albright-Knox Art Gallery, Buffalo. New York 1982 (cat.).– Conzen-Meairs, I. et al. (ed.): F. L. The Later Years. Whitechapel Art Gallery, London et al. London 1987 (cat.).– Cooper, D.: F. L. et le nouvel espace. London, Paris and Geneva 1949.– Derouet, C. (ed.): F. L. La Poésie de l'objet 1928-1934. Centre Georges Pompidou. Paris 1981 (cat.).– Derouet, C. (ed.): F. L. Léger och Norden. Museet för Finländsk Konst Ateneum et al. Stockholm 1992 (cat.).– Derouet, C. (ed.): F. L. Centre Georges Pompidou, Paris et al. Paris 1997 (cat.).– Descargues, P.: F. L. Paris 1955.– Francia, P. d.: F. L. New Haven (CT) and London 1983.– Green, C.: L. and the Avant-Garde. New Haven (CT) and London 1976.– Kosinski, D. (ed.): F. L. 1911-1924. Der Rhythmus des modernen Lebens (Le rythme de la vie moderne). Kunstmuseum Wolfsburg et al. Munich 1994 (cat.) / F. L. 1911-1924. The Rhythm of Modern Life. Kunstmuseum Wolfsburg et al. New York 1994 (cat.).– Lanchner, C. (ed.): F. L. The Museum of Modern Art. New York 1998 (cat.).– Lasalle, H. (ed.): F. L. Palazzo Reale. Milan 1989 (cat.) / F. L. Musée d'Art Moderne de la Communauté Urbaine de Lille, Villeneuve d'Ascq. Milan 1990 (cat.).– Laugier, C. and M. Richet: Le Œuvres de F. L. 1881-1955. Centre Georges Pompidou. Paris 1981 (cat.).– F. L. Musées des Beaux-

Arts de Montreal et al. New York 1982 (cat.).– F. L. Musée des Arts Décoratifs. Paris 1956 (cat.).– Le Noci, G.: F. L. Sa Vie, son œuvre, son rêve. Milan 1971.– Leymarie, J. and M. Richet (ed.): F. L. Grand Palais. Paris 1971 (cat.).– Néret, G.: F. L. Paris 1992, London 1993.– Prat, J.-L. (ed.): F. L. Rétrospective. Fondation Maeght. Saint-Paul 1988 (cat.).– F. L. Staatliche Kunsthalle Berlin. Berlin 1980 (cat.).– Schmalenbach, W.: F. L. New York 1976, Cologne 1977.– Schmalenbach, W. and M. Moeller (ed.): F. L. Kunsthalle der Hypo-Kulturstiftung. Munich 1988 (cat.).– Schneede, U. (ed.): F. L. Gouachen, Aquarelle, Zeichnungen. Kunsthalle Tübingen et al. Stuttgart 1983 (cat.).– Serota, N. (ed.): F. L. Zeichnungen, Bilder, Zyklen. 1930-1955. Staatsgalerie Stuttgart. Munich 1988 (cat.)

LEHMBRUCK Wilhelm
1880 Meiderich (near Duisburg) – 1919 Berlin
German sculptor. **1895–1899** Studied at the Düsseldorf School of Arts and Crafts and **1901–1907** at the Düsseldorf Academy. **1905** Scholarship for a study trip to Italy. **1910** Moved to Paris. Acquainted with Archipenko, Brancusi, Modigliani and Derain. **1911** Modelled his first Kniende (Kneeling figures). Took up copperplate engraving and lithography. **1912** Participated at the Sonderbund exhibition. Second trip to Italy. **1914** Moved to Berlin, and exhibited with the German Werkbund that same year. **1916** First major solo-exhibition at the Kunsthalle Mannheim. **1917/18** Spent a year in Zurich. **1919** Elected to the Prussian Academy of Fine Arts. Suicide. Lehmbruck, whose attenuated, dynamic figures stem from the symbolist-existentialist tradition founded by Adolf von Hildebrand and Rodin, is seen as a key figure in the history of sculpture.
CATALOGUES RAISONNÉS: Lahusen, M. C. (ed.): W. L. Gemälde und großformatige Zeichnungen. Munich 1997.– Petermann, E. (ed.): Die Druckgraphik von W. L. Stuttgart 1964
MONOGRAPHS, CATALOGUES: Betthausen, P. and C. Brockhaus (ed.): W. L. 1881-1919. Plastik. Malerei. Graphik. Aus den Sammlungen des W.-L.-Museums der Stadt Duisburg. Museen der Stadt Gotha et al. Duisburg 1987 (cat.).– Bock, H. et al. (ed.): W. L. Nationalgalerie. Berlin 1973 (cat.).– Franz, E. (ed.): W. L. Zeichnungen aus dem W.-L.-Museum Duisburg. Kunsthaus Zurich et al. Zurich 1990 (cat.).– Güse, E. G.: L. und Italien. Duisburg 1979.– Heller, R. (ed.): W. L. Die Zeichnungen der Reifezeit. Stuttgart 1985.– Heller, R. (ed.): The Art of W. L. National Gallery of Art, Washington et al. Washington 1972 (cat.).– Hofmann, W.: W. L. Cologne 1957, New York 1959, Munich 1964.– Hoff, A.: W. L. Leben und Werk. Berlin 1933, 1961 / W. L. Life and Work. Washington 1969.– Holländer, G.: L. in Duisburg. Eine rezeptionsgeschichtliche Studie. Bonn 1995.–

Markin, J. P. and J. V. Bugoevc: Vil'gel'm Lembruk. Moscow 1989.– Pfeiffer, A. (ed.): W. L. Städtische Museen, Heilbronn et al. Heilbronn 1981 (cat.).– Riden, G. (ed.): W. L. Sieben Beiträge zum Gedenken seines 50. Todestages. Duisburg 1969.– Salzmann, S. (ed.): W. L. 1881-1919. National Gallery, Edinburgh et al. Edinburgh 1979 (cat.).– Salzmann, S. and K.-E. Vester (ed.): Hommage à L. / L. in seiner Zeit. Wilhelm-Lehmbruck-Museum. Duisburg 1981 (cat.).– Schubert, D.: Die Kunst L.'s. Worms 1981, Dresden 1990.– Syamken, G.: W. L. Hamburg 1991

LEIBOWITZ Annie
born **1949** Warterbury (CT)
American photographer. **1970** Studied photography and painting in San Francisco, and worked for the magazine Rolling Stone. **1971** Bachelor of Fine Arts at the Art Institute of San Francisco. **1973** Head of photography at Rolling Stone. **1975** Accompanied the group The Rolling Stones on a concert tour. From **1983** photographed for Condé Nast at Vanity Fair. Won the Granny Award for photography for the Album Cover of the Year. **1984** Nominated Photographer of the Year by the American Society of Magazine Photographers. **1987** Portrait and advertising campaign for American Express, for which she won the Campaign of the Decade prize. Prize for Innovation and Photography from the Society of Magazine Photographers. **1989** Did portraits of the American Ballet Theater. Received the Infinity Award for Applied Photography from the International Center of Photography, New York.

LE MOAL Jean
born **1909** Authon-du-Perche (Eure-et-Loire)
French painter. **1926–1929** Studied at the Ecole des Beaux-Arts in Lyon and **1934–1938** at the Académie Ranson in Paris under Bissière. **1939** Travelled to the USA. Took up abstract painting. **1941** Together with Bazaine, Manessier, Lapicque and Singier, founded the group "Mouvement des jeunes peintres de la tradition française" and took part in their joint-exhibitions at the Galerie Braun in Paris. From **1943** exhibitions in the Salon de Mai, and from **1944** joint exhibitions with Manessier and Singier at the

Galerie de France. **1950** Awarded the Prix de la critique. **1959** Participation in documenta 2 in Kassel. Le Moal's rhythmically organised colour structures are representative of the Ecole de Paris.
MONOGRAPHS, CATALOGUES: J. L. M. Galerie Beyeler. Basel 1956 (cat.).– J. L. M. Overbeck-Gesellschaft. Lübeck 1961 (cat.).– J. L. M. Museum. Metz 1963 (cat.).– J. L. M. Galerie Appel und Fertsch. Frankfurt-on-Main 1967 (cat.).– J. L. M. Galerie de France. Paris 1974 (cat.)

LEMPICKA Tamara de
1898 Warsaw – **1980** Cuernavaca
Polish painter. **1917** Fled with her husband to Paris, where she took private lessons with Denis and Lhote. Developed an independent style, combining elements of Neo-Classicism and Post-Cubism in which she painted erotic motifs. **1925** Completed her best-known work, the self-portrait *Tamara in Bugatti*, where she presents herself as a vamp. Became known to a wider public through her participation in the first Art Deco exhibition in Paris and was subsequently the most sought-after portraitist in Parisian high society. **1928** Portrait of Baron Raoul Kuffner's mistress *Nana de Herrera*. **1933** Married Kuffner. **1939** Moved to Beverley Hills in the USA, where she painted portraits of numerous Hollywood stars. **1973** Retrospective in Paris. **1974** Moved to Mexico.
WRITINGS: Ishioka, E. (ed.): Five Days with T. de L. Tokyo 1980
CATALOGUE RAISONNE: Blondel A. (ed.): T. de L. Catalogue raisonné 1921-1979. Lausanne 1998
MONOGRAPHS, CATALOGUES: Bazin, G.: T. de L. Paris 1980.– Calvesi, M. and A. Borghese (ed.): T. de L. Tra eleganza e trasgressione. Accademia di Francia, Villa Medici. Roma 1994 (cat.).– T. de L. 1925 à 1935. Galerie de Luxembourg. Paris 1972 (cat.).– Lempicka-Foxhall, K. d. and C. Phillips: Passion by Design. The Art and Times of T. de L. Oxford and New York 1987 / T. d. L. Malerin aus Leidenschaft, Femme Fatale der 20er Jahre. Munich 1987.– Marmori, G. (ed.): T. de L. The Major Works of T. de L. 1925-1935. Parma 1977.– Mori, G.: T. de L. Parigi 1920-1938. Florence 1994 / T. de L. Paris 1920-1938. Paris 1995.– Néret, G.: T. de L. 1898-1980. Cologne 1991.– Parco View: T. de L. Tokyo 1980.– Thormann, E.: T. de L. Kunstkritik und Künstlerinnen. Berlin 1993

LE PARC Julio
born **1928** Mendoza
Argentinian kinetic artist. Began studying at the age of 15 at the Escuela de Bellas Artes in Buenos Aires. **1958/59** Grant from the French government and assistantship with Victor Vasarely. Together with artist friends, undertook an analysis of the works of famous avant-garde artists, which led to his abandoning a freestyle formal language and beginning to work with sequences and

series. **1960** Founded the Groupe de Recherche d'Art Visuel, whose aim was to encourage active viewer participation. This Le Parc achieved by creating special environments such as labyrinths, playrooms, street events or mobile objects, affecting the viewer's body awareness. From **1965** participated in numerous exhibition of Groupe de Recherche d'Art Visuel and Tendances Nouvelles in Europe, North and South America and Japan. **1968** Participation in documenta 4 in Kassel.
MONOGRAPHS, CATALOGUES: Elia, A. (ed.): J. L. P. Experiencias 30 años 1958-1988. Buenos Aires 1988 (cat.).– Mari, E.: J. L. P. Milan 1960.– J. L. P. Galerie Buchholz. Munich 1968 (cat.).– J. L. P. Experiment plats för upplevelse av ögats, kroppens och tingens rörelser. Konst Museum, Göteborg et al. Stockholm 1969 (cat.).– J. L. P. Kinetische Objekte. Museum. Ulm 1970 (cat.).– J. L. P. Recherches 1959-1971. Städtische Kunsthalle Düsseldorf et al. Düsseldorf 1972 (cat.).– J. L. P. Pinturas recientes. Museo de Arte Moderno. Bogotá 1976.– Popper, F. and J. Clay (ed.): L. P. Museo de Bellas Artes. Caracas 1967 (cat.)

LEROY Eugène
born **1910** Tourcoing
French painter. **1931–1932** Attended the Ecole des Beaux-Arts in Lille and Paris. **1936–1956** Went to Brussels and Amsterdam to study the works of Rembrandt and Malevich, to Italy where he developed a passion for Bellini and Giorgione, and to Munich where he visited exhibitions of Klee and Kandinsky. From **1958** lived and worked in Wasquehal, a remote spot that became his *point de fixation*. Between **1965** and **1972**, in search of a mode of painting, he produced numerous graphic works, especially gouaches and later acrylic and oil paintings in which figures and landscapes appear to emerge from a brown-coloured substance like clay or earth. **1972–1974** Trips to New York and Washington, where Rothko's paintings had a profound effect on him. Also went to Leningrad and Moscow. **1977** Exhibition at the Ecole des Beaux-Arts in Lille. **1980** Retrospective at the Museum van Hedendaagse Kunst in Ghent. **1992** Took part in documenta 9 in Kassel.
MONOGRAPHS, CATALOGUES: Hergott, F. (ed.): E. L. Le retour d'Ulysse / Ulysses

Returns. Stedelijk Van Abbe Museum, Eindhoven et al. Eindhoven 1988 (cat.).– E. L. Museum van Hedendaagse Kunst. Ghent 1982 (cat.).– E. L. Musée d'Art Moderne de la Communauté Urbaine de Lille. Villeneuve d'Ascq 1987 (cat.).– E. L. Dessins. Musée de Poitiers. Poitiers 1990 (cat.).– E. L. Kunsthalle Basel. Basel 1997 (cat.).– E. L. Galerie B.: E. L. Paris 1994.– Pleynet, M. (ed.): E. L. Rétrospective. Musée d'Art Moderne et d'Art Contemporain. Nice 1993 (cat.)

LEVINE Les
born **1935** Dublin
Irish-born American multimedia artist. Studied at the Central School of Arts and Crafts in London and first worked as a designer and photographer. **1958** Moved to Canada, where he produced his first sculptures. From **1965** incorporated videos into his works. **1967–1969** Projects involving video, film, telephones and other media leading to the series *Disposable Art* and *Software Art*. **1970** Set up the Museum of Mott Art offering careers advice to artists. From **1972** taught at New York University. **1974** Received the National Endowment for the Arts and was made Professor of Video Art at William Patterson College Wayne in New York. **1975** Broadcasting of Les Levine Festival by the cable TV station Cable Arts. **1977** and **1987** took part in documenta 6 and 8 in Kassel. **1990** Solo-exhibition at the Centraal Museum in Utrecht.
MONOGRAPHS, CATALOGUES: Gisler, V. and L. Kurmann (ed.): L. L. Media Projects and Public Advertisements. Mai 36 Galerie. Lucerne 1988 (cat.).– Nahas, D. (ed.): Public Mind. L. L.'s Media Sculpture and Mass Ad Campaigns 1969-1990. Everson Museum of Art. Syracuse (NY) 1990 (cat.).– Schmidt, J.-K. (ed.): L. L. Medienskulptur. Galerie der Stadt Stuttgart. Stuttgart 1997 (cat.).– Video-As Art-By L. L. Plattsburg (NY) 1979

LEWITT Sol
born **1928** Hartford (CT)
American object and concept artist. **1945-1949** Studied at Syracuse University, New York. **1953** Attended the Cartoonist and Illustrator School in New York. **1955/56** Worked as a graphic artist for the architect

I. M. Pei. **1960–1965** Instructor at the Museum of Modern Art in New York. Became acquainted with Mangold, Ryman and Flavin. **1963/64** First sculptures, influenced by Bauhaus and De Stijl. **1964–1971** Taught at the Cooper Union and the Education Department of New York University. **1965** First solo-exhibition at the Daniels Gallery in New York. **1966** First open structures with cuboid modules. From **1968** numerous wall drawings: strictly schematic compositions with rhythmic lines painted directly onto walls. **1968–1982** Participation in documenta 4–7 in Kassel. From **1970** concentrated on printing techniques. LeWitt designed serial systems, based on geometric and mathematical laws, that could be transformed into sculptural structures through a third modifier. This approach to art makes him one of the leading exponents of Concept Art in America.
WRITINGS: S. L.: Autobiography. New York and Boston 1980.– Zevi, A. (ed.): S. L. Critical Texts. New York 1995
CATALOGUES RAISONNES: Fuchs, R. and W. Kaiser (ed.): S. L. Drawings 1958-1992. Haags Gemeentemuseum, The Hague et al. The Hague 1992 (cat.).– Lewison, S. (ed.): S. L. Prints 1970-1986. Tate Gallery. London 1986 (cat.).– S. L. Books 1966-1990. Portikus. Frankfurt-on-Main 1990 (cat.).– Singer, S. (ed.): S. L. Wall Drawings 1968-1984. Stedelijk Museum, Amsterdam et al. Amsterdam 1984 (cat.).– Singer, S. (ed.): S. L. Wall Drawings 1984-1992. Kunsthalle Bern. Bern 1992 (cat.)
MONOGRAPHS, CATALOGUES: Batchelor, D. and R. Krauss (ed.): S. L. Structures 1962-1993. Museum of Modern Art, Oxford et al. Oxford and Munich 1993 (cat.).– Haenlein, C. (ed.): S. L. Walldrawings. Kestner-Gesellschaft. Hanover 1988 (cat.).– Legg, A. et al. (ed.): S. L. The Museum of Modern Art. New York 1978 (cat.).– Lewison, J. (ed.): S. L. Prints 1970-1996. Tate Gallery. London 1986 (cat.).– S. L. Gemeentemuseum. The Hague 1970 (cat.).– S. L. Structures. Museum of Modern Art, Oxford et al. Oxford 1993 (cat.) / S. L. Structures. Museum Villa Stuck, Munich et al. Munich 1993 (cat.).– Paoletti, J. T. (ed.): No Title (The Collection of S. L.) Wesleyan University Art Gallery et al. Middletown 1981 (cat.).– Reynolds, J. (ed.): S. L. Twenty-Five Years of Wall Drawings 1968-1993. Addison Gallery of American Art. Andover 1993 (cat.).– Rose, B. et al. (ed.): S. L. The Museum of Modern Art, New York et al. New York 1978 (cat.)

LHOTE André
1885 Bordeaux – **1962** Paris
French painter and art critic. Self-taught. Studied sculpture at the Ecole des Beaux-Arts in Bordeaux. **1908** Moved to Paris. **1910** First solo-exhibition at the Galerie Drouet in Paris. Co-founder of the journal *Nouvelle Revue française*, for which he worked until **1940** as an art critic. **1911**

M. A Catalogue Raisonné 1943-1990. New York 1990
MONOGRAPHS, CATALOGUES: Arnason, H. H.: R. M. New York 1977, 1982.– Ashton, D. et al. (ed.): R. M. Albright-Knox Art Gallery. Buffalo 1983 (cat.).– Carmean, E. A. (ed.): R. M. The Reconciliation Elegy. Geneva and New York 1980.– Caws, M. A.: R. M. What Art Holds. New York 1996.– Flam, J.: R. M. Oxford and New York 1991, Paris 1991, Recklinghausen 1992.– Harten, J. et al. (ed.): R. M. Eine Retrospektive. Städtische Kunsthalle Düsseldorf et al. Düsseldorf 1976 (cat.).– Mattison, R. S.: R. M. The Formative Years. Ann Arbor (MI) 1986.– R. M. Kunsthalle Kiel. Kiel 1971 (cat.).– R. M. Kunstmuseum und Kunstforening. Aarhus 1980 (cat.).– R. M. Fundació Antoni Tàpies, Barcelona et al. Barcelona 1996 (cat.).– O'Hara, F. et al. (ed.): R. M. A Retrospective. The Museum of Modern Art, New York et al. New York 1965 (cat.).– Pleynet, M.: R. M. Paris 1989.– Rosand, D. (ed.): R. M. on Paper. Drawings, Prints, Collages. New York et al. New York 1996.– Terenzio, S. (ed.): R. M. & Black. William Benton Museum of Art. New York 1980 (cat.)

MUCHE Georg
1895 Querfurt – **1987** Lindau
German painter and craftsman. **1913** Studied painting in Munich. **1914** Moved to Berlin. **1915** First non-figurative paintings inspired by the works of Kandinsky. **1916-1919** Taught at the art school attached to Der Sturm in Berlin. **1920-1927** Head teacher of the wood sculpture and weaving classes at the Bauhaus. **1927-1931** Taught at Itten's art school in Berlin. From **1931** teaching post at the Breslau Academy. **1933** Dismissed. **1934** Trip to Italy. **1937** His works displayed as part of the exhibition of "degenerate art" in Munich. **1939-1958** Directed his own school of textile engineering in Krefeld. **1944-1949** Painted frescoes for the Institute of Silk Industry in Krefeld. **1950** Participated at documenta 1 in Kassel. **1960** Moved to Lindau on Lake Constance. **1963** Guest of honour at Villa Massimo in Rome. Solo-exhibition at the Kunstverein in Mannheim. **1974** Retrospective at the Nationalgalerie Berlin. **1979** Awarded the Lovis Corinth Prize by the City of Regensburg.
WRITINGS: Ackermann, U. (ed.): G. M.: Der alte Maler. Briefe 1945-1984. Tübingen 1992.– G. M.: Buonfresco. Briefe aus Italien über Handwerk und Stil der echten Frescomalerei. Berlin 1938.– G. M.: Blickpunkt Sturm, Dada, Bauhaus, Gegenwart. Munich 1961, Tübingen 1965
CATALOGUES RAISONNES: Droste, M. et al. (ed.): G. M. Das künstlerische Werk 1912-1927. Bauhaus-Archiv. Berlin 1980 (cat.).– Schiller, P. H. (ed.): G. M. Das druckgraphische Werk. Darmstadt 1970
MONOGRAPHS, CATALOGUES: Brüggemann, E. W. and U. Ackermann

(ed.): G. M. Sturm – Bauhaus – Spätwerk. Retrospektive. Bad Homburg v. d. Höhe 1995 (cat.).– Busch, L.: G. M. Dokumente zum malerischen Werk der Jahre 1915 bis 1920. Tübingen 1984.– Heinz, M. and A. Burger (ed.): G. M. Leise sagen. Neue Galerie, Staatliche und Städtische Kunstsammlungen. Kassel 1986 (cat.).– Linder, G.: G. M. Friedrichshafen 1983.– G. M. Gemälde, Zeichnungen, Graphik. Städtische Galerie im Lenbachhaus. Munich 1965 (cat.).– G. M. Das malerische Werk 1928-1982. Bauhaus-Archiv. Berlin 1983 (cat.).– Richter, H.: G. M. Recklinghausen 1960.– Thiem, G. (ed.): G. M. Der Zeichner. Staatsgalerie Stuttgart. Stuttgart 1977 (cat.)

MUELLER Otto
1874 Liebau – **1930** Breslau
German painter and graphic artist. **1890-1894** Trained as a lithographer in Görlitz. **1894-1896** Studied at the Dresden Academy and, after graduating, travelled with Gerhard Hauptmann through Switzerland and France. **1898/99** Studied at the Munich Academy under Stuck. Admired Böcklin, Hans von Marées and Ludwig von Hofmann. Returned to Dresden. **1908** Moved to Berlin. Came to know Lehmbruck and Rilke. **1910** Joined the Brücke group and helped to found the New Secession. **1912** Took part in the Sonderbund exhibition in Cologne. Travelled with Kirchner to Bohemia. While fighting in the war **1916-1918** he did many sketches for later paintings. **1918** Returned to Berlin. **1919** Member of the Arts Advisory Council. Taught at the Breslau Academy. **1920** and **1923** Spent the summers with Heckel on the Baltic Sea. **1924-1930** Numerous trips to Dalmatia, Hungary, Romania and Bulgaria. Mueller's favourite theme was gypsy life. His palette was more subdued than that of most Brücke painters.
WRITINGS: Pachnicke, G. (ed.): O. M. Briefe an Lotte und Gerhart Hauptmann in den Jahren 1897-1899. Nuremberg 1986
CATALOGUES RAISONNES: Buchheim, L.-G.: O. M. Leben und Werk. Mit einem Werkverzeichnis der Graphik. Feldafing 1963, 1968.– Karsch, F. (ed.): O. M. Das graphische Gesamtwerk. Holzschnitte, Radierungen, Lithographien, Farblithographien. Berlin 1974
MONOGRAPHS, CATALOGUES: Billeter, F.: Der Plastiker O. M. Zurich 1983.– Decker, M.: Gestaltungselemente im Bildwerk von O. M. Dortmund 1993.– Lüttichau, M.-A. v.: O. M. Ein Romantiker unter den Expressionisten. Cologne 1993.– Moeller, M. (ed.): O. M. Brücke-Museum, Berlin et al. Berlin 1996 (cat.).– O. M. 1874-1930. Kunsthalle Bremen. Bremen 1956 (cat.).– O. M. Gemälde, Zeichnungen und Druckgraphik. Städtisches Museum Mülheim/Ruhr 1974 (cat.).– Schmeller, A.: O. M. Mädchenbilder und Zigeunerleben. Munich 1959

MUNCH Edvard
1863 Løten (Hedmark) – **1944** Ekely (near Oslo)
Norwegian painter and graphic artist. Tragic childhood: Both his mother and his sister Sophie died of consumption, while his father was melancholy and dementedly pious. First attended technical college. From **1881** studied at the Royal School of Drawing in Oslo. Painted human figures and naturalistic landscapes full of light, under the supervision of Christian Krohg. **1883** Attended the Thaulows Academy, where classes were held in the open air. **1885** First trip to Paris and development of a highly personal and colourful, expressive style. **1889** First solo-exhibition. State scholarship. During his stay in Paris **1889-1892** he studied Old Masters, Impressionism and the paintings of the Pont-Aven School and Nabis, and began to paint Pointillist landscapes. **1892** Trip to Berlin, where his exhibition at the Verein der bildenden Künstler (Artists' Union) caused a scandal. Founded the Berlin Secession. Contact with Strindberg, Meier-Graefe, Przybyszewski, Botho-Graeff. **1893** Began work on his *Frieze of Life*. From **1894** publication of graphic reproductions. In the 1890's made many long visits to France, Italy and Germany. Around **1900** did numerous illustrations. **1896-1898** Participated in the exhibitions at the Salon des Indépendants in Oslo. **1916** Wall paintings for the University of Oslo. Moved to Ekely near Oslo. **1921/22** Design for the canteen of the Freia Chocolate Factory in Oslo. Munch, one of the founding fathers of Expressionism, had a decisive influence on the development of modern art, especially in Germany.
WRITINGS: Schiefler, G. (ed.): E. M. Briefwechsel. 2 vols. Hamburg 1987-1990.– Torjusen, B. (ed.): Words and Images of E. M. London 1989
CATALOGUE RAISONNE: Schiefler, G. (ed.): Verzeichnis des graphischen Werks E. M.'s. 2 vols. Berlin 1907-1928, Oslo 1974, Cologne 1995
MONOGRAPHS, CATALOGUES: Benesch, O.: E. M. London 1960.– Bjørnstad, K.: E. M. Oslo 1993, Frankfurt-on-Main 1996.– Bock, H. and G. Busch: E. M. Probleme, Forschungen, Thesen. Munich 1973.– Boulton Smith, J.: E. M. 1863-1944. Berlin 1962.– Carlsson, A.: E. M. Leben und Werk. Stuttgart and Zurich 1984.– Deknatel, F.: E. M. New York 1950.– Eggum, A.: E. M. malerier, skisser og studier. Stockholm 1983/E. M. peintures, esquisses, études. Paris 1983/E. M. Paintings, Sketches and Studies. New York 1984/E. M. Gemälde, Zeichnungen und Studien. Stuttgart 1986.– Eggum, A.: M. and Photography. New Haven (CT) 1989/M. und die Photographie. Bern 1991.– Eggum, A. and R. Repetti (ed.): M. et la France. Musée d'Orsay. Paris 1992 (cat.).– Eggum, A. et al. (ed.): M. und Deutschland. Kunsthalle der Hypo-Kulturstiftung, Munich et al. Stuttgart 1994 (cat.).– Fahr-Becker-Sterner, G. (ed.): E. M. Museum

Villa Stuck. Munich 1987 (cat.).– Gauguin, P.: E. M. Oslo 1946.– Gerlach, H. E.: E. M. Sein Leben und sein Werk. Hamburg 1955.– Gierløff, C.: E. M. selv. Oslo 1953.– Heller, R.: M. His Life and Work. Chicago and London 1984/E. M. Leben und Werk. Munich et al. 1993.– Hodin, J. P.: E. M. Berlin and Mainz 1963, London and New York 1972, Paris 1991.– Hougen, P. (ed.): E. M. Haus der Kunst, Munich et al. Munich 1973 (cat.).– Keiner, M. (ed.): E. M. und seine Modelle. Galerie der Stadt Stuttgart. Stuttgart 1993 (cat.).– Kneher, J.: E. M. in seinen Ausstellungen zwischen 1892 und 1912. Worms 1994.– Langaard, J. H.: E. M. Modningsår. Oslo 1960.– Langaard, J. H. and R. Revold: E. M. som tegner. Oslo 1958.– Langaard, J. H. and R. Revold: E. M. fra år til år. Oslo 1961.– Langaard, J. H. and R. Revold.: E. M. Mesterverker i Munch-museet. Oslo 1963.– Magnaguagno, G. (ed.): E. M. 1863-1944. Museum Folkwang, Essen et al. Bern 1987 (cat.).– Messer, T.: E. M. Cologne 1989.– Moen, A.: E. M. 3 vols. Oslo 1956-1958.– E. M. Liebe, Angst, Tod. Kunsthalle Bielefeld. Bielefeld 1980 (cat.).– Rosenblum, R. et al. (ed.): E. M. Symbols and Images. National Gallery of Art. Washington 1978 (cat.).– Sarvig, O.: E. M. Grafik. Copenhagen 1948.– Schneede, U. M.: E. M. Höhepunkte des malerischen Werks im 20. Jahrhundert. Hamburger Kunstverein. Hamburg 1984 (cat.).– Schneede, U. M.: E. M. Die frühen Meisterwerke. Frankfurt-on-Main 1992.– Schütz, M. B.: Farbe und Licht bei E. M. Saarbrücken 1985.– Stang, R.: E. M. The Man and His Art. New York 1979, 1988/E. M. Der Mensch und Künstler. Königstein 1979.– Stenersen, R.: E. M. Närbild av ett geni. Stockholm 1944, Oslo 1945, Zurich 1949.– Thiis, J.: E. M. og hans samtid. Oslo 1933.– Timm, W.: E. M. Graphik. Stuttgart 1969.– Væring, R. and J. H. Langaard: E. M. selvportretter. Oslo 1947.– Willoch, S.: E. M. raderinger. Oslo 1950.– Wood, M.-H. (ed.): E. M. The Frieze of Life. New York 1993

MUNKACSI Martin
1896 Kolozsvar – **1963** New York
Hungarian painter and photographer. First focused on painting. **1923** Discovered photography by chance and in a very short time became one of the most sought-after photojournalists in Hungary. From **1927** worked for the publishers Ullstein in Berlin and for the newspaper *Berliner Illustrirte Zeitung*. Commissions took him all over the world. In the 30s he emigrated to America, where, among other things, he photographed for *Harper's Bazaar*. Munkacsi not only broke through the strict conventions of formal fashion photography but also set a new trend in photojournalism with his dynamic, spontaneous pictures and unusual snapshots.
MONOGRAPHS, CATALOGUES: Hoghe, R. (ed.): Retrospektive Fotografie. M. M. Bielefeld and Düsseldorf 1980.– White, N. and J. Esten (ed.): M. Photographs of the '20s, '30s and '40s. New York 1979

MÜNTER Gabriele
1877 Berlin – **1962** Murnau
German painter. **1898-1900** Spent two years with her sister in the USA. **1902** Studied painting at the Phalanx School under Kandinsky. **1903** Became engaged to Kandinsky although he was still married. **1904-1908** Travelled with Kandinsky to Italy, France, Switzerland, Holland and Tunisia, and made many trips to Russia. **1908** First stay in Murnau. **1909** Inherited a house in Murnau and became friends with Jawlensky and von Werefkin. Joined the

Neue Künstlervereinigung (New Artists' Association) in Munich. **1911/12** Exhibited with the Blauer Reiter group. **1911** Out of solidarity with Kandinsky broke away from the Neue Künstlervereinigung. On the outbreak of war in **1914**, moved to Switzerland with Kandinsky, but went back to Murnau when he travelled on to Russia. **1915** Last meeting with Kandinsky in Stockholm. **1916** Told by Kandinsky that he wanted a separation, she was unable to work for a whole year. **1917** Moved to Copenhagen. **1920** Returned to Murnau. **1927** Took up painting again. Trip to Paris. **1933–1945** Retired to her house in Murnau. **1957** Donated many of her own paintings as well as those of Kandinsky to the Städtische Galerie in Lenbachhaus in Munich WRITINGS: Hoberg, A. (ed.): Kandinsky, W. und G. M. in Murnau und Kochel 1902-1914. Briefe und Erinnerungen. Munich 1994/Kandinsky, W. and G. M. Letters and Remnsciences 1902-1914. Munich 1994
CATALOGUES RAISONNES: Helms, S. (ed.): G. M. Das druckgraphische Werk. Munich 1967.– Pfeiffer-Belli, E. (ed.): G. M. Zeichnungen und Aquarelle. Mit einem Katalog von S. Helms. Berlin 1979
MONOGRAPHS, CATALOGUES: Eichner, J.: Kandinsky und G. M. Vom Ursprung moderner Kunst. Munich 1957.– Gollek, R. (ed.): G. M. 1877-1962. Städtische Galerie im Lenbachhaus. Munich 1977 (cat.).– Gollek, R.: G. M. Hinterglasbilder. Munich and Zurich 1981.– Gollek, R. (ed.): Das Münter-Haus in Murnau. (n. p.) 1984.– Heller, R. (ed.): G. M. The years of Expressionism 1903-1920. Milwaukee Art Museum et al. Milwaukee 1997.– Hoberg, A. and H. Friedel (ed.): G. M. 1877-1962. Retrospektive. Städtische Galerie im Lenbachhaus, Munich et al. Munich 1992 (cat.).– Kleine, G.: G. M. und Wassily Kandinsky. Biographie eines Paares. Frankfurt-on-Main 1990.– Mochon, A.: G. M. Between Munich and Murnau. Cambridge (MA) 1980.– G. M. Schirn Kunsthalle. Frankfurt-on-Main 1992 (cat.).– Röthel, H. K.: G. M. Munich 1957.– Vester, E. (ed.): G. M. Kunstverein Hamburg et al. Hamburg 1988 (cat.).– Windecker, S.: G. M. Eine Künstlerin aus dem Kreis des Blauen Reiter. Berlin 1991

NAUMAN Bruce
born **1941** Fort Wayne (IN)
American artist. **1960–1964** Studied mathematics, physics and art at the University of Wisconsin, Madison. **1964–1966** Studied at the University of California, Davis. **1965** First solo-exhibition of fibreglass sculptures at the Nicholas Wilder Gallery, Los Angeles. Began in **1966** to do films and body performances. From **1966–1968** gave courses at the San Francisco Art Institute. **1967** Moved to Mill Valley, California. **1968** First solo-exhibition in the Leo Castelli Gallery, New York and in the Galerie Konrad Fischer in Düsseldorf. Between **1968** and **1982** participation in

documenta 4–7 in Kassel. **1969** Moved to Pasadena. Journey to Paris. **1970** Lectureship in sculpture at the University of California, Irvine. **1972/73** Installations like *Wall Sound Piece* or *Green Light Corridor*. **1979** Moved to Pecos, New Mexico. **1991** Received the Max Beckmann Prize from the City of Frankfurt. **1992** Participation in documenta 9 in Kassel. **1993–1996** Important touring retrospective at the Centro de Arte Reina Sofia, Madrid and the Kunsthaus, Zurich. Nauman's multimedia works revolve around two central aspects of art: body experience – which is why he is often called the pioneer of Body Art – and sensory perceptions and their distortion. WRITINGS: B. N. Interviews 1967-1988. Newark (NJ) 1996.– Hoffmann, C. (ed.): B. N. Interviews 1967-1988. Dresden 1996
CATALOGUES RAISONNES: Benezra, N. et al. (ed.): B. N. Exhibition Catalogue and Catalogue Raisonné. Walker Art Center, Minneapolis et al. Minneapolis 1994 (cat.).– Bruggen, C. v. et al. (ed.): B. N. Zeichnungen. 1965-1986. Museum für Gegenwartskunst, Basel et al. Basel 1986 (cat.).– Cordes, C. (ed.): B. N. Prints 1970-1989. A Catalogue Raisonné. New York 1989.– Snyder, J. and I. Shaffner (ed.): B. N. Prints and Related Works 1985-1996. Ridgefield et al. Ridgefield 1997 (cat.)
MONOGRAPHS, CATALOGUES: Ammann, J.-C. et al. (ed.): B. N. Kunstmuseum Basel et al. Basel 1986 (cat.)/B. N. Musée d'Art Moderne de la Ville de Paris, Paris et al. Paris 1986 (cat.)/B. N. Whitechapel Art Gallery, London et al. London 1986 (cat.).– Bruggen, C. v.: B. N. New York 1988, Basel 1989.– Halbreich, K. (ed.): B. N. Museo Nacional Centro de Arte Reina Sofia, Madrid et al. Madrid 1993 (cat.).– Labaume, V. et al. (ed.): B. N. Image/Text 1966-1996. Kunstmuseum Wolfsburg. Stuttgart 1997 (cat.).– Livingstone, J. and M. Tucker: B. N. Works from 1965-1972. Los Angeles County Museum et al. Los Angeles 1972 (cat.).– B. N. The Museum of Modern Art, New York et al. New York 1995 (cat.).– Richardson, B. (ed.): B. N. Neons. The Baltimore Museum of Art. Baltimore 1982 (cat.).– Schmidt, K. et al. (ed.): B. N. 1972-1981. Rijksmuseum Kröller-Müller, Otterlo et al. Amsterdam 1981 (cat.).– Simon, J. (ed.): B. N. Walker Art Center, Minneapolis et al. Minneapolis 1994 (cat.).– Zutter, J. and F. Meyer (ed.): B. N. Skulpturen und Installationen 1985-1990. Museum für Gegenwartskunst, Basel et al. Cologne 1990 (cat.)

NAY Ernst Wilhelm
1902 Berlin – **1968** Cologne
German painter. **1925–1928** Studied at the Berlin Academy under Hofer, among other teachers. **1931** Awarded the Rome Prize by the Prussian Art Academy. Turned to Surrealism. **1933** First solo-exhibition at the Galerie Flechtheim in Berlin. **1936** Barred from exhibiting. **1937** His works shown in the exhibition of "degenerate art". Visited Lofoten in Norway, where the barren land-

scape inspired him to do abstractions, the so-called *Lofoten* paintings. **1945–1951** Lived in Hofheim near Frankfurt am Main. **1951** Moved to Cologne. Around **1955** first disk compositions in decorative, occasionally nervously shifting colours. **1955–1964** Participation in documenta 1–3 in Kassel. **1956** Received the first prize for painting from the state of North Rhine-Westphalia and became a member of the Berlin Academy. **1960** Awarded the Guggenheim prize. From **1963** his works show the influence of L'art informel. Nay is one of the most important transitional figures between the pre-war abstractionists, such as Kandinsky and Klee, and the post-war generation of abstract painters. WRITINGS: E. W. N.: Vom Gestaltwert der Farbe: Fläche, Zahl, Rhythmus. Munich 1955
CATALOGUES RAISONNES: Gabler, K. (ed.): E. W. N. Die Druckgraphik 1923-1968. Stuttgart and Zurich 1975.– Gohr, S. and A. Scheibler (ed.): E. W. N. Werkverzeichnis der Ölgemälde 1922-1968. 2 vols. Cologne 1991.– Haftmann, W.: E. W. N. Cologne 1960, 1991
MONOGRAPHS, CATALOGUES: Cassou, J.: N. Cologne 1969.– Gallwitz, K. (ed.): E. W. N. Die Hofheimer Jahre 1945-1951. Städelsches Kunstinstitut und Städtische Galerie, Frankfurt-on-Main. Stuttgart 1994 (cat.).– Gohr, S. and W. Haftmann (ed.): E. W. N. Eine Retrospektive. Josef-Haubrich-Kunsthalle. Cologne 1990 (cat.).– Haftmann, W. and H. Fuchs (ed.): E. W. N. Akademie der Künste. Berlin 1967 (cat.).– Hofmann, W. (ed.): E. W. N. Museum des 20. Jahrhunderts. Vienna 1967 (cat.).– E. W. N. 1902-1968. Bilder und Dokumente. Germanisches Nationalmuseum, Nuremberg. Munich 1980 (cat.).– E. W. N. 1902-1968. Bilder kommen aus Bildern. Museum Haus Lange, Krefeld et al. Krefeld 1985 (cat.).– Nay, E.: Ein strahlendes Weiß. Meine Zeit mit E. W. N. Berlin 1984.– Usinger, F.: E. W. N. Recklinghausen. 1961

NEUSÜSS Floris
born **1937** Lennep
German photographer. Studied photography, painting, and graphic art in Wuppertal, Munich, and Berlin. **1958** Began experimental photography. **1960** Nudograms and Body photographs (Körperfo-

togramme). **1963** Went to Vienna and worked with St. Stephan gallery group. **1964** Studio of her in own in Munich. Chemical paintings on body photograms. From **1971** lectured in experimental photography at the Kassel Werkakademie. **1972** Founded the Fotoforum Kassel and organized art and photographic exhibitions. **1971–1975** Photographic syntax projects. From **1976** *Körperauflösungen* and photogram performances. **1982** First photogram portraits. **1984** Large-format photograms and first Nachtbilder (night pictures). **1989** ULO-photograms.
WRITINGS: F. N.: Fotografie als Kunst – Kunst als Fotografie. Cologne 1979.– F. N.: Fotogramme, die lichtreichen Schatten. Munich and Kassel 1983.– F. N.: Das Fotogramm in der Kunst des 20. Jahrhunderts. Cologne 1990
MONOGRAPHS, CATALOGUES: F. N. Fotogramme. Düsseldorf 1963.– F. N. Figuren und Maßstäbe. London 1976 (cat.).– F. N. Fotografie 1957-1977. Kunstverein Kassel. Kassel 1977 (cat.).– F. N. Nachtstücke. Fotogramme 1957-1997. Rheinisches Landesmuseum. Bonn 1997 (cat.)

NEVELSON Louise
1900 Kiev – **1988** New York
Russian-born American sculptress and painter. **1905** Emigration to the USA. **1920** Moved to New York. **1929/30** Studied at the Art Students League, New York. **1931/32** European trip. Developed an enthusiasm for African sculpture, which she saw in Paris at the Musée de l'Homme, as well as for the artists Boccioni, Brancusi and Picasso. Studies under H. Hofmann in Munich. **1932** Collaboration with Rivera on murals in the US. **1933** First solo-exhibition in New York. **1941** First solo-exhibition in the Nierendorf Gallery, New York. **1957** Sculptures made from single pieces of wood. **1960** First European solo-exhibition in the Galerie Daniel Cordier, Paris. **1962** Exhibited in the American Pavilion at the Venice Biennale. In **1964** and **1968** Participation in documenta 3 and 4 in Kassel. **1969** Solo-exhibition in the Museum of Fine Arts, Houston, **1973** in Moderna Museet, Stockholm and **1974** in the Nationalgalerie, Berlin. **1977** Participation in the exhibition "Boîtes" in Paris. Nevelson became known at the end of the 50s for her wooden constructions, painted in single colours, in which ordinary wooden pieces (chair legs, panels, parts of banisters) were displayed like holy relics. WRITINGS: MacKown, D. (ed.): L. N. Dawns and Dusks. Taped Conversations with D. MacKown. New York 1976
CATALOGUE RAISONE: Baro, G. (ed.): L. N. The Prints. New York 1974
MONOGRAPHS, CATALOGUES: Albee, E. (ed.): L. N. Atmosphere and Environments. Whitney Museum of American Art. New York 1980 (cat.).– Bober, N.: Breaking Tradition: The Story of L. N. New York 1984.– Cain, M.: L. N. New York 1989.– Celant, G.: L. N. Milan and Munich 1973.–

Celant, G. (ed.): N. Palazzo delle Esposizioni, Roma. Milan 1994 (cat.).– Friedman, M. (ed.): N. Wood Sculptures. Walker Art Center, Minneapolis. New York 1973 (cat.).– Glimcher, A. B.: L. N. New York and London 1972, 1976.– Gordon, J. (ed.): L. N. Whitney Museum of American Art. New York 1967 (cat.).– Johnson, V. E. (ed.): L. V. Prints and Drawings 1953-1966. New York 1967.– Kramer, H. and J. Lipman (ed.): N's World. Whitney Museum of American Art. New York 1983 (cat.).– Lisle, L.: L. N. A Passionate Life. New York 1990.– L. N. Centre National d'Art Contemporain. Paris 1974 (cat.).– Roberts, C.: N. Paris 1964.– Wilson, L.: L. N. Iconography and Sources. New York 1981

NEWMAN Barnett
1905 New York – **1970** New York
American painter and sculptor. **1922–1930** Studied philosophy and ornithology, then art at the Art Students League in New York. Around **1930** became acquainted with Still, Pollock, Gottlieb and Avery. Worked from **1931–1939** as an art teacher in the New York high school system. After destroying of his early artworks, he published essays in **1947/48** in *Tiger's Eye* magazine (of which he was co-publisher), including his two most important treatises on painting: *The First Man was an Artist* and *The Sublime is Now*. **1948** Founded the art school Subject of the Artist with Baziotes, Motherwell and Rothko. **1959** Lectureship at the University of Saskatchewan in Saskatoon, Canada. **1959** and **1968** participation in documenta 1 and 4 in Kassel. **1962–1964** Lecturer at the University of Pennsylvania in Philadelphia. Not until the age of 43 did Newman discover his own painting style in mystical abstraction. With his variations on thin vertical colour stripes on a monochrome background, he became one of the most important exponents of Color Field Painting.
WRITINGS: Heynen, J. (ed.): B. N. Texte zur Kunst. Hildesheim 1979.– O'Neill, J. P. (ed.): B. N. Selected Writings and Interviews 1925-1970. New York 1990, Berkeley 1992/ B. N. Schriften und Interviews 1925-1970. Bern and Berlin 1996
CATALOGUES RAISONNES: Richardson, B. (ed.): B. N. The Complete Drawings 1944-1969. Baltimore Museum of Art. Baltimore 1979 (cat.).– Schor, G. (ed.): The Prints of B. N. 1961-1969. New York 1997/ B. N. The Prints 1961-1969. Stuttgart 1997
MONOGRAPHS, CATALOGUES: Bois, Y.-A. (ed.): B. N. Paintings. Pace Gallery. New York 1988 (cat.).– Brockhaus, C. and B. Vogelsang (ed.): B. N. Das zeichnerische Werk. Museum Ludwig. Cologne 1981 (cat.).– Hess, T. B.: B. N. New York 1969.– Hess, T. B. (ed.): B. N. The Museum of Modern Art, New York et al. Greenwich (CT) 1971 (cat.).– Heynen, J.: B. N.'s Texte zur Kunst. Hildesheim 1979.– Hommage à B. N. Nationalgalerie. Berlin 1982 (cat.).– B. N. Stedelijk Museum, Amsterdam et al. 1972 (cat.).– B. N. Das druckgraphische

Werk. Städtisches Museum Abteiberg. Mönchengladbach 1986 (cat.).– B. N. Gemälde und Skulpturen. Kunstsammlung Nordrhein-Westfalen, Düsseldorf. Stuttgart 1997 (cat.).– Paskus, B.: The Theory, Art and Critical Reception of B. N. Diss. Chapel Hill 1974.– Quick, D. M.: Meaning in the Art of B. N. and Three of His Contemporaries. Ann Arbor (MI) 1983.– Richardson, B. (ed.): B. N. The Complete Drawings 1944-1969. Detroit Institute of Arts et al. Detroit 1979 (cat.).– Read, H.: B. . 2 vols. London 1948 and 1956.– Reid, N. (ed.): B. N. Tate Gallery. London 1969 (cat.).– Rosenberg, H.: B. N. Broken Obelisk and Other Sculptures. Seattle 1971.– Rosenberg, H.: B. N. New York 1978, 1994.– Russel, J.: B. N. New York 1969.– Stecker, R.: The Stations of the Cross Lema Sabachthani von B. N. Bochum 1993.– Strick, J. (ed.): The Sublime is Now. The Early Work of B. N. Paintings and Drawings 1944-1949. Pace Wildenstein Gallery, New York et al. New York 1994 (cat.).– Vall, R. v. d.: Een subliemgevoel van plaats. Een filosofische interpretatie van het werk van B. N. Groningen 1994.– Zweite, A. (ed.): B. N. Bilder, Skulpturen, Graphik. Kunstsammlung Nordrhein-Westfalen. Düsseldorf 1997 (cat.)

NEWTON Helmut
born **1920** Berlin
German-born Australian photographer. **1936–1938** Apprenticed to the Berlin photographer Yva. Lived from **1938–1940** in Singapore. **1940–1944** Military service in the Australian army. **1956** Lived in London. **1957** Moved to Paris. **1975** First solo-exhibition in the Galerie Nikon, Paris. **1976** Art Directors Club Prize in Tokyo. Solo-exhibition in the Nicholas Wilder Gallery, Los Angeles. **1981** Moved to Monte Carlo. **1984/85** Retrospective in the Musée d'Art Moderne de la Ville de Paris. **1985** Participation in the "Shots of Style" exhibition in the Victoria und Albert Museum, London. **1989** Was made Chevalier des Arts et des Lettres by the French culture minister. Participation in the "The Art of Photography" exhibition at the Museum of Fine Arts, Houston. Received the World Image Award for the best portrait photo in **1991** in New York. **1992** Awarded the German Service Cross. **1994** Retrospective at the Deichtorhallen, Hamburg.
MONOGRAPHS, CATALOGUES: Felix, Z. (ed.): H. N. Aus dem Photographischen Werk. Deichtorhallen, Hamburg. Munich 1993 (cat.).– Lagerfeld, K.: H. N. Munich 1982.– Lagerfeld, K. (ed.): H. N. Centre National de la Photographie. Paris 1986 (cat.).– Newton, J. (ed.): H. N. in Moskau. Pushkin Museum, Moscow. Munich 1989 (cat.)

NICHOLSON Ben
1894 Denham (Buckinghamshire) – **1982** London
English painter and object artist. Studied at

the Gresham School in Holt and at the Slade School of Art in London. After a stay in Paris in **1921**, where he saw paintings by Braque, Matisse and Picasso for the first time, he developed, through Cubism, his own novel concept of the pictorial image as an autonomous object. **1933** First completely abstract reliefs: fibreboard pieces cut into geometric shapes, painted in different colours and glued in layers. Until **1937** member of Abstraction-Création. Moved back to Cornwall in **1940** with his second wife, the sculptress Barbara Hepworth, and, along with the sculptor Gabo, attracted a circle of artists who became known as the St. Ives Painters. After **1945** returned to using representational elements in his pictures; alongside severe geometric abstractions he produced landscapes and still lifes reduced to little more than a few sketched lines. Nicholson became the principal exponent of Concrete Art in England. **1955 –1964** Participation in documenta 1 – 3 in Kassel.
WRITINGS: B. N.: Appliance House. Chicago and Cambridge 1990
CATALOGUES RAISONNES: Browse, L.: B. N. London 1956.– Read, H. (ed.): B. N. Paintings, Reliefs, Drawings. 2 vols. London 1955-1956.– Russel, J. (ed.): B. N. Drawings, Paintings and Reliefs 1911-1968. Bern 1969
MONOGRAPHS, CATALOGUES: Aley, R.: B. N. London 1963.– Baxandall, D.: B. N. Art in Progress. London 1962.– Harrison, C. (ed.): B. N. Tate Gallery. London 1969 (cat.).– Hodin, J. P.: B. N. The Meaning of His Art. London 1957.– Lewison, J. (ed.): B. N. The Years of Experiment 1919-1939. Kettle's Yard. Cambridge 1983 (cat.).– Lewison, J.: B. N. London and New York 1991.– Lewison, J. (ed.): B. N. Fondation Pierre Gianadda. Martigny 1992 (cat.).– Lewison, J. (ed.): B. N. Tate Gallery, London et al. London 1993 (cat.).– Lynton, N.: B. N. London 1993, 1998, Paris 1993.– Nash, S. A. (ed.): B. N. Fifty Years of His Art. Albright-Knox Art Gallery, Buffalo et al. New York 1978 (cat.).– Read, H.: B. N. Paintings, Reliefs, Drawings. 2 vols. London 1955-1956.– Russel, J. et al. (ed.): B. N. Drawings, Paintings, Reliefs 1911-1968. London 1969/ B. N. Zeichnungen, Gemälde, Reliefs 1911-1968. Stuttgart 1969.– Summerson, J.: B. N. Harmondsworth 1948

NITSCH Hermann
born **1938** Vienna
Austrian action artist. **1957** Created the idea of the Orgies-Mysteries Theatre. **1960 –1966** Exhibitions and actions using naked people; several prison sentences. **1960** First solo-exhibition in the Loyality Club, Vienna, and **1961** at the Galerie Fuchs, Vienna. After **1969**, publication of articles on the theory of the Orgies-Mysteries Theatre. **1971** Appointed professor at the Frankfurt School of Art. Bought Prinzendorf Castle. **1972** Participation in documenta 5 in Kassel. **1973** Founded a benefit

organization for the Orgies-Mysteries Theatre. **1981** Participation in the "Westkunst" exhibition in Cologne. **1972** and **1982** participation in documenta 5 and 7 in Kassel. **1984** Three-day long performance of the 80th Action at Prinzendorf Castle. **1989** Termination of his professorship at the Städelschule in Frankfurt on the Main. Nitsch, one of the exponents of Vienna Actionism, tried to shake the complacency of bourgeois society through his happening-style ritualised performances (sacrificial rites such as animal slaughter).
WRITINGS: H. N.: Orgien Mysterien Theater/ Orgies Mysteries Theatre. Darmstadt 1969.– H. N.: Die Architektur des Orgien-Mysterien-Theaters. Munich 1987.– H. N.: Das Orgien-Mysterien-Theater. Manifeste, Aufsätze, Vorträge. Salzburg and Vienna 1990.– H. N.: Zur Theorie des Orgien Mysterien Theaters. Zweiter Versuch. Salzburg 1995
CATALOGUES RAISONNES: H. N. Das Orgien Mysterien Theater. Die Partituren aller ausgeführten Aktionen 1960-1979. Naples, Munich, Vienna 1979.– Rychlik, O. and C. Gargele (ed.): H. N. Das früheste Werk 1955-1960. Vienna 1986
MONOGRAPHS, CATALOGUES: Eccher, D. (ed.): H. N. Galleria Civica di Arte Contemporanea, Trento. Milan 1991 (cat.).– Fuchs, R. (ed.): H. N. Das Orgien Mysterien Theater 1960-1983. Stedelijk Van Abbe Museum. Eindhoven 1983 (cat.).– Hegyi, L. et al. (ed.): H. N. Das Orgien Mysterien Theater. Museum Moderner Kunst Stiftung Ludwig. Vienna 1996.– H. N. Das Orgien Mysterien Theater. Theoretische Schriften. Partiturentwurf des 6 Tage Spieles. Naples, Reggio Emilia. Munich 1976 (cat.).– H. N. Das Orgien Mysterien Theater. 80. Aktion in Prinzendorf. Vienna 1984.– H. N. Das rote Tuch: der Mensch das unappetitlichste Vieh. H. N. Das Orgien-Mysterien-Theater im Spiegel der Presse 1960-1988. Vienna 1988.– H. N. Museum Moderner Kunst. Passau 1996 (cat.).– Ronte, D. and A. Zweite (ed.): N. Das bildnerische Werk. Städtische Galerie im Lenbachhaus, Munich et al. Munich, Salzburg and Vienna 1988 (cat.).– Rychlik, O. (ed.): H. N. Das früheste Werk 1955-1960. Vienna 1986.– Weiermair, P. (ed.): H. N. Expo '92. Seville 1992 (cat.)

NOLAN Sidney
1917 Carlton (Victoria) – **1992** London
Australian painter. Studied under Charles Wheeler at the National Gallery Art School in Melbourne. Began to paint at the end of the 30s. During his military service **1942– 1945**, he discovered the landscapes of northern Victoria. From **1945** he created the *Ned Kelly* series, the first of a set of picture sequences on the 19th century Australian bandit and folk hero. **1947/48** European trip. Series of paintings telling the story of *Mrs. Fraser*, who was shipwrecked and lived among the Australian aborigines. **1957** Travelled to England. **1959** Participation in documenta 2 in Kassel.

MONOGRAPHS, CATALOGUES: Adams, B.: S. N. Such Is Life. A Biography. London 1987.– Clark, K. and C. MacInnes (ed.): S. N. Catalogue of an Exhibition of Paintings from 1947-1957. Whitechappel Art Gallery. London 1957 (cat.).– Clark, J. (ed.): S. N. Landscapes and Legends. National Gallery of Victoria. Cambridge and New York 1987 (cat.).– Clark, K. et al. (ed.): S. N. London 1961.– Gilchrist, M.: N. at Lanyon. Canberra 1976, 1985.– Haese, R. et al. (ed.): S. N. The City and the Plain. National Gallery of Victoria. Melbourne 1983 (cat.).– Krimmel, B. and E. (ed.): S. N. Gemälde und Druckgraphik. Kunsthalle Darmstadt. Darmstadt 1971 (cat.).– Lynn, E.: S. N. Myth and Imagery. London and Melbourne 1967.– Lynn, E.: S. N. Australia. Sydney 1979.– Lynn, E. and B. Semler: S. N.'s Ned Kelly. Canberra 1985.– McInnes, C. and B. Robertson: S. N. London 1961.– Melville, R. (ed.): Ned Kelly. 27 Paintings by S. N. London 1964.– Missingham, H. (ed.): S. N. Retrospective Exhibition. Paintings from 1937-1967. Art Gallery of New South Wales. Sydney 1967 (cat.).– Sayers, A. (ed.): S. N. The Ned Kelly Story. Metropolitain Museum of Art. New York 1994 (cat.)

NOLAND Kenneth
born **1924** Asheville (NC)
American painter. **1946–1948** Studied at Black Mountain College in Beria (NC) and **1948/49** under Ossip Zadkine in Paris. Taught until **1956** at various institutes in Washington, including the Institute of Contemporary Art and the Catholic University. **1968** Participation in documenta 4 in Kassel. **1977** Made a member of the American Academy and Institute of Art and Letters. **1985** Became Milton Avery Professor at Bard College, Annandale-on-Hudson (NY). Worked with the architect I. M. Pei on the design of the Wiesner Building at the Massachusetts Institute of Technology. **1986/87** Guest-artist at the Pratt Institute in New York in the departments of computer and video art. **1992** Participation in documenta 9 in Kassel. Noland's works are representative of Hard-Edge- and Minimal Art. Along with Louis he developed Color Field Painting with thinned paints. At first he worked with disk-like colour fields, then gradually began to use horizontally laid colour bands in

soft, harmonious tones. In the mid-80s, he became involved in computer art.
MONOGRAPHS, CATALOGUES: Agee, W. C. (ed.): K. N. The Circle Paintings 1956-1963. Museum of Fine Arts. Houston 1993 (cat.).– Fenton, T. (ed.): K. N. An Important Exhibition of Paintings from 1958 through 1989. Salander-O'Reilly Galleries 1989. New York 1989 (cat.).– Goldman, J.: K. N. Handmade Papers. Bedford Village 1978.– Moffet, K.: K. N. New York 1977.– Waldman, D. (ed.): K. N. A Retrospective. Solomon R. Guggenheim Museum. New York 1977 (cat.).– Wilkin, K.: K. N. New York 1990, Paris 1994

NOLDE Emil
1867 Nolde (near Tondern) – **1956** Seebüll (near Neukirchen)
German painter and graphic artist. **1884– 1888** Apprenticeship as furniture designer and woodcarver. Later worked in furniture factories in Munich, Karlsruhe and Berlin. **1889** Teacher at the Karlsruhe School of Arts and Crafts. **1892–1897** Taught ornamental drawing and modelling in the Arts and Crafts School in St. Gallen. **1899** Attended Hoelzel's School in Dachau and the Académie Julian in Paris. **1906/07** Member of the Brücke; met Munch. Dedicated himself from **1909** to religious themes. **1910** Controversy with Liebermann. Co-founder of the New Secession. **1913/14** Travelled with a scientific expedition to New Guinea via Russia, China, and Japan. **1919–1921** Member of the Arbeitsrat für Kunst (Arts Advisory Council). **1926** Moved to Seebüll. From **1931** member of the Prussian Art Academy. **1937** As part of the Nazi "degenerate art" operation, 1,052 of his works were seized from German museums. **1941** Ejected from the Reichskunstkammer (National Arts Council) and banned from painting. **1944** His Berlin studio was destroyed in a bombing raid. **1946** Awarded a professor's title by the state of Schleswig-Holstein. **1956** Founding of the Seebüll Ada and Ernst Nolde Foundation. Nolde's painting, through its subject matter and style, belongs to the more sensual form of Expressionism.
WRITINGS: E. N.: Brief aus den Jahren 1894-1926. Berlin 1929.– E. N.: Jahre der Kämpfe. Berlin 1934.– E. N.: Welt und Heimat. Cologne 1965.– E. N.: Reisen – Ächtung – Befreiung. Cologne 1967.– E. N.: Mein Leben. Berlin 1931, Cologne 1976
CATALOGUES RAISONNES: Schiefler, G. and C. Mosel (ed.): E. N. Das graphische Werk. 2 vols. Berlin 1927, Cologne 1966-1967, 1995.– Urban, M. (ed.): E. N. Werkverzeichnis der Gemälde. 2 vols. Munich 1987-1990/E. N. Catalogue Raisonné of the Oil-Paintings. 2 vols. London 1987-1991
MONOGRAPHS, CATALOGUES: Ackley, C. S. et al. (ed.): N. The Painter's Prints. Museum of Fine Arts, Boston et al. Boston 1995 (cat.).– Bradley, W. S.: The Art of E. N. In The Context of North German Painting and Volkish Ideology. Ann Arbor (MI) 1983.– Bradley, W. S.: E. N. and German

Expressionism. Ann Arbor (MI) 1986.– Brugger, I. and M. Reuther (ed.): E. N. Kunstforum Bank Austria. Vienna 1994 (cat.).– Busch, G.: E. N. Aquarelle. Munich and Zurich 1987.– Chiappini, R. (ed.): E. N. Museo d'arte Moderna, Lugano. Milan 1994 (cat.).– Fehr, H.: E. N. Ein Buch der Freundschaft. Cologne 1957.– Haftmann, W.: E. N. Cologne 1958, New York 1959.– Haftmann, W.: E. N. Ungemalte Bilder. Cologne 1963/E. N. Unpainted Pictures. New York 1963.– Hoffmann, K. (ed.): E. N. Kunstverein Wolfsburg. Wolfsburg 1991 (cat.).– Holeczek, B. (ed.): E. N. Gemälde, Aquarelle und Druckgraphik. Verzeichnis der Bestände. Kunstmuseum Hannover mit Sammlung Sprengel. Hanover 1980.– E. N. Ungemalte Bilder 1938-1945. Seebüll 1981/E. N. Unpainted Pictures. Neukirchen 1987.– Osten, G. v. de (ed.): E. N. Gemälde, Zeichnungen und Druckgraphik. Josef-Haubrich-Kunsthalle. Cologne 1973 (cat.).– Osterwold, T. (ed.): E. N. Württembergischer Kunstverein. Stuttgart 1987 (cat.).– Pois, R.: E. N. Washington 1982.– Reuther, M.: Das Frühwerk E. N. Vom Kunstgewerbler zum Künstler. Cologne 1985.– Roters, E. and M. M. Möller (ed.): E. N. in Berlin. Brücke Museum. Berlin 1988 (cat.).– Selz, P. (ed.): E. N. The Museum of Modern Art. New York 1980 (cat.).– Urban, M. (ed.): E. N. Aquarelle und Handzeichnungen. Seebüll 1967, 1982.– Urban, M. (ed.): Die Stiftung Seebüll Ada und E. N. Neukirchen 1991.– Vergo, P. and S. Lunn (ed.): E. N. Whitechappel Art Gallery. London 1995 (cat.)

NOTHHELFER Gabriele and **Helmut**
born **1945** Berlin (Gabriele)
born **1945** Bonn (Helmut)
German photographers. **1967–1969** Studied at the Lette School in Berlin and **1969/70** at the Folkwangschule in Essen. They have lived in Berlin since **1970** and work as technical employees at the Technical University and the Free University in Berlin. **1977** Participation in documenta 6 in Kassel. Their photography centres on contemporary themes, often showing people in unusual situations.
MONOGRAPH, CATALOGUE: G. and H. N. Galerie Breiting. Berlin 1980 (cat.)

O'KEEFFE Georgia
1887 Sun Prairie (WI) – **1986** Santa Fe (NM)
American painter. **1905/06** Studied at the Art Institute of Chicago under J. Vanderpoel and **1907/08** at the Art Students League, New York, under W. M. Chase. **1909–1911** Did advertising drawing in Chicago. **1912** Took a summer course in painting under A. Bement at the University of Virginia, Charlottesville. **1912–1914** Taught art in Amarillo (TX). **1914/15** Moved to New York; studying at Columbia University under Arthur Dove. **1916** Participation in a group exhibition in Stieglitz' 291

gallery, New York. **1917** First solo-exhibition in the 291 gallery. **1917/18** Taught in Canyon (TX). **1924** Married the photographer Stieglitz. Exhibited large-format floral paintings alongside photographs by Stieglitz at the Anderson Galleries in New York. **1927** Retrospective at the Brooklyn Museum, New York. From **1929** regular trips to New Mexico. **1932** Summer stay in Canada. **1943** Retrospective in the Art Institute of Chicago. **1946** Stieglitz died; she moved to New Mexico. **1950** First European trip. **1966** Retrospective at the Amon Carter Museum, Fort Worth (TX), and **1970** at the Whitney Museum, New York. O'Keeffe's painting is mostly concerned with nature motifs like landscapes and plants, and has elements of both realism and Surrealism.
WRITINGS: Giboire, C. (ed.): Lovingly Georgia. The Complete Correspondence of G. O'K. and Anita Pollitzer. New York 1990
MONOGRAPHS, CATALOGUES: Benke, B.: G. O'K. 1887-1986. Flowers in the Desert. Cologne 1995.– Bry, D. and N. Callaway (ed.): G. O'K. The New York Years. New York 1991/G. O'K. Die New Yorker Jahre. Munich 1991.– Bry, D. and L. Goodrich (ed.): G. O'K. Whitney Museum of American Art. New York 1970 (cat.).– Callaway, N. (ed.): G. O'K. One Hundred Flowers. New York and London 1987.– Castro, J. G.: The Art and Life of G. O'K. London and New York 1986.– Cowart, J. et al. (ed.): G. O'K. Art and Letters. The Museum of Modern Art, New York et al. New York 1987 (cat.).– Cowart, J. et al.: G. O'K. Ihr Leben und Werk. Bern 1989.– Eldredge, C. C.: G. O'K. New York 1991.– Eldredge, C. C. (ed.): G. O'K. American and Modern. Hayward Gallery, London et al. London 1993 (cat.).– Goodrich, L.: G. O'K. Drawings. New York 1968.– Haskell, B.: G. O'K. Works on Paper. Museum of New Mexico. Santa Fe 1985.– Hassrick, P. H. (ed.): The G. O'K. Museum New York 1997.– Kastro, J. G.: The Art and Life of G. O'k. New York 1985.– Kristeva, J. et al. (ed.): G. O'K. Paris 1989.– Lisle, L.: Portrait of an Artist. A Biography of G. O'K. Albuquerque 1986/G. O'K. Das Leben der großen amerikanischen Malerin. Munich 1989.– Merrill, C. (ed.): From the Faraway Nearby: G. O'K. as Icon. Reading (MA) 1990, Albuquerque (NM) 1998.– Messinger, L. M. (ed.): G. O'K. Metropolitan Museum of Art. New York 1988 (cat.).– Robinson, R.: G. O'K. A Life. New York and London 1989.– Whitaker Peter, S.: G. O'K. and Photography. Diss. New York 1987.– Whitaker Peter, S.: G. O'K. The Early Years. New York and London 1991.– Winter, J.: My Name is Georgia. San Diego 1998

ODENBACH Marcel
born **1953** Cologne
German video artist. **1974–1979** Studied history of art, architecture, and semiotics at Aachen Technical College. **1976** First solo-

exhibition in the Galerie Hinrichs, Lohmar. Began to work in video with installations and performances. **1981** One-man show at the Folkwang Museum, Essen. **1982** Awarded a Glockengasse grant in Cologne. **1983** Karl-Schmidt-Rottluff grant, Darmstadt. **1987** Participation in documenta 8 in Kassel. **1989** Took part in the "Video-Skulptur" exhibition in Cologne and **1993** in the Mediale at the Deichtorhallen in Hamburg. **1994** Solo-presentation at the Federal Art and Exhibition Centre in Bonn. In his installations, Odenbach uses video as means of creating collages dealing with social themes.
MONOGRAPHS, CATALOGUES: Damsch-Wiehager, R. (ed.): M. O. Video-Arbeiten, Installationen, Zeichnungen 1988-1993. Galerie der Stadt Esslingen. Stuttgart 1993 (cat.).– Dziewior, Y. and F. Malsch (ed.): M. O. Zeichnungen 1975-1977. Vaduz et al. Vaduz 1997 (cat.).– Felix, Z. (ed.): M. O. Videoarbeiten. Folkwang Museum, Essen et al. Essen 1981 (cat.).– M. O. Stehen ist nicht Umfallen. Badischer Kunstverein, Karlsruhe et al. Karlsruhe 1988 (cat.).– Sand, G. (ed.): M. O. Besenrein. Video-Installationen. Sprengel Museum. Hanover 1997 (cat.)

OEHLEN Albert
born **1954** Krefeld
German painter. Trained in publishing. **1978-1981** Studied at the Hamburg School of Fine Arts. Displayed a strong element of social criticism in his first large-format paintings. **1984** Participation in the "Wahrheit ist Arbeit" exhibition at the Folkwang Museum in Essen (with W. Büttner, G. Herold and Kippenberger) leading to international exhibitions: **1984** "Von hier aus", Düsseldorf; **1988** "German/American Art of the Late 80s", Düsseldorf and Boston; **1989** "Bilderstreit", Cologne; **1991** "Metropolis", Berlin. At the end of the 80s, he produced his first abstract paintings. **1991** First visit to Los Angeles, where he did abstract oil paintings, painted-over pictures with figurative themes, and computer-generated graphics. Further exhibitions: **1993** "Der zerbrochene Spiegel", Vienna and Hamburg; **1995** Wexner Center, Columbus (OH); **1994** retrospective at the Deichtorhallen, Hamburg.
WRITINGS: A. O. im Gespräch mit W. Dickhoff und M. Prinzhorn. Cologne 1991
CATALOGUE RAISONNE: A. O. Linolschnitte. Graz and Cologne 1989
MONOGRAPHS, CATALOGUES: Ammann, J.-C. (ed.): A. O. Abortion of the Cool. Gesellschaft für Gegenwartskunst. Augsburg 1995 (cat.).– A. O. Abräumung. Prokuristische Malerei 1982-1984. Cologne 1987.– A. O. Salzburger Kunstverein. Salzburg 1993 (cat.).– A. O. Malerei. Deichtorhallen. Hamburg 1994 (cat.).– A. O. and Christopher Williams. Wexner Center for the Arts. Columbus (OH) 1995 (cat.).– A. O. Kunsthalle Basel. Basel 1997 (cat.).– Riemschneider, B. (ed.): A. O. Cologne 1995.– Rivas, F. et al. (ed.): A. O.

Institut Valenciano de Arte Moderna. Valencia 1996 (cat.)

OELZE Richard
1900 Magdeburg – **1980** Posteholz
German painter. **1921-1926** Studied under Johannes Itten at the Weimar Bauhaus. **1926-1929** Lived in Dresden. **1929** Exhibited with the Dresden Secession. **1930/31** Lived in Ascona, then moved to Berlin. **1933** Moved to Paris; contact with the Surrealist artists grouped around Breton. **1934** Took part in the Surrealist "Minotaure" exhibition. **1936** Participation in the "International Surrealist Exhibition" in London and "Fantastic Art, Dada, Surrealism" exhibition at the Museum of Modern Art in New York. Lived from **1936-1938** in Switzerland. **1940** Military service. **1945** Held by the Americans as a prisoner-of-war. **1946-1962** Lived in Worpswede. **1950** Solo-exhibition in the Moderne Galerie, Cologne, and **1952** at the Kunstkabinett in Bremen. **1959** Participation in documenta 2 in Kassel. **1962** Moved to Posteholz. **1964** Awarded the Karl Ernst Osthaus Prize by the City of Hagen. Participation in documenta 3. Solo-exhibition at the Kestner Society, Hanover. **1966** First prize in an exhibition given by the state of North Rhein-Westphalia. **1968** Participation at the Venice Biennale. **1973** Solo-exhibition at the Hamburg Kunsthalle. **1978** Max Beckmann Prize awarded by the City of Frankfurt.
CATALOGUE RAISONNE: Schmied, W. (ed.): R. O. 1900-1980. Gemälde und Zeichnungen. Werkverzeichnis. Berlin 1987
MONOGRAPHS, CATALOGUES: Damsch-Wiehager, R.: R. O. Ein alter Meister der Moderne. Munich and Lucerne 1989.– Damsch-Wiehager, R.: R. O. Erwartung. Die ungewisse Gegenwart des Kommenden. Frankfurt-on-Main 1993.– Jaguer, E.: R. O. Paris 1990.– Küster, B. (ed.): R. O. Landschaften. Kunsthalle Wilhelmshaven. Lilienthal 1994 (cat.).– R. O. Kraft der Stille. Galerie Brockstedt. Hamburg 1995 (cat.).– Schmied, W. (ed.): R. O. Gemälde und Zeichnungen 1925-1962. Kestner-Gesellschaft. Hanover 1964 (cat.).– Schmied, W.: R. O. Göttingen et al. 1965.– Schmied, W. (ed.): R. O. 1900-1980. Akademie der Künste, Berlin et al. Berlin 1987 (cat.)

OLDENBURG Claes
born **1929** Stockholm
Swedish-American artist. **1936** Moved with his family to Chicago. **1946-1950** Studied art and literature at Yale University, New Haven (CT). **1950/51** Worked as a newspaper reporter. **1953/54** Studied at the Art Institute of Chicago. **1956** Moved to New York, where he painted compositions heavily influenced by Abstract Expressionism. Met Dine. **1958** Met Kaprow, Segal and R. Whitman. Took part in happenings. **1958/59** First assemblages and environments. **1959** First solo-exhibition at the Judson Gallery, New York. From **1965**

worked on colossal monuments. **1964** Solo-exhibition at the Ileana Sonnabend gallery, Paris. **1964** and **1968** participation at the Venice Biennale. **1968-1982** Took part in documenta 4, 6 and 7 in Kassel. **1969** One-man exhibition at the Museum of Modern Art, New York. **1970** Retrospective at the Stedelijk Museum, Amsterdam. **1972** Arranged the *Mouse Museum*. Starting in **1976** produced large-format projects with C. van Bruggen, whom he married in **1977**. Retrospective of drawings in Stockholm and Tübingen. **1979** Installation of the *Mouse-Museum/Ray Gun Wing* at the Museum Ludwig in Cologne. **1984/85** *The Course of the Knife* project at the Campo dell' Arsenale, Venice. **1996** Retrospective at the Federal Art and Exhibition Centre, Bonn. Oldenburg, one of the main exponents of American Pop Art, started by making models of edibles like hamburgers, ice cream cones, and cakes, before he began to reproduce hard objects like basins, telephones, and vacuum cleaners in soft materials (*Soft Objects*).
WRITINGS: C. O.: Store Days. New York 1967.– C. O.: Raw Notes. Documents and Scripts of the Performances. Halifax 1973.– C. O. and L. Bruggen: Large-Scale Projects 1977-1996. New York 1980
CATALOGUES RAISONNES: Axsom, R. et al. (ed.): Printed Stuff. Prints, Posters and Ephemery by C. O. A Catalogue Raisonné 1958-1996. New York 1996.– Baro, G. (ed.): C. O. Drawings and Prints. London and New York 1969.– Hentschel, M. (ed.): C. O. Multiples 1964-1990. Portikus, Frankfurt-on-Main et al. Frankfurt-on-Main 1992 (cat.).– Lawson, T. et al. (ed.): C. O. Multiples in Retrospect 1964-1990. New York 1991
MONOGRAPHS, CATALOGUES: Adriani, G. et al. (ed.): C. O. Zeichnungen. Kunsthalle Tübingen et al. Tübingen 1975 (cat.).– Bruggen, C. v. (ed.): C. O. Mouse Museum /Ray Gun Wing. Rijksmuseum Kröller-Müller, Otterlo et al. Otterlo 1979 (cat.).– Bruggen, C. v.: C. O. Nur ein anderer Raum. Frankfurt-on-Main 1991.– Celant, G. (ed.): A Bottle of Notes and Some Voyages. C. O., Coosje v. Bruggen. Northern Centre for Contemporary Art, Sunderland et al. London 1988 (cat.).– Celant, G. (ed.): C. O. and Coosje v. Bruggen. Large Scale Projects. London 1995.– Celant, G. et al. (ed.): C. O. An Anthology. National Gallery of Art, Washington et al. New York 1995 (cat.)/C. O. Eine Anthologie. Kunst- und Ausstellungshalle der Bundesrepublik Deutschland, Bonn et al. Stuttgart 1996 (cat.).– Friedman, M. (ed.): O.: Six Themes. Walker Art Center. Minneapolis 1975 (cat.).– Fuchs, R. (ed.): C. v. Bruggen and C. O. Large-Scale Projects 1977-1980. New York 1980.– Glimcher, A.: C. O. New York 1992.– Haskell, B. (ed.): C. O. Object into Monument. Pasadena Art Museum. Pasadena 1971 (cat.).– Johnson, E. H.: C. O. Harmondsworth and Baltimore 1971.– Koepplin, D. (ed.): C. O. Die frühen Zeichnungen. Kupferstichkabinett. Basel 1992 (cat.).– C. O. Proposals for Monu-

ments and Buildings 1965-1969. Chicago 1969.– C. O. Raw Notes. Documents and Scripts of the Performances. Nova Scotia College of Art and Design. Halifax 1973 (cat.).– C. O. Multiples. Musée d'Art Moderne de Saint-Etienne. Saint-Etienne 1993.– Rose, B. (ed.): C. O. The Museum of Modern Art. New York 1969 (cat.).– Rose, B.: C. O. New York 1970, Stuttgart 1976.– Rose, B. et al. (ed.): Large-Scale Projects. C. O. and Coosje van Bruggen. New York 1994.– Ruhrberg, K. (ed.): C. O. Städtische Kunsthalle Düsseldorf. Düsseldorf 1970 (cat.).– Solway, A. and T. Lawson (ed.): C. O. Multiples in Retrospect 1964-1990. New York 1991

OLITSKI Jules
born **1922** Snovsk
Russian-born American painter. **1924** Moved to the USA. **1939-1942** Studied at the National Academy of Design and at the Beaux-Arts Institute, New York. **1942** Became an American citizen. **1942-1945** Military service. **1949-1951** Studied in Paris, attending the Académie de la Grande Chaumière and the sculpture school under Zadkine. Early works were influenced by Dubuffet, Fautrier and de Staël. **1950** First solo-exhibition at the Galerie Huit, Paris. **1952-1955** Trained as an art teacher at New York University. **1956-1967** Teaching jobs in New York and at Bennington College (VT). Under the influence of Noland and Frankenthaler, took a new direction and, in **1959**, using bright, thinly laid-on colours and biomorphic forms, created his *stained paintings*. From **1964** produced large-format Color Field and spray paintings. **1966** Participation at the Venice Biennale and **1967** at the Tokyo Biennale. **1968** Participation in documenta 4 in Kassel. **1973** and **1977** Solo-exhibition at the Museum of Fine Arts, Boston. Olitski, one of the most important Color Field painters, works with minimal colour contrast and chromatic colour ranges.
CATALOGUE RAISONNE: Wilkin, K. and S. Long (ed.): The Prints of J. O. A Catalogue Raisonné 1954-1989. Associated American Artists. New York 1989
MONOGRAPHS, CATALOGUES: Geldzahler, H. et al. (ed.): J. O. Salander-O'Reilly Galleries. New York 1990 (cat.).– Fenton, T.: J. O. and the Tradition of Oil Painting. Edmonton Art Gallery. Edmonton 1979 (cat.).– Fried, M.: J. O. Paintings. Corcoran Gallery. Washington 1967 (cat.).– Krauss, R. E. (ed.): J. O. Recent Paintings. Philadelphia Institute of Contemporary Art. Philadelphia 1968 (cat.).– Moffet, K. (ed.): J. O. Museum of Fine Arts. Boston 1973 (cat.).– Moffett, K.: J. O. New York 1981

OPALKA Roman
born **1931** Hocquincourt (Abbéville)
Polish-born French painter. **1940** Family forcibly moved to Coburg. **1946** Returned to Poland. **1949/50** Studied at the Lodz Art

School. **1951-1956** Studied at the Warsaw Art Academy. **1962** First participation at the Venice Biennale. **1965** Started to incorporate sequences of numbers in his paintings. **1966** First solo-exhibition at the Artysty Plastyka gallery in Warsaw. **1973** Solo-exhibition at the Museum Folkwang, Essen. **1974** Solo-exhibition at the John Weber Gallery, New York. **1976/77** DAAD scholarship to Berlin. **1977** Participated in the documenta 6 in Kassel and moved to France. **1984** Became a French citizen. **1987** Participation at the São Paulo Biennale. **1993** Solo-exhibition at the Musée d'Art Moderne, Paris. As his work progresses, a biographical series of sequentially numbered paintings is being built up, which he supplements with photographic self-portraits.
WRITINGS: R. O.: Begegnung durch Trennung. Munich 1991
MONOGRAPHS, CATALOGUES: Kowalska, B.: R. O. Kraków 1976.– Mason, R. M. (ed.): R. O. Musée d'Art et d'Histoire. Geneva 1977 (cat.).– Noël, B. et al. (ed.): R. O. Paris 1996.– R. O. Museum Haus Lange. Krefeld 1977 (cat.).– R. O. Neue Nationalgalerie. Berlin 1994 (cat.).– R. O. Anti-Sisyphos. Mit einem kritischen Apparat von C. Schlatter. Stuttgart 1994.– Schlatter, C. (ed.): O. Paris 1992 (cat.).– Shapiro, D.: O. Paris 1986

OPPENHEIM Dennis
born **1938** Mason City (WA)
American artist. Until **1965** studied at the California College of Arts and Crafts and at Stanford University. **1969** Began to work as a land artist, whereby he frequently altered the surface of the earth or its structure (*Annual Rings*). **1970** Began to involve his own body as well as nature in his works; in *Reading Position for Second Degree Burn* he used sunshine. **1972** and **1977** Participation in documenta 5 and 6 in Kassel. **1979** One-man show at the Basel Kunsthalle, **1995** at the Munich Kunstbunker Tumulka. Oppenheim documents his Land Art and Body Art in photographics, film and video.
CATALOGUE RAISONNE: Celant, G. (ed.): D. O. La Biennale di Venezia. Venice 1997 (cat.)
MONOGRAPHS, CATALOGUES: Gandini, M. (ed.): D. O. New York 1996.– Heiss, A. (ed.): D.O. Selected Works 1967-

1990. Institute of Contemporary Art, P. S. 1 Museum. New York 1991 (cat.).– Joyaux, A. G.: D. O. Accelerator for Evils Thoughts. Ball State University Museum of Art. Muncie (IN) 1985 (cat.).– D. O. Stedelijk Museum Amsterdam 1974.– D. O. Palais des Beaux-Arts. Brussels 1975 (cat.).– D. O. Retrospective. Works 1967-1977. Musée d'Art Contemporain. Montreal 1978 (cat.).– D. O. Kunsthalle Basel. Basel 1979 (cat.).– D. O. Musée d'Art Moderne de la Communauté Urbaine de Lille. Villeneuve d'Ascq 1994 (cat.).– D. O. Mannheimer Kunstverein. Mannheim 1996 (cat.).– Pagé, S. and J.-M. Poinsot (ed.): D. O. Musée d'Art Moderne de la Ville de Paris. Paris 1979 (cat.).– Spooner, P. F.: D. O. Drawings and Selected Sculpture. Illinois State University Galleries. 1992

OPPENHEIM Meret
1913 Berlin – **1985** Basel
Swiss painter and object artist. **1932** Moved to Paris, where she studied at the Académie de la Grande Chaumière. Acquaintance with Giacometti and Arp. **1936** First solo-exhibition at the Galerie Schulthess, Basel. Participation in the "Fantastic Art, Dada, Surrealism" exhibition at the Museum of Modern Art, New York. Her *Déjeuner en Fourrure* was a sensation and was bought by the Museum of Modern Art. **1937-1939** Attended the Basel School of Arts and Crafts. **1938** Tour of Italy. **1942** Participation in the "First papers of surrealism" exhibition in New York. **1952** Solo-exhibition at the Galerie d'Art Moderne, Basel, and **1956** at the A l'Etoile Scellée gallery in Paris. Began in **1958** to work in sculpture. **1959** At the international surrealist exhibition in Paris she showed her famous *Festmahl* (Banquet), on the body of a naked woman with a golden face. **1972** Participation at the "Artistes suisses contemporains" exhibition in the Grand Palais in Paris and at the "Le Surréalisme" show at the Musée des Arts Décoratifs. **1975** Art prize of the City of Berne. **1982** First prize from the City of Berlin. Oppenheim was the leading female member of the Surrealist movement, transforming Surrealist ideas into art in a witty, dadaist way.
WRITINGS: Meyer-Thoss, C. (ed.): M. O. Aufzeichnungen 1928-1985. Träume. Bern and Berlin 1986.– M. O: Poèmes et carnet 1928-1985. Paris 1993
CATALOGUES RAISONNES: Curiger, B. (ed.): M. O. Spuren durchstandener Freiheit. Zurich and Frankfurt-on-Main 1989/ M. O. Defiance in the Face of Freedom. Cambridge (MA) 1990
MONOGRAPHS, CATALOGUES: Burckhardt, J. et al. (ed.): M. O. Beyond the Teacup. Solomon R. Guggenheim Museum, New York et al. New York 1996 (cat.).– Burckhardt, J. et al. (ed.): M. O. Eine andere Retrospektive. Vienna 1997 (cat.).– Curiger, B.: M. O. Zurich 1982.– Gianelli, I. (ed.): M. O. Palazzo Bianco, Genoa et al. Florence 1983 (cat.).– Helfenstein, J. (ed.): M. O. Legat an das Kunst-

museum Bern. Bern 1987 (cat.).– Helfenstein, J.: M. O. und der Surrealismus. Stuttgart 1993.– Meyer-Thoss, C.: M. O. Buch der Ideen. Zurich 1996.– M. O. Kunsthalle Bern et al. Bern 1984 (cat.).– M. O. Musée d'Art Moderne de la Ville de Paris. Paris 1984 (cat.).– M. O. Institute of Contemporary Arts. London 1989 (cat.).– Reuterswärd, C. F. et al. (ed.): M. O. Moderna Museet. Stockholm 1967 (cat.).– Schulz, I.: Edelfuchs und Morgenrot. Studien zum Werk von M. O. Munich 1993.– Tavel, H. C. v. and H. Heisenbüttel (ed.): M. O. Museum der Stadt Solothurn et al. Solothurn 1974 (cat.)

OROZCO José Clemente
1883 Ciudat Guzmán – **1949** Mexico City
Mexican painter. As a boy, he was already fascinated by the pictures of the folk art printmaker J. G. Posada. **1897-1900** Trained at the Agricultural School in Mexico City. **1904-1908** Studied architecture. **1908-1914** Drawing courses at the San Carlos Art Academy in Mexico City. Strongly influenced by the folk art of the Indios and Mestizos. From **1911** he worked as a political cartoonist for the opposition; among others for *La Vanguardia* magazine. Loose contact with Rivera and Siqueiros. **1917/18** Trips to San Francisco and New York. From **1922** onwards did large murals. **1923** Founder member of the Union of Technical Workers, Painters, and Sculptors. **1927-1934** Lived in the USA, mostly in New York. **1932** European trip. **1934** Mural for the Palacio de Bellas Artes, Mexico City. **1940** Six panel paintings for the Museum of Modern Art, New York. **1946** Awarded the Mexican National Prize. **1947** Retrospective at the Palacio de Bellas Artes, Mexico City. Along with Rivera and Siqueiros, Orozco is considered as one of the founders, of contemporary Mexican painting, of which murals are the outstanding feature.
WRITINGS: J. C. O.: Textos de O. Mexico City 1955.– J. C. O.: An Autobiography. Austin 1962
CATALOGUES RAISONNES: Hopkins, J. H. (ed.): O. A Catalogue of His Graphic Work. (o. O) 1967.– Marrozini, L. (ed.): Catálogo completo de la obra gráfica de O. San Juan 1970
MONOGRAPHS, CATALOGUES: Cardoza y Aragón, L.: O. Mexico City 1986.– Cardoza y Aragón, L. et al. (ed.): J. C. O. Musée d'Art Moderne de la Ville de Paris. Paris 1979 (cat.).– Conde, T. del (ed.): J. C. O. Antología critica. Mexico City 1982.– Conde, T. del et al. (ed.): O. Una relectura. Mexico City 1983.– Elliott, D. (ed.): O. 1883-1949. Museum of Modern Art. Oxford 1980 (cat.).– Helm, M.: Man of Fire. J. C. O. An Interpretative Memoir. Institute of Contemporary Art. New York 1953, Westport (CT) 1971 (cat.).– Lynch, J.: J. C. O.: The Easel Paintings and the Graphic Art. Diss. Cambridge 1960.– Manrique, J. A.: O. Mural Paintings. (n. p.) 1991.– Münzberg, O. and M. Nungesser

(ed.): J. C. O. Berlin 1981.– Reed, A.: O. New York 1956, 1985.– Reed, A. and M. Valladares de Orozco: O. Dresden 1979.– Zuno, J. G.: O. y la ironía plástica. Mexico City 1953

OURSLER Tony
born **1957** New York
American artist. **1979** Finished his training at the California Institute of the Arts, Valencia, then taught at the Massachusetts College of Art in Boston. **1981** First solo-exhibition "Video Viewpoints" at the Museum of Modern Art in New York. **1986** "Spheres of Influence" exhibition at the Pompidou Centre in Paris. **1988/89** Video performances with Constance DeJong in Los Angeles, New York and Chicago. Participation at the World Wide Video Festival in The Hague. **1992** Participation in documenta 9 in Kassel. **1994** Participation at the Media Biennale in Leipzig. **1997** Took part in documenta 10 in Kassel. In his multimedia works, Oursler examines the effects of the modern media on the human body and psyche.
MONOGRAPHS, CATALOGUES: Balkenhol, B. (ed.): T. O. My Drawings. Kassel 1997 (cat.).– Malsch, F. (ed.): T. O. Portikus, Frankfurt-on-Main et al. Frankfurt-on-Main 1995 (cat.).– T. O. Sphères d'influence. Centre Georges Pompidou. Paris 1986 (cat.).– T. O. Judy. Salzburger Kunstverein. Salzburg 1994.– T. O. Kunstverein Hannover. Hanover 1998 (cat.)

OZENFANT Amédée
1886 St. Quentin – **1966** Cannes
French painter. **1906** Moved to Paris. **1909** -**1913** Trips to Russia, Italy, Belgium, and Holland. **1910/11** and **1914** Participation at the Salon d'Automne. **1915** Started the magazine *L'Elan*. **1918** With Le Corbusier, he invented Purism and published the Purist manifesto *Après le Cubisme*. **1920**-**1925** Published magazine *L'Esprit nouveau* together with Le Corbusier. **1921** "Jeanneret and Ozenfant" exhibition at the Galerie Druet, Paris. **1924** Shared a studio with Léger in Paris. **1927** First solo-exhibition at the Galerie Barbazanges, Paris. **1928** Participation in the exhibition of contemporary French painting in Moscow. **1925** Started to work on murals for the Musée

d'Art Moderne, Paris. **1935–1938** Lived in London. **1938** Moved to New York, where he established the Ozenfant School of Fine Arts. **1954** Returned to France. Ozenfant, co-founder of Purism, hoped to protect synthetic Cubist painting from becoming merely decorative, but in his own clichéd painting style, he fell victim to a certain aestheticism.
WRITINGS: A. O. and Le Corbusier: Après le cubisme. Paris 1918.– A. O. and Le Corbusier: La Peinture moderne. Paris 1927.– A. O.: A foundation of Modern Art. London 1931.– A. O.: Memoires 1886-1962. Paris 1968
MONOGRAPHS, CATALOGUES: Ball, S. L.: O. and Purism. The Evolution of a Style 1915-1930. Ann Arbor (MI) 1978.– Debrée, C. and F. Ducrois (ed.): A. O. Musée Antoine Lécuyer, Saint Quentin et al. Saint Quentin 1985 (cat.).– Ducrois, F.: A. O. Dijon 1985.– Golding, J.: O. New York 1985

PAIK Nam June
born **1932** Seoul
Korean composer and artist. **1950** Moved to Hongkong, then to Japan. Until **1956** she studied music, art history and philosophy at the University of Tokyo. **1956/57** Studied music history in Munich; acquaintanceship with K. Stockhausen. **1957/58** Studied composition at the Musikhochschule in Freiburg. Friendship with Cage. Worked from **1958–1963** at the Studio for Electronic Music at WDR, the West German Radio station in Cologne. **1962** Took part in the *Fluxus* Festival, Wiesbaden. **1963** First solo-exhibition with television sets at the Galerie Parnass, Wuppertal. **1963/64** Lived in Japan; experimented with electromagnetic manipulation of television pictures. **1964** Moved to New York; began collaborating with Charlotte Moorman. **1965** Solo-exhibition at the Galleria Bonino, New York. **1966** First installations with TV monitors. **1969/70** Developed a video synthesizer along with S. Abe. **1971** Solo-exhibition at the Museum of Modern Art, New York. **1975** Took part in the São Paulo Biennale. **1977** Participation in documenta 6 in Kassel. **1979** Became professor at the Art Academy in Düsseldorf. **1982** Retrospective at the Whitney Museum, New York. **1977** and **1987** participation in documenta 6 and 8 in Kassel. **1991/92** Important travelling exhibition "Video Time – Video Space" in Düsseldorf, Basel, Zurich and Vienna. **1993** Representative at the German pavilion at the Venice Biennale. **1995** Retrospective at the Wolfsburg Kunstmuseum. Paik, who experiments with the artistic possibilities inherent in electronic media, is one of the pioneers of video art.
WRITINGS: Decker, E. (ed.): N. J. P. Niederschriften eines Kulturnomaden. Cologne 1992.– N. J. P.: Du cheval à Christo et autres écrits. Brussels 1993
MONOGRAPHS, CATALOGUES: Block, R. (ed.): Art for Twenty-Five Million

People. Daadgalerie. Berlin 1984 (cat.).– Bußmann, K. and F. Matzner (ed.): N. J. P. Eine Database. La Biennale di Venezia. Deutscher Pavillon. Stuttgart 1993 (cat.).– Decker, E.: P. Video. Cologne 1988.– Fargier, J.-P.: N. J. P. Paris 1989.– Hanhardt, J. G. (ed.): N. J. P. Whitney Museum of American Art. New York 1982 (cat.).– Herzogenrath, W. (ed.): N. J. P. Werke 1946-1976. Musik, Fluxus, Video. Kölnischer Kunstverein. Cologne 1976 (cat.).– Herzogenrath, W.: N. J. P. Fluxus – Video. Munich 1983.– Herzogenrath, W. (ed.): N. J. P. Video Works 1963-1988. Hayward Gallery. London 1988 (cat.).– Kellein, T. and T. Stoos (ed.): N. J. P. Video Time – Video Space. Kunsthalle Basel et al. Stuttgart 1991 (cat.).– Matzner, F. (ed.): N. J. P. Baroque Laser. Münster 1995.– Restany, P. (ed.): N. J. P. La Fée électronique. Musée d'Art Moderne de la Ville de Paris. Paris 1989 (cat.).– N. J. P. et al.: N. J. P. Eine Data Base. Stuttgart 1994.– Rosebush, I. (ed.): N. J. P.: Videa'n Video 1959-1973. Everson Museum of Art. Syracuse (NY) 1979 (cat.).– Sayag, A. (ed.): N. J. P. Tricolor Video. Centre Georges Pompidou. Paris 1982 (cat.)

PALADINO Mimmo
born **1948** Paduli (near Benevent)
Italian painter. Studied from **1964–1968** at the Liceo Artistico di Benevento. **1977** First solo-exhibition at the Galleria Lucio Amelio in Naples; a year later he covered its walls with a monumental pastel painting. **1978–1980** Monochrome paintings in primary colours with geometric elements and found objects attached. **1980** Technical experiments with printing; produced archetypal figures in acquatint, woodblock and linocut prints. **1982** Participation in documenta 7 in Kassel. **1982–1985** Trips to Brazil; the blend of African and Catholic culture fascinated him and afterwards found its way into his work. Along with Clemente, Chia and Cucchi, Paladino, who projects archetypes and symbols onto the canvas, belongs to the Transavanguardia group.
WRITINGS: M. P.: En De Re. Modena 1980.– M. P. Milan 1990
MONOGRAPHS, CATALOGUES: Braun, E. and N. Rosenthal: M. P. Milan 1993.– Crutchfield, M. A. and H. Risatti (ed.): M. P. Recent Painting and Sculpture 1982-1986. Virginia Museum of Fine Arts. Richmond 1986 (cat.).– Dorflès, G.: M. P. Milan 1982.– Eccher, D. (ed.): M. P. L'opera su carta 1970-1992. Galleria Civica di Arte Contemporanea, Trento. Milan 1992 (cat.).– Friedel, H. (ed.): M. P. Arbeiten von 1977-1985. Städtische Galerie im Lenbachhaus. Munich 1985 (cat.).– Koepplin, D. et al. (ed.): M. P. Zeichnungen 1976-1981. Kunstmuseum Basel et al. Basel 1981 (cat.).– Oliva, A. B. and N. Rosenthal (ed.): M. P. Forte Belvedere, Florence. Milan 1993 (cat.).– M. P. Kunsthalle Basel et al. Basel 1980 (cat.).– M. P. Arbeiten auf Papier. Works on Paper. 1973-

1987. Moderne Galerie, Salzburg et al. Salzburg 1987 (cat.).– Pohlen, A. (ed.): M. P. Bilder und Zeichnungen 1981-1982. Von der Heidt-Museum, Wuppertal et al. Wuppertal 1982 (cat.).– Raspail, T. et al. (ed.): M. P. Musée St. Pierre. Lyon 1984 (cat.).– Schwarz, A. et al. (ed.): M. P. Naples 1995 (cat.).– Schwarz, M. et al. (ed.): M. P. Badischer Kunstverein. Karlsruhe 1980 (cat.).– Tidholm, T.: M. P. Drawings. Stockholm 1991

PALERMO Blinky
(Peter Heisterkamp)
1943 Leipzig – **1977** Sri Lanka
German painter. **1952** Moved to Munster. **1961** Studied at the Munich School of Arts and Crafts. **1962–1967** Studied at the Düsseldorf Art Academy under Bruno Goller and Beuys. From **1964**, he went under the name of Blinky Palermo. **1966** First solo-exhibition at the Friedrich Dahlem gallery in Munich. From **1968** shared a studio with Knoebel, then with Rückriem. **1970** Travelled to New York with Gerhard Richter. **1972** and **1977** participation in documenta 5 and 6 in Kassel. Moved in **1973** to New York with his second wife Kristin. **1974** Travelled around America with Knoebel. **1975** Participation in the São Paulo Biennale. **1976** Again set up a studio in Düsseldorf and exhibited in the German pavilion at the Venice Biennale. **1980** Retrospective at the Galerie-Verein in Munich. Palermo, who can be considered a Minimalist and Hard-Edge artist, invokes a new spatial experience by making subtle optical and sculptural changes to a room.
CATALOGUES RAISONNES: Jahn, F. (ed.): P. Die gesamte Grafik und alle Auflageobjekte 1966-1975. Städtisches Museum Abteiberg, Mönchengladbach et al. Munich 1983 (cat.).– Moeller, T. (ed.): P. Bilder und Objekte, Zeichnungen. 2 vols. Stuttgart 1995.– Werner, K. (ed.): B. P. Leipziger Galerie für Zeitgenössische Kunst. Stuttgart 1993 (cat.)
MONOGRAPHS, CATALOGUES: Bürgi, B. and E. Franz (ed.): P. Werke 1963-1977. Kunstmuseum Winterthur et al. Winterthur 1984 (cat.).– Dahlem, F. et al. (ed.): B. P. 1964-1976. Staatsgalerie moderner Kunst. Munich 1980 (cat.).– Dahlem, F. et al. (ed.): B. P. Munich 1989.– Maas, E. and D. Greenidge (ed.): B. P. 1943-1977. New York 1989.– Moeller, T. (ed.): P. Städtisches Kunstmuseum Bonn. Bonn 1994 (cat.).– B. P. Kunstmuseum. Winterthur 1984 (cat.).– B. P. Centre Georges Pompidou. Paris 1985 (cat.).– B. P. Städtisches Kunstmuseum Bonn. Bonn 1994 (cat.).– Schwenk, B.: Gleichnisse des Unerklärlichen. Zur Malerei des B. P. Frankfurt-on-Main 1990.– Schwenk, B.: Studien zur Person und zum Werk des Malers B. P. Bonn 1991.– Stemmler, D. (ed.): P. Städtisches Kunstmuseum Bonn. Bonn 1981 (cat.).– Storck, G. (ed.): P. Stoffbilder 1966-1972. Museum Haus Lange. Krefeld 1977 (cat.)

PANAMARENKO
born **1940** Antwerp
Belgian artist. **1955–1960** Studied at the Art Academy in Antwerp. **1961/62** Military sevice. **1962–1964** Worked at the National Hoger Institute. **1963** First solo-exhibition at the Antwerp Art Academy. **1964/65** First happenings. Published the *Happening News* magazine. **1967** Built his first airplane. **1969** Solo-exhibition at the René Block gallery in Berlin and the Konrad Fischer gallery in Düsseldorf. **1972** and **1977** Participation in documenta 5 and 6 in Kassel. **1972/73** Tour exhibition at the Kunstmuseum in Lucerne, at the Düsseldorf Kunsthalle, and at the Württembergischer Kunstverein in Stuttgart. **1976** Took part in the Venice Biennale. **1981** Solo-exhibition at the Pompidou Centre, Paris. **1987** Participation in the "Brennpunkt Düsseldorf" exhibition at the Düsseldorf Kunstmuseum. **1989** Retrospective at the Museum van Hedendaagse Kunst, Antwerp. **1992** Took part in documenta 9 in Kassel. Panamerenko's technically perfectly constructed flying objects, which do not fly, are a parody on contemporary Icarian illusions of progress.
WRITINGS: P.: Der Mechanismus der Schwerkraft. Bielefeld 1975.– Theys, H.: P. Brussels 1992.– Theys, H. (ed.): P. Multiples 1966-1994. Galerie Jamar. Antwerp 1995 (cat.)
MONOGRAPHS, CATALOGUES: Baudson, M.: P. Paris 1996.– Bex, F. and L. Dewachter (ed.): P. Een overzicht 1965-1985. Museum van Hedendaagse Kunst. Antwerp 1989 (cat.).– Grisebach, L. and P. Hefting (ed.): P. Nationalgalerie, Berlin et al. Berlin 1978 (cat.).– Grisebach, L. and J. Hoet (ed.): P. Haus der Kunst, Munich et al. Munich 1982 (cat.).– P. Objekte. Städtisches Museum Abteiberg. Mönchengladbach 1973 (cat.).– P. Musée d'Art Moderne de la Ville de Paris. Paris 1973 (cat.).– P. Stedelijk Van Abbe Museum. Eindhoven 1974 (cat.).– P. The Aeromodeller. Centre Georges Pompidou. Paris 1981 (cat.).– P. Werke 1963-1977. Kunstmuseum Winterthur et al. Munich 1984 (cat.).– P. Kunstverein Hannover. Hanover 1991 (cat.).– Tittel, L. et al. (ed.): P. Arbeiten 1966-1985. Kunstverein Friedrichshafen. Friedrichshafen 1985 (cat.)

PAOLINI Giulio
born **1940** Genua
Italian artist. First worked on stage designs. **1964** First solo-exhibition at the Galleria La Salita, Rome. **1967** Took part in the Arte Povera exhibition at the Galleria La Bertesca, Genoa with works focusing on the relationship between the artist, his subject and the observer (*Young Man observes Lorenzo Lotto*). **1971** Took part in the Arte Povera exhibition at the Munich Kunstverein. Between **1972** and **1992** participation in documenta 5, 6, 8 and 9 in Kassel. **1975/76** Creation of *Mimesi*, two copies of a Roman copy of the Medici Venus, facing each other so that the gaze

into the past is met by a look into the future. **1981** DAAD scholarship to Berlin. **1984** Took part in the Venice Biennale. **1985** Solo-exhibition at the Guggenheim Museum, New York. **1986** Retrospective at the Stuttgart Staatsgalerie. **1991** Solo-exhibition at the Castello di Rivoli, Turin. Paolini has a special position in the Arte Povera movement. His works are visual essays on art which transcend language; with him, they define art as a place to think about art.
WRITINGS: G. P.: IDEM. Torino 1975.– G. P.: Hortus clausus. Werke und Schriften 1960-1980. Lucerne 1981.– G. P.: Suspense. Breve storia del vuoto in tredici stanze. Florence 1988
CATALOGUE RAISONNE: G. P. L'opera grafica 1967-1992. Torino 1992
MONOGRAPHS, CATALOGUES: Bandini, M. et al. (ed.): G. P. Tutto qui. Pinacoteca Communale. Ravenna 1985 (cat.).– Celant, G.: G. P. New York and Paris 1972.– Cladders, J. (ed.): G. P. Städtisches Museum. Mönchengladbach 1977 (cat.).– Cousseau, H. C. et al. (ed.): G. P. Musée des Beaux-Arts. Nantes 1987 (cat.).– Fagiolo, M. and A. Carlo: G. P. Parma 1980.– Faust, W. M. and E. Franz (ed.): G. P. Del bello intelligibile. Kunsthalle Bielefeld et al. Bielefeld 1982 (cat.).– Inboden, G. et al. (ed.): G. P. 4 vols. Staatsgalerie Stuttgart. Stuttgart 1986 (cat.).– Isler, S.: Del bello intelligibile: semiotische Analyse zu sechs Werken von G. P. Zurich 1983.– Kunz, M. (ed.): G. P. Werke und Schriften 1960-1980. 2 vols. Kunstmuseum. Lucerne 1981.– Maubant, J.-L. and D. Soutif (ed.): P. Melanconia ermetica. Galerie Maeght-Lelong. Paris 1985 (cat.).– Monferini, A. et al. (ed.): G. P. Galleria Nazionale d'Arte Moderna, Roma. Milan 1988 (cat.).– G. P. 2 vols. Le Nouveau Musée. Villeurbanne 1984 (cat.).– Poli, F.: G. P. Torino 1990.– Szeemann, H. et al. (ed.): G. P. Stedelijk Museum, Amsterdam et al. Amsterdam 1980

PAOLOZZI Eduardo
born **1924** Leith (near Edinburgh)
English sculptor and graphic artist. **1943** Studied art at Edinburgh College of Art. **1944-1947** Studied at the Slade School of Fine Arts, London. **1947** First solo-exhibition at the Mayor Gallery, London. **1947-**

1950 Lived in Paris. Met Arp, Brancusi, Giacometti, Dubuffet, T. Tzara. **1949-1955** Taught fabric design at the Central School of Arts and Crafts, London. **1952** Founded the Independent Group at the Institute of Contemporary Arts in London. **1955-1958** Lectureship in sculpture at St. Martins School of Arts, London. **1959-1977** Took part in documenta 2-4 and 6 in Kassel. **1960** Participation in the Venice Biennale. **1962** First silkscreen prints. **1964** Solo-exhibition at the Museum of Modern Art, New York. **1974** DAAD scholarship to Berlin. **1979** Honorary doctorate bestowed by the Royal College of Art, London. **1981-1989** Professor of sculpture at the Munich Art Academy. **1981** Took part in the "West-kunst" exhibition in Cologne. **1985** Solo-exhibition at Museum Ludwig, Cologne. **1989** Guest-professorship at the Royal College of Art, London.
WRITINGS: E. P.: Metafisikal Translations. London 1962
CATALOGUE RAISONNE: Miles, R. (ed.): The Complete Prints of E. P. Prints, Drawings, Collages 1944-1977. Victoria and Albert Museum. London 1977 (cat.)
MONOGRAPHS, CATALOGUES: Frayling, C. and M. McLeod (ed.): E. P. Lost Magic Kingdoms. Museum of Mankind. London 1985 (cat.).– Grisebach, L. and F. Whitford (ed.): E. P. Nationalgalerie Berlin et al. Berlin 1975 (cat.).– Kirkpatrick, D.: E. P. London 1970.– Kirkpatrick, D. (ed.): E. P. Musée Nationaux du Canada. 1976 (cat.).– Konnertz, W.: E. P. Cologne 1984.– Middleton, M.: E. P. London 1963.– E. P. Laing Art Gallery, Newcastle et al. London 1976 (cat.).– E. P. Kölnischer Kunstverein. Cologne 1979 (cat.).– Schneede, U. M.: P. Stuttgart 1970, London and New York 1971.– Spencer, R. et al. (ed.): E. P. Recurring Themes. Royal Scottish Academy, Edinburgh et al. Edinburgh 1984 (cat.)/E. P. Wiederkehr der Themen. Städtische Galerie im Lenbachhaus, Munich et al. Munich 1984 (cat.).– Whitford, F.: E. P. Tate Gallery. London 1971 (cat.).– Whitford, F. et al. (ed.): E. P. Sculpture, Drawings, Collages and Graphics. The Arts Council of Great Britain, London et al. London 1976

PARKS Gordon
(Alexander Buchanan)
born **1912** Fort Scott (KS)
American photographer, film director and writer. Self-taught. Worked in several fields before deciding to become a photographer in **1937**. First specialised in fashion photography. **1942/43** Took pictures for the project Farm Security Administration. **1943-1945** War correspondent for the Office of War Information in Washington. **1948-1961** While working for *Life* magazine as a photojournalist, did a photoseries on streetgangs in Harlem and the civil rights movement and, at the same time, composed music and wrote poetry. Thereafter became a freelance photographer. **1962-1971** Wrote scripts and directed various films, including

---

Shaft (1971). **1977** Participation in documenta 6 in Kassel. Published several books of his photographs, to which he wrote poems. Parks is one of the few successful black photographers.
MONOGRAPHS, CATALOGUES: Berry, S.: G. P. New York 1991.– Buchsteiner, T. and K. Steinorth (ed.): G. P. 40 Jahre Fotografie. Tübingen 1989 (cat.).– Donloe, D.: G. P. Photographer, Writer, Composer, Film Maker. Los Angeles 1993.– G. P. Half Past Autumn. A Retrospective. Boston 1997 (cat.)

PASCIN Jules
(Julius Pincas)
1885 Vidin (Bulgaria) – **1930** Paris
Bulgarian painter and draughtsman, whose father was a Spanish Jew and whose mother was Italian. Moved to Vienna in **1900**. **1903** Worked as a cartoonist for *Simplicissimus* magazine in Munich. **1905** Lived in Paris. In **1914** he moved to London, and finally settled in New York, where he became an American citizen. **1916/17** Resided in Cuba. **1920** Returned to Paris. **1924** Travelled in Tunisia. **1927/28** Lived in New York. **1930** Committed suicide shortly before the opening of his solo-exhibition in the Galerie Georges Petit, Paris. Pascin, who was an extraordinary cartoonist, produced drawings of women ranging from the charming to the frivolous; inspired by Toulouse-Lautrec, they also show a Fauvist influence.
CATALOGUE RAISONNE: Hémin, Y. et al. (ed.): J. P. Catalogue raisonné. 4 vols. Paris 1984-1992
MONOGRAPHS, CATALOGUES: Bay, A. (ed.): P. Malerier, Tegninger, Grafikk. Nasjonalgalleriet. Oslo 1980 (cat.).– Diehl, G.: P. Haus der Kunst, Munich et al. Munich 1969.– Dubreuil, P. (ed.): P. Œuvre gravé. Paris 1981.– Fels, F.: Dessins de P. Paris 1966.– Freudenheim, T. (ed.): P. University Art Museum. Berkeley 1966 (cat.).– Kobry, Y. and E. Cohen (ed.): P. 1885-1930. Musée-Galerie de la Seita. Paris 1995 (cat.).– Lang, L. (ed.): J. P. Berlin 1981.– Leeper, J. P.: J. P.'s Carbbean Sketchbook. Austin 1964.– Warnod, A.: P. Monte Carlo 1954.– Werner, A. (ed.): P. New York 1959, 1972, Hamburg 1963

PASMORE Victor
1908 Chesham – **1998** Malta
English painter and sculptor. Self-taught. **1927-1938** Government clerk in London; evening classes in art at the Central School. Started by doing impressionist style landscapes, then turned to Cubism. **1933** Joined the London Group. **1934** Took part in the "Objective Abstraction" exhibition. **1937** Co-founder of the Euston Road School, where he worked as a teacher. **1947/48** Friendship with Nicholson. Gradually developed an individual abstract painting style. **1954-1961** Lectureship at Durham University. **1954** Solo-exhibition at the Institute of Contemporary Art, London.

1956 Participation in the "This Is Tomorrow" exhibition at the Whitechapel Art Gallery, London. **1960** Honoured as a leading English artist at the Venice Biennale. **1962** Solo-exhibition at the Kestner Society, Hanover. **1964** Participation in documenta 3 in Kassel. **1965** Retrospective at the Tate Gallery, London. **1983** Appointed to the Royal Academy. Pasmore was originally a determined proponent of representational painting, but later became a pioneer, both in theory and practice, of abstract art in England.
CATALOGUE RAISONNE: Bowness, A. and L. Lambertini (ed.): V. P. A Catalogue Raisonné of the Paintings, Constructions and Graphics 1926-1979. London and New York 1980
MONOGRAPHS, CATALOGUES: Alley, R. (ed.): V. P. Retrospective Exhibition 1925-1965. Tate Gallery. London 1965 (cat.).– Bell, C.: V. P. Harmondsworth 1945.– Gowing, L. and L. Sjöberg (ed.): V. P. Yale Center for British Art. New Haven 1988 (cat.).– Grieve, A. (ed.): V. P. Royal Academy of Arts. London 1980 (cat.).– Lynton, N. (ed.): V. P. Paintings and Graphics 1980-1992. London 1992.– V. P. National Gallery. London 1990 (cat.).– Reichardt, J.: V. P. London 1962

PEARLSTEIN Philip
born **1924** Pittsburgh (PA)
American painter. **1946-1949** Studied at the Carnegie Institute of Technology, Pittsburgh. **1951-1955** Studied art history at the Institute of Fine Arts, New York. Began to work as a graphic designer. **1955** First solo-exhibition at the Tanager Gallery, New York. **1959-1963** Taught at the Pratt Institute, New York. **1963-1968** Taught at Brooklyn College, New York. **1970** Retrospective at the Georgia Museum of Art, Athens. **1972** Solo-exhibiton at the Hanover Kunstverein and at the Kupferstichkabinett, Berlin. **1974** Prizewinner at the Tokyo Biennale. Typical characteristics of Pearlstein's pictures are a photographic point of view combined with a photorealist style of representation. His figures and motifs, which are often cut off at the edges of the pictures, seem to have been captured there by chance. He frequently paints nudes, mostly in pairs.

CATALOGUE RAISONNE: Bowman, R. (ed.): P. P. The Complete Paintings. New York and London 1983
MONOGRAPHS, CATALOGUES: Boatright, K. (ed.): P. P. Paintings and Watercolours. The University of Iowa Museum of Art. Iowa City 1983 (cat.).– Dückers, A. (ed.): P. P. Zeichnungen und Aquarelle, die Druckgraphik. Berlin 1972.– Kramer, L. K. (ed.): The Graphic Works of P. P. 1978-1994. Springfield Art Museum. Springfield 1995 (cat.).– Landwehr, W. C. (ed.): The Lithographs and Etchings of P. P. Springfield Art Museum. Springfield 1978 (cat.).– Nochlin, L. (ed.): P. P. Gorgia Museum of Art. Athens 1970 (cat.).– Perreault, J. (ed.): P. P. Drawings and Watercolors. New York 1988.– Viola, J.: The Painting and Teaching of P. P. New York 1982

PECHSTEIN Max
1881 Eckersbach – **1955** Berlin
German painter. **1896–1900** Apprenticeship in decorative painting in Zwickau. **1900–1902** Studied at the Dresden School of Arts and Crafts. **1902–1906** Studied at the Dresden Academy. **1906** Joined the Brücke artists. Prize for Painting from the State of Saxony. **1907** Summer visit to Kirchner in Goppeln. **1908** Moved to Berlin, where he became a member of the Berlin Secession. **1910** Co-founder of the New Secession. Visited the Moritzburger lakes with Heckel and Kirchner. **1911** Founded with Kirchner the MUIM Institute (Moderner Unterricht in Malerei – Modern Teaching of Painting). **1912** Left the Brücke group because of his involvement in the Secession exhibition in Berlin. **1914** Trip to the Palau islands. Developed a simpler, more primitive stye. **1915/16** Military service on the western front. **1918** Co-founder of the Arbeitsrat für Kunst (Arts Advisory Council). **1922** Member of the Prussian Academy of the Arts. **1933** Banned from painting or exhibiting. **1937** His art is classified as "degenerate" and 326 works confiscated from German museums. **1944** Destruction of his Berlin apartment and loss of the greater part of his works. **1945** Professorship at the School of Fine Arts in Berlin.
WRITINGS: M. P.: Gedichte und Aufzeichnungen aus Palau, Künstlerbekenntnisse. Potsdam 1921.– M. P.: Ruf an die Jugend. Lorch and Stuttgart 1946.– Reidemeister, L. (ed.): M. P. Erinnerungen. Wiesbaden 1960, Munich 1963, Stuttgart 1993
CATALOGUES RAISONNES: Fechter, P. (ed.): Das graphische Werk M. P.'s. Berlin 1921.– Krüger, G. (ed.): Das druckgraphische Werk M. P.'s. Tökendorf 1988
MONOGRAPHS, CATALOGUES: Dieterich G. et al. (ed.): M. P. Das ferne Paradies. Städtisches Kunstmuseum Spendhaus. Reutlingen 1995 (cat.).– Lemmer, K.: M. P. und der Beginn des Expressionismus. Berlin 1949.– Möller, M. (ed.): M. P. Brücke-Museum. Berlin et al. Berlin 1996 (cat.).– Möller, M. (ed.): M. P. Sein

malerisches Werk. Kunsthalle Tübingen et al. Tübingen 1997 (cat.).– Reidemeister, L. (ed.): M. P. 1881-1955. Zeichnungen und Aquarelle. Stationen seines Lebens. Brücke-Museum. Berlin 1981 (cat.).– Schilling, J. (ed.): M. P. Kunstverein Braunschweig et al. Brunswick 1982 (cat.).– Schilling, J. (ed.): M. P. Zeichnungen und Aquarelle. Kunstverein Wolfsburg et al. Hamburg 1987 (cat.).– Timm, W. (ed.): M. P. Druckgraphik. Ostdeutsche Galerie. Regensburg 1989 (cat.).– Timm, W. (ed.): M. P. Ostsee-Bilder. Ostdeutsche Galerie. Regensburg 1981 (cat.)

PEDERSEN Carl-Henning
1913 Copenhagen – **1993** Copenhagen
Danish painter. Self-taught. **1933** Inspired by Miró and Klee, began to paint in abstract style. **1936** Exhibition at the Copenhagen Autumn Salon. **1939** Trip to Paris. **1940** Contact with the artists' group Host. Worked on the *Helhesten* magazine; in the first issue, he published essays by Klees. **1948** Founded the Cobra group, which included Jorn and Appel; worked on its magazine. **1959/60** Trips to Turkey, Ceylon, India, and Israel. **1962** UNESCO Prize at the Venice Biennale. Worked on large mosaics in Copenhagen and Herning. **1963** Exhibition at the Galerie de France, Paris. **1968** Retrospective at the Carnegie Museum, Pittsburgh. **1976** Opening of the Carl-Henning Pedersen and Else-Alfelt Museum in Denmark. **1983** Designed stained-glass windows for the Museum of the Danish Resistance Movement in Copenhagen. **1986** Produced mosaics, frescoes, and stained-glass windows for the cathedral in Ribe, Denmark.
MONOGRAPHS, CATALOGUES: C.-H. P.: P. Milan 1985.– Andreasen, E. (ed.): C.-H. P. Copenhagen 1965.– Dotremont, C.: C.-H. P. Brussels 1950.– Ninka: Portraet af maleren C.-H. P. Copenhagen 1980.– Paquet, M.: C.-H. P. Paris 1986.– C.-H. P. Tegninger, Akvareller og Gouacher 1936-1983. Copenhagen 1983 (cat.).– Schade, V.: C.-H. P. Copenhagen 1966

PENALBA Alicia
born **1918** Buenos Aires
Argentinian sculptress. **1935** Began her studies at the Academy of Fine Arts in

Buenos Aires. **1943** Apprenticeship at E. Centurio's studio. **1947** Received a prize at the Salon Nacional. **1948** Grant to study in Paris and continuation of her training under Ossip Zadkine. **1952** Systematically destroyed her earlier works. In a period of withdrawal, she produced *Love Totems* and *Plant Liturgies*: narrow tubular sculptures which open out from the inside. **1956** In her sculpture entitled *The Spark*, she turned from figures reaching upwards to sawtooth and jagged forms. **1957** First solo-exhibition at the Galerie du Dragon in Paris. **1961** Exhibition at the Charles Lienhard gallery in Zurich. **1964** Took part in documenta 3 in Kassel.
MONOGRAPHS, CATALOGUES: Alva Negri, T.: A. P O de la cadencia musical en la escultura. Buenos Aires 1986.– A. P. Musée des Beaux-Arts. La Chaux-de-Fonds 1982 (cat.).– Joffroy, A. B. et al. (ed.): P. Musée d'Art Moderne de la Ville de Paris. Paris 1977 (cat.).– Seuphor, M.: A. P. Amriswil 1960.– Seuphor, M. (ed.): A. P. Otto Gerson Gallery. New York 1960 (cat.).– Waldberg, P.: P. Paris 1957.– Waldberg, P. (ed.): A. P. Schloß Morsbroich, Städtisches Museum. Leverkusen 1964 (cat.)

PENCK A. R.
(Ralf Winkler)
born **1935** Dresden
German painter. **1956** Apprenticeship as a draughtsman with an advertising agency in Dresden. Taught himself the fundamentals of painting at the same time. Constantly at odds with the East German regime, he managed to survive by working as a postman, stoker and nightwatchman. **1960/61** First paintings of Stick Figures, which from then on became his trademark. **1965** A preoccupation with mathematics, cybernetics, and information theory led to his *System- und Weltbildern* (Systems and World Pictures). **1966** First *Standart* pictures; from **1968** *Standart* models out of sticking plaster. Started using the pseudonym A. R. Penck out of fear of government repression (A. Penck, who lived from 1858 – 1949 was a geologist and ice age expert). **1970** Founded the Lücke artists' group. **1972–1992** Participation in documenta 5, 7 and 9 in Kassel. **1977** First wooden sculptures, which from **1982** were also cast in bronze. After leaving East Germany in **1980**, he first settled in the Rhineland, then moved to London in **1983**, and from there went on to Dublin and New York. **1982** Published the first issue of *Krater und Wolke* magazine. **1985/86** Small bronzes and marble statuary. **1988** Lectureship at the Düsseldorf Academy. Penck fills his large canvases with archaic characters, symbols, and stick figures, which has given him the reputation of being a modern cave painter.
WRITINGS: A. R. P.: Standart Making. Munich 1970.– A. R. P.: Was ist Standart. Cologne and Munich 1970.– A. R. P.: Ich – Standart Literatur. Paris 1971.– A. R. P.: Der Begriff Modell. Erinnerungen an 1973.

Cologne 1978.– A. R. P. (mit J. Immendorf): Immendorf besucht Y. Munich 1979.– A. R. P.: Ende im Osten. Berlin 1981.– A. R. P. im Gespräch mit W. Dickhoff. Cologne 1990
MONOGRAPHS, CATALOGUES: Beeren, W. A. L. et al. (ed.): A. R. P. Museum Boymans-van Beuningen. Rotterdam 1979 (cat.).– Calvocoressi, R. (ed.): A. R. P. Waddington Galleries. London 1982 (cat.).– Calvocoressi, R. (ed.): A. R. P. Tate Gallery. London 1984 (cat.).– Dalbajewa, B. (ed.): A. R. P. Analyse einer Situation. Gemäldegalerie Neue Meister. Dresden 1992 (cat.).– Fuchs, R. and M. J. Jitta (ed.): Tekeningen A. R. P. Haags Gemeentemuseum. The Hague 1988 (cat.).– Gachnang, J. and M. Schmidt-Miescher (ed.): A. R. P. Kunsthalle Bern. Bern 1981 (cat.).– Gohr, S. (ed.): A. R. P. Gemälde, Handzeichnungen. Josef-Haubrich-Kunsthalle. Cologne 1981 (cat.).– Grisebach, L. et al. (ed.): A. R. P. Nationalgalerie, Berlin et al. Munich 1988 (cat.).– Guidieri, R. and C. Haenlein (ed.): A. R. P. Skulpturen und Zeichnungen 1971-1987. Kestner-Gesellschaft, Hanover et al. Hanover 1988 (cat.).– Guidieri, R. (ed.): A. R. P. Sculptures. Paris 1988 (cat.).– Koepplin, D. (ed.): A. R. P. Zeichnungen bis 1975. Kunstmuseum Basel. Basel 1978 (cat.).– Marcadé, B.: A. R. P. Paris 1988.– A. R. P. Musée d'Art Moderne de Saint-Etienne. Saint-Etienne 1985 (cat.).– A. R. P. Skulpturen. Cologne 1983.– A. R. P. Zeichnungen 1958-1985. Gachnang & Springer. Bern and Berlin 1986 (cat.).– A. R. P. Sculptures in Bronze. Waddington Galleries. London 1986 (cat.).– Schmidt, M. et al. (ed.): A. R. P. Kunsthalle Bern. Bern 1975 (cat.).– Yau, J: A. R. P. New York 1993

PENN Irving
born **1917** Plainfield (NJ)
American photographer. Studied at the Philadelphia Museum School of Industrial Art under A. Brodovitch. Worked at first as a painter and was art director of various magazines, including the *Junior League Magazine*. **1942** Travelled to Mexico. **1943** First jobs for *Vogue*. **1944** Worked for the *American Field Service*. Trips to Europe and India. **1953** Opened a photographic studio in New York. **1974** Appearance of *Worlds in a Small Room*, a book in which he puts together a series of portraits taken during his travels in Africa, Italy, New Guinea, and other countries. Penn was one of the leading fashion photographers of the 50s. He is well known for his portraits of celebrities as well as of anonymous contemporary characters.
MONOGRAPHS, CATALOGUES: Foresta, M. A. (ed.): I. P. Master Images. National Museum of American Art. Washington 1990 (cat.).– Geldzahler, H. (ed.): I. P. Street Material. Metropolitan Museum of Art. New York 1977 (cat.).– Krauss, R. (ed.): I. P. Earthly Bodies. Marlborough Gallery. New York 1980 (cat.).– Szarkowski, J. (ed.): I. P. Recent Works. The Museum

of Modern Art. New York 1975 (cat.).–
Szarkowski, J. (ed.): I. P. The Museum of
Modern Art. New York 1986 (cat.).–
Westerbeck, C. et al. (ed.): I. P. A Retro-
spectice. The Art Institute of Chicago et
al. Chicago 1997 / I. P. Eine Retrospektive.
Munich 1997 (cat.)

PENONE Giuseppe
born **1942** Garessio Ponte
Italian artist. **1960–1968** Studied at the
Accademia delle Belle Arti in Turin with
Anselmo and Pistoletto. **1968** First solo-
exhibition at the Deposito d'Arte Presente
and **1969** at the Galleria Gian Enzo
Sperone in Turin. From **1970** he taught at
the Liceo Artistico, Turin. Began to experiment with his own body (e.g. body prints).
1972–1987 Participation in documenta 5, 7
and 8 in Kassel. **1977** Solo-exhibition at
the Lucerne Kunstmuseum. **1978** Solo-
exhibition at the Museum Folkwang,
Essen, and participation at the Venice
Biennale. **1984** Solo-exhibition at the
Museum of Contemporary Art, Chicago.
1992 Retrospective at the Castello di Rivoli,
Turin. Penone, one of the Arte Povera
artists, frequently examines the relationship
between body and space in his art, for
example by projecting enlarged fingerprints
on the walls or by using mirroring contact
lenses which reflect the room as image on
the artist's eye.
WRITINGS: G. P.: Rovesciare gli occhi.
Torino 1977
CATALOGUE RAISONNE: Recht, R. (ed.):
P. L'Espace de la main. Musée de la Ville
de Strasbourg. Strasbourg 1991 (cat.)
MONOGRAPHS, CATALOGUES:
Ammann, J. C. (ed.): G. P. Bäume, Augen,
Haare, Wände, Tongefässe. Kunstmuseum.
Lucerne 1977 (cat.).– Barilli, R. et al. (ed.):
G. P. Staatliche Kunstalle. Baden-Baden
1978 (cat.).– Bradley, J. (ed.): G. P.
National Gallery of Canada. Ottawa 1983
(cat.).– Celant, G. and Z. Felix (ed.): G. P.
Museum Folkwang. Essen 1978 (cat.).–
Celant, G. (ed.): G. P. Stedelijk Museum.
Amsterdam 1980 (cat.).– Celant, G. (ed.):
G. P. Arnolfini Gallery, Bristol et al. Milan
1989 (cat.).– Gianelli, I. and G. Verzotti
(ed.): P. Castello di Rivoli, Museo d'Arte
Contemporanea. Torino 1992 (cat.).– G.
P. Städtisches Museum Abteiberg,
Mönchengladbach. Cologne 1982 (cat.).–
G. P. Musée des Beaux-Arts. Nantes 1986
(cat.).– Peters, H. A. (ed.): G. P. Staat-
liche Kunsthalle Baden-Baden. Baden-
Baden 1978 (cat.).– Schreier, C. (ed.):
G. P. Die Adern des Steins. Städtisches
Kunstmuseum Bonn. Bonn 1997 (cat.).–
Torsato, G. (ed.): G. P. Nîmes et al. Nîmes
1997 (cat.)

PERMEKE Constant
1886 Antwerp – **1952** Oostende
Belgian painter and sculptor. **1903–1906**
Studied at the Academies in Bruges and
Ghent. Met the artists Servaes, van den
Berghe, and the de Smet brothers. **1909**

Moved into the artists' colony in Laethem-
Saint-Martin. From **1912** lived in Ostend,
where he painted numerous landscapes
showing the influence of Breughel. **1913**
Forms became simplified to sharp-edged
areas of colour. **1914** Wounded in the war
and evacuated to England. **1916** Moved
from London to Chardstock, Devonshire.
1918 Returned to Ostend. **1925** Moved to
Jabbeke (near Bruges). **1920** Co-founder of
the art magazine *Sélection*. First exhibition
at the Cercle Royal Artistique et Littéraire,
Antwerp. From **1936** he took up sculpture.
1945/46 Director of the Académie Royale
des Beaux-Arts, Antwerp. **1947** Retrospective at the Musée d'Art Moderne, Paris.
1950 and **1952** participation at the Venice
Biennale. **1959** Retrospective at the
Museum voor Schone Kunsten, Antwerpen. In addition to landscapes, Permeke
produced monumental figure compositions, whose tendency towards the geometric reveals the influence of the Cubists
and Léger.
MONOGRAPHS, CATALOGUES: Avermaete, R.: P. Brussels 1958, 1970.–
Bussche, W. v. de (ed.): C. P. Provinciaal
Museum. Jabbeke 1972 (cat.).– Bussche,
W. v. de: P. Antwerp 1986.– Bussche, W.
v. de (ed.): C. P. 1886-1952. Kunstverein
Hannover. Brussels 1987 (cat.).– Fierens,
P.: P. Paris 1930.– Haesaerts, P.: P. ou la
volonté de grandeur. Antwerp 1938.–
Haesaerts, P.: P. sculpteur. Brussels
1939.– Langui, E.: C. P. Brussels 1947,
1952.– C. P. Rétrospective. Koninklijk
Museum voor Schone Kunsten. Antwerp
1959 (cat.).– C. P. Rétrospective. Provinciaal Museum voor Moderne Kunst. Oostende 1986 (cat.).– Ridder, A. d.: C. P.
1886-1952. Brussels 1947, 1952.– Stubbe,
A.: C. P. Leuven 1931

PETROV Alexander
born **1947** Kujbyschew
Russian painter. **1961–1966** Studied at the
Painting Academy Penzensk, **1967–1971**
at the Painting and Industry School in
Moscow. Lives in Moscow.

PETRUSSOV Georgi
1903 Rostov-on-Don – **1971** Moscow
Russian photographer. Self-taught.
Worked **1920–1924** for the Rostov Industrial Bank, and from **1924** until he died as
a press photographer in Moscow: **1926–
1928** as a staff member for *Pravda*, **1928–
1930** as chief photographer for the Magnitogorsk Foundries, **1930–1941** on a pictorial documentation of the new Russia, **1941
–1945** as a photographic war-correspon-
dent for the Soviet Information Bureau as
well as for the newspaper *Isvestia*, and **1957
–1971** as a photojournalist for the Novosty
Agency. One of the most important Soviet
press photographers of the 30s and 40s.
His emphasis was on industrial and war
photography.
MONOGRAPHS, CATALOGUES: Var-
tanov, A.: G. P. Moscow 1979

PEVSNER Antoine
(Nathan Borisovic Pevsner)
1886 Orel (Russia) – **1962** Paris
Russian artist and constructivist theoretician. **1902–1911** Studied at the Art Academies in Kiev and St. Petersburg. **1911**
Moved to Paris. **1913** Became acquainted
with Archipenko, Brancusi and Modigliani.
First abstract encaustic paintings. **1915–
1917** Lived in Oslo with his brother Gabo.
1917 Moved to Moscow, where he worked
together with Malevich and Tatlin and
taught at the WChUTEMAS art school.
1920 Published the *Realist Manifesto* with
Gabo. **1921** Moved to Germany. **1923**
Returned to Paris; took part in the Salon
des Réalités Nouvelles. **1924** Exhibition
with Gabo in the Percier gallery, Paris.
1929/30 Member of the Cercle et Carré
group. Became a French citizen. **1937**
Acquaintanceship with Kandinsky. **1938**
Exhibition at the Le Niveau gallery, Paris.
1946 Became a leading member of the
Salon des Réalités Nouvelles. **1947** Solo-
exhibition at the René Drouin gallery, Paris
and, **1957**, at the Musée National d'Art
Moderne, Paris. **1955** and **1959** participation
in documenta 1 and 2 in Kassel. **1962** Took
part in the Venice Biennale. **1970** Retrospective at the National d'Art Moderne,
Paris. Pevsner's multi-dimensional constructions, which deliberately use oxidation
processes as part of their visual effect, had a
stimulating influence on Kinetic Art and
light environments.
WRITINGS: Pradel, M.-N. (ed.): P. au
Musée National d'Art Moderne. Les écrits
de P. Paris 1964
MONOGRAPHS, CATALOGUES: Dorival,
B.: Le Dessin dans l'œuvre d'A. P. Paris
1965.– Giedion-Welcker, C. and P. Peissi:
A. P. Huldigung eines Freundes. Neuchâtel
1961 / A. P. Hommage d'un ami. Neuchâtel
1961.– Joray, M. (ed.): A. P. Neuchâtel
1961.– Massat, R. A. P. et le constructivisme. Paris 1956.– A. P. Musée National
d'Art Moderne. Paris 1957 (cat.)

PEZOLD Friederike
born **1945** Vienna
Austrian video and multimedia artist.
Studied at the Munich Academy. **1971** First
video works. From **1973** incorporated
video, photography and drawings in a new
female pictorial language, best represented

by her **1976** work *Die neue leibhaftige
Zeichensprache eines Geschlechts* (The new
incarnate Sign Language of a Sex). **1977**
Started an independent radio station *Radio
freies Utopia* in Munich. Participation in
documenta 6 in Kassel. **1978** Produced a
video film *Die schwarz-weiße Göttin* (The
Black and White Goddess) for WDR (West
German Broadcasting Station). **1980** Participation at the Venice Biennale. From **1984**
use of collages. Through her multimedia
works and performances, Pezold aims to
create a new social awareness and provoke
her viewers into interacting more positively
with their environment.
MONOGRAPHS, CATALOGUES: Haber,
H. G. et al. (ed.): F. P. Städtische Galerie
im Lenbachhaus, Munich. Graz 1975
(cat.).– F. P. Die schwarz-weiße Göttin und
ihre leibhaftige Zeichensprache. Staatliche
Kunsthalle Baden-Baden. Baden-Baden
1977 (cat.).

PHILLIPS Peter
born **1939** Birmingham
English painter. **1953–1955** Attended the
Moseley Road Secondary School of Art.
1955–1959 Studied at the Birmingham
College of Art. **1959–1962** Continued his
studies at the Royal College of Art,
London. Contact with Kitaj, Jones and
Hockney. **1962/63** Lectured at Coventry
College of Art and Birmingham College of
Art. **1963** Participation at the Paris Biennale. **1964** Took part in the Pop Art exhibition in The Hague, Vienna, and Berlin.
1964–1966 Lived in New York. Toured
the USA with A. Jones. **1965** Solo-exhibition at the Kornblee Gallery, New York.
1966 Created the *Hybrid Project*, a survey
set up to establish the ideal work of art.
1968/69 Guest-professor at the Hamburg
School of Fine Arts. **1972** Retrospective at
the Westfälischer Kunstverein in Münster
and **1976** at the Tate Gallery in London.
1981 Australian trip. Pop artist Phillips
quotes the modern culture of the mass
media and consumer goods in his picture
collages.
MONOGRAPHS, CATALOGUES:
Crispoli, E.: P. P. Works/Opere 1960-1974.
Milan 1977.– Finch, C. and K. Honnef
(ed.): P. P. Westfälischer Kunstverein.
Münster 1972 (cat.).– Livingstone, M. (ed.):
P. P. Retrovision. Paintings 1960-1982.
Walker Art Gallery, Liverpool et al. Liverpool 1982 (cat.)

PICABIA Francis
1879 Paris – **1953** Paris
French painter with a Spanish father. Until
1908 painted in Impressionist style, then
fell under the spell of the Fauves and
Cubists. In his search for new modes of
expression, he became one of the forerunners of abstract art with his work *Rubber*
(Paris, Musée National d'Art Moderne),
painted in **1909**. He continued on this
path from **1913–1915**, which he spent
mostly in the USA. Out of these sharp-

edged, abstract compostions grew a series of machine paintings, whose very lack of functionality challenges faith in technical progress. **1916** Moved back to Europe and joined the Dada group in Paris. He made collages out of buttons, matches, feathers and other materials. After **1927**, the second important phase in his work began: a series of transparent paintings, in which superimposed, linear images blend into each other. From **1931–1939** lived on a boat near Cannes, **1939–1945** in Golfe-Juan. After returning to Paris, took up Colour Field Painting. **1947** Took part in the "Le Surréalisme en 1947" exhibition. In his art, Picabia experimented with many styles: Impressionism, Cubism, Orphism, Dadaism, and Surrealism. Due to this artistic diversity, he found it hard at first to make an impact, however, his overall influence on the development of 20th century art has proved significant and long-lasting.
WRITINGS: Orth, E.: Das dichterische Werk von F. P. Frankfurt-on-Main 1994.– F. P.: Ecrits. Paris 1975-1978/Schriften. 2 vols. Hamburg 1981.– F. P.: Lettres à Christine 1945-1951. Paris 1988
MONOGRAPHS, CATALOGUES: Armero, G. (ed.): F. P. 1879-1953. Salas Pablo Ruiz Picasso, Madrid et al. Madrid 1985 (cat.).– Arthaud, C. (ed.): P. et la Côte d'Azur. Musée d'Art Moderne et d'Art Contemporain. Nice 1991 (cat.).– Bois, Y.-A.: P. Paris 1975, 1985.– Borràs, M. L.: P. London and New York 1985, Nortford 1993.– Calvocoressi, R. et al. (ed.): P. 1879-1953. National Gallery of Scotland, Edinburgh et al. Edinburgh 1991 (cat.).– Camfield, W. A.: F. P. His Art, Life and Times. Princeton (NJ) 1979.– Christians, U.: Studien zu F. P. Diss. Berlin 1980.– Faggiolo, P. Milan 1976.– Fauchereau, S.: P. Paris 1996.– Felix, Z. (ed.): F. P. Das Spätwerk 1933-1953. Deichtorhallen, Hamburg et al. Stuttgart 1997 (cat.).– Granath, O. and N. Öhmann (ed.): F. P. Moderna Museet. Stockholm 1984 (cat.).– Heinz, M. and O. Schuldt (ed.): F. P. Städtische Kunsthalle Düsseldorf et al. Düsseldorf 1983 (cat.).– Heinz, M. (ed.): P. 1879-1953. Galerie Neuendorf, Frankfurt-on-Main et al. Frankfurt-on-Main and Stuttgart 1988 (cat.).– Labia, P. et al. (ed.): F. P. Antology. Lisbon 1997 (cat.).– Le Bot, M.: F. P. et la crise des valeurs figuratives 1900-1925. Paris 1968.– Martin, J.-H. and H. Seckel (ed.): F. P. Grand Palais. Paris 1976 (cat.).– Mohler, O.: Album F. P. Torino 1975.– F. P. Solomon R. Guggenheim Museum. New York 1970 (cat.).– F. P. Kunsthaus Zürich. Zurich 1984 (cat.).– F. P.: "Il n'y a pas d'idéal sans passion et la passion n'est pas un idéal objectif". Musée des Beaux-Arts. Nîmes 1986 (cat.).– F. P. Didier Imbert Fine Art. Paris 1990 (cat.).– F. P. Máquinas y Españolas. IVAM Centro Julio González, Valencia et al. Paris 1995 (cat.).– Sanouillet, M. (ed.): F. P. et "391". 2 vols. Paris 1960-1966.– Wilson, S. (ed.): F. P. Accomodations of Desire 1924-1932. Kent Gallery. New York 1991 (cat.)

PICASSO Pablo
1881 Málaga – **1973** Mougins (near Cannes) Spanish artist. **1891** Moved with his family to La Coruña. First painting lessons from his father. **1895** Attended the La Lonja art school in Barcelona. **1896** First studio in Barcelona. **1899** Frequented the intellectuals' café El Quatre Gats. **1900** First stay in Paris, where he painted scenes from variety shows and circus life. From **1901**, he signed his works *Picasso*, his mother's name. His paintings from this time tend to be an almost monochrome blue-green (his Blue Period). **1904** Moved to Paris and set up a studio in the Bateau-Lavoir district. Met Matisse, Derain and Gertrude Stein, who was his first collector. His palette changed to reddish tones (the Red Period). **1906** Intensive involvement in the works of Cézanne. **1907**, even before he met Braque and the dealer and writer Kahnweiler, his style took a dramatic, revolutionary turn: with his painting *Les Demoiselles d'Avignon*, he broke definitively with the formal and aesthetic mores of the 19th century and paved the way for Cubism. **1909** Development of Analytical Cubism together with Braque. **1912** Began three-dimensional "paintings", incorporating sheet metal and wire as construction elements, as well as his first *papiers collés*. **1917** Stage designs for Diaghilev's Ballets Russes. **1920–1924** Neo-classical period. **1930** Set up a sculpture studio at Boisgeloup castle. **1937** For the Spanish pavilion at the Paris World Fair, he painted the mighty *Guernica*, employing abstraction, deformation, and anatomical mutilation to protest against the bombing of the Basque city by the German Condor Legion. **1939** Completion of the *Suite Vollard* series of etchings. **1940** Returned to Paris, where he was forbidden to exhibit. **1944** Joined the French Communist Party. From **1946**, he lived on the Côte d'Azur. From **1950** became especially interested in ceramics. In the 50s he began to explore the Old Masters, and painted variations on works by Velázquez, Delacroix and Manet. In his impressive late period from **1960** until his death, Picasso fought strongly and angrily against the growing predominance of abstraction. He donated all the works belonging to his family to the Picasso Museum in Barcelona, which opened in **1970**. **1985** Opening of the Musée Picasso in Paris.
WRITINGS: Bernadac, M. L. and C. Piot (ed.): P. écrits. Paris 1989, Munich 1989
CATALOGUES RAISONNES: Besnard-Bernadac, M. L. et al. (ed.): Le Musée Picasso. Catalogue sommaire illustré des collections. 2 vols. Paris 1985-1987/The Picasso Museum, Paris. 2 vols. London and New York 1986-1987/Picasso-Museum Paris. Bestandskatalog. Munich 1985.– Bloch, G. (ed.): P. P. Katalog des graphischen Werkes 1904-1967/Catalogue of the Printed Graphic Work 1904-1967/Catalogue de l'œuvre gravé et lithographié. 4 vols. Bern 1968-1979.– Chip, H. B. (ed.): P. P. Catalogue Raisonné of His Works. Vol. 1-6. San Francisco 1995-1998.– Daix, P.

and G. Boudaille (ed.): P. 1900-1906. Catalogue raisonné de l'œuvre peint. Neuchâtel 1966/P. The Blue and Rose Periods. A Catalogue Raisonné. of the Paintings 1900-1906. Greenwich (CT) 1967/P. Blaue und Rosa Periode 1900-1906. Munich 1966.– Daix, P. and J. Rosselet (ed.): Le Cubisme de P. Catalogue raisonné de l'œuvre peint 1907-1916. Neuchâtel 1979/The Cubist Years 1907-1916. A Catalogue Raisonné of the Paintings and Related Works. New York 1979.– Geiser, B. and B. Baer (ed.): P. Peintre-Graveur. Catalogue illustré de l'œuvre gravé et lithographié (et des monotypes). 1899-1965. 5 vols. Bern 1933-1992.– Glimcher, A. and M. (ed.): Je suis le cahier. Die Skizzenbücher P.'s. Reinbek 1986/Je Suis le Cahier. The Sketchbooks of P. New York 1986.– Goeppert, S. et al. (ed.): P. P. Catalogue raisonné des livres illustrés. Geneva 1983/P. P. The Illustrated Books. Geneva 1983.– Mourlot, F. (ed.): P. Lithographe. 4 vols. Monte Carlo 1949-1964/P. Lithograph. 4 vols. Geneva 1970.– Museu Picasso. Catàleg de pintura i dibuix. Textos de M. A. Capmany et al. Barcelona 1985.– Palau i Fabre, J. (ed.): P. The Early Years. New York 1981/P. Kindheit und Jugend eines Genies 1881-1907. Munich 1981.– Palau i Fabre, J. (ed.): P. Cubism 1907-1917. Barcelona and New York 1990.– Ramié, G. (ed.): Céramique de P. Paris 1974, 1984/P. Keramik. Bern 1980/P. Catalogue of the Edited Ceramic Works. Vallauris 1988.– Rau, B. (ed.): P. P. Die Lithographien. Stuttgart 1988, 1993.– Rodrigo, L. C. (ed.): P. in His Posters. Image and Work. 4 vols. Madrid 1992.– Spies, W. and C. Piot (ed.): P. Das plastische Werk. Werkverzeichnis der Skulpturen 1983/Les Sculptures de P. Lausanne 1971/P. Sculpture. London 1972.– Zervos, C. (ed.): P. P. 1895-1972. 33 vols. Paris 1932-1978

PIENE Otto
born **1928** Laasphe (Westphalia) German painter and object artist. **1944** Military service. **1948–1950** Studied at the Munich Academy, and from **1950–1953** at the Düsseldorf Academy. **1953–1957** Studied philosophy at Cologne University. **1955** Began to work artistically with light. **1957** Founder member, with Mack, of the Zero group. **1959** Solo-exhibition at the Schmela gallery, Düsseldorf. **1964** Guest-professor at the University of Pennsylvania. Took part in documenta 3 in Kassel. **1965** Solo-exhibition at the Kestner Society, Hanover. From **1968** lectureship at Massachusetts Institute of Technology in Cambridge, where he became director of the Center for Advanced Visual Studies in **1974**. **1972** Created the *Olympia Regenbogen* (Olympia Rainbow) in Munich. Exterior decoration of a factory building with monumental frescoes (commissioned by Rosenthal). **1977** Took part in documenta 6 in Kassel. **1981–1983** Organisation of the Sky Art conferences in Cambridge (MA), Linz and Munich. Became known for his kinetic light works (especially the "light

ballet"), which represent an attempt to reconcile modern technology with nature.
WRITINGS: O. P. and H. Mack: Zero. 3 vols. Düsseldorf 1958-1961/Zero. Cambridge (MA) 1973.– O. P.: More Sky I. Betrachtungen und Skizzen zum Environment. Cambridge (MA) 1970.– O. P.: Migrant Apparition. Cambridge (MA) 1971.– O. P.: Rainbows. Cambridge (MA) 1971.– Piene-Texte. Munich and Frankfurt-on-Main 1961
CATALOGUE RAISONNE: Mahlow, D. et al. (ed.): O. P. Werkverzeichnis der Druckgraphik 1960-1976. Karlsruhe 1977
MONOGRAPHS, CATALOGUES: Alloway, L. (ed.): O. P. Massachusetts Institute of Technology. Cambridge (MA) 1975 (cat.).– Claus, J. and H. Stachelhaus (ed.): O. P. Galerie Heimeshoff. Essen 1985 (cat.).– Herzogenrath, W. (ed.): O. P. Kölnischer Kunstverein. Cologne 1993 (cat.).– O. P. Retrospektive. Kölnischer Kunstverein. Cologne 1974 (cat.).– O. P. and J. Wissmann (ed.): O. P. Arbeiten auf Papier. Galerie Löhrl. Mönchengladbach 1986 (cat.).– Seaman, B. (ed.): Sonderausstellung O. P. und das CAVS, 20 Jahre Arbeit am Center for Advanced Visual Studies des Massachusetts Institutes of Technology, Cambridge (MA) Badischer Kunstverein, Karlsruhe. Berlin 1988 (cat.).– Wiese, S. v. and S. Rennert (ed.): O. P. Retrospektive 1952-1996. Kunstmuseum und Kunstpalast. Cologne 1996 (cat.).– Wißmann, J.: O. P. Recklinghausen 1976

PISTOLETTO Michelangelo
born **1933** Biella
Italian artist. Worked from **1947–1958** as an art restorer in his father's workshop. **1958** Enthousiastic discovery of the works of Francis Bacon. **1960** First solo-exhibition at the Galleria Galatea, Turin. **1961** First paintings with reflecting areas. **1964** Solo-exhibition at Ileana Sonnabend gallery in Paris. **1967** Major prize at the São Paulo Biennale. **1968** Gave his exhibition space at the Venice Biennale to other artists. Participation in documenta 4 in Kassel and at the "Arte povera azioni povere" in Amalfi. **1968–1970** Actions with the Lo Zoo group. **1971** Took part in the Arte Povera exhibition at the Munich Kunstverein. **1977** Directed the opera *Neither* in Rome. **1978** DAAD scholarship to Berlin. **1980** Solo-exhibition at the Museum of Modern Art, San Francisco. **1981** Participation in the "Westkunst" exhibition in Cologne. Sculptures out of polyurethane foam. **1982** Took part in documenta 7 in Kassel. First marble sculptures. **1985** Began covering sculptures with cloth and then painting them. **1989** Solo-exhibition at the Museo Capodimonte, Naples. **1992** and **1997** participation in documenta 9 and 10 in Kassel. **1994** Retrospective at the National Museum of Contemporary Art, Seoul. **1996** Solo-exhibition at the Lenbachhaus, Munich. Pistoletto, a multimedia artist whose work includes painting, photography, sculpture, and action art,

emphasises creative cooperation with other artists.
WRITINGS: M. P.: A Minus Artist. Florence 1988
MONOGRAPHS, CATALOGUES: Boatto, A.: P. Roma 1960.– Boatto, A,: M. P. dentro-fuori lo specchio. Roma 1969.– Celant, G. (ed.): M. P. Forte di Belvedere, Florence. Milan 1984 (cat.).– Celant, G. and A. Heiss (ed.): P. Division and Multiplication of the Mirror. Institute of Contemporary Art, P. S. 1 Museum, New York. New York 1988 (cat.).– Celant, G.: P. New York 1989, Milan 1990.– Corà, B.: M. P. Lo spazio della riflessione nell'arte. Ravenna 1986.– Dercon, C. (ed.): M. P. e la fotografia. Fundación de Serralves, Porto et al. Porto 1993 (cat.).– Felix, Z. (ed.): M. P. Gli oggetti in meno, lo specchio, la gabbia. Deichtorhallen. Hamburg 1992 (cat.).– Garcia, A. et al. (ed.): M. P. Palacio de Cristal, Parque del retiro. Madrid 1983 (cat.).– Krimmel, B. (ed.): M. P. Mathildenhöhe. Darmstadt 1974 (cat.).– Monferini, A. et al. (ed.): M. P. Galleria Nazionale d'Arte Moderna, Roma. Milan 1990 (cat.).– M. P. Centre National d'Art Contemporain. Grenoble 1987 (cat.).– Poetter, J. and R. E. Pahlke (ed.): M. P. Staatliche Kunsthalle Baden-Baden. Baden-Baden 1988 (cat.).– Schmied, W. (ed.): M. P. Kestner-Gesellschaft. Hanover 1973 (cat.).– Schott, F. and M. Schibig (ed.): M. P. Oggetti in meno 1965-1966. Kunsthalle Bern et al. Bern 1989 (cat.)

PLESSI Fabrizio
born **1940** Reggio Emilia
Italian video artist and stage designer. Studied at the Venice Academy of Fine Arts, where he later held master classes in painting. From **1968** his obsession with water led to installations, films, videos and performances on that theme. **1980** Took part in the Venice Film Festival with his *Liquid movie*. Awarded the City of Milan Prize. From **1982** devised myriad variations on the various mechanical and electronic possibilities of reproducing the element water. **1987** Received the international prize for *L'immagine elettronica* in Bologna. Created an electronic stage set for E. Cosimi's ballet *Sciame* at the Rovereto Festival. Participation in documenta 8 in Kassel. **1989** Designed sets and costumes for the opera *The Fall of Icarus* at the National Opera in Brussels. **1990** Professorship at the Media Arts Academy in Cologne.
CATALOGUE RAISONNE: Koelen, D. v. de (ed.): F. P. Opus Video-Skulptur. Werkverzeichnis der Video-Skulpturen 1976-1997. Mainz 1998
MONOGRAPHS, CATALOGUES: Bartsch, I. (ed.): F. P. Retrospektive. Museum am Ostwall. Dortmund 1993 (cat.).– Fagone, V. et al. (ed.): P. Water Video Projects. Heidelberger Kunstverein. Heidelberg 1983 (cat.).– Fagone, V. et al. (ed.): P. Milan 1985.– Goddrow, G. A. (ed.): F. P. Progetti del Mondo. Cologne 1997.– Kubisch, C.: F. P.

Aachen 1979.– Oliva, A. B. and O. Calabrese (ed.): P. Civici Musei, Reggio Emilia. Treviso 1990 (cat.).– F. P. Kunsthalle Kiel. Kiel 1977 (cat.).– F. P. Bombay Bombay. Museum Ludwig. Cologne 1993 (cat.).– F. P. Zeichnungen. Neue Galerie. Linz 1994 (cat.).– Reitbauer, R. (ed.): P. Museum Moderner Kunst, Stiftung Ludwig. Vienna 1991 (cat.).– Schepers, J. (ed.): F. P. La Rocca Elettronica. Rocca Paolina. Perugia 1995 (cat.).– Zweite, A. (ed.): F. P. Aquabiographie. Städtische Galerie im Lenbachhaus. Munich 1974 (cat.)

POIRIER Anne and **Patrick**
born **1942** Marseille (Anne)
born **1942** Nantes (Patrick)
French artists. **1963**–**1966** Studied at the Académie des Arts Décoratifs in Paris. **1967** – **1971** Lived in Rome on Villa Medici grants. **1970** First solo-exhibition in Rome. **1972** Solo-exhibition at the Maenz gallery, Cologne. **1974** Took part in the "Spurensicherung" (Trace- and Clue-Finding Art) exhibition at the Kunstverein, Hamburg. **1976**, **1980** and **1984** participants at the Venice Biennale. **1977** Took part in documenta 6 in Kassel. Solo-exhibition at the Neue Berliner Kunstverein. **1979/80** P.S.1 grants for New York. **1988** Solo-exhibition at the Lenbachhaus and at the Dany Keller gallery, Munich. **1977/78** DAAD scholarship to Berlin. **1973** Solo-exhibition at the Neue Galerie, Aachen. **1977** Participation in documenta 6 in Kassel. **1984** Solo-exhibition at the Brooklyn Museum, New York. **1988** Solo-presentation at the Kunstforum in the Lenbachhaus, Munich. **1994** Solo-exhibition at the Museum Moderner Kunst, Vienna. The Poiriers are proponents of trace- and clue-finding art and individual mythology.
WRITINGS: A. and P. P.: Domus Aurea, archéologie, fiction. Paris 1977
MONOGRAPHS, CATALOGUES: Barzel, A. (ed.): A. & P. P. Decouvertes et rapports. Villanova University. Villanova (PA) 1991 (cat.).– Lascaut, G. et al. (ed.): A. et P. P. Domus Aurea, fascination des ruines. Centre Georges Pompidou, Paris et al. Paris and Bonn 1978 (cat.).– Foray, J.-M. et al. (ed.): A. und P. P. Museum Moderner Kunst Stiftung Ludwig, Vienna et al. Milan 1994 (cat.).– Marchi, S. (ed.): A. and P. P. Architettura e mitologica. Chiesa di S. Carpoforo. Milan 1984 (cat.).– Metken, G. et al. (ed.): A. and P. P. Galerie der Stadt Esslingen. Esslingen 1987 (cat.).– A. and P. P. Ruines sur ruines. Musée des Beaux-Arts de Caen. Caen 1985 (cat.)

POLIAKOFF Serge
1906 Moscow – **1969** Paris
Russian-born French painter. **1918** Fled the Russian Revolution and moved to Paris in **1923**. Studied music and first earned his living as a guitarist. **1929/30** Attended the Académie Frochot, the Académie Bilbul and the Grande Chaumière in Paris. **1935**–**1937** Studied at the Slade School of Art in

London, afterwards moving back to Paris, where he made friends with Kandinsky, Sonia and Robert Delaunay and Freundlich. **1946** Awarded the Kandinsky Prize and, in **1956**, the Lissone Prize. In the late 40s he created his first monumental compositions while, in the 50s, he painted primarily diptychs and triptychs. **1959** and **1964** participation in documenta 2 and 3 in Kassel. **1962** Took French citizenship. **1965** International Prize at the Tokyo Biennale. **1966** first prize at the Menton Biennale. Via the colour theories of the Orphists, he developed a form of synthetic Cubism: a patchwork structure of highly intense colour areas that becomes denser towards the middle.
WRITINGS: S. P.: Enluminures. St. Gallen 1972
CATALOGUES RAISONNES: Poliakoff, A. (ed.): S. P. Catalogue raisonné (in preparation).– Rivière, Y. (ed.): S. P. Les Estampes. Paris 1974
MONOGRAPHS, CATALOGUES: Brütsch, F.: S. P. 1900-1969. Neuchâtel 1993.– Cassou, J.: S. P. Amriswil 1963.– Durozoi, G. et al. (ed.): S. P. Eine Übersicht. Museum Würth. Künzelsau 1997 (cat.).– Lassaigne, J.: P. Gouaches. Paris 1957.– Marchiori, G.: S. P. Paris 1976.– S. P. Musée National d'Art Moderne de la Ville de Paris. Paris 1970 (cat.).– S. P. Les Estampes. Paris 1974.– S. P. Fondation Dina Vierny, Musée Maillol. Paris 1996 (cat.).– Ragon, M.: P. Paris 1956.– Vallier, D.: S. P. Paris 1959.– Vallier, D. (ed.): S. P. Rétrospective. Galerie Melki. Paris 1991 (cat.).– Vierny, D. et al. (ed.): S. P. Paris 1995 (cat.)

POLKE Sigmar
born **1941** Oels (Lower Silesia)
German painter. **1953** Moved to West Berlin, then to Düsseldorf. **1959/60** Apprenticeship as a glass painter. Studied from **1961**–**1967** under Götz, Hoehme and Beuys at the Düsseldorf Art Academy. **1963** With K. Fischer-Lueg and G. Richter developed, Kapitalistischer Realismus a highly polemical version of Pop Art. From **1965** detailed study of historical and contemporary art works: variations on paintings by Dürer and Kandinsky, imitations of Arte Povera and Concept Art works. **1970/71** and **1977** guest-professor at the Hamburg School of Fine Arts. **1972**–**1982**

Participation in documenta 5 – 7 in Kassel. **1974** Travelled to Pakistan and Afghanistan. **1978** Moved to Cologne. Began to incorporate cartoons and, in the early 80s, addressed political themes. **1982** Received the Will Grohmann Award, **1984** the Kurt Schwitters Award, **1986** first prize for painting at the Venice Biennale, **1987** the Lichtwark Award in Hamburg, and **1988** the Baden-Württemberg State Award. **1989** Appointed professor at the Hamburg School of Fine Arts. **1991** *Neue Bilder* (New Pictures) series. Again and again, Polke comments ironically on the effects of manipulation by the mass media. He adheres to a classical modernist style, but employs unusual techniques and materials taken partly from trival and sub-cultures.
WRITINGS: S. P.: Höheres Wesen befehlen. Berlin 1968.– S. P.: Bizarre. Heidelberg 1972
MONOGRAPHS, CATALOGUES: Beeren, W. et al. (ed.): S. P. Museum Boymans-van Beuningen, Rotterdam et al. Rotterdam 1983 (cat.) / S. P. Städtisches Kunstmuseum Bonn et al. Bonn 1984 (cat.).– Beeren, W. (ed.): S. P. Stedelijk Museum. Amsterdam 1992 (cat.).– Belting, H. et al. (ed.): S. P. Die drei Lügen der Malerei. Kunst- und Ausstellungshalle der Bundesrepublik Deutschland, Bonn. Stuttgart 1997 (cat.).– Curiger, B. and H. Liberknecht (ed.): S. P. Musée d'Art Moderne de la Ville de Paris 1988 (cat.).– Erfle, A.: S. P. Der Traum des Menelaos. Cologne 1997.– Ferguson, R. (ed.): S. P. Photoworks. Museum of Contemporary Art, Los Angeles et al. Zurich, Berlin and New York 1995 (cat.).– Gachnang, J. (ed.): S. P. Zeichnungen 1963-1969. Bern and Berlin 1987 (cat.).– Gohr, S. et al. (ed.): S. P. Kunsthalle, Zurich et al. Zurich and Cologne 1984 (cat.).– Groot, E. d. (ed.): S. P. Museum Boymans-van Beiningen, Rotterdam et al. Rotterdam 1983.– Hentschel, M.: Die Ordnung des Heterogenen. S. P.'s Werk bis 1986. Darmstadt 1991.– Heubach, F. W. and B. H. D. Buchloh (ed.): S. P. Bilder, Tücher, Objekte. Werkauswahl 1962-1971. Kunsthalle Tübingen et al. Tübingen 1976 (cat.).– Lamarche-Vadel, B. et al. (ed.): S. P. Musée d'Art Moderne de la Ville de Paris. Paris 1988 (cat.).– Nesbit, J. (ed.): S. P. Join the Dots. Tate Gallery, Liverpool. London 1995 (cat.).– Poetter, J. (ed.): S. P. Fotografien. Staatliche Kunsthalle Baden-Baden. Stuttgart 1990 (cat.).– S. P. San Francisco Museum of Modern Art et al. San Francisco 1990 (cat.).– Schimmel, P. and M. Morris Hambourg (ed.): S. P. Photowork. Museum of Contemporary Art. Los Angeles 1995 (cat.).– Schjeldahl, P. (ed.): S. P. Mary Boone Gallery, New York 1986 (cat.).– Schmidt, K. (ed.): S. P. Zeichnungen, Aquarelle, Skizzenbücher 1962-1988. Städtisches Kunstmuseum Bonn. Bonn 1988 (cat.).– Schmidt, K. and G. Schweikhart (ed.): S. P. Städtisches Kunstmuseum Bonn. Bonn 1988 (cat.).– Schulz-Hoffmann, C. and U. Bischoff (ed.): S. P. Schleifenbilder. Stuttgart 1992.– Stemmler, D. (ed.): S. P. Neue Bilder. Städtisches Museum Abteiberg. Mönchengladbach 1992 (cat.).– Szeemann, H. and T. Stooss (ed.): S. P. Josef-Haubrich-Kunsthalle, Cologne et al. Cologne 1984 (cat.).– Thistlewood, D. (ed.): S. P. Back to Postmodernity. Liverpool 1996.– Tosatto, G. and B. Marcadé (ed.): S. P. Carré d'Art, Musée d'Art Contemporain, Nîmes et al. Paris 1994 (cat.)

POLLOCK Jackson
1912 Cody (WY) – **1956** East Hampton (NY)
American painter. **1925**–**1929** Studied at the Manual Arts School in Los Angeles and

from **1929/30** at the Art Students League in New York under Benton, the most important representative of American Scene Painting, whom he assisted in painting murals. **1936–1943** Created murals as part of a government programme. **1939** During a period of treatment for alcoholism, he began to study the teaching of C. G. Jung, especially his theory of archetypes. From **1942** friendship with Motherwell, a leading Abstract Expressionist, and with the Surrealist Matta, who encouraged him to write Surrealist poems. At first, he painted non-representational pictures, whose stylised forms were borrowed from primitive art, especially Indian art. **1945** Married the artist L. Krasner. **1946** First *Drip Painting*, whereby paint from perforated paint cans was allowed to drip onto canvases laid on the floor; at the same time he was experimenting with a heavy impasto made of sand, glass fragments, and other materials, and used sticks, knives, and spatulas instead of brushes. **1950/51** Rebelled against the anti-abstract art policies of the Art Institute of Chicago. **1951** Underwent further therapy for alcoholism and, in **1955**, psychoanalysis. **1956** Died in an automobile accident. Pollock developed Action Painting out of the Surrealist technique of Automatism. This gestural approach later led to the happening.
CATALOGUE RAISONNE: O'Connor, F. V. et al. (ed.): J. P. A Catalogue Raisonné of Paintings, Drawings and Other Works. 4 vols. New Haven (CT) and London 1978
MONOGRAPHS, CATALOGUES: Abadie, D. et al. (ed.): J. P. Centre Georges Pompidou. Paris 1982 (cat.).– O.: J. P. Lucerne 1971.– Busignani, A.: P. Florence, London and New York 1971.– Cernuschi, C. (ed.): J. P. Psychoanalytic Drawings. Duke University Museum of Art, Durham et al. Durham 1992 (cat.).– Cernuschi, C.: J. P. Meaning and Significance. New York 1992.– Clark, T. J.: J. P. Abstraktion und Figuration. Hamburg 1994.– Frank, E.: J. P. New York 1983, Munich 1984.– Frascina, F. (ed.): P. and After. The Critical Debate. New York 1985.– Friedman, B. H.: J. P. Energy Made Visible. New York 1972.– Fujieda, T.: J. P. Tokyo 1979.– Landau, E.: J. P. New York 1989.– Naifeh, S. and G. W. Smith: J. P. An American Saga. London and New York 1989, London 1992.– Namuth, H.: L'Atelier de J. P. Paris 1978.– O'Connor, F. V. (ed.): J. P. The Museum of Modern Art. New York 1967 (cat.).– O'Connor, F. V. (ed.): J. P. The Black Pourings 1951-1953. Institute for Contemporary Art. Boston 1980 (cat.).– O'Hara, F.: J. P. New York 1959.– J. P. Bilder. Städtische Galerie im Städelschen Kunstinstitut. Frankfurt-on-Main 1982 (cat.).– Potter, J.: To a Violent Grave. An Oral Biography of J. P. New York 1985.– Putz, E.: J. P. Theorie und Bild. Hildesheim 1975.– Ratcliff, C.: The Fate of a Gesture. J. P. and Postwar American Art. New York 1996.– Robertson, B.: J. P. New York 1960.– Rohn, M. L.: Visual Dynamics in J. P.'s Abstractions. Ann Arbor (MI)

1987.– Rose, B. (ed.): J. P. Drawings into Paintings. The Museum of Modern Art. New York 1980 (cat.).– Solomon, D.: J. P. A Biography. New York 1987.– Tomassoni, I.: P. Florence, London and New York 1969.– Wayup, C. L. (ed.): J. P. Psychoanalytical Drawings. New York 1970

POMODORO Arnaldo
born **1926** Morciano di Romagna
Italian sculptor. Brother of G. Pomodoro. First studied architecture and was then apprenticed to a goldsmith. **1954** Moved to Milan, where he had his first solo-exhibition in **1955**. **1957** Signatory of the *Manifesto Against Style*. **1959** Took part in documenta 2 in Kassel. From the 60s, he produced geometric, usually spherical metal sculptures, whose smooth surfaces are broken in places to reveal graceful, intricate interiors. **1965** Solo-exhibition at the Marlborough Gallery, Rome. **1965–1968** Design and production of the open-air sculpture *Grande Disco* in front of the theatre in Darmstadt. **1969** Solo-exhibition at the Boymans-van Beuningen Museum, Rotterdam, and at the Kunstverein in Cologne. Pomodoro set a new course for the plastic arts by taking the principles of L'art informel and applying them to sculpture.
MONOGRAPHS, CATALOGUES: Ballo, G.: A. e Gio Pomodoro. Milan 1962.– Hunter, S.: A. P. New York 1982.– Hunter, S.: A. P. Milan 1995.– Mussa, I. (ed.): Luoghi fondamentali. Sculture di A. P. Forte di Belvedere, Florence. Milan 1984 (cat.).– Krimmel, E. (ed.): A. P. Großplastiken. Freiräume und Foyers des Staatstheaters. Darmstadt 1972 (cat.).– A. P. Museum Boymans-van Beuningen, Rotterdam et al. Rotterdam and Cologne 1969 (cat.).– Quintavalle, A. C.: A. P. Opere dal 1956 al 1960. Milan 1990.– Rosenthal, M. (ed.): A. P. A Quarter Century. Columbus Museum of Art. Columbus (OH) 1983 (cat.)

POONS Larry
born **1937** Tokyo
American painter. **1955–1957** Studied in Boston at the New England Conservatory of Music, **1958** at the Museum School of Fine Arts. **1958/59** Returned to New York, where he had lived as a boy. Met Louis, Newman, Noland, Kelly and F. Stella. In the early 60s, he produced his first *Dot Pictures*: paintings with oval or round dots of colour in a regular pattern on a monochrome background. **1963** Solo-exhibition at the Green Gallery and, **1967**, at the Leo Castelli Gallery, New York. **1968** Took part in documenta 4 in Kassel. From the early 70s, used viscous paint, dripped or thrown onto the canvas. **1978/79** Exhibition with M. Steiner at the Wuppertal Kunstverein and at Amerika Haus in Berlin. **1981/82** Retrospective at the Museum of Fine Arts, Boston. **1986** Solo-exhibition at the André Emmerich Gallery, New York. Poon's meditative Color Field style is coupled with a

gestural actionism, showing the influence of Pollock's Action Painting.
MONOGRAPHS, CATALOGUES: Fenton, T.: (ed.): L. P. Recent Paintings. Edmonton Aret Gallery. Alberta 1974 (cat.).– Moffet, K. and T. Fenton (ed.): L. P. Paintings 1971-1981. Museum of Fine Arts. Boston 1981 (cat.).– Steiner, M. (ed.): L. P. Skulpturen und Gemälde aus New York. Wuppertal 1978 (cat.)

POPOVA Lyubov
1889 Ivanovskoye – **1924** Moscow
Russian painter. **1907–1909** Studied painting in Moscow under Joukovski, Joun and Dudin. **1910** Travelled in Italy. **1912** Took part in the artists' meeting in the Basnia (Tower) gallery in Moscow; meeting with Tatlin. **1912/13** Lived in Paris, where she worked in the studios of Metzinger and Le Fauconnier and painted her first Cubist pictures. **1913** Returned to Moscow. **1916** Under the influence of Malevich, produced her first non-representational pictures, displayed in a joint exhibition with Tatlin and Malevich in Moscow. **1917** Co-founded *Supremus* magazine. **1918** Member of the leftist federation of the Union of Moscow Artists, which included Rodchenko and Stepanova. **1919** Took part in the national exhibition "Non-Representational Art and Suprematism", **1921** in the "5 x 5 = 25" exhibition in Moscow. **1920–1923** Taught at the WChUTEMAS art school; did stage set designs. **1922** Took part in the exhibition of Russian art at the van Diemen gallery, Berlin. **1924/25** Posthumous retrospective at the Stroganov Institute, Moscow. In her various creative phases, Popova showed the influences of Cubism, Suprematism, and Constructivism. Out of her close association with Tatlin and Malevich, she developed her own non-representational style, known as Painterly Architectonics.
MONOGRAPHS, CATALOGUES: Adaskina, N. and D. Sarabianov: L. P. Paris 1989.– Dabrowski, M. (ed.): L. P. The Museum of Modern Art, New York et al. New York 1991 (cat.).– Sarabianov, D. V. and N. L. Adaskina: L. P. New York 1990.– Weiss, E. (ed.): L. P. 1889-1924. Museum Ludwig, Cologne et al. Munich 1991 (cat.)

PRAGER Heinz-Günther
born **1944** Herne (Westphalia)
German sculptor. **1964–1968** Studied at the School of Arts and Crafts in Münster. Regular study trips to Paris. From **1967** experimented with forms in wood, bronze and iron. **1970** First sculptures out of steel and pig iron, exploring the relationship between the viewer and the object viewed. **1973** Won a Villa Romana scholarship to Florence. **1974** Developed an anthropometric theory of sculpture. **1975** First solo-exhibition at the Museum Folkwang, Essen. Experiments on the variability of cylinders and plates. **1977** Took part in documenta 6 in Kassel. **1982/83** Stayed at the Villa Massimo in Rome. **1983** Professor of Sculp-

ture at the Braunschweig School of Art. Many commissions for sculptures in public places.
MONOGRAPHS, CATALOGUES: Cladders, J.: H.-G. P. Skulpturen. Galerie Kunst & Architektur. Hamburg 1986 (cat.).– Mennekes, S. J. F. (ed.): H.-G. P. Skulpturen, Arbeiten auf Papier. Skulpturenmuseum Glaskasten. Marl 1990 (cat.).– Nowald, K. (ed.): H.-G. P. Skulpturen. Museum Folkwang. Essen 1975 (cat.).– Oelschlägel, P.: H.-G. P. Distanz und Nähe. Hanover 1995.– Peters, U. (ed.): H.-G. P. Bodenskulpturen. Germanisches Nationalmuseum. Nuremberg 1990 (cat.).– Schneckenburger, M.: P. Skulpturen. Palais Liechtenstein, Vienna et al. Stuttgart 1983 (cat.).– Schnell, W.: H.-G. P. Skulpturen 1967-1978. Städtisches Museum, Schloß Morsbroich. Leverkusen 1978 (cat.).– Schwarz, M. (ed.): H.-G. P. Skulpturen und Zeichnungen. Badischer Kunstverein. Karlsruhe 1974 (cat.).– Uelsberg, G.: H.-G. P. Skulpturen. Cologne 1996.– Wedewer, R.: H.-G. P. Zeichnungen und Skulpturen. Cologne 1977

PRAMPOLINI Enrico
1894 Modena – **1956** Rome
Italian painter and stage designer. **1911** Studied at the Rome Art Academy. **1912/13** Rejected by the Academy, he joined the Futurist movement. **1913** Wrote the manifesto We Want to *Bomb the Academy* and *Atmosfera struttura*. **1914** Took part in the Futurist exhibition at the Galleria Sprovieri, Rome. **1916** Met T. Tzara; took part in the Dada exhibition in Zurich. **1917** Founded *Noi* magazine. **1922** Joined the Section d'Or. Contact with the Bauhaus and De Stijl. **1923** Published his manifesto *Mechanical Art*. **1924** Took part in the Futurist Congress in Milan. **1925–1937** Long stays in Paris. Met Mondrian, Vantongerloo, and others. Worked on theatre sets. **1931** Member of Abstraction-Création. **1934** Published the *Stile futurista* magazine with Fillia. **1941** Moved to Rome for good. **1961** Posthumous retrospective at the Galleria Nazionale d'Arte Moderna, Rome. Prampolini's painting went through many changes over the years. His avant-garde style is part Futurist, part Cubist, but his compositions also display elements of Purism and Geometric Abstraction.

MONOGRAPHS, CATALOGUES: Ballo, G. (ed.): P. verso i polimaterici. Galleria Fonte d'Abisso. Modena 1989 (cat.).– Bucarelli, P. (ed.): E. P. Galleria Nazionale d'Arte Moderna. Roma 1961 (cat.).– Courthion, P.: E. P. Roma 1957.– Crispolito, E. and G. d. Marco (ed.): E. P. Galleria Civica, Modena. Florence 1991 (cat.).– Crispolito, E. et al. (ed.): P. Dal futurismo all' informale. Palazzo delle Esposizioni. Roma 1992 (cat.).– Lista, G. (ed.): E. P. Carteggio futurista. Roma 1992.– Menna, F.: E. P. Roma 1967.– Oliva, A. B. (ed.): P. 1913-1956. Galleria Fonte d'Abisso. Modena 1985 (cat.).– Oliva, A. B.: P. Opere dal 1913-1956. Bologna 1986.– Pfister, E.: E. P. Milan 1940.– Siligato, R. (ed.): P. Carteggio 1916-1956. Palazzo delle Esposizioni. Roma 1992 (cat.).– Sinisi, S.: "Varieté". P. e la scena. Torino 1974

Gangs, images taken from special magazines for truckers, surfers, motorcyclists, etc. **1986** Reproductions, redrawing and manual transfers of cartoons and puns. **1988** Took part in the Venice Biennale and in the BiNationale in Boston and Düsseldorf. **1992** Participation in documenta 9 in Kassel.
WRITINGS: R. P. Why I Go to the Movies Alone. New York 1983, Cologne 1994
MONOGRAPHS, CATALOGUES: Diserens, C. and V. Todoli (ed.): R. P. Spiritual Amerca. IVAM Centro Julio González. Valencia 1989 (cat.).– Haenlein, C. (ed.): R. P. Photographien 1977-1993. Kestner-Gesellschaft. Hanover 1994 (cat.).– Linker, K. (ed.): R. P. Le Nouveau Musée. Lyon 1983 (cat.).– Phillips, L. (ed.): R. P. Whitney Museum of American Art, New York et al. New York 1992 (cat.).– R. P. Magasin-Centre National d'Art Contemporain. Grenoble 1988 (cat.).– R. P. IVAM Centre del Carme. Valencia 1989 (cat.).– R. P. Inside World. Kent Fine Art. New York 1989.– R. P. San Francisco Museum of Modern Art et al. San Francisco 1993 (cat.)

PRIGOV Dimitri
born **1940** Moscow
Russian painter. **1967** Finished studying sculpture at the Stroganov Art Institute in Moscow. Wrote poetry, dramas, and essays after a course in visual and concrete poetry. Took part in music performances with jazz and rock musicians. **1989** First solo-exhibition at the Struve Gallery, Chicago, and at the St. Louis Gallery of Contemporary Art. **1990** DAAD scholarship to Berlin. Prigov attempts in his art to distance himself from the cultural mainstream. His critical view of stereotyped images is underlined by his deliberate use of Soviet clichés in visual and verbal combination.
MONOGRAPHS, CATALOGUES: D. P. Struve Gallery. Chicago 1989 (cat.).– D. P. Saint Louis Gallery of Contemporary Art. Saint Louis 1989 (cat.)

PRINCE Richard
born **1949** in the Panama Canal Zone
American painter and photographer. **1976** First solo-exhibition at the Ellen Sragrow Gallery in New York. **1980** Became known for his rephotographing of printed pictures like advertising photos and magazine illustrations, including the Malboro Cowboys. Solo-exhibitions at Artists Space gallery in New York and at the CEPA Gallery in Buffalo, to which he added short texts on horror films, sex and war. **1984** Created the

PUNI Ivan
(Jean Pougny)
1892 Konokkala (Finnland) – **1956** Paris
French painter of Russian-Finnish extraction, also known as Jean Pougny. **1910**-**1912** Studied art at the Académie Julian, Paris. At the end of **1912** he returned to St. Petersburg, where he had contact with Burlyuk, Malevich and Tatlin. **1914** Took part in the Salon des Indépendants, Paris. **1915** Organized the "0,10" exhibition, in which Malevich and Tatlin were also involved. Signatory of the *Suprematist Manifesto*. **1917** Participation in the "Karo Bube" exhibition. **1918** Lectured at the SWOMAS. **1919** Moved to Finland, **1920** to Berlin. **1921** Solo-exhibition at the Sturm gallery in Berlin. From **1923** he lived in Paris. Contact with Léger, Ozenfant, Severini, etc. **1924** Took part in the Salon des Tuileries. **1940** Travelled with Delaunay to the South of France, settling in Antibes. **1942** Returned to Paris. **1946** Became a French citizen. Puni was at first influenced by the Cubists but became one of the most important Suprematist artists. In later years he developed a more sensitive, figurative, atmospheric style of painting.
CATALOGUE RAISONNE: Berninger, H. and J.-A. Cartier (ed.): J. P. 1892-1956. Catalogue de l'œuvre. 2 vols. Tübingen 1972-1992
MONOGRAPHS, CATALOGUES: Cartier, J. A.: I. P. Paris 1956.– Gindertael, R. V. (ed.): P. Geneva 1957.– Marcade, J.-C. et al. (ed.): I. P. 1892-1956. Musée d'Art Moderne de la Ville de Paris. Paris 1993 (cat.).– Merkert, J. et al. (ed.): I. P. 1892-1956. Berlinische Galerie, Berlin et al. Stuttgart 1993 (cat.).– I. P. 1894-1956. Stedelijk Museum. Amsterdam 1961 (cat.).– I. P. Kunsthaus Zürich. Zurich 1975 (cat.)

PURRMANN Hans
1880 Speyer – **1966** Basel
German painter. Took lessons from his father. **1898**-**1900** Studied at the Karlsruhe School of Arts and Crafts. **1900**-**1905** Studied art at the Munich Academy under Franz von Stuck. **1906** Moved to Paris; met Matisse in Gertrude Stein's salon. **1908** Founded the Matisse School in Paris with Levy and Moll. **1916** Moved to Berlin. **1935** Became director of the Villa Romana in Florence. **1937** Works were banned as degenerate. Lived from **1943** in Montagnola, near Lugano. **1950** Was made an honorary citizen of the City of Speyer. **1960** Solo-exhibition at the Hanover Kunstverein. **1962** Solo-exhibition at the Haus der Kunst and **1976/77** at the Villa Stuck museum in Munich. Purrmann's bright, colourful painting, mostly of landscapes, is reminiscent of that of his French idol Matisse.
WRITINGS: Göpel, B. and E.: Leben und Meinungen des Malers H. P. Erzählungen, Schriften und Briefe. Wiesbaden 1961
CATALOGUE RAISONNE: Heilmann, A. (ed.): H. P. Das druckgraphische Werk. Gesamtverzeichnis. Langenargen 1981
MONOGRAPHS, CATALOGUES: Gerke, E. and H.-J. Imiela: H. P. Mainz 1966.– Hausen, E.: Der Maler H. P. Berlin 1950.– Heilmann, A. (ed.): H. P. Stilleben, Akte, Interieurs. Kunstverein Speyer et al. Heidelberg 1990 (cat.).– Hindelang, E. (ed.): H. P. zum 100. Geburtstag. Museum Langenargen. Langenargen 1980 (cat.).– Ludwig, H.-J. (ed.): H. P. Akademie der Künste der DDR. Berlin 1982 (cat.).– H. P. Landschaften. Saarland Museum, Saarbrücken et al. Saarbrücken 1996 (cat.).– Roland, B. (ed.): Der Maler H. P. Landesmuseum Mainz et al. Mainz 1987 (cat.).– Rudloff, M. (ed.): H. P. Im Licht der Farbe. Gerhard-Marx-Haus, Bremen. Heidelberg 1995 (cat.).– Schumacher, E. (ed.): H. P. Haus der Kunst. Munich 1962 (cat.).– Weber, W. (ed.): H. P. zum 100. Geburtstag. Pfalzgalerie, Kaiserslautern et al. Mainz 1982 (cat.)

PUSENKOFF Georgi
born **1953** Krasnopolie (White Russia)
Russian painter. **1968** Moved with his family to Moscow. **1976** Ended his studies at the College of Electronic Technology in

Moscow. **1983** Course of studies in graphic art at the Academy of Polygraphy in Moscow. Worked as a graphic artist for book publishers. From **1984** exhibitions in the USSR and abroad. **1987** Member of the Hermitage association and of the Artists' Union. Lives and works since **1990** in Moscow and Cologne. **1993** Solo-exhibition at the Hans Mayer gallery, Düsseldorf, and at the Tretyakov gallery in Moscow. **1995** Exhibition at the Russian State Museum in St. Petersburg.
MONOGRAPHS, CATALOGUES: G. P. Russian State Museum, St. Petersburg, and U.-Blickle-Stiftung, Kraichtal. Kraichtal 1995 (cat.)

RÄDERSCHEIDT Anton
1892 Cologne – **1970** Cologne
German painter. **1910** Began his studies at the Cologne School of Arts and Crafts, **1911**-**1914** continued at the Düsseldorf Academy. Trained as a drawing teacher. **1914**-**1917** Military service. **1917**-**1919** Trainee teacher in Cologne, then worked as a freelance artist. **1919** Co-founder and member of the Stupid group in Cologne. **1925** Worked together with Hoerle and Seiwert in the Group of Progressive Artists. Took part in the "Neue Sachlichkeit" exhibition at the Mannheim Kunsthalle. **1934/35** Moved to Berlin. **1936** Fled to France. **1937** Participation in the Salon des Surindépendants. **1938** Took part in the exhibition "Freie Deutsche Kunst" mounted by the Freie Künstlerbund (FKB) at the Maison de la Culture in Paris, a counterpart to the National Socialist propaganda exhibition of "degenerate art". **1939**-**1942** Held prisoner in Toulon and Les Milles; his Paris studio was confiscated. **1942** Fled to Switzerland. **1947** Moved to Paris. **1949** Returned to Cologne. **1952** Retrospective at the Kunstverein in Cologne. **1960** Participation in the exhibition of the German Artists' Association at the Kunsthalle in Baden-Baden. **1962** Exhibition at the Cologne Kunstverein. Räderscheidt's early painting was closely related to Magic Realism, but in later years became more abstract.
MONOGRAPHS, CATALOGUES: Arand, W. (ed.): A. R. Niederrheinischer Kunstverein und Städtisches Museum Wedel. Cologne 1988 (cat.).– Eimert, D. (ed.): A. R. Das Spätwerk. Leopold-Hoesch-Museum. Düren 1978 (cat.).– Feldenkirchen, T. (ed.): A. R. Kölnischer Kunstverein. Cologne 1967 (cat.).– Herzog, G.: A. R. Cologne 1991.– Richter, H.: A. R. Recklinghausen 1972.– Schäfke, W. and M. Euler-Schmidt (ed.): A. R. 1892-1970. Josef-Haubrich-Kunsthalle. Cologne 1993 (cat.)

RADZIWILL Franz
1895 Strohhausen – **1983** Varel-Dangast
German painter. **1909**-**1913** Apprenticeship as a bricklayer. Studied architecture at the Technical College, and did evening courses in commercial drawing and design at the

School of Arts and Crafts in Bremen. **1915 -1917** Military service. **1919** Returned from prisoner-of-war camp. **1920-1923** Lived in Berlin, where he was a member of the Free Secession and the Novembergruppe. **1923** Moved to Dangast. **1925** Travelled to Holland. First solo-exhibition in Oldenburg. **1927** Exhibition at the Paul Cassirer gallery in Berlin. **1927/28** Worked in Dix's studio in Dresden. **1929** Took part in the Neue Sachlichkeit exhibition at the Stedelijk Museum in Amsterdam. **1933** Succeeded Klee as professor at the Düsseldorf Academy. **1935** Was dismissed from his post and forbidden to work. Travelled to Africa and South America. **1937** Was among the artists labelled "degenerate" by the Third Reich. **1939-1945** Called up for military service. **1963** Was awarded the Prix de Rome and a scholarship to the Villa Massimo. Became known for his landscapes and paintings of harbours, which rekindled the mystical feeling towards nature of German Romanticism through Magic Realism.
WRITINGS: Wietek, G. (ed.): F. R. – Wilhelm Niemeyer. Dokumente einer Freundschaft. Oldenburg 1990
CATALOGUES RAISONNÉS: Firmenich, A. and R. W. Schulze (ed.): F. R. 1895-1983. Werkverzeichnis der Ölgemälde. Cologne 1995.– Presler, G. (ed.): F. R. Die Druckgraphik. Weingarten 1993
MONOGRAPHS, CATALOGUES: Adelsbach, K. (ed.): F. R. 1895-1983. Das größte Wunder ist die Wirklichkeit. Kunsthalle Emden. Cologne 1995 (cat.).– Augustiny, W.: F. R. Göttingen 1963.– Hoffmann, J. and B. Sonnenschein (ed.): F. R. Staatliche Kunsthalle Berlin et al. Berlin 1981 (cat.).– Keiser, H. W. and R. W. Schulze: F. R. Der Maler. Munich 1975.– Radziwill, K. and H. et al. (ed.): F. R. Gemälde, Aquarelle, Handzeichnungen. Kunsthalle Bremen. Bremen 1970 (cat.).– Küster, B.: F. R. Oldenburg 1981.– Maaß-Radziwill, H. H.: F. R. im Dritten Reich: der andere Widerstand. Vol. 1. Bremen 1995.– März, R.: F. R. Berlin 1975.– Radziwill, K. and H. Maaß-Radziwill (ed.): F. R. Raum und Haus. F.-R.-Haus, Varel. Munich and Lucerne 1987 (cat.).– Soiné, K. (ed.): F. R. Bilder der Seefahrt. Bremen 1992 (cat.).– Wietek, G. (ed.): F. R. Aquarelle und Zeichnungen. Landesmuseum Oldenburg 1975 (cat.).– Wietek, G.: F. R., Wilhelm Niemeyer. Dokumente einer Freundschaft. Oldenburg 1990

RAINER Arnulf
born **1929** Baden (near Vienna)
Austrian painter. Studied from **1947-1949** at the Villach School of Arts and Crafts. **1950** Left the School of Applied Arts after one day, and the Vienna Academy of Fine Arts after only three days. First drawings influenced by the Surrealists. **1951** After intensive involvement with Abstract Expressionism and Tachisme, began to paint pictures almost devoid of form or division into colour areas (*Atomisationen* and *Blind-*

zeichnungen). **1953** He developed the over-painting technique which formed the basis of his later work. **1964** Experimented with hallucinogenic drugs and was involved in studies in psychiatric clinics. Investigated his own psyche using Action and Body Art. **1969** He began to take pictures of his own face and body, which he then painted over; he used the same technique on the paintings of Old Masters as well as contemporary artists. **1972-1983** Participation in documenta 5 – 7 in Kassel. After **1977** he also painted over pictures of death masks and death portraits. **1978** Exhibited finger paintings and foot paintings at the Curtze gallery in Vienna and Düsseldorf. In the 80s he took up religious themes again; a series of crucifixions, martyrdoms, massacres and portrayals of angels. **1985** Over-painting of botanical and zoological drawings from 18th and 19th century textbooks. **1987** Overpainting of snake and plant pictures. Rainer, the inventor of overpainting, uses the formal techniques of Viennese Actionism as a form of exhibitionism and to break down the barriers between art and life.
WRITINGS: Breicha, O. (ed.): A. R. Hirndrang. Selbstkommentar und andere Texte zu Werk und Person. Salzburg 1980.– A. R.: Proportionsordnungen 1953/54. Vienna 1988
CATALOGUES RAISONNÉS: Breicha, O. (ed.): A. R. Überdeckungen. Werkkatalog sämtlicher Radierungen, Lithographien und Siebdrucke 1950-1971. Vienna 1972.– Catoir, B.: A. R. Übermalte Bücher. Munich 1989
MONOGRAPHS, CATALOGUES: Aigner, C. et al. (ed.): A. R. Abgrundtiefe. Perspektieve. Krems 1997 (cat.).– Berswordt-Wallrabe, H.-L. A. v. (ed.): A. R. Malerei auf Kreuzen. Bochum 1988.– Breicha, O.: A. R. Überdeckung. Munich 1971.– Catoir, B. and A. Saura (ed.): A. R. Campus Stellae. Santiago 1996 (cat.).– Fuchs, R. et al. (ed.): A. R. Solomon R. Guggenheim Museum, New York et al. Munich 1989 (cat.).– Güse, E.-G. (ed.): A. R. Saarland Museum, Saarbrücken et al. Stuttgart 1990 (cat.).– Haenlein, C.-A. (ed.): A. R. Retrospektive 1950-1977. Kestner-Gesellschaft. Hanover 1977 (cat.).– Hofmann, W. et al. (ed.): A. R. Museum des 20. Jahrhunderts. Vienna 1968 (cat.).– Hofmann, W. et al. (ed.): A. R. A. R. Mort et sacrifice. Centre Georges Pompidou. Paris 1984 (cat.).– Hofmann, W. and A. R.: A. R. Totenmasken. Salzburg 1985.– Honisch, D. (ed.): A. R. Nationalgalerie, Berlin et al. Berlin 1980 (cat.).– Heynen, J. (ed.): A. R. Werke der 50er bis 80er Jahre. Museen Haus Lange and Haus Ester, Krefeld et al. Krefeld 1988 (cat.).– Kussin, T. (ed.): A. R. Naturgeschichte – Fauna, Flora etc. Schloß Grafenegg. Vienna 1987 (cat.).– Mennekes, F. (ed.): A. R. Umkreisen und Durchdringen. Christusgesichter. Stuttgart 1986 (cat.).– Mennekes, F.: A. R. Weinkreuz. Frankfurt-on-Main 1990.– A. R. Stedelijk Van Abbe Museum. Eindhoven 1984 (cat.).– A. R. Centre National d'Art Con-

temporain. Grenoble 1987 (cat.).– A. R. Young Cross. The Menil Foundation. Houston 1992 (cat.).– Rodiek, T. and H. Schulz (ed.): A. R. Kunsthalle Dominikanerkirche, Osnabrück et al. Osnabrück 1993 (cat.).– Rychlik, O. (ed.): Raineriana. Aufsätze zum Werk von A. R. Vienna and Cologne 1989.– Rychlik, O. (ed.): Die Titenmaskenüberarbeitungen von A. R. Vienna 1991.– Sandner, O. (ed.): A. R. Enzyklopädie und Revolution. Bregenz 1990 (cat.).– Schmidt, H. M. (ed.): A. R. Arbeiten 1948-1975. Hessisches Landesmuseum, Darmstadt et al. Darmstadt 1975 (cat.).– Schmidt, H. M. et al. (ed.): A. R. Retrospektive 1950-1976. Städtische Galerie im Lenbachhaus, Munich et al. Bern and Munich 1977 (cat.).– Schütt, J.: A. R. Überarbeitungen. Berlin 1994.– Schwaiger, B.: A. R. Malstunde. Vienna and Hamburg 1980.– Ullrich, F. (ed.): A. R. Städtische Kunsthalle Recklinghausen. Recklinghausen 1994 (cat.).– Wedewer, R. et al. (ed.): A. R. Zeichnungen 1949-1985. Museum Morsbroich, Leverkusen et al. Munich 1988 (cat.).– Wimmer, G. (ed.): A. R. verdeckt – entdeckt. Vienna 1987 (cat.)

RAMOS Mel
born **1935** Sacramento (CA)
American painter. **1953-1958** Studied art and art history at Sacramento Junior College and at California State University under Thiebaud. **1958** Taught at Elk Grove High School and at California State University. **1961** Began to draw in comic strip style, at first imitating the the *Batman* series. **1963** Took part in the exhibition "Pop Goes the East" at the Contemporary Art Museum, Houston. **1964** First solo-exhibition at the Bianchini Gallery, New York. From **1965** began to draw single female figures; drew pin-up girls from advertising pictures and magazine ads. **1967** Solo-exhibition at the Museum of Modern Art, San Francisco. **1972** Exhibition at the Utah Museum of Fine Arts, Salt Lake City. **1974** Participation in the Pop Art exhibition at the Whitney Museum, New York. **1977** Retrospective at the Oakland Museum (CA). From **1980** taught at California State University, Hayward. Took up landscape painting and self-portraits. **1986** Awarded the Visual Artists Fellowship Grant from the National Endowment for the Arts. Ramos' poster-style Pop Art lays the marketing strategies of the advertising industry bare by quoting their images.
MONOGRAPHS, CATALOGUES: Belz, C. (ed.): M. R. A Twenty Year Survey. Rose Art Museum, Brandeis University. Waltham 1980 (cat.).– Claridge, E.: The Girls of M. R. London and Chicago 1975.– Claridge, L.: M. R. Gemälde, Zeichnungen und Projekte der Jahre 1969-1972. Darmstadt 1975.– M. R. Watercolours. Berkeley 1979.– M. R. The Artist's Studio. Louis K. Meisel Gallery. New York 1989 (cat.).– Rosenblum, R.: M. R. Pop Art Images. Cologne 1994.– Wember, P. (ed.): M. R. Museum Haus Lange. Krefeld 1975 (cat.)

RAUSCHENBERG Robert
born **1925** Port Arthur (TX)
American painter and object artist. **1947** Attended the Académie Julian in Paris. **1948/49** Studied at Black Mountain College in Beria (NC) under Albers, **1949/50** at the Art Students League in New York under Kline, Motherwell, and others. **1951** First solo-exhibition at the Betty Parsons's Gallery, New York. Period of *All-White Paintings* and *All-Black Paintings*. **1952/53** Travelled around Spain, North Africa, and Italy. Following his return to New York he put on happenings with Cage, Merce Cunningham and David Tudor and began work on *Combine Paintings* made up of the most varied materials and found objects and in which painted elements are combined with objects and fragments. Also did collages and assemblages. **1959-1977** Participation in documenta 2, 4 and 6 in Kassel, at the São Paulo Biennale and at the Biennale in Paris. **1960** Took part in the exhibition "Le Nouveau Réalisme à Paris et à New York". **1966** Along with Billy Klüver, an engineer, he founded the company Experiments in Art and Technology (E. A. T.). From **1970** he preferred working with cardboard in Minimal Art style; in the 80s he created sculptures out of found metal parts and pictures made by etching with acid on metal plates. Since **1984** he has headed the *Rauschenberg Overseas Cultural Interchange* (ROCI) project, which supports cooperation between artists around the globe. He goes on tour with dance and theatre groups, for whom he designs sets. Rauschenberg is recognised as a pioneer of American Pop Art.
WRITINGS: Rose, B. (ed.): R. An Interview. New York 1987/R. R. im Gespräch mit B. Rose. Cologne 1989
CATALOGUE RAISONNÉ: Foster, E. (ed.): R. R. Prints 1948-1970. Minneapolis Institute of Arts. Minneapolis 1970 (cat.)
MONOGRAPHS, CATALOGUES: Adriani, G. and W. N. Greiner (ed.): R. R. Zeichnungen, Gouachen, Collagen 1949-1979. Kunsthalle Tübingen. Munich 1979 (cat.).– Alloway, L. (ed.): R. R. National Collection of Fine Arts, Smithsonian Institution, Washington et al. Washington 1976 (cat.).– Alloway, L. et al.: R. R. Werke 1950-1980. Staatliche Kunsthalle Berlin et al. Berlin 1980 (cat.).– Carow, B. (ed.): R. R. Kunstverein Hannover. Hanover 1970 (cat.).– Cowart, J. et al. (ed.): ROCI – R. Overseas Culture Interchange. National Gallery of Art, Washington. Munich 1991 (cat.).– Craft, C.: R. R. Haywire. New York 1997.– Feinstein, R. (ed.): R. R. The Silkscreen Paintings 1962-1964. Whitney Museum of American Art. New York 1990 (cat.).– Feinstein, R.: Random Order: The First Fifteen Years of R. R. Diss. New York University. New York 1990.– Forge, A.: R. New York 1969.– Geldzahler, H. et al. (ed.): R. R. Paintings, Drawings and Combines 1949-1964. Whitechappel Art Gallery. London 1964 (cat.).– Hopps, W. (ed.): R. R. The Early 1950's. The Corcoran Gallery of Art, Washington et al. Houston 1991

(cat.).– Hopps, W. and S. Davidson (ed.): R. R. A Retrospective. Solomon R. Guggenheim Museum, New York et al. New York 1997.– Hulten, P.: R. R. Photographs. New York 1981.– Kotz, M. L.: R. Art and Life. New York 1990.– R. R. National Collection of Fine Arts, Smithsonian Institution. Washington 1976 (cat.).– R. R. Tate Gallery. London 1981 (cat.).– Rose, B.: R. New York 1987.– Smith, M. L.: Image and World in the Prints of R. R. 1951-1981. Diss. University of Texas. Austin 1992.– Tomkins, C.: Off the Wall. R. R. and the Art World of our Time. Garden City 1980.– Turrell, J. B. (ed.): R. Sculpture. Fort Worth Art Museum. Fort Worth 1995 (cat.).– Wissmann. R. R. Black Maket. Stuttgart 1970.– Yakush, M. (ed.): R. Overseas Culture Interchange. National Gallery of Art. Washington 1991 (cat.).– Zemter, W. R.: R. R. Untersuchungen zur Bildstruktur. Diss. Bochum 1974.– Zweite, A. (ed.): R. R. Kunstsammlung Nordrhein-Westfalen, Düsseldorf. Cologne 1994 (cat.)

RAY Man
(Emanuel Rudnitzky)
1890 Philadelphia **– 1976** Paris
American painter, photographer, and object artist. Was part of the avant-garde circles in New York, especially at Stieglitz' gallery. After meeting Duchamp and Picabia, he took part in Dada events, participating between **1916–1921** in demonstrations and exhibitions in New York and working for *391* and New York Dada magazines. In Paris, where he followed Duchamp in **1921**, he joined the group around Tristan Tzara, André Breton and Picabia. He did experimental photography and film, created collages and produced objects. **1925** He joined the Surrealist movement, became its official photographer, and took up painting again. **1927** Exhibition of photographs in New York. **1926** and **1928** Film projects. **1930–1940** Maintained contacts to artists and writers. **1940–1951** Worked in Hollywood. **1951** Returned to Paris; concentrated on painting and drawing. As one of the most productive and imaginative figures between Dada and Surrealism, Man Ray could never decide on which of his myriad talents he should concentrate: sculpture, painting, photography, film, literature, or architecture.
WRITINGS: M. R.: Selfportrait. London and Boston 1963/M. R. Selbstporträt. Eine illustrierte Autobiographie. Munich 1983.– M. R.: Objets de mon affection. Paris 1983
CATALOGUES RAISONNES: Anselmino, L. and B. Pilat (ed.): M. R. opera grafica. 2 vols. Florence 1973/M. R.'s Graphic Work. Catalogue Raisonné. San Francisco 1984.– Foresta, M. et al. (ed.): M. R. 1890-1976. Sein Gesamtwerk. Schaffhausen et al. 1989, 1994.– Hermann, B. (ed.): M. R. Objets de mon affection. Paris 1989.– Martin, J. H. (ed.): Catalogue raisonné

des sculptures et des objets. Paris 1983.– M. R. 1890-1976. Sein Gesamtwerk. Kilchberg 1994.– Sers, P. (ed.): M. R. Sculptures et objets. Catalogue raisonné. Paris 1983
MONOGRAPHS, CATALOGUES: Argan, G. C. et al. (ed.): M. R. Università. Parma 1981 (cat.).– Arigoni, C. (ed.): M. R. Cent' anni di libertà. 1890-1990. Palazzo Fortuny, Venice. Paris 1990 (cat.).– Baldwin, N.: M. R. American Artist. New York and London 1988, 1991.– Baum, T.: M. R.'s Paris. Washington 1989.– Bouhours, J.-M. and P. d. Haas (ed.): M. R. Directeur du mauvais movie. Paris 1997.– Bourgeade, P.: Bonsoir, M. R. Paris 1972.– Bramly, S.: M. R. Paris 1980.– Bussmann, G. (ed.): M. R. Frankfurter Kunstverein. Frankfurt-on-Main 1979 (cat.).– Ceuleers, J. (ed.): M. R. 1890-1976. Galerie Ronny van de Velde, Antwerp. Ghent 1995 (cat.).– Esten, J. (ed.): M. R. Bazaar Years. New York 1988/M. R. in Harper's Bazaar. Munich 1989.– Fagiolo, M. (ed.): M. R. Opere 1914-1973. Il Collezionista d'Arte Contemporanea. Roma 1973 (cat.).– Foresta, M. (ed.): Perpetual Motif. The Art of M. R. National Museum of American Art, Smithsonian Institution, Washington et al. New York 1988, 1994 (cat.).– Guadagnini, W. (ed.): M. R. L'età della luce. Galleria Civica, Modena. Bologna 1989 (cat.).– Hartshorn, W. and M. Foresta (ed.): M. R. in Fashion. International Center of Photography, New York et al. New York 1990 (cat.).– Jahn, A. et al. (ed.): M. R. Galerie der Stadt Stuttgart et al. Stuttgart 1998 (cat.).– Janus (ed.): M. R. L'immagine fotografica. Venice 1976 (cat.).– Janus (ed.): M. R. Photographien, Gemälde, Objekte. Munich 1991.– Leymarie, J. et al. (ed.): M. R. Musée National d'Art Moderne, Paris et al. Paris 1972 (cat.).– Martin, J.-H. (ed.): M. R. photographe. Centre Georges Pompidou. Paris 1982, London 1982, Munich 1982 (cat.).– Penrose, R.: M. R. London 1975.– Perl, J. (ed.): M. R. New York 1979.– Perlin, G. and D. Palazzoli (ed.): M. R. Rétrospective 1912-1976. Nice 1997 (cat.).– Sayag, A. d' (ed.): M. R. La photographie à l'envers. Grand Palais. Paris 1997 (cat.).– Schlüter, B. (ed.): M. R. Neues wie Vertrautes. Kunstmuseum Wolfsburg. Stuttgart 1994 (cat.).– Schwarz, A.: M. R. The Rigour of Imagination. London and New York 1977.– Schwarz, A.: M. R. Munich 1980.– Seta, C. d.: M. R. Udine 1989

RAYSSE Martial
born **1936** Golfe-Juan (near Nice)
French painter and object artist. **1957** First solo-exhibition at the Longchamp gallery, Nice. **1960** Signatory to the *Nouveau Réalisme* manifesto and took part in the activities of the group. **1961** Took part in the Biennale des Jeunes in Paris and in the exhibition "The Art of Assemblage" in New York. **1962** First use of neon. Soloexhibition at the Iolas Gallery, New York. **1965** Retrospective at the Stedelijk Museum, Amsterdam. **1966** Awarded the

David Bright Prize at the Venice Biennale. **1967** Stage design for the ballet *Paradis perdu* by Roland Petit. **1968** and **1977** participation in documenta 4 and 6 in Kassel. In the 70s, he worked with simple materials like tempera on cardboard and painted mythological themes in a style related to Tachisme. Later turned to film-making. **1981** Retrospective at the Pompidou Centre, Paris. **1992** Participation in documenta 9 in Kassel. Raysse stood out, especially in the 60s, with assemblages using varied materials and techniques that showed consumer society as if through a distorting mirror.
MONOGRAPHS, CATALOGUES: Hulten, P. (ed.): M. R. 1970-1980. Centre Georges Pompidou. Paris 1981 (cat.).– Jouffroy, A.: M. R. Paris 1996.– Petersen, A. (ed.): M. R. Stedelijk Museum. Amsterdam 1981 (cat.).– M. R. Národní Galerie. Prague 1969 (cat.).– M. R. Musée Picasso. Antibes 1982 (cat.).– M. R. Maître et esclave de l'imagination. Stedelijk Museum. Amsterdam 1965 (cat.).– Semin, D. and V. Dabin (ed.): M. R. Rétrospective. Galerie National du Jeu de Paume, Paris et al. Paris 1992 (cat.).– Todoroff, U. et al. (ed.): M. R. Museum Moderner Kunst Stiftung Ludwig, Vienna et al. Vienna 1993 (cat.)

REDON Odilon
(Bertrand-Jean Redon)
1840 Bordeaux **– 1916** Paris
French painter and graphic artist. Largely self-taught. Studied in Bordeaux and Paris. **1867** Etchings displayed at the Salon. Admired E. Delacroix, and later became acquainted with C. Corot, G. Courbet, and H. Fantin-Latour. **1881** First exhibition at the gallery of *La Vie moderne*. **1884** Co-founder of the Salon des Indépendants. Took part in **1886** in the VIII Impressionist exhibition. **1890** Friendship with Gauguin. **1891** Close contact to the poet Mallarmé, to the Nabis group and to Gauguin; began to work using symbols. **1899** Exhibition of Symbolist painters in his honour at the Durand-Ruel gallery. Began to do paintings and pastels again in loosely applied, strong colours. **1909–1916** Lived meditative and withdrawn in Bièvres near Paris.
WRITINGS: Levy, S. (ed.): Lettres inédites d'O. R. à Bonger, Jourdain, Vines. Paris 1987.– O. R.: Lettres d'O. R. Brussels and Paris 1923.– O. R.: A soi-même: Journal (1867-1915). Paris 1961, 1989.– O. R.: Selbstgespräch. Tagebücher und Aufzeichnungen 1867-1915. Munich 1971.– O. R.: Critiques d'Art. Bordeaux 1987.– O. R. and C. Terrasse: Conversations avec O. R. Paris 1993
CATALOGUES RAISONNES: Harisson, S. R. (ed.): The Etchings of O. R. A Catalogue Raisonné. New York 1986.– Mellerio, A. (ed.): O. R. Complete Illustrative Catalogue of Lithographs and Etchings. New York 1968.– Mellerio, A. (ed.): O. R. Peintre, dessinateur et graveur. Paris 1923.– Wildenstein, A. et al. (ed.): O. R. Cata-

logue raisonné de l'œuvre peint et dessiné. 3 vols. Paris 1992-1996
MONOGRAPHS, CATALOGUES: Bacou, R.: O. R. 2 vols. Geneva 1956.– Bacou, R. (ed.): O. R. Pastels. London and New York 1987/O. R. Pastelle. Cologne 1988.– Berger, K.: O. R. Phantasie und Farbe. Cologne 1964/O. R. Fantasy and Color. New York 1965.– Cassou, J.: O. R. Paris 1974, Munich 1974.– Christ, O.: O. R. Visionen eines Künstlerpoeten. Berlin 1994.– Coustet, R.: L'Univers d'O. R. Paris 1984.– Daulte, F. and J. Jones (ed.): O. R. Fondation de l'Hermitage. Lausanne 1992 (cat.).– Druick, D. W. (ed.): O. R. Prince of Dreams (1840-1916). The Art Institute of Chicago et al. New York and London 1994 (cat.).– Eisenman, S. F.: The Temptation of Saint R. Biography, Ideolgy and Style in the Noirs of O. R. Chicago 1992.– Gamboni, D.: La Plume et le pinceau. O. R. et la littérature. Paris 1989.– Gowing, L. (ed.): O. R. Collección Ian Woodner. Barcelona 1990 (cat.).– Hobbs, R.: O. R. London and Boston 1977.– Klockenbring, G.: O. R. Wege zum Tor der Sonne. Stuttgart 1986.– Koella, R. (ed.): O. R. Kunstmuseum Winterthur et al. Winterthur 1983 (cat.).– Martin-Méry, G. (ed.): O. R. 1840-1916. Galerie des Beaux-Arts. Bordeaux 1985 (cat.).– Mellerio, A.: O. R. Peintre, dessinateur et graveur. Paris 1923, New York 1968.– Motoé, K. and K. Takahashi (ed.): O. R. 1840-1916. The National Museum of Modern Art, Tokyo et al. Tokyo 1989 (cat.).– Piel, F. (ed.): O. R. Meisterwerke aus der Sammlung Ian Woodner. Museum Villa Stuck. Munich 1986 (cat.).– O. R. La Natura dell'invisible. Musée Cantonale d'Art, Lugano. Geneva 1996 (cat.).– Sandstrom, S.: Le Monde imaginaire d'O. R. Lund 1955.– Schatz, M.: Der Betrachter im Werk von O. R. Hamburg 1988.– Selz, J.: O. R. Paris 1971.– Vialla, J.: La Vie et l'œuvre d'O. R. Paris 1988.– Wilson, M.: Nature and Imagination. The Work of O. R. London 1978

REED David
born **1946** San Diego (CA)
American painter. **1966** Attended the Skowhegan School of Painting and Sculpture. **1966/67** Lived in New York. Studied at the New York Studio School and **1968** at Reed College in Portland. **1975** First soloexhibition at the Susan Coldwell Gallery, New York. **1977–1995** Exhibited regularly at the Max Protech Gallery, New York. **1992** Solo-exhibition at the San Francisco Art Institute and **1995** at the Württembergischer Kunstverein, Stuttgart. **1997** Participation in documenta 10 in Kassel.
MONOGRAPHS, CATALOGUES: Hentschel, M. and U. Kittelmann (ed.): D. R. Kölnischer Kunstverein et al. Stuttgart 1995.– Holler-Schuster, G. and P. Weibel (ed.): D. R. Neue Malereien für den Spiegelsaal. Graz 1996 (cat.).– D. R. San Francisco Art Institute. San Francisco 1993 (cat.).– D. R. Kölnischer Kunstverein et al. Münster 1995 (cat.)

REINHARDT Ad

1913 Buffalo – **1967** New York
American painter. **1931–1937** Studied art
history at Columbia University in New
York under Meyer Schapiro and others.
1936 Began studying painting at the
National Academy of Design and at the
American Artists School. **1937–1947** Joined
the American Abstract Artists group.
During the war, worked as an art critic for a
magazine in New York and photographed
for the Marines. Continued his art history
studies after the war at the Institute of Fine
Arts in New York and specialised in Far
Eastern art. From **1947** taught at Brooklyn
College and other American schools and
universities. **1952/53** First European trip.
1955 First exhibition of *Black Paintings*.
From **1960** painted nothing else but black
squares, all of the same size. **1965** Became
active in the peace movement, protesting
against the Vietnam War. **1967** Awarded a
Guggenheim grant. **1968** Participation in
documenta 4 in Kassel. In a logical contin-
uation of Mondrian's abstract painting style
and using a minimal palette, Reinhardt
strove to achieve a purist, self-sufficient art.
His black paintings are the product of this
endeavour.
WRITINGS: Kellein, A. (ed.): A. R.
Schriften und Gespräche. Munich 1984.–
Rose, B. (ed.): Art as Art. The Selected
Writings of A. R. New York 1975
MONOGRAPHS, CATALOGUES: Bois,
Y.-A. (ed.): A. R. Los Angeles Museum of
Contemporary Art et al. New York 1991
(cat.).– Heere, H.: A. R. und die Tradition
der Moderne. Frankfurt-on-Main 1986.–
Hess, R. (ed.): The Art Comics and Satire
of A. R. Städtische Kunsthalle Düsseldorf.
Düsseldorf 1975 (cat.).– Inboden, G. and A.
Kellein (ed.): A. R. Staatsgalerie Stuttgart.
Stuttgart 1985 (cat.) / A. R. New York 1987.–
Jenderko, I. and M. Imdahl (ed.): Epitaphe
für A. R. Staatliche Kunsthalle Baden-
Baden. Baden-Baden 1977 (cat.).– Kosuth,
J. and C. Kozlov: A. R. Education into
Darkness. New York 1966.– Lippard, L.:
A. R. New York 1981, Stuttgart 1984.–
McConathy, D. (ed.): A. R. Städtische
Kunsthalle Düsseldorf et al. Düsseldorf
1972 (cat.).– Rowell, M. (ed.): A. R. and
Color. Solomon R. Guggenheim Museum.
New York 1980 (cat.).– Schjeldahl, P. (ed.):
A. R. Art Comics and Satires. Truman
Gallery. New York 1976 (cat.)

RENGER-PATZSCH Albert

1897 Würzburg – **1966** Wamel
German photographer. **1916–1918** Military
service, then studied chemistry at Dresden
Technical College. **1922–1925** Press photographer for the *Chicago Tribune*. Worked
together with E. Fuhrmann on the book
series *The World of Plants*. **1924/25** Plant
studies and essays for the *Deutschen
Kamera Almanach*. **1925** Worked as a freelance photographer. First exhibitions.
Member of the Deutsche Werkbund. **1928**
Had his own studio in the Museum Folkwang in Essen. Book of photographs, *Die*
Welt ist schön (The World is Beautiful),
published by K. Wolff. Worked as an
industrial photographer and for advertising.
After the destruction of his archives in the
war, he moved to Wamel in **1944**. Renger-
Patzsch was one of the most outspoken
proponents of Neue Photographie, a movement which insisted that photographs
should speak for themselves.
MONOGRAPHS, CATALOGUES: Heise,
C. G.: A. R.-P. der Photograph. Berlin
1942.– Honnef, K. and G. Kierblewsky
(ed.): Industrielandschaften, Industriearchi-
tektur, Industrieprodukt. Fotografien 1925-
1960 von A. R.-P. Rheinisches Landesmu-
seum, Bonn. Cologne 1977 (cat.).– Kempe,
F. (ed.): A. R.-P. Der Fotograf der Dinge.
Ruhrland- und Heimatmuseum. Essen
1967 (cat.).– Kempe, F. and C. G. Heise
(ed.): A. R.-P. 100 Photos. Centre Georges
Pompidou, Paris et al. Paris 1979 (cat.).–
Kuspit, D. (ed.): A. R.-P. Joy Before the
Object. The J. Paul Getty Museum,
Malibu. New York 1993 (cat.).– Pfingsten,
C.: Aspekte zum fotografischen Werk A.
R.-P. Witterschlick/Bonn 1992.– A. R.-P.
Museum Ludwig. Cologne 1993 (cat.).– A.
R.-P. Städtisches Kunstmuseum Bonn.
Stuttgart 1996 (cat.).– A. R.-P. Meisterw-
erke. Haus der Kunst. Munich 1998 (cat.)

RENOIR Pierre-Auguste

1841 Limoges – **1919** Cagnes-sur-Mer
(near Nice)
French painter. **1854–1858** Apprenticeship
as a porcelain painter in Paris. **1860–1864**
Studied at the Ecole des Beaux-Arts and
entered the studio of Gleyre with Monet,
Sisley and Bazille. **1863** Painted *en plein air*
with these friends in the Barbizon district;
met Pissarro and Cézanne. **1864/65** Exhibited at the Salon. In **1866** and **1867** his light
and natural portraits were rejected by the
Salon. **1868–1870** Shared a studio with
Bazille; met Manet. **1869** Together with
Monet in Bougival on the Seine, laid the
foundations of the Impressionist style. **1872**
Rejected again by the Salon, he insisted on
the setting-up of a Salon des Refusés.
Durand-Ruel exhibited one of his paintings
for the first time in London. **1874, 1876** and
1877 Participation in Impressionist exhibitions. **1879** Solo-exhibition at the gallery at
Charpentier's magazine *La Vie moderne*.
1882 Visited Cézanne in L'Estaque.

Durand-Ruel showed his paintings at the
7th Impressionist Exhibition and in
London. **1889** Refused to take part in the
Paris World Fair. **1890** Married Aline.
Returned to using bright colours and loose
brushstrokes and, over the following years,
painted mostly nudes and landscapes. **1892**
First purchase of one of his paintings by the
French nation. **1900** Took part in the cen-
tennial show of French art at the Paris
World Fair. **1902** His health began to fail
and his hands became crippled by rheuma-
tism. **1904** First participation in the Paris
Autumn Salon. **1910** Retrospective at the
9th Venice Biennale. **1913** Began to
produce sculpture, with the help of R.
Guinos. **1919** Was made Commander of the
Legion of Honour and one of his paintings
was hung in the Louvre. Beside Monet one
of the greatest Impressionists.
CATALOGUES RAISONNES: Dauberville,
G.-P. and M. (ed.): Catalogue raisonné de
l'œuvre de P.-A. R. (in preparation).–
Daulte, F. (ed.): A. R. Catalogue raisonné
de l'œuvre peint. Vol. 1: Figures 1860-1890.
Vol. 2: Figures 1891-1905. 2 vols. Lausanne
and Paris 1971-1996.– Fezzi, E. (ed.): Das
gemalte Gesamtwerk von R. aus der
impressionistischen Periode 1869-1883.
Lucerne 1973 / Tout l'œuvre peint de R.
Periode impressionniste 1869-1883. Paris
1985.– Roger-Marx, C.: Les Lithographies
de R. Monte Carlo 1951.– Stella, J. G.
(ed.): The Graphic Work of R. Catalogue
Raisonné. Bradford and London (n. d.).–
Tancock: The Sculpture of R. Philadelphia
1976.– Vollard, A.: P.-A. R. Tableaux,
pastels et dessins. Paris 1918, 1954 / R.'s
Paintings, Pastels and Drawings. Tableaux,
pastels et dessins de P.-A. R. San Francisco
1989
MONOGRAPHS, CATALOGUES: Adriani,
G. (ed.): R. Gemälde 1860-1917. Kunsthalle
Tübingen. Cologne 1996 (cat.).– André, A.:
L'Atelier de R. 2 vols. Paris 1931, San Fran-
cisco 1989.– Bacou, R.: P. R. 2 vols. Geneva
1956.– Bailes, C. B. et al. (ed.): R.'s Por-
traits. The Art Institute of Chicago.
Chivago 1997 (cat.).– Bailey, C. et al. (ed.):
R. Portraits. National Gallery of Canada,
Ottawa. New Haven (CT) 1997 (cat.).–
Barnes, A. C. and V. d. Mazia: The Art of
R. Merion (PA) 1986.– Baudot, J.: R.: Ses
amis, ses modèles. Paris 1949.– Daulte, F.:
P.-A. R. Basel 1958.– Daulte, F.: P.-A. R.
Watercolours, Pastels and Drawings in
Colour. London 1959.– Daulte, F.: A. R.
Paris 1974.– Distel, A. et al. (ed.): R. Grand
Palais, Paris et al. Paris 1985 (cat.) / Hayward
Gallery, London et al. London and New
York 1985 (cat.).– Fezzi, E.: R. Paris 1972.–
Fosca, F.: R. London and Paris 1961.–
Gaunt, W.: R. Oxford 1982.– Gowing, L.:
R. Paintings. London 1947.– Haesaerts, P.:
R. sculpteur. Brussels 1947 / R. Sculptor.
New York 1947.– Hoog, M. and N.
Wadley: R. Un peintre, une vie, une œuvre.
Paris 1989.– Keller, H.: A. R. Munich
1987.– Monneret, S.: R. Cologne 1990.–
Perruchot, H.: La Vie de R. Paris 1964.–
Renoir, J.: R. My Father. Boston 1958 /
Mein Vater A. R. Munich 1962.– Rewald J.
(ed.): R. Drawings. New York 1946.–
Rouart, D.: R. Geneva 1954, London 1985.–
White, B. E.: R. His Life, Art and Letters.
New York 1984

REUSCH Erich

born **1925** Wittenberg (Elbe)
German sculptor and architect. **1947–1953**
Studied at the School of Fine Arts in Berlin
under R. Scheibe and Uhlmann. From **1953**
worked as an architect in Düsseldorf.
Designed housing estates in Düsseldorf,
Hanover, and Frankfurt am Main. From
1964 worked as a freelance artist. **1966**
Solo-exhibition at the Von der Heydt-

Museum, Wuppertal. **1971** Project for the
Ruhr University in Bochum. **1975–1988**
Professorship at the Düsseldorf Academy.
1976 Solo-exhibition at the Düsseldorf
Kunsthalle. **1977** Took part in documenta 6
in Kassel. **1986/87** Exhibition at the City
Museum in Lüdenscheid. **1998** Retrospective at the Kunstmuseum, Bonn. From the
60s, he designed kinetic objects using new
materials and techniques.
MONOGRAPHS, CATALOGUES:
Adolphs, V. et al. (ed.): E. R. Arbeiten 1954-
1998. Kunstmuseum Bonn. Bonn 1998
(cat.).– Jensen, J. C. (ed.): E. R. Elektrosta-
tische Objekte. Kunsthalle zu Kiel. Kiel
1973 (cat.).– Kerber, B. (ed.): Hommage à
Mc Cready. E. R. Museum am Ostwall.
Dortmund 1972 (cat.).– Schneckenburger,
M. (H.): E. R. Kunstverein Arnsberg. Arnsberg 1993 (cat.).– Weyergraf, C. and M.
Imdahl: E. R. Kunsthalle Düsseldorf.
Düsseldorf 1976 (cat.).– Weyergraf, C.
(ed.): E. R. Karl Ernst Osthaus-Museum.
Hagen 1978 (cat.).– Wissmann, J. (ed.): E.
R. Städtische Galerie Lüdenscheid. Lüden-
scheid 1986 (cat.)

RHEIMS Bettina

born **1952** Paris
French photographer. Began to photograph
while still at school. **1972/73** Worked as a
fashion model in New York. **1975–1978**
Ran a gallery of modern painting. **1978**
Publication of her animal photographs in
book form. From **1982** worked as a fashion
photographer for J.-C. de Castelbajac.
From **1984** numerous portraits of celebrities
and important public figures. **1987** First
exhibition devoted solely to her works put
on by Espace Photographique de Paris.
MONOGRAPHS, CATALOGUES: Mon-
teroso, J.-L.: B. R. Paris 1987.– B. R. and B.
Lamarche-Vadel: Les Espionnes. Munich
1992

RIBOUD Marc

born **1923** Lyons
French photographer. Self-taught. **1943–
1945** Was active in the French Resistance
and the Free French Army. **1945–1948**
Studied engineering at the Ecole Centrale
in Lyons. **1948–1952** Industrial engineer in
Lyons. From **1952** worked for the Magnum
agency and as a freelance photographer and

photojournalist in Paris. **1957–1971** Several trips to China. **1958–1975** Vice-president of Magnum Photos in Paris, **1975/76** president in Paris and New York. Became known for his pictures of China and North Vietnam, in which he emphasised the contrast between the single figure and the group.
MONOGRAPHS, CATALOGUES: Daniel, J. (ed.): M. R. in China. New York 1997.– M. R. Photos choisies 1953-1985. Musée d'Art Moderne de la Ville. Paris 1985 (cat.).– M. R. Centre National de la Photographie. Paris 1993 (cat.)

RICHIER Germaine
1904 Arles – **1959** Montpellier
French sculptress. Started her studies at the Ecole des Beaux-Arts, Montpellier. **1925** Moved to Paris. **1925–1929** Student and assistant in E. Bourdelle's studio. **1934** Blumenthal prize. **1937** Awarded the Diplom d'Honneur de Sculpture at the Paris World Fair. **1939–1945** Lived in Switzerland. From **1940** came under the influence of Giacometti. **1946** Returned to Paris. **1948–1954** Regular participation at the Venice Biennale. **1950** Her Christ sculpture for the church in Assy caused a controversy. **1951** Sculpture prize at the São Paulo Biennale. From **1951** she worked together with the painters Vieira da Silva and Hartung. **1956** Retrospective at the Musée National d'Art Moderne, Paris. **1959** and **1964** participation in documenta 2 and 3 in Kassel. Richier's figures, whose limbs are often tied together with wire, are bizarre creatures somewhere between human and animal, and with references to apocalyptic symbolism and Surrealist fantasy.
CATALOGUE RAISONNE: Guiter, F. (ed.): G. R. Catalogue raisonné (in preparation)
MONOGRAPHS, CATALOGUES: Cassou, J.: G. R. Cologne and Berlin 1961.– Cassou, J. et al. (ed.): G. R. Sculpteur 1904-1959. Paris 1966.– Crispolti, E.: G. R. Milan 1968.– Lammert, A. and J. Merkert (ed.): G. R. Akademie der Künste. Berlin 1997 (cat.).– Paulhan, J.: G. R. Paris 1957.– Ponge, F.: G. R. Montrouge 1948.– Prat, J.-L. (ed.): G. R. Rétrospective. Fondation Maeght. Saint-Paul 1996 (cat.).– G. R. Musée National d'Art Moderne. Paris 1955 (cat.).– G. R. Kunsthalle Bern. Bern 1958 (cat.).– G. R. 1904-1959. Kunsthaus Zürich. Zurich 1963 (cat.).– G. R. Galerie Creuzevault. Paris 1966 (cat.).– G. R. 1904-1959. Retrospective. Gallery Gimpel Fis. London 1973 (cat.)

RICHTER Gerhard
born **1932** Dresden
German painter. First worked as a stage designer and poster artist in Zittau. **1952–1955** Studied at the Dresden Academy and, after moving to West Germany in **1961**, at the Düsseldorf Academy. **1963** Satirical introduction of *Capitalist Realism into Art* together with K. Fischer-Lueg and Polke.

1964 Painted his first pictures based on magazine photographs and snapshots. **1967** Awarded the *Junger Westen* art prize in Recklinghausen; guest-professorship at the Hamburg School of Fine Arts. **1968** Began a series of large-format abstract paintings with great intensity of colour. **1969** Worked as an art teacher. **1971** Professorship at the Düsseldorf Academy. **1972** Took part in the Venice Biennale with *48 Portraits*. **1972–1997** Participation in documenta 5 – 10 in Kassel. **1974** Exhibition of the *Graue Bilder* (Grey Pictures) at the Municipal Museum in Mönchengladbach. **1978** Guest-professor at Nova Scotia College of Art and Design in Halifax. **1981** Arnold Bode Prize, **1985** Kokoschka Prize. **1991** Important retrospective at the Tate Gallery, London, and **1993** at the Musée d'Art Moderne de la Ville de Paris. Richter painted out-of-focus paraphrases of famous paintings and historical portrait photos in monochrome grey tones, enlarging them considerably. The originals, either his own pictures or ones from other sources, were then collected in an *Atlas*. In addition to these works, which lie stylistically between photorealism and Pop Art, he did colourful landscapes and cloud formations, candlelit still lifes, crudely painted aerial views of cities, and paintings based on RAL-colour charts.
WRITINGS: G. R.: Text. Frankfurt-on-Main 1993.– Obrist, H.-U. (ed.): G. R. Text. Schriften and Interviews. Frankfurt-on-Main and Leipzig 1993
CATALOGUES RAISONNES: Buchloh, B. H. D. (ed.): G. R. Catalogue Raisonné 1965-1993. Stuttgart 1993.– Harten, J. and D. Elger (ed.): G. R. Gemälde 1962-1985. Städtische Kunsthalle Düsseldorf. Cologne 1986 (cat.).– G. R. Editionen 1965-1993. Kunsthalle Bremen. Munich 1993 (cat.).
MONOGRAPHS, CATALOGUES: Buchloh, B. H. D. (ed.): G. R. Centre Georges Pompidou. Paris 1977 (cat.).– Buchloh, B. H. D. and R. Fuchs (ed.): G. R. Stedelijk Van Abbe Museum, Eindhoven et al. Eindhoven 1978 (cat.).– Buchloh, B. H. D. et al. (ed.): G. R. Art Gallery of Ontario, Toronto et al. Toronto 1988 (cat.).– Butin, D.: Zu R.'s Oktober-Bildern. Cologne 1991.– Butin, D. (ed.): G. R. Editionen 1965-1993. Kunsthalle Bremen. Munich 1993 (cat.).– Ehrenfried, S.: Ohne Eigenschaften. Das Portrait bei G. R. Vienna 1997.– Friedel, H. and U. Wilmes (ed.): G. R. Atlas der Fotos, Collagen und Skizzen. Cologne 1997.– Honnef, K.: G. R. Recklinghausen 1976.– Jahn, F. (ed.): G. R. Atlas. Städtische Galerie im Lenbachhaus, Munich et al. Munich 1989 (cat.).– Loers, V. (ed.): G. R. Shapes and Positions. Kunsthalle Ritter, Klagenfurt et al. Klagenfurt 1992 (cat.).– Loock, U. (ed.): G. R. Äquarelle. Staatsgalerie Stuttgart. Stuttgart 1985 (cat.).– Loock, U. and D. Zacharopoulos: G. R. Munich 1985.– Nasgaard, R. (ed.): G. R. Paintings. Museum of Contemporary Art, Chicago et al. London 1988 (cat.).– Neff, T. A. et al. (ed.): G. R.

Art Gallery of Ontario, Toronto. London 1988 (cat.).– Obrist, H.-U. (ed.): G. H. 100 Bilder. Stuttgart 1996.– Petzet, M. and A. Zweite (ed.): G. R. Städtische Galerie im Lenbachhaus. Munich 1973 (cat.).– Rainbird, S. and J. Severne (ed.): G. R. Tate Gallery. London 1991 (cat.).– G. R. Kunst- und Ausstellungshalle der Bundesrepublik Deutschland, Bonn. Stuttgart 1993, 1996 (cat.)./ G. R. Musée d'Art Moderne de la Ville de Paris et al. Stuttgart 1993 (cat.).– Salzmann, S. (ed.): G. R. Editionen 1965-1993. Kunsthalle Bremen. Bremen 1993 (cat.).– Thomas-Netik, A.: G. R. Mögliche Aspekte eines postmodernen Bewusstseins. Essen 1986.– Tilroe, A. and B. H. D. Buchloh (ed.): G. R. Museum Boymans-van-Beuningen. Rotterdam 1989 (cat.)

RICHTER Hans
1888 Berlin – **1976** Locarno
German artist. **1906–1909** Studied architecture. Attended the Berlin Academy and the Weimar School of Art. **1912/13** Contact with the Sturm group in Berlin. **1916** Member of the Dada movement in Zurich. **1917** First abstract works. **1918** Took part in the Dada exhibition "Die neue Kunst" in Zurich. **1921** Contributed to *De Stijl* magazine. **1922** Was one of the organisers of the Dada Contructivists Congress in Weimar. **1923–1926** Along with Mies van der Rohe and W. Graeff, published the magazine *G*. **1931** Fled from the Nazis to Russia, then to France, Holland, and Switzerland. **1936** Took part in the exhibition "Cubism and Abstract Art" in New York. **1941** Moved to the USA; was director of the Film Institute at City College in New York. **1944–1947** Worked on the film *Dreams that Money Can Buy*. **1952** Solo-exhibition at the Stedelijk Museum, Amsterdam. **1954–1958** Made films such as *8x8* and *Dadascope*. From **1960** took up painting again and made collages. Richter attempted very early on to use film in art. With his abstract film experiments, he was the most important early practitioner of the art of film-making.
WRITINGS: Gray, C. (ed.): H. R. by H. R. London 1971.– H. R.: Dada Profile. Zurich 1961.– H. R.: Dada. Kunst und Antikunst. Cologne 1964.– H. R.: Dada. Art and Anti-Art. London and New York 1965.– H. R.: H. R. London 1971.– H. R.: Begegnungen von Dada bis heute. Cologne 1973.– H. R.: Der Kampf um den Film. Munich 1976
MONOGRAPHS, CATALOGUES: Fifield, C.: True Artist and True Friend. A Biography of H. R. New York 1993.– Hoffman, J. (ed.): H. R. Malerei und Film. Deutsches Filmmuseum. Frankfurt-on-Main 1989 (cat.).– Hoßmann, G.: H. R. 1888-1976. Das bildnerische Werk. Diss. Cologne 1985.– Read, H.: H. R. Neuchâtel 1965.– Read, H. (ed.): H. R. Painter and Film-maker. Goethe Institut. London 1978 (cat.).– Volkmann, B. and R.-F. Raddatz (ed.): H. R. 1888-1976. Dadaist, Filmpionier, Maler, Theoretiker. Akademie der Künste, Berlin et al. Berlin 1982 (cat.)

RICKEY George
born **1907** South Bend (IN)
American sculptor. **1926–1929** Studied in Oxford, **1929/30** at the Academy Lhote in Paris. **1945** First mobile. From **1949** kinetic glass sculptures; later mobiles in bare steel. **1962** Solo-exhibition at the Düsseldorf Kunstverein. **1964–1977** Participation in documenta 3, 4 and 6 in Kassel. **1966** Exhibition at the Corcoran Gallery of Art, Washington. **1967** Published *Constructivism, Origins and Evolution*. **1971** Solo-exhibition at the Museum of Art, San Francisco. Exhibitions: **1973** at the Kestner Society, Hanover, **1976** at the Kunsthalle in Bielefeld and **1992** at the Berlinische Galerie. Rickey's kinetic sculptures and steel mobiles are mostly Minimalist in style, being reduced to a few right-angled, reflecting elements.
WRITINGS: G. R.: Constructivism, Origins and Evolution. New York 1967
CATALOGUE RAISONNE: Eggeling, U. (ed.): G. R. Kinetische Skulpturen. Werkeverzeichnis und Bibliographie. Galerie Utermann. Dortmund 1990 (cat.)
MONOGRAPHS, CATALOGUES: Buchholz, A. and K. Gallwitz (ed.): G. R. Kinetische Skulpturen. Städtische Galerie im Städelschen Kunstinstitut. Frankfurt-on-Main 1977 (cat.).– Merkert, J. (ed.): G. R. in Berlin. 1967-1992. Berlinische Galerie. Berlin 1992 (cat.).– G. R. Retrospective Exhibition. UCLA Art Council. Los Angeles 1971 (cat.).– G. R. Kestner-Gesellschaft. Hanover 1973 (cat.).– G. R. Artcurial. Paris 1990 (cat.).– Riedl, P. A.: G. R. Kinetische Objekte. Stuttgart 1970.– Rosenthal, M.: G. R. New York 1977.– Selz, P. (ed.): G. R. Sixteen Years of Kinetic Sculpture. Corcoran Gallery of Art. Washington 1966 (cat.).– Tafel, V. (ed.): G. R. Skulpturen. Galerie Pels-Leusden, Villa Griesebach und Skulpturengarten. Berlin 1987 (cat.).– Weisner, U. (ed.): G. R. Kinetische Objekte. Kunsthalle Bielefeld. Bielefeld 1976 (cat.).– Zielske, H. (ed.): G. R. Sieben kinetische Skulpturen. Galerie Utermann. Dortmund 1994 (cat.)

RILEY Bridget
born **1931** London
English painter. **1949–1952** Studied at Goldsmith's College of Art and **1952–1955** at the Royal College of Art, London. **1959–**

1961 Taught at Hornsey College of Art. Around **1960** explored Seurat's pointillism. After **1961** taught at Croydon Art College. **1962** First solo-exhibition at Gallery One, London. **1965** Participation in the exhibition "Responsive Eye" at the Museum of Modern Art, New York. **1968** and **1977** Awarded first prize for painting at the Venice Biennale and participated in documenta 4 in Kassel. **1971** Retrospective at the Düsseldorf Kunsthalle and **1978** at the Albright-Knox Art Gallery, Buffalo. **1983** Design sketches for the Royal Liverpool Hospital and *Colour Movements* for Ballet Rambert, Edinburgh. **1985** Retrospective at the Goldsmith's College Gallery, London. Influenced by Vasarely, Riley's pictures explore the optically irritating effects of colour patterns which evoke the illusion of movement on the picture surface.
MONOGRAPHS, CATALOGUES: Carow, B. (ed.): B. R. Kunstverein Hanover et al. Hanover et al. 1970 (cat.).– Kudielka, R. (ed.): B. R. Works 1959-1978. The National Museum of Modern Art. Tokyo 1980 (cat.).– Kudielka, R. (ed.): B. R. Gemälde 1982-1992. Kunsthalle Nürnberg et al. Nuremberg 1992 (cat.).– B. R. Paintings and Drawings 1951-1971. Hayward Gallery. London 1971 (cat.).– B. R. The Arts Council of Great Britain. London 1973 (cat.).– B. R. Works 1959-1978. Albright-Knox Art Gallery. Buffalo 1978 (cat.).– B. R. The Artist's Eye. National Gallery. London 1989 (cat.).– B. R. Recent Works. Spacex Gallery. Exeter 1993 (cat.).– Sausmarez, M. d.: B. R. London 1970

RINKE Klaus
born **1939** Wattenscheid
German artist. **1954–1957** Apprenticeship as poster painter in Gelsenkirchen. **1957–1960** Studied painting at the Folkwangschule, Essen. **1965–1968** Polyester figures. From **1968** worked with water. **1968** Solo-exhibition at the Kunsthalle Bern. From **1969** body events, which he called *Primärdemonstrationen*. **1972** Participation in documenta 5 in Kassel and **1973** at the São Paulo Biennale. From **1974** professorship at the Düsseldorf Academy. **1977** Participation in documenta 6 in Kassel. **1978–1980** Lived in Australia. **1981** Retrospective of drawings at the Stuttgart Staatsgalerie and **1992** of his complete works at the Düsseldorf Kunsthalle. Rinke gave up painting early in order to dedicate himself to more natural modes of expression, such as water sculptures.
CATALOGUE RAISONNE: Schmidt, H.-W. (ed.): K. R. retro aktiv. 1954-1991. Werkverzeichnis der Malerei, Skulptur, Primärdemonstrationen, Fotografie und Zeichnungen ab 1980. Städtische Kunsthalle Düsseldorf 1992 (cat.).
MONOGRAPHS, CATALOGUES: Adriani, G. (ed.): K. R. Zeit/Time, Raum/Space, Körper/Body, Handlungen/Transformationen. Kunsthalle Tübingen. Cologne 1972 (cat.).– Gauss, U. and A. Rave (ed.): R. – Hand – Zeichner. Die autonomen Werke

---

von 1957-1980. Staatsgalerie Stuttgart et al. Stuttgart 1981 (cat.).– Hofmann, W. and H. R. Leppien (ed.): K. R. Meine Plastik ist Zeichnung. Hamburger Kunsthalle. Hamburg 1978 (cat.).– Leppien, H. R. (ed.): K. R. Meine Plastik ist Zeichnung. Hamburger Kunsthalle. Hamburg 1978 (cat.).– K. R. Musée d'Art Moderne de la Ville de Paris. Paris 1976 (cat.).– K. R. Palais du Tau. Rheims 1986 (cat.)

RIOPELLE Jean-Paul
born **1923** Montreal
Canadian painter. **1940–1942** Studied mathematics at the Polytechnic, Montreal. Inspired to take up painting by André Breton's essay *Surrealism and Painting*. **1946** Participation at the International Surrealist exhibitions in New York and Paris. European travels and acquaintanceship with Breton. **1947** Moved to Paris; contact with P. Waldberg, Soulages, Mathieu, Wols and others. **1949** Solo-exhibition at the Nina Dausset gallery, Paris. **1951** and **1955** participation at the São Paulo Biennale and, **1954**, at the Venice Biennale. **1959** and **1964** participation in documenta 2 and 3 in Kassel. **1962** Art prize awarded by UNESCO in Paris. **1972** Solo-exhibition at the Musée d'Art Moderne de la Ville de Paris. **1981** Retrospective at the Musée National d'Art Moderne, Paris. Riopelle's main influences were P.-E. Borduas and the Surrealists. The main body of his work can be placed between Abstract Expressionism and the Ecole de Paris.
CATALOGUE RAISONNE: Riopelle, Y. (ed.): J.-P. R. Catalogue raisonné (in preparation)
MONOGRAPHS, CATALOGUES: Billy, H. d.: R. Montreal 1996.– Bordier, R. et al. (ed.): R. Œuvres 1966-1977. Paris 1991 (cat.).– Erouart, G.: Entretiens avec J.-P. R. Montreal 1993.– Gagnon, D.: R. grandeur nature. Saint-Laurent 1988.– Prat, J.-L. (ed.): J.-P. R. "D'hier et d'aujourd'hui". Fondation Maeght. Saint-Paul 1990 (cat.).– Prat, J.-P. (ed.): J.-P. R. Museum of Fine Arts. Montreal 1991 (cat.).– J.-P. R. National Gallery of Canada. Ottawa 1962 (cat.).– R.-P. R. Autour d'une œuvre. Musée des Beaux-Arts de Rennes. Rennes 1988 (cat.).– Schneider, P.: R. Signes mêlés. Paris 1972.– Schneider, P. (ed.): J.-P. R. Musée d'Art et d'Industrie de Saint-Etienne. Saint-Etienne 1980 (cat.).– Schneider, P. (ed.): J.-P. R. Peinture 1946-1977. Centre Georges Pompidou, Paris et al. Paris 1981 (cat.).– Vigneault, G. et al. (ed.): J.-P. R. Montreal Museum of Fine Arts. Montreal 1991 (cat.)

RIST Pipilotti
born **1962** Rheintal (Switzerland)
Swiss video and computer artist. Studied commercial art, graphic illustration, and photography at the School of Applied Arts in Vienna and attended the class on audiovisual design at the Design School in Basel. Worked for Dig it, the Laboratory for

---

Image and Sound in Zurich, and was a member of the music ensemble Les Reines Prochaines. She works mostly with video installations, because, as she says, "everything fits in there, like in a compact handbag". Her tapes are often played at festivals and in museums, as well as being broadcast on television. **1988** Won the prize at the Feminale Cologne for her video *Japsen* (Gasping). **1989** Received and award from VIPER in Lucerne for her video installation *Die Tempodrosslerin saust* (The Speed Limiter is Racing). **1994** Awarded the video art prize of the Swiss Banking Federation. **1997** Received the Premio 2000 at the Venice Biennale.
CATALOGUE RAISONNE: P. R. Remake of the Weekend. Hamburger Bahnhof, Berlin et al. Cologne 1998 (cat.)
MONOGRAPHS, CATALOGUES: P. R. I Am Not the Girl Who Misses Much. Cologne 1994

RIVERA Diego
1886 Guanajuato – **1957** Mexico City
Mexican painter. **1907** Grant to travel to Europe and study in Madrid and Paris. Inspired by the works of Cézanne and Picasso, began to paint in a Cubist style. After a stay of several months in Italy, during which he studied Renaissance frescoes, he returned to Mexico in **1921**, where he received commissions for large murals. The historical cycle that he produced for the Ministry of Education in Mexico City from **1923–1928** already bears the hallmarks of his personal style: simply-told monumental compositions depicting the lives and social conflicts of the Mexican people. **1927/28** Travelled to the Soviet Union. **1929–1935** Decorated the interior of the Mexican National Palace with a history of his country from the Indios and the Aztecs to modern times. **1933** A mural for the Rockefeller Center in New York, featuring a portrait of Lenin, caused a scandal. From **1951** decoration of exteriors. **1952** Mosaic for the Olympic Stadium in Mexico City. Rivera, who was married to the artist F. Kahlo, is one of the Big Three (along with Orozco and Siqueiros) of the Mexican mural movement.
WRITINGS: D. R. and G. March: My Art, My Life. New York 1960, 1990
CATALOGUES RAISONNES: Favela, R.

(ed.): Catalogue Raisonné of Works of D. R. (in preparation).– D. R. Catálogo general de obra de caballete. Mexico City 1989
MONOGRAPHS, CATALOGUES: Azuela, A.: D. R. en Detroit. Mexico City 1985.– Burrus, C. (ed.): D. R. & Frida Kahlo. Fondation Pierre Gianadda. Martigny 1990 (cat.).– Craven: D. R. As Epic Modernist. Thorndike 1997.– Downs, L. and E. Sharp (ed.): D. R. A Retrospective. Detroit Institute of Arts et al. New York 1986 (cat.).– Downs, L. and E. Sharp (ed.): D. R. Retrospectiva. Museo Nacional Centro de Arte Reina Sofía, Madrid et al. Madrid 1992 (cat.).– Eder, R. et al. (ed.): D. R. Exposición nacional de homenaje. Palacio de Bellas Artes. Mexico City 1977 (cat.).– Favela, R. (ed.): D. R. The Cubist Years. Phoenix Art Museum. Phoenix 1984 (cat.).– Gonzáles, D.: D. R. His Art, His Life. Springfield 1996.– Holland, G.: D. R. Chatham 1997.– Larrera, I. H. d. (ed.): D. R. Paradise Lost at Rockefeller Center. Mexico City 1987.– Larrera, I. H. d. (ed.): D. R.'s Murals at the Rockefeller Center. Mexico City 1990.– López Rangel, R.: D. R. y la arquitectura mexicana. Mexico City 1986.– Marín, G. R.: Encuentros con D. R. México 1993.– Münzberg, O. (ed.): D. R. Retrospektive. Detroit Institute of Arts, Detroit et al. Berlin 1987 (cat.).– Newman Helms, C. (ed.): D. R. A Retrospective. Detroit Institute of Arts, Detroit et al. New York 1986 (cat.).– O'Gorman, J.: La técnica de D. R. en la pintura mural. Mexico City 1954.– Paine, F. E.: D. R. North Stratford 1979.– Reyero, M.: D. R. Mexico City 1983.– Rosci, M.: Die Fresken von D. R. Herrsching 1989.– Secker, H. F.: D. R. Dresden 1957.– Tibbs, T. (ed.): J. de R. Retrospective Exhibition 1930-1971. La Jolla Museum of Contemporary Art. La Jolla 1972 (cat.).– Tibol, R. (ed.): Arte y politica: D. R. Mexico City 1979.– Tibol, R.: D. R. ilustrador. Mexico City 1986.– Wolfe, B.: The Fabulous Life of D. R. New York 1969, 1990/La Vie fabuleuse de D. R. Paris 1994

RIVERS Larry
born **1923** New York
American painter. **1944/45** Studied composition at the Juillard School of Music, New York. Earned his living at first as a jazz saxophonist. **1947/48** Studied art under Hofmann and **1948–1951** at New York University. Became enthusiastic about Bonnard and De Kooning. **1949** First solo-exhibition at the Jane Street Gallery, New York. **1950** Lived in Europe. **1964–1977** Participation in documenta 3, 4 and 6 in Kassel. **1966** Set design for Stravinsky's *Oedipus Rex*. **1967/68** Television production *Africa* with Gaisseau. **1968** Participation in documenta 4 in Kassel. **1970–1972** Production of the semi-documentary film *Tits*. **1970** Retrospective at the Art Institute of Chicago. **1975** Travelled through East Africa. **1980** Retrospective at the Kestner Society, Hanover. **1981** Exhibition at the Hirshhorn Museum, Washington. In the

60s, Rivers combined his Abstract Expressionist style with motifs from consumer society or from art history, which links him with the beginnings of Pop Art.
WRITINGS: L. R. and A. Weinstein: What Did I Do? The Unauthorized Autobiography. New York 1992
MONOGRAPHS, CATALOGUES: Brightman, C. (ed.): Drawings and Digressions by L. R. New York 1979.– Haenlein, C. (ed.): L. R. Retrospektive. Bilder und Skulpturen. Kestner-Gesellschaft. Hanover et al. Hanover 1980 (cat.).– Harrison, H. A.: L. R. New York 1977, 1984.– Hunter, S. (ed.): L. R. Rose Art Museum, Brandeis University. Waltham (MA) 1965 (cat.).– Hunter, S.: L. R. New York 1969, 1972.– Hunter, S.: L. R. New York 1989, Paris 1990.– Koriath, H.: L. R. Bildende Kunst in Beziehung zur Dichtung Frank O'Haras. Frankfurt-on-Main 1990.– Rosenzweig, P. (ed.): L. R. Hirshorn Museum. Washington 1981 (cat.).– Rouart, D.: R. New York 1985

RODIN Auguste
1840 Paris – **1917** Meudon
French sculptor. Studied at the Ecole des Arts Décoratifs and later at the Ecole des Beaux-Arts in Paris. **1864** First independent sculptures. **1875** Created *The Age of Bronze.* **1876** Travelled to Florence and Rome; fell under the spell of Michelangelo. **1877** Visited French cathedrals, to study Gothic art. **1881** Visited London. **1883** Met Camille Claudel. **1884–1886** Worked on the *Burghers of Calais.* **1894** Moved to Meudon. Met G. Clemenceau, Cézanne, Monet. **1898** Broke off relations with Claudel. **1900** Had his own pavilion at the Paris World Fair. **1916** Set up the Rodin Museum at the Hôtel Biron, Paris. **1917** Married M. Beuret. Rodin's sculptures are habitually sketchy, even fragmentary. Rodin, who initiated the modern era in sculpture, tended to create only a torso and often carved his work out of the block using very few cuts. This was a reaction to the restrictive conformity of traditional sculpture and allowed his successors to explore new pathways.
WRITINGS: Beausire, A. and H. Pichet (ed.): Correspondance de R. 2 vols. Paris 1985-1992.– Gsell, P. (ed.): A. R. Die Kunst. Gespräche des Meisters. Leipzig 1913 / R. on Art. New York 1971
CATALOGUES RAISONNES: Goldscheider, C.: A. R. Vie et œuvre. Catalogue raisonné de l'œuvre sculpté. Vol. 1: 1860-1886. Lausanne and Paris 1989.– Grappe, C. (ed.): Catalogue du Musée R. Paris 1944.– Judrin, C. (ed.): Musée Rodin. Inventaire des dessins. 6 vols. Paris 1984.– Tancock, J. L: The Sculpture of A. R. The Collection of the Rodin Museum, Philadelphia. Boston 1976, 1989.– Thorson, V. (ed.): R. Graphics. A Catalogue Raisonné of Drypoints and Book Illustrations. Fine Arts Museums of San Francisco. San Francisco 1975 (cat.)
MONOGRAPHS, CATALOGUES: Anders, G.: Obdachlose Skulptur. Über R. Munich 1994.– Barbier, N. (ed.): Marbres de R.

Collection du Musée Rodin. Paris 1987.– Barbier, N. (ed.): R. Sculpteur. Œuvres méconnues. Musée Rodin. Paris 1992 (cat.).– Beausire, A.: Quand R. exposait. Paris 1988.– Bonnet, A.-M. (ed.): A. R. Erotic Watercolors. New York 1995 / Erotische Aquarelle. Munich 1995.– Bothner, R.: A. R. Die Bürger von Calais. Frankfurt-on-Main and Leipzig 1993.– Butler, R.: R. The Shape of Genius. New Haven (CT) and London 1993.– Butler, R. et al. (ed.): A. R. Eros und Leidenschaft. Tübingen 1996.– Caso, J. d. and P. B. Sanders (ed.): R.'s Sculpture. A Critical Study of the Spreckels Collection. The Fine Arts of San Francisco. Rutland 1977 (cat.).– Crone, R. and S. Salzmann. (ed.): R. Eros und Kreativität. Kunsthalle Bremen et al. Munich 1991 (cat.).– Daix, P. R. Paris 1988.– Descharnes, R. and J.-F. Chabrun: A. R. New York 1967.– Elsen, A. E. (ed.): R. The Museum of Modern Art. New York 1963 (cat.).– Elsen, A. and K. Varnedoe: The Drawings of R. New York 1971.– Elsen, A. E. (ed.): R. Rediscovered. National Gallery of Art. Washington 1981 (cat.).– Elsen, A. E.: R.'s Thinker and the Dilemmas of Modern Public Sculpture. New Haven (CT) 1985.– Grunfeld, F. V.: R. A Biography. London and New York 1987.– Grunfeld, F. V.: Rodin. Berlin 1993.– Güse, E.-G. (ed.): A. R. Zeichnungen und Aquarelle. Westfälisches Landesmuseum, Münster et al. Stuttgart 1984 (cat.) / A. R. Drawings and Watercolors. Westfälisches Landesmuseum, Münster. New York 1984 (cat.).– Jarrassé, D.: R. La Passion du mouvement. Paris 1993 / R. A Passion for Movement. New York 1995.– Jianou, I. and C. Goldscheider: A. R. Paris 1967.– Laurent, M.: R. Paris 1988, Cologne 1989.– Lavrillier, C.-M.: R. La Porte de l'enfer. Lausanne 1988.– Martinez, R.-M.: R. L'Artiste face à l'état. Paris 1993.– Miller Vita, J. and G. Marotta (ed.): R. Metropolitan Museum of Modern Art. New York 1986 (cat.).– Mirbeau, O.: Correspondance avec A. R. Tusson 1988.– Pinet, H. (ed.): Les Photographes de R. Paris 1986.– Schmoll gen. Eisenwerth, J. A.: R.-Studien. Persönlichkeit, Werke, Wirkung, Bibliographie. Munich 1983.– Schmoll gen. Eisenwerth, J. A.: R und Camille Claudel. Munich 1994.– Taillandier, Y.: R. Paris 1983 (cat.)

RODCHENKO Alexander
1891 St. Petersburg – **1956** Moscow
Russian artist. **1911–1914** Trained at the art school in Kasan. **1914–1916** Studied at the Stroganoff Institute in Moscow. **1915** Founded the school of Non-objective Art. Contacts with Malevich and Tatlin. **1916** Participated in the exhibition "Magazin" in Moscow. **1918** Decorated the Moscow cabaret Café Pittoresque with Tatlin and G. Jakulov. **1920** Founder member of the Inkhuk cultural institute. Began to do photomontages and mobile-like hanging sculptures. **1921–1930** Professor at the School of Technological Art in Moscow. **1921** Period of monochrome pictures. Participation in

the exhibition "5 x 5". **1922** Participation in the Constructivist exhibition in Berlin. Gave up painting to dedicate himself to typographic work, poster and stage design. From **1924** concentrated on photography. **1925** Awarded special honours at the International Exhibition of Art and Industry in Paris. Worked from **1933** as a photojournalist, compiling a pictorial record of the new Russia. **1940–1944** Second non-representational phase. Among the successors to the Suprematists around Malevich, it was Rodchenko, the artist-engineer and production artist, who was chiefly responsible for the theoretical development and practical, artistic realisation of Constructivism.
WRITINGS: Khan-Magomedov, S. O. (ed.): A. R. Aufsätze, Erinnerungen, autobiographische Notizen, Briefe. Dresden 1993.– Lavrentiev, A. et al. (ed.): R.: Ecrits complets sur l'art, l'architecture et la révolution. Paris 1988
CATALOGUES RAISONNES: Elliot, D. and A. Lavrentiev (ed.): A. R. Works on Paper 1914-1920. London 1991.– Karginow, G.: R. Budapest 1979.– Khan-Magomedov, S. O. et al. (ed.): R. The Complete Work. London and Cambridge (MA) 1986 / R. L'œuvre complet. Paris 1987
MONOGRAPHS, CATALOGUES: Elliott, D. (ed.): A. R. 1891-1956. Museum of Modern Art. Oxford 1979 (cat.).– Gallissaires, P. (ed.): A. R. Alles ist Experiment. Der Künstler-Ingenieur. Hamburg 1993.– Gaßner, H. (ed.): R. Fotografien. Munich 1982.– Gaßner, H.: A. R. Konstruktion 1920 oder die Kunst, das Leben zu organisieren. Frankfurt-on-Main 1984.– Karginov, G.: R. Paris 1977, London 1979.– Larentiev, A. (ed.): R. Grafico, designer, fotografo. Milan 1992 (cat.).– Larentiev, A. N. (ed.): A. R. Photography 1924-1954. New York 1995 / A. R. Photographie 1924-1954. Cologne 1995.– Linhart, L.: A. R. Prague 1964.– Noever, P. (ed.): A. M. R., W. F. Spenanowa. Die Zukunft ist unser einziges Ziel. Munich 1991.– A. R. und W. Stepanowa. Wilhelm Lehmbruck Museum, Duisburg et al. Duisburg 1982 (cat.).– Unverfehrt, G. and T. Böttger (ed.): R. Fotograf. Münchner Stadtmuseum et al. Göttingen 1989 (cat.) / R. Der Fotograf. Städtische Galerie. Wolfsburg 1990 (cat.).– Volkov-Lannite, L.: A. R. Moscow 1968.– Weiss, E. (ed.): A. R. Fotografien 1920-1938. Cologne 1978

ROHLFS Christian
1849 Niendorf – **1938** Hagen
German painter and graphic artist. **1864** Serious knee injury, which later led to the amputation of his leg. **1870** Began to study art in Weimar, continuing from **1874–1884.** Independently of the French Impressionists, he developed his own naturalistic style which was soon heavily criticised. **1895** Lived in Berlin. **1901** Appointed to teach at the Folkwang School in Hagen, which was being set up by K. E. Osthaus, but the school was not opened. Met Renoir, Signac, Seurat, Cézanne and van Gogh,

who influenced his painting for a short time. From **1900** member of the Berlin Secession. In the summers of **1905/06**, he painted in Soest and met Nolde. From **1910** he turned to Expressionism. **1911** Joined the New Secession; **1914** member of the Free Secession. **1924** Member of the Prussian Academy of Arts in Berlin. From **1927– 1938** lived most of the year in Ascona for health reasons. **1937** Expelled from the Berlin Academy and his works confiscated.
CATALOGUES RAISONNES: Elger, D. and A. Meseure (ed.): C. R. Das druckgraphische Gesamtwerk. Museum am Ostwall, Dortmund et al. Dortmund (cat.).– Gädeke, T.: C. R. Bestandkatalog seiner Werke im Schleswig-Holsteinischen Landesmuseum. Schleswig 1990.– Utermann, W. (ed.): C. R. Das druckgraphische Werk. Dortmund 1987.– Vogt, P. (ed.): C. R. Œuvrekatalog der Druckgraphik. Göttingen 1950.– Vogt, P.: C. R. Aquarelle, Wassertempera, Zeichnungen (mit Werkverzeichnis). Recklinghausen 1958.– Vogt, P. (ed.): C. R. Das graphische Werk. Recklinghausen 1960.– Vogt, P. and U. Köcke (ed.): C. R. Œuvrekatalog der Gemälde. Recklinghausen 1978
MONOGRAPHS, CATALOGUES: Bußmann, K. et al. (ed.): C. R. Westfälisches Landesmuseum, Münster et al. Stuttgart 1989 (cat.).– Gleisberg, D.: C. R. Dresden 1978.– Happel, R. (ed.): C. R. Kunstverein Braunschweig et al. Brunswick 1992 (cat.).– C. R. Aquarelle und Zeichnungen. Westfälisches Landesmuseum. Münster 1974 (cat.).– C. R. 1849-1938. Gemälde zwischen 1877 und 1935. Museum Folkwang. Essen 1978 (cat.).– Scheidig, W.: C. R. Dresden 1965.– Schmidt, K. J. and H.-G. Kerkhoff (ed.): C. R. 1849-1938. Lyrische Expressionen. Artforum, Düsseldorf et al. Düsseldorf 1995 (cat.).– Vogt. P.: C. R. Cologne 1953, 1967.– Vogt, P. (ed.): C. R. Das Spätwerk. Museum Folkwang. Essen 1967 (cat.).– Vogt, P. (ed.): C. R. Folkwang Museum, Essen et al. Recklinghausen 1988 (cat.).– Vogt, P.: C. R. 1849-1938. Aquarelle, Wassertemperablätter, Zeichnungen. Recklinghausen 1988

ROSAI Ottone
1895 Florence – **1957** Ivrea
Italian painter. Studied at the Institute of Decorative Art and the Art Academy in Florence. **1913** First solo-exhibition in Florence. Met the Futurists Boccioni, Carrà and Severini while participating in an exhibition organised by *Lacerba* magazine. **1914 –1916** Contributed to the Futurist magazine *Lacerba.* The Futurist influence was very much in evidence in his still lifes and collage-like mixtures of painting and *papiers collés* from this period. From **1920** he distanced himself from Futurism and turned to a warmly coloured, naturalist Neo-primitivism, painting popular themes with wit and naiveté. **1925–1930** Took part in the exhibition of the Novecento group and worked for *Il Selvaggio* magazine. In the early 40s he did paintings of the cruci-

fixion and war, displaying great expressive intensity.
WRITINGS: O. R.: Il libro del Teppista. Florence 1919.– O. R.: Via Toscanella. Florence 1930
CATALOGUE RAISONNE: O. R.: I disegni del "Bargello". Florence 1990
MONOGRAPHS, CATALOGUES: Cavallo, R.: O. R. Milan 1973.– Santini, P. C.: R. Florence 1960.– Santini, P. C. et al. (ed.): O. R. Opere dal 1911 al 1951. Galleria Nazionale d'Arte Moderna, Romaa et al. Florence 1983 (cat.)

ROSENBACH Ulrike
born **1949** Bad Salzdefurth
German video artist. **1964–1969** Studied at the Düsseldorf Academy under Beuys and others. **1972** First video works. Solo-exhibition at the Ernst gallery in Hanover. **1973** Produced the live video event *isolation is transparent.* **1973–1976** Lived in the USA, taught at California Institute of the Arts, Valencia. **1976** Started the School of Creative Feminism in Cologne. **1977** and **1987** participation in documenta 6 and 8 in Kassel. **1978** Solo-exhibition at the Kunstmuseum Düsseldorf. **1980** and **1984** Participation at the Venice Biennale. **1984** Took part in the exhibition "Von hier aus" (From Here) in Cologne. Received the Festival Prize at the Locarno Video Festival and a Western Front working grant for Vancouver. **1989** Took part in the exhibition "Video-Skulptur" in Cologne. From **1989** was professor for New Media at the Saarbrücken Art Academy. **1995** Retrospective at the Freiburg video-forum. Rosenbach pioneered video art in Germany. Her work focuses on feminist issues.
WRITINGS: U. R.: Video, Performance, Feministische Kunst und Foto. Cologne 1978
MONOGRAPHS, CATALOGUES: Hirner, R. (ed.): U. R. Last Call für Engel. Kunstmuseum Heidenheim et al. Heidenheim 1996 (cat.).– Lupri, C.: U. R. Video, Performance, Installation. Art Gallery of York University. Toronto 1989 (cat.).– Schulz, B. (ed.): U. R. Arbeiten der 80er Jahre: Video, Installation, Performance, Fotografie. Stadtgalerie. Saarbrücken 1990 (cat.).– U. R. (ed.): U. R. Videokunst, Foto, Aktion/ Performance, feministische Kunst. Cologne 1982.– U. R. Spuren des Heiligen in der Kunst heute. Neue Galerie, Sammlung Ludwig. Aachen 1986 (cat.)

ROSENQUIST James
born **1933** Grand Forks (ND)
American painter. **1952–1955** Studied at the University of Minnesota in Minneapolis and **1957–1959** in New York at the Art Students League, where he met George Grosz and Robert Indiana. At first he worked as a designer, poster artist, and shop window dresser before he set up his own studio in the neighbourhood of Indiana and Ellsworth Kelly and started to produce banners with billboard images in fluores-

cent colours. **1963** Commission for a mural for the New York State Pavilion. **1965** Gigantic mural *F III* (3 x 26 m), a spatially interlocking composition, portraying the interplay of the human, commercial and mechanized aspects of American society. **1968** and **1977** participation in documenta 4 and 6 in Kassel. **1969** Experiments with film techniques. **1970** First video works. In the 70s, he was active in the anti-war movement and for the rights of the artist in a democratic society. From **1983** the mechanical elements in his paintings were there to mock a naive faith in technology. Rosenquist, one of the leading representatives of American Pop Art, assembles his monumental canvases out of fragmentary images taken from everyday life and elements of commercial advertising.
CATALOGUE RAISONNE: Glenn, C. W. (ed.): J. R. Time Dust. The Complete Graphics 1962-1992. Walker Art Center, Minneapolis et al. New York 1993 (cat.)
MONOGRAPHS, CATALOGUES: Adcock, C. E. et al. (ed.): J. R. IVAM Centro Julio González. Valencia 1991 (cat.).– Brundage, S. (ed.): J. R. The Big Paintings. Leo Castelli Gallery. New York 1994 (cat.).– Damiani, R.: J. R. The Nineties. New York 1996.– Goldman, J. (ed.): J. R. Denver Art Museum et al. New York 1985 (cat.).– Goldman, J.: J. R. The Early Pictures 1961-1964. New York 1992.– J. R. Whitney Museum of American Art. New Yok 1986 (cat.).– Tucker, M.: J. R. Whitney Museum of American Art. New Yok 1972 (cat.).– Varian, E. H. (ed.): J. R. Graphics Restrospective. The John and Mabel Ringling Museum of Art. Sarasota (FL) 1979 (cat.).– Weiss, E.: J. R. Gemälde, Räume, Graphik. Josef-Haubrich-Kunsthalle. Cologne 1972 (cat.)

ROSSO Medardo
1858 Turin – **1928** Milan
Italian sculptor. **1881** Moved to Milan. **1882** Studied sculpture at the Brera Academy in Milan. **1884** Worked in J. Dalous studio in Paris, and was influenced by Impressionism and the works of Rodin. **1885** Lived in Vienna. **1886** Exhibition at the Salon des Indépendants in Paris; began to work on cemetery statuary. From **1889** lived in Paris again, where he met Degas, Robin and the collector Rouart.

1900 Took part in the Paris World Fair. **1904** Solo-exhibition at the Salon d'Automne in Paris; further solo-exhibitions in Vienna and Milan. **1929** Retrospective at the Salon d'Automne in Paris. **1950** Retrospective at the Venice Biennale. A characteristic of Rosso's work is the mobility of his figures, evoking an Impressionist sense of movement with a psychological dimension. Many of his sculptures are purposely left in the wax model stage.
WRITINGS: Fezzi, E. (ed.): M. R. Scritti e pensieri 1889-1927. Cremona 1994
MONOGRAPHS, CATALOGUES: Barbantini, N.: M. R. Venice 1950.– Barr, M. S. (ed.): M. R. The Museum of Modern Art. New York 1963 (cat.).– Barr, M. S.: M. R. New York 1972.– Borghi, M.: M. R. Milan 1950.– Caramel, L and Mola Kirchmayr, P. (ed.): Mostra di M. R. Palazzo della Permanente. Milan 1979 (cat.).– Caramel, L. (ed.): M. R. Impressions in Wax and Bronze. 1882-1906. Kent Fine Art, New York et al. New York and London 1988 (cat.).– Caramel, L. (ed.): M. R. Whitechappel Art Gallery. London 1994 (cat.).– Fagioli, M. and L. Minunno (ed.): M. R. 2 vols. Florence 1993 (cat.).– Lista, G (ed.): M. R. La Sculpture impressionniste. Paris 1994.– Lista, G.: M. R. Destin d'un sculpteur. 1858-1928. Paris 1994.– Marchiori, G.: M. R. Milan 1966.– Papini, G.: M. R. Milan 1945.– M. R. Whitechapel Art Gallery. London 1994 (cat.).– Sanna, J. d.: M. R. o la creazione dello spazio moderno. Milan 1985.– Weiermair, P. et al. (ed.): M. R. 1858-1928. Frankfurter Kunstverein. Frankfurt-on-Main 1984 (cat.)

ROTELLA Mimmo
born **1918** Catanzaro
Italian artist. **1945** Finished studies at the Art Academy in Naples. **1945** Moved to Rome. **1951** First solo-exhibition at the Galleria Chiurazzi, Rome. **1951/52** Studied in the USA on a scholarship from the University of Missouri, Kansas City. From **1954** produced decollages often including film and advertising posters. **1961** Joined the Nouveaux Réalistes. Met Jacques de la Villeglé and Raymond Hains. **1964** Moved to Paris. **1965** Took part in the exhibition "Hommage à Nicéphore Nièpce" at the Galerie J in Paris. **1972** Publication of his book *Autorotella.* **1975** Produced a record of his phonetic poems. **1980** Moved to Milan. **1985** Solo-exhibition at the Reckermann gallery in Cologne. **1986** Invited to lecture in Cuba. Rotella, with his torn-poster paintings, is a typical exponent of Nouveau Réalisme.
MONOGRAPHS, CATALOGUES: Appella, G.: Colloquio con R. Roma 1984.– Barilli, R. and T. Sicoli: R. Milan 1996 (cat.).– Fagiolo dell'Arco, M.: M. R. Milan 1977.– Hunter, S. (ed.): R. Décollages 1954-1964. Milan 1986.– Oliva, A. B. et al.: M. R. L'Amière. Milan 1989.– Restany, P.: R. Dal décollage alla nuova immagine. Milan 1963.– Restany, P. et al. (ed.): M. R. Württembergischer Kunstverein, Stuttgart et al.

Stuttgart 1998 (cat.).– M. R. Autorotella. Milan 1972, Paris 1990.– Trini, T.: R. Milan 1974

ROTH Dieter
1930 Hanover – **1998** Basel
Also known as Diter Rot. German painter and action artist. **1943** Moved to Switzerland. **1947** Trained as a graphic artist. Lived from **1957–1964** in Reykjavik. Travelled to Amsterdam, Basel, New York, Paris. **1958** First solo-exhibition in Reykjavik. **1964** Solo-exhibition at the Museum School of Art, Philadelphia. Collaborated with A. Knowles, D. Higgins, Brecht, C. Moorman and Paik. **1967** Returned to Reykjavik. **1968** and **1977** took part in documenta 4 and 5 in Kassel. From **1968** taught at the Düsseldorf Academy. **1981** Participation in the "Westkunst" exhibition in Cologne and **1982** at the Venice Biennale. **1984** Solo-exhibition at the Museum of Contemporary Art, Chicago. **1985** Took part in the exhibition "Livres d'Artistes" at the Pompidou Centre, Paris. Lived from **1990** in Basel. **1998** Prize at the Art Multiple, Düsseldorf. Roth can be categorised under the Fluxus and Eat-Art movements. He is best known for his book works, displaying an individual style of typography, and for his chocolate and mould objects.
WRITINGS: D. R.: Scheisse. Providence 1966.– D. R.: Die blaue Flut. Stuttgart 1967.– D. R.: mundunculum. Cologne 1968.– D. R.: Gesammelte Werke. Bücher und Grafik. 2 vols. Stuttgart 1971-1979.– D. R.: Frühe Schriften und typische Scheiße. Stuttgart, London 1975.– D. R.: Ein Tagebuch aus dem Jahre 1982. Basel 1984
CATALOGUES RAISONNES: D. R. Werkverzeichnis Graphik und Bücher. 2 vols. Stuttgart et al. 1972-1979.– Oberhuber, K. et al. (ed.): D. R. Das druckgraphische Werk. Cologne 1998
MONOGRAPHS, CATALOGUES: Broos, K. (ed.): D. R. Centre Régional d'Art Contemporain Midi-Pyrénées, Labege. 1987 (cat.).– Goldstein, A. (ed.): D. R. Museum of Contemporary Art. Chicago 1984 (cat.).– Helms, D. (ed.): D. R. Arbeiten auf Papier. Herzog Anton Ulrich-Museum. Brunswick 1985 (cat.).– Hohl, H. and A. Kamber (ed.): D. R. Zeichnungen. Hamburger Kunsthalle et al. Hamburg 1987 (cat.).– D. R. Bücher. Kestner-Gesellschaft. Hanover 1974 (cat.).– D. R. Bonner Kunstverein. Bonn 1983 (cat.).– D. R. Bilder, Zeichnungen, Objekte. Basel 1989 (cat.).– D. R. Museum Moderner Kunst. Passau 1992 (cat.).– Schneede, U. M. (ed.): D. R. Originale 1946-1976. Hamburger Kunstverein. Hamburg 1974 (cat.).– Schwarz, D.: Auf der Bogen Bahn. Studien zum literarischen Werk von D. R. Zurich 1981

ROTHENBERG Susan
born **1945** Buffalo (NY)
American painter and draughtswoman. **1962–1967** Studied at the Fine Arts School at Cornell University. **1964** Graduate

studies at State University, New York. **1965** Lived in Greece. **1971** Married the sculptor Trakas. **1975** First solo-exhibition with *Three Large Paintings* at the gallery 112 Greene Street in New York. **1979** Participation at the Whitney Biennale, New York. Separation from Trakas. Travelled to Mexico. **1980** Participation at Venice Biennale. **1981** Solo-exhibition at the Basel Kunsthalle. **1982** Participation at the exhibition "Zeitgeist" in Berlin. Solo-exhibition at the Stedelijk Museum, Amsterdam. **1988** Travelled in China. **1989** Married Naumann. **1990** Retrospective at the Rooseum Centre of Contemporary Arts, Malmö, and **1992** at the Albright-Knox Art Gallery, Buffalo and participation in documenta 9 in Kassel. Besides paintings Rothenberg has produced some very fine drawings.
MONOGRAPHS, CATALOGUES: Auping, M. (ed.): S. R. Paintings and Drawings. Albright-Knox Art Gallery, Buffalo et al. New York 1992 (cat.).– Blum, P. (ed.): S. R. Kunsthalle Basel et al. Basel 1981 (cat.).– Grevenstein, A. v. (ed.): S. R. Recente Schilderijen. Stedelijk Museum. Amsterdam 1982.– Nittve, L. and R. Storr (ed.): S. R. 15 Years – A Survey. Malmö Konsthall. Malmö 1990 (cat.).– Rathbone, E. (ed.): S. R. The Phillips Collection, Washington et al. Washington 1985 (cat.).– Tuchman, M. (ed.): S. R. Los Angeles County Museum of Art et al. Los Angeles 1983 (cat.).– Simon, J.: S. R. New York 1991

ROTHKO Mark
(Markus Rothkowitz)
1903 Dvinsk (Lithuania) – **1970** New York
Lithuanian-born American painter. **1910** Moved with his family to Oregon. **1921–1923** Studied at Yale University, New Haven, and **1924–1929** under M. Weber at the Art Students League in New York. **1935** Founded the Expressionist group with Adolf Gottlieb The Ten. **1938** Showed interest in Surrealism and studied Greek mythology, metaphysics, C. G. Jung's theory of archetypes, and primitive art. **1947** First paintings with floating forms. **1949** With Baziotes, Motherwell and Newman, started the Subject of the Artist School, which closed in **1950**. Taught at the successor to this school (Studio 35) until **1955**, and at Brooklyn College as an assis-

tant professor from **1951–1954**. **1959** Participation in documenta 2 in Kassel. From **1960** he began to use ever darker colours. **1964** He decorated a chapel designed by Philip Johnson for the De Menil family in Houston. **1970** Suicide. With his meditative paintings, Rothko is among the most important of the Color Field painters.
CATALOGUE RAISONNE: Sandler, I. and B. Clearwater (ed.): M. R. Catalogue Raisonné (in preparation)
MONOGRAPHS, CATALOGUES: Ashton, D.: About R. New York 1983, 1996.– Barnes, S.: The R. Chapel. An Act of Faith. Austin 1989.– Breslin, J. E. B.: M. R. A Biography. Chicago 1993/M. R. Eine Biographie. Klagenfurt 1995.– Chave, A. c.: M. R. Subjects in Abstraction. New Haven (CT) and London 1989, 1991.– Clearwater, B. (ed.): M. R. Works on Paper. National Gallery of Art, Washingtonn. New York 1984 (cat.).– Clearwater, B. (ed.): M. R. Œuvres sur papier. Paris 1993.– Glimcher, M. (ed.): The Art of M. R. Into an Unknown World. New York and London 1991.– Kellein, T. (ed.): M. R. Kunsthalle Basel. Basel 1989 (cat.).– McKinney, D. et al. (ed.): M. R. Kunsthaus Zurich et al. Zurich 1971 (cat.).– Nodelman, S.: The R. Chapel Paintings. Form as Meaning in the American Abstract Sublime. Austin 1997.– Rosenblum, R. et al. (ed.): M. R. Tate Gallery. London 1987, 1996 (cat.).– Seldes, L.: The Legacy of M. R. New York 1978, 1996.– Waldman, D. and B. Malamud (ed.): M. R. 1903-1970. A Retrospective. Solomon R. Guggenheim Museum, New York et al. New York 1978 (cat.).– Waldman, D.: M. R. in New York. Solomon R. Guggenheim Museum. New York 1994.– Weis, J. (ed.): M. R. National Gallery of Art, Washington et al. Washington 1998 (cat.).– Weiss, E. (ed.): M. R. 1903-1970. Retrospektive der Gemälde. Museum Ludwig. Cologne 1988 (cat.)

ROUAULT Georges
1871 Paris – **1958** Paris
French painter and engraver. During his apprenticeship in a stained-glass workshop, he restored some medieval windows. Later studied with G. Moreau, whose influence is visible in his works up to **1903**. After Moreau's death, H. Daumier and Toulouse-Lautrec encouraged him to portray scenes and characters from real life. Before gravitating towards Fauvism around **1905**, he painted in dark, heavy colours. He then began to use wild, strong brush slashes, presenting his figures – clowns, prostitutes, farmers, workers, judges – in sombre but vivid, glowing colours with darkly outlined faces. The contrast between the broad, black lines and the pulsing, luminous colours is reminiscent of the stained-glass techniques he knew. **1917–1927** Produced important series of engravings, including illustrations for C. Baudelaire's *Fleurs du Mal* and the *Miserere*. **1932** Devoted himself increasingly to religious art, a development culminating in **1945** in his

stained-glass windows for the church in Assy.
WRITINGS: G. R.: Souvenirs intimes. Paris 1926.– G. R.: Paysages légendaires. Paris 1929.– G. R.: Petite banlieue. Paris 1929.– G. R.: Divertissements. Paris 1943.– G. R.: Soliloques. Neuchâtel 1944.– G. R.: Miserere. Paris 1991
CATALOGUES RAISONNES: Chapon, F. and I. Rouault (ed.): G. R. Œuvre gravé. 2 vols. Monte Carlo 1978-1979/R.'s Complete Graphic Work. San Francisco 1979.– Chapon, F. (ed.): Le Livre des livres de R. Monaco 1992/R.'s Illustrated Books. Catalogue Raisonné. San Francisco 1993.– Courthion, P.: G. R. Paris 1962, New York 1962, Cologne 1962.– Dorival, B. and I. Rouault (ed.): G. R. L'œuvre peint. 2 vols. Monte Carlo 1988/R.'s Complete Paintings. San Francisco 1988.– Molinari, D. (ed.): G. R. 1871-1958. Catalogue raisonné. Collections de la Ville de Paris. Paris 1983
MONOGRAPHS, CATALOGUES: Bellini, P.: G. R. Uomo e artista. Milan 1972.– Chiappini, R. (ed.): G. R. Museo d'Arte Moderna. Lugano 1997 (cat.).– Dorival, B. (ed.): G. R. Haus der Kunst, Munich et al. Munich 1974 (cat.).– Gohr, S. (ed.): G. R. Josef-Haubrich-Kunsthalle. Cologne 1983 (cat.).– Hergott, F. r.: R. Paris 1991.– Hergott, F. et al. (ed.): R. Première période 1903-1920. Centre Georges Pompidou. Paris 1992 (cat.)/G. R. The Early Years 1903-1920. Royal Academy. London 1993 (cat.).– Hopf, E. (ed.): G. R. 1871-1958. Kunstamt Wedding. Berlin 1988 (cat.).– Koja, S. (ed.): G. R. Malerei und Graphik. Landessammlungen Rupertinum, Salzburg. Munich 1993 (cat.).– Leymarie, J. and M. Hoog (ed.): G. R. Exposition du centenaire. Musée National d'Art Moderne. Paris 1971 (cat.).– Marcoulesco, I.: G. R. The Inner Light. Houston 1996

ROUSSEAU Henri
1844 Laval – **1910** Paris
French painter. Self-taught. **1863/64** Military musician; claimed to have served in Mexico. **1869** Began to work for the Paris customs office, where he earned his nickname *The Customs Officer*. During the Franco-Prussian war, he was a low-ranking officer in the French army. **1880** First exhibition of paintings. **1885** Exhibited at the Salon des Champs-Elysées in Paris. **1896–1910** Regular participation in the Salon des Indépendants, from **1905** also at the Salon d'Automne. **1890** Met Toulouse-Lautrec, Gauguin, Redon, Seurat and Pissarro. First exotic paintings. **1906** Met Delaunay, Picasso and Apollinaire and, in **1907**, made friends with Wilhelm Uhde, who published the first monograph on him in **1911**. Rousseau's portraits, still lifes, landscapes, and fantasy scenes are the first examples of a style termed "naive". Naive, because their subject matter is portrayed in a highly individual manner, without realistic analysis or intellectual reflection.
CATALOGUES RAISONNES: Artieri, G. (ed.): L'opera completa di R. il Doganiere.

Milan 1969.– Bouret, J.: H. R. Neuchâtel 1961, Greenwich (CT) 1961, Herrsching 1974.– Certigny, H. (ed.): Le Douanier R. et son temps. Biographie et catalogue raisonné. 2 vols. Tokyo 1984-1989.– Vallier, D.: H. R. Paris 1961, Cologne 1961, New York and London 1964, Munich 1981.– Vallier, D. (ed.): Tout l'œuvre peint de H. R. Paris 1970
MONOGRAPHS, CATALOGUES: Abé, Y. (ed.): H. R. et l'univers des naïfs français. Grande Galerie, Odakyu. Tokyo 1981 (cat.).– Alley, R.: Portrait of a Primitive. The Art of H. R. Oxford 1978.– Bihalji-Marin, L. and O.: H. R. Leben und Werk. Cologne 1976.– Broadskaya, N.: H. R. New York 1983.– Certigny, H.: La Vérité sur le douanier R. Lausanne, Paris 1961, 1971.– Elgar, F.: R. Paris 1980.– Hoog, M. (ed.): Le Douanier R. Grand Palais, Paris et al. Paris 1984 (cat.).– Keay, C.: H. R. Le Douanier. London and New York 1976.– Le Pichon, Y.: Le Monde du douanier R. Paris 1981/The World of H. R. New York 1982.– Perruchot, H.: H. R. Eine Biographie. Eßlingen a. N. 1957.– Plazy, G.: Le Douanier R. Un naïf dans la jungle. Paris 1992.– Rich, D. C.: H. R. Museum of Modern Art Publications in Reprint. New York 1969.– Schneede, M.: H. R. Dortmund 1994.– Shattuck, R. et al. (ed.): H. R. The Museum of Modern Art. New York 1985 (cat.).– Stabenow, C. (ed.): H. R. Die Dschungelbilder. Munich 1984.– Stabenow, C.: H. R. Cologne 1991.– Vallier, D.: H. R. Paris 1979, New York 1979.– Vitiello, R.: R. e l'alienazione. Roma 1981

ROZANOVA Olga
1886 Malenkach – **1918** Moscow
Russian artist. **1904–1910** Studied applied arts in Moscow. **1911** Moved to St. Petersburg, where she attended the Svanseva art school, and took part in exhibitions given by the Young People's Union. **1912–1914** Cubist-Futurist period. **1913** Published her essay *Concerning the Principles of a New Art*. **1915** Joined the Suprematist movement and worked on their magazine. Took part in the exhibitions "Streetcar WITH", "Zero-Ten", "Magazin", and "Karo Bube". Did book illustrations for Futurist poets and wrote her own *Transcendancy Poems*. **1919** Posthumous retrospective in Moscow. Several of her works were shown in **1922** at the Russian art exhibition at the Diemen gallery in Berlin. Rozanova revolutionised the art of book printing by breaking away from traditional typesetting; through the integration of collage technique she created a new union of words and pictures.
MONOGRAPHS, CATALOGUES: Rubinger, K. et al. (ed.): Künstlerinnen der russischen Avantgarde. 1910-1930. Galerie Gmurzynska. Cologne 1979 (cat.)

RÜCKRIEM Ulrich
born **1938** Düsseldorf
German sculptor. **1957–1959** Apprenticeship as a stonemason in Düren. **1959–1961**

Worked as a mason at Cologne Cathedral. **1962** Travelled through southern Europe, Morocco, and Tunisia and, after his return, decided to become a sculptor. **1964** First solo-exhibition at the Leopold Hoesch Museum, Düren. From **1968** he developed his own working technique, in which the material and the working process itself are characterised by doubling, reducing, and slighty changing to the raw materials. **1969** Moved to Mönchengladbach where he shared a studio with Palermo. **1970** Solo-exhibition at the Museum Haus Lange in Krefeld. **1972–1992** Participation in documenta 5, 7, 8 and 9 in Kassel. **1975–1984** Professor at the Hamburg Academy of Fine Arts. **1978** Participation at the Venice Biennale with four split Dolomite stones. **1981** Participation at the "Westkunst" exhibition in Cologne. **1984** Professor of sculpture at the Düsseldorf Academy and **1988** Professor at the Frankfurt Academy. Rückriem has made an important contribution to Process Art with his stone, iron, and wooden sculptural works which reflect the creative processes and his working methods.
CATALOGUE RAISONNE: Meschede, F. et al. (ed.): U. R. Multiples und Druckgraphik 1969-1985. Freiburg 1986 (cat.)
MONOGRAPHS, CATALOGUES: Barker, B. et al. (ed.): U. R. Arbeiten. Stuttgart 1994.– Bußmann, K. et al. (ed.): U. R. Skulpturen, Zeichnungen. Westfälisches Landesmuseum. Münster 1985 (cat.).– Deecke, T. (ed.): U. R. Skulpturen 1977/78. Westfälischer Kunstverein, Münster et al. Mannheim 1979 (cat.).– Erhardt, H. (ed.): U. R. Städtische Galerie im Lenbachhaus. Munich 1995 (cat.).– Fuchs, R. (ed.): U. R. Skulpturen 1968-1970. Stedelijk Van Abbe Museum, Eindhoven et al. Eindhoven 1977 (cat.).– Gallwitz, K. et al. (ed.): Biennale 78, Venice. Deutscher Pavillon – U. R. Stuttgart 1978 (cat.).– Goldwater, M. et al. (ed.): U. R. New Works. The Fort Worth Art Museum. Fort Worth 1981 (cat.).– Heubach, F. et al. (ed.): U. R. Sculptures. Centre Georges Pompidou. Paris 1983 (cat.).– Hohmeyer, J.: U. R. Munich 1988.– Kersting, H. and U. R. (ed.): U. R. Skulpturen. Städtische Galerie im Städel. Frankfurt-on-Main 1984 (cat.).– Kersting, H.: U. R. Kunstsammlung Nordrhein-Westfalen, Düsseldorf et al. Düsseldorf 1987 (cat.).– Meschede, F.: Der Stein drängt nach draußen. Untersuchungen zur Skulptur von U. R. und ihre Entwicklung als Kunst im öffentlichen Raum. Diss. Münster 1987.– Meschede, F. et al. (ed.): U. R. Skulpturen-Zeichnungen. Kunstsammlung Nordrhein-Westfalen, Düsseldorf et al. Düsseldorf 1987 (cat.).– U. R. Museum of Modern Art. Oxford 1976 (cat.).– Ulbricht, G.: U. R. Skulpturen 1968-1973. Cologne 1973

RUETZ Michael
born **1940** Berlin
German photographer. Came from a publishing family in Riga. Studied Chinese,

Japanese and journalism in Freiburg, Munich and Berlin. Doctoral thesis on a Chinese novelist. **1969 – 1973** Worked as an editor for *Stern* magazine in Hamburg and, since then, as a freelance photographer. **1975** Examen at the Folkwang Art School, Essen, under Steinert and W. Fleckhaus. Since **1983** contracted author with Little, Brown and Company in Boston. Professorship at an art academy in Braunschweig. Won the Otto Steinert Award for Photography and **1981** the Villa Massimo Prize in Rome. Spent several years in Italy, America and Australia.
WRITINGS: M. R.: Christo verpackt Monschau. Cologne 1971.– M. R.: Auf Goethes Spuren. Zurich 1978.– M. R.: Nekropolis. Munich 1978.– M. R.: APO Berlin 1966-1969. Frankfurt-on-Main 1980.– M. F.: Luna. Nördlingen 1986.– M. F.: Über Berlin. Munich 1991.– M. F.: Library for the Eye 1993-1996. Berlin 1993-1996.– M. F.: Bibliothek der Augen I, II. Göttingen 1997-1998
MONOGRAPHS, CATALOGUES: M. R. Fotograf der Revolte. Galerie Mikro. Berlin 1970 (cat.)

RUFF Thomas
born **1958** Zell am Harmersbach (Black Forest)
German photographer. **1977–1985** Studied photography at the Düsseldorf Academy under Becher. **1985** and **1987** Portraits of his parents, relatives, and friends, as well as a serie of large colour portraits of heads in a sober, documentary style. From **1987** he photographed new buildings built during the German economic miracle of the 50s, selecting individual buildings that interested him rather than particular styles or categories. **1988** Received a grant for young artists from the state of North Rhine-Westphalia. **1989** Black and white photos of the night sky using existing material from the European Southern Observatory. **1992** Took part in documenta 9 in Kassel and in the **1995** Venice Biennale. In the mid-90s, he began to produce synthetic portraits using computer manipulation.
MONOGRAPHS, CATALOGUES: Brauchitsch, B. v.: T. R. Frankfurt-on-Main 1992.– Durand, R. (ed.): T. R. Paris 1997 (cat.).– Levene, U. (ed.): T. R. Rooseum Center for Contemporary Art. Malmö 1996

(cat.).– T. R. Porträts. Museum Schloß Hardenberg, Velbert et al. Cologne 1988 (cat.).– T. R. Portretten, Huizen, Sterren, Stedelijk Museum, Amsterdam et al. Amsterdam and Grenoble 1989 (cat.).– T. R. Bonner Kunstverein. Bonn 1991 (cat.).– T. R. and A. Giese (ed.): T. R. andere Portraits + 3 D. Deutscher Pavillon, Biennale von Venedig. Stuttgart 1995 (cat.)

RUSCHA Edward
born **1937** Omaha (NE)
American painter. **1942** Moved to Oklahoma City. **1947** Began to draw comics. **1949** Travelled to California. **1955** Trip to Mexico. **1956–1960** Studied at the Chouinard Art Institute and at the school of the Walt Disney cartoonists in Los Angeles. **1963** Solo-exhibition at the Ferus Gallery, Los Angeles. **1963–1966** Publication of his books *Twenty-Six Gasoline Stations* and *Every Building on the Sunset Strip.* **1964** Participation at the exhibition "American Drawings" at the Guggenheim Museum, New York. **1967** Participation at the Saõ Paulo and Paris Biennale and **1970** at the Venice Biennale. **1972–1992** Took part in documenta 5 – 7 and 9 in Kassel. **1982** Exhibition entitled "I don't want no Retrospective – The Works of Edward Ruscha" at the San Francisco Museum of Modern Art. **1985** Mural for the Miami Dade public library. **1989** Retrospective at the Pompidou Centre, Paris. **1993** Solo-exhibition at the Gagosian Gallery, New York. Ruscha's alphabetic works represent the complex relationship between text and typography. In the 70s, he used organic substances (like foodstuffs) in place of paints.
MONOGRAPHS, CATALOGUES: Bogle, A. (ed.): E. R. Graphic Works by E. R. City Art Gallery. Auckland 1978 (cat.).– Bois, Y.-A. (ed.): E. R. Romance with Liquids. Paintings 1966-1969. Gagosian Gallery. New York 1993 (cat.).– Bois, Y.-A.: E. R. The Word Paintings. New York 1993.– Cathcart, L. L. (ed.): E. R. Albright-Knox Art Gallery. Buffalo 1976 (cat.).– Clearwater, B. and C. Knight (ed.): E. R. Words Without Thoughts Never to Heaven Go. Lannan Museum, Lake Worth. New York 1988 (cat.).– Foster, E. A.: E. R. Minneapolis 1972.– Groot, E. d. (ed.): E. R. Paintings. Museum Beuymans-van Beuningen, Rotterdam et al. Rotterdam 1989 (cat.).– Hickey, D. et al. (ed.): The Works of E. R. San Francisco Museum of Modern Art et al. New York 1982 (cat.).– Hulten, P. and D. Cameron (ed.): E. R. Centre Georges Pompidou, Paris et al. Paris 1989 (cat.)

RUSSOLO Luigi
1885 Pertogruaro – **1947** Cerro di Laveno
Italian painter and musician. Studied music. **1909** Encouraged by Bonzagni and Romani to take up painting. Friendship with Boccioni. **1910** Co-founder of the Futurist movement with Balla, Boccioni, Carrà and Severini. Took part between **1910**

–1913 in Futurist exhibitions and signed the painting manifestos of the group. **1913** Issued the *Manifesto of Noise Art,* in which he coined the term Bruitism. Gave up painting in favour of music and together with U. Piatti constructed the *Intonarumori,* a musical instrument for producing noises. **1917** Wounded in the war. **1918** Moved to Paris. **1941** Took up figurative painting again.
WRITINGS: Maffina, G. F.: L. R. e l'arte dei rumori. Con tutti gli scritti musicali. Torino 1978.– L. R.: L'arte dei rumori. Milan 1916.– L. R.: Al di là della materia. Milan 1938
CATALOGUE RAISONNE: Maffina, G. F. (ed.): L'opera grafica di L. R. Varese 1977
MONOGRAPHS, CATALOGUES: Bartsch, I. (ed.): R. Die Geräuschkunst. 1913-1931. Museum. Bochum 1985 (cat.).– Zanovello Russolo, M. et al. (ed.): L. R. L'uomo, l'artista. Milan 1958

RUTHENBECK Reiner
born **1937** Velbert
German sculptor. Studied photography and from **1962** sculpture at the Düsseldorf Academy, as a student of Beuys. **1965** First sculptures, influenced by Surrealism, made out of clay, iron, wire and wood. Towards the end of the 60s, he tried to imbue his sculptures and objects with a sense of stillness. His interest in a purely existential objectivity led finally to his famous *Aschehaufen* (Ashheap) of **1968/69** and the *Papierhaufen* (Pile of Paper) of **1970**, two works which link him with the Arte Povera movement. Since the mid-70s he has used fabrics to create environments out of rooms. **1972–1992** Participation in documenta 5 – 7 and 9 in Kassel. **1975** Taught at the Hamburg School of Fine Arts. **1976** Participation at the Venice Biennale. From **1980** professorship at the Düsseldorf Academy in the Department of Art Education, Münster. **1982** Table installations. Konrad von Soest Prize for the Plastic Arts, awarded by the Westphalen-Lippe landscape association. His works explore the diverse interrelationships of rigid, elastic and flexible materials and the tensions that emerge between object and space. He thereby bridges the gap between Material and Kinetic Art.
MONOGRAPHS, CATALOGUES: Bee, A. (ed.): R. R. Frankfurt-on-Main 1997

(cat.).– Blume, D. (ed.): R. R. Arbeiten 1965-1983. Kunstverein Braunschweig. Brunswick 1983 (cat.).– Grinten H. v. d. and J. Cladders (ed.): R. R. Städtisches Museum Abteiberg. Mönchengladbach 1972 (cat.).– Harten, J. (ed.): R. R. Objekte. Städtische Kunsthalle Düsseldorf. Düsseldorf 1974 (cat.).– Honnef, K. and J. Cladders (ed.): R. R. Westfälischer Kunstverein. Münster 1971 (cat.).– Potter, J. (ed.): R. R. Staatliche Kunsthalle Baden-Baden. Baden-Baden 1993 (cat.).– Wontorra, B. (ed.): R. R. Fotografie 1956-1976. Kunstverein für die Rheinlande und Westfalen, Düsseldorf. Stuttgart 1991 (cat.)

RYMAN Robert
born **1930** Nashville (TN)
American painter. **1948/49** Trained as a teacher at Tennessee Polytechnic Institute in Cookville and **1949/50** at George Peabody College for Teachers in Nashville. **1950–1952** Served in the American Army. **1952** Settled in New York, where he became interested in painting. Worked until **1960** as a museum warden at the Museum of Modern Art, where he met the artists Flavin and LeWitt, both proponents of Minimal Art. **1961** Married the art critic L. Lippard. Between **1972** and **1982** took part in documenta 5 – 7 in Kassel. **1993** Important retrospective at the Tate Gallery, London. Since the early 50s Ryman, the concept artist, has painted almost nothing but square format monochrome pictures, seeking a way to reveal the creative process itself and the gradual unfolding of a work. From the 60s he became interested in the visual effects created by fixing his canvases to the wall with hooks.
CATALOGUE RAISONNE: Baker Sandbock, A. (ed.): R. R. Prints 1969-1993. New York 1993
MONOGRAPHS, CATALOGUES: Bois, Y.-A. and C. Sauer (ed.): S. R. Centre Georges Pompidou, Paris et al. Paris 1981 (cat.).– Frémont, J.: R. R. Le paradoxe absolu. Caen 1991.– Huber, C. (ed.): R. R. Kunsthalle Basel. Basel 1975 (cat.).– R. R. Paintings and Reliefs. INK, Hallen für internationale neue Kunst. Zurich 1980 (cat.).– R. R. Espace d'Art Contemporain. Paris 1992 (cat.).– Sauer, C. and U. Raussmüller (ed.): R. R. Hallen für Neue Kunst. Schaffhausen 1991 (cat.).– Spector, N. (ed.): R. R. Stedelijk Museum. Amsterdam 1974 (cat.).– Spector, N. (ed.): R. R. Whitechapel Art Gallery. London 1977 (cat.).– Storr, R. (ed.): R. R. Tate Gallery, London et al. London and New York 1993 (cat.).– Waldman, D. (ed.): R. R. Solomon R. Guggenheim Museum. New York 1972 (cat.)

SAINT PHALLE Niki de
born **1930** Neuilly-sur-Seine (near Paris) French sculptress and painter. **1933** Moved to New York. **1951** Returned to France. **1956** First assemblages. Solo-exhibition in St. Gallen. From **1961** staged happenings

with her husband Jean Tinguely, and did *Shot Paintings*. Contact with the Nouveaux Réalistes in Paris. Participated in the exhibition "The Art of Assemblage" at the Museum of Modern Art, New York. **1964** Began to model Nanas, voluptuous, garishly coloured female figures. **1966** Installation of the giant, walk-through Nana figure *Hon* at the Moderna Museet, Stockholm. Design of further *Sculptural Houses*. **1967** Solo-exhibition at the Stedelijk Museum, Amsterdam. **1968** Participated in the exhibition "Dada, Surrealism and their Heritage" at the Museum of Modern Art, New York. **1976** Solo-exhibition at the Boymans-van Beuningen Museum, Rotterdam. **1979** Began construction of a sculptural park *Giardino dei Tarocchi* (Tarot Garden) near Florence. **1982** Created *La Fontaine Strawinsky*, a fountain in Paris, with Tinguely. **1988** Participated at the Venice Biennale. **1993** Solo-exhibition at the Musée d'Art Moderne de la Ville de Paris. The spectacular, monumental and garish character of de Saint Phalle's sculptures has much in common with Pop Art.
MONOGRAPHS, CATALOGUES: Boulez, P. (ed.): J. Tinguely and N. de S. P. La Fontaine Igor Strawinsky über dem I. R. C. A. M. Centre Georges Pompidou. Bern 1983.– Bourdon, D. (ed.): N. at Nassau. Nassau County Museum of Fine Arts. Roslyn (NY) 1987 (cat.).– Chenivesse, D. (ed.): N. de S. P. Das graphische Werk 1968-1980. Figuren. Ulmer Museum. Ulm 1980 (cat.).– Hering, K.-H. (ed.): N. de S. P. Werke 1962-1968. Düsseldorfer Kunstverein. Düsseldorf 1969 (cat.).– Hulten, P. et al. (ed.): N. de S. P. Centre Georges Pompidou. Paris 1980 (cat.).– Hulten, P. et al. (ed.): N. de S. P. Kunst- und Ausstellungshalle der Bundesrepublik Deutschland, Bonn et al. Stuttgart 1992 (cat.).– Hulten, P. (ed.): N. de S.-P. Tableaux éclatés. Musée d'Art Moderne de la Ville de Paris. Paris 1993 (cat.).– N. de S. P. Stedelijk Museum. Amsterdam 1967 (cat.).– N. de S. P. Retrospektive 1954-1980. Wilhelm Lehmbruck Museum. Duisburg 1980 (cat.).– N. de S. P. Moderna Museet. Stockholm 1981 (cat.).– Schulz-Hoffmann, C. (ed.): N. de S. P. Bilder, Figuren, Phantastische Gärten. Kunsthalle der Hypo-Kulturstiftung. Munich 1987 (cat.)

SALGADO Sebastião Ribeiro
born **1944** Aimoóres (Minas Gerais) Brazilian photographer. **1964–1967** Studied economics at the University of São Paulo, graduating with a Master's degree in **1968**. From **1969–1971** wrote his doctoral thesis in Paris. **1971–1973** Worked for a coffee import company in London. **1973** First pieces of photojournalism. From **1979** member of the photographic agency Magnum in Paris. Photographic documentation of the living conditions of immigrant workers in European countries.
MONOGRAPHS, CATALOGUES: Buarque de Hollanda, C.: Terra by S. S. New York 1997.– Galeano, E. and F.

Ritchin: S. S. An Uncertain Grace. New York 1990

SALLE David
born **1952** Norman (OK)
American painter. Studied until **1975** at the California Institute of the Arts, Valencia. **1975** First solo-exhibition as part of "Project" in Cambridge (MA) and at the Claire Copley Gallery, Los Angeles. **1976** Solo-exhibition in the Foundation Corps de Garde, Groningen. **1981** Participated in the "Westkunst" exhibition in Cologne. **1982** Took part in documenta 7 in Kassel and in the exhibition "Zeitgeist" in Berlin. **1985** Participated in the Nouvelle Biennale de Paris. **1986** Solo-exhibition at the Whitney Museum of American Art, New York. Participated in the exhibition "Europa/Amerika" at the Museum Ludwig, Cologne. **1988** Retrospective at the Staatsgalerie Moderner Kunst, Munich, and at the Tel Aviv Museum of Art. **1994** Solo-exhibition at the Mary Boone Gallery, New York.
WRITINGS: Schjeldahl, P.: S An Interview with D. S. New York 1987
MONOGRAPHS, CATALOGUES: Beeren, W. A. L. (ed.): D. S. Museum Boymans-van Beuningen. Rotterdam 1983 (cat.).– Busche, E. A. (ed.): D. S. Arbeiten auf Papier. 1974-1986. Museum am Ostwall, Dortmund et al. Dortmund 1986 (cat.).– Kardon, J. and L. Phillips (ed.): D. S. Institute of Contemporary Art, University of Pennsylvania, Pittsburgh et al. Pittsburgh 1986 (cat.).– Kögel, R.: D. S. Malerei. Ein kunstwissenschaftlicher Meta-Ansatz Hamburg 199.– Liebmann, L. (ed.): D. S. 1979-1994. New York 1994.– Power, K. and C. Schulz-Hoffmann (ed.): D. S. Staatsgalerie moderner Kunst, Munich et al. Munich and Madrid 1988 (cat.).– Rosenblum, R. (ed.): D. S. Zurich 1986.– D. S. Whitney Museum of American Art. New York 1986 (cat.).– Whitney, D. (ed.): D. S. New York 1994

SALOMON Erich
1886 Berlin – **1944** Auschwitz
German photographer. First studied law. Was a prisoner of war in France. **1918–1925** Worked as a photojournalist for Ullstein Verlag. **1927–1933** Reportages for the

Berliner Illustrirte Zeitung, Time and the *New York Tribune*. **1934** Fled to Holland, but was later arrested by the Nazis. **1971** Posthumously awarded the Erich Salomon Prize – the first time the prize had gone to a photojournalist. **1981** Retrospective at the Stedelijk Museum, Amsterdam. With his photographic documentation of great political events, Salomon laid the foundations of modern photojournalism.
MONOGRAPHS, CATALOGUES: Barents, E. and W. H. Roobol (ed.): Dr. E. S. 1886-1944. Aus dem Leben eines Fotografen. Munich 1981.– Forberg, G.: Die unbestechliche Kamera des Dr. E. S. Düsseldorf 1976.– Frecot, J. (ed.): E. S. Berlinische Galerie. Berlin 1986 (cat.).– Hassner, R. (ed.): E. S. Fotografiska Museet. Stockholm 1974 (cat.).– E. S. Berlinische Galerie. Berlin 1983 (cat.).– Vries, H. d. and P. Hunter-Salomon (ed.): E. S. Portrait of an Age. New York 1967

SAMARAS Lucas
born **1936** Kastoria
Greek-born American artist. **1948** Moved to the USA. **1955–1959** Studied art history at Rutger's University (NJ), and at Columbia University, New York. **1955** First solo-exhibition at Rutger's University. **1966** Retrospective at the Pace Gallery, New York. **1968 – 1977** Participated in documenta 4 – 6 in Kassel. **1969** Taught at Yale University, New Haven, and **1970/71** at Brooklyn College, New York. Solo-exhibition at the gallery Der Spiegel in Cologne. **1971** Retrospective at the Museum of Contemporary Art, Chicago. **1978** Trips to England and Greece. **1980** Participated at the Venice Biennale and **1983** in the exhibition "New Art" at the Tate Gallery, London. **1984, 1985** and **1987** Solo-exhibition at the Pace Gallery. Samaras' early works, furniture-like objects covered with thousands of needles, are closely related to Fluxus. In his later environments he uses mirrors to evoke the illusion of unlimited space.
WRITINGS: L. S.: S. Album, Autointerview, Autobiography, Utopolaroid. New York 1971
MONOGRAPHS, CATALOGUES: Alloway, L. (ed.): L. S. Selected Works 1960-1966. Pace Gallery. New York 1966 (cat.).– Glenn, C. and A. Glimcher (ed.): L. S. Phototransformations. University Art Museum. Long Beach 1975 (cat.).– Glenn, C. (ed.): L. S. Sketches, Drawings, Doodles and Plates. New York 1987.– Glimcher, A.: L. S.'s Photo-Transformations. New York 1975.– Idiana, G. (ed.): L. S. Chairs and Drawings. Pace Gallery. New York 1987 (cat.).– Levin, K.: L. S. New York 1974.– Lifson, B.: The Photographs of L. S. New York 1987.– McEvilley, T. et al. (ed.): L. S. Objects and Subjects 1969-1986. Denver Art Museum et al. New York 1988 (cat.).– L. S. Whitney Museum of American Art. New York 1973 (cat.).– L. S. Self 1961-1991. Yokohama Museum of Art. Yokohama 1991 (cat.).– Schjedahl, P. (ed.): S. Pastells. Denver Art Museum. Denver 1981 (cat.)

SANDER August
1876 Herford – **1964** Cologne
German photographer. **1890-1896** As a
boy, worked on the dump at the Herford
mine. **1896** Employed by the photographer
G. Jung in Trier. **1898-1900** Worked here
and there as a photographic assistant.
Attended the Dresden Academy of Painting. **1901** Employee at the Photographic
Art Institute Greiff in Linz on the Danube
which he took over in **1902** together with
F. Stuckenberg. In **1904** awarded a gold
medal and special honours at an exhibition
at the Palais des Beaux-Arts in Paris. **1910**
Moved to Cologne. **1914** Took part in the
exhibition of the Deutsche Werkbund.
1920 Had the idea of compiling an artistic
documentary register of different types of
people. **1929** Publication of *Antlitz der
Zeit* (Face of our Time), a preview of the
complete work *Menschen des 20. Jahrhunderts* (People of the 20th Century)
containing about 550 photographs. **1934**
Antlitz der Zeit taken out of circulation
by the Nazis and the printing blocks
destroyed. **1939** Found a safe place for his
photographs and moved to Kuchhausen.
1944 Cologne apartment destroyed in a
bombing raid. **1950** Exhibited at the first
Photokina in Cologne. **1954** Participated
in the exhibition "Family of Man" at the
Museum of Modern Art in New York.
1960/61 Received the Federal Service
Cross and the Cultural Prize of the
German Photographic Society. **1962**
Publication of his book of photographs
Deutschenspiegel.
MONOGRAPHS, CATALOGUES: Hartz,
J. v.: A. S. Millerton 1977/A. S. Paris 1977.–
Kramer, R. (ed.): A. S. Photographs of an
Epoch. New York 1980.– Lange. S. (ed.):
A. S. Visages d'une époque. Centre
National de la Photographie. Paris 1995
(cat.).– Sachse, R. (ed.): A. S. Köln wie es
war. Cologne 1988.– A. S. V fotografijach
net nejasnych tenej! Pushkin Museum.
Moscow 1994 (cat.).– Sander, G.: A. S.
Leipzig 1982.– Sander, G. (ed.): A. S. In
der Photographie gibt es keine ungeklärten
Schatten! August-Sander Archiv. Berlin
1994 (cat.).– Schreier, C. (ed.): A. S.
National Portrait Gallery. London 1997
(cat.).– Wilde, A. et al. (ed.): A. S. Die
Reise nach Sardinien. Sprengel Museum.
Hanover 1995 (cat.)

SANTOMASO Giuseppe
1907 Venice – **1990** Venice
Italian painter. Studied at the Venice Art
Academy. **1928** First public exhibition. **1937**
Travelled to Holland. From **1940** solo-exhi-
bitions at the Rive Gauche gallery in Paris
and in the Hanover Gallery, London. **1945**
Publication of 27 of his drawings in P.
Eluard's Anthology *Grand Air* by the
Milanese gallery Santa Radegonda. **1947**
Founder member of the group Fronte
Nuovo delle Arti. **1952** First purely abstract
painting. **1953** Intensive study of the paint-
ings of Hans Hartung. **1954** Won first prize
for painting at the Venice Biennale. San-

tomaso achieved a form of abstraction that
never completely betrays its relation to the
object. The lyrical, somewhat hermetic elements that appear in his paintings of the
50s are evidence of Hartung's influence.
CATALOGUES RAISONNES: Alfieri (ed.):
S. Catalogo ragionato 1931-1974. Venice
1975.– Calderoni, F. (ed.): S. Opera grafica
1938-1975. Roma 1975.– G. S. Catalogue
raisonné 1931-1974. Venice 1975
MONOGRAPHS, CATALOGUES: Apollonio, U.: G. S. Amriswil 1959.– Ballo, G.
(ed.): S. Opere 1939-1982. Museo Correr,
Venice. Milan 1982 (cat.).– Daminato, L.
(ed.): S. Opere 1939-1986. Palazzo Reale.
Milan 1986 (cat.).– Francastel, P.: S. Cicale
e cattedrali. Amriswil 1962.– Messer, T.
(ed.): S. Opere 1939-1986. Palazzo Reale.
Milan 1986 (cat.).– Ponente, N. (ed.): S.
Pitture. Venice 1968.– Rasekhschaffe-Aras,
A. and M. Bärmann (ed.): G. S. Ravens-
burg 1988 (cat.).– Steingräber, E. and C.
Schulz-Hoffmann (ed.): S. Staatsgalerie
moderner Kunst. Munich 1979 (cat.).–
Steingräber, E.: S. Langenhagen 1992.–
Venturi, L.: S. Roma 1955

SAURA Antonio
1930 Huesca – **1998** Cuenca
Spanish painter. Self-taught. **1943-1947**
Began to paint during a long period of
illness. **1950** First solo-exhibition in the
book shop Libros de Zaragoza in Madrid.
1953-1955 Lived in Paris and had contact
with the Surrealists. **1956** Returned to
Madrid. **1957** Founded the group El Paso
with Tàpies, Millarès and Canogar in
Madrid. **1958** First *Imaginary Portraits*.
Participated at the Venice Biennale. **1959-
1977** Took part in documenta 2, 3 and 6 in
Kassel. **1960** Participated in the exhibition
"Spanish Painting" at the Museum of
Modern Art, New York. Won the Guggenheim Award and **1966** the main prize for
graphic reproductions at the Lugano Biennale. **1967** Lived in Paris until his expulsion
from France in **1977**. **1979** Touring retrospective, starting at the Stedelijk Museum,
Amsterdam. **1983** Led the committee
"Artists of the World against Apartheid".
1985 Taught at Circulo de Bellas Artes,
Madrid. **1987** Painted the ceiling of the new
town hall in Huesca. **1990** Retrospective at
the Centro de Arte Reina Sofia, Madrid,
and at Lenbachhaus in Munich.

WRITINGS: A. S.: Libreta 1958-1980.
Madrid 1982
CATALOGUES RAISONNES: Galfetti, M.
(ed.): A. S. L'œuvre gravé 1958-1984. Paris
1985/A. S. La obra grafica. Paris 1990.–
Galfetti, M. (ed.): A. S. L'œuvre imprimé
1958-1984. Geneva 1985
MONOGRAPHS, CATALOGUES: Ayllon,
J.: A. S. Barcelona 1969.– Chiappini, R.
(ed.): A. S. Museo d'Arte Moderna della
Città di Lugano, Villa Malpensata. Milan
1994 (cat.).– Circi-Pellicier, A. (ed.): A. S.
Fundació Joan Miró, Barcelona et al.
Barcelona 1980 (cat.).– Cohen, M. and T.
Llorens (ed.): A. S. Peintures 1956-1985.
Musée Rath, Geneva et al. Geneva 1989.–
Cortanze, G. de (ed.): A. S. Paris 1994.–
Köb, E. (ed.): A. S. La quinta del sordo.
Secession. Vienna 1989 (cat.).– Mason, R.
M. (ed.): A. S. Musée d'Art et d'Histoire,
Geneva 1989 (cat.)/A. S. Städtische Galerie
im Lenbachhaus, Munich 1990 (cat.).–
Oliver, G.: S. in Cuenca. Copenhagen
1983.– Vázque de Parga, A. (ed.): S. Dese-
nari 1890-1990. Barcelona 1991 (cat.).–
Sarduy, S.: A. S. Barcelona 1987.– A. S.
Desenari. 1980-1990. Palau de la Virreina.
Barcelona 1991 (cat.).– Söderberg, L. (ed.):
A. S. Imagina 1956-1997. Malmö Konsthall.
Malmö 1997 (cat.)

SCHAD Christian
1894 Miesbach – **1982** Stuttgart
German painter and experimental photographer. **1913** Studied at the Munich
Academy. **1915** Participated in an exhibition
of the New Munich Secession. **1915-1920**
Lived in Zurich and Geneva. Participated
in Dada events. **1919** First photograms enti-
tled *Schadographien*. **1920-1927** Lived in
Italy. **1925** Moved to Vienna where, in **1927**,
he had his first solo-exhibition at the
Galerie Würthle. **1929** Took part in the
exhibition "Neue Sachlichkeit" at the
Stedelijk Museum, Amsterdam. **1936** Participated in the exhibition "Fantastic Art,
Dada, Surrealism" at the Museum of
Modern Art, New York. **1942** Moved to
Aschaffenburg and, in **1962**, to Keilheim.
1968 Participated in the exhibition "Dada-
Surrealism and their Heritage" at the
Museum of Modern Art. Major retrospec-
tives: **1972** at the Palazzo Reale in Milan,
1980 at the Kunsthalle Berlin and **1997** at
Lenbachhaus, Munich. Schad is best
known for his invention of Schadographie,
by which images of objects are produced on
light-sensitive plates without the use of a
camera.
WRITINGS: C. S. Mein Lebensweg.
Galerie Würthle. Vienna 1926 (cat.)
CATALOGUES RAISONNES: Richter,
M.-L. and T. Helmert-Corvey (ed.): C. S.
Druckgraphiken und Schadographien in
Einzelblättern und Mappenwerken 1913-
1981. Herford et al.– Testori, G. (ed.):
C. S. Werkverzeichnis 1920-1930. Galleria
del Levante. Milan and Munich 1970 (cat.)
MONOGRAPHS, CATALOGUES: Bezzola,
T. (ed.): C. S. Kunsthaus Zurich et al.
Zurich 1997 (cat.).– Eberle, M. and H.

Bergius (ed.): C. S. Staatliche Kunsthalle
Berlin. Berlin 1980 (cat.).– Gravenkamp,
C.: C. S. Das Gesicht des 20. Jahrhunderts im
Werk des Malers C. S. Kassel 1959.– Hartl,
C. (ed.): C. S. 1894-1982. Oberhausmu-
seum. Passau 1989 (cat.).– Heesemann-
Wilson, A.: C. S. Expressionist, Dadist und
Maler der Neuen Sachlichkeit. Göttingen
1978.– Laszlo, C.: C. S. Basel 1972.–
Osborn, M.: Der Maler C. S. Berlin 1927.–
Richter, G. A. (ed.): C. S. Zeichnungen
und Legenden. Rottach-Egern 1990 (cat.).–
Schad, B. et al. (ed.): C. S. Die späten
Jahre. 1942-1982. Galerie der Stadt Aschaf-
fenburg et al. Aschaffenburg 1994 (cat.).–
R. S. Schadographien 1918-1975. Von der
Heydt-Museum. Wuppertal 1975 (cat.).–
Tassi, R. (ed.): C. S. Palazzo Reale. Milan
1972 (cat.).– Testori, G.: C. S. Werke von
1920 bis 1930. Milan and Munich 1970

SCHAPIRO Miriam
born **1923** Toronto
Canadian-born American painter and
collage artist. Studied **1943-1949** at the
University of Iowa, where she later met her
husband, the painter P. Brach. Her abstract
gestural paintings of the 50s developed into
Hard-Edge painting with calmer, more
orderly forms. In the 70s, the artist combined found objects and materials from the
world of a housewife into collages, assemblages and paintings, calling this procedure
femmage. **1971-1975** Collaboration with J.
Chicago, as director of the Department of
Feminist Art at the California Institute of
Art in Valencia. Her works became connected with decorative Pattern-Art. In the
80s she took up figurative acrylic painting
on the theme of dance.
WRITINGS: M. S.: Women and the Creative Process. Manchester 1974
MONOGRAPHS, CATALOGUES: Goma-
Peterson, T. (ed.): M. S. A Retrospective.
College of Wooster Art Museum. Wooster
(OH) 1980 (cat.).– M. S. Femmages 1971-
1985. Brentwood Gallery. St. Louis 1985
(cat.).– M. S. Bernice Steinbaum Gallery.
New York 1986

SCHIELE Egon
1890 Tulln (Lower Austria) – **1918** Vienna
Austrian painter and draughtsman. **1906-
1909** Studied at the Vienna Academy. **1909**
Co-founder of the Neukunstgruppe (New
Artists' Group). Collaboration with the
Vienna workshops. **1907** Met Klimt. **1911**
Joined the artists' association Sema in
Munich. **1912** Took part in the exhibition of
the Blauer Reiter. Given a three-day sentence for disseminating pornographic drawings. **1914** Participated in the exhibition of
the Werkbund in Cologne. **1915** Called up
for military service. **1918** Died of Spanish
influenza. Schiele's career as an artist, cut
short by his untimely death, falls squarely
within the period of Viennese Jugendstil.
However, his works have marked Expressionist traits. He contorts his figures and
selects daring perspectives and glowing

colours: colour, for him, being the most potent medium of expression.
WRITINGS: E. S.: Ich ewiges Kind. Gedichte. Vienna and Munich 1985
CATALOGUES RAISONNES: Kallir, O. (ed.): E. S. The Complete Works. London, New York, Paris and Cologne 1990.– Kallir, O. (ed.): E. S. Das druckgraphische Werk. Vienna 1970.– Leopold, R. (ed.): E. S. Gemälde, Aquarelle, Zeichnungen. Salzburg 1972 / E. S. Paintings, Watercolours, Drawings. London 1973.– Malafarina, G. (ed.): Tout l'œuvre peint de S. Paris 1983
MONOGRAPHS, CATALOGUES: Comini, A.: E. S. London 1976.– Comini, A.: Nudes. E. S. New York 1995.– Comini, A.: E. S.'s Portraits. Berkeley 1990.– Fischer, W. G.: E. S. 1890-1918. Desire and Decay. Cologne 1995.– Fournier, J.-F.: E. S. La Décadence de Vienne 1890-1918. Paris 1992.– Kallir, J. (ed.): E. S. National Gallery, Washington et al. New York 1994 (cat.).– Knafo, D.: E. S. A Self in Creation. Rutherford 1993.– Kuchling, H.: E. S. und sein Kreis. Ramerding 1982.– Mitsch, E.: E. S. 1890-1918. Salzburg 1974.– Mitsch, E.: E. S. Salzburg and Vienna 1987.– Mitsch, E.: The Art of E. S. Oxford 1989, San Francisco 1995.– Mitsch, E. (ed.): E. S. in der Albertina. Vienna 1990 (cat.).– Müller-Tamm, P. (ed.): E. S. Inszenierung und Identität. Cologne 1995.– Nebehay, C. M.: E. S. 1890-1918. Leben, Briefe, Gedichte. Salzburg and Vienna 1979.– Nebehay, C. M.: E. S. Leben und Werk. Salzburg and Vienna 1980.– Nebehay, C. M.: E. S. Von der Skizze zum Bild. Die Skizzenbücher. Vienna and Munich 1989.– Sabarsky, S. (ed.): E. S. Pinacoteca Capitolina, Roma. Milan 1984 (cat.).– Sabarsky, S. (ed.): E. S. Hamburger Kunsthalle. Hamburg 1985 (cat.).– Sabarsky, S. (ed.): E. S. New York 1985.– Sabarsky, S. (ed.): E. S. 1890-1918. A Centennial Retrospective. Los Angeles County Museum of Art. Nassau 1990 (cat.).– Schröder, K. A. and H. Szeemann (ed.): E. S. und seine Zeit. Sammlung Leopold. Kunsthaus Zurich et al. Munich 1989.– Schröder, K. A.: E. S. Eros und Passion. Munich 1995.– Steiner, R.: E. S. 1890-1918. The Midnight Soul of the Artist. Cologne 1991.– Thomas, K. (ed.): E. S. Die Sammlung Leopold, Wien. Cologne 1995 (cat.).– Walrod, S. T.: E. S. A Psychobiography. Ann Arbor (MI) 1980.– Werkner, P. (ed.): E. S. Art, Sexuality and Viennese Modernism. Palo Alto 1994.– Whitford, F.: E. S. London 1981.– Wilson, S.: E. S. Ithaca (NY) 1980

SCHLEMMER Oskar
1888 Stuttgart – **1943** Baden-Baden
German painter, sculptor and stage designer. After an apprenticeship in an intarsia workshop, studied **1905-1909** at the School of Arts and Crafts and the Art Academy in Stuttgart. **1910** Lived in Berlin. **1912** Master classes under Hoelzel in Stuttgart. **1920** Invited to the Bauhaus in Weimar by Walter Gropius and appointed director of the workshop for mural paint-

ings and later for wood and stone sculpture. Became famous for his Constructivist designs for his *Triadic Ballet*, first performed in **1922** in Stuttgart, in which figures in costumes made up of basic geometric forms represent people in space. **1923** Took over the theatre workshop at the Bauhaus and, after moving to Dessau, set up an experimental theatre there. **1928-1930** Painted murals for the Folkwang Museum in Essen. **1929** Took up an appointment at the Breslau Academy. **1932** Professorship at the American School in Berlin, terminated in **1933** by the Nazis. **1938/39** Camouflaged military installations. **1940** Worked with Baumeister and Muche at the Wuppertal Institute of Painting Materials. **1942** Series of small-scale *Fensterbilder* (Window Paintings). Throughout his career, in all his various works, Schlemmer explored the relationships and effects of space, form, colour, sound, movement and light.
WRITINGS: Bärmann, M. (ed.): J. Bissier und O. S. Briefwechsel. St. Gallen 1988.– Hüneke, A. (ed.): O. S. Idealist der Form. Briefe, Tagebücher, Schriften 1912-1943. Leipzig 1990.– O. S.: Die Bühne am Bauhaus. Bauhausbuch. Munich 1925 / The Theatre of the Bauhaus. Middletown (CT) 1961 / Théâtre et abstraction. Paris 1978.– O. S.: Briefe und Tagebücher. Munich 1958, Stuttgart 1977.– Schlemmer, T. (ed.): The Letters and Diaries of O. S. Middletown (CT) 1972
CATALOGUES RAISONNES: Grohmann, W. and T. Schlemmer (ed.): Zeichnungen und Graphik. Œuvrekatalog. Stuttgart 1965, San Francisco 1982.– Hildebrandt, H. (ed.): O. S. Munich 1952.– Maur, K. v. (ed.): O. S. Monographie und Œuvrekatalog der Gemälde, Aquarelle, Pastelle und Plastiken. 2 vols. Munich 1979.– Schlemmer, T. (ed.): O. S. Zeichnungen und Graphik. Œuvrekatalog. Stuttgart 1965
MONOGRAPHS, CATALOGUES: Bender, B. et al. (ed.): O. S. Wand – Bild. Bild – Wand. Städtische Kunsthalle Mannheim: Mannheim 1988 (cat.).– Gauss, U. (ed.): O. S. Aquarelle. Staatsgalerie Stuttgart. Stuttgart 1988 (cat.).– Grohmann, W. and T. Schlemmer: O. S. Zeichnungen und Graphiken. Stuttgart 1965.– Herzogenrath, W.: O. S. Die Wandgestaltung der neuen Architektur. Munich 1973.– Hohl, R. (ed.): O. S. Die Fensterbilder. Kunstmuseum Basel. Frankfurt-on-Main 1990.– Kahn-Rossi, M. (ed.): O. S. Les Noces. Museo Cantonale d'Arte, Lugano. Milan 1988 (cat.).– Lehman, A. L. and B. Richardson (ed.): O. S. The Baltimore Museum of Art et al. Baltimore 1986 (cat.).– Maur, K. v.: O. S. Munich 1979.– Maur, K. v. (ed.): O. S. Staatsgalerie Stuttgart. Munich 1977, 1982 (cat.).– Maur, K. v. (ed.): O. S. Der Folkwang-Zyklus. Malerei um 1930. Staatsgalerie Stuttgart et al. Stuttgart 1993 (cat.).– Meyer-Ellinger, H. (ed.): O. S. 1888-1943. Jahrhunderthalle, Hoechst et al. Frankfurt-on-Main 1984 (cat.).– Scheper, D.: O. S. Das triadische Ballett und die Bauhausbühne. Berlin 1988.– Schlemmer, C. R. and U. J. (ed.): O. S. Tanz, Theater, Bühne. Kunstsammlung Nordrhein-Westfalen, Düsseldorf et al. Stuttgart 1994 (cat.).– O. S. Staatsgalerie Stuttgart et al. Stuttgart 1977 (cat.).– Svestka, J. et al. (ed.): O. S. Das Lackkabinett. Düsseldorfer Kunstverein. Düsseldorf 1987 (cat.)

SCHLICHTER Rudolf
1890 Calw – **1955** Munich
German painter. **1904** Apprenticeship as an enamel painter in a factory in Pforzheim. **1907-1910** Attended the Stuttgart School of Arts and Crafts. **1910** Began studies at the Karlsruhe Academy. **1916** Called up for

military service, but prematurely dismissed for staging a hunger strike. **1919** Co-founder of the group Rih in Karlsruhe. Moved to Berlin, where he joined the Novembergruppe. **1920** Participated in the First International DADA Trade Fair. Worked as an illustrator for various publishers. **1925** Participated in the "Neue Sachlichkeit" exhibition at the Kunsthalle Mannheim. **1927** Solo-exhibition at the Neumann-Nierendorf gallery in Berlin. **1929** Took part in the "Neue Sachlichkeit" exhibition at the Stedelijk Museum in Amsterdam. **1931** Publication of his novel *Zwischenwelt*. **1932/33** Moved to Rottenburg am Neckar. Publication of his autobiography in two volumes. **1939** Confiscation of his works, classified as "degenerate" by the Nazis. **1939** Moved to Munich. **1942** Loss of his studio through a bombing raid. **1949** Publication of an article entitled *Das Abenteuer der Kunst* (The Adventure of Art). **1998** Major retrospective at Lenbachhaus, Munich.
WRITINGS: Heißerer, D. (ed.): R. S. Das Abenteuer der Kunst. Hamburg 1949, 1998.– Heißerer, D. (ed.): R. S. Die Verteidigung des Panoptikums. Autobiographische, zeit- und kunstkritische Schriften sowie Briefe 1930-1955. Berlin 1995.– Heißerer, D. (ed.): R. S. Drohende Katastrophe. Gedichte 1931-1936. Warmbronn 1997.– Heißerer, D. (ed.): R. S. und Ernst Jünger. Briefwechsel. Stuttgart 1997.– R. S.: Autobiographie. 2 vols. Hamburg 1932-1933, Berlin 1991.– R. S.: Das Abenteuer der Kunst. Hamburg 1949
MONOGRAPHS, CATALOGUES: Adriani, G. (ed.): R. S. Gemälde, Aquarelle, Zeichnungen. Kunsthalle Tübingen et al. Munich 1997 (cat.).– Grützmacher, C. (ed.): R. S. Das widerspenstige Fleisch. Berlin 1991.– Grützmacher, C. (ed.): R. S. Tönerne Füße. Berlin 1992.– Horn, G. et al. (ed.): R. S. 1890-1955. Staatliche Kunsthalle Berlin et al. Berlin 1984 (cat.).– Metken, G.: R. S. Blinde Macht. Frankfurt-on-Main 1990.– R. S. Von der Heydt-Museum, Wuppertal et al. Munich 1997 (cat.).– Testori, G. (ed.): R. S. 1890-1955. Galleria del Levante. Milan 1970 (cat.)

SCHMIDT-ROTTLUFF Karl
(Karl Schmidt)
1884 Rottluff (near Chemnitz) – **1976** Berlin
German painter and graphic artist. **1901** Friendship with Heckel. **1905** Began to study architecture at the technical college in Dresden. Together with Bleyl, Kirchner and Heckel, founded the Brücke group. **1906** Brought Nolde into the group. **1907-1912** Spent the summers in Dangast. **1910** Abandoned Impressionist Valeur painting and restricted himself to pure colours. **1911** His gradual simplification of form and structure led to Cubist-style figures. **1912** Moved to Berlin; friendship with Feininger. Participated in the "Sonderbund" exhibition in Cologne. Travelled to Italy, Paris and Dalmatia. **1913** Brücke disbanded. **1915**

-1918 Fought in Lithuania and Russia. **1918-1921** Joined the Arbeitskreis für Kunst and worked for the magazine *Die Aktion*. **1918-1943** Lived in Berlin, spending summers on the Baltic Sea. **1931-1933** Member of the Prussian Academy of Arts. **1937** 608 of his works declared "degenerate" by the Nazis and confiscated from German museums. **1943** Moved to Rottluff after the loss of his Berlin studio. **1946** Returned to Berlin where, from **1947-1954**, he was professor at the School of Fine Arts. Responsible for the founding of the Brücke-Museum in Berlin in **1964**. Schmidt-Rottluff's extensive œuvre includes not only paintings but also graphic works, including many woodcuts.
CATALOGUES RAISONNES: Grohmann, W.: K. S.-R. (mit Werkverzeichnis der Gemälde 1905-1954). Stuttgart 1956.– Rathenau, E. (ed.): K. S.-R. Das graphische Werk seit 1923. New York and Berlin 1964.– Schapire, R. (ed.): K. S.-R.'s graphisches Werk bis 1923. 2 vols. Berlin 1924, 1970, New York 1987.– K. S.-R. Zum 100. Geburtstag. Schleswig-Holsteinisches Landesmuseum. Schleswig 1984 (cat.).– K. S.-R. Gemälde und Aquarelle. Ausstellung zum 100. Geburtstag des Künstlers. Brücke-Museum. Berlin 1984 (cat.).– K. S.-R. Der Maler. Städtische Kunstsammlungen. Chemnitz 1993 (cat.)
MONOGRAPHS, CATALOGUES: Anna, S. (ed.): K. S.-R. Malerei und Grafik. Bestandskatalog der Städtischen Kunstsammlungen Chemnitz. Stuttgart 1993.– Brix, K.: K. S.-R. Leipzig and Munich 1972.– Grohmann, W.: K. S.-R. Stuttgart 1956.– Moeller, M. M.: K. S.-R. Aquarelle. Brücke-Museum, Berlin et al. Munich 1991 (cat.).– Moeller, M. M. and H.-W. Schmidt (ed.): K. S.-R. Der Maler. Städtische Kunsthalle Düsseldorf et al. Stuttgart 1992 (cat.).– Moeller, M. M. (ed.): K. S.-R. Tuschpinselzeichnungen. Galerie Jahrhunderthalle, Hoechst et al. Munich 1995 (cat.).– Moeller, M. M. (ed.): K. S.-R. Kunsthalle der Hypo-Kulturstiftung, Munich et al. Munich 1997 (cat.).– Reidemeister, L. (ed.): K. S.-R. Brücke-Museum. Berlin 1984 (cat.).– Schilling, J. and D. Blume (ed.): K. S.-R. Werke 1905-1961. Kunstverein Braunschweig. Brunswick 1979 (cat.).– Thiem, G.: K. S.-R. Aquarelle und Zeichnungen. Munich 1963.– Thiem, G. and A. Zweite (ed.): K. S.-R. Retrospektive. Städtische Galerie im Lenbachhaus, Munich et al. Munich 1989 (cat.).– Wietek, G.: S.-R. Graphik. Munich 1971.– Wietek, G.: K. S.-R. in Hamburg und Schleswig-Holstein. Neumünster 1984.– Wietek, G.: S.-R. Oldenburger Jahre 1907-1912. Mainz 1995

SCHNABEL Julian
born **1951** New York
American painter. **1965** Moved with his family from New York to Texas, where he studied from **1969-1972** at the University of Houston. **1973/74** Took part in the Independent Study Program run by the

Whitney Museum in New York. **1978** Travelled to Spain, Italy and Germany, where he exhibited for the first time at the December gallery in Düsseldorf. **1979** Achieved recognition in the art world with his solo-exhibition at the Mary Boone Gallery in New York. **1980** Participated at the Venice Biennale, **1981** in the exhibition "A New Spirit in Painting" at the Royal Academy in London and in the "Westkunst" exhibition in Cologne. **1982** Major solo-exhibition at the Stedelijk Museum, Amsterdam. **1983** First sculptures made of heterogeneous materials. **1985** Represented at the Nouvelle Biennale in Paris. **1987** Major retrospective at the Pompidou Centre in Paris and at the Whitney Museum of American Art in New York. **1987/88** *Recognitions*, projections of the names of saints and religious or clerical symbols, the tarpaulin of military vehicles onto projections. In his mostly large-format paintings Schnabel combines unusual grounds with found objects such as broken pieces of china or antlers.
WRITINGS: J. S.: C. V. J. Nicknames of Maitre D's and Other Excerpts from Life. New York 1987
MONOGRAPHS, CATALOGUES: Ammann, J.-C. and M. Suter (ed.): J. S. Kunsthalle Basel et al. Basel 1981 (cat.).– Barzel, A. (ed.): J. S. Museo d'Arte Contemporaneo. Prato 1989 (cat.).– Blistène, B. et al. (ed.): J. S. Centre Georges Pompidou. Paris 1987 (cat.).– Collings, M. et al. (ed.): J. S. Paintings 1975-1986. Whitechapel Art Gallery, London et al. London 1986 (cat.).– Eccher, D. and N. Rosenthal (ed.): J. S. Bologna 1996 (cat.).– Eccher, D.: J. S. New York 1997.– Francis, R. (ed.): J. S. Tate Gallery. London 1982 (cat.).– Grevenstein, R. and A. v. (ed.): J. S. Stedelijk Museum. Amsterdam 1982.– Kuspit, D. B. (ed.): J. S. Waddington Galleries. London 1985 (cat.).– Landau, S. and G. Politi (ed.): J. S. Israel Museum. Jerusalem 1988 (cat.).– McEvilley, T. (ed.): J. S. Paintings 1975-1986. Whitechapel Art Gallery. London 1986 (cat.).– Ricard, R. and A. v. Grevenstein (ed.): J. S. Stedelijk Museum. Amsterdam 1982 (cat.).– J. S. CVJ. New York 1988 (cat.).– J. S. Musée d'Art Contemporain de Bordeaux. Bordeaux 1989 (cat.).– J. S. Sculpture 1987-1989. New York 1990.– J. S. Works on Paper 1976-1992. Matthew Marks Gallery. New York 1994 (cat.).– J. S. Galleria d'Arte Moderna. Bologna 1996 (cat.).– Syring, M. L. (ed.): J. S. Bilder 1975-1986. Städtische Kunsthalle Düsseldorf 1987 (cat.).– Zutter, J. et al. (ed.): J. S. Arbeiten auf Papier 1975-1988. Museum für Gegenwartskunst, Basel et al. Munich 1989 (cat.)

SCHNEIDER Gérard
1898 Sainte-Croix (Waadt) – **1986** Paris
Swiss-born French painter. **1916/17** Studied at the Ecole des Arts Décoratifs in Neuchâtel. **1918** Moved to Paris, where he entered Cormon's studio at the Ecole des Beaux-Arts. **1920** Moved back to Switzerland. First exhibition in Neuchâtel. From

1922 lived in Paris again. **1926** Participated in the Salon d'Automne and, in **1936**, in the Salon des Surindépendants. **1944** Became an abstract painter. **1946** Exhibited at the Salon des Réalités Nouvelles. **1947** First solo-exhibition at the Lydia Conti gallery in Paris. **1948** Participated at the Venice Biennale. **1955** Exhibition at the Palais des Beaux-Arts, Brussels. **1955** and **1959** participation in documenta 1 and 2 in Kassel. **1957** Prix des la Peinture Abstraite in Lissone. **1959** Won a prize at the International Art Exhibition in Tokyo, **1966** major prize at the Venice Biennale. **1970** Retrospective at the Galleria Civica d'Arte, Turin. **1983** Solo-exhibition at the Musée des Beaux-Arts, Neuchâtel.
MONOGRAPHS, CATALOGUES: Dunoyer, J.-M. (ed.): G. S. Musée d'Art et d'Histoire de Neuchâtel. Neuchâtel 1983 (cat.).– Gindertaël, R. v.: G. S. Galleria Lorenzelli, Bergamo. Venice 1967 (cat.).– Orizet, J.: S. Peintures. Paris 1984.– Pobé, M.: S. Paris 1959.– Ragon, M.: G. S. Amriswil 1961.– G. S. Städtische Kunsthalle Düsseldorf. Düsseldorf 1962 (cat.)

SCHÖFFER Nicolas
1912 Kalocsa – **1992** Paris
Hungarian-born French sculptor and object artist. Studied at the Budapest School of Arts. **1936** Moved to Paris and continued his studies at the Ecole des Beaux-Arts. **1948** First exhibition at the Galerie Breteau. Developed the theoretical basis for his later kinetic sculptures involving audiovisual effects such as reflected light, movement, sound and music. **1950** First public exhibition of kinetic sculptures at the Galerie des Deux-Iles, Paris. **1954** Constructed sound installations, with the engineer J. Bureau and the composer P. Henry. **1956** and **1964** Created *Cysp I*, the first cybernetic sculpture. **1959** and **1964** participation in documenta 2 and 3 in Kassel. **1961** Built a 52 metre-high kinetic tower in La Boverie Park, Liège. In the same year, participated at the São Paulo Biennale and, in **1964**, in documenta 3 in Kassel. **1965** First major presentations in America as part of the exhibition "Kinetic and Optic Art Today" at the Albright-Knox Art Gallery, Buffalo. **1968** Designed a cybernetic stage set for the Hamburg Opera. Major prize at the Venice Biennale. **1973** Constructed the automobile sculpture *Scam*. **1986** Awarded the Leonardo Prize in San Francisco. Schöffer, a leading exponent of Kinetic Art, developed a new art form out of a combination of sculpture, projected light, movement and film.
WRITINGS: N. S.: La Ville cybernétique. Paris 1969.– N. S.: Le nouvel esprit artistique. Paris 1970.– N. S.: Perturbation et Chronocratie. Paris 1978
MONOGRAPHS, CATALOGUES: Aknai, T.: N. S. Budapest 1975.– Cassou, J. et al.: N. S. Neuchâtel 1963.– Habasque, G. and J. Cassou: N. S. Neuchâtel 1963.– Haas, A.: N. S. Paris 1975.– Hoornart, P.: N. S. Liège 1985.– N. S. Kinetische Plastik. Licht,

Raum, Bewegung. Städtische Kunsthalle Düsseldorf. Düsseldorf 1968.– N. S. Musée d'Art Moderne. Paris 1974 (cat.).– Sers, P.: Entretiens avec N. S. Paris 1971

SCHOLZ Georg
1890 Wolfenbüttel – **1945** Waldkirch
German painter. **1908** Studied painting under H. Thoma and W. Trübner at the regional school of art in Karlsruhe. **1914–1918** Military service. **1919** Joined the Communist Party. Together with Hubbuch and Schlichter founded the group Rih, that merged with the Novembergruppe. From **1920** realist paintings in Berlin Dada style. Became acquainted with Dix, Grosz and Kanoldt. From **1923** taught at the regional school of art in Karlsruhe. **1925/26** Contributed to *Simplicissimus*. **1925** Participated in the "Neue Sachlichkeit" exhibition at the Kunsthalle Mannheim. **1933** Dismissed from his teaching post. **1937** Confiscation of his paintings, classified as "degenerate art". **1975** Retrospective at the Badische Kunstverein, Karlsruhe. Scholz was one of the most energetic proponents of Critical Realism in the early 20s.
CATALOGUE RAISONNE: Bessel, B. (ed.): G. S. Das druckgraphische Werk. Künstlerhaus-Galerie. Karlsruhe 1982 (cat.)
MONOGRAPHS, CATALOGUES: Holsten, S.: G. S. Karlsruhe 1990.– Leibinger, R. (ed.): G. S. 1890-1945. Waldkirch (ed.).– Mück, H.-D. (ed.): G. S. 1890-1945. Malerei, Zeichnung, Druckgraphik. Stuttgart 1991.– G. S. Ein Beitrag zur Diskussion realistischer Kunst. Badischer Kunstverein. Karlsruhe 1975 (cat.)

SCHOONHOVEN Jan
born **1914** Delft
Dutch painter and sculptor. **1930-1934** Studied at the Academy of Arts in The Hague, and from **1946** worked for the postal service there. **1949** First solo-exhibition at the Arts Centre in The Hague. In the early 50s, made contact with the Cobra artists. **1955** Started to make reliefs out of *papier mâché*. **1958** Co-founder of the Nederlandse informele Groep. **1960** Founded the group Nul together with Armando, Henk and Peeters. **1967** Won a second prize at the São Paulo Biennale and took part in the World Fair in Montreal.

1968 Exhibited at documenta 4 in Kassel. **1972/73** Major solo-exhibitions at Abteiberg Museum, Mönchengladbach and the Hamburg Kunsthalle. **1977** Participated in documenta 6 in Kassel and, in **1981**, in the "Westkunst" exhibition, Cologne. **1984** David Röell Award. **1989** Retrospective at the Stedelijk Museum, Amsterdam. Schoonhoven's conception of objectivity, as manifested in his series of *papier mâché* relief works, aligns him with artists of the Zero group.
MONOGRAPHS, CATALOGUES: Bool, F. et al. (ed.): J. S. Retrospectief. Haags Gemeentemuseum et al. The Hague 1984 (cat.).– Imdahl, M. et al. (ed.): J. S. Retrospektiv. Essen et al. Essen 1995 (cat.).– Lemoine, S. (ed.): J. S. Retrospektive. Institut Néederlandais, Paris et al. Paris 1988 (cat.).– J. S. Zeichnungen 1940-1975. Städtische Kunsthalle Düsseldorf et al. Düsseldorf 1975 (cat.).– J. S. Städtisches Museum, Schloß Morsbroich. Leverkusen 1981 (cat.).– J. S. A Retrospective. Ritter Art Gallery. Boca Raton 1987 (cat.).– Wesseling, J.: S. Beeldend kunstenaar. s'-Gravenhage 1990

SCHRIMPF Georg
1889 Munich – **1938** Berlin
German painter. Self-taught. **1902** Apprenticeship as a baker. **1915** Military service. Early discharge owing to illness. **1915–1917** Lived in Berlin and began to work as a freelance artist. **1918** Moved to Munich. **1921** Joined the New Secession. **1922** Went to Italy where he came in contact with the group Valori plastici. **1924** Publication of a short article on Schrimpf by Carrà. **1925** Participated in the "Neue Sachlichkeit" exhibition at the Kunsthalle Mannheim. From **1927** professor at the Munich School of Decorative Arts. **1929** Participated in the "Neue Sachlichkeit" exhibition at the Stedelijk Museum in Amsterdam. **1932** Spent a year in Rome. **1933–1938** Professor at the Teacher Training College for the Arts in Berlin. **1933** Participated in the exhibition "Neue Deutsche Romantik" at the Kestner Society in Hanover. **1937** Resigned voluntarily from his professorship.
CATALOGUE RAISONNE: Storch, W. (ed.): G. S. und Maria Uhden. Leben und Werk. Mit einem Werkverzeichnis. Museum Villa Stuck, Munich et al. Munich and Berlin 1985 (cat.)
MONOGRAPHS, CATALOGUES: Hartleb, R.: G. S. Dresden 1984.– Pförtner, M. G. S. Berlin 1940

SCHULTZE Bernard
born **1919** Schneidemühl
German painter and object artist. **1934–1936** and **1938/39** Studied at the Teacher Training College for the Arts in Berlin. **1936–1938** Studied at the Düsseldorf Academy. **1939–1944** Military service. **1945** After losing all his early works in the war, began to paint in a Surrealist style. Went to France. **1947–1968** Lived in Frankfurt am

Main. **1951** Experimented with Tachisme.
1952 Founder member of the group
Quadriga. From **1956** made reliefs by sticking torn photographs to the canvas. **1959**–
1977 Participation in documenta 2, 3 and 6
in Kassel. From **1961** *Migof* constructions
and *Zungen* (tongue)-collages: three-
dimensional works in which the sculptural
elements project out of the surface of the
painting far into the surrounding space.
From **1964** repeated trips to New York.
1966 Solo-exhibition at the Kestner Society
in Hanover. **1968** Moved to Cologne. **1976**
Large-format oil paintings, watercolours
and drawings. **1980** Major solo-exhibition
at the Kunsthalle Düsseldorf. **1986** Lovis
Corinth Prize. In the late 50s, as his Expressionist and Surrealist periods drew to a
close, he turned to abstraction and L'art
informel, and applied the principles of this
approach to his sprawling sculptures that
seem to reach out and capture space.
WRITINGS: B. S.: Migof-Reden, Zeichnungen und Texte. Stierstadt 1971.– B. S.:
Im Sieb die gelbroten Körner. Heidelberg
1972.– B. S.: Sperriger Zaun aus Zeit.
Düsseldorf 1976
CATALOGUES RAISONNES: Heuer, E.
and W. Zemter (ed.): B. S. Die Druckgrafik. Märkisches Museum. Witten 1990
(cat.)
MONOGRAPHS, CATALOGUES:
Honnef, K. (ed.): B. S. Papier-Arbeiten.
1946-1983. Rheinisches Landesmuseum,
Bonn et al. Bonn 1984 (cat.).– Leo, P. (ed.):
B. S. Städtisches Museum. Bochum 1970
(cat.).– Leppien, H. R. (ed.): B. S. Zerbrochene Verstecke. Hamburger Kunsthalle. Hamburg 1980 (cat.).– Romain, L.
and R. Wedewer: B. S. Munich 1991.–
Schmied, W. (ed.): B. S. Kestner-Gesellschaft. Hanover 1966 (cat.).– Roters, E.
and C. Schneegans (ed.): B. S. Im Labyrinth. Werke von 1947-1990. Gemäldegalerie. Dresden 1991 (cat.).– Volkmann, B.
and R.-F. Raddatz (ed.): B. S. Im Labyrinth. Werke von 1940-1980. Städtische
Kunsthalle Düsseldorf et al. Berlin 1980
(cat.).– Wedewer, R. and P. W. Jansen
(ed.): B. S. Städtisches Museum Leverkusen, Schloß Morsbroich. Leverkusen
1966 (cat.).– Weis, E. (ed.): B. S. Das
große Format. Arbeiten aus dem letzten
Jahrzehnt. Museum Ludwig, Cologne et
al. Munich 1994 (cat.)

SCHUMACHER Emil
1912 Hagen (Westphalia) – **1999** Ibiza
German painter. **1932**–**1935** Taking his
parents' advice, studied graphic art at the
Dortmund School of Arts and Crafts. First
worked as a painter and lithographer. **1939**–
1945 Employed as a technical draughtsman
in an armaments factory. After the war,
inspired by the paintings of Rohlfs, he
began to paint Cubist landscapes. However, after going to Paris in **1951**, where he
met Wols, he developed a graffiti-like pictorial language related to L'art informel.
He treated his colours as autonomous raw
materials, and gave them depth by applying

the paint so thickly that it almost formed a
relief. **1958**–**1960** Professor at the Hamburg
School of Fine Arts. **1959**–**1977** Participa-
tion in documenta 2, 3 and 6 in Kassel.
1966–**1977** Professor at the Karlsruhe
Academy and **1967/68** at the Minneapolis
School of Art. Made several tours of the
USA and, from **1971**, spent summer and
winter holidays in Ibiza. On one trip to
Morocco, in **1983**, he painted the series
Maroc. **1987** Awarded the Jörg Ratgeb
Prize and made an honorary citizen of the City of
Hagen. By incorporating materials such as
lead, asphalt, sisal and paper, and altering
the painting surface through hammering,
Schumacher produced works of art that are
half-paintings, half-reliefs.
WRITINGS: E. S.: Ein Buch mit sieben
Siegeln. Heidelberg 1972
MONOGRAPHS, CATALOGUES:
Bretschneider, K. (ed.): E. S. und das
Materialbild. Hamburger Kunsthalle et al.
Hamburg 1998 (cat.).– Brunner, R.: E. S.
Das informelle Werk. Gießen 1992.– Chris-
tian, J. C. (ed.): E. S. Werke 1989-1992.
Kunstsammlung Nordrhein-Westfalen.
Düsseldorf 1992 (cat.).– Fehr, M. (ed.): E.
S. Zeichen und Farbe. Cologne 1987.–
Franzke, A. et al. (ed.): E. S. 2 vols. Museo
d'Arte Moderna della Città di Lugano.
Lugano 1994 (cat.).– Fuchs, E.-G.: E. S.
Arbeiten auf Papier. Augsburger Kunstver-
ein. Augsburg 1985 (cat.).– Güse, E.-G.: E.
S. Djerba. Stuttgart 1983.– Güse, E.-G.: E.
S. Die Gouachen der 80er Jahre. Munich
1992.– Herrmann, M. (ed.): E. S. Späte
Bilder. Nationalgalerie. Berlin 1988 (cat.).–
Jensen, J. C. et al. (ed.): E. S. Arbeiten auf
Papier. Museumsberg Flensburg. Flensburg
1997 (cat.).– Holeczek, B. (ed.): E. S.
Arbeiten auf Papier 1957-1982. Kunstmu-
seum Hanover et al. Hanover 1982 (cat.).–
Klant, M. and C. Zuschlag: E. S. im
Gespräch. "Der Erde näher als den
Sternen". Stuttgart 1992.– Meyer zu Eissen,
A. (ed.): E. S. Kunsthalle Bremen et al.
Bremen 1984 (cat.).– Ruhrberg, K.: E. S.
Zeichen und Farbe. Cologne 1984 (cat.).–
Schilling, J. (ed.): E. S. Gemälde und
Werke auf Papier. 1946-1990. Kunstverein
Wolksburg. Wolfsburg 1990 (cat.).–
Schmalenbach, W. (ed.): E. S. Kunstverein
für die Rheinlande und Westfalen. Düssel-
dorf 1971 (cat.).– Schmalenbach W.: E. S.
Cologne 1981.– E. S. Arbeiten auf Papier.
Städtisches Museum, Mülheim et al.
Mülheim 1987 (cat.).– E. S. Malerei 1936-
1991. Museum der bildenden Künste.
Leipzig 1993 (cat.).– E. S. Pinacoteca
Comunale, Casa Rusca, Locarno. Lugano
1994 (cat.).– E. S. Retrospektive. Haus der
Kunst, Munich et al. Munich 1998 (cat.).–
Sylvanus, E.: E. S. Recklinghausen 1959.–
Wißmann, J.: E. S. Documenta III.
Formlos und doch Form. Cologne 1992.–
Wißmann, J. (ed.): E S. Ein Künstler und
seine Stadt. Karl-Ernst-Osthaus-Museum.
Hagen 1997 (cat.)

SCHÜTTE Thomas
born **1954** Oldenburg
German sculptor. **1973**–**1981** Studied
under Gerhard Richter at the Düsseldorf
Academy. **1977** Created the *Mauer* (Wall)
at the Düsseldorf Academy. **1979** Solo-
exhibitions at the gallery La Vitrine in Paris
and at the Arno Kohnen gallery in Düsseldorf. **1981** Participated in the "Westkunst"
exhibition, Cologne. Solo-exhibition at the
Konrad Fischer gallery, Düsseldorf. **1986**
Solo-exhibition at Museum Haus Lange,
Krefeld and participation in the Jehnisch
Park sculpture exhibition, Hamburg. **1987**
and **1997** took part in documenta 8 and 10
in Kassel. **1990** Solo-exhibition at the
Kunsthalle Bern und **1992** at the Raum
für Kunst, Hamburg. **1994** Solo-exhibitions
at the Hamburg Kunsthalle and at the
Württembergische Kunstverein, Stuttgart.
Schütte's approach to art is that of a con-
cept artist, except that he emphasises the
quality of experience evoked by his modified spaces. His best-known works are
architectural models that appear monumental.
WRITINGS: T. S.: Aufzeichnungen aus der
2. Reihe. Düsseldorf 1991
MONOGRAPHS, CATALOGUES: Barth,
F. (ed.): T. S. Figur. Hamburger Kunsthalle,
Hamburg et al. Hamburg 1994 (cat.).–
Bußmann, K. and U. Wilmes (ed.): T. S.
Obst und Gemüse. Westfälisches Landesmuseum. Münster 1987 (cat.).– Dürr, B.
et al. (ed.): Hier 88 – T. S. Staatliche Kunsthalle Baden-Baden. Baden-Baden 1988
(cat.).– Glozer, L. and U. Look (ed.): T. S.
Pläne I-XXX. Produzentengalerie. Hamburg 1985 (cat.).– Heynen, J. et al. (ed.): T.
S. London 1998 (cat.).– Loock, U. et al.
(ed.): T. S. Sieben Felder. Kunsthalle Bern
et al. Bern 1990 (cat.).– Osterwold, T. (ed.):
T. S. Kassel 1996 (cat.).– T. S. Musée d'Art
Moderne de la Ville de Paris. Paris 1990
(cat.).– T. S. Skizzen und Gedichte. Kunstraum, Munich et al. Düsseldorf 1995
(cat.).– Wilmes, U. and T. S.: T. S. Portikus. Frankfurt-on-Main 1989 (cat.)

SCHWARZKOGLER Rudolf
1940 Vienna – **1969** Vienna
Austrian action artist. **1957**–**1961** Studied
applied graphics at the Lehr- und Versuchsanstalt in Vienna. **1958** Became acquainted
with Hermann Nitsch. **1964** Participated in

Otto Muehl's happening *Luftballkonzert*,
and afterwards worked with him on the
adaptation of the text *Sanitäre Kunst*. **1965**
Active participant in Nitsch aktions. **1966**
Participated in the action-concert for Al
Hansen at the gallery next to St. Stephan's
church in Vienna. Self-wounding and
maiming actions, aimed at freeing himself
from taboos connected with the body.
1967/68 Made films with Günter and Anni
Brus and Muehl. First depressions and
health problems. **1969** Killed himself by
jumping out of the window of his apartment.
MONOGRAPHS, CATALOGUES: Badura-
Triska, E. and H. Klocker: R. S. Leben und
Werk. Museum Moderner Kunst Stiftung
Ludwig, Vienna et al. Klagenfurt 1992
(cat.).– Nitsch, H. (ed.): R. S. Galerie
nächst St. Stephan. Vienna 1970 (cat.).–
Weiermair, P. and H. Nitsch (ed.): R. S.
Galerie Krinzinger. Innsbruck 1976 (cat.)

SCHWITTERS Kurt
1887 Hanover – **1948** Ambleside
German artist. **1909**–**1914** Studied at the
Dresden Academy and **1914** in Berlin. **1915**
Returned to Hanover. **1918** First public
exhibition at the gallery Der Sturm in
Berlin. Worked on the magazine of the
same name. **1919** Labelled his dadaist works
MERZ. **1920** Met Arp and T. Tzara. Exhibition at the Société Anonyme in New York.
1921 First meetings with Hausmann and
Höch. **1922** Participated in the Dada congress in Weimar. Acquaintanceship and collaboration with Doesburg. **1923**–**1932** Published the magazine *MERZ*. **1923** Spent the
summer with Arp on the Island of Rügen.
1924 Started work on his first Merz building in his house in Hanover. **1924** Première
of *Ursonate*. Exhibition at the Kestner
Society, Hanover. **1932** Joined the group
Abstraction-Création. **1933** Emigrated to
Norway and began his second Merz building. **1940** Escaped to England, where he
began his last Merz building in Ambleside.
Among the Dadaists, Schwitters stood
apart, his goal being to develop a new synthetic art form combining painting, sculpture and architecture. For a long time he
was not accepted by the other Berlin
Dadaists. In his Merz buildings, collages
and assemblages he gave found objects new
value by incorporating them into pictures.
WRITINGS: Hausmann, R and K. S.: Pin.
Gießen 1986.– Lach, F. (ed.): K. S. Das
literarische Werk. 5 vols. Cologne 1973-
1981, 1998.– Nundel, E. (ed.): K. S. Briefe
aus fünf Jahrzehnten. Frankfurt-on-Main
1975.– Rothenberg, J. and P. Joris (ed.): K.
S. Poems, Performances, Pieces, Proses,
Plays, Poetics. Philadelphia 1993
CATALOGUE RAISONNE: Schwitters, E.
and I. Bodesohn-Vogel (ed.): K. S. Werk-
verzeichnis der Collagen, Assemblagen,
Ölbilder, Aquarelle, Plastiken. 2 vols.
Freren 1991.– S.-Archiv der Stadtbibliothek
Hannover. Bestandsverzeichnis. Hanover
1986
MONOGRAPHS, CATALOGUES: Bailly,
C.: K. S. Paris 1993.– Bazzoli, F.: K. S.

L'Art m'amuse beaucoup. Marseille 1991.–
Büchner, J. and N. Nobis (ed.): K. S.
1887-1948. Sprengel Museum, Hanover.
Berlin 1986 (cat.).– Dietrich, D.: The Col-
lages of K. S. Tradition and Innovation.
Cambridge 1993.– Elderfield, J. (ed.): K.
S. The Museum of Modern Art. New York
and London 1985, Düsseldorf 1987 (cat.).–
Elger, D.: K. S. Der Merzbau. Cologne
1984.– Erfurth, E. (ed.): Kalter Hund oder
Der Skandal um K. S. Ursonate. Obern-
burg 1993.– Gohr, S. and D. Elger (ed.):
K. S. Die späten Werke. Museum Ludwig.
Cologne 1985 (cat.).– Homayr, R.: Montage
als Kunstform. Opladen 1991.– Lach, F.:
Der Merzkünstler K. S. Cologne 1971.–
Lemoine, S. nd D. Semin (ed.): K. S.
Centre Georges Pompidou, Paris et al.
Paris 1994 (cat.).– Nobis, B.: K. S. und
die romantische Ironie. Alfter 1993.–
Nobis, B. et al. (ed.): K. S. IVAM Centro
Julio González, Valencia 1995 (cat.).–
Nündel, E.: K. S. in Selbstzeugnissen und
Bilddokumenten. Reinbek 1981.– Ratte-
meyer, V. and D. Helms (ed.): "Typogra-
phie kann unter Umständen Kunst sein" –
K. S. Typographie und Werbegestaltung.
Landesmuseum Wiesbaden et al. Wies-
baden 1990 (cat.).– Remerson, S.: K. S.
in England 1940-1948. London 1958.–
Schaub, G. (ed.): K. S. "Bürger und Idiot".
Berlin 1993.– Schmalenbach, W.: K. S.
Cologne 1967, Munich 1984, New York
1967, 1984.– Schreck, J. (ed.): K. S. Anna
Blume und andere Literatur und Grafik.
Berlin 1985.– Stadtmüller, K. (ed.): K. S.
in Norwegen. Hanover 1997.– Steinitz, K.
T.: K. S. Erinnerungen aus den Jahren
1918-1930. Zurich 1963.– Steinitz, K. T.: K.
S. A Portrait from Life. Berkeley 1968.–
Themerson, S.: K. S. in England 1940-1948.
London 1958.– Webster, G.: Kurt Merz
Schwitters. A Biographical Study. Cardiff
1997

SEAMAN Bill
born **1956** Kennet (MS)
American video artist. **1975**–**1977** Studied
at the Rhode Island School of Design in
Providence. **1979** Bachelor of Fine Arts at
San Francisco Art Institute. **1985** Master of
Science in Visual Studies at Massachusetts
Institute of Technology, Cambridge (MA)
where, from **1987**, he also held classes in
film and video. Grant from the National
Endowment for the Arts, Washington. **1992**
and **1995** special awards for Interactive Art
at Ars Electronica, Linz. **1994/95** Guest-
artist at ZKM in Karlsruhe. **1995** International Video Art Prize from Southwest
German Radio in Baden-Baden and the
ZKM, Karlsruhe. **1996** Awards at the
Videonale and the Federal Art and Exhibition Centre in Bonn. From **1966** professor
at the Department of Arts at the University
of Maryland, Baltimore. Up until **1983**
Seaman worked mostly as a perfomance
artist, but after that began to make videos
as well. His interactive installations of the
90s combine texts, static images and film
sequences.

MONOGRAPHS, CATALOGUES: B. S.
The Design of the Grip. Institute of Contemporary Arts. Boston 1989 (cat.).– B. S.
Passage Sets/One Pulls Pivots at the Tip of
the Tongue. Art Gallery of New South
Wales. Sydney (cat.).– B. S. Passagen Kom-
binationen. Man manövriert Drehungen
auf der Zungenspitze. Kunst- und Ausstellungshalle der Bundesrepublik Deutschland, Bonn. Bonn 1996 (cat.)

SEGAL Arthur
1875 Jassy (Romania) – **1944** London
Romanian painter. **1892** First studied in
Berlin then, in **1896**, transferred to Munich
where he attended Hoelzel's classes.
1902/03 Study trips to Paris and Italy.
1904 Returned to Berlin and participated
in the exhibition of the Berlin Secession.
1914–**1920** Moved to Ascona. Became
acquainted with Arp and Javlensky. **1916**
Exhibited and took part in Cabaret
Voltaire. **1920** Returned to Berlin and
became a member of the Novembergruppe.
1925 Refused the offer of a teaching position at the Bauhaus. **1932** Exhibited with
the Novembergruppe and in the "Juryfreie
Kunstschau" (Art Show without a Jury).
1933 Emigrated to Mallorca. **1936** Moved
to London. Segal was a key figure in the
Zurich Dada movement and one of the
main organisers of Cabaret Voltaire.
WRITINGS: A. S.: Über das Licht in der
Malerei. Berlin 1924
MONOGRAPHS, CATALOGUES: Exner,
H.: A. S. Dresden 1985.– Friedman, M.
and G. W. J. Beal (ed.): G. S. Walker Art
Center. Minneapolis 1978 (cat.).– Herzogenrath, W. and P. Liska (ed.): A. S. 1875-
1944. Kölnischer Kunstverein et al. Berlin
1987 (cat.).– Nathanson, R.: A Collection
of Woodcuts by A. S. London 1972

SEGAL George
born **1924** New York
American sculptor. **1940** Moved with his
family to South Brunswick (NJ). **1941/42**
Attended the Cooper Union of Art and
Architecture in New York. **1942**–**1946**
Trained as an art teacher and studied philosophy and literature at Rutgers University
in New Brunswick (NJ). **1947**–**1949** Continued his studies at Pratt Institute of
Design in Brooklyn and New York Univer-

sity. **1953** Friendship with Kaprow. From
1955 taught at Highland Park Community
Center. **1956** First solo-exhibition at the
Hansa Gallery, New York. **1957/58** Staged
happenings with Oldenburg and Kaprow.
1960 Began work on plaster-casts of life-
size human figures and environments. **1963**
Solo-exhibition at the Galerie Sonnabend,
Paris. **1964** Taught at Hunter College. **1968**
and **1972** participated in documenta 4 and
5 in Kassel. Solo-exhibition at the Museum
of Contemporary Art, Chicago. **1971/72**
Retrospectives in European cities. **1978**
Major retrospective at the Walker Art
Center, Minneapolis. **1981/82** Tours and
exhibitions in China and Japan. **1988** Participated at the Venice Biennale. Segal
places his anonymous white plaster figures
in realistic settings, giving the impression
that they have been turned to stone while
going about their daily business.
MONOGRAPHS, CATALOGUES: Barrio-
Garay, J. L. (ed.): G. S. Environments.
Philadelphia Institute of Contemporary
Art. Philadelphia 1976 (cat.).– Finkeldey,
B.: G. S. Situationen. Kunst und Alltag.
Frankfurt-on-Main 1990.– Friedman, M.
and G. W. J. Beal (ed.): G. S. Sculptures.
Walker Art Center. Minneapolis 1978
(cat.).– Hunter, S. and D. Hawthorne: G.
S. Paris 1988, New York 1988.– Kreyten-
berg, G.: G. S. Ruth in Her Kitchen. Stutt-
gart 1970.– Marck, J. v. d.: G. S. New York
1975, 1979.– Price, M. (ed.): G. S. Modern
Art Museum of Fort Worth. Fort Worth
1990 (cat.).– G. S. Kunsthaus Zürich.
Zurich 1971 (cat.).– G. S. Städtische Galerie
im Lenbachaus, Munich et al. Munich 1972
(cat.).– G. S. Museum Boymans-van
Beuningen. Rotterdam 1972 (cat.).– Seitz,
W. C.: S. London and New York 1972,
Stuttgart 1972.– Teuber, D.: G. S. Wege zur
Körperüberformung. Frankfurt-on-Main
and Bern 1987.– Tuchman, P.: G. S. New
York 1983, Munich 1984.– Viatte, G. (ed.):
G. S. Centre National d'Art Contemporain.
Paris 1972 (cat.)

SEGALL Lasar
1889 Vilnius – **1957** São Paulo
Lithuanian painter. **1906**–**1909** Studied at
the Berlin School of Arts and the Dresden
Academy. **1909** Exhibited with the Berlin
Secession. **1910** Came to know Grosz, Dix
and Schwitters. **1911**–**1913** Trips to Holland
and Brazil. **1914** Internment in Meißen.
1917 Went to Vilnius. **1919** Co-founder of
the Dresden Secession. **1920** Solo-exhibition at the Museum Folkwang in Hagen
and **1922** at the Kupferstichkabinett
attached to Leipzig Museum. **1923** Moved
to São Paulo. **1926** Exhibition at the Kunstkabinett Stuttgart. Lived **1931** in Paris, **1934**
in Rom and **1943** in New York. **1954** Major
Retrospective in São Paulo. Segall originally
tended to paint expressive figures, and
during World War II he did several paintings depicting the persecution of the Jews.
In the course of his career he progressed
from Expressionism to geometric abstraction.

WRITINGS: L. S. Antologia de textos
nacionais sobre a obra e o artista. Rio de
Janeiro 1982
MONOGRAPHS, CATALOGUES: Bardi,
P. M.: L. S. Milan 1959.– Beccari, V. D'H.:
L. S. e o modernismo paulista. Sao Paulo
1984.– Fierens, P.: L. S. Paris 1938.– From-
mold, E.: L. S. Milan 1975.– Gullar, F. et al.
(ed.): L. S. Museu de Arte Moderna. Rio de
Janeiro 1967.– Horn, G. and V. d'Horta
Beccari (ed.): L. S. 1891-1957. Malerei,
Zeichnungen, Druckgrafik, Skulptur. Staat-
liche Kunsthalle Berlin. Berlin 1990 (cat.).–
Levi, L.: Os temas judáicos de L. S. São
Paulo 1979.– Naves, R. and M. Mattos
Araújo (ed.): O desenho de L. S. Museu
Lasar Segall. São Paulo 1991 (cat.)

SEIWERT Franz Wilhelm
1894 Cologne – **1933** Cologne
German painter. **1910**–**1914** Attended the
Cologne School of Arts and Crafts. **1917**
Contributed to the magazine *Die Aktion*.
1919 Participated in Dada events, but
never exhibited with the Dadaists. Joined
the artists' group Stupid. **1923** First major
solo-exhibition at the Kunstverein in
Cologne. **1924** Publication of his treatise
*Technik, Produktionsorganisation, Kultur
and die neue Gesellschaft* (Technology,
Production Management, Culture and the
New Society). **1929** Published the magazine
a–z for the Gruppe progressiver Künstler
(Group of Progressive Artists). Participated
in the exhibition "asb (architectuur,
schilderwerk, beeldhouwwerk)" at the
Stedelijk Museum, Amsterdam. **1930** Took
part in the exhibition "Socialistische kunst
heden" at the Stedelijk Museum. **1931/32**
Helped to set up the Kunstgewerbe-
museum (Museum of Arts and Crafts) in
Cologne. **1933** Glass mosaic representing
the life of the working classes destroyed by
the Nazis. Though formally influenced by
Cubism and Dada, Seiwert's paintings
mainly reflect his Marxist view of the
world, showing the relationships of workers
to operating systems and to each other in
an ideal, technological society.
WRITINGS: Bohnen, U. and D. Backes:
Der Schritt, der einmal getan wurde, wird
nicht zurückgenommen. F.-W. S. Schriften.
Berlin 1978
CATALOGUE RAISONNE: Bohnen, U.
(ed.): F.-W. S. 1894-1933. Leben und Werk.
Werkverzeichnis. Kölnischer Kunstverein.
Cologne 1978 (cat.)
MONOGRAPHS, CATALOGUES:
Bohnen, U. (ed.): F.-W. S. 1894-1933.
Brunswick 1978.– Jatho, C. O.: F. W. S.
Recklinghausen 1964

SEKINE Nobuo
born **1942** Imiya
Japanese sculptor. **1964**–**1968** Studied
painting at the School of Arts in Tama, and
took additional courses in sculpture from
1967 in Tokyo. **1965** First solo-exhibition at
the Tokyo Gallery. **1970** Participated at the
Venice Biennale. **1972** Commission for a

sculpture for the town hall in Saitama. **1976** Various works for the sculpture garden of the Louisiana Museum in Humlebæk, Denmark. From **1980** flat reliefs in steel. Since **1987** he has been working on *Phase Conceptions*, a series of works incorporating painterly and sculptural elements. Sekine combines natural materials such as sponges, water and mud with steel or sculpted paving stones, in an attempt to discover and reveal their material and structural properties.
MONOGRAPHS, CATALOGUES: Sculpture of Scenery. Works of N. S and Environment. Art Studio. Tokyo 1987.– N. S. Louisiana Museum. Humblebæk 1978 (cat.)

SERAPHINE de Senlis
(Séraphine Louis)
1864 Assy – **1934** Senlis
French naïve painter. Spent her youth working as a shepherdess, and later entered domestic service in Senlis. **1912** Her artistic talent was discovered by Wilhelm Uhde. Throughout her hardworking but sheltered life, she painted flowers, leaves and fruits. These paintings in which human figures are linked to nature in a bizarre, surreal fashion are not representations of any particular natural order but rather the fantastic products of a heavenly dream. **1927** First exhibition at the Galerie Quatre Chemins in Paris. **1934** Died, mentally deranged, in a home for the aged in Senlis.
MONOGRAPHS, CATALOGUES: Gunther, T. M. (ed.): La Réalité intérieure. S. de Senlis et quelques peintres autodidactes. Musée d'Art et d'archéologie. Senlis 1989 (cat.).– S. L. Galerie de France. Paris 1945 (cat.).– S. L. Ancienne Abbaye Saint-Vincent. Senlis 1972 (cat.).– Vircondelet, A.: S. L. Paris 1986

SERRA Richard
born **1939** San Francisco
American sculptor. **1957–1961** Studied at the University of California in Berkeley and in Santa Barbara (CA). **1964** Completed his studies at Yale University, New Haven (CT) where he came in contact with Albers. **1964/65** Fulbright scholarship to Paris. Encountered Arte Povera. **1966**

Visited Florence. First solo-exhibition at the Galleria La Salita in Rome. Moved to New York. **1968** Produced his *Splashing Series*: examples of Process Art in which molten lead is flung into the corners of a room. Made 16 mm films of everyday occurences and encounters. **1969** Solo-exhibition at the Castelli Warehouse, New York. From the 70s onwards produced monumental open-air sculptures out of steel plates that seem to intersect their surroundings. **1972–1987** Participated in documenta 5 – 8 in Kassel. **1975** Awarded the Skowhegan Medal for Sculpture. **1980** Participated at the Venice Biennale and, **1982** and **1987**, in documenta 7 and 8 in Kassel. **1983** Major retrospective at the Pompidou Centre in Paris, **1986** at the Museum of Modern Art, New York and **1990** at the Stedelijk Van Abbe Museum, Eindhoven. In Serra's labile, precariously balanced sculptural configurations of steel, sheer weight – a basic material property – becomes the central binding element of the work.
WRITINGS: R. S.: Ecrits et entretiens 1970-1989. Paris 1990/R. S.: The Hours of the Day. Schriften und Interviews 1970-1989. 2 vols. Kunsthaus Zürich. Bern 1990 (cat.).– R. S.: Writings, Interviews. Chicago 1994.– Weyergraf, C. (ed.): R. S. Interviews etc. 1970-1980. Hudson River Museum. Yonkers (NY) 1980 (cat.) CATALOGUES RAISONNES: Breitenbach, S. (ed.): R. S. Das druckgraphische Werk 1972-1988. Berlin 1989.– Güse, E.-G. (ed.): R. S. Westfälisches Landesmuseum, Münster et al. Stuttgart 1987, New York 1988 (cat.).– Janssen, H. (ed.): R. S. Zeichnungen 1969-1990. Bern 1990 MONOGRAPHS, CATALOGUES: Berg, K. v. d.: Der leibhafte Raum. Das Terminal von R. S. in Bochum. Stuttgart 1995.– Bois, Y.-A. and R. E. Krauss (ed.): R. S. Centre Georges Pompidou. Paris 1983 (cat.).– Brockhaus, C. et al. (ed.): R. S. Props. Wilhelm Lehmbruck Museum. Duisburg 1994 (cat.).– Buskirk, M.: R. S. Intersection. New York 1996.– Galerie m (ed.): R. S. Neue Skulpturen in Europa 1977-1985. Bochum 1985.– Krauss, R. E. and L. Rosenstock (ed.): R. S. Sculpture. The Museum of Modern Art. New York 1986, 1988 (cat.).– Krempel, U. et al. (ed.): R. S. Running Arcs, Weight and Measure, Drawings. Kunstsammlung Nordrhein-Westfalen. Düsseldorf 1993 (cat.).– Pacquement, A.: R. S. Paris 1993.– Reinartz, D.: R. S. La Mormaire. New York 1996.– Rosenstock, L. (ed.): R. S. Sculpture. The Museum of Modern Art. New York 1986 (cat.).– Rouse, Y. (ed.): R. S. Museo Nacional Centro de Arte Reina Sofia. Madrid 1992 (cat.).– Schwandner, M. (ed.): R. S. Intersection Basel. Düsseldorf 1996.– R. S. Drawings 1969-1990. Bonnefantenmuseum. Maastricht 1990 (cat.).– R. S. Weight and Measure. Tate Gallery, London et al. London and Seattle 1992 (cat.).– Weyergraf, C. et al. (ed.): R. S. Arbeiten 66-77. Kunsthalle Tübingen et al. Tübingen 1978 (cat.).– Weyergraf-Serra, C. and M. Buskirk (ed.): The Destruction of Titled Arc. Cambridge (MA) 1991

SERUSIER Paul
1864 Paris – **1927** Morlaix
French painter and theoretician. **1888** Assistant at the Académie Julian in Paris. Met Gauguin in Pont-Aven and learnt about Synthetism. Introduced Gauguin to Denis, Bonnard and Vuillard. **1889** Organised the group of Symbolist artists, the Nabis. Visited Gauguin and, like him, painted Breton peasant women and landscapes. **1891** Under the influence of J.

Verkade, a fellow-member of the Nabis, his ideas began to be permeated with elements of mysticism. **1892** Long stay in Pont-Aven. **1893** Went to Italy with Bernard. **1893–1896** Worked at the Lugné-Poe Theatre. **1897** Visited Verkade for the first time at the Benedictine monastery of Beuron in Germany. **1914–1927** Went back to work in Brittany. The influence of his role model Gauguin and his love of Japanese woodcuts find expression in Sérusier's blocks of colour and linear outlines.
WRITINGS: P. S.: ABC de la peinture. Suivi d'une correspondance inédite. Paris 1921,1950
CATALOGUE RAISONNE: Guicheteau, M. and P. H. Boutaric (ed.): P. S. 2 vols. Paris 1976-1989
MONOGRAPHS, CATALOGUES: Boyle-Turner, C.: P. S. Diss. Ann Arbor (MI) 1983.– Denis, M.: P. S. Sa Vie, son œuvre. Paris 1942.– Guicheteau, M.: P. S. Paris 1976.– Guicheteau, M.: P. S. Pontoise 1989.– Masson, H.: P. S. De Pont-Aven à Châteauneuf-du-Faou. Saint-Brieuc 1991.– P. S. Musée des Jacobins. Morlaix 1987 (cat.).– P. S. et la Bretagne. Musée de Pont-Aven. Pont-Aven 1991 (cat.)

SERVRANCKX Victor
1897 Dieghem – **1965** Vilvorde
Belgian painter. **1912–1917** Studied at the Académie des Beaux-Arts in Brussels. **1917** First solo-exhibition at the Galerie Giroux in Brussels. From **1932** professor at the Ecole des Arts Industriels et Décoratifs in Bruxelles. **1920** Joined the group of Paris artists L'Effort moderne, promoted by L. Rosenberg. **1925** Influence of Mondrian and Moholy-Nagy on his work. **1926** Represented at the exhibition of the Société Anonyme in America. **1947** Retrospective at the Palais des Beaux-Arts, Brussels. Servranckx was one of Belgium's first abstract painters. Originally influenced by the Futurist machine aesthetic, he later tended toward Surrealism and finally practised strictly formal Abstraction.
MONOGRAPHS, CATALOGUES: Bilcke, M: S. Antwerp 1959, Brussels 1964.– Hommage à S. Galerie Contemporaine. Brussels 1957 (cat.).– V. S. Musée d'Ixelles. Brussels 1965 (cat.).– V. S. en de abstracte kunst. Koninklijke Musea voor Schone Kunsten van België. Brussels 1989 (cat.)

SEURAT Georges
1859 Paris – **1891** Paris
French painter and theoretician. **1878/79** Studied at the Ecole des Beaux-Arts in Paris; read many treatises on colour theory. **1880** Military Service. **1883** First large work, an outdoor scene painted according to a new colour-splitting method termed Divisionism or Pointillism. **1884** Rejected by the official Salon. Came to know Signac and, together with him and other artists, founded the Société des Artistes Indépendants who held their own Salon. **1885** Painted works on the island of La Grande Jatte, in Paris and at Grancamp on the coast of Normandy. **1886** *La Grand Jatte* caused a sensation at the VIII Impressionist exhibition. Exhibited with Pissarro and Signac in Nantes. Met the theoretician and art critic C. Henry and made contact with the Symbolists and Anarchists. **1887** Participated in the exhibition of the Les XX group in Brussels. **1888** Painted at Port-en-Bessin, **1889** on the beach at Crotoy and **1890** in Gravelines, where he wrote down his theories of painting. Died of diphtheria. Seurat's colour theories and scientific approach to painting had a profound effect on modern painting and theoretical developments in 20th century art.
WRITINGS: Seurat, P.: Notes sur Delacroix. Caen 1987.– G. S.: Correspondance, témoignages, notes inédites, critiques. Paris 1991
CATALOGUES RAISONNES: Chastel, A. (ed.): L'opera completa di S. Milan 1972.– Dorra, H. and J. Rewald (ed.): S. L'œuvre peint, biographie et catalogue critique. Paris 1959.– Grenier, C. (ed.): S. Catalogo completo dei dipinti. Florence 1990.– Haucke, C.-M. d. (ed.): S. et son œuvre. 2 vols. Paris 1961.– Kahn, G. (ed.): Dessins. 2 vols. Paris 1920.– Minervino, F. (ed.): Das Gesamtwerk des S. Lucerne 1972/Tout l'œuvre peint de S. Paris 1973.– Zimmermann, M. F.: S. Sein Werk und die kunsthistorische Debatte seiner Zeit. Weinheim 1991/S. His Complete Works. San Francisco 1991

SEVERINI Gino
1883 Cortona – **1966** Paris
Italian painter. **1899** Went to Rome, where he attended evening classes at the Villa

Medici. **1901** After meeting Balla and Boccioni he decided to devote himself to art. From **1906** lived in Paris, where he encountered the paintings of Seurat and met Modigliani. Signed the *Technical Manifesto of Painting* issued by the Futurists on 11 February **1910**. Produced his first paintings of dancers and cabarets during this period. **1912** Took part in Futurist exhibitions in Paris, London and Berlin and organised exhibitions for the Milan Futurists in Paris. **1915–1921** Cubist period: numerous still lifes with musical instruments. **1924–1935** Carried out several commissions for mosaics and murals. **1950** Important prize at the Venice Biennale. Severini combined divisionist principles of composition with a cubo-futurist approach. He was chiefly concerned with conveying a sense of movement and the connection between events, separated in time but linked in the mind.
WRITINGS: G. S.: Du cubisme au classicisme. Paris 1921.– G. S.: Tempo de "l'effort moderne". La vita di un pittore. Florence 1968.– G. S.: Dal cubismo al classicismo e altri saggi sulla divina proporzione e sul numero d'oro. Florence 1972.– G. S.: La vita di un pittore. Milan 1946, 1983/The Life of a Painter. The Autobiography of G. S. Princeton (NJ) 1995.– G. S.: Ecrits sur l'art. Paris 1987.– G. S.: Lezioni sul mosaico. Ravenna 1988
CATALOGUES RAISONNES: Fonti, D. (ed.): G. S. Catalogo ragionato. Milan 1988.– Meloni, F. (ed.): Tutta l' opera grafica. Reggio Emilia 1982
MONOGRAPHS, CATALOGUES: Barilli, R. (ed.): G. S. (1883-1966). Palazzo Pitti, Florence. Milan 1983 (cat.).– Benzi, F. (ed.): G. S. Affreschi, mosaici, decorazioni, monumentali 1921-1941. Galleria Arco Farnese. Roma 1992 (cat.).– Dorfles, G. and P. L. Siena, P. L. (ed.): S. Castel Mareccio, Bolzano. Milan 1987 (cat.).– Eco, U. et al. (ed.): G. S. dal 1916 al 1936. Palazzo Cuttica. Alessandria 1987 (cat.).– Fagiolo dell'Arco, M. (ed.): G. S. Prima e dopo l'opera. Documenti, opere ed imagini. Palazzo Casali, Cortona. Milan 1983 (cat.).– Hanson, A. C. (ed.): S. Futurista 1912-1917. New Haven (CT) et al. 1995 (cat.).– Mascherpa, G. (ed.): S. e il mosaico. Ravenna 1985 (cat.).– Pacini, P.: G. S. Florence 1966.– Pacini, P.: S. 1913. Prato 1977.– Ruggeri, G.: Il tempo di G. S. Bologna 1981.– G. S. Musée National d'Art Moderne. Paris 1967 (cat.).– Venturi, L.: G. S. Roma 1961.– Vescovo, M. (ed.): G. S. La regola, la maschera, il sacro. Bologna 1993

SEYMOUR David
1911 Warsaw – **1956** Suez Canal
Polish-born American photographer. From **1933** worked as a freelance photographer in Paris. **1936–1938** Documented the Spanish Civil War. **1939** Reportage on Spanish refugees being shipped to Mexico. Emigrated to the USA and volunteered for military service in the American army. Photoseries on postwar Germany and the founding of the State of Israel. **1947** Together with Capa, Cartier-Bresson and others, founded the photographic agency Magnum, and was its president from **1954 –1956**. Seymour became famous for his moving pictures of neglected, starving and crippled children. He was killed while covering the Suez Canal crisis.
MONOGRAPHS, CATALOGUES: Capa, C. and B. Karia (ed.): D. S. Chim. 1911-1956. New York and London 1974.– Cartier-Bresson, H. et al. (ed.): D. S. 1911-1956. New York and London 1974.– Fárová, A. (ed.): D. S. New York 1967.– Friedberg, J.: D. S.-Chim. Prague 1966

SHAHN Ben
1898 Kowno (Lithuania) – **1969** New York
Lithuanian-born American painter and photographer. **1906** Moved to New York. **1913–1917** Trained as a lithographer. **1919–1922** Studied biology. **1922** Attended the National Academy of Design, New York. **1924/25** and **1927–1929** Toured North Africa and Europe. **1929** Inspired through his friendship with Evans to take up photography. **1930** Solo-exhibition at the Downtown Gallery, New York. **1931/32** Completed the series *Sacco and Vanzetti*. **1932** Assisted Rivera with murals for the Rockefeller Center. Solo-exhibition at the Harvard Society for Contemporary Art in Cambridge (MA). **1947** Taught at the Museum of Fine Arts, Boston. Solo-exhibition at the Museum of Modern Art, New York. **1954** Participated at the Venice Biennale. **1956** Professorship at Harvard University. **1959** and **1964** participation in documenta 2 and 3 in Kassel. **1960** Retrospective at the Museum of Modern Art, New York, and **1962** at the Kunsthalle Baden-Baden. In that he used his art to speak out against social and political injustice, Shahn can be regarded as an exponent of social realism.
WRITINGS: Pohl, F. K.: B. S. with B. S.'s Writings. San Francisco 1993.– B. S.: The Biography of a Painting. Cambridge (MA) 1956, New York 1966.– B. S.: The Shape of Content. Cambridge (MA) 1957, 1963
CATALOGUES RAISONNES: Prescott, K. W. (ed.): The Complete Graphic Works of B. S. New York 1973.– Soby, J. T. (ed.): B. S. Catalogue Raisonné 2 vols. New York 1963
MONOGRAPHS, CATALOGUES: Bentivoglio, M.: B. S. Roma 1963.– Bryson Shahn, B.: B. S. New York 1972.– Morse, J. D. (ed.): B. S. London and New York 1972.– Pohl, F. K.: B. S. New Deal Artist in a Cold War Climate. 1947-1954. Austin 1989.– Pratt, D. (ed.): The Photographic Eye of B. S. Cambridge 1975.– Rodman, S.: Portrait of the Artist as an American: B. S. New York 1951.– Shan, B. B.: B. S. New York 1972.– B. S. Prefectural Museum of Arts. Hiroshima 1970 (cat.).– Soby, J. T. (ed.): B. S. His Graphic Art. New York 1963 / B. S. Grafik. Frankfurt-on-Main 1963.– Soby, J. T.: B. S. Malerei Frankfurt-on-Main 1964.– Weiss, M. R. (ed.): B. S. Photographer. An Album from the Thirties. New York 1973

SHAIKHET Arkadi
1898 Nikolajev – **1959** Moscow
Soviet photojournalist. **1918** Moved to Moscow. **1922** Worked as a retoucher for a portrait photographer. From **1924** worked as a photojouranlist for *Rabotschaja* and *Oronek* and other organisations. Member of the Union of Russian Proletarian Photojournalists (ROPF). **1931** Together with M. Alpert and S. Tules produced the photodocumentary *24 Hours in the Life of the Filppov Family*, potraying a day in the life of a metal worker. **1928** Received a first

prize for works displayed at the exhibition "10 Years of Soviet Photography". During World War II, took photographs at the front. Co-founder of Soviet photojournalism.

SHAW Jeffrey
born **1944** Melbourne
Australian action and multimedia artist. **1958–1964** Studied architecture and history of art at the University of Melbourne and **1965/66** sculpture at the Accademia di Brera in Milan and at St. Martin's School of Art in London. **1987** Presented the video-installation *Heavens Gate* at the Felix Meritis gallery in Amsterdam. **1989** Taught at the Academy in Rotterdam and **1990** at the Rietveld Academy in Amsterdam. From **1991** director of the Institute for Visual Media at ZKM in Karlsruhe. **1992** Presentation of his *Virtual Museum* at Ars Electronica in Linz. Until **1995** professor at the Karlsruhe School of Design. Shaw uses digital media such as computers and beam projectors in an attempt to involve the public in the creation and modification of a work. Their reactions then become a constituent part of the artwork.
MONOGRAPHS, CATALOGUES: J. S. Going to the Heart of the Center of the Garden of Delights. De Vleeshal. Middelburg 1986 (cat.).– Weibel, P. u. H. Klotz (ed.): J. S. A User's Manuel – Eine Gebrauchsanweisung. Vom Expanded Cinema zur Virtuellen Realität. ZKM Karlsruhe. Stuttgart 1997 (cat.)

SHEELER Charles
1883 Philadelphia – **1965** Dobbs Ferry (NY)
American painter and photographer. **1902–1906** Studied art at Pennsylvania Academy of Fine Arts in Philadelphia. **1904/05** Trip to Europe. **1907** First solo-exhibition in Philadelphia. **1908/09** Long stays in Italy and Paris. Came to know the Cubists and Fauves. **1912** First professional work as a photographer. **1913** Participated in the Armory Show in New York. **1918** Moved to New York. **1920** Worked on films with Strand. From **1923** photographed for *Vogue*. **1927** Photo-documentary of the Ford plants in Michigan. **1929** Photoseries of Chartres Cathedral. **1933** Moved to Connecticut. Participated at the Biennale of

American Art at the Whitney Museum, New York. **1939** Solo-exhibition at the Museum of Modern Art, New York. **1959** A stroke put an end to his artistic career. Sheeler's activities as a photographer and painter influenced and enhanced one another. Architecture was his central theme.
MONOGRAPHS, CATALOGUES: Dochterman, L.: The Stylistc Development of the Work of C. S. Diss. The University of Iowa. Iowa City 1963.– Fillin-Yeh, S.: C. S. and the Machine Age. Diss. New York 1981, Ann Arbor (MI) 1983.– Fillin-Yeh, S. (ed.): C. S. American Interiors. Yale University Art Gallery. New Haven (CT) 1987 (cat.).– Friedman, M. et al. (ed.): C. S. Smithsonian Institution. Washington 1968 (cat.).– Friedman, M. (ed.): C. S. Paintings, Drawings, Photographs. New York 1975.– Lucic, K.: C. S. and the Cult of the Machine. London and Cambridge (MA) 1991.– Rourke, C.: C. S. Artist in the American Tradition. New York 1938, 1969.– C. S. Smithsonian Institution, Washington et al. Washington 1962.– C. S. The Photographs. Museum of Fine Arts. Boston 1988 (cat.).– Troyen, C. and E. E. Hirshler (ed.): C. S. 2 vols. Museum of Fine Arts, Boston et al. New York 1987 (cat.)

SHERMAN Cindy
born **1954** Glen Ridge (NJ)
American artist. **1972–1975** Studied art at the State University of New York, Buffalo. **1975** Photoseries *Cutouts*. **1976** First Solo-exhibition at the Hallwals Gallery. **1977** Moved with her friend Robert Longo to New York, where she made her first untitled film stills. **1980** Colour photographs with backscreen projections. Solo-exhibition at Metro-Pictures, New York. **1982** Solo-exhibition at the Stedelijk Museum in Amsterdam. Participated in documenta 7 in Kassel and at the Venice Biennale. **1983** Received a Guggenheim grant. **1984–1986** Touring retrospective organised by the Akron Art Museum (OH). **1989** Awarded the Skowhegan Medal for Photography. Participated in the exhibition "Bilderstreit" in Cologne. **1989/90** Worked on *History Portraits* in Rome. **1991** Solo-exhibition at the Kunsthalle Basel. **1997** Made her first film *Office Killer*. Most of Cindy Sherman's photographs are pictures of herself, transformed and integrated into typical styles and images of the mass media.
WRITINGS: C. S. im Gespräch mit W. Dickhoff. Cologne 1995
MONOGRAPHS, CATALOGUES: Barendt, E. (ed.): C. S. Stedelijk Museum, Amsterdam. Munich 1982 (cat.).– Barendt, E. and P. Schjeldahl (ed.): C. S. Whitney Museum of American Art. New York 1987, Munich 1987.– Cathcart, L. (ed.): C. S. Photographs. Contemporary Arts Museum. Houston 1985 (cat.).– Cruz, A. et al. (ed.): C. S. Museum of Contemporary Art, Chicago et al. Los Angeles and London 1997 (cat.).– Felix, Z. and M. Schwandner (ed.): C. S. Photoarbeiten 1975-1995. Deich-

torhallen. Hamburg 1995 (cat.).– Foster, H. et al. (ed.): C. S. Museum Boymans-van Beuningen, Rotterdam et al. Rotterdam 1996 (cat.).– Gravel, B. v.: C. S. New York 1996.– Kellein, T. (ed.): C. S. Kunsthalle Basel et al. Stuttgart 1991 (cat.).– Krauss, R. and N. Bryson (ed.): C. S. 1979-1993. New York 1993, Munich 1994.– Meneguzzo, M.: C. S. Milan 1990.– Schjedahl, P.: C. S. New York 1984.– Schjedahl, P. and L. Phillips (ed.): C. S. Whitney Museum of American Art. New York 1987 (cat.).– Schneider, C.: C. S. History Portraits. Die Wiedergeburt des Gemäldes nach dem Ende der Malerei. Munich 1995.– C. S. Staatliche Kunsthalle Baden-Baden. Baden-Baden 1997 (cat.)

SIEVERDING Katharina
born **1945** Prague
German artist. **1949** Moved to Castrop-Rauxel. **1962** Studied at the Hamburg School of Fine Arts, and **1967-1974** at the Düsseldorf Academy under T. Otto. **1969** Masterclasses with Beuys. From **1969** concentrated on photography and film. **1972-1982** Participated in documenta 5 – 7 in Kassel. **1976** DAAD scholarship to New York. **1977** Solo-exhibition at the Museum Folkwang, Essen. From **1975** large-format photography. **1980** Solo-exhibition at the Mattildenhöhe exhibition centre in Darmstadt. Sieverding's photography focuses on social and political issues such as role conflicts between men and women and questions of identity.
MONOGRAPHS, CATALOGUES: Crone, R. et al. (ed.): S. Bonner Kunstverein. Bonn 1992 (cat.).– Fuchs, R. et al. (ed.): K. S. Kunstsammlung Nordrhein-Westfalen, Düsseldorf et al. Cologne 1997 (cat.).– Inboden, G. and R. Schmitz (ed.): K. S. Biennale di Venezia 1997. Venice 1997 (cat.).– Schneider, A. and K. S.: K. S. Kristallisationsbilder. Staatliche Museen, Neue Nationalgalerie. Berlin 1992 (cat.).– K. S. Städtisches Museum Abteiberg. Mönchengladbach 1984 (cat.).– K. S. Kunstverein Bonn et al. Stuttgart 1992 (cat.).– K. S. Städtische Galerie. Erlangen 1993 (cat.).– Solomon-Godeau, A. (ed.): K. S. Eine Installation. Museum Ostdeutsche Galerie. Regensburg 1993 (cat.)

SIGNAC Paul
1863 Paris – **1935** Paris
French painter. Studied for a short while at Bing's Académie libre. **1884** Co-founder of the Société des Artistes Indépendants. Became friends with Seurat, and adopted his divisionist method of painting. **1886** Participated in the VIII Impressionist exhibition. Represented by Durand-Ruel in New York and exhibited with Seurat and Pissarro in Nantes. **1887** Travelled with Seurat to Brussels and to the Mediterranean. **1889** Visited van Gogh in Arles. Illustrated the theoretical works of C. Henry and was politically aligned with the Anarchists. His harbour scenes and sea

paintings, in oils and watercolours, are like mosaics made up of tiny squares of pure, brilliant colour. **1893** Bought a house in Saint-Tropez that became the favourite seaside retreat of many modern painters. **1896** First trip to Holland. **1899** Published his theoretical treatise on Neo-impressionism, *D'Eugène Delacroix au néo-impressionnisme*. **1908** Elected president of the Indépendants. Like his friend Seurat, Signac was an artist whose method of painting and theoretical writings were fundamental to Neo-Impressionism.
WRITINGS: P. S.: D'Eugène Delacroix au néo-impressionnisme. Paris 1899, 1987.– P. S.: Jongkind. Paris 1927
CATALOGUES RAISONNES: Cachin, F. (ed.): P. S. Catalogue raisonné (in preparation).– Kornfeld, E. W. and P. A. Wick (ed.): Catalogue raisonné de l'œuvre gravé et lithographié de P. S. Bern 1974
MONOGRAPHS, CATALOGUES: Cachin, F. P. S. Milan 1970, Paris 1971, Greenwich (CT) 1971.– Lemoyne de Forges, M. T. (ed.): Catalogue de l'exposition du centenaire de P. S. Musée National du Louvre. Paris 1963 (cat.).– Monery, J.-P. (ed.): S. et Saint-Tropez. Musée de l'Annonciade, Saint-Tropez et al. Saint-Tropez 1992 (cat.).– Ratcliff, F.: P. S. and Color in Neo-Impressionism. New York 1992.– P. S. Musée National d'Art Moderne. Paris 1951 (cat.).– P. S. und die Befreiung der Farbe in Europa. Westfälisches Landesmuseum, Münster et al. Münster 1996 (cat.).– P. S. La Libération des couleurs. Musée de Grenoble. Paris 1997 (cat.)

ŠIMA Josef
1891 Jaroměř – **1971** Paris
Czech painter. **1911-1914** Studied at the Academy of Art in Prague under J. Preisler, and later at the Vienna Academy. **1921** Moved to Paris. Member of the group Devětsil and founder-member, together with Lecomte, Daumal and Reneville, of Group du Grand Jeu. **1923** First solo-exhibition at the gallery Topič in Prague. From **1925** paintings influenced by Surrealism and geometric abstraction. Around **1930** became interested in mythological themes. **1959** Participation in documenta 2 in Kassel. **1968** Retrospective at the Musée d'Art Moderne in Paris, **1974** at the Kunst-verein Bochum and **1992** at the Musée

d'Art Moderne, Paris. Sima experimented with a variety of painting styles in the course of his career. In Czechoslovakia he was celebrated as the "Painter of Things Imaginary". His late works from the mid-50s onwards are mostly geometric compositions with pronounced light-dark contrasts.
MONOGRAPHS, CATALOGUES: Leymarie, J. et al. (ed.): S. Musée National d'Art Moderne. Paris 1968 (cat.).– Linhartová, V.: J. S., ses amis, ses contemporains. Brussels 1974.– Machalick_, J.: J. S. Prague 1991.– Munck, J. (ed.): S. Le grand jeu. Musée d'Art Moderne. Paris 1992 (cat.).– Peyré, Y.: Les Leçons de la lumière. Caen 1992.– S. et Le Grand Jeu. Musée d'Art Moderne de la Ville de Paris et al. Paris 1992 (cat.).– Smejkal, F. J. S. Prague 1988, Paris 1992.– Spielmann, P. (ed.): J. S. Neue Galerie am Landesmuseum Joanneum, Graz. Bochum 1974 (cat.).– Starobinski, J. (ed.): S. œuvres récentes. Galerie le Point cardinal. Paris 1971 (cat.)

SIMONDS Charles
born **1945** New York
American object artist. **1963-1969** Studied at the University of California in Berkeley and Rutgers University in New Brunswick (NJ). **1969-1971** Employed as a teacher. From **1970** sculptural works on walls of buildings on Lower East Side, New York. **1971** *Landscape Body Dwelling*: an example of Body Art, in which the naked, mud-covered body of the artist is presented as a derelict landscape. This action led on to a series of portable models of ruins that became his *Pompeii Complex*. **1970-1974** Worked on various film projects and carried out actions. **1976** Publication of his book *Three Peoples*. **1977** Participation in documenta 6 in Kassel. **1994** Exhibition at the Fundació la Caixa in Barcelona. Simond's attempts to symbolically visualize cultural and historical developments and social decline are in some respects related to the works of the Spurensicherer (trace- and clue-finding artists).
WRITINGS: C. S. Three Peoples. Genoa 1975
MONOGRAPHS, CATALOGUES: Abadie, D. and G. Celant (ed.): C. S. Galerie Nationale du Jeu de Paume, Paris et al. Paris 1994 (cat.).– Neff, J. H. (ed.): C. S. Circles and Towers Growing. Museum of Contemporary Art, Chicago et al. Chicago 1982 (cat.).– Lascaut, G.: S. Paris, New York and Zurich 1986.– Molderings, H. (ed.): C. S. Schwebende Städte und andere Architekturen. Westfälischer Kunstverein. Münster 1978 (cat.).– Sauquet, S. (ed.): C. S. Fundació Caixa de Pensiones. Barcelona 1994 (cat.).– C. S. Albright-Knox Art Gallery. Buffalo 1977 (cat.).– C. S. Circles and Towers Growing. Museum Ludwig, Cologne et al. Cologne 1979 (cat.).– C. S. Galerie Maegt Lelong. Paris 1986 (cat.)

SINGIER Gustave
1909 Warneton – **1984** Paris
Belgian-born French painter. **1919** Moved

to Paris where he trained as an interior decorator. **1936** His meeting with C. Walch stimulated him to take up abstract painting. **1945** Founded the Salon de Mai. **1946** Joint-exhibition with Le Moal and Manessier at the Galerie Drouin, Paris. First tapestry design. **1949** Solo-exhibition at the Galerie Billiet-Caputo, Paris. **1951-1954** Taught at the Académie Ranson. **1955** and **1959** participation in documenta 1 and 2 in Kassel. **1957** Solo-exhibition at the Kestner Society, Hanover. From **1967** professor at the Ecole Nationale des Beaux-Arts, Paris. **1973** Solo-exhibition at the Musée des Beaux-Arts in Caen. **1992** Retrospective at the Centre Noroit in Arras. Singier's simplified abstract forms and warm, glowing colours have strong similarities to Manessier's paintings.
CATALOGUE RAISONNE: Schmücking, R. (ed.): G. S. Das graphische Werk. Brunswick 1958
MONOGRAPHS, CATALOGUES: Charbonier, G.: S. Paris 1957.– Lescure, J. (ed.): S. Musée des Beaux-Arts. Caen 1973 (cat.).– Lescure, J.: G. S. Paris 1988.– G. S. Städtisches Museum. Wuppertal 1957 (cat.)

SIQUEIROS David Alfaro
1886 San Rosalía de Camargo – **1974** Mexico City
Mexican painter. **1911-1913** Studied at the San Carlos Art Academy in Mexico City. **1919** Received a scholarship enabling him to work in Paris and Barcelona for three years. Friendship with Rivera. **1924** Painted frescoes in the Escuela Nacional Preparatoria. **1930** Banished to Tasco for political reasons and in **1932** officially exiled. Designed a mural for the Plaza Art Center in Los Angeles. **1934** Spent a year in New York. **1935** Organised a workshop, with pupils including Pollock. **1937** Took part in the Spanish Civil War. **1944** Founded the Centro Realista de Arte Moderna. **1950** Frescoes for the Palacio de Bellas Artes. **1955** Visits to Poland and the Soviet Union. **1962** Sentenced to eight years' imprisonment but granted a reprieve in **1964**. From **1964-1969** worked on a monumental fresco entitled *The March of Humanity*, for which he was awarded the Mexican National Prize for Art. Along with Rivera and Orozco, Siqueiros is regarded as one of the great Mexican fresco painters.

WRITINGS: D. A. S.: Esculto-pintura: Cuarta etapa del muralismo en México. New York 1968.– D. A. S.: L'Art et la révolution. Paris 1973/Art and Revolution. London 1975.– D. A. S.: Me llamaban el Coronelazo. Mexico City 1977/Man nannte mich den "Großen Oberst". Erinnerungen. Berlin 1988.– Tibol, R. (ed.): Textos de D. A. S. Mexico City 1974/D. A. S. Der neue mexikanische Realismus. Reden und Schriften zur Kunst. Dresden 1975
MONOGRAPHS, CATALOGUES: Arenal de Siqueiros et al. (ed.): Vida y obra de d. A. S.: Juicios criticos. Mexico City 1975.– De Micheli, M.: S. New York 1968.– Folgarait, L.: So Far from Heaven. D. A. S.'s "The March of Humanity" and Mexican Revolutionary Politics. Cambridge (MA) 1987.– Grigulevic, I. R.: S. Moscow 1980.– Rochfort, D.: The Development of a Revolutionary Public Mural Art in the Work of D. A. S. Diss. London 1986.– Rodríguez, A.: S. Mexico City 1974.– Semenov, O. S.: D. A. S. Moscow 1980.– Stein, P.: S. His Life and Works. New York 1994.– Tibol, R.: S.: Introductor de realidades. Mexico City 1961/D. A. S. Dresden 1966.– White, D. A.: S. Encino 1990

SIRONI Mario
1885 Sassari (Sardinia) – **1961** Milan
Italian painter. **1900** Moved to Rome. **1905** Began to study mathematics but stopped after one year. Came to know Severini and Boccioni, and entered the studio of Balla. **1914** Participated in the international Futurist exhibition in Rome. **1915** Became an official member of the Futurists. **1915–1918** Signed up for military service. **1918** Settled in Milan where he worked as an art critic. Sironi's paintings display a close affinity to Pittura metafisica. **1919** Participated in the Futurist exhibition at the Palazzo Cova, Milan. **1922** Founder-member of the Novecento Italiano group. **1926** and **1929** organised two Novecento exhibitions. **1935–1940** Worked on murals for the Turin Triennale and for the University of Rome. After World War II, designed stage sets and took up easel painting again. **1956** Honorary membership of the Accademia di San Luca. Sironi's paintings bridge three of the great art movements of his time, Futurism, Pittura metafisica and Neo-Classicism.
WRITINGS: Camesasca, E. (ed.): M. S. Scritti editi e inediti. Milan 1980
CATALOGUES RAISONNES: Bellonzi, F. (ed.): Catalogue raisonné de l'œuvre gravé. Milan 1985.– Benzi, F. and A. S. (ed.): S. illustratore. Catalogo ragionato. Roma 1988
MONOGRAPHS, CATALOGUES: Bartolini, S.: M. S. Reggio Emilia 1976.– Bellonzi, F.: S. Milan 1985.– Benzi, F. (ed.): M. S. Astrazione e materia. Galleria Arco Farnese. Roma 1989 (cat.).– Benzi, F. (ed.): M. S. 1885-1961. Galleria Nazionale d'Arte Moderna, Roma. Milan 1993 (cat.).– Bucci, M. and C. Bartoletti (ed.): M. S. per il teatro. Gabinetto Disegni e Stampe degli

Uffizi. Florence 1991 (cat.).– Gian Ferrari, C. (ed.): S. 1885-1961. Palazzo Reale. Milan 1985 (cat.).– Harten, J. and J. Poetter (ed.): M. S. 1885-1961. Städtische Kunsthalle Düsseldorf et al. Cologne 1988 (cat.).– Penelope, M. (ed.): S. Opere 1902-1960. Padiglione dell'Artigiano Sardo. Sassari 1985 (cat.).– Penelope, M.: S. Dal Futurismo al Dopoguerra. Roma 1990.– Pica, A.: M. S. pittore. Milan 1955, 1962/M. S. Painter. London 1955.– Sartoris, A.: M. S. Milan 1946.– M. S. Il mito dell' architettura. Padiglione d'Arte Contemporanea. Milan 1990 (cat.).– Traversi, G.: M. S. Disegni. Milan 1968

SLEVOGT Max
1868 Landshut – **1932** Neukastel
German painter and graphic artist. **1884–1890** Studied at the Munich Academy of Fine Arts under J. Herterich and W. Diez. Strongly influenced by W. Leibl and W. Trübner. **1889** Went to Paris and studied French Impressionism at the Académie Julian. **1890** Study trip to Italy. **1893** Joined the Munich Secession and the Freie Vereinigung (Association of Free Painters). From **1896** contributed to the magazine *Simplizissimus*. **1900** Went to Paris for the World Fair. **1901** Stayed in Frankfurt am Main, where he did his zoo paintings. From **1901** lived in Berlin and concentrated on portrait painting. Directed a master class at the Academy. **1914** Travelled to Egypt and painted landscapes in a new light, under the blazing sun. **1915** Did war paintings in Belgium, and in **1918** moved to Neukastel in the Palatinate. In the 20s he took up religious themes again, producing the graphic series *Passion*. Did over 500 illustrations for Goethe's *Faust*. **1924** Painted a music room at Neukastel, another in Berlin and a third **1927** in Bremen. His last work, completed in **1932**, was a fresco of *Golgotha* in the Friedenskirche at Ludwigshafen. Along with Liebermann and Corinth, Slovegt is one of the leading exponents of German Impressionism.
CATALOGUES RAISONNES: Sievers, J. and E. Waldmann (ed.): M. S. Das druckgraphische Werk 1890-1914. Heidelberg and Berlin 1962/M. S. The Graphic Work 1890-1914. San Francisco 1991
MONOGRAPHS, CATALOGUES: Blinn, H.: M. S. und seine Wandmalereien. Landau 1983.– Dieckmann, F. (ed.): W. A. Mozart: Die Zauberflöte. M. S. Randzeichnungen zu Mozarts Handschrift. Berlin 1984.– Esser, K.-H. (ed.): M. S. Nachlaß aus Neukastel. Mainz 1972.– Imiela, H.-J.: M. S. Karlsruhe 1968.– Imiela, H.-J. and B. Roland: S. und Mozart. M.-S.-Galerie, Schloß "Villa Ludwigshöhe" et al. Mainz 1991 (cat.).– Güse, E.-G. et al. (ed.): M. S. Gemälde, Aquarelle, Zeichnungen. Saarland Museum, Saarbrücken et al. Stuttgart 1992 (cat.).– Heffels, M.: Die Buchillustrationen von M. S. Bonn 1952.– Mosel, C.: M. S. Graphik und Handzeichnungen. Hanover 1965.– Passarge, W.: S. Wand- und Deckengemälde auf Neukastel. Hei-

delberg and Berlin 1961.– Roland, B.: M. S. Der Nachlass auf Schloß "Villa Ludwigshöhe". Dortmund 1982.– Roland, B. (ed.): M. S. Ägyptenreise 1914. Landesmuseum, Mainz et al. Mainz 1989 (cat.).– Roland, B.: S.-Graphik. 3 vols. Edenkoben 1990.– Roland, B. (ed.): M. S. Pfälzische Landschaften. Max-Slevogt-Galerie, Schloß Ludwigshöhe. Munich 1991 (cat.).– Weber, W.: Die religiösen Werke von M. S. Kaiserslautern 1966

SMET Gustave de
1877 Ghent – **1943** Deurle-sur-Lys
Belgian painter. First apprenticed to his father, a decorative painter. **1888–1895** Studied at the Art Academy in Ghent. **1901** Moved to Laethem-Saint-Martin, where Permeke, Berghe, Servaes and his brother Léon were working, and adopted a Neo-Impressionist style. **1914** Emigrated with Berghe to Holland. Influenced by Le Fauconnier, he took up Expressionist painting. **1918** Returned to Laethem and, together with P.-G. Hecke and A. de Ridder, set up the studio Sélection. **1927** Moved to Deurle. Co-founder of the Flemish Expressionist movement.
CATALOGUE RAISONNE: Hecke, P.-G. v. and E. Langui (ed.): G. de S. Sa Vie et son œuvre. Brussels 1945
MONOGRAPHS, CATALOGUES: Boysen, P.: G. d. S. Antwerp 1989.– Langui, E.: G. d. S. De mensch en zijn werk. Brussels 1945.– Puyvelde, L. v.: G. d. S. Antwerp 1949.– G. de S. Exposition rétrospective. Koninklijk Museum voor Schone Kunsten. Antwerp 1961 (cat.).– G. d. S. Rétrospective. Provinciaal Museum voor Moderne Kunst. Oostende 1989 (cat.)

SMITH David
1906 Decatur (IN) – **1965** Albany (NY)
American sculptor. Worked originally as a welder and solderer at the Studebaker automotive plant in South Bend (IN). There he learned various basic techniques that he later applied in his sculptures. **1926-1931** Studied at the Art Students League in New York. **1930** Met J. Graham. **1932** First wood sculptures. **1933/34** Began to work in steel. **1937** Exhibition at the Willard Gallery, New York. **1941** Moved to Bolton Landing where he set up his own workshop Terminal

Iron Works. **1950/51** Received a Guggenheim grant. Participated **1951** at the São Paulo Biennale and **1954** at the Venice Biennale. **1957** Solo-exhibition at the Museum of Modern Art, New York. **1958** Exhibited again at the Venice Biennale. **1959-1977** Took part in documenta 2–4 and 6 in Kassel. **1962** Worked on 27 sculptures for the "Festival of Both Worlds in Spoleto". **1986** Major retrospective at the Kunsthalle, Düsseldorf. Though there are many parallels between Smith's works and those of Calder and González, especially in terms of style and motif, his mastery of industrial manufacturing techniques sets him apart and introduces an important new material element to his sculpture.
WRITINGS: Gray, C. (ed.): D. S. by D. S. Sculpture and Writings. New York and London 1968, 1972
CATALOGUES RAISONNES: Krauss, R. E. (ed.): Terminal Iron Work/The Sculpture of D. S. Cambridge (MA) 1971, New York and London 1977.– Schwartz, A. and P. Cummings (ed.): D. S. The Prints. New York 1987
MONOGRAPHS, CATALOGUES: Carmean, E. A. (ed.): D. S. National Gallery of Art. Washington 1982 (cat.).– Cone, J. H. and M. Paul (ed.): D. S. 1906-1965. A Retrospective Exhibition. Fogg Art Museum. Cambridge et al. Cambridge (MA) 1966 (cat.).– Cummings, P. (ed.): D. S. The Drawings. Whitney Museum of American Art. New York 1979 (cat.).– Fry, E. F. (ed.): D. S. Solomon R. Guggenheim Museum. New York 1969 (cat.).– Fry, E. F. (ed.): D. S. Painter, Sculptor, Draftsman. Hirshhorn Museum and Sculpture Garden, Washington. New York 1982 (cat.).– Gimenez, C. (ed.): D. S. 1906-1965. IVAM Centro Julio González, Valencia et al. Valencia 1996 (cat.).– Lewison, J. et al. (ed.): D. S. Medals for Dishonor. 1937-1940. Imperial War Museum, London et al. Leeds 1991 (cat.).– McCoy, G. (ed.): D. S. From Life of the Artist. New York, Washington and London 1973.– Marcus, S. E.: The Working Methods of D. S. Diss. Columbia University. New York 1972.– Marcus, S. E.: D. S. The Sculptor and His Work. Ithaca (NY) and London 1983.– Merkert, J. (ed.): D. S. Skulpturen, Zeichnungen. Kunstsammlung Nordrhein-Westfalen, Düsseldorf et al. Munich 1986 (cat.)/D. S. Sculptures, Drawings. Whitechappel Art Gallery. London 1987 (cat.).– Rikhoff, J.: D. S. I Remember. Glenns Falls (NY) 1984.– D. S. Solomon R. Guggenheim Museum. New York 1969 (cat.).– D. S. Zeichnungen. Staatsgalerie Stuttgart et al. Stuttgart 1976 (cat.).– D. S. Medals for Dishonor. Columbus Museum of Art. Columbus (OH) 1996 (cat.).– D. S.: D. S. in Italy. New York 1996.– Wilkin, K.: D. S. New York 1984

SMITH Kiki
born **1954** Nuremberg
American sculptress, painter and installation artist. **1976** Went to New York where she met the film producer C. Ahearn who

introduced her to the artists' group Collaborative. **1979** First paintings in the series Severed Limbs. Began to use Gray's Anatomy as source material. **1980–1983** Involved in various projects, including books and videos. Trips to Europe. **1985** Trained as an emergency medical technician. **1987** First paper sculptures, taking the body as her central theme. **1991** Participated at the Whitney Biennale in New York. **1993** Invited to the Whitney and the Venice Biennale. **1997** Took part in documenta 10 in Kassel.
MONOGRAPHS, CATALOGUES: Ackley, C. et al. (ed.): K. S. The Unique Print 70s into 90s. Museum of Fine Arts. Boston 1990 (cat.).– Brown, E. A. (ed.): K. S. Sojourn in Santa Barbara. University Art Museum. University of California. Santa Barbara 1991 (cat.).– Bradley, J. (ed.): K. S. The Power Plant. Toronto 1994 (cat.).– Colombo, P. et al. (ed.): K. S. Institute of Contemporary Art. Amsterdam 1990 (cat.).– Fuchs, A. (ed.): K. S. Lousiana Museum of Modern Art. Humblebæk 1995 (cat.).– Isaak, A.(ed.): K. S. Whitechapel Gallery. London 1995 (cat.).– Landau, S. (ed.): K. S. The Israel Museum. Jerusalem 1994 (cat.).– Morin, F. and M. Vignelli (ed.): K. S. The Interrupted Life. New Museum of Contemporary Art. New York 1991 (cat.).– Noever, P. (ed.): K. S. Silent Works. MAK – Museum für angewandte Kunst. Graz 1992 (cat.).– Shearer, L. and C. Gould (ed.): K. S. Williams College Museum, Williamstown et al. Williamstown 1992 (cat.).– K. S. New Work. Pace Wildenstein. New York 1995 (cat.).– K. S. Whitechappel Art Gallery. London 1995 (cat.).– K. S. Montreal Museum of Fine Arts et al. Montreal 1996 (cat.).– Spapen, M. (ed.): K. S. Prints and Multiples 1985-1993. Barbara Krakow Gallery. Boston 1994 (cat.).– Stoops, S. L. (ed.): K. S. Unfolding the Body. Rose Art Museum. Brandeis University 1992 (cat.).– Théberge, P. (ed.): K. S. The Montreal Museum of Fine Arts. Montreal 1996 (cat.)

SMITH Tony
1912 South Orange (NJ) – **1980** New York
American sculptor, painter and architect. **1933–1936** Studied at the Art Students League, Chicago. **1937/38** Continued his studies at the New Bauhaus in Chicago. **1938/39** Assistant to F. L. Wright. Became friends with Newman, Rothko, Pollock and Still. **1953–1955** Spent two years in Germany. **1950–1953** and **1957/58** taught at the Pratt Institute, New York. **1960** First minimalist sculptures. **1966** First solo-exhibition in Hartford (CT). **1968** Participated in documenta 4 in Kassel. **1969** Taught at the University of Hawaii in Honolulu. **1974** Solo-exhibition at the University of Maryland Art Gallery. **1988** Retrospective at the Westfälische Landesmuseum, Münster, and at Museum Abteiberg in Mönchengladbach. His simple geometric sculptures of almost architectonic dimensions can be termed site-specific sculptures, since their

design is very much determined by the place at which they are destined to stand.
MONOGRAPHS, CATALOGUES: Lippard, L. R.: T. S. New York 1971 / T. S. Stuttgart 1971.– McShine, K. (ed.): T. S. The Museum of Modern Art. New York 1971 (cat.).– Meschede, F. (ed.): T. S. Skulpturen und Zeichnungen. 1961-1969. Westfälisches Landesmuseum, Münster et al. Münster et al. 1988 (cat.).– T. S. Ten Elements and Throwback. Pace Gallery. New Yok 1979 (cat.).– T. S. Paintings and Sculpture. The Pace Gallery. New York 1983 (cat.).– Wagstaff, S. (ed.): T. S. Two Exhibitions of Sculpture. Wadsworth Antheneum, Hartford (CT), Philadelphia Institute of Contemporary Art. Philadelphia 1966 (cat.)

SMITH William Eugene
1918 Wichita (KS) – **1979** Tuscon (AZ)
American photographer. **1936/37** Studied photography at the University of Notre Dame, Indiana. First photographs for newspapers in Wichita and **1937/38** for *Newsweek*, New York. From **1938** worked as a freelance photographer for *Life* magazine, *Harper's Bazaar* and the *New York Times*. **1944/45** and **1947–1954** employed again by *Life* magazine as a war correspondent. **1949** Elected president of the Photo League. **1954** Joined the agency Magnum. **1959** Honorary award from the American Society of Magazine Photographers. **1966–1969** Taught photography at the New School for Social Research in New York, and subsequently at the School of Visual Arts, New York, and the University of Arizona, Tuscon. **1971** National Endowment for the Arts Award. Smith specialized in human interest photography: reportages on social issues.
WRITINGS: Lamb, C. and A. Stark (ed.): W. E. S. Papers. Tucson (AZ) 1983
MONOGRAPHS, CATALOGUES: Bunnell, P. C. and L. K. (ed.): W. E. S. His Photographs and Notes. New York 1969, 1993.– Hansen, H.: Myth and Vision. On the Walk to Paradise Garden and the Photography of W. E. S. Lund 1987.– Hughes, J.: W. E. S. Shadow and Substance. New York 1989.– Johnson, W. S. (ed.): W. E. S. Early Work. Tucson (AZ) 1980.– Johnson, W. S.: W. E. S. Master of the Photographic Essay. Millerton (NY) 1981, London 1990.– Kirstein, L.: W. E. S. His Photographs and Notes. New York 1993.– Maddow, B. et al. (ed.): Let Truth Be The Prejustice. W. E. S. His Life and Photographs. Philadelphia Museum of Art. New York 1985 (cat.).– W. E. S. Milan 1983.– Willumson, G. G.: W. E. S. and the Photograhic Essay. Cambridge (MA) 1992

SMITHSON Robert
1938 Passaic (NJ) – **1973** near Tecovas Lake (TX)
American artist. **1953–1956** Studied at the Art Students League, New York, and **1956** at Brooklyn Museum School. **1957** Travelled through the USA and Mexiko. First

paintings in Abstract Expressionist style. **1959** First solo-exhibition at the Artist's Gallery, New York. **1960** Came to know LeWitt. **1961** First solo-exhibition at the Galleria George Lester, Rome. In the mid-60s took up "Minimal Art". Close contact with other minimal artists. **1966** Participated in the exhibition "Primary Structures" at the Jewish Museum, New York, and soon afterwards produced his first Land Art projects, some in collaboration with Heizer. **1968** Participated in the Minimal Art exhibition at the Gemeentemuseum in The Hague. **1970** Created *Spiral Jetty* in the Great Salt Lake at Utah: earthworks forming an enormous spiral, turning the landscape into a huge geometric figure. **1972** and **1977** participated in documenta 5 and 6 in Kassel. **1973** Guggenheim grant. Killed in a plane crash while surveying his work *Amarillo Ramp* near Tecovas Lake. **1974** Solo-exhibition at the New York Cultural Center. **1993** Retrospective at the Centro Julio González, Valencia. In his best-known works Smithson used natural landscapes to form geometric figures.
WRITINGS: Holt, N. (ed.): The Writings of R. S. New York 1979, Berkeley 1994.– Tsai, E. (ed.): R. S. Unearthed. Drawings, Collages, Writings. Wallach Gallery at Columbia University. New York 1991 (cat.)
MONOGRAPHS, CATALOGUES: Boulan, M.-S. (ed.): R. S. Une rétrospective. IVAM Centro Julio González, Valencia et al. Valencia 1993 (cat.).– Casanova, M. et al. (ed.): R. S. El paisaje entrópico. Una retrospectiva 1960-1973. IVAM Centro Julio González, Valencia et al. Valencia 1993 (cat.).– Halley, P. (ed.): R. S. The Early Works 1959-1962. Diana Brown Gallery. New York 1985 (cat.).– Hobbs, R. et al. (ed.): R. S. Sculpture. Ithaca (NY) and London 1981.– Hobbs, R. et al. (ed.): R. S. Retrospective. Musée d'Art Moderne de la Ville de Paris, Paris et al. Paris 1982 (cat.)/R. S. A Retrospektive. Wilhelm Lehmbruck Museum. Duisburg 1983 (cat.).– Meschede, F. and B. Kalthoff (ed.): R. S. Zeichnungen aus dem Nachlaß. Westfälisches Landemuseum, Münster et al. Münster 1989 (cat.).– Schmidt, E.: Zwischen Kino, Landschaft und Museum: Erfahrung und Fiktion im Werk von R. S. Frankfurt-on-Main 1995.– Shapiro, G: Earthwards. R. S. and Art After Babel. Berkeley 1995, 1998.– R. S. Das Frühwerk 1959-1962. Kunstmuseum. Lucerne 1988 (cat.).– R. S. Une Rétrospective. Le Paysage entropique 1960-1973. Palais des Beaux-Arts, Brussels et al. Brussels 1994 (cat.).– Sobieszek, R. (ed.): R. S. Photo Works. Los Angeles County Museum of Art. Albuquerque 1993 (cat.)

SNELSON Kenneth
born **1927** Pendleton (OR)
American sculptor. **1946/47** Studied at the University of Oregon in Eugene, **1947/48** at Black Mountain College in Beria (NC) under Albers and De Kooning, and **1949** at the Académie Montmartre under Léger.

1960 Moved to New York. **1962** First solo-exhibition at the Pratt Institute, Brooklyn. Taught at the Cooper Union and the School of Visual Arts in New York and also at Yale University in New Haven (CT). **1966** Exhibition at the Dwan Gallery in New York. **1974** Received a grant from the National Endowment for the Arts, and in **1975**, a DAAD scholarship to Berlin. **1977** Participation in documenta 6 in Kassel. **1987** Honorary award from the American Institute of Architects and Letters. With his forceful, dynamic constructions of metal piping and taut ropes, Snelson can be regarded as one of the leading abstract sculptors in America during the 60s and 70s.
MONOGRAPHS, CATALOGUES: Fox, H. N. (ed.): K. S. Hirshhorn Museum, Washington et al. Washington 1981 (cat.).– Glozer, L. (ed.): K. S. Struktur und Spannung. Kunstverein Hannover. Hanover 1971 (cat.).– Schneider, A. and K. S. (ed.): K. S. Skulpturen. Nationalgalerie. Berlin 1977 (cat.).– Weider, L.: Full Circle. Panoramas by K. S. New York 1990

SOLANO Susana
born **1946** Barcelona
Spanish sculptress. Painted up to the end of the 70s, and then took up abstract sculpture, first working with curved iron plates. **1980** First solo-exhibition at the Fundació Joan Miró, Barcelona. **1983** Solo-exhibition at the Galeria Ciento, Barcelona. **1987** Participated in documenta 8 in Kassel and at the São Paulo Biennale. Solo-exhibition at the Musée d'Art Contemporain, Bordeaux. **1988** and **1993** Participated at the Venice Biennale. **1989** Solo-presentations at the Abteiberg Museum, Mönchengladbach, and at the Hirshhorn Museum, Washington. **1992** Participated in documenta 9 in Kassel and had a solo-exhibition at the Whitechapel Art Gallery, London. Solano's works are mostly installations in steel, reminiscent of enclosures or cages.
MONOGRAPHS, CATALOGUES: Blanch, T. and D. Stemmler (ed.): S. S. Städtisches Museum Abteiberg. Mönchengladbach 1989 (cat.).– Blanch, T. et al. (ed.): S. S. Museo Nacional Centro de Arte Reina Sofia, Madrid et al. Madrid 1992 (cat.).– Froment, J.-L. and J.-M. Poinsot: S. S. Sculptures de 1981 à 1987. Musée d'Art

Contemporain. Bordeaux 1987.– García, A. and A. Himmelreich (ed.): S. S. Bonnefantenmuseum. Maastricht 1988 (cat.).– García, A. et al. (ed.): S. S. Skulpturen und Fotografien. Neuer Berliner Kunstverein et al. Wechmar 1996 (cat.).– Logrono, M.: El templo escultórico de S. S. Madrid 1987.– Martínez-Garrido, S. (ed.): S. S. Museo Nacional Centro de Arte Reina Sofía. Madrid 1992 (cat.).– Navarro, J. R. (ed.): S. S. Fundació Joan Miró. Barcelona 1980 (cat.).– Poinsot, J.-M. (ed.): S. S. Musée d'Art Contemporain de Bordeaux. Bordeaux 1987 (cat.).– Poinsot, J.-M. (ed.): S. S. Museum of Modern Art, San Francisco et al. San Francisco 1991 (cat.).– Queralt, R. (ed.): S. S. Galleria Giorgio Persano. Torino 1987 (cat.).– S. S. Centre National d'Art Contemporain. Grenoble 1993 (cat.)

SOLDATI Atanasio
1896 Parma – **1953** Milan
Italian painter. Studied architecture up until **1922**. First solo-exhibition in Parma. **1925** Moved to Milan. Developed a strictly geometric abstract painting style, closely related to that of Mondrian. **1930** Moved closer to Pittura metafisica. **1933** Solo-exhibition at the Galleria Il Milione, Milan. After World War II, joined Dorfles, Monnet and Munari in founding the movement Movimento Arte Concreta. **1954** Posthumous retrospective at the Galleria Bergamini, Milan. **1969** Solo-exhibition at the Galleria Civica d'Arte Moderna, Turin. Soldati aimed to achieve a synthesis of metaphysics and abstraction through his painting.
MONOGRAPHS, CATALOGUES: Bianchino, G. (ed.): A. S. Università di Parma. Parma 1993 (cat.).– Garau, A. (ed.): A. S. Milan 1990.– Mallé, L. and N. Ponente (ed.): A. S. Galleria Civica d'Arte Moderna. Torino 1970 (cat.).– Santini, P. C. (ed.): A. S. Centro Cult. Olivietti. Ivrea 1965 (cat.)

SONDERBORG K. R. H.
(Kurt Rudolf Hoffmann)
born **1923** Sonderborg
German painter. **1939–1941** Business studies. **1941/42** Interned in the concentration camp Fuhlsbüttel. **1947–1949** Studied at the Hamburg School of Art. **1951** Trip to

Italy. **1953** Worked in Hayter's graphic studio Atelier 17 in Paris. Member of the Zen 49 group. **1955** Karl-Ernst Osthaus Prize from the City of Hagen. **1956** Joint-exhibition with Götz at the Kestner Society, Hanover. **1957** Went to England. **1958** Participated at the Venice Biennale and **1959** and **1964** in documenta 2 and 3 in Kassel. **1960** Prize for graphic art at the Tokyo Biennale and **1963** major prize for drawing at the São Paulo Biennale. **1965** Solo-exhibition at the Stedelijk Museum, Eindhoven. **1966** Taught at the Stuttgart Academy. **1970** Participated at the Venice Biennale. **1985** Scholarship to the Villa Massimo, Rome. **1988** Retrospective at the City Gallery in Stuttgart. Sonderborg's spontaneous, expressive style of painting is closely related to French Tachisme, although his mode of expression is often quite graphic, being limited to black-and-white contrasts.
MONOGRAPHS, CATALOGUES: Gauss, U. (ed.): K. R. H. S. Arbeiten auf Papier. Staatsgalerie Stuttgart. Stuttgart 1985 (cat.).– Hahn, O.: K. R. H. S. Stuttgart 1964, London 1964.– Költzsch, G.-W. (ed.): K. R. H. S. Werke 1948-1986. Moderne Galerie des Saarland Museums. Saarbrücken 1987 (cat.).– Labarthe, A. S.: S. Tuer un rat. Paris 1974.– Meyer, W. and T. Osterwold (ed.): K. R. H. S. Württembergischer Kunstverein. Stuttgart 1993 (cat.).– Motte, M. d. la (ed.): K. R. H. S. Galerie Georg Nothelfer. Berlin 1991 (cat.).– Nusser, U. et al. (ed.): K. R. H. S. Württembergischer Kunstverein. Stuttgart 1993 (cat.).– Poetter, J. (ed.): K. R. H. S. Staatliche Kunsthalle Baden-Baden. Baden-Baden 1993 (cat.).– Reinhardt, B. (ed.): K. R. H. S. Galerie der Stadt Stuttgart 1988 (cat.).– K. R. H. S. Kölnischer Kunstverein. Cologne 1965 (cat.)

SONNIER Keith
born **1941** Mamou (LA)
American artist. **1959–1963** Studied at the University of Southwestern Louisana in Lafayette. **1963/64** Lived in France. **1964–1966** Studied at Rutgers University, New Brunswick (NJ). Began to work in glass and neon. **1968** Solo-exhibition at the Ricke gallery in Cologne. From **1970** film and video installations. **1970** Solo-exhibition at the Steledijk Museum, Eindhoven, and at the Leo Castelli Gallery, New York. **1972** Participated in documenta 5 in Kassel and at the Venice Biennale. **1974** Guggenheim grant and first prize at the Tokyo Graphic Biennale. **1977** Participation in documenta 6 in Kassel. **1979** Solo-presentation at the Pompidou Centre, Paris. **1987** Retrospective at the Alexandria Museum of Art (LA). **1989** Solo-exhibition at the Hirshhorn Museum, Washington, and at the Douglas Hyde Gallery, Dublin. Since the mid-60s, most of Sonnier's best-known works have been objects constructed out of neon and glass. They are examples of Material Art.
MONOGRAPHS, CATALOGUES: Elger, D. (ed.): K. S. Sprengel Museum, Hanover

et al. Stuttgart 1993 (cat.).– Kuspit, D. (ed.): K. S. Hyde Gallery. Dublin 1989 (cat.).– O'Brien, G. (ed.): K. S. Leo Castelli Gallery. New York 1992 (cat.).– Puvogel, R. (ed.): K. S. Projekt Flughafen Munich 1989-1992. Stuttgart 1992.– Raben, H. et al. (ed.): K. S. Lichtweg/Lightway. Stuttgart 1992.– K. S. Stedelijk Van Abbe Museum. Eindhoven 1970 (cat.).– K. S. Argon-und-Neon-Arbeiten. Museum Haus Lange. Krefeld 1979 (cat.).– K. S. Kunsthalle. Nuremberg 1994 (cat.).– Zilczer, J. (ed.): K. S. Hirshhorn Museum and Sculpture Garden. Washington 1989 (cat.)

SOTO Jesús Rafael
born **1923** Ciudad Bolivar
Venezuelan painter and sculptor. **1942–1947** Studied at the Art Academy in Caracas. **1947–1950** Director of the Maracaibo Academy. **1950** Moved to Paris where he exhibited at the Salon des Réalités Nouvelles and met Tinguely and Agam. **1956** Solo-exhibition at the Galerie Denise René, Paris. **1958** Participated at the Venice Biennale. **1963** Received the Premio Wolf prize at the São Paulo Biennale and exhibited at the Museum Haus Lange in Krefeld. **1964** Awarded the David Bright Prize at the Venice Biennale and participation in documenta 3 in Kassel. **1968** Solo-exhibition at the Kunsthalle Bern and **1971** at the Museum of Contemporary Art, Chicago. **1981** Participated in the "Westkunst" exhibition, Cologne. **1990** Won the UNESCO Picasso Medal. **1992** Retrospective at the Museo de Bellas Artes, Caracas. **1993** Nominated Commandeur des Arts et Lettres in France. Soto uses optical illusions, reminiscent of Vasarely's Op Art, but also explores the possibilities of technologically produced vibrations.
WRITINGS: S. Textos. Madrid 1990
MONOGRAPHS, CATALOGUES: Balza, J.: J. S. el niño. Caracas 1981.– Boulton, A.: S. Caracas 1973.– Boulton, A. et al. (ed.): S. Palacio de Velázquez, Parque del Retiro. Madrid 1982 (cat.).– Boulton, A. and M. Homma (ed.): J. R. S. Museum of Modern Art. Kamakura 1990.– Butor, M. et al. (ed.): J. R. S. Galerie Nationale du Jeu de Paume. Paris 1996 (cat.).– Clay, J. (ed.): S. Musée d'Art Moderne de la Ville de Paris. Paris 1969 (cat.).– Joray, M.: J. R. S. Neuchâtel 1984.– Lemaire, G.-G.: J.-R. S. Paris 1997.– Renard, C.-L. (ed.): S. A Retrospective Exhibition. Solomon R. Guggenheim Museum. New York 1974 (cat.).– Renard, C.-L. (ed.): S. Œuvres actuelles. Centre Georges Pompidou. Paris 1979 (cat.).– Somaini, L.: S. Milan 1991.– S. Cuarenta años de creación 1943-1983. Museo de Arte Contemporáneo. Caracas 1983.– S. Space Art. Center for the Fine Arts and the Hispanic Heritage Festival Committee. Miami 1985 (cat.)

SOULAGES Pierre
born **1919** Rodez (Aveyron)
French painter. **1938** Went to Paris to study

at the Ecole des Beaux-Arts but returned home after a short time without completing the course. **1943** Discovered abstract art, and came to know Sonia Delaunay. **1946** Moved to Courbevoie. **1947** Set up his own studio in Paris. Became acquainted with Picabia, Hartung and Léger. First works exhibited at the Salon des Surindépendants. **1949** First solo-exhibition at the Galerie Lydia Conti, Paris. **1949–1951** Stage and costume designs. **1953** Prize for Painting at the São Paulo Biennale. **1955** and **1964** participation in documenta 1 and 2 in Kassel. **1960/61** First retrospective at the Kestner Society, Hanover, the Folkwang Museum, Essen, and the Gemeentemuseum in The Hague. **1967** Retrospective at the Musée d'Art et d'Industrie, Saint-Etienne. From **1979** painted mostly in dark colours. **1987** Designed a monumental tapestry for the new Ministry of Finance in Paris. Awarded a major national prize for painting in Paris. **1993** Retrospective in Seoul. **1995** Completed a series of stained-glass windows for the Abbey of Conques in France. In many of Soulage's paintings, broad swaths of black or dark brown hover over a pale or lightly washed ground.
CATALOGUES RAISONNÉS: Daix, P. and J. J. Sweeney (ed.): P. S. L'œuvre 1947-1990. Neuchâtel 1991.– Encrevé, P. (ed.): S. L'œuvre complet. Peintures. 3 vols. 1946-1996. Paris 1994-1998.– Rivière, Y. (ed.): S. Eaux-fortes, litographies 1952-1973. Paris 1974
MONOGRAPHS, CATALOGUES: Ceysson, B.: P. S. Paris 1979.– Ceysson, B. (ed.): P. S. 40 Jahre Malerei. Stuttgart 1989.– Duby, S. et al. (ed.): P. S. Musée Saint-Pierre, Lyon et al. Lyon 1987, Reutlingen 1987 (cat.).– Heck, C. et al. (ed.): Conques. Les vitraux de S. Paris 1994.– Juliet, C.: Entretien avec P. S. Caen 1990.– Labbaye, C.: S. Eaux-fortes, lithographies 1952-1973. Paris 1974.– Loers, V. (ed.): S. 40 Jahre Malerei. Museum Fridericianum, Kassel et al. Kassel 1989 (cat.).– Pacquement, A. et al. (ed.): S. Peintures récentes. Centre Georges Pompidou. Paris 1979 (cat.).– Ragon, M.: Les Ateliers de S. Paris 1990.– Rivière, Y. (ed.): S. Eaux-fortes, lithographies 1952-1973. Paris 1974.– P. S. Musée d'Art Moderne de la Ville de Paris. Paris 1996 (cat.).– Sweeney, J. J.: P. S. Neuchâtel 1972, Greewich 1972, London 1973

SOUTINE Chaïm
1893 Smilovitchy (near Minsk) – **1943** Paris
Lithuanian-born French painter. **1910–1913** Studied at the Art Academy in Vilnius, and then went to Paris. **1916** Took a studio at the artists' colony La Ruche where he lived with Modigliani and Chagall. Introduced by Modigliani to the art dealer Zborowski who in **1919** persuaded him to go to Céret to paint landscapes. His numerous landscapes, painted there over the next three years in a thick impasto and garish colours, betray a tortured and restless spirit. **1923** Returned to Paris and sold all the paintings in his studio to the American art collector

A. Barnes. His newly acquired affluence calmed Soutine's vehemence somewhat, but did not prevent a second triumph: paintings of animal carcasses in which he pays homage to Rembrandt. People in uniform were another favourite theme of his. **1937** Came to know Gerda Groth, who was trying to escape from the Germans. Lived with her in Civry-sur-Serein near Auxerre and in Paris, until she was deported to a concentration camp. **1940** Met the former wife of Ernst, who hid him from the Nazis in Paris. **1943** Died from internal bleeding caused by a stomach ulcer. Became famous in the mid-20s for his paintings of slaughtered oxen. In the early 30s, after a short lyrical period, his paintings once again became powerfully expressive, as he portrayed the suffering of uprooted, homeless people.
CATALOGUES RAISONNES: Lanthemann, J. (ed.): S. Catalogue raisonné de l'œuvre dessinée. Paris 1981.– Tuchman, M., E. Dunow and K. Perls (ed.): C. S. (1893-1943). Catalogue Raisonné. Werkverzeichnis. 2 vols. Cologne 1993
MONOGRAPHS, CATALOGUES: Chiappini, R. (ed.): C. S. Museo d'Arte Moderna della Città di Lugano. Milan 1995 (cat.).– Cogniat, R.: S. Paris 1979, New York 1984.– Courthion, P.: S. Peintre du déchirant. Lausanne 1972.– Güse, E.-G. (ed.): C. S. 1893-1943. Westfälisches Landesmuseum, Münster et al. Stuttgart 1981 (cat.).– Lassaigne, J.: S. Paris 1954.– Michaelis, G.: Mes années avec S. Paris 1973.– Nicoïdski, C. (ed.): S. ou la Profanation. 1993, l'année Soutine. Orangerie des Tuileries. Paris 1993 (cat.).– Szittya, E.: S. et son temps. Paris 1955.– Tuchman, M. (ed.): C. S. Los Angeles County Museum. Los Angeles 1968 (cat.).– Vallès-Bled, M. (ed.): S. Musée. Chartres 1989 (cat.).– Werner, A.: C. S. New York 1985, Paris 1986.– Wheeler, M.: S. New York 1950, 1967

SOUTTER Louis
1871 Morges (Waadt) – **1942** Ballaigues (Waadt)
Swiss painter. **1888–1890** Studied natural sciences and engineering in Lausanne. **1892–1894** Studied music at the Conservatoire in Brussels. **1895** Took painting lessons, first in Lausanne and Geneva and then in Paris. **1897** Moved to the USA. **1898**

Directed the art department at Colorado College in Colorado Springs. **1904** Returned to Morges. **1906** Admitted to a psychiatric clinic for the first time. **1923** Permanently committed to a mental asylum. **1936** First solo-exhibition at the Wadsworth Atheneum in Hartford (CT). **1937** Solo-exhibition at the Paul Vallotton gallery, Lausanne. **1939** Solo-exhibition at the Weyhe Gallery, New York. Soutter painted and drew in a desperate attempt to earn money and usually used the simplest materials (chalk and school notebooks). The themes of his expressive drawings were often taken from the Bible.
CATALOGUE RAISONNE: Thévoz, M. (ed.): L. S. Catalogue de l'œuvre. Lausanne and Zurich 1976
MONOGRAPHS, CATALOGUES: Bader, A.: L. S. Eine pathologische Studie. Stuttgart 1968.– Berger, R. and E. Manganel: L. S. Lausanne 1961.– Hachmeister, H. (ed.): L. S. Zeichnungen und Fingermalereien. Hachmeister Galerie. Münster 1991 (cat.).– Kuenzi, A. and A. Ferrari (ed.): L. S. Fondation Pierre Gianadda. Martigny 1990 (cat.).– Morax, R. (ed.): L. S. Illustrationen zum Tell. Bern 1994.– L. S. Rétrospective. Musée Cantonal des Beaux-Arts, Lausanne et al. Lausanne 1974.– Thévoz, M.: L. S. Lausanne 1970.– Thévoz, M.: L. S. ou l'écriture du désir. Lausanne and Zurich 1974.– Thévoz, M.: Détournement d'écriture. Paris 1989.– Zweite, A. (ed.): L. S. (1871-1942). Zeichnungen, Bücher, Fingermalereien. Städtische Galerie im Lenbachhaus, Munich et al. Munich 1985 (cat.)

SPENCER Stanley
1891 Cookham – **1959** Cookham
English painter. **1908–1912** Studied under Tonks at the Slade School of Art in London. **1912** Participated in the second Post-Impressionist exhibition in London. **1914–1918** Military service. **1922** Lived in Yugoslavia. **1926–1932** Worked on murals for the Burghclere Chapel. **1927** First solo-exhibition at the Goupil Gallery, London. **1932** Moved to Cookham. **1932** and **1939** participated at the Venice Biennale. **1932–1935** Elected to the Royal Academy but resigned when two of his works were rejected. **1933–1936** Spent two years in Switzerland. **1939–1945** Engaged as an official war artist. **1946** Took part in the competition *The Temptation of St. Anthony*. **1950** Elected to the Royal Academy. **1954** Trip to China. **1955** Retrospective at the Tate Gallery and **1980** at the Royal Academy, London. Spencer's striking but finely executed figurative paintings were usually based on religious themes. His later works depict sexual tensions and problems associated with old age or illness.
WRITINGS: Rothenstein, J. (ed.): S. S. The Man. Correspondence and Reminiscences. London 1979
CATALOGUE RAISONNE: Bell, K. (ed.): S. S. A Complete Catalogue of the Paintings. London and New York 1992
MONOGRAPHS, CATALOGUES: Alison,

J. (ed.): S. S. The Apotheosis of Love. Barbican Art Gallery. London 1991 (cat.).– Bell, K. (ed.): S. S. Royal Academy of Arts. London 1980 (cat.).– Carline, R.: S. S. at War. London 1978.– Collis, M.: S. S. A Biography. London 1962.– Collis, M.: A private View on S. S. London 1972.– Nesbitt, J. (ed.): S. S. A Sort of Heaven. Tate Gallery, London. Liverpool 1992 (cat.).– Pople, K.: S. S. A Biography. London 1991, New York 1997.– Robinson, D.: S. S. Visions from a Berkshire Village. Oxford 1979.– Robinson, D.: S. S. Oxford 1990, San Francisco 1993.– Spencer, G.: S. S. London 1961.– S. S. War Artist on Clydeside. Scottish Arts Council. Edinburgh 1975 (cat.).– S. S. 1891-1959. The Arts Council of Great Britain. London 1976 (cat.)

SPERO Nancy
born **1926** Cleveland (OH)
American painter. **1945–1949** Studied at the Art Institute of Chicago. **1949/50** Went to Paris and attended the Ecole des Beaux-Arts. **1951** Married Leon Golub. Worked in New York, Chicago, Ischia, Florence and Paris on compositions with reduced forms. **1962** First solo-exhibition in Paris. **1964** Moved to New York. **1966–1970** Inspired by the horror of the Vietnam War and the fixation of the New York art scene on Pop and Minimal Art to produce her *War Series*. Actively engaged in artistic and political activities of the Art Workers Coalition. **1969** Joined the group Women Artists in Revolution. **1971** Founder-member of the New York Artists in Residence Gallery. From **1974** concentrated on the subject of women, producing feminist works portraying the torture of femal political prisoners. After **1978** Spero created large-scale murals, installations and designs of whole rooms, using stamps rather than traditional methods of painting. **1997** Participation in documenta 10 in Kassel.
MONOGRAPHS, CATALOGUES: Bird, J. and L. Tickner (ed.): N. S. Institute of Contemporary Arts. London 1987 (cat.).– Bird, J. et al. (ed.): N. S. London 1996 (cat.).– King, E. A. (ed.): N. S. The Black Paris Paintings 1959-1966. Carnegie-Mellon University Art Gallery. Pittsburgh 1985 (cat.).– Pohlen, A. (ed.): N. S. Bilder 1958-1990. Haus am Waldsee, Berlin et al. Berlin 1990 (cat.).– N. S. Rebirth of Venus. Kyoto 1989.– Storr, R. (ed.): N. S. Works Since 1950. Everson Museum of Art, Syracuse (NY) et al. New York 1987 (cat.).– Tickner, L.: N. S. Inscribing Woman Between The Lines. Institute of Contemporary Arts. London 1987 (cat.).– Vierneisel, K. et al. (ed.): N. S. Women Breathing. Ulmer Museum. Stuttgart 1992.– Weskott, H. et al. (ed.): N. S. in der Glyptothek. Arbeiten auf Papier. Glyptothek am Königsplatz. Munich 1991

SPOERRI Daniel
(Daniel Isaak Feinstein)
born **1930** Galati (Romania)

Romanian object artist. **1942** Moved to Switzerland. **1950–1954** Trained as a dancer. **1955–1957** Danced at the Bern Opera. **1957** Assistant to K. Bremer at the theatre in Darmstadt. Wrote articles on experimental theatre. **1959** Moved to Paris. **1960** Founder-member of the Nouveaux Réalistes. Began his *Trap Pictures*, in which random arrangements of objects are affixed to their chance support, for instance a table, tipped into a vertical position and declared a work of art. Contact with the Fluxus movement in New York. **1961** First solo-exhibition at the Galleria Schwarz, Milan. Participated in the exhibition "The Art of Assemblage" at the Museum of Modern Art, New York. **1968** Opened his Eat-Art-Restaurant in Düsseldorf and issued the magazine *Eat-Art-Edition*. **1972** Retrospective at the Centre National d'Art Contemporain, Paris. Participated **1976** at the Venice Biennale, **1977** in documenta 6 in Kassel and **1981** in the "Westkunst" exhibition in Cologne. **1983** Professorship at the Munich Academy. **1990** Solo-exhibition at the Musée d'Art Moderne de la Ville de Paris and the Museum Moderner Kunst, Vienna, and **1994** at the Musée de l'Assistance publique, Paris. Spoerri is one of the leading exponents of Nouveau Réalisme. As he put it himself, he "shapes life into a work of art", and thereby bridges the gap, often with a touch of irony, between art and trivial, day-to-day culture.
WRITINGS: D. S.: Topographie anecdotée du hasard. Paris 1962, 1990/Anekdoten zu einer Topographie des Zufalls. Neuwied and Berlin 1968.– D. S.: "Ja, Mama, das machen wir". Egnach 1962.– D. S.: L'optique moderne. Paris 1963.– D. S.: Gastronomisches Tagebuch. Neuwied and Berlin 1970.– D. S.: The Mythological Travels of a Modern Sir Mandeville. New York 1970
MONOGRAPHS, CATALOGUES: Bremer, C. et al. (ed.): D. S. Zürcher Kunstgesellschaft. Zurich 1972 (cat.).– Dufrêne F. and D. S. (ed.): D. S. Centre National d'Art Contemporain. Paris 1972 (cat.).– Hahn, O.: D. S. Paris 1990.– Huber-Greub, B. and S. Andreae (ed.): D. S. Musée sentimental de Bâle. Basel and Bern 1989 (cat.).– Kamber, A. (ed.): D. S. Kosta Theos: "Dogma I am god". Kunstmuseum Solothurn. Dieterswil, Brussels 1987 (cat.).– Kamber, A. et al. (ed.): Petit lexique sentimental autour de D. S. Centre Georges Pompidou, Paris et al. Paris and Solothurn 1990 (cat.).– Schmidt, P. (ed.): Salute. D. S. Freunde und Studenten, Munich 1983-1989. Künstlerwerkstatt Lothringerstraße. Munich 1990 (cat.).– D. S. Hommage à Isaac Feinstein. Stedelijk Museum. Amsterdam 1971 (cat.).– D. S. Städtisches Kunstmuseum Spendhaus. Reutlingen 1985 (cat.)

STAEL Nicolas de
1914 St. Petersburg – **1955** Antibes (Côte d'Azur)
Russian-born French painter. Became a page-boy at the royal court in St. Peters-

burg at the age of two. After the revolution in **1919** fled with his family to Poland, and from there to exile in Belgium. **1933-1936** Studied at the Académie des Beaux-Arts in Brussels. First worked as a stage designer. From **1938** lived in Paris, where he was a pupil of Léger. **1942** Painted his first abstract compositions that were hung **1944** beside the paintings of Kandinsky, Domela and Magnelli in the exhibition "Peintures Abstraites" at the Galerie L'Esquisse in Paris. From **1950** clearly recognisable, figurative forms appear in his paintings. **1955** Committed suicide. De Staël began by painting still lifes and portraits, but destroyed most of these early works. After a long period of experimenting with ideas related to Tachisme and L'art informel, he took to painting abstract Color Field compositions.
WRITINGS: N. de S.: Lettres à Pierre Lecuire. Paris 1966.– N. de S.: Lettres à Jacques Dubourg. London 1981
CATALOGUE RAISONNE: Chastel, A. et al. (ed.): N. de S. Catalogue raisonné de l'œuvre peint. Neuchâtel 1996
MONOGRAPHS, CATALOGUES: Cassou, J. (ed.): Musée National d'Art Moderne. Paris 1956 (cat.).– Cooper, D.: N. de S. London 1961.– Dobbels, D.: S. Paris 1994.– Dumur, G.: N. de S. Paris 1975, New York 1985.– Granville, P. and D. Sutton (ed.): N. de S. Grand Palais, Paris et al. Paris 1981 (cat.).– Jouffroy, J. P.: La Mesure de N. de S. Neuchâtel 1981.– Lévy, D. A. et al. (ed.): N. de S. Fondazione Magnani Rocca, Parma. Milan 1994 (cat.).– Mansar, A. S.: N. de S. Paris 1990.– Messer, T. M. (ed.): N. de S. Retrospektive. Schirn Kunsthalle, Frankfurt-on-Main. Stuttgart 1994 (cat.).– Monod-Fontaine, I. (ed.): N. de S. Centre Georges Pompidou. Paris 1981 (cat.).– Prat, J.-L. (ed.): N. de S. Rétrospective de l'œuvre peint. Fondation Maeght. Saint-Paul 1991 (cat.).– Prat, J.-L. (ed.): N. de S. Fondation Pierre Gianadda. Martigny 1995 (cat.).– Rathbone, E. E. (ed.): N. de S. in America. The Phillips Collection, Washington et al. Washington 1990 (cat.).– N. de S. Galleria Civica. Torino 1960 (cat.).– N. de S. Fondation Maeght. Saint-Paul 1972 (cat.).– Sutton, D. (ed.): N. de S. Whitechappel Art Gallery. London 1956 (cat.).– Tudal, A.: N. de S. Paris 1951

STAMOS Theodoros
1922 New York – **1997** New York
Greek-born American painter. **1936-1939** Studied sculpture at the American Artists School, New York. **1943** First solo-exhibition at the Wakefield Gallery, New York. **1948/49** Trips to France, Italy and Greece. **1948** Participated at the Venice Biennale. **1950** Taught at Black Mountain College in Beria (NC). **1955** Participated in the exhibition "Cinquante ans d'Art aux Etats Unis" at the Musée d'Art Moderne, Paris. **1959** Participated in documenta 2 in Kassel. **1970** Took part in the exhibition "Trends in 20s Century Art" at the Santa Barbara

Museum (CA) and **1978** in the exhibition "Abstract Expressionism: The Formative Years" at the Whitney Museum, New York. In contrast to most Abstract Expressionist works, Stamos' paintings often prompt associations in the viewer and have an atmospheric quality, reminiscent of landscapes.
MONOGRAPHS, CATALOGUES: Cavaliere, B. and T. F. Wolff (ed.): T. S. Werke 1945-1984. Galerie Knoedler. Zurich 1984 (cat.).– Pomeroy, R.: S. New York 1974.– Ronte, D. (ed.): S. Kouros Gallery. New York 1989 (cat.).– Sawyer, K. B.: S. Paris 1960.– Schneidler, H. (ed.): T. S. Malerei 1947-1987. Schloß Morsbroich. Leverkusen 1987 (cat.).– N. S. Corcoran Gallery of Art. Washington 1958 (cat.)

STAZEWSKI Henryk
1894 Warsaw – **1988** Warsaw
Polish painter. **1913-1919** Studied at the Academy of Fine Arts in Warsaw. **1924** A founder-member of the Constructivist, Suprematist and Cubist group Blok, and editor of their magazine. Friendships with M. Seuphor and Mondrian. After an early Cubist and Purist phase, he adopted the geometric abstract style of Mondrian. **1926** Collaborated with the avant-garde group Praesens. Interior decorations and book designs in a Neo-Plastic style. **1929** Member of the a. r.group. Joined Cercle et Carré in **1932** and Abstraction-Création in **1930**. From **1929-1933** experimental phase, in which he tried to combine the styles of Neo-Plasticism and Unism. After World War II, resumed geometric abstract painting. **1959-1964** Series of white metal reliefs: systematic variations on a square. **1974** Developed the idea of a series of white paintings with arrangements of black lines. **1980** Set up an artists' exchange programme between Poland and America.
MONOGRAPHS, CATALOGUES: Kowalska, B.: H. S. Warsaw 1985.– Piga, S. (ed.): H. S. 1894-1988. Rilievi e dipinti. Roma 1991 (cat.).– Stanislawski, R. and J. Ladnowska (ed.): H. S. Muzeum Sztuki. Lodz 1969 (cat.).– Stanislawski, R. (ed.): H. S. Pionero polaco del arte concreto. Centro Atlántico de Arte Moderno. Las Palmas de Gran Canaria 1990 (cat.)

STEICHEN Edward
1879 Luxemburg – **1973** West Wedding (CT)
American photographer, originally from Luxemburg. **1881** Moved to Hancock (MI). **1894-1898** Trained as a lithographer in Milwaukee. **1899** Participated in the second Philadelphia Photographic Salon. **1900** Came to know Stieglitz in New York. Visited the Paris World Fair. **1901** So impressed by Rodin that he offered to take portraits of him. **1902** First solo-exhibition of photographs and paintings at the Maison des Artistes, Paris. Joined the Photo Secession. Returned to New York. **1904** First prize at the international exhibition in La Haye. **1905** Opened Gallery 291 in New York with Stieglitz. **1906** Second stay in Paris. **1908** First colour photographs. **1913** Issues 42/43 of the journal *Camera Work* dedicated to him. **1917** Leading American war photographer in France. In the 20s and 30s was chief photographer for *Vogue and Vanity Fair*. **1936** Solo-exhibition at the Museum of Modern Art, New York. From **1947** director of photography at the Museum of Modern Art, New York. **1952-1955** Organised the exhibition "The Family of Man". **1961** Major retrospective at the Museum of Modern Art, New York.
WRITINGS: E. S.: A Life in Photography. New York 1963 / Ein Leben für die Fotografie. Düsseldorf 1965
MONOGRAPHS, CATALOGUES: Kelton, R.: E. S. New York 1978, Munich 1978.– Liberman, A. et al. (ed.): S. the Photographer. The Museum of Modern Art. New York 1961 (cat.).– Longwell, D. (ed.): S. The Master Prints. 1895-1914. The Symbolist Period. The Museum of Modern Art. New York 1978 (cat.)/S. Meisterphotographien 1895-1914. Die symbolistische Periode. New York and Tübingen 1978.– Mayer, G. (ed.): E. S. The Photographer. New York 1961 (cat.).– Phillips, C.: S. at War. New York 1981.– Sandburg, C.: S. the Photographer. New York 1929.– Shoenfeld, A. (ed.): The Paintings of E. S. The Heckscher Museum. Huntington 1985 (cat.)

STEINBACH Haim
born **1944** Rechovott (Israel)
American sculptor of Israeli origins. **1962** Took American citizenship. **1962-1968**

Studied at the Pratt Institute in Brooklyn and **1971-1973** at Yale University, New Haven (CT). **1969** First solo-exhibition at the Panoras Gallery, New York. **1988** Solo-exhibition at the Musée d'Art Contemporain, Bordeaux. Participated in the group exhibition "Schlaf der Vernunft" (The Deadening of Reason), Kassel. **1991** Took part in the exhibition "Metropolis" in Berlin. **1992** Participated in documenta 9 in Kassel. Steinbach places objects of various origins in surprising combinations on shelf-like stands. A form of wordless theatre with material objects as players, presented with biting irony.
MONOGRAPHS, CATALOGUES: Celant, G. et al. (ed.): H. S. Œuvres récentes. Musée d'Art Contemporain de Bordeaux. Bordeaux 1986 (cat.).– Dubost, P. et al. (ed.): H. S. Kärtner Landesgalerie. Klagenfurt 1994 (cat.).– Hegyi, L. et al. (ed.): H. S. Vienna et al. Vienna 1997 (cat.).– No Rocks Allowed: A Book for an Exhibition by H. S. Rotterdam 1992

STEINERT Otto
1915 Saarbrücken – **1978** Essen
German photographer. Self-taught. **1934-1939** Studied medicine, and worked until **1948** as a doctor. **1948-1951** Head of the department of photography at the Saarbrücken School of Arts and Crafts. **1949** Founded the group fotoform to which Keetman and Hajek-Halke belonged. **1951** Organised the first of three programmatic exhibitions of photography entitled Subjektive *Fotografie*, developing the principles set down in the Bauhaus publication *Neue Fotografie* and providing an important stimulus to photography in Germany. **1952-1959** Director of the School of Arts and Crafts in Saarbrücken. Specialised in artistic portraits and live-photography. **1959-1978** As director of the Folkwang School in Essen, set up a department of photography and organised numerous exhibitions. **1974** Awarded the National Service Cross. Steinert was one of the most influential teachers of photography in the postwar era.
WRITINGS: O. S.: Subjektive Fotografie. Bonn 1952, Munich 1955.– O. S.: Teaching Methods. Essen 1965.– O. S.: das Technische Bild- und Dokumentationsmittel Fotografie. Essen 1973
MONOGRAPHS, CATALOGUES: Eskildsen, U. and R. Knodt (ed.): Sammlung O. S. Folkwang Museum. Essen 1981.– Eskildsen, U. and T. Koenig (ed.): O. S. und Schüler. Fotografie und Ausbildung 1948-1978. Folkwang Museum. Essen 1990 (cat.).– Kempe, F. and H. Schardt: O. S. und seine Schüler. Essen 1965.– Kempe, F. (ed.): O. S., der Initiator einer fotografischen Bewegung. Folkwang Museum, Essen et al. Essen 1976 (cat.).– Koenig, T.: O. S.'s Konzept "Subjektive Fotografie" 1951-1953. Munich 1988.– Plunien, E. (ed.): O. S. und Schüler. Essen 1967 (cat.).– Schmoll gen. Eisenwerth, J. A. (ed.): O. S. Der Initiator einer fotografischen Bewegung. Museum Folkwang. Essen 1959

(cat.).– Tamms, F.: Gestaltung des Bildteils. O. S. Düsseldorf 1966

STELARC
born **1948** Victoria
Australian performance, multimedia and Internet artist. From **1968** first appearances as an artist. From **1970** *Amplified Body Events*, from **1976** *The Third Hand Project*, **1992** *Virtual Arm Project* and **1995** *Ping Body*. He uses robots and medical systems in his works to reinforce his effects. **1994** Presented *Bodies and Machines* in the exhibition "Mutations d'Image" in Paris and at the Charleroi Dance Biennale. In his performances he interacts with a third hand, a virtual arm, a virtual body and a magnetic sculpture.

STELLA Frank
born **1936** Malden
American painter. **1950**–**1954** Visited the-Attended Phillips Academy, Andover (MA). Came to know Carl Andre. **1954**–**1958** Studied art and art history under S. Greene and W. C. Seitz at Princeton University (NJ). Came to know Jasper Johns. **1959** While living in New York, he began his strictly geometric series of black pinstripe paintings. **1961** Trip to Europe. Around **1966** first works in copper and aluminium paints, and compositions in which a tension is set up between the compact inner pattern and the surrounding frame. In his *Shaped Canvases* he cut the painted form out of the canvas. **1968** and **1977** participation in documenta 4 and 6 in Kassel. Around **1975** he abandoned this stringently geometric approach and produced multi-coloured montages made up of curved shapes cut out of sheets of aluminium and painted in bright colours. **1983** Guest-professor at Harvard University. **1990** Produced his first three-dimensional works and, in **1992**, his first architectural designs, including plans for a museum of modern art in Dresden. Major retrospectives: **1987** at the Museum of Modern Art, New York, and **1996** at the Haus der Kunst, Munich. Stella set out to develop a style of Color Field Painting free of any trace of expressiveness. To avoid creating any artificial impressions or evoking emotional associations, he used the paints, brushes and tools

of an ordinary house-painter and usually confined his art to symmetrical patterns.
WRITINGS: F. S.: Working Space. The Charles Norton Eliot Lectures 1983-1984. Cambridge (MA) and London 1986
CATALOGUES RAISONNES: Axsom, R. H. (ed.): The Prints of F. S. A Catalogue Raisonné 1967-1982. New York 1983.– Rubin, L. and R. Rosenblum (ed.): F. S. Paintings 1958-1965. A Catalogue Raisonné. New York 1986
MONOGRAPHS, CATALOGUES: Boehm, G. et al. (ed.): F. S. Werke 1958-1976. Kunsthalle Bielefeld. Bielefeld 1977 (cat.).– Geelhaar, C. (ed.): F. S. Zeichnungen 1956-1970. Kunstmuseum Basel. Basel 1980 (cat.).– Goldman, J. et al. (ed.): F. S. Museo Nacional Centro de Arte Reina Sofía. Madrid 1995 (cat.).– Goldman, J. et al. (ed.): F. S. Haus der Kunst, Munich et al. Munich 1996 (cat.).– Guberman, S.: F. S. An Illustrated Biography. New York 1995.– Imdahl, M.: F. S. Sanbornville II. Stuttgart 1970.– Inboden, G. (ed.): F. S. Black Paintings 1958-1960. Staatsgalerie Stuttgart. Stuttgart 1988 (cat.).– Leider, P. (ed.): F. S. Since 1970. Fort Worth Art Museum. Fort Worth 1978 (cat.).– Meier, R.: Shards by F. S. London and New York 1983.– Pacquement, A.: F. S. La création contemporaine. Paris 1988.– Reinhardt, B. (ed.): F. S. Moby Dick Series. Stuttgart 1993.– Rosenblum, R.: F. S. Harmondsworth and Baltimore 1971.– Rubin, W. S. (ed.): F. S. The Museum of Modern Art. New York 1970 (cat.).– Rubin, W. (ed.): F. S. 1970-1987. The Museum of Modern Art, New York et al. New York 1987 (cat.)/F. S. 1970-1987. Centre Georges Pompidou. Paris 1987 (cat.).– F. S. Working Space. Cambridge 1986

STELLA Joseph
1877 Muro Lucano – **1946** New York
Italian-born American painter. **1896** Emigrated with his brother to the USA and settled in New York, where he studied medicine for one year. **1898**–**1901** Studied at the New York School of Arts under William M. Chase. **1907/08** Worked for the magazine *Survey*. First industrial townscapes. **1909/10** Returned to Italy and made contact with the Futurists. **1911/12** Went to Paris where he met Modigliani and Matisse. **1912** Saw the Futurist exhibition and exhibited his own works at the Salon des Indépendants in Paris. **1913** Returned to New York and took part in the Armory Show. **1915** Met Duchamp and Picabia. **1920** First solo-exhibition at the Montross Gallery in New York. Joined the Société Anonyme and participated in their exhibition. **1923** Painted his most famous work entitled *New York Interpreted*. **1930**–**1934** Second stay in Paris. **1940** Trip to India. **1939** Retrospective at the Newark Museum (NJ). **1963** Retrospective at the Whitney Museum of American Art, New York. Many of Stella's paintings show the industrial and urban face of America.
MONOGRAPHS, CATALOGUES: Baur, J.

I. H.: J. S. New York et al. 1971, 1991.– Gerdts, W. H. (ed.): Drawings of J. S. Newark (NJ) 1962.– Haskell, B. (ed.): J. S. Whitney Museum of American Art. New York 1994 (cat.).– Jaffe, I. B.: J. S. Cambridge (MA) 1970.– Jaffe, I. B.: J. S.'s Symbolism. San Francisco 1994.– Moser, J. (ed.): Visual Poetry. The Drawings of J. S. National Museum of American Art, Washington et al. Washington 1990 (cat.).– J. S. Whitney Museum of American Art. New York 1963 (cat.).– Zilczer, J. (ed.): J. S. Hirshhorn Museum and Sculpture Garden Collection. Washington 1983 (cat.)

STEPANOVA Varvara
1884 Kowno (Lithuania) – **1958** Moscow
Russian artist. **1910**–**1913** Attended art school in Kasan. Met Rodchenko, her later professional partner and husband. Took private lessons from I. Maschkov. **1913/14** Studied at the Stroganov School of Art in Moscow. **1914**–**1917** Worked for the leftist Federation of Artists and in the department of fine arts of NARKOMPROS in Moscow. **1918** Co-founder of the Constructivist movement. **1921**–**1925** Taught at the College of Social Education in Moscow, and from **1924/25** also in the textile department of WChUTEMAS. **1922** Stage design for the comedy *The Death of Tarelkin* by A. Suchowo-Kobylin. Did fabric designs, designed magazine and book covers and, together with her husband, produced picture books.
WRITINGS: Lavrentiev, A. (ed.): S. Moscow 1994
CATALOGUES RAISONNES: Lavrentiev, A. N. (ed.): V. S. The Complete Work. Cambridge 1988 / W. S. Ein Leben für den Konstruktivismus. Weingarten 1988
MONOGRAPHS, CATALOGUES: Holsten, S. et al. (ed.): Alexander Rodtschenko und W. S. Wilhelm-Lehmbruck-Museum. Duisburg 1982 (cat.).– Noever, P. (ed.): Alexander M. Rodtschenko und W. S. Die Zukunft ist unser einziges Ziel. Munich 1991.– Quilici, V. (ed.): Rodcenko e S. Alle origini del costruttivismo. Palazzo dei Priori e Palazzo Cesaroni, Perugia. Milan 1984 (cat.)

STIEGLITZ Alfred
1864 Hoboken (NJ) – **1946** New York
German-born American photographer and gallery owner. **1871** Moved to New York. **1881** Moved to Berlin. **1882**–**1890** Studied mechanical enginering and photochemistry at the College of Technology in Berlin. **1883** Took up photography. **1890** Returned to New York. **1890** Published the magazine *American Amateur Photographer*. **1896** First night exposures. **1897**–**1902** Founded and published the journal *Camera Notes*. **1899** First solo-exhibition at the Camera Club, New York. **1902** Together with Coburn and Steichen founded the Photo-Secession. **1903** Founded and published the magazine *Camera Work*. **1904** Met the photographer Kühn. **1907** Trip to Germany.

1905 Ran Gallery 291, where in **1908** he exhibited drawings by Rodin. **1916** Published the Dada-oriented magazine *291*, to which Picabia, Duchamp and Man Ray contributed. **1917** Stopped working for *Camera Work* and *291*. **1924** Married Georgia O'Keeffe. **1925** Organised the exhibition "Seven Americans", and opened The Intimate Gallery and in **1929** its successor An American Place. After **1937** gave up photography owing to severe illness. **1942** Solo-exhibition at the Museum of Modern Art, New York, and **1944** at the Philadelphia Museum of Art. As a representative of Art Photography Stieglitz was one of the most important champions of photography as an art form and of the avant-garde in America in the early 20th century.
WRITINGS: Seligmann, H. J.: A. S. Talking. Notes from Some Conversations 1925-1931. New Haven (CT) 1966.– A. S.: Photo-Secessions and ist Opponent. Five Letters. New York 1910
MONOGRAPHS, CATALOGUES: America and A. S. A Collective Portrait. Millerton 1979.– Arrowsmith, A. and B. Rathbone (ed.): Georgia O'Keeffe and A. S. Two Lives. The Phillips Collection, Washington et al. London 1992 (cat.).– Bunnell, P. C.: A. S. Photographs from the Collection of Georgia O'Keeffe. Santa Fe 1993.– Bry, D.: A. S. Photographer. Essay. New York 1965, 1996.– Doty, R.: Photo-Secession. S. and the Fine-Art Movement in Photography. New York 1978.– Dufek, A.: A. S. Prague 1990.– Gee, H. (ed.): S. and the Photo-Secession. Pictorialism to Modernisme 1902-1917. New Jersey State Museum. Trenton 1978 (cat.).– Greenough, S. and J. Hamilton (ed.): A. S. Photographs and Writings. Metropolitan Museum of Art, New York et al. New York 1983 (cat.).– Greenough, S.: A. S.'s Photographs of Clouds. Diss. Albuquerque 1984.– Frank, W. et al. (ed.): America and A. S. A Collective Portrait. New York 1934.– Haines, R. E.: The Inner Eye of A. S. Washington 1982.– Homer, W. I.: A. S. and the American Avant-garde. Boston 1977.– Homer, W. I.: A. S. and the Photo-Secession. Boston 1983.– Kiefer, G. W. A. S. New York 1991.– Lowe, S. D.: S. A Memoir/Biography. New York 1983.– Lynes, B. B.: O'Keeffe, S. and the Critics 1916-1929. Ann Arbor (MI) 1989.– Norman, D. (ed.): A. S. Introduction to an American Seer. New York 1960, 1973.– Peterson, C. (ed.): A. S.'s Camera Notes. New York 1996.– Porter, A. (ed.): Camera Work: A. S. Zurich 1985.– Seligman, H. J.: A. S. Talking. Notes on Some of His Conversations. 1925.-1931. New Haven (CT) 1966.– Szarkowski, J.: A. S. at Lake George. New York 1995.– Weber, E.: A. S. New York 1994.– Whelan, R.: A. S. A Biography. Boston 1995

STILL Clyfford
1904 Grandin (ND) – **1980** New York
American painter. Studied **1926/27** and **1931**–**1933** at Spokane University in Washington, where he later became an art

teacher himself. His pupils at colleges and universities in California, Virginia and New York included Tobey and Rothko and many other Abstract Expressionist painters. **1943** First solo-exhibition at the San Francisco Museum of Art. In the 30s, inspired by the works of Cézanne and van Gogh, he painted abstract figures and landscapes, while his works of the 40s are more Surrealist in character, being based on mythological themes and the workings of the subconscious. Around **1947** he developed his last painting style: large canvases, usually covered in a thick, monochrome-black layer of paint and framed by bright contrasting colours. **1959** Participated in documenta 2 in Kassel and in the exhibition at the Albright-Knox Art Gallery in Buffalo (NY). **1979** Retrospective at the Metropolitan Museum of Modern Art, New York, and **1992** at the Kunsthalle Basel. Out of the principles of Abstract Expressionism Still created works of a calm, meditative character.
MONOGRAPHS, CATALOGUES: Anfam, D.: C. S. Diss. London 1984.– Jonas-Edel, J.: C. S.'s Bild vom Selbst und vom Absoluten. Studien zur Intention und Entwicklung seiner Malerei. Cologne 1995.– Kellein, T. (ed.): C. S. Albright-Knox Art Gallery, Buffalo et al. Munich 1992 (cat.)/C. S. Kunsthalle Basel. Munich 1992 (cat.).– Kellein, T. (ed.): C. S. New York 1995.– O'Neill, J. P. O. and K. Kuh (ed.): C. S. Metropolitan Museum of Art. New York 1979 (cat.).– C. S. Thirty-Three Paintings in the Albright-Knox Art Gallery. Buffalo 1966 (cat.).– C. S. Marlborough-Gerson Gallery Inc. New York 1969 (cat.).– C. S. San Francisco Museum of Contemporary Art. San Francico 1976 (cat.)

STÖHRER Walter
1937 Stuttgart – **2000** Berlin
German painter. **1957–1959** Studied at the Karlsruhe Academy under HAP Grieshaber. **1959** Moved to Berlin. Participated at the Young Artists Biennale in Paris. **1961** First solo-exhibition at the Kellergalerie in Schloß Darmstadt. **1964** Critics Award from the City of Berlin. **1965** Solo-exhibition at the Galerie St. Stefan, Vienna. **1973** Studied at the Cité des Arts, Paris. **1977** Villa Romana Award, Florence. **1979** Solo-exhibition at the DAAD gallery in Berlin,

and **1980** at the Württembergische Kunstverein, Stuttgart. **1981/82** Guest-professor at the Berlin School of Arts. **1984** Retrospective at the Kunsthalle in Düsseldorf and at the Saarland Museum, Saarbrücken. From **1986** professor at the Berlin School of Arts. **1989** Solo-exhibition at the Berlinische Galerie. Stöhrer's paintings, executed with an impulsive, passionate brush stroke, are reminiscent of Écriture automatique (automatic writing) and the spontaneity of L'art informel.
CATALOGUE RAISONNE: Bose, G. (ed.): W. S. Werkverzeichnis der Druckgraphik. Radierungen 1960-1966. Berlin 1994
MONOGRAPHS, CATALOGUES: Bose, G. (ed.): W. S. Bilder 1961-1988. Museum für moderne Kunst, Photographie und Architektur. Berlin 1989 (cat.).– Jensen, J. C. (ed.): W. S. Neue Bilder. Kunsthalle Kiel. Kiel 1990 (cat.).– Jensen, J. C. et al. (ed.): W. S. Kunstverein Hannover. Hannover 1998 (cat.).– Meyer zu Eissen, A. (ed.): W. S. Arbeiten 1962-1983. Kunsthalle Bremen et al. Bremen 1983 (cat.).– Motte, M. d. la (ed.): W. S. Weissglut. Galerie Nothelfer. Berlin 1993 (cat.).– Reising, G. (ed.): W. S. Werke auf Papier 1959-1995. Staatliche Kunsthalle. Karlsruhe 1995 (cat.).– Schaart, J. (ed.): W. S. Bilder 1961-1988. Berlinische Galerie. Berlin 1989 (cat.).– Schmidt, J.-K. (ed.): W. S. Stuttgart 1995 (cat.).– W. S. Arbeiten 1962-1983. Kunstmuseum. Düsseldorf 1984 (cat.).– W. S. Frühe Druckgrafik. Kunsthalle Bremen. Bremen 1994 (cat.).– W. S. Neue Arbeiten. Kunstverein Augsburg et al. Augsburg 1994 (cat.).

STRAND Paul
1890 New York – **1976** Paris
American photographer. **1904–1909** Studied at the Ethical Culture School in New York under Hine. **1909** Joined the Camera Club in New York. **1911** Trip to Europe. **1912** Set up his own studio, specialising first of all in portraits, street scenes and architecture. **1915** Documentary series on the Southern States of America. **1916** Photoseries on depressed areas of New York. Experiments with abstract compositions. First solo-exhibition at the 291 gallery and first photographs published in *Camera Work*. **1919–1921** Collaborated with Sheeler on the film *Manahatta*. **1922** Made further expeimental films and wrote articles on photography. Taught at C. H. White's School of Photography. **1935** Travelled to Russia where he met Sergei M. Eisenstein. **1943/44** Photomontages on the election campaign of F. D. Roosevelt. **1945** Retrospective at the Museum of Modern Art, New York. **1950** Moved to Paris. Photoseries in various countries, including a series of portraits of contemporary artists in France. **1971** Retrospective at the Philadelphia Museum of Art. Strand, whose abstract photography is an attempt to reveal the underlying structure of the viewed object, can be considered the first modern photographer in America.
MONOGRAPHS, CATALOGUES: Butor, M. et al. (ed.): P. S. Centre Georges Pompidou. Paris 1977 (cat.).– Duncan, C.: P. S. The World on My Doorstep, the Years 1850 to 1976. New York 1994/P. S. Die Welt vor meiner Tür. Museum Folkwang, Essen. New York and Frankfurt-on-Main 1994 (cat.)/P. S. Le Monde à ma porte. Paris 1994.– Greenough, S. (ed.): P. S. An American Vision. National Gallery of Art, Washington et al. New York 1990 (cat.).– Hoffman, H. and M. E. Hofman: P. S. A Retrospective Monograph. 2 vols. New York 1972.– Lloyd, V. (ed.): P. S. A Retrospective Exhibition of His Photographs 1915-1968. National Portrait Gallery.

London 1976 (cat.).– Newhall, N. (ed.): P. S. Photographs 1915-1945. The Museum of Modern Art. New York 1945 (cat.).– Peters, G. P.: P. S. An Extraordinary Vision. Santa Fe 1994.– Rosenblum, N.: P. S. The Early Years. Diss. New York. Ann Arbor (MI) 1983.– Stange, M. et al. (ed.): P. S. Essays on His Life and Work. New York 1990

STRELOW Liselotte
1908 Redel (near Polzin) – **1981** Hamburg
German photographer. **1924–1929** Agricultural work. From **1930** studied photography at the Lette School in Berlin, and then entered the studio of S. Byk. **1938** Employed as a photographer by Kodak in Berlin. **1945** Opened a new photographic studio in Detmold. **1950** Moved to Düsseldorf, where she made her name taking portraits of artists, actors and stage celebrities. **1957** Received a prize for photography at the Venice Biennale. **1961** Publication of her book on portrait photography entitled Das manipulierte Menschenbild (Manipulation of the Human Image). **1977** Retrospective at the Rheinisches Landesmuseum, Bonn, and participation in documenta 6 in Kassel.
WRITINGS: L. S.: Das manipulierte Menschenbildnis. Düsseldorf and Vienna 1961.– L. S.: Photogenic Portrait Management. London 1966
MONOGRAPHS, CATALOGUES: Honnef, K. et al. (ed.): L. S. Porträts 1933-1972. Rheinisches Landesmuseum, Bonn. Cologne 1977 (cat.)

STRUTH Thomas
born **1954** Geldern (Lower Rhineland)
German photographer. **1973–1980** Studied painting under Gerhard Richter and photography under Becher at the Düsseldorf Academy. From **1976** large-scale documentary series in black-and-white of architecture and municipal buildings in their cultural and social context, a favourite theme being empty streets, deserted inner-city areas and derelict factories. **1978** Scholarship from the Düsseldorf Academy to New York, where his first solo-exhibition was held. **1980–1982** Community service in a citizens' advice bureau. **1982** Took up professional photography, with a special focus on urban life and city centres in metropo-

lises as varied as Naples, Tokyo, Chicago and Berlin. International exhibitions in Munich, Cologne, Brussels, Amsterdam, Paris, Washington and New York. **1993** Professor at Karlsruhe School of Design.
MONOGRAPHS, CATALOGUES: Belting, H. (ed.): T. S. Museum Photographs. Hamburger Kunsthalle. Munich 1993 (cat.).– Buchloh, B. H. D. (ed.): T. S. Photographs. Chicago 1990 (cat.).– Buchholz, B. et al. (ed.): T. S. Portraits. Hanover 1997 (cat.).– Lingwood, J. and M. Teitelbaum (ed.): T. S. Strangers and Friends. Photographs 1986-1992. Institute of Contemporary Arts, London. Cambridge 1994.– T. S. Unbewußte Orte. Kunsthalle Bern et al. Cologne 1987 (cat.).– T. S. Portraits. Krefelder Kunstmuseum, Museum Haus Lange. Krefeld 1992 (cat.).– T. S. Stranger and Friends. Photographs 1986-1992. Institute of Contemporary Arts, Boston et al. Munich 1994.– T. S. Straßen. Fotografie 1976-1995. Städtisches Kunstmuseum Bonn. Cologne 1995 (cat.)

STRZEMINSKI Vladislav
1893 Minsk – **1952** Lodz
Polish painter and theoretician. **1918/19** Studied at WChUTEMAS in Moscow. **1922** Moved to Poland. Joined the artists' groups Blok a. r. and Praesens. **1924–1927** Together with his wife Kobro, developed the theory of Unism, with the aim of achieving an absolute pictorial balance, i.e. perfect homogeneity of all the constituent parts of a composition. **1930–1933** Unistic compositions devoid of all forms of colour contrast. **1945–1950** Taught at the School of Applied Arts in Lodz. **1958** Posthumous publication of his treatise Learning by Seeing. Strzemiński's ideas are a logical extension of Malevich's theories of Suprematism. Unism was chiefly manifested in white paintings , divided up into minute fields that produce a vibrating effect.
WRITINGS: W. S.: Unizm w malarstwie. Warsaw 1928.– W. S.: Teoria widzenia. Kraków 1974.– W. S.: Pisma. Warsaw 1975.– W. S. and K. Kobro: L'Espace uniste. Ecrits du constructivisme polonais. Lausanne 1977
MONOGRAPHS, CATALOGUES: Adolphs, V. et al. (ed.): W. S. 1893-1952. Städtisches Kunstmuseum Bonn. Cologne 1994 (cat.).– Baranowicz, Z.: W. S. Warsaw 1984.– Turowski, A. (ed.): W. S. Städtische Kunsthalle Düsseldorf. Düsseldorf 1980 (cat.).– Zagrodzkiego, J. (ed.): W. S. In Memoriam. Lodz 1988

SUGAI Koumi
1919 Kobe – **1996** Paris
Japanese painter and graphic artist. **1933–1937** Studied at the Art Academy in Osaka. Worked from **1937** as a poster designer. **1947** Took painting lessions from T. Nakamura. **1948/49** Became especially interested first in Surrealism and then in the works of Pollock and Calder. **1952** Moved to Paris. **1953** First solo-exhibition at the Craven

gallery in Paris. **1956** Participated in the Salon des Réalités Nouvelles and **1957** in the Salon de Mai in Paris. **1959** Prize for graphic art at the Ljubljana Biennale. Participated in documenta 2 in Kassel. **1960** Retrospective at the Art Museum in Leverkusen. **1961** Prize for painting at the Tokyo Biennale, **1962** David Bright Prize at the Venice Biennale and **1965** prize for painting at the São Paulo Biennale. **1963** Solo-exhibition at the Kestner Society, Hanover. **1964** Participated in documenta 3 in Kassel. **1969** Retrospective at the National Museum of Modern Art, Kyoto. **1981** Solo-exhibition at the Satani Gallery, Tokyo. Sugaï's lyrical form of Abstract Expressionism is closely related to the painting style of the Ecole de Paris, but is also threaded through with traces of traditional Japanese calligraphy.
MONOGRAPHS, CATALOGUES: Chalumeau, J.-L.: K. S. Paris 1995.– Lambert, J.-C.: S. Paris 1990, Geneva 1992.– K. S. Städtisches Museum, Schloß Morsbroich. Leverkusen 1960 (cat.).– K. S. Retrospektive 1952-1963. Kestner-Gesellschaft. Hanover 1963 (cat.).– Mandiargues, A. P. d. et al. (ed.): K. S. Seibu Museum of Art. Tokyo 1983 (cat.)

SURVAGE Léopold
(Leopoldij Sturzwasgh)
1879 Willmanstrand – **1968** Paris
French painter of Finnish and Danish origins. **1901** Studied at the Moscow Art Academy. **1908** Went to Paris to study under Matisse. Came to know Cézanne, under whose influence he adopted a Cubist approach to painting. **1911** Contact with Archipenko. Participated in the Salon d'Automne, and **1912** in the Salon des Indépendants. **1917** First solo-exhibition in Paris at Galerie Bongard. **1919** Founder-member of Section d'Or. **1920** Solo-exhibition at the gallery of Léonce Rosenberg. **1922** Stage design for Diaghilev's production of the I. Stravinsky ballet *Mavra* in Paris. **1927** Took French citizenship. From **1933** numerous stage designs, wall decorations and tapestries. **1937** Monumental murals for the Paris World Fair. **1960** Guggenheim Award. **1965** Illustrations for books by J. Cocteau and H. de Balzac. **1966** Retrospective at the Musée Galliéra, Paris and **1993** at the Musée d'Art Moderne, Troyes. Survage's

large, decorative paintings display elements of Cubism but have a poetic style of their own.
WRITINGS: Seyres, H. (ed.): L. S. Ecrits sur la peinture. Paris 1992
CATALOGUE RAISONNE: Brosset, E. (ed.): L. S. Catalogue raisonné (in preparation)
MONOGRAPHS, CATALOGUES: Abadie, D. (ed.): S. Les Années héroïques. Musée d'Art Moderne, Troyes et al. Arcueil 1993 (cat.).– Fournet, C. (ed.): S. Rythmes colorés. Musée d'Art et d'Industrie. Saint-Etienne 1973 (cat.).– Gauthier, M.: S. Paris 1953.– Putnam, S.: The Glistening Bridge. L. S. and the Spatial Problem in Painting. New York 1929.– L. S. Musée des Beaux-Arts. Lyon 1968 (cat.).– L. S. Musée d'Art Moderne et d'Art Contemporain. Nice 1975 (cat.).– Warnod, J.: L. S. Brussels 1983

SUTHERLAND Graham
1903 London – **1980** London
English painter. **1921**–**1926** Studied graphic art at Goldsmith's College, London, and then worked as a book illustrator and poster designer. From **1926** taught at Chelsea School of Art in London. Towards the mid-30s he took up oil painting and, influenced by Surrealism, painted semi-abstract landscapes with a weird, haunting quality. **1941**–**1945** Worked as an official war painter, depicting bomb damage in London and towns in southern England. **1944** Commission for a *Crucifixion* for St. Matthew's church in Northampton, completed after the war, when he embarked on a series of religious paintings. **1947** Visited the Côte d'Azur, where he painted more landscapes. **1952** Represented England at the Venice Biennale. **1955**–**1964** Participation in documenta 1 – 3 in Kassel. In the late 50s he painted portraits of famous politicians including W. Churchill and K. Adenauer. In his fantastic, sombre landscape paintings Sutherland was aiming to portray the brutality of nature and the dark forces underlying all beauty. With Bacon, he is one of the main representatives of surrealist-visionary painting in England.
CATALOGUES RAISONNES: Man, F. H. (ed.): G. S. Das graphische Werk 1922-1970. Munich 1970 / G. S. The Graphic Work. 1922-1970. San Francisco 1970.– Tassi, R. (ed.): G. S. Complete Graphic Work. London and New York 1978 / G. S. Tout l'œuvre gravé (1922-1978). Paris 1980
MONOGRAPHS, CATALOGUES: Alley, R. (ed.): G. S. Tate Gallery, London et al. London 1982 (cat.).– Arcangeli, F.: G. S. New York 1975.– Berthoud, R.: G. S. A Biography. London 1982.– Bruno, G. (ed.): G. S. Storia segreta 1922-1979. Museo dell'Accademia Ligustica di Belle Arti. Genoa 1991 (cat.).– Chiappini, R. (ed.): S. Pinacoteca comunale, Casa Rusca, Locarno. Milan 1988 (cat.).– Cooke, G.: G. S. Early Etchings. Brookfield 1993.– Cooper, D.: The Work of G. S. London and New York 1961, Oxford 1980.– Cooper, D. (ed.): G. S. Haus der Kunst, Munich et al. Munich

1967 (cat.).– Hayes, J. (ed.): Portraits by G. S. National Portrait Gallery. London 1977 (cat.).– Hayes, J.: The Art of G. S. Oxford and New York 1980.– Krimmel, B. (ed.): G. S. Mathildenhöhe. Darmstadt 1982 (cat.).– Melville, R. (ed.): G. S. London 1950.– Nicholls, P. et al. (ed.): Bestiari di G. S. Milan 1985 (cat.).– Sanesi, R. (ed.): G. S. Palazzo dell Albere. Trento 1981 (cat.).– G. S. Galleria Civica d'Arte Moderna. Torino 1965 (cat.).– Tassi, R. (ed.): S. Disegni di guerra. Milan 1979 (cat.).– Thuillier, R.: G. S. Inspirations. Guildford, Surrey 1982

TAAFFE Philip
born **1955** Elisabeth (NJ)
American painter. **1977** Finished his studies at the Cooper Union, New York. In the early 80s he incorporated elements of Op Art from the works of artists like Riley in his novel pictorial constructions. Besides Op Art techniques, he was particularly interested in the works of Newman. **1988**–**1992** Lived in Naples, studying ornamental designs from various cultures. In the late 80s he experimented with colour printing techniques and produced increasingly abstract acrylic paintings with sections of collage. **1982** Regular exhibitions in galleries throughout Europe and America, including "German and American Art of the Late 80s", Düsseldorf and Boston (1988), "Post Abstract Abstraction", Aldrich (1987), "Doubletake", Vienna and London (1992), "ARS 95", Helsinki (1995). **1987**, **1991** and **1995** invitations to the Whitney Biennale in New York.
MONOGRAPHS, CATALOGUES: Adams, B. (ed.): P. T. Wiener Secession. Vienna 1996 (cat.).– P. T. Mary Boone Gallery. New York 1981 (cat.).– P. T. Gagosian Gallery. New York 1991 (cat.).– P. T. Center for the Fine Arts. Miami 1993 (cat.).– P. T. Thomas Ammann Fine Art. Zurich 1998 (cat.)

TAEUBER-ARP Sophie
1889 Davos – **1943** Zurich
Swiss painter and sculptress. **1908**–**1910** Attended the St. Gallen School of Arts and Crafts. **1911**–**1913** Studied at the Debschitz College of Education and Research in Munich. **1915** Met Arp. **1916**–**1928** Taught at the School of Arts and Crafts in Zurich.

1916–**1920** Took part in Dada events in Zurich, primarily as a dancer. **1921** Married Arp. **1926**–**1928** Interior decoration of the Aubette restaurant in Strasbourg with Arp and Doesburg. **1928** Moved to Meudon, near Paris. **1930** Joined Cercle et Carré and then Abstraction-Création. **1936** Participated in the exhibition "Fantastic Art, Dada and Surrealism" at the Museum of Modern Art, New York. **1937** Founded the magazine *Plastique* and joined the Swiss Alliance group. **1941**–**1943** Lived in Grasse, near Nice, along with Arp, Magnelli and Sonia Delaunay. **1943** Returned to Zurich; close contact with Bill. Taeuber-Arp's abstract art combines geometric elements in rhythmic formation with the expressive force of pure colour. She had a considerable influence on Arp.
CATALOGUE RAISONNE: Schmidt, G. and H. Weber (ed.): S. T.-A. Basel 1948
MONOGRAPHS, CATALOGUES: Fauve, J. L. et al. (ed.): S. T.-A. Musée d'Art Moderne. Strasbourg 1977 (cat.).– Gohr, S. (ed.): S. T.-A. 1889-1943. Bahnhof Rolandseck. Stuttgart 1993 (cat.).– Lanchner, C. (ed.): S. T.-A. The Museum of Modern Art. New York 1981 (cat.).– Pagé, S. et al. (ed.): S. T.-A. Musée d'Art Moderne de la Ville de Paris et al. Paris 1989 (cat.).– Seuphor, M.: Mission spirituelle de l'art. A propos de l'œuvre de S. T.-A. Paris and Liège 1953.– Staber, M.: S. T.-A. Lausanne 1970.– S. T.-A. Musée National d'Art Moderne. Paris 1964 (cat.).– S. T.-A. Kunstmuseum Winterthur. Winterthur 1977 (cat.).– S. T.-A. zum 100. Geburtstag. Aarauer Kunsthaus et al. Aarau 1989 (cat.).– S. T.-A. Kunsthalle Bern et al. Stuttgart 1993 (cat.).– Wasmuth, J. (ed.): Hans Arp und S. T.-A. Ein Künstlerpaar der Moderne. Stuttgart 1996 (cat.)

TAKIS
(Takis Vassilakis)
born **1925** Athens
Greek-born French sculptor. Self-taught. **1946** First sculptural works. **1953/54** Lived in London. **1954** Moved to Paris. **1955** First solo-exhibition at the Furstenberg gallery, Paris. **1958/59** Began to work with magnetic fields. **1960** Solo-exhibition at the Iolas Gallery, New York. **1966/67** Lived in London. **1968** Took part in documenta 4 in Kassel. **1969** Took part in the exhibition "The Machine as Seen at the End of the Mechanical Age" at the Museum of Modern Art, New York. **1972** Solo-exhibition at the Centre National d'Art Contemporain, Paris, and **1974** at the Hanover Kunstverein. **1977** Took part in documenta 6 in Kassel. **1981**, **1984** and **1985** projects at the Pompidou Centre, Paris. **1988** Grand Prix de sculpture in Paris. **1993** Retrospective at the Galerie Nationale du Jeu de Paume, Paris. Takis's kinetic sculptures, combining mechanical movement with the optical illusions of Op Art, reached their peak with his *Firework sculptures*.
WRITINGS: V. T.: Estafilades. Paris 1961.– V. T.: Musique Magnétique. Paris 1975
MONOGRAPHS, CATALOGUES: Calas,

H. and N.: T. Monographies. Paris 1984.–
Lebel, J. J. et al. (ed.): T. Centre National
d'Art Contemporain. Paris 1972 (cat.).– Pac-
quement, A. (ed.): T. Galerie Nationale du
Jeu de Paume, Paris et al. Paris 1993 (cat.).–
T. Les Magnétrons de T. Galerie Alexandre
Iolas. Paris 1966 (cat.).– T. Städtisches
Museum. Leverkusen 1970 (cat.).– T. Trois
totems. Espace musical. Centre Georges
Pompidou. Paris 1981 (cat.).– Vieville, D.:
T. Paris 1993

TAL-COAT Pierre
(Pierre Jacob)
1905 Clohars-Carnoët – **1985** Saint-Pierre
de Bailleul
French painter. Self-taught. Lived in Paris
1924–1926. **1925** Did designs for the
Henriot porcelain factory in Quimper.
1927 First solo-exhibition at the A. G.
Fabre gallery, Paris. **1930** Studied at the
Scandinavian Academy. **1931** Moved to
Paris. **1935/36** Exhibited with the group
Forces Nouvelles as well as Nouvelle
Génération in Paris. **1936–1939** Worked on
the series *Massacre*: paintings inspired by
the Spanish Civil War. **1940–1944** Lived in
Aix-en-Provence. **1947** Masson introduced
him to Chinese landscape painting. **1954**
Solo-exhibition at the Galerie Maeght. **1955**
and **1959** took part in documenta 1 and 2 in
Kassel. **1968** Grand Prix National des arts.
1976 Solo-exhibition at the Grand Palais,
Paris. **1980** Took part in the exhibition
"Forces nouvelles" at the Musée d'Art
Moderne de la Ville de Paris. The central
theme of Tal-Coat's art is the countryside,
however, he transforms his landscapes into
abstract, lyrical colour visions.
WRITINGS: P. T.-C.: Libre regard. Paris
1991
MONOGRAPHS, CATALOGUES: Blot-
tière, S. (ed.): T.-C. Rétrospective des
dessins et œuvres sur papier. Musée des
Beaux-Arts. Rennes 1988 (cat.).– Greff, J.-P.
(ed.): T.-C. Musée Matisse. Le Cateau-
Cambrésis 1991 (cat.).– Leymarie, J.: T.-C.
Geneva 1992.– Maldiney, H. and R. J.
Moulin (ed.): T. C. Grand Palais. Paris 1976
(cat.).– Mason, R. M. (ed.): T-C. Gravures
1970-1986. Musée d'Art et d'Histoire.
Geneva 1985 (cat.).– Schneider, J.-C. et al.:
T. C. Lavis et aquarelles. Paris 1991

TAMAYO Rufino
1899 Oaxaca – **1991** Mexico City
Mexican painter. **1917/18** Studied at the
Academy in Mexico City. **1921** Director of
the Department of Ethnological Drawing
at the Museum of Anthropology. **1926–
1928** Lived in New York. **1929/30** Taught at
the Art Academy in Mexico City and **1938**
at the Dalton School, New York. **1943**
Worked on frescoes for Smith College,
Northampton. **1948** Retrospective at the
Instituto Nacional de Bellas Artes, Mexico
City. Took part in the Venice Biennale. **1951** Retrospective at the Palais des
Beaux-Arts in Brussels. **1953** First Prize at
the São Paulo Biennale. **1958** Frescoes for

the UNESCO building in Paris. **1979** Solo-
exhibition at the Guggenheim Museum,
New York. **1981** Opening of the Tamayo
Museums in Mexico City. **1987** Retrospec-
tive at the art museum and at the Tamayo
Museum in Mexico City and **1990** at the
Berlin Kunsthalle. Tamayo was not one of
the great revolutionaries of Mexican mural
painting, but found his inspiration in pre-
Columbian folk art, which he combined
with elements of Cubism and Surrealism.
WRITINGS: R. T.: Antología critica.
Mexico City 1987.– Tibol, R. (ed.): Textos
de R. T. Mexico City 1987
MONOGRAPHS, CATALOGUES:
Cardoza y Aragón, L. et al. (ed.): R. T. Pinturas. Museo Nacional Centro de Arte
Reina Sofía. Madrid 1988 (cat.).– Conde, T.
del et al. (ed.): R. T. 70 años de creación.
Museo de Arte Contemporáneo Interna-
cional Rufino Tamayo. Mexico City 1987
(cat.).– Corredor-Matheos, J.: T. Barcelona
1982, 1991.– Genauer, E.: R. T. New York
1974.– Goldwater, R.: R. T. New York
1947.– Lynch, J. B. (ed.): T. Phoenix Art
Museum. Phoenix 1968 (cat.).– Lynch, J.
B. (ed.): R. T. Fifty Years of His Painting.
Phillips Collection. Washington 1978
(cat.).– Moyssén, X. (ed.): R. T. Mexico
City 1980.– Paz, O. (ed.): R.
T. Peintures 1960-1974. Musée d'Art
Moderne de la Ville de Paris. Paris 1974
(cat.).– Paz, O. (ed.): R. T. Myth and
Magic. Solomon R. Guggenheim Museum.
New York 1979 (cat.).– Paz, O. and J. Las-
saigne: R. T. New York 1983, Paris 1983,
Munich 1986.– Ruckhaberle, D. and E.
Coldewey (ed.): R. T. Staatliche Kunsthalle
Berlin. Berlin 1990 (cat.).– Westheim, P.: T.
Mexico City 1957

TANGUY Yves
1900 Paris – **1955** Woodbury (CT)
American painter of French origin. Self-
taught. Joined the French merchant marine
and between **1918–1920** sailed on a
freighter to England, Spain, Portugal, and
South America. **1920–1923** Military
service. He decided to become a painter
1923 after seeing a painting by De Chirico
in a window at the Galerie Paul Guillaume
in Paris. In his first pictures he extended De
Chirico's spatial confinement into an unend-
ing vista: eliminating facades, architecture,

faces, and monuments and taking up his
favourite subject, the infinite panorama of
the sea. **1925** Met André Breton and the
Surrealist painters, and showed his fantastic
landscapes peopled with amorphous,
unidentifiable object and weird sculptural
constructions in their exhibitions. **1939**
Emigrated, along with many of the Surrealists, to America and settled in Woodbury,
where he lived on a farm. **1942** Took part in
the exhibition "Artists in Exile" at the Pierre
Matisse Gallery, New York, and in the Surrealist exhibition organised by Breton and
Duchamp at the Reid Mansion. **1948**
Became an American citizen. **1982** Impor-
tant retrospectives at the Baden-Baden
Kunsthalle and at the Pompidou Centre,
Paris.
WRITINGS: Y. T.: Lettres de loin.
Adressées à Marcel Jean. Paris 1993
CATALOGUES RAISONNES: Sage, K. et
al. (ed.): Y. T. Un Recueil de ses œuvres. A
Summary of His Works. New York 1963.–
Wittrock, W. (ed.): Y. T. Das druckgraphi-
sche Werk. Staatsgalerie Stuttgart. Düssel-
dorf 1976 (cat.)
MONOGRAPHS, CATALOGUES:
Marchesseau, D.: Y. T. Paris 1973.–
Penrose, R. et al. (ed.): Y. T. Centre
Georges Pompidou. Paris 1982 (cat.).– Sage,
K.: Y. T. A Summary of His Works. New
York 1963.– Schmidt, K. (ed.): Y. T. Staatli-
che Kunsthalle Baden-Baden et al. Munich
1982 (cat.).– Soby, J. T.: Y. T. The
Museum of Modern Art. New York 1972
(cat.).– Tanguy, G.-M.: Y. T. Druide sur-
réaliste. Paris 1995.– Y. T. A Retrospective.
Solomon R. Guggenheim Museum. New
York 1983 (cat.).– Waldberg, P.: Y. T. Brus-
sels 1977

TAPIES Antoni
born **1923** Barcelona
Spanish painter, graphic and object artist.
Self-taught. **1943–1946** Studied law in
Barcelona and attended the Academy for
just two months. **1948** Co-founder of the
Dau al Set group and of their magazine.
1951 Visited Picasso. **1952** First abstractions.
1956 Travelled in Italy, and studied
Vedanta, Taoism and Zen Buddhism. **1959
–1977** Participation in documenta 2, 3 and
6 in Kassel. **1966** Arrested and convicted
for holding illegal meetings in a monastery
near Barcelona. **1970** Retreats with Miró to
Montserrat Cloister out of solidarity with
those who had not betrayed Catalan leftists
and communists on trial. First sculptural
objects. **1981** Awarded the Gold Medal for
Fine Arts by King Juan Carlos and received
an honorary doctorate from the Royal
College of Art in London. Important retrospectives: **1993** at the Schirn art museum,
Frankfurt am Main, **1994** at the Galerie
Nationale du Jeu de Paume and **1995** at the
Guggenheim Museum, New York. Involved
himself very early with the work of the Surrealists, and was inspired by Picasso, Miró
and Klee. He quickly moved into abstraction and began to produce collages out of a
never-ending variety of materials. His late

works are characterised by mythological
and philosophical themes. The runes and
symbols that appear, scratched onto or in
his paintings, have a magical, cosmic
meaning.
WRITINGS: Catoir, B. (ed.): Gespräche
mit A. T. Munich 1987, 1998 / Conversations avec A. T. Paris 1988 / Conversations
with A. T. Munich 1991.– A. T.: La Pratique
de l'art. Paris 1974 / Die Praxis der Kunst. St.
Gallen 1976.– A. T.: L'Art contre l'esthétique. Paris 1978 / Kunst kontra Ästhetik. St.
Gallen 1983.– A. T.: Mémoire. Autobiographie. Paris 1981 / Erinnerungen. Fragment
einer Autobiographie. St. Gallen 1988.–
A. T.: La Réalité comme art. Paris 1989
CATALOGUES RAISONNES: Agustí, A.
et al. (ed.): T. Obra completa. 4 vols.
Barcelona 1988-1992 / T. Catalogue
raisonné. 4 vols. Paris 1988-1997 / A. T. The
Complete Works. 4 vols. New York 1988-
1997.– Galfetti, M. (ed.): T. Das graphische
Werk 1947-1978. 2 vols. Sankt Gallen 1974-
1984 / T. L' œuvre gravé 1947-1978. 2 vols.
Paris 1974-1984 / T. The Graphic Work 1947-
1978. 2 vols. San Francisco 1984
MONOGRAPHS, CATALOGUES: Abadie,
D. (ed.): T. ouvrage collectif. Galerie
Nationale du Jeu de Paume. Paris 1994
(cat.).– Ballo, G. (ed.): T. Milano. Milan
1985.– Bärmann, M. and G. Fischer (ed.):
T. El libre. Das Buch. Stadtmuseum, Sieg-
burg et al. Siegburg 1994 (cat.).– Borja, M.
J.: A. T. The Matter Paintings. Ann Arbor
(MI) 1990.– Borja-Villel, M. J. (ed.): T.
Comunicació sobre el mur. Fundació
Antoni Tàpies, Barcelona et al. Valencia
1992 (cat.).– Cirici, A.: T. Zeuge des
Schweigens. Düsseldorf 1971 / T. Witness of
Silence. New York 1972.– Cirlot, J.-E.: T.
Barcelona 1960.– Cirlot, J.-E.: Signifi-
cación de la pintura de T. Barcelona 1962.–
Combalia Dexeus, V.: T. Paris 1984,
Brunswick 1990.– Dauber, G. (ed.): A. T.
Kunsthalle Bremen. Bremen 1977 (cat.).–
Davvetas, D.: A. T. Paris 1994.– Franzke, A.
and M. Schwarz (ed.): A. T. Werk und Zeit.
Stuttgart 1979 (cat.).– Franzke, A.: T.
Munich 1992, Paris 1993, New York 1995.–
García, J.-M. (ed.): T. und die Bücher.
Schirn Kunsthalle, Frankfurt-on-Main.
Barcelona 1991 (cat.).– Gatt, G.: A. T.
Bologna 1967.– Giménez, C. and D.
Ashton (ed.): T. Solomon R. Guggenheim
Museum, New York et al. New York and
Paris 1995 (cat.).– Gimferrer, P.: A. T. i
l'esprit català. Barcelona 1974 / A. T. and the
Catalan Spirit. New York 1975 / A. T. und
der Geist Kataloniens. Frankfurt-on-Main
and Berlin 1976.– Malet, R. M.: Los carte-
les de T. Barcelona 1984 / T. affiches. Paris
1988.– Messer, T. M. (ed.): T. Eine Retrospektive. Schirn Kunsthalle. Frankfurt-on-
Main 1993 (cat.).– Moure, G.: T. Objets du
temps. Paris 1994 / T. Objects of Time.
Cologne 1995.– Penrose, R.: A. T. London
1978, New York 1993.– Permanyer, L.: T.
and the New Culture. New York 1986 / T. et
la nouvelle culture. Paris 1986.– Raillard,
G.: T. Paris 1976.– Raillard, G.: La Syllabe
noire de T. Marseille 1994.– Schmalenbach,
W.: A. T. Zeichen und Strukturen. Frankfurt-on-Main and Berlin 1974.– Schmalenbach, W. (ed.): T. Die achtziger Jahre.
Kunstsammlung Nordrhein-Westfalen,
Düsseldorf 1989 (cat.).– Wye, D. (ed.): A.
T. in Print. The Museum of Modern Art.
New York 1992 (cat.)

TATLIN Vladimir
1885 Moscow – **1958** Norodevichi
Russian artist. **1902/03** and **1909–1911**
Studied at the School of Painting, Sculpture, and Architecture in Moscow. **1907/08**
Lessons from Larionow. **1912** Took part in
the "Donkey Tail" exhibition in Moscow.
1913 Travelled to North Africa, Berlin, and

Paris. Became acquainted with the work of the Fauves and the Cubists. Met Picasso. **1915** Took part in the exhibitions "Streetcar 5" and "0.10" in St. Petersburg. **1916** Took part in the exhibition "Magazin" in Moscow. **1917** Designed the interior of the Café Pittoresque in Moscow with Rodchenko and Jakulov. **1918/19** Director of the IZO NARKOMPROS in Moscow. **1919/20** Tower model construction for the Monument to the Third International. **1921–1925** Taught at the GINChUK in Leningrad. **1922** Took part in the Russian Art exhibition in Berlin. **1923** Stage design for Chlebnikov's play *Zangezi*. **1925–1927** Professor at the Art Institute in Kiev. **1927–1933** Taught at UTEMAS in Moscow. **1929–1932** Construction of the experimental flying machine *Letatlin*. **1934** Returned to classic painting and worked as a stage set designer. **1937** Assisted with the ceremonial decorations in Moscow for the 20th anniversary of the October Revolution. **1948** Officially declared an "Enemy of the People" by the Communist Party. **1993** Retrospective at the Kunsthalle Düsseldorf. Tatlin was one of the most important members of the Eastern European avant-garde. With his counter-reliefs, the new icons of a functional social order, he laid the cornerstone of Constructivism.
CATALOGUE RAISONNE: Andersen T. et al. (ed.): W. T. 1885-1953. Moderna Museet, Stockholm et al. Stockholm 1968 (cat.).
MONOGRAPHS, CATALOGUES: Davenport, G.: T. New York 1974.– Harten, J. and A. Strigalev (ed.): V. T. Retrospektive. Städtische Kunsthalle Düsseldorf et al. Cologne 1993 (cat.).– Harten, J. (ed.): W. T. Leben, Werk, Wirkung. Ein internationales Symposium. Cologne 1993.– Körner, E.: T. Outlines Of a Career in the Context of Contemporary Russian Avant-Garde Art as Related to Eastern and Western Tendencies. Budapest 1985.– Milner, J.: V. T. and the Russian Avant-Garde. New Haven (CT) and London 1983.– Ray, M.: T. e la cultura del Vchutemas. 1885-1953, 1920-1930. Roma 1992.– Rowell, M.: V. T. Form, Faktura. Cambridge (MA) 1978.– Shadova, L. A. (ed.): T. Budapest 1980, Dresden 1984, Weingarten 1987, London and New York 1988.– W. T. Moderna Museet. Stockholm 1968 (cat.)

TELEMAQUE Hervé
born **1937** Port-au-Prince (Haiti)
Haitian-born French painter. **1957–1960** Studied at the Art Students League, New York and, during this time, was strongly influenced by Gorky and De Kooning. **1962** Moved to Paris and participated in the Salon Latino-Américain. **1964** Solo-exhibition at the Matthias Fels gallery in Paris. **1964** Joint-exhibition with Geissler at the Hanover Gallery, London. **1964** and **1968** took part in documenta 3 and 4 in Kassel. **1968** Was represented at the exhibition "Painting in France 1900–1967" at the Metropolitan Museum of Art, New York. Took part in documenta 4 in Kassel. **1976**

Retrospective at the Musée d'Art Moderne de la Ville de Paris. Telemaque's geometrically composed pictures integrate elements of Pop Art and Nouveau Réalisme such as comics and commonplace objects.
MONOGRAPHS, CATALOGUES: Gassiot-Talabot, G. (ed.): H. T. Galleria Arte Borgogna. Milan 1973 (cat.).– Noël, B. (ed.): H. T. Musée d'Art Moderne de la Ville de Paris. Paris 1976 (cat.).– Noël, B. and C. Thieck (ed.): H. T. Galerie Adrien Maeght. Paris 1981 (cat.).– H. T. Dérive graphique. Musée de Maubeuge 1993 (cat.).– H. T. Espace Electra. Paris 1995 (cat.)

THEK Paul
1933 Brooklyn (NY) – **1988** New York
American object artist. **1951–1954** Studied at the Cooper Union, the Art Students League and at the Pratt Institute in New York. Lived from **1955–1962** in Florida and Italy and **1962–1968** in New York, before going to Europe again. **1964** Solo-exhibition at the Stable Gallery, New York, and **1966** at the Pace Gallery, New York. **1968** Took part in documenta 4 in Kassel. **1972** Solo-exhibition at the Moderna Museet, Stockholm, and at the Lucerne Kunstmuseum. **1976** and **1980** took part in the Venice Biennale. **1981** Participated in the "Westkunst" exhibition in Cologne. **1984** Solo-exhibition at the Barbara Gladstone Gallery, New York. **1986** Took part in the Chambre d'Amis exhibition in Ghent. **1991** Retrospective of drawings at the Brooke Alexander Gallery, New York. Thek's early works are provocative environments with a neo-Dadaist anti-aesthetic, which is evident especially in his selection of unusual materials. His mythical environments of the 70s are manifestations of his form of Individual Mythology.
MONOGRAPHS, CATALOGUES: Franke, M.: "Work in Progress – Art is Liturgy". Das historische-prozessuale und betrachterbezogene Ausstellungskonzept von P. T. Frankfurt-on-Main and 1993.– P. T. Kunstmuseum. Lucerne 1973 (cat.).– P. T. Procession. Institute of Contemporary Art, University of Pennsylvania. Philadelphia 1977 (cat.).– Wilson, A. et al. (ed.): P. T. Snap! Pop! Was! Touch me not! Witte de With Center for Contemporary Art, Rotterdam et al. Rotterdam 1995, Berlin 1996 (cat.)

THIEBAUD Wayne
born **1920** Mesa (AZ)
American painter. First worked as a sign painter, caricaturist, and designer. **1942–1945** Served in the US Air Force and designed murals for the US Army. **1949–1953** Studied at San José State University (CA) and at California State University in Sacramento. **1951** First solo-exhibition at the Crocker Art Gallery, Sacramento. **1951–1961** Taught at Sacramento City College. **1954–1957** Produced educational films. Travelled around Mexico and Europe. **1961** Awarded the Scholastic Art prize. **1960–**

1976 Taught at the University of California in Davis. **1965** Solo-exhibition at the Galleria Schwarz, Milan. **1967** Took part in the São Paulo Biennale. **1972** Took part in documenta 5 in Kassel. **1981** Solo-exhibition at the Walker Art Center in Minneapolis and **1985** at the San Francisco Museum of Modern Art. Thiebaud made his name with his ironically exaggerated paintings of commonplace objects like lipstick and pies. In his individual form of Pop Art, he uses heavy impasto and garish colours and emphasises the painting process.
MONOGRAPHS, CATALOGUES: Berkson, B.: Vision and Revision: Hand Colored Prints by W. T. The Fine Art Museum. San Francisco 1991 (cat.).– Cooper, G. (ed.): W. T. Survey 1947-1976. Art Museum. Phoenix 1976 (cat.).– Coplans, J. (ed.): W. T. Pasadena Art Museum. Pasadena 1968 (cat.).– Glenn, C. and J. (ed.): W. T. Private Drawings. The Artist's Sketchbook. New York 1987.– Tsujimoto, K. (ed.): W. T. San Francisco Museum of Modern Art. San Francisco 1985 (cat.)

THIELER Fred
1916 Königsberg – **1999** Berlin
German painter. Member of the Zen 49 group and the Neue Gruppe. **1937–1941** Studied medicine. **1946–1948** Studied at the Munich Art Academy under K. Caspars. **1951/52** Lived in Paris. **1951** First solo-exhibition at the Le Canard gallery, Amsterdam. **1952** Returned to Munich. **1959** and **1964** took part in documenta 2 and 3 in Kassel. **1960–1981** Taught at the Berlin Art Academy. **1983** Solo-exhibition at the Nothelfer gallery, Berlin, and **1986** at the Saarland Museum, Saarbrücken and the Berlin Academy. **1988** Took part in the exhibition "Stationen der Moderne" at the Berlinische Galerie. **1989** Designed the ceiling of the Residenz theatre in Munich. **1991** Retrospective at the Emden Kunsthalle. Thieler is a proponent of abstract Neo-Expressionism.
CATALOGUE RAISONNE: Firmenich, A. and J. Merkert (ed.): F. T. Monographie und Werkverzeichnis. Bilder von 1942-1993. Cologne 1994
MONOGRAPHS, CATALOGUES: Firmenich, A. (ed.): F. T. Dialog mit der Farbe.

Kunsthalle Emden et al. Emden 1991 (cat.).– Motte, M. d. la (ed.): F. T. Städtische Kunstsammlungen. Bonn 1968.– Motte, M. d. la (ed.): F. T. Galerie Nothelfer. Berlin 1983 (cat.).– Orff, H. (ed.): F. T. Haus am Walsee. Berlin 1962 (cat.).– Roters, E. et al. (ed.): F. T. Akademie der Künste, Berlin et al. Berlin 1986 (cat.).– Volkmann, B. and R.-F. Raddatz (ed.): F. T. Arbeiten 1940-1986. Akademie der Künste, Berlin et al. Berlin 1986 (cat.)

THORN-PRIKKER Jan
1868 The Hague – **1932** Cologne
Dutch painter and stained-glass artist. **1883–1887** Studied at the Academy in The Hague. **1910** First stained-glass window for the train station in Hagen, Westphalia. **1913–1918** Taught at the Essen School of Arts and Crafts, and worked on mosaics, glass paintings, murals, furniture design and tapestries. **1920–1923** Took over a professorship at the School of Arts and Crafts in Munich. **1923–1926** Taught in Düsseldorf at the Art Academy and from **1926–1932** at the Cologne School of Arts and Crafts. He was a leading exponent of Dutch Jugendstil, but was also influenced by Pointillism and Symbolism. The greater part of his work was in the crafts: stained-glass, ceramics and batik, at which he excelled.
WRITINGS: J. T. P.: Die Brieven van J. T. P. aan Henri Borel en anderen. Nieuwkoop 1980
MONOGRAPHS, CATALOGUES: Heynen, J. (ed.): J. T. P. Kaiser Wilhelm Museum. Krefeld 1982 (cat.).– Hoff, A.: J. T. P. Recklinghausen 1958.– J. T.-P. Stedelijk Museum. Amsterdam 1968 (cat.).– Wember, P. (ed.): J. T. P. Glasfenster, Wandbilder, Ornamente 1891-1932. Kaiser Wilhelm Museum. Krefeld 1966 (cat.).– Wex, J. L.: J. T. P. Abstraktion und Konkretion in freier und angewandter Kunst. Bochum 1984

THURSZ Frederic
born **1930** Casablanca
Moroccan-born American painter. **1953–1957** Studied in New York and Paris. **1992** Participation in documenta 9 in Kassel. Professorship at City University in New York. With his paintings based on the color field tradition of Rothko and Newman, and

emphasising colour effects, Thursz is representative of the new radical painting movement. Multi-layered, semi-transparent overpainting of the ground using pigment and metallic colours intensify the sheen and illumination effects of the picture surface.
MONOGRAPHS, CATALOGUES: F. M. T. University of Kentucky Gallery of Art. Lexington 1965 (cat.).– F. M. T. Musée d'Art Moderne. St. Etienne 1989 (cat.).– Wahl, K. (ed.): F. M. T. Galerie Lelong. Paris and New York 1991 (cat.)

TILLMANS Wolfgang
born **1968** Remscheid
German photographer. **1987–1990** Lived in Hamburg. **1988** Exhibited his graphic works, produced with a Canon laser copier and entitled *Approaches*, at the Fabrik-Foto-Forum in Hamburg. **1990–1992** Studied photography at the Bournemouth & Poole College of Art and Design in England. Produced photo diptychs which were exhibited at the PPS Galerie F. C. Gundlach in Hamburg. **1992–1994** Worked in London, and **1994/95** in New York. Focused on the themes of young people and subcultures. Photographed for the young fashion magazine *i-D. Interview und Spex*. **1995** Solo-exhibition at the Zurich Kunsthalle and **1996** exhibition of his *Faltenwürfe* at the Daniel Buchholz gallery in Cologne. Tillmans is an important representative of close-to-life photography in Germany.
MONOGRAPHS, CATALOGUES: Lütgens, A. et al. (ed.): W. T. Stuttgart 1996 (cat.).– Riemschneider, B. (ed.): W. T. Cologne 1995.– W. T. Portikus. Frankfurt-on-Main 1995 (cat.).– W. T. Kunsthalle Zürich. Zurich 1995 (cat.).– W. T. Concorde. Cologne 1997

TILSON Joe
born **1928** London
English painter. Worked at first as a carpenter. **1946–1949** Worked for the Royal Air Force. **1949–1952** Studied at St. Martin's School of Art and **1952–1955** at the Royal College of Art. **1955–1957** Lived in Italy. **1958–1963** Taught at St. Martin's School of Art, London. **1960** Received a Gulbenkian Foundation grant. **1962** Solo-exhibition at the Marlborough Fine Art Gallery, London.

1964, **1976** and **1988** took part in the Venice Biennale. **1965** and **1983** awarded the Graphic Prize in Ljubljana. **1968** Participation in documenta 4 in Kassel. **1971/72** Guest-professor at the Hamburg School of Fine Arts. **1972** Moved to Wiltshire. **1973** Retrospective at the Boymans-van Beuningen museum, Rotterdam. **1976** DAAD grant to Berlin. **1985** Appointed a member of the Royal Academy of Arts, London. **1992** Retrospective at Waddington Graphics, London. Tilson, whose work stems from the Pop Art movement, achieved a remarkable synthesis of image and typography in his *Combination Pictures*.
WRITINGS: J. T.: A-Z Box. Fragments of an Oneiric Alphabet. London 1970.– J. T.: Alchera 1970-1976. London 1976
MONOGRAPHS, CATALOGUES: Compton, M. and M. Livingstone: T. Milan 1993.– Gilmour, P. (ed.): J. T. Graphics. Vancouver Art Gallery. Vancouver 1979 (cat.).– Hammacher-v. d. Brande, R. (ed.): J. T. Museum Boymans-van Beuningen. Rotterdam 1973 (cat.).– Quintavalle, A. C.: J. T. Milan 1977.– J. T. Pages. Marlborough Fine Art Ltd. London 1970 (cat.)

TINGUELY Jean
1925 Fribourg – **1991** Bern
Swiss sculptor. **1940–1945** Studied at the Basel School of Arts and Crafts. **1944** Began to experiment with moving objects. **1951** Moved to Paris. **1954** Solo-exhibition at the Arnaud gallery and participation in the Salon des Réalités Nouvelles in Paris. Joined the group Le Mouvement. **1955** Began his *Métamatics*, a series of kinetic sculptures. **1959** Took part in the Paris Biennale. Contact with the group Zero. **1961** Collaboration with Niki de Saint Phalle. **1964–1977** Took part in documenta 3, 4 and 6 in Kassel. **1966** Together with Saint Phalle installed the kinetic female figure *Hon* in the Moderna Museet, Stockholm. Took part in the exhibition "The Machine" at the Museum of Modern Art, New York. **1967** Took part in Expo' 67 in Montreal and **1968** in the exhibition "Dada, Surrealism and their Heritage" at the Museum of Modern Art, New York. Retrospective at the Museum of Contemporary Art, Chicago. **1972/73** Touring retrospective, starting at the Kunsthalle in Basel. **1980/81** Together with Saint Phalle, designed the fountain *La Fontaine Stravinsky* in Paris. **1988** and **1997** Retrospective at the Pompidou Centre, Paris. Tinguely's constructions work like machines but have no meaningful function and can therefore be seen as satirical comments on technological society.
WRITINGS: Hahnloser, M. (ed.): Briefe von J. T. an Maja Sacher. Bern 1992.– Hahnloser, M. (ed.): J. T. Briefe an Paul Sacher und gemeinsame Freunde. Bern 1996
CATALOGUES RAISONNES: Bischofberger, C. (ed.): J. T. Werkkatalog Skulpturen und Reliefs 1954-1985. 2 vols. Zurich 1982-1990

MONOGRAPHS, CATALOGUES: Althaus, P. F. (ed.): J. T. Kunsthalle Basel. Basel 1972 (cat.).– Bezzola, L.: J. T. Zurich 1974.– Bezzola, L. and M. Hahnloser-Ingold (ed.): J. T. Fribourg – Moscou – Fribourg. Zurich 1992.– Botta, M. et al. (ed.): J. T. Die Sammlung. The Collection. Bern 1997.– Calvocoressi, R. (ed.): J. T. Kunsthaus Zurich et al. Zurich 1982 (cat.).– Conil Lacoste, M.: T. L'énergétique de l'insolence. Paris 1989.– Hulten, P. (ed.): J. T. Méta. Frankfurt-on-Main and Vienna 1972, Boston 1972, 1975, Paris 1973.– Hulten, P.: J. T. A Magic Stronger than Death. Milan 1987 / J. T. Une magie plus forte que la mort. Paris 1987.– Hulten, P. (ed.): J. T. Centre Georges Pompidou. Paris 1988 (cat.).– Keller, J.-P.: T. et le mystère de la roue manquante. Carouge 1992.– Lacoste, M.: T. L'énergetique de l'insolence. 2 vols. Paris 1989.– Michaud, E.: J. T. Chronologie, expositions, bibliographie. Paris 1970.– Museum Jean Tinguely (ed.): Museum J. T., Basel. Die Sammlung. Bern 1996.– Poley, S. and S. Salzmann (ed.): J. T. Meta-Maschinen. Wilhelm-Lembruck-Museum. Duisburg 1979 (cat.).– Poley, S. and C. Schulz-Hoffmann (ed.): J. T. Kunsthalle der Hypo-Kulturstiftung. Munich 1985 (cat.).– Schmied, W. and P. F. Althans (ed.): J. T. Kestner-Gesellschaft. Hanover 1972 (cat.).– Schulz-Hoffmann, C. (ed.): J. T. Nachtschattengewächse. Kunsthaus Wien. Munich 1991 (cat.).– Stumm, R. and K. Wyss: J. T. Basel 1985.– J. T. Machines de T. Centre National d'Art Contemporain. Paris 1971 (cat.).– J. T. Stedelijk Museum. Amsterdam 1973 (cat.).– J. T. Centre Georges Pompidou. Paris 1997 (cat.).– Violand-Hobi, H. E.: J. T. Biographie und Werk. Munich 1995

TOBEY Mark
1890 Centerville – **1976** Basel
American painter. **1906–1908** Studied at the Art Institute of Chicago. First worked as a draughtsman in a fashion studio. **1917** First solo-exhibition of portrait drawings at the Knoedler Gallery in New York. **1922** Became interested in Chinese calligraphy and East Asian philosophies, especially the religion of Baha'i. **1922–1925** Taught art in Seattle and **1930–1937** at Dartington Hall in Devonshire. Travelled through Europe, the Orient and the Far East, staying in **1935** in a Zen monastery in Japan, where he studied calligraphy. **1938** Composed his own music. **1959** and **1964** participation in documenta 2 and 3 in Kassel. **1960** Moved to Basel, and felt at home with the humanist tradition there, but continued his travels around the USA. Retrospectives **1974** at the Smithsonian Institution, Washington, **1984** in the National Gallery, Washington, and **1990** "A Centennial Exhibition" at the Beyeler gallery, Basel. Tobey's *White Writings*, networks of fine calligraphic figures, were originally quite easy to interpret but became increasingly abstract and unintelligible, reflecting his introverted, contemplative way of life.

WRITINGS: M. T.: The World of Market. Seattle et al. 1981
CATALOGUE RAISONNE: Heidenheim, H. H. (ed.): M. T. Das druckgraphische Werk. Radierungen und Serigraphien 1970-1975. Düsseldorf 1975
MONOGRAPHS, CATALOGUES: Bärmann, M. et al. (ed.): M. T. Werke 1935-1975. Museum Folkwang. Essen 1989 (cat.).– Bärmann, M. (ed.): M. T. Between Worlds. Museo d'Arte, Mendrisio et al. Mendrisio 1989 (cat.).– Bärmann, M. et al. (ed.): M. T. Museo Nacional Centro de Arte Reina Sofia. Madrid 1997 (cat.).– Choay, F.: M. T. Paris 1961.– Cummings, P. (ed.): M. T. Paintings 1920-1960. Yoshii Gallery. New York 1994 (cat.).– Dahl, A. L. et al. (ed.): M. T. Art and Belief. Oxford and St. Petersburg (FL) 1984.– Ixmeier, E.: M. T. Bochum 1981.– Rathbone, E. E. (ed.): M. T. City Paintings. National Gallery of Art. Washington 1984 (cat.).– Roberts, C.: M. T. New York 1959, Paris 1959.– Schmied, W.: T. Stuttgart 1966, London and New York 1966.– Seitz, W. C. (ed.): M. T. The Museum of Modern Art. New York 1962 (cat.).– Taylor, J. C. (ed.): M. T. Tribute to M. T. National Collection of Fine Arts, Smithsonian Institution. Washington 1974 (cat.).– Thomas, E. B. (ed.): M. T. A Retrospective Exhibition from Northwest Collections. Seattle Art Museum. Seattle 1959 (cat.).– M. T.'s 80. A Retrospective. Seattle Art Museum. Seattle 1970 (cat.).– M. T. Between Worlds. Opere 1935-1975. Museo d'Arte. Mendrisio 1989 (cat.).– M. T. A Centennial Exhibition. Galerie Beyeler. Basel 1990 (cat.).– Yao, M.-C.: The Influence of Chinese and Japanese Calligraphy on M. T. San Francisco 1983

TOMLIN Bradley Walker
1899 Syracuse (NY) – **1953** New York
American painter. **1917–1921** Studied at the College of Fine Arts at Syracuse University, New York. **1921** Moved to New York. **1922** First solo-exhibition put on by Skaneateles and Cazenovia, New York. **1923/24** Studied at the Académie Colarossi and at the Académie de la Grande Chaumière in Paris. **1924** Returned to New York. **1932–1941** Taught at Sarah Lawrence College. **1941** Came to know Gottlieb and was highly impressed by Abstract Expressionism. **1948** Became friends with Motherwell, Pollock and Gorky. **1952** Took part in the exhibition "Fifteen Americans" at the Museum of Modern Art, New York. **1957** Retrospective at the Whitney Museum of American Art, New York. **1959** Posthumous participation in documenta 2 in Kassel. **1975** Retrospective at the Albright-Knox Art Gallery, Buffalo. Tomlin was a leading exponent of Action Painting in America. His most important works were created in the last few years of his life.
MONOGRAPHS, CATALOGUES: Baur, J. I. H. (ed.): B. W. T. Whitney Museum of American Art. New York 1957 (cat.).– Chenault, J. (ed.): B. W. T. A Retrospective

View. The Emily Lowe Gallery, Hofstra University, Hempstedt et al. Buffalo 1975 (cat.)

TORRES-GARCIA Joaquín

1874 Montevideo – **1949** Montevideo
Uruguayan painter of Spanish origins. **1891** Emigrated to Spain. **1894–1908** Studied at the Art Academy in Barcelona. Worked on Gaudí's cathedral the *Sagrada Familia*. **1920/21** Lived in New York and came to know Duchamp and Joseph Stella. **1922** First solo-exhibition at the Hanfstengel Gallery, New York. **1924** Moved to Paris. Friendly relations with Mondrian, Doesburg and Vantongerloo. **1926** Solo-exhibition at the Fabre gallery in Paris. **1928** First participation in the Salon des Indépendants. **1930** Exhibited with Cercle et Carré and helped with the publication of their magazine. **1933** Returned to Montevideo. From **1936** published and edited the journal *Círculo y Cuadrado*. **1935** Co-founder of the Asociación de Arte Constructivo. **1944** Publication of his article *Universalismo Constructivo*, which had a profound influence on other artists and the South American art scene as a whole. Torres-Garcia was an artist who bridged the gap between the pre-Columbian culture of South America and modern European art movements, especially Cubism and Neo-Plasticism.
WRITINGS: Fló, J. (ed.): T.-G. Escritos. Montevideo 1974.– J. T.-G.: Historia de mi vida. Barcelona 1939, 1990.– J. T.-G.: Universalismo constructivo. 2 vols. Buenos Aires 1944, 1984
CATALOGUE RAISONNE: Jardí, E.: T.-G. Barcelona 1974
MONOGRAPHS, CATALOGUES: Brandao, L. (ed.): J. T.-G. Museo de Monterrey. Monterrey 1981 (cat.).– Buzio de Torres, C. et al. (ed.): T.-G. Grid-Pattern-Sign. Paris-Montevideo. Hayward Gallery. London 1985 (cat.).– Buzio de Torres, C. et al. (ed.): T.-G. IVAM Centro Julio Gónzales, Valencia et al. Valencia 1991 (cat.).– Cassou, J.: T.-G. Paris 1955.– Gradowcyk, M. H.: J. T.-G. Buenos Aires 1985.– Jardí, E.: T.-G. New York 1973.– Kalenberg, A. and J. Lassaigne (ed.): T.-G.: Construction et symboles. Musée d'Art Moderne de la Ville de Paris. Paris 1975 (cat.).– Llorens, T. (ed.): J. T.-G. Museo Nacional Centro de Arte Reina Sofía. Madrid 1991 (cat.).– Pereda, R.: T. G. Montevideo 1991.– Robbins, D. (ed.): J. T.-G. 1874-1949. Museum of Art, Rhode Island School of Design et al. Providence 1970 (cat.).– Toys, A. (ed.): Les Joguines de T.-G. IVAM Centro Julio González. Valencia 1997 (cat.)

TOULOUSE-LAUTREC Henri de

1864 Albi – **1901** Chateau Malromé (Gironde)
French painter and graphic artist. **1882–1886** Trained in the studio of Cormon, where he came to know Bernard and van Gogh. Frequented theatres, music-halls,

cafés and the haunts of the Paris demi-monde. **1886** First publication of drawings in magazines. **1889** Exhibited for the first time at the Salon des Indépendants. **1890** Travelled with Signac to Brussels to the exhibition of the Les XX group and to Spain. **1891** Began to design stylised posters with strong outlines and large areas of colour, for restaurants, cabarets, and publishers. **1892** Travelled to Brussels and London. **1893** First important solo-exhibition at Goupil. Lived from time to time in a bordello, where he drew and painted. **1894–1897** Travels to Belgium, Holland, Spain, London, Lisbon. Exhibition at the Salon of the Libre Esthétique group in Brussels. Contact with the Nabis and contributions to *La Revue Blanche*. **1899** After suffering a nervous breakdown, he was committed to the sanatorium in Neuilly. **1901** Became partially paralysed and died in his mother's castle. Toulouse-Lautrec, whose lithographs and posters are still reprinted today, was equally talented in drawing and painting. This double talent allowed him to create a unique style, combining elements of Impressionism, Symbolism and Japanese colour prints.
WRITINGS: Goldschmidt, L. and H. Schimmel (ed.): Unpublished Correspondance of H. de T.-L. London 1969.– Goldschmidt, L. and H. Schimmel (ed.): T.-L. Lettres 1871-1901. Paris 1972./– Schimmel, H. D. (ed.): The Letters of H. de T.-L. Oxford 1991.– Schimmel, H. D. (ed.): Die Briefe von H. de T.-L. Munich 1994
CATALOGUES RAISONNES: Adhémar, J. (ed.): T.-L. Lithographies. Paris 1965/T.-L. His Complete Lithographs and Drypoints. New York 1965.– Adriani, G. (ed.): T.-L. Das gesamte graphische Werk. Sammlung Gerstenberg. Cologne 1986/T.-L. The Complete Graphic Works. Gerstenberg Collection. London 1988.– Dortu, M.-G. (ed.): T.-L. et son œuvre. 6 vols. Paris and New York 1971.– Julien, E. (ed.): Les Affiches de T.-L. Catalogue complet et raisonné. Paris 1992.– Mourlot, F. (ed.): Les Affiches de T.-L. Paris 1992.– Sugana, G. M. and G. Caproni (ed.): The Complete Paintings of T.-L. London 1973/Tout l'œuvre peint de T.-L. Paris 1986.– Wittrock, W. (ed.): T.-L. The Complete Prints. 2 vols. London 1985/T.-L. Catalogue raisonné des estampes. 2 vols. Paris 1985

TOYEN

(Marie Germínová)
1902 Prague – **1980** Paris
Czech painter. **1918** Studied at the Prague Art Academy. **1920** Founder-member of the Devetsil group in Prague. **1923** Exhibited with the Modern Art Bazar group. Took the pseudonym Toyen. **1925** Moved to Paris. **1929** Returned to Prague. **1934** Together with Nezval, Styrsky and Teige founded the Surrealist movement in Prague. **1935** At the Prague Surrealist exhibition, he met André Breton and Paul Eluard, who were also taking part. Travelled to Paris where he met other Surrealists. **1947** Emigrated to

France. **1968** Retrospective in Aquila, Italy. In the mid-30s, after periods devoted to naive and Cubist styles of painting, Toyen became an enthusiastic proponent of Surrealism.
MONOGRAPHS, CATALOGUES: Bischof, R.: T. 1902-1980. Eigenschaften ohne Frau. Frankfurt-on-Main 1987.– Breton, A. et al.: T. Paris 1953.– Breton, A. et al. (ed.): T. Das malerische Werk. Frankfurt-on-Main 1987.– Holten, R. v.: T. En surrealistik visionär. Köping 1984.– Ivsic, R.: T. Paris 1974.– Péret, B.: T. Paris 1953

TRAKAS George

born **1944** Quebec
Canadian sculptor and installation artist. After **1972** installed bridges and corridors through landscapes and gallery spaces. **1977** Exhibited his work *Union Pass* at documenta 6 in Kassel, in which two model bridges, a modern one of steel and an old-style one of wood, were installed facing each other and then melted together into a single new construction through an explosion. **1987** Participation in documenta 8 in Kassel.

TRIER Hann

1915 Düsseldorf – **1999** Castiglione della Pescaia (Tuscany)
German painter. Member of the Zen 49 group. **1934–1938** Studied at the Düsseldorf Art Academy. **1952–1955** Lived and travelled for long periods in South America. **1955/56** Guest-professorship at the Hamburg School of Fine Arts. **1955** Participation in documenta 1 in Kassel. **1957–1980**

Taught at the Berlin School of Fine Arts. **1958** Solo-exhibition at the Cologne Kunstverein and **1959** at the Kestner Society, Hanover. **1959** and **1964** took part in documenta 2 and 3 in Kassel. Retrospectives: **1972** at the Rheinische Landesmuseum in Bonn, **1985** at the Saarland Museum, Saarbrücken, **1990** at the Von der Heydt-Museum, Wuppertal, and again at the Rheinische Landesmuseum in Bonn. Trier's early paintings are Neo-Expressionist in character. After his travels in South America, he developed a linear compositional style which culminated in his *Vibration* paintings.
WRITINGS: H. T.: Wie ich ein Bild male. Berlin 1963.– H. T.: Ut poesis pictura? Einige Betrachtungen zur Malerei der griechischen Antike. Heidelberg 1985
CATALOGUES RAISONNES: Euler-Schmidt, M. (ed.): H. T. Werkverzeichnis der Gemälde 1990-1995. Cologne 1995.– Fehlemann, S. (ed.): H. T. Monographie und Werkverzeichnis der Gemälde bis 1989. Cologne 1990.– Gerlach-Laxner, U. (ed.): H. T. Druckgraphik. Werkverzeichnis und Monographie. Cologne 1994 (cat.)
MONOGRAPHS, CATALOGUES: Fehlemann, S. (ed.): H. T. Retrospetektive. Bilder 1949-1989. Von der Heydt-Museum, Wuppertal. Cologne 1990 (cat.).– Költzsch, G.-W. (ed.): H. T. Tatort Malerei. Moderne Galerie des Saarland Museums, Saarbrücken et al. Saarbrücken 1985 (cat.).– Költzsch, G.-W. (ed.): H. T. Archimedes. Folkwang Museum. Essen 1990 (cat.).– Motte, M. d. la (ed.): Dokumentation H. T. Bonn 1980.– Osterodt, I.: H. T. Zur Genese des Malens mit beiden Händen im künstlerischen Werk 1947-1959. Bramsche 1984.– Roters, E.: H. T. Die Deckengemälde in Berlin, Heidelberg and Cologne. Berlin 1981.– Schmalenbach, W. (ed.): H. T. Kestner-Gesellschaft. Hanover 1959 (cat.).– Schmidt, H. M. (ed.): H. T. Im Handumdrehen. Rheinisches Landesmuseum, Bonn et al. Cologne 1990 (cat.).– Schwinzer, E. et al. (ed.): H. T. Metamorphose der Farbe. Gustav-Lübke-Museum, Hamm et al. Hamm 1995 (cat.).– H. T. Gemälde, Zeichnungen, Graphiken 1951-1972. Rheinisches Landesmuseum, Bonn. Bonn 1972 (cat.).– H. T. Gemälde, Zeichnungen, Graphiken. Kölnischer Kunstverein. Cologne 1979 (cat.)

TROCKEL Rosemarie

born **1952** Schwerte (Westphalia)
German artist. First studied mathematics and theology. **1974–1978** Studied painting at the School of Industrial Arts in Cologne. **1983** First solo-exhibition at the Monika Sprüth gallery, Cologne. **1984** Solo-exhibitions at the Stampa gallery in Basel and at the Ascan Crone gallery in Hamburg. **1985** Solo-exhibition at the Rheinische Landesmuseum in Bonn. **1988** Took part in the BiNationale exhibition in Düsseldorf and Boston. Exhibitions at the Institute of Contemporary Arts, London, and at the Basel Kunsthalle. **1991** Exhibition at the Institute

of Contemporary Art, Boston, and **1992** at the Ludwig Museum, Cologne. **1997** Participation in documenta 10 in Kassel. Trockel is difficult to categorise. She uses a broad range of techniques and styles. Often her work makes reflective or ironic statements about the role of women in contemporary society and about styles of presentation in museums.
CATALOGUE RAISONNE: Theewen, G. (ed.): R. T. Herde. Werkverzeichnis. Cologne 1997
MONOGRAPHS, CATALOGUES: Ammann, J.-C. et al. (ed.): R. T. Kunsthalle Basel et al. Basel 1988 (cat.).– Ammann, J.-C. and U. Panhans-Bühler: R. T. White Carrot. Frankfurt-on-Main 1997.– Burke, G. (ed.): R. T. City Gallery. Wellington 1993 (cat.).– Dickhoff, W. (ed.): R. T. Bilder, Skulpturen, Zeichnungen. Rheinisches Landesmuseum, Bonn. Cologne 1985 (cat.).– Dickhoff, W. (ed.): R. T. Kunsthalle Basel et al. Basel and London 1988 (cat.).– Dickhoff, W.: R. T. Eine Einführung in ihr Werk und Schaffen. Frankfurt-on-Main 1992.– Koepplin, D. (ed.): R. T. Papierarbeiten. Museum für Gegenwartskunst, Basel et al. Basel and Stuttgart 1991 (cat.).– Noever, P. (ed.): R. T. Anima. Österreichisches Museum für Angewandte Kunst, Vienna. Stuttgart 1994 (cat.).– Stich, S. (ed.): R. T. The Insitute of Contemporary Art, Boston et al. Munich 1991 (cat.).– R. T. The Museum of Modern Art. New York 1988 (cat.).– R. T. Museo Nacional Centro de Arte Reina Sofia, Madrid et al. Madrid 1992 (cat.).– R. T. Museum of Contemporary Art. Sydney 1994 (cat.).

TÜBKE Werner
born **1929** Schönebeck (near Magdeburg)
German painter. **1948–1953** After serving an apprenticeship as a painter and graduating from the Master School of German Craftsmanship in Magdeburg, he studied at the Leipzig School of Graphic Art and Book Design. Did yet another course of studies, this time in art education and psychology at the University of Greifswald. From **1954**, he worked as a painter in Leipzig. **1964** Became a lecturer, and in **1972** professor at the Leipzig School of Graphic Art and Book Design, and stayed on as rector for a number of years. As a State Artist of the GDR, he exhibited in **1977** in documenta and 6 in Kassel. At the beginning of the 70s, he was allowed to travel to Italy; this contact with the classic Italian masters was to become an important influence in his work. **1984** He taught at the Summer Academy in Salzburg. From **1983–1989** he and his assistants created the Peasants' War Panorama in Bad Frankenhausen, whose 1,722 square metres of painted surface make it the largest oil painting in the world. With his monumental paintings and murals dealing with historical themes in a classic style, Tübke made an inspiring contribution to socialist history painting.
CATALOGUE RAISONNE: Meißner, G. (ed.): W. T. Gemälde, Aquarelle, Druckgraphik (mit Werkverzeichnis). Gemäldegalerie Neue Meister, Dresden et al. Dresden 1976 (cat.).– Tübke, B. (ed.): W. T. Das graphische Werk. 1950–1990. Düsseldorf 1991
MONOGRAPHS, CATALOGUES: Beaucamp, E.: W. T. Arbeiterklasse und Intelligenz. Frankfurt-on-Main 1985.– Betthausen, P. and C. Bube (ed.): W. T. Nationalgalerie der Staatlichen Museen. Berlin 1989 (cat.).– Emmrich, I.: W. T. Schöpfertum und Erbe. Berlin 1976.– Kober, K. M.: Reformation, Revolution. Panorama Frankenhausen. Monumentalbild von W. T. Dresden 1988.– Kober, K. M.: W. T. Monumentalbild Frankenhausen. Dresden 1989.– Lindner, G. and M. Wollenheit (ed.): W. T. Handzeichnungen und Aquarelle. Panorama, Bad Frankenhausen. Leipzig 1992 (cat.).– Meißner, G.: W. T. Leben und Werk. Leipzig 1989.– Raum, W. (ed.): W. T. Malerei, Grafik, Zeichnung. Staatliche Galerie Moritzburg, Halle et al. Halle 1979 (cat.)

TUCKER William
born **1935** Cairo
English sculptor. **1955–1958** Studied history at Oxford University. **1959/60** Attended the Central School of Art and Design and St. Martin's School of Art, London. **1962** First solo-exhibition at the Grabowski Gallery, London. **1968** Took part in documenta 4 in Kassel. **1974** Published the theoretical paper *The Condition of Sculpture*. **1976** Professorship at the University of Western Ontario. **1978–1982** Taught at Columbia University and **1978–1980** at the New York Studio School of Painting and Sculpture. **1980** Guggenheim grant for sculpture. **1987** Exhibition at the Tate Gallery, London. With his abstract, colourful rod constructions in steel, fibreglass and wood, Tucker belongs, along with King and I. Witkin, to those sculptors of the British avant-garde who have freed sculpture of its representational function and concentrated on materials and structures.
WRITINGS: W. T.: The Language of Sculpture. London and New York 1974
MONOGRAPHS, CATALOGUES: Ashton, D. (ed.): W. T. Gods. Five Recent Sculptures. Tate Gallery. London 1987 (cat.).– Forge, A. (ed.): W. T. Sculpture 1970-1973. Serpentine Gallery. London 1973 (cat.)

TUTTLE Richard
born **1941** Rahway (NJ)
American sculptor and painter. **1959–1963** Studied at Trinity College, Hartford (CT), and **1963/64** at the Cooper Union in New York. **1963** First paper constructions. **1965** First solo-exhibition at the Betty Parsons Gallery, New York. **1967** Began to produce monochrome dyed polygonal linen cloths, which could be turned, hung, or laid at will. **1968** Travelled to Japan. **1970** Solo-exhibition at the Albright-Knox Art Gallery, Buffalo, and **1972** at the Museum of

Modern Art, New York. **1972–1982** Participation in documenta 5 – 7 in Kassel. **1975** Retrospective at the Whitney Museum of American Art, New York. **1979** Solo-exhibition at the Stedelijk Museum, Amsterdam. Tuttle's works are made mostly of a few simple materials – paper, wood, or cloth. With this minimal range of materials, he explores the boundaries between painting and sculpture.
MONOGRAPHS, CATALOGUES: Elger, D. (ed.): R. T. Sprengel Museum. Hanover 1990 (cat.).– Harris, S. et al. (ed.): R. T. Institute of Contemporary Art. Amsterdam 1991 (cat.).– Harris, S. et al. (ed.): The Poetry of Form. R. T. Drawings from the Vogel Collection. Indianapolis Museum of Art. Indianapolis 1994 (cat.).– Hutchinson, J. et al. (ed.): R. T. London et al. London 1996 (cat.).– Johnen, J.: Poetische Punkte. Der Zufall als Erkennungsprinzip im Werk von R. T. Cologne 1982.– Poetter, J. (ed.): R. T. Chaos, die Form / The Form. Staatliche Kunsthalle Baden-Baden. Stuttgart 1993 (cat.).– Smith, H. (ed.): R. T. From 210 Collage-Drawings. Pasadena Institute of Technology. Pasadena 1989 (cat.).– Stemmler, D. et al. (ed.): R. T. Städtisches Museum Abteiberg. Mönchengladbach 1985 (cat.).– Tucker, M. (ed.): R. T. Whitney Museum of American Art, New York et al. New York 1975 (cat.).– R. T. Stedelijk Museum. Amsterdam 1979 (cat.).– R. T. Musée des Beaux-Arts. Calais 1982 (cat.).– R. T. Two Pinwheel Works 1964-1985. Institute of Contemporary Arts. London 1985 (cat.).– R. T. Musée d'Art Contemporain de Bordeaux. Bordeaux 1986 (cat.).– R. T. Oxyderood / Red Oxide. Museum Boymans-van Beuningen. Rotterdam 1994 (cat.).– Verna, G. and A. (ed.): List of Drawing Material of R. T. Zurich 1979

TUYMANS Luc
born **1958** Mortsel
Belgian painter. **1976–1979** Studied painting at the Sint Lukas Institute in Brussels. **1979/80** at the Ecole Nationale Supérieure des Arts Visuels de la Cambre in Brussels and **1980–1982** at the Académie Royale des Beaux Arts in Antwerp. **1982–1986** Studied history of art at the Free University in Brussels. **1989** First solo-exhibition in Antwerp. **1992** Participation in documenta 9 in

Kassel. **1993** Represented at an exhibition of contemporary art at the Hamburg Deichtorhallen and **1994** at the Hayward Gallery at the "Unbound" exhibition. Tuymans combines traditional painting with frames taken from post-war films and amateur snapshots. The unobtrusive, mostly monochrome colours contrast effectively with the brutality of his subject matter.
MONOGRAPHS, CATALOGUES: Busche, W. v. d. et al. (ed.): L. T. Provinciaal Museum voor Moderne Kunst. Oostende 1990 (cat.).– Helfenstein, J. et al. (ed.): L. T. Premonition. Kunstmuseum Bern et al. Bern 1997 (cat.).– Loock, U. (ed.): L. T. Kunsthalle Bern. Bern 1992 (cat.).– Loock, U. (ed.): L. T. London 1996.– Salzman, G. et al. (ed.): L. T. Chicago et al. 1995 (cat.).– L. T. Museum Haus Lange. Krefeld 1993 (cat.)

TWOMBLY Cy
born **1929** Lexington (VA)
American painter. **1948/49** Studied at the Boston School of Fine Art and **1950–1952** at the Art Students League, New York, and at Black Mountain College in Beria (NC), where he attended courses given by Kline and Motherwell. Travelled with Rauschenberg to Italy, Spain, and North Africa. **1953** After his first solo-exhibition at the Kootz Gallery in New York he exhibited for the first time in Europe at the Galeria d'Arte Contemporanea in Florence. In subsequent years he commuted between Europe and America. **1955/56** Taught in the Art Department of Southern Seminary Junior College, Buena Vista (VA). **1957** Settled in Rome. **1977** and **1982** participation in documenta 6 and 7 in Kassel. Important retrospectives: at the Pompidou Centre, Paris in **1988**, and **1994** at the Museum of Modern Art, New York; the latter was also shown at the Nationalgalerie in Berlin. Most of Twombly's paintings have been produced in series and he likes to group his paintings into cycles. Out of Abstract Expressionism he has developed his own complex and script-like pictorial language. His faint allusive signs and marks are dispersed over a more or less monochrome background, with smudging and delicate hints of colour.
CATALOGUES RAISONNES: Bastian, H. (ed.): C. T. Zeichnungen 1953-1973. Frankfurt-on-Main, Berlin and Vienna 1973.– Bastian, H. (ed.): C. T. Das graphische Werk 1953-1984. Munich 1984 / C. T. A Catalogue Raisonné of the Printed Graphic Work. New York 1984.– Bastian, H. (ed.): C. T. Catalogue Raisonné der Gemälde. 4 vols. Munich 1992-1996.– Lambert, Y. (ed.): C. T. Catalogue raisonné des œuvres sur papier. 1973-1982. 2 vols. Milan 1979-1992.– Roscio, N. del (ed.): C. T. Catalogue Raisonné of Sculpture. Vol. 1: 1946-1997. New York and Munich 1997
MONOGRAPHS, CATALOGUES: Barthes, R.: C. T. Berlin 1983.– Bastian, H.: C. T. Bilder 1952-1976. Frankfurt-on-Main, Berlin and Vienna 1978.– Blistène, B. and

H. Szeemann (ed.). C. T. Centre Georges Pompidou. Paris 1988 (cat.).– Busse, K.-P.: Erzählung, Landschaft und Text im Werk von C. T. Cologne 1997.– Göricke, J.: C. T. Spurensuche. Munich 1994.– Heyden, T.: Zu sehen und zu lesen. Anmerkungen zum Verständnis des Geschriebenen bei C. T. Nuremberg 1986.– Schmidt, K. (ed.): C. T. Malerei, Arbeiten auf Papier 1955-1983. Staatliche Kunsthalle Baden-Baden. Baden-Baden 1984 (cat.).– Schmidt, K. and G. Boehm (ed.): C. T. Serien auf Papier 1957-1987. Städtisches Kunstmuseum Bonn et al. Bonn 1987 (cat.).– Schmidt, K. (ed.): C. T. The Menil Collection. Houston 1989 (cat.).– Szeemann, H. et al. (ed.): C. T. Paintings, Works on Paper, Sculpture. Whitechapel Art Gallery. London 1987 (cat.)/C. T. Bilder, Arbeiten auf Papier, Skulpturen. Kunsthaus Zurich et al. unich 1987 (cat.).– C. T. Paintings and Drawings. Whitney Museum of American Art. New York 1979 (cat.).– C. T. Souvenirs of d'Arros and Gaeta. Thomas Ammann Fine Art. Zurich 1992 (cat.).– Varnedoe, K. (ed.): C. T. A Retrospective. The Museum of Modern Art, New York et al. New York 1994 (cat.)/C. T. Eine Retrospektive. Nationalgalerie, Berlin et al. Munich 1995 (cat.)

TWORKOV Jack
1900 Biala (Poland) – **1982** Provincetown (MA)
Polish-American painter. **1913** Moved to the USA. **1920–1923** Studied at Columbia University, New York and **1923–1925** at the Art Students League in New York. **1928** Took American citizenship. Worked from **1936–1941** as part of the Works Progress Administration Federal Art Project. **1940** First solo-exhibition at the A. C. A. Gallery, New York. **1946** His painting became influenced by De Kooning and the Abstract Expressionists. **1948–1955** Taught at Queens College, New York. **1948–1953** Shared a studio with De Kooning. From **1954** he painted in an abstract style. **1959** Took part in documenta 2 in Kassel. **1963–1969** Taught at Yale University, New Haven (CT). **1964** Retrospective at the Whitney Museum of American Art, New York. After **1969** many of his compostions have a grid-like structure. Retrospectives: **1982** at the Guggenheim Museum, New York, and **1987** at the Pennsylvania Academy of the Fine Arts, Philadelphia. Proponent of Abstract Expressionism and Action Painting. His lyric abstractions are imbued with a strongly atmospheric character, calling up associations with landscapes.
MONOGRAPHS, CATALOGUES: Armstrong, R. and C. Baker (ed.): J. T. Paintings 1928-1982. Pennsylvania Academy of the Fine Arts, Philadelphia et al. Philadelphia 1987 (cat.).– Bryant, E. (ed.): J. T. Whitney Museum New York 1964 (cat.).– Demarco, R. et al. (ed.): J. T. Paintings 1950-1978. Third Eye Centre. Glasgow 1979 (cat.).– Forge, A. (ed.): J. T. Fifteen Years

of Painting. Solomon G. Guggenheim Museum. New York 1982 (cat.)

UECKER Günther
born **1930** Wendorf
German artist. **1949–1953** Studied in Wismar and at the Academy of Arts in East Berlin. **1953–1957** Continued his training at the Düsseldorf Academy. **1957** First nailworks. **1958** Joint-exhibitions with Mack and Piene. Created spirals out of nails, called *Clouages*. **1959** First solo-exhibition at the Azimuth gallery, Milan. First turning discs. **1960** Joined the Zero group. **1962** Took part in the exhibition "nul" at the Stedelijk Museum, Amsterdam, and at "ZERO-Festival" in Düsseldorf. The Zero group tied with the group "N" for first prize at the San Marino Biennale. **1964** Award from the state of North Rhine-Westphalia. **1964–1977** Participation in documenta 3, 4 and 7 in Kassel. **1967** Zero group disbanded. **1970** Participated at the Venice Biennale. **1971** Retrospective at the Moderna Museet, Stockholm. Participation at the São Paulo Biennale. **1972** Made the film *Schwarzraum-Weißraum*. **1974** Stage design for Beethoven's opera *Fidelio* in Bremen. From **1976** professor at the Düsseldorf Academy. **1983** Solo-exhibition at the Kunsthalle Düsseldorf. **1984** Travelled on the Trans-Siberian Express. **1987** Retrospective at the Wilhelm-Hack-Museum, Ludwigshafen, and **1992** at the Museum des 20. Jahrhunderts in Vienna. The rhythmic effects created by the highly differentiated play of light and shade in Uecker's *Great Spiral* works, align him closely with Kinetic Art. The painstaking work of setting the thousands of nails in place one by one was, for the artist, a form of Zen-Buddhist meditation.
WRITINGS: G. U.: Kölnisch – Klause – (Phobien). Cologne 1983.– Wiese, S. v. (ed.): G. U. Schriften. St. Gallen 1979
CATALOGUES RAISONNES: Helms, D. (ed.): G. U. Recklinghausen 1970.– Honisch, D. (ed.): Ü. Mit einem Werkverzeichnis von M. Haedecke (1955-1980). Stuttgart 1982, New York 1986
MONOGRAPHS, CATALOGUES: Gassen, R. W. and B. Holeczek: U. Heidelberg 1987 (cat.).– Helms, D.: G. U. Recklinghausen 1970.– Holeczek, B. et al. (ed.): G. U. Retrospektive. Wilhelm-Hack-Museum, Ludwigshafen. Heidelberg 1987 (cat.).– Honisch, D.: M. Skulpturen. Düsseldorf and Vienna 1986.– Honisch, D.: G. U. eine Retrospektive. Kunsthalle der Hypo-Kulturstiftung. Munich 1993 (cat.).– Jocks, N. (ed.): G. U. Archäologie des Reisens. Cologne 1997.– Schmied, W. (ed.): G. U. Kestner-Gesellschaft, Hanover et al. St. Gallen 1972 (cat.).– Sharp, W.: G. U. New York 1966.– Storms, W. (ed.): U. in Wien. Museum Moderner Kunst, Stiftung Ludwig, Vienna. Stuttgart 1992 (cat.).– Strelow, H. G. U. Cologne 1955.– G. U. Bild-Objekte 1957-1970. Moderna Museet. Stockholm 1971 (cat.).– G. U. Staatsgalerie Stuttgart. Stuttgart 1976 (cat.).– G. U.

Kunstverein Braunschweig. Brunswick 1979 (cat.).– Wolleh, L.: G. U. Eine Dokumentation. Cologne 1971

UHLMANN Hans
1900 Berlin – **1975** Berlin
German sculptor. **1919–1924** Studied at the Technical College in Berlin. **1925** First sculptures. **1926–1933** Taught at the Berlin Academy of Fine Arts. **1929** Visit to France. **1930** First solo-exhibition at the Gurlitt gallery, Berlin. **1933–1935** Imprisoned for "conspiracy". Until **1945** worked as an engineer. **1947** Berlin Art Award. **1950** Taught again at the Berlin Academy. **1952** Prize for drawing at the São Paulo Biennale. **1954** Participation at the Venice Biennale and completion of the sculpture *Concerto* for the foyer of the Berlin Music Academy. Between **1955** and **1977** took part in documenta 1 – 3 and 6 in Kassel. **1968** Retrospective at the Berlin Academy, Berlin. **1975** Solo-exhibition of drawings at the Nationalgalerie, Berlin. Uhlmann's early sculptures, slender, abstract constructions of wire or steel, are reminiscent of the works of the Russian Constructivists such as Gabo. After World War II, his three-dimensional works acquired more elasticity and lightness. The fixed, static sculptures were replaced by free forms articulating space.
CATALOGUES RAISONNES: Brockhaus, C. and J. Merkert (ed.): H. U. 1900-1975. Die Aquarelle und Zeichnungen. Mit einem Werkverzeichnis. Wilhelm-Lehmbruck-Museum, Duisburg et al. Duisburg 1990 (cat.).– Haftmann, W.: H. U. Leben und Werk. Mit einem Werkverzeichnis der Skulpturen von U. Lehmann-Brockhaus. Berlin 1975
MONOGRAPHS, CATALOGUES: Baumgart, F. (ed.): U. Handzeichnungen. Frankfurt-on-Main 1960.– Fuchs, H. (ed.): H. U. Plastik und Zeichnungen. Städtische Kunsthalle Mannheim. Mannheim 1978 (cat.).– Killy, H. E. (ed.): H. U. Akademie der Künste. Berlin 1968 (cat.)

ULLMAN Micha
born **1939** Tel Aviv
Israeli sculptor and object artist. **1960–1964** Studied art at the Bezalel Academy of Art in Tel Aviv. **1973** Participated at the

São Paulo Biennale and **1987** in documenta 8 in Kassel. **1988** Exhibition at the Israel Museum in Jerusalem and **1990** at the Nationalgalerie, Berlin. **1992** Took part again in the documenta in Kassel.
MONOGRAPHS, CATALOGUES: Barzel, A. and J. Sartorius (ed.): M. U. Nationalgalerie. Berlin 1990 (cat.).– Scheps, M. and S. Breitenberg-Semel (ed.): M. U. The Surface. Drawings 1970-1980. Tel Aviv Museum. Tel Aviv 1980 (cat.).– Zamona, Y. and A. Ofek (ed.): M. U. Israel Museum. Jerusalem 1988 (cat.)

UMBO
(Otto Umbehr)
1902 Düsseldorf – **1980** Hanover
German photographer. Self-taught. **1921–1923** Studied at the Bauhaus in Weimar under Itten, Gropius, Kandinsky and Klee. **1924** Took the pseudonym Umbo. Worked as clown, camera man and whitewasher. Co-founder of the Deutscher Fotodienst (German Photographic Service). **1938–1943** Worked for the Ullstein Verlag, Berlin. He was one of the most important photojournalists worldwide in the 20s. **1965–1974** Taught at the Hanover School of Arts and Crafts. Umbo had an avant-garde approach to photography and experimented a great deal. He also made montages.
CATALOGUE RAISONNE: Molderings, H.: U. 1902-1980. Düsseldorf 1996
MONOGRAPHS, CATALOGUES: Holeczek, B. and G. Reinhard (ed.): U. Photographien 1925-1933. Spectrum-Photogalerie im Kunstmuseum Hannover. Hanover 1979 (cat.).– Molderings, H. (ed.): U. Vom Bauhaus zum Bildjournalismus. Kunstverein für die Rheinlande und Westfalen, Düsseldorf et al. Düsseldorf 1995 (cat.)/U. Vom Bauhaus zum Bildjournalismus. Kunstmuseum Bern. Bern 1997 (cat.).– Molderings, H. (ed.): U. Centre National de la Photographie. Paris 1996 (cat.).– U. Kunsthalle Darmstadt. Darmstadt 1981 (cat.)

URSULA
(Ursula Schultze-Bluhm)
1921 Mittenwalde (Mark Brandenburg) – **1999** Cologne
German painter and object artist. **1938** Wrote her first prose before moving to

Berlin. **1945–1953** Worked for the American Cultural Institute in Berlin. **1950** Took up painting and wrote accompanying texts. **1954** Dubuffet discovered her work and exhibited her paintings in his Musée de l'art brut. First solo-exhibition at the Zimmer gallery in Frankfurt am Main. **1955** Married the painter Bernhard Schultze. **1960** Neo-Dadaist assemblage of *objets trouvés*. Exhibitions **1974** at the Kunsthalle Düsseldorf. **1977** Participation in documenta 6 in Kassel. **1979** at the Museum Bochum and **1992** at the Von der Heydt-Museum, Wuppertal.
MONOGRAPHS, CATALOGUES: Fehlemann, S. et al. (ed.): U. Retrospektive. Werke 1951-1992. Von der Heydt-Museum, Wuppertal. Munich 1992 (cat.).– U. Musée des Arts Décoratifs. Paris 1972 (cat.).– U. Städtische Kunsthalle Düsseldorf. Düsseldorf 1974 (cat.).– U. Bilder, Objekte, Zeichnungen. Museum Bochum 1979 (cat.).– U. Kunsthalle Bremen. Bremen 1992 (cat.).

UTRILLO Maurice
(Maurice Valadon)
1883 Paris – **1955** Dax (Landes)
French painter. Illegitimate son of the painter Suzanne Valadon. He lived a dissolute life and was an alcoholic. **1902** A doctor advised his mother to encourage him to take up painting. Though this did not cure his drinking problem, it at least unearthed his natural talent as a painter. Despite continual interruptions for treatment, he was soon able to sell his paintings of picturesque places such as Montmartre in Paris. From **1909** onwards he seldom painted from nature but used postcards as his starting material. **1924** Attempted suicide and then moved in to his mother's apartment in Chateau St.-Bertin (Ain). Encouraged by his publisher, Frapier, took up graphic work. In the 30s Utrillo began to overcome his alcoholism. He married and organised numerous exhibitions, but his new-found success only tempted him to produce more paintings in the same vein as his popular city scenes. **1983** Exhibition "Centenaire de la naissance de M. U." at the Musée Jacquemart-André in Paris.
CATALOGUE RAISONNE: Pétridès, P. (ed.): L'œuvre complet de M. U. 5 vols. Paris 1959-1974
MONOGRAPHS, CATALOGUES: Basler, A.: M. U. Paris 1931.– Carco, F.: U. Paris 1956/M. U. Legende und Wirklichkeit. Zurich 1958.– Coquiot, G.: M. U. Berlin 1925.– Courthion, P.: U. e Montmartre. Milan 1969.– Crespello, J.-P.: U. La bohème et l'ivresse à Montmartre. Paris 1970.– Fabris, J.: U. Sa Vie, son œuvre. Paris 1982.– Fabris, J.: L'Exposition rétrospective de M. U. Odakyu Grande Galerie, Tokyo et al. Tokyo 1985 (cat.).– Fabris, J.: M. U. Paris 1992.– Mac Orlan, P.: U. Paris 1952.– Valore, L.: M. U. mon mari. Paris 1956.– Warnod, J.: U. Paris 1983, New York 1984, Munich 1984.– Werner, A.: M. U. New York 1981

VALLOTTON Félix
1865 Lausanne – **1925** Paris
Swiss painter and graphic artist. Came to Paris at the age of 17 to study at the Académie Julian and was fascinated by the paintings of van Gogh, Gauguin and the Symbolists. **1885** Exhibited for the first time at the Salon des Artistes français in Paris. **1894** Worked as a graphic artist for *La Revue Blanche* and *Rire*. **1902** Participation at the exhibition of the group création at the Salon d'Automne, and exhibited there every year from **1919** to **1925**. **1921–1924** Painted southern landscapes. **1925** Retrospective at the Museum Arlaud, Lausanne. **1929** Organised an exhibition entitled "Vallotton inconnu" at the Drouet gallery in Paris **1992** Exhibitions at the Musée Cantonal des Beaux-Arts, Lausanne and **1995** at the Kunsthalle der Hypo-Kulturstiftung, Munich. An important principle in Vallotton's approach to painting was to avoid merely "copying" nature. His works contain elements of Symbolism and Art Nouveau. The realist style of his paintings anticipates Neue Sachlichkeit.
CATALOGUES RAISONNES: Vallotton, M. and C. Goerg (ed.): F. V. Catalogue raisonné de l'œuvre gravé et lithographié. Geneva 1972/F. V. Catalogue Raisonné of the Printed Graphic Work. Geneva 1972
MONOGRAPHS, CATALOGUES: Brodskaia, N.: F. V. Le Nabi étranger. Bornemouth 1996.– Busch, G. et al. (ed.): F. V. Leben und Werk. Frauenfeld 1982/V. Vie et œuvre. Lausanne 1985.– Ducrey, M.: F. V. La Vie, la technique, l'œuvre peint. Lausanne 1989/V. His Life, His Technique, His Paintings. Lausanne 1989.– Ducrey, M. et al. (ed.): F. V. Kunsthalle der Hypo-Kulturstiftung, Munich et al. Munich 1995 (cat.).– Friedrich, A.: F. V. Zurich 1979.– Guisan, G. and D. Jakubec (ed.): F. V. Documents pour une biographie et pour l'histoire d'une œuvre. 3 vols. Paris 1973-1975.– Hahnloser-Bühler, H.: F. V. et ses amis. Paris 1936.– Horn, U. (ed.): F. V. Berlin 1987.– Jourdain, F.: F. V. Geneva 1953.– Jover, M. (ed.): F. V. Gravures sur bois. Monaco 1993.– Koella, R.: Das Bild der Landschaft im Schaffen von F. V. Zurich 1970.– Koella, R. (ed.): F. V. Bilder, Zeichnungen, Graphik. Kunstmuseum Winterthur et al. Winterthur 1978 (cat.).– Koella, R. (ed.): F. V. Kunsthalle der Hypo-Kulturstiftung, Munich et al. Munich 1995 (cat.).– Monnier, J.: F. V. Lausanne 1970.– Newman, S. M. (ed.): F. V. A Retrospective. Yale University Art Gallery, New Haven et al. New Haven (CT) 1991 (cat.).– Newman, S. M. et al.: F. V. New York 1992, Paris 1992.– Saint-James, A.: V. Dessinateur de presse. Paris 1979.– Schultze, J. et al. (ed.): F. V. Das druckgraphische Werk. Kunsthalle Bremen. Bremen 1981 (cat.)/F. V. Das druckgraphische Werk. Rupertinum. Salzburg 1987 (cat.).– F. V. Musée Cantonal des Beaux-Arts. Lausanne 1992 (cat.).– Vierney, D. et al. (ed.): Le nu dans l'œuvre de F. V. Musée Maillol. Paris 1997 (cat.)

VALMIER Georges
1885 Valmier – **1937** Paris
French painter. **1905** Studied at the Académie des Beaux-Arts in Paris. **1913/14** Participated in the Salon des Indépendants in Paris. **1914** Military service. **1919** First solo-exhibition at the Galerie de l'Effort Moderne run by the art dealer Rosenberg in Paris. **1920** Exhibited with the Section d'Or. **1921** Designed the front cover of the journal *Bulletin de l'Effort Moderne*. **1922/23** Stage designs for M. Jacob, Marinetti and others. **1925** Took part in the exhibition "L'Art d'Aujourd'hui" in Paris. **1926** Participated in the exhibition of the Société Anonyme at the Brooklyn Museum, New York. **1929/30** Participated in the Salon des Surindépendants and **1935** in the Abstraction-Création exhibition in Paris. **1937** Decorations for the Paris World Fair. Valmier's style has close links to Cubist painting, his fragmented images becoming increasingly abstract in the course of his career.
CATALOGUE RAISONNE: Bazetoux, D. (ed.): G. V. Catalogue raisonné. Paris 1991
MONOGRAPHS, CATALOGUES: Bettex-Cailler, N.: G. V. Geneva 1956.– Pillement, G. (ed.): G. V. Œuvres de 1917 à 1935. Galerie Melki. Paris 1973 (cat.)

VANTONGERLOO Georges
1886 Antwerp – **1965** Paris
Belgian painter, sculptor and architect. Studied at the Antwerp and Brussels Academies of Art. **1914–1917** Military service. **1916** Went to Holland and met Mondrian and van Doesburg. **1917** Founder-member of the group De Stijl, and until **1920** contributor to the journal of the same name. **1923** Took part in the De Stijl exhibition at the Galerie de l'Effort Moderne in Paris and **1926** in the exhibition of the Société Anonyme at the Brooklyn Museum, New York. **1924** Publication of his article *L'art et son avenir*. **1927** Moved to Paris. **1931–1937** Founder-member and vice-president of the group Abstraction-Création. **1936** Participated in the exhibition "Cubism and Abstract Art" at the Museum of Modern Art, New York. **1943** Solo-exhibition at the Galerie de Berri, Paris. Participated **1946** in the first Salon des Réalités Nouvelles in Paris, **1949** in a joint-exhibition with Bill and Pevsner at the Kunsthaus Zurich and **1952** in the De Stijl exhibition at the Museum of Modern Art, New York. Retrospectives: **1962** at the Marlborough Gallery, London and **1981** at the Kunsthaus Zurich and at the Musées Royaux des Beaux-Arts de Belgique, Brussels. His plastic, mathematically constructed works are an attempt to apply scientific thinking to art. In his abstract sculpture, Vantongerloo extends the formal theories developed by Mondrian to three dimensions, anticipating the Bauhaus approach to architecture. However, after **1937** Vantongerloo introduced rhythmic curving lines, rejecting Mondrian's idea that only rectangular constructions reflect the harmony of the universe.

WRITINGS: G. V.: L'Art et son avenir. Antwerp 1924
MONOGRAPHS, CATALOGUES: Bill, M. (ed.): G. V. Paintings, Sculptures, Reflections. Marlborough Fine Arts Ltd. New York 1948 (cat.).– Ceuleers, J. v. (ed.): G. V. Antwerp et al. Antwerp 1996 (cat.).– Livingston, J. (ed.): G. V. Corcoran Gallery of Art, Washington et al. Washington and Brussels 1980 (cat.).– Thomas, A.: Denkbilder. Materialien zur Entwicklung von G. V. bis 1921. Düsseldorf 1987.– G. V. Musées Royaux des Beaux-Arts de Belgique. Brussels 1981 (cat.).– G. V. Kunsthaus Zürich. Zurich 1981 (cat.).– G. V. Akademie der Künste, Berlin et al. Berlin 1986 (cat.)

VASARELY Victor
(Gyözö Vásárhelyi)
1908 Pécs (Hungary) – **1997** Paris
Hungarian-born French painter and graphic artist. **1928–1930** Entered Sandor Bortnyik's private school of graphic art where he encountered the works of the Russian Constructivists. **1930** Settled in Paris, doing mostly graphic work. From **1944** devoted himself to painting again and from his systematic observations of optical illusions developed a method of geometric abstraction in which an impression of movement is created through visual ambiguity. **1951** First kinetic paintings. From **1955** he designed murals and reliefs in ceramic, aluminium and other metals, mostly for buildings in France. **1955–1968** Participation in documenta 1–4 in Kassel. From **1961** lived in Annet-sur-Marne. **1970** Opening of a museum dedicated to his works in Gardes (Vaucluse). There are two further Vasarely museums in Pécs and Budapest. **1976** Inauguration of the Fondation Vasarely in Aix-en-Provence, which provided the financial backing for the Institute of Contemporary Design and Architecture, opened in **1981**. **1982** Opening of the Vasarely Centre in Oslo. Vasarely is the most creative representative of Op Art. The different hues and arrangements of his brightly coloured geometric shapes create an impression of perpetual movement.
WRITINGS: Ferrier, J.-L.: Entretiens avec V. V. Paris 1969/Gespräche mit V. V. Cologne 1971.– V. V.: Plasticité. Paris 1969.– V. V.: Notes brutes. Paris 1972.– V. V.: Gea. Budapest 1986
CATALOGUE RAISONNE: Joray, M. et al. (ed.): V. V. 4 vols. Neuchâtel 1965-1980
MONOGRAPHS, CATALOGUES: Blomstedt, J.: V. Helsinki 1960.– Brück, A.: V.-Analysen. Hamburg 1970.– Dahhan, B.: V. V. ou La connaissance d'un art moléculaire. Paris 1979.– Diehl, G.: V. V. Paris 1973, Bindlach 1984.– Joray, M. (ed.): V. V. 3 vols. Neuchâtel 1969-1974.– Knierim, R.: V. und der Konstruktivismus. Diss. Bochum 1978.– Motte, M. d. la and A. Tolnay (ed.). V. Werke aus sechs Jahrzehnten. Stuttgart 1986 (cat.).– Schmied, W.: V. V. Wegebereiter zur Modernen Kunst. Hanover 1967.– Schröder, K. A. (ed.): V. V. Kunst-

forum Wien der Bank Austria, Vienna. Munich 1992 (cat.).– Spies, W.: V. V. Cologne 1958.– Spies, W.: V. Teuffen 1969, New York 1971.– V. V. inconnu / The Unknown V./ Der unbekannte V. Neuchâtel 1977.– Weikert, H.: V. V. Begegnung mit Kunstwerken. Munich 1971

VASULKA Steina and Woody
born **1940** Reykjavik (Steina)
born **1937** Brno (Woody)
Steina Vasulka: Icelandic musician and video artist. **1959** Scholarship from the Czechoslovakian Ministry of Culture to study at the Conservatory of Music in Prague. **1964** Married Woody Vasulka and, for a short time, played with the Iceland Symphony Orchestra. **1965** Moved with Woody to New York, where she worked as a freelance musician. From **1969** made videos with Woody. **1973 – 1975** Began the project *Machine Vision*, an on-going exploration of spatial effects created with mechanical systems and electronic imaging techniques. **1979** Faculty member at the Center for Media Study, State University of New York, Buffalo. **1980** Moved to Santa Fe. **1992** Together with Woody, won the American Film Institute Maya Deren Award and **1995** the Siemens Prize for Media Art from the ZKM in Karlsruhe.
Woody Vasulka: Czechoslovakian media artist. Studied engineering in Brno. **1964** Diploma in film production and direction from the School of Performing Arts in Prague. **1965** Founded the electronic media theatre The Kitchen with A. Mannik. **1973 – 1979** Lived in Buffalo, teaching at the Center for Media Study. From **1993** professor at the Polytechnic in Brno.
MONOGRAPHS, CATALOGUES: Sturken, M. (ed.): S. and W. V. Machine Media. San Francisco Museum of Modern Art. San Francisco 1996 (cat.).– Willoughby, D. (ed.): S. and W. V. Vidéastes 1969-1984. Ciné-MBXA/Cinédoc. Paris 1984 (cat.).– Youngblood, G. (ed.): Video by S. and W. V. Denver Art Museum. Denver 1992 (cat.)

VEDOVA Emilio
born **1919** Venice
Italian painter. Self-taught. **1937–1940** Lived in Rome and Florence. **1942** Joined the artists' group Corrente. First solo-exhibition at the Galleria Spiga in Milan. **1943-1945** Active in the resistance movement. **1946** Joined the group Fronte Nuovo delle Arti. **1947** Participation at the Venice Biennale. **1951** Solo-exhibition at the Catherine Viviano Gallery, New York. **1954** Trip to Brazil. **1955 – 1982** Took part in documenta 1–3 and 7 in Kassel. **1957** Guggenheim Award, and **1960** major prize at the Venice Biennale. **1961** Stage design for L. Nono's Opera *Intolleranza* in Venice. **1964/65** Visited Berlin and the USA. From **1975** taught at the Accademia di Belle Arti in Venice. **1984** Retrospective at the Museo Correr, Venice, and **1986** at the Staatsgalerie Moderner Kunst, Munich. **1993** Solo-exhibition at the Museo d'Arte Moderna, Lugano. Many of Vedova's paintings depict violent political upheavals and were intended as protests against injustice and repression. Since the 60s he has been regarded as the leading exponent of L'art informel in Italy.
WRITINGS: Haftmann, W. (ed.): E. V. Blätter aus dem Tagebuch. Munich 1960
MONOGRAPHS, CATALOGUES: Argan, G. C. and M. Calvesi: V. Compresenze 1946-1981. Milan 1981.– Cela, C. J. et al.: La pintura de V. Palma de Mallorca 1962.– Celant, G. (ed.): V. 1935-1984. Museo Correr, Venice. Milan 1984 (cat.).– Chiappini, R. (ed.): E. V. Museo d'Arte Moderna, Lugano. Milan 1993 (cat.).– Eccher, D. (ed.): E. V. Gallerie Civica d'Arte Contemporaneo. Trento 1996 (cat.).– Haftmann, W.: E. V. Munich 1960.– Mahlow, D. et al. (ed.): E. V. Staatliche Kunsthalle Baden-Baden. Baden-Baden 1965 (cat.).– Marchiori, G.: E. V. Venice 1951.– Schilling, J. (ed.): E. V. Kunstverein Braunschweig. Brunswick 1981 (cat.).– Schmied, W. (ed.): V. und Salzburg. Salzburg 1988.– Schulz-Hoffmann, C. et al. (ed.): E. V. Staatsgalerie moderner Kunst, Munich et al. Munich 1986 (cat.).– E. V. Malerei. Wiener Sezession. Vienna 1987 (cat.)

VELDE Bram van
1892 Zoeterwoude – **1981** Grimaud
Dutch painter. **1907–1914** Apprenticed to a decorator in The Hague. **1922/23** Moved to the artists' colony in Worpswede where he began to do paintings. **1924** Went to Paris where he encountered Impressionism and contemporary art. **1932** Moved to Mallorca, but returned to Paris in **1936**, at the outbreak of the Spanish Civil War. **1937** Friendship with S. Beckett. **1946** First solo-exhibition at the Galerie de Mai von Pierre Loeb in Paris. **1952** Solo-exhibition at the Galerie Maeght, Paris. **1964** Participation in documenta 3 in Kassel. **1958** Retrospective at the Kunsthalle Bern. **1959** Moved to Geneva. Retrospectives **1960** at the Stedelijk Museum in Amsterdam, **1966** at the Wallraf-Richartz Museum in Cologne, **1989** at the Musée National d'Art Moderne in Paris and **1996** at the Musée Rath, Geneva. Velde developed a highly individual pictorial language with some Expressionist and Fauvist elements but also close affinities to L'art informel.
CATALOGUES RAISONNES: Mason, R. M. and J. Putman (ed.): B. v. V. Les Lithographies 1923-1981. 3 vols. Paris and Geneva 1973-1984.– Putman, J. and C. Juliet (ed.): B. v. V. Catalogue raisonné de l'œuvre peint 1907-1960. Paris 1975
MONOGRAPHS, CATALOGUES: Beckett, S. et al. (ed.): B. v. V. Paris 1958, New York 1960.– Becket, S. and F. Meyer (ed.): B. v. V. Albright-Knox Art Gallery. Buffalo 1968 (cat.).– Greshoff, J. et al. (ed.): B. v. V. 1895-1981. Bonnefantenmuseum, Maastricht et al. The Hague 1989 (cat.).– Gribaudo, E. (ed.): B. v. V. Torino 1970.– Juliet, C.: Rencontres avec B. v. V. Saint-Clement-de-Rivière 1995 / Begegnungen mit B. v. V. Tübingen 1989.– Mason, R. M. (ed.): B. v. V. 1895-1981. Retrospective du centenaire. Musée Rath, Geneva 1996 (cat.).– Peyré, Y.: D'un accès de vision. B. v. V. Paris 1994.– Slagter, E.: B. v. V. Een hommage. Leyden 1994.– Stoullig, C. et al. (ed.): B. v. V. Centre Georges Pompidou, Paris et al. Paris 1989 (cat.).– B. v. V. Musée National d'Art Moderne. Paris 1970 (cat.).– B. v. V. Fondation Maeght. Saint-Paul 1973 (cat.).– B. v. V. Musée d'Art et d'Industrie de Saint-Etienne. Saint-Etienne 1985 (cat.)

VEREFKIN Marianne von
1860 Tula (Russia) – **1938** Ascona
Russian painter. **1883** Began to study at the Moscow School of Art. **1886** Moved with her family to St. Petersburg where she took private lessons from Repin. **1888** Shot herself in the right hand while hunting and never recovered the use of it. **1891** Came to know Javlensky with whom she moved to Munich in **1896**. Gave up her own painting for nine years. **1906** Met Franz von Lenbach and Franz von Stuck. **1908** Painted with Kandinsky, Münter and Javlensky in Murnau. **1909–1912** Joined the Neue Künstlervereinigung in Munich. **1912** Exhibited with the Blauer Reiter. **1913** Participated in the First German Autumn Salon in Berlin. **1914** Moved with Javlensky to Switzerland and **1919** to Ascona. **1921** Separated from Javlensky. **1924** Founded the artists' group Der Große Bär, organising a group exhibition in **1928** with Schmidt-Rottluff and Rohlfs at the Berlin gallery Nierendorf. Verefkin was originally influenced by the Nabis and Fauves but over the years moved closer to German Expressionism.
WRITINGS: Weiler, C. (ed.): M. v. W. Briefe an einen Unbekannten 1901-1905. Cologne 1960
MONOGRAPHS, CATALOGUES: Brögmann, N. (ed.): M. v. W. Œuvres peintes 1907-1936. Fondation Neumann. Gingis 1996 (cat.).– Fäthke, B.: M. v. W. Leben und Werk 1860-1938. Munich 1988.– Federer, K. (ed.): M. v. W. Zeugnis und Bild. Zurich 1975.– Hahl-Koch, J.: M. v. W. und der russische Symbolismus. Munich 1967.– Russ, S. et al. (ed.): M. v. W. Gemälde und Skizzen. Landesmuseum Wiesbaden. Wiesbaden 1980 (cat.)

VIEIRA DA SILVA Maria Elena
1908 Lisbon – **1992** Paris
Portuguese painter. Originally wanted to be a sculptress and took lessons from E. Bourdelle and C. Despiau in Paris. First worked as an industrial designer and illustrator. **1928/29** Entered the studios of Friesz and Léger, and **1932** studied at the Académie Ranson under Bissière. **1933** First solo-exhibition at the Jeanne Bucher gallery in Paris. **1936** Took part in the exhibition "Ecole de Paris". **1940–1947** Moved to Portugal, then on to Brazil, returning to Paris after the war. **1954** Participated at the Venice Biennale and, between **1955** and **1964**, in documenta 1 – 3 in Kassel. Major retrospectives in Paris and Lisbon. Vieira da Silva's sophisticated networks of subtle, grey-toned lines are like labyrinthine urban visions. In her later works, her structures and tones became more lyrical.
CATALOGUES RAISONNES: Duval, V. et al. (ed.): M. E. V. d. S. Monographie und Catalogue raisonné. 2 vols. Geneva 1993-1994.– Weelen, G. (ed.): V. D. S. Les Estampes 1929-1976. Paris 1977.– Weelen, G. and J.-F. Jaeger: V. D. S. Catalogue raisonné. Geneva 1994
MONOGRAPHS, CATALOGUES: Brouwer, C. d. and A. Mommens (ed.): V. d. S. dans les collections portugaises. Musée d'Art Moderne, Brussels. Tervuren 1991 (cat.).– Butor, M.: V. d. S. Peintures. Paris 1983.– Cesariny, M.: V. d. S. Lisbon 1984.– Descargues, P.: V. d. S. Paris 1950.– Esteban, C. (ed.): V. d. S. Peintures 1935-1969. Musée National d'Art Moderne, Paris et al. Paris 1969 (cat.).– Grynpas N. A. (ed.): V. d. S. Fundação Calouste Gulbenkian, Lisbon et al. Paris and Geneva 1988 (cat.).– Jaeger, J.-F. (ed.): V. d. S. La Densité de la transparence. Galerie J. Bucher. Paris 1986 (cat.).– Lassaigne, J. (ed.): V. d. S. Musée de Peinture et de Sculpture, Grenoble et al. Grenoble 1980 (cat.).– Lassaigne, J. and G. Weelen: V. d. S. Paris 1987, 1992, New York 1979.– Luís, A. B.: Longos dias têm cem anos presença de V. d. S. Lisbon 1982.– Terrasse, A.: L'Univers de V. d. S. Paris 1977.– Vallier, D.: V. d. S. Paris 1971.– Vallier, D.: Chemins d'approche. V. d. S. Paris 1982.– V. d. S. Fundação Calouste Gulbenkian. Lisbon 1977 (cat.).– Weelen, G.: V. d. S. Œuvres sur papier. Paris 1983

VILLEGLE Jacques de la
born **1926** Quimper (Brittany)
French artist. **1944–1946** Studied at the Ecole des Beaux-Arts in Rennes. **1945** Came to know Raymond Hains and worked with him until **1950**. From **1947–1949** studied architecture in Nantes. **1949** Moved to Paris. From **1950** carried out various film projects. **1953** Published the book *Hépérile éclaté* with Hains. **1957** Organised the exhibition "Affiches

lacérées", displaying torn posters. **1959** First solo-exhibition at the studio of François Dufrêne in Paris. Participation at the Biennale des Jeunes in Paris. **1960** Co-founder of the group Nouveaux Réalistes. Solo-exhibitions **1965** at the Museum Haus Lange, Krefeld, **1971** at the Moderna Museet, Stockholm, and **1977** at the Pompidou Centre, Paris. **1986** Took part in the exhibition "1960 les Nouveaux Réalistes" at the Musée d'Art Moderne de la Ville de Paris. Villeglé is an affichist or "poster ripper" and a representative of Nouveau Réalisme.
WRITINGS: J. d. la V.: Les Volantes du ravisseur. La Louvière 1974.– J. d la V.: L'Innocence du choix. Nice 1982
CATALOGUE RAISONNE: Fornet, C. et al. (ed.): J. d. la V. Catalogue thématique des affiches lacérées de V. 14 vols. Paris 1988ff.
MONOGRAPHS, CATALOGUES: Hahn, O. and J. d. la Villeglé (ed.): V. retrospektivt 1949-1971. Moderna Museet. Stockholm 1971 (cat.).– Lamarche-Vadel, B.: V. La Présentation en jugement. Paris 1990.– Restany, P. (ed.): V. Témoin de notre temps. Galerie Beaubourg. Paris 1974 (cat.).– J. d. la V. Lacéré anonyme. Centre Georges Pompidou. Paris 1977 (cat.).– J. d. la V. Le Retour de l'hourloupe. Maison de la Culture. Rennes 1985 (cat.).– J. d. la V. Galerie du Génie. Paris 1988 (cat.)

VILLON Jacques
(Gaston Duchamp)
1875 Damville – **1963** Puteaux
French painter. Brother of Marcel Duchamp and Raymond Duchamp-Villon. **1894** Moved to Paris and trained at the Atelier Cormon. **1905** Joint-exhibition with Duchamp-Villon in Rouen. **1911/12** Founder-member of Section d'Or with Picabia, Léger and Metzinger. **1914–1918** Military service. **1919** Took up abstract painting. From **1920** worked mainly as a graphic artist. **1922** Exhibited with the Société Anonyme in New York. From **1931** resumed abstract painting. **1935** Went to the USA. **1939** Participated in the first Salon des Réalités Nouvelles in Paris. **1950** Carnegie Award. **1951** Retrospective at the Musée National d'Art Moderne, Paris. **1955–1964** Participation in documenta 1–3 in Kassel. **1956** Major prize at the Venice

Biennale. Retrospectives **1960** at the Moderna Museet, Stockholm, **1963** at the Kunsthaus Zurich and **1975** at the Musée des Beaux-Arts, Rouen. Villon's painting is rooted in Cubism, but developed into an individual style with bright colours and simplified forms.
WRITINGS: J. V.: Couleurs et construction. Caen 1985
CATALOGUES RAISONNES: Auberty, J. and C. Perusseaux (ed.): J. V. Œuvre gravé. Paris 1954.– Ginestet, C. d. and C. Pouillon (ed.): V. Les Estampes et les illustrations. Paris 1979
MONOGRAPHS, CATALOGUES: Groot, I. M. d. (ed.): J. V. Grafiek uit een particuliere verzameling. Rijksmuseum. Amsterdam 1984 (cat.).– Lassaigne, J.: J. V. Paris 1950.– Lassalle, H. and O. Popovitch (ed.): J. V. Musée des Beaux-Arts, Rouen et al. Paris 1975 (cat.).– Mellquist, J.: Les Caricatures de J. V. ou la marge de l'indulgence. Geneva 1960.– Pressat, R. et al. (ed.): J. V. L'œuvre gravé. Musée du Dessin et de l'Estampe originale. Gravelines 1989 (cat.).– Robbins, D. (ed.): J. V. Fogg Art Museum, Cambridge (MA). Boston 1976 (cat.).– J. V. Kunsthaus Zürich. Zurich 1963 (cat.).– J. V. Musée Campredon. L'Isle-sur-la-Sorgue 1992 (cat.).– Wick, P. A. (ed.): J. V. Master of Graphic Art 1875-1963. Museum of Fine Arts, Boston. New York 1964 (cat.)

VIOLA Bill
born **1951** Flushing (NY)
American video artist. Up to **1973** studied at the College of Visual and Performing Arts at Syracuse University in New York. **1973–1980** Collaborated with M. Cunningham D. Tudor on the work *Rainforest*. **1974** First solo-presentation of video installations at The Kitchen, New York. **1974–1976** Technical director of Art/Tapes/22 in Florence. **1976–1980** Artist-in-residence at the TV station WNET, New York. **1977** Took part in documenta 6 in Kassel. **1980/81** Visited Japan. **1981** Moved to Long Beach (CA). **1983** Solo-exhibition at the Musée d'Art Moderne de la Ville de Paris. **1987** Retrospective at the Museum of Modern Art, New York, and **1992** at the Kunsthalle Düsseldorf. Took part in documenta 9 in Kassel. **1995** Participation at the Venice Biennale. Viola exploits the technical possibilities of modern media with a high degree of perfection, but uses technology purely to serve his artistic ends and put across the central theme of his works: the basic human experiences of birth and death.
WRITINGS: Violette, R. and B. V. (ed.): B. V. Reasons for Knocking at an Empty House. Writings 1973-1994. Cambridge (MA) 1994, London 1995
CATALOGUE RAISONNE: Pühringer, A. (ed.): B. V. Salzburger Kunstverein. Klagenfurt 1994 (cat.)
MONOGRAPHS, CATALOGUES: Boyle, D. et al. (ed.): B. V. Musée d'Art Moderne de la Ville de Paris. Paris 1983 (cat.).– Boyle, D. et al. (ed.): B. V. Survey of a Decade.

Contemporary Arts Museum. Houston 1988 (cat.).– Brown, J. (ed.): B. V. Museum of Contemporary Art. Los Angeles 1985 (cat.).– Hentschel, M. and H. Paflik-Huber (ed.): B. V. Stations. Württembergischer Kunstverein. Stuttgart 1996 (cat.).– London, B. et al. (ed.): B. V. Installations and Video-tapes. The Museum of Modern Art. New York 1987 (cat.).– Mayes, C. S. (ed.): B. V. The City of Man. Brockton Art Museum. Brockton 1989 (cat.).– Ross, D. et al. (ed.): B. V. Los Angeles County Museum of Art, Los Angeles et al. New York 1997.– Syring, M. L. (ed.): B. V. Nie gesehene Bilder. Städtische Kunsthalle Düsseldorf et al. Düsseldorf 1992 (cat.).– Vierny, D. et al.: V. Paris 1979.– B. V. Slowly Turning Narrative. Institute of Contemporary Art, Philadelphia et al. Philadelphia 1992 (cat.).– B. V. Solomon R. Guggenheim Museum (Soho). New York 1997 (cat.).– B. V. Mas allas de la mirada. Museo Nacional Centro de Arte Reina Sofía. Madrid 1993 (cat.).– Wallace, I. (ed.): B. V. Institute of Contemporary Arts, London et al. London 1984.– Zeitlin, M. A. (ed.): B. V. Buried Secrets. The United States Pavillon 46th Venice Biennale, Venice/Arizona State University Art Museum, Tempe. Tempe 1995 (cat.).– Zutter, J. (ed.): B. V. Museum für Gegenwartskunst. Basel 1987 (cat.)

VIRNICH Thomas
born **1957** Eschweiler (near Aachen)
German painter and object artist. **1978–1981** Studied at the Technical College in Aachen under J. Bandau. **1981–1985** Studied painting at the Düsseldorf Academy under A. Hüppi and E. Gomringer. **1983** First solo-exhibition at the Rosenthal gallery in Selb. Travel grant and award from the City of Aachen. Given a special promotion stand at the art fair Art Cologne in Cologne. **1985** Grant from the state of North Rhine-Westphalia and exhibition at the Museum Abteiberg, Mönchengladbach. **1987** Took part in documenta 8 in Kassel.
MONOGRAPHS, CATALOGUES: Gercke, H. et al. (ed.): T. V. Kunstverein Bonn et al. Bonn 1988 (cat.).– Tacke, C. (ed.): T. V. Kunstraum. Munich 1986 (cat.).– T. V. Kunstverein Braunschweig. Brunswick 1966 (cat.)

VISSER Carel
born **1928** Papendrecht
Dutch sculptor. **1948/49** Studied architecture at the Technical College in Delft. **1949–1951** Studied art at the Royal Academy of Fine Arts in The Hague. **1952** Moved to Amsterdam. **1954** First solo-exhibition at the art dealer's Martinet in Amsterdam. **1958–1962** Taught at the Royal Academy in The Hague. **1962** Guest-professor at the University of Washington. From **1966** taught at Atelier '63 in Haarlem. **1968** Represented the Netherlands at the Venice Biennale and took part in documenta 4 in

Kassel. **1972** Awarded the Dutch national prize for architecture and sculpture and, in **1992**, the art prize from the City of Amsterdam. **1985** Retrospective at the Boymans-van Beuningen Museum, Rotterdam, and **1990** at the Sprengel Museum, Hanover.
MONOGRAPHS, CATALOGUES: Blees, F. (ed.): C. V. Van Reekum Museum. Apeldoorn 1992 (cat.).– Blok, C.: C. V. Amsterdam 1968.– Blotkamp, C.: C. V. Utrecht and Antwerp 1989.– Elger, D. (ed.): C. V. Sprengel Museum. Hanover 1990 (cat.).– Fuchs, R. (ed.): C. V. Beelden, tekeningen, collages. Stedelijk Van Abbe Museum. Amsterdam 1975 (cat.).– Sculptor's Work by C. V. Whitechappel Art Gallery. London 1978 (cat.).– C. V. Neuere Skulpturen und Zeichnungen. Städtische Kunsthalle Düsseldorf. Düsseldorf 1977 (cat.).– C. V. Werken 1975-1985. Museum Boymans-van Beuningen. Rotterdam 1985 (cat.).– C. V. Gemeentemuseum. The Hague 1994 (cat.)

VIVIN Louis
1861 Hadol – **1936** Paris
French painter. Self-taught. **1879–1922** Worked for the post office. **1889** Exhibited at the Salon of the Postal Ministry. **1898** Moved to Paris. After his retirement in **1922**, he devoted himself entirely to painting until paralysis of his right arm prevented him from working anymore. Around **1925** met the art historian Wilhelm Uhde, who recognised his talent and promoted him. **1955** Posthume participation in documenta 1 in Kassel. The naive painter Vivin specialised in hunting scenes, still lifes with flowers and, above all, street scenes and paintings of buildings, which he faithfully reconstructed on paper in minute detail. He often used postcards as his starting material, but gave the pictures a strange, somewhat bleak atmosphere.
MONOGRAPHS, CATALOGUES: Hommage à L. V. Musée du Vieux-Château. Laval 1985 (cat.).– Jakovsky, A.: L. V. Peintre de Paris. Paris 1953.– V. His Paris. Perls Gallery. New York 1971 (cat.)

VLAMINCK Maurice de
1876 Paris – **1958** Rueil-la-Gadelière (Eure-et-Loir)
Flemish-born French painter. **1892** Left home and went to live on the island of

Chatou on the Seine. Was a racing cyclist for a time, and earned his living playing violin in a provincial orchestra. Around **1900** he began to paint, sharing a studio in Chatou, near Paris, with Derain. After seeing the **1901** van Gogh exhibition in Paris he became intoxicated with colour. Up to **1907** applied pure unmixed paints with violent brush strokes. Works exhibited by Vollard in Paris. His style was even bolder than that of the other Fauves. **1908** The Fauves began to disband, and Vlaminck aligned himself more with Cézanne and the Cubists. Following Derain's example, he began to paint sombre, dramatic compositions in a romantic realist style. After **1918** he retired to the country and became something of a recluse. **1943** Publication of his highly controversial book *Portraits avant décès*, drawing the attention of the German occupying forces to several other artists. **1944** Acquitted by a special French court.
WRITINGS: Sauvage, M. (ed.).: M. de V. Mein Testament. Gespräche und Bekenntnisse. Zurich 1959.– M. de V.: Tournant dangereux. Souvenirs de ma vie. Paris 1929.– M. de V.: Les Pensées et la voix. Paris 1983
CATALOGUES RAISONNES: Walterskirchen, K. v. (ed.).: M. d. V. Verzeichnis des graphischen Werkes. Bern 1974.– Wildenstein Institute (ed.): M. de V. Catalogue raisonné (in preparation)
MONOGRAPHS, CATALOGUES: Carco, F.: M. d. V. Paris 1925.– Crespelle, J.-P.: V. Fauve de la peinture. Paris 1958.– Genevoix, M.: M. V. l'homme. Paris 1954.– MacOrlan, P.: V. Peintures 1900-1945. Paris 1945, New York 1958.– Perls, K.: G. V. New York 1941.– Pollag, S.: Mes souvenirs sur V. Geneva 1958.– Rey, R.: M. d. V. Munich 1956.– Sauvage, M.: V. Sa Vie et son message. Geneva 1956.– Selz, J.: V. Paris 1963.– Vallès-Bled, M. and M.-L. Imhoff (ed.): V. Il pittore e la critica. Milan 1988 (cat.).– M. V. Kunstmuseum Bern. Bern 1961 (cat.)

sculpture at the Technical College in Hanover. First abstract paintings. **1922–1924** Entered the studio of Vierthaler. **1923** Studied at the Weimar Bauhaus. **1924** Trip to London. Co-founder of the group "k". Came to know Arp, Schwitters and Doesburg, and subsequently joined the De Stijl group. **1926** Exhibited with the Société Anonyme at the Museum of Modern Art, New York. **1927** Co-founder of the group die abstrakten hannover. **1929** First solo-exhibition at the Povolozky gallery, Paris. **1930** Contact with the Cercle et Carré artists in Paris. **1936/37** Long stays in Berlin and Zurich. **1937** Moved to Amsterdam. **1939** Participation in the exhibition "Réalités Nouvelles" in Paris. **1941** Came to know Beckmann. **1942** Director of Edition Duwaer in Amsterdam. From **1954** taught at the Ulm School of Design. **1955** and **1959** participation in documenta 1 and 2 in Kassel. Retrospectives: **1974** at the Juda Gallery, London, and **1985** at the Wilhelm-Hack-Museum, Ludwigshafen. With his abstract compositions reduced to the most elementary forms, Vordemberge-Gildewart is representative of the Constructivist movement initiated by Doesburg.
WRITINGS: Helms, D. (ed.): F. V.-G.: Schriften und Vorträge. St. Gallen 1976.– F. V.-G.: Millimeter und Geraden. Amsterdam 1940.– F. V.-G.: "abstract-concrett-absolut". Baden-Baden 1954
CATALOGUE RAISONNE: Helms, D. and A. Valstar-Verhoff (ed.): F. V.-G. The Complete Works. Munich 1990
MONOGRAPHS, CATALOGUES: Helms, D.: V.-G. Göttingen 1972.– Helms, D. (ed.): V.-G. Baugestaltung. Landesmuseum Wiesbaden. Wiesbaden 1993 (cat.).– Jaffé, H. L. C.: V.-G. Mensch und Werk. Cologne 1971.– Lohse, R. P. (ed.): V.-G. Eine Bild-Biografie. Teufen 1959.– Partsch, S. (ed.): F. V.-G. 1899-1962. Wilhelm-Hack-Museum, Ludwigshafen. Münsterschwarzach 1986.– Rattemeyer, V. et al. (ed.): Typographie kann unter Umständen Kunst sein. V.-G. Typographie und Werbegestaltung. Landesmuseum Wiesbaden et al. Wiesbaden 1990 (cat.).– Rotzler, W.: V.-G. St. Gallen 1979.– Schäfer, J.: F. V.-G. Studien zu einer beschreibenden Werkanalyse. Frankfurt-on-Main et al. 1984.– F. V.-G. Städtische Kunsthalle Mannheim. Mannheim 1970 (cat.).– F. V.-G. Remembered. Annely Juda Fine Art. London 1974 (cat.).– Wijsenbeek, L. J. F. et al. (ed.): V.-G. Haags Gemeentemuseum et al. The Hague 1966 (cat.)

Studied at the Düsseldorf Academy. **1962–1969** Published the magazine *Dé-coll/age*. **1962** As a co-founder of Fluxus, helped to organise Fluxus events in Wiesbaden, Copenhagen and Paris, followed by New York in **1963** and Berlin and Ulm in **1964**. **1965** Publication of the review *Happening, Fluxus, Pop Art, Neuer Realismus*. **1966** Retrospective at the Kunstverein in Cologne. **1968** Participation at the Venice Biennale. **1969** First covering of cars with concrete, in Cologne. **1971** Moved to Berlin. Made the film *Désastres*. **1974** Retrospective at the Musée d'Art Moderne de la Ville de Paris. **1976** Founded the Museo Vostell Malpartida de Cáceres in Spain. **1977** Took part in documenta 6 in Kassel. **1981** Took his Fluxus train, a mobile museum, to 15 different cities. **1985** Retrospective at the Musée d'Art Moderne, Strasbourg. **1990** Participation at the Venice Biennale. **1992** Retrospectives in Cologne, Bonn and Mannheim. **1997** Hannah Höch Prize for his complete works. After establishing Video Art, Vostell found happenings the most effective way of expressing his political views. With his torn-poster works and smudged, over-painted photo-montages he can also be regarded as a Nouveau Réaliste.
WRITINGS: W. V. and J. Becker (ed.): Happenings: Fluxus, Pop Art, Nouveau Réalisme. Reinbek 1965.– W. V.: Miss Vietnam and Texts of Other Happenings. San Francisco 1969.– W. V.: dé-coll/agen 1954-1969. Berlin 1969.– W. V.: Happening & Leben. Neuwied and Berlin 1970.– W. V.: Aktionen. Reinbek 1970
CATALOGUES RAISONNES: W. V. Œuvre-Verzeichnis. Galerie René Block. Berlin 1970.– Schilling, J. (ed.): W. V. Das plastische Werk 1953-1987. Milan 1987
MONOGRAPHS, CATALOGUES: Domínguez, A. F. (ed.): Museo V. Malpartida de Cáceres 1994.– Gottberg, D. (ed.): V. Fluxus-Zug. Das mobile Museum. Berlin 1981 (cat.).– Lehni, N. et al. (ed.): W. V. Environnement, vidéo, peintures, dessins 1977-1985. Musée d'Art Moderne. Strasbourg 1985 (cat.).– Merkert, J. (ed.): V. Retrospektive. 1958-1974. Neue Nationalgalerie. Berlin 1975 (cat.).– Rüdiger, U. (ed.): V. Leben = Kunst = Leben. Kunstgalerie Gera. Leipzig 1993 (cat.).– Schilling, J. (ed.): W. V. Dé-coll/agen. Verwischungen, Schichtenbilder, Bleibilder, Objektbilder 1955-1979. Kunstverein Braunschweig. Brunswick 1980 (cat.).– Schmied, W. et al. (ed.): V. Retrospektive 1958-1974. Neue Nationalgalerie. Berlin 1975 (cat.).– Schmied, W. et al. (ed.): V. und Berlin. Leben und Werk 1971-1981. Daadgalerie. Berlin 1982 (cat.).– Schmied, W.: Die fünf Hämmer des W. V. Berlin 1992.– Simon, S.: W. V.'s Aktions-Bildsprache. Eine Dokumentation 1954-1969. Berlin 1969.– W. V. Kestner-Gesellschaft. Hanover 1977 (cat.).– W. V. Museum am Ostwall, Dortmund et al. Dortmund 1977 (cat.).– V. Leben = Kunst = Leben. Orangerie. Gera 1993 (cat.).– Wedewer, R. et al. (ed.): W. V. Rheinisches Landesmuseum, Bonn et al. Heidelberg 1992 (cat.).– Wick, R.: V. soziologisch. Bonn 1969

VUILLARD Edouard
1868 Cuiseaux (Saône) – **1940** La Baule (Loire-Atlantique)
French painter. **1886–1889** Studied at the Paris Ecole des Beaux-Arts under Gérôme. **1888** Attended the Académie Julian, where he made friends with Bonnard, Denis and Sérusier. **1889** First and only exhibition of his works at the Salon. **1890** Co-founder of the Symbolist group, the Nabis. Shared a studio with Bonnard and Denis. **1891** Contact with Toulouse-Lautrec. Inspired by Japanese colour woodcuts, he began to

paint intimate interiors. **1892** First of a series of decorative scenes as wall paintings. **1893** Stage designs for the Théâtre de l'Œuvre, run by his old school friend Lugné-Poe. **1900** Trip to Switzerland with Vallotton. Exhibited for the first time with the Berlin Secession and **1901** with the Unabhängigen. **1903** Co-founder of the Deutsche Herbstsalon. **1909** Taught for a short time at the Académie Ranson. **1914–1916** Worked as a military painter. In the 20s and 30s he painted numerous traditional-style portraits, interiors and cityscapes. **1937** Was killed fleeing from German troops. **1990** Retrospective at the Musée des Beaux-Arts in Lyon. Alongside Bonnard and Sérusier, Vuillard is regarded as one of the leading members of the Nabis. He uses sensitive patterning and planes of colour to convey his mystical and religious meaning.
WRITINGS: E. V.: Sous la dir. Paris 1990
CATALOGUES RAISONNES: Chastel, A. et al. (ed.): V. Catalogue des œuvres. Paris 1990.– Roger-Marx, C. (ed.): E. V. L'œuvre gravé. Monte Carlo 1948, Paris 1984/The Graphic Work of E. V. San Francisco 1990
MONOGRAPHS, CATALOGUES: Dumas, A. and G. Cogeval (ed.): V. Musée des Beaux-Arts, Lyon et al. Paris 1990 (cat.).– Easton, E. W. (ed.): The Intimate Interiors of E. V. The Museum of Fine Arts, Houston et al. Washington 1989 (cat.).– Groom, G. L.: E. V. Painter-Decorator. London and New Haven (CT) 1994.– Preston, S.: E. V. New York 1972, 1984.– Ritchie, A. C. (ed.): E. V. The Museum of Modern Art. New York 1954, 1969 (cat.).– Roger-Marx, C.: V. Paris 1945, London 1946.– Russell, J. (ed.): V. 1868-1940. Art Gallery of Toronto et al. Greenwich (CT) 1971 (cat.).– Salomon, J.: Auprès de V. Paris 1953, 1968.– Schweicher, C.: Die Bildraumgestaltung, das Dekorative und das Ornamentale im Werk von E. V. Trever 1949.– Thomson, B.: V. Oxford and New York 1988, Paris 1988.– Thomson, B. (ed.): E. V. South Bank Center, London et al. London 1991 (cat.).– Warnod, J.: V. Paris 1988

VORDEMBERGE-GILDEWART Friedrich
1899 Osnabrück – **1962** Ulm
German painter. First apprenticed to a joiner. **1919** Attended the School of Arts and Crafts, then studied architecture and

VOSTELL Wolf
1932 Leverkusen – **1998** Berlin
German artist. **1950–1953** Trained as a lithographer. **1954/55** Studied art at the Wuppertal School of Arts and Crafts and at the Ecole des Beaux-Arts in Paris. Described his work as "décollage", a term he discovered in an article about a plane crash in the French newspaper *Figaro*. Met the composer Karl-Heinz Stockhausen. **1957/58**

WAGEMAKER Jaap
(Adriaan Barend)
1906 Haarlem – **1972** Amsterdam
Dutch painter. **1919–1925** Studied at the

Haarlem School of Arts and Crafts. **1926** Joined the group of Haarlem artists known as Kunst Zij Ons Doel. First works influenced by Permeke. **1930–1934** Painted numerous still lifes with flowers in the style of Redon. **1946** Moved to Amsterdam. Inspired by Picasso's works. From **1956/57** material paintings incorporating sacking, slate, sand, wood and found objects. **1972** Retrospective at the Kunsthalle in Bremen. The materials Wagemaker used often give the surface of the canvas the appearance of a fissured landscape.
MONOGRAPHS, CATALOGUES:
Doelman, C.: De informele kunst van J. W. Amsterdam 1962.– Heyer, S. d. and M. v. d. Knaap: J. W. Zwolle 1995.– Schultze, J. (ed.): J. W. Kunsthalle Bremen. Bremen 1972 (cat.).– Wagemaker-v. d. Mer, D. et al.: J. W. Amsterdam 1978.– J. W. Stedelijk Museum. Amsterdam 1967 (cat.).– J. W. Aarde in verf. Göttingen 1995 (cat.).

WALL Jeff
born **1946** Vancouver
Canadian photo-artist. **1964–1970** Studied art history at the Department of Fine Arts at the University of British Columbia. Took part in several group exhibitions of Conceptual Art. **1970–1973** Research at the Courtauld Institute of Art in London and wrote his doctoral thesis in art history. **1976** After holding various teaching posts he obtained a professorship at the Center of the Arts at the Simon Fraser University in Vancouver. **1982–1997** took part in documenta 7, 8 and 10 in Kassel. From **1987** Professor of Fine Arts at the University of British Columbia. **1995** Major retrospective in Chicago, Paris, Helsinki and London and **1997** at the Museum of Contemporary Art, Los Angeles. Wall's photographic works reveal his thorough knowledge of the classical genres (landscapes, portraits etc.). His large-format Cibachrome pictures presented in light boxes illuminated with fluorescent lighting are references to key works in the history of art.
WRITINGS: Stemmrich, G. (ed.): J. W. Szenarien im Bildraum der Wirklichkeit. Essays und Interviews. Dresden 1997.– J. W.: Landscape Manual. Vancouver 1970.– J. W. Transparencies. Mit einem Gespräch zwischen Els Barents und J. W. Munich 1986
MONOGRAPHS, CATALOGUES:
Ammann, J.-C. (ed.): J. W. The Storyteller. Frankfurt-on-Main 1992.– Barents E. and F. Migayrou (ed.): J. W. Le Nouveau Musée. Villeurbanne 1988 (cat.).– Brougher, K. (ed.): J. W. Museum of Contemporary Art. Los Angeles 1997 (cat.).– Dufour, G. (ed.): J. W. Vancouver Art Gallery. Vancouver 1990 (cat.).– Duve, T. d. and B. Groys (ed.): J. W. London 1996.– Linsley, R. and V. Auffermann: J. W. The Storyteller. Frankfurt-on-Main 1992.– Schwander, M. and J. W. (ed.): J. W. Dead Troops Talk. Kunstmuseum Luzern. Basel 1993 (cat.).– Thielmann, A. and J. W. (ed.): J. W. West-fälischer Kunstverein. Münster 1988 (cat.).–

Tuyl, G. v. et al. (ed.): J. W. Landscapes and Other Pictures. Kunstmuseum Wolfsburg. Wolfsburg 1996 (cat.).– J. W. Musée d'Art Moderne de la Ville de Paris 1988 (cat.).– J. W. Städtische Kunsthalle Düsseldorf. Düsseldorf 1994 (cat.).– J. W. Galerie Nationale du Jeu de Paume, Paris et al. Paris 1995 (cat.).– J. W. Kunstbau des Lenbachhauses. Munich 1996 (cat.)

WALTHER Franz Erhard
born **1939** Fulda
German artist. **1957–1959** Studied at the Offenbach School of Arts and Crafts, **1959–1961** at the Städelschule in Frankfurt am Main and **1962–1964** at the Düsseldorf Academy under Götz. **1963–1969** Produced 1. Werksatz, action objects with textiles. **1967** Solo-exhibition at the H. Friedrich gallery in Munich. Moved to New York. **1969–1972** 2. Werksatz: walk-through metal objects. **1969** Solo-exhibitions at the Museum Haus Lange in Krefeld and at the Kunsthalle Düsseldorf, **1970** at the Museum of Modern Art, New York. **1971** Returned to Germany and was appointed professor of sculpture at the Hamburg School of Fine Arts. **1972** and **1977** participation in documenta 5 and 6 in Kassel. **1977** Solo-exhibition at Museum Ludwig in Cologne. **1981** Participated in the "Westkunst" exhibition in Cologne. **1982** and **1987** took part in documenta 7 and 8 in Kassel. **1984/85** Professor at the Städelschule in Frankfurt am Main. **1985** Günter Fruhtrunk Prize from the Munich Academy. **1992** Solo-exhibition at the Kunstmuseum in Lucerne. Walther's objects and working constructions, that have no function but still force the viewer to try to work out how they operate, are representative of Process Art.
WRITINGS: König, K. (ed.): F. E. W. Objekte benutzen. Cologne and New York 1968.– F. E. W.: Prozeßmaterial. Cologne 1970.– F. E. W.: Tagebuch. Cologne 1971.– F. E. W.: Organon. Klagenfurt 1983.– F. E. W.: Wortwerke. 1974-1986. Klagenfurt 1987.– F. E. W.: Das Haus in dem ich wohne. Klasgenfurt 1990.– F. E. W.: Denkraum, Werkraum. Über Akademie und Lehre. Regensburg 1993
MONOGRAPHS, CATALOGUES: Adriani, G.: F. E. W. Arbeiten 1955-1963. Material zum 1. Werksatz 1963-1969. Cologne 1972.– Adriani, G. and K. Vogel (ed.): F. E. W. Arbeiten 1969-1976. Tübigen and Hamburg 1977.– Bojescul, W. (ed.): F. E. W. Ich bin die Skulptur. Wandformationen 1978-1985. Kunstverein Braunschweig. Brunswick 1986 (cat.).– Damsch-Wiehager, R. (ed.): F. E. W. Antwort der Körper. Galerie Villa Merkel, Esslingen. Stuttgart 1993 (cat.).– Dückers, A. et al. (ed.): F. E. W. Zeichnungen-Werkzeichnungen 1957-1984. Staatliche Museen, Kupferstichkabinett. Berlin 1989 (cat.).– Lange, S.: Der 1. Werksatz 1963-1969 von F. E. W. Frankfurt-on-Main 1991.– Lingner, M. (ed.): Das Haus in dem ich wohne. Die Theorie zum Werkentwurf von F. E. W. Klagenfurt 1990.– Pauseback,

W. (ed.): F. E. W. Handlung Werk. Nationalgalerie. Berlin 1981 (cat.).– Stemmler, D. and G. Seng (ed.): F. E. W. Arbeiten 1959-1963. Städtisches Kunstmuseum Bonn. Bonn 1980 (cat.).– F. E. W. and H. Kern (ed.): F. E. W. Diagramme zum 1. Werksatz. Kunstraum. Munich 1976 (cat.).– F. E. W. and M. Pauseback (ed.): F. E. W. Handlung. Werk. Nationalgalerie. Berlin 1981 (cat.).– F. E. W. Gelenke im Raum. Deichtorhallen. Hamburg 1998 (cat.)

WANG Cheng
born **1965** Wuhu (Province of Anhui)
Chinese painter. Up to **1991** Studied art at the Jiangsu College of Education. Painted over photographs and texts from newspapers, making pictures that are part-collage and part-painting.

WARHOL Andy
(Andrej Warhola)
1928 Pittsburgh (PA) – **1987** New York
American artist born to Czech immigrant parents. **1945–1949** Studied graphic design at the Carnegie Institute of Technology in Pittsburgh. On graduating, went to New York where he worked as an illustrator and commercial artist. Invented the blotted line technique, a precursor of reproduction methods such as the serigraph technique. From **1960** did paintings based on images from comic strips, or using icons of American advertising and consumerism, like Coca-Cola bottles, dollar bills, Campbell's soup cans, as his motifs. From **1962** he and his team at his New York studio The Factory produced a steady stream of portraits of celebrities, often consisting of rows of repeated images, as well as photographic works, films and music. Brought out the celebrity magazine *Interview* and organised TV shows and multimedia concerts with the pop group Velvet Underground. **1968** Travelled to Stockholm for his first European exhibition and participated in documenta 4 in Kassel. In the same year, the man-hater and feminist writer V. Solanas forced her way into the Factory, fired three revolver shots at Warhol and hit him twice. He was hospitalized for two months. In his later years he often took the works of Old Masters such as Leonardo's *Last Supper* as starting material. **1989** Major retrospective

at the Museum of Modern Art, New York, and at the Museum Ludwig, Cologne. Warhol was and remains the most famous and controversial figure in Pop Art. The mass-production of works through his Factory radically diminished the importance placed on original works in conventional art circles.
WRITINGS: Hackett, P. (ed.): The A. W. Diaries. London 1989 / A. W. Das Tagebuch. Munich 1989.– A. W.: Ladies and Gentlemen. Milan 1975.– A. W.: The Philosophy of A. W. (A to B and Back Again). New York 1975.– A. W. and P. Hackett: POPism: The Warhol Sixties. New York 1980
CATALOGUES RAISONNES: Ammann, T. E. (ed.): A. W. Werkverzeichnis. Band I: Gemalte Bilder und erste Siebdrucke 1960-1962. Munich 1992.– Crone, R. (ed.): A. W. Catalogue Raisonné. New York and Washington 1970, Berlin 1976.– Feldman, F. and J. Schellmann (ed.): A. W. Prints. A Catalogue Raisonné 1962-1987. New York and Munich 1997.– Wünsche, H. (ed.): A. W. Das graphische Werk 1962-1980. Bonn 1981
MONOGRAPHS, CATALOGUES: Angell, C. et al. (ed.): The Inaugural Publication. The A. W. Museum. Pittsburgh 1994 / The A. W. Museum. Stuttgart et al. 1994.– Baudrillard, J.: A. W. Paintings 1960-1986. New York 1996.– Billeter, E. et al. (ed.): A. W. Kunsthaus Zürich. Bern 1978 (cat.).– Blistène, B. and J.-M. Bouhours (ed.): A. W. Cinema. Centre Georges Pompdou. Paris 1990 (cat.).– Bockris, V.: The Life and Death of A. W. New York 1989 / A. W. Düsseldorf 1989 / A. W. Paris 1990.– Bourdon, D.: W. New York 1989, Paris 1989, Cologne 1989.– Cagle, V. M.: Reconstructing Pop / Subculture, Art, Rock and A. W. Thousand Oaks 1995.– Colacello, B.: Holy Terror. A. W. Close-up. New York 1990.– Coplans, J. A. W. Paasadena Art Museum. New York 1970 (cat.).– Coplans, J. and J. Baudrillard: A. W. Silkscreens from the Sixties. Munich 1990.– Crone, R.: A. W. Düsseldorf 1970, New York 1970.– Crone, R. and W. Wiegand: Die revolutionäre Ästhetik A. W.'s. Darmstadt 1972.– Crone, R.: Das bildnerische Werk A. W. Berlin 1976.– Crone, R.: A. W. Die frühen Werke. Stuttgart 1987.– Crone, R. (ed.): A. W. A Picture Show by the Artist. New York 1987.– Felix, Z. (ed.): A. W. Retrospektive. Deichtorhallen, Hamburg. Stuttgart 1993 (cat.).– Francis, M. et al. (ed.): The W. Lok. Glamour, Style, Fashion. Whitney Museum of American Art, New York et al. New York 1997 (cat.).– Garrels, G. (ed.): The Work of A. W. Seattle 1989.– Geldzahler, H.: A. W. Portraits of the Seventies and Eighties. London 1993.– Gidal, R. (ed.): A. W. Films and Paintings. London and New York 1989.– Guiles, F. L.: A. W. Voyeur des Lebens. Munich 1989.– Haenlein, C. A. (ed.): A. W. Bilder 1961-1981. Städtische Galerie im Lenbachhaus, Munich et al. Hanover 1981 (cat.).– Kornbluth, J. (ed.): Pre-Pop W. New York 1988.– Lüthy, M.: A. W. Thirty Are Better Than One. Frankfurt-on-Main 1995.– MacCabe, C. (ed.): Who is A. W.? Bloomington (IN) 1998.– McShine, K. (ed.): A. W. A Retrospective. The Museum of Modern Art, New York et al. New York 1989 (cat.) / A. W. Retrospektive. Museum Ludwig, Cologne et al. Munich 1989 (cat.).– Nochlin, L.: A. W. Nudes. New York 1996.– O'Connor, J. and B. Liu (ed.): Unseen W. New York 1996.– O'Pray, M. (ed.): A. W. Film Factory. London 1989.– Pratt, A. R. (ed.): The Critical Response to A. W. Westport 1997.– Ratcliff, C.: A. W. New York 1983, Munich and Lucerne 1983.– Romain, L.: A. W. Munich 1993.–

Rosenblum, R. (ed.): A. W. Portraits of the 70's. Whitney Museum of American Art. New York 1979 (cat.).– Sabin, S.: A. W. Mit Selbstzeugnissen und Bilddokumenten. Reinbek 1992.– Schellmann, J. (ed.): A. W. Art from Art. Cologne, Munich 1994 (cat.).– Schwander, M.: A. W. Paintings 1960-1986. Kunstmuseum Luzern. Stuttgart 1995 (cat.).– Smith, P. S.: A. W.'s Art and Films. Ann Arbor (MI) 1986.– Smith, P. S.: W. Conversations about the Artist. Ann Arbor (MI) 1988.– Spies, W.: A. W. Cars. Die letzten Bilder. Kunstmuseum Bern. Stuttgart 1990 (cat.).– Stucky, C. (ed.): A. W. Heaven and Hell are Just One Breath Away. Late Paintings and Related Works 1984-1986. New York 1992.– A. W.'s Exposure. New York 1979.– A. W. Wilhelm-Hack-Museum. Ludwigshafen 1996 (cat.).– Wilcock, J.: The Autobiography and Sex Life of A. W. New York 1971

WEEGEE
(Arthur Fellig)
1866 Zloczew (Poland) – **1968** New York
Polish-born American photographer. **1876** Moved to New York. **1915–1935** Worked as an assistant in a photographic laboratory. From **1935** photographed for the police force, taking some sensational pictures of accidents and scenes of crime. **1945** Publication of *Naked City*. First exhibition at the Museum of Modern Art, New York. From **1947** worked for *Vogue, Harper's Bazaar, Life* and other magazines. **1977** Posthume participation in documenta 6 in Kassel. Weegee means Famous One, and Arthur Fellig did indeed become notorious for his photographs of the dark side of New York, night scenes of sex and violence, exposed and captured in the glare of his flash.
WRITINGS: W. by W. An Autobiography. New York 1961, 1975
MONOGRAPHS, CATALOGUES: Coplans, J. and C. Capa (ed.): W. the Famous. Center of Photography. New York 1977 (cat.).– Coplans, J. (ed.): W.: Täter und Opfer. Munich 1978.– Nothhelfer, G. and H.: Bildinterpretationen zu Fotografien von W. Berlin 1978.– Porter, D. (ed.): W. 1899-1968. Zurich 1991.– Stettner, L.: W. The Famous. New York 1977.– Talmey, A. and M. Israel (ed.): W. New York and London 1978

WEGMAN William
born **1942** Holyoke (MA)
American photo and video artist. **1961–1967** Studied at Massachusetts College of Art in Boston and at the University of Illinois in Urbana. **1967–1971** Taught at various universities in the USA. **1971** First solo-exhibition of video tapes at the Pomona College Art Gallery and at the Sonnabend gallery in Paris. **1975** Guggenheim-Fellowship and **1975–1977** National Endowment for the Arts Grant. Many of Wegman's works are parodies centering around his dog Man Ray.
MONOGRAPHS, CATALOGUES: Kunz,

M. (ed.): W. W. Malerei, Zeichnung, Fotografie, Video. Kunstmuseum Luzern et al. Cologne 1990 (cat.)/W. W. Paintings, Drawings, Photographs, Videotapes. New York 1990 (cat.).– Paul, F. (ed.): W. W. L'œuvre photographique. Fonds Régional d'Art Contemporain Limousin. Limoges 1991 (cat.).– Paul, F. (ed.): W. W. Drawings 1973-1997. Limoges 1997 (cat.).– Lyons, L. and K. Levin (ed.): W.'s World. Corcoran Gallery, Washington et al. Washington 1983 (cat.)

WEI Guangqing
born **1963** Huangshi (Province of Hubei)
Chinese painter. Up to **1985** studied oil painting at the Academy of Art in Zhejiang. Since **1995** he has taught oil painting at the Art Academy in Wuhan. Wei's aim is to bridge the gap between the traditional and the modern through art.

WEIBEL Peter
born **1944** Odessa
Austrian video artist. **1946** Moved with his parents to Vienna. **1964** Studied literature at the Sorbonne in Paris. **1965** Made linguistic films. **1966** Wrote articles on conceptual photography and criticisms of theories of ideology. **1967** Actions, plays, texts and audible objects. **1968** Put together action films with Muehl, Brus and Valie Export and carried out actions and film projects in collaboration with Export. Alongside these activities he continued to study logic and wrote a doctoral thesis on mathematical logic. **1970** Took part in the first International Underground Festival in

London, and afterwards produced several linguistic video works. **1977** Took part in documenta 6 in Kassel and **1979** in "Videowochen" at the Museum Folkwang in Essen. **1981** Guest-professorship in Halifax, Canada. **1982** Professor of Design at the Vienna School of Applied Arts. Weibel is an exponent of Expanded Cinema.
WRITINGS: P. W.: Die Beschleunigung der Bilder in der Chronokratie. Bern 1987.– P. W.: Das Ich und die Dinge. Frankfurt-on-Main 1991
MONOGRAPHS, CATALOGUES: Breicha, O. (ed.): P. W. Mediendichtung. Vienna 1982.– Fleck, R. (ed.): P. W. Zur Rechtfertigung der hypothetischen Natur der Kunst und der Nicht-Identität in der Objektwelt. Galerie Tanja Grunert. Cologne 1992 (cat.).– Noever, P. (ed.): P. W. Inszenierte Kunstgeschichte. Österreichisches Museum für angewandte Kunst. Vienna 1988 (cat.).– Schuler, R. (ed.): P. W. Bildwelten 1982-1996. Vienna 1996.– Steinle, C. (ed.): P. W. Malerei zwischen Anarchie und Forschung. Neue Galerie am Landesmuseum Joanneum. Graz 1992 (cat.)

WESSELMANN Tom
born **1931** Cincinnati (OH)
American painter. **1951–1955** Studied psychology at the Cincinnati University and then attended the Art Academy of Cincinnati and the Cooper Union in New York. **1959** Made small abstract collages, combining the contrasting influences of Matisse and De Kooning. **1960** Painted still lifes and landscapes. **1961** First solo-exhibition at the Tanager Gallery in New York. **1963** Took part in the exhibition "Pop Goes the East" at the Contemporary Arts Museum, Houston, and **1965** in the exhibition "Young America 1965" at the Whitney Museum of American Art, New York. **1967** Participated in the São Paulo Biennale and, **1968** and **1977**, in documenta 4 and 6 in Kassel. In the 70s Wesselmann produced free-standing canvases, incorporating elements of collage and actual objects to create a third dimension. From **1983** painted enlargements of spontaneous sketches in garish colours on aluminium and steel. Wesselmann is one of the leading figures in American Pop Art. He became famous in the early 60s for his series *Great American Nudes*.
MONOGRAPHS, CATALOGUES: Buchsteiner, T. and O. Letze (ed.): T. W. Kunsthalle Tübingen et al. Stuttgart 1994 (cat.).– Glenn, C. W. (ed.): T. W. The Early Years, Collages 1959-1962. California State University Art Galleries. Long Beach 1974 (cat.).– Hunter, S.: T. W. New York 1994.– Livingstone, M. (ed.): T. W. A Retrospective Survey 1959-1992. Tokyo et al. Tokyo 1993 (cat.).– McEwen, J. (ed.): T. W. Paintings 1962-1986. The Mayor Gallery, Mayor Rowan Gallery. London 1988 (cat.).– Stealingworth, S.: T. W. New York 1980.– Ward, M.: T. W. Studie zur Matisse-Rezeption in Amerika. Hamburg 1992.– T. W. Galerie de France. Paris 1987 (cat.)

WESTON Edward
1886 Highland Park (IL) – **1958** Carmel (CA)
American photographer. Studied at Illinois College of Photography. **1911** Opened a portrait studio in California and produced his first abstract photographs. **1923** Set up a studio in Mexico City with his son Brett. Came to know Rivera. **1927** Returned to the USA. **1932** Founded the group f/64 with Ansel Adams. **1937** Guggenheim Award. From **1947** suffered from Parkinson's disease. **1948** Photoseries of Point Lobos. **1950** Solo-exhibition at the Museum of Modern Art, New York. **1956** Retrospective at the Stedelijk Museum, Amsterdam. Through his own technical mastery and the influence of Stieglitz, Sheeler and Strand, Weston became a key representative of photographic realism.
WRITINGS: Bunnell, P. (ed.): E. W. on Photography. Salt Lake City 1983.– Newhall, N. (ed.): The Daybooks of E. W. 2 vols. New York 1990, 1996
MONOGRAPHS, CATALOGUES: Armitage, M. (ed.): The Art of E. W. New York 1932.– Baldinger, W. (ed.): The Heritage of E. W. University of Oregon. Eugene 1965 (cat.).– Bunnell, P. C. (ed.): Centennial Essays in Honor of E. W. Carmel 1986.– Conger, A.: E. W. in Mexico. Albuquerque 1983.– Conger, A. (ed.): E. W. Photographs from the Collection of the Center for Creative Photography. Tucson (AZ) 1992.– Danly, S. (ed.): E. W. in Los Angeles. Huntington Library. San Marino 1986 (cat.).– Green, E.: E. W. Washington Gallery of Modern Art. Washington 1966 (cat.).– Maddow, B.: E. W. His Life and Photographs. New York 1979.– Mora, G.: E. W. Form of Passion. New York 1995/Mora, G.: E. W. Formes de la passion. Paris 1995.– Newhall, N. (ed.): E. W. Photographer. The Flame of Recognition His Photographs. Accompanied by Excerpts from the Daybooks and Letters. New York 1965, 1993.– Newhall, B. (ed.): Supreme Instants: The Photography of E. W. Boston 1986.– Stebbins, E. (ed.): E. W.' Portraits and Nudes. Museum of Fine Arts, Boston et al. Boston 1989 (cat.)

WILSON Robert
born **1941** Waco (TX)
American artist. Took lessons from the

American painter G. McNeil in Paris before studying interior design, **1962–1965**, at the Pratt Institute in New York. **1966** Joint projects with the architect P. Soleri in Scottesdale (AZ). Staged public performances in the 70s, combining written texts, music, dance and design and breaking away from the conventional concept of a work as a narrative unfolding in a linear sequence from beginning to end. **1976** Staging at the Avignon Festival of his best-known work, the opera *Einstein on the Beach*, now considered a crowning example of Minimal music. **1984** Wrote a twelve-hour opera entitled *The CIVIL wars*, intending to involve performers from all over the world assembled for the Olympic Games in Los Angeles. However, the piece was never performed.
WRITINGS: R. W. (ed.): R. W. RWWM. Zurich 1997
MONOGRAPHS, CATALOGUES: Ambasz, E.: R. W. Paris 1991.– Bertoni, F. et al. (ed.): R. W. Stuttgart 1997.– Birnie Danzker, J.-A. (ed.): R. W. Steel Velvet. Museum Villa Stuck. Munich 1998 (cat.).– Fairbrother, T. (ed.): R. W.'s Vision. Museum of Fine Arts, Boston et al. Boston, New York 1991 (cat.).– Graff, B.: Das Geheimnis der Oberfläche. Der Raum der Postmoderne und die Bühnenkunst von R. W. Tübingen 199.– Haenlein, C. A. (ed.): R. W. Monuments. Kestner-Gesellschaft. Hanover 1991 (cat.).– Holmberg, A.: The Theatre of R. W. New York 1997.– Lehmann, H.-T.: Collaboration R. W. Zurich 1988.– Reinhardt, B. (ed.): R. W. Erinnerungen an eine Revolution. Environment. Stuttgart 1987 (cat.).– Rockwell, J. and R. Stearns (ed.): R. W. From a Theater of Images. Contemporary Arts Center. Cincinnati 1980 (cat.).– Wachsmann, M. and G. Lohnert (ed.): R. W. Die goldenen Fenster. Städtische Galerie im Lenbachhaus, Munich et al. Munich 1982 (cat.).– R. W. Mr. Bojangles' Memory. Centre Georges Pompidou. Paris 1991 (cat.)

WINTER Fritz
1905 Altenbögge – **1976** Dießen-St. Georgen
German painter. Originally worked as a miner. **1927–1930** Studied at the Bauhaus in Dessau under Klee, Kandinsky and Schlemmer. **1930–1933** Lived in Berlin where he met Gabo. **1933** Moved to Dießen on the Ammersee. During the Third Reich his paintings were classified as "degenerate art" and banned. **1939–1949** Military service. Fought and was taken prisoner in Russia. **1944** Produced his 40-part worked *Triebkräfte der Erde* (Driving Forces of the Earth) while convalescing. **1953** Guest-lecturer at the Hamburg School of Art. From **1955** taught at the Academy of Arts and Crafts in Kassel. **1955** and **1959** participation in documenta 1 and 2 in Kassel. Painted on lighter grounds. From **1961** modulations of space through colour effects. Inspired by the ideas of the

Blauer Reiter movement, Winter saw art as a direct expression of the elementary forces of nature. From the 30s onwards he gradually abandoned figurative painting and after the war became more closely aligned with the Ecole de Paris.
WRITINGS: Haftmann, W. (ed.): F. W. Aus Briefen und Tagebüchern. 1932-1950. Bern 1951
CATALOGUES RAISONNES: Gabler, K. (ed.): Das graphische Werk von F. W. Frankfurter Kunstkabinett. Frankfurt-on-Main 1968 (cat.).– Lohberg, G.: F. W. Leben und Werk. Mit einem Werkverzeichnis der Gemälde. Munich 1986.– Tutsch C. (ed.): F. W. 1905-1976. Verzeichnis sämtlicher Werke F. W. im Besitz der Staatlichen Museen Kassel. Kassel 1992
MONOGRAPHS, CATALOGUES: Boess, C. and C. Schulz-Hoffmann (ed.): F. W. Munich 1988.– Büchner, J.: F. W. Recklinghausen 1963.– Gabler, K.-H.: Das graphische Werk von F. W. Frankfurt-on-Main 1968.– Gausling, H. (ed.): F. W. Städtisches Gustav-Lübcke-Museum, Hamm et al. Ahlen 1985.– Haftmann, W.: F. W. Triebkräfte der Erde. Munich 1957.– Keller, H.: F. W. Munich 1976.– Kricke-Güse, S. and E.-G. Güse (ed.): F. W. Triebkräfte der Erde. Westfälisches Landesmuseum. Münster 1981 (cat.).– Schmidt, J.-K. et al. (ed.): F. W. Galerie der Stadt. Stuttgart 1990 (cat.).– Steingräber, E. (ed.): F. W. Staatsgalerie moderner Kunst und Galerie-Verein, Munich et al. Munich 1976 (cat.).– F. W. Kunstverein für die Rheinlande und Westfalen. Düsseldorf 1966 (cat.).– F. W. Neue Galerie. Kassel 1992 (cat.)

WINTERS Terry
born **1949** Brooklyn (NY)
American artist. Studied art at Pratt Institute, New York, graduating in **1971** with a Bachelor of Fine Arts degree. **1982** First solo-exhibition at the Ileana Sonnabend Gallery in New York. Major solo-exhibitions: **1985** Kunstmuseum, Lucerne, **1986** Tate Gallery, London, **1987** Saint Louis Art Museum and Walker Art Center, Minneapolis, **1991** Museum of Contemporary Art, Los Angeles, and Whitney Museum of American Art, New York, and **1998** at the IVAM Centro Julio González, Valencia.
WRITINGS: T. W. and R. Smith: Schema. New York 1987
MONOGRAPHS, CATALOGUES: Kane, M. L. (ed.): T. W. Currents 33. The St. Louis Art Museum. St. Louis 1987 (cat.).– Kertess, K. and M. Kunz (ed.): T. W. Kunstmuseum. Lucerne 1985 (cat.).– Lewison, J. (ed.): T. W. Tate Gallery. London 1986 (cat.).– Phillips, E. and K. Kertess (ed.): T. W. Museum of Contemporary Art, Los Angeles et al. New York 1991 (cat.).– Plous, P. and C. Knight (ed.): T. W. Painting and Drawing. University Art Museum, Santa Barbara et al. Seattle 1987 (cat.).– T. W. IVAM Centro Julio González, Valencia 1998 (cat.)

WITKIEWICZ Stanislaw
1885 Warsaw – **1939** Jeziory
Polish painter, theoretician and writer. **1904** Trip to Italy. **1905/06** Studied art at the Cracow Academy. **1907** Took private painting lessons from W. Slewinski. **1908** Encountered avant-garde art movements in Paris, but his painting style was chiefly influenced by Jugendstil and Expressionism. **1910** Began writing his novel *The 622 Downfalls of Bungo, or The Demonic Woman.* **1914** Went on a scientific expedition to New Guinea. Signed up at the outbreak of war. From **1917** painted again in an abstract style retaining elements of Symbolism. **1918** Returned to Zakopane and wrote a theoretical treatise and the first of thirty plays. Invited to join the Cracow artists' group The Formalists. **1925** Concentrated on portrait painting. First successful stage designs. **1931** Published numerous articles on his philosophical theories and gradually abandoned painting.
WRITINGS: I. S. W.: Pisma filozoficzne i estetyczne. Warsaw 1974.– I. S. W.: Les Formes nouvelles en peinture et les malentendus qui en découlent. Lausanne 1979
CATALOGUE RAISONNE: Micinska, A.: S. I. W. Life and Work. Warsaw 1990
MONOGRAPHS, CATALOGUES: Crugten, A. (ed.): W. et la peinture. Lausanne 1979.– Hommage à S. I. W. Städtische Kunsthalle Düsseldorf. Düsseldorf 1980 (cat.).– Jakimowicz, I.: W. Warsaw 1985.– Jakimowicz, I. (ed.): S. I. W. Muzeum Narodowe. Warsaw 1990 (cat.).– Lingwood, J. (ed.): S. I. W. Photographs 1899-1939. Third Eye Centre. Glasgow 1989 (cat.).– Manthey, E. and B. v. Schleyer (ed.): S. I. W. 1885-1939. Neue Gesellschaft für Bildende Kunst, Berlin et al. Berlin 1990 (cat.).– Micinska, A.: S. I. W. Warsaw 1991.– Piasecki, Z.: S.W. Warsaw 1983.– Piotrowski, P.: Metafizika obrazu. O teorii sztuki i postawie artystycznej S. I. W. (Metaphysics of Picture. On the Theory of Art and Artistic Attitude of S. I. W.). Poznan 1985.– Piotrowski, P.: S. I. W. Warsaw 1989.– Schmidt, A.: Form und Deformation: zum kunsttheoretischen und dramatischen Werk von S. I. W. Munich 1992.– Sztaba, W.: S. I. W. Warsaw 1985.– S. I. W. Génie multiple de Pologne. Lausanne 1981

WÖLFLI Adolf
1864 Bern – **1930** Waldau
Swiss painter. Was originally a goatherd and farm-labourer in Emmental. **1890** Imprisoned for two years for molesting children. **1895** Arrested again for raping a young girl. Kept for the rest of his life under high security at the psychiatric hospital in Waldau near Bern. **1899** First drawings. Drew with wax crayons and wrote prose and poetry. **1922** Completed his most famous work *Große Wandschirm* (Large Screen) **1976/77** Retrospectives in the Kunstverein in Bern and in Cologne. Over the years, Wölfli's compositions, which were first confused and chaotic, became

clearer and more disciplined. The rampant, intensely coloured images of his disturbed fantasy were seen as exemplary by the Surrealists and taken as examples of Art Brut, a term coined by Dubuffet for the art of outcasts from society.
WRITINGS: A. W.: Von der Wiege bis zum Grab. Schriften 1908-1912. Kunstmuseum Bern. 2 vols. Frankfurt-on-Main 1985
MONOGRAPHS, CATALOGUES: Hunger, B. (ed.): Porträt eines produktiven Unfalls. A. W. Basel and Frankfurt-on-Main 1993.– Longhauser, E. et al. (ed.): The Other Side of the Moon. The World of A. W. Moore Collection of Art and Design, Philadelphia et al. Philadelphia 1988 (cat.).– Morgenthaler, W.: Ein Geisteskranker als Künstler. A. W. Vienna and Berlin 1985/Madness and Art. The Life and Works of A. W. Lincoln 1992.– Spoerri, E. and J. Glaesemer (ed.): A. W. Zeichnungen 1904-1906. Kunstmuseum Bern et al. Bern 1976 (cat.).– Spoerri, E. (ed.): Der Engel des Herrn im Küchenschurz. Über A. W. A. W. Städtische Galerie im Städelschen Kunstinstitut, Frankfurt-on-Main. Stuttgart 1987 (cat.).– Spoerri, E. et al. (ed.): A. W. Dessinateur, compositeur. Lausanne 1991/A. W. Draftsman, Writer, Poet, Composer. Ithaca (NY) 1997.– A. W. Rupertinum. Salzburg 1996 (cat.).– A. W. Schreiber, Dichter, Zeichner. Ed. by Adolf-Wölfli-Stiftung, Kunstmuseum Bern. Basel 1997

WOLS
(Alfred Otto Wolfgang Schulze)
1913 Berlin – **1951** Paris
German painter and photographer. **1919** Moved with his family to Dresden. **1932** Went to Berlin to apply to study at the Bauhaus. However, Moholy-Nagy advised him to go to Paris. There he wrote, painted and worked as a portrait photographer, becoming friends with Ernst, Léger, Domela, Arp, Giacometti, and Ozenfant. **1937** First major commission as official photographer at the Paris World Fair. **1939** Interned at the outbreak of war. **1940** Escaped and went into hiding in Cassis near Marseille, where he did drawings and watercolours. **1942** Fled from the Germans to Montélimar and met the writer H.-P. Roché, who promoted him. **1945** A first

exhibition of his watercolours at the Galerie Drouin was a failure. Returned to Paris one year later, and in **1947** had sensational success with an exhibition in the same gallery. Came to know Jean-Paul Sartre and Simone de Beauvoir, who promised to help him. Shared many artistic ideas with Giacometti and Mathieu. **1955–1964** Participation in documenta 1 – 3 in Kassel. Inspired by Surrealist theories of psychic automatism, Wols produced many of his early drawings, watercolours and oil paintings under the influence of drugs and alcohol. Later, he used thick brush strokes and heavy impasto to create paintings with a relief structure, and sometimes inscribed lines and shapes into the paint.
WRITINGS: W.: Aphorismes. Amiens 1989
MONOGRAPHS, CATALOGUES: Damme, C. v.: Kunst als catharsis en psychogenese … W. Ghent 1985.– Glozer, L. (ed.): W. Photograph. Kestner-Gesellschaft, Hanover. Munich 1978 (cat.).– Götze, G. (ed.): W. sa vie … Goethe-Institut, Paris et al. Paris 1986 (cat.).– Inch, P. (ed.): Circus W. The Life and Work of W. S. Todmorden 1978.– Haftmann, W. et al. (ed.): W. Aufzeichnungen, Aquarelle, Aphorismen, Zeichnungen. Cologne 1963/ W. en personne. Paris 1963.– Haftmann, W. (ed.): W. Stedelijk Van Abbe Museum. Eindhoven 1966 (cat.).– Haftmann, W. (ed.): W. Gemälde, Aquarelle, Zeichnungen. Nationalgalerie. Berlin 1973 (cat.).– Karabelnik-Matta, M. and T. Abt (ed.): W. Bilder, Aquarelle, Zeichnungen, Photographien. Kunsthaus, Zurich et al. Zurich 1989 (cat.).– Osterwold, T. and T. Knubben (ed.): W. Aquarelle 1937-1951. Ravensburg 1997 (cat.).– Petersen, H. J.: W. Leben und Werk im Spiegel gewandelter Wahrnehmung. Frankfurt-on-Main and Berlin 1994.– Rathke, E. and S. (ed.): W. Bilder, Aquarelle, Zeichnungen, Photographien, Druckgraphik. Kunstsammlung Nordrhein-Westfalen. Düsseldorf 1989 (cat.).– Rathke, E. (ed.): W. Fotografias, acuarellas y grabados. Sala Parpalló/Palau des Scala. Valencia 1993 (cat.).– Salden, H. A. F.: W.'s Bildkonzept. Thesis. Giessen 1991.– W. Musée d'Art Moderne de la Ville de Paris. Paris 1973 (cat.).– W. Kunsthaus Zurich et al. Bern 1989 (cat.).– Wols photographe. Centre Georges Pompidou. Paris 1980 (cat.)

WOOD Grant
1892 Anamosa (IA) – **1942** Iowa City (IA) American painter. **1910/11** Studied at the Minneapolis School of Design and Handicraft. **1913–1916** Went to evening classes at the Art Institute in Chicago. From **1913** worked as a designer. **1914–1916** Helped to run the silver workshop of C. Haga in Chicago. **1920** Trip to Paris. **1923/24** Attended the Académie Julian in Paris. **1926** Exhibition at the Carmine gallery, Paris. **1928** Visited Munich. Founded the Little Gallery in Cedar Rapid. **1932** Opening of the Stone City Colony and Art School (IA).

1934–1941 Taught at the University of Iowa, Ames. **1942** Received special honours at the Annual American Exhibition at the Art Institute of Chicago. **1959** Major posthumous retrospective at the University of Kansas, Kansas City. Wood's early paintings have strong Impressionist elements. However, a combined interest in German Renaissance art and Neue Sachlichkeit led him to develop a strictly veristic style. His landscapes and true-to-life portraits of farmers and ordinary people in mid-West America make him an important exponent of American realism and regionalism.
WRITINGS: G. W.: Revolt Against the City. Iowa City 1935
CATALOGUE RAISONNE: Cole, S. (ed.): G. W. The Lithographs. A Catalogue Raisonné. New York 1984
MONOGRAPHS, CATALOGUES: Corn, W. M. (ed.): G. W. The Regionalist Vision. Whitney Museum of American Art, New York et al. New Haven (CT) 1983 (cat.).– Dennis, J. M.: G. W. A Study in American Art and Culture. New York 1975.– Dennis, J. M. (ed.): G. W. Still Lives as Decorative Abstractions. Elvehjem Museum of Art. Madison 1985 (cat.).– Garwood, D.: Artist in Iowa. A Life of G. W. New York 1944.– Liffring-Zug, J. (ed.): Ths is G. W. Country. Davenport Municipal Art Gallery. Davenport (IA) 1977

WOODROW Bill
born **1948** Henley (Oxfordshire) English sculptor. **1967/68** Went to Winchester School of Art. **1968–1971** Studied at St. Martin's School of Art and **1971/72** at Chelsea School of Art in London. **1972** First solo-exhibition at the Whitechapel Art Gallery in London. He made his name in the early 80s as a representative of the New British Sculpture with his assemblages of found objects, used materials and bits of rubbish. In the 90s he began to cast his works in steel and bronze, giving his *objets trouvés* an unusual elegance reminiscent of the ideal aesthetics of classical sculpture. **1987** Participation in documenta 8 in Kassel. **1996** Retrospective at the Tate Gallery in London.
MONOGRAPHS, CATALOGUES: Cooke, L.: B. W. Sculpture 1980-1986. Fruitmarket Gallery. Edinburgh 1986 (cat.).– Roberts, J. (ed.): B. W. Fool's Gold. Tate Gallery, London et al. London 1996 (cat.).– B. W. Positive Earth – Negative Earth. Münchner Kunstverein. Munich 1987 (cat.).– B. W. An American Master Revealea. Davenport Museum of Art. Davenport 1995 (cat.)

WOOL Christopher
born **1955** Chicago American painter. **1984** First solo-exhibition at the Cable Gallery, New York. **1989** Solo-exhibition at the San Francisco Museum of Modern Art, **1991** at the Boyman van Beuningen Museum, Rotter-

dam, and at the Kunsthalle Bern. **1991** Took part in the exhibition "Metropolis" at the Martin-Gropius-Bau in Berlin. **1992** Participation in documenta 9 in Kassel.
MONOGRAPHS, CATALOGUES: New Work: C. W. San Francisco Museum of Modern Art. San Francisco 1989 (cat.).– O'Brien, G. (ed.): C. W. Cats in Bag – Bags in River. Museum Boymans-van Beuningen, Rotterdam et al. Rotterdam 1991 (cat.)

WOTRUBA Fritz
1907 Vienna – **1976** Vienna Austrian sculptor. **1921–1924** Trained as an engraver. **1926–1929** Studied sculpture at the Vienna School of Arts and Crafts. **1928** First *Torso*. **1930** Trip to Germany. Came to know Lehmbruck and Maillol. **1931** Solo-exhibition at the Museum Folkwang, Essen. **1932** Solo-exhibition at the Würthle gallery, Vienna. **1934** and **1948** participation at the Venice Biennale. **1938** Emigrated to Switzerland, settling in Zug. **1945** Returned to Austria and was appointed professor at the Vienna Academy. **1947** Met Giacometti, Daniel-Henri Kahnweiler and Zadkine in Paris. **1955/56** Touring exhibition starting at the Institute of Contemporary Art, Boston. **1959** and **1964** took part in documenta 2 and 3 in Kassel. **1967** Retrospective at the Haus der Kunst, Munich. **1977** Took part in documenta 6 in Kassel. **1980** Opening of the Fritz-Wotruba-Haus in Vienna. **1992** Retrospective at the Kunsthaus in Zug. After World War II, Wotruba abandoned the classical naturalistic style of his early works and moved towards abstraction, producing simple block-like structures with a rough surface. His works had a formative influence on various art movements of the 50s.
WRITINGS: Breicha, O. (ed.): Um W. Schriften zum Werk. Vienna 1968.– F. W.: Überlegungen. Gedanken zur Kunst. Oprecht and Zurich 1945
MONOGRAPHS, CATALOGUES: Besset, M. (ed.): F. W. Palais des Beaux-Arts. Brussels 1951 (cat.).– Breicha, O. (ed.): Um W. Schriften zum Werk. Vienna 1968.– Breicha, O.: F. W. Figur als Widerstand. Salzburg 1977, 1995.– Breicha, O. et al. (ed.): F. W. St. Gallen 1993.– Canetti, E.: F. W. Vienna 1955.– Demus, K.: F. W.

Vienna 1955.– Feuchtmüller, R. et al. (ed.): F. W. Die Kirche in Wien-Mauer. Vienna et al. 1977.– Heer, F.: F. W. Neuchâtel 1961, St. Gallen 1977.– Hofmann, F. W. Museum des 20. Jahrhunderts. Vienna 1963 (cat.).– Hofmann, W. (ed.): F. W. St. Gallen 1984.– Mitsch, E. (ed.): F. W. Druckgraphik 1950-1975. Graphische Sammlung Albertina. Vienna 1989 (cat.).– Peichl, G. (ed.): W. Hommage à W. Akademie der Bildenden Künste. Vienna 1985 (cat.).– Rudloff, M. (ed.): F. W. Der Bildhauer als Bühnenbildner. Gerhard-Marcks-Haus, Bremen. Vienna and Bremen 1992 (cat.).– Salis, J. R.: F. W. Zurich 1948.– F. W. Forte di Belvedere. Florence 1976 (cat.)

WYETH Andrew
born **1917** Chadds Ford (PA) American painter. Was taught to paint by his father, the illustrator N. C. Wyeth. **1937** Illustrated *Robin Hood*. From **1939**, with almost photographic accuracy, he painted landscapes, mainly in Pennsylvania and Maine where he spent most summers. He used tempera paints, depicting desolate scenes with the odd lonely figure. **1955** Made an Honorary Doctor of Fine Arts by Harvard University in Cambridge (MA). **1966** Retrospective at the Pennsylvania Academy of the Fine Arts, Philadelphia. **1971–1985** Series of 200 portraits entitled the *Helga Picture*. **1976** Retrospective at the Metropolitan Museum of Art, New York. Wyeth takes his motifs from his immediate surroundings. His works, which display many elements of Magic Realism, are full of veristic detail.
WRITINGS: A. W.: Autobiography. Boston 1995
CATALOGUE RAISONNE: Allen, D. and D. Jr. (ed.): W. The Collected Paintings, Illustrations and Murals. New York 1972
MONOGRAPHS, CATALOGUES: Corn, W. M. et al. (ed.): The Art of A. W. De Young Memorial Museum. San Francisco 1973 (cat.).– Dempsey, B. H. (ed.): A. W. Sozheastern Collections. Jacksonville Art Museum. Jacksonville 1992 (cat.).– Duff, J. H.: An American Vision. Three Generations of Wyeth Art. New York 1989.– Jur'eva, T. S.: A. W. Moscow 1986.– McCord, D. (ed.): A. W. Museum of Fine Arts, Boston. Greenwich (CT) 1970.– Meryman, R.: A. W. A Secret Life. New York 1996.– Richardson, E. P. (ed.): A. W. Temperas, Watercolors, Dry Brush Drawings. 1938-1966. The Pennsylvania Academy of Fine Arts, Philadelphia et al. Philadelphia 1966 (cat.).– Wilmerding, J. (ed.): A. W. The Helga Pictures. New York 1987.– A. W. Albright-Knox Art Gallery. Buffalo 1962 (cat.).– A. W. Two Worlds of A. W. Kuerners and Olsons. Metropolitan Museum of Art. New York 1976 (cat.).– A. W. Royal Academy of Arts. London 1980 (cat.).– A. W. Temperas, aquarelles, drybrush, dessins. Galerie C. Bernard. Paris 1980 (cat.).– Wyeth, B. J.: W. at Kuerners. Boston 1976

ZADKINE Ossip
1890 Smolensk – **1967** Paris
Russian-born French sculptor. **1905** Moved to England and from **1907** studied in London. **1909** Met Chagall in Vitebsk. Moved to Paris where, from **1911**, he studied at the Ecole des Beaux-Arts and exhibited for the first time at the Salon des Indépendants and the Salon d'Automne. **1912** Joined the Cubists and met Apollinaire, Archipenko, Picasso and Survage. **1913** Friendship with Modigliani. **1914–1917** Fought in the war and was poisoned by nerve gas. War drawings. **1921** Solo-exhibition at the Galerie Barbazanges. **1931** Trip to Greece. **1938** Long stay in New York. **1941** Moved to New York. **1945** Returned to Paris and taught at the Académie de la Grande Chaumière. **1949** Retrospective at the Musée National d'Art Moderne, Paris. **1950** Awarded a major prize for sculpture at the Venice Biennale. **1953** Memorial to the destruction of the City of Rotterdam. **1959** Participation in documenta 2 in Kassel. **1992** Exhibition at the Musée Réattu, Arles. Zadkine was one of the first artists to apply the principles of Cubism to sculpture.
WRITINGS: O. Z.: Comment je suis devenu sculpteur. Brussels 1951.– O. Z.: Le Maillet et le ciseau. Souvenirs de ma vie. Paris 1968
CATALOGUES RAISONNES: Czwiklitzer, C. (ed.): O. Z. Le Sculpteur-graveur de 1919 à 1967. Paris 1967.– Jianou, I. (ed.): O. Z. Catalogue raisonné des sculptures. Paris 1979.– Lecombre, S. (ed.): O. Z. L'œuvre sculpté. Paris 1994
MONOGRAPHS, CATALOGUES: Beranová, J. and J. Postma: Z. Rotterdam 1985.– Buchanan, D.: The Secret World of Z. Paris 1966.– Cassou, J.: O. Z. Amriswil 1962.– Cogniat, R.: O. Z. Paris 1958.– Gertz, U.: Z. Duiburg 1965.– Hammacher, A. M.: O. Z. Munich 1958, London and New York 1958.– Jianou, I.: Z. Paris 1964, 1979.– Lecombre, S. (ed.): Catalogue Musée Z. Sculptures. Paris 1989.– Lichtenstern, C.: O. Z. 1890-1967. Der Bildhauer und seine Ikonographie. Berlin 1980.– Marchal, G.-L. and S. Lecombre (ed.): O. Z. La Sculpture … toute une vie. Rodez 1992.– Moutashar, M. (ed.): Z. Bois et pierres. Musée Réattu, Arles et al. Arles 1992 (cat.).– Prax, V.: Avec Z. Souvenirs de notre vie. Lausanne, Paris 1973

ZAO WOU-KI
born **1921** Peking
Chinese-born French painter. **1935–1941** Studied at the Academy of Art in Hangzhou. **1940** Detailed analysis of the works of Klee, Matisse and Picasso. **1941–1947** Professor at the Academy of Art in Hangzhou. **1941** First solo-exhibition at the Sino-Soviet Society in Tongking. **1948** Moved to Paris. **1950** Solo-exhibition at the Galerie Pierre, Paris. Met Michaux and P. Loeb. **1953** Stage design for the ballet La Perle by R. Petit. **1955** Received the Carnegie Award in Pittsburgh. **1957/58**
Tour of the USA. **1965** Retrospective at the Museum Folkwang, Essen, and at the Albertina, Vienna. **1971–1975** Lived in China. **1981** Exhibition at the Grand Palais, Paris. **1990** Solo-exhibition at the Musée des Beaux-Arts, Tours. Zao Wou-ki is a representative of the Ecole de Paris, combining elements of Far Eastern calligraphy and lyrical landscape painting with Tachisme.
CATALOGUES RAISONNES: Agerup, J. (ed.): Z. W.-K. The Graphic Work. A Catalogue Raisonné 1937-1995. Skorping 1995.– Jacometti, N.: Catalogue raisonné de l'œuvre gravée et lithographiée de Z. W.-K. 1949-1954. Berne 1955.– Leymarie, J. and F. Marquet (ed.): Z. W.-K. Catalogue raisonné des peintures. Paris 1978-1986.– Marquet, F. and R. Callois (ed.): Z. W.-K. Les Estampes 1937-1974. Paris 1975
MONOGRAPHS, CATALOGUES: Daix, P. (ed.): Z. W.-K. L'œuvre 1935-1993. Neuchâtel 1994.– Join-Lambert, S. (ed.): Z. W.-K. Musée des Beaux-Arts. Tours 1990 (cat.).– Laude, J.: Z. W.-K. Brussels 1974.– Leymarie, J.: Z. W.-K. New York 1979.– Ragon, M.: Z. W.-K. Madrid 1962.– Roy, C.: Z. W.-K. Paris 1992.– Schneider, P. (ed.): Z. W.-K. Centre d'Art plastique contemporain. Paris 1988 (cat.).– Z. W.-K. and F. Marquet: Autoportrait. Paris 1988

ZENIUK Jerry
born **1945** Hamburg
German-born American painter. **1950** Moved to the USA. **1969** Graduated from the University of Boulder (CO), and then began to paint with pigments mixed with hot wax and graphite powder. **1971** First solo-exhibition in New York. **1973/74** Went to Hamburg and exhibited his encaustic wax paintings in a number of German cities. **1976** Stopped using wax and began to paint exclusively with natural pigments applied to the canvas in several layers to achieve contrasts of form and colour. **1977** Participation in documenta 6 in Kassel. **1977/78** DAAD scholarship to Berlin. **1981** Fellowship for painting from the National Endowment for the Arts. **1996** Retrospective at the Kunsthalle Karlsruhe.
MONOGRAPHS, CATALOGUES: Salzmann, S. (ed.): J. Z. 1971-1989. Kunsthalle
Bremen et al. Bremen 1990 (cat.).– J. Z. Palmenhaus. Städtische Galerie Villa Zanders. Bergisch-Gladbach 1994 (cat.).– J. Z. Staatliche Kunsthalle Karlsruhe. Karlsruhe 1996 (cat.)

ZHANG Xiaogang
born **1958** Kunming (Province of Yunnan) Chinese painter. **1982** Completed his course in oil painting at the Academy of Fine Arts in Sichuan. **1986** Founder-member of the Society for Research into Western Art. Taught at the Academy of Fine Arts in Sichuan, Chongqing.

ZORIO Gilberto
born **1944** Adorno Micca
Italian Arte Povera artist. **1963–1970** Studied sculpture and painting at the Accademia Albertina di Belle Arti, Turin. **1967** First solo-exhibition at the Galleria Sperone, Turin. Took part in the exhibition "Arte Povera" at the University of Genoa. **1968** Participated in the exhibition "Prospect '68" at the Kunsthalle Düsseldorf. **1969** Solo-exhibition at the Sonnabend gallery, Paris. **1971** Took part in the Arte Povera exhibition at the Kunstverein Munich and **1972** in documenta 5 in Kassel. **1976** Solo-exhibition at the Kunstmuseum in Lucerne and **1985** at the Württembergische Kunstverein, Stuttgart. **1986** Participation at the Venice Biennale and solo-exhibition at the Pompidou Centre, Paris. **1987** Solo-exhibition at the Stedelijk Van Abbe Museum, Eindhoven. Zorio uses many different materials in all sorts of combinations. His sculptures, that seem to shatter space, are as dynamic as his performances.
MONOGRAPHS, CATALOGUES: Ammann, J. C. et al. (ed.): G. Z. Kunstmuseum. Lucerne 1976 (cat.).– Ammann, J. C. (ed.): G. Z. Stedelijk Museum. Amsterdam 1979 (cat.).– Ammann, J. C. et al. (ed.): G. Z. Opere 1967 al 1984. Galleria Civica. Modena 1985 (cat.).– Celant, G. (ed.): G. Z. Galleria Christian Stein. Torino 1987 (cat.).– Celant, G. and R. H. Fuchs (ed.): G. Z. Stedelijk Van Abbe Museum. Eindhoven 1987 (cat.).– Celant, G. (ed.): IVAM Centro del Carme. Valencia 1991 (cat.).– Celant, G. (ed.): G. Z. Florence 1992 (cat.).– David, C. et al. (ed.):
G. Z. Centre Georges Pompidou. Paris 1986 (cat.).– Dimitrijevic, N. and M. Bertoni (ed.): G. Z. Institute of Contemporary Arts, Amsterdam et al. Amsterdam 1991 (cat.).– Merz, B. and D. Zaccharopoulos (ed.): G. Z. Pinacoteca Comunale. Ravenna 1982 (cat.).– Merz, B. et al. (ed.): G. Z. Au fond de la cour à droite. Galerie Pietro Sparta. Chagny 1984 (cat.).– G. Z. Württembergischer Kunstverein, Stuttgart et al. Stuttgart 1985 (cat.).–

Acknowledgments, copyrights, credits

The editor, the authors and the publisher wish to thank the artists, museums and public collections, galleries and private collectors, archives, photographers and all other institutions and individuals who have helped us in compiling this publication over a period of three years. The editor and the publisher have made every effort to ensure that all copyrights were respected for the works illustrated and that the necessary permission was obtained from the artists, their heirs, representatives or estates. Given the large number of artists involved, this was not possible in every case, in spite of intensive research. Should any claims remain outstanding, the copyright holders or their representatives are requested to contact the publisher.

© VG BILD-KUNST, BONN 1998: Abakanowicz, Abramovic, Adler, Agam, Albers, Alechinsky, Andre, Antes, Anuszkiewicz, Archipenko, Arman, Arp, Arroyo, Artschwager, Atlan, Balla, Balthus, Baranov-Rossiné, Barceló, Basquiat, Bauchant, Baumeister, Bazaine, Beckmann, Belling, Bellmer, Benton, Bernard, Beuys, Bill, Bissier, Bissière, Blumenfeld, Boltanski, Bombois, Bonnard, Bourgeois, Brancusi, Braque, Brauner, Broodthaers, Brüning, Buchheister, Buffet, Bulatov, Buren, Bury, Calder, Campendonk, Campigli, Capogrossi, Carrà, Casorati, Caulfield, César, Chagall, Chaissac, Chamberlain, Charchoune, Chia, Chillida, Claasen, Coburn, Constant, Corneille, Crotti, Cruz-Diez, Csáky, Dado, Davis D., Davis S., De Chirico, De Kooning, Denis, Depero, Derain, Dewasne, Diller, Dix, Doesburg, Domela, Dominguez, Dongen, Dorazio, Dubuffet, Duchamp, Dufy, Ensor, Erfurth, Ernst, Erró, Estève, Etienne-Martin, Export, Fahlström, Fautrier, Feininger L., Felixmüller, Fetting, Fischer, Flavin, Francis, Friesz, Gargallo, Gerz, Giacometti, Girke, Gleizes, Goncharova, González, Gorky, Graves, Gromaire, Grosz, Gruber, Gursky, Guttuso, Haacke, Hains, Hamilton, Hartung H., Hausmann, Heiliger, Heisig, Held, Hélion, Herbin, Hérold, Hirshfield, Höch, Hödicke, Hoehme, Hoerle, Horn, Itten, Jacobsen, Jacquet, Janco, Javlensky, Jensen, Johns, Judd, Kabakov, Kahlo, Kandinsky, Kanoldt, Kanovitz, Kisling, Klapheck, Klee, Klein Y., Kokoschka, Kosuth, Kramer, Kudo, Kupka, Lakner, Lam, Lanskoy, Lapicque, Lardera, Larionov, Laurencin, Laurens, Lavier, Leck, Léger, Le Moal, Le Parc, Leroy, Levine, LeWitt, Lhote, Lichtenstein, Liebermann, Lindner, Lissitzky, Lohse, Mack, Magnelli, Magritte, Maillol, Manessier, Mangold, Manguin, Manzoni, Marcoussis, Marden, Marini, Marquet, Masson, Matta, Mattheuer, Metzel, Metzinger, Michaux, Miotte, Miró, Moholy-Nagy, Monory, Morandi, Morellet, Morris, Mortensen, Mueller, Münter, Nauman, Nevelson, Newman, Nicholson, Nitsch, Noland, Nothhelfer, O'Keeffe, Odenbach, Olitski, Opalka, Oppenheim M., Ozenfant, Palermo, Paolozzi, Pascin, Permeke, Pevsner, Picabia, Poirier, Poliakoff, Pollock, Poons, Prager, Puni, Purrmann, Räderscheidt, Radziwill, Ramos, Rauschenberg, Raysse, Reinhardt, Richier, Rickey, Riopelle, Rivera, Rivers, Rodchenko, Rohlfs, Rosenbach, Rosenquist, Rotella, Rothko, Rouault, Ruff, Ruthenbeck, Saint Phalle, Salle, Saura, Schmidt-Rottluff, Schneider, Schöffer, Schoonhoven, Schumacher, Schütte, Schwitters, Segal G., Séraphine, Serra, Servranckx, Severini, Shahn, Signac, Simonds, Singier, Slevogt, Smith D., Solano, Sonnier, Soto, Soulages, Soutine, Spencer, Spoerri, Staël, Stella F., Stepanova, Stöhrer, Strelow, Survage, Sutherland, Taeuber-Arp, Takis, Tal-Coat, Tanguy, Tatlin, Thieler, Tilson, Tinguely, Tobey, Torres-García, Trier, Trockel, Tübke, Umbo, Valmier, Vantongerloo, Vasarely, Vieira da Silva, Villeglé, Villon, Virnich, Visser, Vivin, Vlaminck, Vostell, Vuillard, Walther, Wesselmann, Winter, Wols, Zadkine, Zao Wou-ki. Adams: © 1998 by the Trustees of the Ansel Adams Publishing Rights Trust, Mill Valley (CA). All Rights Reserved.– Altenbourg: © 1998 Nachlaß Altenbourg/Galerie Brusberg Berlin.– Appel: © 1998 K. Appel Foundation/VG Bild-Kunst, Bonn.– Auerbach: © 1998 Marlborough Fine Art Ltd., London.– Bacon: © 1998 Estate of Francis Bacon, Marlborough Fine Art Ltd., London.– Barlach: © 1998 Ernst und Hans Barlach Lizenzverwaltung, Ratzeburg.– Beaton: © 1998 Cecil Beaton Archive, courtesy of Sotheby's, London.– Blake: c/o Waddington Galleries Ltd., London.– Blossfeldt: © 1998 Karl Blossfeldt-Archiv/Ann und Jürgen Wilde/VG Bild-Kunst, Bonn.– Boeckl: © 1998 Oskar Boeckl, Fuschel am Berg.– Borofsky: © 1998 Paula Cooper Gallery, New York.– Brandt: © 1998 Bill Brandt Archive Ltd., London.– Buchloh: © 1998 Nachlaß Buchholz, Königstein.– Burri: © 1998 Fondazione Palazzo Albizzini, Città di Castello, Perugia.– Byars: © 1998 Estate James Lee Byars.– Dalí: © 1998 Salvador Dalí, Fundación Gala-Salvador Dalí/VG Bild-Kunst, Bonn.– Davringhausen: © 1998 Galerie Wildbrand, Cologne.– Delaunay, Delaunay-Terk: © 1998 L & M Services B. V., Amsterdam.– Delvaux: © 1998 Fondation Paul Delvaux S. Idesbald, Belgium/VG Bild-Kunst, Bonn.– Dexel: © 1998 Bernhard Dexel, Hamburg.– Dine: © 1998 Pace Wildenstein Gallery, New York.– Di Suvero: © 1998 Oil & Steel Gallery, Long Island City.– Doisneau: The Estate of Robert Doisneau/Rapho agence de presse photographique, Paris.– Drtikol: © 1998 Ervina Boková-Drtikolová, Podolsky.– Eisenstaedt, A. Feininger: © 1998 Time Life Syndication, New York.– Evans: © 1998 Estate of Walker Evans, The Metropolitan Museum of Art, New York.– Fontana: © 1998 Fondazione Fontana, Milan.– Freundlich: © 1998 Les amis de Jeanne et Otto Freundlich, Pontoise.– Gabo: © 1998 Nina and Abraham Williams, Biddenden.– Gidal: © 1998 Pia Gidal, Jerusalem.– Glarner: © 1998 Fritz Glarner Estate, Locarno.– Gormley: © 1998 Jay Joplin/White Cube Gallery, London.– Gottlieb: © 1998 Adolph and Esther Gottlieb Foundtion/VG Bild-Kunst, Bonn.– Graeser: © 1998 Camille Graeser-Stiftung, Zurich.– Haas: © 1998 Tony Stone/Getty Communication, London.– Hanson: © 1998 Wesla Hanson, Davie (FL).– Haring: © 1998 Keith Haring Estate, New York.– Heartfield: © 1998 The Heartfield Community of Heirs/VG Bild-Kunst, Bonn.– Heckel: © Nachlaß Erich Heckel, Hemmenhofen.– Heizer: © 1998 Xavier Fourcade Inc., New York.– Henri: © 1998 Galleria Martini e Rocchetti, Genoa.– Hesse: © 1998 The Estate of Eva Hesse, New York.– Hirst: © 1998 Jay Joplin/White Cube Gallery, London.– Hockney: © 1998 The David Hockney No. 1 U. S. Trust, Los Angeles.– Hofer: © 1998 Nachlaß Hofer, c/o Kunsthandlung Köhrmann, Cologne.– Hofmann: © 1998 The Estate of Hans Hofmann, Courtesy Andre Emmerich Gallery, New York.– Horst: © 1998 Richard J. Horst, New York.– Hoyningen-Huene: © 1998 Richard J. Horst, New York.– Hundertwasser: © 1998 Joram Harel Management, Vienna.– Immendorff, Kirkeby, Lüpertz, Penck: © 1998 Galerie Michael Werner, Cologne and New York.– Jorn: © 1998 Estate of Asger Jorn, Copenhagen.– Kertész: © 1998 Ministère de la Culture, France.– Kienholz: © 1998 Estate of Edward Kienholz, Nancy Kienholz, Hope (ID).– Kippenberger: © 1998 Galerie Gisela Capitain, Cologne.– Kirchner: © 1998 Ingeborg und Dr. Wolfgang Henze-Ketterer, Wichtrach/Bern.– Kitaj: © 1998 Marlborough Fine Art Ltd., London.– Kline: © 1998 VAGA Inc., New York.– Kobro: © 1998 Muzeum Sztuki,

Lodz.– Kricke: © 1998 Sabine Kricke-Güse, Saarbrücken.– Krull: © 1998 Germaine-Krull-Stiftung, Braunfels.– Kühn: © 1998 Kühn-Nachlaß, Birgitz.– Kushner: © 1998 D. C. Moore Gallery, New York.– Lange: © 1998 The Estate of Dorothea Lange, Oakland Museum, Oakland (CA).– Le Corbusier: © 1998 FLC/VG Bild-Kunst, Bonn.– Lempicka: © 1998 Kizette de Lempicka-Foxhall, Houston.– Lipchitz: © 1998 The Estate of Jacques Lipchitz, courtesy, Marlborough Gallery, New York.– Louis: © 1998 Estate of Morris Louis, Washington.– McLean: © 1998 Anhony d'Offay Gallery, London.– Mantz: © 1998 Grete Mantz-Schmidt, Maastricht.– Manzù: © 1998 Inge Manzù, Rome.– Marcks: © 1998 Brigitte Marcks-Geck, Hamburg.– Matisse: © 1998 Succession H. Matisse/VG Bild-Kunst, Bonn.– Matta-Clark: © 1998 Courtesy Holly Solomon Gallery, New York.– Meidner: © 1998 Ludwig Meidner-Archiv, Jüdisches Museum der Stadt Frankfurt/Main.– Meistermann: © 1998 Georg-Meistermann-Nachlaßverwaltung, Cologne/VG Bild-Kunst, Bonn.– Merz: © 1998 Archivio Mario Merz, Torino.– Moholy: © 1998 Friedrich Karsten, London.– Mondrian: © 1998 Mondrian/Holtzman Trust, c/o Beeldrecht, Amsterdam/VG Bild-Kunst, Bonn.– Moore: © 1998 The Henry Moore Foundation, Much Hadham, Hertfordshire.– Morley: © 1998 Mary Boone Gallery, New York.– Motherwell: © 1998 Dedalus Foundation/Society VG Bild-Kunst, Bonn.– Munch: © 1998 The Munch Museum/The Munch Ellingsen Group/VG Bild-Kunst, Bonn.– Munkacsi: © 1998 Joan Munkacsi, Woodstock (NY).– Nay: © 1998 Nachlaß Ernst Wilhelm Nay, Frau Elisabeth Nay-Scheibler, Cologne.– Newton: © 1998 Helmut Newton/Galerie Rudolf Kicken, Cologne.– Nolde: © 1998 Stiftung Seebüll Ada und Emil Nolde, Neukirchen-Seebüll.– Oelze: © 1998 Richard Oelze Archiv, Aerzen.– Oursler: © 1998 Metro Pictures, New York.– Pechstein: © 1998 Max Pechstein Urheberrechtsgemeinschaft, Hamburg.– Penn: Courtesy Vogue. © 1950 (renewed 1978) by The Condé Nast Publications Inc., New York.– Picasso: © 1998 Succession Picasso/VG Bild-Kunst, Bonn.– Polke: © 1998 Sigmar Polke/Galerie Klein, Bad Münstereifel.– Pomodoro: © 1998 Arnoldo Pomodoro, courtesy, Marlborough Gallery, New York.– Ray: © 1998 Man Ray Trust, Paris/VG Bild-Kunst, Bonn.– Renger-Patzsch: © 1998 Albert-Renger-Patzsch-Archiv/Ann und Jürgen Wilde/VG Bild-Kunst, Bonn.– Rheims: © 1998 Gina Kehayoff Verlag, Munich.– Rosai: © 1998 Ottone Rosai, Prato.– Ryman: © John Weber Gallery, New York.– Salomon: © 1998 Peter Hunter, Den Haag.– Sander: © 1998 Photograp. Sammlung/SK Stiftung Kultur-A. Sander Archiv, Cologne/VG Bild-Kunst, Bonn.– Schad: © 1998 Günter A. Richter Edition, Rottach-Egern.– Schlemmer: © 1998 C. Ramon Schlemmer, Oggebbio.– Schlichter: © 1998 Viola Roehr-v. Alvensleben, Munich.– Schrimpf: © 1998 Nachlaß Georg Schrimpf, Munich.– Seymour: © 1998 David Seymour Estate, Washington.– Steichen: © 1998 Steichen Carousel, New York.– Steinert: © 1998 Stefan Steinert, Essen/Museum Folkwang, Essen.– Stieglitz: © 1998 The Georgia O'Keefe Foundation, Albiquiu (NM).– Still: © 1998 Mrs. Clyfford Still, New Windsor (MD).– Strand: © 1998 Aperture Foundation Inc., Paul Strand Archive, Millerton (NY).– Tapies: © 1998 Fondation Antoni Tapies Barcelona/VG Bild-Kunst, Bonn.– Tuymans: © 1998 Zeno X Gallery, Antwerp.– Twombly: © 1998 Cy Twombly Archives of Painting and Drawings, Heiner Bastian, Berlin.– Uhlmann: © 1998 Nachlaß Hans Uhlmann, Hanover.– Utrillo: © 1998 Association Maurice Urillo/VG Bild-Kunst, Bonn.– Vordemberge-Gildewart: © 1998 Stiftung Vordemberge-Gildewart, Lachen.– Wall: © 1998 Marian Goodman Gallery, New York.– Warhol: © 1998 The Andy Warhol Foundation for the Visual Art/VG Bild-Kunst, Bonn.– Weegee (Arthur Fellig): © 1998 reproduced with permission of the InternatIonal Center of Photography, New York.– Weston: © 1998 Center for Creative Photography, Tucson (AZ).– Wood: © 1998 VAGA Inc., New York.

© 1998 THE ARTISTS: Acconci, Albright, Almy, Anderson, Anselmo, Arakawa, Arcangelo, Armajani, Armitage, Aycock, Baj, Baldessari, Baselitz, Baziotes, Becher, Berghe, Berlewi, Birnbaum, Blais, Bleckner, Blume, Botero, Brecht, Brisley, Bruch, Brus, Bruskin, Burden, Campus, Caro, Chadwick, Chaldei, Charlton, Christo & Jeanne-Claude, Clemente, Close, Colville, Corpora, Cottingham, Cragg, Cucchi, Dai Guangyu, Darboven, De Maria, Duncan, Eddy, Emshwiller, Estes, Fabro, Fischl, Flanagan, Förg, Frank, Frankenthaler, Freud, Frize, Garouste, Garrin, Geiger, Gertsch, Gilbert & George, Gober, Goings, Goldin, Golub, Götz, Graubner, Green, Grützke, Gundlach, Günther, Hajek, Halley, Hantaï, Heerich, Hegedüs, Helnwein, Hill, Holzer, Hoover, Indiana, Jenney, Jetelová, Jochims, Jonas, Jones, Kantor, Kaprow, Karavan, Kawamata, Kawara, Keetman, Kelley, Kelly, Kiefer, King, Klauke, Knoebel, Koons, Kosoff, Kounellis, Krims, Kruger, Kubota, Lafontaine, Lang, Lasker, Lassnig, Lebeck, Liu Wei, Long, Longo, Luginbühl, McBride, McCollum, Marioni, Martens, Martin, Mathieu, Michals, Neusüss, Oehlen, Oldenburg, Oppenheim D., Paik, Paladino, Panamarenko, Paolini, Parks, Pearlstein, Pedersen, Penone, Petrov, Pezold, Phillips, Piene, Pistoletto, Plessi, Prigov, Prince, Pusenkoff, Rainer, Reed, Reusch, Richter G., Riley, Rinke, Rist, Roth, Rothenberg, Rückriem, Ruscha, Samaras, Schapiro, Schnabel, Schultze, Seaman, Sekine, Shaw, Sherman, Sieverding, Smith K., Smithson, Snelson, Sonderborg, Spero, Stamos, Steinbach, Stelarc, Storch, Sugái, Taaffe, ThIemaque, Thek, Thiebaud, Thursz, Tillmans, Trakas, Tucker, Tuttle, Uecker, Ullman, Vasulka, Vedova, Viola, Wang Cheng, Weibel, Wei Guangquing, Wegman, Wilson, Winters, Woodrow, Wool, Wyeth, Zeniuk, Zhang Xiaogang, Zorio.

© 1998 THE HEIRS OF THE ARTISTS OR THEIR ESTATES: Afro, Albright, Armagnac, Baertling, Baziotes, Berghe, Berlewi, Birolli, Butler, Calderara, Cornell, Crippa, Demuth, Diebenkorn, Disler, Dove, Epstein, Exter, Filatov, Filliou, Fleischmann, Freund, Fruhtrunk, Gnoli, Goller, Grandma Moses, Grossberg, Guston, Hartley, Hartung K., Hausner, Hepworth, Hine, Hoelzel, Hubbuch, Huszár, Ignatovich, Kassák, Kemény, Kliun, Kudojarov, Macdonald-Wright, MacIunas, Malevich, Meyer, Miller, Moche, Nolan, Orozco, Pasmore, Penalba, Petrussov, Prampolini, Richter H., Russolo, Santomaso, Schwarzkogler, Segal A., Segall, Seiwert, Shaikhet, Sheeler, Sima, Siqueiros, Sironi, Smet, Smith T., Soldati, Soutter, Stazewski, Strzeminski, Tamayo, Thorn-Prikker, Tomlin, Toyen, Tworkov, Ursula, Velde, Verefkin, Wagemaker, Witkiewicz, Wölfli, Wotruba.

PHOTO CREDITS. The locations and owners of the works illustrated are noted in the respective captions unless these wished to remain anonymous or were not known to the editor. The archives, photographers and copyright holders who gave us their support are listed below. We wish to thank them for their kind assistance. The editor and the publisher would be grateful for notification of any omissions or errors in this respect. The numbers refer to the book pages.

Abbrevations: t = top, tr = top right, tl = top left, c = centre, b = bottom, bl = bottom left, br = bottom right. Aachen: Ludwig Forum für Internationale Kunst 396 t (Photo: Anne Gold), 514 (Photo: Anne Gold), 563 t, 566 t; Sammlung Niescher 413 t.– Ahlen: Fritz-Winter-Haus 236.– Amsterdam: Heiting Collection 642 br, 648, 660 t, 660 b, 661 t, 661 b, 662 t, 665 t, 669 b, 675 t, 676 tr, 678 b.– Archives of the authors: 20, 26 t, 183 t, 248 t, 257 tl, 263 br, 379 bl, 438 t, 445, 446 b, 474 b, 478 tl, 483 t, 497 t, 499, 502 t, 504 t, 506 t, 512 b, 523 t, 528 t, 530 tr, 532 t, 535 t, 537 t, 538 bt, 559 t, 562 t, 562 bl, 566 b, 569 t, 572 t.– Archives of the artists: 238 t, 240 b, 247 tl, 263 bl, 264o, 264 bl, 264 br, 265 tl, 265 tr, 296 b (Photo: Octavian Stacescu), 297, 307 t, 336, 340 t, 342 t, 342 b, 343 b, 354 b, 366 t, 367 b (Photo: Joachim Rosse), 372 t, 375 t, 381 b, 395 br, 475 tr, 475 br, 490 tl, 493 b, 495 t, 502 b, 503, 530 b, 538 bl, 545, 548 t, 548 c, 548 b, 552 b, 553 t, 564 t, 564 b, 567 t, 567 b, 570 t, 570 c, 591, 597 t, 597 c, 601 t (Photo: Werner Schulz), 602 t, 603 t, 603 b, 604, 605 br (Photo: Ilja Schnorr), 608 t, 609 t, 609 b (Photo: Lothar Schnepf), 610 b, 613 t, 615 l, 616 b, 617 t, 662 b, 679 t, 679 b, 680 tl, 680 tr.– Bad Münstereifel: Courtesy Galerie Klein 388, 678 tr.– Basel: Courtesy Galerie Beyeler 351 t; Courtesy Galerie Buchmann 363; Öffentliche Kunstsammlung Basel (Photo: Martin Bühler) 465 b, 556 t.– Belen (NM): Donald Woodman 551.– Berlin: Archiv für Kunst und Geschichte (AKG) 2, 10, 27, 35, 38, 41 t, 45, 46 bl, 47 t, 49, 57, 62, 64 t (Photo: Erich Lessing), 65 c, 69, 77 t, 80 t, 82, 90 t, 91 b, 93, 100, 111 tl, 111 tr (Photo: Erich Lessing), 115, 118, 121 b, 125 (Photo: David Heald), 128 t, 138, 143, 150 b, 156 tl, 159, 160 (Photo: Erich Lessing), 163 tl, 163 tr (Photo: Erich Lessing), 163 b, 164 tr, 165 tr, 168, 169, 174 tl, 178 t, 178 b, 181 t, 200 b, 202 tr, 204 tr, 208 tl, 210, 215, 216/217, 230 tr, 247 tr (Photo: Erich Lessing), 249, 270, 275, 276 tl, 291, 292 bl, 303 b, 311 t, 312 t, 313 b, 320 t, 321 b, 324 t, 325, 341 b, 345, 352 t; Brücke-Museum (Photo: R. Friedrich) 424 t; Courtesy Busche Galerie 359 b; Courtesy Galerie Brusberg 367 t, 368 b; Courtesy Galerie Max Hetzler 360, 375 br, 391 b, 392 t, 392 b, 393 tr; Courtesy Ladengalerie 367 tl; Fine Art Rafael Vostell 584.– Bochum: c Bochum Kunstvermittlung 542 t, 542 l, 542 r (Photo: Gerd Geyer), 606.– Bonn: Kunst- und Ausstellungshalle der Bundesrepublik Deutschland (Photo: P. Oszwald) 597 b, 599 br, 614 t; Rheinisches Landesmuseum 637 b, 640 tl, 642 tl, 642 tr, 652, 658, 659 t, 659 b, 670 tr, 674 b; Stiftung für Kunst und Kultur und Kunstmuseum (Photos: Norbert Faehling) 398, 399.– Boston: C. O. White 590 tr.– Cologne: 235 Media 601 bl, 613 c, 613 b, 617 b (Photo: Seaman); Courtesy Galerie Reckermann 328 br; Courtesy Galerie Ricke 393 tl, 394 t; Courtesy Jablonka Galerie 394 br; Elisabeth Jappe 602 br, 603 c; Elisabeth Nay-Scheibler 237; Friedrich Rosenstiel 596, 602 bl; Internationale Kunstmesse (Photo: Elmar Thomas) 608 bl; Klemens Gasser und Tanja Grunert GmbH 618; Michael Konze 416 t; Rheinisches Bildarchiv 54, 110 bl, 207 t, 251, 255, 261 t, 299, 301 t, 308 br, 310 t, 314, 315, 316/317, 319 t, 323 b, 339 b, 340 br, 361 t, 361 b, 362 b, 369 b, 370 t, 370 b, 371 t, 371 b, 412 b, 436 br, 441 b, 462, 464 t, 481, 485 b, 492 b, 511 t, 512 t, 518, 520, 523 b, 527 br, 528 b, 530 tr, 536 b, 536 br, 537 b, 612 t, 620, 622 t, 622 b, 623, 624, 625, 626, 627, 629, 630 t, 630 b, 631 t, 631 b, 632 t, 632 bl, 632 br, 633 t, 633 b, 634, 635, 636 t, 636 b, 637 t, 637 c, 638 t, 638 bl, 638 br, 639, 640 t, 640 b, 641 t, 641 b, 642 bl, 643 t, 643 b, 644, 645 tl, 645 tr, 645 b, 646 t, 646 b, 647, 649, 650 t, 650 b, 651 t, 651 b, 653, 654, 655 t, 655 b, 656 t, 656 c, 656 b, 657, 663 l, 663 r, 664 t, 664 b, 665 b, 666 t, 666 c, 666 b, 667 t, 667 b, 668 b, 669 t, 670 bl, 670 br, 671 t, 671 b, 672 t, 672 b, 673 t, 673 bl, 673 br, 674 t, 675 b, 676 b; Westdeutscher Rundfunk (WDR) 595.– Darmstadt: Hessisches Landesmuseum (Photo: S. Althöfer) 554.– Duisburg: Wilhelm Lehmbruck Museum 414 t, 418, 496 t, 557 bl.– Düren: Sammlung Renker 539 t.– Düsseldorf: Courtesy Galerie Gmyrek 375 bl; Courtesy Galerie Hans Mayer 386 t; Courtesy Galerie Karin Fesel 180 tr, 366 b; Courtesy Galerie Konrad Fischer 552 tl; Kunstsammlung Nordrhein-Westfalen (Photo: Walter Klein), 262, 326; Monika Baumgartl (photo) 540 br, 600; Walter Vogel (photo) 577; Wolfgang Volz 540, 549, 550.– Emden: Kunsthalle in Emden 397 tl, 397 tr.– Esslingen: Fingerle 113 t.– Frankfurt-on-Main: Lufthistorische Gesellschaft am Flughafen Frankfurt am Main 446 t.– Fuschel am Berg: Oskar Boeckl 246 b.– Haigerloch: Sammlung Sabine Schwenk 391 t.– Hamburg: Barlach Haus 413 b; Hamburger Kunsthalle (Photo: Elke Walford) 475 tr, 575 t; Sammlung F. C. Gundlach 677 tr.– Hanover: Ponton European Media Art LAB 617 c; Sprengel Museum Hannover 461, 468.– Heidelberg: Edition Staeck (Photo: Giancarlo Pancaldi) 605 bl.– Hempstead (NY): Eric Politzer 552 tr.– Herrsching: Ehemaliges Archiv Schuler 94 b, 157 b.– Humblebæk: Louisiana Museum of Modern Art 199 c, 453, 473, 483 b, 489, 490 tl, 540 bl, 558 t.– Kassel: Documenta-Archiv 533 b (Photo: Dirk Bleicher), 560, 611 r; Frank Mihm 544 t, 563 b, 565, 598 t; Georg Memec 541; Neue Galerie Kassel 590 b.– Küsnacht: Walter Bechtler-Stiftung 506 b.– Lodz: Muzeum Sztuki 449.– London: Courtesy Annely Juda Fine Art 355 t, 355 b, 447 b, 531 t; Kasmin Ltd. 531 br, 532 t; Lund Humpries 89; Marlborough International Fine Art 332, 333, 379 br; Saatchi Collection 572 c, 573 br; Tate Gallery 435, 491 bl (Photo: F. L. Kenett); Time Life 310 b.– Lucerne: Courtesy Galerie Rosengart 218 t.– Mannheim: Städtische Kunsthalle Mannheim 415 t, 443 t.– Mexico City: Rafael Doniz 205 tl, 206 b.– Much Hadham, Hertfordshire: Henry Moore Foundation 402, 476.– Milan: Collection Panza di Biumo 535 c, 535 b, 598 b; Edizione Beatrice d'Este 40 b; Fabbri 78 tl, 78 bl, 87 t, 88 tr, 88 br, 98 t, 122 t, 143 b, 154 tr, 174 tr, 184 b, 239 tl, 439 tl, 467 b; Galleria Schwarz 459; Le Arti 417.– Mulhouse: Braun 47 br.– Munich: Archiv Alexander Koch 43 b, 53, 60, 96, 112 tl, 113 b, 116, 182, 188, 190 l, 196 b; Archiv Bruckmann 79 tl, 226 bl; Archiv KML 30; Courtesy Barbara Gross Galerie 383 b; Courtesy Galerie Walser 356 b; Courtesy Sammlung Goetz 362 t, 390, 395 bl, 614 b, 676 tl (Photo: Raimund Koch); Galerie Heiner Friedrich 547 b; Marc Weis & Martin De Mattia 573 bl.– Münster: Westfälisches Landesmuseum für Kunst und Kulturgeschichte 539 b; Napa (CA): Hess Collection 158 bl, 222 tl, 223 tr, 240 t, 288 b, 292 br, 340 bl, 343 t, 364, 376 t, 441 b, 538 t.– Neuchâtel: Ides et Calendes 212.– Neukirchen-Seebüll: Stiftung Seebüll Ada und Emil Nolde 51 b.– Neuss-Selikum: Gerhard Hoehme Archiv (Photo: Olaf Bergmann) 266 b.– New York: Courtesy Barbara Gladstone Gallery 611 l; Courtesy Blum Helman Gallery 544 bl; Courtesy Byard Hoffman Foundation 612 bl; Courtesy D. C. Moore Gallery 353 l; Courtesy Lelong Gallery 393 b; Courtesy Leo Castelli Gallery 385 bl, 605 t; Courtesy Pace Wildenstein 574 t; Courtesy Sperone Westwater 557 br; Harry Shunk 578 t, 580 c, 581 t; New York Graphic Society 107, 203 t; Performing Art Services 583 t; Perls Galleries 431 l; Silvermann Collection (Photo: Rolf Jährling) 587 t, 588 b; The Museum of Modern Art 438 l.– Otterlo: Rijksmuseum Kröller-Müller 516.– Paris: Collection Ninon Robelin 522 b; Courtesy Galerie Denise René 171 br; Courtesy Galerie Louise Leiris 218 b; Courtesy Galerie Yvon Lambert 385 br; Courtesy Marianne et Pierre Nahon, Galerie Beaubrug 576; Galerie de France 470 b, 471 b; Galerie Durand-Dessert (Photo: Adam Rzepka) 570 b; Galerie Flinker 495; Marc Vaux 440; Musée National d'Art Moderne, Centre Georges Pompidou 444, 466; Musée Rodin (Photo: Bruno Jarret) 408.– Remscheid: Sammlung Feelisch 583 (Photo: Robert R. McElroy), 587 l, 589 t, 614 b.– Rovereto: Museo Fortunato Depero 436 bl.– Saint-Paul-de-Vence: Fondation Maeght 505 b.– Seattle: Charles Adler 497 b.– Stuttgart: Archiv Kohlhammer 150 t; Sammlung Südwest LB 353 b; Staatsgalerie Stuttgart 423 t, 587 r

(Archiv Sohm), 587 b (Archiv Sohm).– Torini: Galleria Galatea 64 b; Paolo Mussat Sartor 557 l.– Venice: Peggy Guggenheim Collection 493 tr.– Vienna: Jaffé 47 bl, 129, 205 b; Museum moderner Kunst 521, 522 tr, 586 b, 599 t; L. Hoffenreich 585 t.– Winterthur: Sammlung Oskar Reinhart 412 t.– Zurich: Alesco AG 559 b, 572 b, 574 b, 601 br; Courtesy Galerie Bruno Bischofberger 324 b, 377 b, 378 b, 384 t, 387 t, 507, 508; Courtesy Galerie Thomas Ammann 276 tr, 285, 378 t, 380 b, 382 tl, 394 bl; Kunsthaus Zurich, Alberto Giacometti Stiftung 488 b. The remaining illustrations belong to the editor's archive and the archive of Benedikt Taschen Verlag, Cologne.

PORTRAITS: Adams, Ansel: Weston.– Adelmann, Marianne: Armitage, César, Hajek, Kricke, Lardera, Penalba, Pomodoro, Schöffer.– Akademie der Kunst, Berlin: Heartfield.– Annely Juda Fine Art, London: Green.– Araiy, JuanVictor: Orozco.– Archiv Sohm, Stuttgart: Macunias.– Archives of American Art: Benton, Louis, Flanagan, Hopper.– Archivio Storico delle Arti Contemporanee della Biennale di Venezia: Boccioni, Morandi, Severini.– Arendt, Karl: Buchholz.– Armstrong, David: Goldin.– Arthur, John: Pearlstein.– ATP Bilderdienst, Zurich: Bill.– August Sander Archiv, Cologne: Seiwert.– Barbara Gross Galerie, Munich: Spero.– Barcellona, Marianne: Graves, Nauman.– Bauer, Karlheinz: Bellmer.– Baumgartl, Monika: Rinke.– BBC Hulton Picture Library: Epstein, O'Keeffe, Spencer, Stieglitz.– Benson, Bob: De Maria.– Bercholt: Le Moal.– Bergmann, Olaf: Hoehme.– Bettex, Ivan: Crotti.– Bezzola, Leonardo: Saint Phalle.– Boelhouwer, H. C.: Schoonhoven.– Boubat, Edouard: Hantaï.– Bravo, Manuel Alvarez: Rivera.– Buchholz, Daniel: Tillmans.– Burckhardt, Rudolph: Diller.– Chevalier, Yvonne: Magnelli.– Cooper, Martha: Fischl.– Crespelle, J.-P.: Gris.– Culer, Ara: Alechinsky.– D'Allesandro, R.: Arcangelo.– Darrow, A.: Gabo.– Deutsche Fotothek, Dresden: Barlach.– Documenta 2 (catalogue): Afro, Appel, Bacon, Baumeister, Bazaine, Bissière, Braque, Brauner, Buchheister, Burri, Capogrossi, De Kooning, Dubuffet, Ernst, Fautrier, Fontana, Geiger, Goller, Gorky, Götz, Guston, Jorn, Kantor, Kemény, Lam, Manessier, Marcks, Masson, Mathieu, Matisse, Mortensen, Motherwell, Nay, Nicholson, Pasmore, Poliakoff, Pollock, Santomaso, Saura, Sima, Soulages, Staël, Sugaï, Sutherland, Tamayo, Tàpies, Thieler, Tobey, Trier, Vasarely, Vedova, Villon.– Documenta 8: Anderson, Aycock, Cage, Günther, Jetelová, Kaprow, Kiefer, Morris, Paik, Penone, Rosenbach, Trakas, Wall.– Eurich, Crispin: Moore.– Feininger, Lotte: Salomon.– Felb, Chris: Wood.– Felver, Chris: Woodrow.– Film Publishers Inc., NewYork: Laurens.– Frank, Stephen: Arbus.– Fricke, Karsten: Claasen, Michaels, Newton, Umbo.– Friters-Drucker, M.: Jacobsen.– Fritz Glarner Estate, Locarno: Glarner.– Füermann, Klaus: Lebeck, Leibowitz.– Galerie Bischofberger, Zurich: Barceló (Photo: Mário Cabrita Gil), Basquiat.– Galerie Gmyrek, Düsseldorf: McLean (Photo: Bernd Janssen).– Galerie Inge Baecker, Cologne: Kabakov.– Galerie Karin Fesel, Düsseldorf: Calderara, Jochims (Photo: Diemar Schneider, Cologne).– Galerie Konrad Fischer, Düsseldorf: Long.– Galerie Louis Carré & Cie, Paris: Estève.– Galerie Maeght, Paris: Giacometti.– Galerie Maeght Lelong, Paris: Velde.– Galerie Nothelfer, Berlin: Lakner (Photo: E. Kiessling).– Galerie Ricke, Cologne: Marioni (Photo: Nicholas Walster), Reed (Photo: PamelaReed).– Galerie Rupert Walser, Munich: Zeniuk.– Galerie Yvon Lambert, Paris: Blais.– Galvin, Guglielmo: Caulfield.– Giacometti: Ruscha.– Gnilka, Ewald: Uhlmann.– Goldblatt, John: King.– Gorgoni, Gianfranco: Andre, Paladino, Smithson, Sonnier.– Grab, Richard de: Tal-Coat.– Greenfield-Sanders, Timothy: Halley.– Greer, Fergus: K. Smith.– Grethe, Arnold: Hoyningen-Huene.– Griffin, Steve: Artschwager.– Grotz, Paul: Evans.– Haas, Marianne: Garouste.– Halsband, Michael: Kanovitz.– Hauert, Roger: Picasso.– Hervochon, Yves: Agam.– Hess: Beckmann.– Higgins, Dick: Brecht.– Hoyningen-Huehne, George: Cartier-Bresson.– Hyde, Jacqueline: Survage.– Institut Belge d'Information et de Documentation: Magritte.– Katz, Benjamin: Baselitz, Beuys, Boltanski, Buren, Byars, Chia, Clemente, Cucchi, Fabro, Förg, Gilbert & George, Grützke, Haacke, Haring, Hödicke, Horn, Immendorff, Kelley, Kirkeby, Knoebel, Kramer, Lasker, LeParc, Leroy, Lüpertz, Marden, Neusüss, Odenbach, Oehlen, Penck, Plessi, Polke, G. Richter, Rückriem, Salle, Schnabel, Sherman, Steinbach, Struth, Trockel, Villeglé, Virnich.– Keystone: Siqueiros.– Kiesling, G.: Vostell.– Klemm, Barbara: Ruetz.– Krolow, Wolfgang: Chaldej.– Kunsthalle in Emden: Bruskin, Filatow.– Kunsthalle Mannheim: Bissier.– Künstlerinnen/Künstler: Antes, Bruch, Burden, Campus, D. Davis, Dorazio, Duncan, Export, Filliou, Fischer, Frize, Garrin, Gertsch, Gerz, Girke (Archiv Brandstetter & Wyss, Zurich), Graubner, Gundlach, Hanson, Heerich, Hegedüs, Karavan, Kippenberger, Klapheck, Klauke, Lichtenstein, Lohse, Luginbühl, Mack, Meistermann, Miotte, Morellet, Prager, Räderscheidt, Rist, Roth, Schultze, Schütte (Photo: Hans Strube), Shaw, Snelson, Stelarc, Tübke, Ursula, Vasulka, Wagemaker, Winters, Wool.– Lacombe, Brigitte: Rothenberg.– Larionov, Mme Larionov.– Lazarus, Marvin P.: Gottlieb.– Lloyd, Gilbert: Diebenkorn.– Lortz, Helmut: Berlewi.– Mapplethorpe, Robert: Kushner.– Marlborough Fine Arts, London: Auerbach.– Mayr, Walter: Schumacher.– McDarrah, Fred W.: Chamberlain, Hesse, Judd, Still.– Mihm, Frank: Hoover, Kawamata, Lafontaine, Lang, Longo, Metzel, Solano.– Miller, W.: Brancusi.– Moholy, Lucia: Henri.– Moholy-Nagy, László: Moholy.– Morgenbaum, Carl: Mantz.– Müller, Gregoire: Jacquet.– Musée Léger, Biot: Léger.– Muzeum Sztuki, Lodz: Kobro.– Namuth, Hans: Cornell, Jensen, Kline.– Natanson, Alfred: Vallotton.– Newhall, Beaumont: Adams, Halsman.– Nguyen, Michel: Thursz.– Norman, Dorothy: Demuth.– Ohlbaum, Isolde: Brus.– Orgel-Köhne, L. und A.: Höch.– Parks, Gordon Jr.: Parks.– Pevsner, Mme: Pevsner.– Pfaffe, Wolfgang: Abramovic, Acconi, Jonas, Kounellis, Levine, Matta-Clark, Poirier.– Pflaum, Barbara: Lassnig.– Phocas, Suzanne: Metzinger.– Pinsard, Laurent: Etienne-Martin.– Price, Penelope: Oursler.– Ramos, Mrs.: Ramos.– Ramson, Sidsel: Pedersen.– Rautert, Timm: Walther.– Reiser: Fruhtrunk.– Riess: Archipenko.– Rowan, Richard: Haas.– Schmied, Erika: Matta, Oelze, Uecker.– Schuh: Doesburg.– Schwabik, Marian: Eisenstaedt.– Schwartz, Marvin W.: Heizer, Flavin.– Schwitters, Ernst: Schwitters.– Seng, Walther: Piene.– Seuphor, Michel: Russolo, Vantongerloo.– Shunk, Harry: Y. Klein.– Steichen, Edward: Sheeler.– Stieglitz, Alfred: Dove, Hartley.– Stiftung für Kunst und Kultur und Kunstmuseum, Bonn: Liu Wei, Wang Cheng, Wei Guangquing, Zhang Xiaogang.– Stocchi, Gabriele: Twombly.– Strelow, Liselotte: Heiliger.– Sunami, Soichi: Miró.– The British Council, London: Freud.– The Pace Gallery, NewYork: Morley, Reinhardt.– Trewyn Studio, St. Ives: Hepworth.– Tyler Graphics: Frankenthaler, Tworkow.– Vandercan, Serge: Fleischmann.– Volz, Wolfgang: Christo & Jeanne-Claude.– Votava, F.: Wotruba.– Wadenoyen, Hugo van: Chadwick.– Waller, Baine: Estes.– Weill, Etienne: Arp.– Weiss, Gerhard: Helnwein, Helnwein.– Wiklund, Lars: Fahlström.– Wilkinson, Kirk C.: Wyeth.– Wolff, Martha: Kandinsky.

Self-portraits: Brandt, Close, Coburn, Drtikol, Baranov-Rossiné, Becher, Blumenfeld, Bourke-White, Doisneau, A. Feininger, Freund, Gidal, Kassák, Keetman, Krims, Krull, Mapplethorpe, McBride, Meyer, Opalka, Prince, Ruff, Sieverding, Steichen, Thiebaud, Weegee, Wegman, Wilson.

Index of Names

Bold numbers indicate illustrations.
Names mentioned in the lexicon of artists are not included in the index of names.